Street by Street

SURREY

PLUS ALDERSHOT, BIGGIN HILL, BRACKNELL, CRAWLEY, CROYDON, EAST GRINSTEAD, EDENBRIDGE, FARNBOROUGH, GATWICK AIRPORT, HORSHAM, KINGSTON UPON THAMES, RICHMOND, SUTTON

Enlarged Areas Farnham, Guildford, Woking

lst edition May 2001

© Automobile Association Developments Limited 2001

This product includes map data licensed from Ordnance Survey® with the permission of the Controller of Her Majesty's Stationery Office. © Crown copyright 2000. All rights reserved. Licence No: 399221.

Published by AA Publishing (a trading name of Automobile Association Developments Limited, whose registered office is Norfolk House, Priestley Road, Basingstoke, Hampshire, RG24 9NY. Registered number 1878835).

Mapping produced by the Cartographic Department of The Automobile Association.

A CIP Catalogue record for this book is available from the British Library.

Printed by G. Canale & C. S.P.A., Torino, Italy

The contents of this atlas are believed to be correct at the time of the latest revision. However, the publishers cannot be held responsible for loss occasioned to any person acting or refraining from action as a result of any material in this atlas, nor for any errors, omissions or changes in such material. The publishers would welcome information to correct any errors or omissions and to keep this atlas up to date. Please write to Publishing, The Automobile Association, Fanum House, Basing View, Basingstoke, Hampshire, RG21 4EA.

Ref: MX118

Key to map pages	ii-iii
Key to map symbols	iv-1
Enlarged scale pages	2-11
Street by Street	12-229
Index – towns & villages	230-231
Index – streets	232-279
Index – featured places	279-287

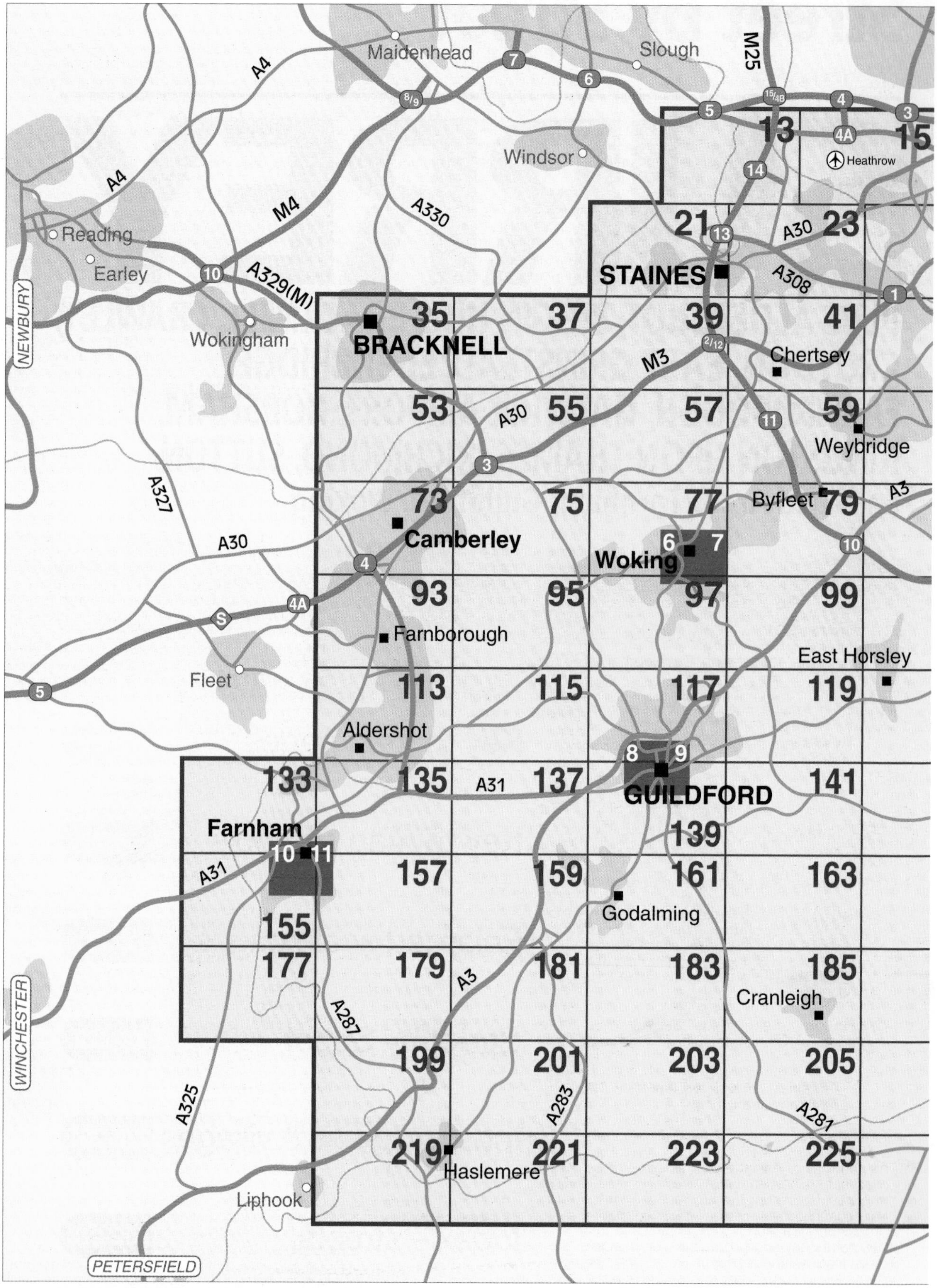

ii

Maidenhead
7
Slough
M25
6
5
15/4B
4
3
8/9
13
4A
15
Windsor
14
Heathrow
A4
M4
A330
21
13
A30
23
Reading
A329(M)
10
STAINES
A308
1
Earley
35
37
39
41
Wokingham
BRACKNELL
M3
Chertsey
2/12
53
55
57
59
A30
11
Weybridge
A327
73
75
77
Byfleet
79
A3
A30
Camberley
6
7
10
4
Woking
93
95
97
99
4A
Farnborough
S
East Horsley
Fleet
113
115
117
119
5
Aldershot
133
135
A31
137
8
9
141
Farnham
GUILDFORD
139
A31
10
11
157
159
161
163
155
Godalming
177
179
A3
181
183
185
Cranleigh
A287
199
201
203
205
A325
A283
A281
219
221
223
225
WINCHESTER
Haslemere
Liphook
PETERSFIELD

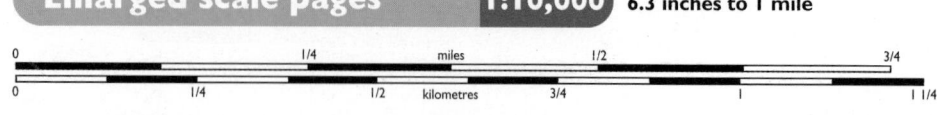

Enlarged scale pages   **1:10,000** 6.3 inches to 1 mile

0   1/4   miles   1/2   3/4
0   1/4   1/2   kilometres   3/4   1   1 1/4

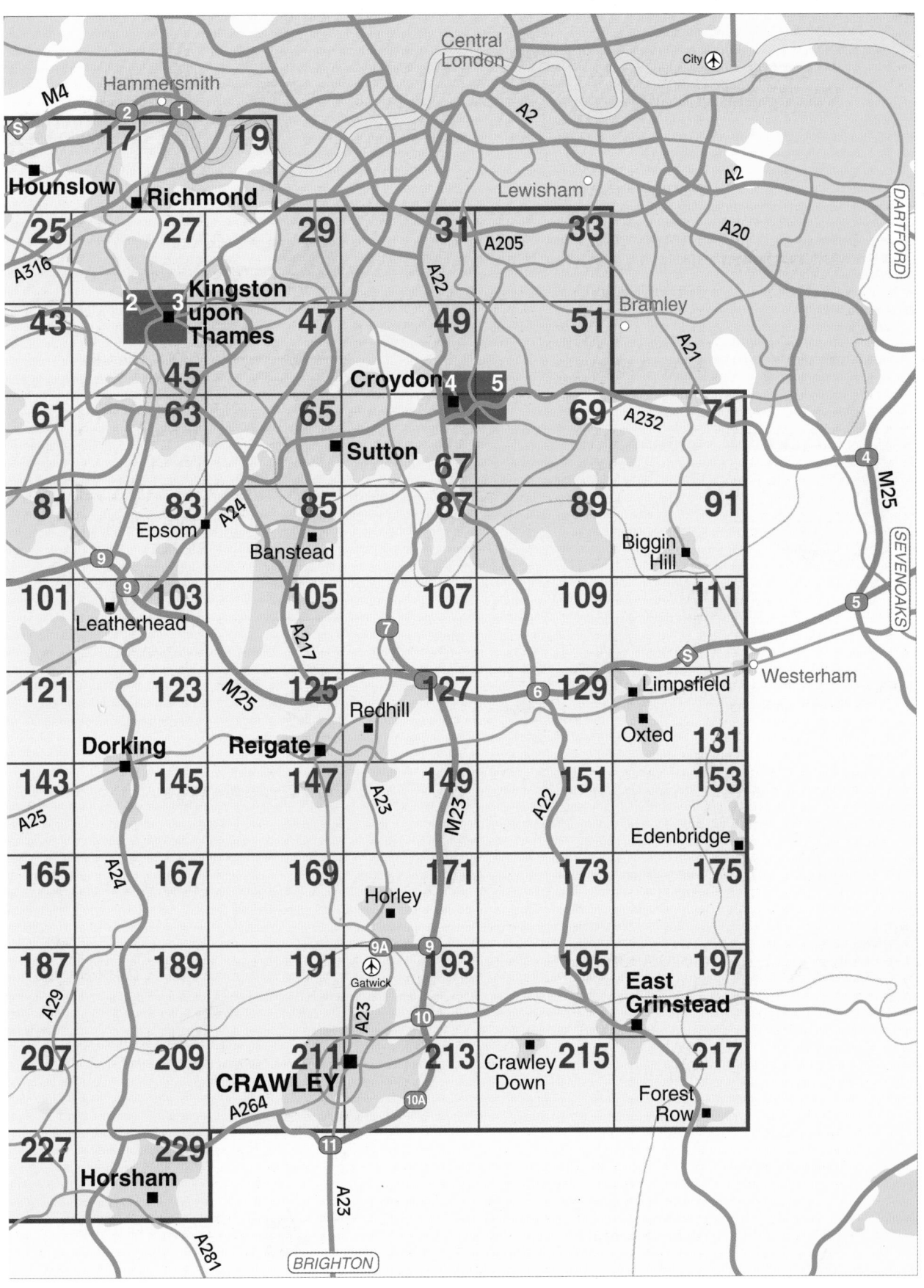

Central London

Hammersmith

City ✈

M4

S

2 1

17   19

Hounslow

Richmond

Lewisham

A2

A2

DARTFORD

25   27   29   31   33

A205

A316

A22

A20

43   Kingston   47   49   51   Bramley

2 3 upon

Thames

A21

45

Croydon 4 5

61   63   65   69   71   A232

Sutton

67

M25

81   83   85   87   89   91   SEVENOAKS

Epsom   A24

Banstead   Biggin

Hill

9

101   9 103   105   107   109   111   5

Leatherhead   A217

7

121   123   125   127   6 129   Limpsfield   Westerham

M25   Redhill   S

Dorking   Reigate   Oxted   131

143   145   147   149   151   153

A25   A23   M23   A22

Edenbridge

165   167   169   171   173   175

A24   Horley

187   189   191   193   195   197

A29   9A   9   East

Gatwick   Grinstead

A23

10

207   209   211   213   215   217

CRAWLEY   Crawley   Forest

A264   Down   Row

10A

227   229

11

Horsham

A23

A281

BRIGHTON

0   1/2   miles   1

0   1/2   1   kilometres   1 1/2   2

Junction 9	Motorway & junction	P+🚌	Park & Ride
Services	Motorway service area	🚌	Bus/coach station
	Primary road single/dual carriageway		Railway & main railway station
Services	Primary road service area		Railway & minor railway station
	A road single/dual carriageway	⊖	Underground station
	B road single/dual carriageway	⊖	Light railway & station
	Other road single/dual carriageway	+++++++++++	Preserved private railway
	Restricted road	*LC*	Level crossing
	Private road	•—•—•—•—	Tramway
← ←	One way street	- - - - - - -	Ferry route
	Pedestrian street	··············	Airport runway
- - - - - - -	Track/ footpath	- · - · - · -	Boundaries- borough/ district
▪▪▪▪▪▪▪▪	Road under construction	⌄⌄⌄⌄⌄⌄⌄⌄	Mounds
[- - - -]	Road tunnel	**93**	Page continuation 1:17,500
P	Parking	**7**	Page continuation to enlarged scale 1:10,000

River/canal lake, pier

Aqueduct lock, weir

465
▲
Winter Hill
Peak (with height in metres)

Beach

Coniferous woodland

Broadleaved woodland

Mixed woodland

Park

Cemetery

Built-up area

Featured building

City wall

A&E
Accident & Emergency hospital

Toilet

Toilet with disabled facilities

Petrol station

PH
Public house

PO
Post Office

Public library

i
Tourist Information Centre

Castle

Historic house/ building

Wakehurst Place NT
National Trust property

M
Museum/ art gallery

†
Church/chapel

Country park

Theatre/ performing arts

Cinema

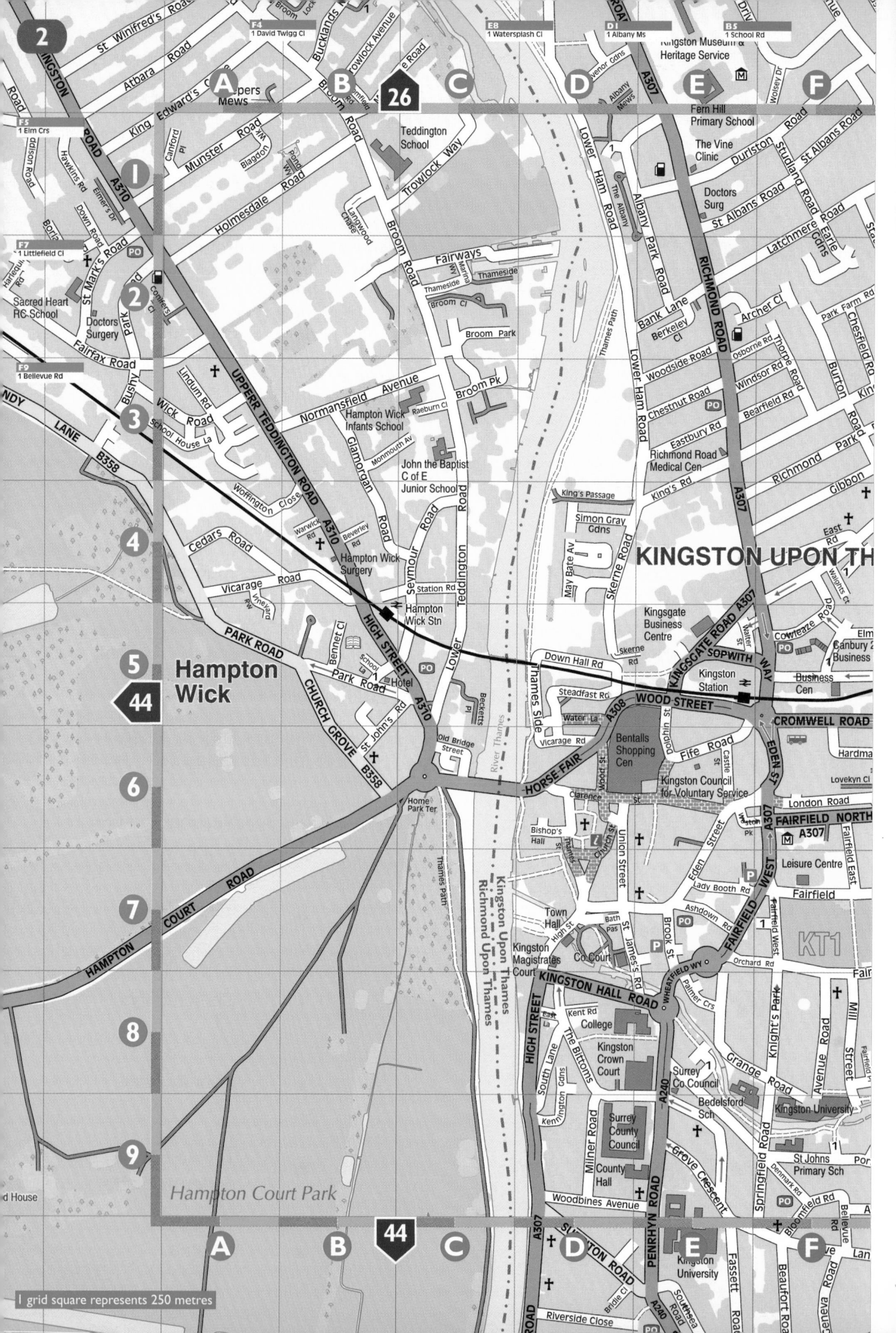

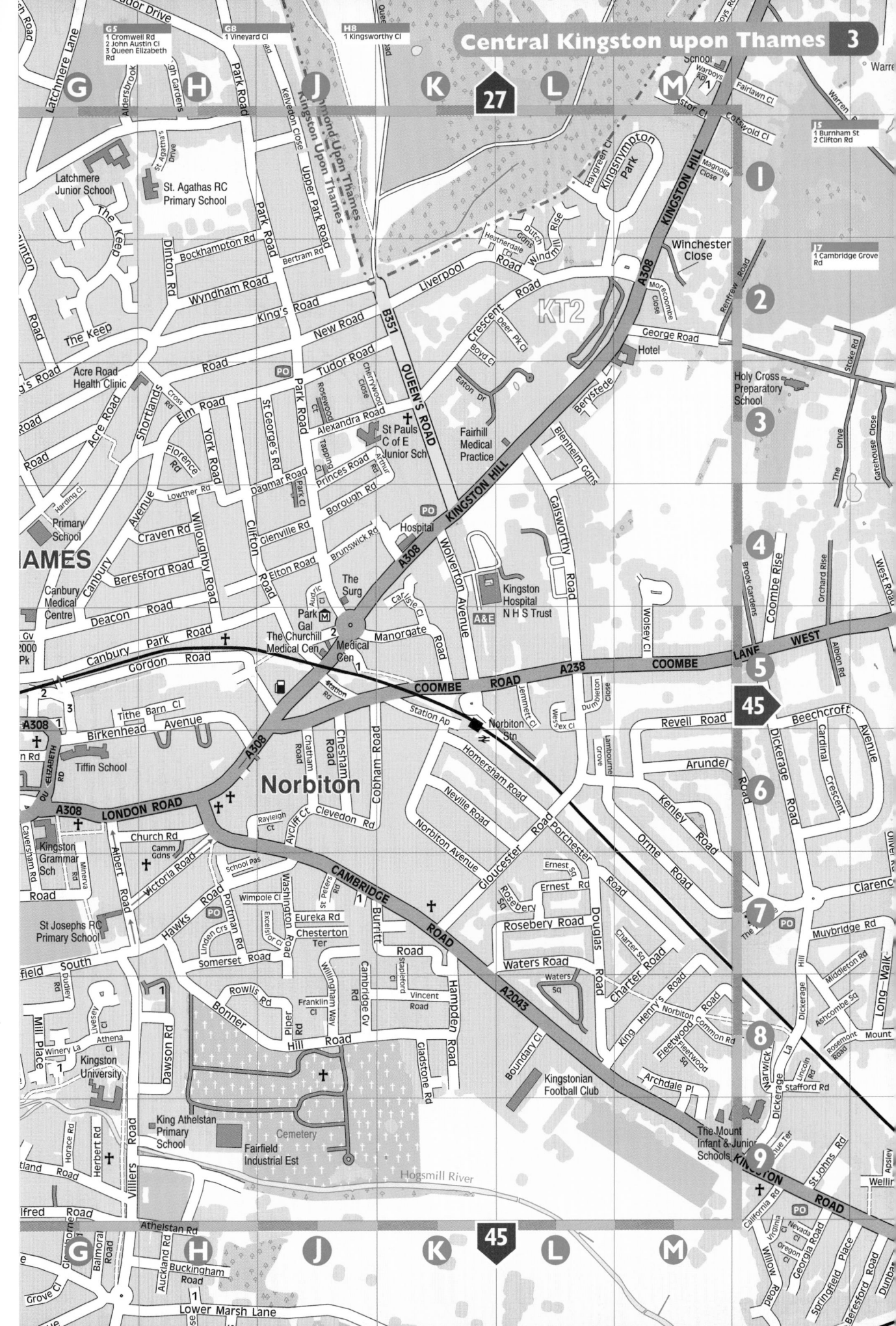

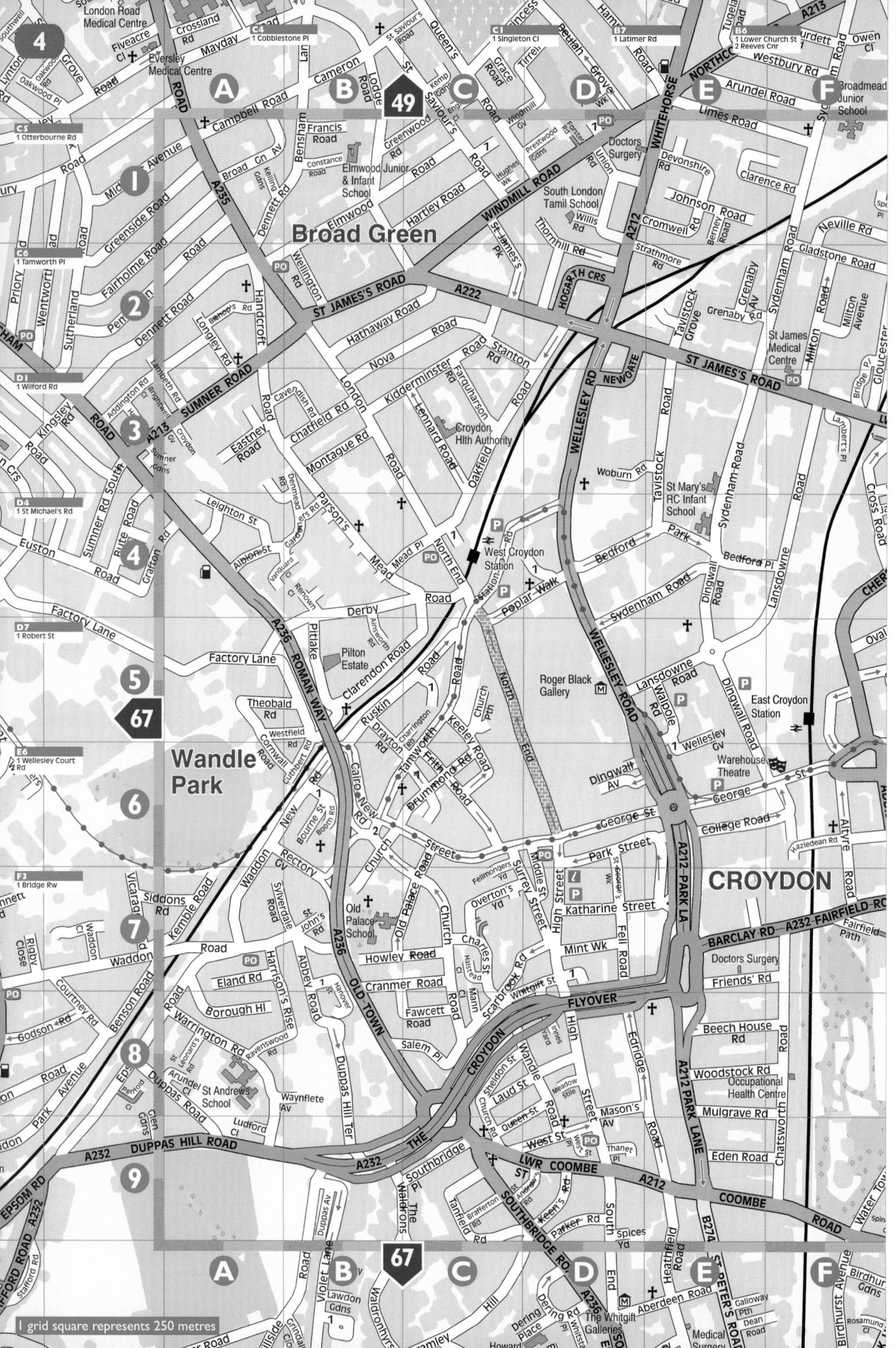

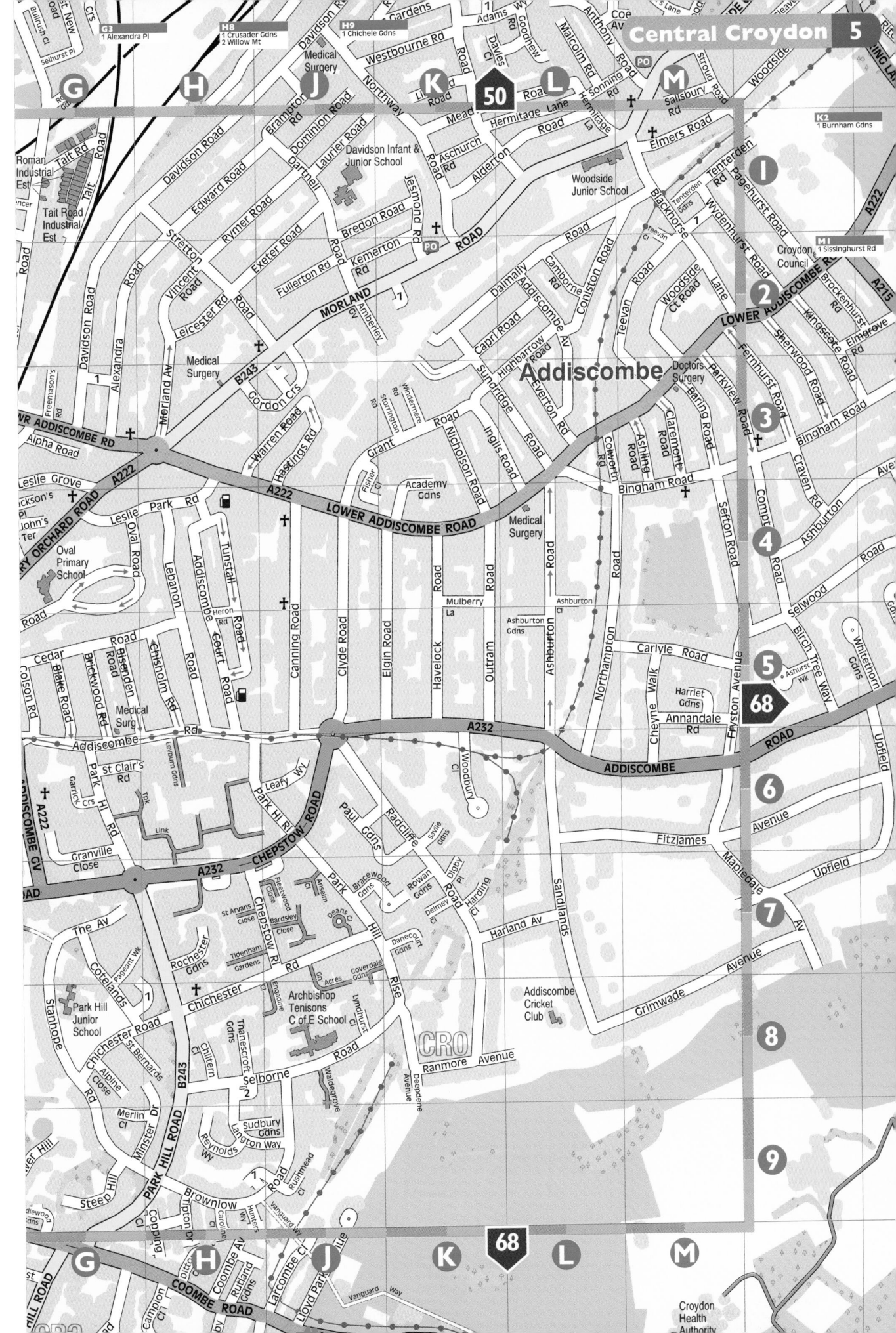

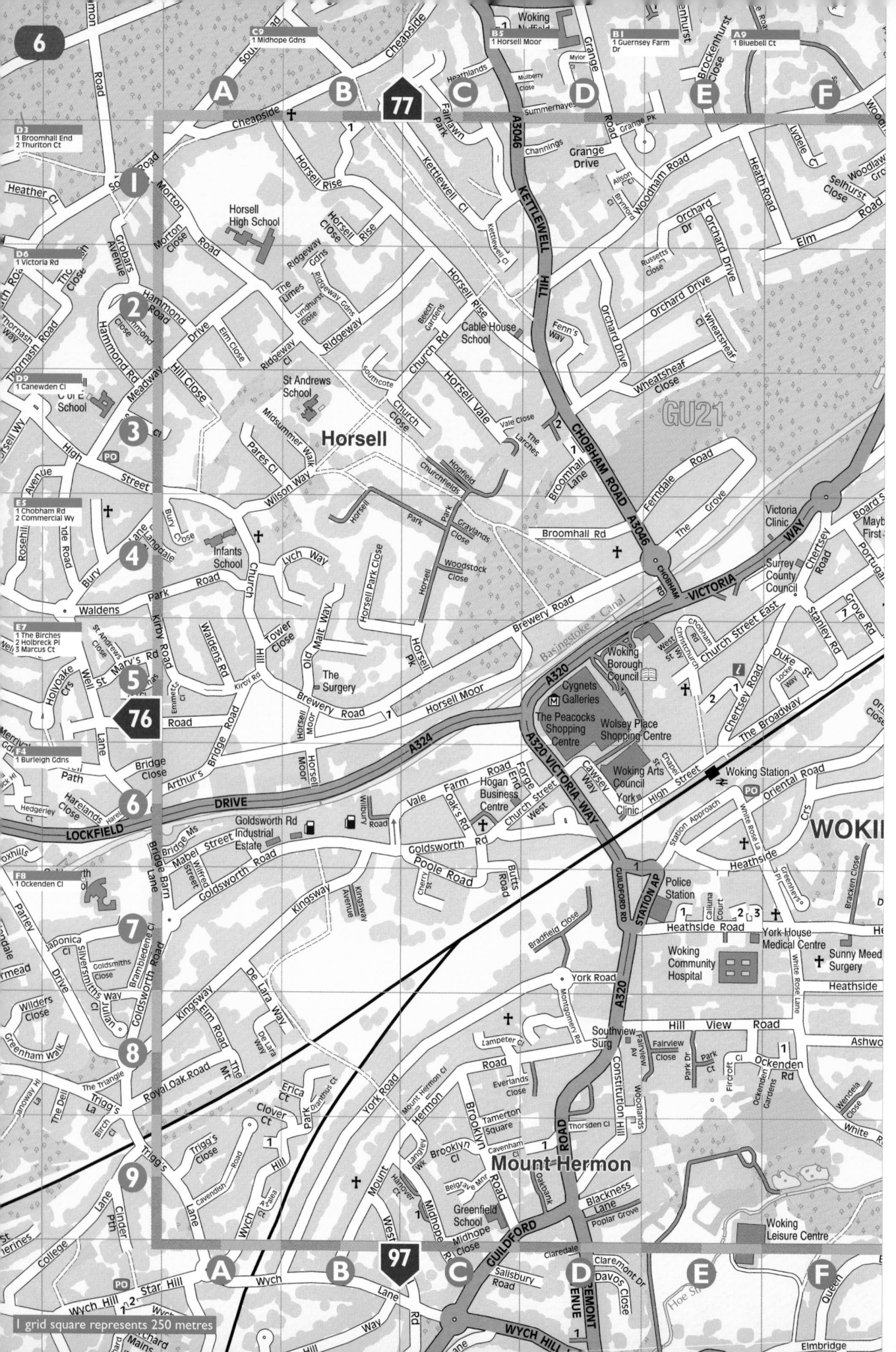

I grid square represents 250 metres

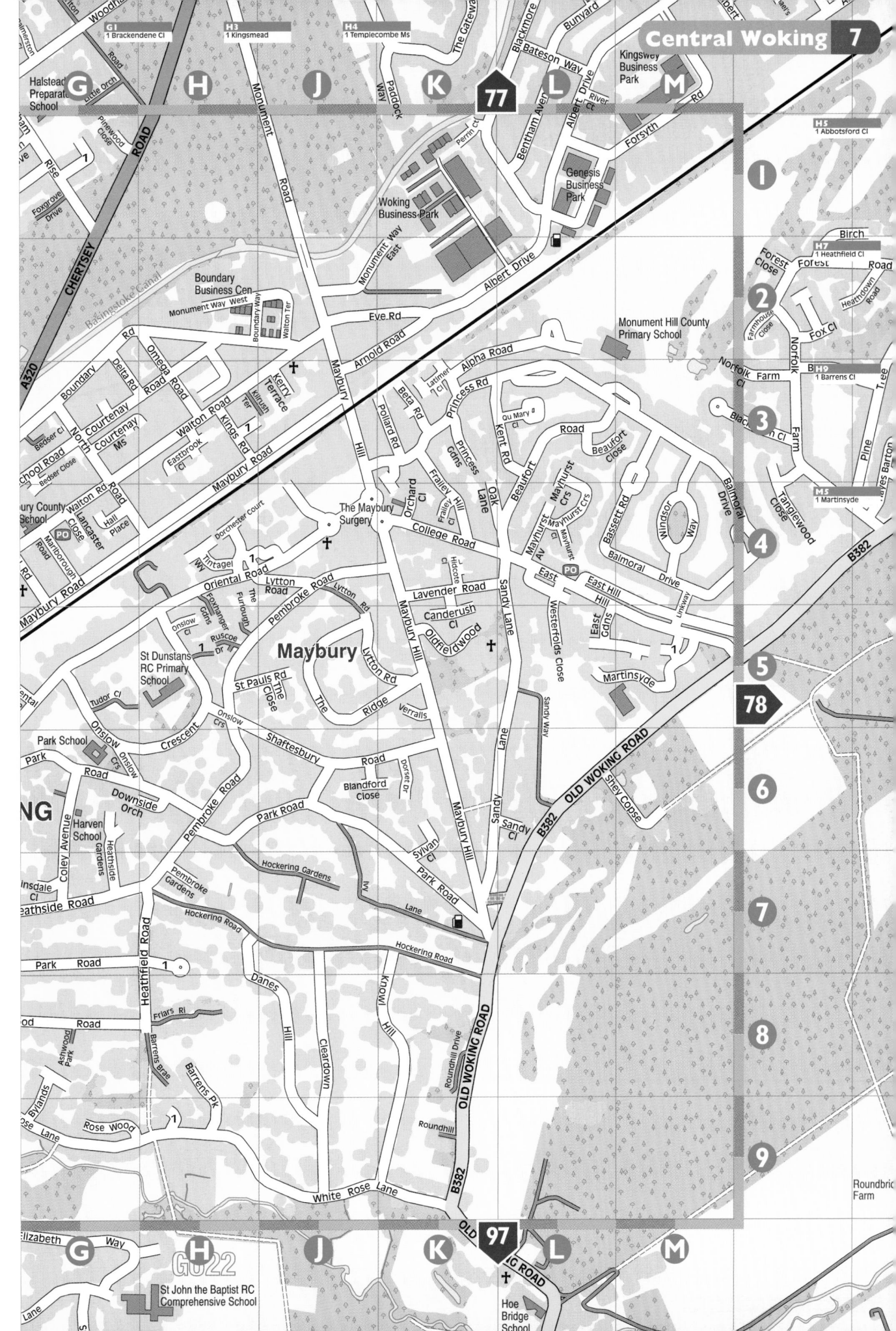

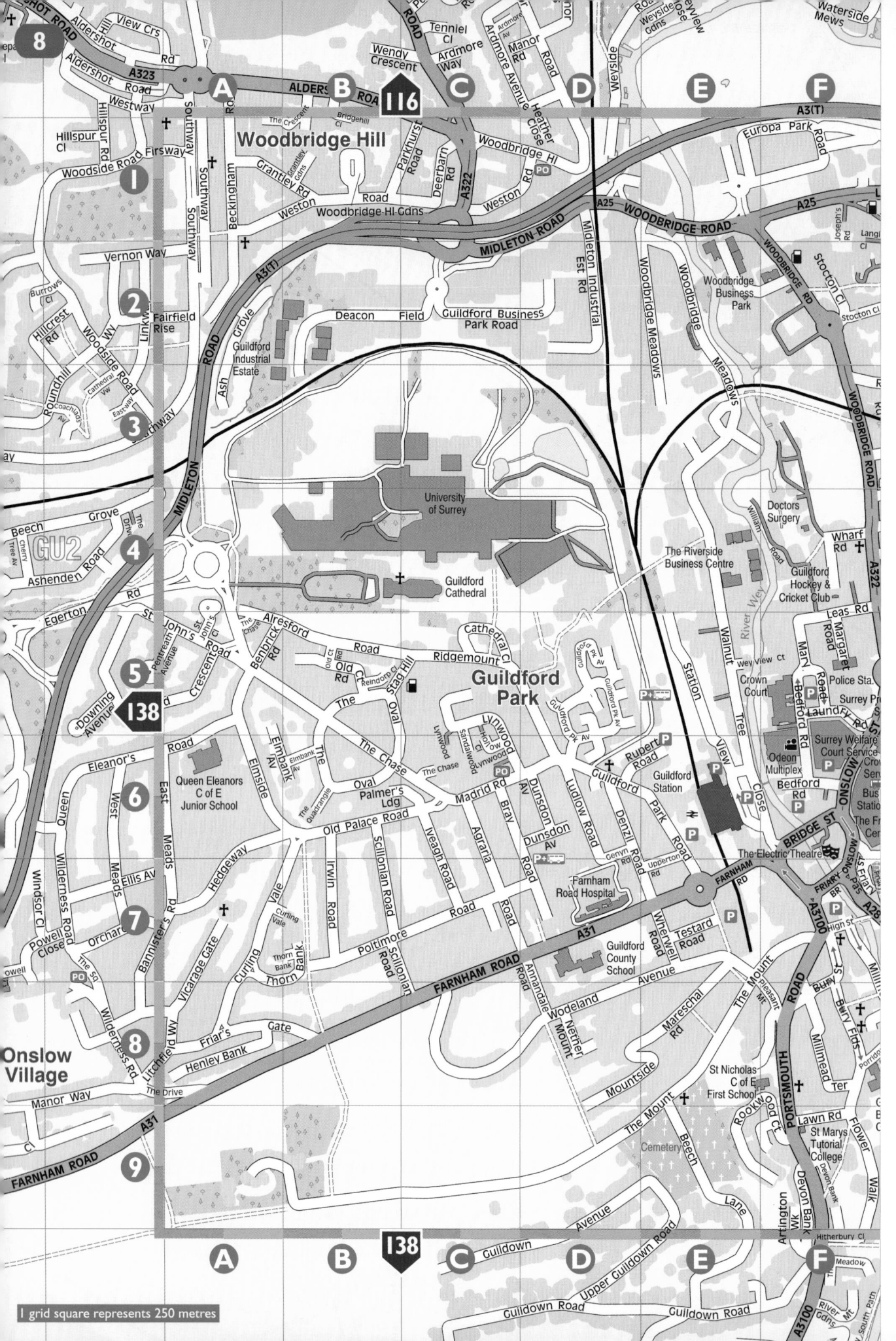

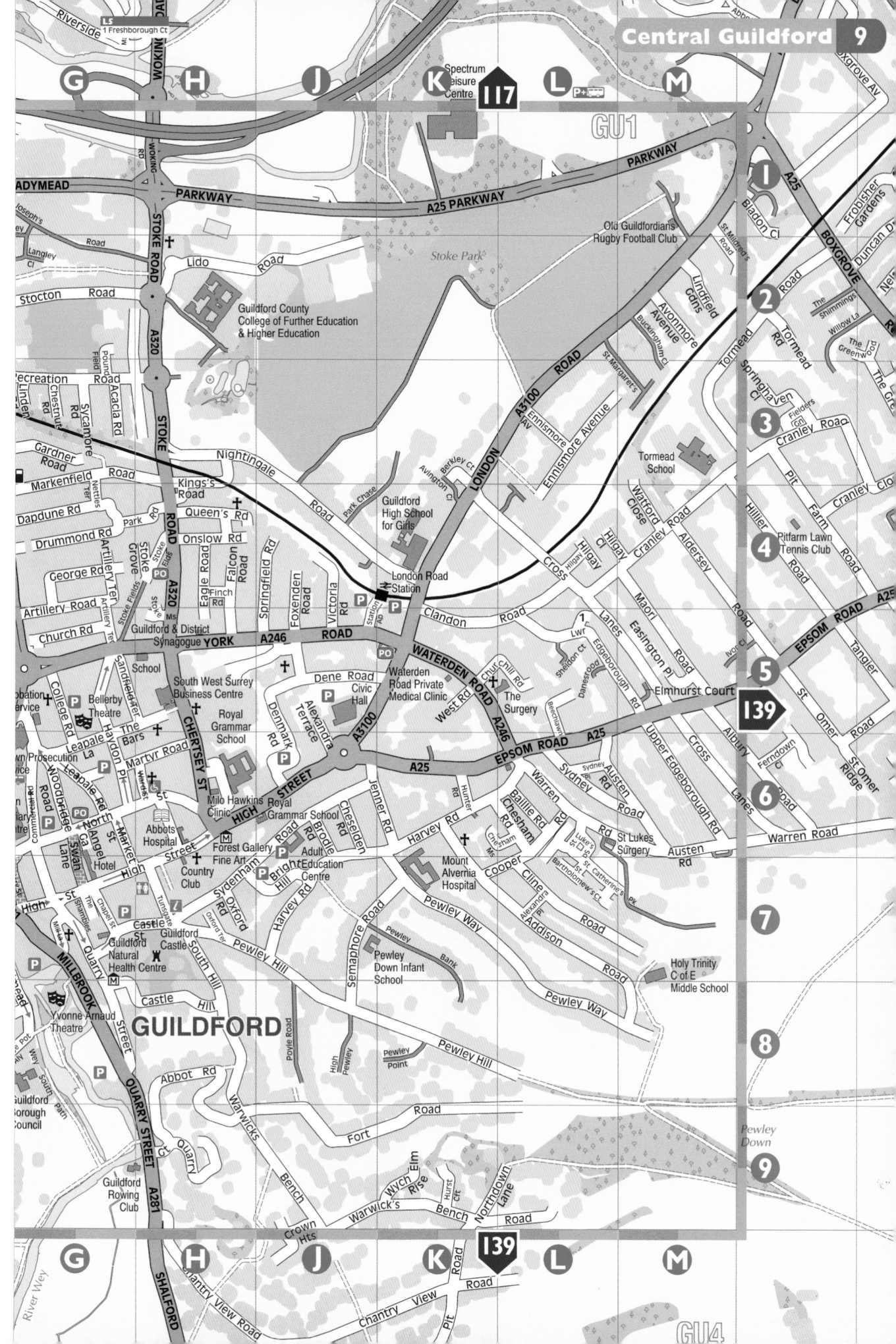

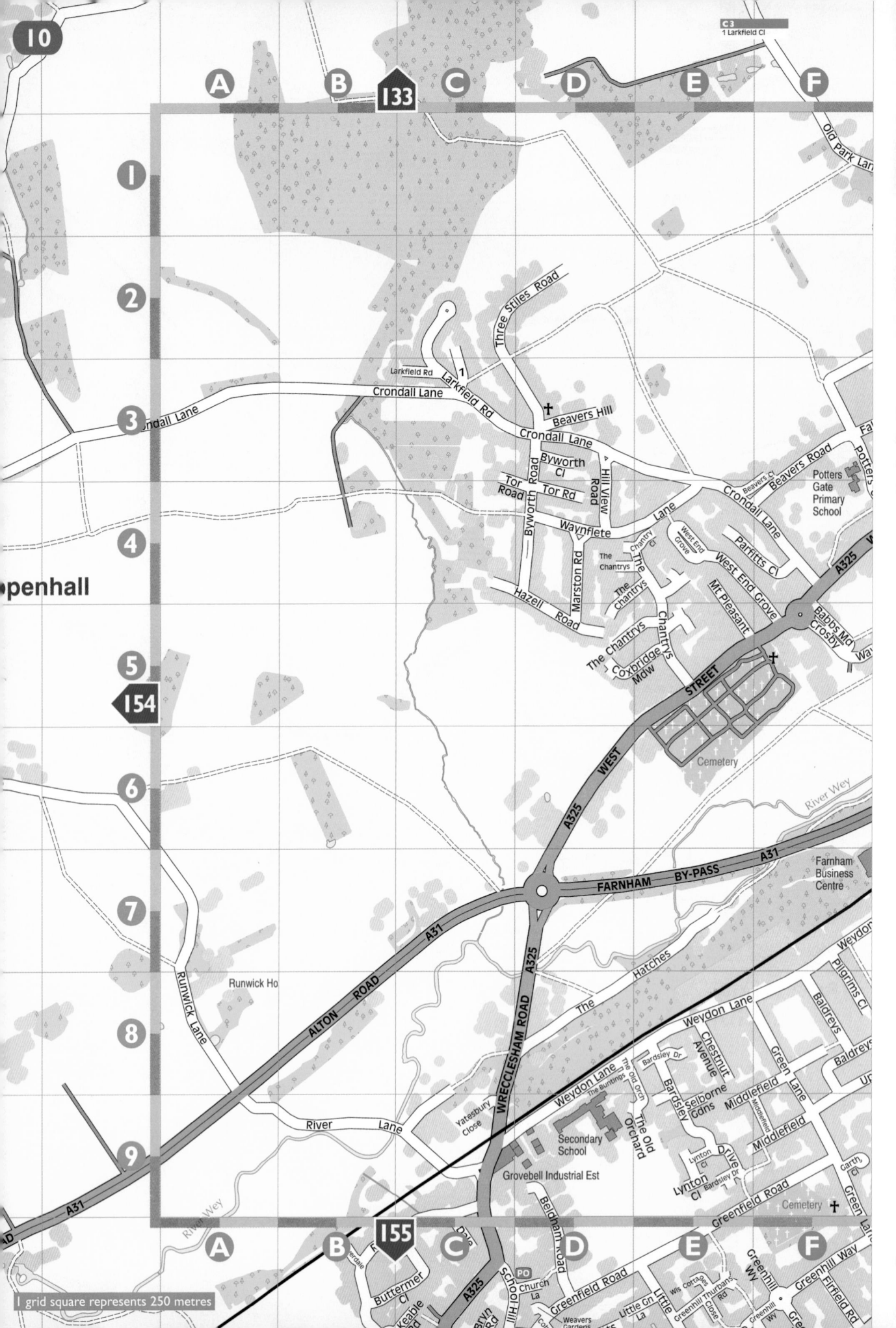

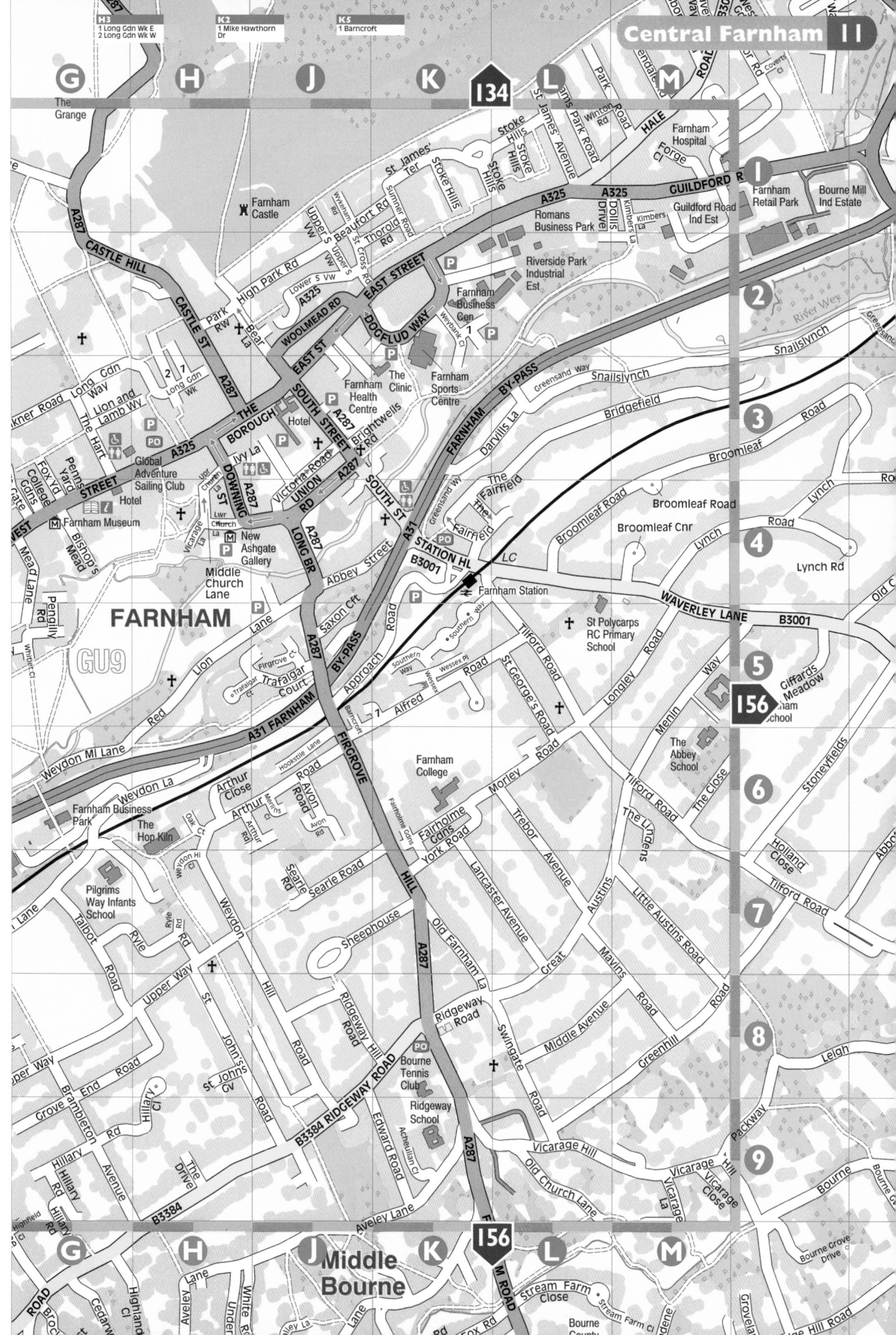

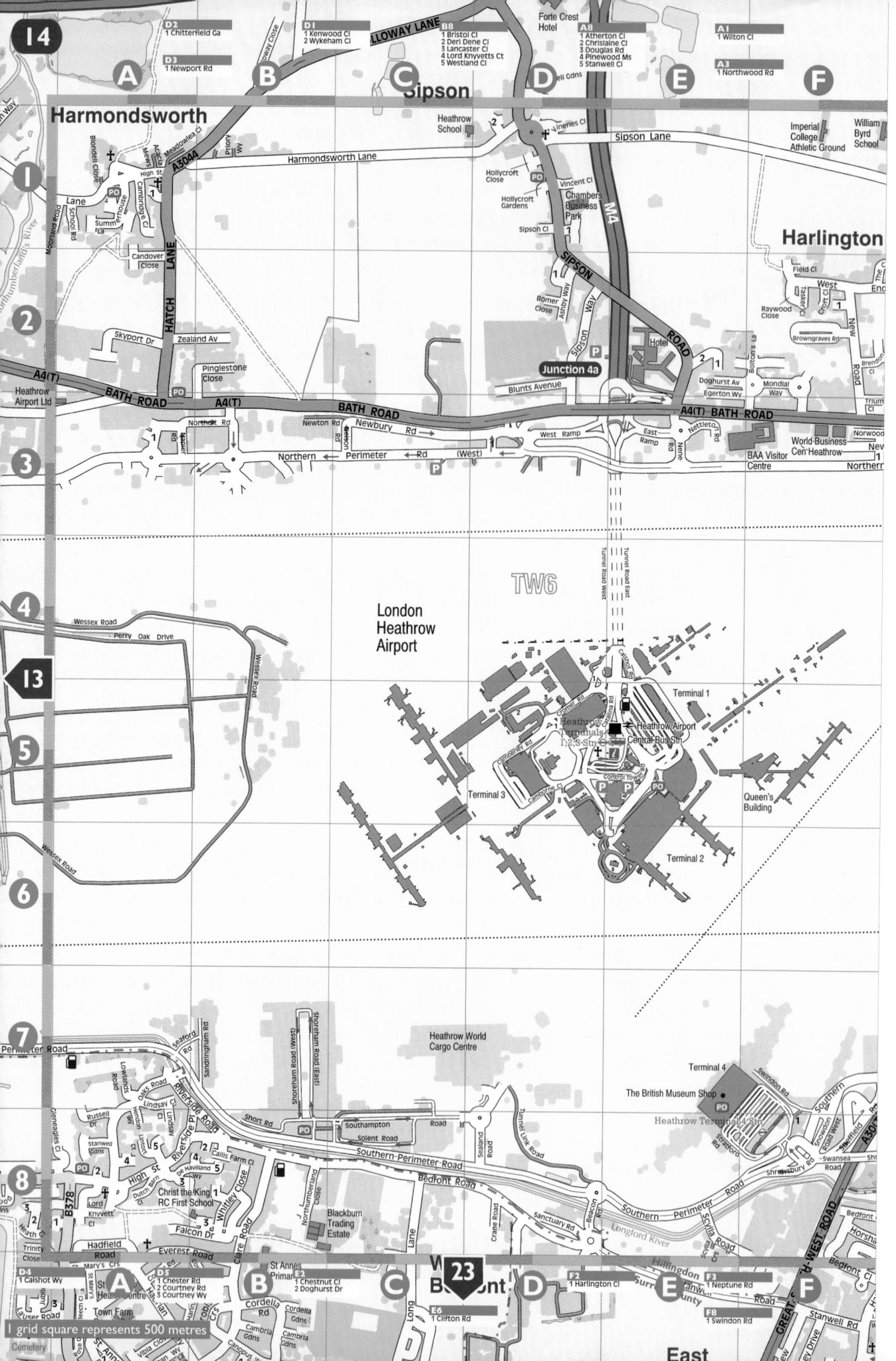

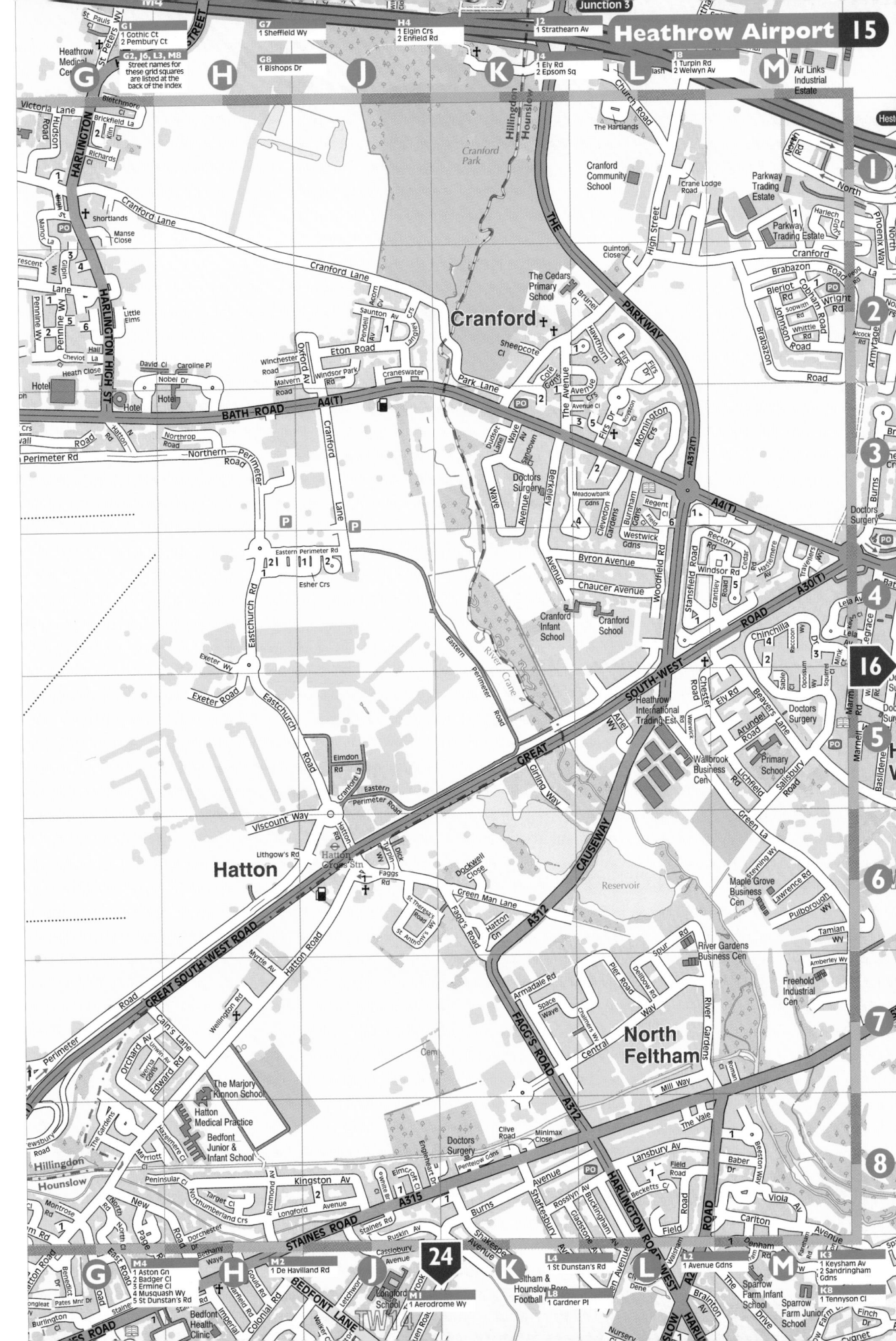

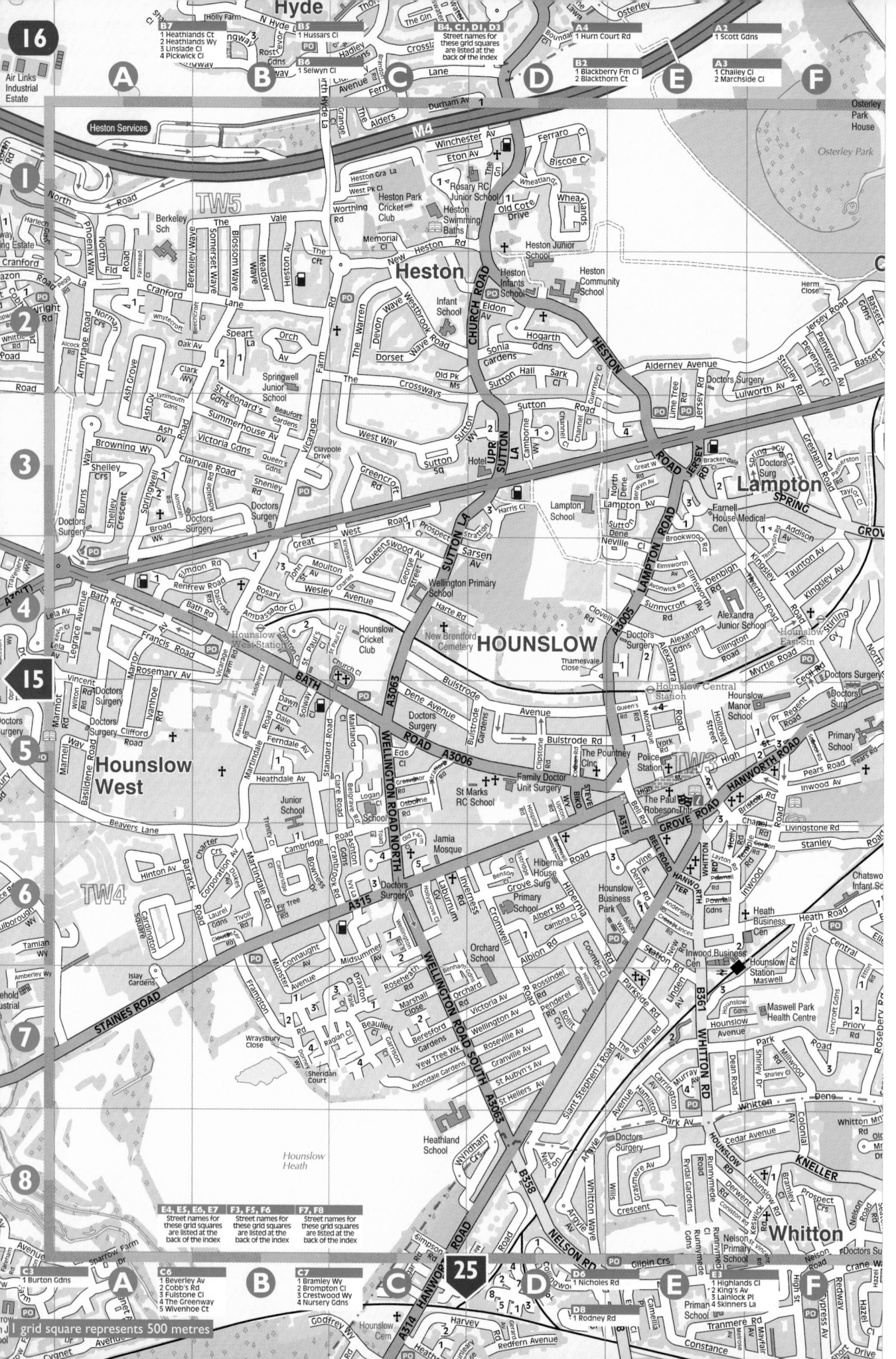

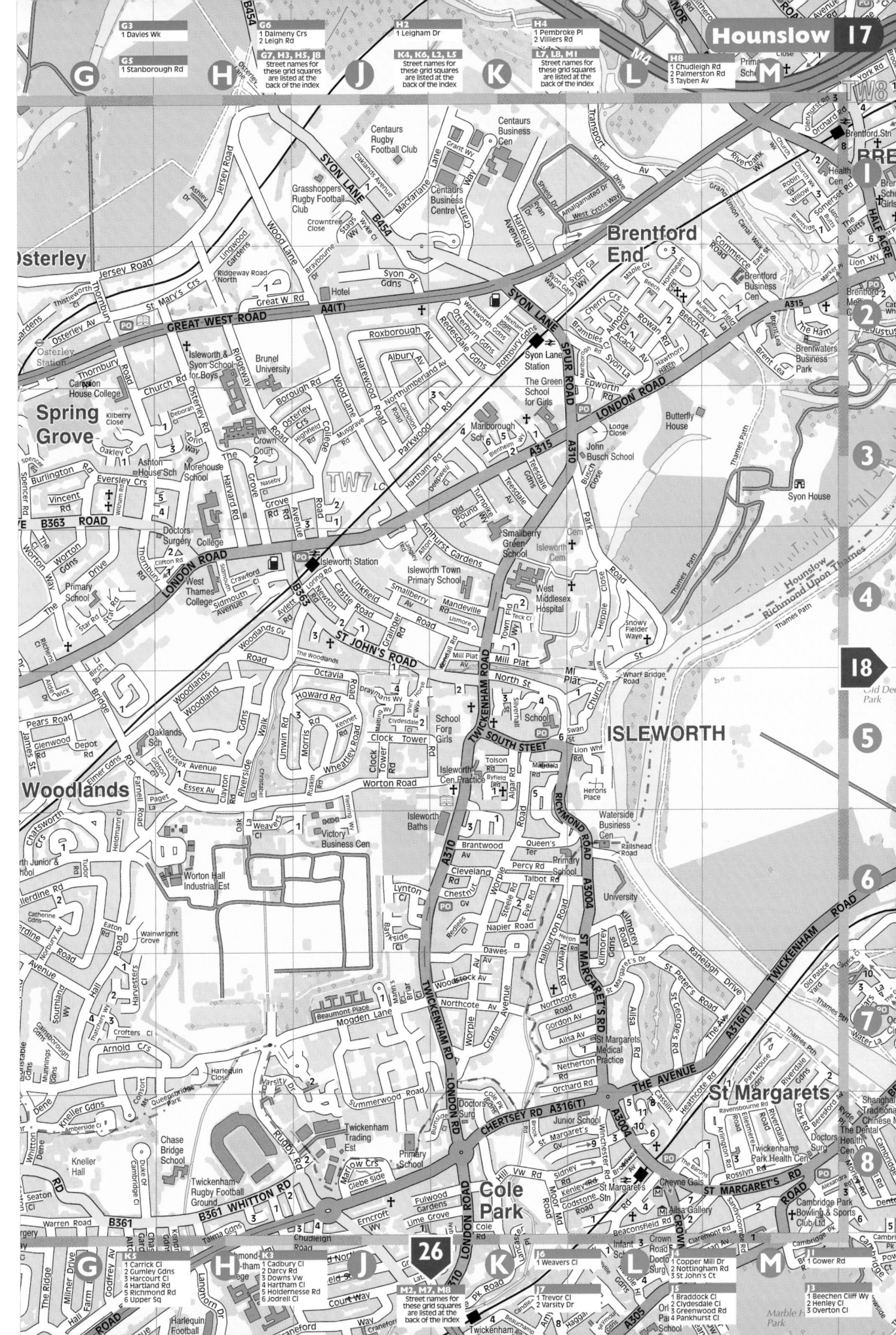

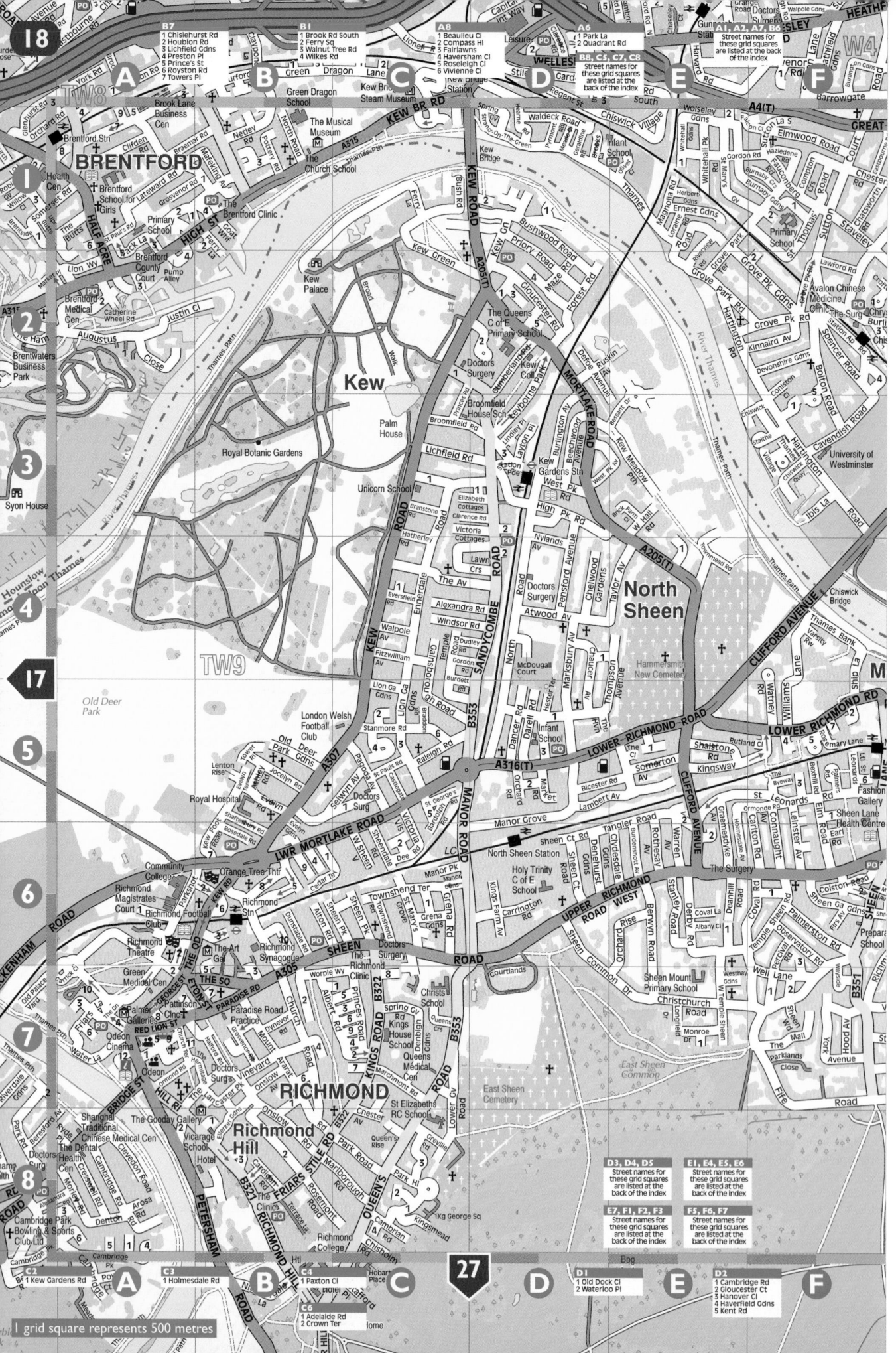

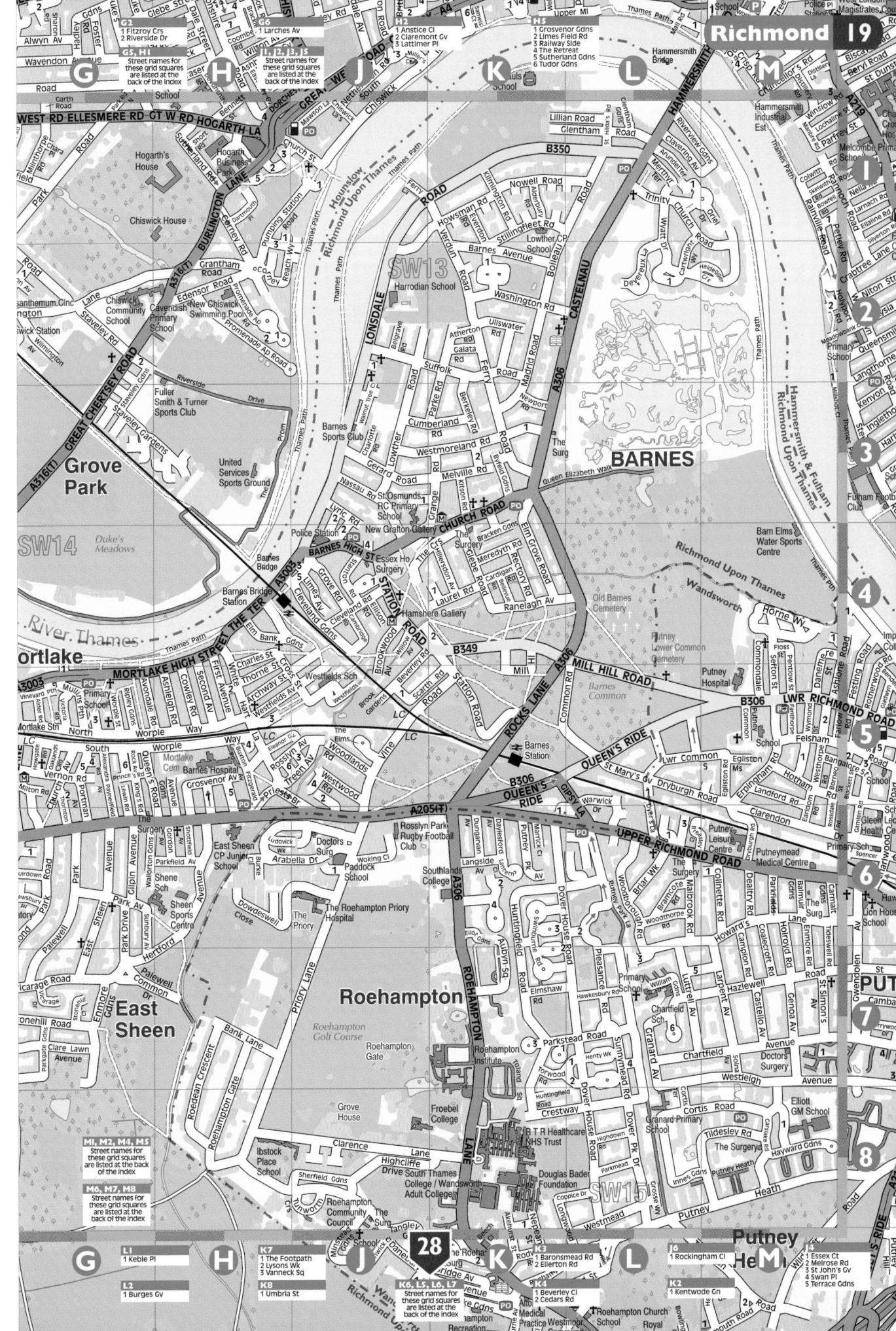

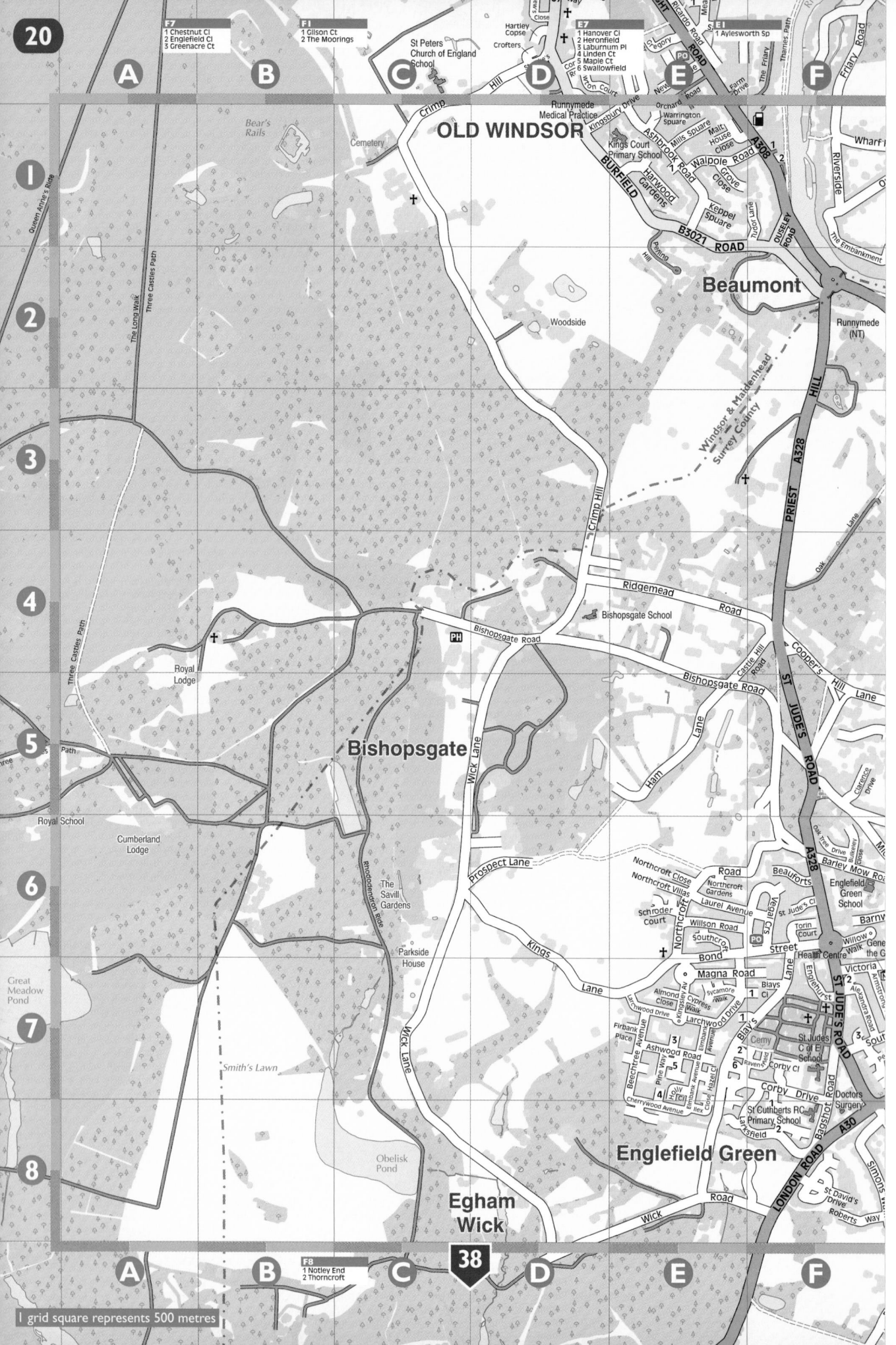

A   B   C   D   E   F

F7
1 Chestnut Cl
2 Englefield Cl
3 Greenacre Ct

F1
1 Gilson Ct
2 The Moorings

E7
1 Hanover Cl
2 Heronfield
3 Laburnum Pl
4 Linden Ct
5 Maple Ct
6 Swallowfield

E1
1 Aylesworth Sp

St Peters
Church of England
School

Hartley
Copse
Crofters

OLD WINDSOR

Runnymede
Medical Practice

Bear's
Rails

Cemetery

Kingsbury Drive
Kings Court
Primary School
Walpole Road
Grove
Close
Keppel
Square

Mills Square
Malt
House
Ashbrook Road
Harwood
Gardens
New
Orchard Road
Warrington
Square

BURFIELD
B3021   ROAD
OUSELEY ROAD
Tudor Lane

Beaumont

Riverside
Wharf Rd
The Embankment

Woodside

Runnymede
(NT)

Windsor & Maidenhead
Surrey County

Crimp
Hill

Crimp Hill

PRIEST   HILL   A328

Oak Lane

Ridgemead   Road

Bishopsgate School

Three Castles Path

Queen Anne's Ride

The Long Walk

Royal
Lodge

Bishopsgate Road
PH
Bishopsgate Road

Castle Hill
Road

Cooper's   Hill   Lane

ST JUDE'S ROAD

Bishopsgate

Wick Lane

Ham
Lane

Clatterice
Drive

Three Castles Path

Path

Royal School

Cumberland
Lodge

Rhododendron Ride

The Savill
Gardens

Prospect Lane

Northcroft Close
Northcroft Villas

Northcroft
Gardens
Road

Beauforts
Barley Mow Rd
Englefield
Green
School
Barnw

Laurel Avenue
Schroder
Court
Willson Road
Southcroft
Bond

PO
Street

Torin
Court

A328

Willow
Walk
Victoria
the G

Great
Meadow
Pond

Parkside
House

Kings
Lane

Magna Road

Almond Cl
Cypress
Kingsley Av
Larchwood Drive

Blays
Cl

Blays
Cl

St Jude's
Lane

Englehurst
Alexandra Road
Armstrong

Wick Lane

Smith's Lawn

Firbank
Place
Beechtree Avenue
Ashwood Road
Pine Way
Holly
Cherrywood Avenue

Sycamore
Walk
Larchwood Drive
Elmbank Avenue
Elm
Ilex
Hazel Cl

Cemy
St Judes
C of E
School
Corby Cl
Raven Field
Corby   Drive

Victoria
Alexandra Road

Doctors
Surgery

St Cuthberts RC
Primary School

Englefield Green

St David's
Drive

LONDON ROAD
BAGSHOT ROAD
A30
Simons La
Roberts Way

Obelisk
Pond

Egham
Wick

Wick   Road

St David's
Drive

38

A   B   C   D   E   F

1 grid square represents 500 metres

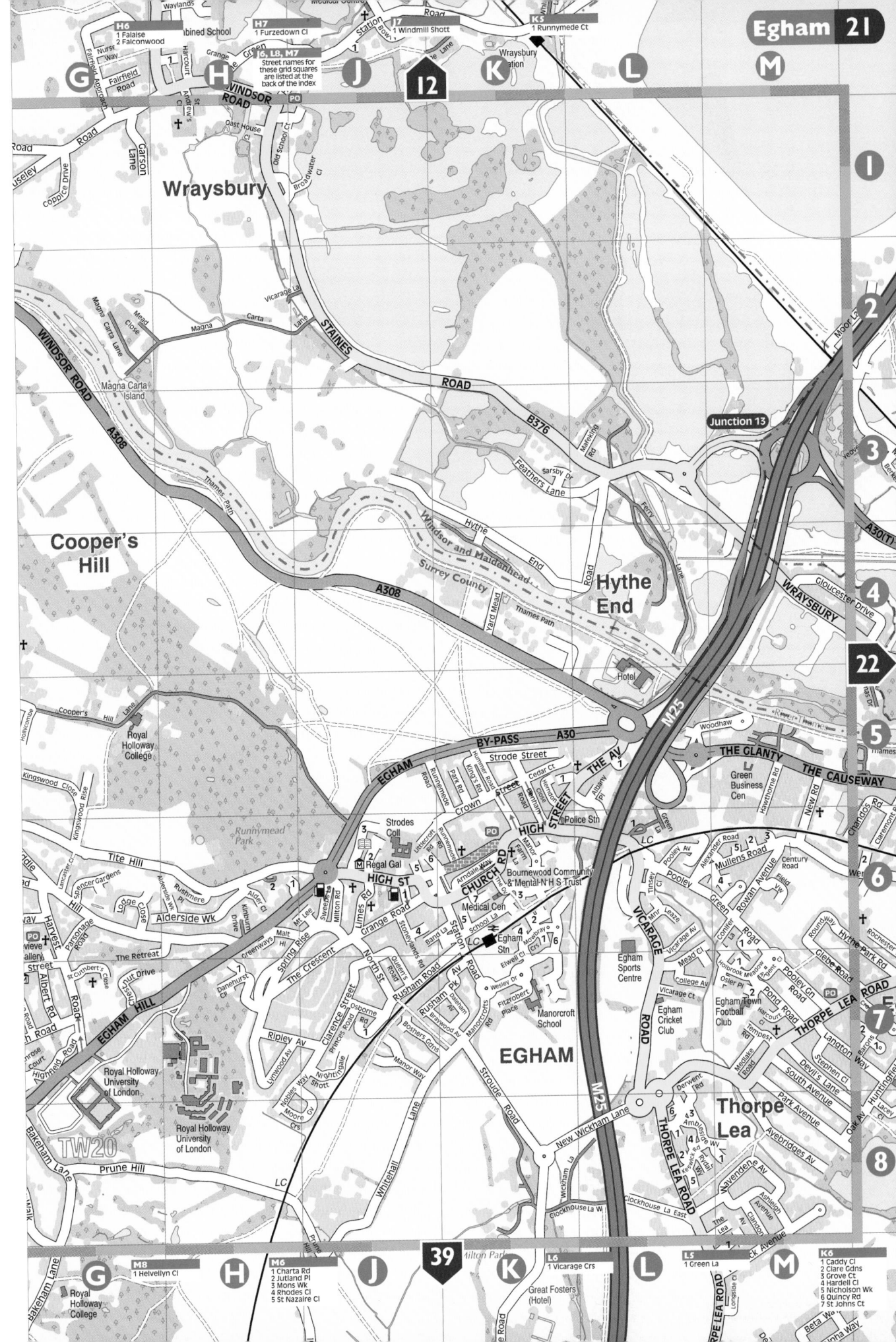

1 grid square represents 500 metres

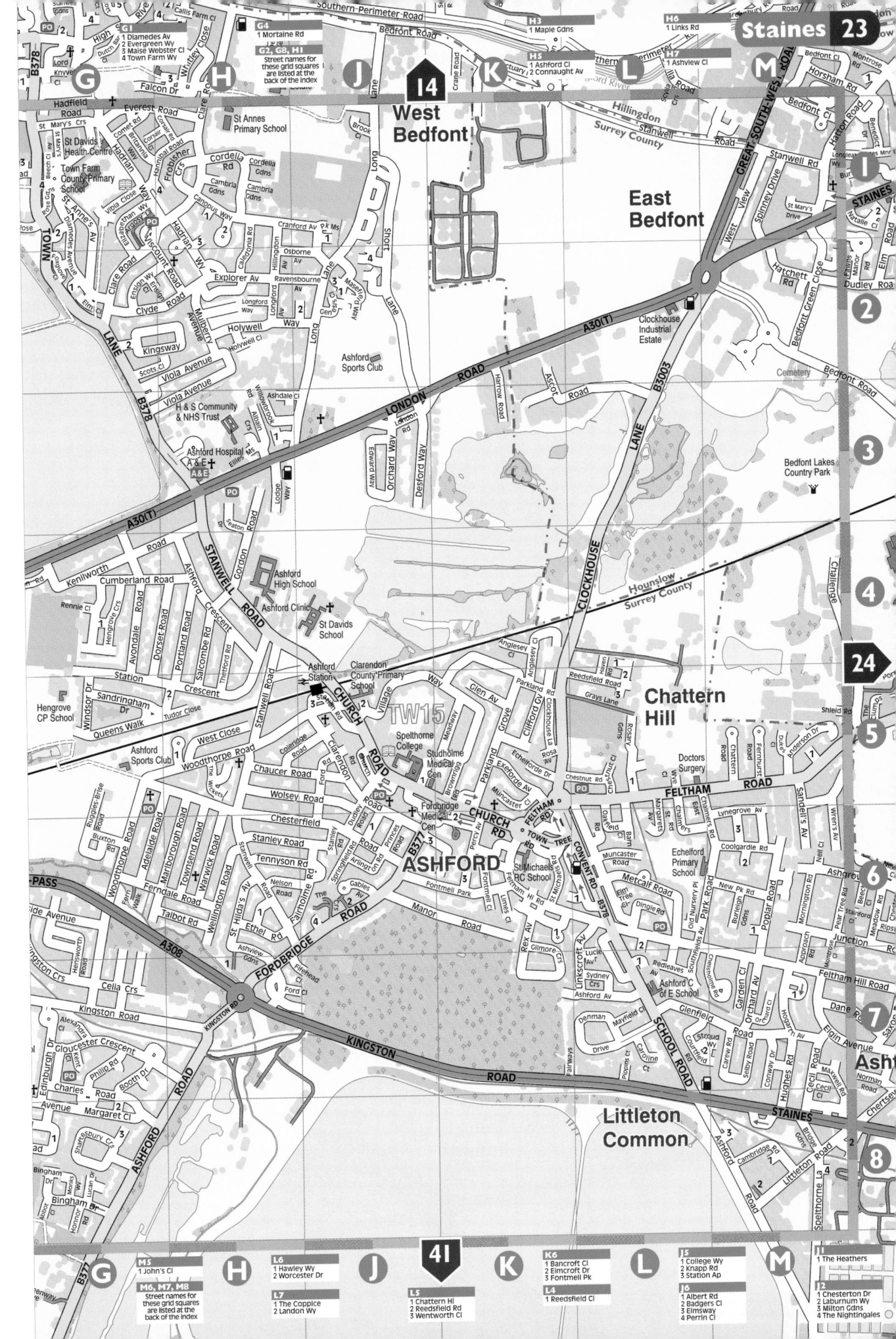

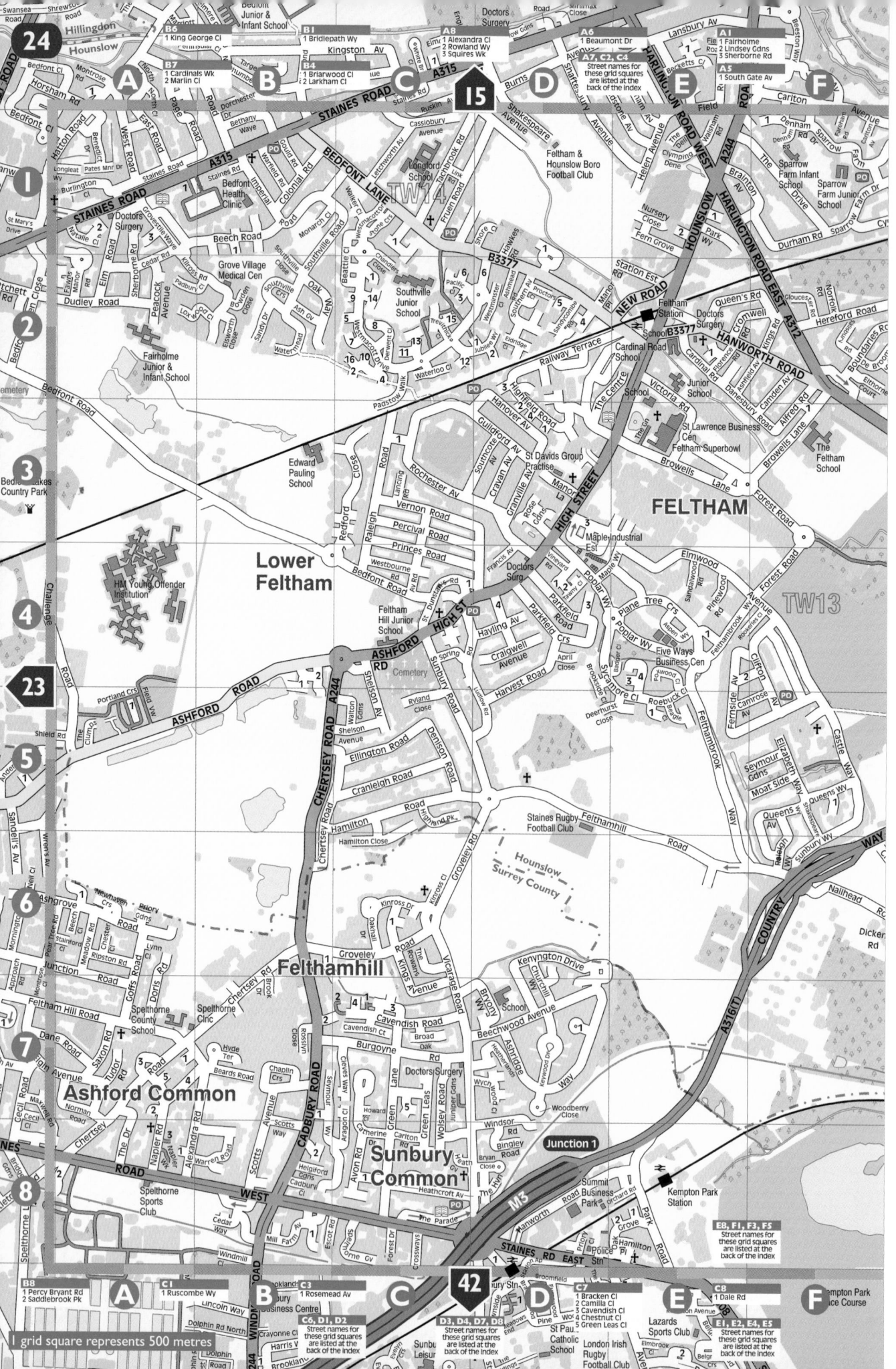

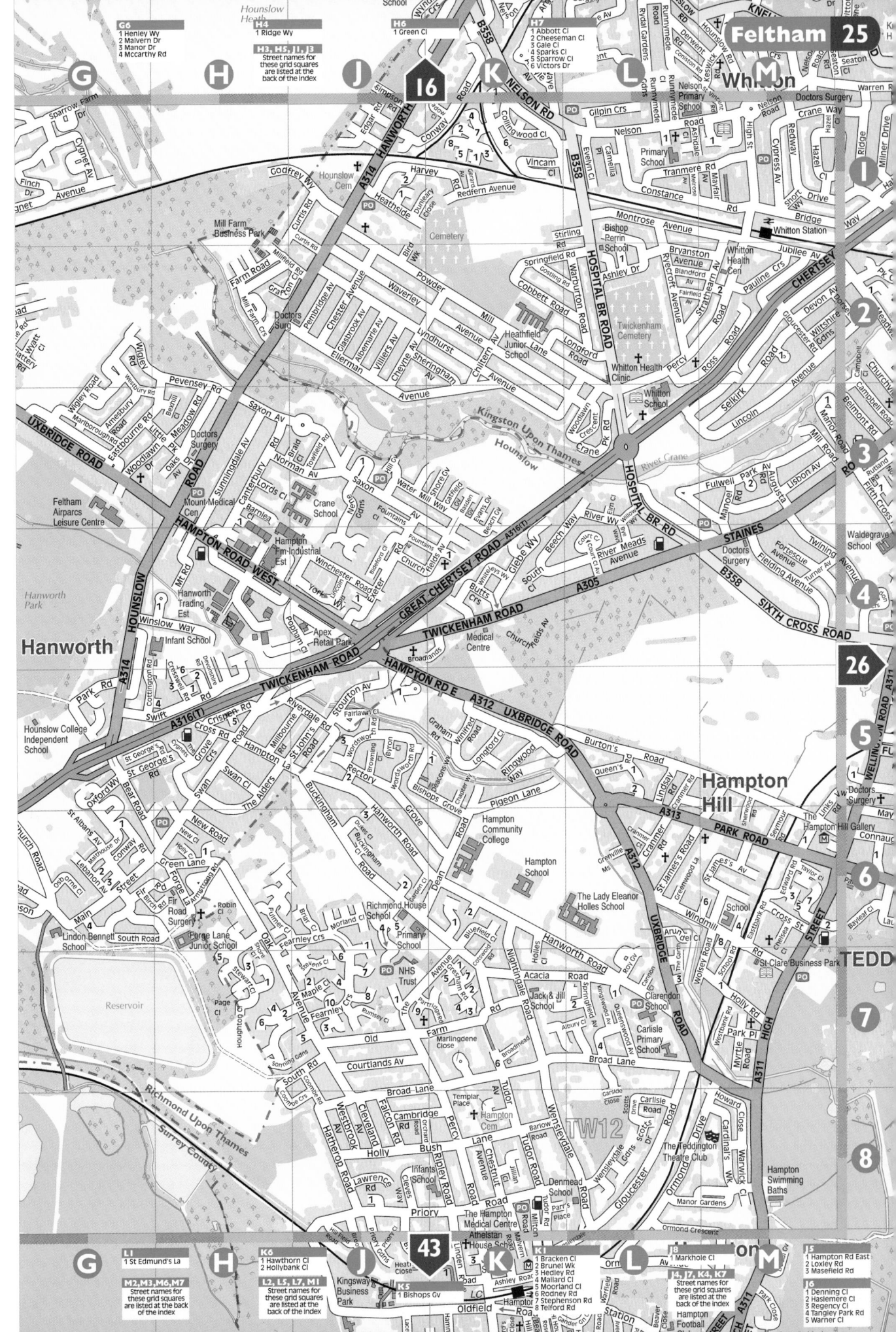

Hanworth

Hampton Hill

TEDD

TW12

16

26

43

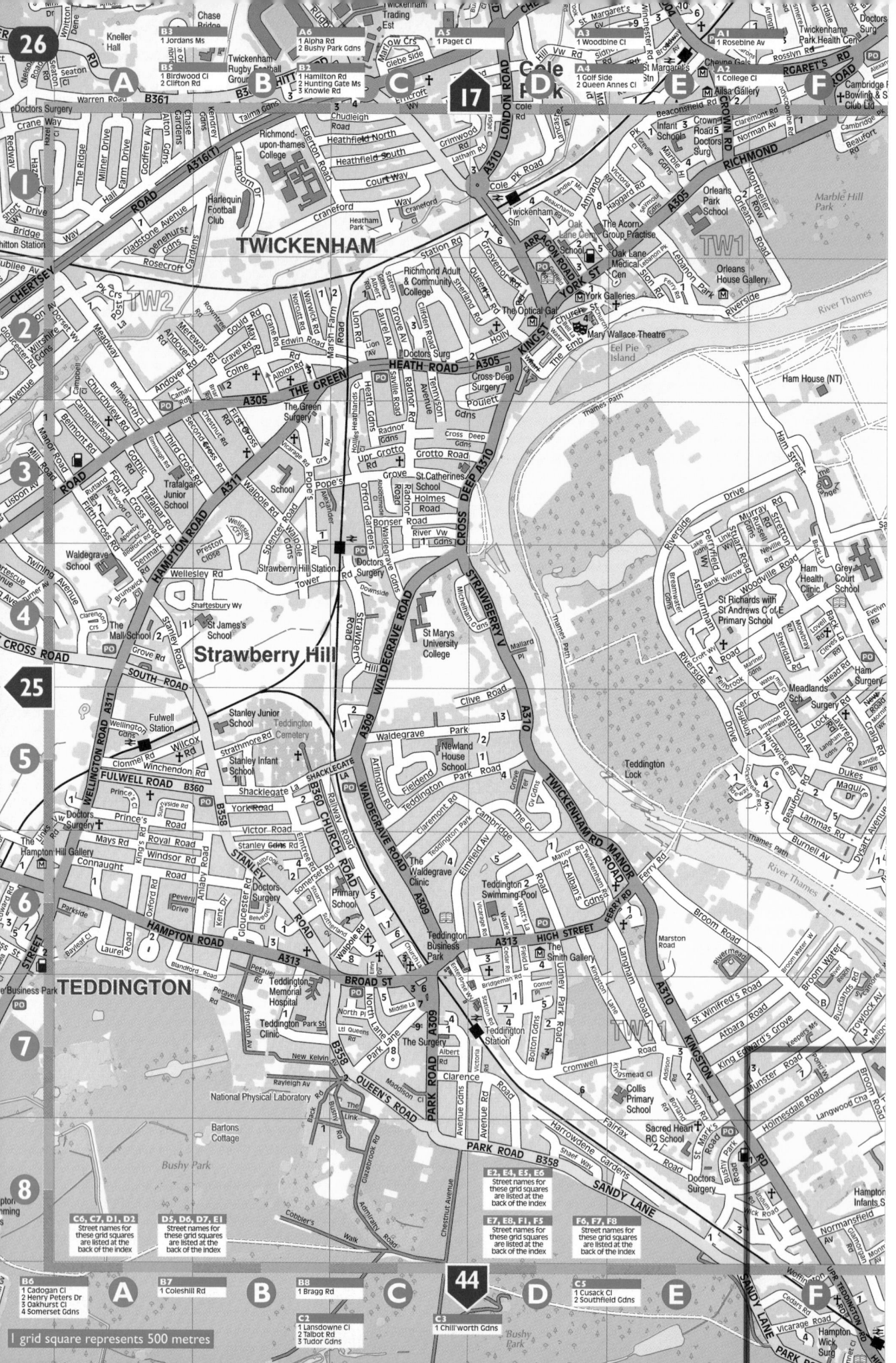

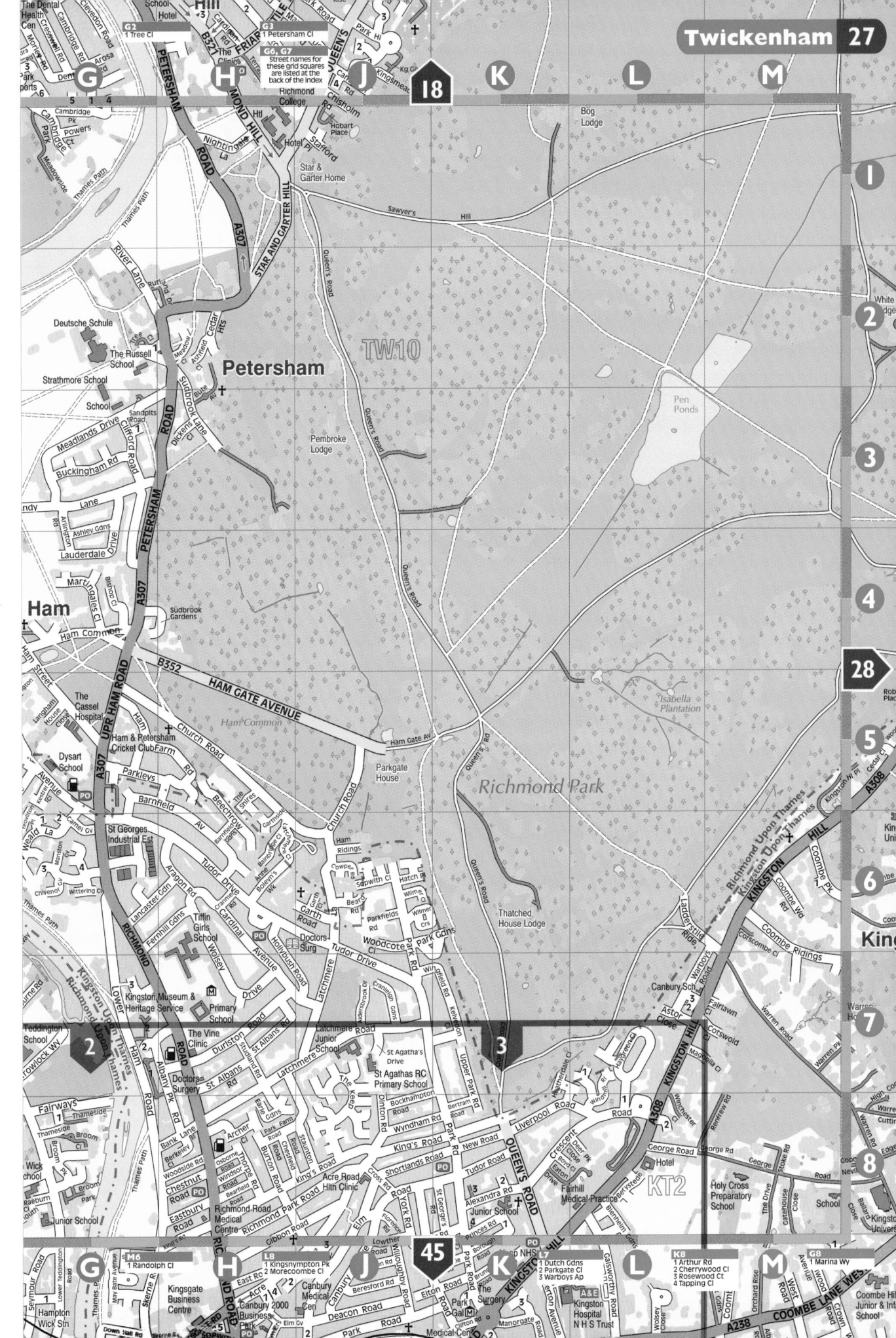

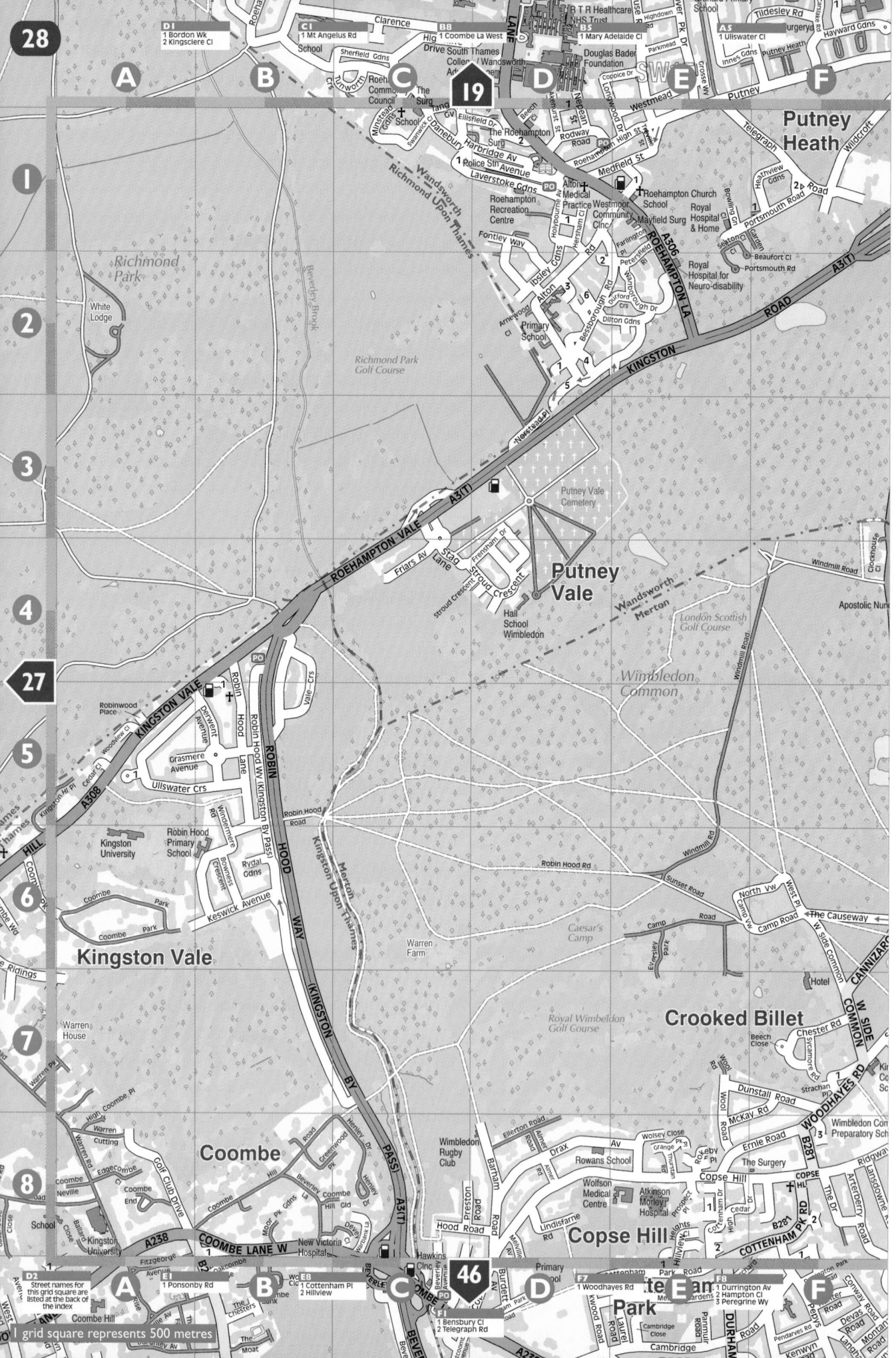

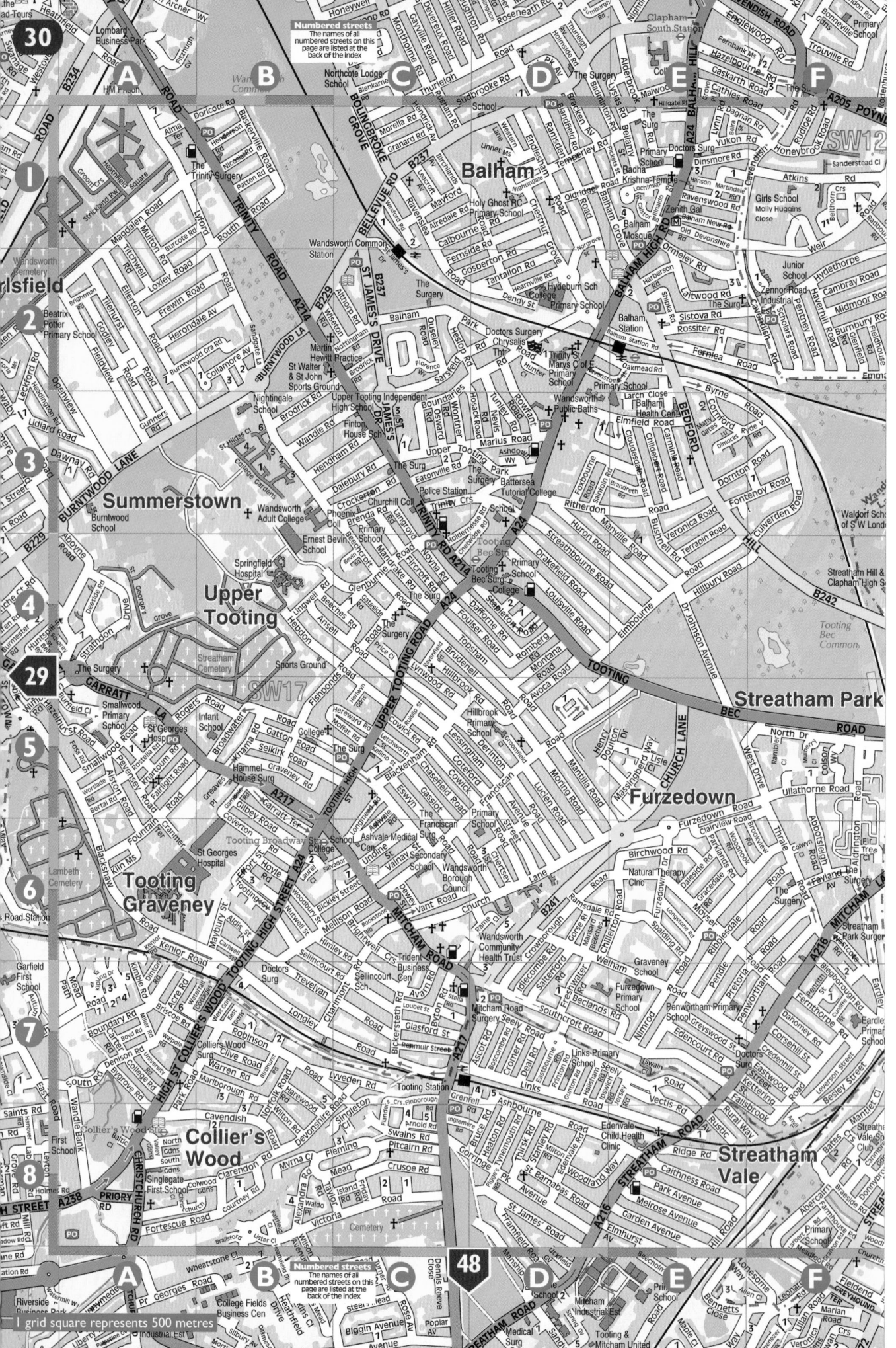

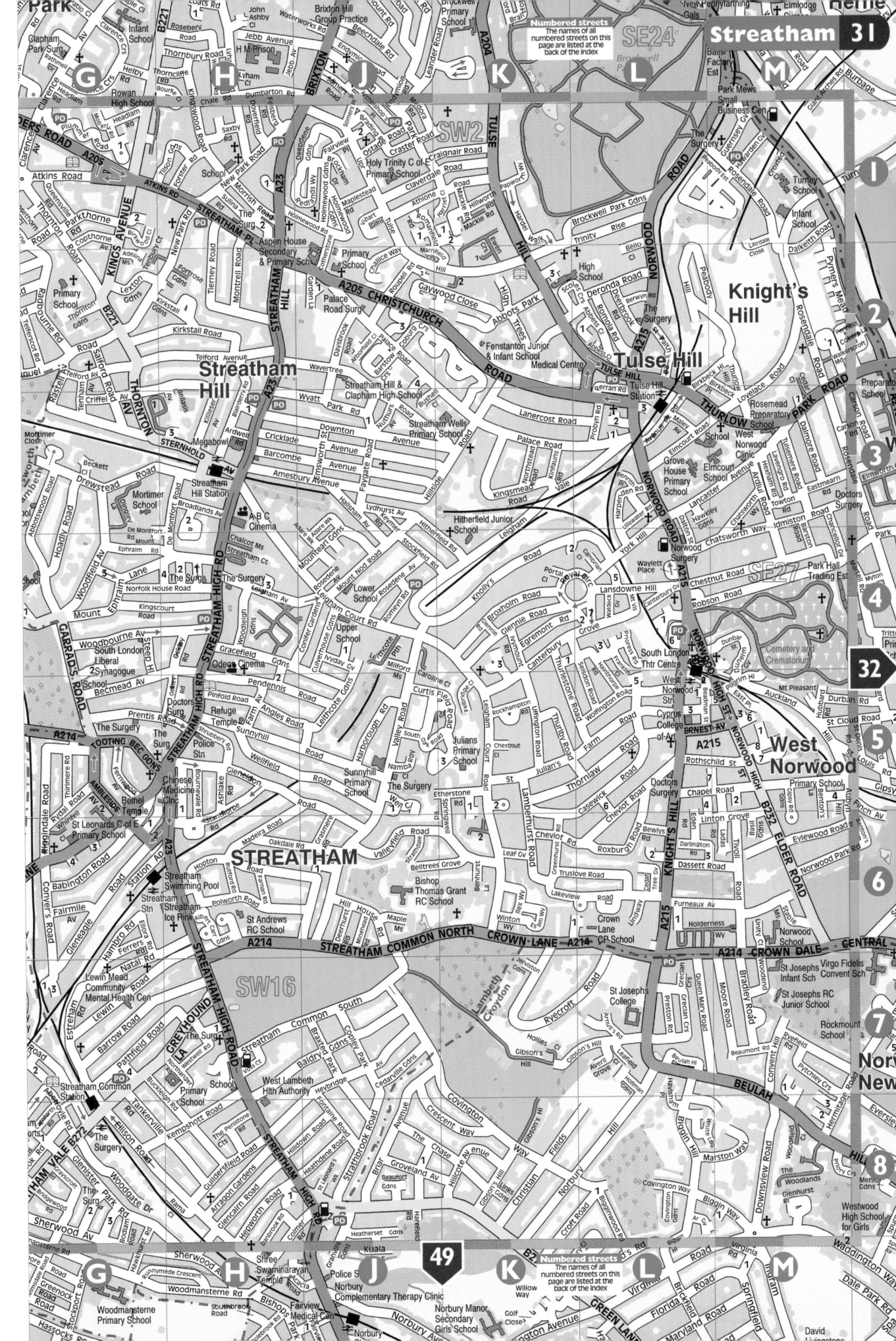

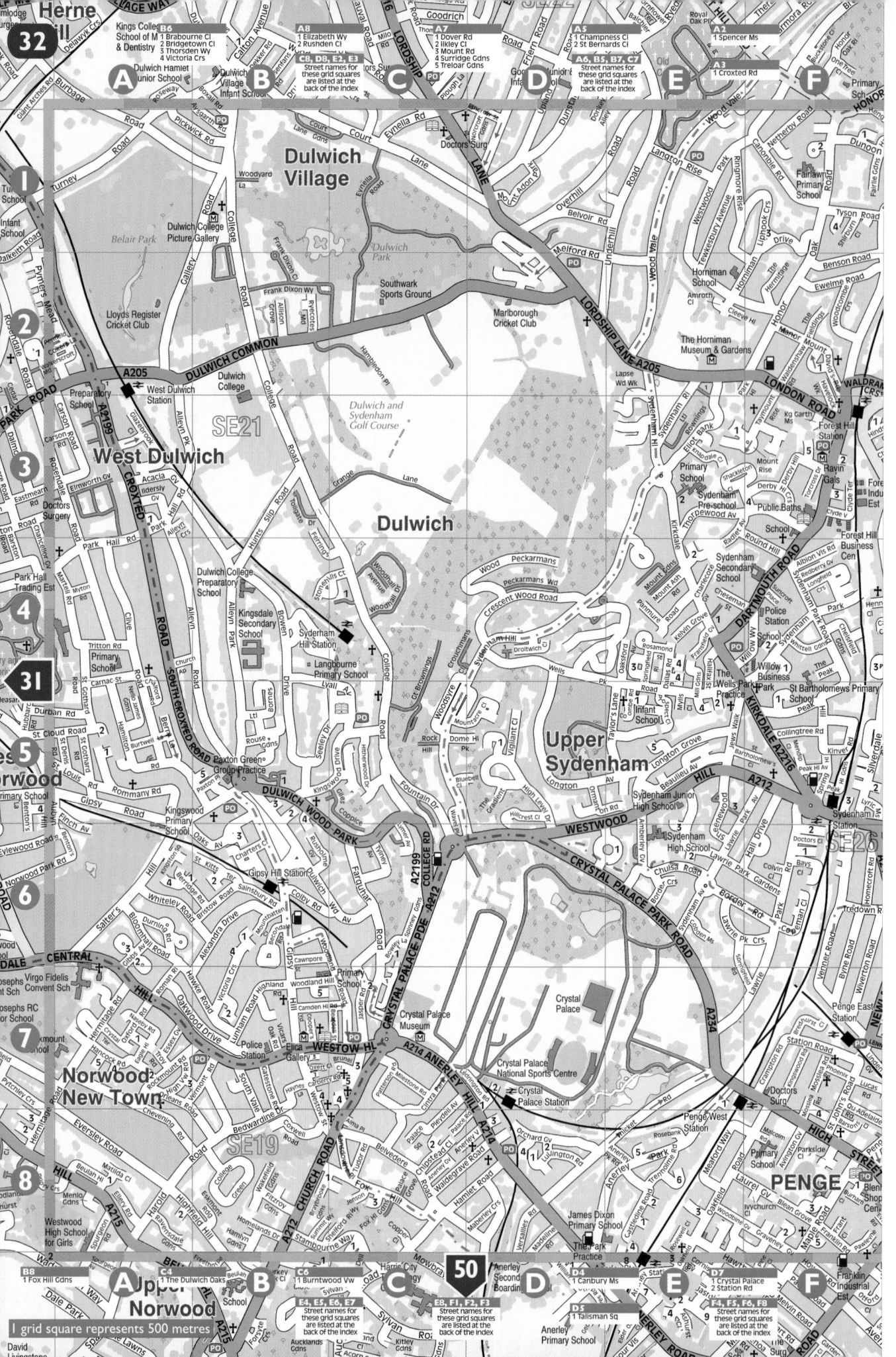

Herne Hill

Kings College B6
School of M & Dentistry
1 Brabourne Cl
2 Bridgetown Cl
3 Thorsden Wy
4 Victoria Crs

A8
1 Elizabeth Wy
2 Rushden Cl

C8, D8, E2, E3
Street names for these grid squares are listed at the back of the index

A7
1 Dover Rd
2 Ilkley Cl
3 Mount Rd
4 Surridge Gdns
5 Treloar Gdns

A5
1 Champness Cl
2 St Bernards Cl

A2
1 Spencer Ms

A6, B5, B7, C7
Street names for these grid squares are listed at the back of the index

A3
1 Croxted Rd

Dulwich Village

West Dulwich

SE21

Dulwich

Upper Sydenham

SE26

Norwood New Town

SE19

PENGE

Upper Norwood

B8
1 Fox Hill Gdns

C4
1 The Dulwich Oaks

C6
1 Burntwood Vw

E4, E5, E6, E7
Street names for these grid squares are listed at the back of the index

E8, F1, F2, F3
Street names for these grid squares are listed at the back of the index

D4
1 Canbury Ms

D7
1 Crystal Palace
2 Station Rd

D5
1 Talisman Sq

E4, F5, F6, F7, F8
Street names for these grid squares are listed at the back of the index

I grid square represents 500 metres

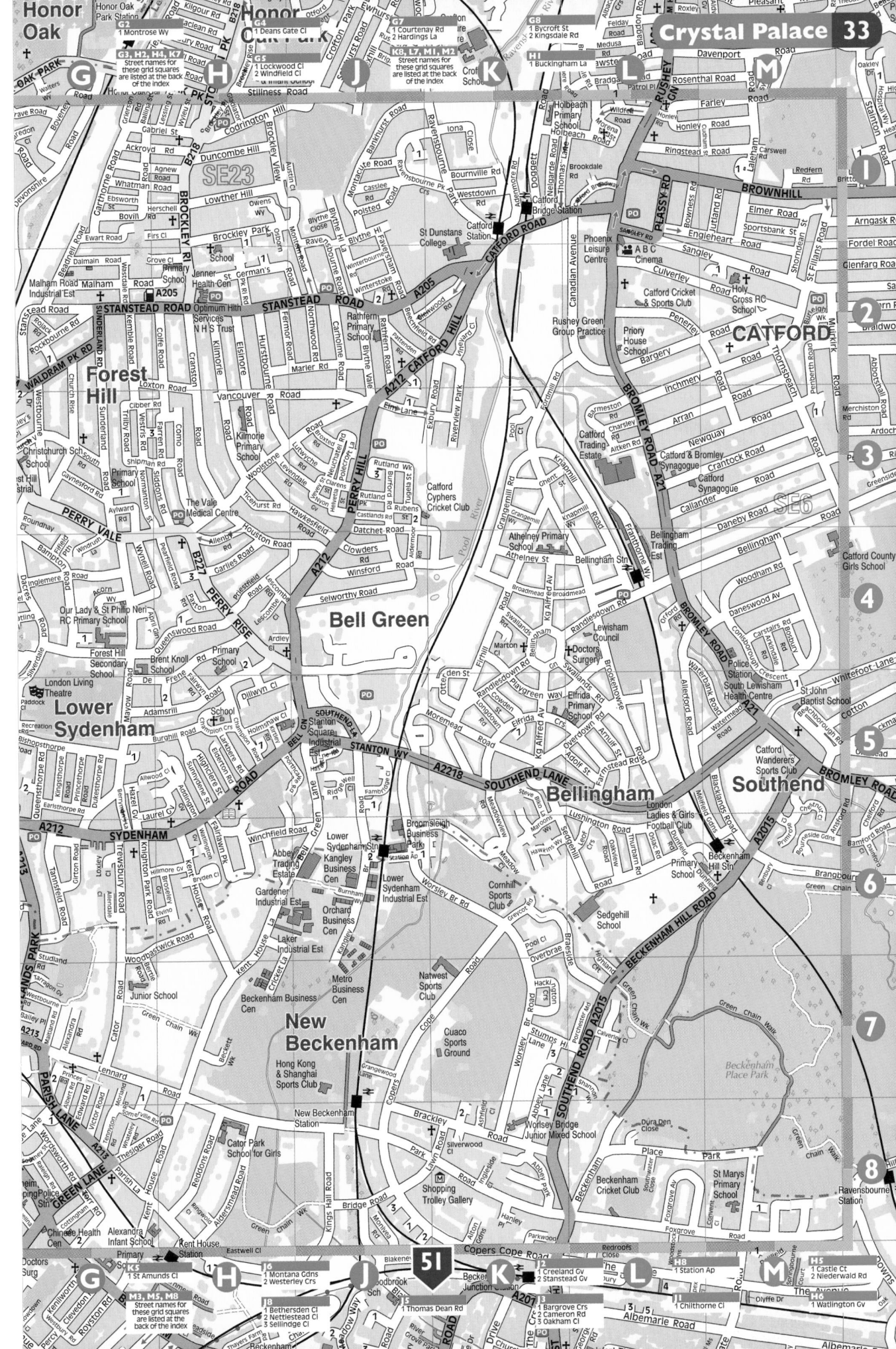

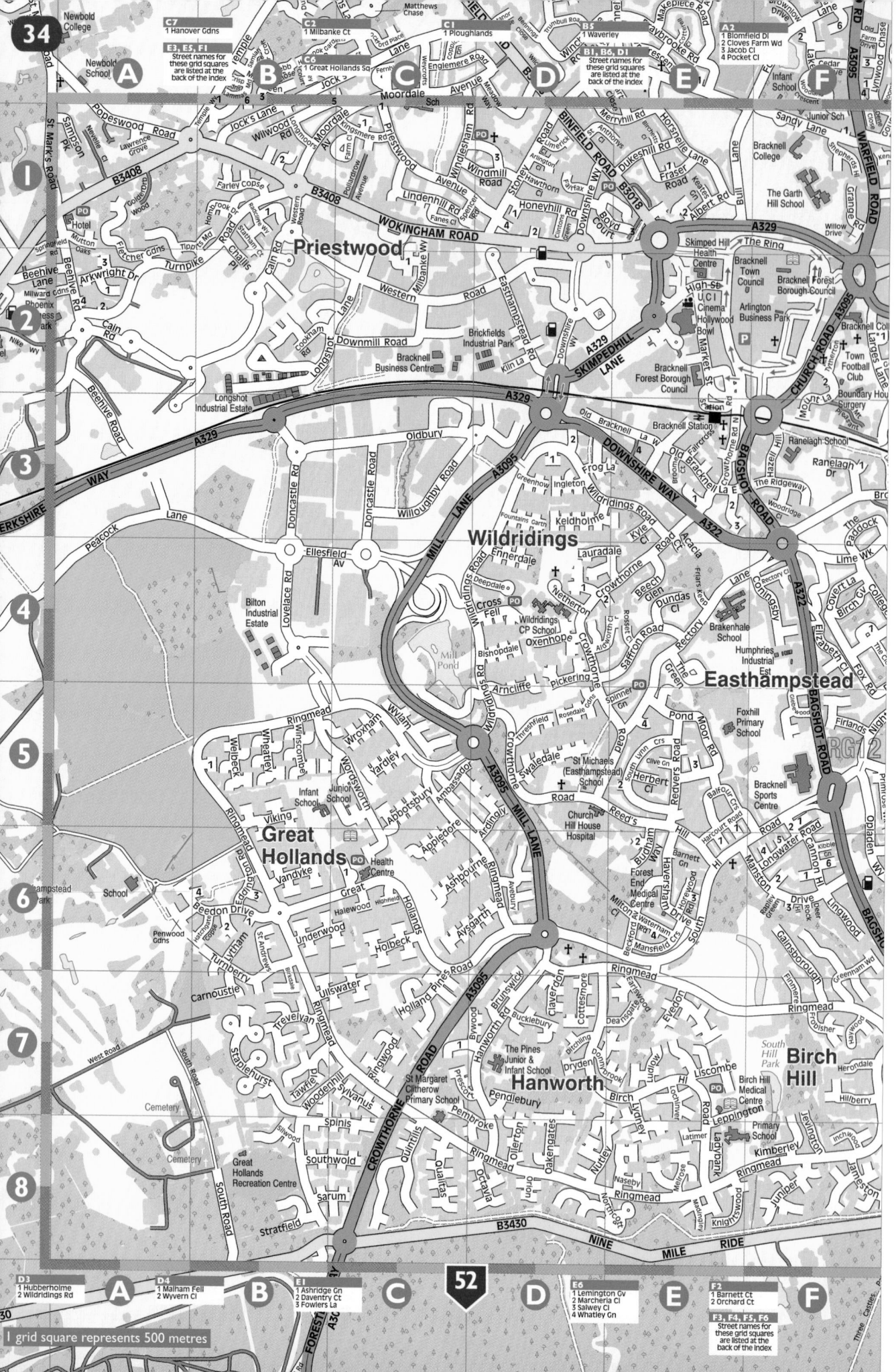

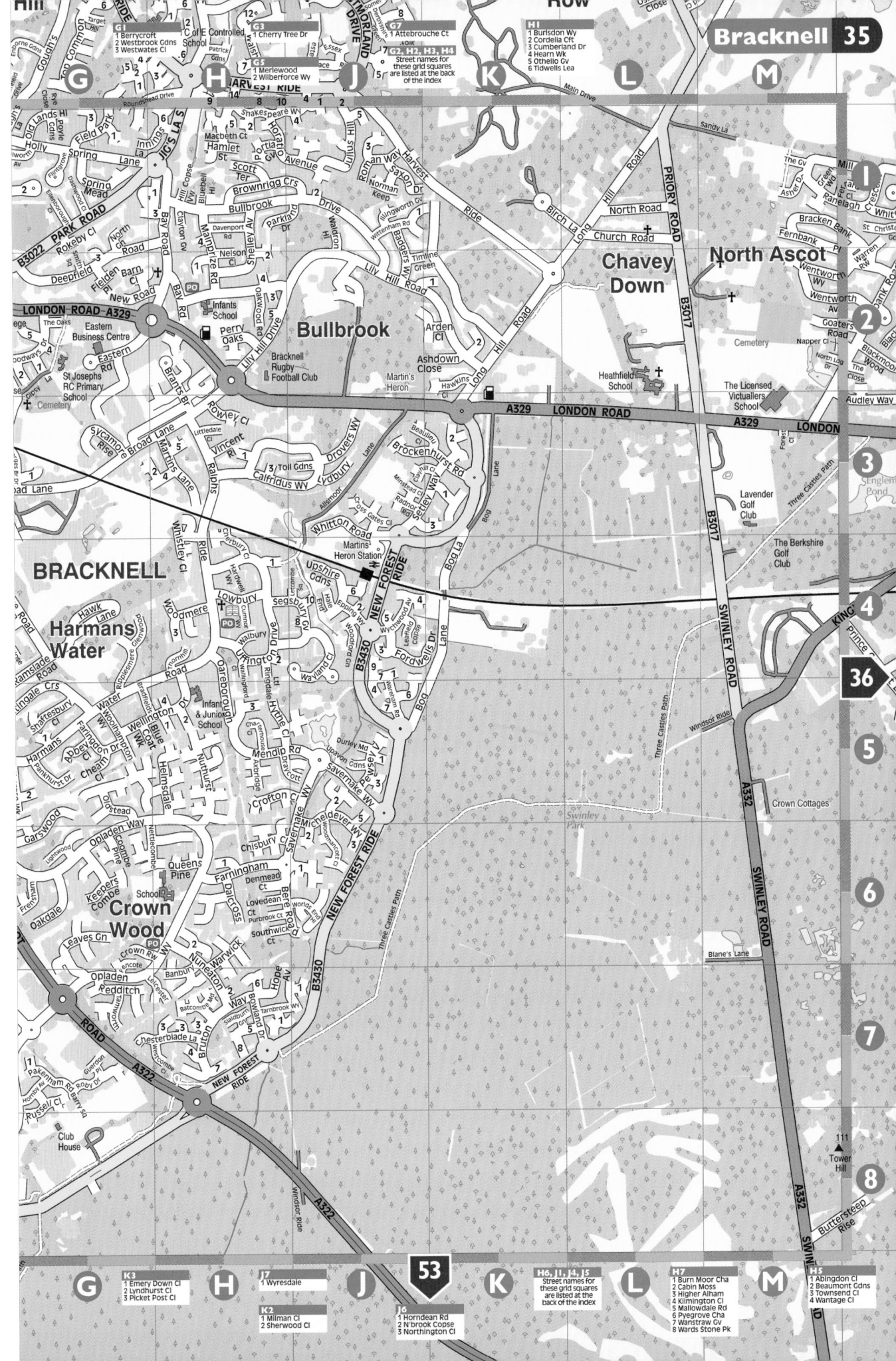

G1
1 Berrycroft
2 Westbrook Gdns
3 Westwates Cl

G3
1 Cherry Tree Dr

G7
1 Attebrouche Ct

H1
1 Burisdon Wy
2 Cordelia Cft
3 Cumberland Dr
4 Hearn Wk
5 Othello Gv
6 Tidwells Lea

G5
1 Merlewood Wy
2 Wilberforce Wy

G2, H2, H3, H4
Street names for
these grid squares
are listed at the back
of the index

G
H
J
K
L
M

North Ascot

Chavey
Down

Bullbrook

BRACKNELL

Harmans
Water

Crown
Wood

LONDON ROAD A329

A329 LONDON ROAD

A329 LONDON

36

53

G
H
J
K
L
M

K3
1 Emery Down Cl
2 Lyndhurst Cl
3 Picket Post Cl

J7
1 Wyresdale

H6, J1, J4, J5
Street names for
these grid squares
are listed at the
back of the index

H7
1 Burn Moor Cha
2 Cabin Moss
3 Higher Alham
4 Kilmington Cl
5 Mallowdale Rd
6 Pyegrove Cha
7 Wanstraw Gv
8 Wards Stone Pk

H5
1 Abingdon Cl
2 Beaumont Gdns
3 Townsend Cl
4 Wantage Cl

K2
1 Milman Cl
2 Sherwood Cl

J6
1 Horndean Rd
2 N'brook Copse
3 Northington Cl

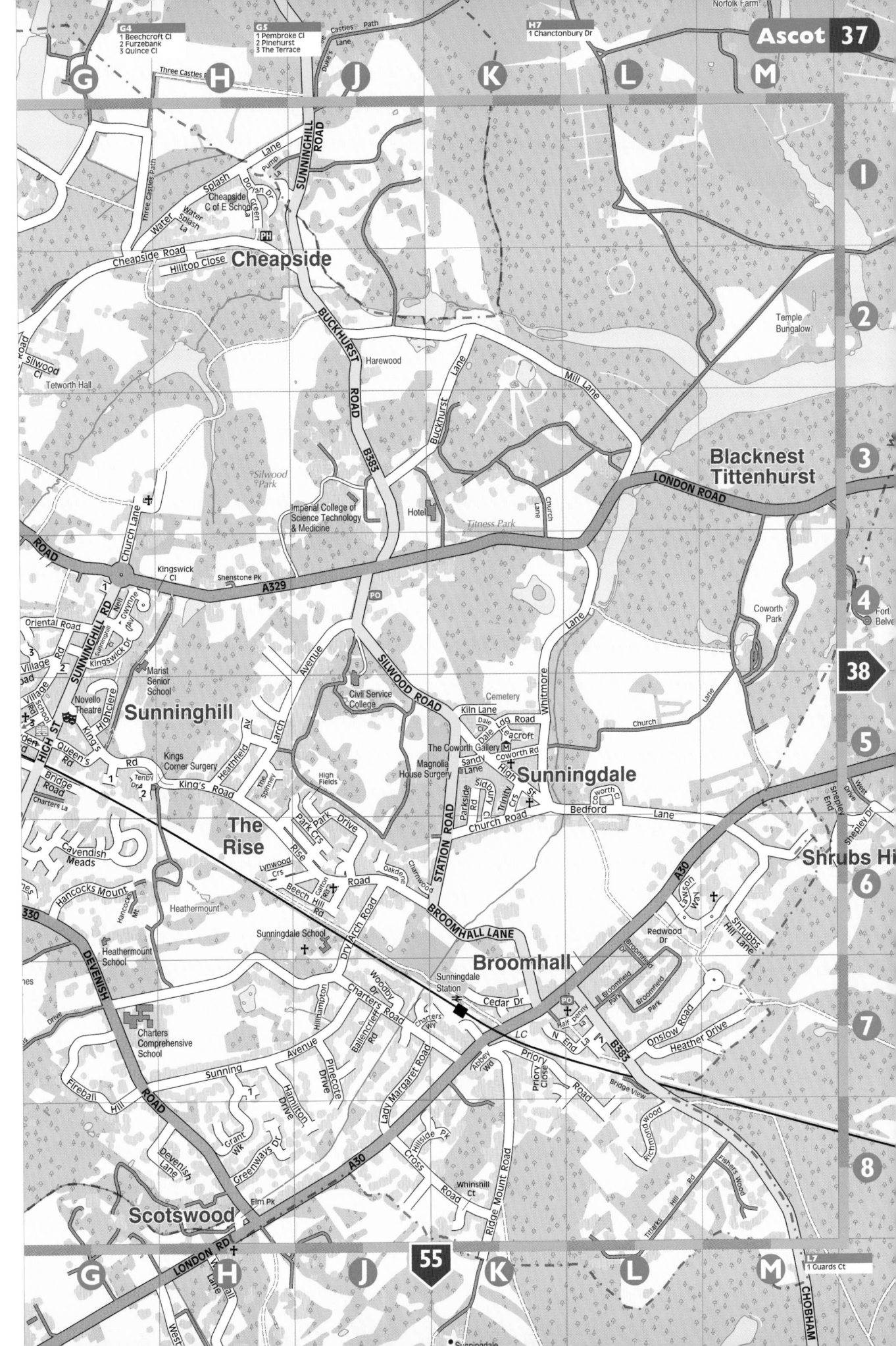

G4
1 Beechcroft Cl
2 Furzebank
3 Quince Cl

G5
1 Pembroke Cl
2 Pinehurst
3 The Terrace

H7
1 Chanctonbury Dr

Norfolk Farm

G **H** **J** **K** **L** **M**

1

Three Castles Path

Castles Path
Dukes Lane

Splash

Pump Lane

Donan Dr
Green Dr

Cheapside
C of E School

Water Splash La

Water La

PH

Cheapside

Cheapside Road

Hilltop Close

Silwood Cl

Tetworth Hall

SUNNINGHILL ROAD

2

Temple Bungalow

Harewood

BUCKHURST ROAD B383

Buckhurst Lane

Mill Lane

LONDON ROAD

Blacknest
Tittenhurst

3

Silwood Park

Imperial College of
Science Technology
& Medicine

Hotel

Titness Park

Church Lane

Coworth Park

Fort Belve

4

CHURCH ROAD

ROAD

Church Lane

Kingswick Cl

Shenstone Pk

A329

PO

Oriental Road

Village Road

SUNNINGHILL RD

Nell Gwynne

Kingswick Dr

Marist Senior School

Highclere

King's Rd

Sunninghill

Avenue

SILWOOD ROAD

Civil Service College

Cemetery

Kiln Lane

Dale Ldg Road

Dale La

Whitmore Lane

Church Lane

38

Novello Theatre

HIGH ST

Queen's Rd

Tenby Dr

King's Road

Kings Corner Surgery

Heathfield Av

Larch Av

The Spinney

High Fields

The Coworth Gallery

Magnolia House Surgery

Sandy Lane

Seacroft

Coworth Rd

Sidbury High St

Trinity Crs

Sunningdale

Church

5

Cavendish Meads

Bridge Road

Charters La

The Rise

Park Crs

Rise

Lynwood Crs

Galton Rd

Beech Hill Rd

Park Drive

Road

Oakdene

Charnwood

STATION ROAD

Parkside Rd

Church Road

Bedford Lane

Coworth Cl

Shepley End

Shepley Dr

West

Shrubs Hi

6

B330

Hancocks Mount

Hancocks Mt

Heathermount

DEVENISH

Heathermount School

Sunningdale School

Dry Arch Road

BROOMHALL LANE

Broomhall

Sunningdale Station

Cedar Dr

LC

Lawson Way

Redwood Dr

Broomfield Park

Broomfield Park

Shrubbs Hill Lane

A30

7

Charters Comprehensive School

Fireball Hill

Devenish Lane

ROAD

Sunning Avenue

Grant Wk

Greenways Dr

Elm Pk

Hamilton Drive

Pinecote Drive

Hillhampton

Charters Road

Ballencrieff Rd

Charters Wy

Appley Wd

N End La

Half penny La

PO

Priory Close

Priory Road

Bridge View

Onslow Road

Heather Drive

Richmondwood

B383

8

Scotswood

LONDON RD

Hillside Pk

A30

Lady Margaret Road

Cross

Whinshill Ct

Ridge Mount Road

Fishers Wood

Titlarks Hill Rd

1 Guards Ct

CHOBHAM

G **H** **J** **K** **L** **M**

Sunningdale

I

2

3

4

5

6

7

8

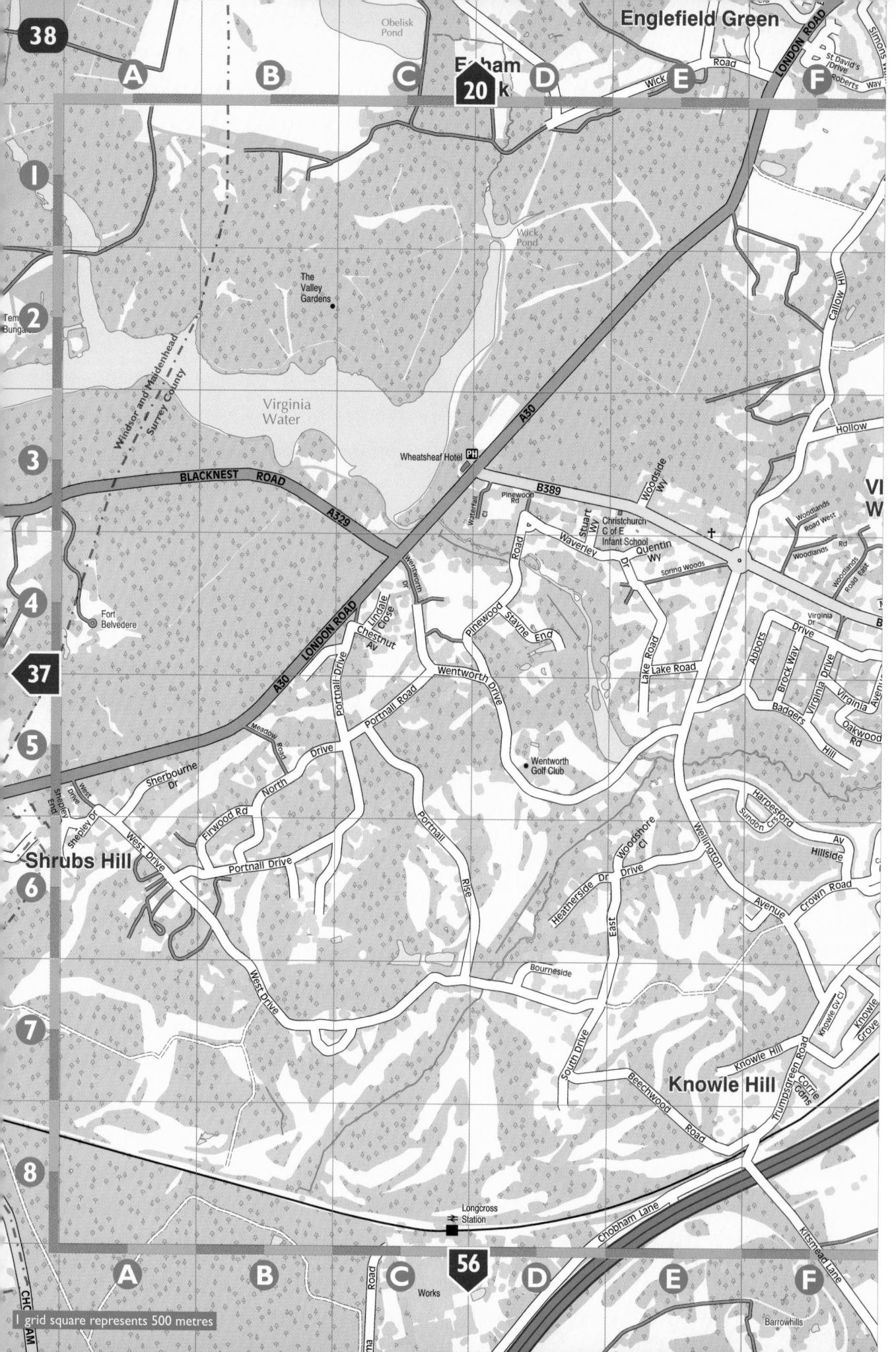

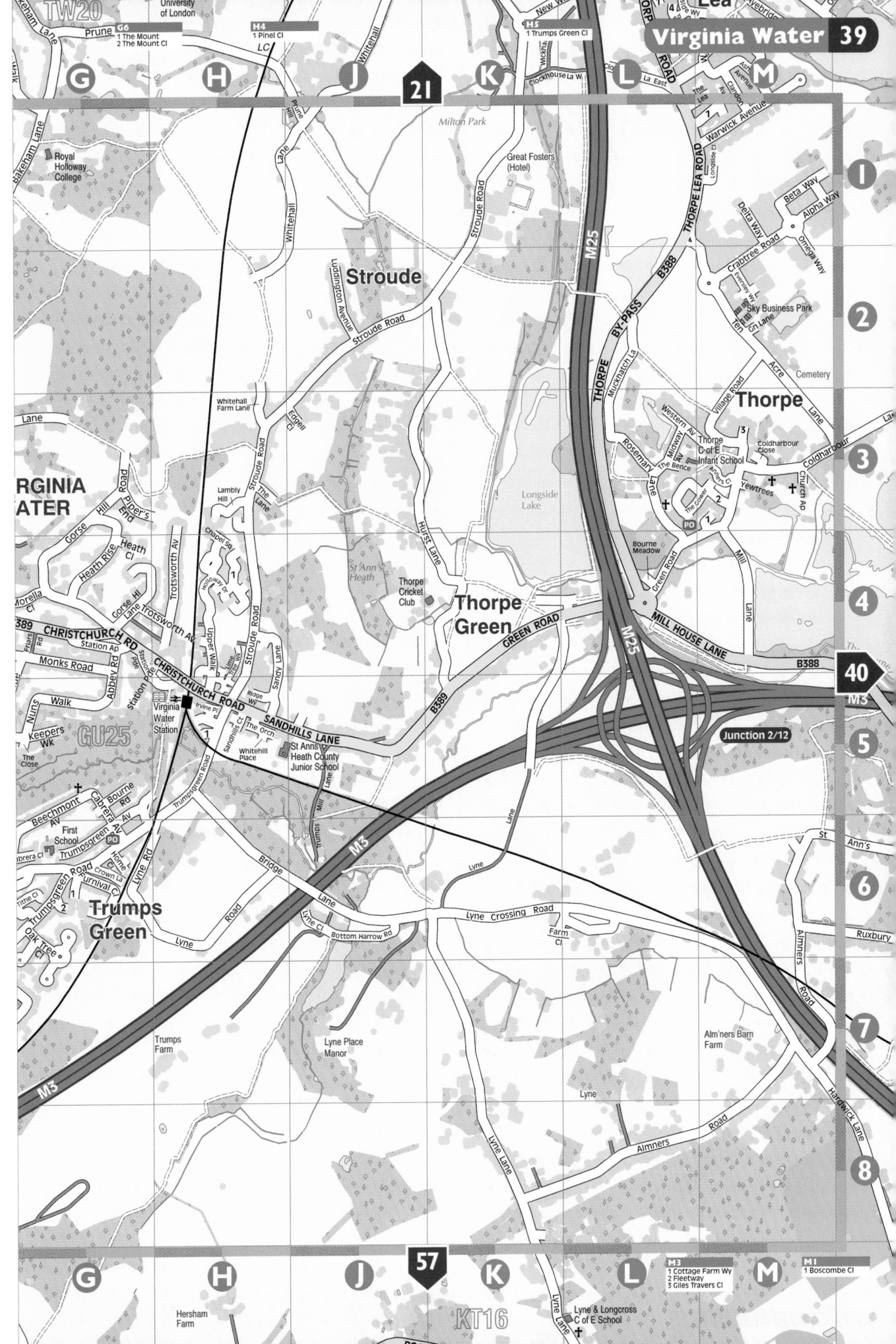

TW20

University of London

G6
1 The Mount
2 The Mount Cl

H4
1 Pinel Cl

LC

H5
1 Trumps Green Cl

New Wa

Lea

Ave

M

Prune

keham Lane

Prune

Whitehall

wickha

Clockhouse La Wy

ROAD

La East

Ash

Warwick Avenue

7

Beta Way

Alpha Way

THORPE LEA ROAD

Delta Way

Crabtree Road

Omega Way

1

2

Milton Park

Royal Holloway College

Great Fosters (Hotel)

B388

Sky Business Park

Stroude

Luddington Avenue

Stroude Road

M25

THORPE BY-PASS

Mucknatch La

Ten

Gn Lane

Acre

Cemetery

Thorpe

3

Whitehall Farm Lane

Edgell Cl

Longside Lake

Western Av

Midway

Village Road

Thorpe C of E Infant School

3

Coldharbour Close

Coldharbour

La

RGINIA ATER

Corse Hill

Piper's End

Heath Rise

Stroude Road

Lambly Hill

The Lane

Rosemary La

The Bence

Arbors Cl

Yewtrees

Church Ap

4

Heath Cl

Chapel Sq

Hurst Lane

St Ann's Heath

Thorpe Cricket Club

Thorpe Green

Green Road

The Tower

2

1

PO

Bourne Meadow

Mill

MILL HOUSE LANE

B388

40
M3

Morella Cl

B389

Friars Rd

CHRISTCHURCH RD

Station Ap

Trotsworth Av

Holloway Dr

1

Upper Walk

Stroude Road

Sandy Lane

GREEN ROAD

B389

M25

Junction 2/12

5

Monks Road

Abbey Rd

Nuns Walk

Keepers Wk

GU25

Station Rd

Virginia Water Station

CHRISTCHURCH ROAD

Irvine Pl

Ridge Wy

Sandhills Ct

The Orch

SANDHILLS LANE

Whitehill Place

St Anns Heath County Junior School

Mill Lane

Lane

St Ann's

Ruxbury

6

The Close

Beechmont Av

Cabrera Av

Bourne Rd

First School

Cabrera Cl

Trumpsgreen Road

PO

Home La

Crown La

Furnival Av

1

Lyne Rd

Trumpsgreen Road

Bridge Lane

Lyne Cl

Bottom Harrow Rd

Lyne Crossing Road

Almners Road

Hardwick Lane

7

Trees Cl

Oak Tree Cl

Trumps Green

Lyne

Lyne Lane

Farm Cl

Alm'ners Barn Farm

8

Trumps Farm

M3

Lyne Place Manor

Lyne

Lyne Lane

Almners Road

G

H

J

57

K

L

M1
1 Boscombe Cl

M

M

1 Cottage Farm Wy
2 Fleetway
3 Giles Travers Cl

Hersham Farm

KT16

Lyne & Longcross C of E School

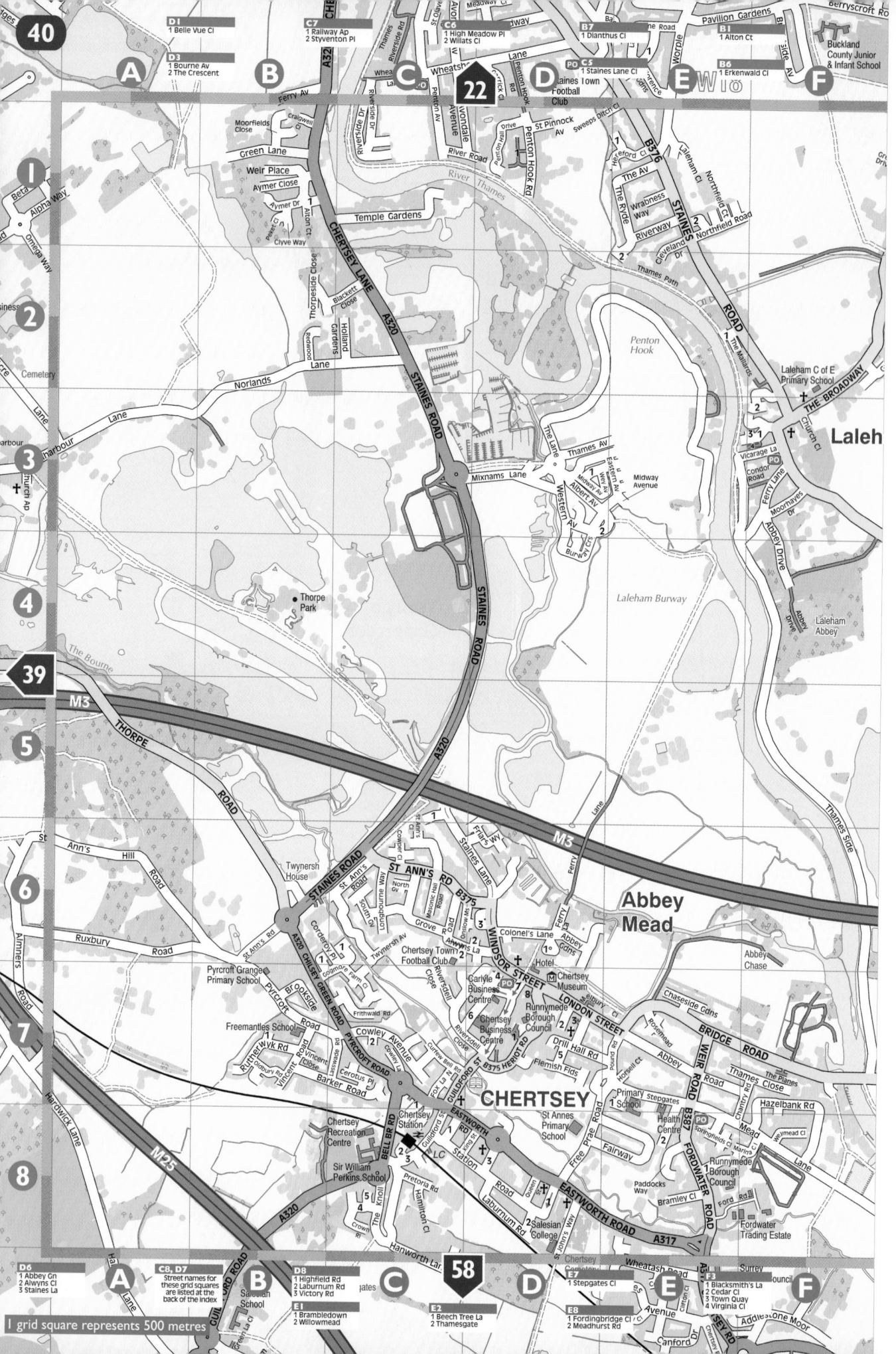

I grid square represents 500 metres

H3
1 Astleham Wy

J3
1 Goddard Cl
2 Wilcox Gdns

K4
1 Barley Mow Wy
2 Burbidge Rd
3 Ford Cl

K5
1 Pool End Cl
2 Roseacre Cl
3 Thornhill Wy

G   H   J   **23**   K   L   M

I

Queen Mary Reservoir

2 Charlt

3

ASHFORD ROAD B377

Greenway Tree

Grange Pl

am

Duggan Wy
Lion Cl
Kordas Cl
Studios Road
Studios Road
Hitchcock Cl
Magdalene Road
Rectory Close

Littleton Church of England Infant School

Littleton

New Road

Chariton

Hetherington Road
Walnut Tree Rd
Almond Close
Walnut Tree Road
Chariton Road
PO

Bingham Dr
Monks Wy
Honnor Rd
Lucan Dr
Talbot

Bridge Road
Stewart Av
Ash Road
Hermitage Close
Horne Road
Winchstone Cl
Squire's
Squire's Road
Cranwell Grove

Stewart Rd
Elliott Gdns
Glen Close
Francis Cl
Wood Road
Petts La
Waterspalsh

Nutty La

Chariton Lane

4

SHEPPERTON ROAD B376

Laleham Rd
Milton Dr
Ashurst Drive
Laleham Rd
Bravington Cl
Fairview Dr
Rosewood Dr
Briar Road
Bush Rd
Saxon CP School

LALEHAM
Wright Gdns
PO
Laleham Road
Mandeville Rd
Acacia Av
Preston Rd
Jessiman Ter
Greeno Crescent

Shepperton Green

TW17

ROAD
Tanglyn Av
B376
Pentland Av
Marion Av
Shepperton Hlth Centre

M3

River Ash

42

Lois Drive
Barbara Close
Chariton Crescent
Old Chariton Road
Linden Wy
Rodd Estate

5

Shepperton Business Park
Station Rd
Shepperton Station
Green Lane
B3366 **GREEN LANE**
Kilmiston Av
Richmond Dr
Nell
Green La
Duppas Close

6

Littleton Lane

Sheepwalk

SS School
Shepherds Cl
Barton Cl
Manor Farm Av
St School
St Nicholas C of E JMI School
Grant Rd
Burchetts Wy
HIGH STREET
Glebeland Gdns
Broadlands Avenue
B376
Bruce Avenue
Grove Rd
Manygate

Thamesmead Co Secondary Scho
Gordon Road
Mitre

Shepperton

M3

RENFREE WAY

Mervyn Rd
Wadham
Church Road
Halliford School
RUSSELL
Halliford Close

ROAD Lo
Ha

7

CHERTSEY BRIDGE ROAD
CHERTSEY ROAD B375

Docket Eddy

Chertsey Road

Cemetery
Farm Close
Range Wy
St Nicholas Dr
Desborough Cl
Church Sq
Church Pth
Thames Path

B3

University Rugby Foo

8

Thames Path
Ferry Lane
Park Rd
Abbey Rd
Towpath
PH

Chertsey Meads

River Thames

Walton Lane

Dorney Grove

G   **M6**   H   **M5**   J   **59**   K   **L7**   L   **L6**   M   **L5, M2, M7**

M6
1 Cliveden Pl
2 Copthorne Cl
3 High St
4 Thurlestone Cl

M5
1 Govett Av
2 Green La
3 Station Ap

L7
1 Cemetery La

L6
1 Claremont Dr
2 Mere Rd
3 Old Forge Crs
4 School La
5 Westbury Cl

L5, M2, M7
Street names for these grid squares are listed at the back of the index

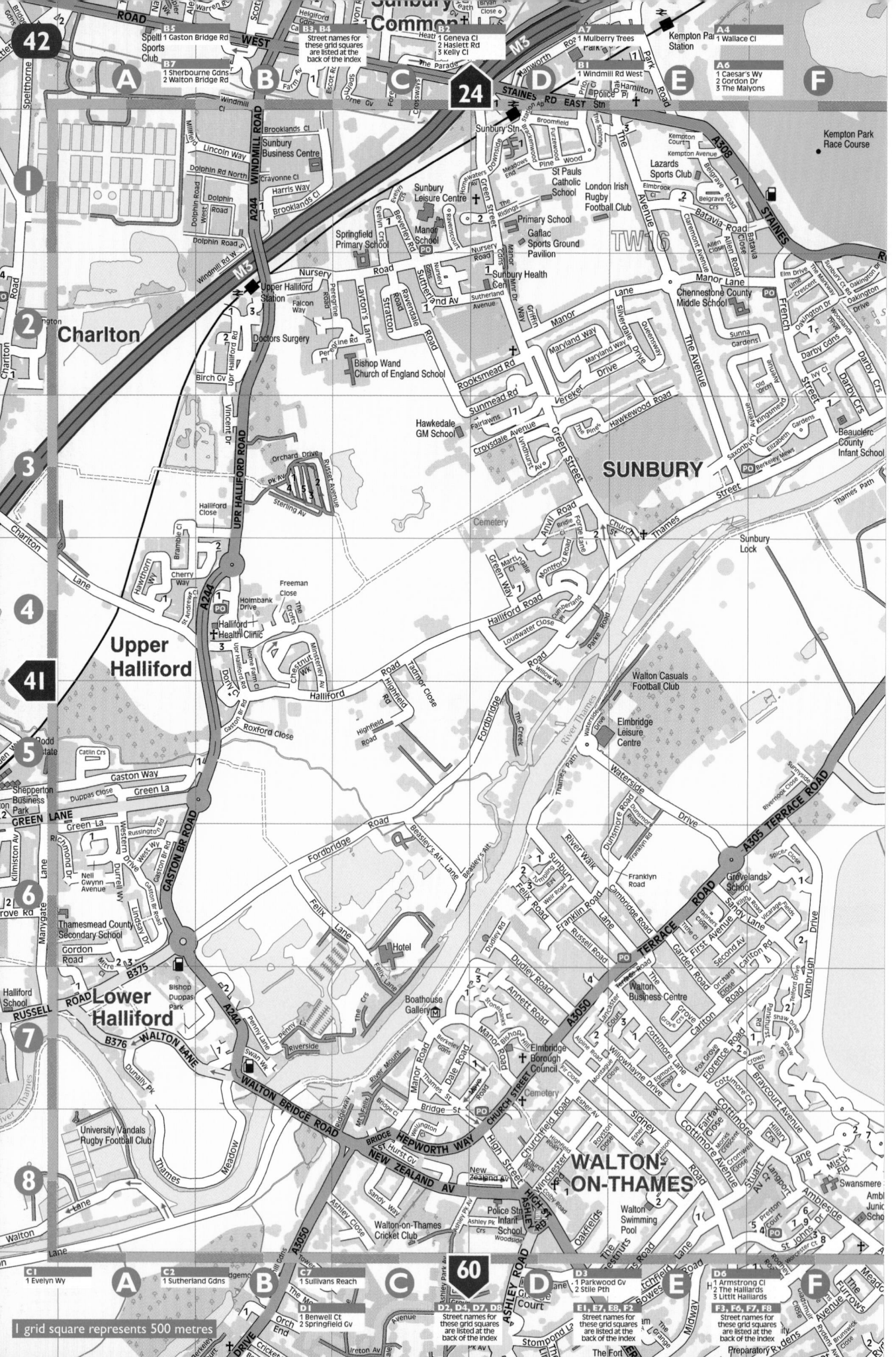

A   B   C   D   E   F

26

I

Bushy Park

Hampton
Wick

2

Hurst
Park

HAMPTON COURT ROAD
A308

East Molesey
Cricket Club

Diana
Fountain

Bushy
Park

HAMPTON COURT

ROAD   A308

3

HURST   ROAD
A3050

Hotel

Hampton
Court Palace

Stud
House

4

KT8

Molesey
Lock

Hotel

RIVERBANK

River Thames

Hampton
Court Station

Thames Path

Hampton
Court
Park

43

St Mary's
Road

East Molesey
Infant School

PO

BRIDGE RD

CREEK RD

HAMPTON CT WAY

LC

5

The Teddington
Theatre Club

Grist Memorial
Sports Club

Old Tiffinians
Sports Ground

Queen's Road

Aragon Avenue

PH

6

Imber Court
Trading Estate

Metropolitan
Police
Football Club

ESHER ROAD
B3379

Broadfields

Orchard Lane

A309

Ennismore Gardens

Summer   Road

St Nicholas Rd

Old School
Sq

Thames
Ditton County
First School

Ashley Rd

Surrey Co
Council

PO

High St

Richmond Upon Thames
Surrey County

Thames Path

Richmond Upon Thames
Kingston Upon Thames

Seething Wells

BRIGHTON

7

EMBER
LANE

B364

St Pauls
RC Primary School

EMBERCOURT ROAD

Thames Ditton Station

Esher College

Thames Ditton
Junior School

STATION ROAD

WATTS ROAD

KT7

Giggs
Hill
Surgery

GIGGS HILL RD

Thames
Ditton

Giggshill

PORTSMOUTH ROAD

Kingston
Liberal
Synagogue

Westville Rd

Southville Road

St Mary's C of E
Primary School

8

Ember Sports
Club

B3379   EMBER LANE   STATION ROAD

A309

Weston
Green

PO

Weston
Green Road

Portsmouth Road

A307

Long
Ditton

A   B   C   D   E   F

Esher
Station

Hinchley Wood
Secondary School

I grid square represents 500 metres

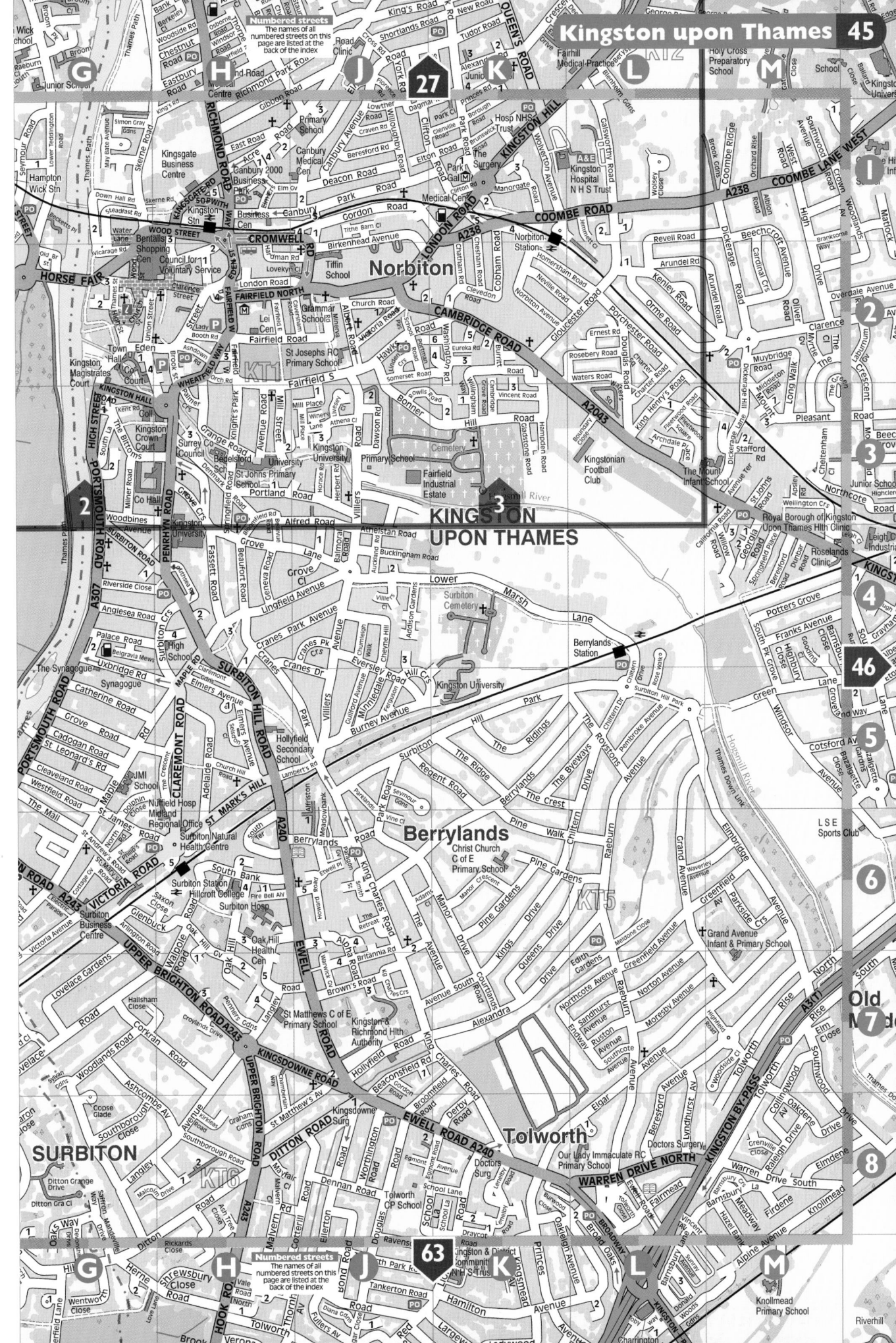

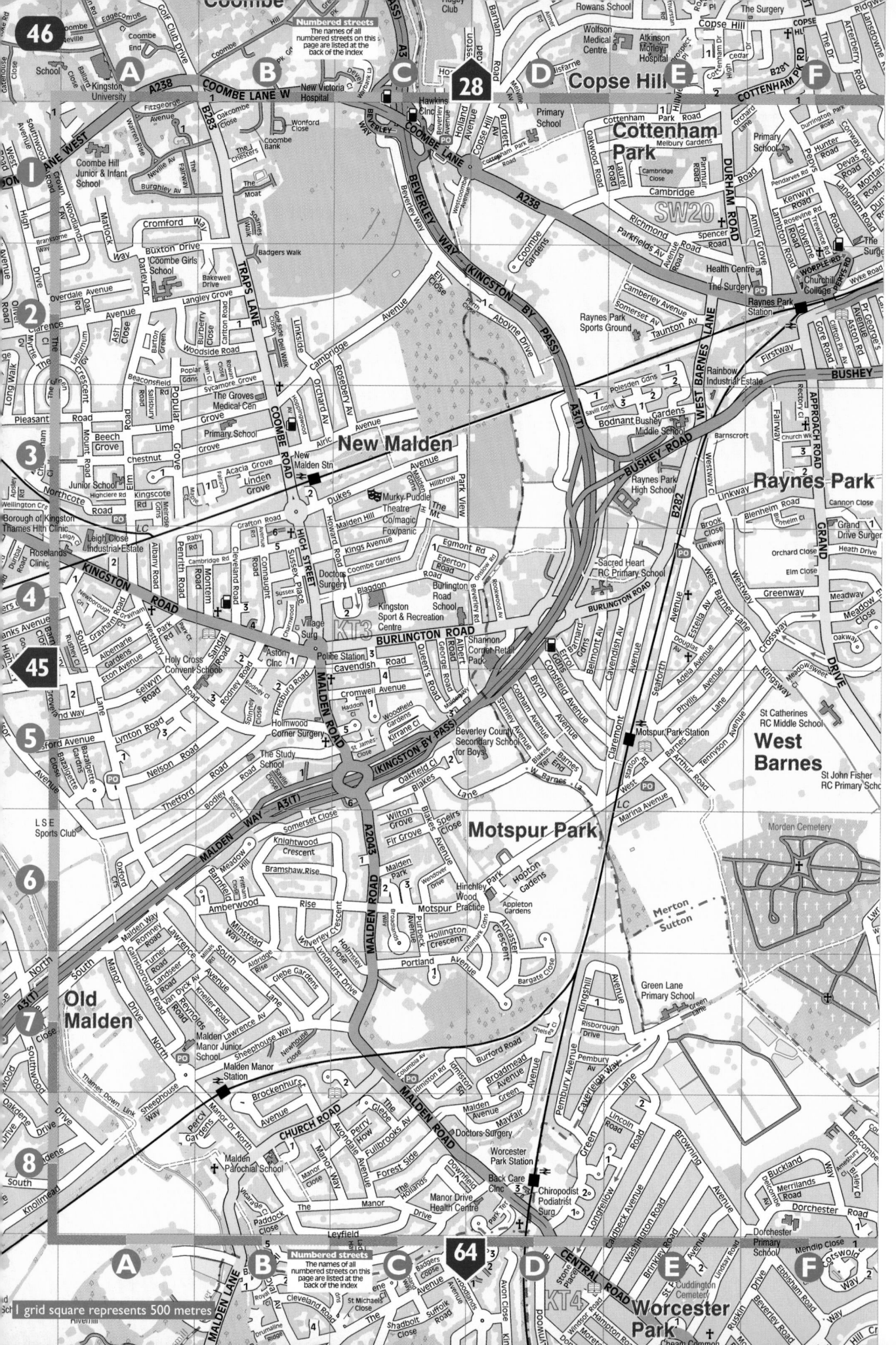

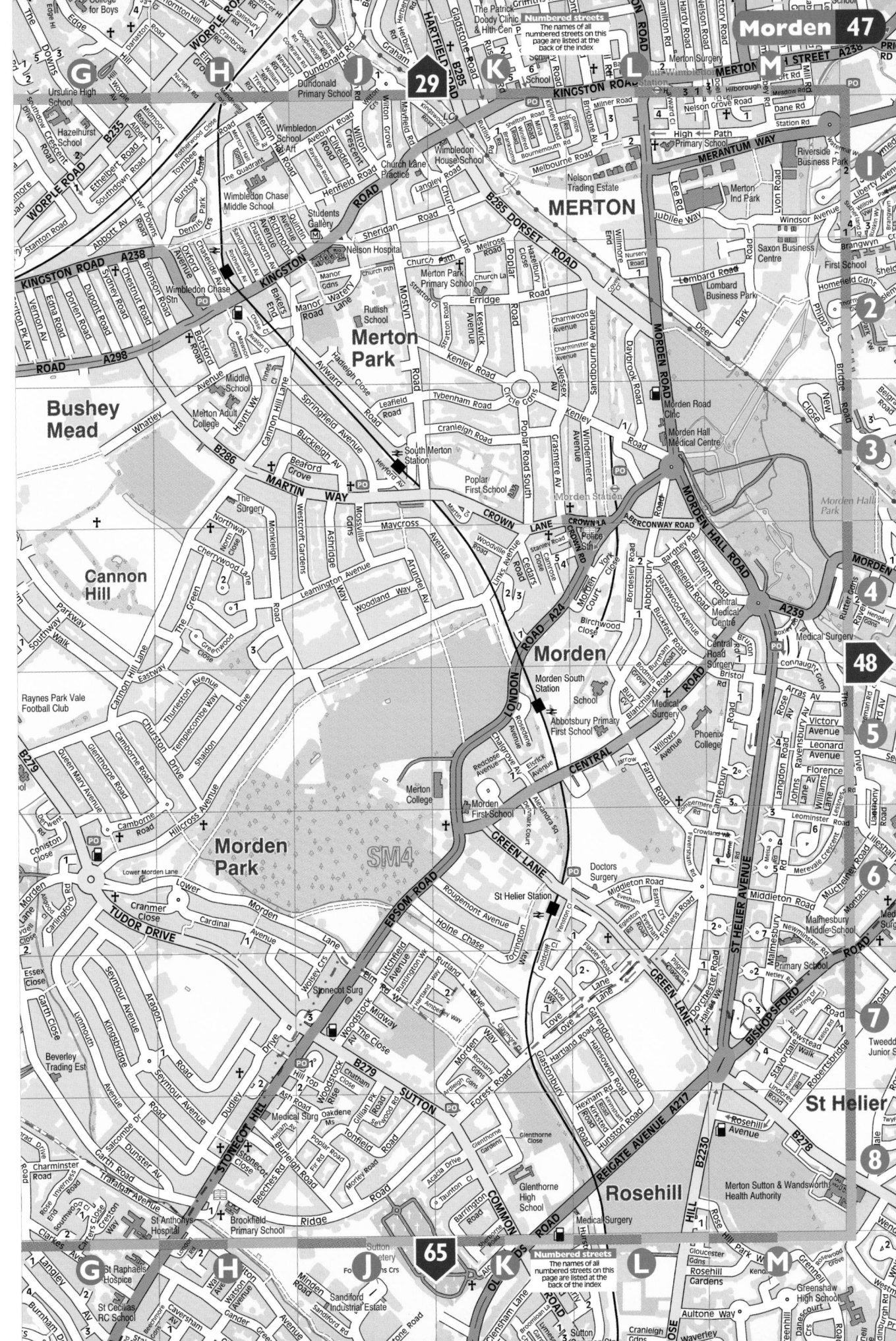

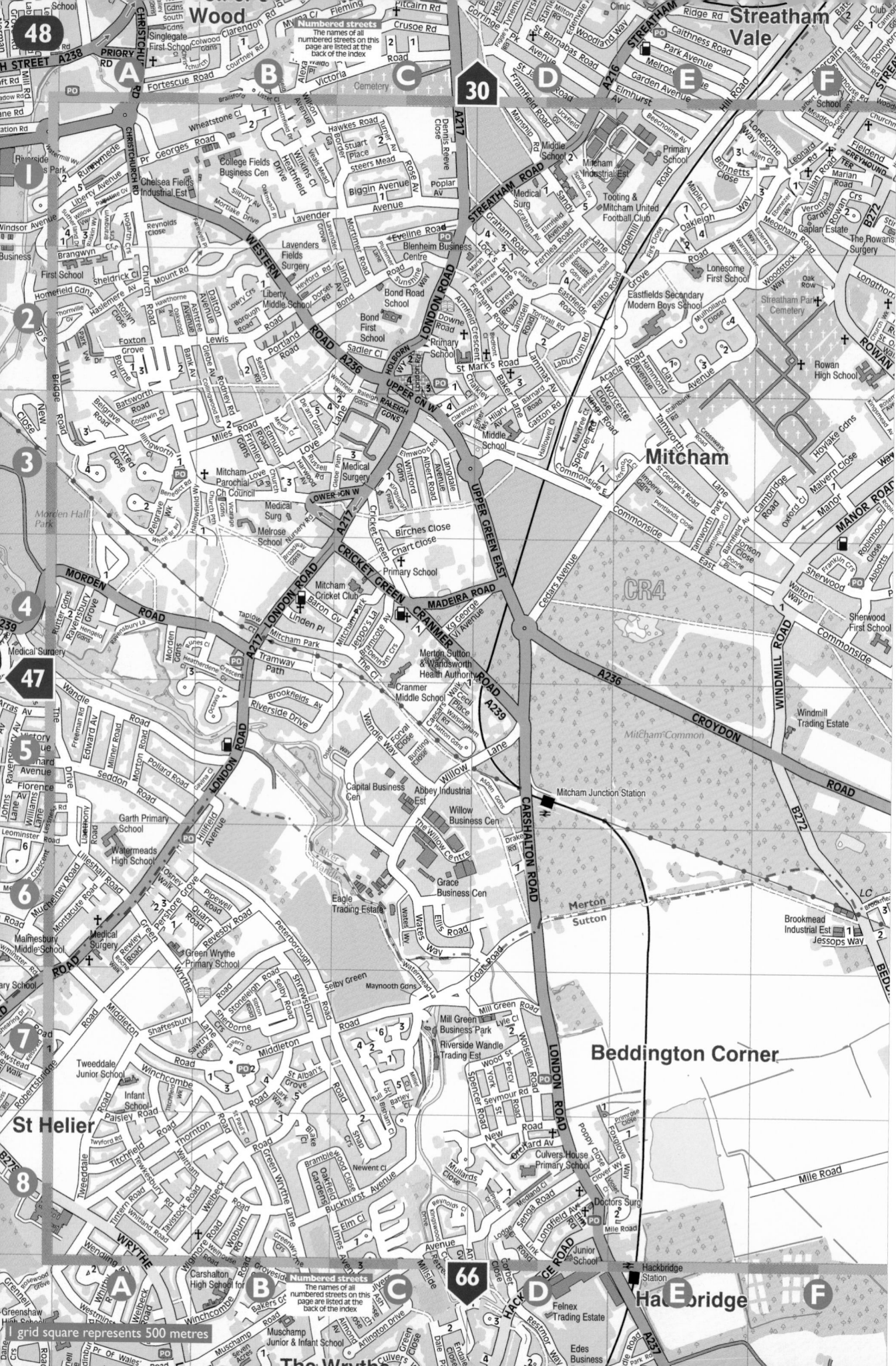

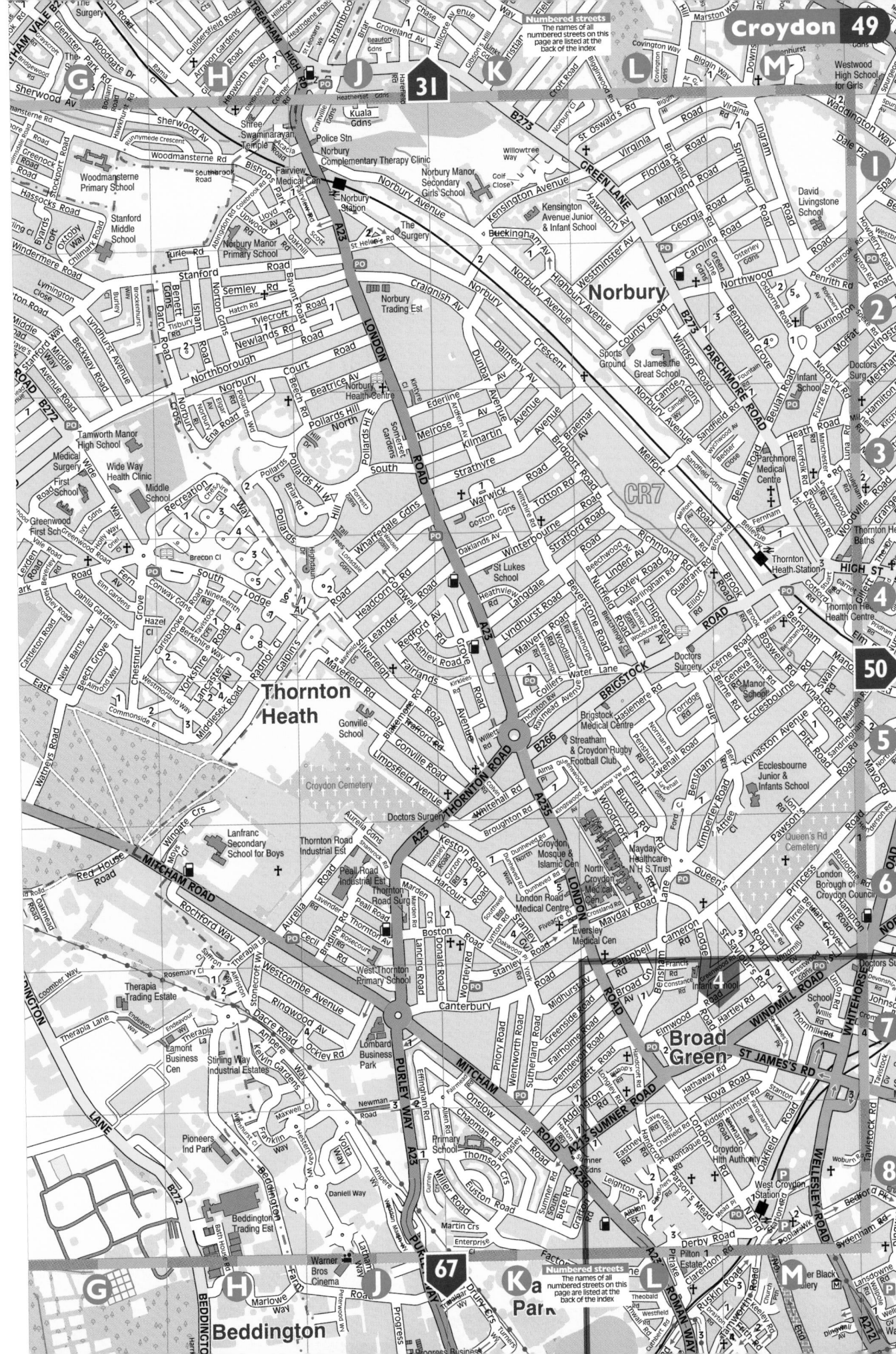

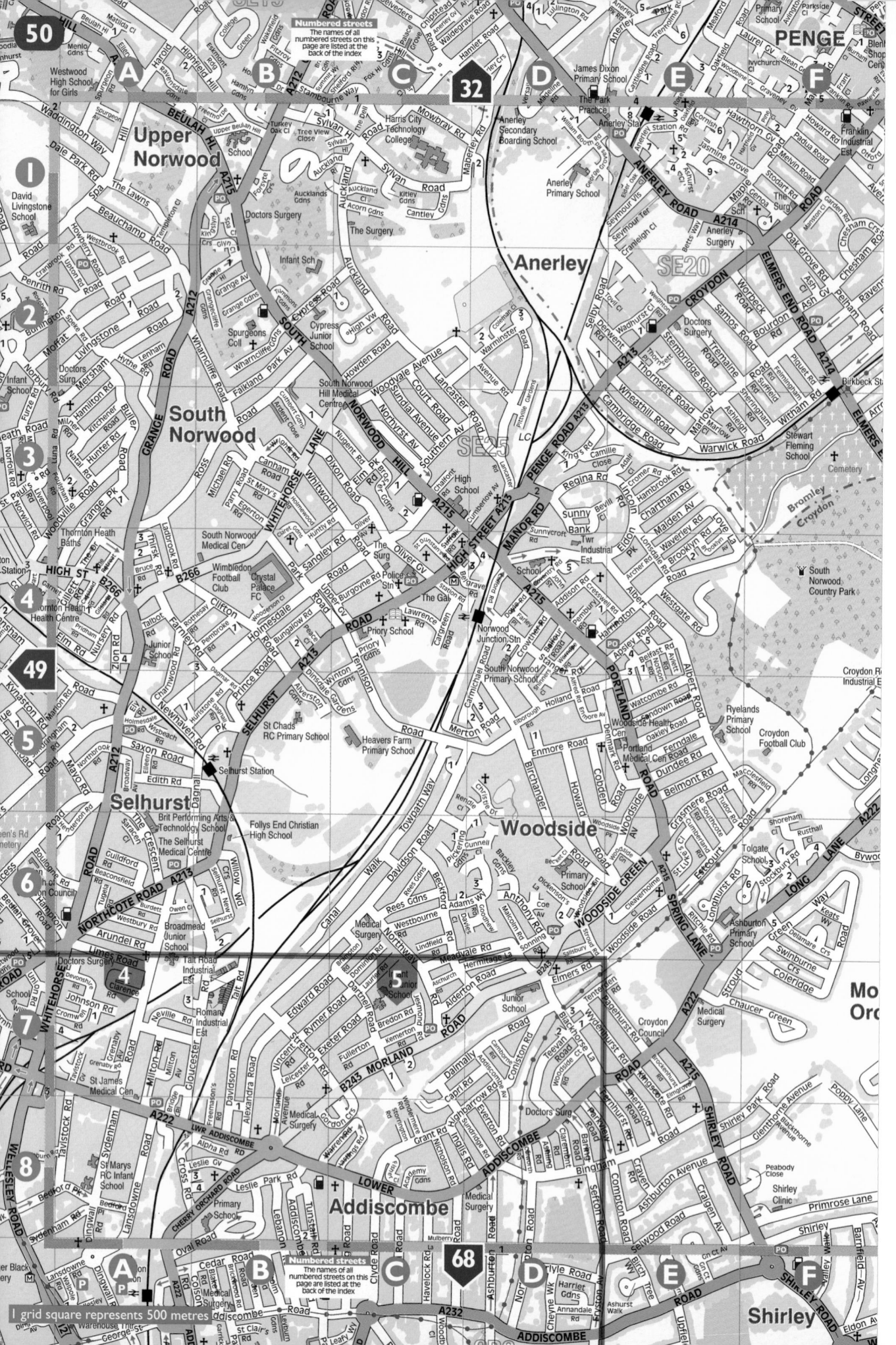

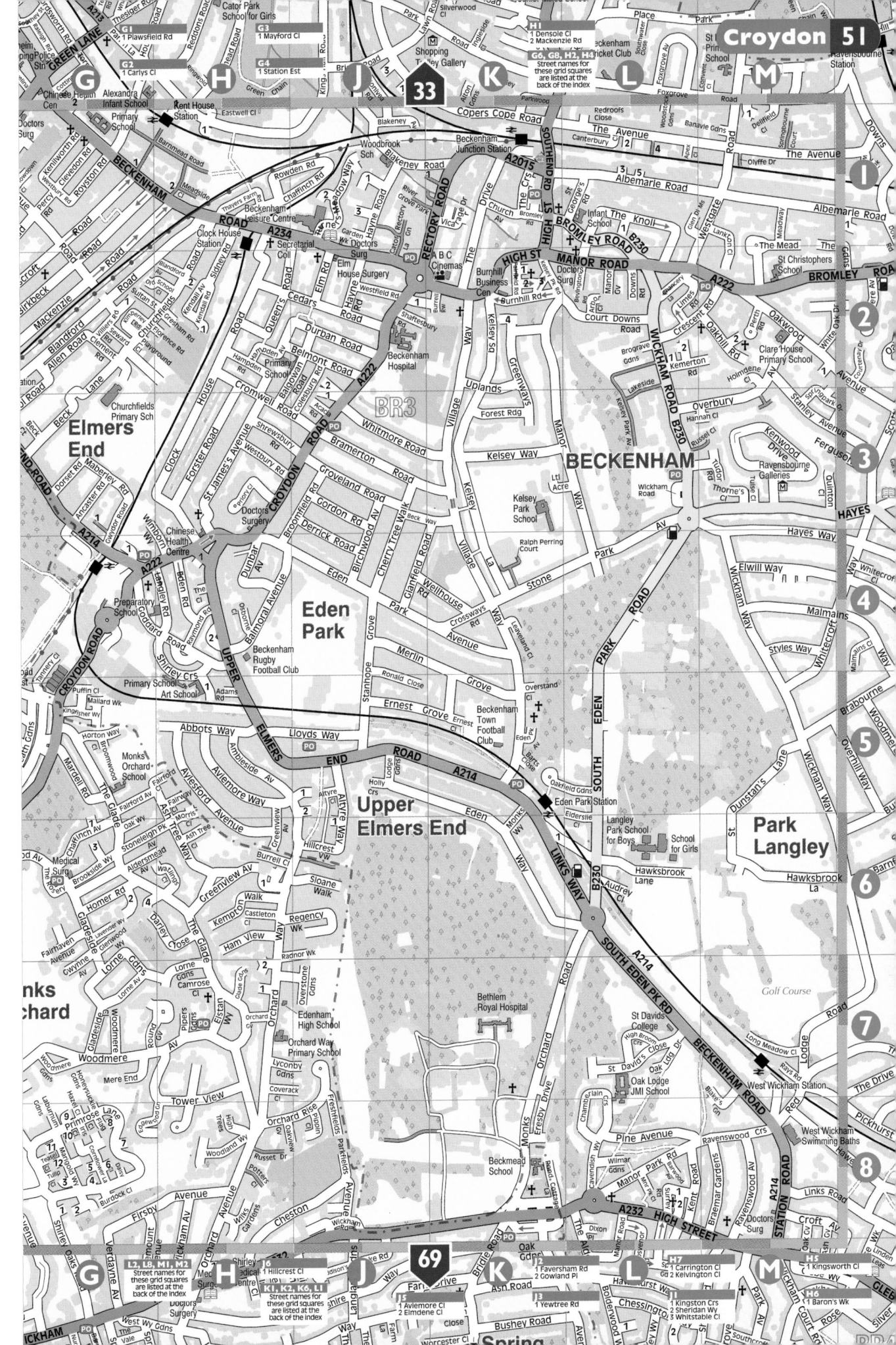

52

B8
1 Crown Pl
2 Grantham Cl
3 Rugby Cl

B7
1 Barkis Mead
2 Frodsham Wy
3 Peggotty Pl
4 Steerforth Copse
5 Trotwood Cl

A8
Street names for
this grid square are
listed at the back of
the index

A7
1 Darleydale Cl
2 Georgeham Rd
3 Kirkham Cl

Cemetery

Great
Hollands
Recreation Centre

Southwold

A   B   C   34   D   NINE   E   MILE   RIDE   F

I

Crowthorne
Business
Centre

2

Ringmead

Octavia

Qualitas

Oak

Nutle

Ringmead

bank

Ringmead

Melrose

Maltby

Juniper

Union

B3430

Knight

3430

FORESTERS WAY

A3095

ROAD

Crowthorne
Wood

BRACKNELL

Brackell Rd

3

Bokers Row

B3348

KNFD RD

RG45

Three Castles Path

Kentigern Drive

White City

4

Upr Broadmoor Rd

Broadmoor Rd

Napier

Club
La

Upper

The Terrace

Cricket Fld Gv

Rd

Road

Furze Hill

Crs

5

Chaplain's

School Hill

Hill

Broadmoor
Hospital

FORESTERS WAY

Broadmoor
County Primary
School

Lower

Broadmoor

Road

Eastern
Lane

Addiscombe Rd

Road

Gordon Rd

South
Meadow

Three Castles Path

Broadmoor Farm

6

South Road

A3095

FORESTERS WAY

ROAD   A3095

7

RACKSTRAW
Way

Way
dale

Rosedale

1   3
Copperfield Av   4

5

Magdalene Road

Merton Cl

Fakenham

Lewsham

Lewsham
Wy

Acacia Av

8

Tottenham
Wk

9

3

Owlsmoor

Union
Cl

Rookwood Av

Durham
Rd

Oxford Rd

Church   Road

Trinity

Owlsmoor
Primary
School

Yale Cl

Peternouse

8

Compton Close

Evesham Wk

Horsham

Apple
Tree
Cl

Avenue

Oak

Culver
Rd

Millin's Cl

Victoria
Rd

Cambridge

Moor

Yeovil

Birkbeck

Balliol
Way

Girton
Cl

Wadham

Road

Windsor

Ride

Matthews

King's

Epsom
Close

Arrebatti Rd

RACKSTRAW ROAD

Cookham

Road

Whitmore
Cl

May

Charlton
Cl

Brook

PO
Rd

Yeovil

The Surgery

Cannon
Close

College
Town

72

Road

Range
Vw

Goodwood
Road

A   B   C   72   D   E   F

Sandhurst
School

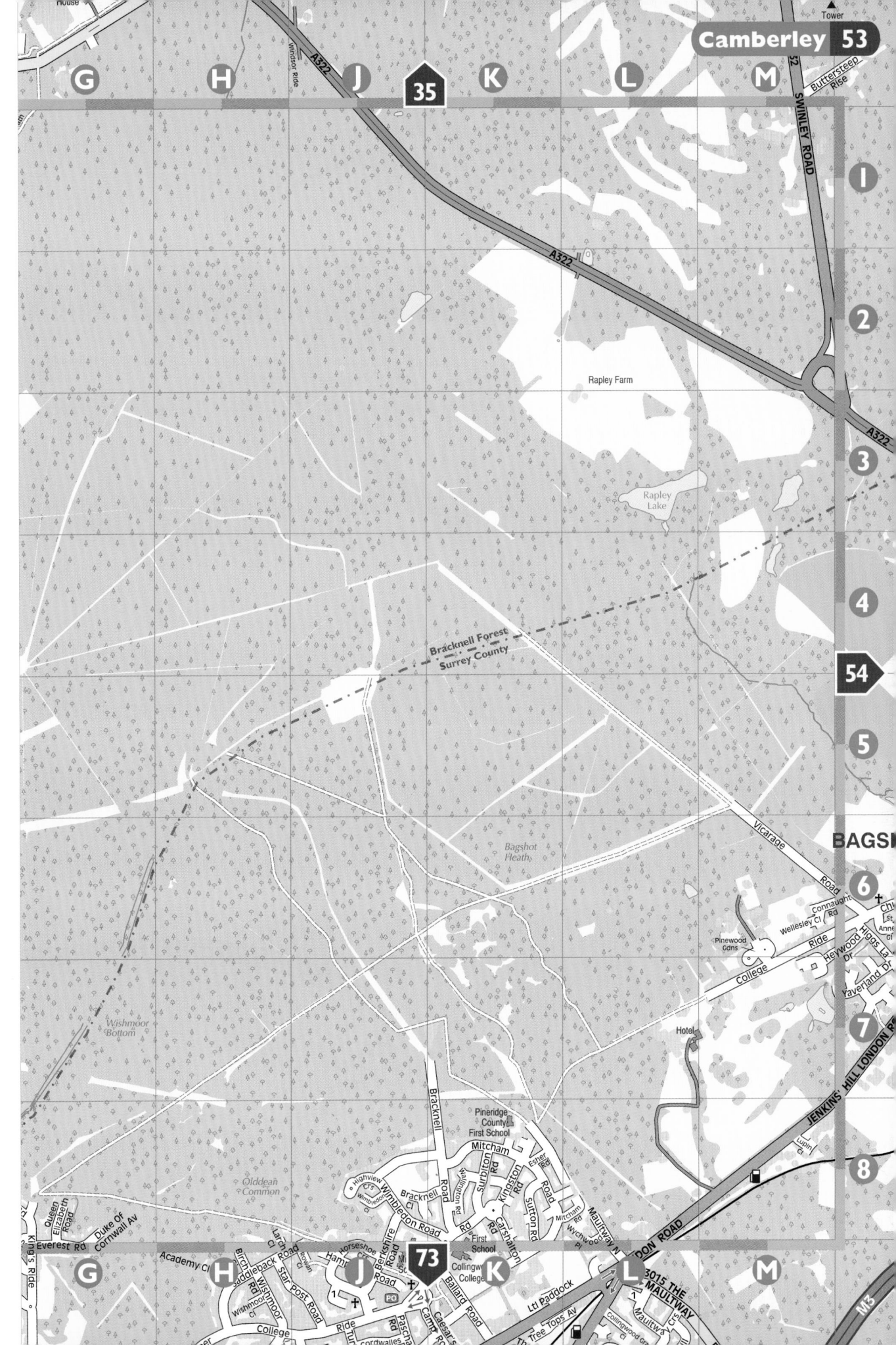

G H J **35** K L M

I
2
3
4
54
5
6
7
8

SWINLEY ROAD

Tower

Buttersteep Rise

A322

A322

Rapley Farm

Rapley Lake

Bracknell Forest
Surrey County

Vicarage Road

BAGS

Connaught Rd

Wellesley Cl

Pinewood Gdns

Heywood Dr

College Ride

Yaverland Dr

Hotel

JENKINS HILL

Wishmoor Bottom

Bracknell Road

Pineridge County First School

Mitcham Rd

Highview Cl

Wimbledon Cl

Surbiton Rd

Kingston Rd

Esher Rd

Sutton Rd

Mitcham Rd

Maultway N

DON ROAD

M3

Olddean Common

Queen Elizabeth Road

Duke of Cornwall Av

King's Ride

Everest Rd

Academy Cl

Birchdaleback Road

Saddleback Road

Larch Cl

Star post Road

Wishmoor Cl

Horseshoe Cl

Rowan

Hamp

Berkshire Road

1

PO

Bracknell Road

Caesar's Rd

Ballard Road

First School

Collingwood College

K

Ltl Paddock

3015 THE MAULTWAY

Tree Tops Av

Collingwood Wa

Maultwa

Lupin

G H J **73** K L M

College Ride Turn Paschal cordwalles

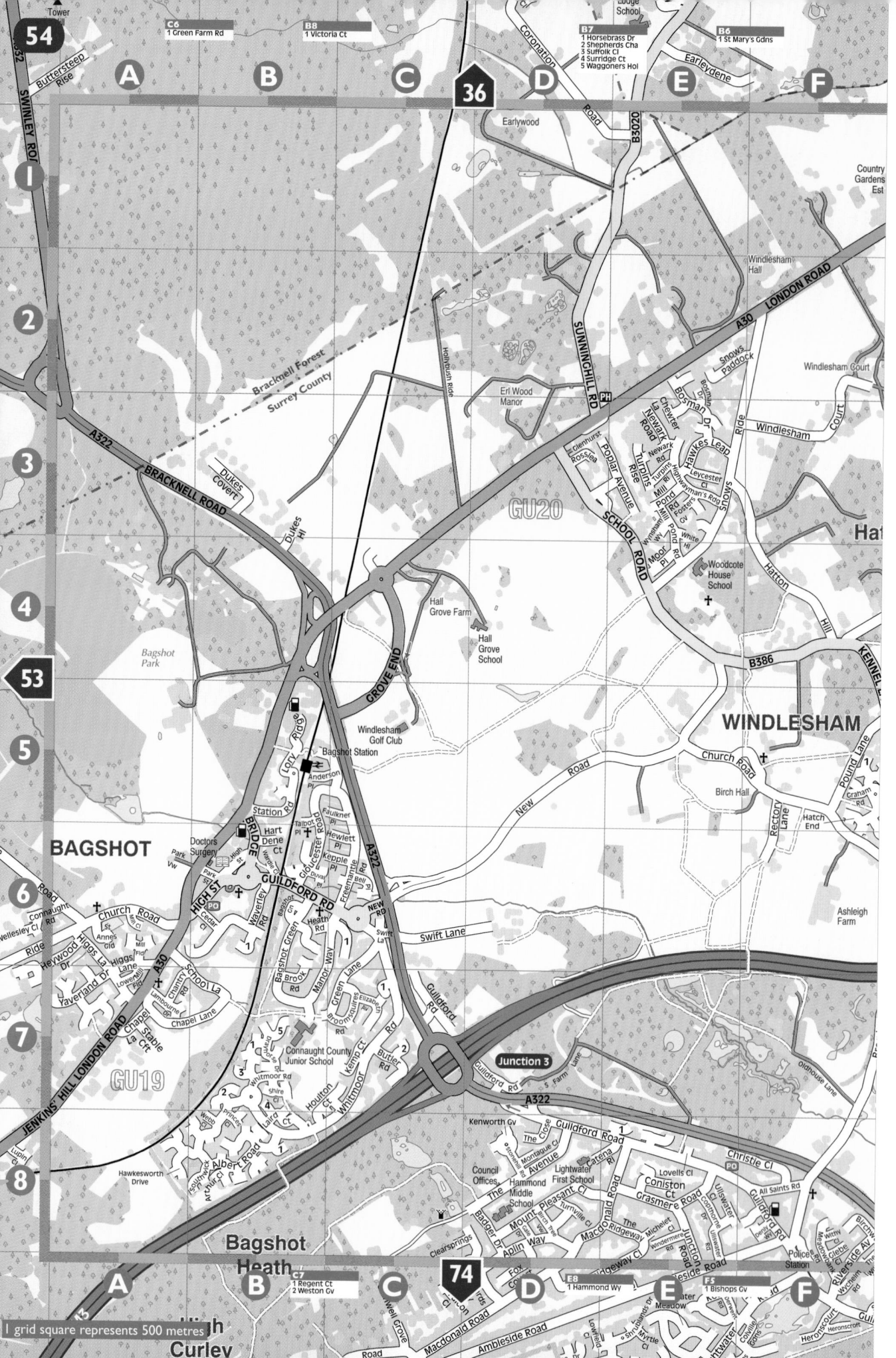

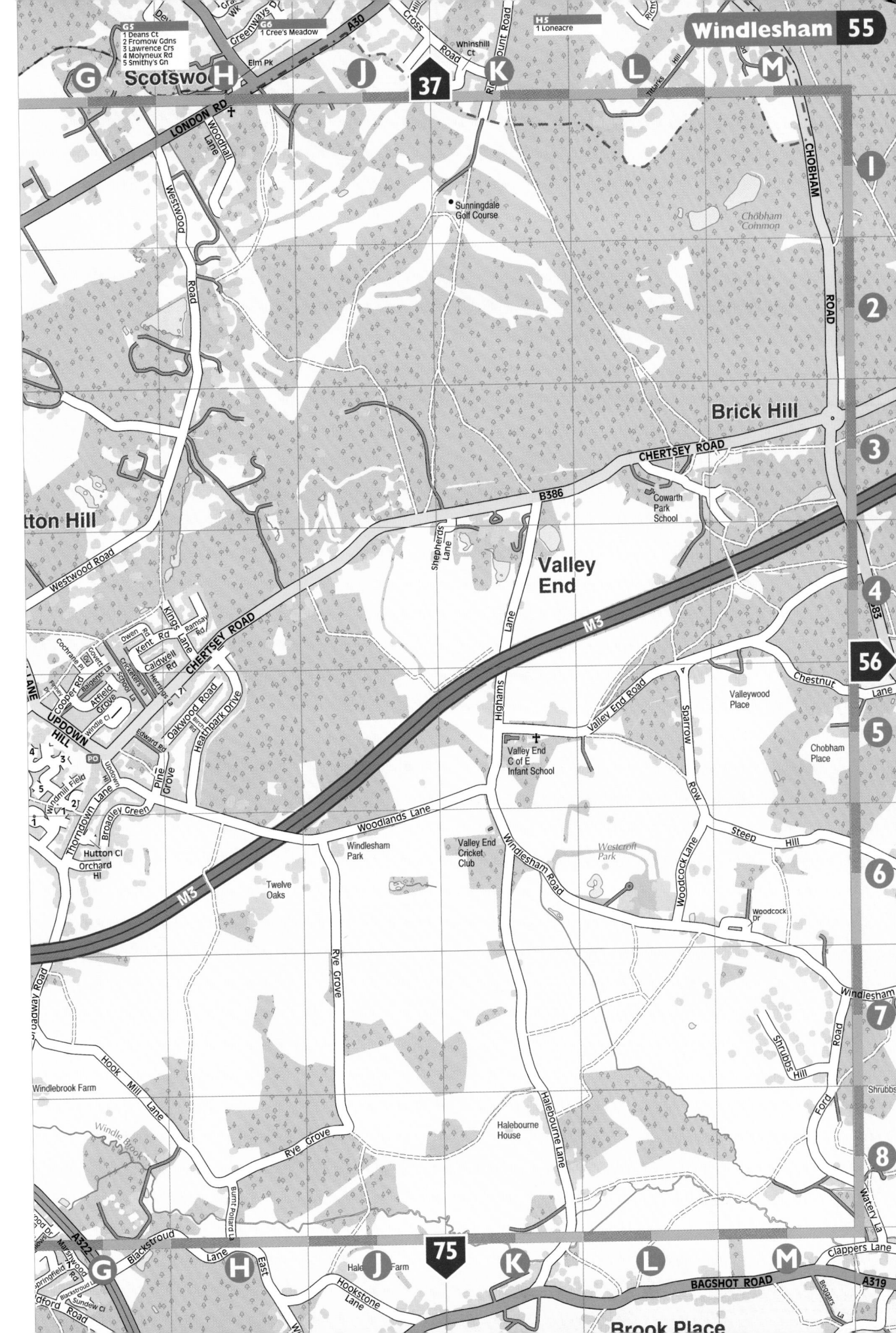

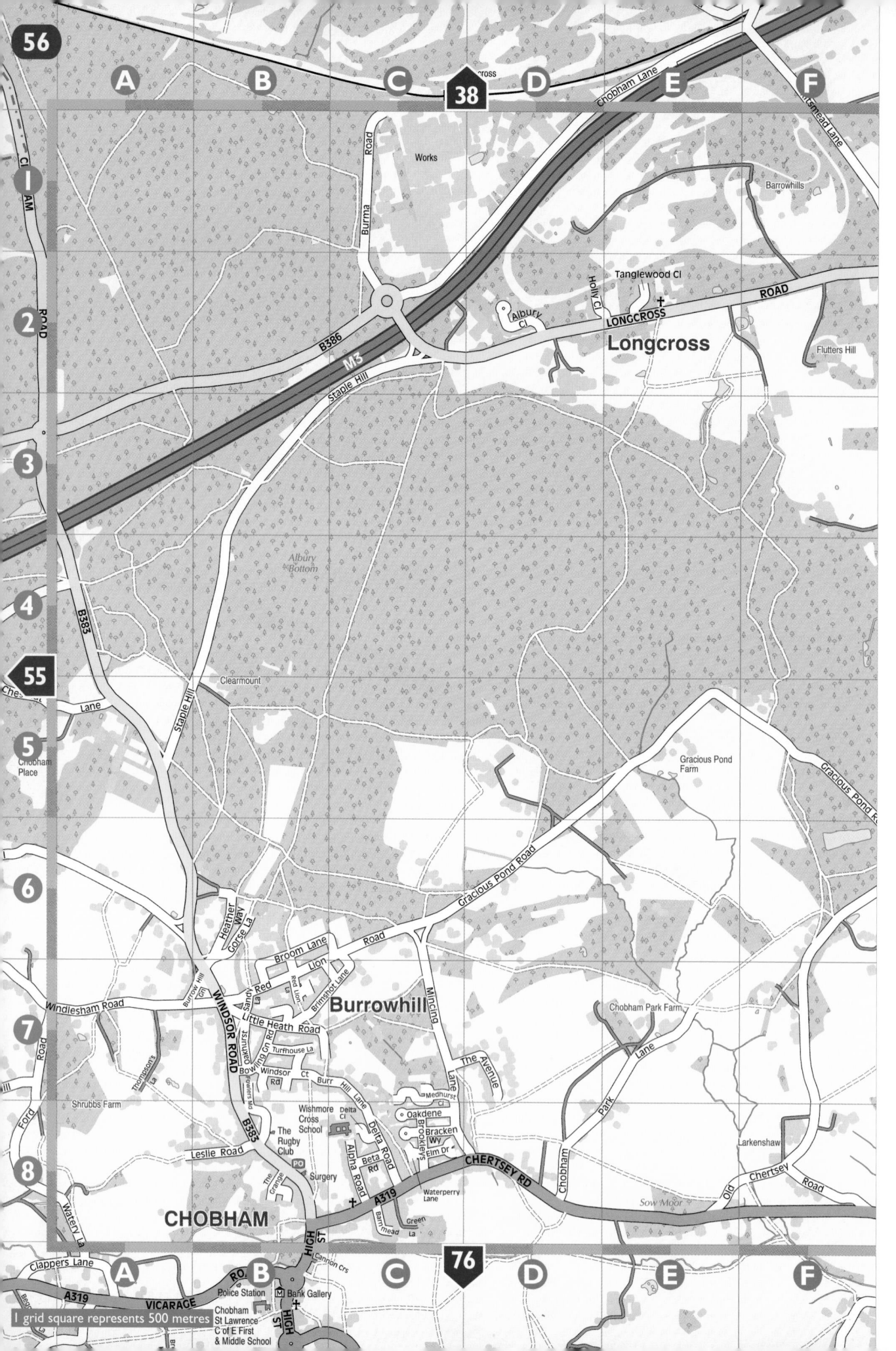

G H J 39 K L M

L5
1 Chobham Cl

M4
1 Brunner Ct
2 Warwick Deeping

M5
1 Cottage Cl
2 Malvern Cl

I

Lyne Lane

KT16

Lyne & Longcross
C of E School

Silverlands

Hersham
Farm

HOLLOWAY HILL

The A...
t Hospi...

B386

Greenlands

2

Kitsmead La

LONGCROSS ROAD

TRYS HILL LONGCROSS ROAD

B386 LONGCROSS ROAD

Stonehill Road

LONGCROSS ROAD

France
Farm

Runn...
Hosp...

Accommodation Rd

3

Fox Hills

Hillswood

Drive

A3...

Accommodation Road

4

GUILDFORD ROAD

Fox

Tringham Cl

Wilson
Dr

Hills

2 1

Ottersh

Road

58

Foxhills

Stonehill Road

Stonehill Crs

Stonehill

BROX

A319

2

Shaw Cl

Escott Pl

...er Rd

4

Ottershaw

Queenwood

Ottet...

The
Maples

Simons Cl

Coach Road

PO

Chaworth Rd

...

5

Slade

Bousle...

Flower
Crs

Cross Lane

Chaworth Cl

Slade

ROAD

A320

CHOBHAM

Brox

Chaworth Cl

Ch...
C...

Stonehill Road

Stannershill Farm

Stanyards

Home Farm Close

Meath
School

Crofton Close

Brox

6

Trelawn Cl

Southwood

Duffins Orch

Avenue

7

CHERTSEY

Bonsey's Lane

ROAD

Youngstroat La

A319

GUILDFORD

Brox

St Chapins Way

Greenwood

ROAD

Road

Woodlands Cl

8

Anningsley Park

Anningsley
Park

Emmetts
Mill

G H Fairoaks
Airport J 77 K L Dunford
Bridge M

Bonsey's
Farm

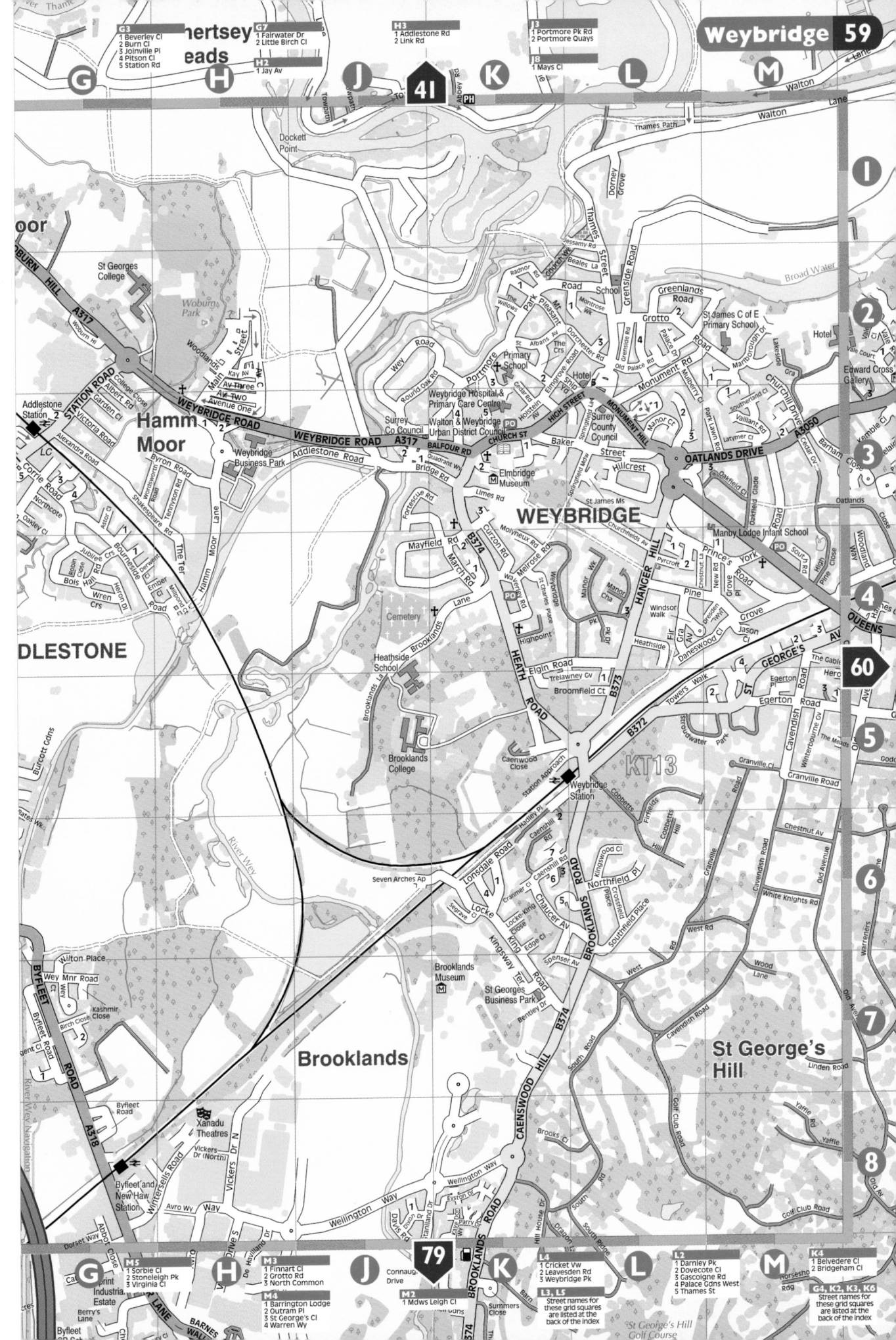

G
H
J
41
K
L
M
I
2
3
4
60
5
6
7
8

Weybridge

Dockett Point

St Georges College

Woburn Park

Addlestone Station

Hamm Moor

DLESTONE

Weybridge Business Park

WEYBRIDGE ROAD A317

Addlestone Road

Weybridge Hospital & Primary Care Centre
Walton & Weybridge Urban District Council

Surrey Co Council

BALFOUR RD

CHURCH ST

Elmbridge Museum

WEYBRIDGE

KT13

Surrey County Council

Manby Lodge Infant School

OATLANDS DRIVE

QUEENS

Cemetery

Heathside School

Brooklands College

HEATH ROAD

Weybridge Station

ST GEORGE'S AV

Seven Arches Ap

River Wey

BYFLEET ROAD A318

Wilton Place

Brooklands Museum

St Georges Business Park

Brooklands

Kingsway

CAENSWOOD HILL

BROOKLANDS ROAD

St George's Hill

Xanadu Theatres

Byfleet and New Haw Station

Wintersells Road

Vickers Dr

Wellington Way

79

Connaught Drive

Golf Club Road

St George's Hill Golf Course

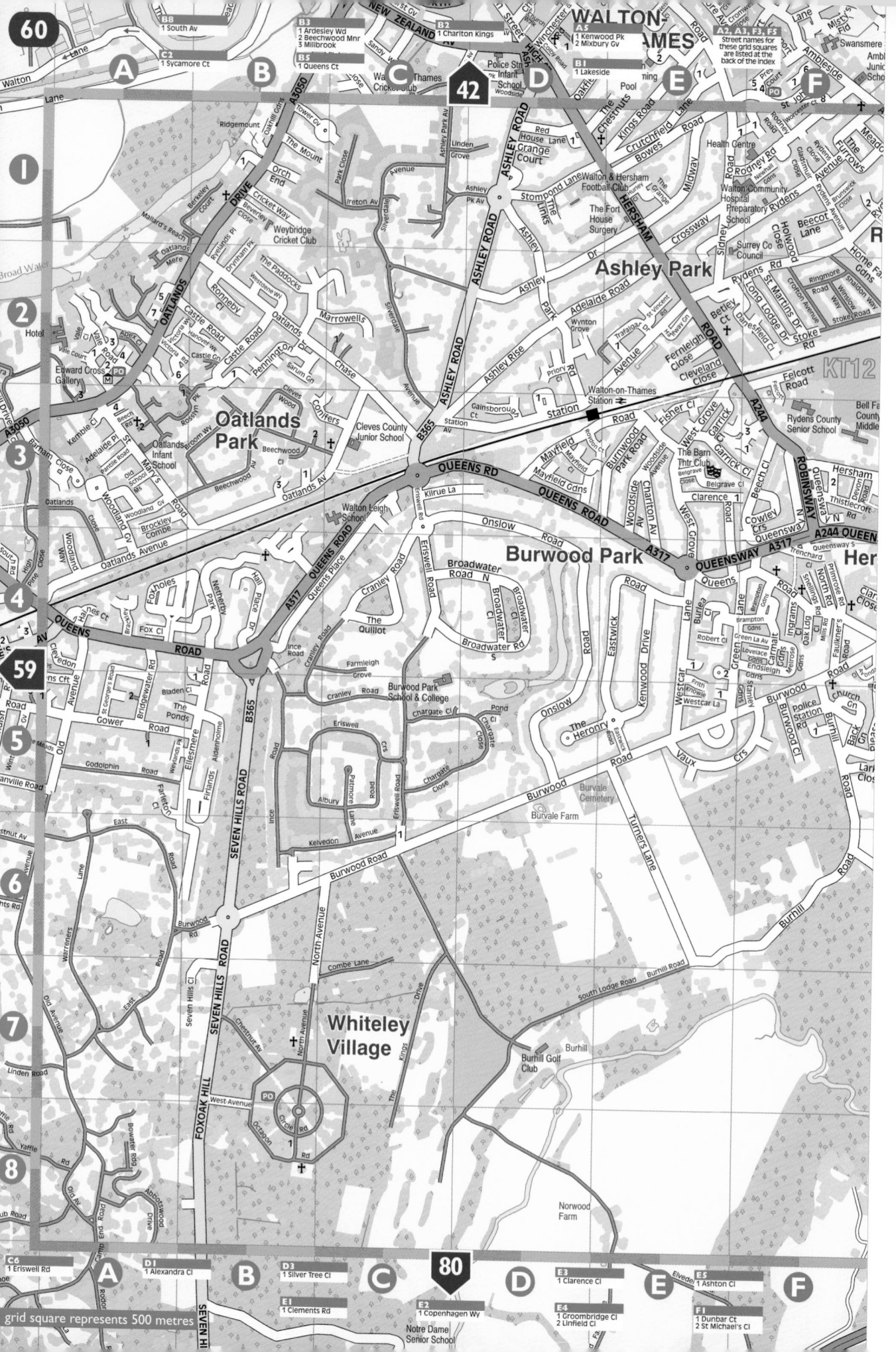

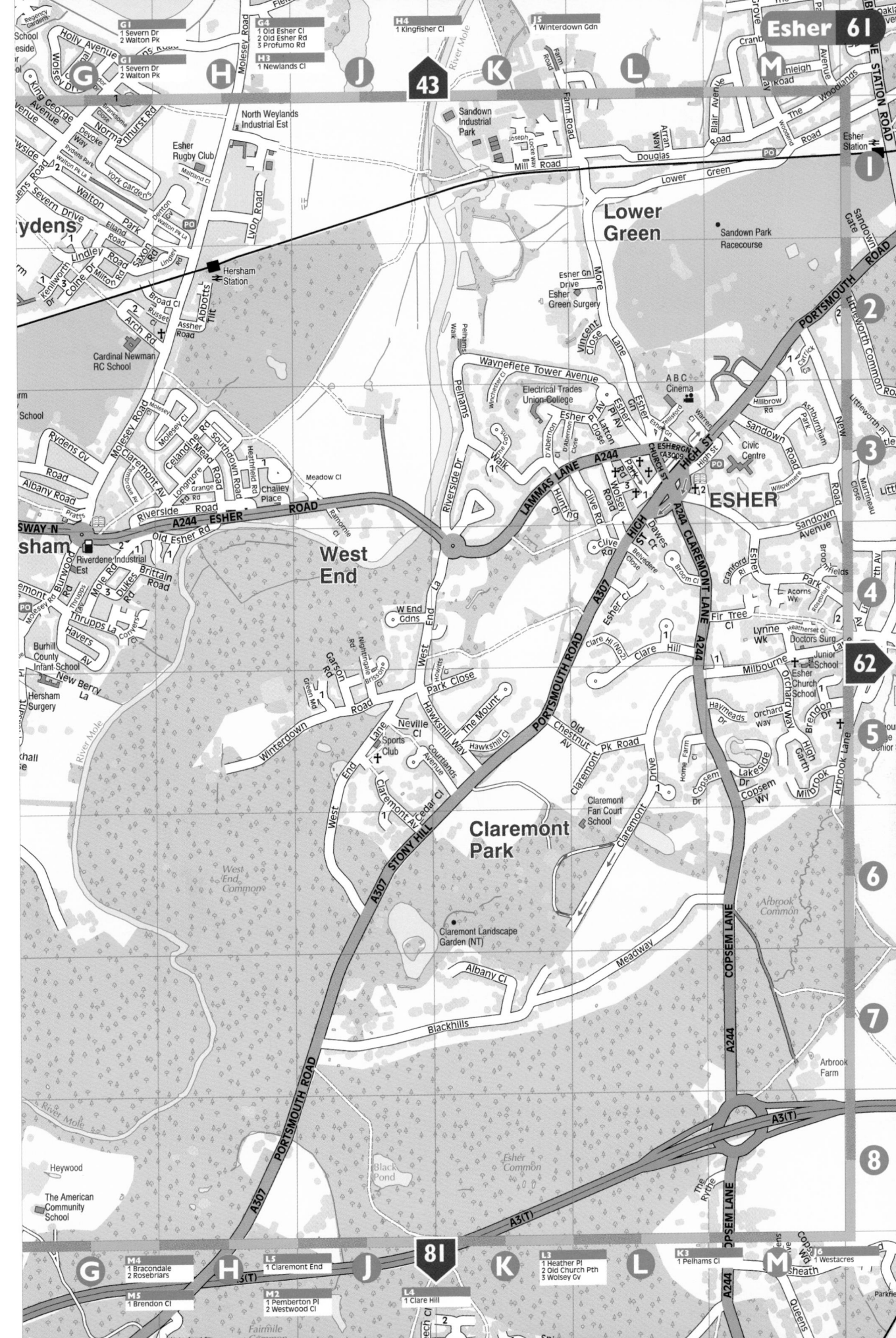

Map grid references (top)

G1
1 Severn Dr
2 Walton Pk

G1
1 Severn Dr
2 Walton Pk

G4
1 Old Esher Cl
2 Old Esher Rd
3 Profumo Rd

H3
1 Newlands Cl

H4
1 Kingfisher Cl

J5
1 Winterdown Gdn

Grid columns

G H J **43** K L M

1

2

3

ESHER

4

62

5

6

7

8

Labels and places

Regency Gardens
School
side
Holly Avenue
Molesey Road
North Weylands Industrial Est
Esher Rugby Club
River Mole
Sandown Industrial Park
Farm Road
Esher Station
Sandown Gate
PORTSMOUTH ROAD
Littleworth Common Road
PO
Esher Station

King George Avenue
Norma nhurst Rd
Devoke Way
Rydens Park
Walton Pk La
York Gardens
Walton Park
Denton Rd
Walton Pk La
Lyon Road
Joseph
Mill Road
Lower Green
Douglas
Arran Way
Blair Avenue
Carrick
Carrick Ca
New

Rydens
Lindley Road
Elland Road
Milton
Lingfield
Broad Cl
Russet
Abbotts Tilt
Hersham Station
Esher Gn Drive
More Lane
Esher Green Surgery
Sandown Road
Ashburnham Park
Littleworth Pl
Littley

Colne Dr
Kenilworth Dr
Arch Rd
Assher Road
Cardinal Newman RC School
Waynflete Tower Avenue
Pelhams Walk
Electrical Trades Union College
Winchester Cl
A B C Cinema
Hillbrow Rd
Warren
Sandown Road
Martineau Close
Little

School
Rydens Gv Road
Molesey Road
Molesey Cl
Celandine Mead
Southdown Road
Heathfield Rd
Meadow Cl
Chailey Place
Riverside Dr
Esher Pl Av
D'Abernon
Esher Pl Av
Esher
Esher Pl
Pelham
Wolsey Road
Park
ESHERGN A3000
Church St
PO
Civic Centre
Esher Avenue
Broom fields

Albany Road
Claremont Av
Longmore
Grange
Rd
Riverside Road
A244 ESHER ROAD
Ramonie
W End La
Hunting
Clive Rd
A244
High St CL
HIGH ST CL
A244
ESHER
Cranford Rd
Acorns Wy
Rosebrook

ham
Old Esher Rd
West End
W End Gdns
West End La
Clive Rd
Clare Hi (No)
Clare Hill
A307
Fir Tree Cl
Lynne Wk
Heatherset Cl
Doctors Surg
Junior School

Riverdene Industrial Est
Burwood Rd
Mole Rd
Dukes Ave
Brittain Road
Garson Rd
Green Md
Nightingale Rd
Briscoe
Park Close
Esher Cl
PORTSMOUTH ROAD
Milbourne
Esher Church School
Orchard Way
High Garth
Esher Church School Senior S

PO
Molesey Rd
Thrupps La
Converts
Havers Av
Winterdown Road
Neville Cl
Sports Club
Courtlands Avenue
Hawkshill Way
The Mount
Hawkshill Cl
Old Chestnut Av
Claremont Pk Road
Copsem Dr
Lakeside Dr
Copsem Wy
Arbrook Lane

Burhill County Infant School
New Berry La
Hersham Surgery
West End Lane
Claremont Av
Cedar Cl
STONY HILL
A307
Claremont Park
Claremont Fan Court School
Claremont Drive
Home Farm
Meadway
Arbrook Common

River Mole
West End Common
Claremont Landscape Garden (NT)
Albany Cl
Blackhills
COPSEM LANE
A244
Arbrook Common
Arbrook Farm

Heywood
PORTSMOUTH ROAD
A307
Black Pond
Esher Common
A3(T)
The Rythe
COPSEM LANE
A3(T)
A3(T)

The American Community School

Map grid references (bottom)

M4
1 Bracondale
2 Rosebriars

M5
1 Brendon Cl

L5
1 Claremont End

M2
1 Pemberton Pl
2 Westwood Cl

L4
1 Clare Hill

L3
1 Heather Pl
2 Old Church Pth
3 Wolsey Gv

K3
1 Pelhams Cl

M
1 Westacres

Grid columns (bottom)

G H J **81** K L M

A3(T)
Fairmile Common
Waterford Cl
Beech La
Spinn
Fairmile Common
Copse Wa
sheath
Queens
Parkfiel

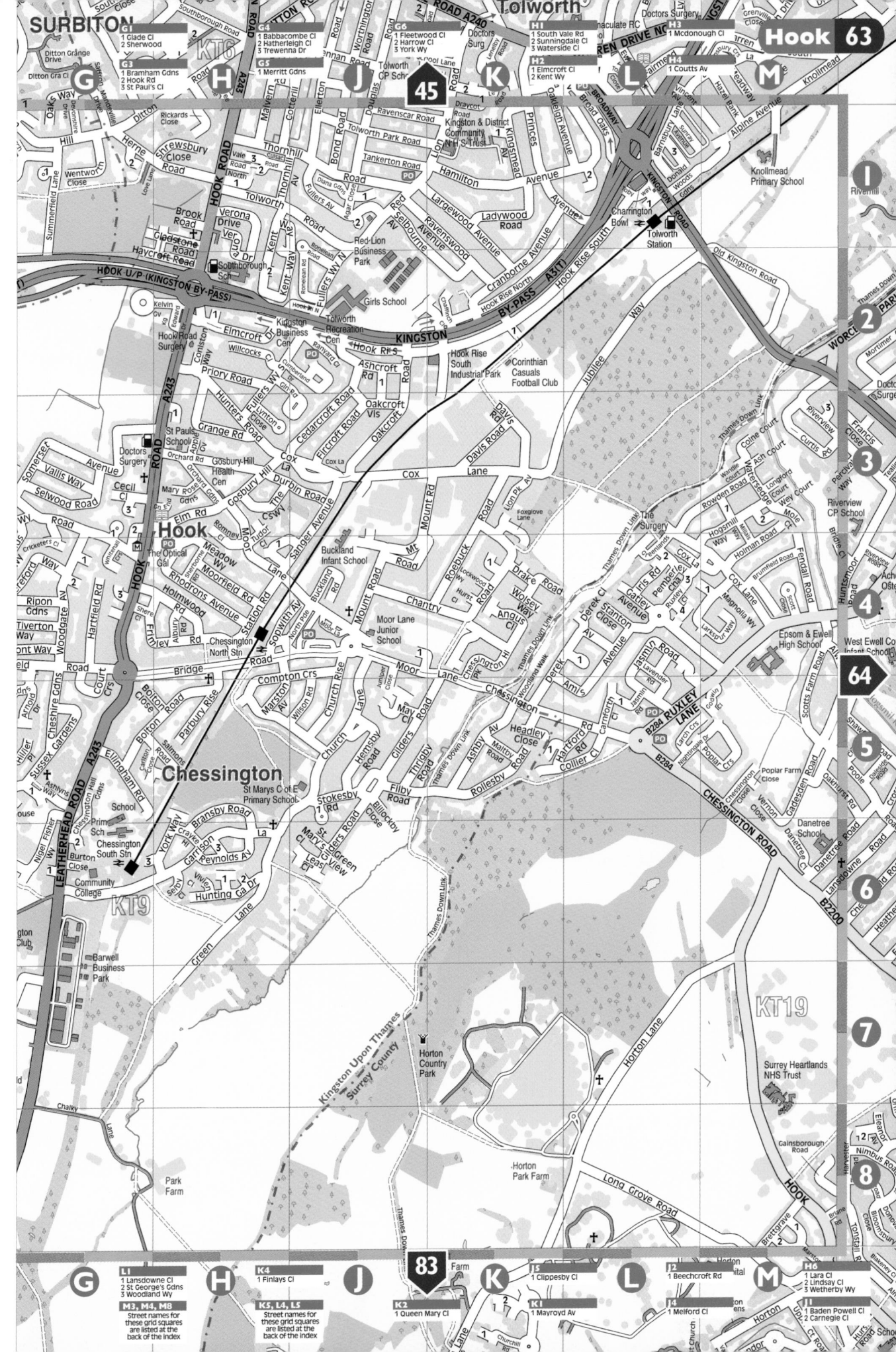

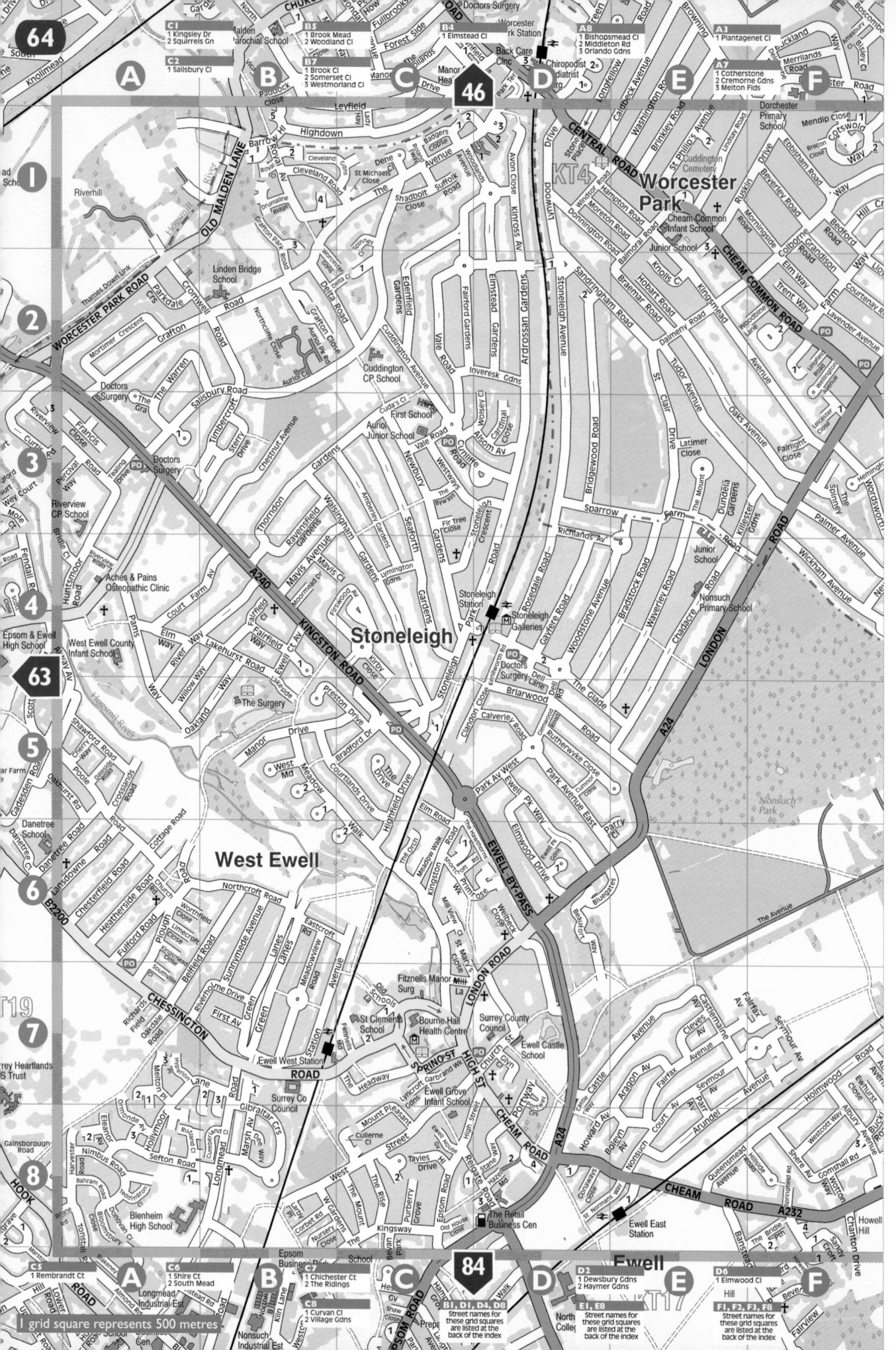

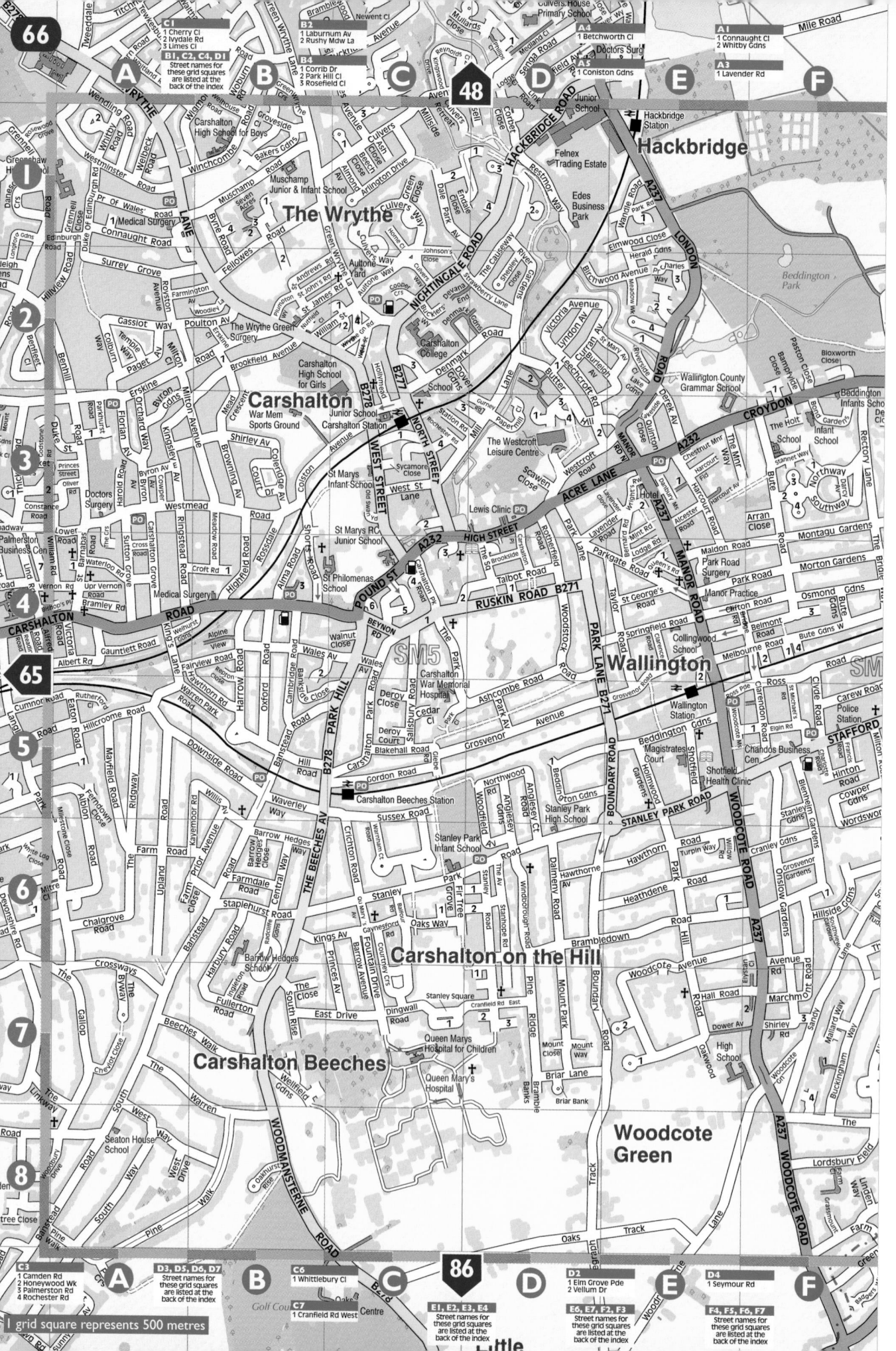

I
2
3
4
5
6
7
8

A
B
C
D
E
F

The Wrythe

Carshalton

Hackbridge

Felnex Trading Estate

Edes Business Park

Beddington Park

Wallington County Grammar School

Wallington

CROYDON

The Westcroft Leisure Centre

STAFFORD

Carshalton on the Hill

Carshalton Beeches

Queen Marys Hospital for Children

Queen Mary's Hospital

Woodcote Green

SM5

A
B
C
D
E
F

1 grid square represents 500 metres

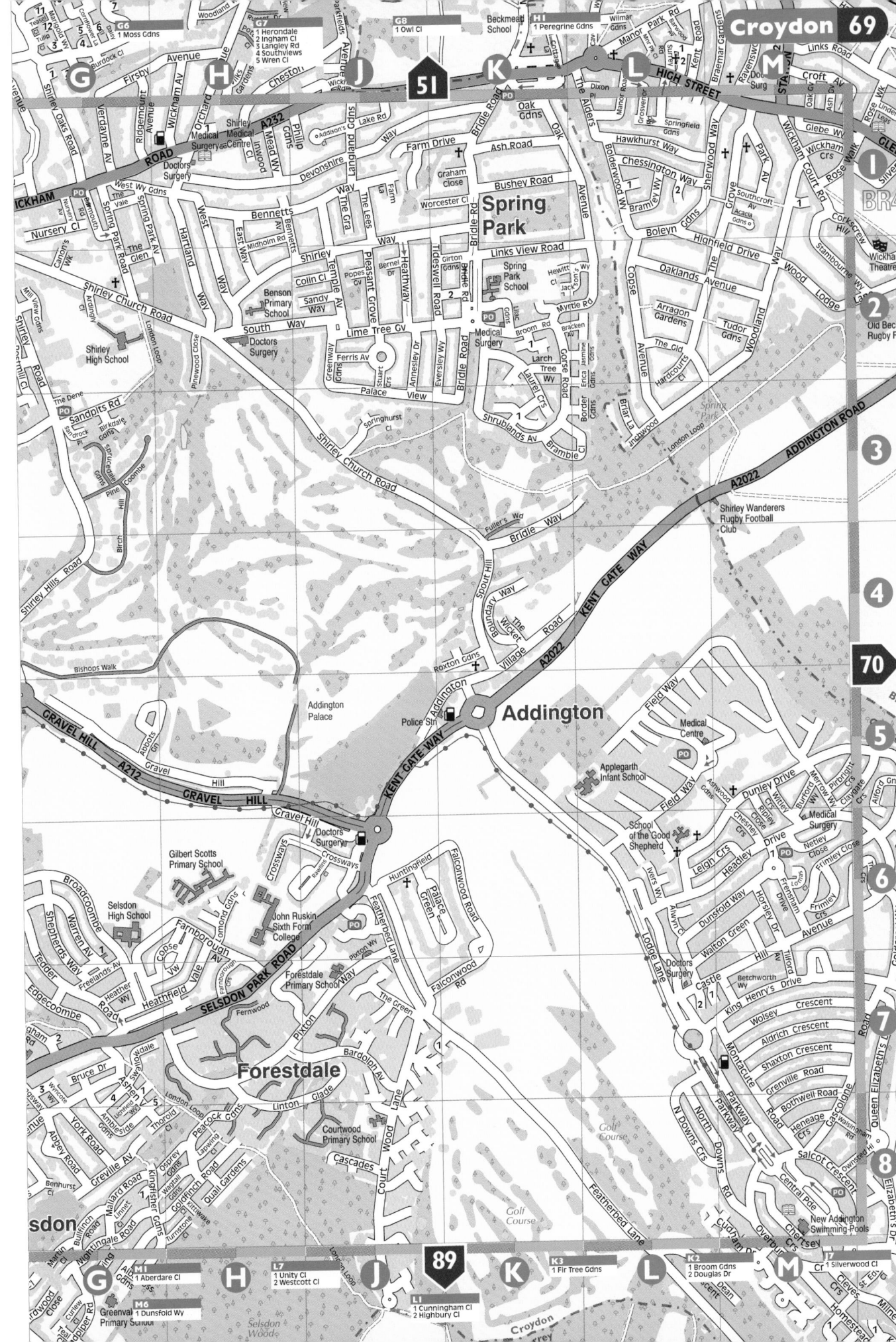

Beckmead School

1 Owl Cl

1 Peregrine Gdns

Wilmar Gdns

Manor Park Rd

HIGH STREET

G7
1 Herondale
2 Ingham Cl
3 Langley Rd
4 Southviews
5 Wren Cl

1 Moss Gdns

G **H** **J** **51** **K** **L** **M**

Wickham Theatre

I

BR4

Medical Surgery Medical Centre

Doctors Surgery

A232

Philip Gdns

Farm Drive

Ash Road

Bushey Road

Worcester Cl

Spring Park

Old Becke Rugby Fo

2

Shirley High School

Bennetts

Shirley

Colin Cl

Benson Primary School

Sandy Way

Lime Tree Gv

Pleasant Grove

Spring Park School

Medical Surgery

3

Arragon Gardens

Tudor Gdns

Oaklands Avenue

The Old

ADDINGTON ROAD

Sandpits Rd

South Way

Doctors Surgery

Ferris Av

Palace View

Springhurst Cl

Shirley Church Road

Fuller's Wd

Bridle Way

A2022

Shirley Wanderers Rugby Football Club

4

Bishops Walk

KENT GATE WAY

Spout Hill

Boundary Way

The Wicket

Village Road

A2022

Roxton Gdns

70

GRAVEL HILL

A212

Gravel Hill

GRAVEL HILL

Abbots Gn

Addington Palace

Police Stn

Addington

Field Way

Medical Centre

Applegarth Infant School

School of the Good Shepherd

Dunley Drive

5

Gilbert Scotts Primary School

Selsdon High School

Crossways

John Ruskin Sixth Form College

Doctors Surgery

Crossways

Huntingfield

Palace Green

Falconwood Road

SELSDON PARK ROAD

Broadcoombe

Warren Av

Shepherds Way

Tedder

Edgecoombe

Heather Wy

Heathfield

Farnborough Av

Forestdale Primary School

Pixton Wy

Featherbed Lane

The Green

Headley Drive

Dunsfold Way

Walton Green

Doctors Surgery

Castle

King Henry's Drive

6

Betchworth Wy

Wolsey Crescent

Aldrich Crescent

Shaxton Crescent

7

Forestdale

Bardolph Av

Linton

Glade

Court Wood Lane

Falconwood Rd

Grenville Road

Bothwell Road

Heneage Crs

Montacute

PARKWAY

N Downs Crs

North Downs

Salcot Crescent

8

York Road

Greville Av

Courtwood Primary School

Cascades

Golf Course

Central Pde

New Addington Swimming Pools

sdon

Nightingale Road

Kingfisher Gdns

Goldfinch Road

Quail Gardens

Golf Course

Croydon

Chertsey

Overpurn

Cudham Crs

Featherbed Lane

M1
1 Aberdare Cl

Greenval Primary School

M6
1 Dunsfold Wy

G **H** **89** **J** **K** **L** **M**

1 Unity Cl
2 Westcott Cl

K3
1 Fir Tree Gdns

K7
1 Broom Gdns
2 Douglas Dr

1 Silverwood Cl

Selsdon Wood

1 Cunningham Cl
2 Highbury Cl

G H J K L M

Keston Mark

Ravenswood School for Boys

1 Thanet Dr `G2`

1 Colliers Wd `G4`

1 Forest Dr `H2`

1 Claremont Cl `K3`

A232

Locksbottom

Darrick Wood

Darrick Wood Junior & Primary School

Darrick Wood Swimming Pool

Bromley Hospitals N H S Trust

Keston

Keston C of E Primary School

FARNBOROUGH COMMON

The Birches

Farnborough

HIGH STREET

Farnborough Primary School

The Larches

Holwood

High Elms Country Park

High Elms Golf Course

Shire Lane

Lower Hook Farm

North End Farm

Holwood Farm

The Rookery

Gorringes

Cuckoo Wood

G
Leaves Green

1 Crabbs Croft Cl `M4`
2 Ladycroft Gdns
3 Starts Hill Av

H

1 La Tourne Gdns `M2`
2 Lysander Wy
3 Sloane Gdns

Street names for this grid square are listed at the back of the index `M3`

J
Downe

D 1 Lyoth Rd `M1`
Primary School

K

1 Ashtree Cl `L3`
2 Bassetts Cl
3 Harlands Gv
4 Paddock Cl
5 Tugmutton Cl

L

1 Grasmere Av `L2`
2 Grasmere Rd
3 Langdale Cl

M

Hazelwood

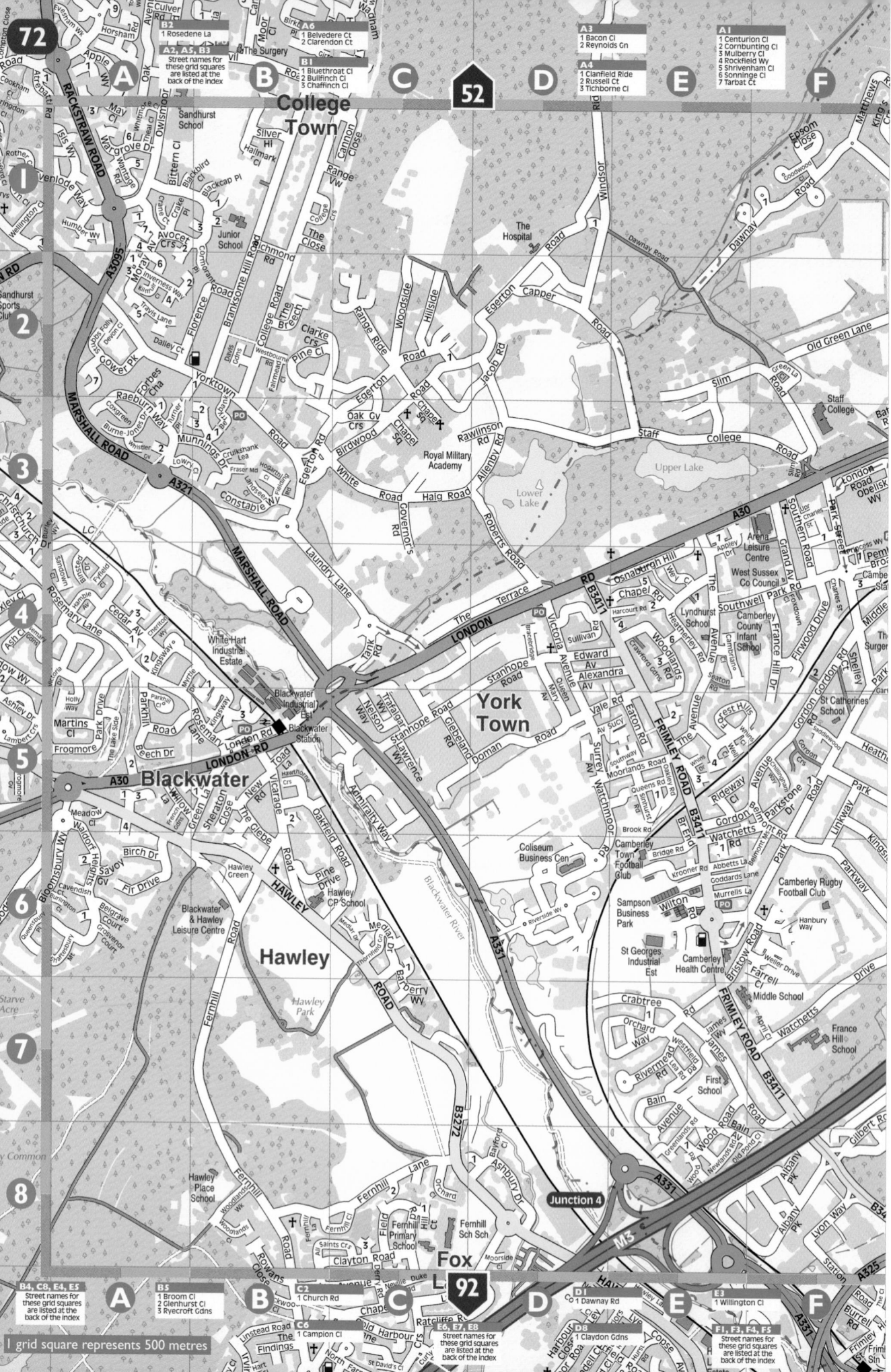

College Town

52

York Town

Blackwater

Hawley

Junction 4

Fox

1 grid square represents 500 metres

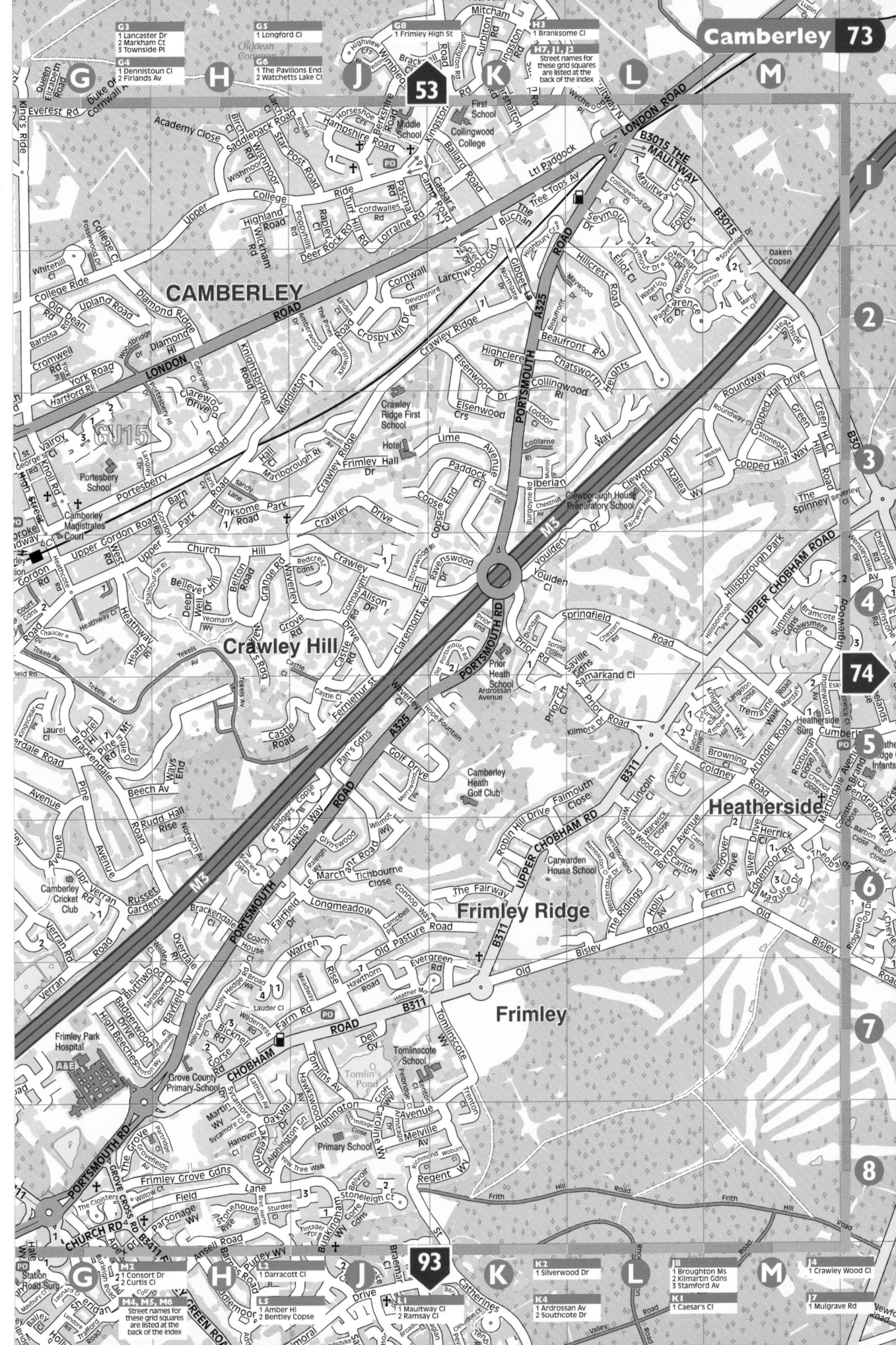

Oldean Common

CAMBERLEY

GU15

Crawley Hill

Heatherside

Frimley Ridge

Frimley

Hawkeswo... Drive
1 Gorse Bank
Albert Road
D1

A7
1 Marshall Cl
2 Myers Wy

Council Offices
Montague Avenue
Lightwater Firs
Catena Rd
Lovells Cl
Christie Cl
Coniston Ct
A4
1 Brackenwood
2 Englesfield
3 Greenholme
Saints Rd

A   **B**   **C**
54
D   **E**   **F**

Bagshot Heath

Hammond Middle School
The
Pleasar
Grasmere Road
Police Station

I

High Curley

M3
High View Road
Maple Cl
Falcon Cl
Mallards
Badger Dr
Aplin Wy
The
Turnville Cl
The Ridgeway
Macdonald Rd
Win...
Junction Road
Ambleside Road
Keswick Dr
Colville Gdns
Heronscroft
Heroncourt
Riverside
Birch...
LIGHTWAT

Macdonald Road
Ambleside Road
Fox Covert
Ridgeway Cl
Rydal
Lowfield Shrubland
Myrtle Cl
Lightwater Meadow
Colville Cl
Colville Cdns

LIGHTWAT

Curley Hill Road
Sorrel Dr
Deer Leap
Quarry Ba
Osborne Dr
Briar
Briar AV
Blackmorne Dr
Burdock Cl

2

Green Hill Cl
B3015
Perry Wy
Corbett Dr
Alsford
Briar
Ivy Dr
Spruce Dr
Broom Fld
1
1

Drive
Miles Pl
Avenue
Barnett Lane
B311
RED ROAD

GU18

Green
The Spinney
Beverley Cl
B311

3

Hook Lane
Bren

OBHAM ROAD
Cherriedale Rd
Wensleydale Rd
AV
Rydal Cl
Ravenstone Rd
Priestley
Lane

4
Inner Gdns
Dawsmere Cl
Ingelwood
2
1
3
Buttermere Dr
Kemal Owl
Keswick Cl

Westend Common

73
Copelands Close
Drive
Cumberland Road

Marca?
wood side
1
Heatherside Sho...
Brandon
Martindale Avenue
PO
Heather Ridge County Infants School

5

Strawberry Bottom

Roxb
Close
Chevron Close
Pendragon Way
Kirkstone Close
Redwood Drive
Lockley
Shildon
Close
THE MAULTWAY

6
ick Rd
Theobalds
Wy
Barton Close
Rixon Close
Dalston Close

Wingfield Gdns

Bisley
Ridgeway Dr
Chevesmore Drive
Road
1
2
Henderson Dr
B3015

7

Colony Gate

8
Hill Road

Minorca
Minorca Road
Aisne Road

Pirbright Common

A   **B**   **C**   **D**   **E**   **F**
Alma Gardens
Bettridge
Newfou...
B1
1 Bluebell Rl
2 Northfield
3 The Orchard
94
Blackdown

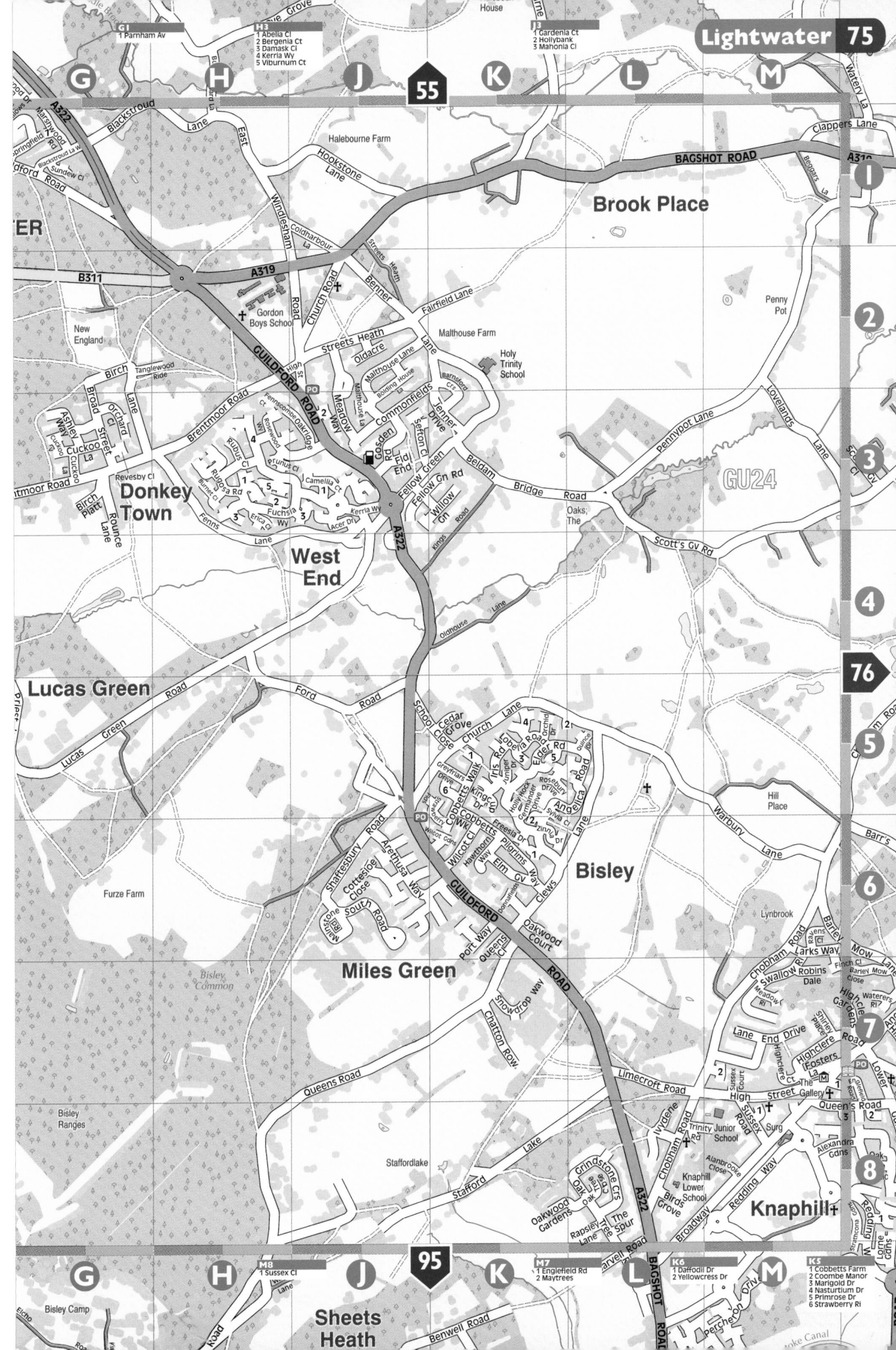

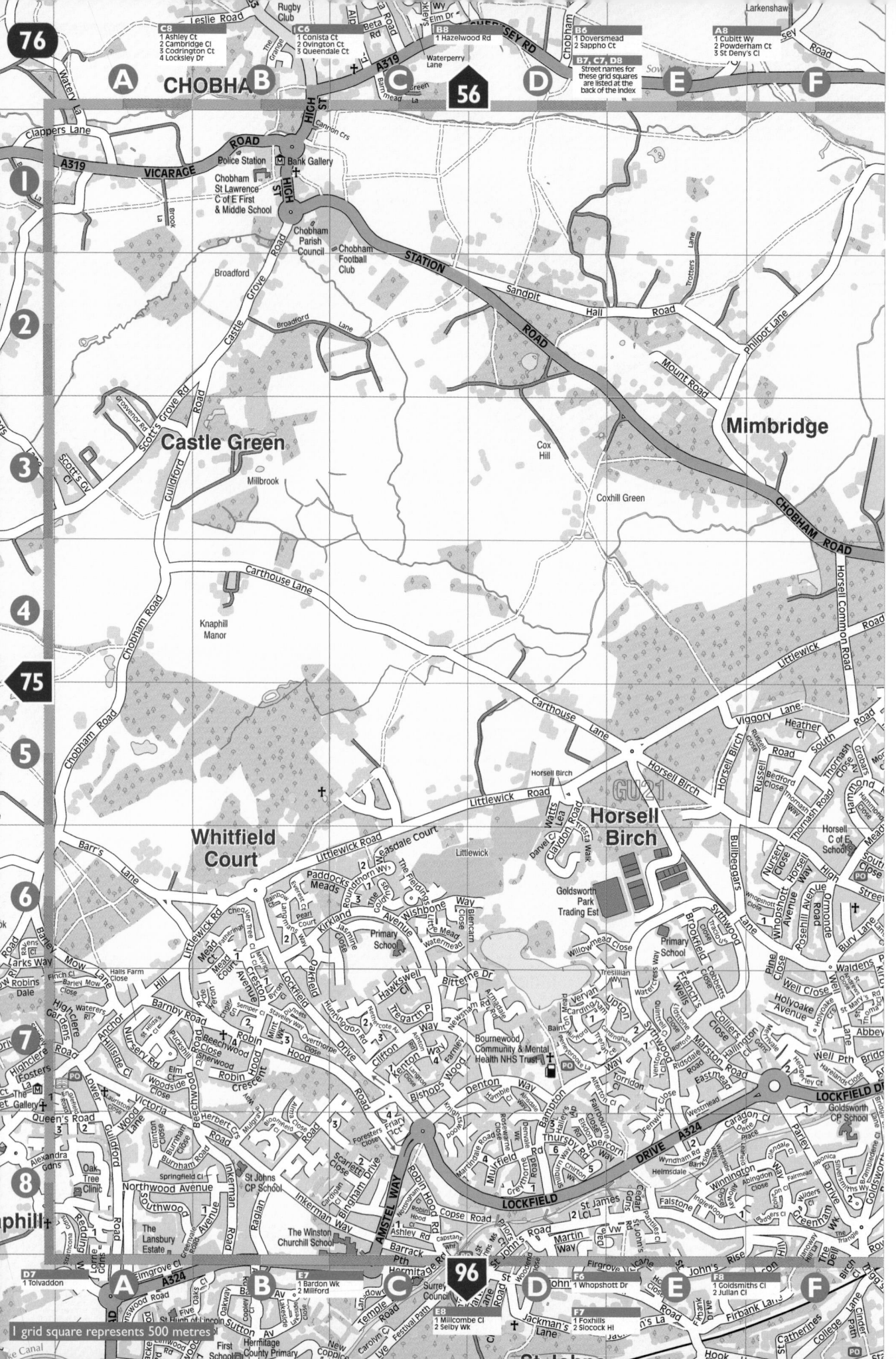

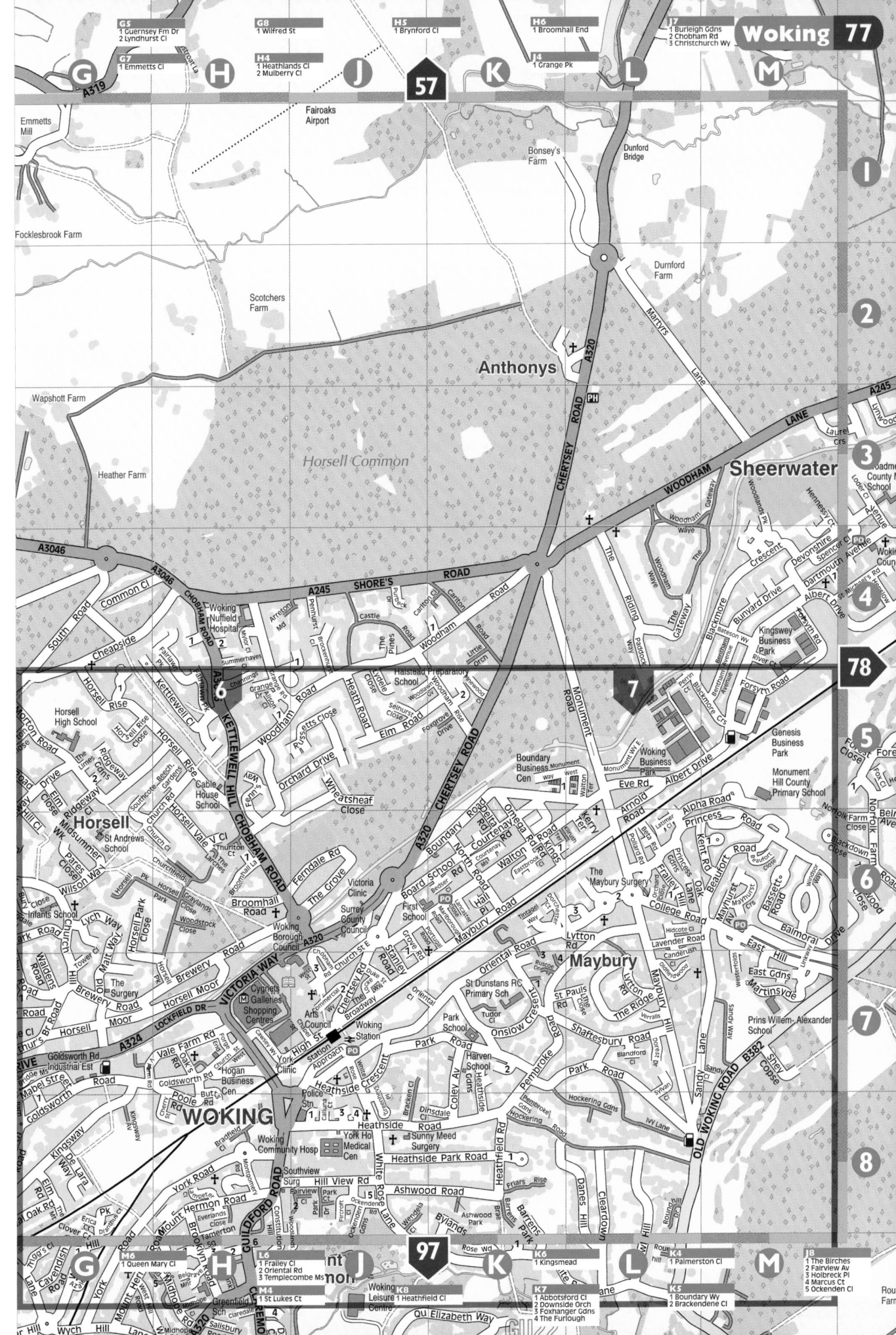

G5
1 Guernsey Fm Dr
2 Lyndhurst Cl

G7
1 Emmetts Cl

G8
1 Wilfred St

H4
1 Heathlands Cl
2 Mulberry Cl

H5
1 Brynford Cl

H6
1 Broomhall End

J7
1 Burleigh Gdns
2 Chobham Rd
3 Christchurch Wy

G A319   H   J   **57**   K   L   M

Emmetts Mill

Fairoaks Airport

Focklesbrook Farm

Bonsey's Farm

Dunford Bridge

Durnford Farm

Scotchers Farm

Anthonys

A320   CHERTSEY ROAD   PH

Martyrs   LANE

WOODHAM   Sheerwater

A245

Roadmead County M... School

Wapshott Farm

Horsell Common

Heather Farm

A3046

A3046   CHOBHAM ROAD

SHORE'S   ROAD   A245

Woking Nuffield Hospital

Halstead Preparatory School

6

7

Woking Business Park

Genesis Business Park

Monument Hill County Primary School

78

Horsell High School

Horsell Rise

Horsell

St Andrews School

KETTLEWELL HILL   CHOBHAM ROAD

Ferndale Rd

The Grove

Victoria Clinic

Surrey County Council

A320

Boundary Business Cen

Woking Business Park

Maybury

Broomhall Road

Woking Borough Council

CHERTSEY ROAD

Board School Rd

Courtenay Rd

Walton Rd

Maybury Road

Oriental Road

"The Maybury Surgery"

College Road

Lavender Road

East Hill

East Gdns

Balmoral Drive

Martinsyde

WOKING

Victoria Way

Cygnets Galleries Shopping Centres

Arts Council

Woking Station

St Dunstans RC Primary Sch

Shaftesbury Road

Maybury Lane

Prins Willem- Alexander School

Goldsworth Rd   A324

Hogan Business Cen

Police

Woking Clinic

Station Approach

Heathside Crescent

Harven School Road

Pembroke Road

OLD WOKING ROAD B382

Goldsworth

Woking Community Hosp

York Ho Medical Cen

Sunny Meed Surgery

Heathside   Road

Southview Surg

Hill View Rd

Heathside Park Road

Ashwood Road

GUILDFORD ROAD

Hermon Road

G   M6
1 Queen Mary Cl   H   L5
1 Fralley Cl
2 Oriental Rd
3 Templecombe Ms   J   **97**   K   L   M   J8
1 The Birches
2 Fairview Av
3 Holbreck Pl
4 Marcus Ct
5 Ockenden Cl

K6
1 Kingsmead

K7
1 Abbotsford Cl
2 Downside Orch
3 Foxhanger Gdns
4 The Furlough

K5
1 Boundary Wy
2 Brackendene Cl

M4
1 St Lukes Ct

Woking Leisure Centre

1 Heathfield Cl

Qu Elizabeth Way

GU22

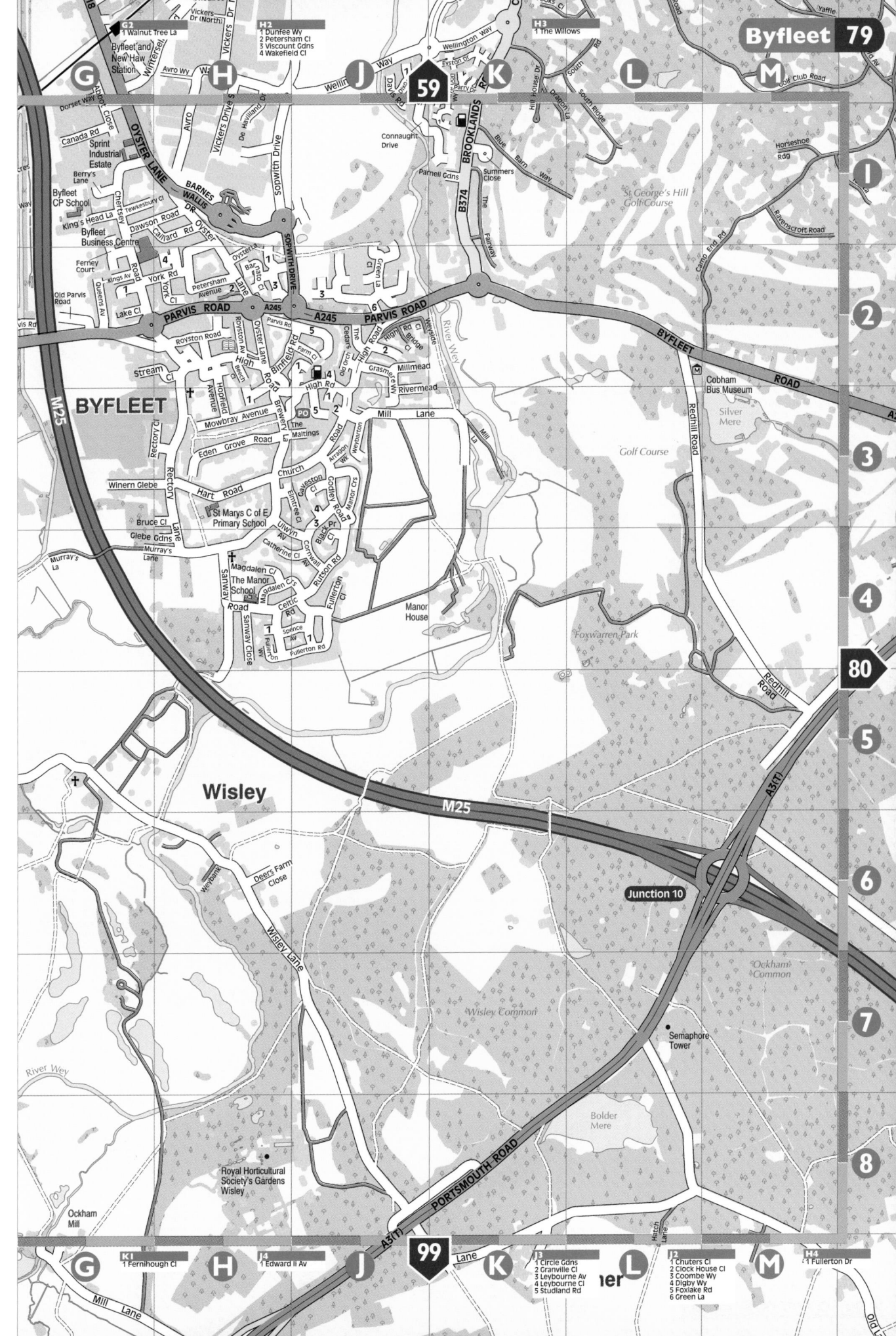

G H J K L M

I

H2
1 Dunfee Wy
2 Petersham Cl
3 Viscount Gdns
4 Wakefield Cl

G2
1 Walnut Tree La

H3
1 The Willows

59

Byfleet and
New Haw
Station

Vickers
Dr (North)

Vickers Dr

Wellington Way

Eyston Cl

Parry Dr

Wolf Club Road

Horseshoe
Rdg

Ravenscroft Road

Canada Rd

Sprint
Industrial
Estate

Berry's
Lane

Byfleet
CP School

King's Head La

Byfleet
Business Centre

Ferney
Court

Old Parvis
Road

OYSTER LANE

BARNES WALLIS DR

SOPWITH DRIVE

Avro Wy

Sopwith Drive

De Havilland Pl

Connaught
Drive

Parnell Gdns

BROOKLANDS

Summers
Close

B374

The Fairway

St George's Hill
Golf Course

Silver
Mere

Cobham
Bus Museum

M

BYFLEET ROAD

A2

Chertsey

Tewkesbury Cl

Dawson Road

Galliard Rd

Kings Av

York Rd

Lake Cl

Queens Av

Parvis Rd

PARVIS ROAD

A245

PARVIS ROAD

Oyster La

Farm Cl

High Rd

Bridge

Green La

The Cedars

Wayside

River Wey

Royston Road

Oyster Lane

Binfield Rd

High Road

Grasmere W

Millmead

Rivermead

BYFLEET

Stream Cl

Hopfield Avenue

High Rd

Mill Lane

Mowbray Avenue

PO

The Maltings

Brewery Road

Arragon Wy

Wenderton

Mill La

Golf Course

Eden Grove Road

Rectory Cl

Rectory Lane

Hart Road

Church Road

Gaveston Rd

Elmtree Cl

Codley Road

Manor Crs

Redhill Road

Winern Glebe

Bruce Cl

Glebe Gdns

St Marys C of E
Primary School

Ulwin Av

Black Pr

Cornwall

Catherine Cl

Rutson Rd

Murray's La

Murray's
Lane

Sanway Road

Magdalen Cl
The Manor
School

Magdalen C's

Celtic Rd

Fullerton Cl

Spence Av

Fullerton Rd

Sanway Close

Manor
House

Foxwarren Park

Redhill Road

A3(T)

80

M25

Junction 10

Ockham
Common

Wisley

Wisley Lane

Deers Farm
Close

Westbank

Wisley Common

Semaphore
Tower

River Wey

Ockham
Mill

Royal Horticultural
Society's Gardens
Wisley

Bolder
Mere

PORTSMOUTH ROAD

A3(T)

99

Hatch La

M25

I

2

3

4

5

6

7

8

G H J K L M

K1
1 Fernihough Cl

H4
1 Edward II Av

99

J1
1 Circle Gdns
2 Granville Cl
3 Leybourne Av
4 Leybourne Cl
5 Studland Rd

J2
1 Chuters Cl
2 Clock House Cl
3 Coombe Wy
4 Digby Wy
5 Foxlake Rd
6 Green La

H4
1 Fullerton Dr

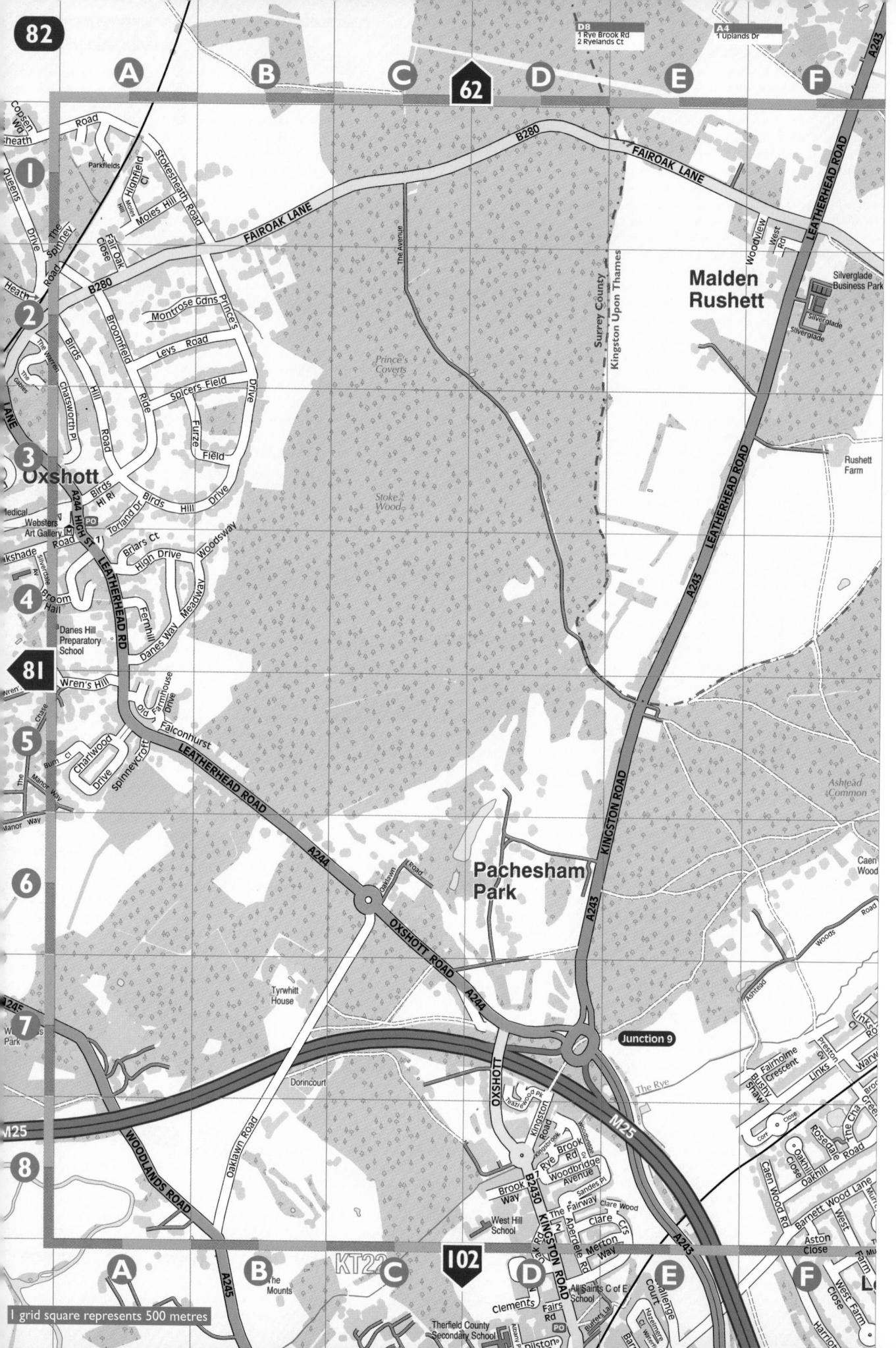

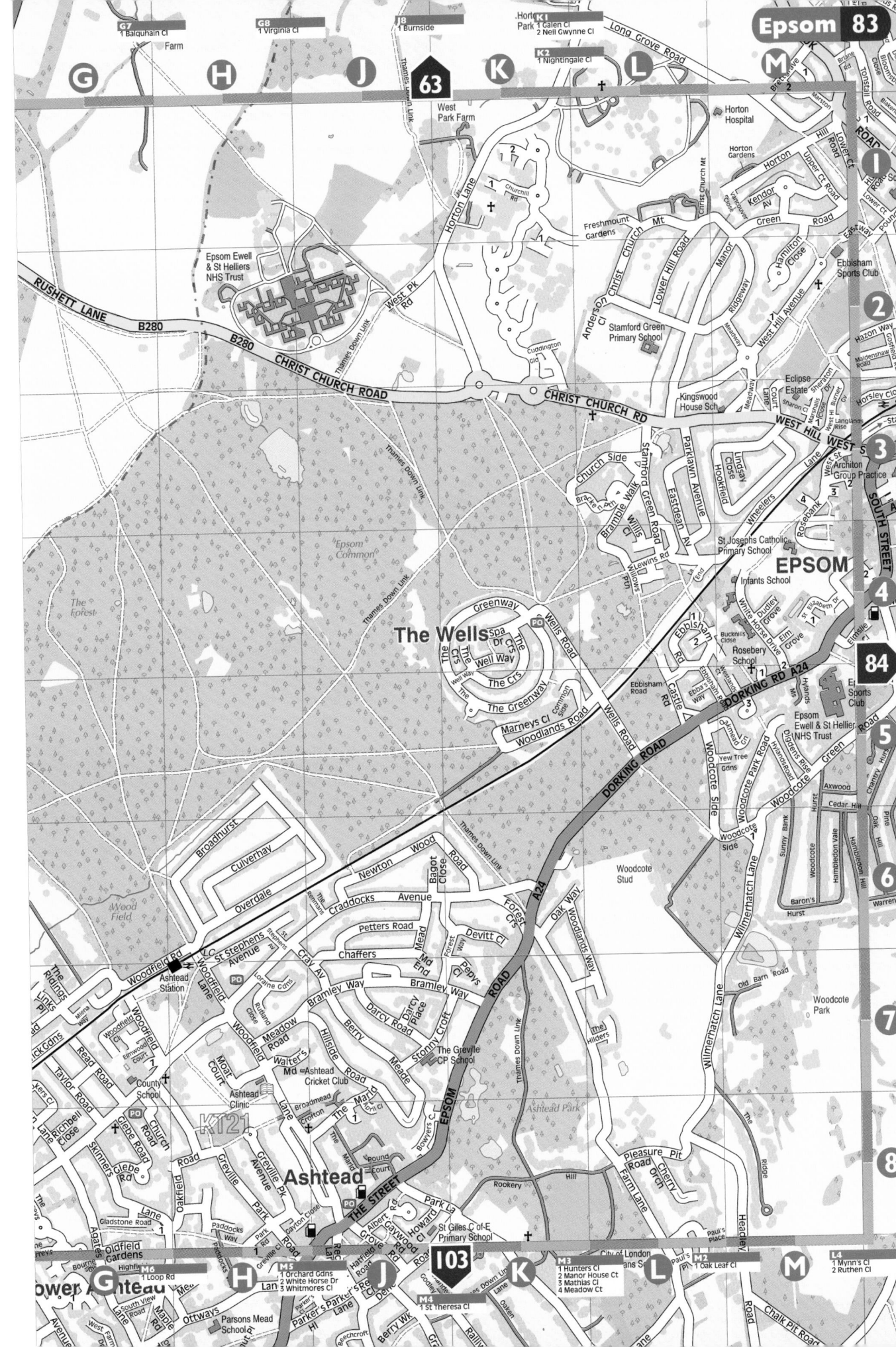

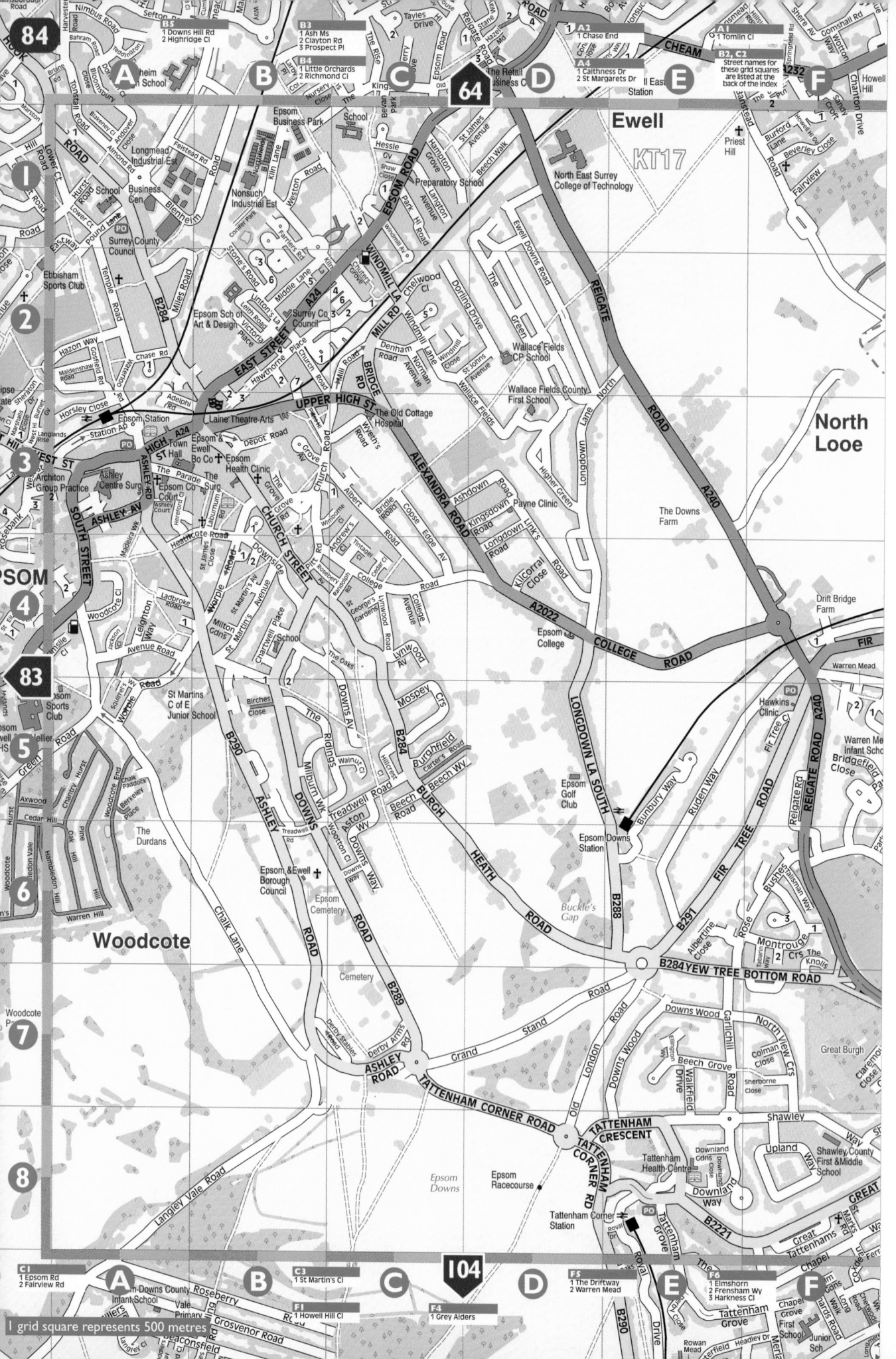

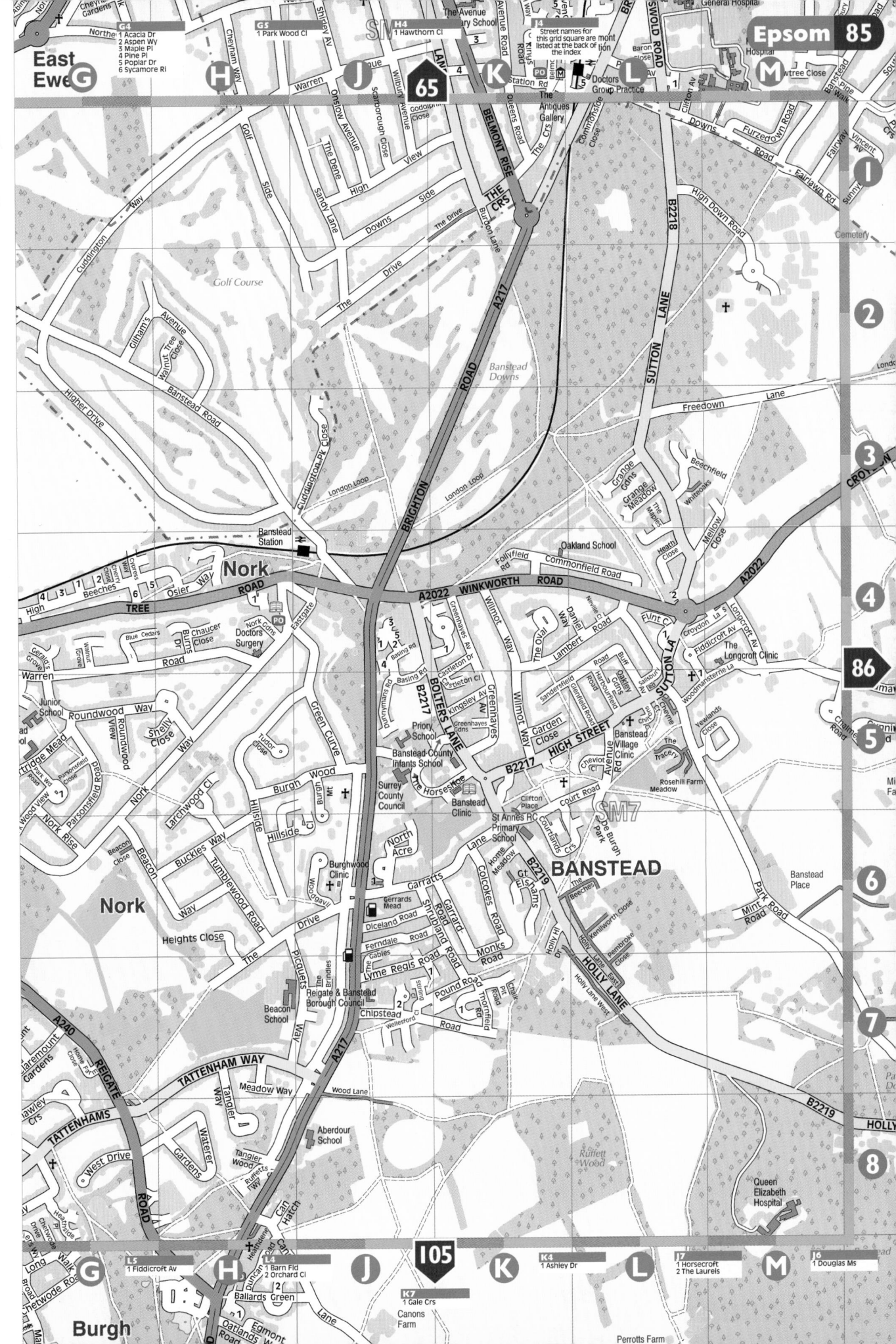

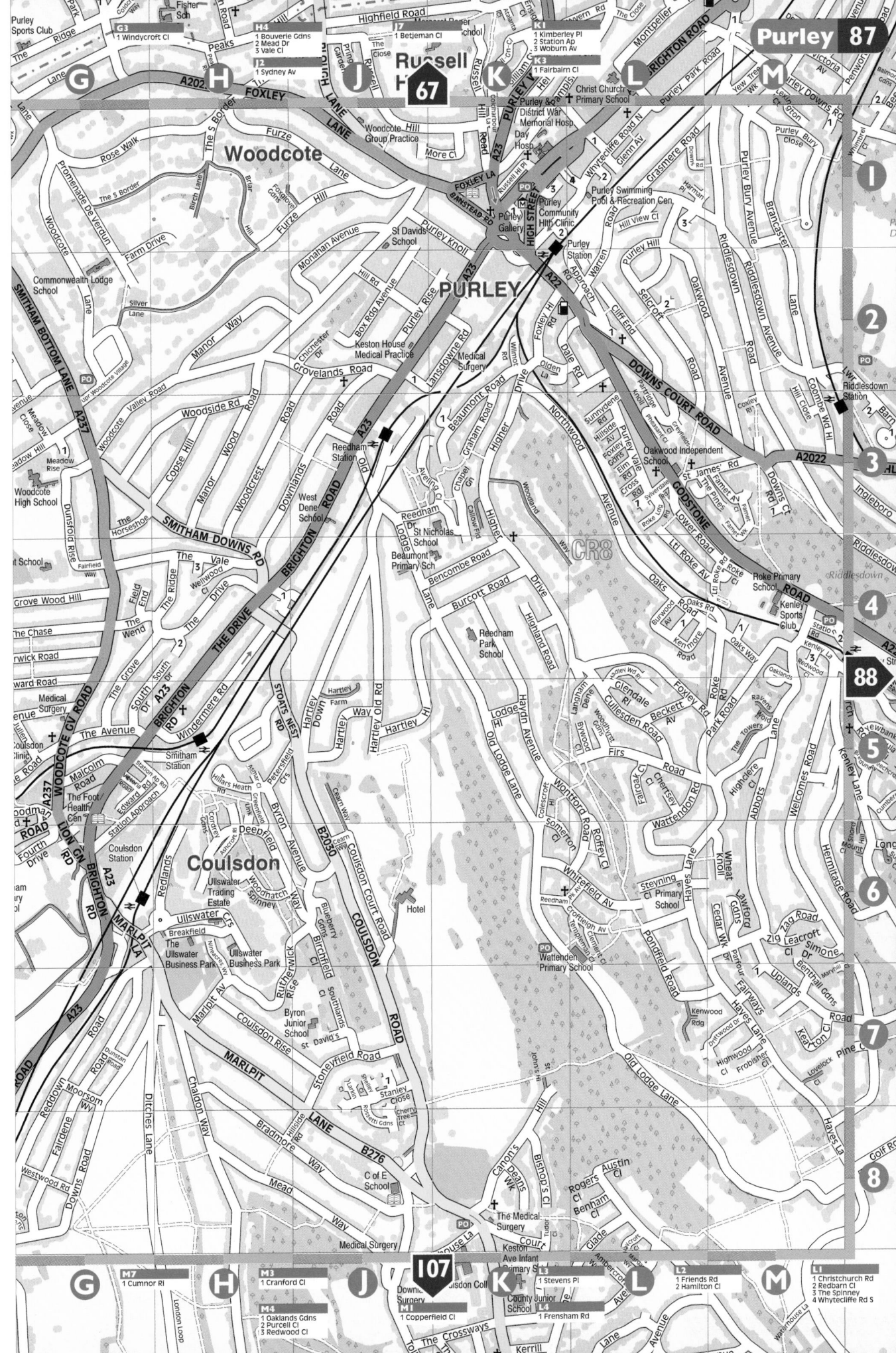

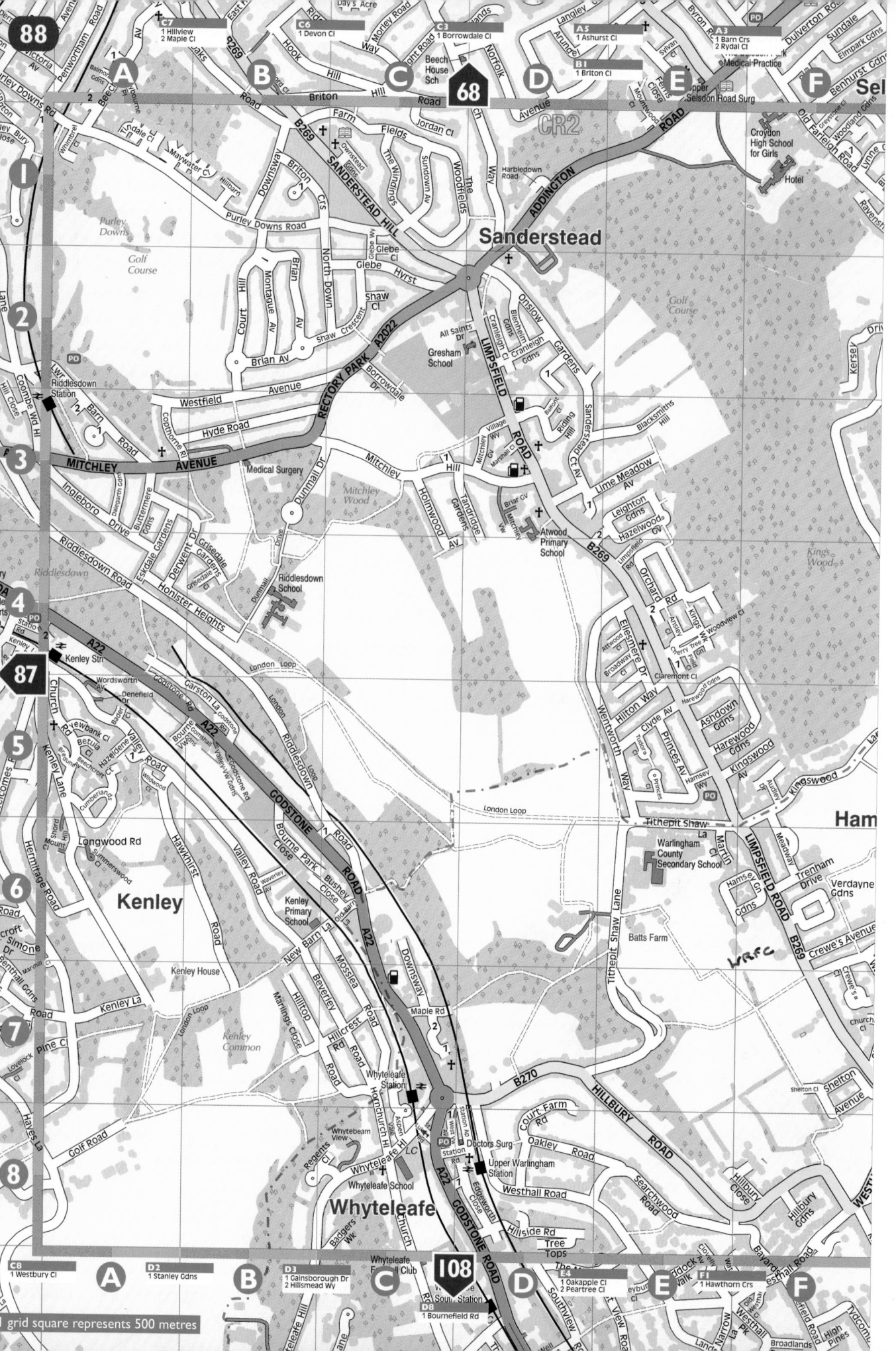

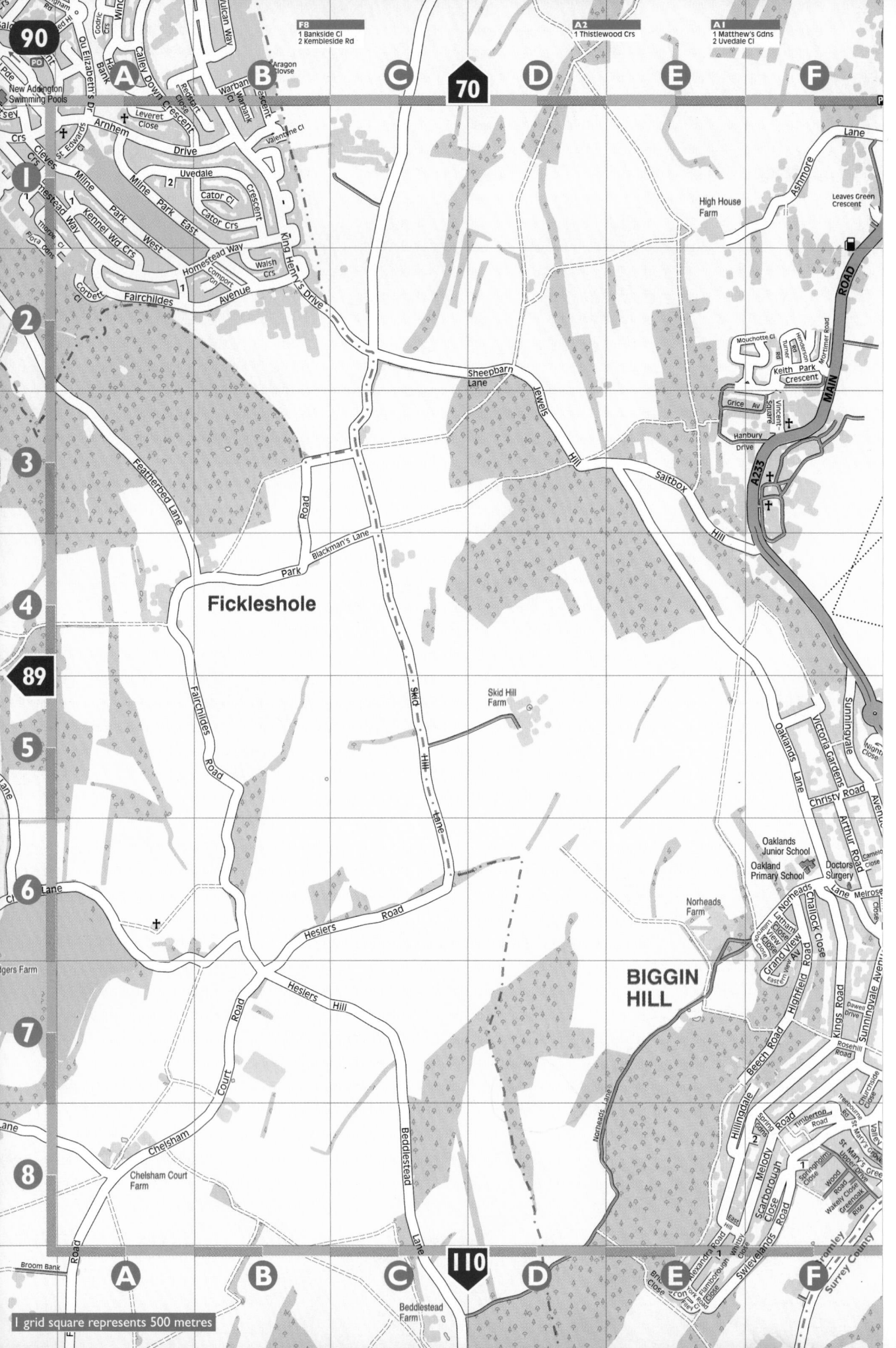

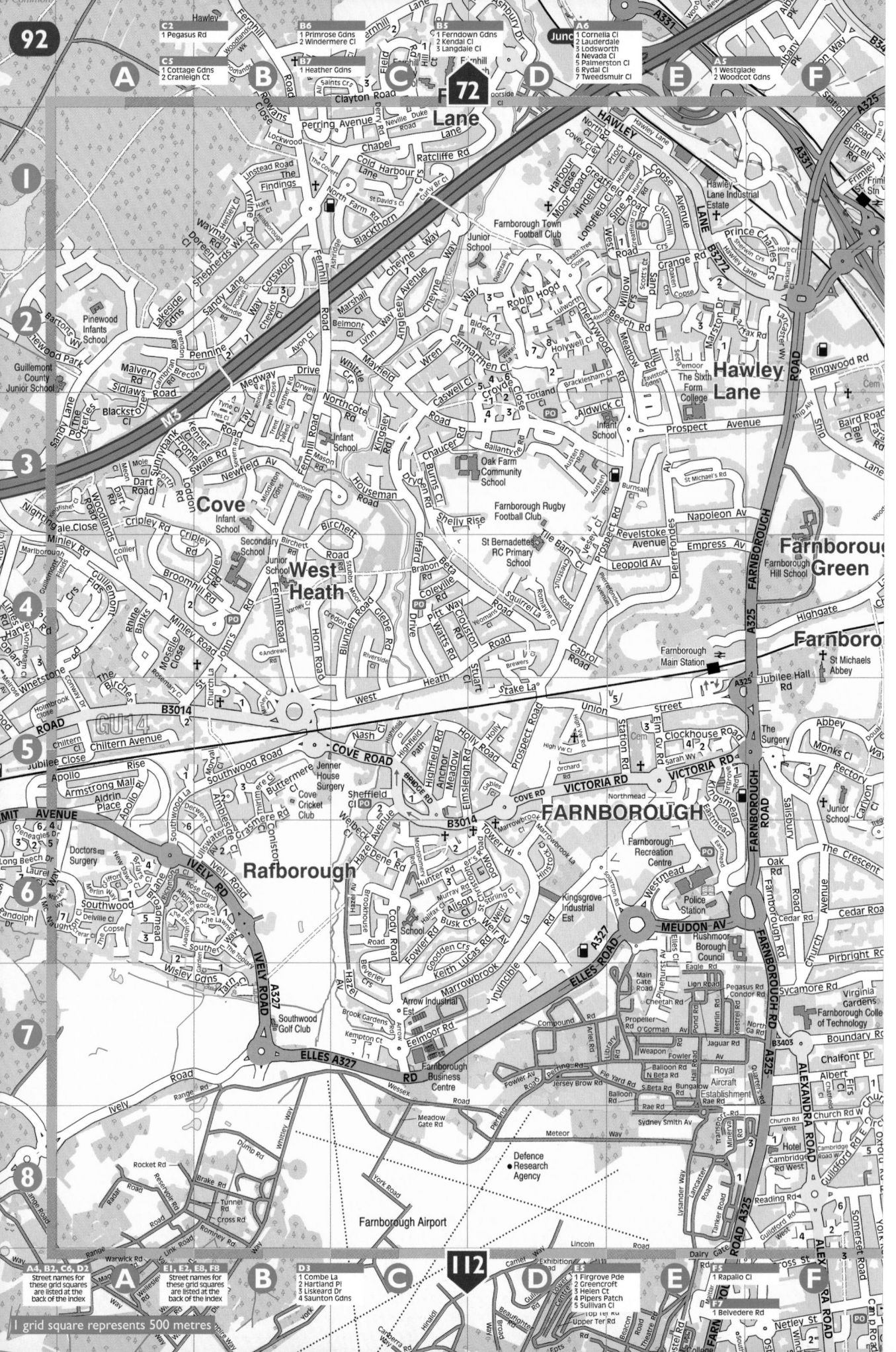

A   B   C   D   E   F

72

72

Lane

I

2

3

4

5

6

7

8

Cove

West Heath

Rafborough

Hawley Lane

Farnborough Green

Farnboro

Farnborough

FARNBOROUGH

112

A   B   C   D   E   F

1 grid square represents 500 metres

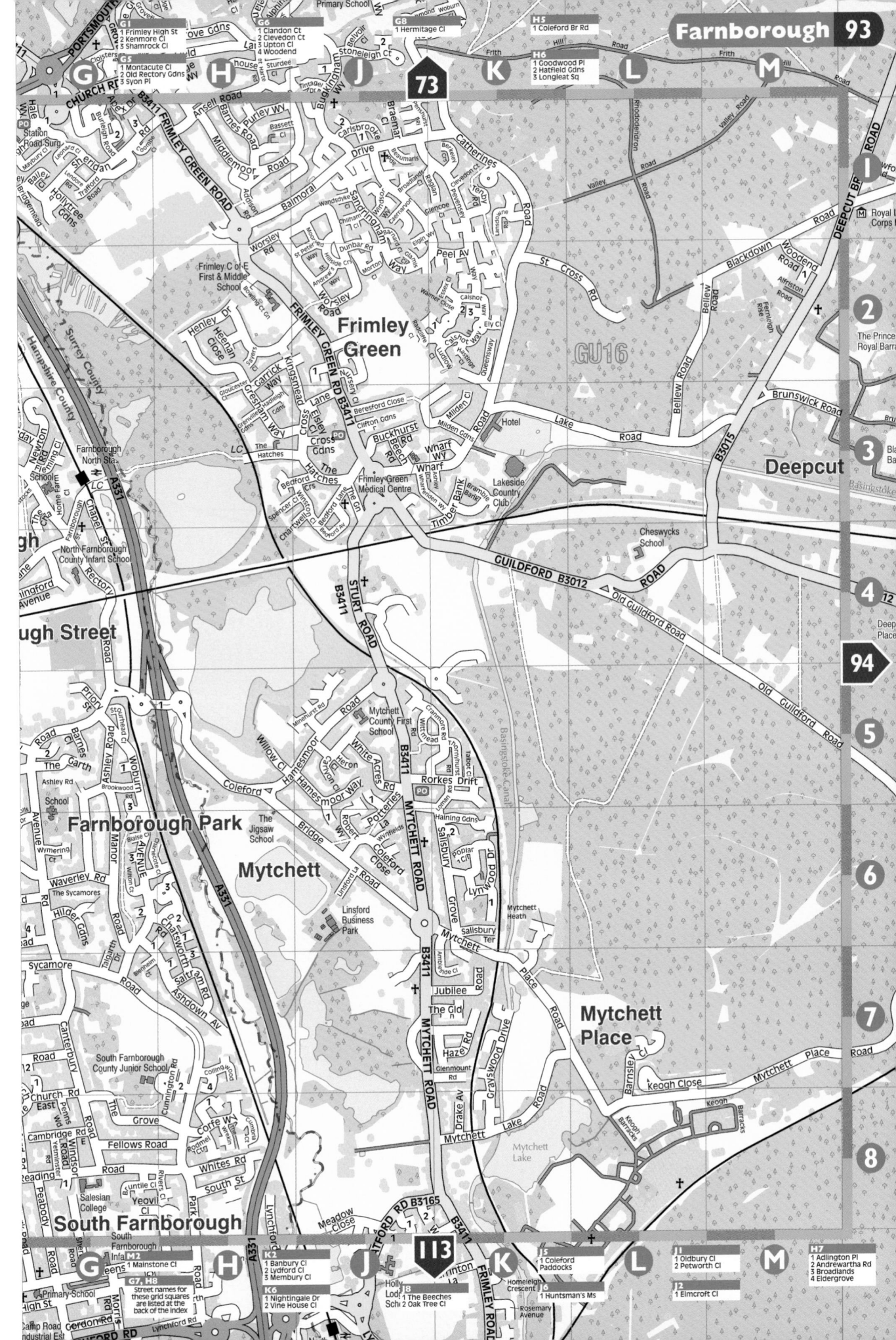

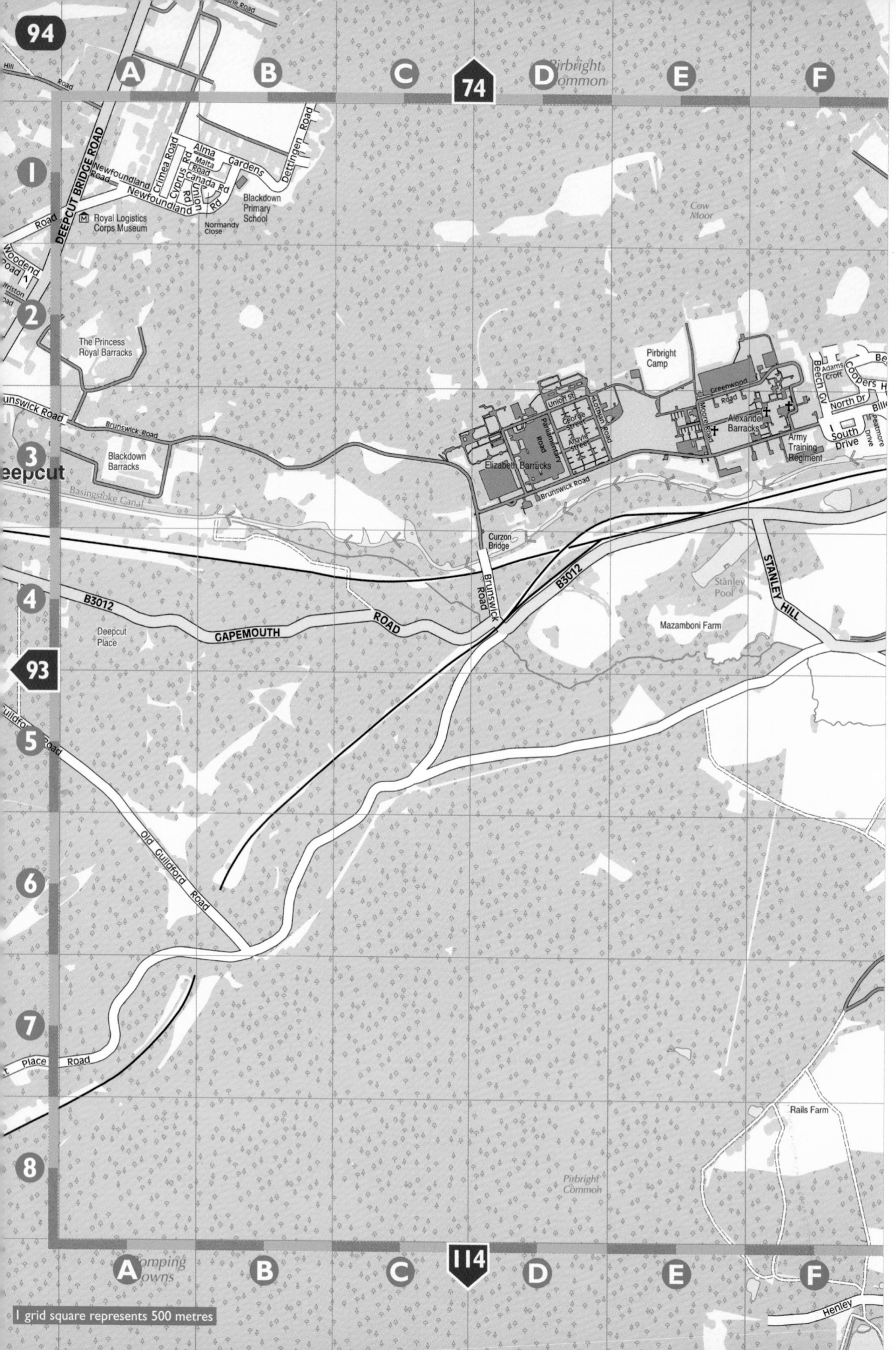

A B C D E F

74

I

2

The Princess
Royal Barracks

Brunswick Road

3
Deepcut

Blackdown
Barracks

Brunswick Road

Basingstoke Canal

4
B3012

Deepcut
Place

GAPEMOUTH ROAD

5

Guildford Road

Old Guildford Road

6

7

t Place Road

8

A B C D E F

114

Newfoundland
Road
Newfoundland

Crimea Road
Cyprus Rd
Malta Rd
Canada Rd
Union Rd
Caution Rd

Alma
Gardens

Dettingen Road

Royal Logistics
Corps Museum

Normandy
Close

Blackdown
Primary
School

Woodend
Road

Christon
Road

Pirbright
Common

Cow
Moor

Pirbright
Camp

Greenwood
Road

Union St
George
Street
Argyle
Street

Penitentiary Road

Aldinah Road

Moore Road

Alexander
Barracks

Army
Training
Regiment

Beech Gv
Adams Croft
North Dr
Coopers H
South
Drive
Beatmore
Drive
Bill

Elizabeth Barracks

Brunswick Road

Curzon
Bridge

Brunswick Road

B3012

STANLEY HILL

Stanley
Pool

Mazamboni Farm

Rails Farm

Pirbright
Common

Tomping
Downs

Henley

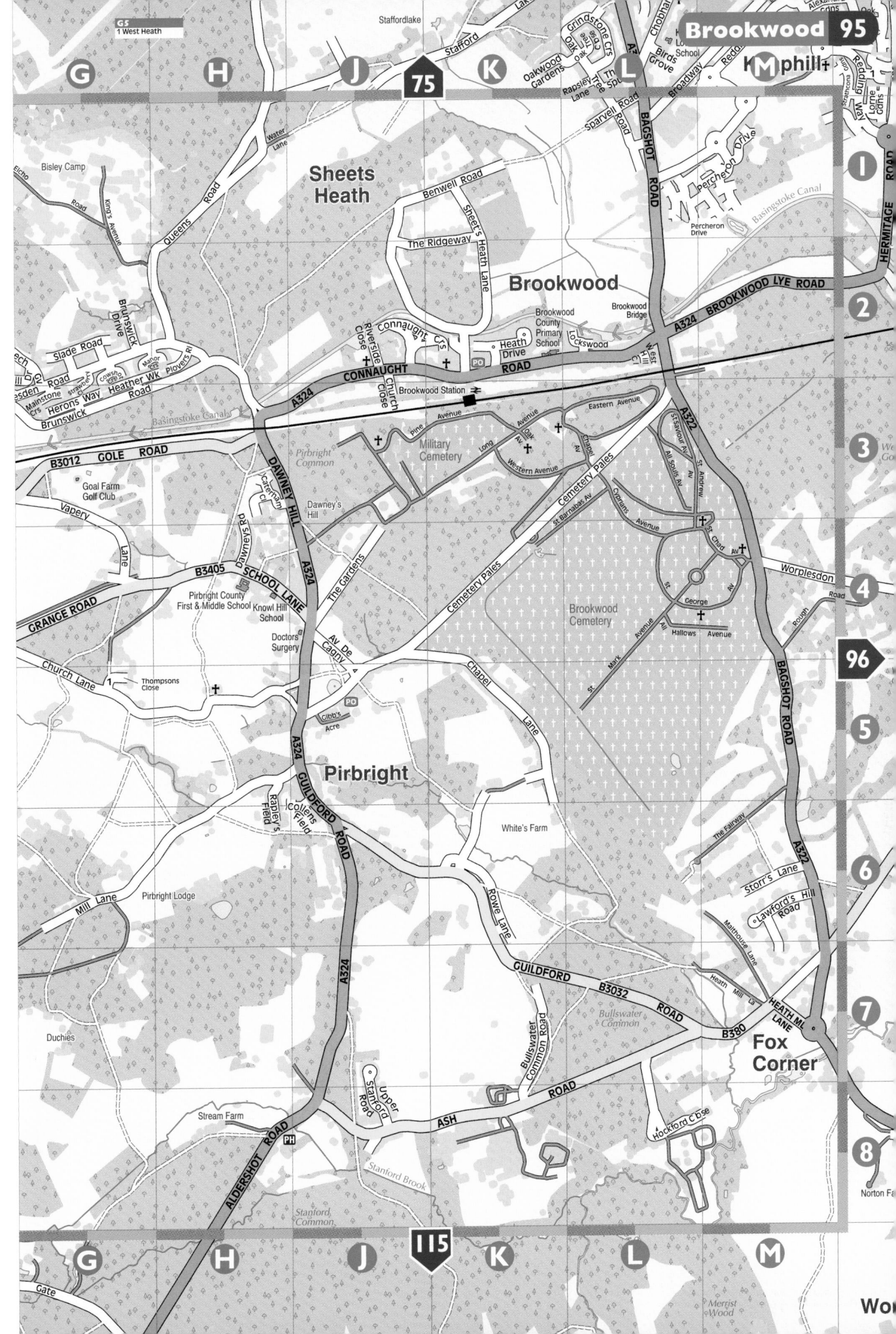

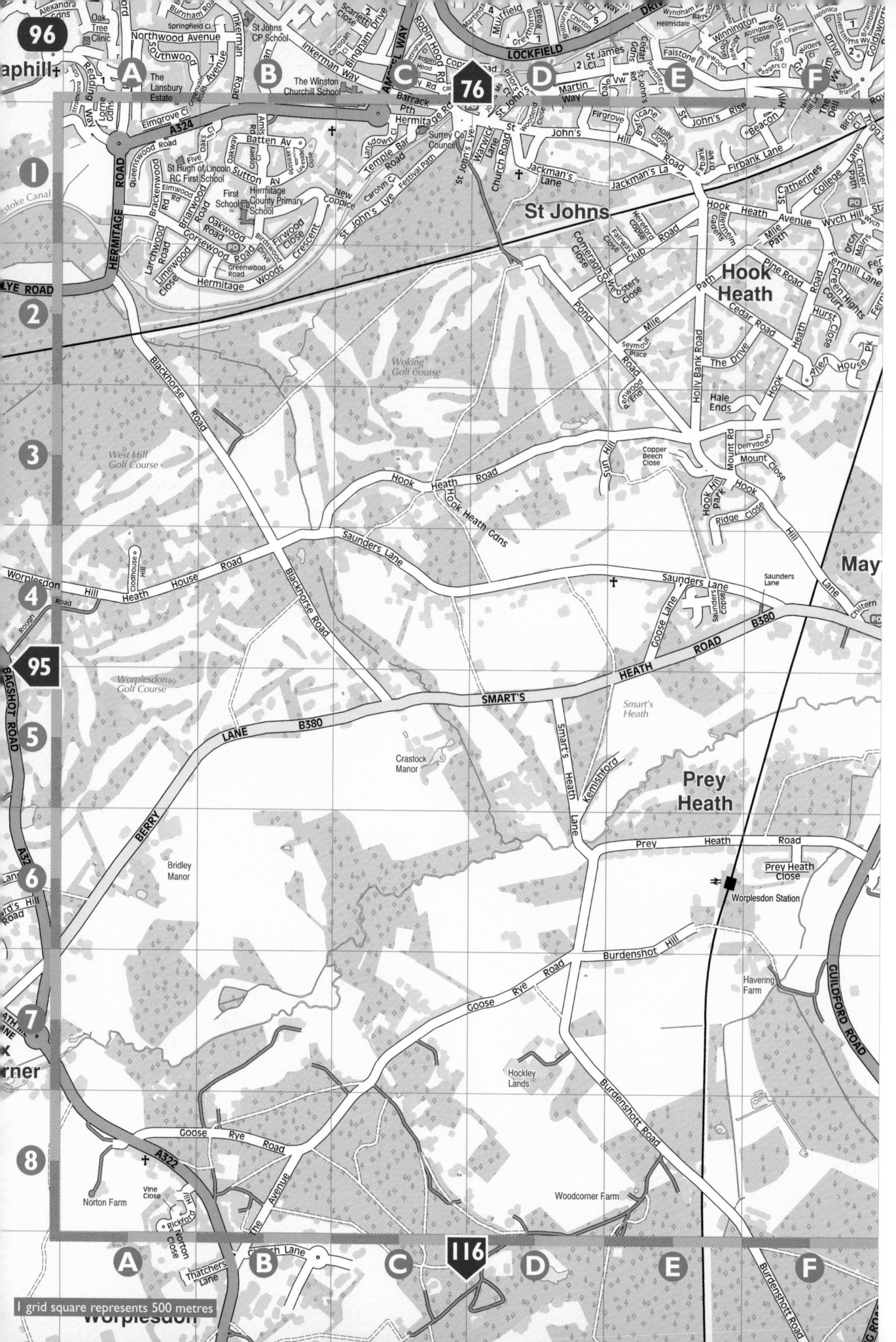

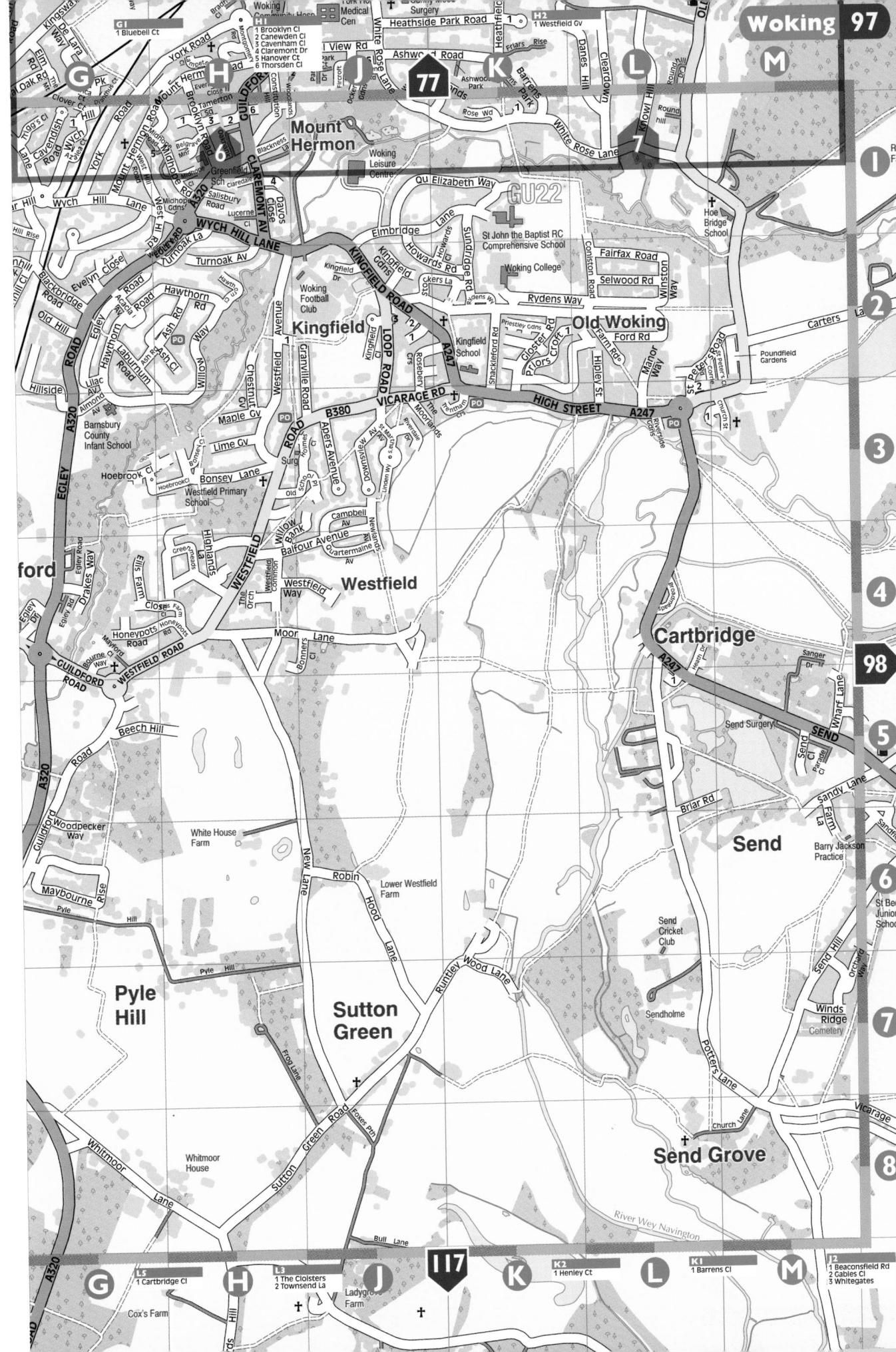

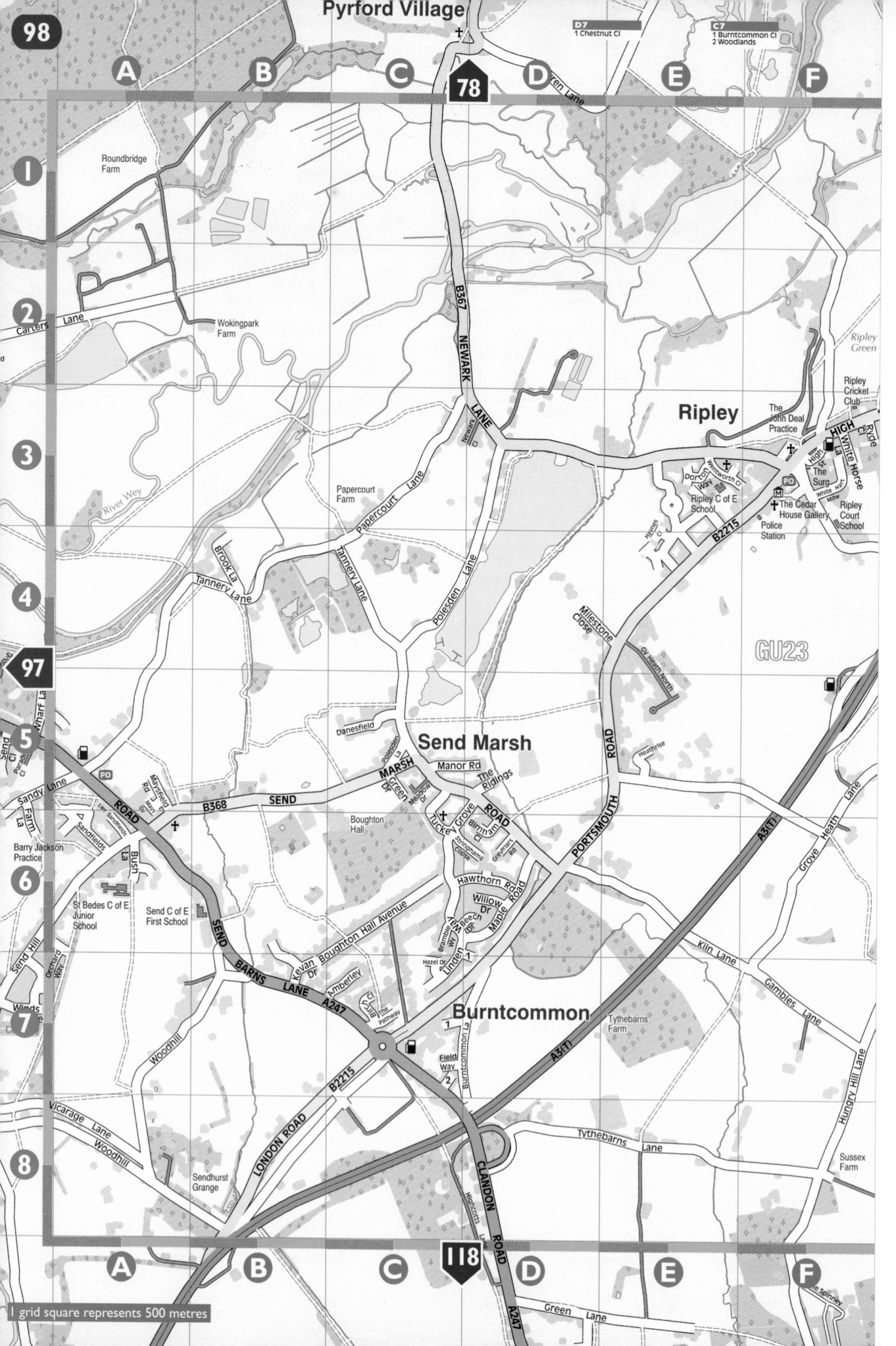

G H J **79** K L M

Royal Horticultural
Society's Gardens
Wisley

Mill

I

Elm Lane

**Elm
Corner**

Mill Lane

2

Ockham Lane

Hatch Lane

**Bridge
End**

Upton
Farm

B2215

A3(T)

**Church
End**

3

SAINT

PORTSMOUTH ROAD

B2039

Alms Heath

School Lane

Ockham

4

Ockham
Park

Guileshill Lane

OCKHAM ROAD NORTH B2039

Slade
Farm

100

Rose Lane

Guileshill Farm

5

Service Area

Whitehill
Lane

Ryde
Farm

Bachelor's Lane

Green Lane

Waterloo
Farm

6

Ripley Lane

Bachelors

Long Reach

Northcote Crs

The Raleigh
School

Nightingale Crs

7

Green Lane West

Northcote Road

Edwin

Edwin Cl

Holly Close

Jury
Farm

Manor
Farm

East Lane

Farleys
Cl

8

Holride
Farm

Silkmore Lane

Kingston Lane

Greta Bank

Woodside

Lollesworth
Farm

Roundtree
Farm

Lollesworth Lane

G H J **119** K L M

100

A   **B**   **C**   **80**   **D**   **E** St Matthews C of E First School   **F**

1

Old Lane

Hatchford Park

Cold Norton Farm

PH Downside Common

Downside

Deacon Close
Middleton Road

2

Ockham Lane

Upton Farm

Martyr's Green

May's Green

Newmarsh Farm

Horsley Road

3

Stumps Grove

4

Blackmoor Farm

Old Lane

Old La Gdns

Surrey Gdns

Bank's Lane

99

Lane

slad
arm

5

Wi

Lane

Forest Road

Howard Road

PO
Effingham Junction Station

Effingham Common

Norwood Farm

Lower Farm Road

Lower Farm

6

The Drift

The Forest

Ockham

Forest La

Orchard Cl

Heathway

Falconwood

Berrington Dr

Heathway

Effingham Cricket Club

Hinterland House

7

Nightingale Crs
Nightingale Av

Weston Lea

Glenesk House Preparatory School

Heathercdene

The Highlands

Wildwood Cl

Parkside Cl
Parkside Pl

Forest Road

Forest Close

Hooke Road

Heath View

The Raleigh School

Edwin Rd
Edwin Cl

cote Crs

Meadow Way
Howard Close

B2039

Horsley Station

The Ridings

Nightingale Road

Heath Vw

Greatlee Wood

Effingham Common

thcote Road

East Lane

8

Lollesworth Farm

Kingston Avenue
PO
The Medical Centre

Cobham Way

Thorncaste Place

Lovelace

The Rise

The Chase

Glendene Avenue

The Birches

Norreis Ride

Norreis Drive

High Park Av

High Park Avenue

Old Rectory La

EAST HORSLEY

sworth Lane

A   **B**   Ockham Dr   **OCKHAM ROAD**   Woodlands   **C**   **120**   **D**   **E**   **F**

Lynx Hill

Horsley Sports

Orestan Farm

restan Lane

1 grid square represents 500 metres

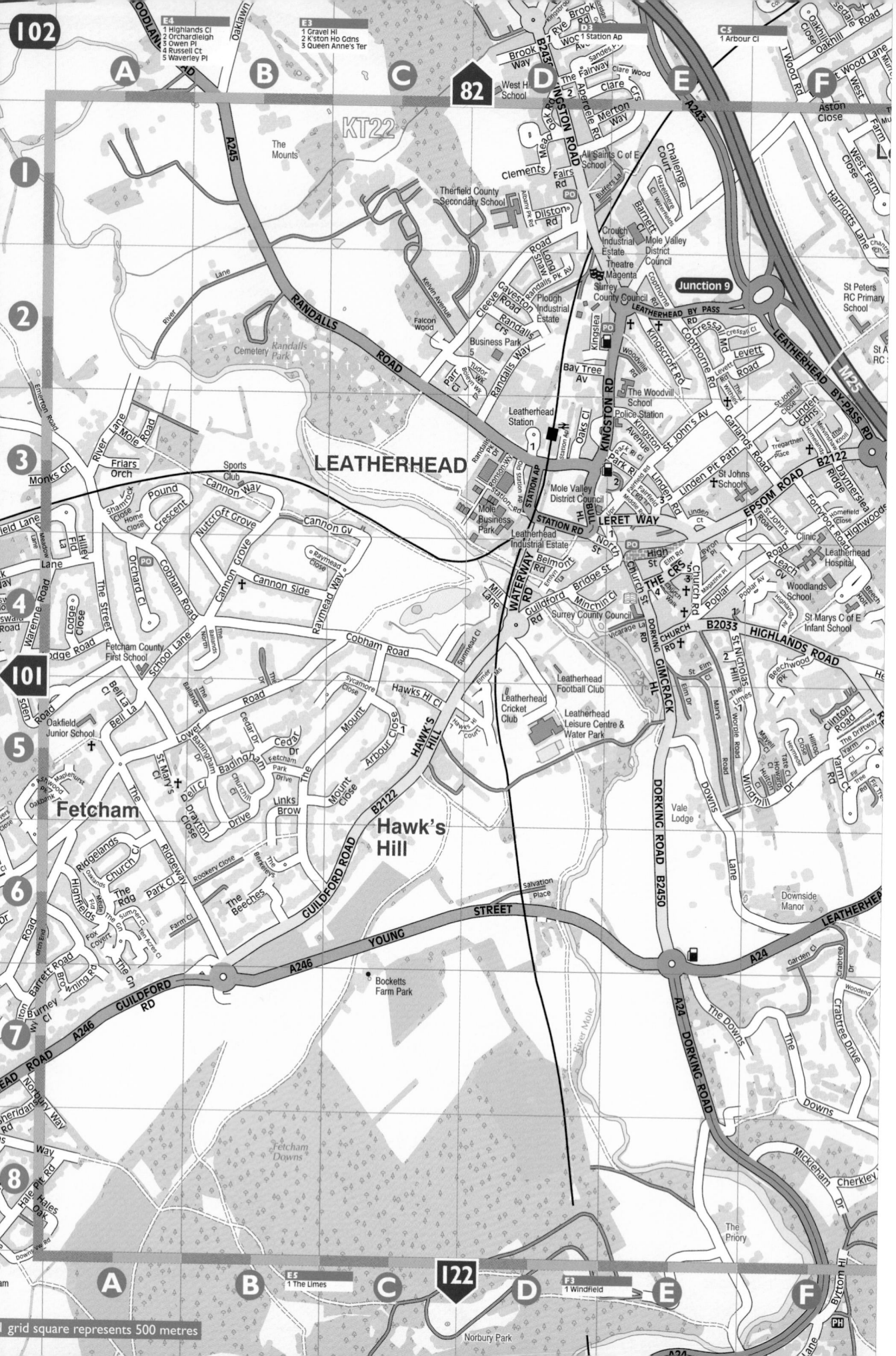

A   B   C   82   D   E   F

E4
1 Highlands Cl
2 Orchardleigh
3 Owen Pl
4 Russell Ct
5 Waverley Pl

E3
1 Gravel Hl
2 K'ston Ho Gdns
3 Queen Anne's Ter

C5
1 Arbour Cl

KT22

1 Station Ap

The Mounts

Clements

All Saints C of E School

Therfield County Secondary School

Challenge Court

Mole Valley District Council

Junction 9

St Peters RC Primary School

Crouch Industrial Estate

Theatre Magenta

Surrey County Council

Plough Industrial Estate

RANDALLS ROAD

Cemetery

Randalls Park

Randalls Business Park

Bay Tree Av

The Woodvill School

Police Station

Kingston Avenue

LEATHERHEAD BY PASS

LEATHERHEAD BY-PASS RD

M25

Friars Orch

Monks Gn

Sports Club

Leatherhead Station

LEATHERHEAD

Mole Business Park

Mole Valley District Council

St Johns School

EPSOM ROAD

B2122

Cannon Way

Nutcroft Grove

Cannon Gv

Cannon Grove

Cannon side

Raymead Way

Raymead Close

LERET WAY

Leatherhead Industrial Estate

St Johns

Leatherhead Hospital

Woodlands Rd

101

Fetcham County First School

Cobham Road

Belmont

Bridge St

Minchin Cl

Surrey County Council

CIMCRACK HL

CHURCH

B2033

HIGHLANDS ROAD

St Marys C of E Infant School

Oakfield Junior School

Bell La

Hawks Hl Cl

Leatherhead Football Club

Leatherhead Cricket Club

Leatherhead Leisure Centre & Water Park

Fetcham

Links Brow

Hawk's Hill

B2122

Vale Lodge

Downside Manor

Ridgelands

Church Cl

The Rdg

The Beeches

GUILDFORD ROAD

salvation Place

DORKING ROAD

B2450

LEATHERHEAD

Bocketts Farm Park

YOUNG STREET

A246 GUILDFORD RD

A246

A24

A24 DORKING ROAD

The Downs

Crabtree Drive

River Mole

Fetcham Downs

The Priory

Mickleham Dr

Cherkley

A   B   122   C   D   E   F

E5
1 The Limes

F3
1 Windfield

Norbury Park

1 grid square represents 500 metres

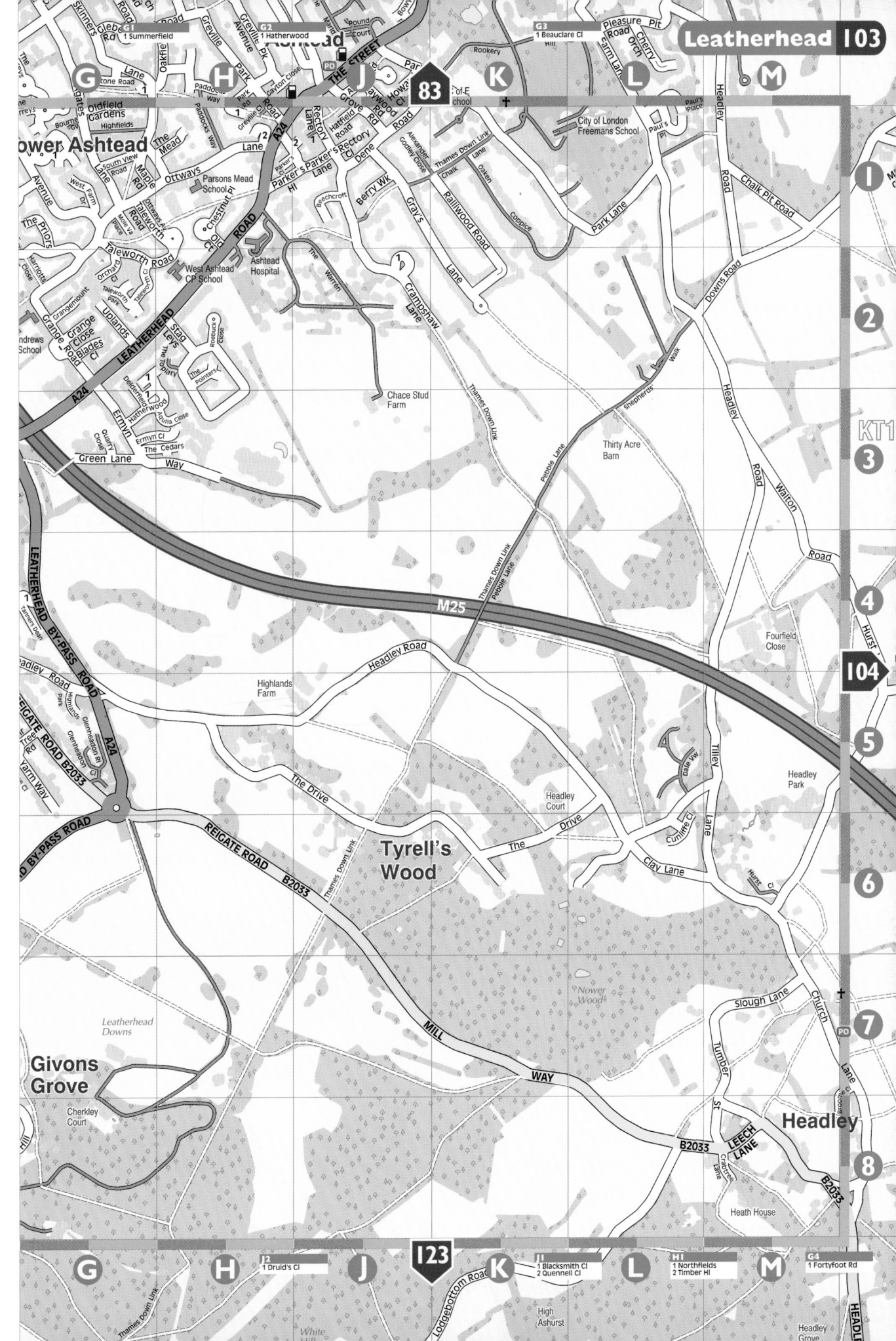

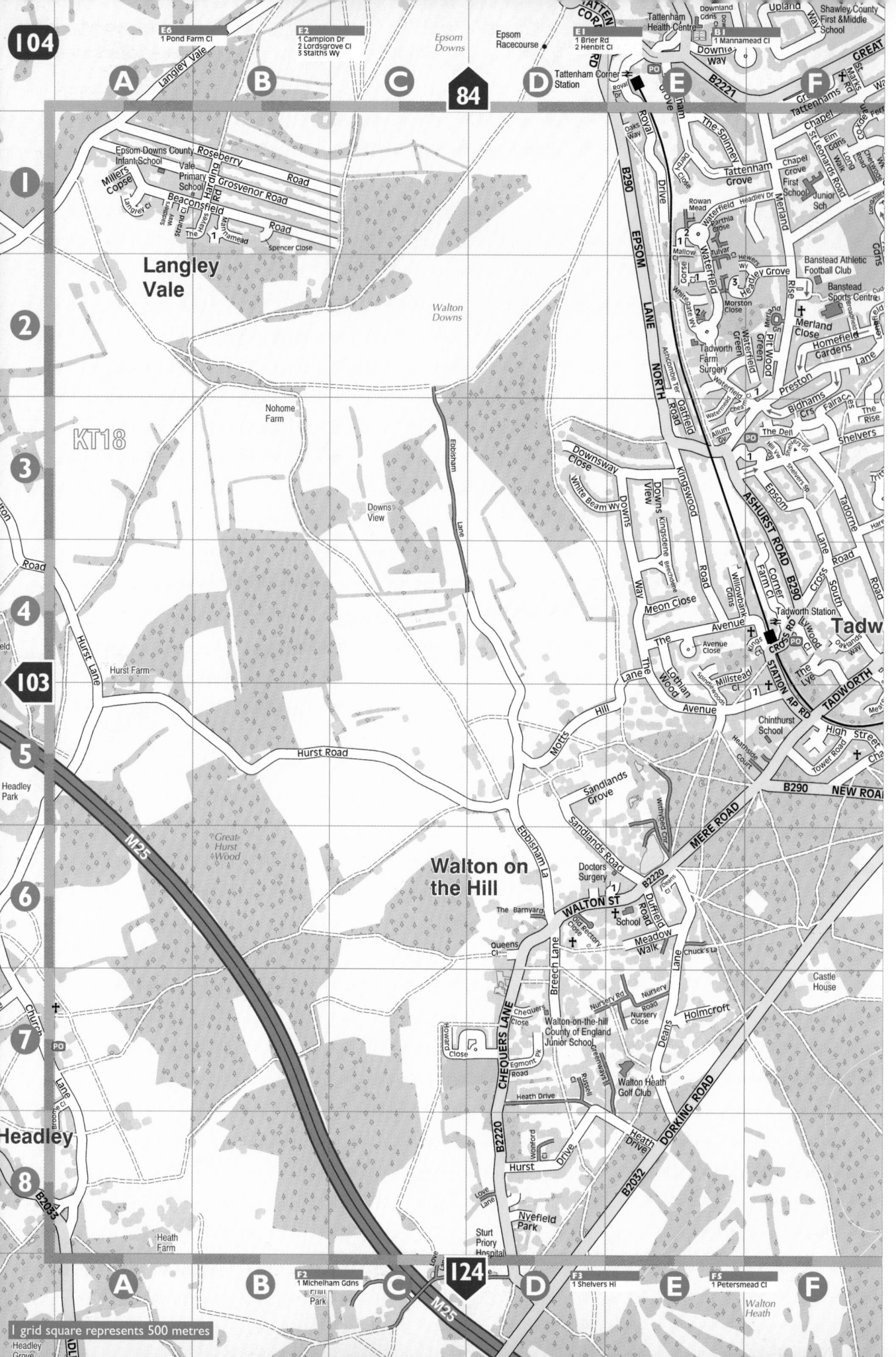

E6
1 Pond Farm Cl

E2
1 Campion Dr
2 Lordsgrove Cl
3 Stalths Wy

Epsom
Downs

Epsom
Racecourse

E1
1 Brier Rd
2 Henbit Cl

Downland
Gdns

Upland
Wy

Tattenham
Health Centre

Shawley County
First & Middle
School

B1
1 Mannamead Cl

GREAT

TATTEN
COR

A   B   C   84   D   Tattenham Corner   E   B2221   F
                          Station

Downs
Way

Gr
Tattenhams

Chapel
La

The Spinney

St Mark's

Tattenham
Grove

Merland

Elm Gdns
St Leonards Rd

Long
Walk

Chapel
Grove
First
School

Junior
Sch

1   Epsom Downs County   Roseberry
     Infant School
Millers
Copse   Epsom Vale   Road

Langley
Vale

Grosvenor Road

Saddlers   Harding Rd
Way   The

Beaconsfield

Langley Cl   Strand Cl

Rowan
Mead

Waterfield Headley Dr
Parthia

Banstead Athletic
Football Club

Banstead
Sports Centre

Merland
Close

Homefield
Gardens

The Hayes

Primary
School

Mannamead
Road   1

Spencer Close

Mallow
Cl

Tulyar

Waterfield

Morston
Close

Preston

Bidhams
Crs

Fairac
s

The
Rise

Shelvers

KT18

Nohome
Farm

Walton
Downs

Downs
View

Ebbisham Lane

Downsway
Close

White Beam Wy

Kingswood

Downs
View

Kingsdene

Breechelea

Willowbank
Gdns

Tadworth
Farm Surgery

Allum
Gr

PO

The Dell

EPSOM   LANE   NORTH

B290

Oatfield

Ashcombe Ter

Whitegate Wy

ASHURST ROAD

Epsom

PO

Corner
Farm Cl

B290

Tadworth Station

Cross Rd

Cross Rd South

Tadorne
Road

3

I

2

3

103

4

5

6

7

8

Headley

Hurst Lane

Hurst Farm

Hurst Road

M25

Great
Hurst
Wood

Headley
Park

Church Lane

PO

Brooms Cl

B2033

Heath
Farm

Walton on
the Hill

Ebbisham La

The Barnyard

Queens
Cl

Chequers
Close

Breech Lane

CHEQUERS LANE

Howard
Close

Egmont
Road

Heath Drive

B2220

Hurst
Drive

Wootford

Love Lane

Nyefield
Park

Sturt
Priory Hospital

Motts

Hill

The
Lane

The
Avenue

Kingswood Road

Meon Close

The
Avenue

Sandlands
Grove

Sandlands Road

Withypool Cl

Doctors
Surgery   1

B2220

WALTON ST

Old Rectory

School

Meadow
Walk

Chuck's La

Nursery Rd

Nursery
Road

Nursery
Close

Russell

Greenway

Deans

Lane

Walton-on-the-hill
County of England
Junior School

Walton Heath
Golf Club

Heath
Drive

DORKING ROAD

B2032

Duffield
Road

Avenue
Close

The
Lothian
Wood

Spindlewood

Millstead
Cl

Chinthurst
School

Heathside
Court

MERE ROAD

B290   NEW ROAD

Tower Road

High Street

Oaklands
Way

The
Lye

Holmcroft

Castle
House

Tadw

Station Ap Rd

STATION AP RD

Lywood Cl

A   B   F2   C   124   D   E   F
         1 Michelham Gdns   M25   F3   F5
         Flint   1 Shelvers Hi   1 Petersmead Cl
         Park

Love La

Walton
Heath

1 grid square represents 500 metres

Headley
Grove

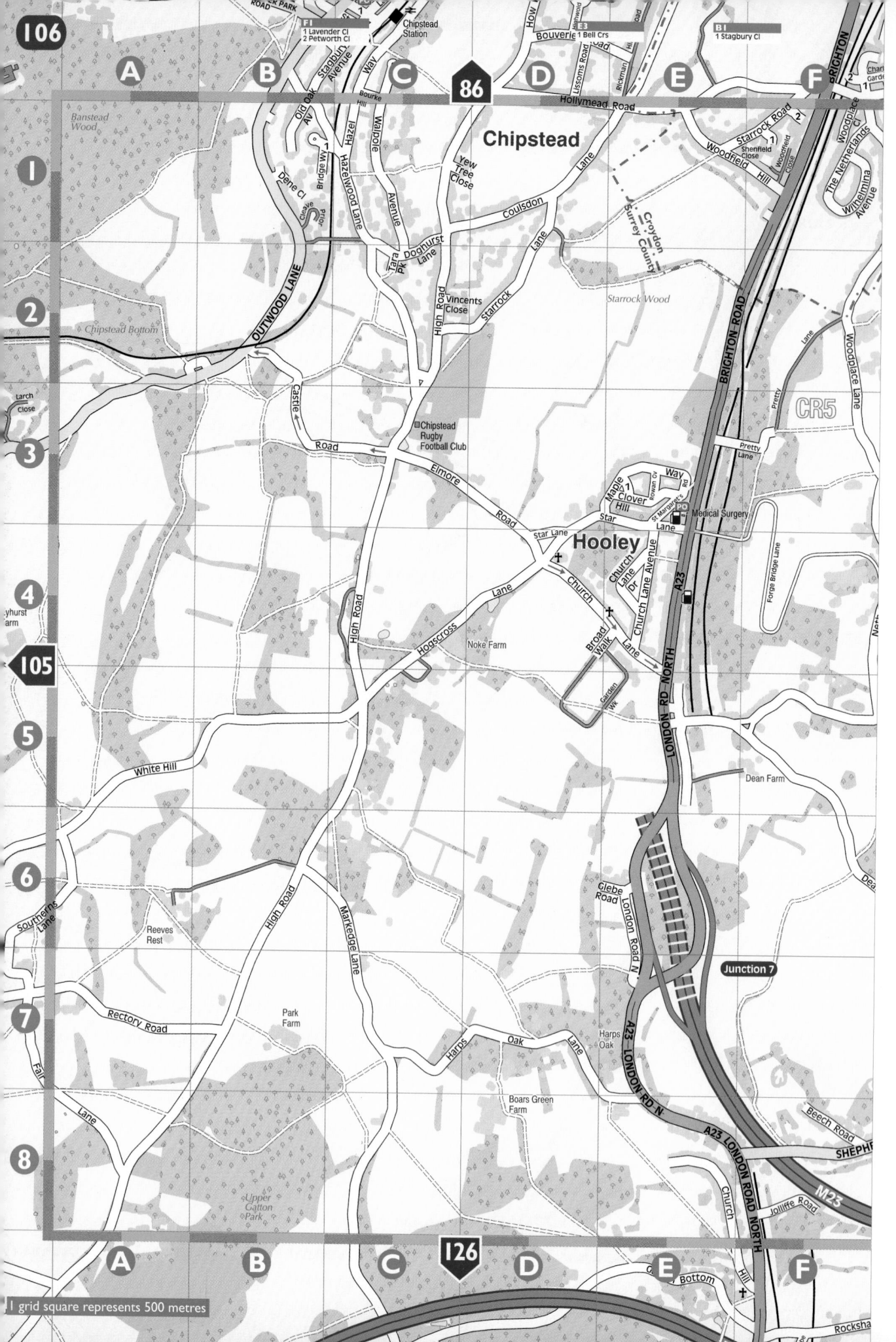

A   B   C   86   D   E   F

Banstead Wood

1 Lavender Cl
2 Petworth Cl

Chipstead Station

F1

Bouverie 1 Bell Crs

E3

How

Highfield

Old

B1

1 Stagbury Cl

BRIGHTON

Hollymead   Road

Chipstead

Lissoms Road

Rickman

Starrock Road

Woodfield

Shenfield Close

Woodfield Hill

Woodplace

The Netherlands

Wilhelmina Avenue

1

Old Oak Av
Bridge Wy
Dene Cl
Priory
Stagbury Avenue
Bourke Hill
Hazel
Walpole
Avenue
Hazelwood Lane
Way
Tara Pk
Doghurst Lane
High Road

Yew Tree Close

Coulsdon   Lane

Vincents Close
Starrock Lane

Croydon Surrey County

Starrock Wood

Woodplace Lane

2

Chipstead Bottom

OUTWOOD LANE

Pretty Lane

CR5

Larch Close

Castle

3

Road

Elmore Road

Chipstead Rugby Football Club

Maple Hill
Rowan Ov
1
Clover
St Margaret's
Way
Rd
PO
Medical Surgery

Pretty Lane

Star Lane
Hooley
star

Lane

4

yhurst Farm

High Road

Church Lane
Dr
Church Lane Avenue
A23

Forge Bridge Lane

Hogscross Lane
Noke Farm
Broad Walk
Garden WK
LONDON RD NORTH

5

White Hill

Dean Farm

6

Southerns Lane

High Road

Markedge Lane

Glebe Road

London Road N.

Junction 7

7

Fall

Rectory Road

Park Farm

Reeves Rest

Harps
Oak
Lane
Harps Oak

A23 LONDON RD N

8

Lane

Upper Gatton Park

Boars Green Farm

Beech Road

A23 LONDON ROAD NORTH

SHEPHE

M23

Church Hill

Jolliffe Road

SHEPH

Rocksha

A   B   126   C   D   E   F
                              Bottom

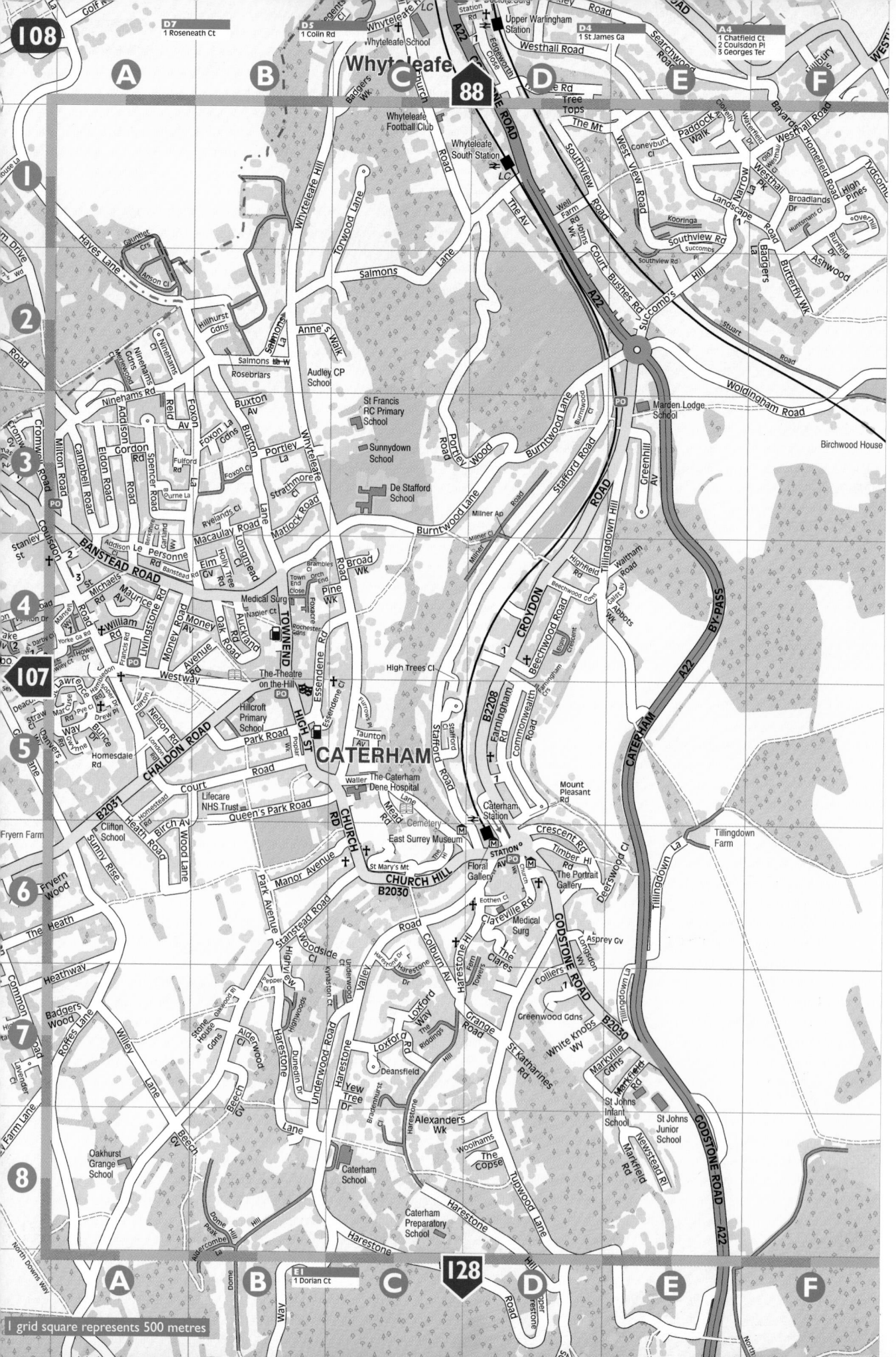

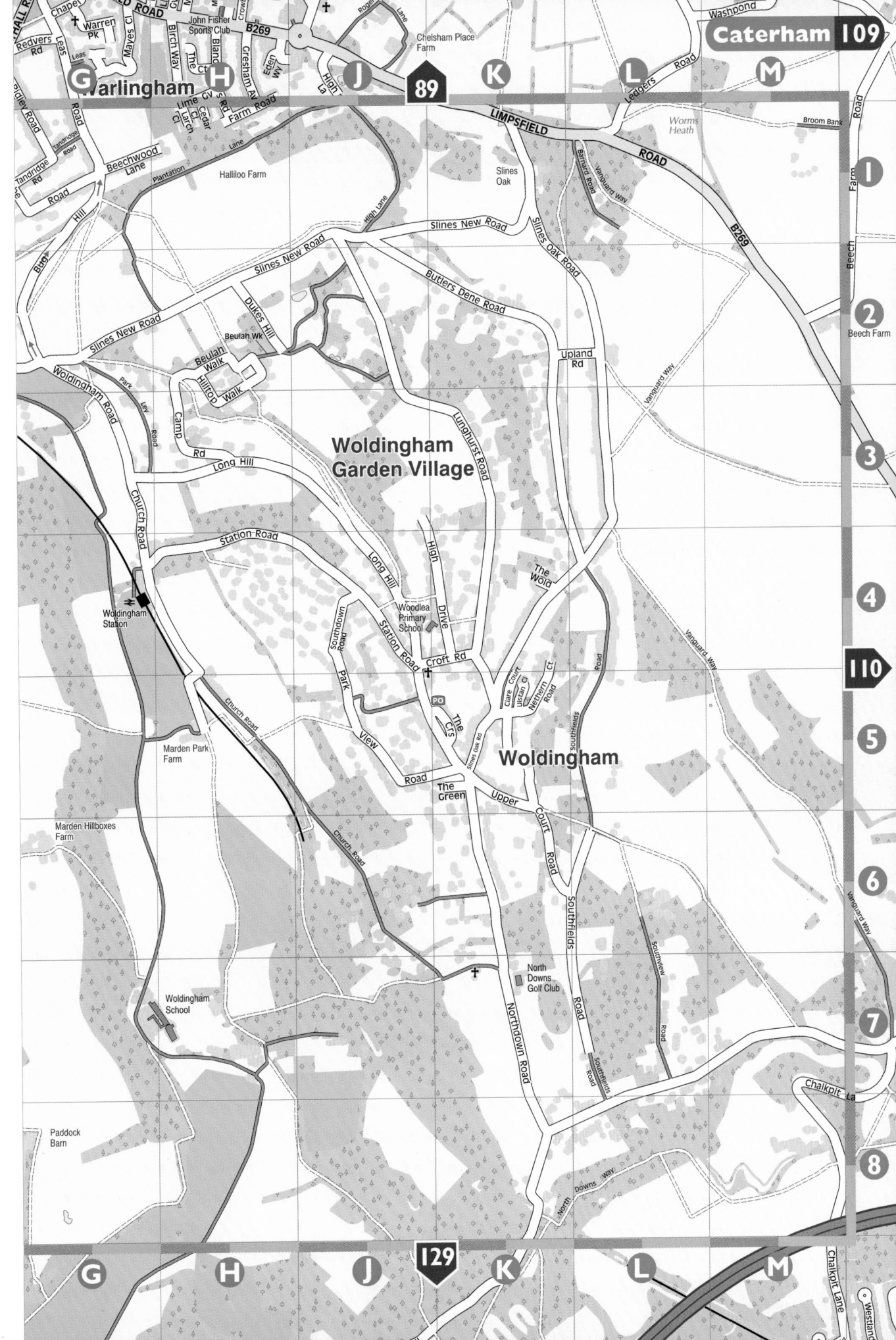

Woldingham
Garden Village

Woldingham

89

129

110

Woldingham
Station

Marden Park
Farm

Marden Hillboxes
Farm

Woldingham
School

Paddock
Barn

North
Downs
Golf Club

Worms
Heath

Beech Farm

Halliloo Farm

Chelsham Place
Farm

Woodlea
Primary
School

Warlingham

John Fisher
Sports Club

Warren
Pk

Chapel

Redvers
Rd

Beechwood
Lane

Plantation

Dukes Hill

Beulah Wk

Beulah
Walk

Hilltop
Walk

Camp
Rd

Long Hill

Station Road

Slines New Road

Slines New Road

Slines New Road

Slines New Road

Butlers Dene Road

Slines Oak Road

Slines
Oak

Upland
Rd

Barnard Road

Vanguard Way

Vanguard Way

Vanguard Way

Vanguard Way

Vanguard Way

Lunghurst Road

Long Hill

High
Drive

Southdown
Road

Station Road

Croft Rd

The Crs

Park
View
Road

The
Green

Upper
Court
Road

Northdown Road

Southfields

Southfields

Southfields

Southview
Road

Nethern
Ct
Road

Clare
Court
Ulstan Cl

The Wold

Ledgers
Road

Broom Bank

Washpond

LIMPSFIELD
ROAD

B269

B269

Church Road

Church Road

Church Road

Woldingham Road

North Downs Way

Chalkpit La

Chalkpit Lane

Westland

G H J K L M

G H J K L M

I
2
3
4
5
6
7
8

A   B   C   90   D   E   F

Broom Bank

Chelsham Court Farm

Beech Farm

1 Wedgwoods
1 Richmond Cl

Springholm Close
Scarbrook Road
St Mary's Green
Upland Drive
Wood
Wakely Close
Greenoak Rise

Surrey County
Bromley

I

Beddlestead Farm

Alexandra Road
York Road
Flamborough Close
White Close
Swievelands Road
Bridlington Close
Lusted Hall Lane

Lusted Hall Farm
Coatsfield Road
Shaw Road
Greenway
Crossways
Crossways Park
Westmore Road
Grove Road
Whitewood Cottages
Redhouse Road
Westmore Road
Ship Field Close
PO

2
Beech Farm

3
Cheverells Farm

New Surgery

Beddlestead Lane

CROYDON ROAD

4

109

B269

Clarks Lane Farm

Approach Road

North Downs Way

5
North Downs Way
Titsey Hill
CLARKS LANE
B2024
White Lane

6
The Ridge
North Downs Way
B269
Pilgrims Lane

Vanguard Way

Titsey

7
Vanguard Way
Flint House
North Downs Way
Titsey Park
Park Farm

Chalkpit La

8
Greensand Way

M25
M25
Greensand Way

Water Lane
Pitchfont Lane
Vanguard Way
TITSEY ROAD

Chalkpit La

A   B   C   130   D   E   F

Limpsfield Grange

1 grid square represents 500 metres

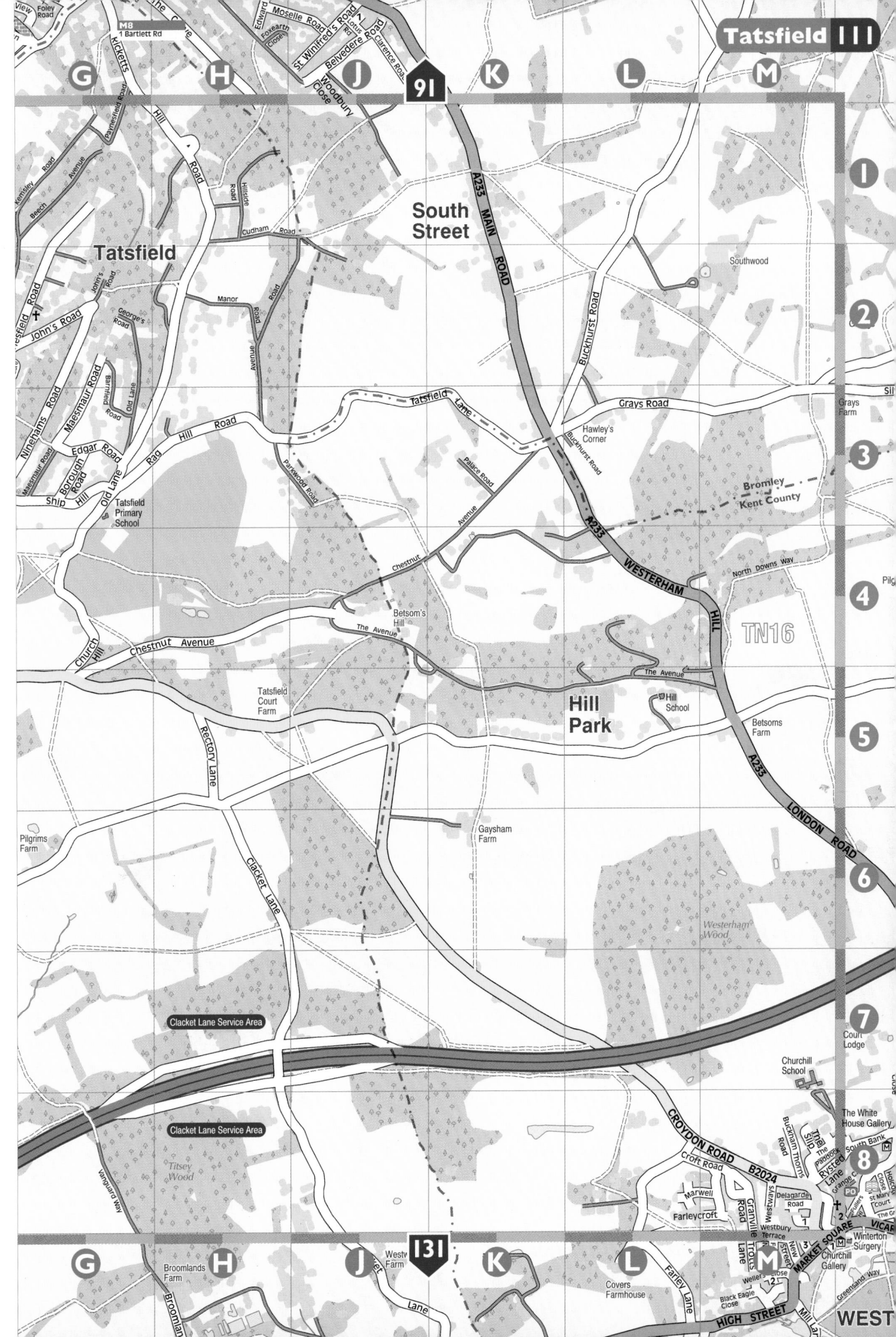

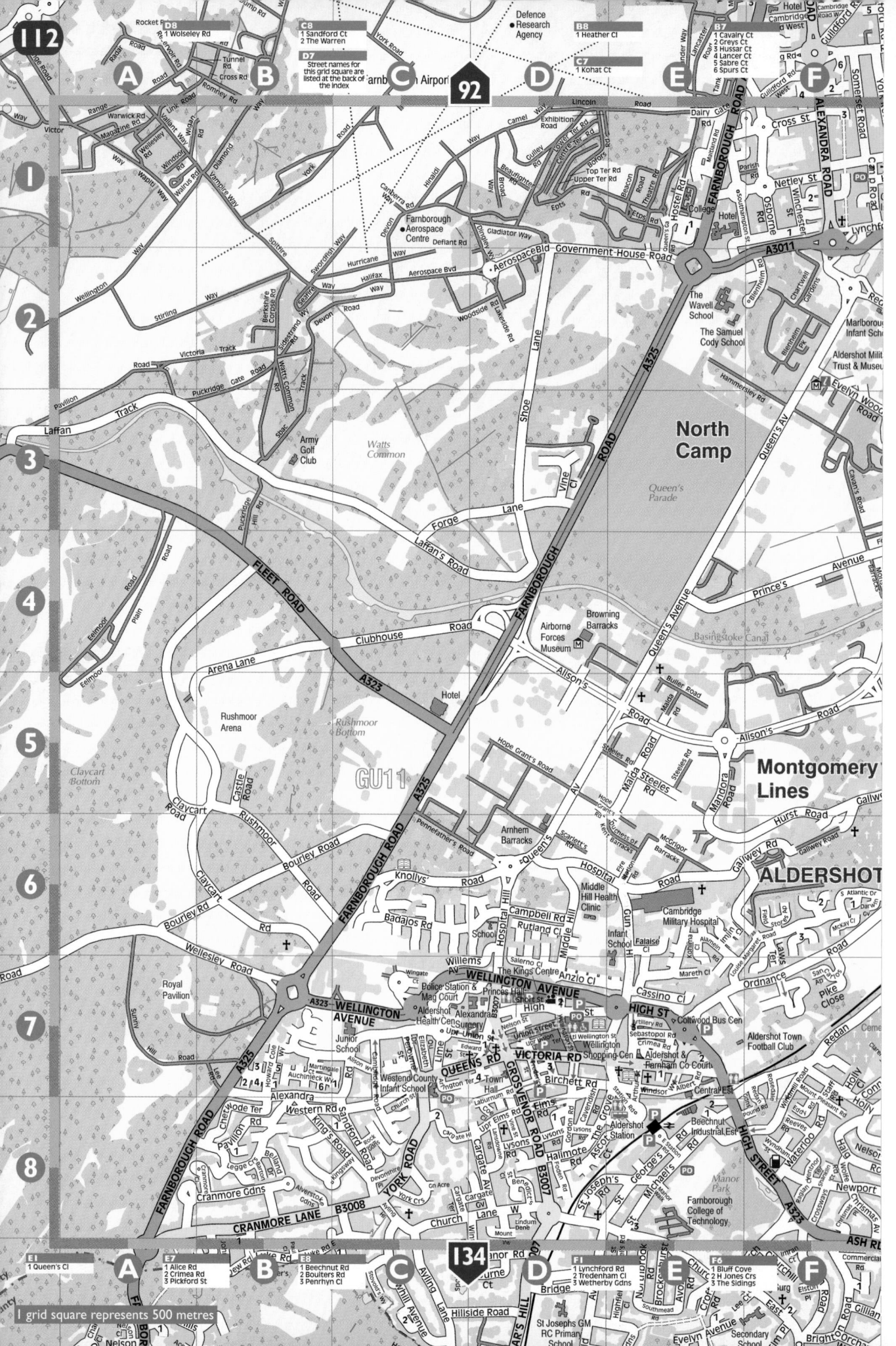

I grid square represents 500 metres

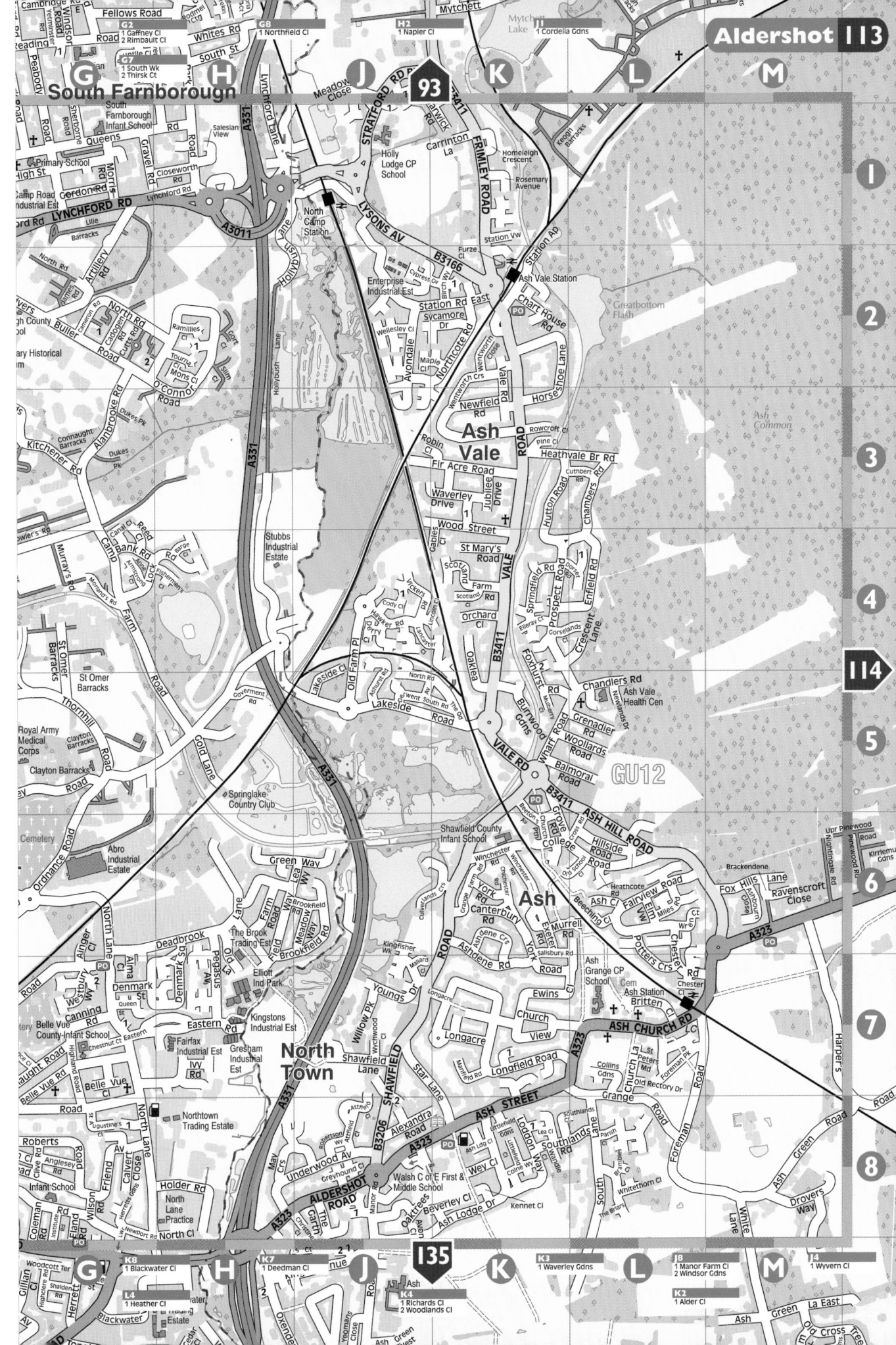

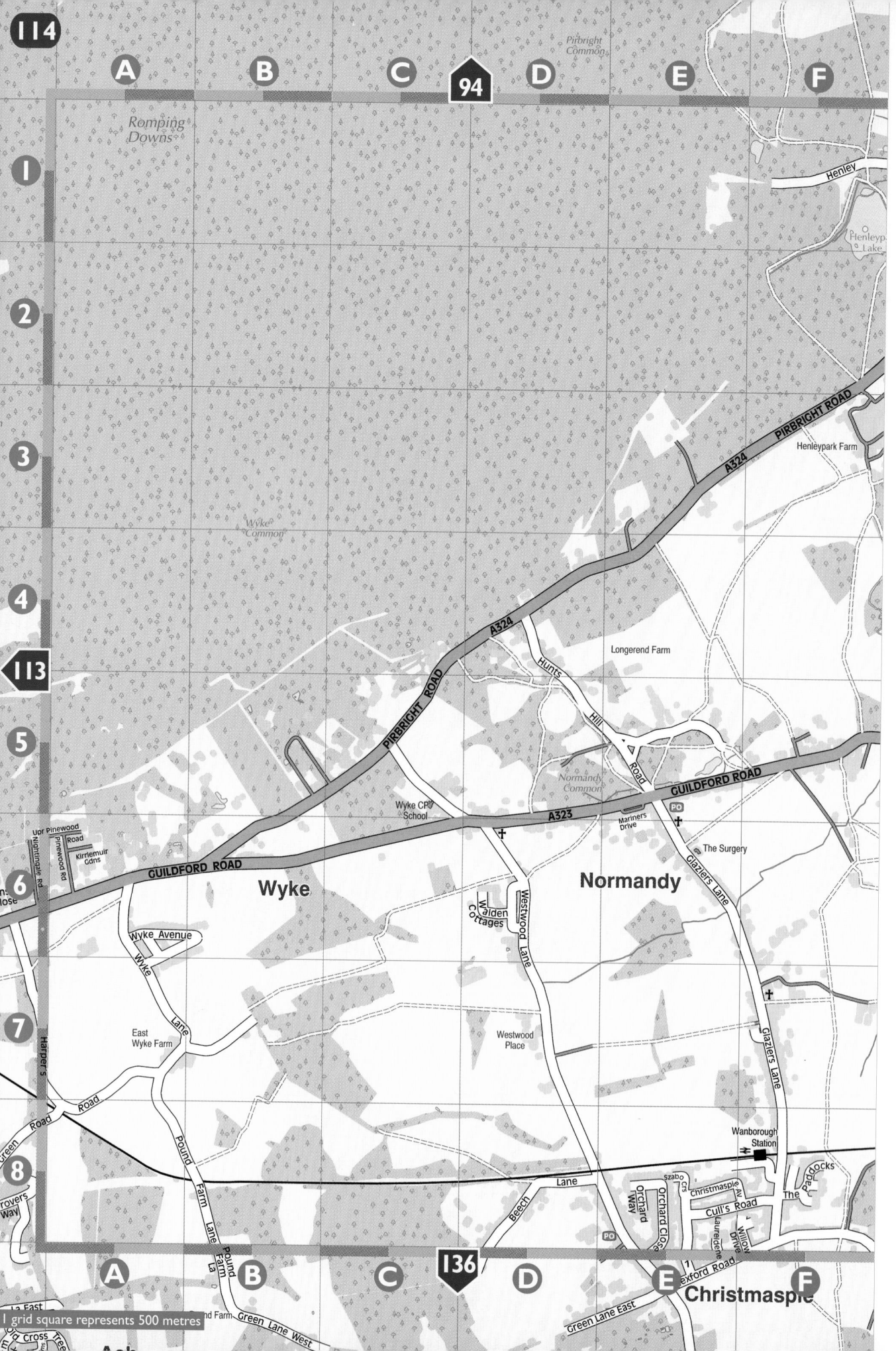

114

A B C 94 D E F

Romping
Downs

Pirbright
Common

Henley

Plenleyp
Lake

1

2

3

Wyke
Common

PIRBRIGHT ROAD A324

Henleypark Farm

4

113

A324

Longerend Farm

Hunts

Hill

Road

PIRBRIGHT ROAD

5

Normandy
Common

GUILDFORD ROAD

A323

Mariners
Drive

PO

The Surgery

Upr Pinewood
Nightingale Rd Road
Pinewood Rd
Kirriemuir
Gdns

GUILDFORD ROAD

6

Wyke

Wyke Avenue

Wyke CP
School

Walden
Cottages

Westwood Lane

Normandy

Glaziers Lane

Close

Wyke Lane

7

Harper's

East
Wyke Farm

Westwood
Place

Glaziers Lane

Green Road
Road

Pound Farm Lane

Wanborough
Station

The
Paddocks

8

rovers
Way

Lane

Beech

Szabo Crs
Christmaspie
Av

Orchard
Way

Cull's Road

Orchard Close

Willow Drive

Laureldene

PO

Pound
La

A B C 136 D E Green Lane East F Christmaspie

La East

Cross Tree

d Farm Green Lane West

exford Road

1 grid square represents 500 metres

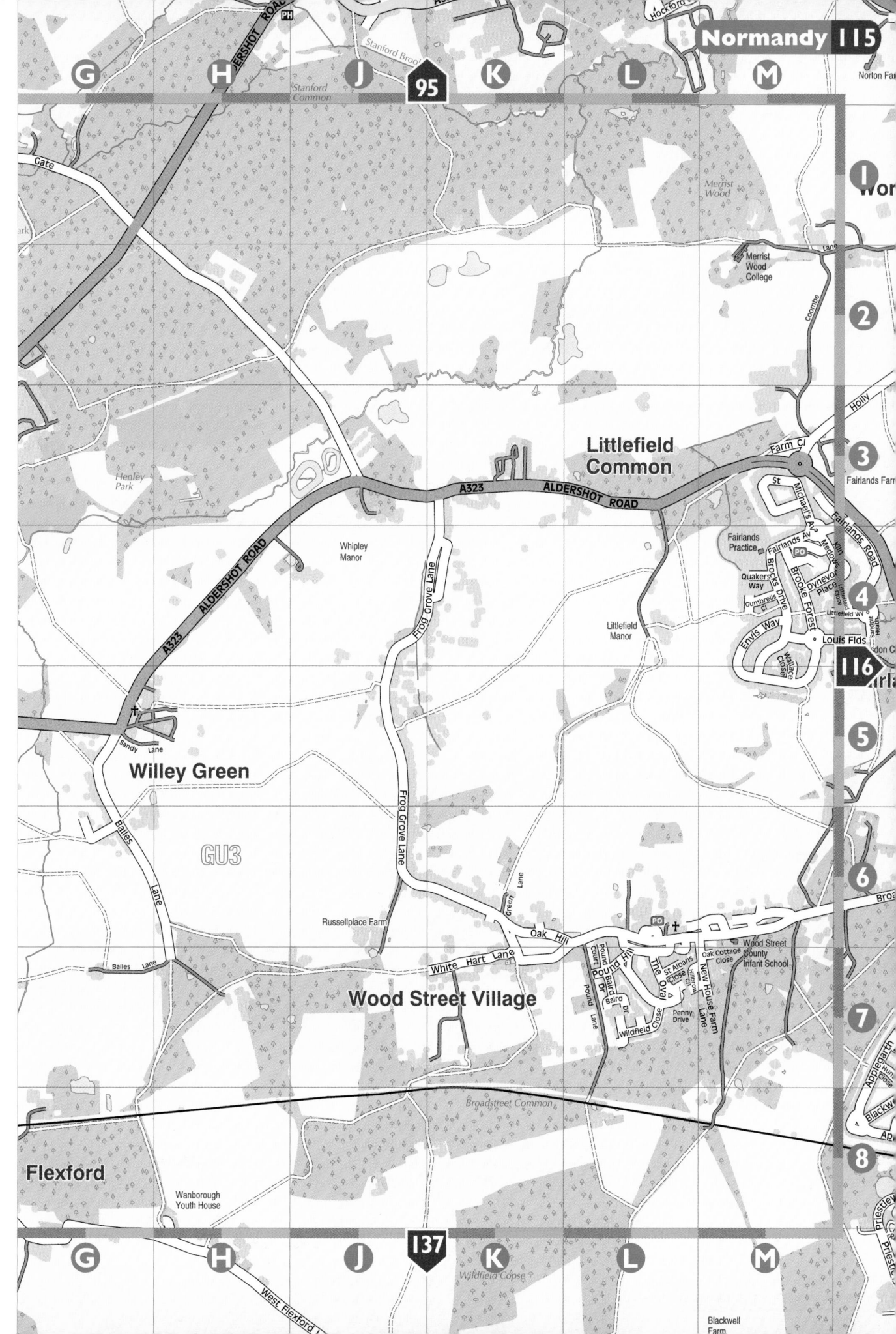

G H J 95 K L M

I Wor

Norton Far

Hockford

2

Stanford Brook

Stanford Common

Merrist Wood

Cate

Merrist Wood College

Farm Cl

Holly

Lane

Coombe

3

Fairlands Farm

Littlefield Common

A323 ALDERSHOT ROAD

St

Michael's Av

Fairlands Road

Henley Park

ALDERSHOT ROAD

Whipley Manor

Frog Grove Lane

A323

Littlefield Manor

Fairlands Practice

Fairlands Av

PO

Brooke Forest

Brooks Drive

Kiln Meadows

Littlefield Close

Dynevor Place

4

Quakers Way

Gumbrells Cl

Littlefield W

Envis Way

Wallace Close

Louis Flds

Sandpit

Idon Cl

116

arla

Willey Green

Sandy Lane

5

GU3

Balles Lane

Frog Grove Lane

6

Bro

Green Lane

Russellplace Farm

Oak Hill

PO

Wood Street County Infant School

Balles Lane

White Hart Lane

Oak Hill

Pound Court

Baird Dr

The Oval

St Albans Close

Oak Cottage Close

New House Farm Lane

Addlegarth

Priestley

Wood Street Village

Pound Lane

Baird Dr

Penny Drive

Wildfield Close

Hillier Way

7

Blackw

Ap

8

Broadstreet Common

Flexford

Wanborough Youth House

Priestley

West Flexford I

Wildfield Copse

Blackwell Farm

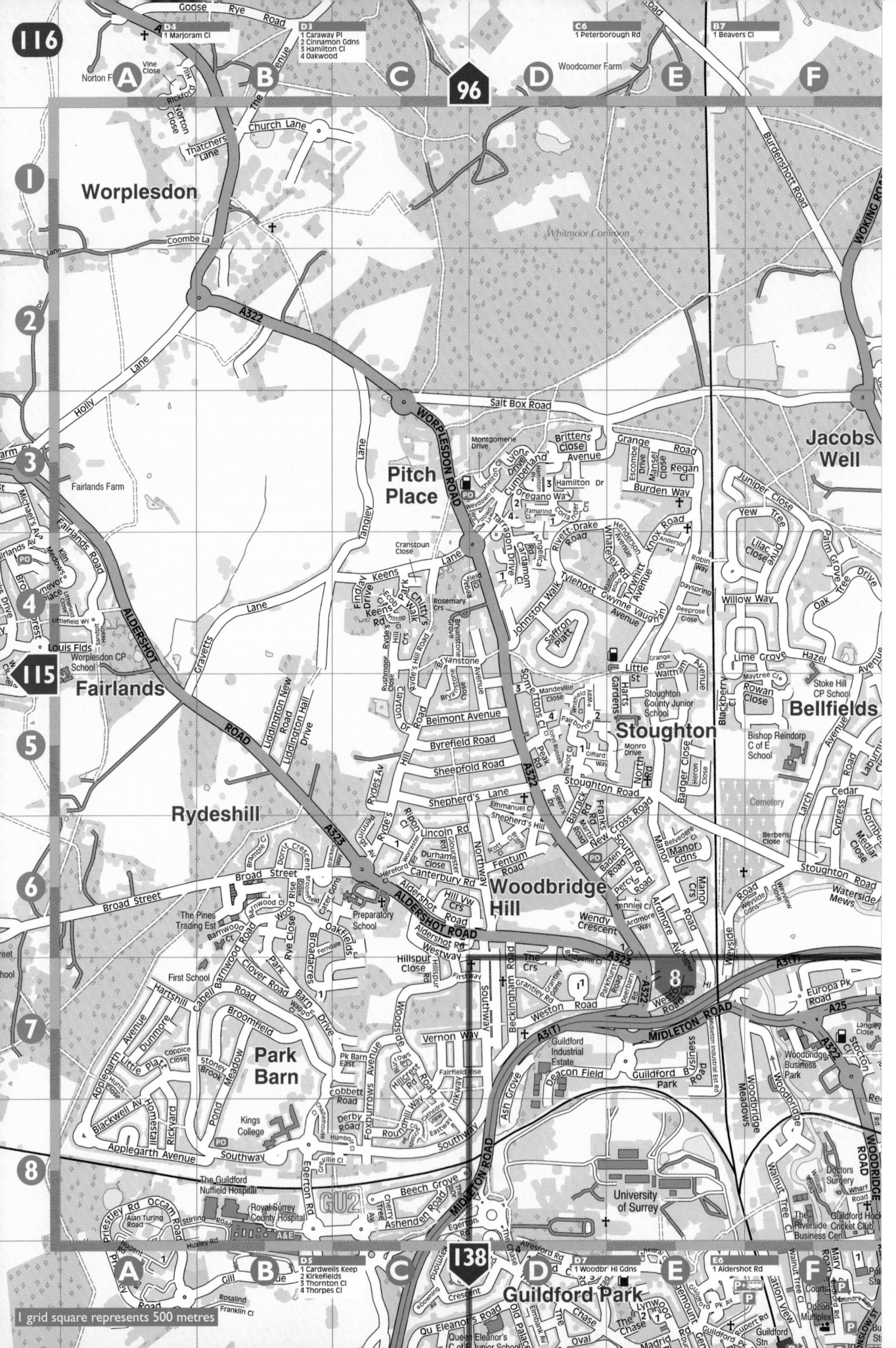

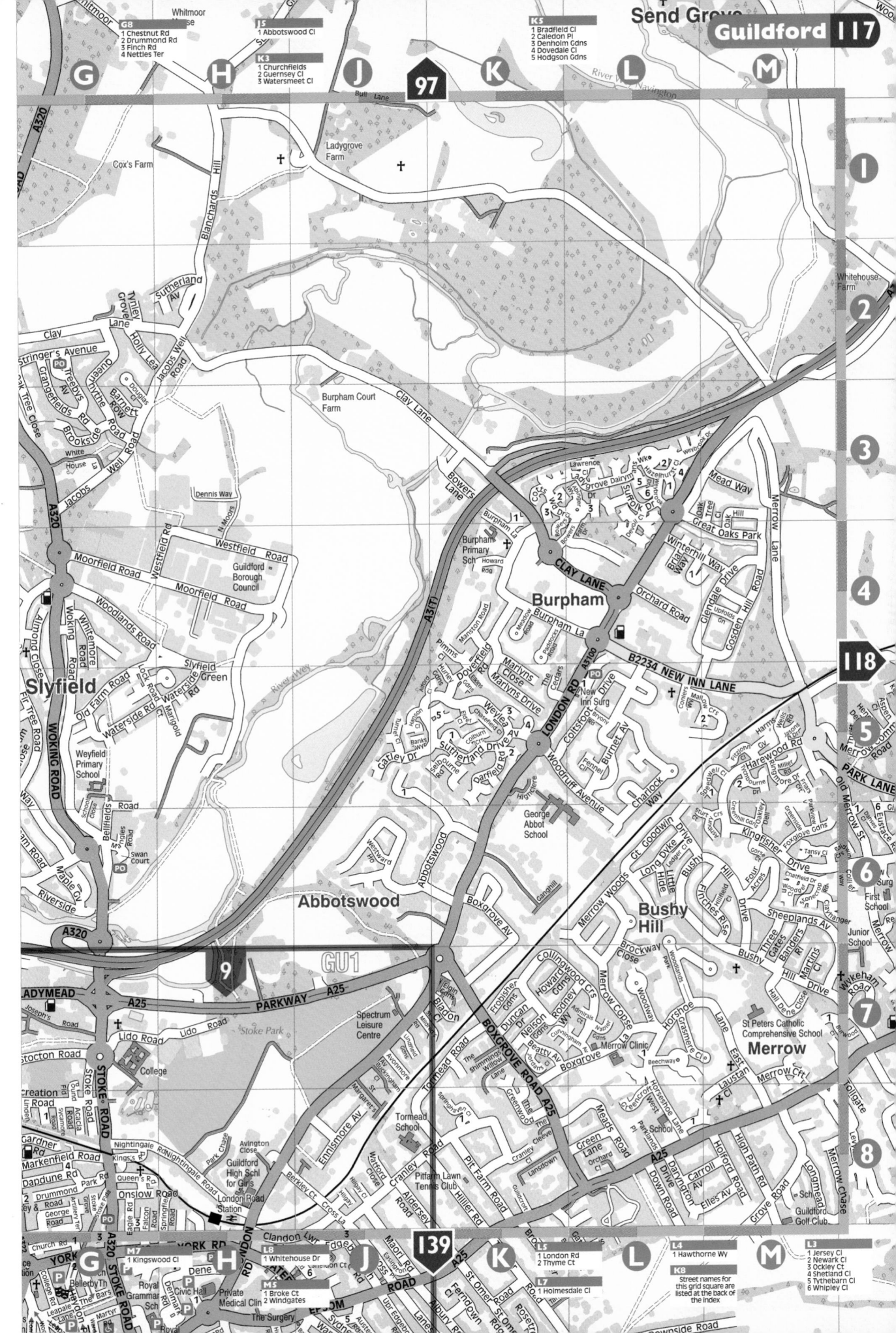

G8
1 Chestnut Rd
2 Drummond Rd
3 Finch Rd
4 Nettles Ter

J5
1 Abbotswood Cl

K5
1 Bradfield Cl
2 Caledon Pl
3 Denholm Gdns
4 Dovedale Cl
5 Hodgson Gdns

K3
1 Churchfields
2 Guernsey Cl
3 Watersmeet Cl

G **H** **J** **97** **K** **L** **M**

I

2

3

4

118

5

6

7

8

River Wey Navigation

Whitehouse Farm

Cox's Farm

Ladygrove Farm

Burpham Court Farm

Clay Lane

Bowers Lane

Burpham

Burpham Primary Sch

CLAY LANE

Orchard Road

Mead Way

Merrow Lane

Great Oaks Park

Winterhill Way

Clandale Drive

Gosden Hill Road

Park Lane

Old Merrow St

Merrow Common Road

B2234 NEW INN LANE

A3100

London Rd

Burnet Av

Charlock Way

Kingfisher Drive

Bushy Hill

Merrow

St Peters Catholic Comprehensive School

Wykeham Road

Tolgate

Merrow Chase

Guildford Golf Club

A3(T)

Manston Road

Pimms

Marlyns Close

Marlyns Drive

Wey Ley

Dovefield

Sutherland Drive

Gatley Dr

George Abbot School

Abbotswood

Boxgrove Av

Abbotswood

Woodruff Avenue

Long Dyke

Bushy Hill Drive

Three Gates

Sheeplands Av

Martins

Brockway Close

Moorfield Road

Westfield Road

Guildford Borough Council

Moorfield Road

Woodlands Road

Woking Road

Whitemore Road

Slyfield

Slyfield Green

River Wey

Weyfield Primary School

Old Farm Road

Waterside Rd

Swan Court

Maple Cv

Riverside

A320

Blanchards Hill

Tynley Grove

Sutherland Av

Holly Lea

Jacobs Well Road

Stringer's Avenue

Crangefields Rd

Treebys Av

Barnett Row

Brookside

Clay Lane

Dennis Way

Westfield Rd

N Moors

Bellfields Rd

A320

Woking Road

9 GU1

LADYMEAD A25 PARKWAY A25

Spectrum Leisure Centre

Stoke Park

Lido Road

Stockton Road

College

Creation Road

Gardner Road

Markenfield Road

Dapdune Rd

Drummond Road

George Road

Church Road

YORK A320 **STOKE ROAD**

Kingswood Cl

Onslow Road

Nightingale Rd

Guildford High Schl for Girls

London Road Station

Park Chase

Avington Close

Ennismore Av

Tormead School

Berkley Ct

Cranley Road

Pit Farm Road

Pitfarm Lawn Tennis Club

Clandon Lwr

Whitehouse Dr

Broke Ct
Wingates

The Surgery

139

BOXGROVE ROAD A25

Boxgrove

Merrow Clinic

Frobisher Gdns

Howard Cl

Collingwood Crs

Woodcock Cl

Rodney

Nelson Gdns

Duncan Dr

Bladon

Merrow Copse

Merrow Woods

Green Lane

Meads Road

Downs Road

Carroll Av

Darlington Rd

Hoford Road

High Path Rd

Grove Road

Longmead

Elles Av

St Omer Rd

Epsom Road

1 Hawthorne Wy **L4**

K8
Street names for this grid square are listed on the back of the index

L3
1 Jersey Cl
2 Newark Cl
3 Ockley Ct
4 Shetland Cl
5 Tythebarn Cl
6 Whipley Cl

G **H** **J** **K** **L** **M**

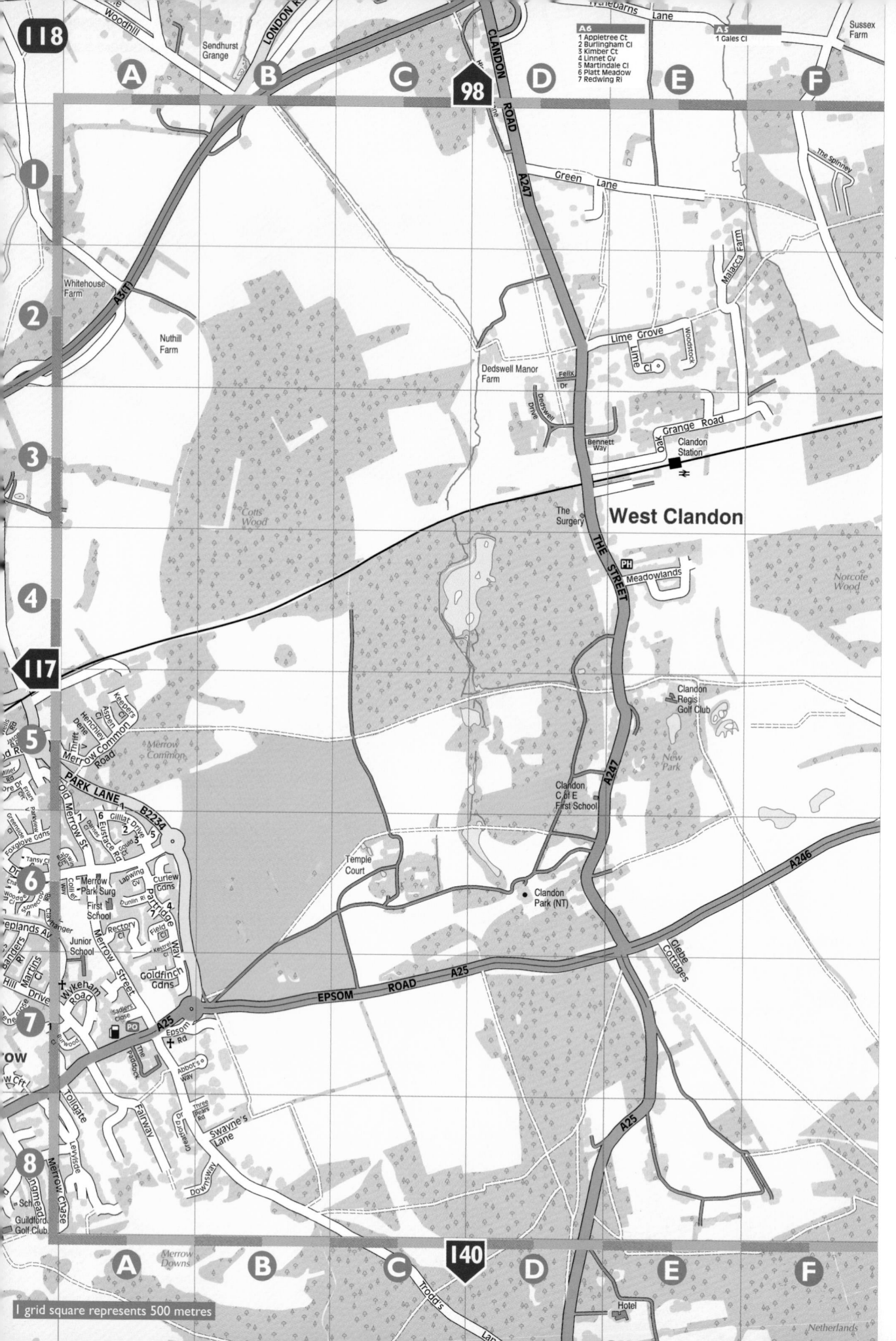

H5
1 St Thomas's Dr

Holride
Farm

G   **H**   Silkmore Lane   **J**   ◆99   **K**   **L**   **M**   Lollesworth Farm

Lollesworth Lane

Roundtree Farm

1

Ripley Road

Silkmore Lane

Rickson's La

Tintells La

Tintells La

Kenyons

West Horsley

2

Ltl Cranmore Lane

The Street

Fairwell Lane

Ripley Lane

Pincott La

School La

Mount Pleasant

Cranmore Lane

3

A246   EF

Gason Wood

Cranmore School

PO

Butlers Hill

Wix Farm

4

120

Hatchlands Park (NT)

Wix Hill

Jeffries Road

Shere Road

Back Lane

Back Lane

East Clandon

The Street

7

New Road

School La

A246

Blake's Lane

5

Epsom Road

Blake's Lane Farm

6

High Clandon

Hook Wood

Hillside Farm

Pebble Hill

7

Fullers Farm

Fullers Farm Road

Clandon Downs

Woodcote Lodge

8

Old Scotland Farm

G   **H**   **J**   ◆141   **K**   **L**   **M**

Staple

Shere Road

Green Dene

Combe Lane

120

EAST HORSLEY

100

119

142

Lollesworth Lane
Lollesworth Farm
East

Kingston Avenue
The Medical Centre
The Birches
Glendene Avenue
Old Rectory La
1 Bishopsmead Dr
The Chase
Rise
High Park Av
High Park Avenue
Drive

C1
1 Woodland Cl

B3
1 Bluebell La
2 Ockham Rd S

Orestan Farm
Orestan Lane

Woodland Drive
1
Oakwood Dr
Oakwood Close
OCKHAM ROAD SOUTH
Frenchlands Hatch
Pennymead Drive
Lynx Hill
Horsley Sports Club
High John Dr
Meadow Bank
Park Corner Dr
Lower Peryers
Lynx Hill
Highfields
Pine Walk
Th Farm La
Manor Cl
Holmwood Close
Bishopsmead Close
St Farm Cl
Nomad Theatre
St Martins House Business Centre
PO
1
Horsley Towers
Chester Road
Calvert Road
Salmons Road
Dirtham Lane

KT24

St Martins Cl
Fearn Cl
2
Longhurst Road
Rowbarns Way
Horsley Park
A246
Warren Farm

A246 EPSOM ROAD

Rowbarns
Oldlands Wood
Outdowns

The Warren

Chalk Lane
Lark Rise
The Sheepleas

Crocknorth Road

Green Dene
Hillside Farm
Pebble Hill
Mountain Wood
Bottom
Honeysuckle
Crocknorth
Crocknorth

Effingham Forest

Green Dene
Road

Dunley Hill Farm

Oaken Grove

1 grid square represents 500 metres

G1 1 Crossways
G2 1 The Crossroads
K1 1 Mayfield Gn

Great Bookham

101

122

143

L1 1 Styles End

G **H** **J** **K** **L** **M**

Preston Cross Hotel & Country Club

St Lawrence CP School
PH
Church
Middle Farm Pl
Chapel
The Surgery
Yew Tree Wk
PO
St Teresas Preparatory School
Effingham Golf Club

Effingham

Howard of Effingham School
Manor House School

Effingham Place

GUILDFORD
A246
Guildford Road
Lindens Clo
Orchard Gdns
Mount Pleasant
Norwood Close
Norwood Road
Meadway
Links Wy
Strathcona Avenue
Woodlands Road
Rectory Lane
Manor House Lane
The St
Browns La
A246
Beech Avenue
Beech Ct

Swanns Meadow
Hawkwood Rise
Hawkwood Dell

Newenham Rd
Oveton Way
White Way
Beales Rd
Dowlans Close
Dowlans
Dowlans Rd
Beech Cv
Kidborough Down
Groveside Close
Grovestone

West Down
Polesden View
Polesden Road

Dawnay Road
Howard Road
Dorking Road
Oakdene Close

South Bookham School

Goldstone Farm

Phoenice Farm

Polesden Lacey (NT)

Chapel Lane

High Barn Road
High Barn

Critten Lane

Effingham Hill Farm
St Teresas School

Yewtree Farm

Tanner's Hatch

Ranmore Common

Pigden Cottage

Dogkennel Green

High Barn Road

North Downs Way

Ranmore Common

I **2** **3** **4** **5** **6** **7** **8**

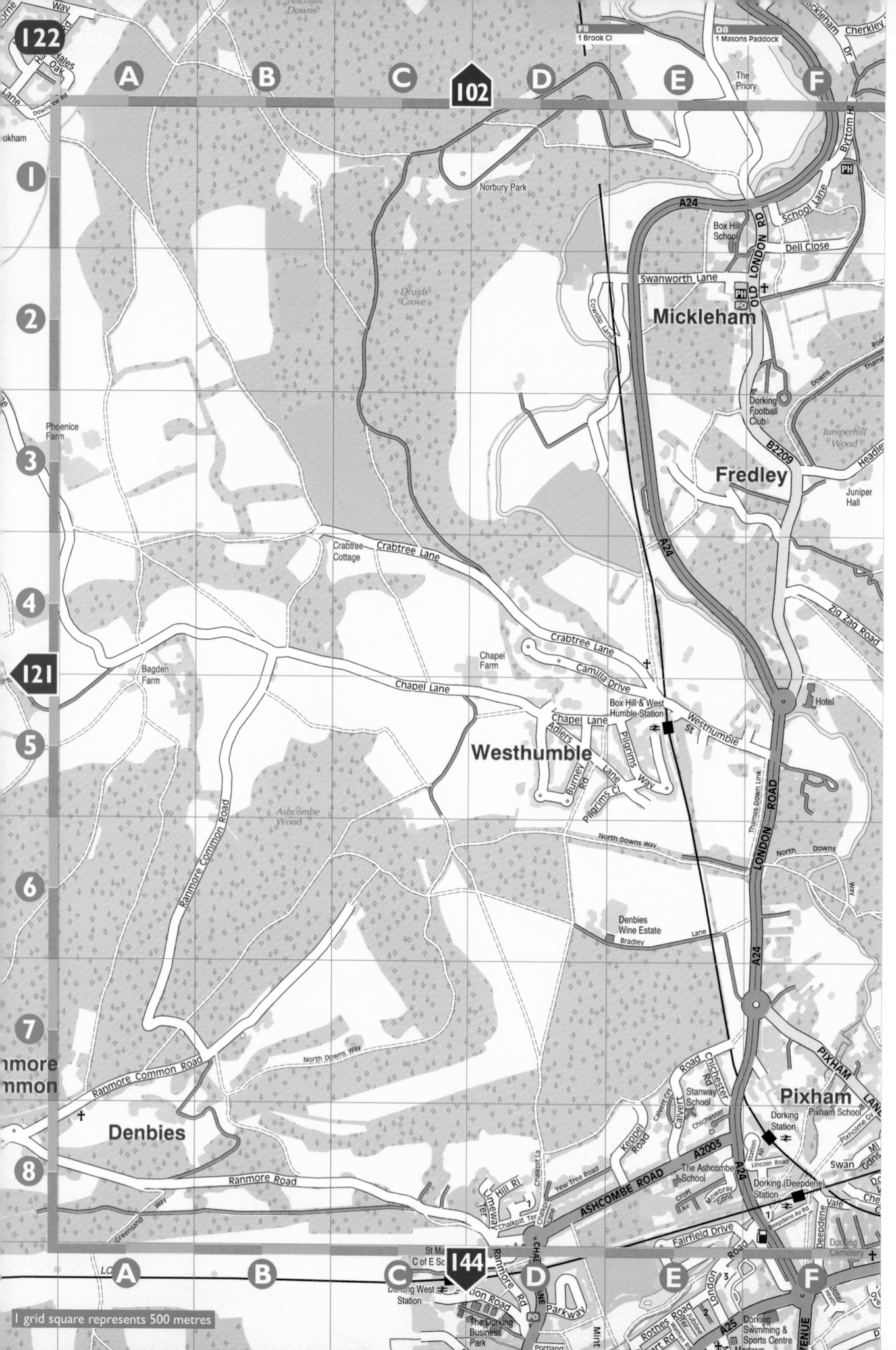

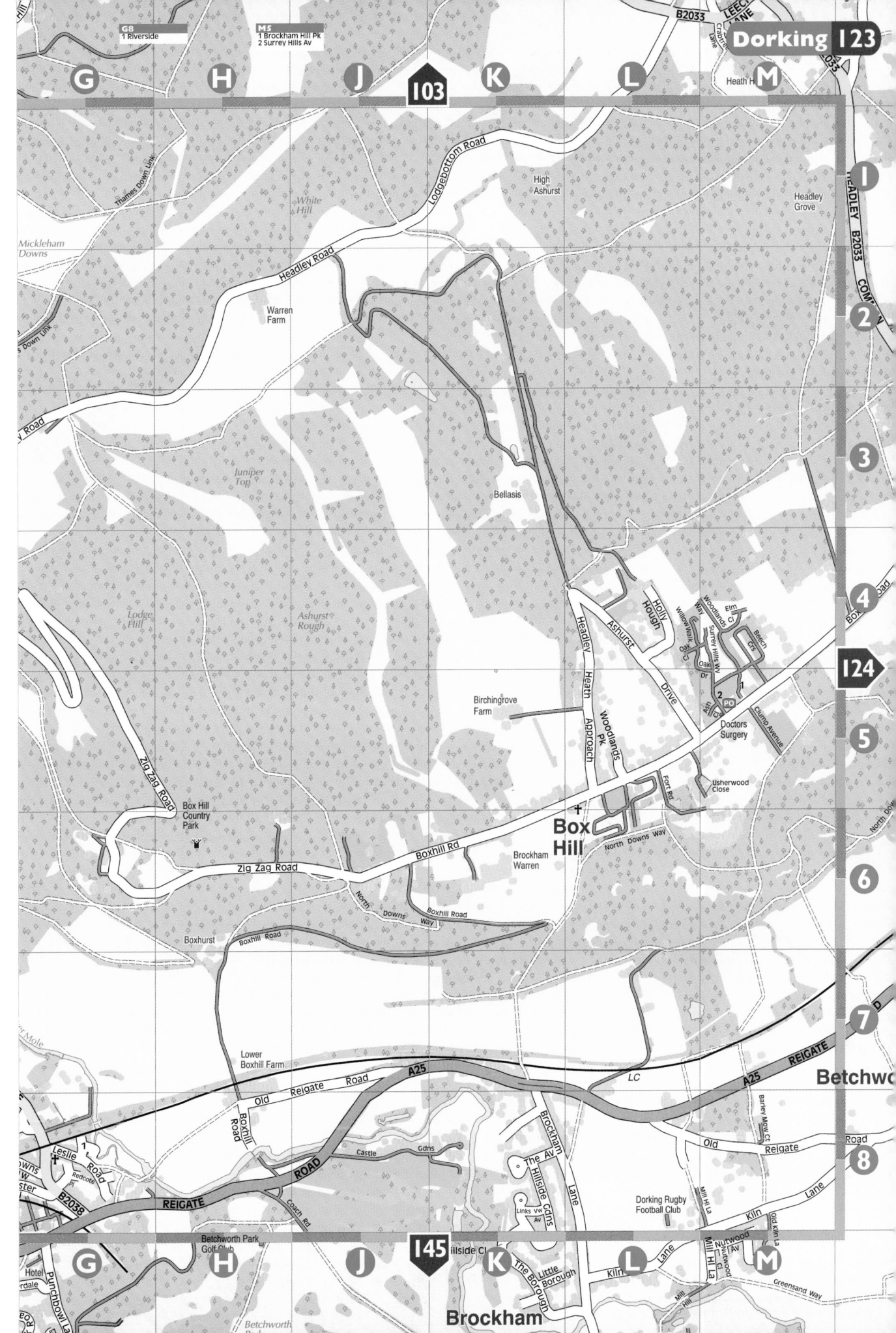

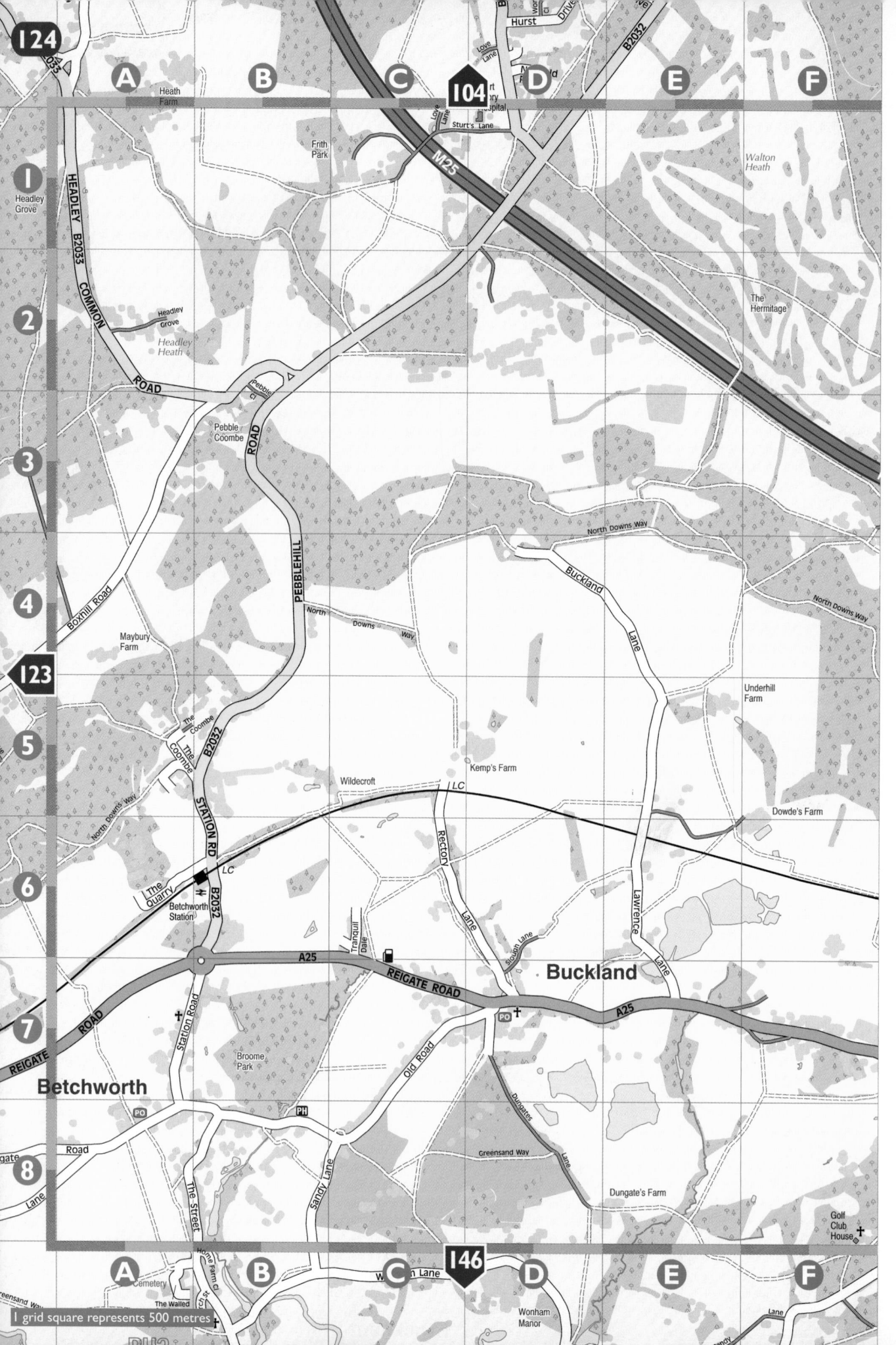

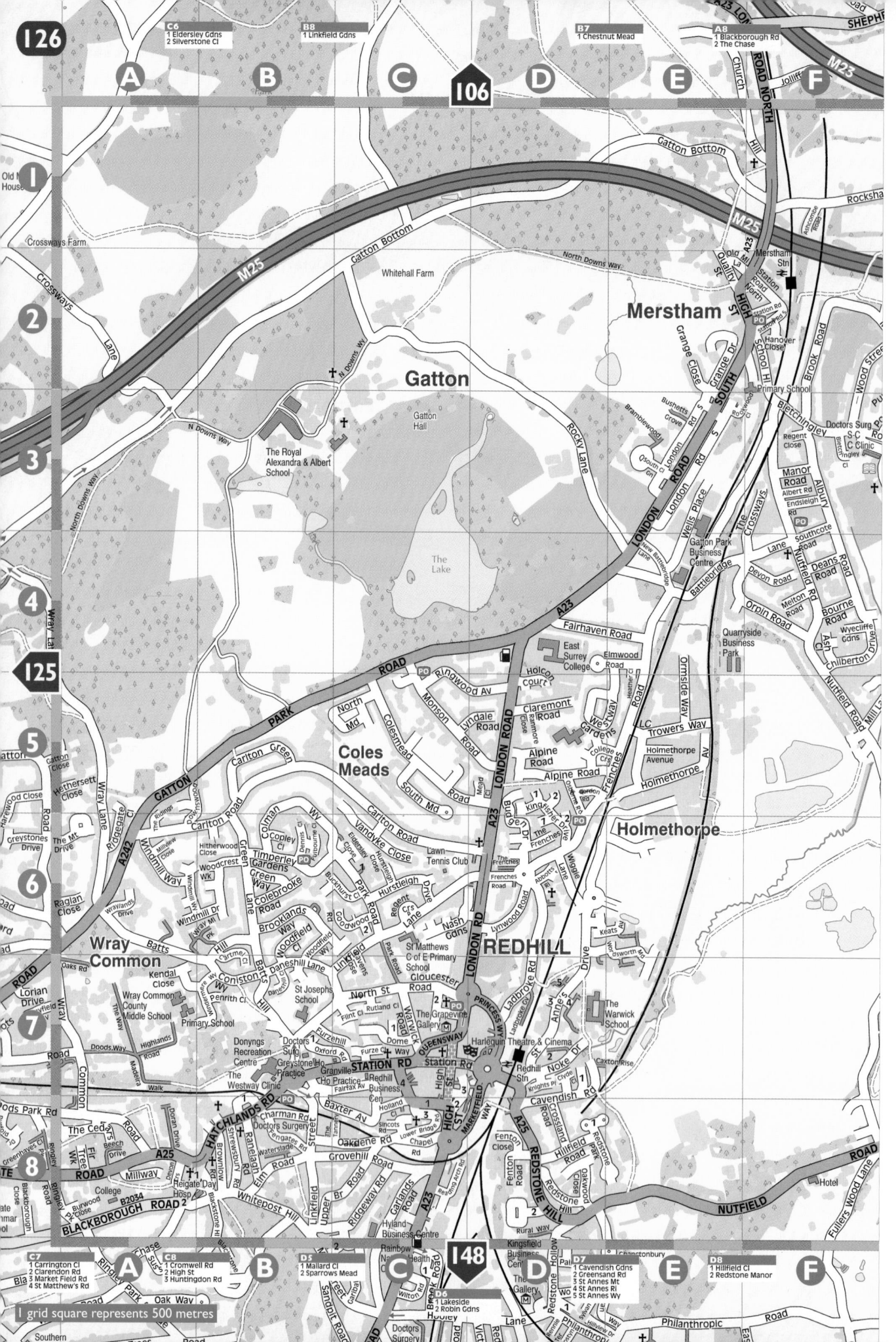

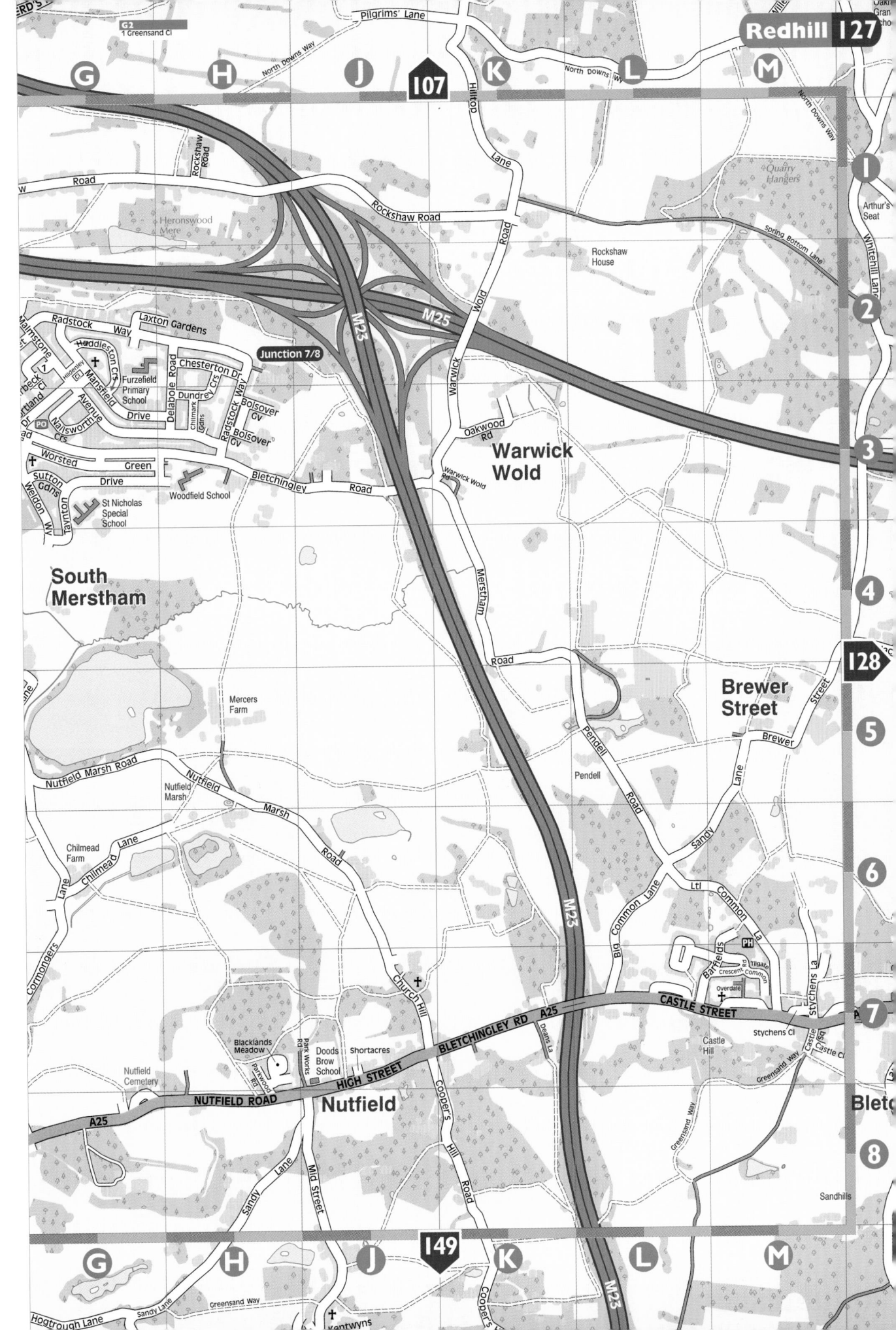

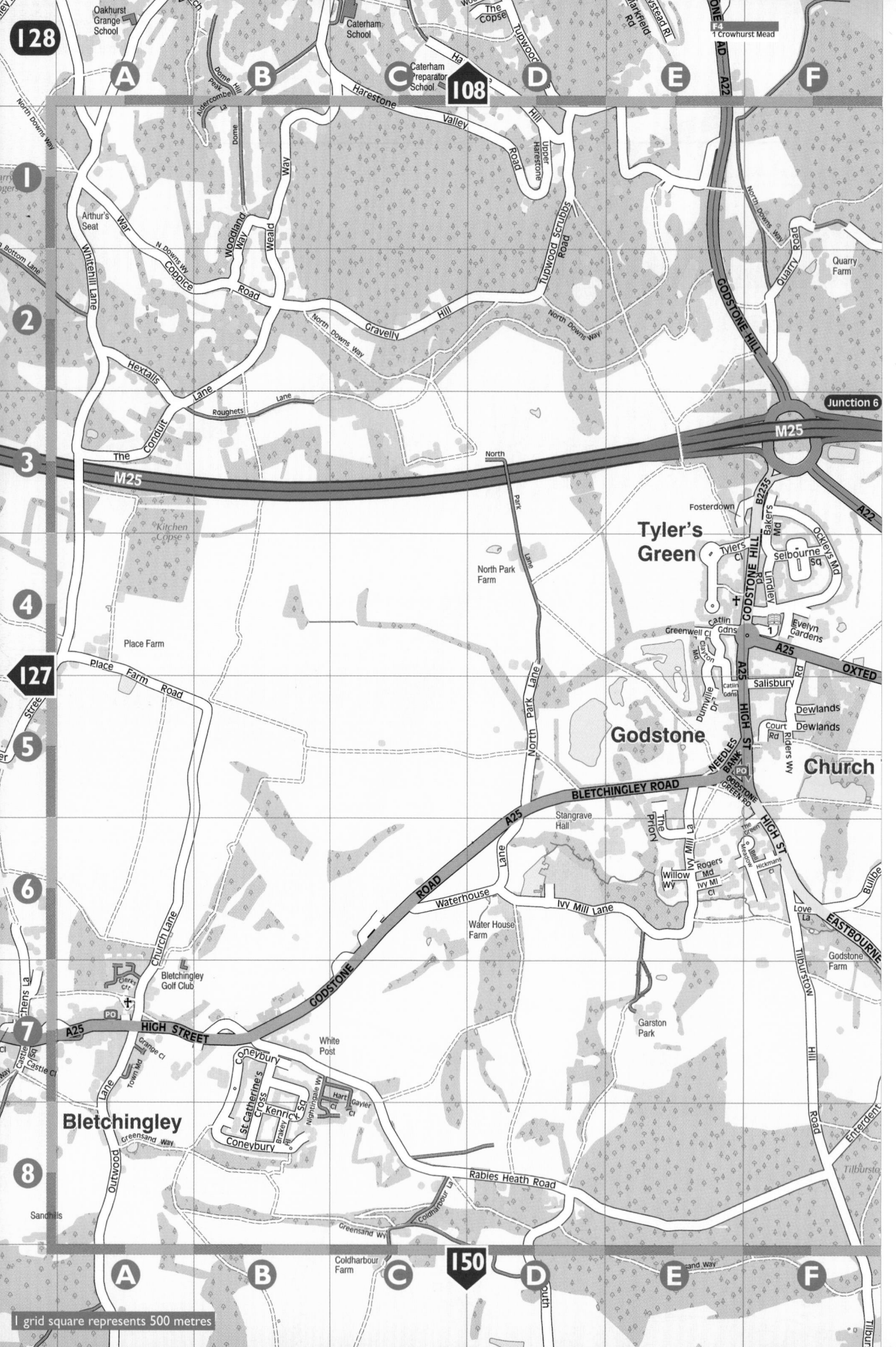

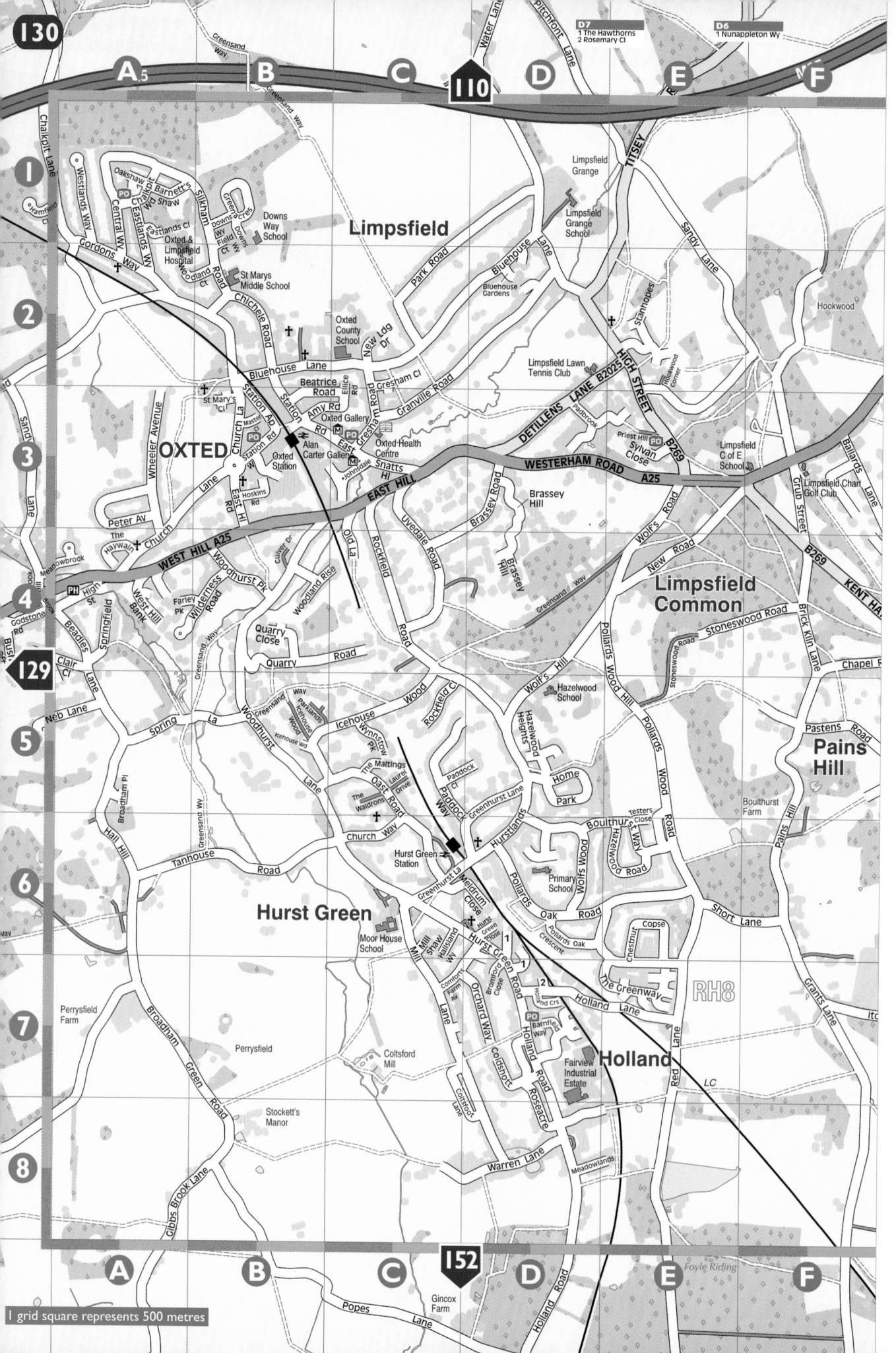

A5   B   C   110   D   E   F

I   Chalkpit Lane   Hamfield   Westlands Way   Oakshaw   Barnett's Shaw   Silkham   Downs Cres   Downs Way School   Central Wy   Gordons Way   Oxted & Limpsfield Hospital   Eastlands Cl   Woodland Ct   Greensand Way   Greensand Way   Limpsfield Grange   Limpsfield Grange School   Hookwood

Limpsfield

2   St Marys Middle School   Chichele Road   Station Ap   Bluehouse Lane   Beatrice Road   Oxted County School   New Ldg Dr   Ellice Rd   Gresham Road   Gresham Cl   Granville Road   Park Road   Bluehouse Lane   Bluehouse Gardens   Limpsfield Lawn Tennis Club   Stanhopes   Hedgecourt Corner   Titsey   Sandy Lane

St Mary's Cl   Wheeler Avenue   Master Rd   St Mary's Cl   PO   Station   Amy Rd   Oxted Gallery   Alan Carter Gallery   Oxted Station   Johnsdale   Snatts Hl

3   **OXTED**   Church La   Station Rd   East Rd   Hoskins Rd   Peter Av   EAST HILL   Oxted Health Centre   Uvedale Road   Rockfield   Brassey Road   Brassey Hill   WESTERHAM ROAD A25   DETILLENS LANE B2025   HIGH STREET   Priest Hill   Sylvan Close   Limpsfield C of E School   B269   Limpsfield C of E School   Crub Street   Limpsfield Chart Golf Club

The Haywain   Church   WEST HILL A25   Woodhurst Pk   Culver Dr   Old La   Rockfield   Road   Greensand Way   New Road   Wolf's Road   B269   KENT HA

4   PH   High St   Godstone Rd   Beadles Lane   Springfield   West Bank   Farley Pk   Wilderness Road   Woodland Rise   Quarry Close   Quarry   Road   Brassey Hill   Wood   Limpsfield Common   Stoneswood Road   Stoneswood Road   Brick Kiln Lane   Chapel R

Meadowbrook

5   Clair Cl   Neb Lane   Spring La   Greensand Way   Woodhurst Lane   Greensand Wy   Parklands   Icehouse   Treehouse Wood   Icehouse Wd   Wynnstow Pk   The Maltings   Oast   Laura Drive   The Waldrons   Paddock Cl   Wood   Rockfield Cl   Hazelwood Heights   Hazelwood School   Pollards Wood Hill   Pollards Wood Road   Pastens Road   **Pains Hill**   Boulthurst Farm

6   Broadham Pl   Hall Hill   Greensand Wy   Tanhouse   Road   Church Way   Paddock Way   Hurst Green Station   Greenhurst Lane   Hurstlands   Home Park   Primary School   Wolfs Wood   Hazelwood Road   Boulthurst Way   Testers Close   Short Lane

Hurst Green   Moor House School   Mill Shaw   Halisland   Contors Farm Av   Greenhurst La   Meldrum Close   Hurst Green Rd   Pollards Oak Road   Pollards Oak Crescent   Chestnut Copse   RH8

7   Perrysfield Farm   Broadham Green Road   Perrysfield   Orchard Way   Coldshott   Mill Lane   Hurst Green Close   1   Bromford Close   1   Holland Lane   The Greenway   Red Lane   Grants Lane   Itc

PO   Barnfield Way   Holland Road   Roseacre   Holland Cres   **Holland**   Fairview Industrial Estate   LC

8   Gibbs Brook Lane   Stockett's Manor   Coltsford Mill   Coldshott Lane   Warren Lane   Meadowlands   Foyle Riding

A   B   C   152   D   E   F

Gincox Farm   Popes Lane   Holland Road

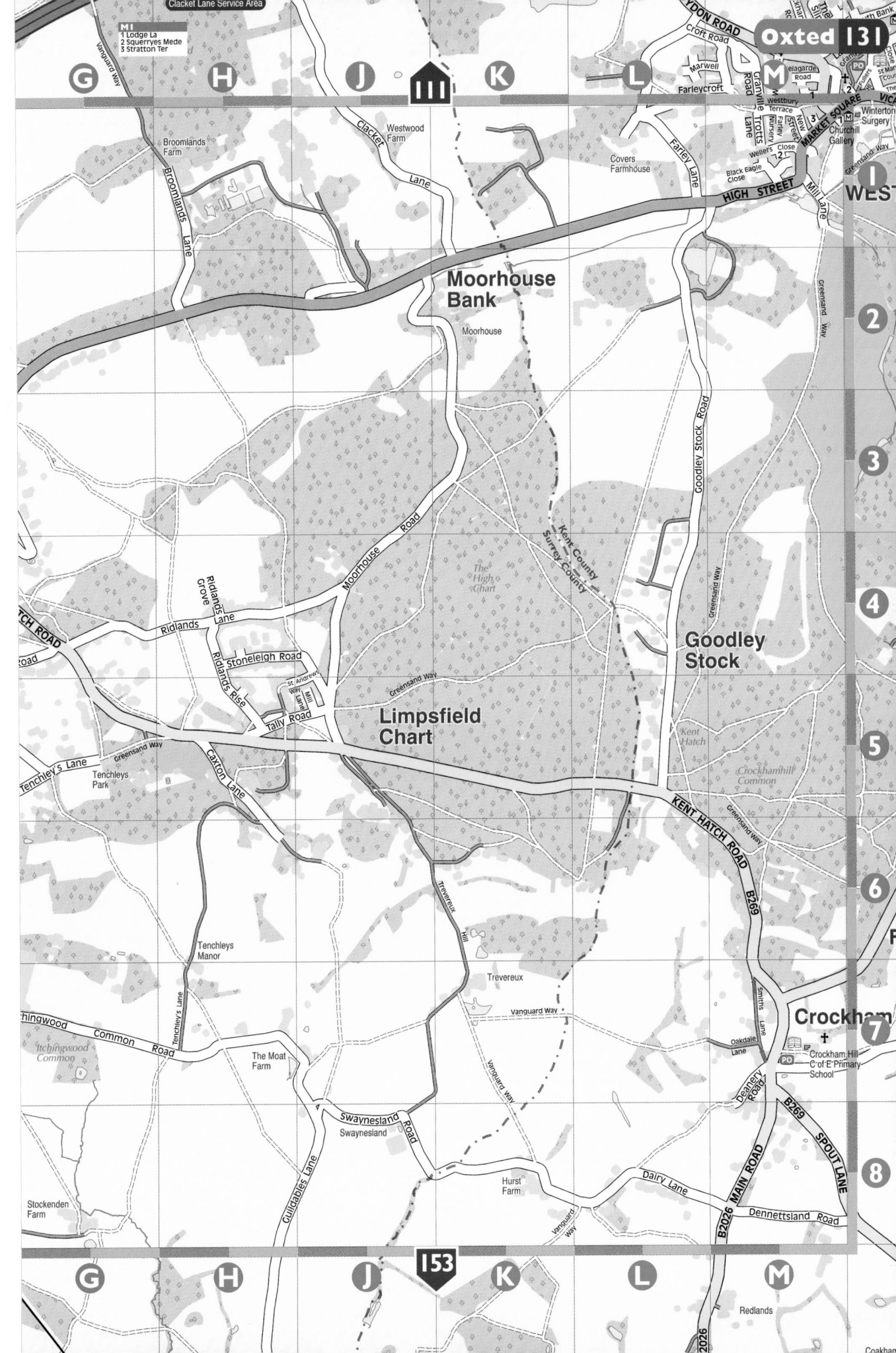

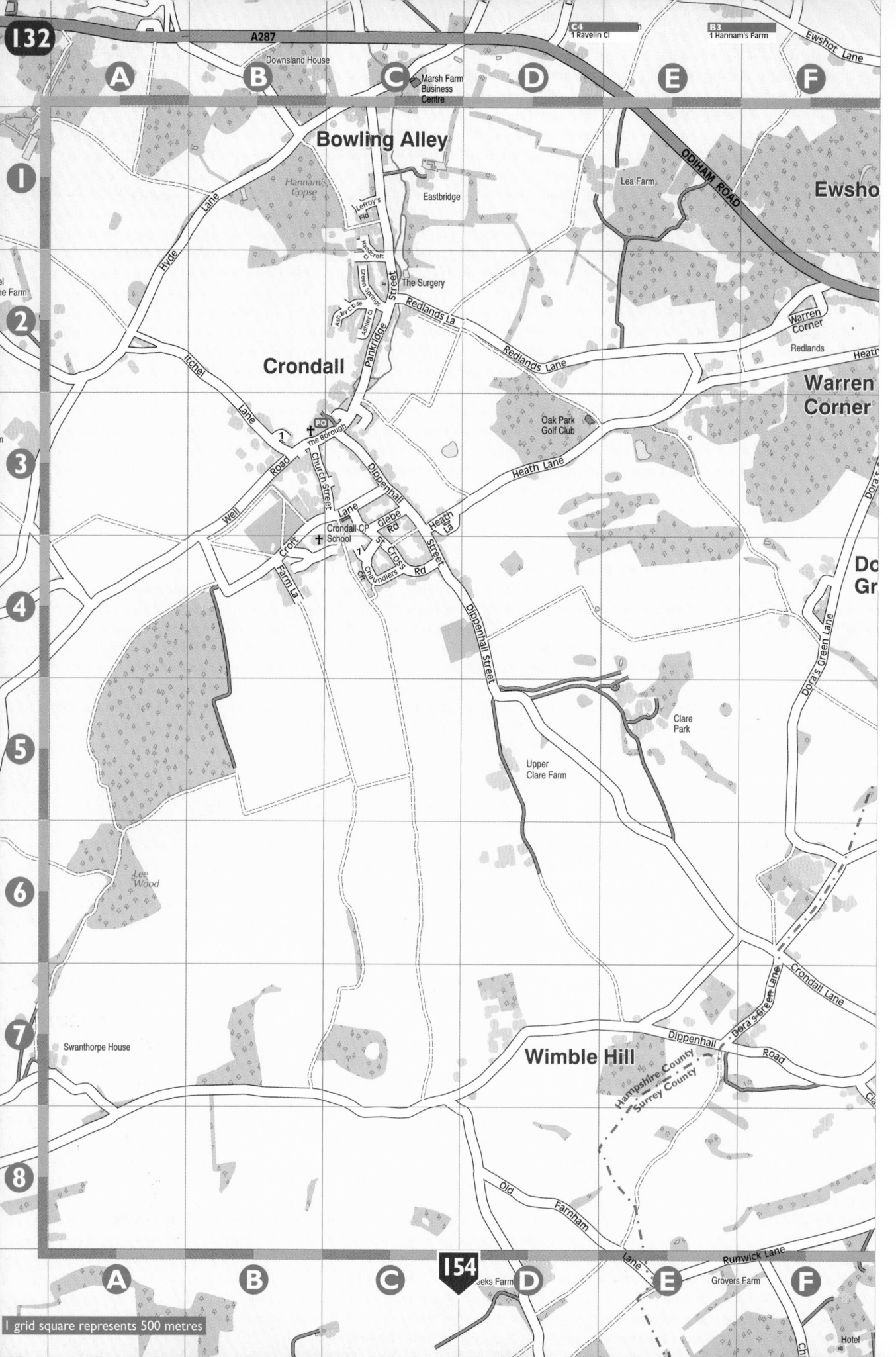

A287

C4
1 Ravelin Cl

B3
1 Hannam's Farm

Ewshot Lane

A   B   C   D   E   F

ODIHAM ROAD

Bowling Alley

Downsland House

Marsh Farm
Business
Centre

1

Lea Farm

Ewsho

Hannam's
Copse

Lefroy's
Fld

Eastbridge

Hyde Lane

Lane

Green Springs

Handcroft Cl

Ashley CP Sch

Asley Cl

Pankridge Street

The Surgery

Redlands La

Redlands Lane

Warren
Corner

Redlands   Heath

2

Crondall

Warren
Corner

Itchel Lane

PO

The Borough

Dippenhall   Lane

Oak Park
Golf Club

Heath Lane

3

Dora's Green Lane

Well Road

Church Street

Crondall CP
School

Glebe Rd

St Cross Rd

Chandlers

Heath Street

Heath La

Do
Gr

4

Croft

Farm La

Dippenhall Street

5

Upper
Clare Farm

Clare
Park

Lee
Wood

6

Dora's Green Lane

Crondall Lane

7

Swanthorpe House

Dippenhall

Dora's Green Lane

Road

Cle

Wimble Hill

Hampshire County
Surrey County

8

Old   Farnham

Lane

Runwick Lane

Grovers Farm

A   B   C   eeks Farm   D   E   F

Hotel

Ch

1 grid square represents 500 metres

G1
1 Magpie Cl
2 Partridge Cl
3 Sparrowhawk Cl
4 Woodpecker Cl

K2
1 Lawday Pl

K3
1 Ambleside Crs
2 Beck Gdns
3 Dukes Cl
4 Folly La S
5 Trinity Flds
6 Ullswater Cl

K7
1 Chantry Cl

L2
1 St Marks Pl

G H J K L M

I

2

3

4

134

5

GU9

10

11

ODIHAM ROAD

Hog Hatch

Upper Old Park

Folly Hill

Middle Old Park

Lower Old Park

Dippenhall

Upper Hale

B3005

Golf Course

Farnham Park

The Grange

Farnham Castle

Riverside Business Park

Park Industrial Estate

Farnham Business Cen

Three Stiles Rd

Crondall Lane

Beavers Hl

Beavers Close

Primary School

Waynflete Lane

The Chantrys

Runwick Lane

Farnham Business Park

Farnham Business

Cemetery

WEST STREET

BY-PASS

155

Ridgway House

Runwick House

G
M8
1 Barncroft
2 Fairholme Gdns
3 Firgrove Ct
4 Merlins Cl
5 Saxon Cft

H
M7
1 Brightwells Rd

J

K

L8
1 Arthur Cl
2 Whitlet Cl

L
L7,M2,M3,M6
Street names for these grid squares are listed at the back of the index

M
L3
1 Balmoral Crs
2 Chatsworth Gv
3 Oaktrees
4 Wings Cl

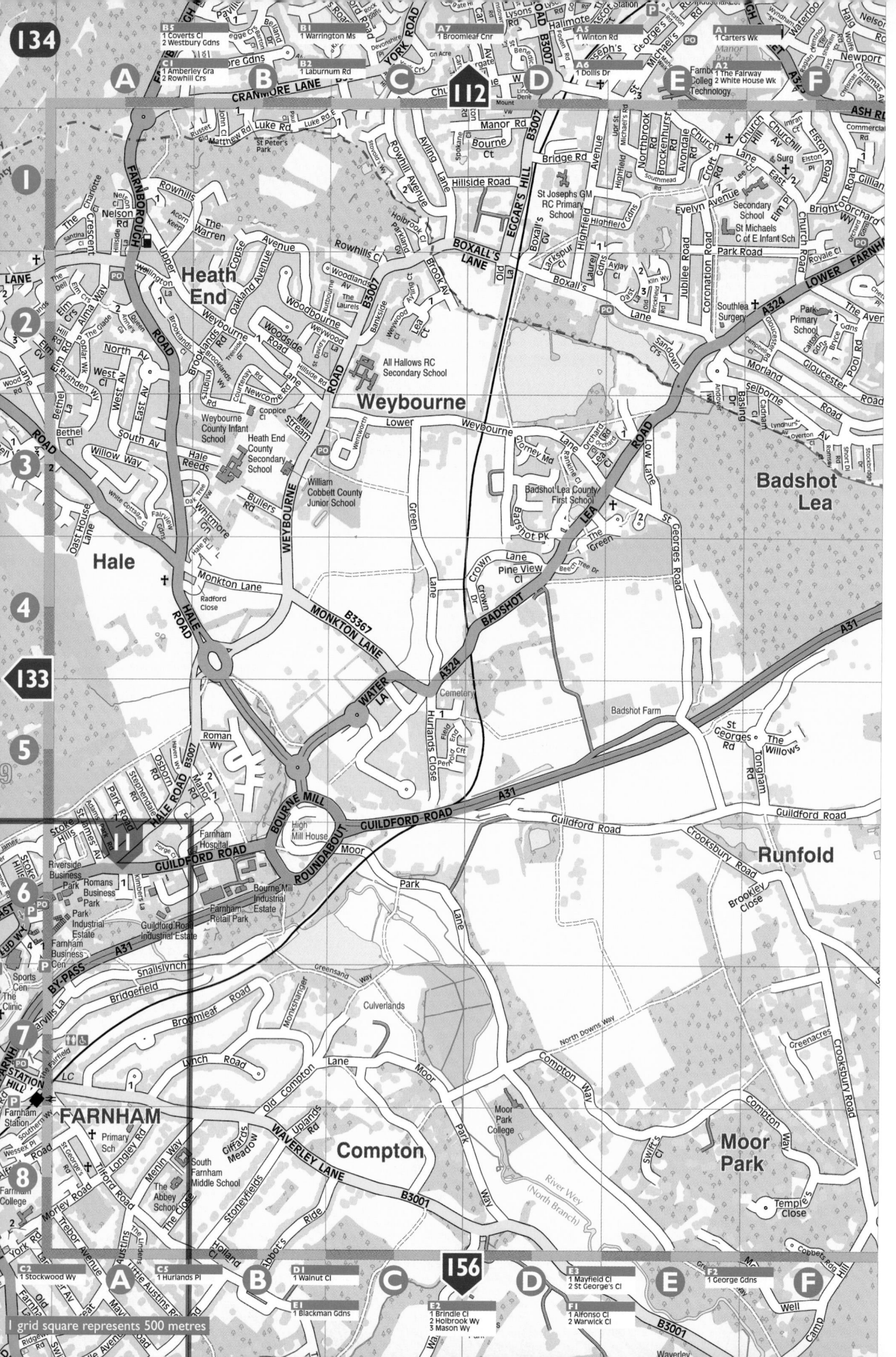

1 grid square represents 500 metres

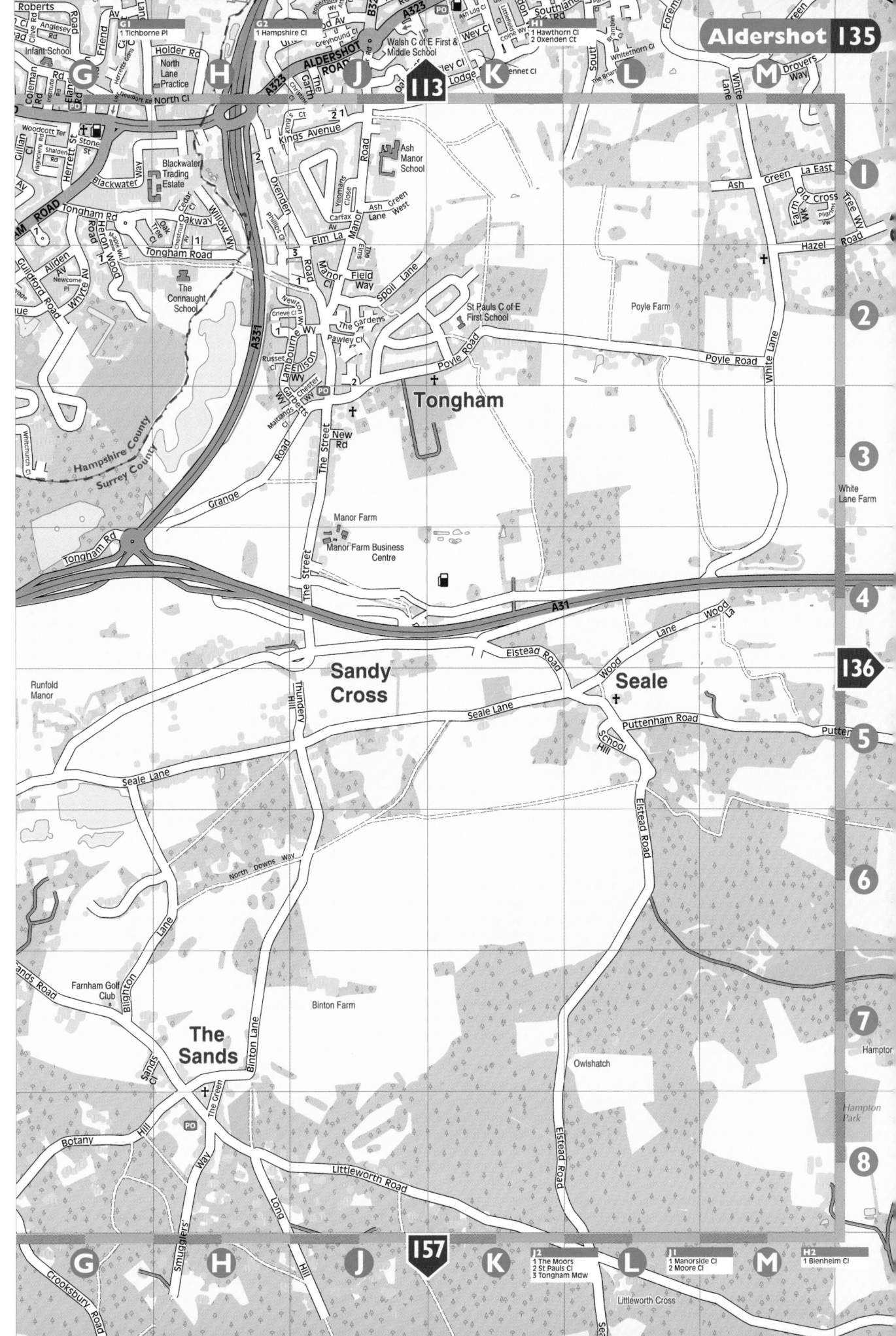

113

136

157

G1
1 Tichborne Pl

G2
1 Hampshire Cl

H1
1 Hawthorn Cl
2 Oxenden Ct

J1
1 The Moors
2 St Pauls Cl
3 Tongham Mdw

L1
1 Manorside Cl
2 Moore Cl

H2
1 Blenheim Cl

Tongham

Sandy
Cross

Seale

The
Sands

Runfold
Manor

Farnham Golf
Club

Binton Farm

Owlshatch

Hampton
Park

White
Lane Farm

Poyle Farm

Manor Farm

Manor Farm Business
Centre

Ash Manor
School

St Pauls C of E
First School

The Connaught
School

Blackwater Trading
Estate

Walsh C of E First &
Middle School

Littleworth Cross

North Downs Way

Hampshire County
Surrey County

A31

A331

A323

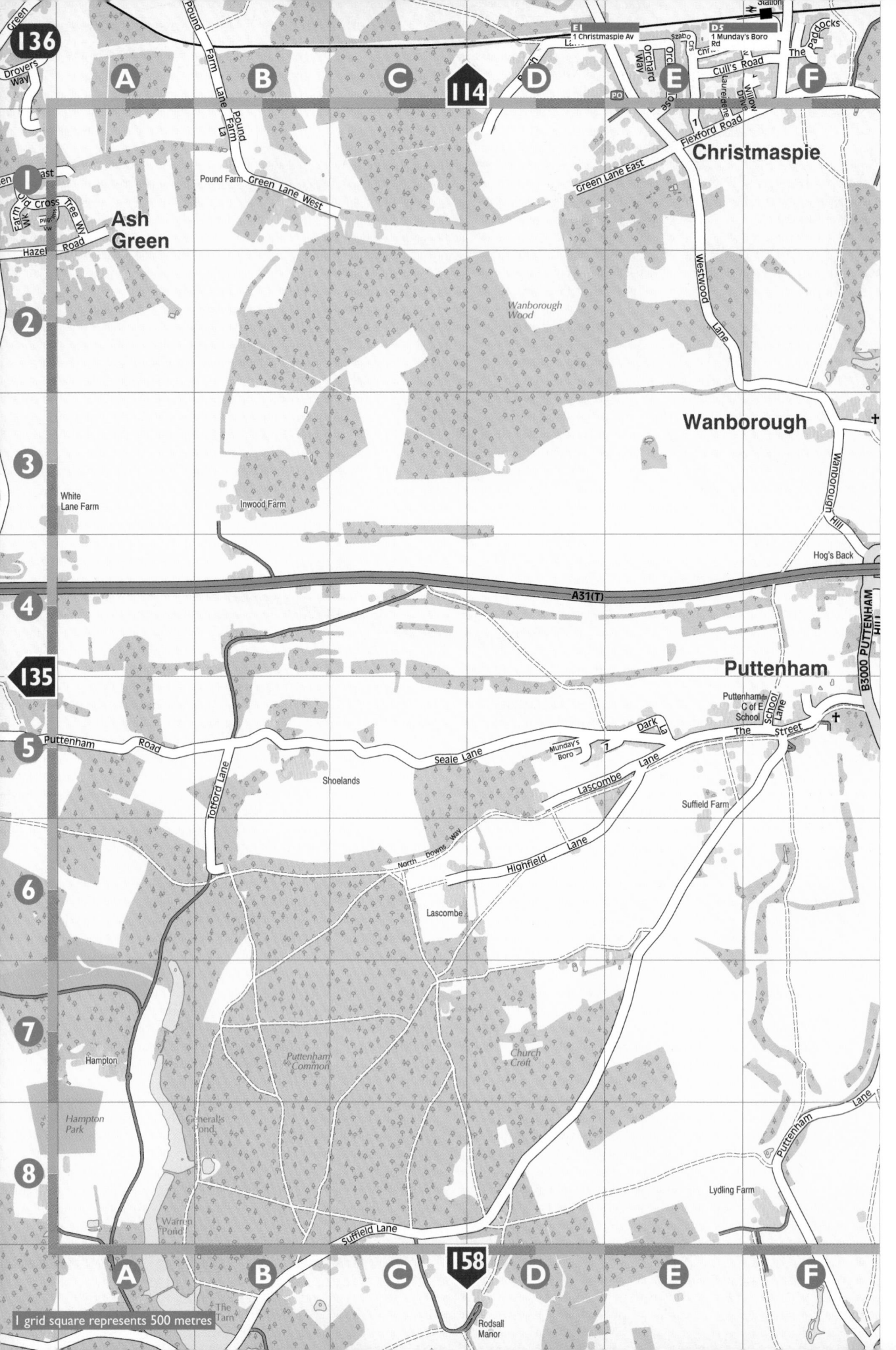

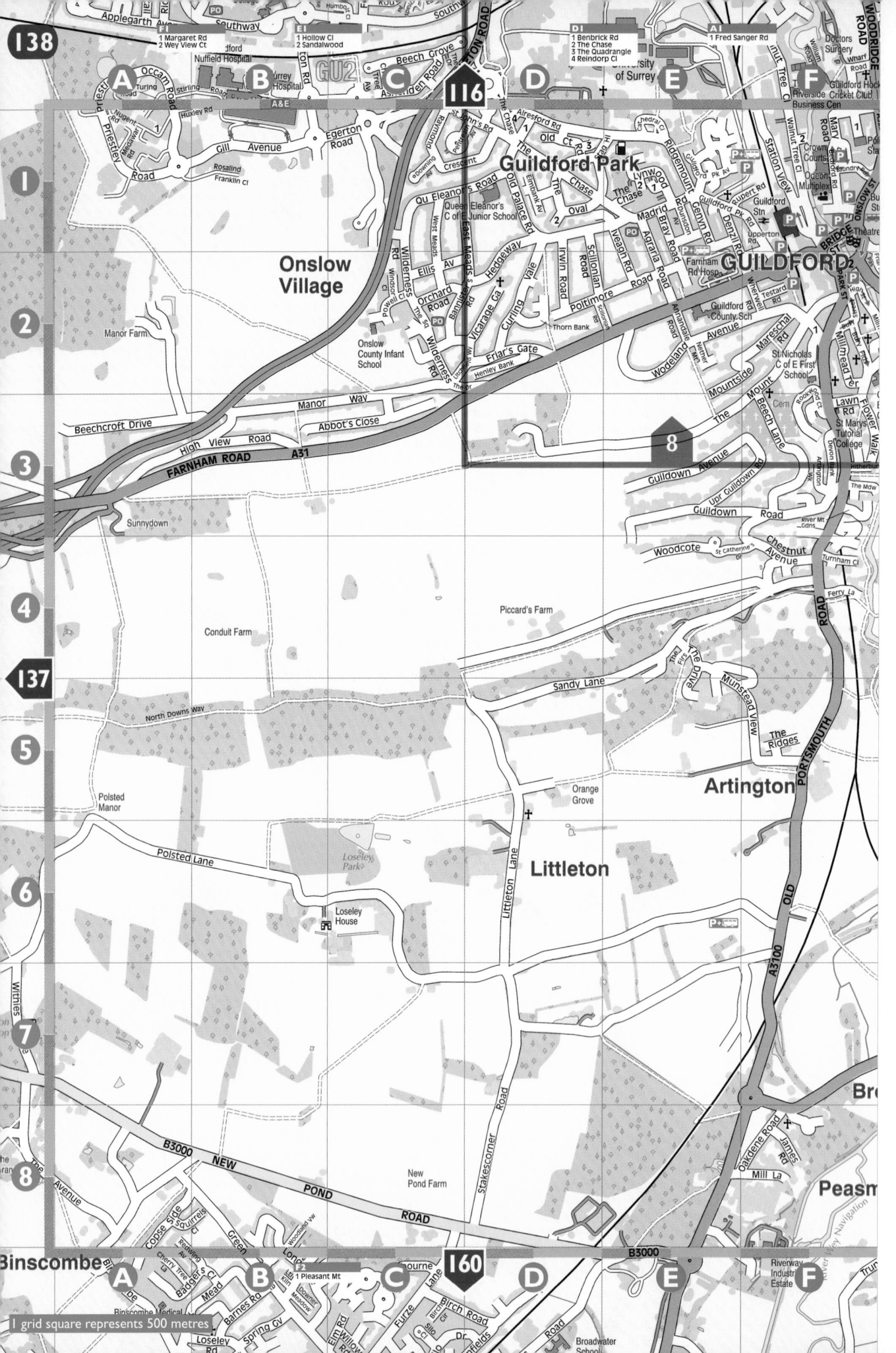

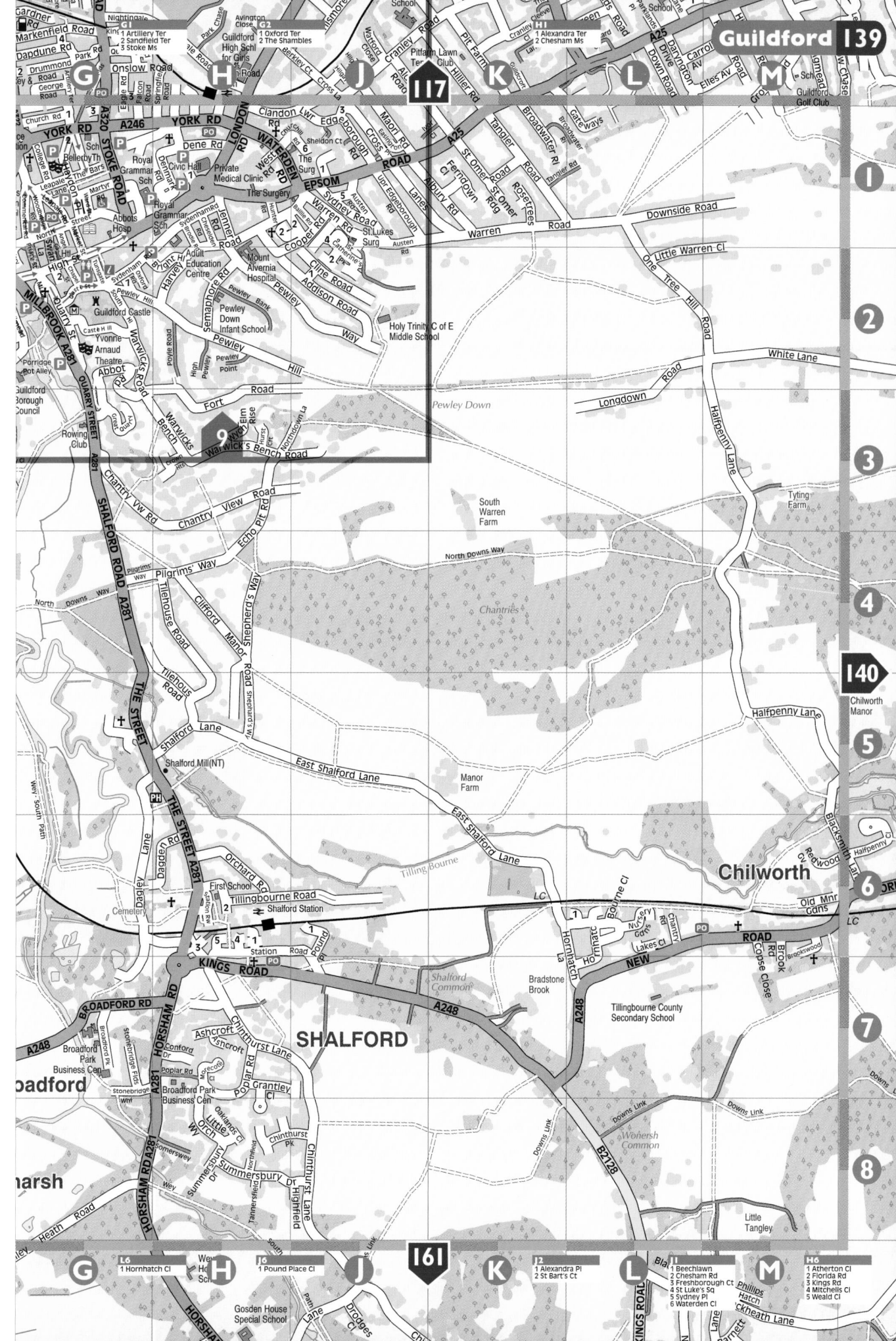

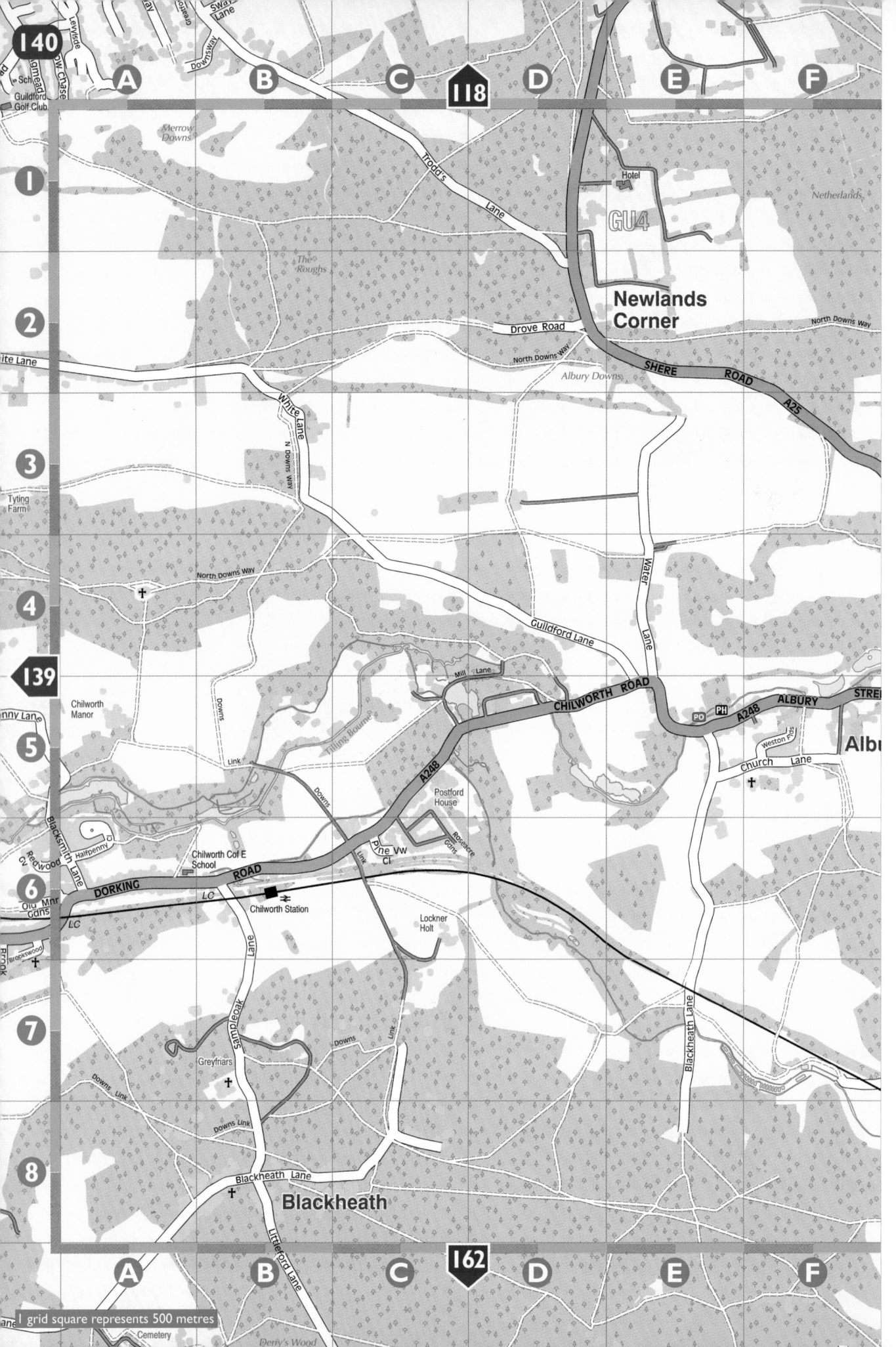

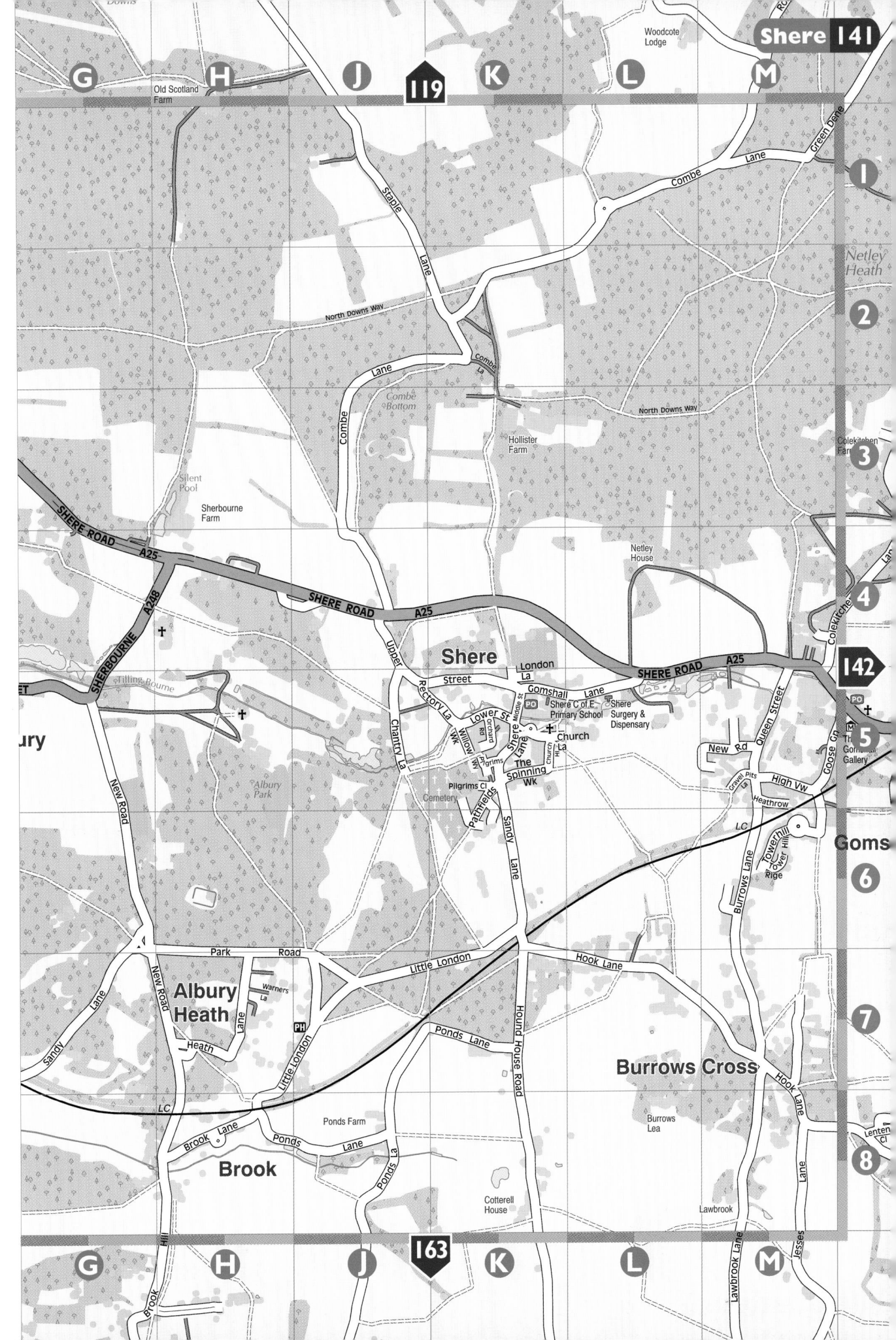

G H J 119 K L M

Woodcote
Lodge

Old Scotland
Farm

I

Green Lane

Combe Lane

Netley
Heath

2

Staple Lane

North Downs Way

Combe Lane

Combe La

Combe
Bottom

Hollister
Farm

North Downs Way

Colekitchen
Farm

3

Silent
Pool

Sherbourne
Farm

Netley
House

Colekitchen La

4

SHERE ROAD A25

A248

SHERE ROAD A25

SHERE ROAD A25

142

PO

†

Sherbourne

Tilling Bourne

†

†

Shere

London
La

Gomshall Lane

The Gomshall
Gallery

5

ury

New Road

Albury
Park

Upper

Street

Rectory La

Lower St

Middle St

Orchard Rd

Willow Wk

Chantry La

Shere Lane

PO

Church La

Shere C of E
Primary School

Shere
Surgery &
Dispensary

Church Hl

New Rd

Queen Street

Goose Gn

High Vw

Gravel Pits La

Heathrow

M

Pilgrims
Wk

Pilgrims Cl

The
Spinning
Wk

†
†

Cemetery

†
†

Pathfields

Burrows Lane

Towerhill

Tower Hill

Rige

LC

Goms

6

Sandy Lane

Park Road

Little London

Hook Lane

7

New Road

Warners
La

Albury
Heath

PH

Heath

Little London Lane

Sandy Lane

Ponds Lane

Hound House Road

Ponds Lane

Burrows Cross

Burrows
Lea

Hook Lane

Lenten Cl

8

LC

Brook Lane

Ponds La

Ponds Lane

Ponds Farm

Cotterell
House

Lawbrook

Lawbrook Lane

Jesses Lane

Brook

Brook Hill

G H J 163 K L M

A   B   C   120   D   E   F

Dunley Hill Farm

1

Green Dene

Netley Heath

Oaken Grove

2

Colekitchen Lane

3

Colekitchen Farm

Hackhurst Downs

North Downs Way

North Downs Way

Beggars Lane

4

Colekitchen Lane

LC

Hackhurst Farm

Leasers Barn

PO

Gomshall Station

The Gomshall Gallery

Mill

5

STATION ROAD

Hackhurst Lane

Abinger Hammer School

Goose Gn

gh Vw

Wonham Way

Gomshall

Abinger Hammer

PO

A25

GUILDFORD ROAD A25

Crossways Farm

6

B2126

FELDAY ROAD

Hammerfield Dr

Paddington Farm

Raikes Lane

7

Rad Lane

Wonham Wy

Wonham Way

Rad La

B2126 HORSHAM ROAD

Fulvens House

Raikes Lane

ok Lane

Lenten Cl

8

Pursers

Rad La

Crest Hl

Fulvens

Annisdowne Cl

164

PH

Raikes Farm

Sutton Abinger

Jesses La

Broadfield R

Sweet La

Hoe

Hoe Lane

Knolfield

Hoe Lane

Westfield

Sutton

Sutton

Water Lane

Sutton

Lane

A   B   C   164   D   E   F

1 grid square represents 500 metres

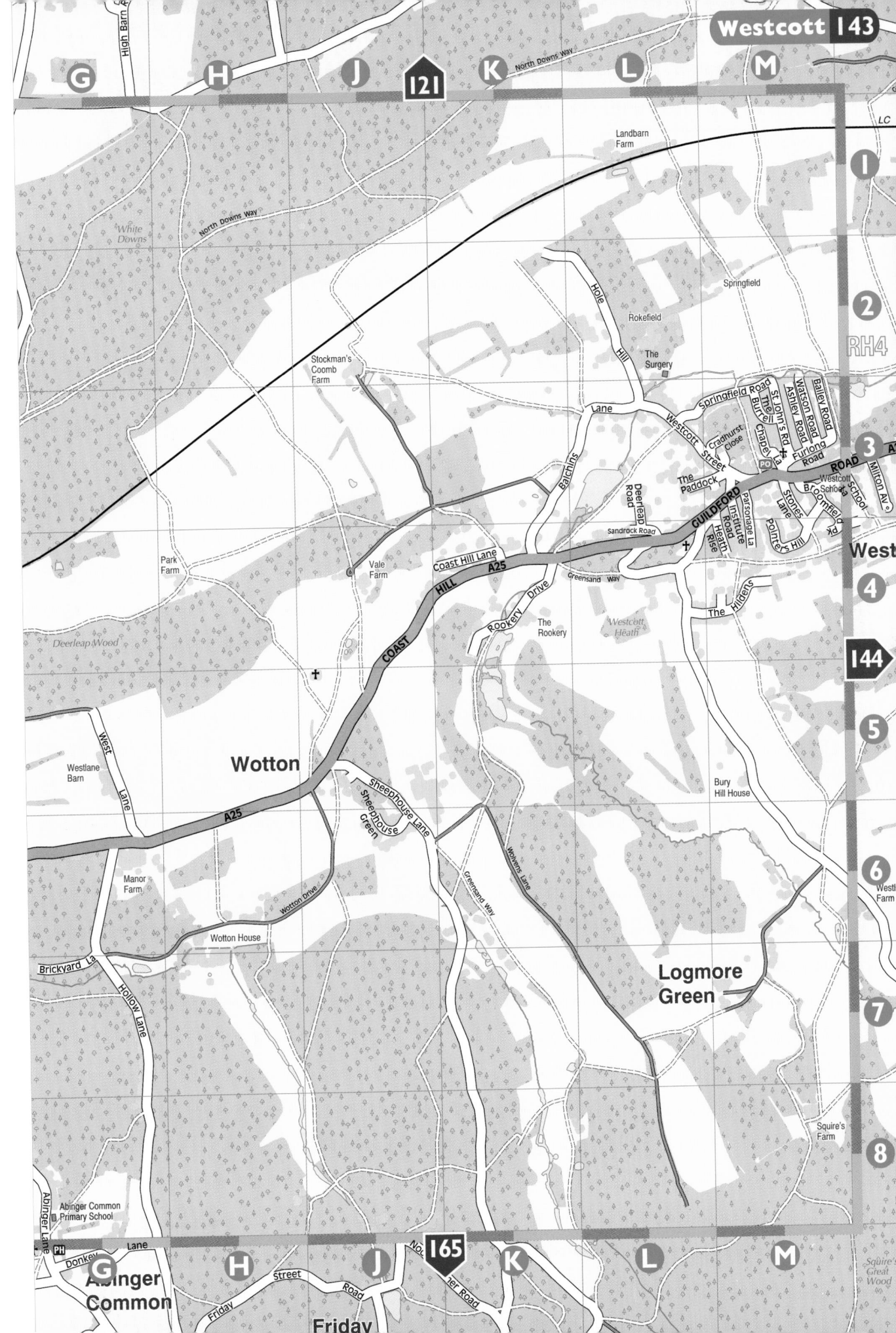

G **H** **J** **121** **K** **L** **M**

North Downs Way

1

LC

Landbarn
Farm

White
Downs

North Downs Way

Springfield

2

RH4

Rokefield

The
Surgery

Stockman's
Coomb
Farm

Springfield Road

Hole

Hill

Lane

Watson Road

Bailey Road

Ashley Road

3

Westcott
Street

The
Burrell

St John's Rd

ROAD

West

Balchins

Cradhurst
Close

Chapel

Furlong
Road

Milton Av

Westcott
School

Lane

The
Paddock

PO

Westcott
School

Park
Farm

Vale
Farm

Coast Hill Lane

A25

Deerleap
Road

GUILDFORD

Institute
Road

Parsonage La

Stones

Broomfield

PK

Sandrock Road

Heath
Rise

Point's Hill

Lane

4

COAST

HILL

Greensand Way

Greensand Way

Westcott
Heath

The
Hildens

Deerleap Wood

†

Rookery Drive

The
Rookery

144

5

Westlane
Barn

West

Wotton

Lane

A25

Sheephouse Lane

Sheephouse
Green

Bury
Hill House

6

Westl
Farm

Manor
Farm

Wotton Drive

Wolvens Lane

Greensand Way

7

Wotton House

Brickyard Lane

Hollow Lane

Logmore
Green

8

Squire's
Farm

Abinger Common
Primary School

Abinger Lane

PH

Donkey

Lane

G **H** Friday Street **J** **165** er Road **K** **L** **M** Squire's
Great
Wood

**Abinger
Common**

Friday

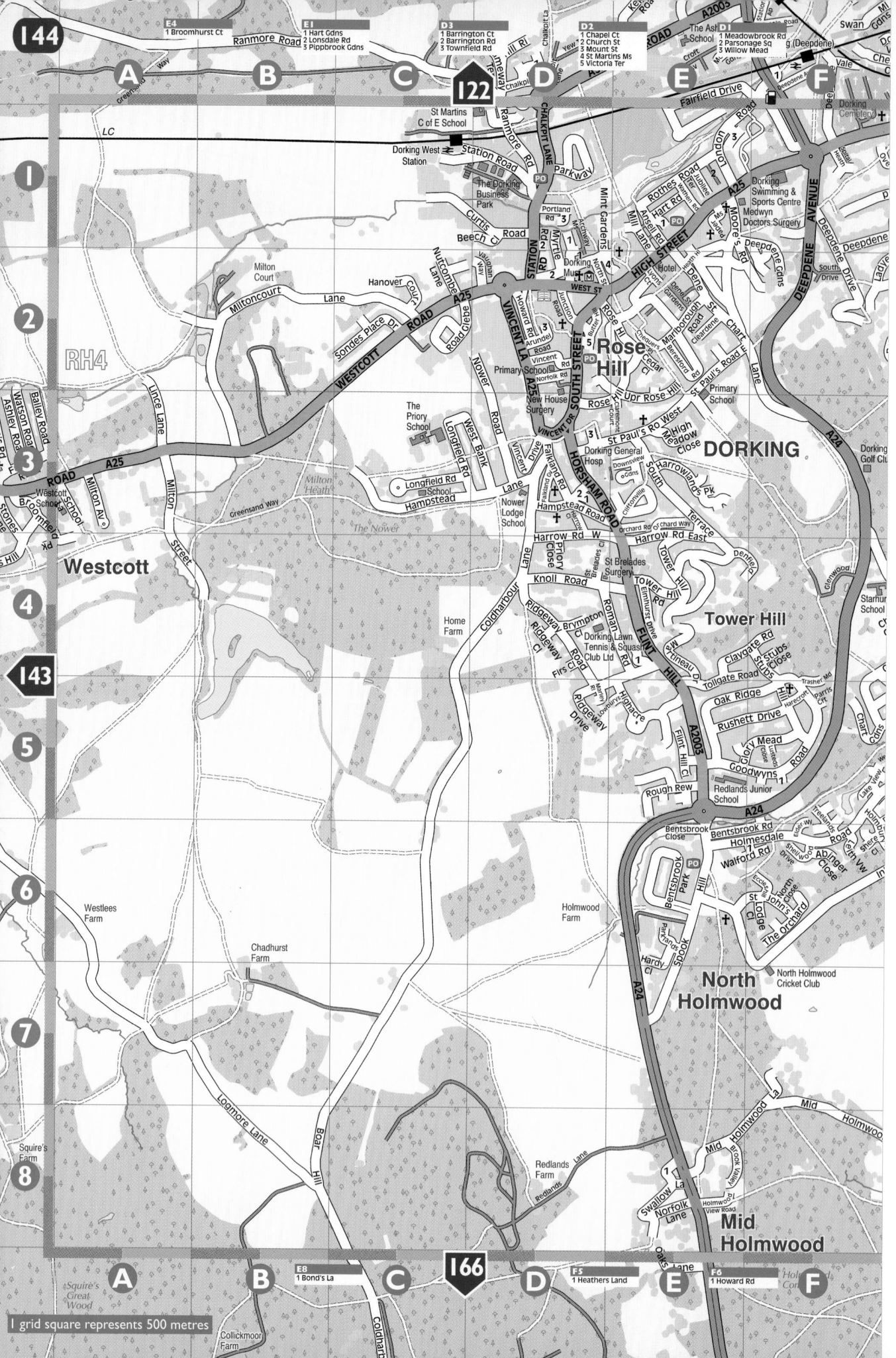

Ranmore Road

A   B   C   D   E   F

Fairfield Drive

1

St Martins
C of E School

Dorking West
Station   Station Road

The Dorking
Business Park

Milton
Court

2

RH4

Hanover   Court
Miltoncourt   Lane

Sondes Place Dr

WESTCOTT   ROAD   A25

The Priory
School

Rose
Hill

DORKING

3

ROAD   A25

Milton
Heath

West Bank

Longfield Rd
School

Greensand Way

Hampstead

Nower
Lodge
School

St Paul's
Primary
School

Dorking General
Hosp

Westcott
School

Bailey Road

Lince Lane

Milton   Street

4

Westcott

The Nower

Home
Farm

Coldharbour

Dorking Lawn
Tennis & Squash
Club Ltd

Tower Hill

5

6

Westlees
Farm

Holmwood
Farm

Bentsbrook
Park

7

Chadhurst
Farm

North
Holmwood

North Holmwood
Cricket Club

8

Squire's
Farm

Logmore Lane

Bear   Hill

Redlands
Farm

Mid
Holmwood

Squire's
Great
Wood

Collickmoor
Farm

1 grid square represents 500 metres

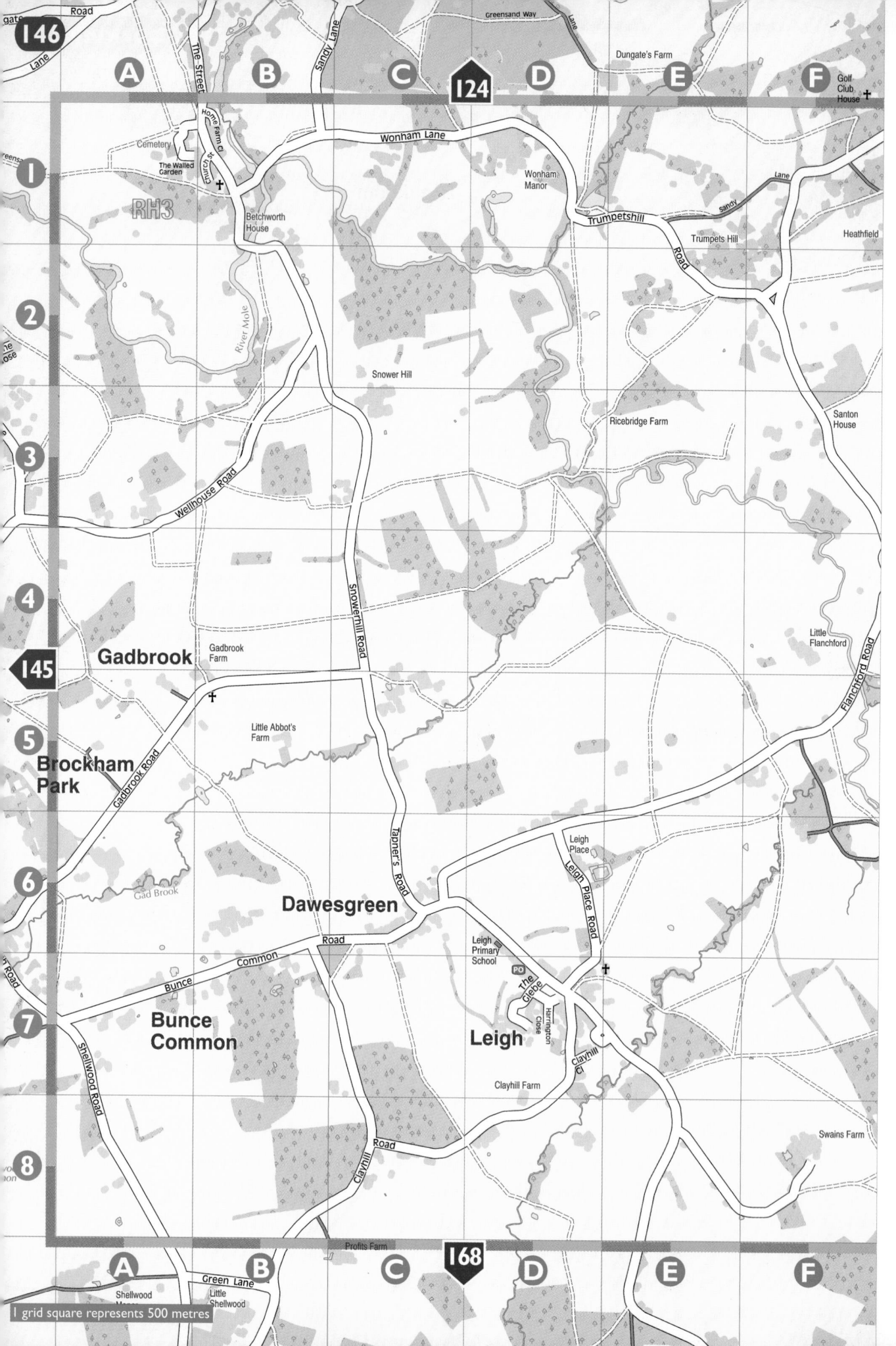

146

A   B   C   124   D   E   F

Greensand Way   Lane   Dungate's Farm   Golf Club House †

Sandy Lane

1   RH3   Cemetery   Wonham Lane
The Walled Garden   Wonham Manor   Lane   Sandy
Betchworth House   Trumpetshill   Trumpets Hill   Heathfield

The Street   Home Farm Cl   Church St   †

2   River Mole   Snower Hill   Ricebridge Farm   Santon House

3   Wellhouse Road

4   Little Flanchford   Flanchford Road

145   Gadbrook   Gadbrook Farm
†
Little Abbot's Farm   Snowerhill Road

5   Brockham Park   Gadbrook Road

6   Gad Brook   Leigh Place   Leigh Place Road
Dawesgreen   Tapner's Road
Road   Leigh Primary School   PO   †

7   Bunce Common   Shellwood Road
Bunce   Common   The Glebe   Harrington Close   Leigh   Clayhill Cl
Clayhill Farm   Swains Farm

8   Clayhill   Road
Profits Farm   168

A   Green Lane   B   C   D   E   F
Shellwood   Little Shellwood

1 grid square represents 500 metres

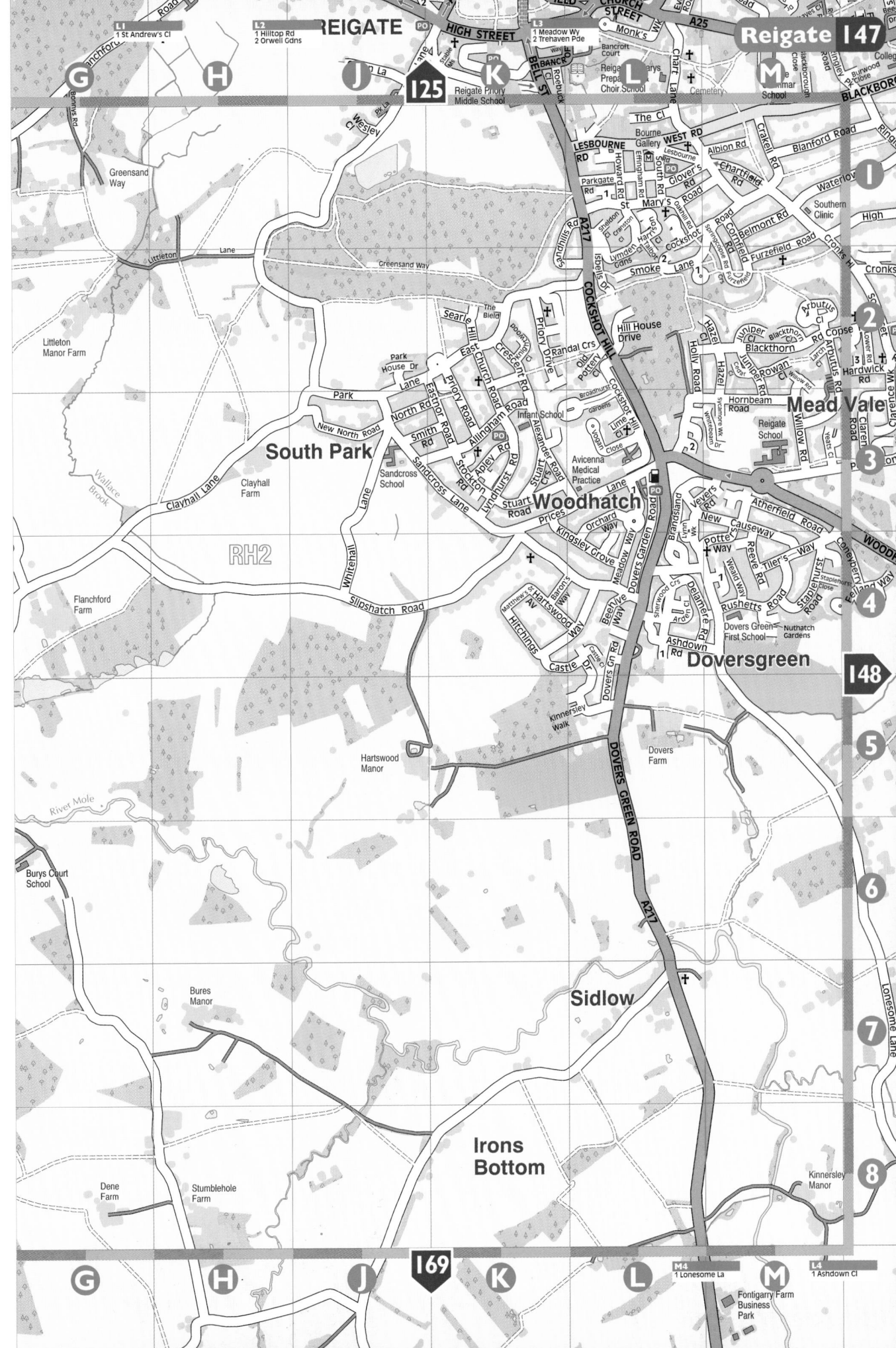

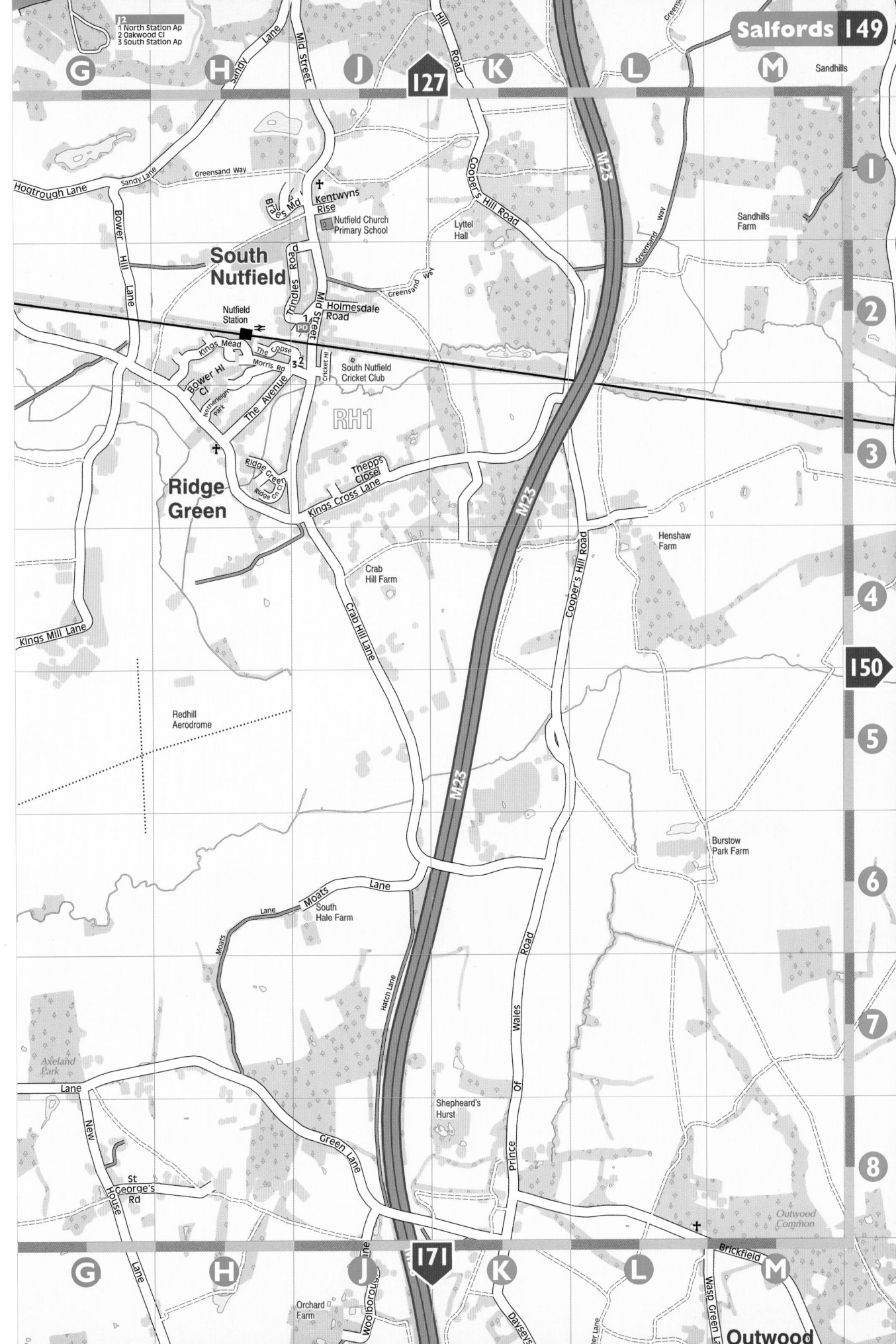

G H J 127 K L M

I

2

3

4

150

5

6

7

8

Sandhills

Sandhills Farm

Hogtrough Lane

Sandy Lane

Greensand Way

Bower Hill Lane

Mid Street

Sandy Lane

Brae's Md

Pindles Road

Kentwyns Rise

Nutfield Church Primary School

South Nutfield

Nutfield Station

PO

Kings Mead

Bower Hl Cl

The Copse

Morris Rd

Netherleigh Park

Holmesdale Road

Cricket Hl

Greensand Way

South Nutfield Cricket Club

RH1

Lyttel Hall

Cooper's Hill Road

M23

Greensand Way

Ridge Green

The Avenue

Ridge Green Cl

Ridge Gn

Kings Cross Lane

Thepps Closel

Crab Hill Farm

Crab Hill Lane

Henshaw Farm

Cooper's Hill Road

M23

Kings Mill Lane

Redhill Aerodrome

M23

Burstow Park Farm

Moats Lane

Lane

South Hale Farm

Moats

Hatch Lane

Wales Road

Axeland Park Lane

New House Lane

St George's Rd

Green Lane

Shepheard's Hurst

Prince Of Wales Road

Outwood Common

Brickfield

G H J 171 K L M

Woolborou

Orchard Farm

The

Dansey's

Daysey's

Wasp Green La

Outwood

Sandhills

A B C 128 D E F

Rabies Heath Road

Tilburstow

Coldharbour Farm

Greensand Wy

Colharbour La

South Park Lane

Greensand Way

Wychroft House

Nash's Farm

I

2

Cuckseys Farm

South Park Farm

South Park Lane

Outwood Lane

Kennels Farm

Lambs Business Park

Terra Cotta

Rush Ave

3

4

149

5

Lower South Park

6

Carlton Road

Lodge Farm

Carlton Road

7

Brown's Hill Lane

Harewood House

8

Hookstile House

Byers Lane

Tile Barn

wood mmon

Outwood Lane

A B C 172 D E F

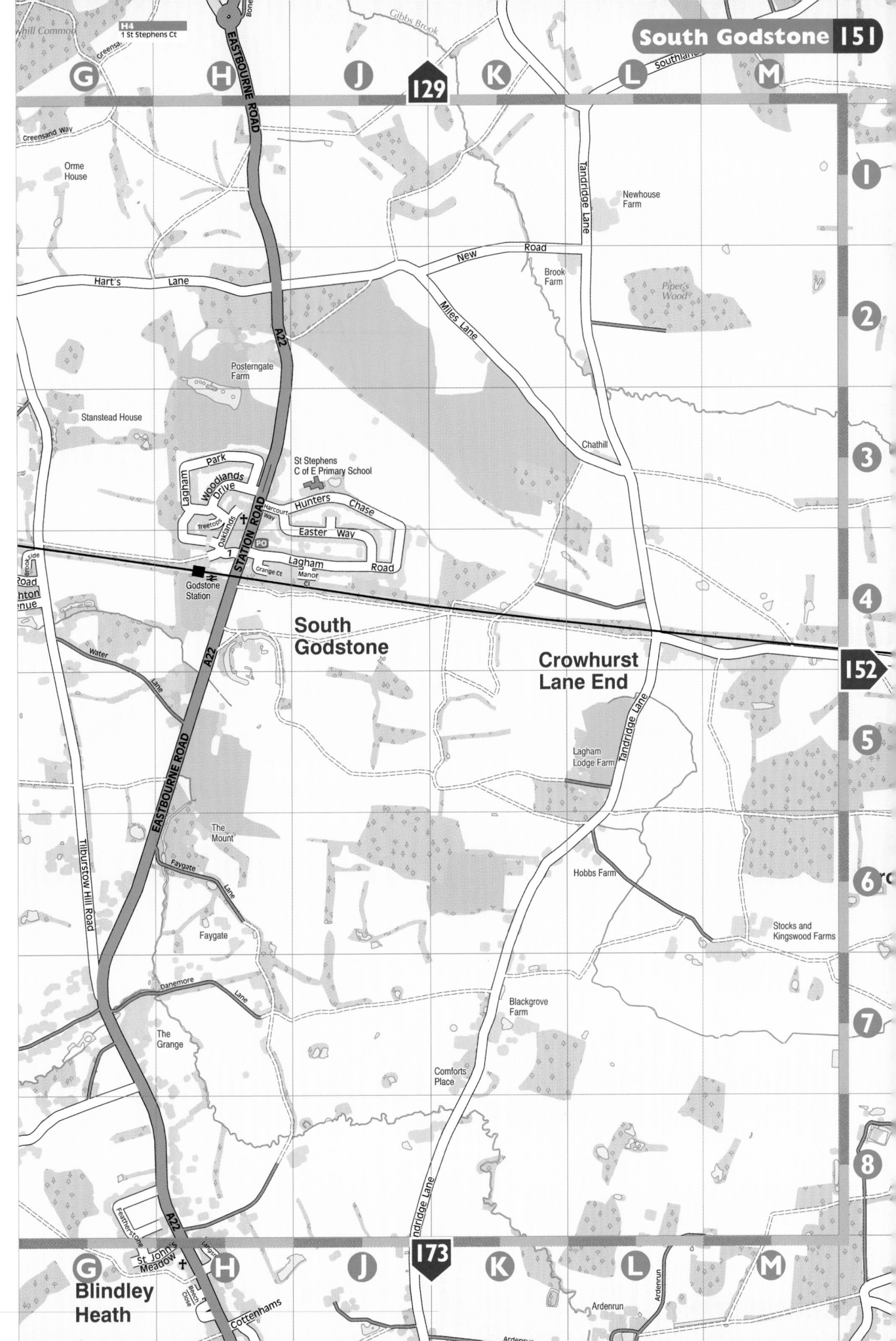

G H J **129** K L M

I

2

3

4

152

5

6

7

8

Whill Common

Greensa.
H4
1 St Stephens Ct

Greensand Way

Orme
House

Hart's   Lane

Gibbs Brook

EASTBOURNE ROAD

Southlan

Tandridge Lane

Newhouse
Farm

New   Road

Miles Lane

Brook
Farm

Piper's
Wood

A22

Posterngate
Farm

Chathill

Stanstead House

Park

Woodlands
Drive

Lagham

St Stephens
C of E Primary School

Treetops

Oaklands

Harcourt
Way

Hunters   Chase

Easter   Way

Lagham   Manor   Road

STATION ROAD

PO

Grange Ct

Brook Side

Road

ighton
enue

Godstone Station

**South
Godstone**

**Crowhurst
Lane End**

Water

Lane

A22

Tandridge Lane

Lagham
Lodge Farm

EASTBOURNE ROAD

Tilburstow Hill Road

The
Mount

Faygate

Lane

Faygate

Hobbs Farm

Stocks and
Kingswood Farms

Danemore   Lane

The
Grange

Blackgrove
Farm

Comforts
Place

Featherstone

A22

Cottenhams

ndridge Lane

St John's
Meadow

Beech Close

Layton

**Blindley
Heath**

Ardenrun

Ardenru

Arden

rc

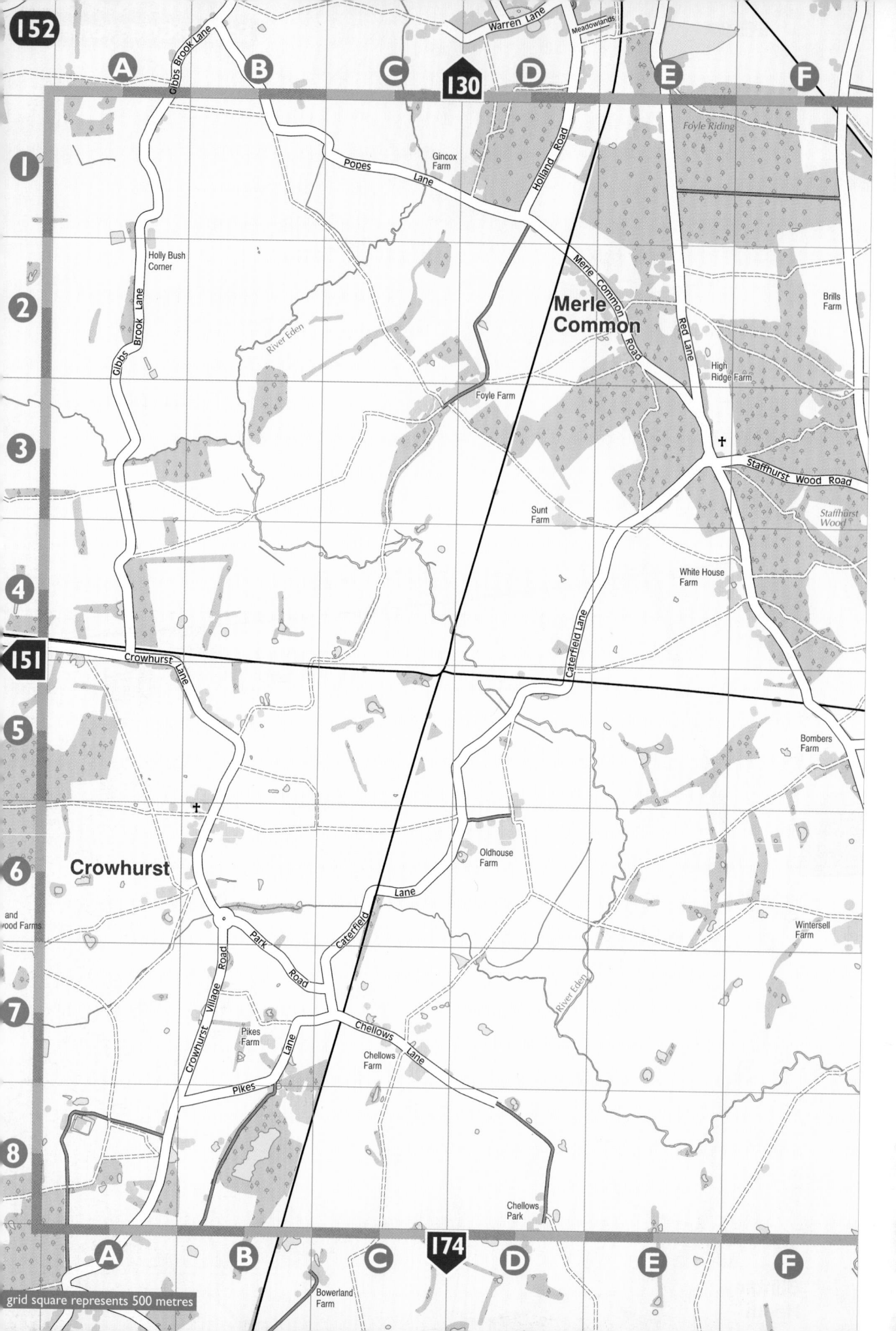

grid square represents 500 metres

A   B   C   **132**   D   E   F

A4
1 Brooklands Cl

I

Old Farnham Lane

Runwick Lane

Cheeks Farm   Grovers Farm

Hotel

Chamber Lane

2

Hill Farm

Willey Place

Perryland

Crondall Road

Northbrook

3

Church Lane

Lane

East Green

Hole

PH   A31

4

Hole Lane   Longcroft   Eggars Fld   Babs Flds   Bonners Fld   School Lane

A31

Gravel Hill Road

PO

Gravel Hill Rd

5

Rectory Lane

Station Road

Holt Pound Inclosure

Holt Pound

Aquarium

dley Farm

6

Wey Bank

Birdworld

Lodge Pond

sington Road

Station Road   Bentley Station

7

sington Close

Blacknest Road

Bentley Hall

park Ct

Alice Holt Lodge

Glenbervie Inclosure

Catham Copse

Lodge Inclosure

Alice Holt Forest

8

The Cross

Back Lane

A   B   C   **176**   D   **Bucks Horn Oak**   E   F

Blacknest Road

Road

1 grid square represents 500 metres

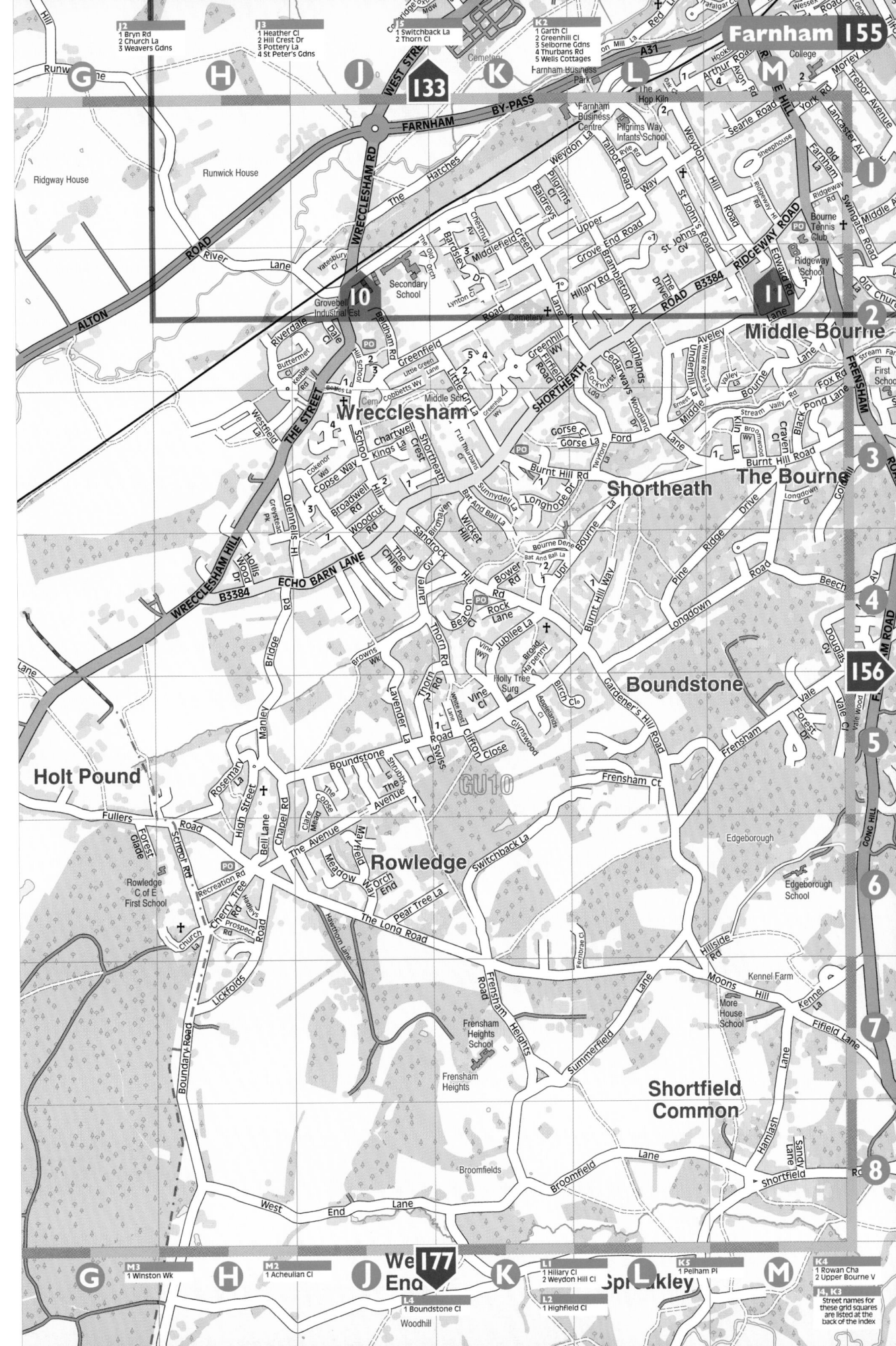

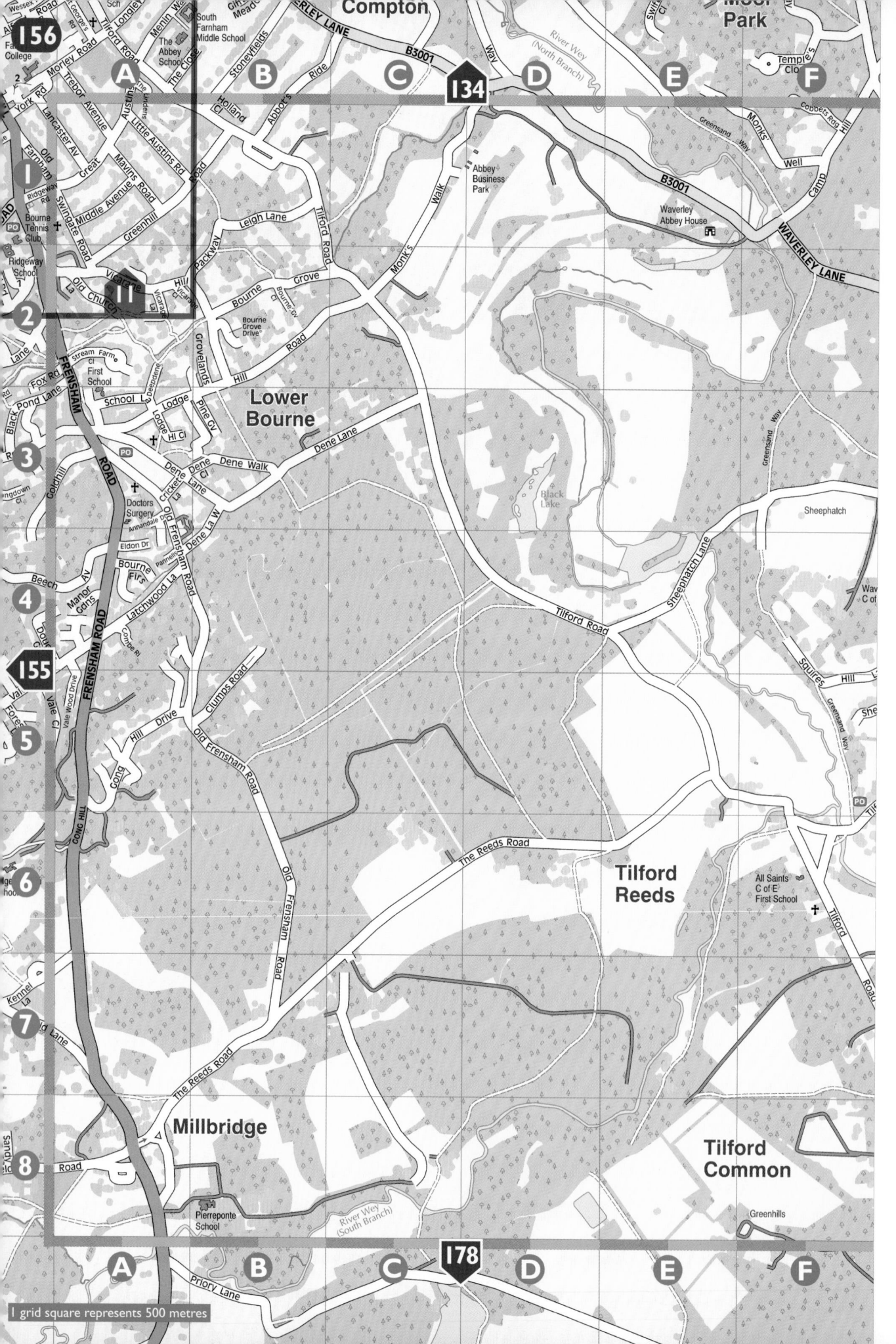

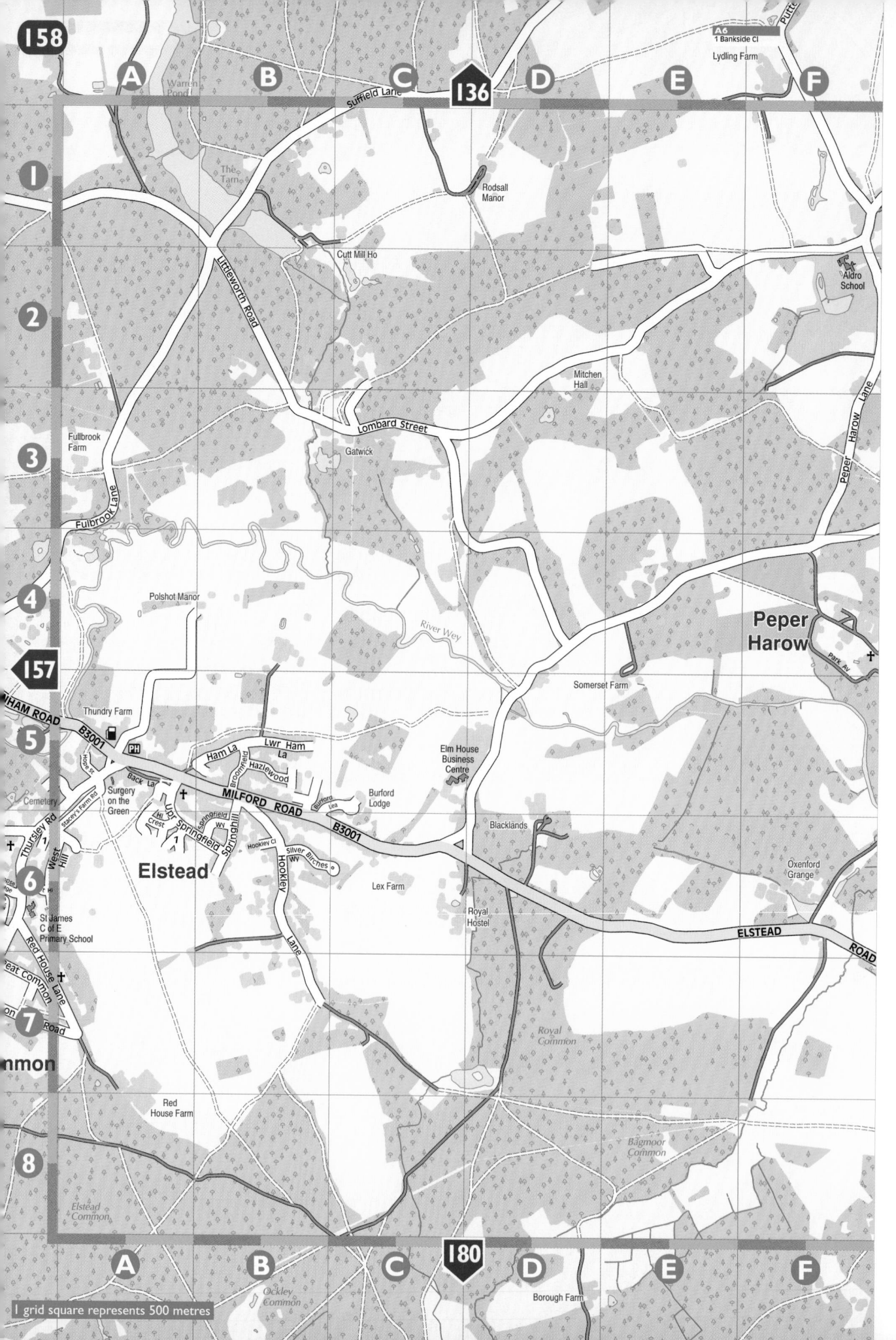

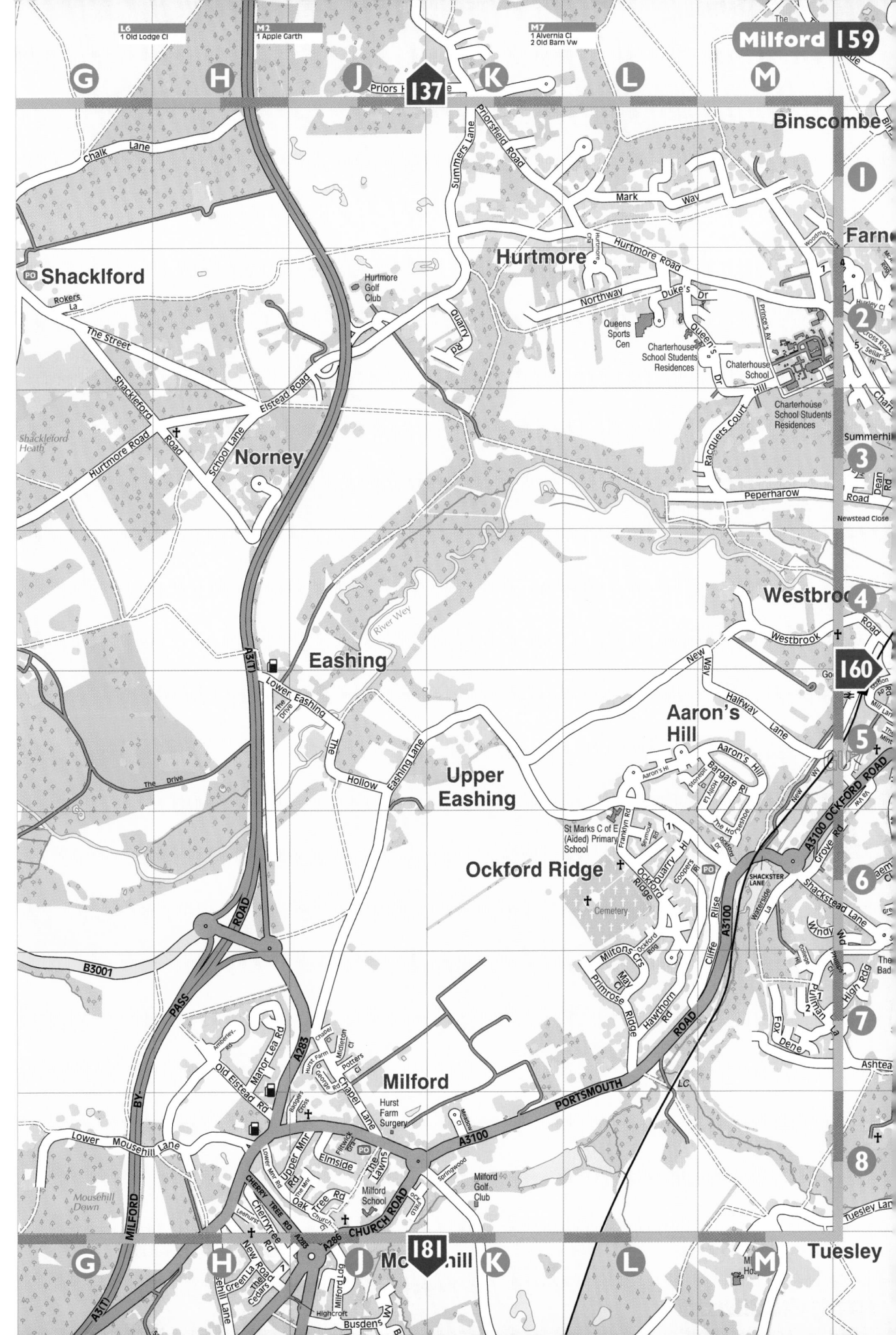

L6
1 Old Lodge Cl

M2
1 Apple Garth

M7
1 Alvernia Cl
2 Old Barn Vw

G   H   J   Priors   137   K   L   M

Binscombe

I

Farnc

Summers Lane

Priorsfield Road

Mark Way

Hurtmore

Hurtmore Cfs

Hurtmore Road

Northway

Duke's Dr

Queen's Dr

Prince's Av

Cross Rd

Sellar Hl

Huxley Cl

Chatt

4

2

Chalk Lane

School Lane

Shackleford Road

PO Shacklford

Rokers La

The Street

Hurtmore Road

Shackleford Road

Elstead Road

Norney

Hurtmore Golf Club

Quarry Rd

Queens Sports Cen

Charterhouse School Students Residences

Chaterhouse School

Charterhouse School Students Residences

Racquets court

Summerhi

3

Dean Road

Peperharow

Newstead Close

Shackleford Heath

River Wey

Westbroc

Westbrook

New Way

Halfway Lane

Goc

Westbrook Road

4

160

5

Eashing

A3(T)

Lower Eashing

The Drive

The Hollow

Eashing Lane

Upper Eashing

Aaron's Hill

Aaron's Hl

Aaron's Hil

Bargate Ri

Stovold

El Holly

The Ho

Cobbe

New Wy

New Wy

Station Rd

Mill Lan

The

5

The Drive

St Marks C of E (Aided) Primary School

Franklyn Rd

Seymour

Ockford Ridge

Ockford Ridge

Quarry Hl

Cooper's Rise

PO

SHACKSTER LANE

Grove Rd

Shackstead Lane

A3100 OCKFORD ROAD

6

Cemetery

Cliffe Rise

A3100

Waterside La

Windy Wd

High Rdg

College Hill

Gre

The Bad

ROAD

PASS

BY-

MILFORD

B3001

Miltons Crs

May

Ockford Rdg

Primrose Ridge

Hawthorn Rd

Fox Dene

Phillips

Pullman

1 2

7

Ashtea

Amberley Rd

Old Elstead Rd

Manor Lea Rd

A283

Hurst Farm

Midleton

St George

Potters Cl

Chapel Rd

Chapel Lane

Badger's Croft

Milford

Hurst Farm Surgery

Meadrow

A3100

PORTSMOUTH

ROAD

LC

7

Lower Mousehill Lane

Mousehill Down

A3(T)

Green La

Cedars

New Road

The

Cherrytree Rd

Upper Mnr Rd

Oak Tree Rd

Lower Mnr Rd

Cherry Tree Rd

Leahurst

A286

Elmside

The Lawns

PO

Fieldway

Milford School

Church

CHURCH ROAD

Springwood

Milford Golf Club

Milford Lodge

Highcroft

8

M
Ho

G   H   J   Mo...hill   181   K   L   M   Tuesley

Tuesley Lan

Busdens

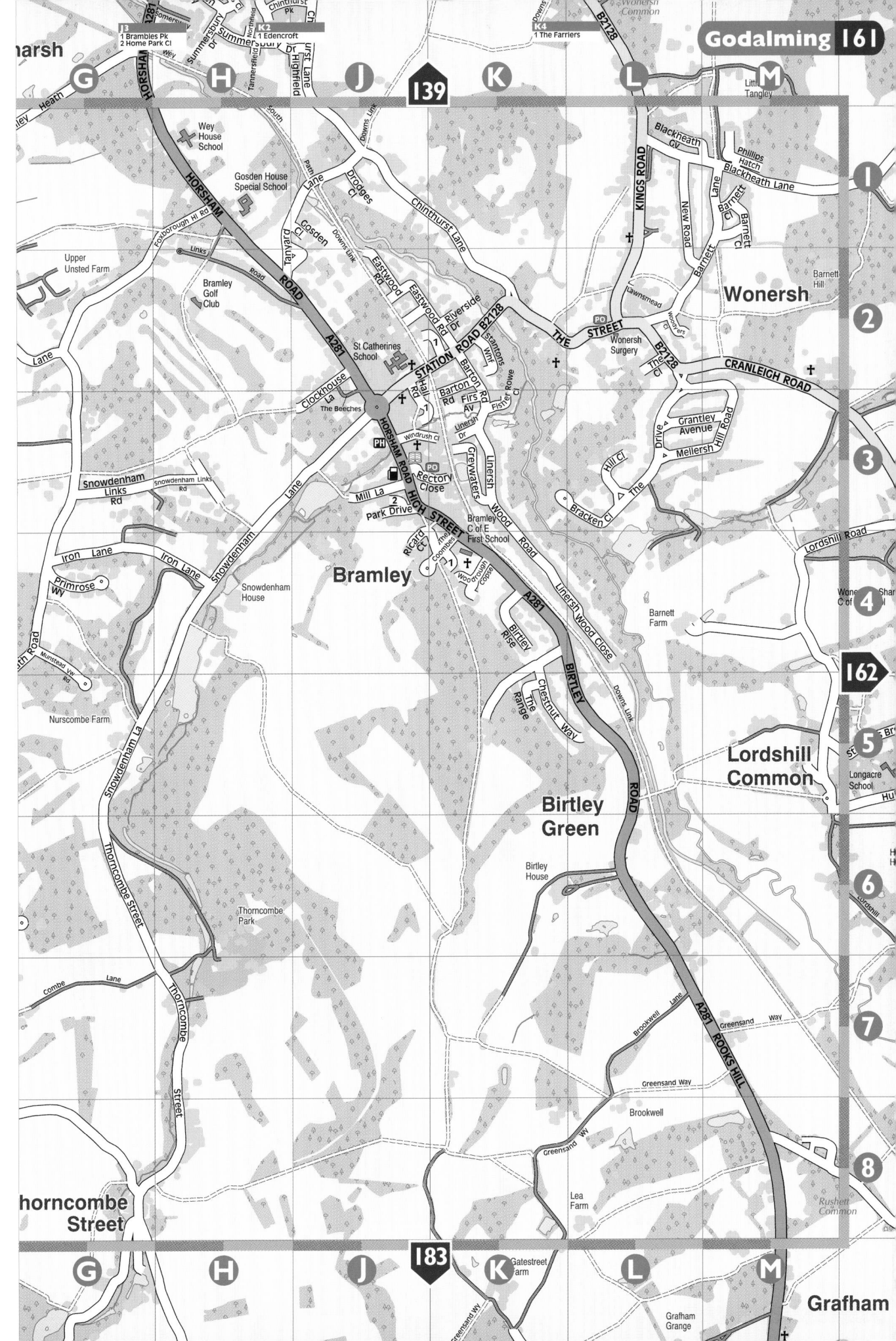

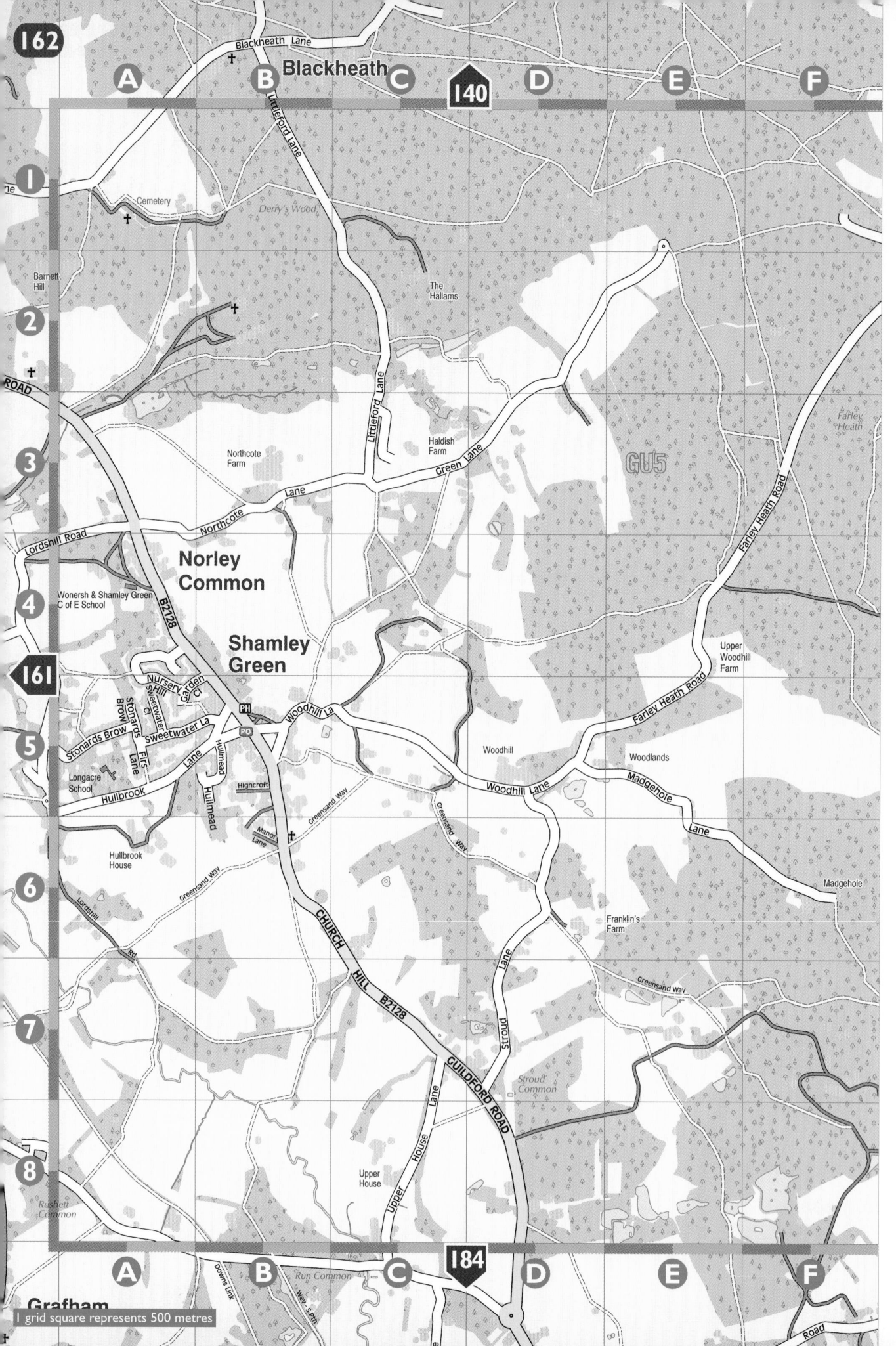

A B **Blackheath** C 140 D E F

Blackheath Lane

1

Cemetery

Derfy's Wood

Barnett
Hill

2

The Hallams

ROAD

*Farley
Heath*

3

Northcote
Farm

Haldish
Farm

GU5

Littleford Lane

Green Lane

Lordshill Road

**Norley
Common**

4 Wonersh & Shamley Green
C of E School

B2128

Upper
Woodhill
Farm

**Shamley
Green**

Farley Heath Road

161

Nursery
Garden Cl

Sweetwater
Cl

Stonards
Brow

PH

Woodhill La

Woodhill

Woodlands

Madgehole
Lane

5 Stonards Brow

Firs
Lane

Sweetwater La

PO

Longacre
School

Hullmead

Lane

Hullbrook

Highcroft

Woodhill Lane

Madgehole

Hullmead

Greensand Way

Manor
Lane

Greensand
Way

6 Lordshill

Hullbrook
House

Greensand Way

Franklin's
Farm

Greensand Way

Stroud Lane

7 Rd

CHURCH
HILL
B2128

GUILDFORD ROAD

Stroud
Common

Upper House
Lane

8

Upper
House

*Rushett
Common*

A B Run Common C 184 D E F

Grafham

Downs Link

Wey S path

Road

1 grid square represents 500 metres

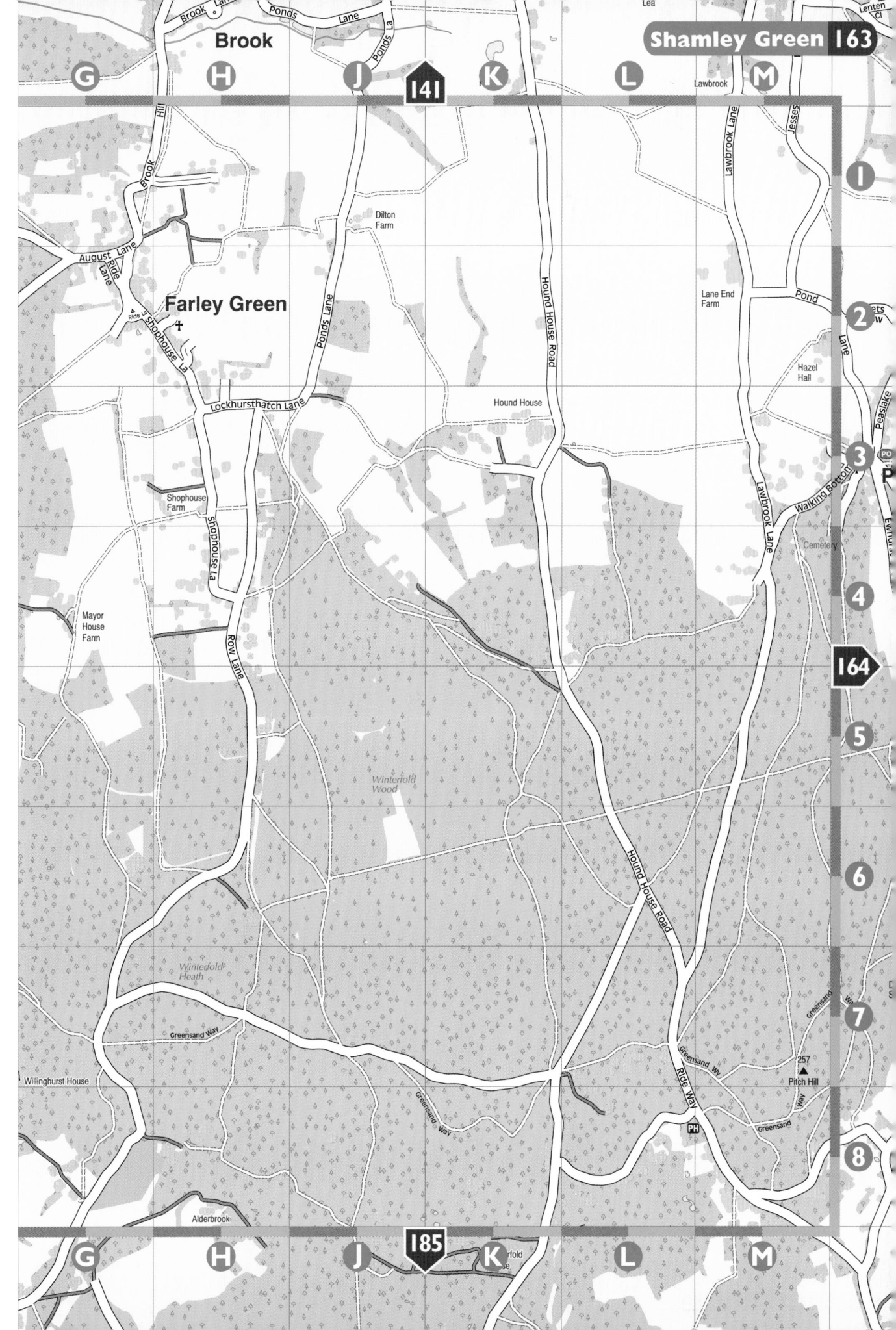

Brook

Farley Green

Dilton Farm

Lane End Farm

Lawbrook

Hazel Hall

Hound House

Shophouse Farm

Hound House Road

Lockhursthatch Lane

Mayor House Farm

Cemetery

Winterfold Wood

Row Lane

Shophouse La

Ponds Lane

Lawbrook Lane

Walking Bottom

Winterfold Heath

Greensand Way

Hound House Road

Greensand Way

Willinghurst House

Greensand Way

Greensand Wy

Ride Way

Pitch Hill

257

Greensand

Alderbrook

G H J K L M

141

185

164

PO

G H I J K L M

2 3 4 5 6 7 8

August Lane

Ride Lane

Brook Hill

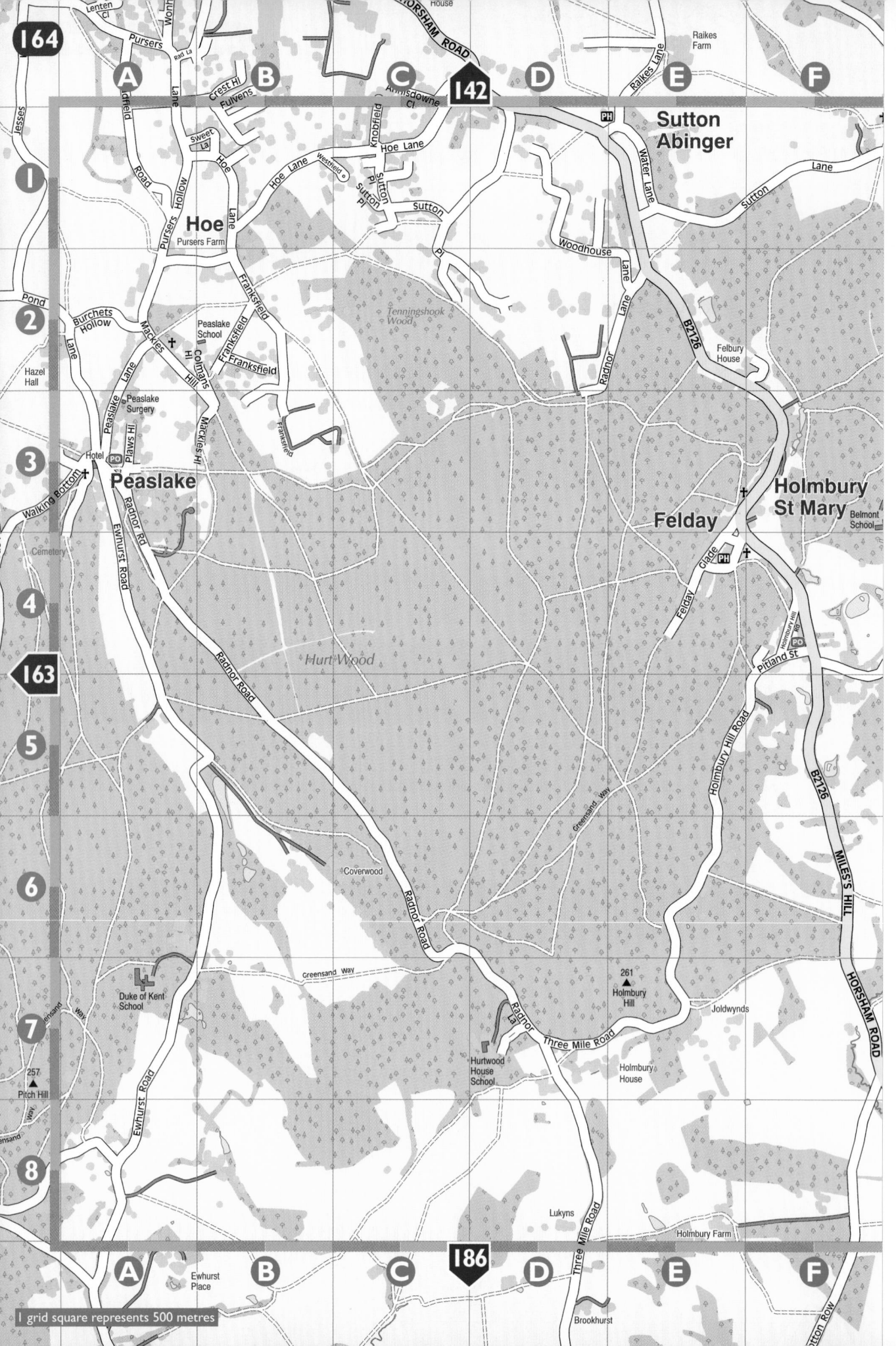

142

186

163

Sutton
Abinger

Hoe

Peaslake

Felday

Holmbury
St Mary

Hurt Wood

Tenningshook
Wood

HORSHAM ROAD

Raikes
Farm

Belmont
School

Felbury
House

Duke of Kent
School

Hurtwood
House School

Holmbury
House

Coverwood

Joldwynds

261
Holmbury
Hill

257
Pitch Hill

Greensand Way

Greensand Way

Three Mile Road

Lukyns

Brookhurst

Holmbury Farm

Ewhurst
Place

Radnor Road

Radnor Road

Ewhurst Road

Holmbury Hill Road

MILES'S HILL

HORSHAM ROAD

B2126

B2126

Water Lane

Radnor Lane

Woodhouse Lane

Sutton Lane

Sutton Lane

Hoe Lane

Hoe Lane

Sutton Pl

Sutton Pl

Knobfield

Annisdowne Cl

Westfield

Fulvens

Crest Hl

Pursers

Lenten Cl

Jesses

Pond La

Burchets Hollow

Hazel Hall

Mackles Lane

Peaslake Lane

Plaws Hl

Colmans Hl

Peaslake School

Peaslake Surgery

Franksfield

Franksfield

Mackles Hl

Walking Bottom

Cemetery

Hotel

PO

Pursers Farm

Pursers Hollow

Sweet La

Hoe Lane

Rad La

Wonham

Felday Glade

Pitland St

Pitland St

Holmbury Hill Rd

PO

PH

PH

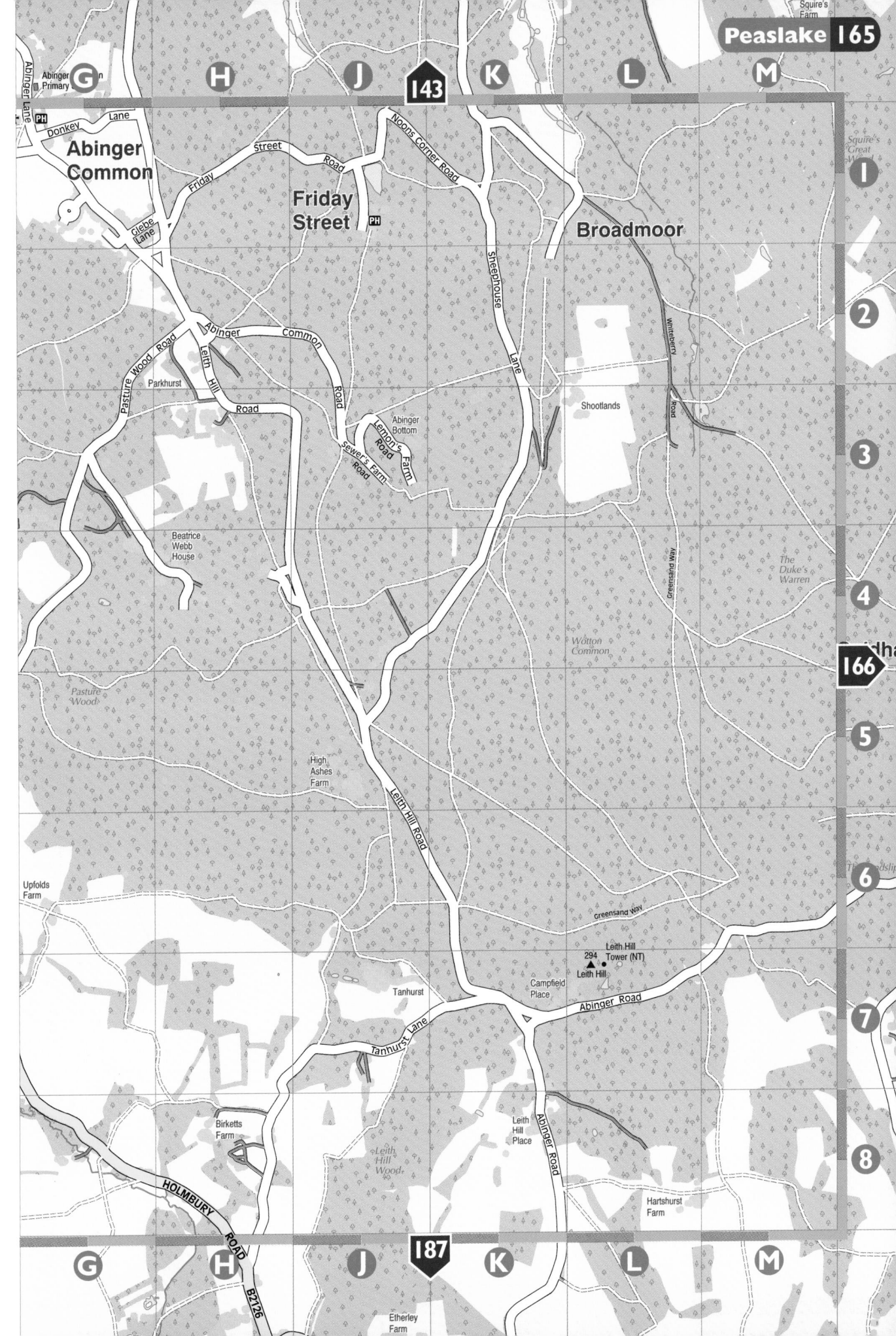

G

H

J

143

K

L

M

Squire's
Farm

Abinger
Primary G

PH

Donkey   Lane

**Abinger
Common**

Glebe
Lane

Friday   Street   Road

Noons Corner Road

Squire's
Great
Wood

1

**Friday
Street**

PH

Abinger   Common   Road

Leith   Hill

Road

Parkhurst

Pasture Wood Road

Sewer's Farm Road

Lemon's Farm Road

Abinger
Bottom

Sheephouse   Lane

Shootlands

Whiteberry   Road

Broadmoor

2

3

Beatrice
Webb
House

Greensand Way

The
Duke's
Warren

4

166

Wotton
Common

5

Pasture
Wood

High
Ashes
Farm

Leith   Hill   Road

Upfolds
Farm

6

Greensand Way

Leith Hill
Tower (NT)

294
Leith Hill

Campfield
Place

Abinger   Road

7

Tanhurst

Tanhurst Lane

Leith
Hill
Place

Abinger   Road

Birketts
Farm

Leith
Hill
Wood

8

HOLMBURY   ROAD

B2126

Hartshurst
Farm

G

H

J

187

K

L

M

Etherley
Farm

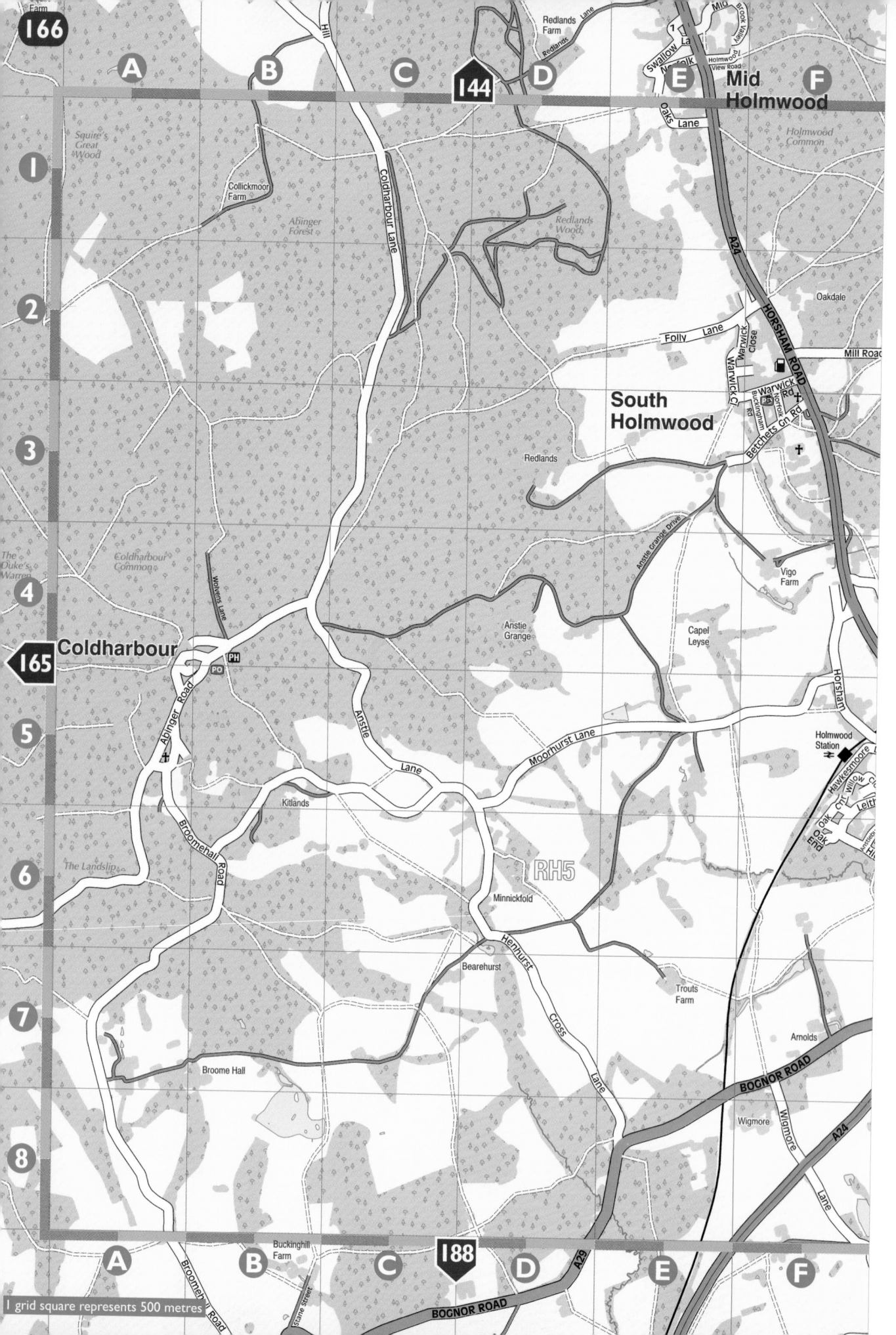

144

165 ◀

Mid Holmwood

A B C D E F

1

2

3

4

5

6

7

8

Squire's Great Wood

Collickmoor Farm

Abinger Forest

Coldharbour Lane

Redlands Farm

Redlands Lane

Redlands

Redlands Wood

Holmwood Common

Oakdale

Folly Lane

Warwick Close

Warwick Cl.

Warwick Rd.

Norfolk Rd.

Buckingham Rd.

Betchets Gn. Rd.

Mill Road

South Holmwood

A24

HORSHAM ROAD

Swallow La.

Oaks Lane

View Road

The Duke's Warren

Coldharbour Common

Wolvens Lane

Coldharbour

PH

PO

Abinger Road

Anstie Lane

Anstie Grange Drive

Anstie Grange

Vigo Farm

Capel Leyse

Horsham Rd.

Holmwood Station

Hawkesmoore

Willow Cl.

Oak Cl.

Oak End

Leith

Broomehall Road

Kitlands

Moorhurst Lane

Minnickfold

RH5

The Landslip

Henhurst Cross Lane

Bearehurst

Trouts Farm

Arnolds

Broome Hall

Buckinghill Farm

188

Staine Street

BOGNOR ROAD

A29

Wigmore

Wigmore Lane

A24

BOGNOR ROAD

A B C D E F

I grid square represents 500 metres

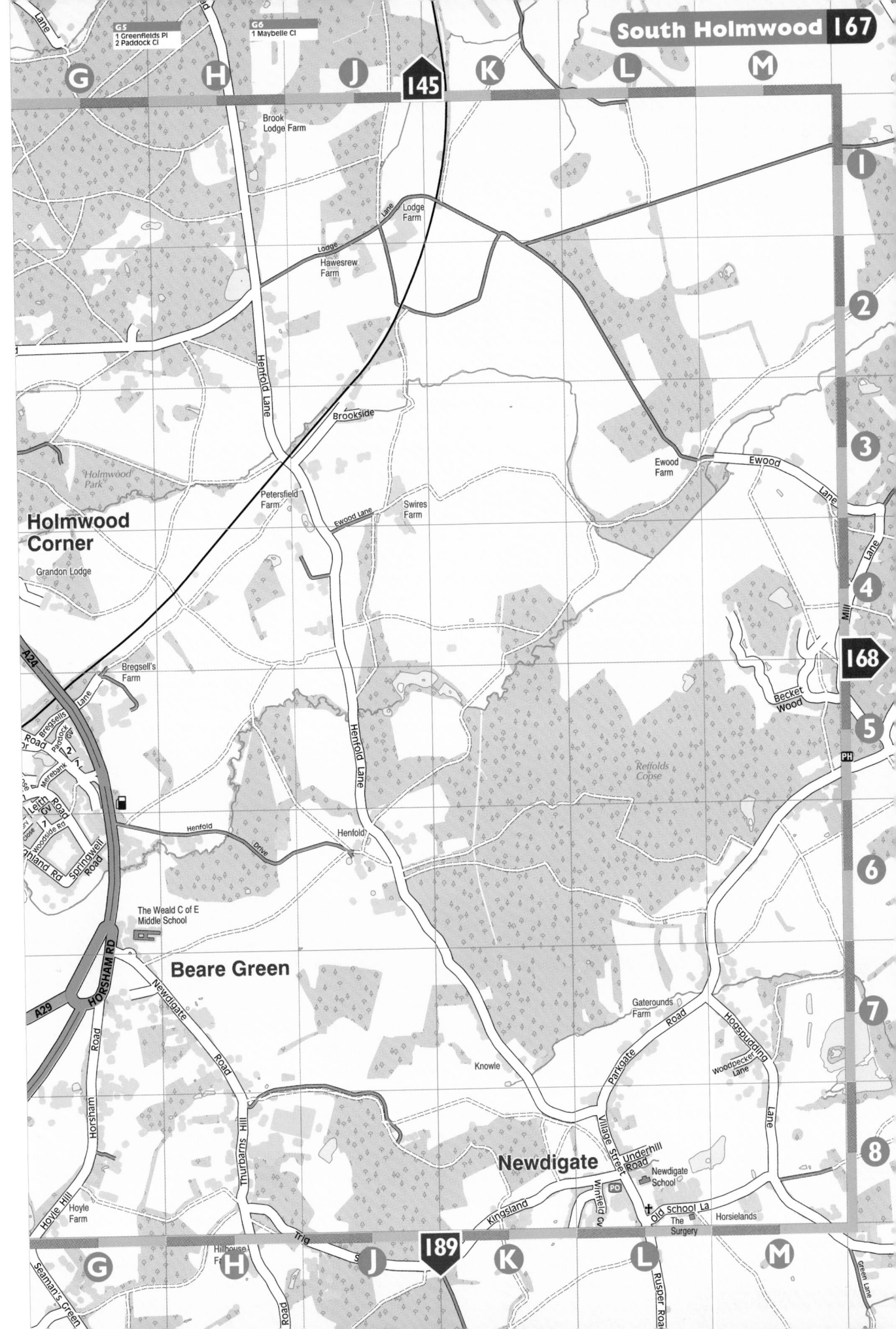

G

H

J

145

K

L

M

I

2

3

168

4

5

PH

6

7

8

G5
1 Greenfields Pl
2 Paddock Cl

G6
1 Maybelle Cl

Brook
Lodge Farm

Lodge
Farm

Lodge

Hawesrew
Farm

Lane

Brookside

Ewood
Farm

Ewood

Lane

'Holmwood'
Park

Petersfield
Farm

Ewood Lane

Swires
Farm

Mill

Lane

Becket
Wood

**Holmwood
Corner**

Grandon Lodge

Henfold Lane

Reifolds
Copse

PH

A24

Bregsell's
Farm

Bregsells
Road

Paddock

Merebank

Leith
Gv

Woodside Rd

hland Rd

Springwell
Road

Henfold

Henfold
Drive

Henfold

Henfold Lane

The Weald C of E
Middle School

Beare Green

A29

HORSHAM RD

Newdigate
Road

Horsham
Road

Thunarns Hill

Knowle

Gaterounds
Farm

Parkgate
Road

Hogspudling
Lane

Woodpecker
Lane

Hoyle Hill

Hoyle
Farm

Trig

189

Newdigate

Village Street

Underhill
Road

Newdigate
School

PO

Winfield Gv

Kingsland

Old School La

The
Surgery

Horsielands

Rusper Road

Green Lane

Seaman's Green

Hillhouse
F

G

H

J

K

L

M

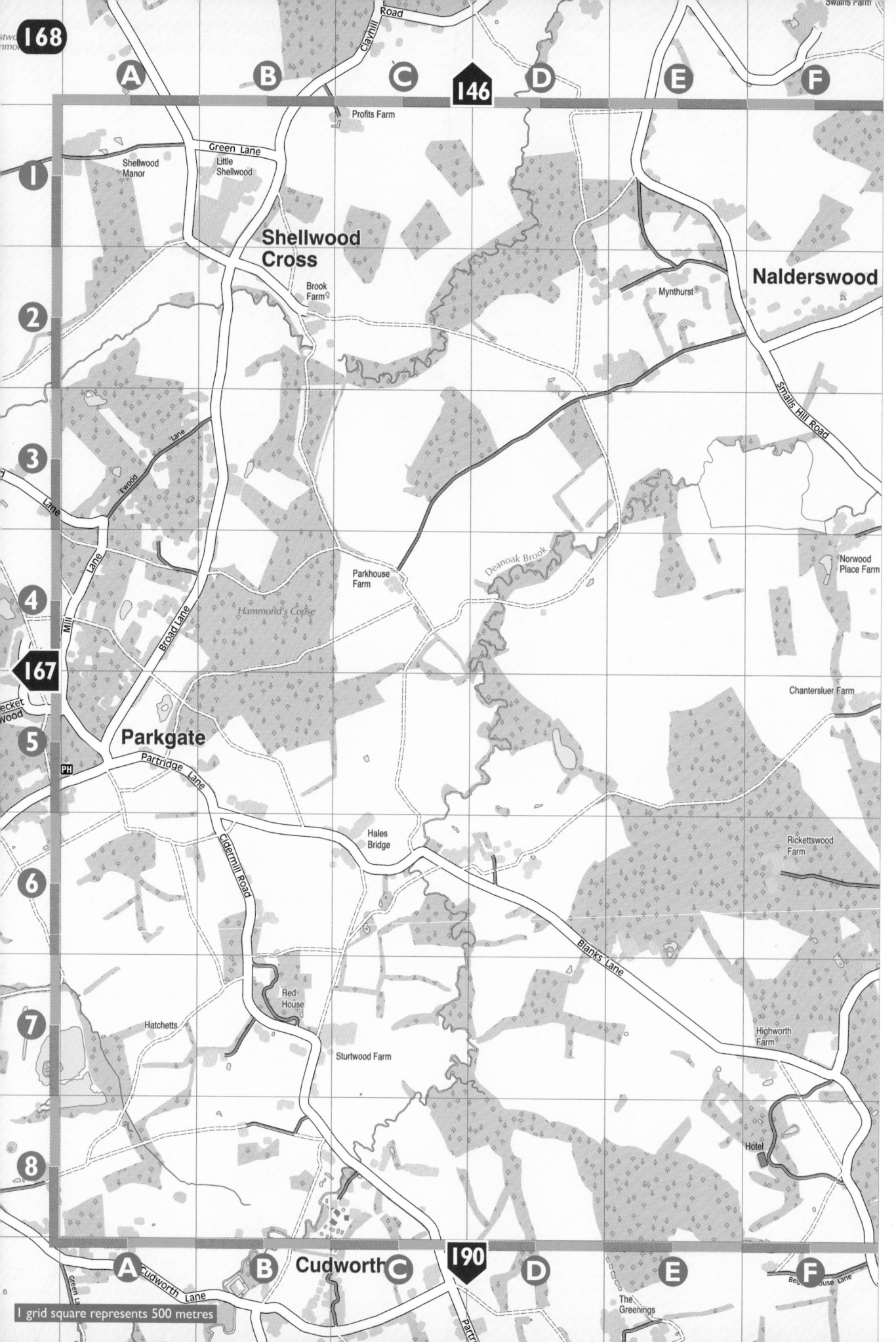

168

A   B   C   **146**   D   E   F

Road

Clayhill

Swains Farm

Profits Farm

Green Lane

1   Shellwood Manor   Little Shellwood

Shellwood Cross

Brook Farm

Mynthurst

Naldeswood

2

Smalls Hill Road

Ewood

Lane

3

Lane

Broad Lane

Mill Lane

Hammond's Copse

Parkhouse Farm

Deanoak Brook

Norwood Place Farm

4

167

ecket wood

Chantersluer Farm

5

Parkgate

Partridge Lane

PH

Cidermill Road

Hales Bridge

Rickettswood Farm

6

Blanks Lane

Red House

7

Hatchetts

Sturtwood Farm

Highworth Farm

8

Hotel

A   Cudworth Lane   B   **Cudworth**   C   **190**   D   E   F   House Lane

Green La

Partr

The Greenings

1 grid square represents 500 metres

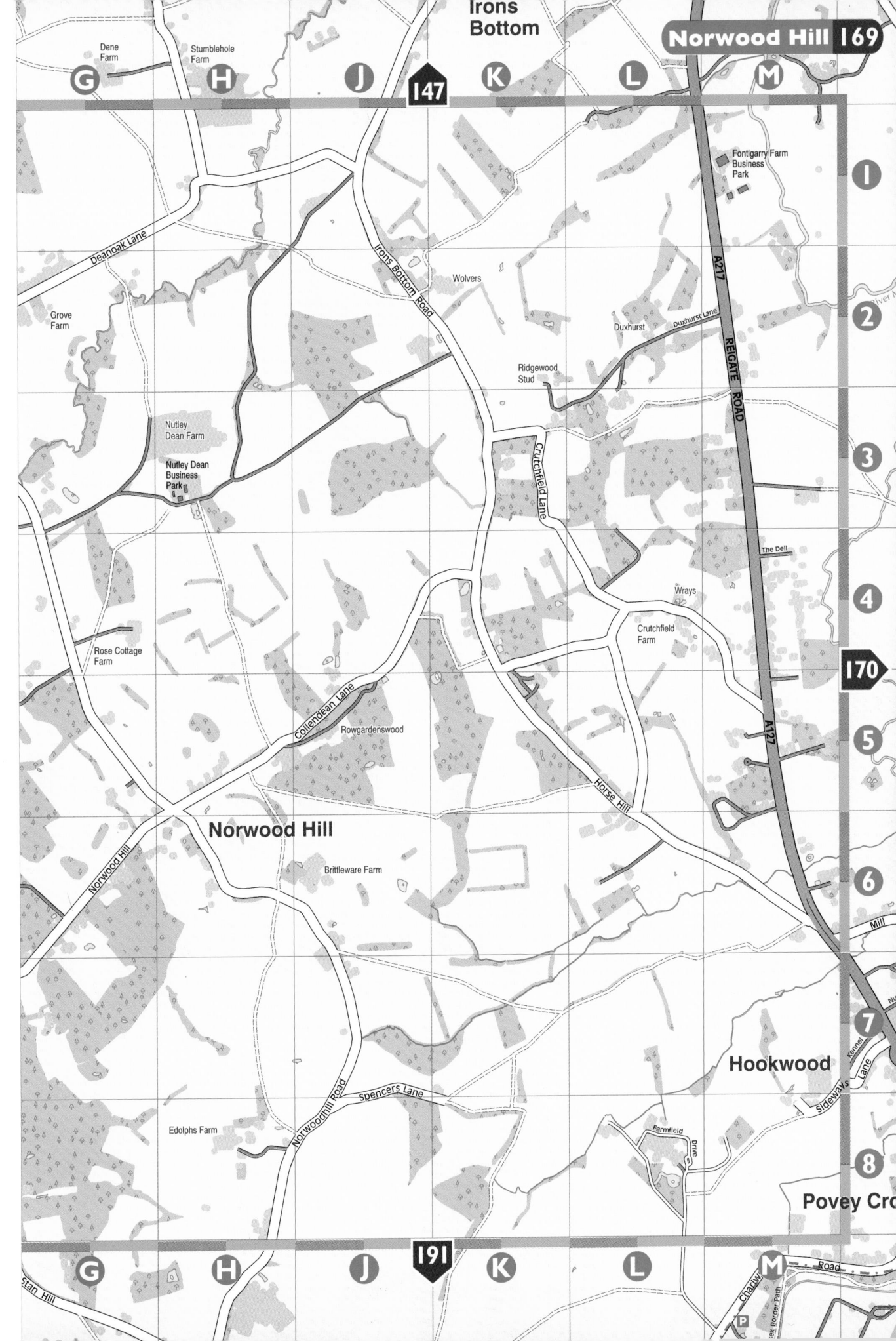

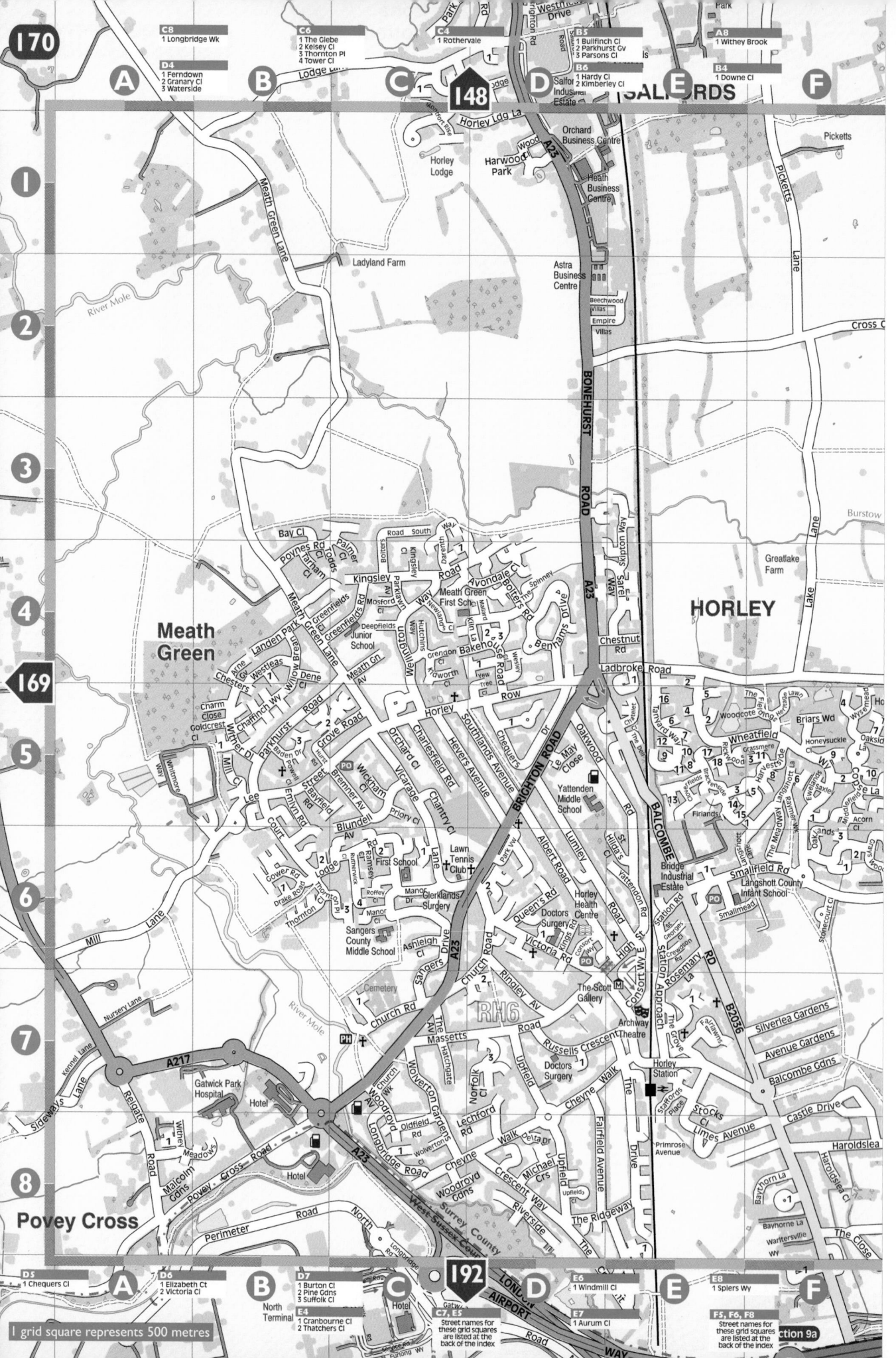

A   B   C   D   E   F

148

I   1   2   3   4   5   6   7   8

169

SALFORDS

HORLEY

Meath Green

Povey Cross

RH6

London Airport

1 grid square represents 500 metres

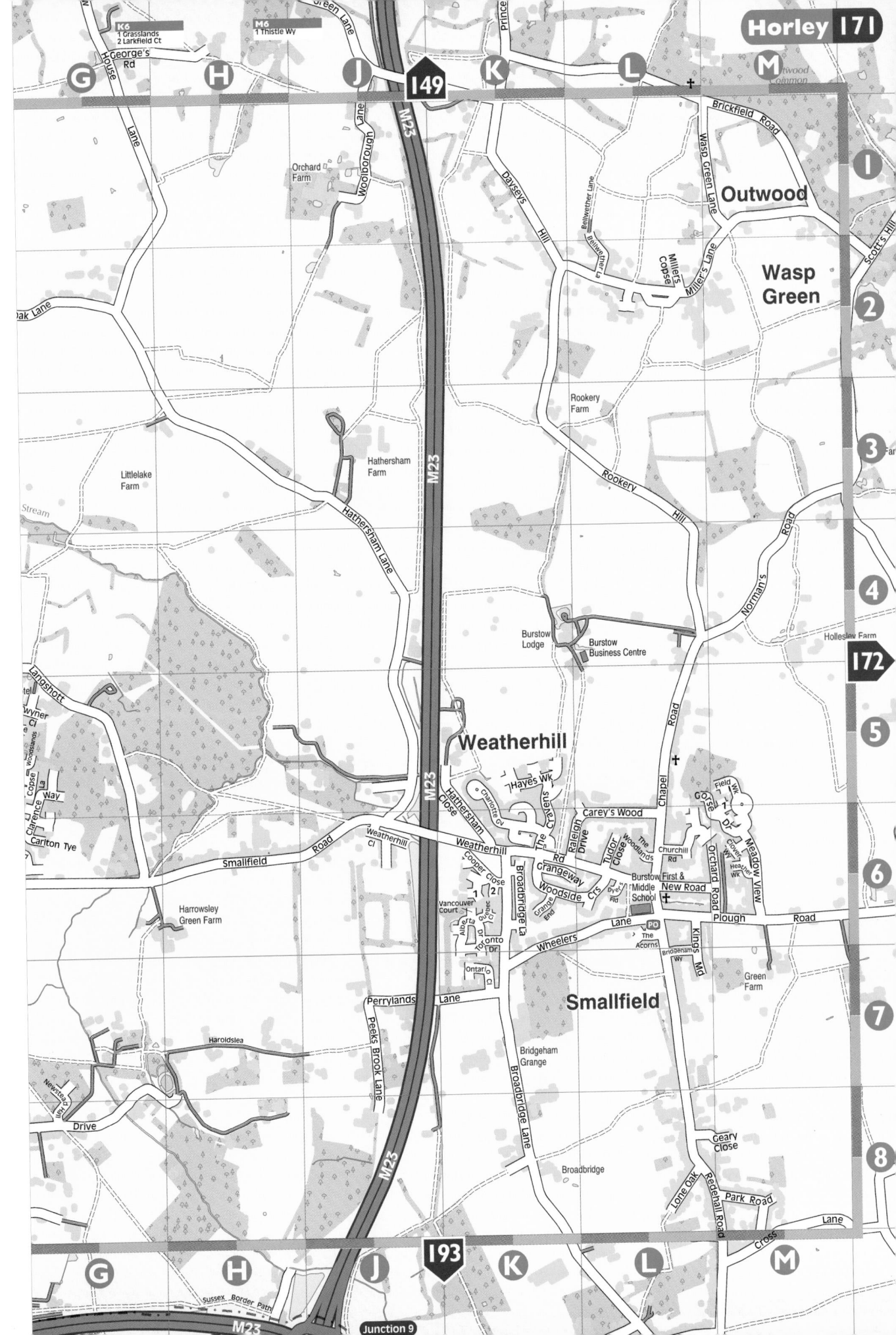

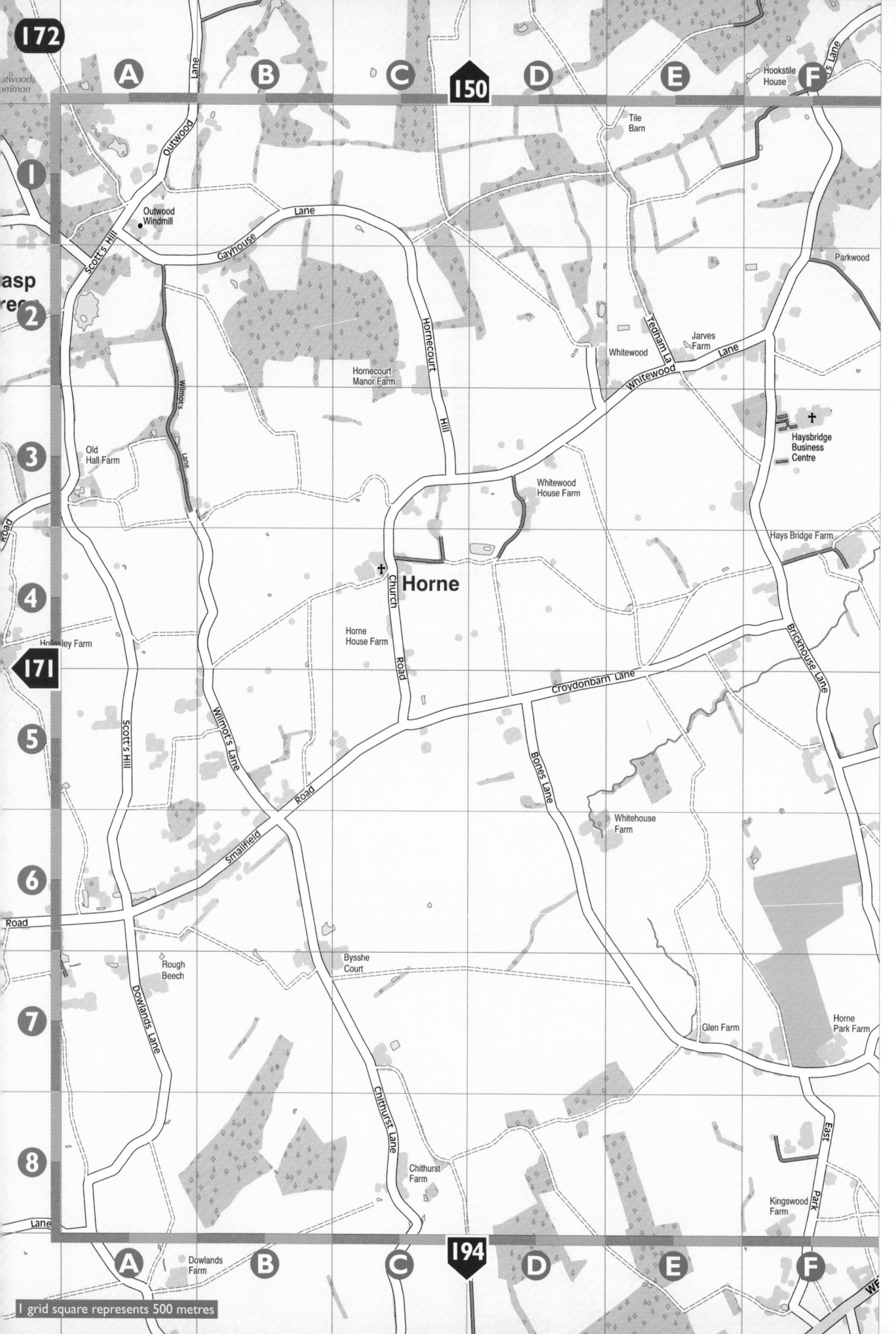

172

A Lane B C 150 D E Hookstile House F 's Lane

1

otwood common

Outwood Lane

Scott's Hill

Tile Barn

asp rea

2

Outwood Windmill

Gayhouse Lane

Hornecourt Hill

Whitewood

Tedham La

Jarves Farm Lane

Whitewood

Parkwood

Hornecourt Manor Farm

3

Old Hall Farm

Wilmot's Lane

Whitewood House Farm

Haysbridge Business Centre

Hays Bridge Farm

Road

4

† Horne

Church Road

Horne House Farm

Hollesley Farm

171

Scott's Hill

Croydonbarn Lane

Brickhouse Lane

5

Wilmot's Lane

Road

Bones Lane

Whitehouse Farm

6

Road

Smallfield

7

Rough Beech

Bysshe Court

Glen Farm

Horne Park Farm

Dowlands Lane

8

Chithurst Lane

Chithurst Farm

East

Park

Kingswood Farm

Lane

A Dowlands Farm B C 194 D E F WF

1 grid square represents 500 metres

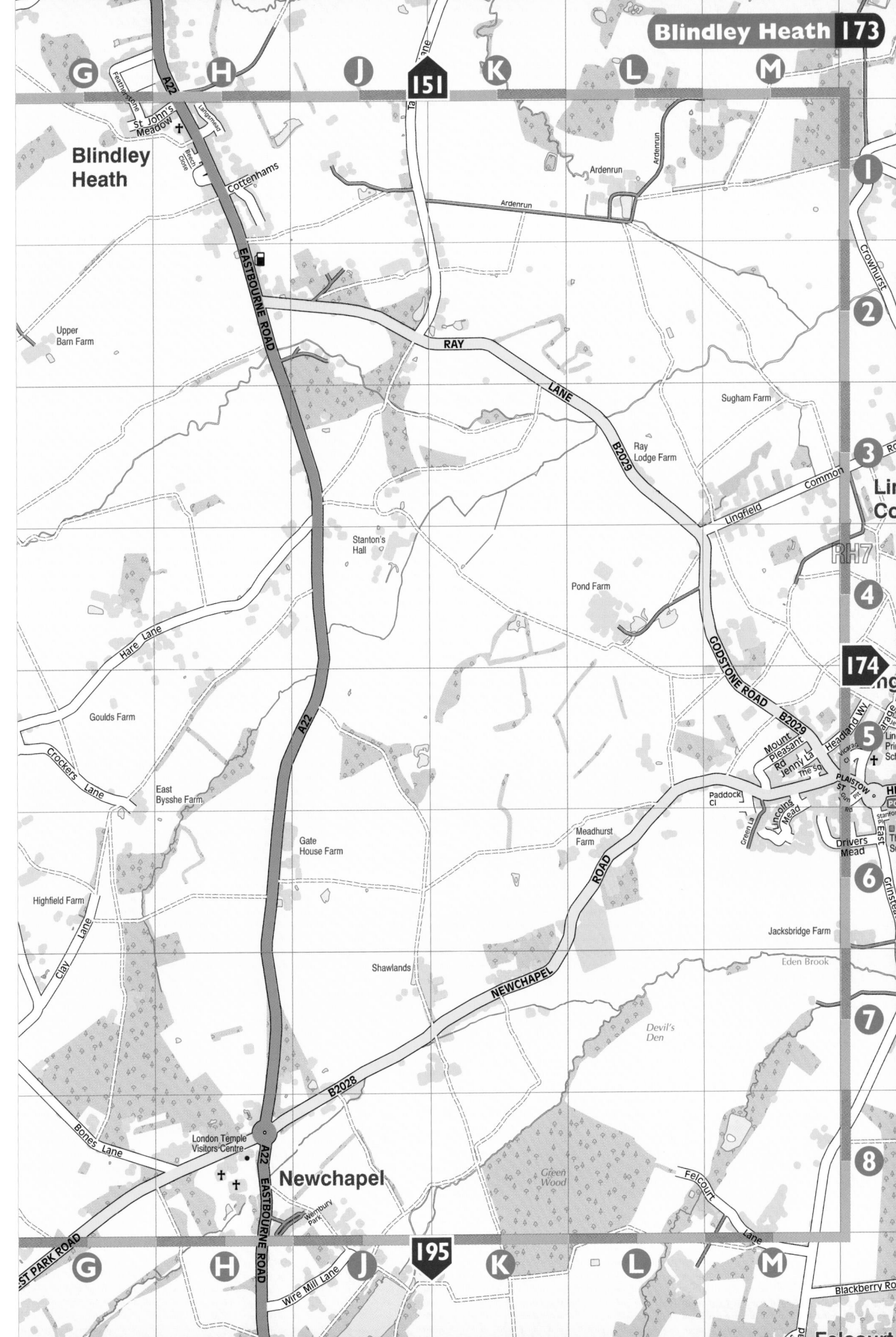

G H J **151** K L M

Blindley Heath

St John's Meadow

Featherbed

Langridge

Cottenhams

Beech Close

EASTBOURNE ROAD

A22

Upper Barn Farm

RAY

LANE

B2029

Ardenrun

Ardenrun

Ardenrun

Sugham Farm

Ray Lodge Farm

Lingfield Common

Lingfield

RH7

Crownhurst

Lin Co

174

Stanton's Hall

Pond Farm

GODSTONE ROAD

B2029

ng

Hare Lane

Goulds Farm

Crockers Lane

East Bysshe Farm

Gate House Farm

Mount Pleasant Rd

Jenny La

The Sq

Vicarag

PLAISTOW ST

Paddock Cl

Lincolns Mead

Green La

Headland Wy

Parade

Lingf Prim Sch

HIG

PO

Drivers Mead

East

Stanfor

Th Su

Grinste

Highfield Farm

Clay Lane

Meadhurst Farm

NEWCHAPEL ROAD

Jacksbridge Farm

Eden Brook

Shawlands

NEWCHAPEL ROAD

Devil's Den

A22

B2028

Bones Lane

London Temple Visitors Centre

Newchapel

Wembury Park

EASTBOURNE ROAD

Green Wood

Felcourt

ST PARK ROAD

G H EASTBOURNE ROAD J **195** K L M

Wire Mill Lane

Blackberry Road

Fe

I

2

3

4

5

6

7

8

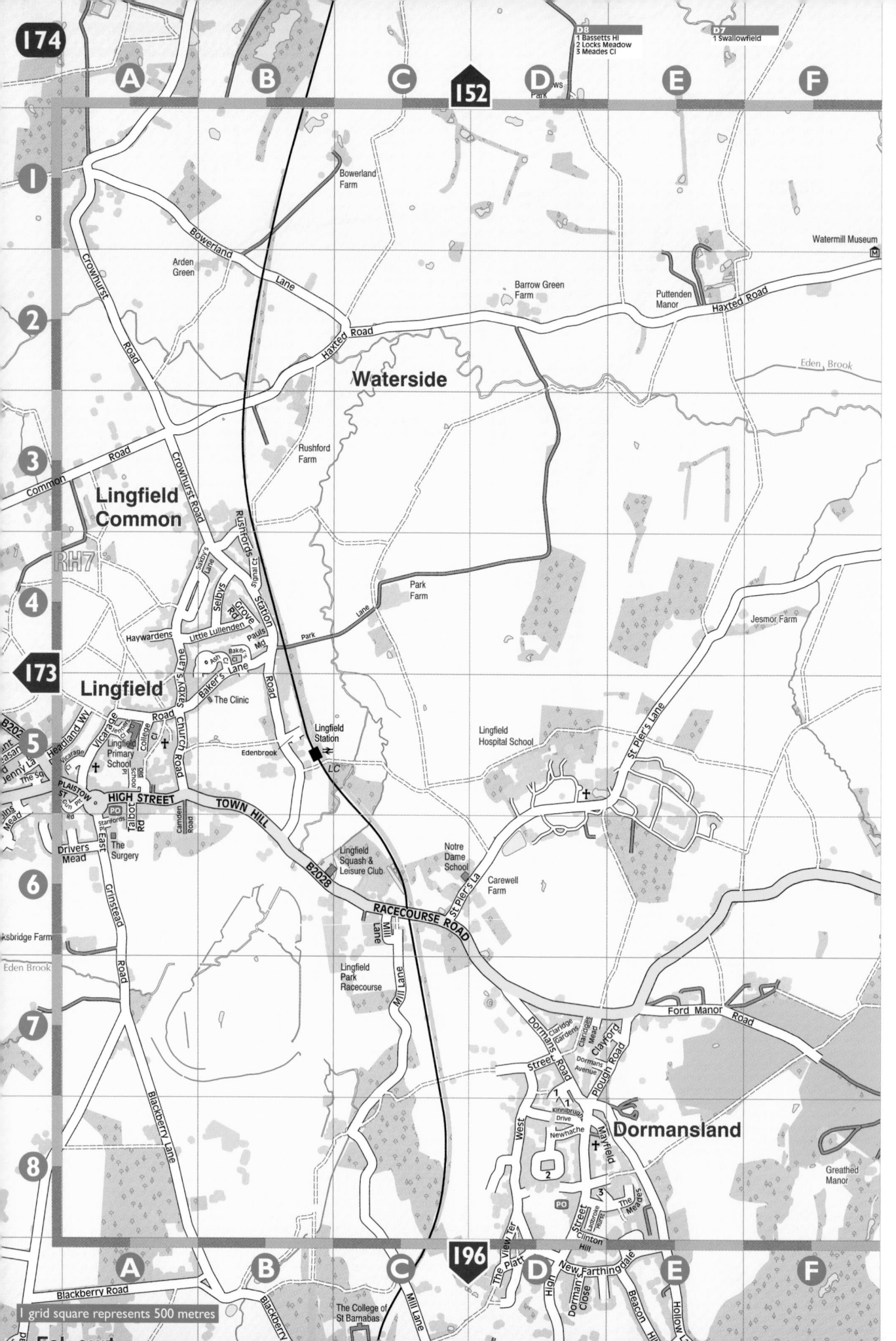

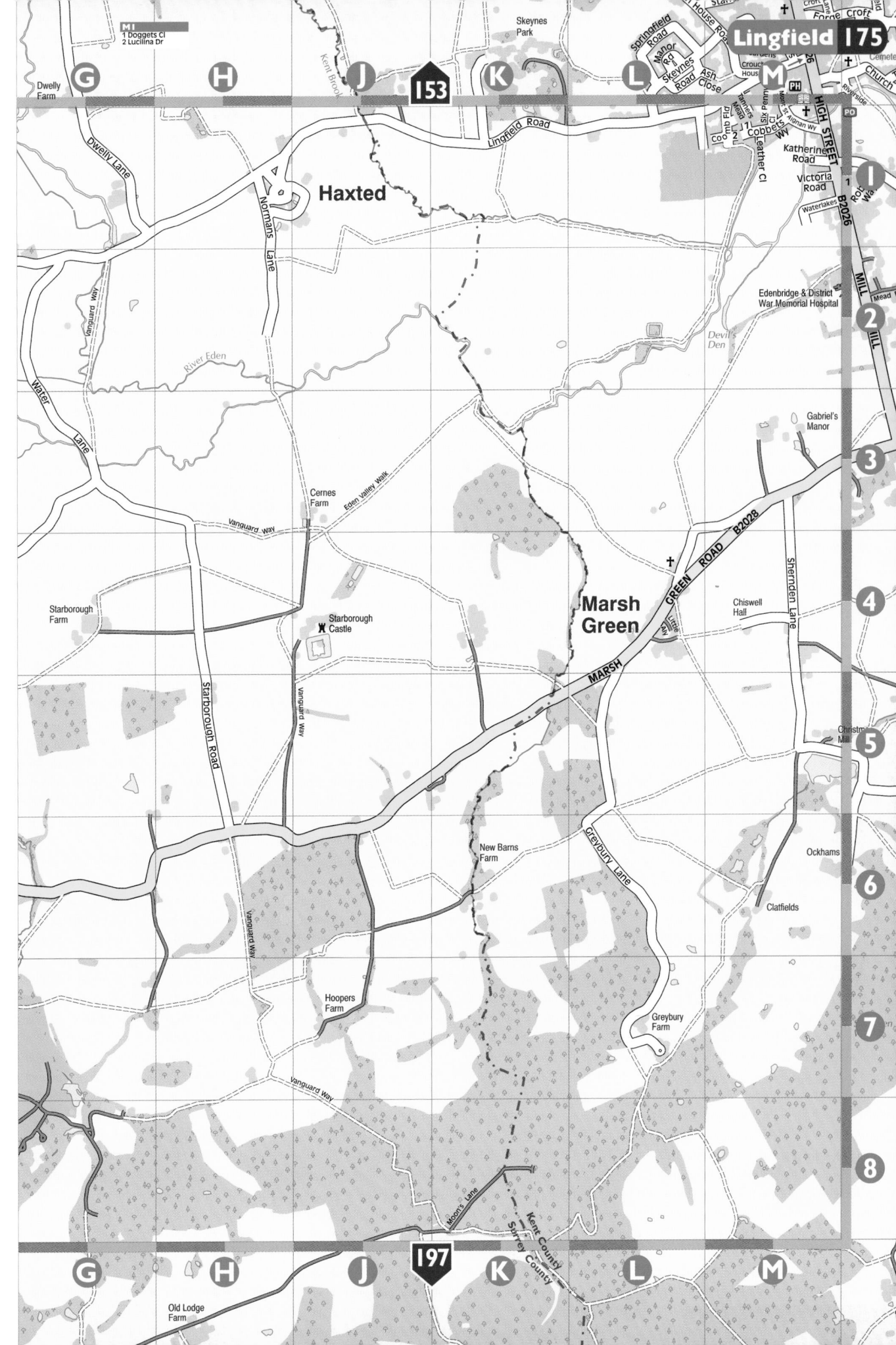

G

H

J **153**

K

L

M

I

1 Doggets Cl
2 Lucillina Dr

Dwelly
Farm

Dwelly Lane

Normans Lane

Haxted

Kent Brook

Lingfield Road

Skeynes
Park

Springfield
Road

Manor
Rd

Skeynes
Road

Ash
Close

Crouch
House

Coomb Flds

Cobbett's

Leather Cl

Katherinee
Road

Victoria
Road

Waterlakes

Mill

Mead Rd

HIGH STREET

B2026

Church

Riverside

PH

PO

2

Edenbridge & District
War Memorial Hospital

Devil's
Den

Gabriel's
Manor

3

Water Lane

River Eden

Cernes
Farm

Eden Valley Walk

Vanguard Way

Starborough
Farm

Starborough
Castle

**Marsh
Green**

MARSH
Little Ham

GREEN ROAD

B2028

Chiswell
Hall

Sherrenden Lane

4

Christm
Mill

5

Starborough Road

Vanguard Way

New Barns
Farm

Greybury Lane

Ockhams

Clatfields

6

Vanguard Way

Hoopers
Farm

Greybury
Farm

7

Vanguard Way

Moon's Lane

Kent County
Surrey County

8

G

H

J **197**

K

L

M

Old Lodge
Farm

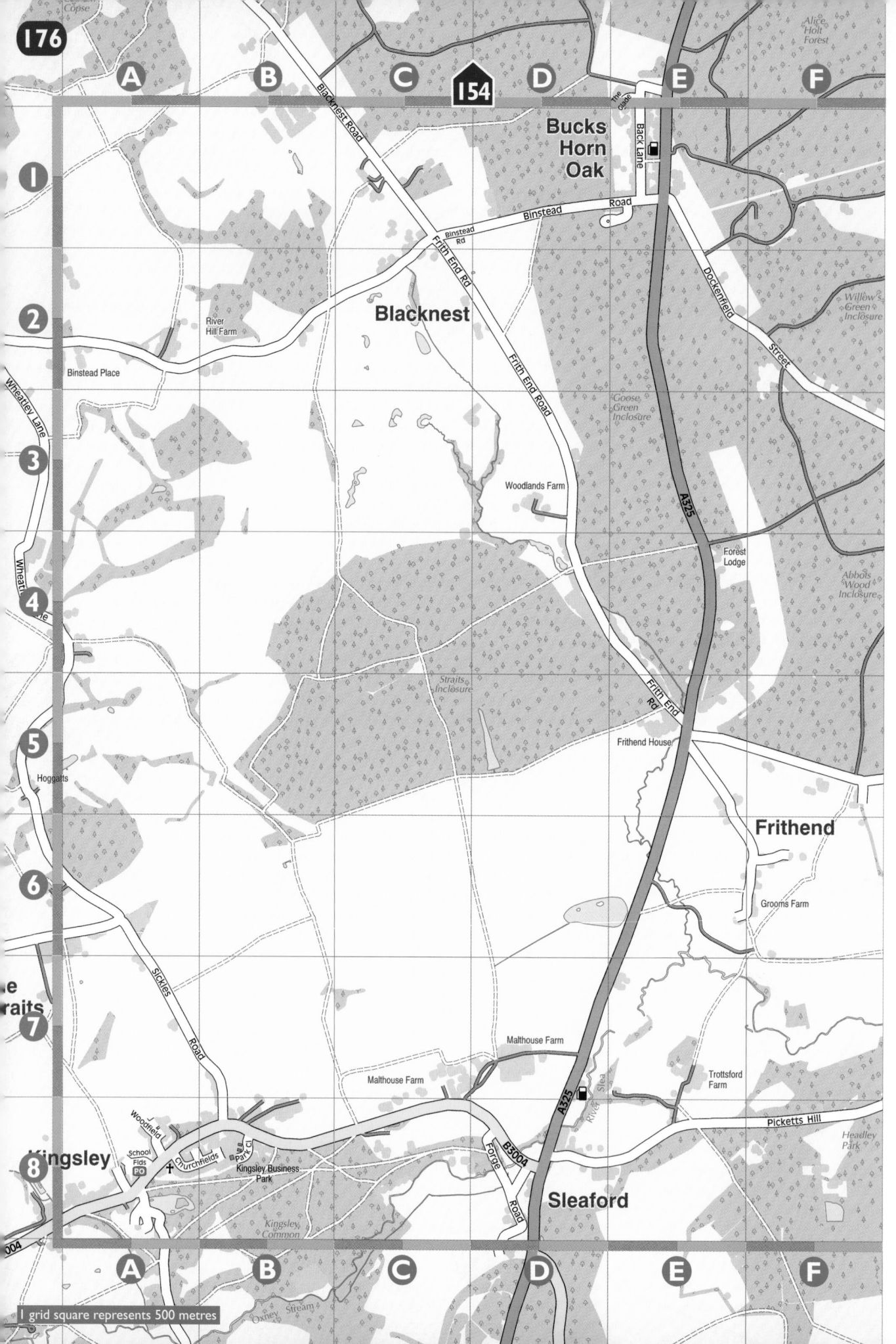

154

Bucks Horn Oak

Blacknest Road

Binstead Road

Binstead Rd

Frith End Rd

Blacknest

River Hill Farm

Binstead Place

Wheatley Lane

Dockenfield Street

Willow's Green Inclosure

Alice Holt Forest

Goose Green Inclosure

Frith End Road

A325

Woodlands Farm

Forest Lodge

Abbots Wood Inclosure

Straits Inclosure

Frith End Rd

Frithend House

Frithend

Hoggatts

Grooms Farm

Sickles Road

Malthouse Farm

Malthouse Farm

Trottsford Farm

A325

River Slea

Picketts Hill

Headley Park

e raits

Woodfield

School Flds PO

Churchfields

Park Cl

Kingsley

Kingsley Business Park

Kingsley Common

B3004

Forge Road

Sleaford

Oxney Stream

004

A B C D E F

M5
1 Pond La

G   H   West   End   J   Lane   K   L   M

Broomfields

Broomfield   Lane

`155`

**West
End**

Spreakley

Woodhill

I

Frensh
C
First Sc

The
Street

Lovers Cr   Peakfield Lane

Pitt Farm   **Frensham**   2

**Batt's
Corner**

Mill   Lane

Boundary Road

Bealeswood Lane   3

Lake Lane   Pitt   Lane   Bacon   Lane

Dockenfield

Dockenfield   4

Street   Green La   The   Street   †   Old   Lane   Frensham
Pond
Sailing Club   `178`

Hampshire County   Surrey County   High Thicket Road   Pond   Lane   5

Manor
Farm   Hotel   Bacon Lane

Old Lane   6

†   Heath Hill   Surrey County   River Wey   Wishanger
Lodge   Frensham Lane

Hampshire County   7

Mellow
Farm   Frensham Lane   Stream Farm   Wishanger Lane   Bacon Lane

Smithy   Lane   Frensham Lane   Simm

Headley Park
Country Club   Smithfield Lane   8

Pickets Hill   Pickets
Hill Farm   Park
View Farm   Smith

G   H   J   K   L   Lane   M   Church Road

Tignals   Spats Lane

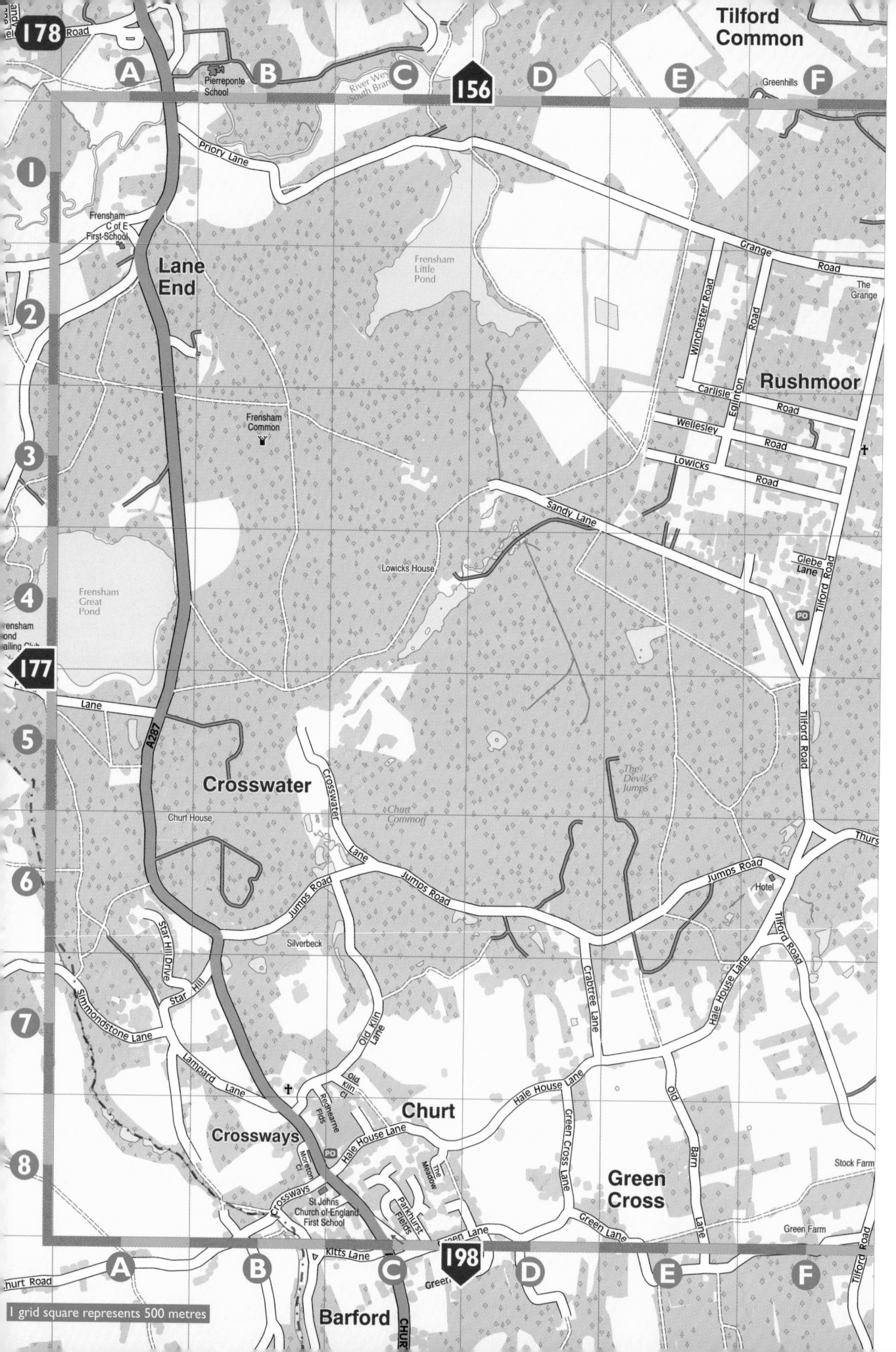

G   H   J   157   K   L   M

Woolfords

Woolford's Farm

Tadmoor Cottage

Elstead Common

I

Pudmore Pond

Abbot's Lodge

Hankley Common

Thursley Road

Woolfords Lane

Greensand Way

The Moat

2

Thursley Common

Truxford

3

Greensand Way

Houndown

Thursley Road

4

180

Dyehouse

Dye House   Road

The Lane

Dyehouse

5

PH

Thursley

Smallbrook

Greensand   way

The Street

Highfield Lane

Greensand Way

6

...ley Road

Churt Place

Thursley Road

Pitch Place

Sailors Lane

Greensand Way

Lower Highfield Farm

PORTSMOUTH

7

Hyde Farm

Hyde Lane

Ridgeway Farm

Highfield Lane

Pitlands Farm

A3(T)

Marchants Farm

Hyde Lane

8

G   H   J   199   K   L   M

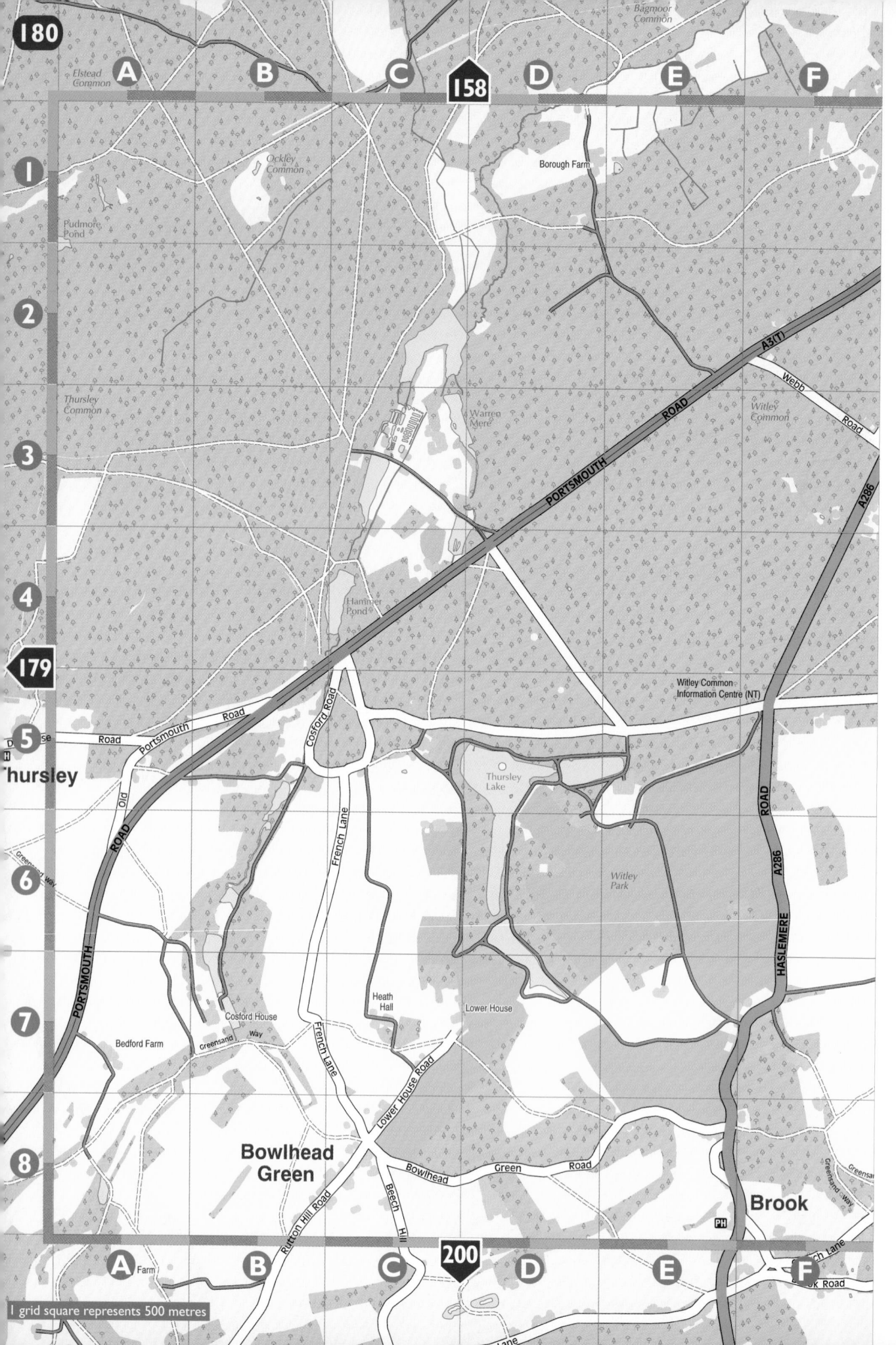

180

A   B   C   **158**   D   E   F

1

2

3

4

179

5

6

7

8

A   B   C   **200**   D   E   F

Elstead Common
Ockley Common
Pudmore Pond
Thursley Common
Borough Farm
Bagmoor Common
Warren Mere
Witley Common
Hammer Pond
A3(T)
Webb Road
PORTSMOUTH ROAD
A286
Witley Common Information Centre (NT)
Portsmouth Road
Old Road
Thursley
Cosford Road
French Lane
Thursley Lake
Witley Park
HASLEMERE ROAD
A286
Greensand Way
PORTSMOUTH ROAD
Heath Hall
Lower House
Cosford House
Bedford Farm
Greensand Way
French Lane
Lower House Road
Bowlhead Green
Bowlhead Green Road
Rutton Hill Road
Beech Hill
Brook
PH
Greensand Way
Farm

1 grid square represents 500 metres

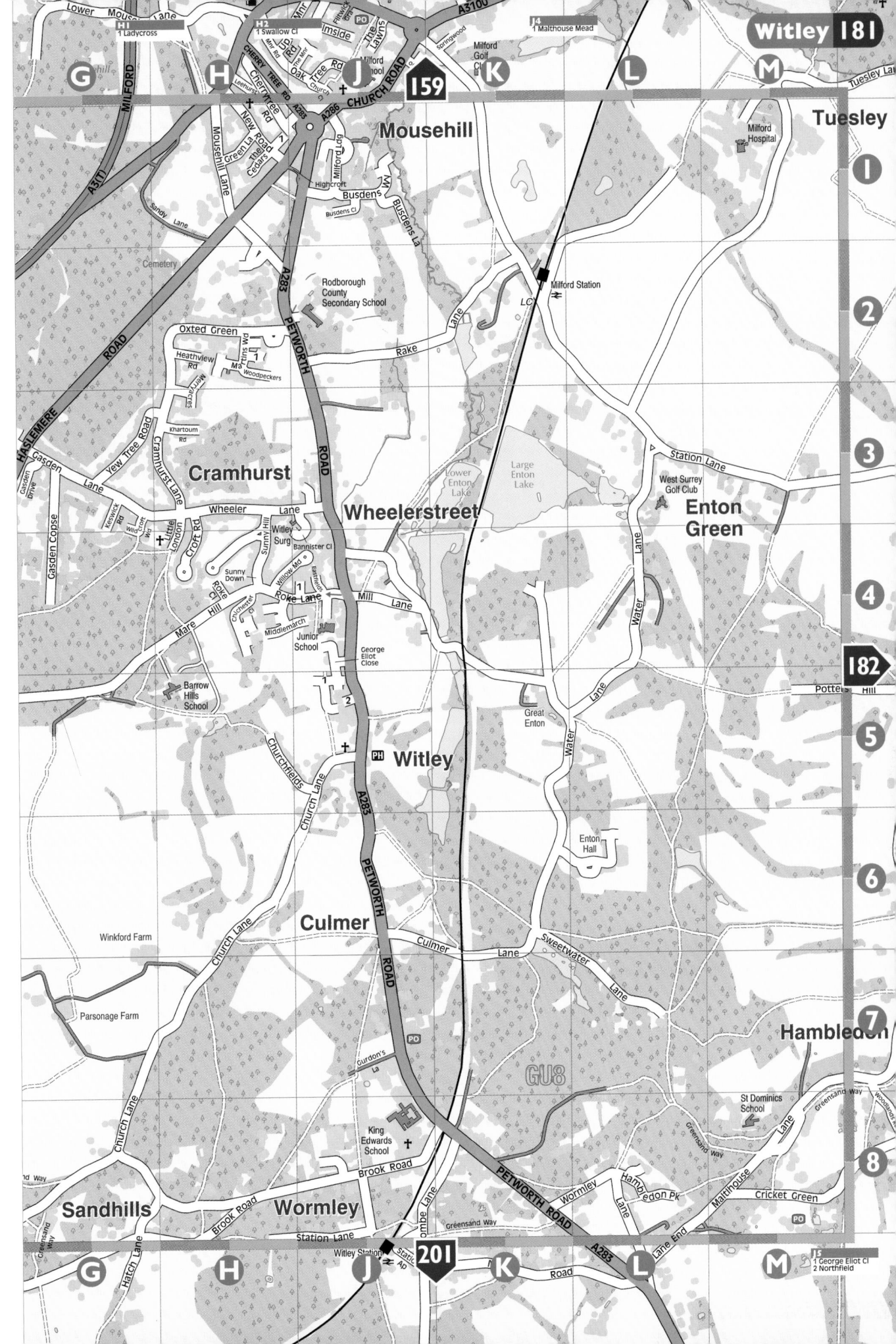

Tuesley

Tuesley La

Busbridge
Hall

Busbridge
Lakes

N Munstead

BRIGHTON ROAD

1

2

Hambledon Road

South Munstead Lane

Winkworth
Arboretum (NT)

South Munstead Farm

3

Hydestile

Clock Barn Lane

Juniper
Valley

New Rd

4

Potters   Hill

Hydon
Heath

Mare   Lane

5

Hambledon Road

Feathercombe   Lane

Great Ho

Marepond
Farm

Markwick Lane

6

Greensand   Way

Little
Burgate Farm

Greensand   Way

Church
Lane

7

Hambledon

Greensand   Way

Greensand   Way

Burgate House

Greensand Way

Woodend Rd

8

Green

Upper   Vann   Lane

PO

Vann Lane

Vann Lane

Vann Lane

Round

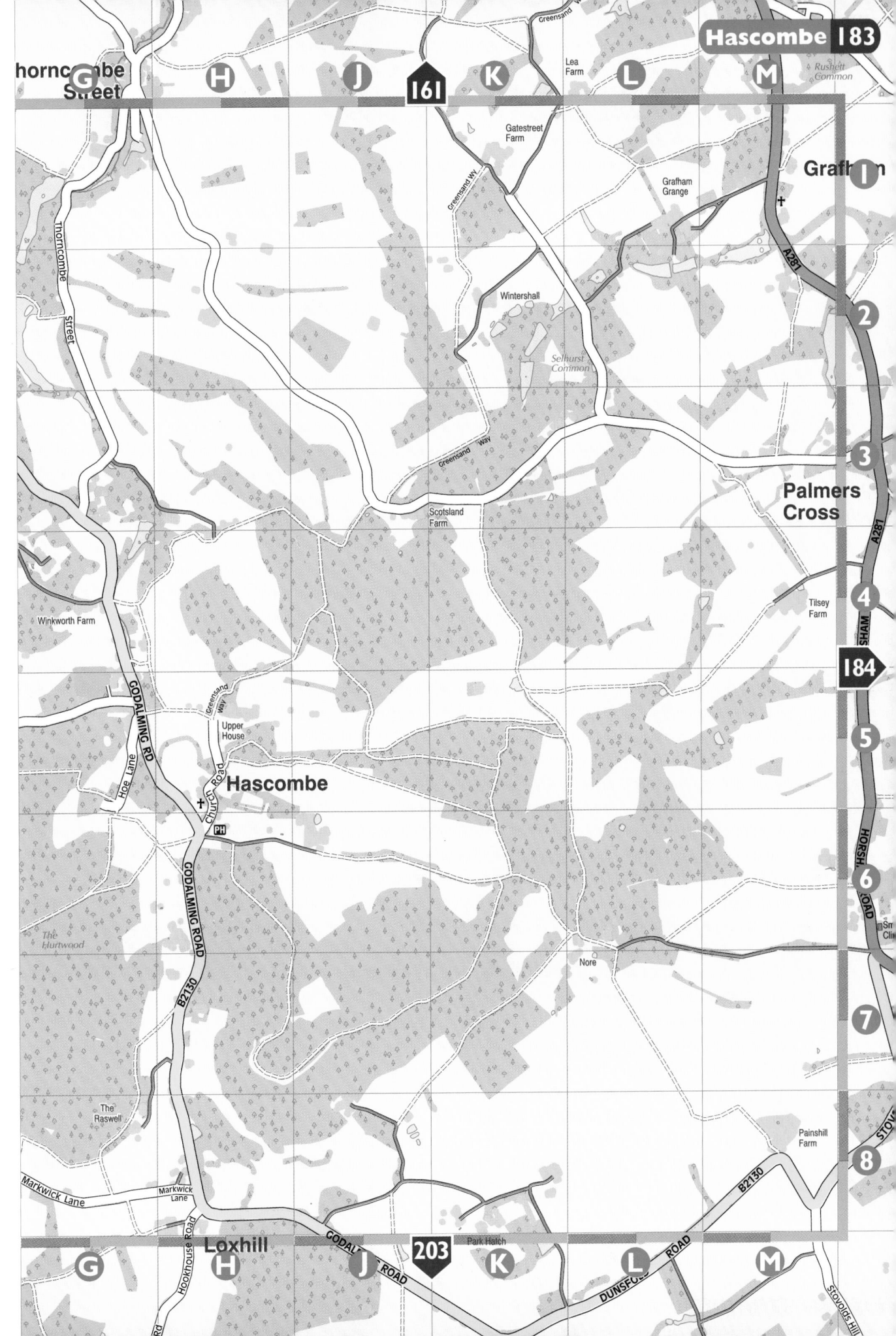

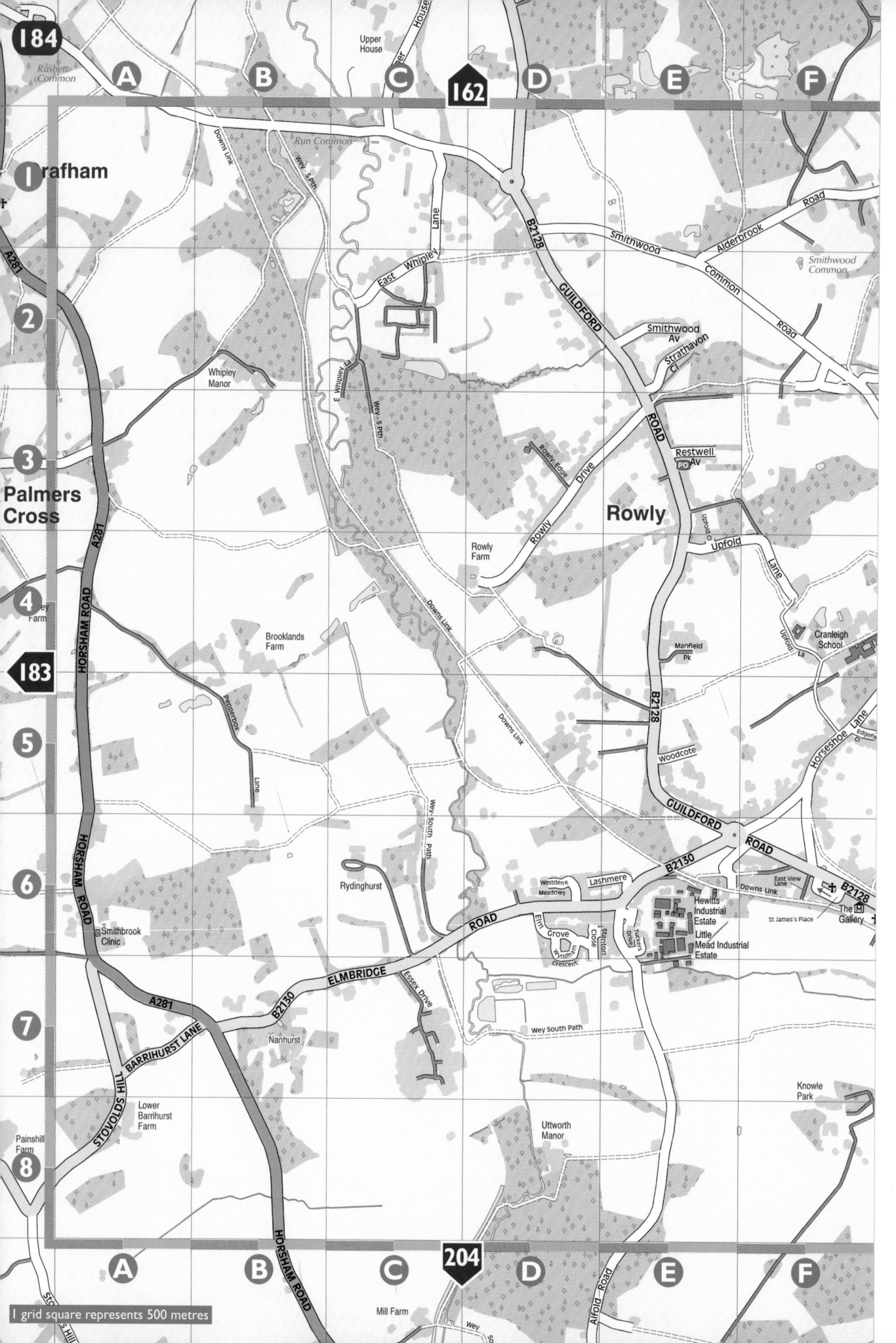

162

183

204

A   B   C   D   E   F

I   rafham

2

3   Palmers Cross

4

5

6

7

8

A   B   C   D   E   F

Rushett Common

Upper House

Run Common

East Whipley Lane

Whipley Manor

E Whipley La

Wey S Pth

Smithwood

Alderbrook Road

Smithwood Common

Smithwood Av

Strathavon Cl

B2128

GUILDFORD

Restwell Av
PO

ROAD

Rowly Edge Drive

Rowly Farm

Rowly Drive

Rowly

Upfold Cl
Upfold Lane

Upfold La

Cranleigh School

Downs Link

Brooklands Farm

Pepperbox Lane

Manfield Pk

B2128

Horseshoe Lane

Edgefie

Downs Link

Wey South Path

Woodcote

GUILDFORD

ROAD

B2130

B2128

Rydinghurst

Westdene Meadows

Lashmere

Elm Grove

Wyndham Crescent

Stanton Close

Tuckers Drive

Hewitts Industrial Estate

Little Mead Industrial Estate

St James's Place

East View Lane

Downs Link

The M Gallery

A281

HORSHAM ROAD

Smithbrook Clinic

ROAD

ELMBRIDGE

B2130

Essex Drive

A281

Nanhurst

BARRIHURST LANE

STOVOLDS HILL

Lower Barrihurst Farm

Painshill Farm

Wey South Path

Uttworth Manor

Knowle Park

HORSHAM ROAD

Mill Farm

Wey So

A281

Wey S Pth

A281

Downs Link

Wey S Pth

Wey S Pth

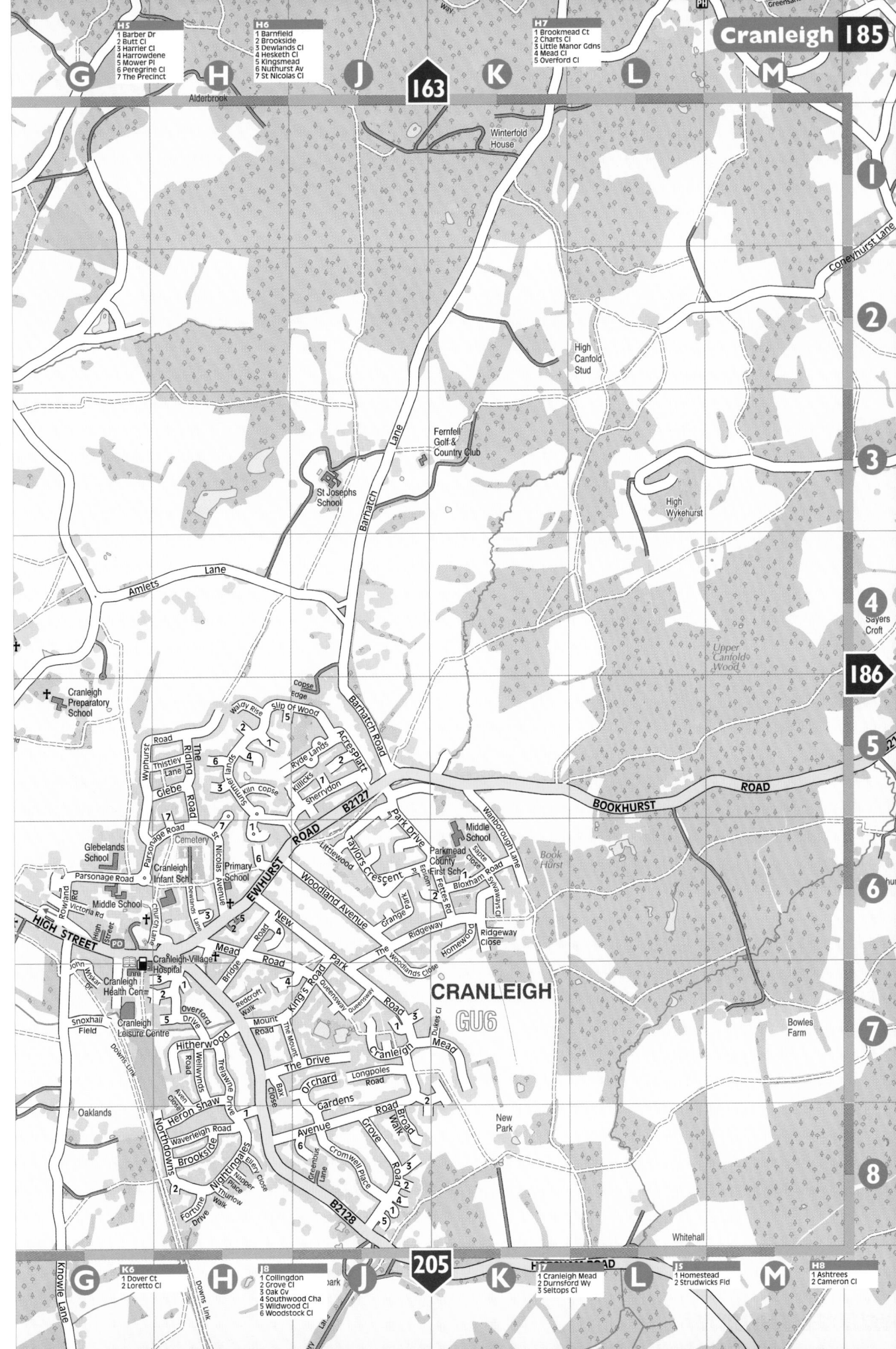

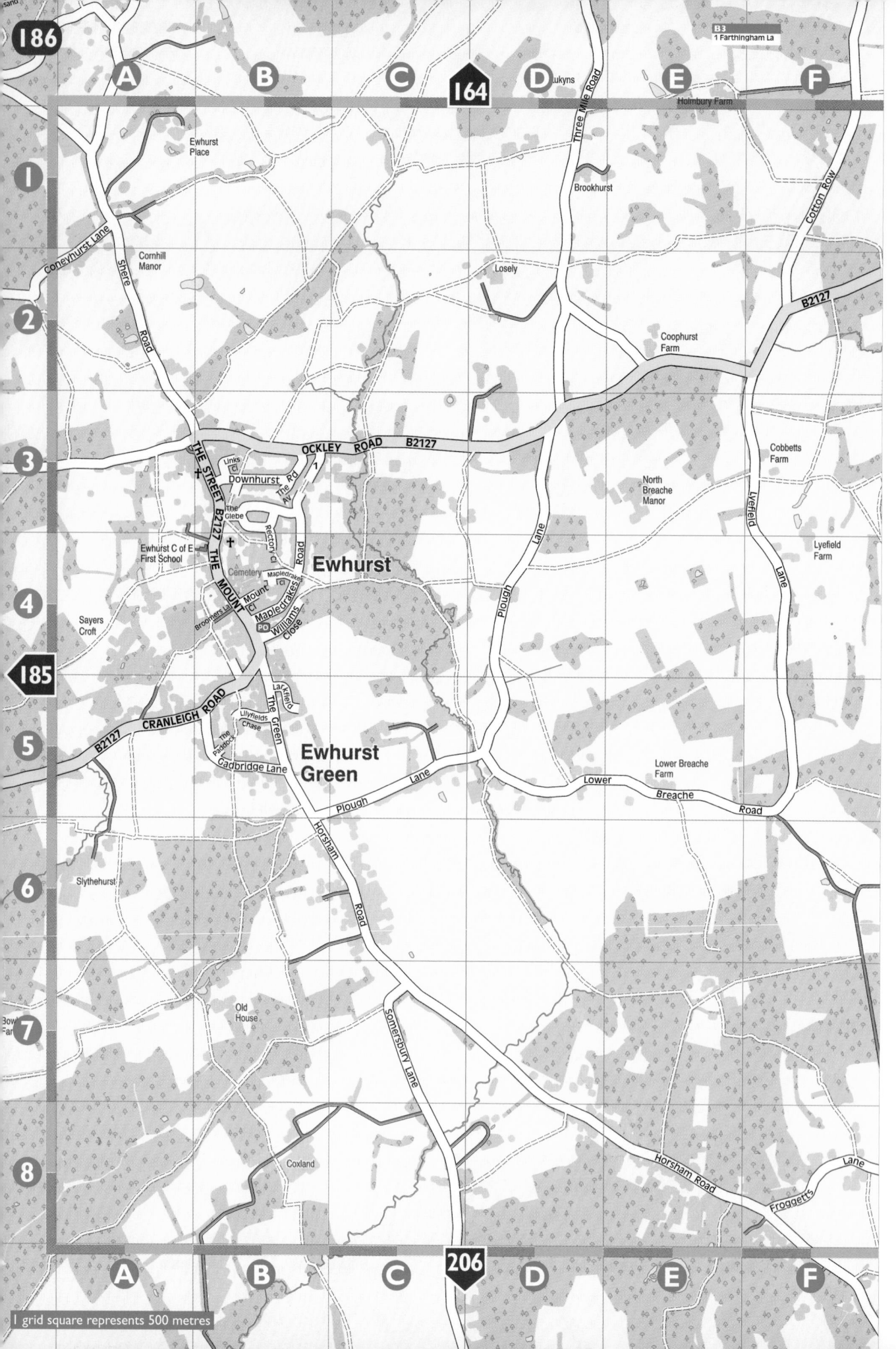

M5
1 Brickyard Copse

HOLMBURY ROAD

B2126

Mill Lane

Wickland Farm

✝

Forest
Green

New Road

Etherley
Farm

Leith
Hill
Wood

Hill
Place

165

ETHERLEY HILL

OCKLEY ROAD   B2126

Mole Street

Hartshurst
Farm

LAKE

Jayes
Park

Ockle

Leith
tice

Horsham Road

Pond Head Lane

Gosterwood
Manor Farm

Pisley Lane

Fishfold
Farm

Pond
Head

Scott Broadwood
School

Club House

188

Cricketer's Close

Elmers
Road

1

PH

Rectory
Close

Mole Street

Parkland
Farmhouse

Pond Head
Lane

Mayes
Green

Parklands

Lowerhouse
Farm

New   Barn   Lane

Cathill   Lane

Standon Lane

Hotel

Leith
Vale

Standon
Homestead

STANE

Horsham Road

Standon Lane

Trap Lane

Walliswood

Walliswood
Farm

PH

Church Lane

✝

Oakwood Mill
Farm

STREET

Waley's
Lan

E
F

Oakfields

207

Hale
House

A29

Raynes

G   H   J   K   L   M

I

2

3

4

5

6

7

8

G   H   J   K   L   M

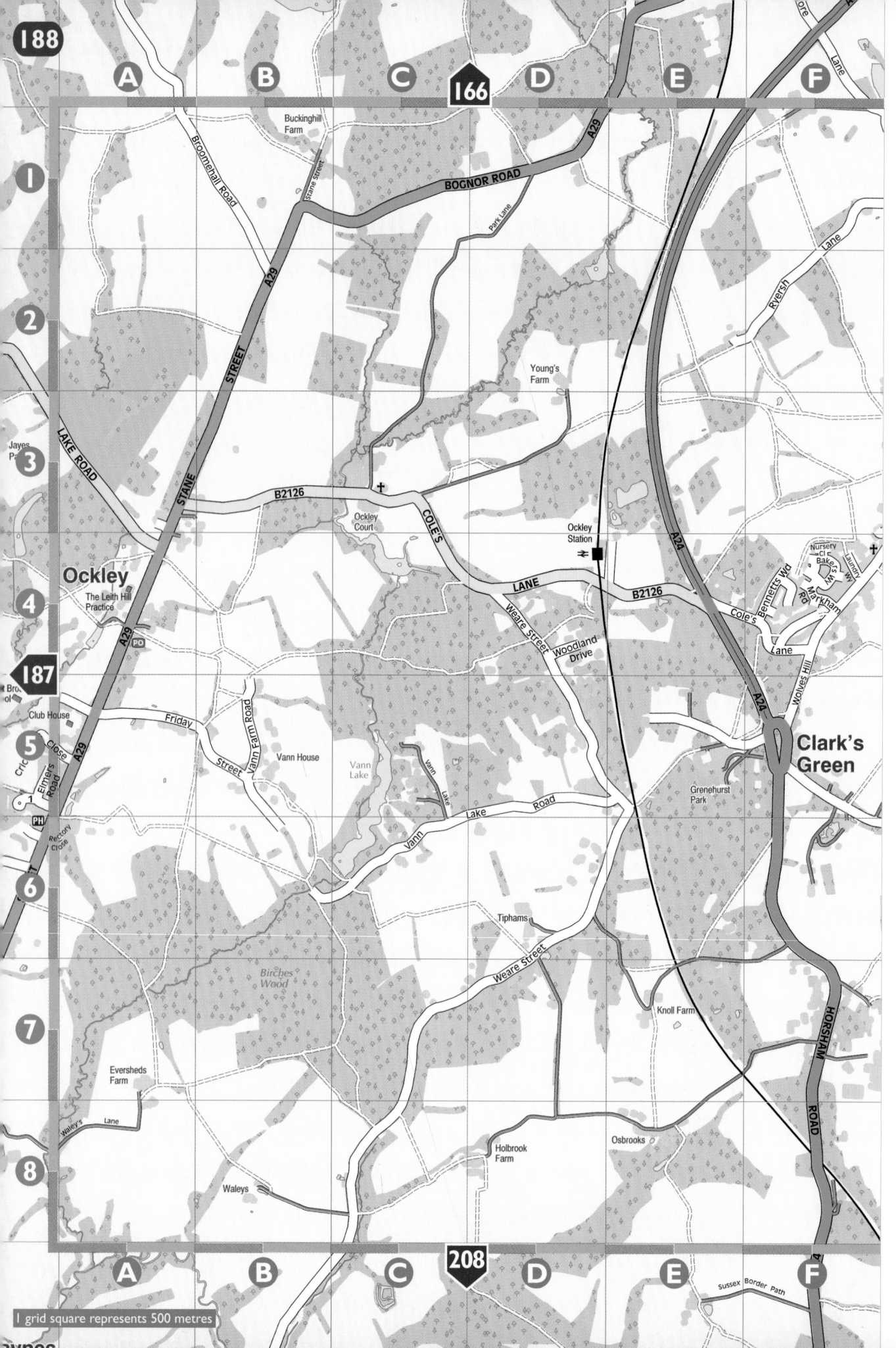

A B C **166** D E F

I

2

3

4

187

5

6

7

8

A B C **208** D E F

Broomehall Road

Buckinghill Farm

Stane Street

BOGNOR ROAD

A29

Park Lane

Young's Farm

LAKE ROAD

Jayes Pa

STANE STREET

A29

B2126

Ockley Court

COLE'S

Ockley Station

A24

Ockley

The Leith Hill Practice

PO

B2126

LANE

Weare Street

Woodland Drive

Cole's

Lane

Nursery Cl
Bake
W

Markham Rd

Ryersh Lane

Wolvers Hill

Bennetts Wa

Bro
ol

Club House

Cric

Elmers Road

Close

A29

Friday Street

Vann Farm Road

Vann House

Vann Lake

Vann Lake

Lake Road

Clark's Green

Grenehurst Park

PH

Rectory Close

Tiphams

HORSHAM ROAD

Birches Wood

Weare Street

Knoll Farm

Eversheds Farm

Waley's Lane

Holbrook Farm

Osbrooks

Waleys

Sussex Border Path

1 grid square represents 500 metres

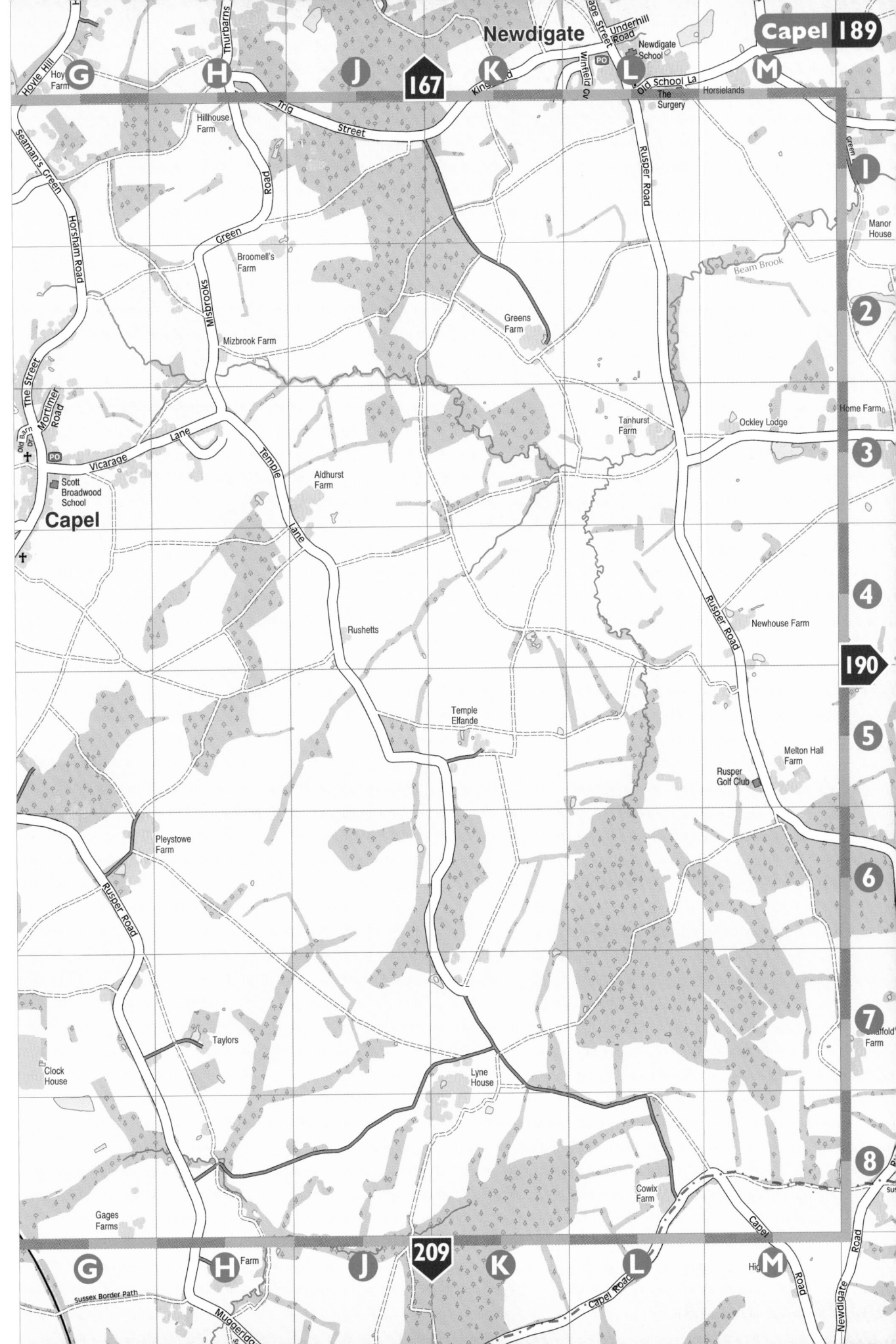

Newdigate

G H J K L M

167

190

209

G H J K L M

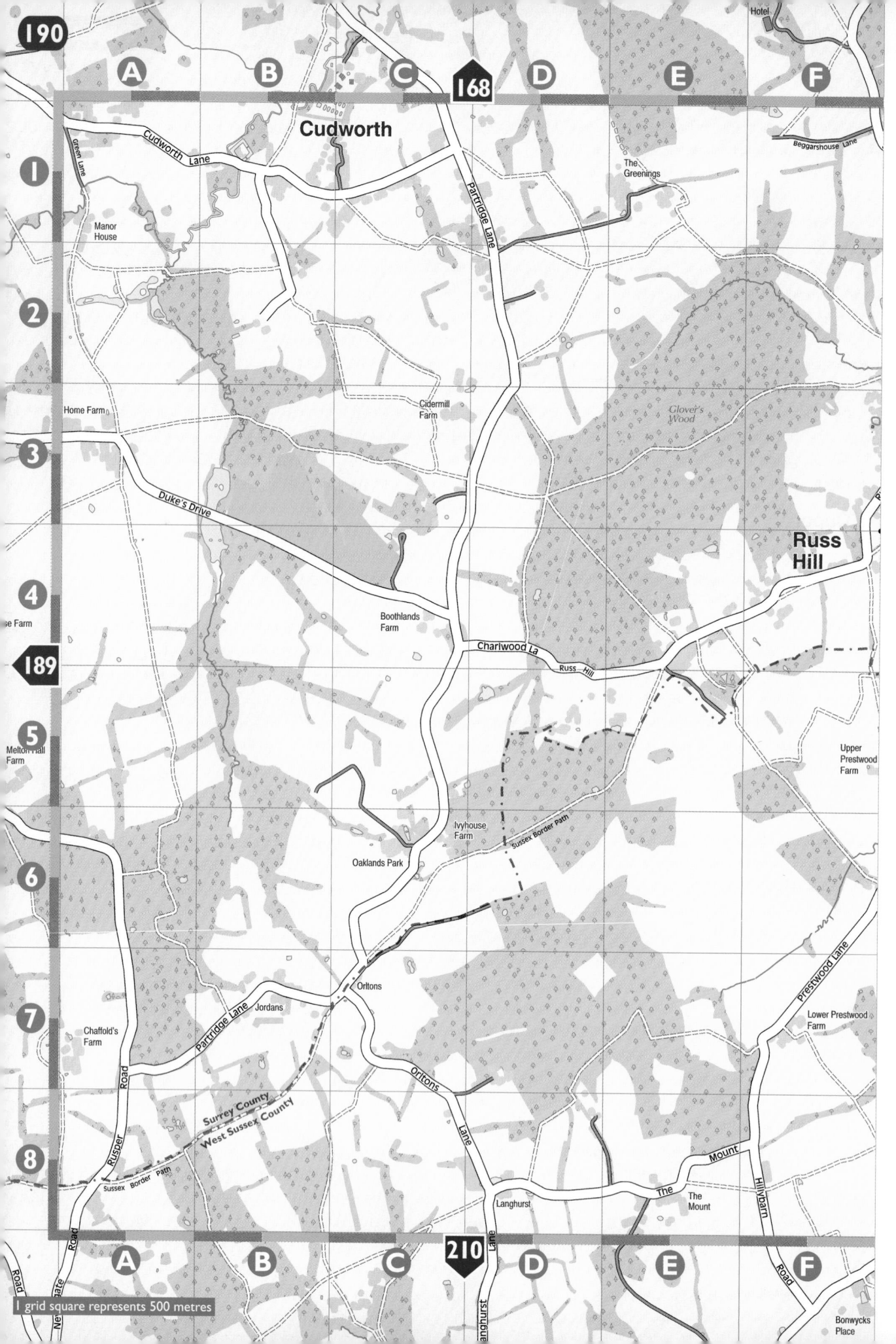

A B C 168 D E F

1

Cudworth

Green Lane
Cudworth Lane

Manor
House

2

Cidermill
Farm

The
Greenings

Beggarshouse Lane

Partridge Lane

Hotel

3

Home Farm

Duke's Drive

Glover's
Wood

Russ
Hill

4

...se Farm

Boothlands
Farm

Charlwood La

Russ Hill

5

Melton Hall
Farm

Upper
Prestwood
Farm

Ivyhouse
Farm

Sussex Border Path

Oaklands Park

6

Partridge Lane

Orltons

Jordans

Lower Prestwood
Farm

7

Chaffold's
Farm

Rusper Road

Orltons
Lane

Prestwood Lane

Hillybarn

Surrey County
West Sussex County

The Mount

8

Sussex Border Path

Newdate Road

Langhurst

The
Mount

Langhurst Lane

A B C 210 D E F

Road

Bonwycks
Place

1 grid square represents 500 metres

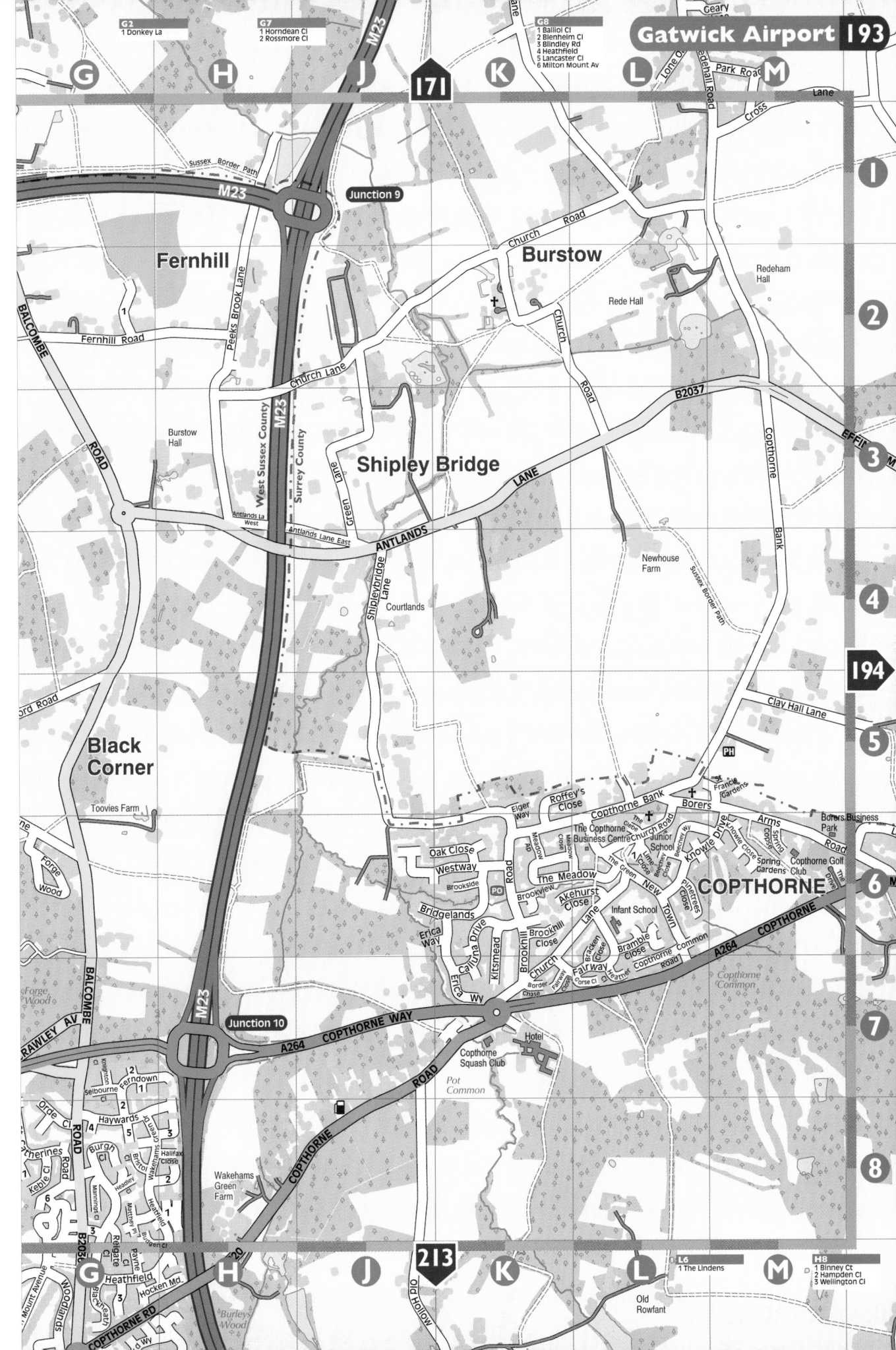

`194`

`213`

G2
1 Donkey La

G7
1 Horndean Cl
2 Rossmore Cl

G8
1 Balliol Cl
2 Blenheim Cl
3 Blindley Rd
4 Heathfield
5 Lancaster Cl
6 Milton Mount Av

L6
1 The Lindens

H8
1 Binney Ct
2 Hampden Cl
3 Wellington Cl

G H J K L M

I 2 3 4 5 6 7 8

Junction 9

Junction 10

Fernhill

Burstow

Redeham Hall

Rede Hall

Church Road
Church Lane
Church Road

M23

Sussex Border Path

Fernhill Road

Peeks Brook Lane

Balcombe Road

Burstow Hall

West Sussex County
Surrey County

Church Lane

Green Lane

Shipley Bridge

Antlands La West
Antlands Lane East
ANTLANDS
LANE

Shipleybridge Lane

Courtlands

B2037

Copthorne Bank

Newhouse Farm

Sussex Border Path

Clay Hall Lane

Black Corner

Toovies Farm

Forge Wood

Eiger Way
Roffey's Close

PH

St France Gardens

Borers Arms

Borers Business Park

Oak Close
Westway
Brookside

The Copthorne Business Centre
Church Road
Junior School

Borers Road

Spring Copse

Spring Gardens

Copthorne Golf Club

COPTHORNE

PO

Bridgelands

Brookview

The Meadow
Akehurst Close

Infant School

New Town

Pinetrees Close

Knowle Drive
Knowle Close

Erica Way

Calluna Drive
Kitsmead
Brookhill Close
Church Lane

Brackenhurst Close
Bramble Close

Copthorne Common

Copthorne Common Road

A264 COPTHORNE

Copthorne Common

M23

Fairway
Border Chase
Corse Cl
Heather

Junction 10
A264 COPTHORNE WAY

Hotel

Copthorne Squash Club

Pot Common

CRAWLEY AV

Balcombe Road

Forge Wood

Wakehams Green Farm

COPTHORNE ROAD

Selbourne
Ferndown
Haywards

Knighton

Catherines
Keble Cl
Burgh Cl
Bristol Cl
Halifax Close

Orde Cl

Mannings

Matthews

Headley

Heathfield

Reigate
Payne

Mount Avenue

B205

Spring

Heathfield
Hocken Md

Burges Cl

COPTHORNE RD

Burleys Wood

Old Hollow

Old Rowfant

EFFIT

M

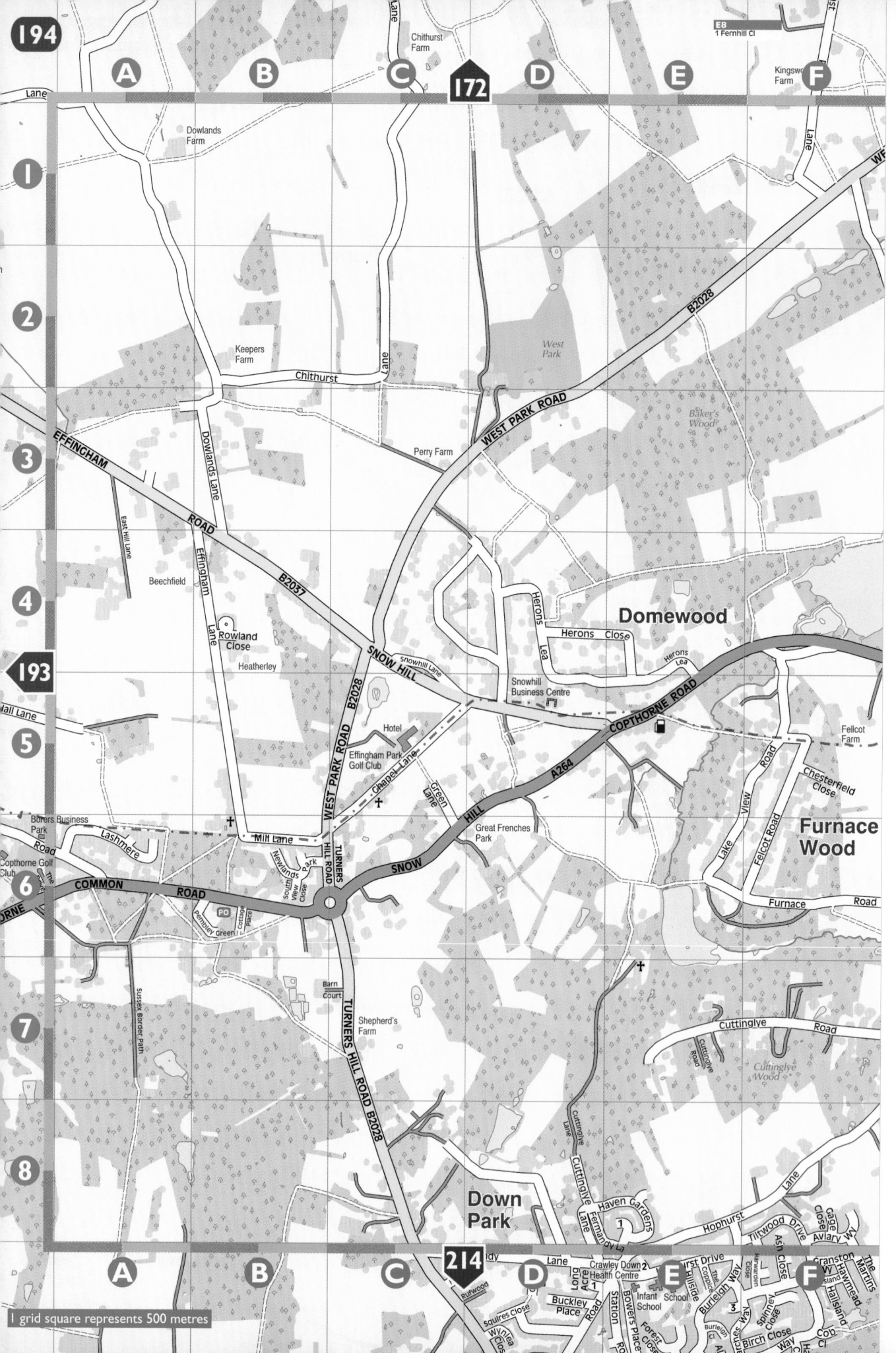

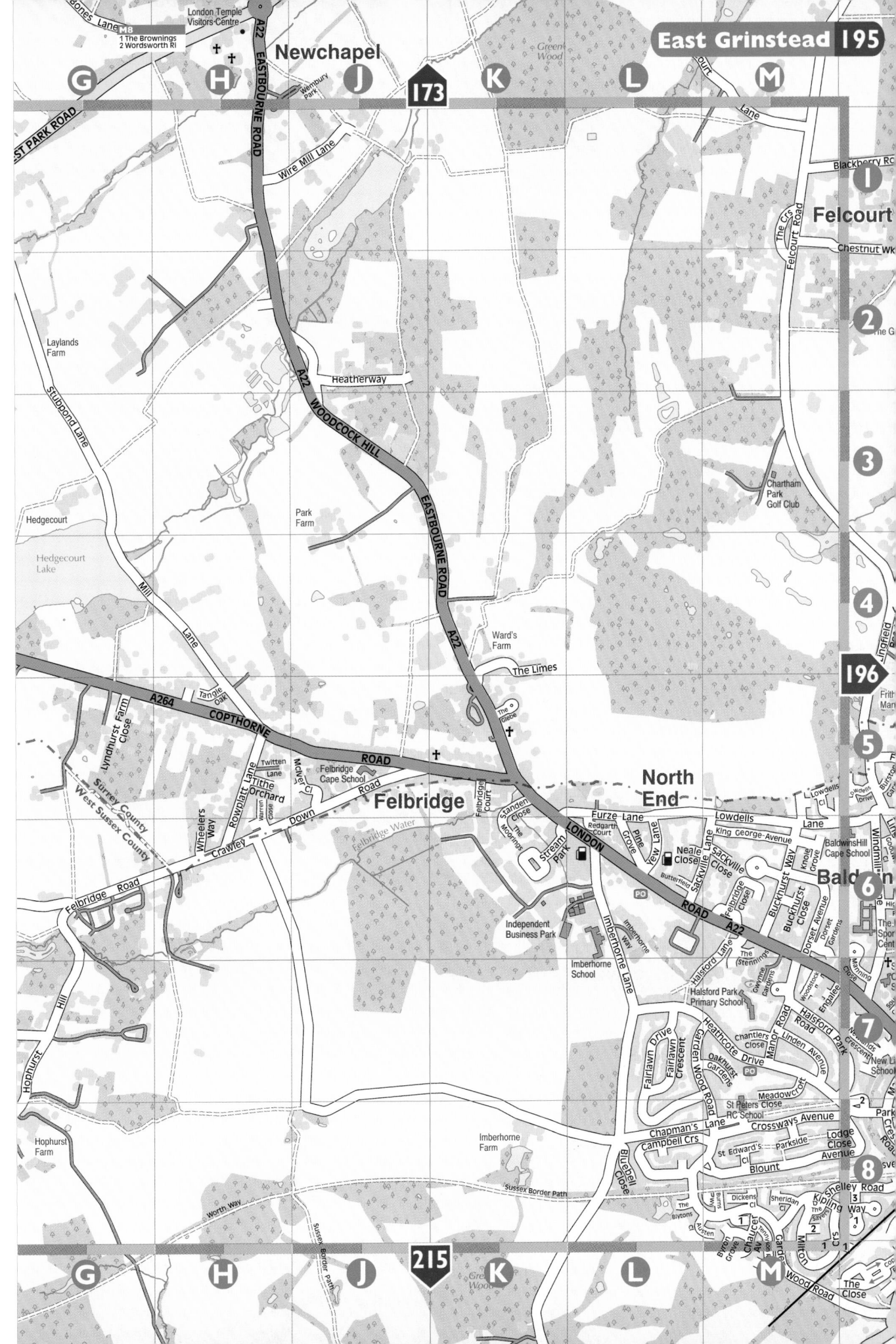

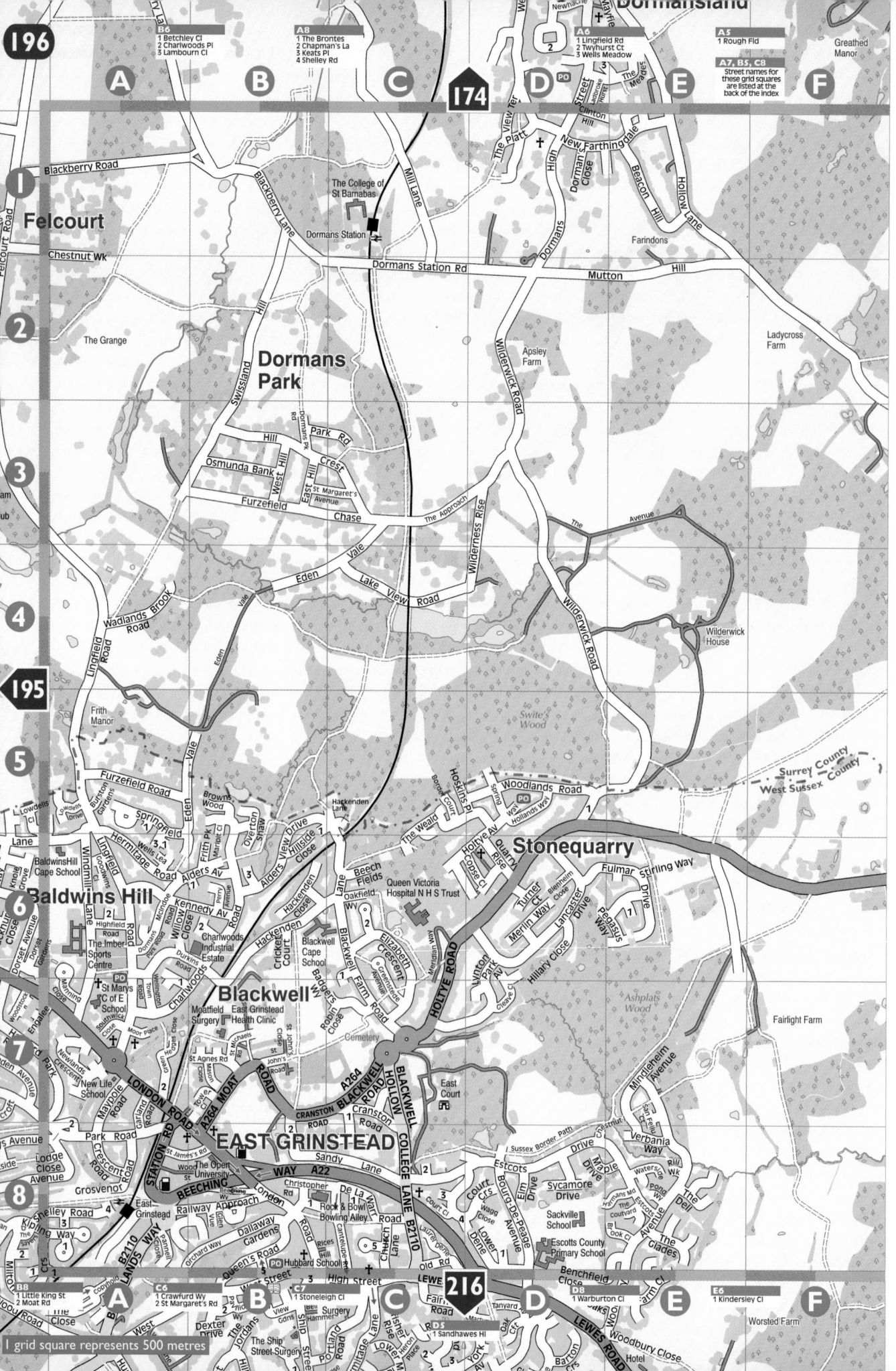

G   H   J   175   K   L   M

1

Old Lodge
Farm

2

Vanguard Way

Beeches
Farm

Sussex Border Path

Moon's Lane

Sussex Border Path

Upper Stonehurst
Farm

Hollow Lane

3

Lower Stonehurst
Farm

Lullenden

Basing
Farm

Scarletts

4

Blockfield
Wood

Sussex Border Path

Shepherdsgrove Lane

Vanguard Way

Gotwick Manor

5

Gotwick Farm

✝

Orchards

East Sussex County
West Sussex County

HOLTYE ROAD   A264

Vanguard Way

Hammerwood

6

Shovelstrode
Lane

Shovelstrode
Manor

Brooklands

Hammerwood
Park

7

Vanguard Way

Homestall
Stud

8

Shovelstrode
Farm

G   H   Hill
Road   J   217   K   L   Owlett's Farm   M

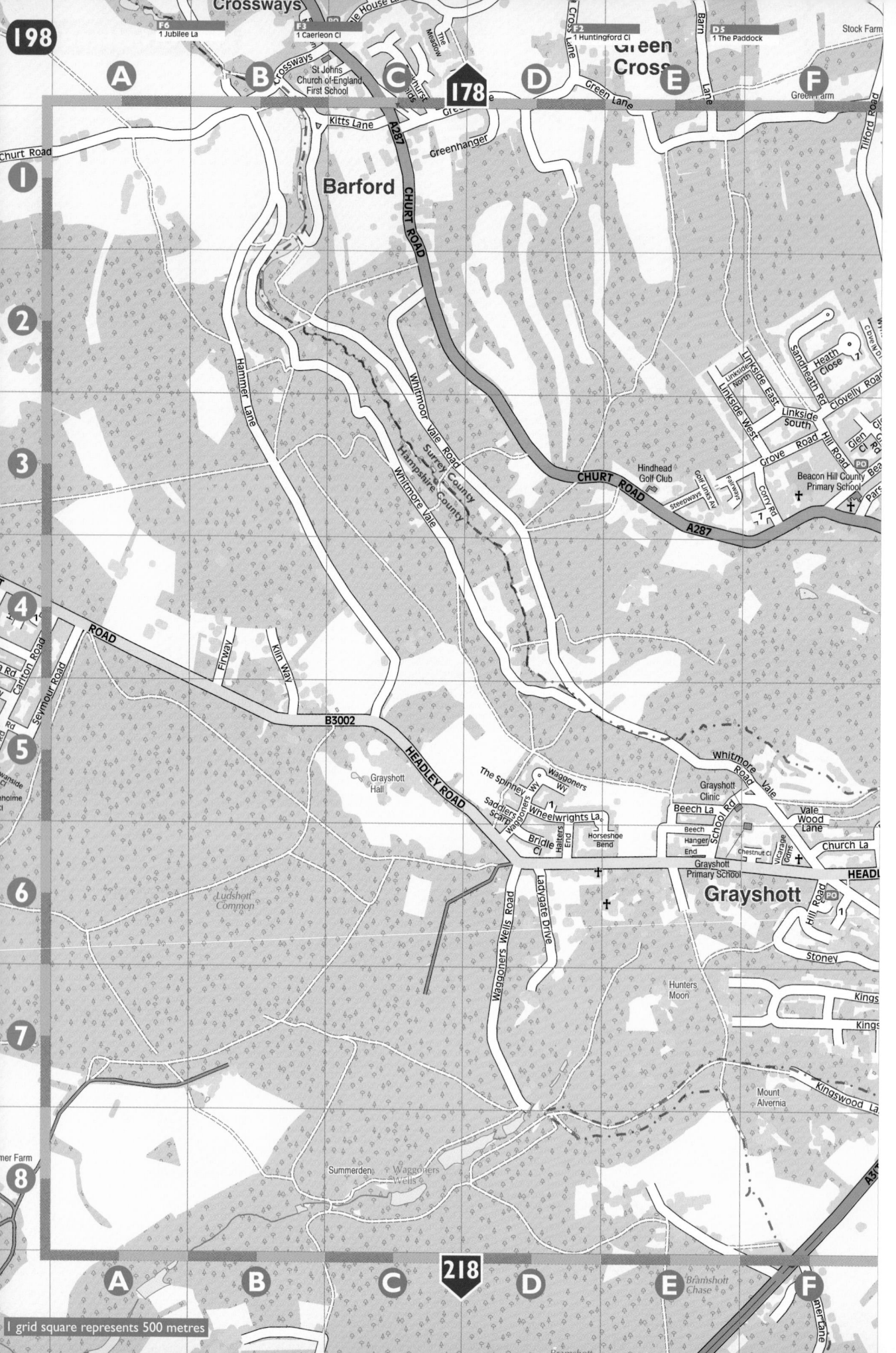

Crossways

F6 1 Jubilee La   F3 1 Caerleon Cl   F2 1 Huntingford Cl   D5 1 The Paddock   Stock Farm

The House La   The Meadow   Green Cross Lane   Barn Lane   Green

A   B   C   178   D   Green Cross   E   F   Green Farm

Kitts Lane   Greenhanger   Tilford Road

St Johns Church of England First School

Churt Road

Barford

1

CHURT ROAD
A287

Hammer Lane

Whitmoor Vale Road   Heath Close

Linkside North   Sandheath Rd   Clovelly Road

2

Surrey County   Linkside East   Linkside West   Linkside South

Hampshire County   Grove Road   Hill Road   Glen   Beacon

Whitmore Vale   CHURT ROAD   Hindhead Golf Club   PO   Beacon Hill County Primary School

3   Golf Links Av   Corry Rd   Pars

Steepways   A287

Firway   Kiln Way

ROAD

4

Carlton Road
Seymour Road

Rd   Rd

5   B3002

The Spinney   Waggoners Wy   Whitmore Road

Grayshott Hall   Waggoners Wy   Grayshott Clinic   Vale Wood Lane

HEADLEY ROAD   Saddlers Scarp   Wheelwrights La.   Beech La   Chestnut Cl   Church La

Waggoners   Beech Hanger End   Vicarage Gdns   HEAD

Bridle Cl   Halters End   Horseshoe Bend   Grayshott Primary School

6   Ludshott Common   Grayshott   PO   1

Waggoners Wells Road   Ladygate Drive   Stoney   Kings

Hunters Moon   Kings

7

Kingswood La

Summerden   Waggoners Wells   Mount Alvernia

mer Farm

8

A   B   C   218   D   E   Bramshott Chase   F   mer Lane

1 grid square represents 500 metres   Bramshott

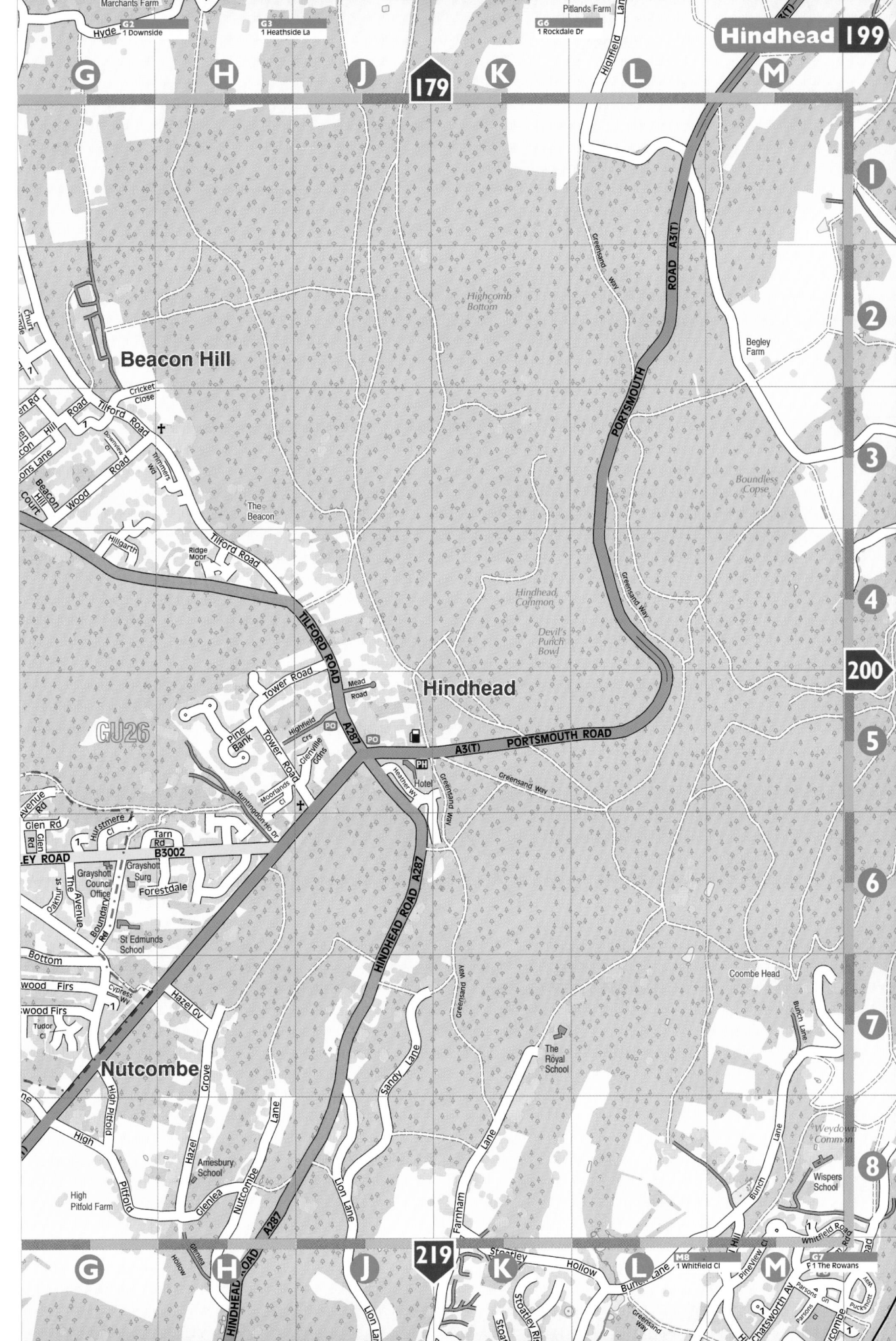

Marchants Farm

Pitlands Farm

G2 Hyde 1 Downside

G3 1 Heathside La

G6 1 Rockdale Dr

G **H** **J** 179 **K** **L** **M**

I

2

Highcomb Bottom

Begley Farm

Beacon Hill

Cricket Close

Green Rd

Tilford Road

Hill

Beacon Lane

Downview Wa

Thirmers

3

Wood Road

Boundless Copse

Beacon Hill Court

Hillgarth

The Beacon

Ridge Moor Cl

Tilford Road

Greensand Way

PORTSMOUTH ROAD A3(T)

Hindhead Common

4

Devil's Punch Bowl

200

Tilford Road

Tower Road

Mead Road

Hindhead

GU26

Pine Bank

Highfield Crs

Glenville Gdns

PO

A287

PO

Greensand Way

A3(T) **PORTSMOUTH ROAD**

5

Tower Road

Moorlands Cl

Huntingdon Ho Dr

PH

Hotel

Heather Wy

Greensand Way

Greensand Way

Avenue Rd

Glen Rd

Glen Rd

Hurstmere Cl

Tarn Rd

Grayshott Council Office

Forestdale

B3002

6

EY ROAD

The Avenue

Boundary Rd

St Edmunds School

HINDHEAD ROAD A287

Coombe Head

Bottom

wood Firs

wood Firs

Cypress Wy

Hazel Gv

Bunch Lane

7

Tudor Cl

Nutcombe

High Pitfold

Hazel Grove

Nutcombe Lane

Sandy Lane

The Royal School

Weydown Common

Wispers School

8

High

Amesbury School

Glenlea

A287

Lion Lane

Farnham Lane

Bunch Lane

Pineview Ct

Whitfield Road

Chatsworth Av

High Pitfold Farm

Glenlea Hollow

HINDHEAD ROAD

Lion Lane

Stoatley Hollow

Bunch Lane

M8 1 Whitfield Cl

G7 1 The Rowans

Wycombe

Parsons

G **H** **J** 219 **K** **L** **M**

Stoat

Stoatley Ri

Greensand Way

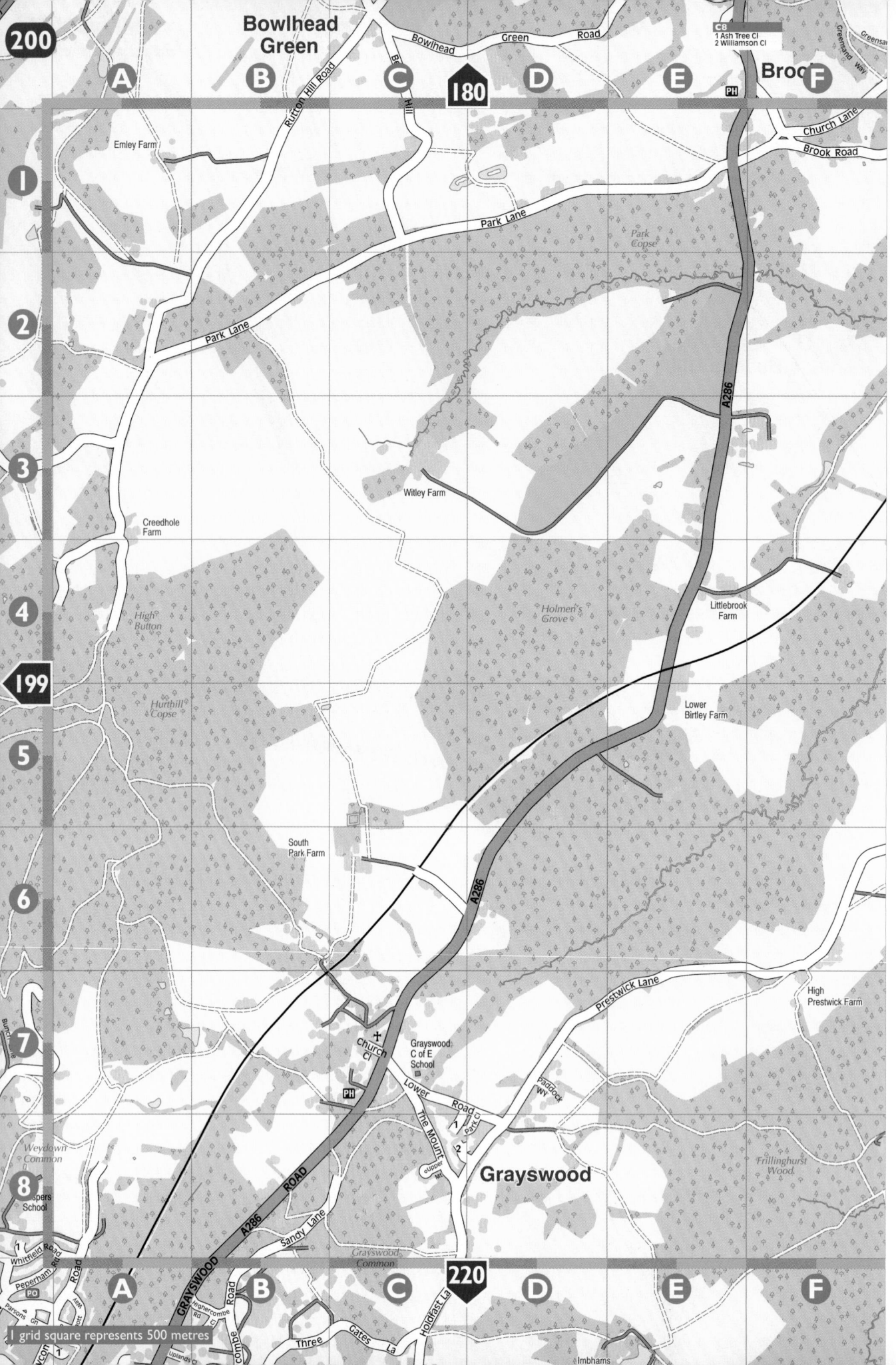

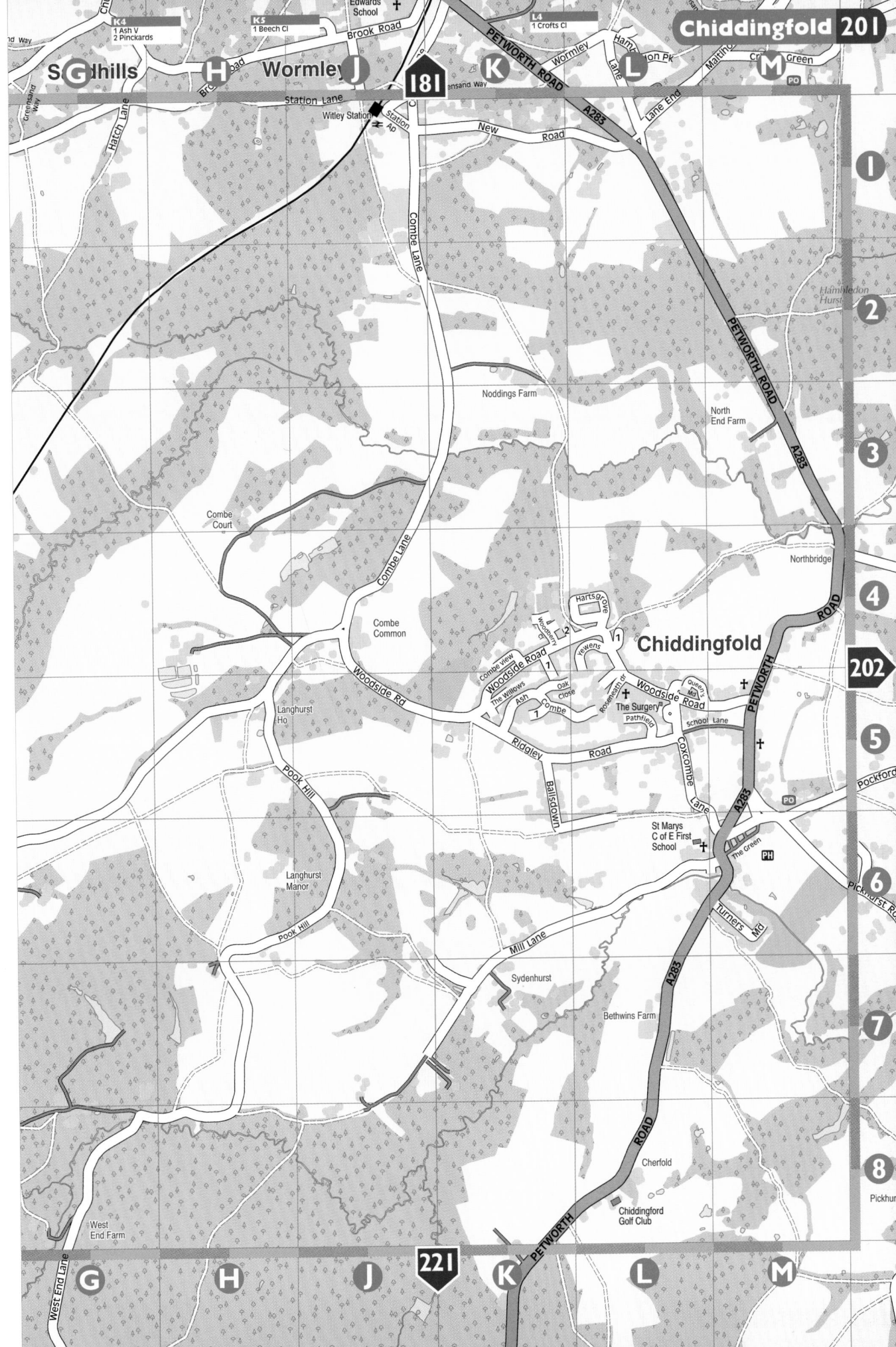

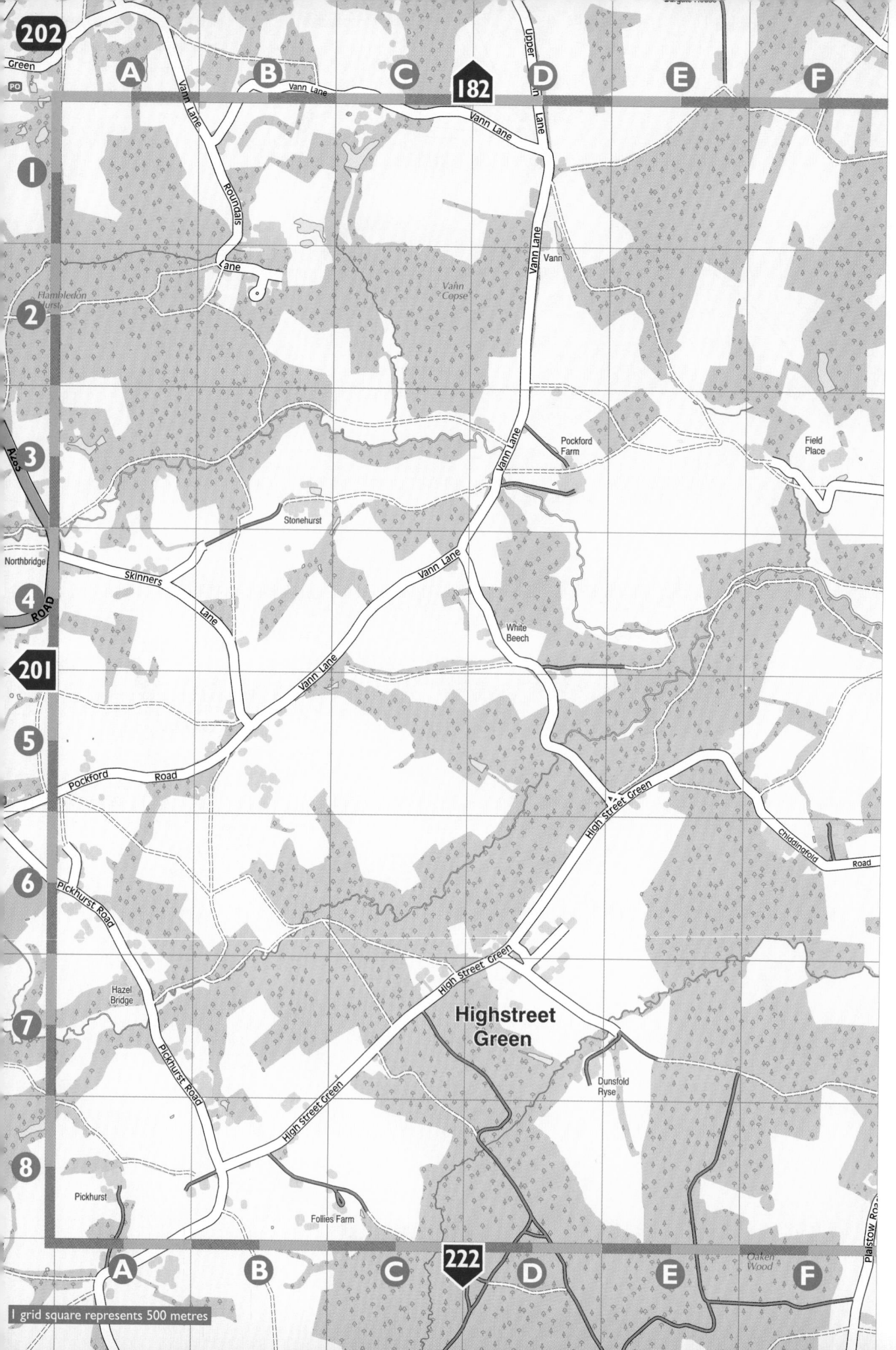

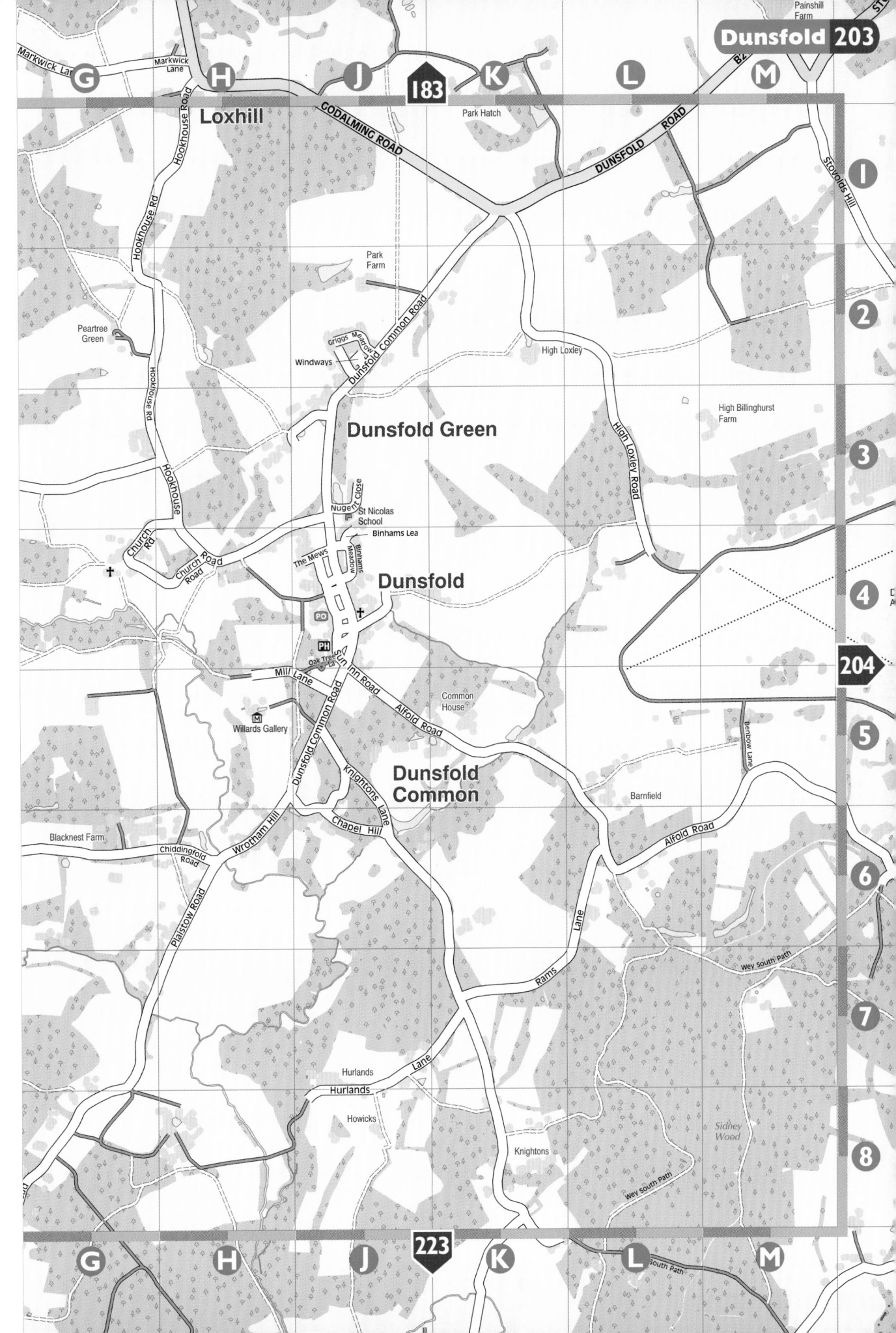

Markwick Lane

G

Markwick Lane

H

J

183

K

L

M

I

Loxhill

Hookhouse Road

GODALMING ROAD

Park Hatch

DUNSFOLD ROAD

Stovolds Hill

2

Park Farm

Hookhouse Rd

Peartree Green

Griggs Meadow

Windways

Dunsfold Common Road

High Loxley

High Billinghurst Farm

3

Dunsfold Green

High Loxley Road

Hookhouse Road

Church Rd

Nugent Close

St Nicolas School

Church Road

The Mews

Binhams Lea

Binhams Meadow

Dunsfold

4

PO

PH

Oak Tree

Sun Inn Road

204

Mill Lane

Willards Gallery

Dunsfold Common Road

Common House

Afold Road

5

Benbow Lane

Knightons Lane

Dunsfold Common

Barnfield

Blacknest Farm

Chiddingfold Road

Wrotham Hill

Chapel Hill

Afold Road

6

Plaistow Road

Rams Lane

Wey South Path

7

Lane

Hurlands

Sidney Wood

Hurlands

Howicks

8

Knightons

Wey South Path

G

H

J

223

K

L

South Path

M

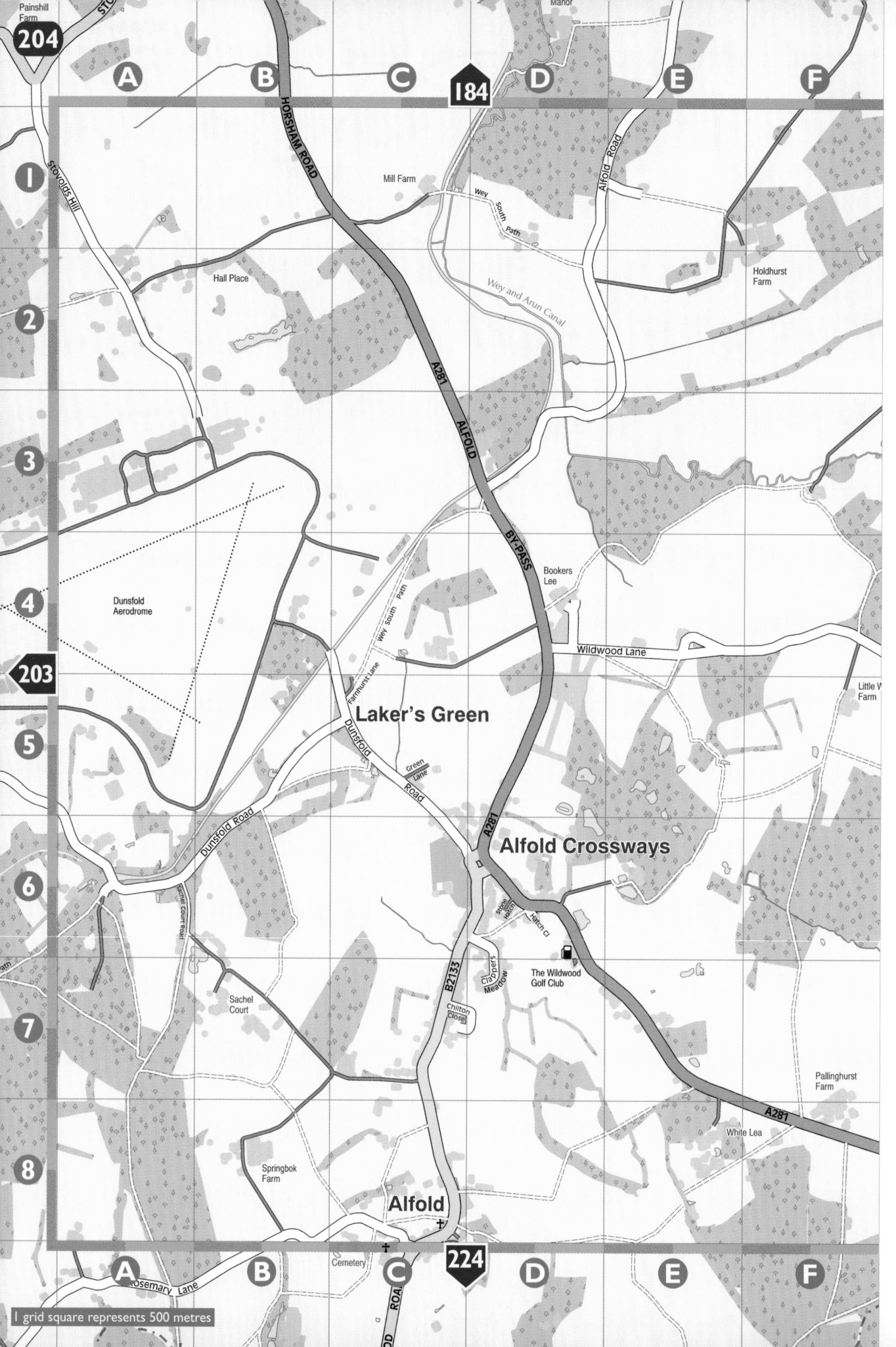

A   B   C   184   D   E   F

I

Stovolds Hill

Painshill
Farm

Mill Farm

HORSHAM ROAD

Wey
South
Path

Holdhurst
Farm

2

Hall Place

Wey and Arun Canal

A281

3

ALFOLD

BY-PASS

Bookers
Lee

4

Dunsfold
Aerodrome

Wey   South   Path

Farmhurst Lane

Wildwood Lane

203

Little W
Farm

ROAD

5

Laker's Green

Alfold Road

Green
Lane

Dunsfold

Road

A281

6

Dunsfold Road

Sachel Court Road

Alfold Crossways

Strood
Hatch

Hatch Cl

7

Sachel
Court

B2133

Clappers
Meadow

The Wildwood
Golf Club

Chilton
Close

Pallinghurst
Farm

A281

White Lea

8

Springbok
Farm

Alfold

Cemetery

A   B   C   224   D   E   F

Rosemary Lane

ROAD

1 grid square represents 500 metres

A B C **186** D E F

I

2

B2128

3 Baynard's Park

acre Drive

Drive

4

205

5

Somersbury Lane

Somersbury Wood

Coxland

Horsham Road

Froggetts Lane

Hillhouse Farm

Pollingfold

Ellen's Green

Ruet

Furzen Lane

Ellens

6 Maybanks Manor

Drive

B2128

Bury St Austen's

7

Hermonger Lane

Cox Green

Lynwick Street

STREET

Sussex Border Path

Highcroft Drive

Hermongers

8

CHURCH

Church St

The Ridge

I grid square represents 500 metres

Kilnfield Road

Pondtail

rze Road

Hyes

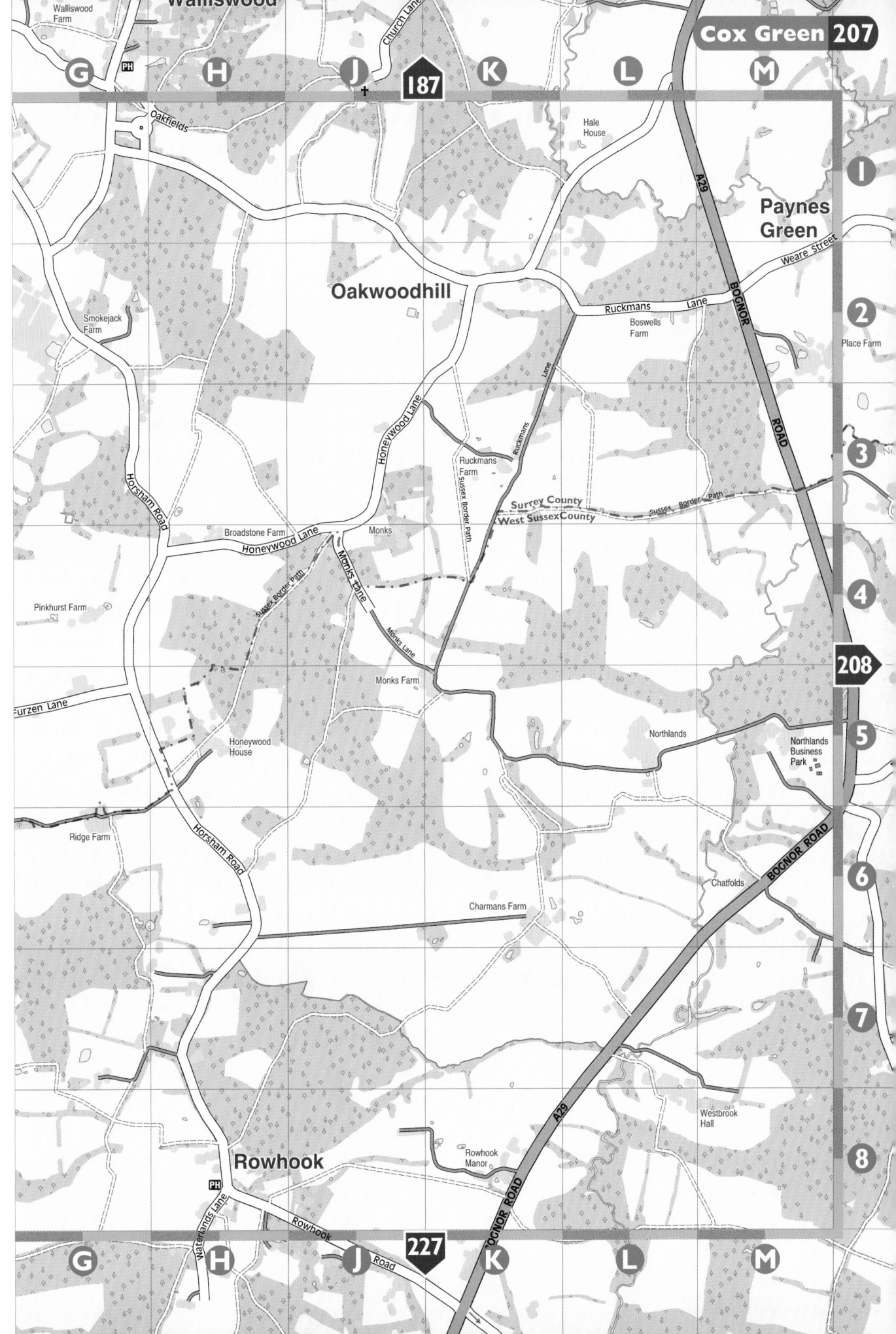

188

A B C D E F

I

aynes
reen

Weare Street

2

Place Farm

Sussex Border Path

3

ROAD

North River

Denne Farm

4

207

5

Business
Park

6

GNOR ROAD

7

8

RH12

1 grid square represents 500 metres

Waley s

Snugglers Lane

Oakdale
Farm

Sussex Border Path

Holbrook
Farm

Osbrooks

Sussex Border Path

A24

Wattlehurst
Farm

Old
Barn

Hewells
Farm

Tickfold
Farm

Kingsfold

DORKING ROAD

Marches Road

The Marches

A24

Boldings Brook

Stone Farm

Marches Road

Joanland
Farm

Mayes Lane

Durfold

Warnham
Lodge

Geerings

Northlands Road

Sands Farm

Cider Mill
Farm

Mayes Lane

Threestile

Knob Hill Road

A24

Andrew's
Farm

Warnham
Station

A B C D E F

228

Warnham
C of E School

Sch

Warnham

Freeman
Rd

Lucas

Greytons

Bell Road

DORKING RD

Westons
Place

Station Road

LC

Road

G H J K L M

189

Gages Farms

Ridge Farm

Sussex Border Path

Muggeridge's

Surrey County
West Sussex County

Sussex Border Path

HH

Friday Street

Stammerham Business Centre

New Barn Farm

Capel Road

Highams

Newgate Road

Sussex Border Path

High Street

Rusper

Rusper School

COOKS Md

Pucks Croft

Cowix

Capel Road

I

2

Sussex Border Path

Dial Post Farm

Steeres Hill

Ashmore La

Gardeners

Horsham Road

3

Friday Street

Great Benhams

The Nunnery

Manns Farm

Baldhorns Park

Wimland Road

4

210

Green Lane

Langhurst Close

Langhurst

Langhurstwood Road

Horsham Road

Old Holbrook

Green Lane

Coombers Farm

5

6

Graylands

Hilltop Farm

Rusper Road

7

The Castle

Benson's Lane

Benson's Farm

Wimla

8

G H J K L M

229

Holbrook Park

Old Holbrook

Moa House Farm

Rusper Road

Owlscastle Farm

190

209

Rusper

Chowles

Lambs
Green

Cobnor

Stumbleholm
Farm

Bonwycks
Place

Normans

Pucks Croft

Axmas Farm

Rusper Court
House

Kilnwood
End

Carylls

Kilnwood

Kilnwood Lane

Wimlands Lane

Carylls
Lea

Wimland
Farm

Faygate
Business
Centre

Oak Wk

Faygate
Station

Holmbush
Farm

Burns
Way

CRAWLEY ROAD

Faygate

Park Road

A264

Beechwood

Holmbush

West Sus

The Mount

Hillybarn

Langh

The

Langhurst Lane

Burnt House Lane

Rusper Road

East Street

Faygate Lane

Lambs Green Road

River Mole

Wimland Hill

Wimland Road

Benson's Lane

Benson's Farm

Newdigate Road

High Street

Rusper Road

Cooks Md

Rusper School

PO

A   B   C   D   E   F
I
2
3
4
5
6
7
8

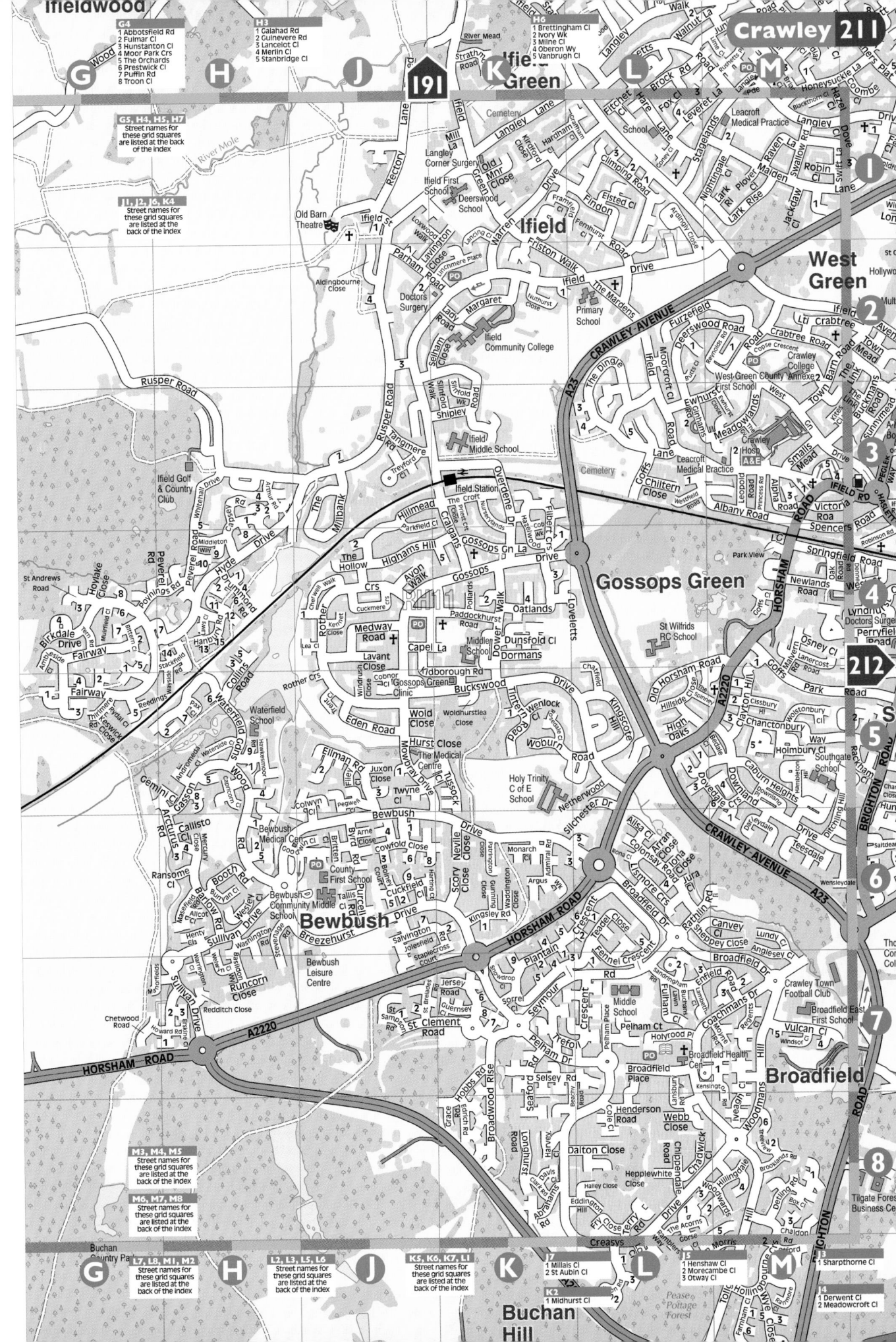

Ifieldwood

G H J K L M

191

**Ifield
Green**

Ifield

**West
Green**

2

3

Gossops Green

4

212

5

6

7

8

Bewbush

Broadfield

**Buchan
Hill**

G H J K L M

193

Wakehams
Green
Farm

Old
Rowfant

Ley
House

Home
Farm

Rowfant

Burleys
Wood

Crabbet
Park

Hayheath

Worth Way

Compasses
Corner

Turners Hill Road

RH10

Worth
Hall

Worth

Worth
Way

214

Junction 10A

Standinghall Lane

Standinghall
Farm

Worthlodge
Forest

Coldharbour
Farm

Standinghall Lane

Oldhouse Warren

CUFFS HILL

B2036

BALCOMBE ROAD

B2036

Whitley Hill

PADDOCKHURST ROAD

Back Lane

**Worth
Abbey**

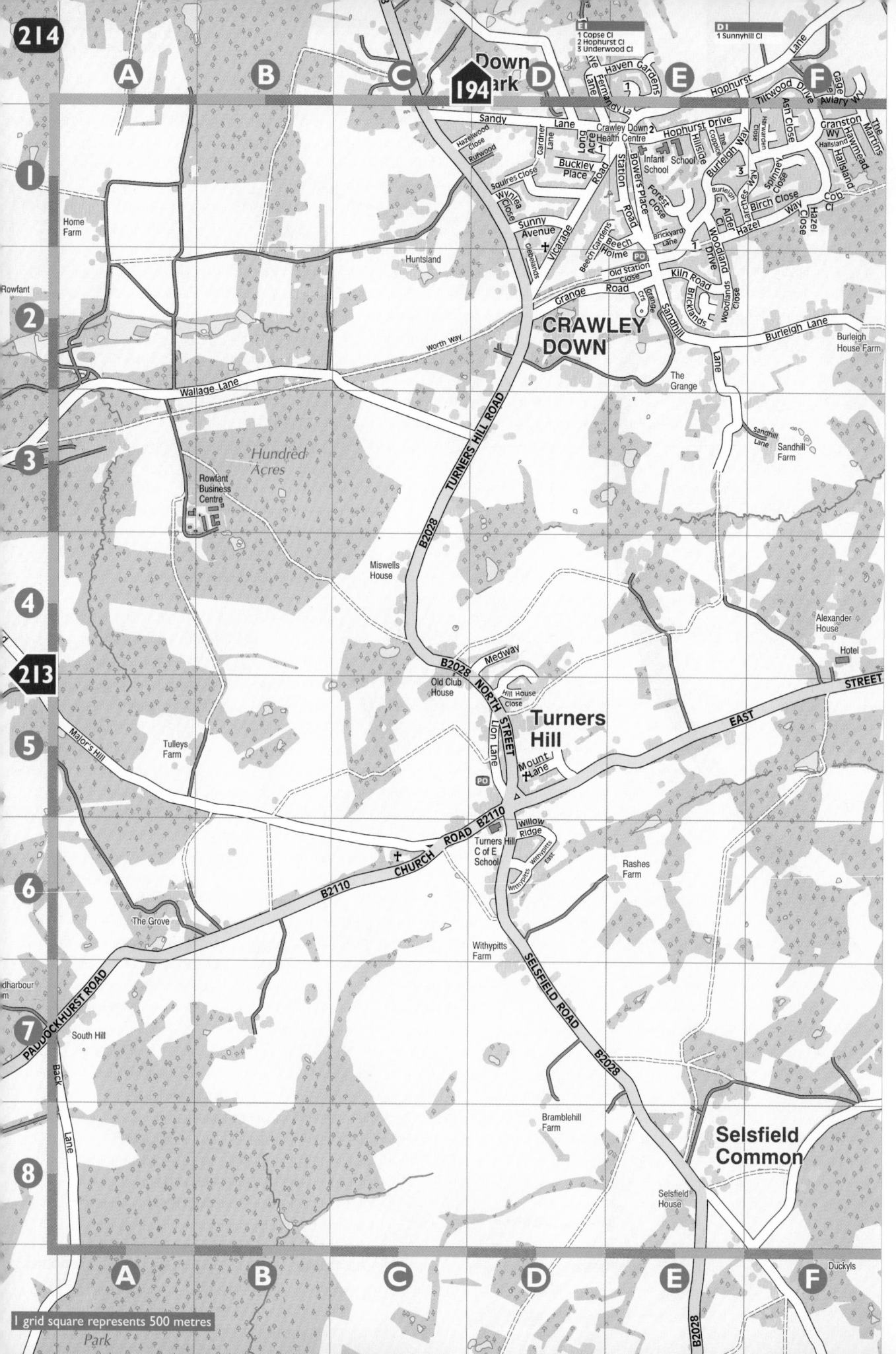

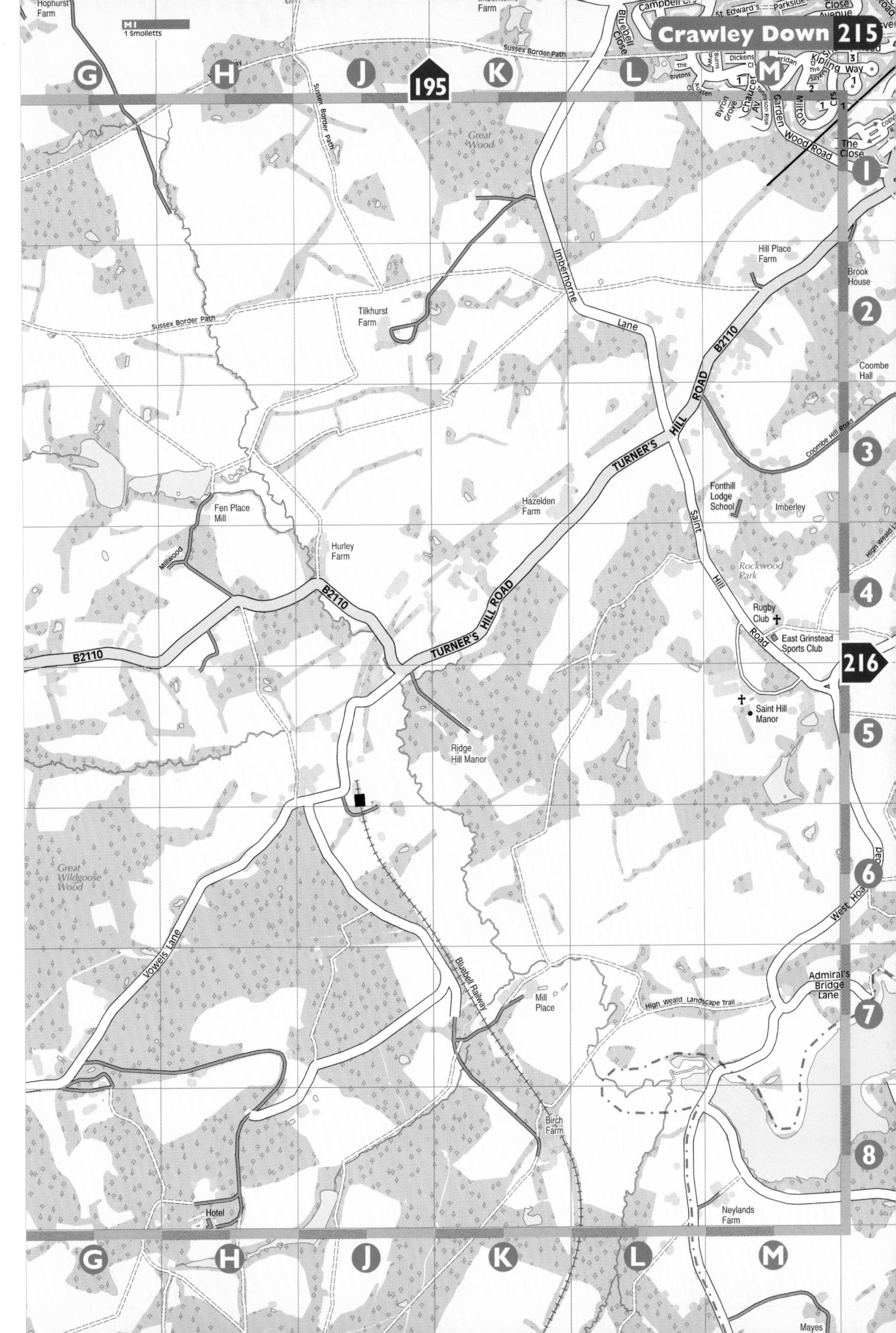

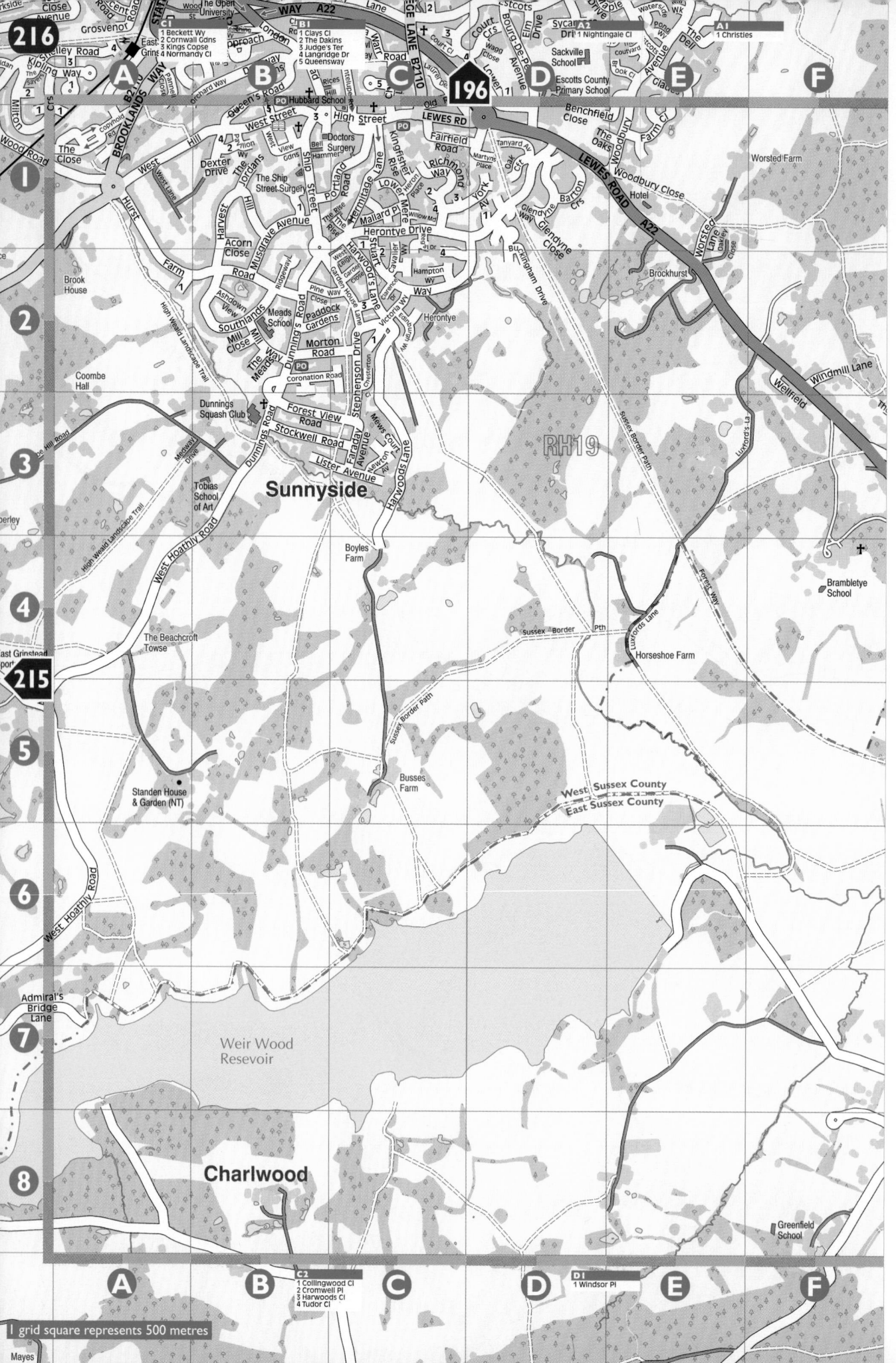

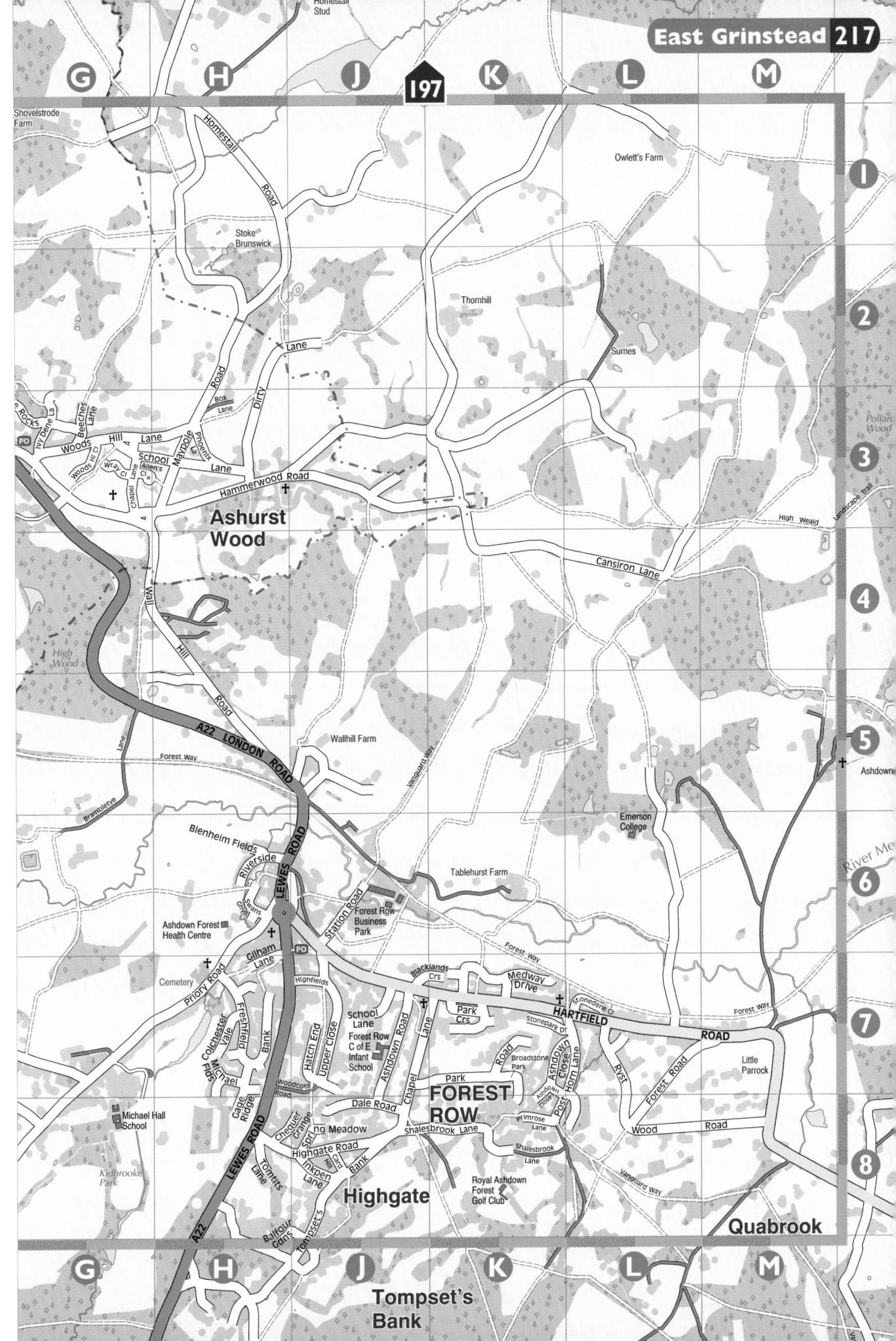

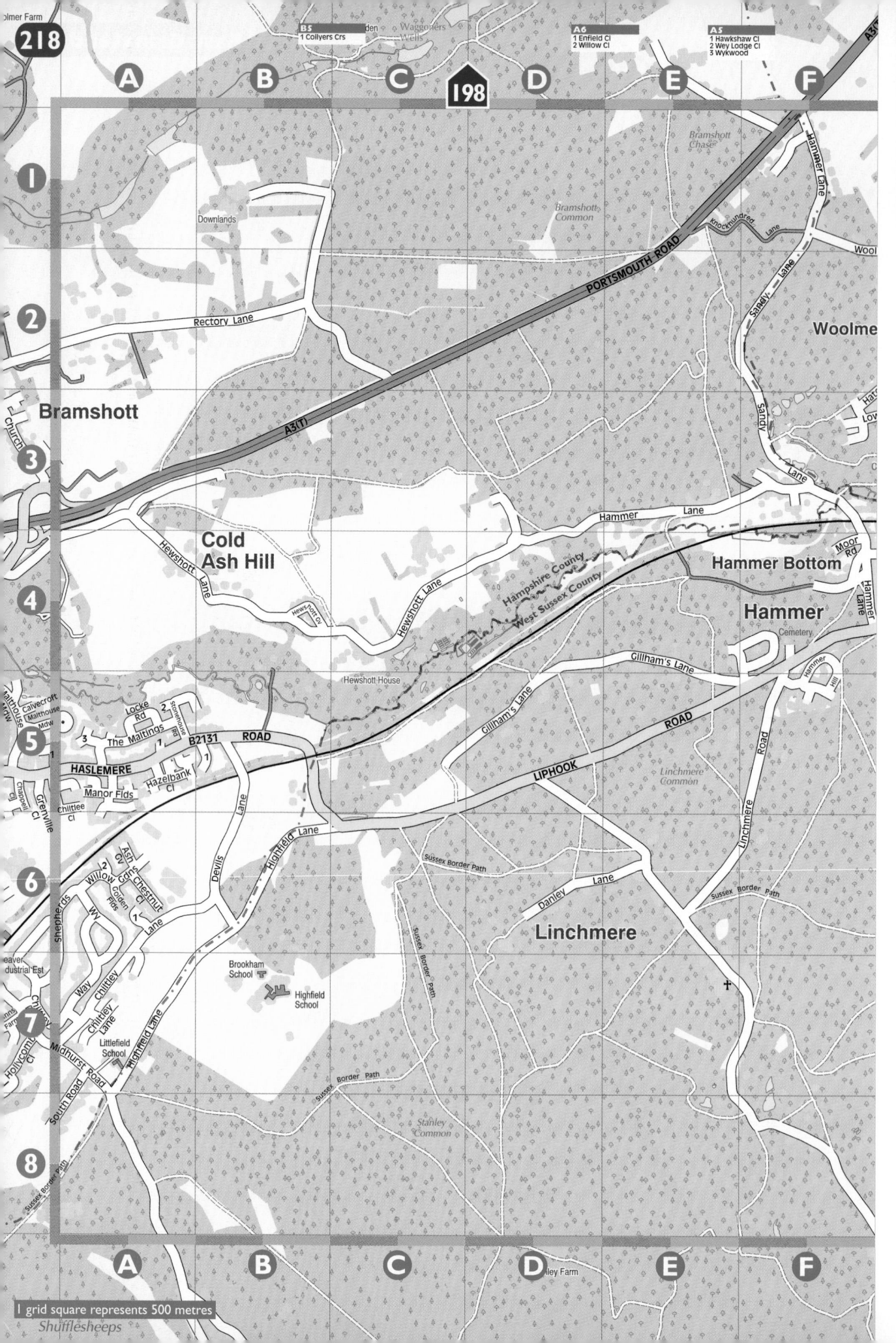

olmer Farm

Shufflesheeps

B5
1 Collyers Crs

A6
1 Enfield Cl
2 Willow Cl

A5
1 Hawkshaw Cl
2 Wey Lodge Cl
3 Wykwood

198

Downlands

Bramshott Chase

Bramshott Common

PORTSMOUTH ROAD

Knocknundred

Hammer Lane

Sandly Lane

Woolme

Rectory Lane

A3(T)

Woo

Church

Bramshott

Sandy

Lane

Low

Har

Hammer Lane

Hewshott Lane

Hammer Bottom

Cold Ash Hill

Hewshott Lane

Hampshire County
West Sussex County

Hammer

Moor Rd

Hammer Lane

Cemetery

Hewshott House

Gillham's Lane

Hammer Hill

Calvecroft
Malthouse Mdw

Locke Rd

The Maltings

B2131

ROAD

Gillham's Lane

ROAD

LIPHOOK

Linchmere
Common

Linchmere Road

HASLEMERE

Hazelbank Cl

Manor Flds

Chiltlee Cl

Grenville Cl

Chapel Cl

Lane

Highfield Lane

Devils

Sussex Border Path

Shepherds Way

Willow Gdns

Ash Gv

Chestnut Cl

Colden Flds

Danley Lane

Linchmere

Chiltley Way

Brookham School

Highfield School

Sussex Border Path

Sussex Border Path

Chiltley Lane

Littlefield School

Highfield Lane

Midhurst Road

South Road

Stanley Common

Hol)/comb

Farm

eaver
dustrial Est

Sussex Border Path

ley Farm

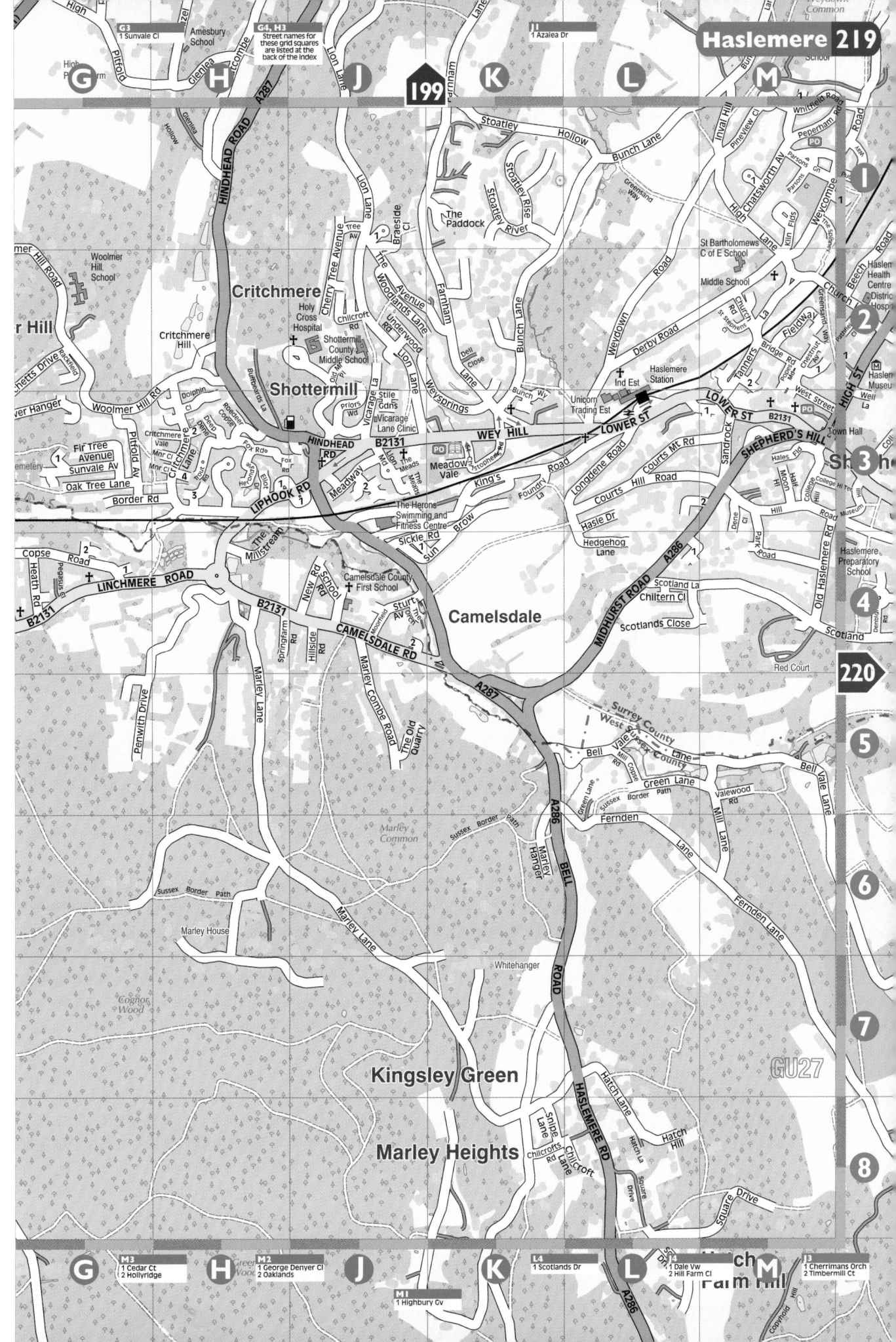

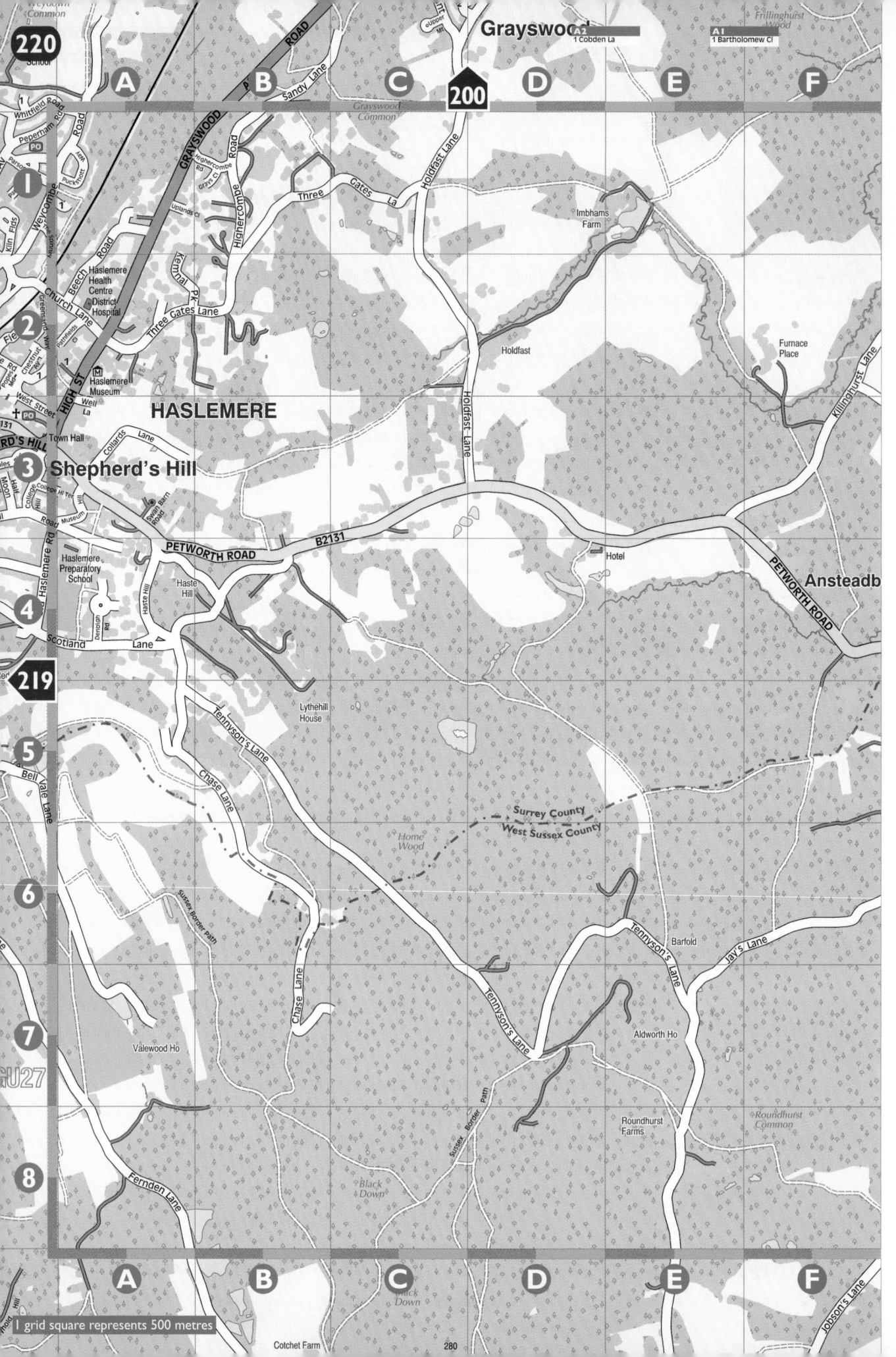

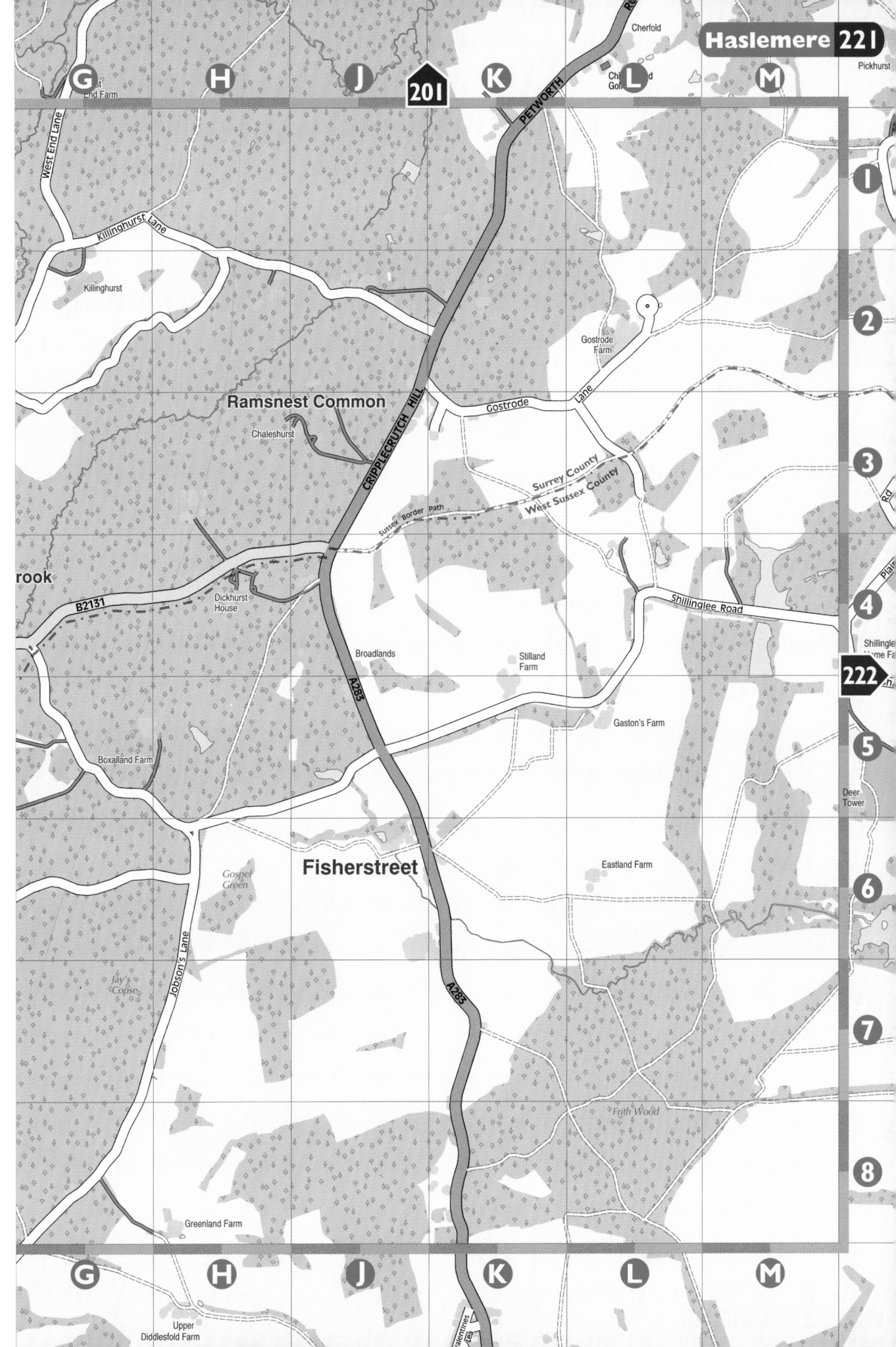

Cherfold

Pickhurst

Chiddingfold Golf Club

PETWORTH

West End Farm

West End Lane

Killinghurst Lane

Killinghurst

Gostrode Farm

Ramsnest Common

Chaleshurst

Gostrode Lane

CRIPPLECRUTCH HILL

Surrey County

West Sussex County

Sussex Border Path

rook

B2131

Dickhurst House

Shillinglee Road

Shillinglee Home Farm

Broadlands

Stilland Farm

A285

222

Boxalland Farm

Gaston's Farm

Deer Tower

Gospel Green

Fisherstreet

Eastland Farm

Jobson's Lane

Jay's Copse

A283

Frith Wood

Greenland Farm

Upper Diddlesfold Farm

Valentines

A   B   C   D   E   F

Pickhurst

Follies Farm

Oaken Wood

Plaistow Road

1

Tugley Wood

Durfold Hall Farm

2

Robins Farm

Fisher Lane

Shillinglee Park Golf Club

3

Fisherlane Wood

Durfold Wood

Sussex Border Path

Durfo

Plaistow Rd

Surrey County

West Sussex County

4

Shillinglee Home Farm

Shillinglee Road

5

Newhouse Farm

East End Farm

Deer Tower

6

The Lake

Haymans Farm

Kingspark Wood

7

Park Mill Farm

Birchfold Copse

8

Dale's Farm

Mitchell Park Farm

A   B   C   D   E   F

Upper

1 grid square represents 500 metres

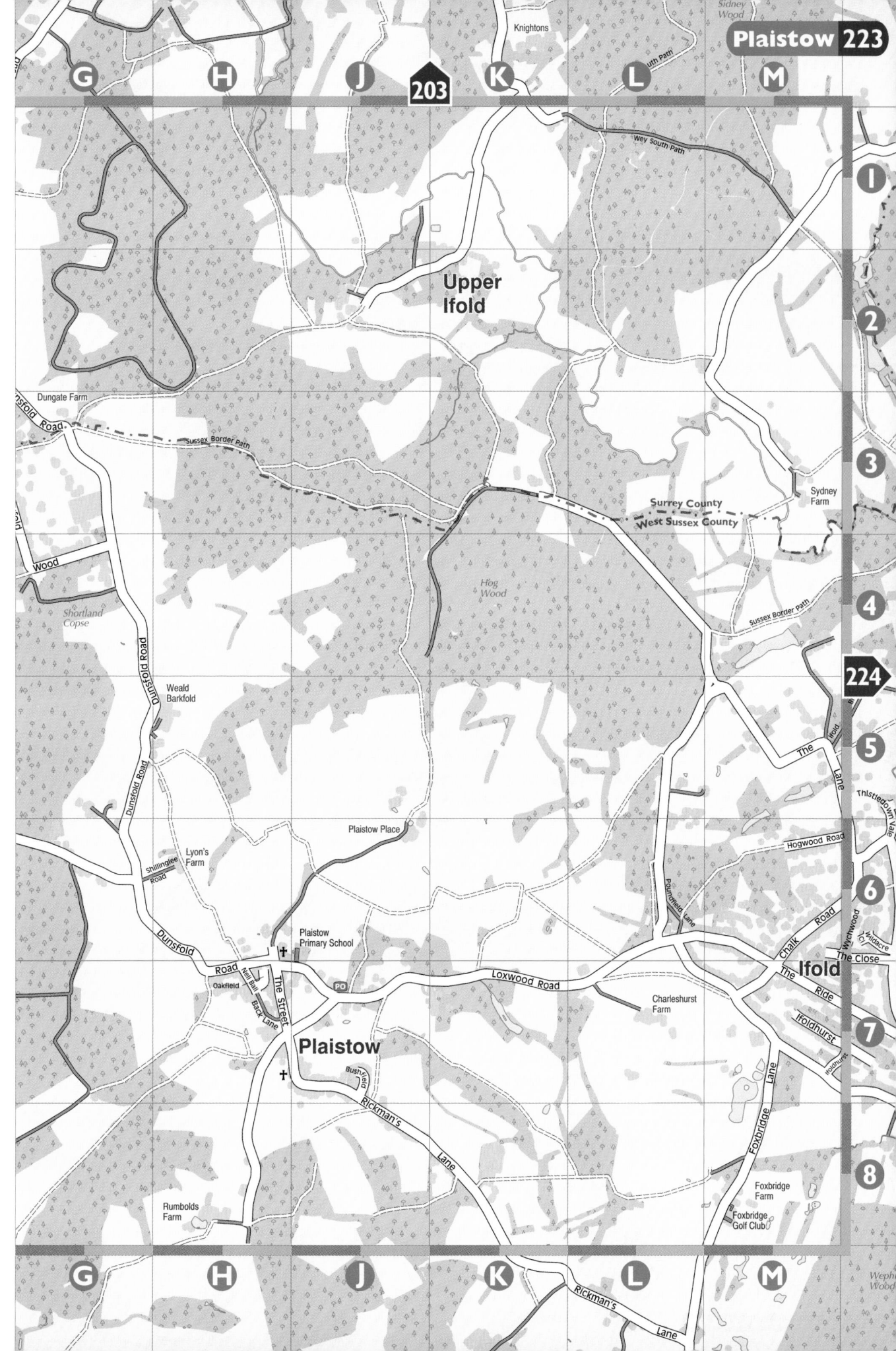

Knightons

Sidney
Wood

uth Path

G

H

J

203

K

L

M

Wey south Path

Upper
Ifold

I

2

Dungate Farm

Dunsfold Road

Sussex Border Path

Surrey County

West Sussex County

Sydney
Farm

3

Wood

Shortland
Copse

Hog
Wood

Sussex Border Path

4

224

Weald
Barkfold

Dunsfold Road

The Ifold Lane

5

Thistledown Vale

Plaistow Place

Hogwood Road

6

Shillinglee
Road

Lyon's
Farm

Poundfield Lane

Chalk Road

Wephurst Ln

Wildacre

The Close

The Ride

Ifold

Dunsfold

Road

Plaistow
Primary School

Oakfield

Neil Ball

Back Lane

The Street

PO

Loxwood Road

Charleshurst
Farm

Ifoldhurst

7

Foxbridge Lane

Ifoldhurst

Plaistow

Bushfield

Rickman's

Lane

Rumbolds
Farm

Foxbridge
Farm

Foxbridge
Golf Club

8

G

H

J

K

Rickman's

L

Lane

M

Wephu
Wood

A B C D E F

Ifold

+ **204**
PO

Rosemary Lane

Springbok
Farm

Cemetery

1

LOXWOOD ROAD

Monckton
Hook

Pigbush   Lane

2

The Walled
Garden

Alfold Bars

Oakhurst   Lane

Loxwood
Hall

Old
Songhurst
Farm

3

Oakhurst
Farm

Sydney
Farm

Wey South Path

Merry
Hills

4

B2133

Merryhills Lane

Pond Close Lane

223

Bridge

Lane

Pound Close

THE PARADE

Spy   Lane

5

Ifold
Lane

Thistledown Vale

Pond Close

Badgers Way

Loxwood

Nicholson

Glebe
lands

2

Loxwood Primary
School

Hogwood Road

Station Road

Wey South Path

Farm Place

PO

3

Farm Close

Farm Close

1

Brewhurst
Mill

Wey South Path

6

Wynwood

Widacre

The Close

Ifold

+

B2133

Brewhurst   Lane

The Ride

7

Hoghurst

The Drive

Plaistow Road

Headfoldswood
Farm

Skiff Lane

8

Weph
Wood

Lakers
Lodge

A B C D E F

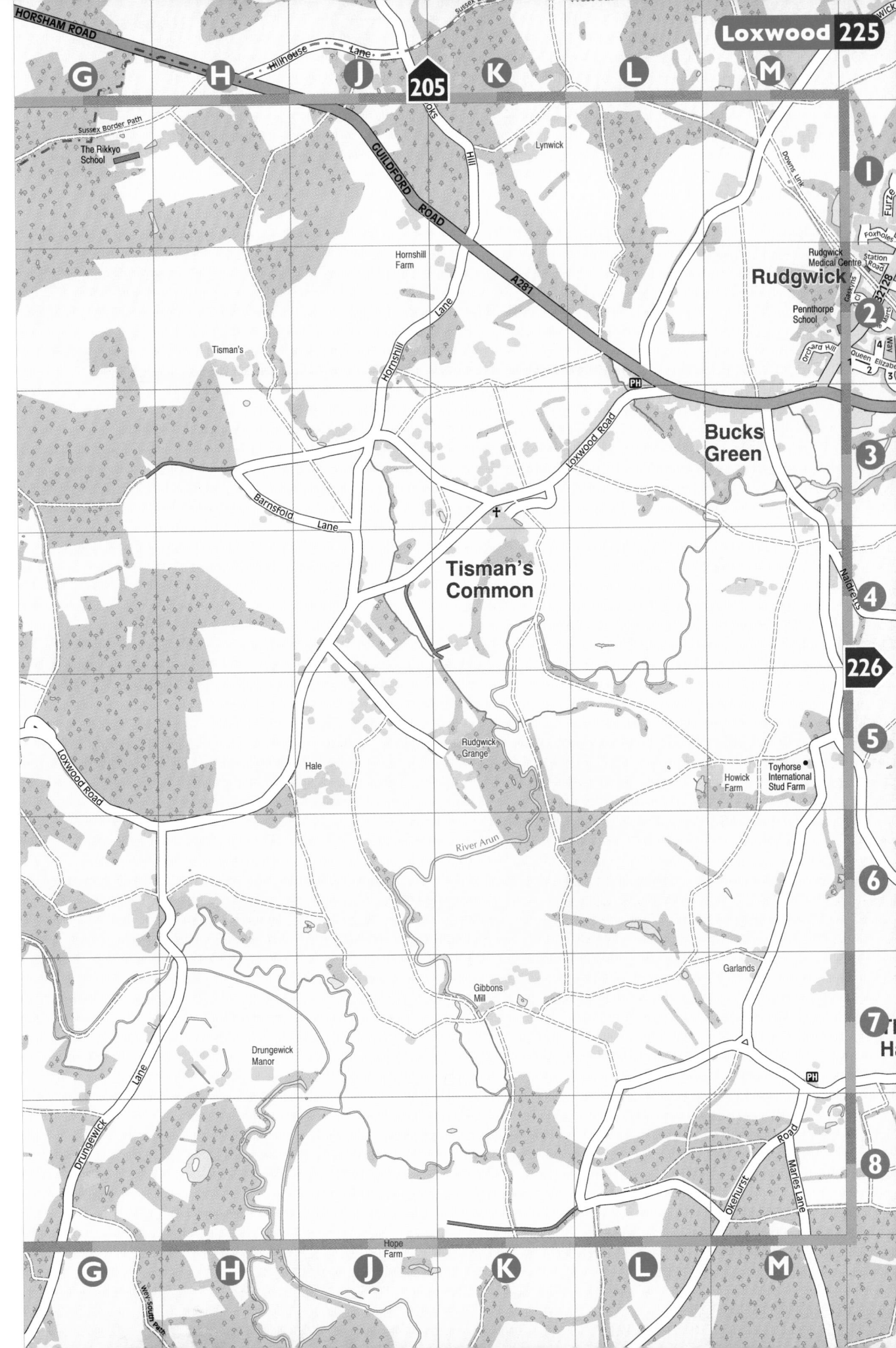

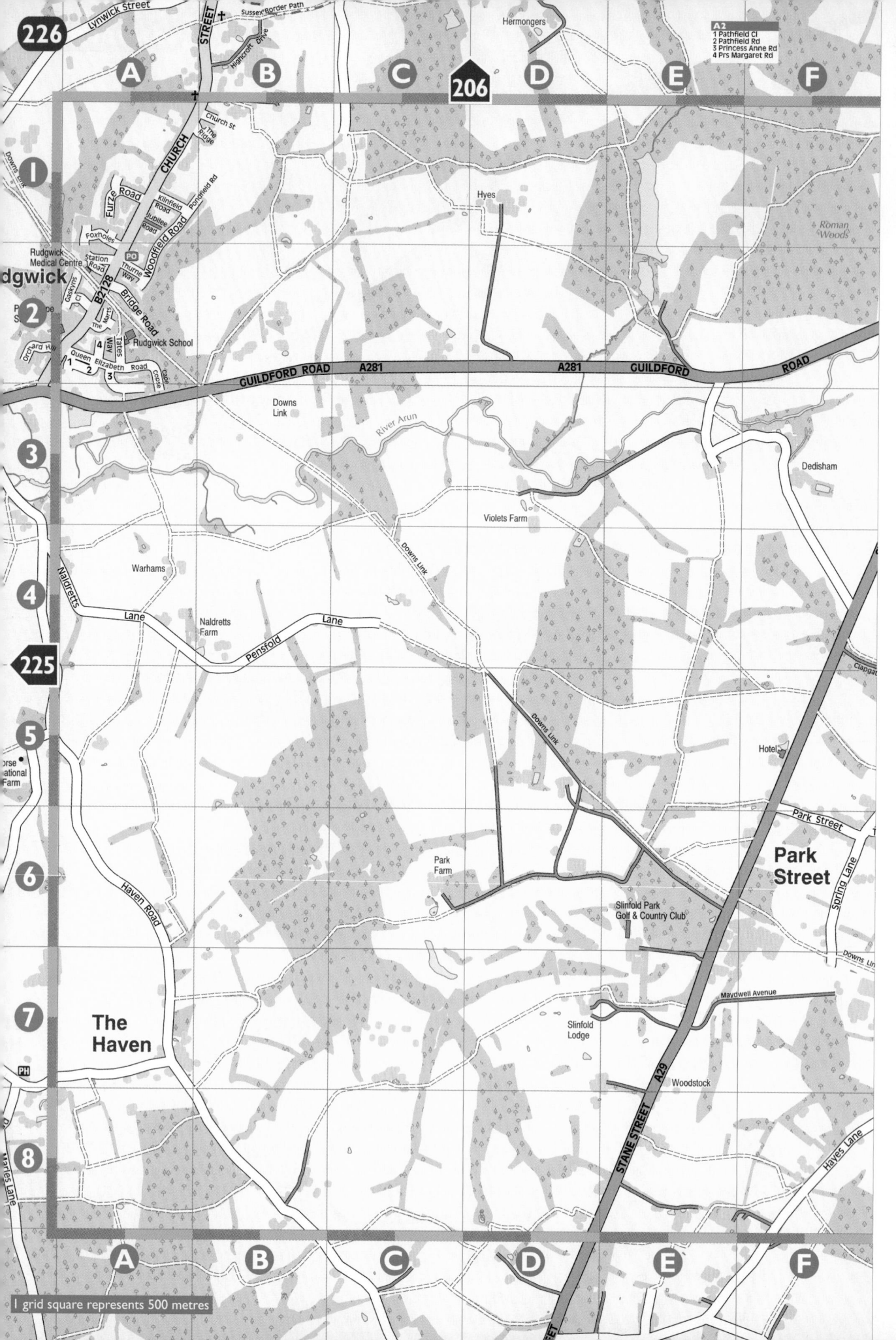

206

225

A2
1 Pathfield Cl
2 Pathfield Rd
3 Princess Anne Rd
4 Prs Margaret Rd

Lynwick Street

STREET

Sussex Border Path

Highcroft Drive

Hermongers

Church st
The Lodge

CHURCH

Furze Road

Church St

Klinfield Road
Jubilee Road

Pondfield Rd

Woodfield Road

Roman Woods

Foxholes

Hyes

PO
Thurne Way

Station Road

Rudgwick Medical Centre

dgwick

B2128

Gaskyns Cl

Bridge Road

The Merts

Rudgwick School

Orchard Hill

Queen Elizabeth Road

Dedisham

GUILDFORD ROAD   A281

A281   GUILDFORD   ROAD

Downs Link

River Arun

Violets Farm

Warhams

Naldretts Lane

Naldretts Farm

Pensfold Lane

Downs Link

Clapgat

Hotel

Naldretts Lane

Park Street

orse
ational
Farm

Downs Link

Park Farm

Park Street

Downs Lin

Spring Lane

Haven Road

Slinfold Park Golf & Country Club

Maydwell Avenue

The Haven

Slinfold Lodge

STANE STREET

A29

Woodstock

PH

Mayes Lane

Hayes Lane

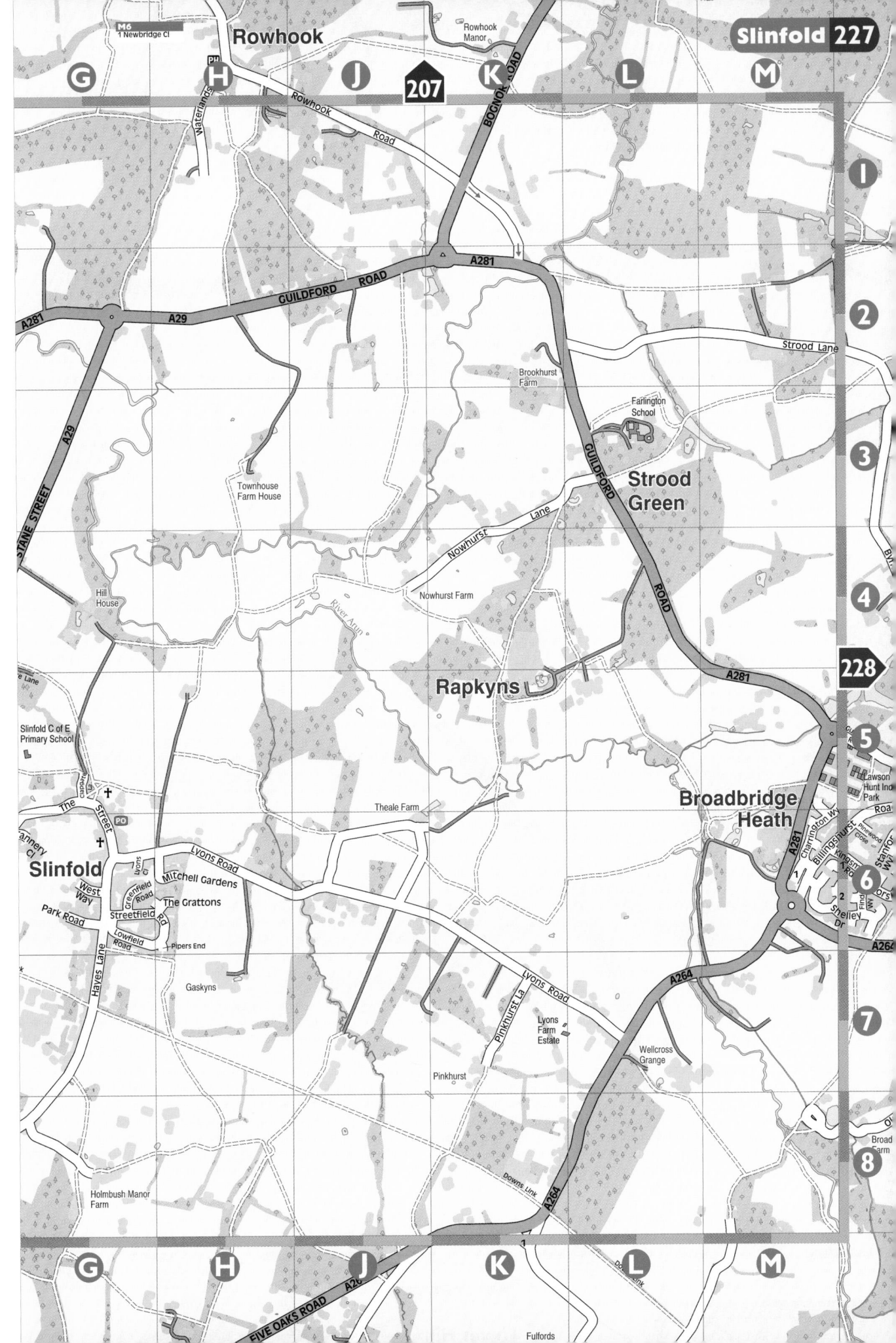

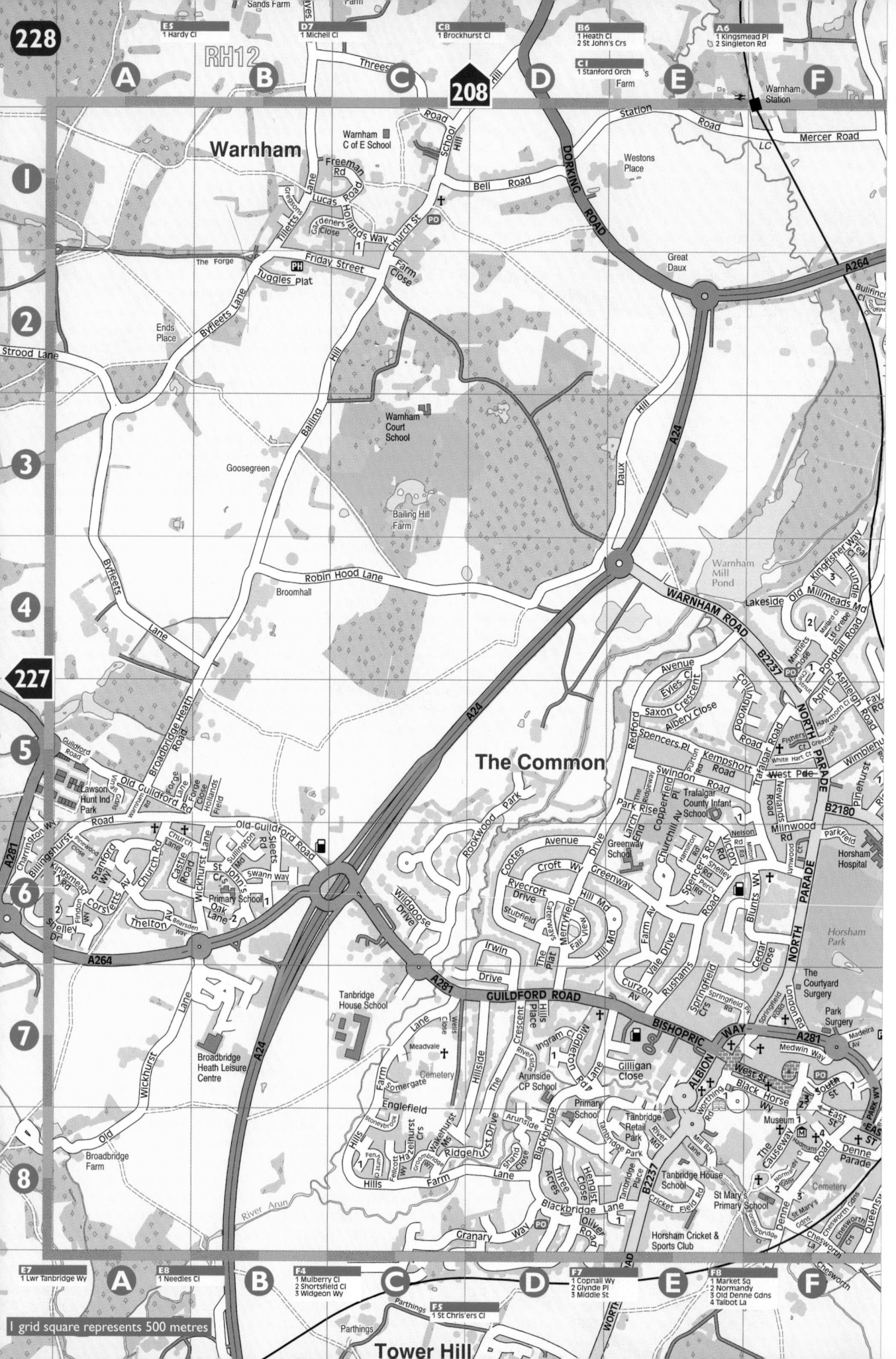

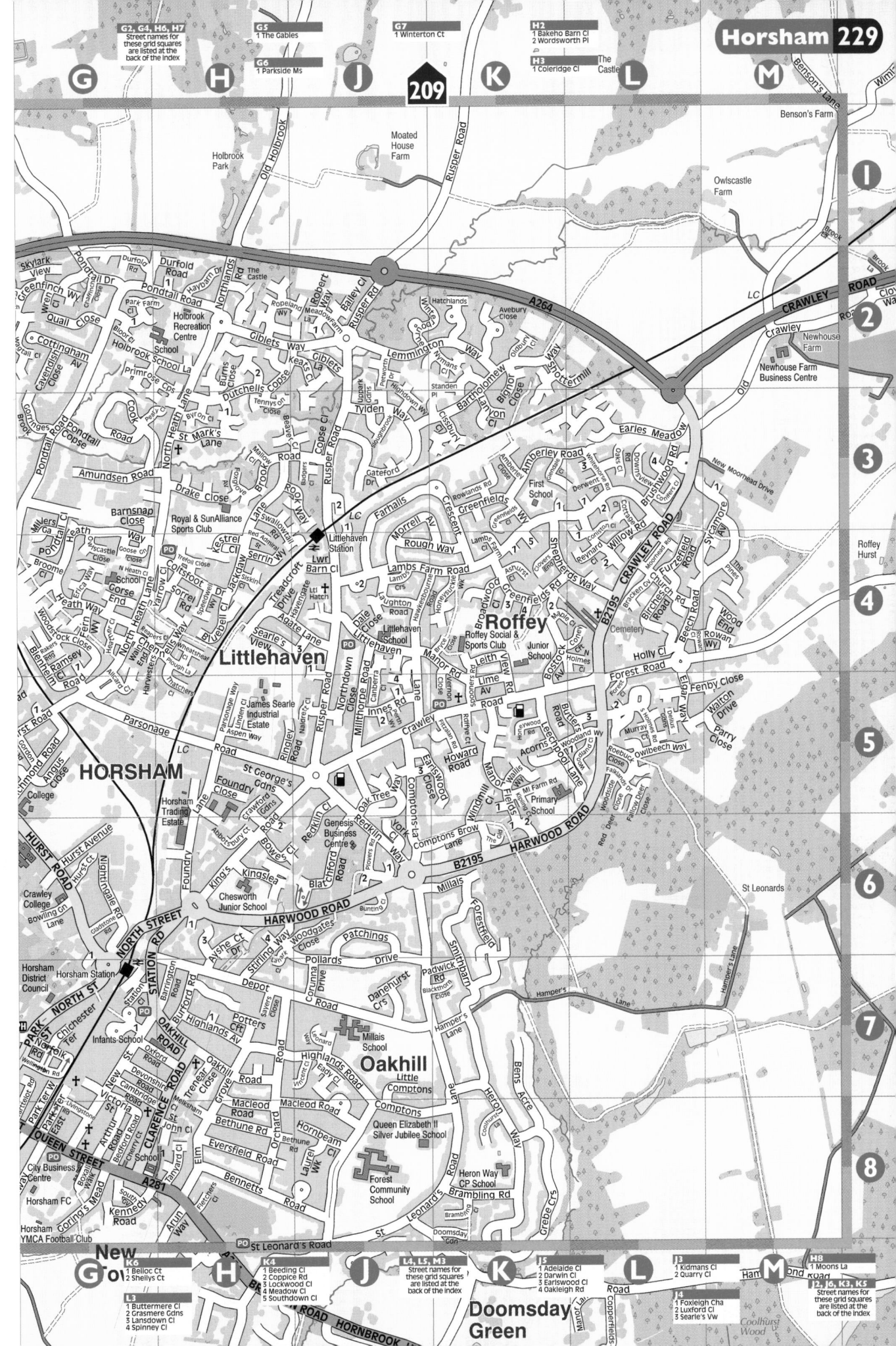

Place	Page	Grid
Aaron's Hill	159	L5
Abbey Mead	40	E6
Abbotswood	117	J6
Abinger Common	165	L5
Abinger Hammer	142	B6
Addington	69	K5
Addiscombe	5	L3
Addlestone	58	F4
Addlestonemoor	58	F1
Albury	140	D7
Albury Heath	141	H7
Aldershot	112	F6
Alfold	204	C8
Alfold Bars	224	C2
Alfold Crossways	204	D6
Anerley	50	D2
Ansteadbrook	220	F4
Anthonys	77	K2
Aperfield	91	J7
Artington	138	E5
Ascot	36	C3
Ash	113	K6
Ashford	23	J6
Ashford Common	24	A7
Ash Green	136	A1
Ashley Park	60	D2
Ashstead	83	H8
Ashurst Wood	217	H3
Ash Vale	113	K3
Badshot Lea	134	F3
Bagshot	53	M6
Bagshot Heath	54	B8
Baldwins Hill	195	M6
Balham	30	C1
Bandonhill	67	G4
Banstead	85	K6
Barford	198	B1
Barnes	19	L3
Barwell	62	F6
Batt's Corner	177	G2
Beacon Hill	199	G2
Beare Green	167	H7
Beaumont	20	E2
Beckenham	51	L3
Beddington	67	H1
Beddington Corner	48	D7
Bellfields	116	F5
Bell Green	33	J4
Bellingham	33	K5
Belmont	65	K7
Benhilton	65	L2
Berrylands	45	J6
Berry's Green	91	K6
Betchworth	123	M7
Bewbush	211	J6
Biggin Hill	90	E7
Binscombe	159	M1
Birch Hill	34	F7
Birtley Green	161	K5
Bishopsgate	20	C5
Bisley	75	L6
Blackbrook	145	H7
Black Corner	193	G5
Blackheath	140	B8
Blacknest	37	H5
Blacknest	176	C2
Blackwater	72	A4
Blackwell	196	B7
Bletchingley	128	B4
Blindley Heath	173	G1
Boundstone	155	L5
The Bourne	11	J8
Bowlhead Green	180	B8
Bowling Alley	132	B4
Box Hill	123	K6
Bracknell	35	G4
Bramley	161	J4
Brands Hill	12	E2
Brentford	18	A1
Brentford End	17	L7
Brewer Street	127	M5
Brick Hill	55	M3
Bridge End	99	L2
Broadbridge Heath	227	L5
Broadfield	211	M7
Broadford	138	F7
Broad Green	4	B1
Broadham Green	129	M6
Broadmoor	165	L1
Brockham	145	K1
Brockham Park	145	M5
Brook	141	H8
Brook	180	F8
Brooklands	59	J7
Brook Place	75	L1
Brookwood	95	K2
Broomhall	37	K7
Buckland	124	D7
Bucks Green	225	L3
Bucks Horn Oak	176	D1
Bullbrook	35	J2
Bunce Common	146	A7
Burgh Heath	105	G1
Burntcommon	98	C7
Burpham	117	K6
Burrowhill	56	C7
Burrows Cross	141	L7
Burstow	193	K2
Burwood Park	60	D4
Busbridge	160	D7
Bushbury	145	K5
Bushey Mead	47	G3
Bushy Hill	117	L6
Byfleet	79	G3
Camberley	73	H2
Camelsdale	219	K4
Cannon Hill	47	G4
Capel	189	G3
Carshalton	66	B3
Carshalton Beeches	66	B7
Carshalton on the Hill	66	C6
Cartbridge	97	L4
Castle Green	76	A3
Caterham	108	B5
Catford	33	M2
Catteshall	160	D3
Chaldon	107	L6
Charleshill	157	K4
Charlton	41	M2
Charlwood	191	J1
Charlwood	216	B8
Chattern Hill	23	L5
Chavey Down	35	L2
Cheam	65	J4
Cheapside	37	H2
Chelsham	89	K7
Chertsey	40	D7
Chertsey Meads	41	H8
Chessington	63	H5
Chiddingfold	201	L4
Chilworth	139	M6
Chipstead	106	D1
Chobham	56	A8
Christmaspie	136	E1
Church End	99	J3
Church Town	128	F5
Churt	178	C8
Claremont Park	61	K6
Clark's Green	188	F5
Claygate	62	C5
Clock House	86	F4
Cobham	80	D4
Cold Ash Hill	218	B4
Coldharbour	166	A4
Cole Park	17	K8
Coles Meads	126	C5
College Town	72	B1
Collier's Wood	30	A8
Colnbrook	12	F3
The Common	228	D5
Compton	134	C8
Compton	137	K6
Coney Hall	70	B3
Coombe	28	B8
Cooper's Hill	21	G4
Copse Hill	28	D8
Copthorne	193	L6
Cottenham Park	46	E1
Coulsdon	87	H6
Cove	92	B3
Cox Green	206	B7
Cramhurst	181	H3
Cranford	15	K2
Cranleigh	185	J7
Crawley	212	B4
Crawley Down	214	D2
Crawley Hill	73	H4
Critchmere	219	H2
Crockham Hill	131	M7
Crondall	132	B2
Crooked Billet	28	E7
Crosswater	178	B5
Crossways	178	B8
Crowhurst	152	A6
Crowhurst Lane End	151	K4
Crownpits	160	B6
Crown Wood	35	G6
Croydon	4	E7
Cudworth	190	B1
Culmer	181	J6
Dawesgreen	146	B6
Deepcut	93	M3
Deepdene	145	G2
Denbies	122	A8
Dippenhall	133	G7
Dockenfield	177	J5
Domewood	194	E4
Donkey Town	75	G3
Dora's Green	132	F4
Dorking	144	E3
Dormansland	174	E8
Dormans Park	196	B2
Doversgreen	147	L4
Downe	91	J1
Down Park	194	D8
Downside	100	E1
Dulwich	32	C3
Dulwich Common	32	E2
Dulwich Village	32	B1
Dunsfold Common	203	J5
Dunsfold Green	203	J3
Dunsford	203	J4
Earlsfield	29	M2
Earlswood	148	C2
Eashing	159	J4
East Bedfont	23	L1
East Clandon	119	H5
East Ewell	65	G8
East Green	154	B3
East Grinstead	196	E4
Easthampstead	34	E4
East Horsley	120	A1
East Molesey	43	M5
East Sheen	19	G7
Eden Park	51	J4
Effingham	121	G1
Egham	21	K7
Egham Hythe	22	A7
Egham Wick	20	C8
Ellen's Green	206	B5
Elm Corner	99	K1
Elmers End	51	G3
Elstead	158	A6
Englefield Green	20	E8
Enton Green	181	L3
Epsom	83	M4
Esher	61	M3
Ewell	84	E1
Ewhurst	186	B4
Ewhurst Green	186	B5
Ewshot	132	F1
Fairlands	116	A5
Fairmile	81	J2
Farleigh	89	J4
Farleigh Court	89	K4
Farley Green	163	H2
Farnborough	71	L4
Farnborough Green	92	D5
Farnborough Park	93	G6
Farnborough Street	92	F4
Farncombe	160	A1
Farnham	10	L1
Faygate	210	B8
Felbridge	195	J5
Felcourt	195	M1
Felday	164	E3
Feltham	24	E3
Felthamhill	24	B6
Fernhill	193	H2
Fetcham	102	A5
Fickleshole	90	B4
Field Common	43	J7
Fisherstreet	221	H6
Flexford	115	G8
Folly Hill	133	K4
Forestdale	69	H7
Forest Green	187	H2
Forest Hill	33	G4
Forest Row	217	J3
Fox Corner	95	M7
Fox Lane	72	C8
Fredley	122	E3
Frensham	177	L2
Friday Street	165	J1
Frimley	73	K7
Frimley Green	93	J2
Frimley Ridge	73	K6
Frithend	176	F6
Frith Hill	160	A3
Furnace Green	212	D5
Furnace Wood	194	D6
Furzedown	30	E5
Gadbrook	146	A4
Gatton	126	C2
Giggshill	44	D7
Givons Grove	103	G7
Godalming	160	C5
Godstone	128	E5
Gomshall	141	M6
Goodley Stock	131	L4
Gossops Green	211	L4
Grafham	183	M1
Grayshott	198	E6
Grayswood	200	D8
Great Bookham	101	L8
Great Hollands	34	B6
Green Cross	178	E8
Grove Park	19	G3
Guildford	9	G8
Guildford Park	8	C5
Hackbridge	66	F1
Hale	134	A4
Ham	27	G4
Hambledon	181	M7
Hammer	218	F4
Hammer Bottom	218	E4
Hammerwood	197	L6
Hamm Moor	59	G3
Hampton	43	L1
Hampton Hill	25	M5
Hampton Wick	2	A5
Hamsey Green	88	F5
Hanworth	25	G4
Hanworth	34	D7
Harlington	14	F1
Harmans Water	35	G4
Harmondsworth	13	M1
Hascombe	183	H5
Haslemere	220	A3
Hatton	15	H6
The Haven	226	A7
Hawk's Hill	102	C6
Hawley	72	B6
Hawley Lane	92	E2
Haxted	175	J1
Hazelwood	91	M1
Headley	103	M8
Heath End	134	A2
Heatherside	73	M5
Hersham	60	F4
Heston	16	C2
High Curley	74	A1
Highgate	217	J8
Highstreet Green	202	C7
Hill Park	111	L5
Hinchley Wood	62	C2
Hindhead	199	J5
Hoe	164	A1
Hog Hatch	133	J3
Holland	130	D7
Holloway Hill	160	B7
Holmbury St Mary	164	F3
Holmethorpe	126	E6
Holmwood Corner	167	G3
Holt Pound	155	L5
Hook	63	H4
Hook Heath	96	E2
Hookwood	169	M7
Hooley	106	D4
Horley	170	E4
Horne	172	C4
Horsell	6	B3
Horsell Birch	76	D5
Horsham	229	G5
Horton	12	D5
Hounslow	16	A4
Hounslow West	16	A5
Hurst Green	130	B6
Hurst Park	43	M2
Hurtmore	159	K2
Hydestile	182	B3
Hythe End	21	L4
Ifield	211	K1
Ifield Green	191	K8
Ifieldwood	191	G8
Ifold	223	M7
Irons Bottom	147	K8
Isleworth	17	L5
Jacobs Well	116	F3
Kenley	88	A6
Keston	71	G3
Keston Mark	71	G2
Kew	18	C2
Kingfield	188	A4
Kingsfold	208	D2
Kingsley Green	219	J7
Kingston upon Thames	2	D4
Kingston Vale	28	A6
Kingswood	105	J5
Knaphill	75	M8
Knight's Hill	31	M2
Knowle Green	22	E4
Knowle Hill	38	E7
Laker's Green	204	C5
Laleham	40	F3
Lambs Green	210	C3
Lampton	16	E3
Lane End	178	A2
Langley Green	191	L7
Langley Vale	104	A2
Leatherhead	102	B3
Leaves Green	91	G1
Leigh	146	D7
Lightwater	74	F1
Limpsfield	130	C1
Limpsfield Chart	131	J5
Limpsfield Common	130	E4
Linchmere	218	D6
Lingfield	174	A5
Lingfield Common	174	A3
Little Bookham	101	H7
Littlefield Common	115	L3
Little Heath	81	J4
Littlehaven	229	H4
Littleton	41	L3
Littleton	138	D6
Littleton Common	23	L8
Little Woodcote	86	D1
Locksbottom	71	L2
Logmore Green	143	L7
Longcross	56	E2
Long Ditton	44	E8
Longford	13	M3
Lordshill Common	161	M5
Lower Ashtead	102	F1
Lower Bourne	11	L7
Lower Feltham	24	B4
Lower Green	61	L1
Lower Halliford	42	A7
Lower Kingswood	105	K8
Lower Sydenham	33	G5
Lowfield Heath	192	C4
Loxhill	203	H1
Loxwood	224	B5
Lucas Green	75	G5
Luxted	91	K4
Maidenbower	212	F5
Malden Rushett	82	E2
Manor Royal	192	B7
Margery	125	K3
Marley Heights	219	J8
Marlpit Hill	153	L5
Marsh Green	175	L4
Martyr's Green	100	B2
Maybury	7	J5
Mayes Green	187	H6
Mayford	96	F4
May's Green	100	C2
Mead Vale	147	M3
Meath Green	170	A4
Merle Common	152	D2
Merrow	117	M2
Merstham	126	E2
Merton	47	L1
Merton Park	47	J2
Mickleham	122	E2
Middle Bourne	11	G6
Mid Holmwood	144	E8
Miles Green	75	J7
Milford	159	J7
Millbridge	156	A8
Mimbridge	76	B3
Mitcham	48	E3
Mogador	125	G3
Monks Orchard	50	F7
Montgomery Lines	112	F5
Moorhouse Bank	131	G2
Moor Park	134	E8
Morden	47	K4
Morden Park	47	H6
Mortlake	18	F4
Motspur Park	46	D6
Mount Hermon	6	C9
Mousehill	181	J1
Mugswell	105	L7
Mytchett	93	H6
Mytchett Place	93	L7
Nalderswood	168	F2
Nash	70	E5
New Addington	70	A6
New Beckenham	33	H7
Newchapel	173	H8
Newdigate	167	K8
New Haw	58	F6
Newlands Corner	140	E2
New Malden	46	C3
Norbiton	3	J6
Norbury	49	L2
Nork	85	G6
Norley Common	162	A4
Normandy	114	D6
Norney	159	H3
North Ascot	35	M2
North Camp	112	E3
North Cheam	65	G2
North End	195	L5
North Feltham	15	L7
Northgate	212	C1
North Holmwood	144	E7
North Looe	84	F3
North Sheen	18	E4
North Town	113	H7
Norwood Hill	169	H6
Norwood New Town	32	A7
Nutcombe	199	G7
Nutfield	127	J8
Oakhill	229	J7
Oakwoodhill	207	J2
Oatlands Park	60	B3
Ockford Ridge	159	K6
Ockham	99	H4
Ockley	188	A4
Old Coulsdon	107	L2
Old Malden	46	A7
Old Windsor	20	C1
Old Woking	97	L2
Onslow Village	138	B2
Osterley	16	F2
Ottershaw	57	M4
Outwood	171	M1
Owlsmoor	52	A7
Oxshott	81	M3
Oxted	130	A3
Pachesham Park	82	D6
Pains Hill	130	F5
Palmers Cross	183	M3
Park Barn	116	B7
Parkgate	168	A5
Park Langley	51	M6
Park Street	226	F6
Paynes Green	207	M1
Peaslake	164	A3
Peasmarsh	138	F8
Penge	32	F8
Peper Harow	158	F4
Petersham	27	H2
Pirbright	95	J5
Pitch Place	116	C3
Pitch Place	179	K6
Pixham	122	F7
Plaistow	223	J7
Pot Common	157	M7
Pound Hill	212	F1
Povey Cross	169	M8
Poyle	13	H3
Prey Heath	96	E5
Priestwood	34	B2
Purley	87	K2
Putney Heath	28	F1
Putney Vale	28	D4
Puttenham	136	E4
Pyle Hill	97	G7
Pyrford	78	C5
Pyrford Green	78	E7
Pyrford Village	78	B8
Quabrook	217	M8
Rafborough	92	B6
Ramsnest Common	221	H3
Ranmore Common	121	M7
Rapkyns	227	K5
Raynes Park	46	F3
Redhill	126	D6
Reigate	125	J8
Reigate Hill	125	J6
Richmond	18	B7
Richmond Hill	18	B8
Ridge Green	149	H3
Ripley	98	E3
The Rise	37	H6
Roehampton	19	J7
Roffey	229	K4
Rosehill	47	L8
Rose Hill	144	D2
Roundshaw	67	J5
Rowhook	207	H8
Rowledge	155	J6
Rowly	184	E3
Row Town	58	C5
Rudgwick	225	M2
Runfold	134	F6
Rushmoor	178	F2
Rusper	209	M2
Russell Hill	67	J8
Russ Hill	190	F4
Rydens	60	F1
Rydeshill	116	A6
St George's Hill	59	M7
St Helier	47	M8
St Johns	96	D1
St Margarets	17	M8
Salfords	148	E8
Sanderstead	88	C2
Sandhills	181	G8
The Sands	135	H7
Sandy Cross	135	J5
Scotswood	37	G8
Seale	135	L5
Seething Wells	44	E6
Selhurst	50	A5
Selsdon	68	F8
Selsfield Common	214	E8
Send	97	M6
Send Grove	97	L8
Send Marsh	98	C5
Shackleford	159	G2
Shalford	139	J7
Shamley Green	162	B4
Sheerwater	77	M3
Sheets Heath	95	J1
Shellwood Cross	168	B1
Shepherd's Hill	219	M3
Shepperton	41	K6
Shepperton Green	41	K4
Shere	141	K4
Shipley Bridge	193	J3
Shirley	68	F1
Shortfield Common	155	L7
Shortheath	10	D8
Shottermill	219	H3
Shrubs Hill	37	M6
Sidlow	147	L2
Sleaford	176	D8
Slinfold	227	G6
Slyfield	117	G5
Smallfield	171	K7
South Ascot	36	D6
South Beddington	67	G4
South Croydon	67	M5
South Earlswood	148	B5
Southend	33	M5
South Farnborough	93	G4
Southfields	29	K2
Southgate	212	A5
South Godstone	151	J4
South Holmwood	166	E3
South Merstham	127	G4
South Norwood	50	A3
South Nutfield	149	H2
South Park	147	H3
South Street	111	J1
South Wimbledon	29	M6
Spitals Cross	153	M6
Spreakley	177	L1
Spring Grove	17	G3
Spring Park	69	K1
Staines	22	C5
Stanwell	13	M8
Stanwell Moor	13	K8
Stoke D' Abernon	81	H5
Stonebridge		

Stonehill 57 H5	Thorpe 39 M3	Upper Ifold 223 K2	West Dulwich 32 A3	Woking 6 F6
Stoneleigh 64 C4	Thorpe Green 39 K4	Upper Norwood 50 A1	West End 61 J4	Woldingham 109 K5
Stonequarry 196 D6	Thorpe Lea 21 M8	Upper Shirley 68 F3	West End 75 J4	Woldingham Garden Village 109 J3
Stoughton 116 E5	Three Bridges 212 C2	Upper Sydenham 32 D5	West End 177 J1	Wonersh 161 M2
Strawberry Hill 26 B4	Thursley 179 M5	Upper Tooting 30 B4	West Ewell 64 B6	Woodbridge Hill 8 A1
Streatham 31 H6	Tilford 157 C6	Valley End 55 K4	Westfield 97 J4	Woodbridge Hill 116 D6
Streatham Hill 31 H2	Tilford Common 156 E8	Virginia Water 38 F3	West Green 211 M2	Woodcote 84 A6
Streatham Park 30 E5	Tilford Reeds 156 E6	Waddon 67 J1	West Heath 92 B4	Woodcote 87 H1
Streatham Vale 30 E8	Tilgate 212 A6	Wallington 66 E4	West Hill 29 H1	Woodcote Green 66 E8
Strood Green 227 L3	Tinsley Green 192 F5	Walliswood 187 H8	West Horsley 119 L2	Woodham 58 D8
Stroude 39 J2	Tisman's Common 225 K4	Walton-on-Thames 42 D8	Westhumble 122 D5	Woodhatch 147 K3
Summerstown 30 A3	Titsey 110 F7	Walton on the Hill 104 C6	West Molesey 43 J4	Woodlands 17 G5
Sunbury 42 D3	Tittenhurst 37 M3	Wanborough 136 E3	West Norwood 31 M5	Woodmansterne 86 A5
Sunbury Common 24 C8	Tolworth 45 K8	Wandle Park 4 A6	Weston Green 44 B8	Woodside 50 D6
Sunningdale 37 K5	Tongham 135 J3	Wandle Park 67 K1	Weybourne 134 C3	Wood Street Village 115 J7
Sunninghill 37 C5	Tooting Graveney 30 A6	Warlingham 89 C3	Weybridge 59 K3	Woolmer Hill 218 F2
Sunnymeads 12 B6	Tower Hill 144 E4	Warnham 228 B1	Wheelerstreet 181 J3	Worcester Park 64 E1
Sunnyside 216 B3	Troy Town 153 J4	Warren Corner 132 F2	Whitebushes 148 E5	Wormley 181 H8
Surbiton 45 C8	Trumps Green 39 C6	Warwick Wold 127 K3	Whiteley Village 60 C7	Worplesdon 116 A1
Sutton 65 K4	Tuesley 181 M1	Wasp Green 171 M2	Whitfield Court 76 A6	Worth 213 H4
Sutton Abinger 164 E1	Tulse Hill 31 L2	Waterside 174 C2	Whitton 16 F8	Worth Abbey 213 L8
Sutton Green 97 J7	Turners Hill 214 D5	Weatherhill 171 K5	Whyteleafe 88 C8	Wotton 143 H5
Tadworth 104 F4	Twickenham 26 B1	The Wells 83 J4	Wildridings 34 C4	Wray Common 126 A6
Tandridge 129 K7	Tyler's Green 128 E4	West Barnes 46 F5	Willey Green 115 G5	Wraysbury 21 H1
Tatsfield 111 G2	Tyrell's Wood 103 J6	West Bedfont 23 J1	Wimbledon 29 H6	Wrecclesham 10 B7
Teddington 26 A7	Upper Eashing 159 K5	Westbrook 159 M4	Wimble Hill 132 D7	The Wrythe 66 B1
Thames Ditton 44 D7	Upper Elmers End 51 J5	West Byfleet 78 E3	Windlesham 54 E5	Wyke 114 B6
Thorncombe Street 160 F8	Upper Hale 133 L3	West Clandon 118 E3	Wisley 79 H5	York Town 72 D5
Thornton Heath 49 H5	Upper Halliford 42 A4	Westcott 144 A4	Witley 181 J5	

USING THE STREET INDEX

Street names are listed alphabetically. Each street name is followed by its postal town or area locality, the Postcode District, the page number, and the reference to the square in which the name is found.

Example: **Abbey Dr** *TOOT* SW17................**30** D6 [1]

Some entries are followed by a number in a blue box. This number indicates the location of the street within the referenced grid square. The full street name is listed at the side of the map page.

GENERAL ABBREVIATIONS

ACC ACCESS	CTYD COURTYARD	HLS HILLS	MWY MOTORWAY	SE SOUTH EAST
ALY ALLEY	CUTT CUTTINGS	HO HOUSE	N NORTH	SER SERVICE AREA
AP APPROACH	CV COVE	HOL HOLLOW	NE NORTH EAST	SH SHORE
AR ARCADE	CYN CANYON	HOSP HOSPITAL	NW NORTH WEST	SHOP SHOPPING
ASS ASSOCIATION	DEPT DEPARTMENT	HRB HARBOUR	O/P OVERPASS	SKWY SKYWAY
AV AVENUE	DL DALE	HTH HEATH	OFF OFFICE	SMT SUMMIT
BCH BEACH	DM DAM	HTS HEIGHTS	ORCH ORCHARD	SOC SOCIETY
BLDS BUILDINGS	DR DRIVE	HVN HAVEN	OV OVAL	SP SPUR
BND BEND	DRO DROVE	HWY HIGHWAY	PAL PALACE	SPR SPRING
BNK BANK	DRY DRIVEWAY	IMP IMPERIAL	PAS PASSAGE	SQ SQUARE
BR BRIDGE	DWGS DWELLINGS	IN INLET	PAV PAVILION	ST STREET
BRK BROOK	E EAST	IND EST INDUSTRIAL ESTATE	PDE PARADE	STN STATION
BTM BOTTOM	EMB EMBANKMENT	INF INFIRMARY	PH PUBLIC HOUSE	STR STREAM
BUS BUSINESS	EMBY EMBASSY	INFO INFORMATION	PK PARK	STRD STRAND
BVD BOULEVARD	ESP ESPLANADE	INT INTERCHANGE	PKWY PARKWAY	SW SOUTH WEST
BY BYPASS	EST ESTATE	IS ISLAND	PL PLACE	TDG TRADING
CATH CATHEDRAL	EX EXCHANGE	JCT JUNCTION	PLN PLAIN	TER TERRACE
CEM CEMETERY	EXPY EXPRESSWAY	JTY JETTY	PLNS PLAINS	THWY THROUGHWAY
CEN CENTRE	EXT EXTENSION	KG KING	PLZ PLAZA	TNL TUNNEL
CFT CROFT	F/O FLYOVER	KNL KNOLL	POL POLICE STATION	TOLL TOLLWAY
CH CHURCH	FC FOOTBALL CLUB	L LAKE	PR PRINCE	TPK TURNPIKE
CHA CHASE	FK FORK	LA LANE	PREC PRECINCT	TR TRACK
CHYD CHURCHYARD	FLD FIELD	LDG LODGE	PREP PREPARATORY	TRL TRAIL
CIR CIRCLE	FLDS FIELDS	LGT LIGHT	PRIM PRIMARY	TWR TOWER
CIRC CIRCUS	FLS FALLS	LK LOCK	PROM PROMENADE	U/P UNDERPASS
CL CLOSE	FLS FLATS	LKS LAKES	PRS PRINCESS	UNI UNIVERSITY
CLFS CLIFFS	FM FARM	LNDG LANDING	PRT PORT	UPR UPPER
CMP CAMP	FT FORT	LTL LITTLE	PT POINT	V VALE
CNR CORNER	FWY FREEWAY	LWR LOWER	PTH PATH	VA VALLEY
CO COUNTY	FY FERRY	MAG MAGISTRATE	PZ PIAZZA	VIAD VIADUCT
COLL COLLEGE	GA GATE	MAN MANSIONS	QD QUADRANT	VIL VILLA
COM COMMON	GAL GALLERY	MD MEAD	QU QUEEN	VIS VISTA
COMM COMMISSION	GDN GARDEN	MDW MEADOWS	QY QUAY	VLG VILLAGE
CON CONVENT	GDNS GARDENS	MEM MEMORIAL	R RIVER	VLS VILLAS
COT COTTAGE	GLD GLADE	MKT MARKET	RBT ROUNDABOUT	VW VIEW
COTS COTTAGES	GLN GLEN	MKTS MARKETS	RD ROAD	W WEST
CP CAPE	GN GREEN	ML MALL	RDG RIDGE	WD WOOD
CPS COPSE	GND GROUND	ML MILL	REP REPUBLIC	WHF WHARF
CR CREEK	GRA GRANGE	MNR MANOR	RES RESERVOIR	WK WALK
CREM CREMATORIUM	GRG GARAGE	MS MEWS	RFC RUGBY FOOTBALL CLUB	WKS WALKS
CRS CRESCENT	GT GREAT	MSN MISSION	RI RISE	WLS WELLS
CSWY CAUSEWAY	GTWY GATEWAY	MT MOUNT	RP RAMP	WY WAY
CT COURT	GV GROVE	MTN MOUNTAIN	RW ROW	YD YARD
CTRL CENTRAL	HGR HIGHER	MTS MOUNTAINS	S SOUTH	YHA YOUTH HOSTEL
CTS COURTS	HL HILL	MUS MUSEUM	SCH SCHOOL	

POSTCODE TOWNS AND AREA ABBREVIATIONS

ADL/WDHM Addlestone/Woodham	CHEAM Cheam	FNM Farnham	LING Lingfield	STMC/STPC St Mary Cray/St Paul's Cray
ALDT Aldershot	CHERT Chertsey	FRIM Frimley	LIPH Liphook	STRHM/NOR Streatham/Norbury
ALTN Alton	CHOB/PIR Chobham/Pirbright	FSTH Forest Hill	LTWR Lightwater	STWL/WRAY Stanwell/Wraysbury
ASC Ascot	CHSGTN Chessington	FUL/PGN Fulham/Parsons Green	MFD/CHID Milford/Chiddingfold	SUN Sunbury
ASHF Ashford (Surrey)	CHSWK Chiswick	GDST Godstone	MORT/ESHN Mortlake/East Sheen	SURB Surbiton
ASHTD Ashtead	CLAP Clapham	GODL Godalming	MRDN Morden	SUT Sutton
ASHV Ash Vale	COB Cobham	GSHT Grayshott	MTCM Mitcham	SWTR Southwater
BAGS Bagshot	COUL/CHIP Coulsdon/Chipstead	GT/LBKH Great Bookham/Little Bookham	NRWD Norwood	SYD Sydenham
BAL Balham	CRAN Cranleigh	GU Guildford	NWMAL New Malden	TEDD Teddington
BARN Barnes	CRAWE Crawley east	GUW Guildford west	ORP Orpington	THDIT Thames Ditton
BECK Beckenham	CRAWW Crawley west	HASM Haslemere	OXTED Oxted	THHTH Thornton Heath
BELMT Belmont	CROY/NA Croydon/New Addington	HAYES Hayes	PETW Petworth	TOOT Tooting
BF/WBF Byfleet/West Byfleet	CTHM Caterham	HEST Heston	PGE/AN Penge/Anerley	TWK Twickenham
BFOR Bracknell Forest/Windlesham	CWTH Crowthorne	HMSMTH Hammersmith	PUR/KEN Purley/Kenley	VW Virginia Water
BH/WHM Biggin Hill/Westerham	DORK Dorking	HNHL Herne Hill	PUT/ROE Putney/Roehampton	WAND/EARL Wandsworth/Earlsfield
BIL Billingshurst	DTCH/LGLY Datchet/Langley	HOR/WEW Horton/West Ewell	RCH/KEW Richmond/Kew	WARL Warlingham
BLKW Blackwater	DUL Dulwich	HORL Horley	RCHPK/HAM Richmond Park/Ham	WDR/YW West Drayton/Yiewsley
BMLY Bromley	E/WMO/HCT East & West Molesey/Hampton Court	HORS Horsham	RDKG Rural Dorking	WDSR Windsor
BNFD Binfield	EBED/NFELT East Bedfont/North Feltham	HPTN Hampton	REDH Redhill	WEY Weybridge
BNSTD Banstead	EDEN Edenbridge	HSLW Hounslow	REIG Reigate	WHTN Whitton
BOR Bordon	EDUL East Dulwich	HSLWW Hounslow west	RFNM Rural Farnham	WIM/MER Wimbledon/Merton
BRAK Bracknell	EGH Egham	HTHAIR Heathrow Airport	RGUE Rural Guildford east	WLGTN Wallington
BRKHM/BTCW Brockham/Betchworth	EGRIN East Grinstead	HYS/HAR Hayes/Harlington	RGUW Rural Guildford west	WNWD West Norwood
BROCKY Brockley	EHSLY East Horsley	ISLW Isleworth	RPLY/SEND Ripley/Send	WOKN/KNAP Woking north/Knaphill
BRXS/STRHMH Brixton south/Streatham Hill	EPSOM Epsom	KUT Kingston upon Thames	RSEV Rural Sevenoaks	WOKS/MYFD Woking south/Mayford
BRYLDS Berrylands	ESH/CLAY Esher/Claygate	KUTN/CMB Kingston upon Thames north/Coombe	RYNPK Raynes Park	WOT/HER Walton-on-Thames/Hersham
BTFD Brentford	EW Ewell	KWD/TDW/WH Kingswood/Tadworth/Walton on the Hill	SAND/SEL Sanderstead/Selsdon	WPK Worcester Park
BTSEA Battersea	EWKG Wokingham east	LEW Lewisham	SHGR Shamley Green	WWKM West Wickham
CAR Carshalton	FARN Farnborough	LHD/OX Leatherhead/Oxshott	SHPTN Shepperton	
CAT Catford	FELT Feltham		SHST Sandhurst	
CBLY Camberley			SNWD South Norwood	
			STA Staines	

10th Av *KWD/TDW/WH* KT20 ...... **105** H8
11th Av *KWD/TDW/WH* KT20 ...... **105** H7
12th Av *KWD/TDW/WH* KT20 ...... **105** H8
13th Av *KWD/TDW/WH* KT20 ...... **105** H8
14th Av *KWD/TDW/WH* KT20 ...... **105** H8
15th Av *KWD/TDW/WH* KT20 ...... **105** J8
16th Av *KWD/TDW/WH* KT20 ...... **105** H7
1st Av *KWD/TDW/WH* KT20 ...... **105** H7
2nd Av *KWD/TDW/WH* KT20 ...... **105** H7
3rd Av *KWD/TDW/WH* KT20 ...... **105** H7
4th Av *KWD/TDW/WH* KT20 ...... **105** H7
5th Av *KWD/TDW/WH* KT20 ...... **105** H7
6th Av *KWD/TDW/WH* KT20 ...... **105** F5
7th Av *KWD/TDW/WH* KT20 ...... **105** H8
8th Av *KWD/TDW/WH* KT20 ...... **105** H7
9th Av *KWD/TDW/WH* KT20 ...... **105** H7

A

Aaron's HI *RGODL* GU7 ...... **159** M5
Abbess CI *BRXS/STRHM* SW2 ...... **31** L2
Abbetts La *CBLY* GU15 ...... **72** E6
Abbey CI *BRAK* RG12 ...... **35** G5
  WOKS/MYFD GU22 ...... **78** B6
Abbey Dr *STA* TW18 ...... **40** F4
  TOOT SW17 ...... **30** D6 [1]
Abbey Gdns *CHERT* KT16 ...... **40** D6 [1]
Abbey Gn *CHERT* KT16 ...... **40** D6 [1]
Abbey La *BECK* BR3 ...... **33** K8
Abbey Pk *BECK* BR3 ...... **33** K8
Abbey Rd *CHERT* KT16 ...... **40** E7
  CROY/NA CR0 ...... **4** B7
  SAND/SEL CR2 ...... **69** G8
  SHPTN TW17 ...... **41** K8
  VW GU25 ...... **39** C5
  WIM/MER SW19 ...... **29** M8
  WOKN/KNAP GU21 ...... **76** F7
Abbey St *FNM* GU9 ...... **11** C1
Abbey Wk *E/WMO/HCT* KT8 ...... **43** L3
Abbey Wy *FARN* GU14 ...... **92** F5
Abbey Wd *ASC* SL5 ...... **37** K7
Abbot CI *BF/WBF* KT14 ...... **59** G8
  STA TW18 ...... **23** G8
Abbot Rd *GU* GU1 ...... **9** H8
Abbotsbury *BRAK* RG12 ...... **34** C5
Abbotsbury Ct *SWTR* RH13 ...... **229** H6
Abbotsbury Rd *MRDN* SM4 ...... **47** L4
  WWKM BR4 ...... **70** C1
Abbot's CI *GUW* GU2 ...... **138** B3
Abbots Dr *VW* GU25 ...... **38** F4
Abbotsfield Rd
  CRAWW RH11 ...... **211** G4 [1]
Abbotsford CI
  WOKS/MYFD GU22 ...... **7** H5 [1]
Abbots Gn *CROY/NA* CR0 ...... **69** G5
Abbots La *PUR/KEN* CR8 ...... **87** M5
Abbotsleigh CI *BELMT* SM2 ...... **65** L6 [1]
Abbotsleigh Rd
  STRHM/NOR SW16 ...... **30** F5
Abbots Pk *BRXS/STRHM* SW2 ...... **31** K2
Abbot's Ride *FNM* GU9 ...... **11** M3
Abbotstone Rd
  PUT/ROE SW15 ...... **19** M5 [1]
Abbots Wk *CTHM* CR3 ...... **108** K4
Abbots Wy *BECK* BR3 ...... **51** H5
  GU GU1 ...... **118** A7
Abbotswood *GU* GU1 ...... **117** J6
Abbotswood CI *GU* GU1 ...... **117** J5 [1]
Abbotswood Dr *WEY* KT13 ...... **60** A8
Abbotswood Rd
  STRHM/NOR SW16 ...... **31** G2
Abbott Av *RYNPK* SW20 ...... **47** G2
Abbott CI *HPTN* TW12 ...... **25** H7 [1]
Abbotts Ri *REDH* RH1 ...... **126** D6
Abbotts Rd *CHEAM* SM3 ...... **65** H3
  MTCM CR4 ...... **48** F4
Abbotts Tilt *WOT/HER* KT12 ...... **61** H2
Abelia CI *CHOB/PIR* GU24 ...... **75** H3 [1]
Abercairn Rd *STRHM/NOR* SW16 ...... **30** F8
Aberconway Rd *MRDN* SM4 ...... **47** L3
Abercorn CI *SAND/SEL* CR2 ...... **89** G2
Abercorn Wy *WOKN/KNAP* GU21 ...... **76** D8
Aberdare CI *WWKM* BR4 ...... **69** M1 [1]
Aberdeen Rd *CROY/NA* CR0 ...... **67** M3
Aberfoyle Rd *STRHM/NOR* SW16 ...... **31** G7
Abingdon CI *BRAK* RG12 ...... **35** H5 [1]
  WIM/MER SW19 ...... **29** M7 [1]
  WOKN/KNAP GU21 ...... **76** E8
Abingdon Rd *STRHM/NOR* SW16 ...... **49** H1
Abinger Av *BELMT* SM2 ...... **64** F7
Abinger CI *RDKG* RH5 ...... **144** F6
  WLGTN SM6 ...... **67** H4
Abinger Common Rd
  RDKG RH5 ...... **165** H2
Abinger Gdns *ISLW* TW7 ...... **17** H5 [1]
Abinger La *RDKG* RH5 ...... **143** G8
Abinger Rd *RDKG* RH5 ...... **165** K8
  REDH RH1 ...... **148** B3
Abinger Wy *RGUE* GU4 ...... **117** L3
Aboyne Dr *RYNPK* SW20 ...... **46** D2
Aboyne Rd *TOOT* SW17 ...... **30** A4
Abrahams Rd *CRAWW* RH11 ...... **211** K8
Acacia Av *BTFD* TW8 ...... **17** L2
  SHPTN TW17 ...... **41** K5
  SHST GU47 ...... **52** A8
  STWL/WRAY TW19 ...... **12** B6
  WOKS/MYFD GU22 ...... **97** G2
Acacia CI *ADL/WDHM* KT15 ...... **58** C8
Acacia Ct *BRAK* RG12 ...... **34** E3
Acacia Dr *ADL/WDHM* KT15 ...... **78** C1
  CHEAM SM3 ...... **47** J8
  EW KT17 ...... **85** G4 [1]
Acacia Gdns *WWKM* BR4 ...... **69** M1
Acacia Gv *DUL* SE21 ...... **32** A3
  NWMAL KT3 ...... **46** B3
Acacia Ms *WDR/YW* UB7 ...... **14** A1
Acacia Rd *BECK* BR3 ...... **51** J3
  GU GU1 ...... **9** G3
  HPTN TW12 ...... **25** K7
  MTCM CR4 ...... **48** D1
  STA TW18 ...... **22** E6
  STRHM/NOR SW16 ...... **49** H1
Academy CI *CBLY* GU15 ...... **73** H1
Academy Gdns *CROY/NA* CR0 ...... **5** K4

Accommodation La
  WDR/YW UB7 ...... **13** M1
Accommodation Rd
  CHERT KT16 ...... **57** G2
Acer Dr *CHOB/PIR* GU24 ...... **75** J3
Acer Rd *BH/WHM* TN16 ...... **91** G6
Acheulian CI *FNM* GU9 ...... **11** H5
Ackroyd Rd *FSTH* SE23 ...... **33** G1
Acorn CI *EGRIN* RH19 ...... **216** B1
  HORL RH6 ...... **170** F5
  HPTN TW12 ...... **25** L7 [1]
Acorn Gdns *NRWD* SE19 ...... **50** C1
Acorn Gv *HYS/HAR* UB3 ...... **15** J2
  KWD/TDW/WH KT20 ...... **105** J6 [1]
Acorn Keep *FNM* GU9 ...... **134** A1
Acorns *SWTR* RH13 ...... **229** K5
The Acorns *CRAWW* RH11 ...... **211** L8
  HORL RH6 ...... **171** L6
Acorn Wy *FSTH* SE23 ...... **33** G4
  ORP BR6 ...... **71** L3
Acre La *CAR* SM5 ...... **66** D3
  WLGTN SM6 ...... **66** D3
Acre Rd *KUTN/CMB* KT2 ...... **3** C3
  WIM/MER SW19 ...... **30** A7
Acres Gdns
  KWD/TDW/WH KT20 ...... **104** F3
Acres Platt *CRAN* GU6 ...... **185** J5
Acuba Rd *WAND/EARL* SW18 ...... **29** L3
Adair CI *SNWD* SE25 ...... **50** E3
Adams CI *BRYLDS* KT5 ...... **45** J4
Adams Cft *CHOB/PIR* GU24 ...... **94** F2
Adams Park Rd *FNM* GU9 ...... **134** A5
Adamsrill Rd *SYD* SE26 ...... **33** G5
Adams Rd *BECK* BR3 ...... **51** H5
Adams Wy *SNWD* SE25 ...... **50** C6
Adare Wk *STRHM/NOR* SW16 ...... **31** J4
Addington Gv *SYD* SE26 ...... **33** H5
Addington Rd *CROY/NA* CR0 ...... **49** K8
  SAND/SEL CR2 ...... **88** D1
  WWKM BR4 ...... **70** A2
Addington Village Rd
  CROY/NA CR0 ...... **69** J5
Addiscombe Av *CROY/NA* CR0 ...... **5** L2
Addiscombe Court Rd
  CROY/NA CR0 ...... **5** H4
Addiscombe Gv *CROY/NA* CR0 ...... **4** F6
Addiscombe Rd *CROY/NA* CR0 ...... **5** G6
Addison Av *HSLW* TW3 ...... **16** F3
Addison CI *CTHM* CR3 ...... **108** A4
Addison Gdns *BRYLDS* KT5 ...... **45** J4
Addison Rd *CTHM* CR3 ...... **108** A3
  FRIM GU16 ...... **93** H1
  GU GU1 ...... **9** L7
  SNWD SE25 ...... **50** D4
  TEDD TW11 ...... **26** E7
Addison's CI *CROY/NA* CR0 ...... **69** J1
Addlestone Moor
  ADL/WDHM KT15 ...... **58** F1
Addlestone Pk
  ADL/WDHM KT15 ...... **58** E4
Addlestone Rd
  ADL/WDHM KT15 ...... **59** H3 [1]
Adecroft Wy *E/WMO/HCT* KT8 ...... **43** M3
Adela Av *NWMAL* KT3 ...... **46** E5
  HORS RH12 ...... **229** J5 [1]
Adelaide CI *CRAWW* RH11 ...... **192** A8 [1]
Adelaide PI *WEY* KT13 ...... **60** A3
Adelaide Rd *ASHF* TW15 ...... **23** G6
  HEST TW5 ...... **16** B3
  RCH/KEW TW9 ...... **18** C6 [1]
  SURB KT6 ...... **45** H5
  TEDD TW11 ...... **26** C7 [1]
  WOT/HER KT12 ...... **60** D2
Adelina Ms *BAL* SW12 ...... **31** G2
Adelphi CI *CRAWE* RH10 ...... **213** G5 [1]
Adelphi Rd *EW* KT17 ...... **84** A3
Adenmore Rd *CAT* SE6 ...... **33** K1
Adlers La *RDKG* RH5 ...... **122** D5
Adlington PI *FARN* GU14 ...... **93** H7 [1]
Admiral Rd *CRAWW* RH11 ...... **211** K6
Admiral's Bridge La
  EGRIN RH19 ...... **215** M7
Admirals Ct *GU* GU1 ...... **117** L7
Admiralty Rd *TEDD* TW11 ...... **26** C8
Admiralty Wy *CBLY* GU15 ...... **72** C5
Adolf St *CAT* SE6 ...... **33** K5
Advance Rd *WNWD* SE27 ...... **31** M5 [1]
Aerodrome Wy *HEST* TW5 ...... **15** M1 [1]
Aerospace Bvd *ALDT* GU11 ...... **112** D2
  FARN GU14 ...... **112** C2
Agar CI *SURB* KT6 ...... **63** J1
Agate La *HORS* RH12 ...... **229** K3
Agates La *ASHTD* KT21 ...... **83** G8
Agincourt PI *ASC* SL5 ...... **36** F3
Agnew Rd *FSTH* SE23 ...... **33** H1
Agraria Rd *GUW* GU2 ...... **8** C6
Ailsa Av *TWK* TW1 ...... **17** K7
Ailsa CI *CRAWW* RH11 ...... **211** L6
Ailsa Rd *TWK* TW1 ...... **17** L7
Ainger CI *ASHV* GU12 ...... **113** G7
Ainsdale Wy *WOKN/KNAP* GU21 ...... **76** D7
Ainsworth Rd *CROY/NA* CR0 ...... **4** B5
Aintree CI *DTCH/LGLY* SL3 ...... **13** H3
Aintree Rd *CRAWE* RH10 ...... **212** D5
Aircraft Esp *FARN* GU14 ...... **92** F8 [1]
Airedale Rd *BAL* SW12 ...... **30** C1
Airport Wy *HORL* RH6 ...... **192** D1
  STWL/WRAY TW19 ...... **13** K6
Aisne Rd *FRIM* GU16 ...... **74** B8
Aitken CI *MTCM* CR4 ...... **48** C7 [1]
Aitken Rd *CAT* SE6 ...... **33** L3
Akabusi CI *SNWD* SE25 ...... **50** D6 [1]
Akehurst La *CRAWE* RH10 ...... **193** K6
Akehurst St *PUT/ROE* SW15 ...... **19** K8
Akerman Rd *SURB* KT6 ...... **44** F6
Alamein Rd *ALDT* GU11 ...... **112** E6
Alanbrooke CI
  WOKN/KNAP GU21 ...... **75** M8
Alanbrooke Rd *ALDT* GU11 ...... **113** G3
Alan Rd *WIM/MER* SW19 ...... **29** H6
Albain Crs *ASHF* TW15 ...... **23** H3
Albany CI *ESH/CLAY* KT10 ...... **61** K7
  MORT/ESHN SW14 ...... **18** E6
Albany Crs *ESH/CLAY* KT10 ...... **62** B5
Albany Ms *KUTN/CMB* KT2 ...... **2** D1 [1]
  SUT SM1 ...... **65** L4 [1]
Albany Pk *DTCH/LGLY* SL3 ...... **13** G2
  FRIM GU16 ...... **72** F8

Albany Park Rd *KUTN/CMB* KT2 ...... **2** D1
  LHD/OX KT22 ...... **102** D1
Albany PI *BTFD* TW8 ...... **18** A1 [1]
  EGH TW20 ...... **21** L5
Albany Rd *BTFD* TW8 ...... **18** A1 [1]
  CRAWW RH11 ...... **211** M3
  NWMAL KT3 ...... **46** A4
  RCHPK/HAM TW10 ...... **18** C7 [1]
  WIM/MER SW19 ...... **29** L6
  WOT/HER KT12 ...... **61** G3
The Albanys *REIG* RH2 ...... **125** K5
The Albany *KUTN/CMB* KT2 ...... **2** D1
Albatross Gdns *SAND/SEL* CR2 ...... **89** G1
Albemarle Av *WHTN* TW2 ...... **25** J2
Albemarle Gdns *NWMAL* KT3 ...... **46** A4
Albemarle Rd *BECK* BR3 ...... **51** L1
Albemarle *RGUW* GU3 ...... **116** C8
Albert Carr Gdns
  STRHM/NOR SW16 ...... **31** H6
Albert Dr *WIM/MER* SW19 ...... **29** H3
  WOKN/KNAP GU21 ...... **7** K2
Albert Gv *RYNPK* SW20 ...... **47** G1
Albertine CI *EW* KT17 ...... **84** E6
Albert Rd *ADL/WDHM* KT15 ...... **59** G2
  ALDT GU11 ...... **112** E7
  ASHF TW15 ...... **23** J6 [1]
  ASHTD KT21 ...... **83** J8
  BAGS GU19 ...... **54** B8
  BNFD RG42 ...... **34** E1
  CBLY GU15 ...... **72** F4 [1]
  EGH TW20 ...... **21** G7
  EW KT17 ...... **84** C3
  FARN GU14 ...... **92** F7
  HORL RH6 ...... **170** D6
  HPTN TW12 ...... **25** M6 [1]
  HSLW TW3 ...... **16** D6
  KUT KT1 ...... **3** C6
  KUTN/CMB KT2 ...... **3** J3
  MTCM CR4 ...... **48** C3
  NWMAL KT3 ...... **46** C4
  PGE/AN SE20 ...... **33** G8
  RCHPK/HAM TW10 ...... **18** B7
  REDH RH1 ...... **126** F3
  SNWD SE25 ...... **50** E4
  SUT SM1 ...... **66** A4
  TEDD TW11 ...... **26** C7
  TWK TW1 ...... **26** C2
  WARL CR6 ...... **89** H7
Albert Rd North *REIG* RH2 ...... **125** J7
Albert Sq *GU* GU1 ...... **9** J5
Albert Ter *GU* GU1 ...... **9** J5
Albery CI *HORS* RH12 ...... **228** E3
Albion CI *CRAWE* RH10 ...... **213** G4 [1]
Albion Rd *BELMT* SM2 ...... **66** A5
  HSLW TW3 ...... **16** D6
  KUTN/CMB KT2 ...... **45** M1
  REIG RH2 ...... **147** M1
  WHTN TW2 ...... **26** B2
Albion St *CROY/NA* CR0 ...... **4** A4
Albion Villas Rd *FSTH* SE23 ...... **32** F4
Albion Wy *EDEN* TN8 ...... **153** M5
  HORS RH12 ...... **228** E7
  SWTR RH13 ...... **229** C8
Albury Av *BELMT* SM2 ...... **64** F7
  ISLW TW7 ...... **17** J2
Albury CI *CHERT* KT16 ...... **56** D2
  HPTN TW12 ...... **25** K7
Albury Keep *HORL* RH6 ...... **170** E5 [1]
Albury Rd *CHSGTN* KT9 ...... **63** H4
  GU GU1 ...... **9** M5
  REDH RH1 ...... **126** F3
  WOT/HER KT12 ...... **60** B5
Albury St *SHGR* GU5 ...... **140** F5
Alcester Rd *WLGTN* SM6 ...... **66** E3
Alcock CI *WLGTN* SM6 ...... **67** G6
Alcock Rd *HEST* TW5 ...... **16** A2
Alcocks CI *KWD/TDW/WH* KT20 ...... **105** K2
Alcocks La *KWD/TDW/WH* KT20 ...... **105** H2
Alcorn CI *CHEAM* SM3 ...... **47** J8
Aldenham Ter *BRAK* RG12 ...... **34** F6 [1]
Aldenholme *WEY* KT13 ...... **60** B5
Alderbrook Rd *CRAN* GU6 ...... **184** E2
Alderbury Rd *BARN* SW13 ...... **19** K1
Alder CI *ASHV* GU12 ...... **113** K2 [1]
  CRAWE RH10 ...... **214** E1
  EGH TW20 ...... **21** H6
Aldercombe La *CTHM* CR3 ...... **128** B1
Aldermoor Rd *CAT* SE6 ...... **33** J4
Alderney Av *HEST* TW5 ...... **16** E2
Alder Rd *MORT/ESHN* SW14 ...... **19** C5
Alders Av *EGRIN* RH19 ...... **196** A6
Aldersbrook Dr *KUTN/CMB* KT2 ...... **27** J7
Aldersey Rd *GU* GU1 ...... **9** M4
Aldersgrove *E/WMO/HCT* KT8 ...... **44** A5
Aldershot Rd *ASHV* GU12 ...... **113** J8
  CHOB/PIR GU24 ...... **95** J4
  GUW GU2 ...... **116** E6 [1]
  RGUW GU3 ...... **115** H4
Alderside Wk *EGH* TW20 ...... **21** C6
Aldersmead Av *CROY/NA* CR0 ...... **51** G6
Aldersmead Rd *BECK* BR3 ...... **33** H8
Alders Rd *REIG* RH2 ...... **125** L6
Alderstead La *REDH* RH1 ...... **107** G7
The Alders *BF/WBF* KT14 ...... **78** F2
  FELT TW13 ...... **25** H6
  NWDGN UB2 ...... **16** C1
  WWKM BR4 ...... **69** M1
Alders View Dr *EGRIN* RH19 ...... **196** B5 [1]
Alderton Rd *CROY/NA* CR0 ...... **5** K1
Alderwick Dr *HSLW* TW3 ...... **17** G5
Alderwood CI *CTHM* CR3 ...... **108** B7
Aldingbourne CI *CRAWW* RH11 ...... **211** J2
Aldis Ms *TOOT* SW17 ...... **30** B6 [1]
Aldis St *TOOT* SW17 ...... **30** B6
Aldren Rd *TOOT* SW17 ...... **29** M4
Aldrich Crs *CROY/NA* CR0 ...... **69** M7
Aldrich Gdns *CHEAM* SM3 ...... **65** J2 [1]
Aldrich Ter *WAND/EARL* SW18 ...... **29** M3 [1]
Aldridge Ri *NWMAL* KT3 ...... **46** B7
Aldrin PI *FARN* GU14 ...... **92** A5
Aldwick CI *FARN* GU14 ...... **92** D3
Aldwick Rd *CROY/NA* CR0 ...... **67** J2
Aldworth CI *BRAK* RG12 ...... **34** C4
Aldwyn PI *NRWD* SE19 ...... **32** C8
Alexander Evans Ms
  FSTH SE23 ...... **33** G3 [1]

Alexander Godley CI
  ASHTD KT21 ...... **103** J1
Alexander Rd *COUL/CHIP* CR5 ...... **86** E5
  EGH TW20 ...... **21** L6
  REIG RH2 ...... **147** K3
Alexanders Wk *CTHM* CR3 ...... **108** C8
Alexandra Av *CBLY* GU15 ...... **72** D4
  SUT SM1 ...... **65** K2
  WARL CR6 ...... **89** J7
Alexandra Ct *ASHF* TW15 ...... **24** A8 [1]
  FARN GU14 ...... **92** F8 [2]
  WOT/HER KT12 ...... **60** D1 [1]
Alexandra Dr *BRYLDS* KT5 ...... **45** K7
  NRWD SE19 ...... **32** B6
Alexandra Gdns *CAR* SM5 ...... **66** D7 [1]
  HSLW TW3 ...... **16** E4
  WOKN/KNAP GU21 ...... **75** M8
Alexandra PI *CROY/NA* CR0 ...... **5** G3 [1]
  GU GU1 ...... **9** L4
  SNWD SE25 ...... **50** A5 [1]
Alexandra Rd *ADL/WDHM* KT15 ...... **59** G3
  ASHF TW15 ...... **24** A8
  ASHV GU12 ...... **113** J8
  BH/WHM TN16 ...... **110** E1
  BTFD TW8 ...... **18** A1 [1]
  CROY/NA CR0 ...... **5** G3
  EGH TW20 ...... **20** F7
  EW KT17 ...... **84** C3
  FARN GU14 ...... **92** F7
  HSLW TW3 ...... **16** E4
  KUTN/CMB KT2 ...... **3** J3
  MORT/ESHN SW14 ...... **19** G5
  RCH/KEW TW9 ...... **18** C4
  SYD SE26 ...... **33** G7
  THDIT KT7 ...... **44** C5
  TWK TW1 ...... **17** M8
  WARL CR6 ...... **89** H7
  WIM/MER SW19 ...... **30** B8
Alexandra Sq *MRDN* SM4 ...... **47** K5
Alexandra Ter *GU* GU1 ...... **9** J5
Alfold By-pass *CRAN* GU6 ...... **204** C3
Alfold Rd *MFD/CHID* GU8 ...... **203** J5
Alfonso CI *ASHV* GU12 ...... **134** F1 [1]
Alford CI *RGUE* GU4 ...... **117** J3
Alford Gn *CROY/NA* CR0 ...... **70** A5
Alfred CI *CRAWE* RH10 ...... **213** H4
Alfred Rd *FELT* TW13 ...... **24** F3
  FNM GU9 ...... **11** H1
  KUT KT1 ...... **2** F9
  SNWD SE25 ...... **50** D5
  SUT SM1 ...... **65** M4
Alfreton CI *WIM/MER* SW19 ...... **29** C4
Alfriston *BRYLDS* KT5 ...... **45** J6
Alfriston Av *CROY/NA* CR0 ...... **49** H7
Alfriston CI *BRYLDS* KT5 ...... **45** J6 [1]
Alfriston Rd *FRIM* GU16 ...... **93** M2
Algar Rd *ISLW* TW7 ...... **17** K5
Algarve Rd *WAND/EARL* SW18 ...... **29** L2
Alice Ms *TEDD* TW11 ...... **26** C6
Alice Rd *ALDT* GU11 ...... **112** E7 [1]
Alice Wy *HSLW* TW3 ...... **16** E6
Alicia Av *CRAWE* RH10 ...... **212** E3
Alington Gv *WLGTN* SM6 ...... **67** G7
Alison CI *CROY/NA* CR0 ...... **51** G8 [1]
  FARN GU14 ...... **92** C6
  WOKN/KNAP GU21 ...... **6** D1
Alison Dr *CBLY* GU15 ...... **73** J4
Alison's Rd *ALDT* GU11 ...... **112** D4
Alison Wy *ALDT* GU11 ...... **112** C7
Allan CI *NWMAL* KT3 ...... **46** A5 [1]
Allbrook CI *TEDD* TW11 ...... **26** B6
Allcard CI *HORS* RH12 ...... **229** G4
Allcot CI *CRAWW* RH11 ...... **211** H6
  EBED/NFELT TW14 ...... **24** C2 [1]
Alden Av *ASHV* GU12 ...... **135** G2
Aldens La *MFD/CHID* GU8 ...... **160** E7
Allenby Av *SAND/SEL* CR2 ...... **67** M7
Allenby Rd *BH/WHM* TN16 ...... **91** H7
  CBLY GU15 ...... **72** D3
  FSTH SE23 ...... **33** H4
Allen House Pk
  WOKS/MYFD GU22 ...... **96** F2
Allen Rd *BECK* BR3 ...... **51** G2
  CROY/NA CR0 ...... **49** J7
  GT/LBKH KT23 ...... **101** L8
  SUN TW16 ...... **42** E1
Allen's CI *EGRIN* RH19 ...... **217** G3
Allerford Rd *CAT* SE6 ...... **33** L5
Alleyn Crs *DUL* SE21 ...... **32** A3
Alleyn Pk *DUL* SE21 ...... **32** A3
Alleyn Rd *DUL* SE21 ...... **32** A4
Allgood CI *MRDN* SM4 ...... **47** G6
All Hallows Av *CHOB/PIR* GU24 ...... **95** L4
Allingham Rd *REIG* RH2 ...... **147** K3
Allington Av *SHPTN* TW17 ...... **42** B3 [1]
Allington CI *WIM/MER* SW19 ...... **29** G6 [1]
Allison Gv *DUL* SE21 ...... **32** B2
Alloway CI *WOKN/KNAP* GU21 ...... **76** E8
All Saints Crs *FARN* GU14 ...... **72** B8
All Saints Dr *SAND/SEL* CR2 ...... **88** C1
All Saints Rd *LTWR* GU18 ...... **54** F8
  SUT SM1 ...... **65** L2
  WIM/MER SW19 ...... **29** M8
Allsmoor La *BRAK* RG12 ...... **35** G1
All Souls Av *CHOB/PIR* GU24 ...... **95** L3
All Souls' Rd *ASC* SL5 ...... **36** D5
Allum Gv *KWD/TDW/WH* KT20 ...... **104** E3
Allwood CI *SYD* SE26 ...... **33** G5
Allyington Wy *CRAWE* RH10 ...... **213** G4
Allyn CI *STA* TW18 ...... **22** C7
Alma CI *ASHV* GU12 ...... **113** G6
  WOKN/KNAP GU21 ...... **76** B7
Alma Crs *SUT* SM1 ...... **65** H4
Alma Gdns *FRIM* GU16 ...... **94** A1
Alma PI *NRWD* SE19 ...... **32** C8
  THHTH CR7 ...... **49** K5
Alma Rd *CAR* SM5 ...... **66** B4
  ESH/CLAY KT10 ...... **44** B8
  REIG RH2 ...... **125** L7
Alma Ter *WAND/EARL* SW18 ...... **30** A1
Alma Wy *FNM* GU9 ...... **134** A2

Almer Rd *RYNPK* SW20 ...... **28** D8
Almners Rd *CHERT* KT16 ...... **39** M6
Almond Av *CAR* SM5 ...... **66** C1
  WOKS/MYFD GU22 ...... **97** G3
Almond CI *CRAWW* RH11 ...... **211** K4 [1]
  EGH TW20 ...... **20** E7
  FARN GU14 ...... **92** D2
  GU GU1 ...... **117** G4
  SHPTN TW17 ...... **41** M2
Almond Gv *BTFD* TW8 ...... **17** L2
Almond Rd *HOR/WEW* KT19 ...... **84** A1
Almond Wy *MTCM* CR4 ...... **49** G5
Almorah Rd *HEST* TW5 ...... **16** A3
Almsgate *RGUW* GU3 ...... **137** M7
Almshouse La *CHSGTN* KT9 ...... **62** F7
Alnwick Gv *MRDN* SM4 ...... **47** L4 [1]
Alphabet Gdns *CAR* SM5 ...... **48** A6 [1]
Alpha Rd *BRYLDS* KT5 ...... **45** J6
  CHOB/PIR GU24 ...... **56** C8
  CRAWW RH11 ...... **211** M3
  CROY/NA CR0 ...... **5** G3
  HPTN TW12 ...... **26** A6 [1]
  WOKS/MYFD GU22 ...... **7** K3
Alpha Wy *EGH* TW20 ...... **39** M1
Alphea CI *WIM/MER* SW19 ...... **30** E1
Alphington Av *FRIM* GU16 ...... **73** J8
Alphington Gn *FRIM* GU16 ...... **73** H8
Alpine Av *BRYLDS* KT5 ...... **63** M1
Alpine CI *CROY/NA* CR0 ...... **5** G8
  FARN GU14 ...... **92** A6
Alpine Rd *REDH* RH1 ...... **126** D5
  WOT/HER KT12 ...... **42** D7
Alpine Vw *SUT* SM1 ...... **66** B4
Alresford Rd *GUW* GU2 ...... **8** A5
Alric Av *NWMAL* KT3 ...... **46** B3
Alsford CI *LTWR* GU18 ...... **74** C2
Alsom Av *HOR/WEW* KT19 ...... **64** C3
Alston CI *THDIT* KT7 ...... **44** E7
Alston Rd *TOOT* SW17 ...... **30** A5
Alterton CI *WOKN/KNAP* GU21 ...... **76** D7
Alt Gv *WIM/MER* SW19 ...... **29** J8
Althorne Rd *REDH* RH1 ...... **148** D2
Althorp Rd *TOOT* SW17 ...... **30** C2
Alton CI *ISLW* TW7 ...... **17** J4
Alton Ct *STA* TW18 ...... **40** B1 [1]
Alton Gdns *BECK* BR3 ...... **33** K8
  WHTN TW2 ...... **26** A1
Alton Rd *CROY/NA* CR0 ...... **67** K2
  NFNM GU10 ...... **155** G2
  PUT/ROE SW15 ...... **28** D2
  RCH/KEW TW9 ...... **18** B6
Altyre CI *BECK* BR3 ...... **51** J5
Altyre Rd *CROY/NA* CR0 ...... **4** F6
Altyre Wy *BECK* BR3 ...... **51** J5
Alvernia CI *RGODL* GU7 ...... **159** M7 [1]
Alverstoke Gdns *ALDT* GU11 ...... **112** B8
Alverstone Av *WAND/EARL* SW18 ...... **29** K3
Alverstone Rd *NWMAL* KT3 ...... **46** C4
Alverston Gdns *SNWD* SE25 ...... **50** B5
Alvia Gdns *SUT* SM1 ...... **65** M3
Alway Av *HOR/WEW* KT19 ...... **63** M4
Alwin PI *FNM* GU9 ...... **133** M2 [1]
Alwyn CI *CROY/NA* CR0 ...... **69** L6
Alwyne Rd *WIM/MER* SW19 ...... **29** J7
Alwyns CI *CHERT* KT16 ...... **40** D6 [1]
Alwyns La *CHERT* KT16 ...... **40** C6
Amalgamated Dr *BTFD* TW8 ...... **17** K1
Ambassador *BRAK* RG12 ...... **34** C5
Ambassador CI *HSLW* TW3 ...... **16** B4
Ambercroft Wy
  COUL/CHIP CR5 ...... **107** L1
Amber HI *CBLY* GU15 ...... **73** L5 [1]
Amberley CI *CRAWE* RH10 ...... **212** F3
  HORS RH12 ...... **229** K3
  RPLY/SEND GU23 ...... **98** C7
Amberley Dr *ADL/WDHM* KT15 ...... **58** C3
Amberley Gdns *HOR/WEW* KT19 ...... **64** C3
Amberley Gra *ALDT* GU11 ...... **134** C1 [1]
Amberley Gv *CROY/NA* CR0 ...... **5** J2
  SYD SE26 ...... **32** E5
Amberley Rd *HORS* RH12 ...... **229** K3
  MFD/CHID GU8 ...... **159** H7
Amberley Wy *HSLWW* TW4 ...... **15** M7
  MRDN SM4 ...... **47** J7
Amberside CI *ISLW* TW7 ...... **17** G8
Amberwood Dr *CBLY* GU15 ...... **73** J2
Amberwood Ri *NWMAL* KT3 ...... **46** B6
Amblecote *COB* KT11 ...... **81** G1
Amblecote CI *BECK* BR3 ...... **51** H5
  STRHM/NOR SW16 ...... **31** G5
  WOT/HER KT12 ...... **42** F8
Ambleside CI *CRAWW* RH11 ...... **211** G4
  FARN GU14 ...... **92** B5
  FRIM GU16 ...... **93** K7
  REDH RH1 ...... **148** E5 [1]
Ambleside Dr
  EBED/NFELT TW14 ...... **24** C2 [1]
Ambleside Gdns *BELMT* SM2 ...... **65** M5 [1]
  SAND/SEL CR2 ...... **69** G8
Ambleside Rd *LTWR* GU18 ...... **74** D1
Ambleside Wy *EGH* TW20 ...... **21** L8
Ambrey Wy *WLGTN* SM6 ...... **67** G7
Amersham Rd *CROY/NA* CR0 ...... **50** A6 [1]
Amesbury Av *BRXS/STRHM* SW2 ...... **31** H3
Amesbury CI *WPK* KT4 ...... **46** F8
Amesbury Rd *FELT* TW13 ...... **25** G3
Amey Dr *GT/LBKH* KT23 ...... **101** M7
Amhurst Gdns *ISLW* TW7 ...... **17** J3
Amis Av *ADL/WDHM* KT15 ...... **78** D1
  HOR/WEW KT19 ...... **63** K5
Amis Rd *WOKN/KNAP* GU21 ...... **96** B1
Amity Gv *RYNPK* SW20 ...... **46** F1
Amlets La *CRAN* GU6 ...... **185** G4
Ampere Wy *CROY/NA* CR0 ...... **49** H7
Amroth CI *FSTH* SE23 ...... **32** E2
Amstel Wy *WOKN/KNAP* GU21 ...... **76** C8
Amundsen Rd *HORS* RH12 ...... **229** C3
Amyand Cottages *TWK* TW1 ...... **17** L8 [1]
Amyand Park Gdns *TWK* TW1 ...... **26** E1 [1]
Amyand Park Rd *TWK* TW1 ...... **26** D1
Amy Rd *OXTED* RH8 ...... **130** B3
Ancaster Crs *NWMAL* KT3 ...... **46** D6
Ancaster Dr *ASC* SL5 ...... **36** B1
Ancaster Rd *BECK* BR3 ...... **51** G3
Anchorage CI *WIM/MER* SW19 ...... **29** K6 [1]

Anchor Hl *WOKN/KNAP* GU21 ...... 76 A7
Anchor Meadow *FARN* GU14 ...... 92 C5
Anderson Av *GUW* GU2 ...... 116 E4
Anderson Cl *HOR/WEW* KT19 ...... 83 L2
Anderson Dr *WHTN* TW15 ...... 23 M1
Anderson Pl *BAGS* GU19 ...... 54 B5
Anderson Wy *WEY* KT13 ...... 60 A2
Anderson's Pl *HSLW* TW3 ...... 16 E6
  HOR/WEW KT19 ...... 84 A1
Andover Cl *EBED/NFELT* TW14 ...... 24 C2
Andover Rd *WHTN* TW2 ...... 26 A2
Andover Wy *ALDT* GU11 ...... 134 E2
Andrewartha Rd *FARN* GU14 ...... 93 H7
Andrew's Cl *EW* KT17 ...... 84 C4
  WPK KT4 ...... 65 G1
Andrews Rd *FARN* GU14 ...... 92 B4
Andromeda Cl *CRAWW* RH11 ...... 211 H5
Anerley Gv *NRWD* SE19 ...... 32 C8
Anerley Hl *NRWD* SE19 ...... 32 C7
Anerley Pk *PGE/AN* SE20 ...... 32 E7
Anerley Park Rd *PGE/AN* SE20 ...... 32 E8
Anerley Rd *NRWD* SE19 ...... 32 D8
  PGE/AN SE20 ...... 50 E1
Anerley Station Rd
  PGE/AN SE20 ...... 50 E1
Anerley V *NRWD* SE19 ...... 32 C8
Anfield Cl *BAL* SW12 ...... 30 F1
Angelfield *HSLW* TW3 ...... 16 E7
Angel Ga *GU* GU1 ...... 9 C6
Angel Hl *SUT* SM1 ...... 65 L2
Angel Hill Dr *SUT* SM1 ...... 65 L2
Angelica Gdns *CROY/NA* CR0 ...... 51 G8
  GUW GU2 ...... 116 D4
Angel Rd *THDIT* KT7 ...... 44 D8
Anglesea Rd *KUT* KT1 ...... 45 G4
Anglesey Av *FARN* GU14 ...... 92 C2
Anglesey Cl *ASHF* TW15 ...... 23 K5
  CRAWW RH11 ...... 211 M6
Anglesey Court Rd *CAR* SM5 ...... 66 D5
Anglesey Gdns *CAR* SM5 ...... 66 D5
Anglesey Rd *ASHV* GU12 ...... 113 G8
Angles Rd *STRHM/NOR* SW16 ...... 31 H5
Angus Cl *CHSGTN* KT9 ...... 63 K4
  HORS RH12 ...... 229 G1
Anlaby Rd *TEDD* TW11 ...... 26 B6
Annandale Dr *NFNM* GU10 ...... 11 K8
Annandale Rd *CROY/NA* CR0 ...... 68 D5
  GUW GU2 ...... 8 D7
Anne Armstrong Cl *ALDT* GU11 ...... 113 G4
Anne Boleyn's Wk *BELMT* SM2 ...... 65 G6
  KUTN/CMB KT2 ...... 27 H6
Anners Cl *EGH* TW20 ...... 39 M3
Annesley Av *CROY/NA* CR0 ...... 69 J2
Anne's Wk *CTHM* CR3 ...... 108 B2
Annett Cl *SHPTN* TW17 ...... 42 B4
Annett Rd *WOT/HER* KT12 ...... 42 D7
Annie Brookes Cl *STA* TW18 ...... 22 A4
Anningsley Pk *CHERT* KT16 ...... 57 L8
Annisdowne Cl *SHGR* GU5 ...... 142 C8
Annsworthy Av *THHTH* CR7 ...... 50 A3
Ansell Gv *CAR* SM5 ...... 48 C8
Ansell Rd *DORK* RH4 ...... 144 E1
  FRIM GU16 ...... 93 H1
  TOOT SW17 ...... 30 B4
Anselm Cl *CROY/NA* CR0 ...... 5 J7
Ansford Rd *BMLY* BR1 ...... 33 M6
Ansley Cl *SAND/SEL* CR2 ...... 88 E4
Anson Cl *PUR/KEN* CR8 ...... 108 A2
Anstice Cl *CHSWK* W4 ...... 19 H2
Anstiebury Cl *RDKG* RH5 ...... 166 F6
Anstie Grange Dr *RDKG* RH5 ...... 166 C5
Anstie La *RDKG* RH5 ...... 166 C5
Anthony Rd *SNWD* SE25 ...... 50 D6
Antlands La *HORL* RH6 ...... 193 H4
Antlands La East *HORL* RH6 ...... 193 H4
Antlands La West *HORL* RH6 ...... 193 H3
Anton Crs *SUT* SM1 ...... 65 K2
Antrobus Rd *STRHM/NOR* SW16 ...... 30 F8
Anvil Cl *STRHM/NOR* SW16 ...... 30 F8
Anvil La *COB* KT11 ...... 80 D5
Anvil Rd *SUN* TW16 ...... 42 D3
Anyards Rd *COB* KT11 ...... 80 E4
Anzio Cl *ALDT* GU11 ...... 112 D7
Apeldoorn Dr *WLGTN* SM6 ...... 67 H7
Aperdele Rd *LHD/OX* KT22 ...... 82 D8
Aperfield Rd *BH/WHM* TN16 ...... 91 H7
Apers Av *WOKS/MYFD* GU22 ...... 97 J3
Apex Cl *BECK* BR3 ...... 51 L1
  WEY KT13 ...... 60 A2
Apex Dr *FRIM* GU16 ...... 73 G8
Apley Rd *REIG* RH2 ...... 147 K3
Aplin Wy *ISLW* TW7 ...... 17 H3
  LTWR GU18 ...... 74 D1
Apollo Rd *FARN* GU14 ...... 92 A5
Appleby Cl *WHTN* TW2 ...... 26 A3
Appleby Gdns
  EBED/NFELT TW14 ...... 24 C2
Appledore *BRAK* RG12 ...... 34 C6
Appledore Cl *TOOT* SW17 ...... 30 C3
Appledore Ms *FARN* GU14 ...... 92 D2
Applefield *CRAWE* RH10 ...... 212 B2
Applegarth *ESH/CLAY* KT10 ...... 62 C4
  Apple Garth *RGODL* GU7 ...... 159 M2
Applegarth Av *GUW* GU2 ...... 116 A8
Apple Gv *CHSGTN* KT9 ...... 63 H3
Applelands Cl *NFNM* GU10 ...... 155 K5
Appleton Gdns *NWMAL* KT3 ...... 46 D6
Apple Tree Cl *GT/LBKH* KT23 ...... 101 M6
Appletree Cl *PGE/AN* SE20 ...... 50 E1
  RGODL GU7 ...... 160 C2
Appletree Ct *RGUE* GU4 ...... 118 A6
Appletree Pl *BNFD* RG42 ...... 34 D1
Apple Tree Wy *SHST* GU47 ...... 52 A8
Apple Ar *CBLY* GU15 ...... 72 E4
Approach Rd *ASHF* TW15 ...... 23 M7
  E/WMO/HCT KT8 ...... 43 K5
  FNM GU9 ...... 11 C1
  PUR/KEN CR8 ...... 87 L2
  RYNPK SW20 ...... 46 F3
  WARL CR6 ...... 110 E4
The Approach *EGRIN* RH19 ...... 196 C3
April Cl *ASHTD* KT21 ...... 83 J8
  CBLY GU15 ...... 72 F7
  FELT TW13 ...... 24 D4
  HORS RH12 ...... 228 F3
April Gln *FSTH* SE23 ...... 33 G4
Aprilwood Cl *ADL/WDHM* KT15 ...... 78 C1

Apsley Rd *NWMAL* KT3 ...... 45 M3
  SNWD SE25 ...... 50 E4
Aquila Cl *ASHTD* KT21 ...... 103 H3
Arabella Dr *PUT/ROE* SW15 ...... 19 H6
Aragon Av *EW* KT17 ...... 64 E7
  THDIT KT7 ...... 44 C5
Aragon Cl *CROY/NA* CR0 ...... 70 B8
  SUN TW16 ...... 24 C8
Aragon Rd *KUTN/CMB* KT2 ...... 27 H6
  MRDN SM4 ...... 47 G7
Arbor Cl *BECK* BR3 ...... 51 L2
Arborfield Cl *BRXS/STRHM* SW2 ...... 31 J2
Arbour Cl *LHD/OX* KT22 ...... 102 C5
Arbrook La *ESH/CLAY* KT10 ...... 61 M5
Arbutus Cl *REIG* RH2 ...... 147 M2
Arbutus Rd *REIG* RH2 ...... 147 M2
Arcadia Cl *CAR* SM5 ...... 66 D3
Archdale Pl *NWMAL* KT3 ...... 3 M8
Archer Av *EW* KT17 ...... 64 E7
Archer Rd *SNWD* SE25 ...... 50 E4
Arch Rd *WOT/HER* KT12 ...... 61 G2
Archway Cl *WIM/MER* SW19 ...... 29 L5
  WLGTN SM6 ...... 67 H2
Archway Ms *DORK* RH4 ...... 144 D1
Archway St *BARN* SW13 ...... 19 H5
Arcturus Rd *CRAWW* RH11 ...... 211 H5
Arden Cl *BRAK* RG12 ...... 35 K2
  REIG RH2 ...... 147 L4
Arden Gv *ORP* BR6 ...... 71 L3
Arden Rd *CRAWE* RH10 ...... 212 C5
Ardenrun *LING* RH7 ...... 173 K1
Ardesley Wd *WEY* KT13 ...... 60 B3
Ardfern Av *STRHM/NOR* SW16 ...... 49 K3
  CROY/NA CR0 ...... 69 G2
Ardingly *BRAK* RG12 ...... 34 D6
Ardingly Cl *CRAWW* RH11 ...... 211 L1
Ardleigh Gdns *CHEAM* SM3 ...... 47 K8
Ardley Cl *FSTH* SE23 ...... 33 H4
Ardlui Rd *WNWD* SE27 ...... 31 M3
Ardmay Gdns *SURB* KT6 ...... 45 H4
  SURB KT6 ...... 45 H5
Ardmore Av *GUW* GU2 ...... 116 E6
Ardmore Wy *GUW* GU2 ...... 116 E6
Ardrossan Av *CBLY* GU15 ...... 73 K4
Ardrossan Gdns *WPK* KT4 ...... 64 D2
Ardshiel Dr *REDH* RH1 ...... 148 B2
Ardwell Rd *BRXS/STRHM* SW2 ...... 31 H3
Arena La *ALDT* GU11 ...... 112 B5
Arethusa Wy *CHOB/PIR* GU24 ...... 75 J6
Argent Cl *EGH* TW20 ...... 21 M7
Argosy Gdns *STA* TW18 ...... 22 C7
Argosy La *STWL/WRAY* TW19 ...... 23 G1
Argus Wk *CRAWW* RH11 ...... 211 K6
Argyle Av *HSLW* TW3 ...... 16 D8
  WHTN TW2 ...... 16 D8
Argyle Rd *HSLW* TW3 ...... 16 E7
Argyle St *CHOB/PIR* GU24 ...... 94 D3
Ariel Rd *FARN* GU14 ...... 92 D7
Ariel Wy *HSLWW* TW4 ...... 15 L5
Arkell Gv *STRHM/NOR* SW16 ...... 31 L8
Arkindale Rd *CAT* SE6 ...... 33 M4
Arkwright Dr *BNFD* RG42 ...... 34 A2
Arkwright Rd *DTCH/LGLY* SL3 ...... 13 H4
  SAND/SEL CR2 ...... 68 C8
Arlington Cl *BNFD* RG42 ...... 34 D1
  SUT SM1 ...... 65 L2
  TWK TW1 ...... 17 M7
Arlington Dr *CAR* SM5 ...... 66 C1
Arlington Ldg *WEY* KT13 ...... 59 L3
Arlington Rd *ASHF* TW15 ...... 23 J6
  RCHPK/HAM TW10 ...... 27 G3
  SURB KT6 ...... 45 G6
  TEDD TW11 ...... 26 C5
  TWK TW1 ...... 17 M8
Arlington Ter *ALDT* GU11 ...... 112 C7
Armadale Rd *EBED/NFELT* TW14 ...... 15 K7
  WOKN/KNAP GU21 ...... 76 D7
Armfield Cl *E/WMO/HCT* KT8 ...... 43 J5
Armfield Crs *MTCM* CR4 ...... 48 C2
Armitage Ct *ASC* SL5 ...... 36 F6
Armitage Dr *FRIM* GU16 ...... 73 J8
Armstrong Ml *WOT/HER* KT12 ...... 42 D6
Armstrong Rd *EGH* TW20 ...... 20 F7
  FELT TW13 ...... 25 H6
Armytage Rd *HEST* TW5 ...... 16 A2
Arnal Crs *WAND/EARL* SW18 ...... 29 H1
Arncliffe *BRAK* RG12 ...... 34 D5
Arndale Wy *EGH* TW20 ...... 21 K6
Arne Cl *CRAWW* RH11 ...... 211 J6
Arne Gv *HORL* RH6 ...... 170 B4
Arnewood Cl *LHD/OX* KT22 ...... 81 L4
  PUT/ROE SW15 ...... 28 D2
Arney's La *MTCM* CR4 ...... 48 D6
Arnfield Cl *CRAWW* RH11 ...... 211 H4
Arnhem Dr *CROY/NA* CR0 ...... 90 A1
Arnison Rd *E/WMO/HCT* KT8 ...... 44 A4
Arnold Crs *ISLW* TW7 ...... 17 G7
Arnold Rd *CHSGTN* KT9 ...... 63 J2
  STA TW18 ...... 22 F8
  TOOT SW17 ...... 30 C8
  WOKN/KNAP GU21 ...... 7 J3
Arnull St *CAT* SE6 ...... 33 L5
Arnull's Rd *STRHM/NOR* SW16 ...... 31 L7
Arosa Rd *TWK* TW1 ...... 18 A8
Arragon Gdns
  STRHM/NOR SW16 ...... 31 H8
  WWKM BR4 ...... 69 L2
Arragon Rd *TWK* TW1 ...... 26 D2
  WAND/EARL SW18 ...... 29 K2
Arragon Wk *BF/WBF* KT14 ...... 79 J3
Arran Cl *CRAWW* RH11 ...... 211 L6
  WLGTN SM6 ...... 66 F3
Arran Rd *CAT* SE6 ...... 33 L3
Arran Wy *ESH/CLAY* KT10 ...... 61 L1
Arras Av *MRDN* SM4 ...... 47 M5
Arreton Md *WOKN/KNAP* GU21 ...... 78 F4
Arrol Rd *BECK* BR3 ...... 50 F3
Arrow Rd *FARN* GU14 ...... 92 C7
Artel Cft *CRAWE* RH10 ...... 212 C3
Arterberry Rd *RYNPK* SW20 ...... 28 F8
Arthur Cl *BAGS* GU19 ...... 54 B8
  FNM GU9 ...... 10 F2
Arthur Rd *BH/WHM* TN16 ...... 90 F5
  CRAWW RH11 ...... 211 H3
  FNM GU9 ...... 10 F2
  KUTN/CMB KT2 3

Arthur's Bridge Rd
  WOKN/KNAP GU21 ...... 6 A4
Arthur St *ALDT* GU11 ...... 112 E8
Artillery Rd *ALDT* GU11 ...... 112 E7
  GU GU1 ...... 9 G5
Artillery Ter *ALDT* GU11 ...... 9 G4
Arundel Av *EW* KT17 ...... 64 E8
  MRDN SM4 ...... 47 J4
  SAND/SEL CR2 ...... 68 D8
Arundel Cl *CRAWE* RH10 ...... 212 F3
  CROY/NA CR0 ...... 4 A8
  HPTN TW12 ...... 25 L6
Arundel Rd *BELMT* SM2 ...... 65 J6
  CBLY GU15 ...... 73 M5
  CROY/NA CR0 ...... 50 A6
  DORK RH4 ...... 144 D2
  HSLWW TW4 ...... 15 M5
  KUT KT1 ...... 3 M6
Arundel Ter *BARN* SW13 ...... 19 L1
Arunside *HORS* RH12 ...... 228 D8
Arun Wy *SWTR* RH13 ...... 229 H8
Aschurch Rd *CROY/NA* CR0 ...... 5 K1
Ascot Ct *ALDT* GU11 ...... 112 D8
Ascot Ms *WLGTN* SM6 ...... 66 F7
Ascot Rd *ASHF* TW15 ...... 23 K2
  TOOT SW17 ...... 30 D7
Ashbourne *BRAK* RG12 ...... 34 C6
Ashbourne Cl *ASHV* GU12 ...... 113 L6
  COUL/CHIP CR5 ...... 86 F8
Ashbourne Rd *MTCM* CR4 ...... 30 D7
Ashbourne Ter
  WIM/MER SW19 ...... 29 K8
Ashbrook Rd *WDSR* SL4 ...... 20 E1
Ashburnham Pk *ESH/CLAY* KT10 ...... 61 M3
Ashburnham Rd *CRAWE* RH10 ...... 212 D5
  RCHPK/HAM TW10 ...... 26 E4
Ashburton Av *CROY/NA* CR0 ...... 50 E8
Ashburton Cl *CROY/NA* CR0 ...... 50 F8
Ashburton Gdns *CROY/NA* CR0 ...... 5 L5
Ashburton Rd *CROY/NA* CR0 ...... 5 L5
Ashbury Crs *RGUE* GU4 ...... 117 M6
Ashbury Dr *FARN* GU14 ...... 72 D8
Ashbury Pl *WIM/MER* SW19 ...... 29 M7
Ashby Av *CHSGTN* KT9 ...... 63 K5
Ashby Wk *CROY/NA* CR0 ...... 49 M6
Ashby Wy *WDR/YW* UB7 ...... 14 D2
Ash Church Rd *ASHV* GU12 ...... 113 L7
Ash Cl *ASHV* GU12 ...... 113 L6
  CAR SM5 ...... 66 C1
  CRAWE RH10 ...... 194 F8
  EDEN TN8 ...... 153 L8
  KWD/TDW/WH KT20 ...... 123 M5
  LING RH7 ...... 174 B4
  NWMAL KT3 ...... 46 A2
  PGE/AN SE20 ...... 50 F2
  REDH RH1 ...... 126 F4
  WOKS/MYFD GU22 ...... 78 D5
  WOKS/MYFD GU22 ...... 97 H2
Ash Combe *MFD/CHID* GU8 ...... 201 K5
Ashcombe Av *SURB* KT6 ...... 45 G7
Ashcombe Dr *EDEN* TN8 ...... 153 L5
Ashcombe Rd *CAR* SM5 ...... 66 D5
  DORK RH4 ...... 122 D8
  REDH RH1 ...... 126 F1
  WIM/MER SW19 ...... 29 L5
Ashcombe Sq *NWMAL* KT3 ...... 45 M3
Ashcombe Ter
  KWD/TDW/WH KT20 ...... 104 E2
Ash Ct *HOR/WEW* KT19 ...... 63 M3
Ashcroft *RGUE* GU4 ...... 139 H7
Ashcroft Pk *COB* KT11 ...... 81 H2
Ashcroft Ri *COUL/CHIP* CR5 ...... 87 H6
Ashcroft Rd *CHSGTN* KT9 ...... 63 J2
Ashdale *GT/LBKH* KT23 ...... 101 M8
Ashdale Cl *STWL/WRAY* TW19 ...... 23 H3
  WHTN TW2 ...... 25 L1
Ashdene Cl *ASHF* TW15 ...... 23 M8
Ashdene Crs *ASHV* GU12 ...... 113 K6
Ashdene Rd *ASHV* GU12 ...... 113 K6
Ashdown Av *FARN* GU14 ...... 93 H7
Ashdown Cl *BECK* BR3 ...... 51 L2
  BRAK RG12 ...... 35 J2
  FROW RH18 ...... 217 K7
  REIG RH2 ...... 147 L4
Ashdown Dr *CRAWE* RH10 ...... 212 B7
Ashdown Gdns *SAND/SEL* CR2 ...... 88 E5
Ashdown Pk *LHD/OX* KT22 ...... 101 M5
  WOKS/MYFD GU22 ...... 7 G8
Ashdown Pl *THDIT* KT7 ...... 44 D6
Ashdown Rd *EW* KT17 ...... 84 C3
  FROW RH18 ...... 217 J7
  KUT KT1 ...... 2 E7
  REIG RH2 ...... 147 L4
Ashdown Vw *EGRIN* RH19 ...... 216 B2
Ashdown Wy *TOOT* SW17 ...... 30 D3
Ash Dr *REDH* RH1 ...... 148 D2
Ashenden Rd *GUW* GU2 ...... 116 C8
Ashen Gv *WIM/MER* SW19 ...... 29 K4
Ashen V *SAND/SEL* CR2 ...... 69 G7
Asher Dr *ASC* SL5 ...... 35 M1
Ashfield Av *FELT* TW13 ...... 24 E2
Ashfield Cl *BECK* BR3 ...... 33 K8
  RCHPK/HAM TW10 ...... 27 H2
Ashford Av *ASHF* TW15 ...... 23 L7
Ashford Cl *ASHF* TW15 ...... 23 H5
Ashford Crs *ASHF* TW15 ...... 23 H4
Ashford Gdns *COB* KT11 ...... 81 G6
Ashford Rd *ASHF* TW15 ...... 24 A5
  SHPTN TW17 ...... 23 M8
  STA TW18 ...... 23 G8
Ash Green La East *ASHV* GU12 ...... 135 M1
Ash Green La West *ASHV* GU12 ...... 135 J1
Ash Green Rd *ASHV* GU12 ...... 113 M8
Ash Gv *EBED/NFELT* TW14 ...... 24 B1
  GUW GU2 ...... 8 A3
  HEST TW5 ...... 16 A2
  LIPH GU30 ...... 218 A6
  PGE/AN SE20 ...... 50 F3
  STA TW18 ...... 22 F7
  WWKM BR4 ...... 69 M1
Ashgrove Rd *ASHF* TW15 ...... 23 M6
Ash Hall Rd *ASHV* GU12 ...... 113 L6
Ash Keys *CRAWE* RH10 ...... 212 B4
Ashlake Rd *STRHM/NOR* SW16 ...... 31 H5
Ash La *MFD/CHID* GU8 ...... 157 M7
Ashleigh Av *EGH* TW20 ...... 21 M8

Ashleigh Cl *HORL* RH6 ...... 170 C6
Ashleigh Gdns *SUT* SM1 ...... 65 L1
Ashleigh Rd *HORS* RH12 ...... 228 F4
  MORT/ESHN SW14 ...... 19 H5
  PGE/AN SE20 ...... 50 E3
Ashley Av *EPSOM* KT18 ...... 47 K5
  MRDN SM4 ...... 47 K5
Ashley Cl *FRIM* GU16 ...... 93 K3
  GT/LBKH KT23 ...... 101 J7
  NFNM GU10 ...... 132 C2
  WEY KT13 ...... 60 C8
Ashley Ct *WOKN/KNAP* GU21 ...... 76 C2
Ashley Dr *BNSTD* SM7 ...... 85 K4
  ISLW TW7 ...... 17 H1
  WHTN TW2 ...... 25 L2
  WOT/HER KT12 ...... 60 D2
Ashley Gdns *RCHPK/HAM* TW10 ...... 27 G4
Ashley La *CROY/NA* CR0 ...... 67 L3
Ashley Park Av *WOT/HER* KT12 ...... 60 D1
Ashley Park Crs *WOT/HER* KT12 ...... 42 C8
Ashley Park Rd *WOT/HER* KT12 ...... 60 D1
Ashley Ri *WOT/HER* KT12 ...... 60 D3
Ashley Rd *DORK* RH4 ...... 143 M3
  EPSOM KT18 ...... 84 C7
  EW KT17 ...... 84 A3
  FARN GU14 ...... 93 G5
  HPTN TW12 ...... 43 K1
  RCH/KEW TW9 ...... 18 B5
  THDIT KT7 ...... 44 C6
  WIM/MER SW19 ...... 29 L7
  WOKN/KNAP GU21 ...... 76 C8
  WOT/HER KT12 ...... 60 C3
Ashley Wy *CHOB/PIR* GU24 ...... 75 G3
Ashling Rd *CROY/NA* CR0 ...... 5 M3
Ash Lodge Cl *ASHV* GU12 ...... 113 K8
Ash Lodge Dr *ASHV* GU12 ...... 113 K8
Ashlyn's Pk *COB* KT11 ...... 81 H3
Ashlyns Wy *CHSGTN* KT9 ...... 63 G5
Ashmead Rd *EBED/NFELT* TW14 ...... 24 D2
Ashmere Cl *CHEAM* SM3 ...... 65 G4
Ash Ms *EPSOM* KT18 ...... 84 B3
Ashmore La *HAYES* BR2 ...... 90 F1
  HORS RH12 ...... 209 M3
Ashridge *FARN* GU14 ...... 92 C2
Ashridge Gn *BNFD* RG42 ...... 34 E1
Ashridge Wy *MRDN* SM4 ...... 47 J4
  SUN TW16 ...... 24 D7
Ash Rd *ASHV* GU12 ...... 134 F1
  CHOB/PIR GU24 ...... 95 K8
  CRAWE RH10 ...... 212 D1
  CROY/NA CR0 ...... 69 K1
  MRDN SM4 ...... 47 K4
  SHPTN TW17 ...... 41 K4
  WOKS/MYFD GU22 ...... 97 G2
Ash St *ASHV* GU12 ...... 113 K8
Ashtead La *RGODL* GU7 ...... 160 A7
Ashtead Woods Rd *ASHTD* KT21 ...... 82 F7
Ashton Cl *SUT* SM1 ...... 65 K3
  WOT/HER KT12 ...... 60 E5
Ashton Gdns *HSLWW* TW4 ...... 16 C6
Ashton Rd *WOKN/KNAP* GU21 ...... 76 C7
Ashtree Av *MTCM* CR4 ...... 48 A2
Ash Tree Cl *CROY/NA* CR0 ...... 51 H6
  HASM GU27 ...... 200 C8
Ashtree Cl *ORP* BR6 ...... 71 L3
Ash Tree Cl *SURB* KT6 ...... 45 H8
Ashtrees *CRAN* GU6 ...... 185 M8
Ashurst Cl *HORS* RH12 ...... 229 K4
  PGE/AN SE20 ...... 50 E1
  PUR/KEN CR8 ...... 88 A5
Ashurst Dr *CRAWE* RH10 ...... 213 G3
  KWD/TDW/WH KT20 ...... 123 L4
  SHPTN TW17 ...... 41 H5
Ashurst Rd *ASHV* GU12 ...... 113 J5
  KWD/TDW/WH KT20 ...... 104 E3
Ashurst Wk *CROY/NA* CR0 ...... 68 E1
Ash V *MFD/CHID* GU8 ...... 201 K4
Ashvale Rd *TOOT* SW17 ...... 30 C6
Ashview Cl *ASHF* TW15 ...... 23 H7
Ashview Gdns *ASHF* TW15 ...... 23 H6
Ashwell Av *CBLY* GU15 ...... 73 J3
Ashwood *WARL* CR6 ...... 108 F2
Ashwood Gdns *CROY/NA* CR0 ...... 69 L5
Ashwood Pk *LHD/OX* KT22 ...... 101 M5
  WOKS/MYFD GU22 ...... 6 F8
Ashwood Rd *EGH* TW20 ...... 20 E7
  WOKS/MYFD GU22 ...... 6 F8
Aslett St *WAND/EARL* SW18 ...... 29 L1
Asmar Cl *COUL/CHIP* CR5 ...... 87 H5
Aspen Cl *COB* KT11 ...... 81 H6
  RGUE GU4 ...... 118 A5
  STA TW18 ...... 22 C4
Aspen Gdns *MTCM* CR4 ...... 48 D5
Aspen V *CTHM* CR3 ...... 88 C8
Aspen Wy *EW* KT17 ...... 85 G4
  FELT TW13 ...... 24 E4
  HORS RH12 ...... 229 H5
Asprey Gv *CTHM* CR3 ...... 108 D6
Assembly Wk *CAR* SM5 ...... 48 B7
Assher Rd *WOT/HER* KT12 ...... 61 H2
Astleham Wy *SHPTN* TW17 ...... 41 H3
Aston Cl *ASHTD* KT21 ...... 82 F8
Aston Gn *HEST* TW5 ...... 15 M4
Aston Rd *ESH/CLAY* KT10 ...... 62 B4
  RYNPK SW20 ...... 46 F2
Astonville St *WAND/EARL* SW18 ...... 29 K2
Aston Wy *EPSOM* KT18 ...... 84 C6
Astor Cl *ADL/WDHM* KT15 ...... 59 G3
  KUTN/CMB KT2 ...... 27 L7
Atalanta Cl *PUR/KEN* CR8 ...... 67 K8
Atbara Rd *TEDD* TW11 ...... 26 E7
Atcham Rd *HSLW* TW3 ...... 16 F6
Atfield Gv *BFOR* GU20 ...... 55 C5
Atheldene Rd *WAND/EARL* SW18 ...... 29 L2
Athelney St *CAT* SE6 ...... 33 K4
Athelstan Cl *CRAWE* RH10 ...... 213 H3
Athelstan Rd *KUT* KT1 ...... 45 J4
Athena Cl *KUT* KT1 ...... 3 K7
Atherfield Rd *REDH* RH1 ...... 147 M3
Atherley Wy *HSLWW* TW4 ...... 25 J7
Atherton Cl *RGUE* GU4 ...... 139 H4
  STWL/WRAY TW19 ...... 14 A8
Atherton Dr *WIM/MER* SW19 ...... 29 G5
Atherton Rd *BARN* SW13 ...... 19 K2
Athlone *ESH/CLAY* KT10 ...... 62 B5
Athlone Rd *BRXS/STRHM* SW2 ...... 31 J1

Atkins Cl *WOKN/KNAP* GU21 ...... 76 D8
Atkins Dr *WWKM* BR4 ...... 70 A2
Atkinson Ct *CRAWE* RH10 ...... 212 F5
Atkins Rd *BAL* SW12 ...... 30 F1
  CLAP SW4 ...... 31 G1
Attebrouche Ct *BRAK* RG12 ...... 35 G7
Attfield Cl *ASHV* GU12 ...... 113 J8
Attlee Cl *CROY/NA* CR0 ...... 49 M6
Attwood Cl *SAND/SEL* CR2 ...... 88 E4
Atwood *GT/LBKH* KT23 ...... 101 H6
Atwood Av *RCH/KEW* TW9 ...... 18 D4
Aubyn Hl *WNWD* SE27 ...... 31 M5
Aubyn Sq *PUT/ROE* SW15 ...... 19 K6
Auchinleck Wy *ALDT* GU11 ...... 112 B7
Auckland Cl *CRAWW* RH11 ...... 192 A8
  NRWD SE19 ...... 50 C1
Auckland Hl *WNWD* SE27 ...... 31 M5
Auckland Ri *NRWD* SE19 ...... 50 B1
Auckland Rd *CTHM* CR3 ...... 108 B4
  KUT KT1 ...... 45 J4
  NRWD SE19 ...... 50 C1
Aucklands Gdns *NRWD* SE19 ...... 50 B1
Audley Cl *ADL/WDHM* KT15 ...... 58 C8
Audley Dr *SAND/SEL* CR2 ...... 88 F5
Audley Firs *WOT/HER* KT12 ...... 60 F3
Audley Pl *BELMT* SM2 ...... 65 L6
Audley Rd *RCHPK/HAM* TW10 ...... 18 C7
Audley Wy *ASC* SL5 ...... 36 A3
Audrey Cl *BECK* BR3 ...... 51 L6
Audric Cl *KUTN/CMB* KT2 ...... 3 J4
Augur Cl *STA* TW18 ...... 22 C6
Augusta Cl *E/WMO/HCT* KT8 ...... 43 J3
Augusta Rd *WHTN* TW2 ...... 25 M3
Augustine Cl *DTCH/LGLY* SL3 ...... 13 H5
August Gdns *SHGR* GU5 ...... 163 G2
Augustus Cl *BTFD* TW8 ...... 18 A2
Augustus Gdns *CBLY* GU15 ...... 73 M4
Augustus Rd *WIM/MER* SW19 ...... 29 H2
Aultone Wy *CAR* SM5 ...... 66 C2
  SUT SM1 ...... 65 M1
Aurelia Gdns *THHTH* CR7 ...... 49 J5
Aurelia Rd *CROY/NA* CR0 ...... 49 J6
Auriol Cl *HOR/WEW* KT19 ...... 64 B2
Auriol Park Rd *WPK* KT4 ...... 64 B2
Aurum Cl *HORL* RH6 ...... 170 E7
Austen Cl *EGRIN* RH19 ...... 195 L8
Austen Rd *FARN* GU14 ...... 92 C3
  GU GU1 ...... 9 M6
Austin Cl *CAT* SE6 ...... 33 H1
  PUR/KEN CR8 ...... 87 L8
Austyn Gdns *BRYLDS* KT5 ...... 45 L8
Autumn Cl *WIM/MER* SW19 ...... 29 M7
Autumn Dr *BELMT* SM2 ...... 65 J7
Avalon Cl *RYNPK* SW20 ...... 47 H2
Avard Gdns *ORP* BR6 ...... 71 M3
Avarn Rd *TOOT* SW17 ...... 30 C7
Avebury *BRAK* RG12 ...... 34 C6
Avebury Cl *HORS* RH12 ...... 229 K2
Avebury Rd *WIM/MER* SW19 ...... 47 J1
Aveley La *FNM* GU9 ...... 133 H4
Aveling Cl *CRAWE* RH10 ...... 212 F5
  PUR/KEN CR8 ...... 87 J3
Avening Rd *WAND/EARL* SW18 ...... 29 K1
Avenue Cl *CRAN* GU6 ...... 185 H7
Avenue C *HEST* TW5 ...... 15 J3
  KWD/TDW/WH KT20 ...... 104 E4
Avenue Crs *HEST* TW5 ...... 15 K3
Avenue De Cagny
  CHOB/PIR GU24 ...... 95 J4
Avenue Gdns *HEST* TW5 ...... 15 L2
  HORL RH6 ...... 170 F7
  MORT/ESHN SW14 ...... 19 H5
  TEDD TW11 ...... 26 C8
Avenue One *ADL/WDHM* KT15 ...... 59 H3
Avenue Park Rd *WNWD* SE27 ...... 31 L3
Avenue Rd *BELMT* SM2 ...... 65 K8
  BH/WHM TN16 ...... 111 H2
  BNSTD SM7 ...... 85 L5
  COB KT11 ...... 81 G6
  CRAN GU6 ...... 185 J8
  CTHM CR3 ...... 108 A4
  EPSOM KT18 ...... 84 A4
  FARN GU14 ...... 93 G5
  FELT TW13 ...... 24 C4
  GSHT GU26 ...... 199 C6
  HPTN TW12 ...... 43 L1
  ISLW TW7 ...... 17 H3
  KUT KT1 ...... 2 F8
  NWMAL KT3 ...... 46 B3
  PGE/AN SE20 ...... 50 F1
  RYNPK SW20 ...... 46 E2
  SNWD SE25 ...... 50 D2
  STA TW18 ...... 22 A6
  STRHM/NOR SW16 ...... 49 G2
  TEDD TW11 ...... 26 D8
  WLGTN SM6 ...... 66 F6
Avenue South *BRYLDS* KT5 ...... 45 J7
Avenue Sucy *CBLY* GU15 ...... 72 D5
Avenue Ter *NWMAL* KT3 ...... 45 M3
The Avenue *ADL/WDHM* KT15 ...... 58 D8
  ALDT GU11 ...... 134 F2
  BECK BR3 ...... 51 L1
  BELMT SM2 ...... 65 J7
  BH/WHM TN16 ...... 111 J4
  BRYLDS KT5 ...... 45 J6
  CAR SM5 ...... 66 D6
  CBLY GU15 ...... 72 E5
  CHOB/PIR GU24 ...... 95 J7
  COUL/CHIP CR5 ...... 87 G5
  CRAN GU6 ...... 186 B3
  CROY/NA CR0 ...... 5 G7
  CTHM CR3 ...... 108 D1
  EGH TW20 ...... 21 L5
  EGRIN RH19 ...... 196 D3
  ESH/CLAY KT10 ...... 62 B5
  EW KT17 ...... 64 F6
  GSHT GU26 ...... 199 G6
  HASM GU27 ...... 219 J2
  HEST TW5 ...... 15 K3
  HORL RH6 ...... 170 C7
  HPTN TW12 ...... 25 J7
  HSLW TW3 ...... 16 E7
  KWD/TDW/WH KT20 ...... 104 E4
  LHD/OX KT22 ...... 82 C2
  LTWR GU18 ...... 54 D8
  NFNM GU10 ...... 155 H6
  RCH/KEW TW9 ...... 18 D5

RDKG RH5 .... **123** K8
REDH RH1 .... **149** H3
RGODL GU7 .... **160** C7
RGUW GU3 .... **116** B1
RGUW GU3 .... **137** M8
STA TW18 .... **40** E1
STWL/WRAY TW19 .... **12** A5
SUN TW16 .... **42** E1
TWK TW1 .... **17** M7
WPK KT4 .... **64** C1
Avenue Three *ADL/WDHM* KT15.. **59** H2
Avenue Two *ADL/WDHM* KT15 ... **59** H3
Averil Gv *STRHM/NOR* SW16 ... **31** L7
Avern Gdns *E/WMO/HCT* KT8 ... **43** L4
Avern Rd *E/WMO/HCT* KT8 ... **43** L4 🔲
Aviary Rd *WOKS/MYFD* GU22 ... **78** D6
Aviary Wy *CRAWE* RH10........ **194** F8
Aviemore Cl *BECK* BR3 .... **51** J5 🔲
Aviemore Wy *BECK* BR3 .... **51** H5
Avington Cl *GU* GU1 .... **9** K3
Avington Gv *PGE/AN* SE20 .... **32** F8
Avoca Rd *TOOT* SW17 .... **30** D5
Avocet Crs *SHST* GU47 .... **72** A1
Avon Cl *ADL/WDHM* KT15 ...... **58** D5
ASHV GU12 .... **113** J8
FARN GU14 .... **92** B2
SUT SM1 .... **65** M3
WPK KT4 .... **64** D1
Avondale *ASHV* GU12 .... **113** J2
Avondale Av *ESH/CLAY* KT10... **62** D2
STA TW18 .... **22** C8
WPK KT4 .... **46** C8
Avondale Cl *HORL* RH6 .... **170** C4
WOT/HER KT12 .... **60** F4
Avondale Gdns *HSLWW* TW4..... **16** C7
Avondale Rd *ALDT* GU11 ...... **134** E1
ASHF TW15 .... **23** C4
MORT/ESHN SW14 .... **19** C5
SAND/SEL CR2 .... **67** M5
WIM/MER SW19 .... **29** L6
Avonmore Av *GU* GU1 .... **9** M2
Avon Rd *FNM* GU9 .... **11** G2
SUN TW16 .... **24** C8
Avonstowe Cl *ORP* BR6 .... **71** M2
Avonwick Rd *HSLW* TW3 .... **16** E4
Avro Wy *WEY* KT13 .... **79** H1
WLGTN SM6 .... **67** H6
Axbridge *BRAK* RG12 .... **35** H5
Axes La *REDH* RH1 .... **148** F7
Axwood *EPSOM* KT18 .... **83** M5
Aycliff Ct *KUT* KT1 .... **3** J6
Ayebridges Av *EGH* TW20 ..... **21** M8
Ayjay Cl *ALDT* GU11 .... **134** E2
Aylesford Av *BECK* BR3 ...... **51** H5
Aylesworth Sp *WDSR* SL4 ..... **20** E1 🔲
SNWD SE25 .... **50** E4
Ayling Cl *FNM* GU9 .... **134** C2
Ayling Hl *ALDT* GU11 .... **112** C8
Ayling La *ALDT* GU11 .... **134** C1
Aylward Rd *FSTH* SE23........ **33** G3
RYNPK SW20 .... **47** J2
Aymer Cl *STA* TW18 .... **40** B1
Aymer Dr *STA* TW18 .... **40** B1
Aysgarth *BRAK* RG12 .... **34** C6
Ayshe Court Dr *SWTR* RH13 ... **229** H7
Azalea Dr *HASM* GU27 .... **219** J1 🔲
Azalea Wy *CBLY* GU15 .... **73** L3

B

Babbacombe Cl *CHSGTN* KT9 .... **63** G4 🔲
Babbs Md *FNM* GU9 .... **10** D1
Baber Dr *EBED/NFELT* TW14 ... **15** M3
Babington Rd
STRHM/NOR SW16 .... **31** G5 🔲
Babylon La
KWD/TDW/WH KT20 .... **125** L1
Bachelor's La *RPLY/SEND* GU23 .. **99** K6
Back Gn *WOT/HER* KT12 .... **60** F5
Back La *BIL* RH14 .... **223** H7
BTFD TW8 .... **18** A2
CRAWE RH10 .... **213** M7
MFD/CHID GU8 .... **158** A3
NFNM GU10 .... **176** E1
RCHPK/HAM TW10 .... **26** F3
RGUE GU4 .... **119** C5
Backley Gdns *SNWD* SE25 ..... **50** D6
Back Rd *TEDD* TW11 .... **26** B8
Bacon Cl *SHST* GU47 .... **72** A3 🔲
Bacon La *NFNM* GU10 .... **177** M5
Badajos Rd *ALDT* GU11 .... **112** C6
Baden Cl *STA* TW18 .... **22** D8
Baden Dr *HORL* RH6 .... **170** B5
Baden Powell Cl *SURB* KT6 ... **63** J1 🔲
Baden Rd *GUW* GU2 .... **116** D6
Bader Ct *PUR/KEN* CR8 .... **88** A5
Badger Cl *FELT* TW13 .... **24** E4
GUW GU2 .... **116** E5
HSLWW TW4 .... **15** M4 🔲
Badger Dr *LTWR* GU18 .... **54** D8
Badgers Cl *ASHF* TW15 .... **23** J6 🔲
HORS RH12 .... **229** J3
RGODL GU7 .... **160** A1
WOKN/KNAP GU21 .... **76** F3
WPK KT4 .... **64** C1
Badgers Copse *CBLY* GU15 .... **73** H6
WPK KT4 .... **64** C1
Badgers Cross *MFD/CHID* GU8 .. **159** J8 🔲
Badgers Hl *VW* GU25 .... **38** F5
Badgers Hollow *RGODL* GU7 ... **160** A3
Badgers La *WARL* CR6 .... **108** F1
Badgers Wk *CTHM* CR3 .... **88** C8
NWMAL KT3 .... **46** B2
PUR/KEN CR8 .... **86** F1
Badgers Wd *BIL* RH14 .... **224** D5
BRAK RG12 .... **35** J1
EGRIN RH19 .... **196** B6
Badger Wy *NFNM* GU10 .... **133** G1
Badgerwood Dr *FRIM* GU16 .... **73** C7
Badingham Dr *LHD/OX* KT22 ... **102** B5
Badshot Lea Rd *FNM* GU9 ..... **134** D4
Badshot Pk *FNM* GU9 .... **134** D3
Bagot Cl *ASHTD* KT21 .... **83** J6

Bagshot Gn *BAGS* GU19 .... **54** B7
Bagshot Rd *ASC* SL5 .... **36** E8
BRAK RG12 .... **34** E3
CHOB/PIR GU24 .... **75** L1
EGH TW20 .... **20** F8
WOKN/KNAP GU21 .... **95** L1
Bahram Rd *HOR/WEW* KT19 ..... **64** A8
Baigents La *BFOR* GU20 ...... **55** G5
Bailes La *RGUW* GU3 .... **115** G7
Bailey Cl *FRIM* GU16 .... **93** G1
HORS RH12 .... **229** J2
Bailey Pl *SYD* SE26 .... **32** F7
Bailey Rd *DORK* RH4 .... **143** M3
Bailing Hl *HORS* RH12........ **228** B3
Baillie Rd *GU* GU1 .... **9** L6
Bain Av *CBLY* GU15 .... **72** E8
Bainbridge Cl *KUTN/CMB* KT2 .. **27** H6
Baines Cl *SAND/SEL* CR2 ..... **68** A4 🔲
Baird Cl *CRAWE* RH10 .... **192** D8
RGUW GU3 .... **115** L7
Baird Dr *RGUW* GU3 .... **115** L7
Baird Gdns *NRWD* SE19 .... **32** B5 🔲
Baird Rd *FARN* GU14 .... **92** F3
Bakeham La *EGH* TW20 .... **20** F8
Bakehouse Barn Cl
HORS RH12 .... **229** H2 🔲
Bakehouse Rd *HORL* RH6 ...... **170** C4
Baker Cl *CRAWE* RH10 .... **212** A5
Baker La *MTCM* CR4 .... **48** D2
Baker's Cl *LING* RH7 .... **174** B4
Bakers End *RYNPK* SW20 ...... **47** H2
Bakers Gdns *CAR* SM5 .... **66** B1
Baker's La *LING* RH7 .... **174** B5
Bakers Md *GDST* RH9 .... **128** F4
Baker's Wy *RDKG* RH5 .... **188** F4
Bakewell Dr *NWMAL* KT3 ...... **46** B2
Balaclava Rd *SURB* KT6 ...... **44** F7
SURB KT6 .... **63** M2
Balchins La *DORK* RH4 .... **143** K3
Balcombe Gdns *HORL* RH6 ..... **170** F7
HORL RH6 .... **170** E5
Baldreys *FNM* GU9 .... **10** D4
Baldry Gdns *STRHM/NOR* SW16 .. **31** H7
Baldwin Cl *CRAWE* RH10 ...... **212** F6 🔲
Baldwin Crs *RGUE* GU4........ **117** M6
Balfont Cl *SAND/SEL* CR2 .... **88** D3
Balfour Av *WOKS/MYFD* GU22 .. **97** H4
Balfour Crs *BRAK* RG12 ...... **34** E5
Balfour Rd *CAR* SM5 .... **66** B6
HSLW TW3 .... **16** E5 🔲
SNWD SE25 .... **50** D4
WEY KT13 .... **59** J3
WIM/MER SW19 .... **29** L8
Balgonie Rd *FUL/PGN* SW6.. **46** B4 🔲
Balgowan Rd *BECK* BR3 .... **51** H3
Balham Gv *BAL* SW12 .... **30** D1
Balham High Rd *BAL* SW12..... **30** D3
Balham Hl *BAL* SW12 .... **30** E1
Balham New Rd *BAL* SW12 ..... **30** E1
Balham Park Rd *TOOT* SW17 ... **30** C2
Balham Station Rd *BAL* SW12.. **30** D2
Balintore Ct *SHST* GU47 ..... **72** A2 🔲
The Ballands North
LHD/OX KT22 .... **102** B4
The Ballands' South
LHD/OX KT22 .... **102** B5
Ball And Wicket La *FNM* GU9 .. **133** M2
Ballantyne Dr
KWD/TDW/WH KT20 .... **105** J3
Ballantyne Rd *FARN* GU14 .... **92** D3
Ballard Cl *KUTN/CMB* KT2 .... **28** A8
Ballard Rd *CBLY* GU15 .... **73** K1
Ballards Farm Rd *SAND/SEL* CR2 .. **68** D5
Ballards Gn
KWD/TDW/WH KT20 .... **105** H1
Ballards La *OXTED* RH8 ...... **130** F3
Ballards Ri *SAND/SEL* CR2 ... **68** D5
Ballater Rd *SAND/SEL* CR2 ... **68** C4
Ballencrieff Rd *ASC* SL5 .... **37** J7
Ballfield Rd *RGODL* GU7 ..... **160** A3
Ballina St *FSTH* SE23........ **33** G1
Balliol Cl *CRAWE* RH10 ...... **193** C8 🔲
Balliol Wy *SHST* GU47 .... **52** B8
Balloon Rd *FARN* GU14........ **92** E7
Balmoral Av *BECK* BR3 .... **51** H4
Balmoral Crs *E/WMO/HCT* KT8 .. **43** K3
FNM GU9 .... **133** L3 🔲
Balmoral Dr *FRIM* GU16 ...... **93** H1
WOKS/MYFD GU22 .... **7** L4
Balmoral Gdns *SAND/SEL* CR2 .. **68** A8
Balmoral Rd *ASHV* GU12 ...... **113** K5
KUT KT1 .... **45** J4
WPK KT4 .... **64** E2
Balmoral Wy *BELMT* SM2 ...... **65** K8
Balmuir Gdns *PUT/ROE* SW15 .. **19** M6
Balquhain Cl *ASHTD* KT21 .... **83** G7 🔲
Baltic Cl *WIM/MER* SW19 ..... **30** A8
Balvernie Gv *WAND/EARL* SW18 . **29** J1
Bampfylde Cl *WLGTN* SM6...... **66** F2
Bampton Rd *FSTH* SE23 .... **33** G4
Bampton Wy *WOKN/KNAP* GU21 .. **76** D8
Banavie Gdns *BECK* BR3 ...... **51** L1
Banbury *BRAK* RG12 .... **35** H7
Banbury Cl *FRIM* GU16 .... **93** K2 🔲
Bancroft Cl *ASHF* TW15 ...... **23** K6 🔲
Bancroft Ct *REIG* RH2 .... **125** L8
Bancroft Rd *CRAWE* RH10 ..... **213** C2
REIG RH2 .... **125** K8
Banders Ri *GU* GU1 .... **117** M7
Band La *EGH* TW20 .... **21** J6
Bandon Rd *WLGTN* SM6 .... **67** G5
Bangalore St *PUT/ROE* SW15 .. **19** M5
Bank Av *MTCM* CR4 .... **48** A2
Bankhurst Rd *CAT* SE6 .... **33** J1
Bank La *CRAWE* RH10 .... **212** A3
KUTN/CMB KT2 .... **2** E1
PUT/ROE SW15 .... **19** H7
Bank Rd *ALDT* GU11 .... **113** G4
Bankside *FNM* GU9 .... **134** C2
SAND/SEL CR2 .... **68** C5
WOKN/KNAP GU21 .... **76** E3
Bankside Cl *BH/WHM* TN16 .... **90** F8 🔲
CAR SM5 .... **66** B4
ISLW TW7 .... **17** J6
MFD/CHID GU8 .... **158** A6 🔲
Bankside Dr *THDIT* KT7 ...... **62** E1

Bank's La *EHSLY* KT24 .... **100** E4
Banks Rd *CRAWE* RH10 .... **212** F4
Banks Wy *GU* GU1 .... **117** J5
Bank Willow *RCHPK/HAM* TW10.. **26** E4
Bannister Cl
BRXS/STRHM SW2 .... **31** K2 🔲
MFD/CHID GU8 .... **181** J4
Bannister's Rd *GUW* GU2 ..... **138** C2
Banstead Rd *BELMT* SM2 ...... **66** A6
BNSTD SM7 .... **85** H3
CAR SM5 .... **66** B5
CTHM CR3 .... **108** A4
EW KT17 .... **64** E8
PUR/KEN CR8 .... **87** K1
Banstead Rd South *BELMT* SM2 . **65** M8
Banstead Wy *WLGTN* SM6 ...... **67** H4 🔲
Barbara Cl *SHPTN* TW17 ...... **41** L5
Barber Cl *CRAWE* RH10 .... **212** F7
Barber Dr *CRAN* GU6 .... **185** H5 🔲
Barberry Wy *BLKW* GU17...... **72** C6
Barbon Cl *CBLY* GU15 .... **74** A6
Barclay Ct *GT/LBKH* KT23 .... **101** L5
Barclay Rd *CROY/NA* CR0 ..... **4** E7
Barcombe Av *BRXS/STRHM* SW2 . **31** H3
Bardney Rd *MRDN* SM4 .... **47** L4
Bardolph Av *CROY/NA* CR0 .... **69** J7
Bardon Wk *WOKN/KNAP* GU21 .. **76** E7 🔲
Bardsley Cl *CROY/NA* CR0 .... **5** J7
Barge Cl *ALDT* GU11 .... **113** H4
Bargery Rd *CAT* SE6 .... **33** L2
Bargate Cl *NWMAL* KT3 .... **46** D7
Bargate Ri *RGODL* GU7 .... **159** M5
Barge Cl *ALDT* GU11 .... **113** H4
Bargrove Cl *PGE/AN* SE20 .... **32** D8 🔲
Bargrove Crs *CAT* SE6 .... **33** J5 🔲
Barham Cl *WEY* KT13 .... **59** M3
Barham Rd *CROY/NA* CR0 ...... **67** M3
RYNPK SW20 .... **28** D8
Barhatch La *CRAN* GU6 .... **185** J3
Barhatch Rd *CRAN* GU6 .... **185** J5
Baring Rd *CROY/NA* CR0 ...... **5** M3
Barker Rd *CHERT* KT16 .... **40** B7
Barkis Md *SHST* GU47 .... **52** B7 🔲
Barley Cl *CRAWW* RH11 .... **212** A4
Barley Mow Cl
WOKN/KNAP GU21 .... **76** A7
Barley Mow Ct
BRKHM/BTCW RH3 .... **123** M8
Barley Mow La
WOKN/KNAP GU21 .... **75** M6
Barley Mow Rd *EGH* TW20 ..... **20** F6
Barley Mow Wy *SHPTN* TW17 .. **41** K4 🔲
Barlow Cl *WLGTN* SM6 .... **67** H5
Barlow Rd *CRAWW* RH11 .... **211** H6
HPTN TW12 .... **25** K8
Barmeston Rd *CAT* SE6 .... **33** L3
Barmouth Rd *CROY/NA* CR0 .... **69** G1
Barnard Cl *FRIM* GU16 .... **93** J1
SUN TW16 .... **24** E8 🔲
WLGTN SM6 .... **67** G6
Barnard Gdns *NWMAL* KT3 ..... **46** D4
Barnard Rd *MTCM* CR4 .... **48** D3
WARL CR6 .... **109** L1
Barnards Pl *SAND/SEL* CR2 ... **67** L7
Barnato Cl *BF/WBF* KT14 ..... **79** H2
Barnby Rd *WOKN/KNAP* GU21 .. **76** A7
Barncroft *FNM* GU9 .... **11** L6
BNSTD SM7 .... **86** A5
*RG12 .... **35** G2
CBLY GU15 .... **73** H3
Barn Ct *CRAWE* RH10 .... **194** B7
Barn Crs *PUR/KEN* CR8 .... **88** A3 🔲
Barncroft *FNM* GU9 .... **11** H7
Barnes Av *BARN* SW13 .... **19** K2
Barnes Br *CHSWK* W4 .... **19** H4
Barnes Cl *FARN* GU14 .... **93** C5
Barnes End *NWMAL* KT3 .... **46** D5
Barnes High St *BARN* SW13 ... **19** J4
Barnes Rd *FRIM* GU16 .... **93** H1
RGODL GU7 .... **160** B1
Barnes Wallis Dr *WEY* KT13 .. **79** H1
Barnet Dr *HAYES* BR2 .... **71** H1
Barnett Cl *LHD/OX* KT22 ..... **102** E1
SHGR GU5 .... **161** M1
Barnett Ct *BRAK* RG12 .... **34** F2 🔲
Barnett Gn *BRAK* RG12 .... **34** E6
Barnett La *LTWR* GU18........ **74** C2
SHGR GU5 .... **161** L2
Barnett Rw *RGUE* GU4 .... **117** C3
Barnett's Shaw *OXTED* RH8 ... **130** A1
Barnet Wood Rd *HAYES* BR2 ... **70** E2
Barn Fld *BNSTD* SM7 .... **85** L4 🔲
Barnfield *CRAN* GU6 .... **185** H6 🔲
Barnfield Av *CROY/NA* CR0 ... **50** F8
KUTN/CMB KT2 .... **27** C5
MTCM CR4 .... **48** E4
Barnfield Cl *COUL/CHIP* CR5 .. **107** M1
Barnfield Gdns *KUTN/CMB* KT2 . **27** H6
Barnfield Rd *BH/WHM* TN16.... **111** C2
CRAWE RH10 .... **212** A2
SAND/SEL CR2 .... **68** B7
Barnfield Wy *OXTED* RH8 ..... **130** D7
Barnlea Cl *FELT* TW13 .... **25** H3
Barnmead *CHOB/PIR* GU24 ..... **56** C8
Barn Meadow La
GT/LBKH KT23 .... **101** J6
Barnmead Rd *BECK* BR3 .... **51** H1
Barn Rd *ADL/WDHM* KT15 ...... **58** E7 🔲
Barnsbury Cl *NWMAL* KT3 ..... **45** M4
Barnsbury Crs *BRYLDS* KT5.... **45** M8
Barnsbury La *BRYLDS* KT5 .... **63** L1
Barnsfold La *HORS* RH12 ..... **225** H3
Barnsford Crs *CHOB/PIR* GU24 . **75** K2
Barnsley Cl *FRIM* GU16 ...... **93** J1
Barnsnap Cl *HORS* RH12 ...... **229** C3
Barnway *EGH* TW20 .... **20** F6
Barnwood Cl *CRAWE* RH10 ..... **212** F2
RGUW GU3 .... **116** B6
Barnwood Ct *GUW* GU2 .... **116** B6
Barnwood Rd *GUW* GU2 .... **116** B7 🔲
The Barnyard
KWD/TDW/WH KT20 .... **104** D6

Baron Cl *BELMT* SM2 .... **65** L8
Baron Gv *MTCM* CR4 .... **48** B4
Baronsfield Rd *TWK* TW1 ..... **17** L8 🔲
Baron's Hurst *EPSOM* KT18.... **83** M6
Baronsmead Rd *BARN* SW13 ... **19** K3 🔲
The Barons *TWK* TW1 .... **17** L8
Baron's Wk *CROY/NA* CR0 ..... **51** H6 🔲
Barons Wy *EGH* TW20 .... **22** A7
REIG RH2 .... **147** K4
Barossa Rd *CBLY* GU15 .... **73** G2
Barrack Pth *WOKN/KNAP* GU21 .. **76** C8
Barrack Rd *ALDT* GU11 .... **112** D7 🔲
GUW GU2 .... **116** D6
HSLWW TW4 .... **16** A6
Barrens Brae *WOKS/MYFD* GU22 . **7** H8
Barrens Cl *WOKS/MYFD* GU22 .. **7** H9 🔲
Barrens Pk *WOKS/MYFD* GU22 .. **7** H8
Barrett Rd *GT/LBKH* KT23 .... **101** M7
Barricane *WOKN/KNAP* GU21 .. **96** E1
Barrie Cl *COUL/CHIP* CR5 .... **86** F6
Barrie Rd *FNM* GU9 .... **133** K2
Barrihurst La *CRAN* GU6 ..... **184** A7
Barringer Sq *TOOT* SW17 ..... **30** D5 🔲
Barrington Ct *DORK* RH4 ..... **144** D3 🔲
Barrington Ldg *WEY* KT13 .... **59** M4 🔲
Barrington Rd *CHEAM* SM3..... **47** K8
CRAWE RH10 .... **212** A5
DORK RH4 .... **144** D3 🔲
PUR/KEN CR8 .... **86** F7
SWTR RH13 .... **229** H7
Barrow Av *CAR* SM5 .... **66** C6
Barrow Green Rd *OXTED* RH8 .. **129** M3
Barrow Hedges Cl *CAR* SM5 ... **66** B6
Barrow Hedges Wy *CAR* SM5 ... **66** B6
Barrow Hl *WPK* KT4 .... **64** B1
Barrow Hill Cl *WPK* KT4 ..... **64** B1 🔲
Barrow Rd *CROY/NA* CR0 ...... **67** K4
STRHM/NOR SW16 .... **31** G7
Barr's La *WOKN/KNAP* GU21 .. **76** A6
Barry Cl *CRAWE* RH10 .... **212** B6
Barry Sq *BRAK* RG12 .... **35** G7
Barsons Cl *PGE/AN* SE20 ..... **32** F8
The Bars *GU* GU1 .... **9** C6
Barston Rd *WNWD* SE27 .... **31** M3
Barstow Crs *BRXS/STRHM* SW2 . **31** J2
Bartholomew Cl *HASM* GU27 .. **220** A1 🔲
Bartholomew Wy *HORS* RH12 .. **229** K3
Bartlett St *SAND/SEL* CR2 ... **68** A4 🔲
Barton Cl *ADL/WDHM* KT15 .... **58** D5
ALDT GU11 .... **112** B8
SHPTN TW17 .... **41** L6
Barton Crs *EGRIN* RH19 ...... **216** D1
Barton Gn *NWMAL* KT3 .... **46** A2
Barton Rd *SHGR* GU5 .... **161** K3
The Barton *COB* KT11 .... **81** C2
Barts Cl *BECK* BR3 .... **51** K5
Barttelot Rd *HORS* RH12 ..... **228** F8
Barwood Av *WWKM* BR4 .... **51** L8
Basden Gv *FELT* TW13 .... **25** K3
Basemoors *BRAK* RG12 .... **35** H2 🔲
Bashford Wy *CRAWE* RH10 ..... **213** C1
Basildene Rd *HSLWW* TW4 ..... **16** A5
Basildon Cl *BELMT* SM2 ...... **65** L7
Basildon Wy *CRAWW* RH11 ..... **211** H6
Basil Gdns *CROY/NA* CR0 ..... **51** C8 🔲
WNWD SE27 .... **31** M6
Basing Cl *THDIT* KT7 .... **44** C7
Basing Dr *ALDT* GU11 .... **134** E2
Basingfield Rd *THDIT* KT7 ... **44** C7
Basinghall Rd *BELMT* SM2 .... **65** L7
Basing Rd *BNSTD* SM7 .... **85** J5
Basing Wy *THDIT* KT7 .... **44** C7
Baskerville Rd
WAND/EARL SW18 .... **30** B1
Basset Cl *ADL/WDHM* KT15 .... **58** E8
Bassett Cl *BELMT* SM2 .... **65** L7
FRIM GU16 .... **93** H1
Bassett Gdns *ISLW* TW7 ...... **16** F2
Bassett Rd *CRAWE* RH10 ...... **213** C6
WOKS/MYFD GU22 .... **7** L4
Bassetts Cl *ORP* BR6 .... **71** L3 🔲
Bassetts Hl *LING* RH7 .... **174** D8 🔲
Bassetts Wy *ORP* BR6 .... **71** L3
Bassingham Rd
WAND/EARL SW18 .... **29** M1
Baston Manor Rd *WWKM* BR4 ... **70** E2
Baston Rd *HAYES* BR2 .... **70** E1
Bat And Ball La *FNM* GU9 .... **10** C8
NFNM GU10 .... **10** D9
Batavia Cl *SUN* TW16 .... **42** E1
Batavia Rd *SUN* TW16 .... **42** E1
Batcombe Md *BRAK* RG12 ...... **35** H7
Batemans Ct *CRAWE* RH10 ..... **212** D6
Bateman Rd *CRAWE* RH10 ...... **212** D6
Bateson Wy *WOKN/KNAP* GU21 .. **77** M4
Bates Wk *ADL/WDHM* KT15..... **58** F5
Bathgate Rd *WIM/MER* SW19 .. **29** H4
Bath House Rd *CROY/NA* CR0 .. **49** H8
Bath Pas *KUT* KT1 .... **2** D7
Bath Rd *CBLY* GU15 .... **72** F3
DTCH/LGLY SL3 .... **13** H3
HEST TW5 .... **15** L3 🔲
HSLWW TW4 .... **15** M5
HTHAIR TW6 .... **14** E3
Bathurst Av *WIM/MER* SW19 .. **47** L1 🔲
Batley Cl *MTCM* CR4 .... **48** C7
Batsworth Rd *MTCM* CR4 ...... **48** A3
Batten Av *WOKN/KNAP* GU21 .. **96** B1
Battlebridge La *REDH* RH1 ... **126** F4
Battle Cl *WIM/MER* SW19 .... **29** M7 🔲
Batts Hl *REDH* RH1 .... **126** A6
The Baulk *WAND/EARL* SW18 .. **29** K1
Bavant Rd *STRHM/NOR* SW16 .. **49** H7
Bawtree Cl *BELMT* SM2 .... **65** M7
Bax Cl *CRAN* GU6 .... **185** H7
Baxter Av *REDH* RH1 .... **126** B8
Baxter Cl *CRAWE* RH10 .... **212** E5 🔲
Bayards *WARL* CR6 .... **88** F8
Bay Cl *HORL* RH6 .... **170** B3
Bayeux Wy *KWD/TDW/WH* KT20... **105** C4
Bayfield Av *FRIM* GU16 ...... **73** H7
Bayfield Rd *HORL* RH6 .... **170** B3
Bayford Cl *FARN* GU14 .... **72** D8
Bayham Rd *MRDN* SM4 .... **47** L4
Bayhorne La *HORL* RH6 .... **170** F8

Bayleaf Cl *HPTN* TW12 .... **26** A6
Baynards Rd *HORS* RH12 ...... **205** K7
Bay Rd *BRAK* RG12 .... **35** H1
Bays Cl *SYD* SE26 .... **32** F6
Baysfarm Ct *WDR/YW* UB7 ..... **13** M3
Baythorn La *ASC* SL5 .... **36** D2
Bay Tree Av *LHD/OX* KT22 .... **102** D2
Bazalgette Cl *NWMAL* KT3..... **45** M5
Bazalgette Gdns *NWMAL* KT3... **46** A5
Beachborough Rd *BMLY* BR1.... **33** M5
Beach Gv *FELT* TW13 .... **25** K4
Beachy Rd *CRAWW* RH11 .... **211** L8
Beacon Cl *BNSTD* SM7 .... **85** G6
GU GU10 .... **155** K4
Beacon Ct *DTCH/LGLY* SL3 .... **12** F2
Beacon HI *LING* RH7 .... **196** E1
WOKN/KNAP GU21 .... **96** F1
Beacon Hill Ct *GSHT* GU26 ... **199** G3
Beacon Hill Rd *GSHT* GU26 ... **198** F3
Beacon Rd *FARN* GU14 .... **112** E1
HTHAIR TW6 .... **14** D8
Beaconsfield Pl *EW* KT17 .... **84** D1 🔲
Beaconsfield Rd *BRYLDS* KT5 .. **45** J7
CROY/NA CR0 .... **50** A6
EPSOM KT18 .... **104** A1
ESH/CLAY KT10 .... **62** B6
NWMAL KT3 .... **46** A2
TWK TW1 .... **26** E1
WOKS/MYFD GU22 .... **97** J2 🔲
Beacon View Rd
MFD/CHID GU8 .... **157** M7
Beacon Wy *BNSTD* SM7 .... **85** G6
Beadles La *OXTED* RH8 .... **130** A4
Beadlow Cl *MRDN* SM4 .... **48** A6 🔲
Beadman Pl *WNWD* SE27 .... **31** L5 🔲
Beadman St *WNWD* SE27 .... **31** L5
Beadnell Rd *FSTH* SE23 ...... **33** G2
Beaford Gv *RYNPK* SW20 ...... **47** H3
Beagle Cl *FELT* TW13 .... **24** E5
Beales La *NFNM* GU10 .... **10** A6
WEY KT13 .... **59** L2
Bealeswood La *NFNM* GU10 .... **177** H3
Beam Hollow *FNM* GU9 .... **133** M2 🔲
Beardell St *NRWD* SE19 ...... **32** C7
Beard Rd *RCHPK/HAM* TW10 .... **27** J6
Beards Hill *HPTN* TW12 ...... **43** K1
Beards Hill Cl *HPTN* TW12 ... **43** K1
Beards Rd *ASHF* TW15 .... **24** B7
Bearfield Rd *KUTN/CMB* KT2 .. **2** E3
Bear La *FNM* GU9 .... **133** L6
Bear Rd *FELT* TW13 .... **25** G5
Bears Den *KWD/TDW/WH* KT20... **105** J4
Bearsden Wy *HORS* RH12 ...... **228** B3
Bearwood Cl
ADL/WDHM KT15 .... **58** D5 🔲
Beasley's Ait *SHPTN* TW17 ... **42** C6
Beasley's Ait La *SUN* TW16 .. **42** C6
Beatrice Av *STRHM/NOR* SW16 . **49** J3
RCHPK/HAM TW10 .... **18** C7 🔲
Beattie Cl *EBED/NFELT* TW14 . **24** C2
GT/LBKH KT23 .... **101** J6
Beatty Av *GU* GU1 .... **117** K7
Beauchamp Rd
E/WMO/HCT KT8 .... **43** L5
SUT SM1 .... **65** K4
THHTH CR7 .... **50** A1
TWK TW1 .... **26** D1
Beauchamp Ter
PUT/ROE SW15 .... **19** L5 🔲
Beauclare Cl *ASHTD* KT21 .... **103** C3 🔲
Beauclerk Cl *FELT* TW13 ..... **24** E2 🔲
Beaufighter Rd *FARN* GU14 ... **112** D1
Beaufort Ct *PUT/ROE* SW15 ... **28** F2
REIG RH2 .... **125** J7
WOKS/MYFD GU22 .... **7** L3
Beaufort Gdns *ASC* SL5 ...... **36** B1
HEST TW5 .... **16** B3
STRHM/NOR SW16 .... **31** J8
Beaufort Rd *FNM* GU9 .... **133** M6
KUT KT1 .... **45** H4
RCHPK/HAM TW10 .... **26** E1
REIG RH2 .... **125** J7
TWK TW1 .... **26** F1
WOKS/MYFD GU22 .... **7** L4
Beauforts *EGH* TW20 .... **20** F6
Beaufort Wy *EW* KT17 .... **64** D6
Beaufront Cl *CBLY* GU15 ..... **73** K2
Beaufront Rd *CBLY* GU15 ..... **73** K2
Beaulieu Av *SYD* SE26 .... **32** E5
Beaulieu Cl *BRAK* RG12 ...... **35** J3
HSLWW TW4 .... **16** C7
MTCM CR4 .... **48** D1 🔲
TWK TW1 .... **18** A8 🔲
Beaumaris Pde *FRIM* GU16 .... **93** J1
Beaumont Av *RCH/KEW* TW9 ... **18** C5 🔲
Beaumont Cl *CRAWW* RH11 ..... **211** H4 🔲
Beaumont Dr *ASHF* TW15 ...... **24** A6 🔲
Beaumont Gdns *BRAK* RG12 ... **35** H5 🔲
Beaumont Pl *ISLW* TW7 .... **17** J7
Beaumont Rd *NRWD* SE19 ...... **31** M7
PUR/KEN CR8 .... **87** K3
WIM/MER SW19 .... **29** H1
Beaumonts *REDH* RH1 .... **148** C8
Beaver Cl *HORS* RH12 .... **229** H3
HPTN TW12 .... **43** L1
PGE/AN SE20 .... **32** D8 🔲
Beavers Cl *FNM* GU9 .... **133** K7
GUW GU2 .... **116** B7 🔲
Beavers Hl *FNM* GU9 .... **133** J7
Beavers La *HSLWW* TW4 .... **15** M5
Beavers Rd *FNM* GU9 .... **133** K7
Beck Ct *BECK* BR3 .... **51** G3
Beckenham Hill Rd *BECK* BR3 . **33** L3
Beckenham Place Pk *BECK* BR3 . **33** L8
Beckenham Rd *BECK* BR3 ...... **51** G1
WWKM BR4 .... **51** L7
Beckenshaw Gdns *BNSTD* SM7 .. **86** B5
Becket Cl *SNWD* SE25 .... **50** D6
Becket Rd *PUR/KEN* CR8 ...... **87** L5
Beckett Cl *CRAWW* RH11 ...... **192** A8
STRHM/NOR SW16 .... **31** C7
Beckett La *CRAWW* RH11 ...... **192** A8
Becketts Cl *EBED/NFELT* TW14 . **15** L3
Becketts Pl *KUT* KT1 .... **2** C5
Beckett Wk *BECK* BR3 .... **33** H7
Beckett Wy *EGRIN* RH19 ...... **216** C1 🔲
Becket Wd *RDKG* RH5 .... **167** M5

Beckford Av *BRAK* RG12 .... 34 E6
Beckford Rd *CROY/NA* CR0 ..... 50 C6
Beckford St *CROY/NA* CR0 ...... 212 E8
Beck Gdns *FNM* GU9 .... 133 K3
Beckingham Rd *GUW* GU2 .... 8 A1
Beck La *BECK* BR3 .... 51 C3
Beck River Pk *BECK* BR3 .... 51 K1
Beck Wy *BECK* BR3 .... 51 J3
Beckway Rd *STRHM/NOR* SW16 . 49 G2
Beclands Rd *TOOT* SW17 .... 30 D7
Becmead Av *STRHM/NOR* SW16 . 31 G5
Becondale Rd *NRWD* SE19 .... 32 B6
Bedale Cl *CRAWW* RH11 .... 211 M5
Beddington Farm Rd *CROY/NA* CR0 49 H8
   WLGTN SM6 .... 66 D5
Beddington Gdns *CAR* SM5 ...... 66 D5
   WLGTN SM6 .... 66 C4
Beddington Gv *WLGTN* SM6 ..... 67 G4
Beddington La *CROY/NA* CR0 ... 67 H1
   MTCM CR4 .... 48 F6
Beddlestead La *WARL* CR6 ...... 90 C8
Bedfont Cl *EBED/NFELT* TW14 .. 14 F8
   MTCM CR4 .... 48 D2
Bedfont Ct *STWL/WRAY* TW19 .. 13 K5
Bedfont Green Cl
   EBED/NFELT TW14 .... 23 M2
Bedfont La *EBED/NFELT* TW14 .. 24 B1
   FELT TW13 .... 24 C4
   STWL/WRAY TW19 .... 14 C8
Bedford Av *BRAK* RG12 .... 35 J4
Bedford Cl *CHSWK* W4 .... 19 H1
   WOKN/KNAP GU21 .... 76 F5
Bedford Crs *FRIM* GU16 .... 93 H3
Bedford Hl *BAL* SW12 .... 30 E3
Bedford La *ASC* SL5 .... 37 L5
   FRIM GU16 .... 93 J3
Bedford Pk *CROY/NA* CR0 .... 4 D4
Bedford Pl *CROY/NA* CR0 .... 4 E1
Bedford Rd *GU* GU1 .... 8 F6
   SWTR RH13 .... 229 G8
   WHTN TW2 .... 26 A4
   WPK KT4 .... 64 F1
Bedgebury Gdns
   WIM/MER SW19 .... 29 H3
Bedlow Wy *CROY/NA* CR0 .... 67 J3
Bedser Cl *THHTH* CR7 .... 49 M3
   WOKN/KNAP GU21 .... 7 C4
Bedster Gdns *E/WMO/HCT* KT8 . 43 L2
Bedwardine Rd *NRWD* SE19 ..... 32 B8
Beech Av *BH/WHM* TN16 .... 111 C1
   BTFD TW8 .... 17 L2
   CBLY GU15 .... 73 C5
   EHSLY KT24 .... 121 G4
   NFNM GU10 .... 11 H9
   SAND/SEL CR2 .... 88 A1
Beech Cl *ASHF* TW15 .... 24 A6
   BF/WBF KT14 .... 79 H2
   CAR SM5 .... 66 C1
   COB KT11 .... 81 K2
   DORK RH4 .... 144 C1
   EHSLY KT24 .... 121 G2
   LING RH7 .... 173 H1
   MFD/CHID GU8 .... 201 K5
   PUT/ROE SW15 .... 28 D1
   RYNPK SW20 .... 28 F7
   STWL/WRAY TW19 .... 23 C1
   SUN TW16 .... 43 G2
   WOT/HER KT12 .... 60 F3
Beech Close Ct *COB* KT11 .... 81 J1
Beech Copse *SAND/SEL* CR2 .... 68 B4
Beech Crs *KWD/TDW/WH* KT20 . 123 M4
Beechcroft *ASHTD* KT21 .... 103 J1
Beechcroft Cl *ASC* SL5 .... 37 G4
   NWMAL KT3 .... 45 M1
   PUR/KEN CR8 .... 88 A5
Beechcroft Cl *ASC* SL5 .... 37 C4
   HEST TW5 .... 16 B2
   STRHM/NOR SW16 .... 31 K6
Beechcroft Dr *RGUW* GU3 .... 138 C3
Beechcroft Rd *CHSGTN* KT9 ..... 63 J2
   MORT/ESHN SW14 .... 18 F5
   TOOT SW17 .... 30 C4
Beech Dell *HAYES* BR2 .... 71 J3
Beechdene
   KWD/TDW/WH KT20 .... 104 F4
Beech Dr *BLKW* GU17 .... 72 A5
   KWD/TDW/WH KT20 .... 105 J4
   REIG RH2 .... 126 A8
   RPLY/SEND GU23 .... 98 C7
Beechen Cliff Wy *ISLW* TW7 .... 17 J3
Beechen La
   KWD/TDW/WH KT20 .... 105 J7
Beechen Pl *FSTH* SE23 .... 32 F3
The Beeches Av *CAR* SM5 .... 66 B6
Beeches Cl *KWD/TDW/WH* KT20 105 K5
   PGE/AN SE20 .... 50 F1
Beeches Crs *CRAWE* RH10 ...... 212 F5
Beeches La *EGRIN* RH19 .... 217 G3
Beeches Rd *CHEAM* SM3 .... 47 H8
   TOOT SW17 .... 30 B4
The Beeches *ASHV* GU12 .... 93 J8
   BNSTD SM7 .... 85 L6
   LHD/OX KT22 .... 102 B6
   SHGR GU5 .... 161 J3
Beeches Wk *CAR* SM5 .... 66 A7
Beeches Wd
   KWD/TDW/WH KT20 .... 105 K4
Beechey Cl *CRAWE* RH10 .... 193 L6
Beechey Wy *CRAWE* RH10 .... 193 L6
Beech Farm Rd *WARL* CR6 ...... 110 A2
Beechfield *BNSTD* SM7 .... 85 L3
Beechfield Rd *CAT* SE6 .... 33 J2
Beech Flds *EGRIN* RH19 .... 196 H6
Beech Gdns *CRAWE* RH10 .... 214 D2
   WOKN/KNAP GU21 .... 6 C2
Beech Gln *BRAK* RG12 .... 34 E4
Beech Gv *ADL/WDHM* KT15 ..... 58 E3
   CHOB/PIR GU24 .... 94 F2
   CTHM CR3 .... 108 A8
   EPSOM KT18 .... 84 E7
   GT/LBKH KT23 .... 121 K1
   GUW GU2 .... 116 C4
   MTCM CR4 .... 49 C5
   NWMAL KT3 .... 46 A3
Beech Hanger End *GSHT* GU26 . 198 E6
Beech Hl *MFD/CHID* GU8 .... 180 C8
   WOKS/MYFD GU22 .... 97 G5
Beech Hill Av *ASC* SL5 .... 37 H6

Beech Holme *CRAWE* RH10 ...... 214 D1
Beech Holt *LHD/OX* KT22 .... 102 F4
Beech House Rd *CROY/NA* CR0 . 4 E7
Beeching Cl *ASHV* GU12 .... 113 L6
Beeching Wy *EGRIN* RH19 .... 196 B8
Beech La *GSHT* GU26 .... 198 D5
   GUW GU2 .... 8 E9
   SHGR GU5 .... 114 D8
Beechlawn *GU* GU1 .... 9 L5
Beechmeads *COB* KT11 .... 81 G3
Beechmont Av *VW* GU25 .... 39 G6
Beechmore Gdns *CHEAM* SM3 .. 65 G1
Beechnut Rd *ASHV* GU12 .... 112 E8
Beecholme Av *MTCM* CR4 .... 48 E1
Beech Rd *BH/WHM* TN16 .... 90 F7
   EBED/NFELT TW14 .... 24 B1
   EPSOM KT18 .... 84 C5
   FARN GU14 .... 92 E2
   FRIM GU16 .... 93 J3
   HASM GU27 .... 220 A2
   HORS RH12 .... 229 L4
   REDH RH1 .... 106 F8
   REIG RH2 .... 125 K5
   STRHM/NOR SW16 .... 49 H2
   WEY KT13 .... 60 A3
Beechrow *KUTN/CMB* KT2 .... 27 H5
Beechside *CRAWE* RH10 .... 212 B4
Beechtree Av *EGH* TW20 .... 20 E7
Beech Tree Cl *CRAWW* RH11 ... 212 A2
Beech Tree Dr *FNM* GU9 .... 134 D4
Beech Tree La *STA* TW18 .... 40 E2
Beech Tree Pl *SUT* SM1 .... 65 L4
Beech Wy *EW* KT17 .... 84 C5
   FELT TW13 .... 25 K4
   RGODL GU7 .... 160 A6
Beechwood Av *COUL/CHIP* CR5 . 86 E5
   KWD/TDW/WH KT20 .... 105 K3
   RCH/KEW TW9 .... 18 D3
   STA TW18 .... 22 E7
   SUN TW16 .... 24 D7
   THHTH CR7 .... 49 L4
   WEY KT13 .... 60 A3
Beechwood Cl *SURB* KT6 .... 44 F7
   ASC SL5 .... 37 G4
   WOKN/KNAP GU21 .... 76 B7
   HAYES BR2 .... 71 G3
Beechwood Gdns *CTHM* CR3 ... 108 D4
Beechwood La *WARL* CR6 .... 109 G1
Beechwood Mnr *WEY* KT13 ..... 60 B3
Beechwood Pk *LHD/OX* KT22 ... 102 F4
   SAND/SEL CR2 .... 68 B7
   VW GU25 .... 38 E7
   WOKN/KNAP GU21 .... 76 B8
Beechwood Vls *REDH* RH1 ...... 170 D2
Beecot La *WOT/HER* KT12 .... 60 F1
Beeding Cl *HORS* RH12 .... 229 K4
Beedon Dr *BRAK* RG12 .... 34 A6
Beehive Ring Rd *CRAWE* RH10 . 192 E5
Beehive Rd *BRAK* RG12 .... 34 A2
   STA TW18 .... 22 C6
Beehive Wy *REIG* RH2 .... 147 L4
Beeken Dene *ORP* BR6 .... 71 M3
Beeleigh Rd *MRDN* SM4 .... 47 L5
Beeston Wy *EBED/NFELT* TW14 . 15 M8
Beeton's Av *ASHV* GU12 .... 113 K5
Begbie Rd *CAT* SE6 .... 33 M2
Beggars La *CHOB/PIR* GU24 .... 75 M1
   SHGR GU5 .... 142 B4
Beggar's Roost La *SUT* SM1 .... 65 K5
Begonia Pl *HPTN* TW12 .... 25 K7
Behenna Cl *CRAWW* RH11 ...... 211 H4
Beira St *BAL* SW12 .... 30 E1
Beldam Bridge Rd
   CHOB/PIR GU24 .... 75 J4
Beldham Gdns *E/WMO/HCT* KT8 . 43 L3
Beldham Rd *NFNM* GU10 .... 10 B5
Belfast Rd *SNWD* SE25 .... 50 E4
Belfield Rd *HOR/WEW* KT19 .... 64 A7
Belgrade Rd *HPTN* TW12 .... 43 L1
Belgrave Cl *BLKW* GU17 .... 72 A6
Belgrave Crs *SUN* TW16 .... 42 E1
Belgrave Mnr *WOKS/MYFD* GU22 . 6 C9
Belgrave Rd *BARN* SW13 .... 19 J2
   HSLWW TW4 .... 16 C5
   MTCM CR4 .... 48 A3
   SNWD SE25 .... 50 C4
   SUN TW16 .... 42 E1
Belgravia Ms *KUT* KT1 .... 45 K2
Bellamy Rd *CRAWE* RH10 .... 212 F7
Bellamy St *BAL* SW12 .... 30 E1
Belland Dr *ALDT* GU11 .... 112 B8
Bellasis Av *BRXS/STRHM* SW2 . 31 H2
Bell Bridge Rd *CHERT* KT16 .... 40 C8
Bell Cl *FARN* GU14 .... 92 E5
Bell Crs *COUL/CHIP* CR5 .... 106 E3
Bell Dr *WAND/EARL* SW18 ...... 29 H1
Bellever Hl *CBLY* GU15 .... 73 H4
Belle Vue Cl *ASHV* GU12 .... 113 G7
   STA TW18 .... 40 D1
Bellevue Pk *THHTH* CR7 .... 49 M3
Belle Vue Rd *ASHV* GU12 .... 113 G8
   ORP BR6 .... 71 K8
Bellevue Rd *BARN* SW13 .... 19 K4
   KUT KT1 .... 2 F9
   TOOT SW17 .... 30 C1
Bellew Rd *FRIM* GU16 .... 93 L3
Bellew St *TOOT* SW17 .... 29 M4
Bellfields Rd *GU* GU1 .... 117 G6
Bell Gn *SYD* SE26 .... 33 H5
Bell Green La *SYD* SE26 .... 33 J6
Bell Hammer *EGRIN* RH19 ...... 216 D1
Bellingham Cl *CBLY* GU15 .... 73 M5
Bellingham Gn *CAT* SE6 .... 33 K4
Bellingham Rd *CAT* SE6 .... 33 M4
Bell La *LHD/OX* KT22 .... 102 A5
   NFNM GU10 .... 155 H6
   TWK TW1 .... 26 C1
Bell Lane End *LHD/OX* KT22 .... 102 A5
Bellmarsh Rd *ADL/WDHM* KT15 . 58 E3
Bell Meadow *GDST* RH9 .... 128 F6
   NRWD SE19 .... 32 B5
Belloc Cl *CRAWE* RH10 .... 212 E4

Belloc Ct *SWTR* RH13 .... 229 K6
Bello Cl *BRXS/STRHM* SW2 ..... 31 L2
Bell Pl *BAGS* GU19 .... 54 C6
Bell Rd *E/WMO/HCT* KT8 .... 44 A5
   HASM GU27 .... 219 K6
   HORS RH12 .... 228 D1
   HSLW TW3 .... 16 C5
Bells La *DTCH/LGLY* SL3 .... 12 E5
Bell St *REIG* RH2 .... 125 K8
Belltrees Gv *STRHM/NOR* SW16 . 31 K1
Bell Vale La *HASM* GU27 .... 219 L6
Bellwether La *REDH* RH1 .... 171 L1
Belmont Av *GUW* GU2 .... 116 C5
   NWMAL KT3 .... 46 D5
Belmont Cl *FARN* GU14 .... 92 C2
Belmont Ms *CBLY* GU15 .... 72 F6
Belmont Ri *BELMT* SM2 .... 65 J6
Belmont Rd *BECK* BR3 .... 51 H2
   BELMT SM2 .... 65 K8
   CBLY GU15 .... 72 F5
   LHD/OX KT22 .... 102 D4
   REIG RH2 .... 147 M1
   SNWD SE25 .... 50 E5
   WHTN TW2 .... 26 A3
Belmore Av *WOKS/MYFD* GU22 . 78 A6
Beloe Cl *PUT/ROE* SW15 .... 19 K6
Belsize Gdns *SUT* SM1 .... 65 L3
Belsize Rd *FARN* GU14 .... 92 F8
Belstone Ms *FARN* GU14 .... 92 D2
Beltane Dr *WIM/MER* SW19 ..... 29 G4
Belthorn Crs *BAL* SW12 .... 30 F1
Belton Rd *CBLY* GU15 .... 73 H8
Belvedere Av *WIM/MER* SW19 .. 29 H6
Belvedere Cl *ESH/CLAY* KT10 .. 61 L4
   GUW GU2 .... 116 E6
   TEDD TW11 .... 26 B6
   WEY KT13 .... 59 K4
Belvedere Ct *BLKW* GU17 .... 72 A6
Belvedere Dr *WIM/MER* SW19 .. 29 H6
Belvedere Gdns
   E/WMO/HCT KT8 .... 43 J5
Belvedere Gv *WIM/MER* SW19 . 29 H6
Belvedere Rd *BH/WHM* TN16 ... 91 L5
   FARN GU14 .... 92 F7
   NRWD SE19 .... 32 C8
Belvedere Sq *WIM/MER* SW19 . 29 H6
Belvoir Cl *FRIM* GU16 .... 73 J8
Belvoir Rd *EDUL* SE22 .... 32 D1
Benbow La *MFD/CHID* GU8 ..... 203 M5
Benbrick Rd *GUW* GU2 .... 8 A5
Benbury Cl *BMLY* BR1 .... 33 M6
The Bence *EGH* TW20 .... 39 L3
Bench Fld *SAND/SEL* CR2 .... 68 C4
Benchfield Cl *EGRIN* RH19 ...... 216 D1
Bencombe Rd *PUR/KEN* CR8 ... 87 K4
Bencroft Rd
   STRHM/NOR SW16 .... 30 F8
Bencurtis Pk *WWKM* BR4 .... 70 A2
Bendon Va *WAND/EARL* SW18 . 29 L1
Benedict Dr *EBED/NFELT* TW14 . 24 A1
Benedict Rd *MTCM* CR4 .... 48 A3
Benedict Whf *MTCM* CR4 .... 48 B3
Benen-stock Rd
   STWL/WRAY TW19 .... 13 K8
Benett Gdns *STRHM/NOR* SW16 . 49 H2
Benfleet Cl *COB* KT11 .... 81 H2
   SUT SM1 .... 65 M2
Benham Cl *CHSGTN* KT9 .... 62 F5
   COUL/CHIP CR5 .... 107 J7
Benham Gdns *HSLWW* TW4 ..... 16 C7
Benhams Dr *HORL* RH6 .... 170 D4
Benhill Av *SUT* SM1 .... 65 L3
Benhill Rd *SUT* SM1 .... 66 A2
Benhill Wood Rd *SUT* SM1 .... 65 M2
Benhilton Gdns *SUT* SM1 .... 65 M1
Benhurst Cl *SAND/SEL* CR2 ..... 69 G8
Benhurst Gdns *SAND/SEL* CR2 . 68 F8
Benhurst La *STRHM/NOR* SW16 . 31 K6
Benjamin Cl *CRAWE* RH10 ...... 213 G5
Benner La *CHOB/PIR* GU24 ..... 75 J2
Bennet Cl *KUT* KT1 .... 1 F8
Bennett Cl *COB* KT11 .... 80 D3
   CRAWE RH10 .... 212 E7
Bennett Ct *CBLY* GU15 .... 72 F4
Bennetts Av *CROY/NA* CR0 ..... 69 H1
Bennetts Cl *MTCM* CR4 .... 48 E1
Bennetts Farm Pl
   GT/LBKH KT23 .... 101 J7
Bennett St *CHSWK* W4 .... 19 H1
Bennetts Wy *CROY/NA* CR0 ..... 69 H1
Bennetts Wd *RDKG* RH5 .... 188 F4
Bennett Wy *RGUE* GU4 .... 118 D3
Bens Acre *SWTR* RH13 .... 229 K7
Bensbury Cl *PUT/ROE* SW15 ... 28 F1
Bensham Cl *THHTH* CR7 .... 49 M4
Bensham Gv *THHTH* CR7 .... 49 M2
Bensham La *CROY/NA* CR0 ..... 4 B1
   THHTH CR7 .... 49 L5
Bensham Manor Rd *THHTH* CR7 . 49 M4
Benson Cl *HSLW* TW3 .... 16 D6
Benson Rd *CROY/NA* CR0 .... 67 K2
   FSTH SE23 .... 32 F2
Benson's La *HORS* RH12 .... 209 M8
Benthall Gdns *PUR/KEN* CR8 ... 87 M6
Bentham Av *WOKN/KNAP* GU21 . 7 L1
Bentley Copse *CBLY* GU15 ...... 73 L5
Bentley Dr *WEY* KT13 .... 59 K7
Benton's La *WNWD* SE27 .... 31 M5
Benton's Ri *WNWD* SE27 .... 32 A6
Bentsbrook Pk *RDKG* RH5 ...... 144 E6
Bentsbrook Pk *RDKG* RH5 ...... 144 E6
Bentsbrook Rd *RDKG* RH5 ...... 144 E6
Benwell Ct *SUN* TW16 .... 42 D1
Benwell Rd *CHOB/PIR* GU24 ... 95 J1
Beomonds Rw *CHERT* KT16 .... 40 D7
Berberis Cl *GU* GU1 .... 116 F6
Bere Rd *BRAK* RG12 .... 35 H6
Beresford Av *BRYLDS* KT5 ...... 45 L8
   TWK TW1 .... 17 M8
Beresford Cl *FRIM* GU16 .... 93 J3
Beresford Gdns *HSLWW* TW4 .. 16 C7
Beresford Rd *BELMT* SM2 .... 65 J6
   DORK RH4 .... 144 E2
   KUTN/CMB KT2 .... 3 G4
   NWMAL KT3 .... 45 M4
   SNWD SE25 .... 50 D4
Bergenia Ct *CHOB/PIR* GU24 ... 75 H3

Berkeley Av *HEST* TW5 .... 15 K3
   KUTN/CMB KT2 .... 2 E2
   STWL/WRAY TW19 .... 22 A3
   WLGTN SM6 .... 66 F2
Berkeley Crs *FRIM* GU16 .... 93 K1
Berkeley Ct *WEY* KT13 .... 60 A1
   ESH/CLAY KT10 .... 62 D6
   WOT/HER KT12 .... 42 C7
Berkeley Dr *E/WMO/HCT* KT8 .. 43 J5
Berkeley Gdns *BF/WBF* KT14 ... 78 C4
   ESH/CLAY KT10 .... 62 D6
   WOT/HER KT12 .... 42 C7
Berkeley Ms *SUN* TW16 .... 42 F3
   WIM/MER SW19 .... 29 G7
Berkeley Pl *EPSOM* KT18 .... 84 A5
   WIM/MER SW19 .... 29 G7
Berkeley Rd *BARN* SW13 .... 19 K3
The Berkeleys *LHD/OX* KT22 ... 102 B6
Berkeley Waye *HEST* TW5 .... 16 B2
Berkley Cl *TWK* TW1 .... 26 B2
Berkshire Cl *CTHM* CR3 .... 108 A4
Berkshire Corpse Rd
   ALDT GU11 .... 112 B2
Berkshire Rd *CBLY* GU15 .... 73 J1
Berkshire Wy *BRAK* RG12 .... 34 D3
   MTCM CR4 .... 49 H4
Bernard Gdns *WIM/MER* SW19 . 29 J6
Bernard Rd *WLGTN* SM6 .... 66 E4
Bernel Dr *CROY/NA* CR0 .... 69 J2
Berne Rd *THHTH* CR7 .... 49 L5
Berney Rd *CROY/NA* CR0 .... 4 E2
Berridge Rd *NRWD* SE19 .... 32 A6
Berrington Dr *EHSLY* KT24 ...... 100 C6
Berrybank *SHST* GU47 .... 72 B3
Berrycroft *BNFD* RG42 .... 35 G3
Berrylands *BRYLDS* KT5 .... 45 K5
   RYNPK SW20 .... 46 F3
Berrylands Rd *BRYLDS* KT5 ..... 45 J6
Berry La *DUL* SE21 .... 32 A5
   RGUW GU3 .... 96 A6
Berryman's La *SYD* SE26 .... 33 G5
Berry Meade *ASHTD* KT21 .... 83 J7
Berrymeade Wk *BH/WHM* TN16 . 91 L6
Berry's Green Rd *BH/WHM* TN16 . 91 L6
Berry's Hl *BH/WHM* TN16 .... 91 L5
Berry's La *BF/WBF* KT14 .... 79 G1
Berry Wk *ASHTD* KT21 .... 103 J1
Bertal Rd *TOOT* SW17 .... 30 A5
Bertie Rd *SYD* SE26 .... 33 G7
Bertram Rd *KUTN/CMB* KT2 ... 3 J2
Bert Rd *THHTH* CR7 .... 49 M5
Berwyn Av *HSLW* TW3 .... 16 E3
Berwyn Rd *HNHL* SE24 .... 31 L2
   RCHPK/HAM TW10 .... 18 E6
Berystede *KUTN/CMB* KT2 ...... 3 L3
Besley St *STRHM/NOR* SW16 ... 30 F7
Bessant Dr *RCH/KEW* TW9 ...... 18 E3
Bessborough Rd *PUT/ROE* SW15 . 28 D2
Beswick Gdns *BRAK* RG12 .... 35 J1
Beta Rd *CHOB/PIR* GU24 .... 56 C8
   FARN GU14 .... 92 C4
   WOKS/MYFD GU22 .... 7 K3
Beta Wy *EGH* TW20 .... 39 M1
Betchets Green Rd *RDKG* RH5 . 166 F3
Betchley Cl *EGRIN* RH19 .... 196 B6
Betchworth Cl *SUT* SM1 .... 66 A4
Betchworth Wy *CROY/NA* CR0 . 69 M7
Bethany Waye
   EBED/NFELT TW14 .... 24 B1
Bethel Cl *FNM* GU9 .... 134 B3
Bethel La *FNM* GU9 .... 134 B3
Bethersden Cl *BECK* BR3 .... 33 J8
Bethune Cl *CRAWE* RH10 .... 213 G4
Bethune Rd *SWTR* RH13 .... 229 H8
Betjeman Cl *COUL/CHIP* CR5 ... 87 J7
Betley Ct *WOT/HER* KT12 .... 60 E2
Betony Cl *CROY/NA* CR0 .... 51 C3
Betts Cl *BECK* BR3 .... 51 H2
Betts Wy *CRAWW* RH11 .... 192 A7
   PGE/AN SE20 .... 50 E2
   THDIT KT7 .... 44 E8
Betula Cl *PUR/KEN* CR8 .... 88 A1
Between Streets *COB* KT11 ...... 80 E4
Beulah Crs *THHTH* CR7 .... 49 M2
Beulah Gv *CROY/NA* CR0 .... 49 M6
Beulah Hl *NRWD* SE19 .... 32 A8
Beulah Rd *SUT* SM1 .... 65 K5
   THHTH CR7 .... 49 M3
   WIM/MER SW19 .... 29 J8
Beulah Wk *CTHM* CR3 .... 109 H2
Bevan Ct *CROY/NA* CR0 .... 67 K4
Bevan Pk *EW* KT17 .... 84 C1
Beverley Av *HSLWW* TW4 .... 16 C6
   RYNPK SW20 .... 46 C1
Beverley Cl *ADL/WDHM* KT15 .. 59 G3
   ASHV GU12 .... 113 J8
   BARN SW13 .... 19 K4
   CBLY GU15 .... 73 M3
   CHSGTN KT9 .... 62 F3
   EW KT17 .... 84 C1
   WEY KT13 .... 60 B1
Beverley Crs *FARN* GU14 .... 92 C6
Beverley Gdns *BARN* SW13 ..... 19 J5
   WPK KT4 .... 46 C8
Beverley Hts *REIG* RH2 .... 125 L6
Beverley La *KUTN/CMB* KT2 .... 28 B8
Beverley Ms *CRAWE* RH10 ...... 212 D4
Beverley Rd *BARN* SW13 .... 19 J5
   CHSGTN KT9 .... 62 F3
   CTHM CR3 .... 88 B7
   HAYES BR2 .... 71 H1
   KUT KT1 .... 2 C7
   MTCM CR4 .... 49 G4
   NWMAL KT3 .... 46 C4
   PGE/AN SE20 .... 50 E2
   SUN TW16 .... 42 C1
   WPK KT4 .... 64 F1
Beverley Wy *NWMAL* KT3 .... 46 C1
Beverley Wy (Kingston By Pass)
   NWMAL KT3 .... 46 C1
Beverstone Rd *THHTH* CR7 ..... 49 K4
Bevill Cl *SNWD* SE25 .... 50 D3
Bevington Rd *BECK* BR3 .... 51 L2
Bevin Sq *TOOT* SW17 .... 30 C4
Bewbush Dr *CRAWW* RH11 ..... 211 J6
Bewlys Rd *WNWD* SE27 .... 31 L6
Bexhill Cl *FELT* TW13 .... 25 K4
Bexhill Rd *MORT/ESHN* SW14 .. 18 F5
Beynon Rd *CAR* SM5 .... 66 C4
Bicester Rd *RCH/KEW* TW9 ..... 18 D5
Bickersteth Rd *TOOT* SW17 ..... 30 C7

Bickley St *TOOT* SW17 .... 30 B6
Bicknell Rd *FRIM* GU16 .... 73 H7
Bickney Wy *LHD/OX* KT22 .... 101 M4
Bicknoller Cl *BELMT* SM2 .... 65 L8
Biddulph Rd *SAND/SEL* CR2 .... 67 M7
Bideford Cl *FARN* GU14 .... 92 D3
   FELT TW13 .... 25 J4
Bidhams Crs
   KWD/TDW/WH KT20 .... 104 F3
The Bield *REIG* RH2 .... 147 K2
Big Common La *REDH* RH1 ..... 127 L7
Biggin Av *MTCM* CR4 .... 48 C1
Biggin Cl *CRAWW* RH11 .... 211 M5
Biggin Hl *STRHM/NOR* SW16 ... 31 L8
Biggin Wy *NRWD* SE19 .... 31 L8
Bigginwood Rd
   STRHM/NOR SW16 .... 31 L8
Bignor Cl *HORS* RH12 .... 229 K3
Bilberry Cl *CRAWW* RH11 .... 211 L6
Billesden Rd *CHOB/PIR* GU24 .. 94 F3
Billingshurst Rd *HORS* RH12 ... 227 M6
Billinton Dr *CRAWE* RH10 .... 212 E3
Billockby Cl *CHSGTN* KT9 .... 63 J5
Binfield Rd *BF/WBF* KT14 .... 79 H2
   BNFD RG42 .... 34 D1
   SAND/SEL CR2 .... 68 C4
Bingham Dr *STA* TW18 .... 23 G8
   WOKN/KNAP GU21 .... 76 C8
Bingham Rd *CROY/NA* CR0 ..... 5 L4
Bingley Rd *SUN* TW16 .... 24 D8
Binhams Lea *MFD/CHID* GU8 ... 203 J4
Binhams Meadow
   MFD/CHID GU8 .... 203 J4
Binney Ct *CRAWE* RH10 .... 193 H8
Binscombe *RGODL* GU7 .... 160 A1
Binscombe Crs *RGODL* GU7 .... 160 B2
Binscombe La *RGODL* GU7 ...... 160 A1
Binstead Cl *CRAWW* RH11 ...... 211 L1
Binstead Rd *ALTN* GU34 .... 176 C1
   NFNM GU10 .... 176 D1
Binsted Dr *BLKW* GU17 .... 72 A4
Binton La *NFNM* GU10 .... 135 H7
Birchanger *RGODL* GU7 .... 160 B5
Birchanger Rd *SNWD* SE25 ..... 50 D5
Birch Av *CTHM* CR3 .... 108 A6
Birch Cir *RGODL* GU7 .... 160 C1
Birch Cl *ADL/WDHM* KT15 .... 59 G7
   BTFD TW8 .... 17 L2
   CBLY GU15 .... 73 H1
   CRAWE RH10 .... 214 F1
   HSLW TW3 .... 17 G5
   NFNM GU10 .... 155 K5
   RPLY/SEND GU23 .... 98 C7
   TEDD TW11 .... 26 D6
   WOKS/MYFD GU22 .... 97 K7
Birchcroft Cl *CTHM* CR3 .... 107 M7
Birchdale Cl *BF/WBF* KT14 ...... 78 F1
Birch Dr *BLKW* GU17 .... 72 A6
Birchend Cl *SAND/SEL* CR2 ..... 68 A5
Birches Cl *EPSOM* KT18 .... 84 B5
   MTCM CR4 .... 48 C3
Birches Rd *HORS* RH12 .... 229 L4
The Birches *CRAWE* RH10 .... 212 D2
   EHSLY KT24 .... 100 F4
   FARN GU14 .... 92 A5
   ORP BR6 .... 71 K3
   WOKS/MYFD GU22 .... 6 F7
Birchett Rd *ALDT* GU11 .... 112 D7
   FARN GU14 .... 92 B4
Birchetts Cl *BNFD* RG42 .... 34 E1
Birchfield Cl *ADL/WDHM* KT15 . 58 E3
   COUL/CHIP CR5 .... 87 J6
Birchfield Gv *EW* KT17 .... 64 F8
Birchfields *CBLY* GU15 .... 72 F5
Birch Gn *STA* TW18 .... 22 C5
Birch Gv *BRAK* RG12 .... 34 F4
Birchgrove *COB* KT11 .... 80 F4
Birch Gv *KWD/TDW/WH* KT20 . 105 J6
   SHPTN TW17 .... 42 B2
   WOKS/MYFD GU22 .... 78 A5
Birch Hl *CROY/NA* CR0 .... 69 G4
Birch Hill Rd *BRAK* RG12 .... 34 E7
Birchington Rd *BRYLDS* KT5 .... 45 J7
Birchlands Av *BAL* SW12 .... 30 C1
Birch La *ASC* SL5 .... 35 K1
   CHOB/PIR GU24 .... 75 C2
   PUR/KEN CR8 .... 87 H1
Birch Lea *CRAWE* RH10 .... 192 D8
Birch Md *HAYES* BR2 .... 71 K1
Birch Platt *CHOB/PIR* GU24 .... 75 G3
Birch Rd *BFOR* GU20 .... 55 H5
   FELT TW13 .... 25 C6
   RGODL GU7 .... 160 C1
Birch Tree Av *WWKM* BR4 .... 70 C4
Birch Tree Vw *LTWR* GU18 ...... 54 D8
Birch Tree Wy *CROY/NA* CR0 ... 68 E1
Birch V *COB* KT11 .... 81 K3
Birch Wy *ASHV* GU12 .... 113 K2
   WARL CR6 .... 89 H4
Birchway *REDH* RH1 .... 148 E2
Birchwood Av *BECK* BR3 .... 51 J4
   CAR SM5 .... 66 D2
Birchwood Cl *CRAWE* RH10 .... 212 F6
   HORL RH6 .... 170 E5
   MRDN SM4 .... 47 L4
Birchwood Dr *BF/WBF* KT14 ... 78 C2
   LTWR GU18 .... 54 F8
Birchwood Gv *HPTN* TW12 ...... 25 J7
Birchwood La *CTHM* CR3 .... 107 L7
Birchwood Rd *ADL/WDHM* KT15 . 58 E3
   TOOT SW17 .... 30 E6
Birdham Cl *CRAWW* RH11 ...... 211 L1
Birdhaven *NFNM* GU10 .... 10 C9
Bird House La *ORP* BR6 .... 91 K4
Birdhurst Av *SAND/SEL* CR2 .... 68 A3
Birdhurst Gdns *SAND/SEL* CR2 . 68 A3
Birdhurst Ri *SAND/SEL* CR2 .... 68 B3
Birdhurst Rd *SAND/SEL* CR2 ... 68 A3
   WIM/MER SW19 .... 30 B7
Bird-in-hand Pas *FSTH* SE23 ... 32 F3
Birds Gv *WOKN/KNAP* GU21 ... 75 L3
Birds Hill Dr *LHD/OX* KT22 ...... 82 A3
Birds Hill Ri *LHD/OX* KT22 ...... 82 A3
Birds Hill Rd *LHD/OX* KT22 ..... 82 A2
Birdswood Dr
   WOKN/KNAP GU21 .... 96 B1
Bird Wk *WHTN* TW2 .... 25 J2

Birdwood Cl SAND/SEL CR2 ....88 F1
  TEDD TW11 ....26 B5
Birdwood Rd CBLY GU15 ....72 C3
Birkbeck Hl DUL SE21 ....31 L3
Birkbeck Pl DUL SE21 ....31 L2
Birkbeck Rd BECK BR3 ....51 G2
  WIM/MER SW19 ....29 L6
Birkdale BRAK RG12 ....34 B6
Birkdale Dr CRAWW RH11 ....211 G4
Birkdale Gdns CROY/NA CR0 ....69 G3
Birkenhead Av KUTN/CMB KT2 ....3 G6
Birkheads Rd REIG RH2 ....125 K7
Birkwood Cl BAL SW12 ....31 G1
Birnam Cl RPLY/SEND GU23 ....98 D6
Birtley Ri SHGR GU5 ....161 K4
Birtley Rd SHGR GU5 ....161 K4
Biscoe Cl HEST TW5 ....16 D1
Bisham Cl CRAWE RH10 ....213 G6
  MTCM CR4 ....48 C7
Bishop Cl RCHPK/HAM TW10 ....27 C4
Bishopdale BRAK RG12 ....34 D4
Bishop Duppas Pk SHPTN TW17 ....42 A7
Bishop Fox Wy E/WMO/HCT KT8 ....43 J4
Bishopric HORS RH12 ....228 C7
Bishop's Cl COUL/CHIP CR5 ....87 K8
  SUT SM1 ....65 K2
Bishops Dr EBED/NFELT TW14 ....15 G8
Bishopsford Rd MRDN SM4 ....47 M7
Bishopsgate Rd WDSR SL4 ....20 D4
Bishops Gv BFOR GU20 ....54 F5
  HPTN TW12 ....25 K5
Bishop's Hall KUT KT1 ....2 D6
Bishops Hl WOT/HER KT12 ....42 D7
Bishop's Md FNM GU9 ....133 L7
Bishopsmead Cl EHSLY KT24 ....120 C2
  HOR/WEW KT19 ....64 A8
Bishopsmead Dr EHSLY KT24 .. 120 C3
Bishops Park Rd
  STRHM/NOR SW16.. ....49 H1
Bishops Pl SUT SM1 ....65 M4
Bishop's Rd CROY/NA CR0 ....4 A2
  FNM GU9.. ....133 J3
Bishopsthorpe Rd SYD SE26.. ....32 F5
Bishop Sumner Dr FNM GU9 .. 133 M3
Bishops Wk CROY/NA CR0 ....69 G4
Bishops Wy EGH TW20.. ....22 A7
Bishops Wd WOKN/KNAP GU21 ....76 C7
Bisley Cl WPK KT4 ....46 F8
Bitmead Cl CRAWW RH11 ....211 H4
Bittams La CHERT KT16 ....58 A3
Bittern Cl CRAWW RH11 ....211 G4
  SHST GU47 ....72 A1
Bitterne Dr WOKN/KNAP GU21 ....76 C7
The Bittoms KUT KT1 ....2 D8
Blackberry Cl GU GU1 ....116 E5
  SHPTN TW17 ....42 B4
Blackberry Farm Cl HEST TW5.. 16 B2
Blackberry La LING RH7 ....174 A7
Blackberry Rd EGRIN RH19 ....195 M1
Blackbird Cl SHST GU47 ....72 A1
Blackborough Cl REIG RH2 ....125 M8
Blackborough Rd REDH RH1 .. 126 A8
  REIG RH2 ....126 A8
Blackbridge Rd
  WOKS/MYFD GU22.. ....97 G2
Blackbook Rd RDKG RH5.. ....145 H7
The Blackburn GT/LBKH KT23 .. 101 J6
Blackburn Wy RGODL GU7 ....160 C4
Blackbush Cl BELMT SM2 ....65 L6
Blackcap Cl CRAWW RH11 ....211 M5
Blackcap Pl SHST GU47 ....72 B1
Black Dog Wk CRAWE RH10 ....212 B1
Blackdown Av
  WOKS/MYFD GU22.. ....78 B5
Blackdown Cl WOKS/MYFD GU22 .. 7 M3
Blackdown Rd FRIM GU16 ....93 M2
Black Eagle Cl BH/WHM TN16 ....131 M1
Blackenham Rd TOOT SW17 ....30 C5
Blackett Cl EGH TW20 ....40 B2
Blackford Rd CRAWE RH10 ....212 D4
Blackford Cl SAND/SEL CR2 ....67 L7
Blackheath CRAWE RH10 ....213 G1
Blackheath Gv SHGR GU5 ....161 L1
Blackheath La SHGR GU5 ....161 M1
Blackheath Rd FNM GU9 ....133 K2
Blackhills ESH/CLAY KT10 ....61 J7
Blackhorse La CROY/NA CR0 ....5 M1
  REIG RH2 ....125 L3
Blackhorse Rd
  WOKS/MYFD GU22.. ....96 A2
Black Horse Wy HORS RH12 ....228 E7
Blacklands Crs FROW RH18.. ....217 J7
Blacklands Meadow REDH RH1.. 127 H7
Blacklands Rd CAT SE6.. ....33 M5
Blackman Gdns ALDT GU11 ....134 E1
Blackman's La WARL CR6 ....90 B4
Blackmeadows BRAK RG12 ....34 F6
Blackmoor Cl ASC SL5 ....36 A2
Blackmoor Wd ASC SL5 ....36 A2
Blackmore Crs
  WOKN/KNAP GU21 ....77 M4
Blackmore's Gv TEDD TW11 ....26 D7
Blackness La HAYES BR2 ....71 C7
  WOKS/MYFD GU22.. ....6 D9
Blacknest Rd ALTN GU34 ....154 B7
  ASC SL5.. ....38 A3
Black Pond La NFNM GU10.. ....11 H7
Black Prince Cl BF/WBF KT14 ....79 J4
Blackshaw Rd TOOT SW17 ....30 A6
Blacksmith Cl ASHTD KT21 ....103 J1
Blacksmith La RGUE GU4 ....139 M5
Blacksmiths Hl SAND/SEL CR2 ....88 E3
Blacksmiths La CHERT KT16 ....40 D7
  STA TW18 ....40 F3
Blackstone Cl FARN GU14 ....92 A3
  REIG RH2.. ....148 B1
Blackstone Hl REDH RH1 ....126 B8
Blackstroud La East LTWR GU18.. 75 G1
Blackstroud La West LTWR GU18.. 75 G1
Blackthorn Cl CRAWW RH11 ....211M1
  REIG RH2.. ....147 M2
  SWTR RH13.. ....229 J2
Blackthorn Crs HEST TW5 ....16 B2
Blackthorn Ct HEST TW5 ....16 B2
Blackthorn Crs FARN GU14 ....92 C1

Blackthorn Dr LTWR GU18 ....74 E2
Blackthorne Av CROY/NA CR0 ....50 F8
Blackthorne Crs DTCH/LGLY SL3 .. 13 H4
Blackthorne Rd DTCH/LGLY SL3 .. 13 H4
  GT/LBKH KT23 ....101 M8
Blackthorn Rd BH/WHM TN16 ....91 H6
  REIG RH2 ....147 M2
Blackwater Cl ASHV GU12 ....113 K8
Blackwater La CRAWE RH10 ....212 F4
Blackwater Wy ASHV GU12.. ....135 G1
Blackwell Av GUW GU2 ....116 A8
Blackwell Farm Rd EGRIN RH19.. 196 C5
Blackwell Hollow EGRIN RH19 ....196 C7
Blackwell Rd EGRIN RH19 ....196 C7
Blackwood Cl BF/WBF KT14 ....78 F2
Bladen Cl WEY KT13 ....60 A5
Blades Cl LHD/OX KT22 ....103 G2
Bladon Cl GU GU1 ....117 K7
Blagdon Rd NWMAL KT3 ....46 C4
Blagdon Wk TEDD TW11 ....2 A1
Blair Av ESH/CLAY KT10 ....61 M1
Blairderry Rd BRXS/STRHM SW2 .. 31 H3
Blaise Cl FARN GU14 ....93 G6
Blake Cl CAR SM5 ....48 B8
  CRAWE RH10 ....212 C7
Blakeden Dr ESH/CLAY KT10 ....62 C6
Blakehall Rd CAR SM5 ....66 C5
Blakemore Rd
  STRHM/NOR SW16.. ....31 H4
  THHTH CR7 ....49 J5
Blakeney Av BECK BR3 ....51 J1
Blakeney Cl HOR/WEW KT19 ....84 A1
Blakeney Rd BECK BR3 ....51 J1
Blake Rd CROY/NA CR0 ....5 G5
  MTCM CR4 ....48 B3
Blakes Av NWMAL KT3 ....46 C5
Blake's Gn WWKM BR4 ....51 M7
Blakes La NWMAL KT3 ....46 C5
  RGUE GU4 ....119 J5
Blakes Ter NWMAL KT3 ....46 D5
Blakewood Cl FELT TW13 ....24 F5
Blanchards Hl RGUE GU4.. ....117 H1
Blanchland Rd MRDN SM4 ....47 L5
Blanchman's Rd WARL CR6 ....89 H8
Blandford Av BECK BR3 ....51 H2
  WHTN TW2 ....25 L2
Blandford Cl CROY/NA CR0 ....67 H2
  WOKS/MYFD GU22.. ....7 J6
Blandford Rd BECK BR3 ....51 G2
  TEDD TW11 ....26 A6
Blane's La ASC SL5 ....35 M6
Blanford Rd REIG RH2 ....147 M1
Blanks La HORL RH6 ....168 D6
Blatchford Rd SWTR RH13 ....229 J6
Blays Cl EGH TW20 ....20 F7
Blay's La EGH TW20 ....20 E7
Blean Gv PGE/AN SE20 ....32 F8
Blegborough Rd
  STRHM/NOR SW16.. ....30 F7
Blencarn Cl WOKN/KNAP GU21 ....76 D6
Blenheim Cl BF/WBF KT14 ....78 C3
  CRAWE RH10 ....193 G8
  EGRIN RH19 ....196 D6
  NFNM GU10 ....135 H2
  RYNPK SW20 ....46 F3
  WLGTN SM6 ....66 F6
Blenheim Ct FARN GU14 ....93 C7
Blenheim Crs FNM GU9 ....133 K3
  SAND/SEL CR2 ....67 M6
Blenheim Flds FROW RH18 ....217 H6
Blenheim Gdns KUTN/CMB KT2 ....3 L3
  SAND/SEL CR2 ....88 D2
  WLGTN SM6 ....66 F5
  WOKS/MYFD GU22.. ....96 E1
Blenheim Pk ALDT GU11 ....112 F2
Blenheim Park Rd
  SAND/SEL CR2.. ....67 M7
Blenheim Rd ALDT GU11 ....112 F2
  HOR/WEW KT19 ....84 A1
  HORS RH12 ....229 C4
  PGE/AN SE20 ....32 E8
  RYNPK SW20 ....46 F3
  SUT SM1 ....65 K2
Blenheim Wy ISLW TW7 ....17 K3
Bleriot Rd HEST TW5 ....15 M2
Bletchingley Cl REDH RH1 ....126 F3
Bletchingley Rd GDST RH9 ....128 D5
  REDH RH1 ....126 F3
Bletchingly Cl THHTH CR7.. ....49 L4
Blewburton Wk BRAK RG12 ....35 H4
Blewfield RGODL GU7 ....160 C7
Blighton La RUNFLD GU10.. ....135 C7
Blincoe Cl WIM/MER SW19 ....29 G3
Blindley Rd CRAWE RH10 ....193 G8
Blomfield Dl BNFD RG42 ....34 A2
Blondell Cl WDR/YW UB7 ....14 A1
Bloomfield Cl WOKN/KNAP GU21.. 76 B8
Bloomfield Rd KUT KT1 ....45 H4
Bloom Gv WNWD SE27 ....31 L4
Bloomhall Rd NRWD SE19 ....32 A6
Bloomsbury Cl HOR/WEW KT19 ....64 A8
Bloor Cl HORS RH12 ....229 C2
Blossom Cl SAND/SEL CR2.. ....68 C4
Blossom Waye HEST TW5 ....16 B1
Blount Av EGRIN RH19 ....195 M8
Bloxham Crs HPTN TW12 ....43 J1
Bloxham Rd CRAN GU6 ....185 K6
Bloxworth Cl BRAK RG12 ....35 J4
  WLGTN SM6 ....66 F2
Blue Ball La EGH TW20 ....21 J6
Blue Barn Wy WEY KT13 ....79 K1
Bluebell Cl CRAWW RH11 ....211 L6
  EGRIN RH19 ....195 L8
  HORS RH12 ....229 H4
  MTCM CR4 ....48 B8
  ORP BR6 ....71 M1
  SYD SE26 ....32 C5
Bluebell Ct WOKS/MYFD GU22 ....6 A9
Bluebell Rd LTWR GU18 ....74 E1
Bluebell La EHSLY KT24 ....120 B3
Bluebell Ri LTWR GU18 ....74 E1
Blueberry Gdns COUL/CHIP CR5 .. 87 K2
Blue Cedars BNSTD SM7 ....85 G4
Blue Cedars Pl COB KT11 ....81 G2
Blue Coat Wk BRAK RG12 ....35 G5
Bluefield Cl HPTN TW12 ....25 K6
Bluegates EW KT17 ....64 D6

Bluehouse Gdns OXTED RH8 ....130 D2
Bluehouse La OXTED RH8 ....130 B2
Bluethroat Cl SHST GU47 ....72 B1
Bluff Cove ALDT GU11 ....112 F6
Blundel La COB KT11 ....81 L4
Blunden Av HORL RH6 ....170 C6
Blunden Rd FARN GU14 ....92 C4
Blunt Rd CROY/NA CR0 ....68 A4
Blunts Av WDR/YW UB7 ....14 D2
Blunts Rd HORS RH12 ....228 F6
Blyth Cl TWK TW1 ....17 J8
Blythe Cl FSTH SE23 ....33 J1
Blythe Hl FSTH SE23 ....33 J1
Blythe Hl La FSTH SE23 ....33 J1
Blythe V FSTH SE23 ....33 J2
Blythewood La ASC SL5 ....36 A3
Blythwood Dr FRIM GU16 ....73 G7
The Blytons EGRIN RH19 ....195 K8
Board School Rd
  WOKN/KNAP GU21.. ....6 F4
Boar Hl RDKG RH5 ....144 B8
Bockhampton Rd
  KUTN/CMB KT2.. ....3 H2
Boddicott Cl WIM/MER SW19 ....29 H3
Bodens Ride ASC SL5 ....36 C8
Bodiam Cl CRAWE RH10 ....212 F3
Bodiam Rd STRHM/NOR SW16 ....49 G1
Bodley Cl NWMAL KT3 ....46 B5
Bodley Rd NWMAL KT3 ....46 B6
Bodmin Gv MRDN SM4 ....47 L4
Bodmin St WAND/EARL SW18 ....29 K2
Bodnant Gdns RYNPK SW20 ....46 D3
Bofors Rd FARN GU14 ....112 D1
Bog La ASC SL5 ....35 K4
  BRAK RG12 ....35 J5
Bognor Rd HORS RH12 ....227 K1
  RDKG RH5 ....188 C3
  RDKG RH5 ....207M2
Boileau Rd BARN SW13 ....19 K2
Bois Hall Rd ADL/WDHM KT15 ....59 G4
Bolderwood Wy WWKM BR4 ....69 L1
Bolding House La
  CHOB/PIR GU24.. ....75 J3
Boleyn Av E/WMO/HCT KT8 ....43 J3
Boleyn Cl CRAWE RH10 ....213 G6
  STA TW18 ....22 B6
Boleyn Dr E/WMO/HCT KT8 ....43 J3
Boleyn Gdns WWKM BR4 ....69 L1
Boleyn Wk LHD/OX KT22 ....102 C7
Bolney Ct CRAWW RH11 ....211 J6
Bolsover Gv REDH RH1 ....127 H3
Bolstead Rd MTCM CR4 ....48 E1
Bolters La BNSTD SM7 ....85 J5
Bolters Rd HORL RH6 ....170 D4
Bolters Rd South HORL RH6 ....170 C4
Bolton Cl CHSGTN KT9 ....63 G5
Bolton Gdns TEDD TW11 ....26 D7
Bolton Rd CHSGTN KT9 ....63 G5
  CHSWK W4 ....18 F2
  CRAWE RH10 ....212 E8
Boltons Cl WOKS/MYFD GU22 ....78 D5
Bolton's La WDR/YW UB7 ....14 F2
  WOKS/MYFD GU22.. ....78 D6
Bomer Cl WDR/YW UB7 ....14 D2
Bonchurch Cl BELMT SM2 ....65 L6
Bond Gdns WLGTN SM6 ....66 F3
Bond Rd MTCM CR4 ....48 C2
  SURB KT6 ....63 J1
  WARL CR6 ....89 G8
Bond's La RDKG RH5 ....144 E8
Bond St EGH TW20 ....20 E7
Bonehurst Rd HORL RH6 ....170 D2
Bone Mill La GDST RH9 ....129 H8
Bones La HORL RH6 ....172 D5
Bonner Hill Rd KUT KT1 ....3 H8
Bonners Cl WOKS/MYFD GU22 ....97 J4
Bonnetts La CRAWW RH11 ....191 K6
Bonnys Rd REIG RH2 ....125 G8
Bonser Rd TWK TW1 ....26 C3
Bonsey Cl WOKS/MYFD GU22 ....97 H3
Bonsey La WOKS/MYFD GU22 ....97 H3
Bonsey's La WDR/YW UB7.. ....57 H7
Bonsor Dr KWD/TDW/WH KT20 ....105 H4
Bookham Ct LHD/OX KT22 ....101 J5
Bookham Gv GT/LBKH KT23 ....101 L8
Bookham Rd COB KT11 ....101 C2
Bookhurst Rd CRAN GU6 ....185 L5
Booth Dr STA TW18 ....23 G7
Booth Rd CRAWW RH11 ....211 H6
  CROY/NA CR0 ....4 B6
Booth Wy SWTR RH13 ....229 H6
Borage Cl CRAWW RH11 ....211 K7
Border Cha EGRIN RH19 ....193 K7
Border Crs SYD SE26 ....32 E6
Border Gdns CROY/NA CR0 ....69 L3
Border Ga MTCM CR4 ....48 B1
Border Rd HASM GU27 ....219 G3
  SYD SE26 ....32 E6
Bordesley Rd MRDN SM4 ....47 L4
Bordon Wk PUT/ROE SW15 ....28 D1
Borers Arms Rd CRAWE RH10 ....193 L5
Borland Rd TEDD TW11 ....26 E7
Borneo St PUT/ROE SW15 ....19 M5
The Borough BH/WHM TN16 ....111 G3
  ISLW TW7 ....17 H3
  KUTN/CMB KT2 ....3 J4
  MTCM CR4 ....48 B2
  RGODL GU7 ....160 A4
The Borough FNM GU9 ....133 L7
  NFNM GU10 ....132 B3
  RDKG RH5 ....145 K1
Borrowdale Cl CRAWW RH11 ....211 L8
  ECH TW20 ....21 L8
  SAND/SEL CR2 ....88 C3
Borrowdale Dr SAND/SEL CR2 ....88 C2
Bosbury Rd CAT SE6 ....33 M4
Boscombe Cl EGH TW20 ....39 M1
Boscombe Rd TOOT SW17 ....30 D7
  WIM/MER SW19 ....47 K1
  WPK KT4 ....46 F8
Bosham Rd CRAWE RH10 ....212 F6
Boshers Gdns EGH TW20 ....21 J7
Bosman Dr BFOR GU20 ....54 E2
Bostock Av HORS RH12 ....229 K5
Boston Gdns CHSWK W4 ....19 H1
Boston Rd CROY/NA CR0 ....49 J6

Boswell Rd CRAWE RH10 ....212 B6
  THHTH CR7 ....49 M4
Botany Hl NFNM GU10 ....135 G8
Bothwell Rd CROY/NA CR0 ....69 M8
Botsford Rd RYNPK SW20 ....47 H2
Bottom Harrow Rd VW GU25 ....39 J6
Boucher Cl TEDD TW11 ....26 C6
Bouldish Farm Rd ASC SL5 ....36 C5
The Boulevard CRAWE RH10 ....212 A3
Boulogne Rd CROY/NA CR0 ....49 M6
Boulters Rd ASHV GU12 ....112 E8
Boulthurst Wy OXTED RH8 ....130 D6
Boundaries Rd BAL SW12 ....30 C3
  FELT TW13 ....24 F2
Boundary Rd ASHF TW15 ....22 F6
  CRAWE RH10 ....212 B2
  FARN GU14 ....92 F7
  GSHT GU26 ....199 G6
  NFNM GU10 ....177 G3
  WIM/MER SW19 ....30 A7
  WLGTN SM6 ....66 D7
  WOKN/KNAP GU21 ....7 G3
Boundary Rd East
  ADL/WDHM KT15.. ....58 E7
Boundary Rd North
  ADL/WDHM KT15.. ....58 E7
Boundary Rd West
  ADL/WDHM KT15.. ....58 E7
Boundary Wy CROY/NA CR0 ....69 K4
  WOKN/KNAP GU21 ....7 J2
Boundstone Cl NFNM GU10 ....10 E9
Boundstone Rd NFNM GU10 ....155 J5
Bourdon Rd PGE/AN SE20 ....50 F2
Bourg-de-peage Av
  EGRIN RH19.. ....196 D8
Bourke Hl COUL/CHIP CR5 ....86 C8
Bourne Av CHERT KT16 ....40 D3
Bourne Cl BF/WBF KT14 ....78 E3
  RGUE GU4 ....139 L6
Bourne Ct ALDT GU11 ....134 D1
Bourne Dene NFNM GU10 ....10 D9
Bournefield Rd CTHM CR3 ....88 D8
Bourne Firs NFNM GU10 ....11 J9
Bourne Gv ASHTD KT21 ....103 G1
  FNM GU9.. ....11 L5
Bourne Grove Cl FNM GU9 ....11 M5
Bourne Grove Dr NFNM GU10 ....11 L6
Bourne La CTHM CR3 ....108 A3
Bourne Meadow EGH TW20 ....39 L1
Bourne Mill Rbt FNM GU9 ....134 B6
Bournemouth Rd
  STRHM/NOR SW16.. ....31 H5
  WIM/MER SW19.. ....47 K1
Bourne Park Cl PUR/KEN CR8 ....88 B6
Bourne Rd ADL/WDHM KT15 ....58 E7
  REDH RH1.. ....126 F4
  RGODL GU7 ....160 C1
  VW GU25 ....39 G6
Bournevale Rd
  STRHM/NOR SW16.. ....31 H5
Bourne Vw PUR/KEN CR8 ....88 B5
Bourne Wy ADL/WDHM KT15 ....58 F4
  HAYES BR2 ....70 D1
  HOR/WEW KT19 ....63 M3
  SUT SM1 ....65 H4
  WOKS/MYFD GU22.. ....97 G4
Bournville Rd CAT SE6 ....33 K1
Bousley Ri CHERT KT16 ....58 A6
Bouverie Gdns PUR/KEN CR8 ....87 H4
Bouverie Rd COUL/CHIP CR5 ....86 C8
Boveney Rd FSTH SE23 ....33 G1
Bovill Rd FSTH SE23 ....33 G1
Bowater Rdg WEY KT13 ....60 A8
Bowater Rd CRAWE RH10 ....212 F6
Bowden Cl EBED/NFELT TW14 ....24 B2
Bowden Rd ASC SL5 ....36 F5
Bowen Dr DUL SE21 ....32 B4
Bower Hill Cl REDH RH1 ....149 H3
Bower Hill La REDH RH1 ....149 G5
Bowerland La LING RH7 ....174 A1
Bower Rd NFNM GU10 ....10 C9
Bowers Cl RGUE GU4 ....117 K4
Bowers Farm Dr RGUE GU4 ....117 K4
Bowers La RGUE GU4 ....117 K3
Bowers Pl CRAWE RH10 ....214 E1
Bowes Cl SWTR RH13 ....229 H6
Bowes Rd STA TW18 ....22 B7
  WOT/HER KT12 ....60 E1
Bowfell Rd HMSMTH W6 ....19 M1
Bowie Cl CLAP SW4 ....31 G1
Bowland Dr BRAK RG12 ....35 H7
Bowley Cl NRWD SE19 ....32 C7
Bowley La NRWD SE19 ....32 C6
Bowlhead Green Rd
  MFD/CHID GU8.. ....180 C3
Bowling Court Gn FRIM GU16 ....93 H2
Bowling Green Cl
  PUT/ROE SW15.. ....28 E1
Bowling Green La HORS RH12 ....229 C6
Bowling Green Rd
  CHOB/PIR GU24.. ....56 B7
Bowman Ms WAND/EARL SW18 ....29 J2
Bowmans Lea FSTH SE23 ....32 F1
Bowman's Meadow
  WLGTN SM6.. ....66 E2
Bowness Crs PUT/ROE SW15 ....28 B6
Bowness Dr HSLWW TW4 ....16 B5
Bowness Rd CAT SE6 ....33 L1
Bowry Dr STWL/WRAY TW19 ....12 C3
Bowsley Ct FELT TW13 ....24 D3
The Bowsprit COB KT11 ....80 F5
Bowyers Cl ASHTD KT21 ....83 J8
Boxall's Gv ALDT GU11 ....134 D2
Boxall's La ALDT GU11 ....134 D2
Boxall Wk SWTR RH13 ....229 K4
Box Cl CRAWW RH11 ....211 M8
Boxford Cl SAND/SEL CR2 ....89 G2
Boxford Rdg BRAK RG12 ....34 E3
Boxgrove Av GU GU1 ....117 K6
Boxgrove La GU GU1 ....117 K7
Boxgrove Rd GU GU1 ....117 K6

Boxhill Rd DORK RH4 ....123 H6
  KWD/TDW/WH KT20 ....123 J6
Boxhill Wy BRKHM/BTCW RH3 ....145 L4
Box La EGRIN RH19 ....217 H3
Boxley Rd MRDN SM4 ....47 M4
Box Ridge Av PUR/KEN CR8 ....87 J2
Boxwood Wy WARL CR6 ....89 G7
Boyd Cl KUTN/CMB KT2 ....3 K2
Boyd Ct BNFD RG42 ....34 D1
Boyd Rd WIM/MER SW19 ....30 A7
Boyle Farm Rd THDIT KT7 ....44 D6
Brabazon Av WLGTN SM6 ....67 H7
Brabazon Rd HEST TW5 ....15 M2
Brabon Rd FARN GU14 ....92 C4
Brabourne Cl NRWD SE19 ....32 B6
Bracebridge CBLY GU15 ....72 D4
Bracewood Gdns CROY/NA CR0 ....5 J7
Bracken Av CROY/NA CR0 ....69 K2
Bracken Bank ASC SL5 ....35 M1
Bracken Cl CRAWE RH10 ....193 L7
  CRAWE RH10 ....212 B1
  GT/LBKH KT23 ....101 J6
  HSLWW TW4 ....25 K1
  SHGR GU5 ....161 L3
  SUN TW16 ....24 C7
  WOKS/MYFD GU22.. ....6 F7
Brackendale Cl FRIM GU16 ....73 H6
  HEST TW5 ....16 E3
Brackendale Rd CBLY GU15 ....73 G5
Brackendene ASHV GU12 ....113M6
Brackendene Cl
  WOKN/KNAP GU21.. ....7 G1
Bracken End ISLW TW7 ....17 G7
Bracken Gdns BARN SW13 ....19 K4
Bracken Gv HORS RH12 ....229 L4
Brackenhill COB KT11 ....81 K1
Brackenlea RGODL GU7 ....160 A2
Bracken Pth EPSOM KT18 ....83 K3
Brackenside HORL RH6 ....170 C5
Bracken Wy CHOB/PIR GU24 ....56 C8
  RGUE GU3 ....116 B6
Brackenwood CBLY GU15 ....74 A1
  SUN TW16 ....42 D1
Brackenwood Rd
  WOKN/KNAP GU21.. ....96 A1
Bracklesham Cl FARN GU14 ....92 D2
Brackley WEY KT13 ....60 A4
Brackley Cl WLGTN SM6 ....67 H6
Brackley Rd BECK BR3 ....33 J8
Bracknell Cl CBLY GU15 ....53 J8
Bracknell Rd BAGS GU19 ....54 A3
  CBLY GU15 ....53 K7
  CWTH RG45 ....52 A3
Bracondale ESH/CLAY KT10 ....61 M4
Bradbury Rd CRAWE RH10 ....212 F6
Braddock Cl ISLW TW7 ....17 J5
Braddon Rd RCH/KEW TW9 ....18 C5
Bradenhurst Cl CTHM CR3 ....108 C8
Bradfield Cl GU GU1 ....117 K5
  WOKS/MYFD GU22.. ....6 D7
Bradfields BRAK RG12 ....35 G5
Bradford Cl SYD SE26 ....32 E5
Bradford Dr HOR/WEW KT19 ....64 C5
Brading Rd BRXS/STRHM SW2 ....31 J1
  CROY/NA CR0 ....49 J6
Bradley La DORK RH4 ....122 F6
Bradley Rd NRWD SE19 ....31M7
Bradmore Wy COUL/CHIP CR5 ....87 H8
Bradshaw Cl WIM/MER SW19 ....29 K3
Bradshaws Cl SNWD SE25 ....50 D3
Bradstock Rd EW KT17 ....64 E4
Braemar Av SAND/SEL CR2 ....67M8
  THHTH CR7 ....49 L3
  WIM/MER SW19 ....29 K3
Braemar Cl FRIM GU16 ....73 J8
  RGODL GU7 ....160 A6
Braemar Gdns WWKM BR4 ....51 M8
Braemar Rd BTFD TW8 ....18 A1
  WPK KT4 ....64 E2
Braeside ADL/WDHM KT15 ....78 E1
  BECK BR3 ....33 K1
Braeside Av WIM/MER SW19 ....47 H1
Braeside Cl HASM GU27 ....219 J1
Braeside Rd STRHM/NOR SW16 ....30 F8
Braes Md REDH RH1 ....149 H1
Brafferton Rd CROY/NA CR0 ....4 C9
Bragg Rd TEDD TW11 ....26 B8
Braid Cl FELT TW13 ....25 J3
Brailsford Cl WIM/MER SW19 ....30 B8
Brainton Av EBED/NFELT TW14 ....24 E1
Brair Bank CAR SM5 ....66 D7
Brakey Hl REDH RH1 ....128 B8
Bramber Cl CRAWE RH10 ....212 B1
Bramble Acres Cl BELMT SM2 ....65 K6
Bramble Bank FRIM GU16 ....93 L6
Bramble Banks CAR SM5 ....66 D7
Bramble Cl CRAWE RH10 ....193 L6
  CROY/NA CR0 ....69 K3
  REDH RH1 ....148 D2
  RGUE GU3 ....116 B6
  SHPTN TW17 ....42 A4
Brambledene Cl
  WOKN/KNAP GU21.. ....76 F8
Brambledown STA TW18 ....40 E1
Brambledown Rd CAR SM5 ....66 D6
  SAND/SEL CR2 ....68 B6
Bramble La HPTN TW12 ....25 J7
Brambles ASHV GU12 ....113 L4
  BTFD TW8 ....17 L2
  CTHM CR3.. ....108 B4
Brambles Pk SHGR GU5 ....161 J3
The Brambles RGODL GU7 ....160 A2
Brambleton Av FNM GU9 ....10 E4
Brambletye FROW RH18 ....217 G6
Brambletye Park Rd REDH RH1.. 148 C2
Brambletye Rd CRAWE RH10 ....212 D4
Bramble Wk EPSOM KT18 ....83 K3
Bramble Wy RPLY/SEND GU23 ....98 C6
Bramblewood REIG RH2 ....126 E3
Bramblewood Cl CAR SM5 ....48 B8
Brambling Rd SWTR RH13 ....229 K8
Bramcote CBLY GU15 ....73 M4
Bramcote Av MTCM CR4 ....48 C4
Bramcote Rd PUT/ROE SW15 ....19 L6
Bramerton Rd BECK BR3 ....51 J3

Bramham Gdns CHSGTN KT9 ..... 63 G3
Bramley Av COUL/CHIP CR5 ..... 86 F5
  SHPTN TW17 ..... 42 B3
Bramley Cl CHERT KT16 ..... 40 E8
  CRAWE RH10 ..... 212 C3
  REDH RH1 ..... 148 B2
  SAND/SEL CR2 ..... 67 L4
  STA TW18 ..... 22 F7
  WHTN TW2 ..... 16 F8
Bramley Hl SAND/SEL CR2 ..... 67 M4
Bramley Rd BELMT SM2 ..... 65 K8
  CBLY GU15 ..... 72 E7
  SUT SM1 ..... 65 A4
Bramley Wk HORL RH6 ..... 170 F6
Bramley Wy ASHTD KT21 ..... 83 J7
  HSLWW TW4 ..... 16 C7
  WWKM BR4 ..... 69 L1
Brampton Gdns WOT/HER KT12 ..... 42 E5
Brampton Rd CROY/NA CR0 ..... 5 J1
Bramshaw Ri NWMAL KT3 ..... 46 B6
Bramswell Rd RGODL GU7 ..... 160 C3
Bramwell Cl SUN TW16 ..... 43 G2
Brancaster La PUR/KEN CR8 ..... 87 M1
Brancaster Rd
  STRHM/NOR SW16 ..... 31 H4
  CBLY GU15 ..... 74 A5
Brandon Cl CBLY GU15 ..... 74 A5
  CRAWE RH10 ..... 213 G5
Brandon Rd SUT SM1 ..... 65 L3
Brandreth Rd TOOT SW17 ..... 30 E6
The Brandries WLGTN SM6 ..... 67 G2
Brandsland REIG RH2 ..... 147 L4
Brands Rd DTCH/LGLY SL3 ..... 12 E1
Brandy Wy BELMT SM2 ..... 65 K6
Brangbourne Rd BMLY BR1 ..... 33 M6
Brangwyn Crs WIM/MER SW19 ..... 48 E1
  WOT/HER KT12 ..... 61 G1
Branksome Cl CBLY GU15 ..... 73 H3
  WOT/HER KT12 ..... 61 G1
Branksome Hill Rd SHST GU47 ..... 72 B2
Branksome Park Rd CBLY GU15 ..... 73 H3
Branksome Wy WIM/MER SW19.. 47 K1
  NWMAL KT3 ..... 45 M2
Bransby Rd CHSGTN KT9 ..... 63 H6
Branstone Rd RCH/KEW TW9 ..... 18 C3
Brantridge Rd CRAWE RH10 ..... 212 C5
Brants Br BRAK RG12 ..... 35 H2
Brantwood Av ISLW TW7 ..... 17 K6
Brantwood Dr BF/WBF KT14 ..... 78 C5
Brantwood Gdns BF/WBF KT14 .. 78 C5
Brantwood Rd SAND/SEL CR2 ..... 67 M7
Brassey Cl EBED/NFELT TW14 ..... 24 D2
Brassey Hl OXTED RH8 ..... 130 D4
Brassey Rd OXTED RH8 ..... 130 D3
Brasted Cl BELMT SM2 ..... 65 K8
  SYD SE26 ..... 32 F5
Brathway Rd WAND/EARL SW18 .. 29 K1
Bravington Cl SHPTN TW17 ..... 41 J5
Braxted Pk STRHM/NOR SW16 .. 31 J7
Braybourne Dr ISLW TW7 ..... 17 J2
Braybrooke Gdns NRWD SE19 .. 32 B8
Bray Cl CRAWE RH10 ..... 213 G5
Braycourt Av WOT/HER KT12 ..... 42 F7
Bray Gdns WOKS/MYFD GU22.. 78 B6
Bray Rd COB KT11 ..... 81 H6
  GUW GU2 ..... 8 C6
Braywood Av EGH TW20 ..... 21 J7
Breakfield COUL/CHIP CR5 ..... 87 H6
Breamore Ct PUT/ROE SW15 ..... 28 D2
Breamwater Gdns
  RCHPK/HAM TW10 ..... 26 L4
Breasley Cl PUT/ROE SW15 ..... 19 L6
Brecon Cl FARN GU14 ..... 92 A2
  MTCM CR4 ..... 49 H4
  WPK KT4 ..... 64 F1
Bredhurst Cl PGE/AN SE20 ..... 32 F7
Bredon Rd CROY/NA CR0 ..... 5 J2
Bredune PUR/KEN CR8 ..... 88 A5
Breech La KWD/TDW/WH KT20 .. 104 D7
The Breech CBLY GU15 ..... 72 B2
Breezehurst Dr CRAWW RH11 .. 211 J6
Bregsells La RDKG RH5 ..... 167 G5
Bremer Rd STA TW18 ..... 22 D4
Bremner Av HORL RH6 ..... 170 C5
Brenda Rd TOOT SW17 ..... 30 C3
Brende Gdns E/WMO/HCT KT8 .. 43 L4
  HYS/HAR UB3 ..... 14 F2
Brendon Cl ESH/CLAY KT10 ..... 61 M5
Brendon Dr ESH/CLAY KT10 ..... 61 M5
Brendon Rd FARN GU14 ..... 92 A2
Brenley Cl MTCM CR4 ..... 48 D3
Brent Lea BTFD TW8 ..... 17 M2
Brentmoor Rd CHOB/PIR GU24 .. 74 A3
Brent Rd BTFD TW8 ..... 17 M1
  SAND/SEL CR2 ..... 68 E7
Brentside BTFD TW8 ..... 17 M1
Brent Wy BTFD TW8 ..... 18 A2
Bret Harte Rd FRIM GU16 ..... 73 H8
Bretlands Rd CHERT KT16 ..... 58 B1
Brettgrave HOR/WEW KT19 ..... 63 M8
Brettingham Cl
  CRAWW RH11 ..... 211 H6
Brewer Rd CRAWE RH10 ..... 212 A5
Brewers La FARN GU14 ..... 92 D4
Brewer St REDH RH1 ..... 127 M5
Brewery Rd BF/WBF KT14 ..... 79 L1
Brewery Rd WOKN/KNAP GU21 .. 6 B5
Brew House Rd
  BRKHM/BTCW RH3 ..... 145 L4
Brewhurst La BIL RH14 ..... 224 D7
Brian Av SAND/SEL CR2 ..... 88 B2
Briane Rd HOR/WEW KT19 ..... 63 M8
Briar Av LTWR GU18 ..... 74 C2
  STRHM/NOR SW16 ..... 31 J8
Briar Cl BF/WBF KT14 ..... 78 E1
  CRAWW RH11 ..... 191 M8
  HPTN TW12 ..... 25 J5
  ISLW TW7 ..... 17 J7
Briar Gv SAND/SEL CR2 ..... 88 D3
Briar Hl PUR/KEN CR8 ..... 87 H1
Briar La CAR SM5 ..... 66 D7
  CROY/NA CR0 ..... 69 L3
Briar Patch RGODL GU7 ..... 160 A3
Briar Rd RPLY/SEND GU23 ..... 97 L6
  SHPTN TW17 ..... 41 J5
  STRHM/NOR SW16 ..... 49 H3
  WHTN TW2 ..... 26 B2
Briars Cl FARN GU14 ..... 92 A6
Briars Ct LHD/OX KT22 ..... 82 A4
The Briars ASHV GU12 ..... 113 L8

STWL/WRAY TW19 ..... 13 K7
Briars Wd HORL RH6 ..... 170 F5
Briarswood Cl CRAWE RH10 ..... 213 G1
Briar Wk BF/WBF KT14 ..... 78 D2
  PUT/ROE SW15 ..... 19 L6
Briar Wy RGUE GU4 ..... 117 L4
Briarwood Cl FELT TW13 ..... 24 B4
Briarwood Rd EW KT17 ..... 64 D5
  WOKN/KNAP GU21 ..... 96 A1
Brick Farm Cl RCH/KEW TW9 .. 18 E3
Brickfield Cl BTFD TW8 ..... 17 M2
Brickfield Farm Gdns
  ORP BR6 ..... 71 M3
Brickfield La HYS/HAR UB3 ..... 15 G1
Brickfield Rd REDH RH1 ..... 171 M1
  THHTH CR7 ..... 49 L1
  WIM/MER SW19 ..... 29 L5
Brickhouse La GDST RH9 ..... 172 F4
Brick Kiln La OXTED RH8 ..... 130 F4
Bricklands CRAWE RH10 ..... 214 E2
Bricksbury Hl FNM GU9 ..... 133 M2
Brickwood Cl SYD SE26 ..... 32 E4
Brickwood Rd CROY/NA CR0 ..... 5 G5
Brickyard Copse RDKG RH5 .. 187 M5
Brickyard La CRAWE RH10 ..... 214 E1
  RDKG RH5 ..... 143 G7
Brideake Cl CRAWW RH11 ..... 211 K6
Bridge Barn La
  WOKN/KNAP GU21 ..... 76 F7
Bridge Cl BF/WBF KT14 ..... 79 J2
  STA TW18 ..... 22 B5
  WOKN/KNAP GU21 ..... 76 F7
  WOT/HER KT12 ..... 42 C7
Bridge End CBLY GU15 ..... 72 E5
Bridgefield FNM GU9 ..... 134 A7
Bridgefield Cl BNSTD SM7 ..... 84 F5
Bridgefield Rd SUT SM1 ..... 65 K5
Bridge Gdns ASHF TW15 ..... 23 M8
  E/WMO/HCT KT8 ..... 44 A4
Bridgeham Cl WEY KT13 ..... 59 K4
Bridgeham Wy HORL RH6 ..... 171 L7
Bridgehill Cl GUW GU2 ..... 116 D6
Bridgelands CRAWE RH10 ..... 193 J6
Bridge La VW GU25 ..... 39 H6
Bridgeman Rd TEDD TW11 ..... 26 D7
Bridgemead FRIM GU16 ..... 93 G1
Bridge Ms WOKN/KNAP GU21 .. 6 A6
Bridge Pl CROY/NA CR0 ..... 4 F3
Bridge Rd ALDT GU11 ..... 134 D1
  ASC SL5 ..... 37 G5
  BAGS GU19 ..... 54 B5
  BECK BR3 ..... 33 J8
  BELMT SM2 ..... 65 L5
  CBLY GU15 ..... 72 E6
  CHERT KT16 ..... 40 E7
  CHSGTN KT9 ..... 63 H4
  COB KT11 ..... 80 E5
  CRAN GU6 ..... 185 H7
  E/WMO/HCT KT8 ..... 44 B4
  EW KT17 ..... 84 C2
  FARN GU14 ..... 92 C5
  HASM GU27 ..... 219 M2
  HORS RH12 ..... 226 A2
  HSLW TW3 ..... 17 G5
  RGODL GU7 ..... 160 B4
  TWK TW1 ..... 17 L8
  WEY KT13 ..... 59 J3
  WLGTN SM6 ..... 66 E4
Bridge Rw CROY/NA CR0 ..... 4 F3
Bridges La CROY/NA CR0 ..... 67 H3
Bridge St DTCH/LGLY SL3 ..... 13 G2
  GU GU1 ..... 8 F6
  LHD/OX KT22 ..... 102 D4
  RGODL GU7 ..... 160 B5
  TWK TW1 ..... 18 A8
  WOT/HER KT12 ..... 42 C8
Bridgetown Cl NRWD SE19 ..... 32 B6
Bridge Vw ASC SL5 ..... 37 L7
Bridgewater Rd WEY KT13 ..... 60 A5
Bridge Wy COUL/CHIP CR5 ..... 106 D1
  WHTN TW2 ..... 25 M1
Bridgewood Cl PGE/AN SE20 .. 32 E8
Bridgewood Rd
  STRHM/NOR SW16 ..... 31 G8
  WPK KT4 ..... 64 D3
Bridgford St
  WAND/EARL SW18 ..... 29 M4
Bridle Cl GSHT GU26 ..... 198 D6
  HOR/WEW KT19 ..... 63 M3
  KUT KT1 ..... 45 G8
  SUN TW16 ..... 42 D3
Bridle La COB KT11 ..... 81 L5
  TWK TW1 ..... 17 L8
Bridle Pth CROY/NA CR0 ..... 67 H2
The Bridle Pth EW KT17 ..... 64 F8
Bridlepath Wy
  EBED/NFELT TW14 ..... 24 B1
Bridle Rd CROY/NA CR0 ..... 69 K2
  ESH/CLAY KT10 ..... 62 E5
  EW KT17 ..... 84 C3
The Bridle Rd PUR/KEN CR8 ..... 67 H8
Bridle Wy CRAWE RH10 ..... 213 G2
  CROY/NA CR0 ..... 69 K4
  ORP BR6 ..... 71 M3
Bridleway Cl EW KT17 ..... 64 F8
The Bridle Wy WLGTN SM6 ..... 66 F3
Bridlington Cl BH/WHM TN16 .. 110 L1
Bridport Rd THHTH CR7 ..... 49 K3
Brier Lea KWD/TDW/WH KT20 .. 105 J8
Brierley Cl SNWD SE25 ..... 50 D4
Brierley Rd BAL SW12 ..... 30 F3
Brierly Cl GUW GU2 ..... 116 D6
Brier Rd KWD/TDW/WH KT20 .. 104 E1
Briggs Cl MTCM CR4 ..... 48 E1
Bright Hl GU GU1 ..... 9 J7
Brightlands Rd REIG RH2 ..... 125 M6
Brightman Rd
  WAND/EARL SW18 ..... 29 M1
Brighton Rd ADL/WDHM KT15 .. 58 F4
Brighton Rd ADL/WDHM KT15 .. 58 F4
  ALDT GU11 ..... 134 F1
  BELMT SM2 ..... 65 L8
  BNSTD SM7 ..... 85 J4
  COUL/CHIP CR5 ..... 86 F8
  CRAWW RH11 ..... 212 A6
  HORL RH6 ..... 170 C6
  KWD/TDW/WH KT20 ..... 105 J8
  KWD/TDW/WH KT20 ..... 125 K1

MFD/CHID GU8 ..... 160 E8
  PUR/KEN CR8 ..... 67 L8
  REDH RH1 ..... 126 C8
  SAND/SEL CR2 ..... 67 M7
  SURB KT6 ..... 44 F6
Brightside Av STA TW18 ..... 22 F8
Brightwell Cl CROY/NA CR0 ..... 49 K8
Brightwell Crs TOOT SW17 ..... 30 C6
Brightwells Rd FNM GU9 ..... 133 M7
Brigstock Rd COUL/CHIP CR5.. 86 E5
  THHTH CR7 ..... 49 L5
Brimshot La CHOB/PIR GU24 .. 56 B7
Brindle Cl ALDT GU11 ..... 134 E2
The Brindles BNSTD SM7 ..... 85 J7
Brinkley Rd WPK KT4 ..... 64 E1
Brinsworth Cl WHTN TW2 ..... 26 A2
Brisbane Av WIM/MER SW19 .. 47 L1
Brisbane Rd CRAWW RH11 .. 192 A8
Briscoe Rd WIM/MER SW19 ..... 30 A7
Brisson Cl ESH/CLAY KT10 ..... 61 J5
Bristol Cl CRAWE RH10 ..... 193 G8
  STWL/WRAY TW19 ..... 14 B8
Bristol Rd MRDN SM4 ..... 47 M5
Bristow Rd CBLY GU15 ..... 72 E6
  CROY/NA CR0 ..... 67 H3
  HSLW TW3 ..... 16 E5
  NRWD SE19 ..... 32 B6
Britannia Rd BRYLDS KT5 ..... 45 J7
Britannia Wy STWL/WRAY TW19 .. 23 G1
Briton Cl SAND/SEL CR2 ..... 88 B1
Briton Crs SAND/SEL CR2 ..... 88 B1
Briton Hill Rd SAND/SEL CR2 .. 68 B8
Brittain Rd WOT/HER KT12 ..... 61 G4
Britten Cl ASHV GU12 ..... 113 L7
  CRAWW RH11 ..... 211 J6
Brittens Cl GUW GU2 ..... 116 D3
Brixton Hill Pl
  BRXS/STRHM SW2 ..... 31 H1
Broadacre STA TW18 ..... 22 D6
Broadacres GUW GU2 ..... 116 B6
Broad Acres RGODL GU7 ..... 160 B1
Broadbridge Heath Rd
  HORS RH12 ..... 228 A5
Broadbridge La HORL RH6 ..... 171 K7
Broad Cl WOT/HER KT12 ..... 61 G2
Broadcoombe SAND/SEL CR2 .. 69 G6
Broadfield Cl
  KWD/TDW/WH KT20 ..... 104 F2
Broadfield Dr CRAWW RH11 .. 211 M7
Broadfield Pl CRAWW RH11 .. 211 L7
Broadfield Rd SHGR GU5 ..... 142 A8
Broadfields E/WMO/HCT KT8 .. 44 A6
Broadford La CHOB/PIR GU24 .. 76 B2
Broadford Pk RGUE GU4 ..... 139 G7
Broadford Rd RGUE GU4 ..... 139 G7
Broadgates Rd
  WAND/EARL SW18 ..... 30 A2
Broad Green Av CROY/NA CR0 .. 4 A1
Broadham Green Rd
  OXTED RH8 ..... 130 A7
Broadham Pl OXTED RH8 ..... 130 A6
Broad Ha'penny RFNM GU10 .. 155 K4
Broad Hwy COB KT11 ..... 81 G4
Broadhurst ASHTD KT21 ..... 83 H6
Broadhurst Gdns REIG RH2 ..... 147 L2
Broadlands FARN GU14 ..... 93 H7
  FELT TW13 ..... 25 J4
  FRIM GU16 ..... 93 J1
  HORL RH6 ..... 170 F5
Broadlands Av SHPTN TW17 .. 41 M6
  STRHM/NOR SW16 ..... 31 H3
Broadlands Cl
  STRHM/NOR SW16 ..... 31 H3
Broadlands Dr ASC SL5 ..... 36 F7
  WARL CR6 ..... 108 F1
Broadlands Wy NWMAL KT3 .. 46 C6
Broad La BRAK RG12 ..... 34 F3
  HPTN TW12 ..... 25 J8
  RDKG RH5 ..... 168 A4
Broadley Gn BFOR GU20 ..... 55 G6
Broadmead ASHTD KT21 ..... 83 H8
  CAT SE6 ..... 33 K4
  FARN GU14 ..... 92 A4
  HORL RH6 ..... 170 F5
Broadmead Av WPK KT4 ..... 46 D8
Broadmead Cl HPTN TW12 ..... 25 K7
Broadmeads RPLY/SEND GU23 .. 97 L4
Broad Oak SUN TW16 ..... 24 C7
Broad Oaks SURB KT6 ..... 45 L8
Broadoaks Crs BF/WBF KT14 .. 78 E4
Broadstone Pk FROW RH18 .. 217 K7
Broad St CHOB/PIR GU24 ..... 75 G2
  RGUW GU3 ..... 116 A6
  TEDD TW11 ..... 26 C7
Broadview Rd
  STRHM/NOR SW16 ..... 31 G8
Broad Wk COUL/CHIP CR5 ..... 106 D4
  CRAN GU6 ..... 185 J4
  CTHM CR3 ..... 108 C4
  FRIM GU16 ..... 73 H7
  HEST TW5 ..... 16 A3
  KWD/TDW/WH KT20 ..... 104 F1
  RCH/KEW TW9 ..... 18 C2
Broadwater Cl
  STWL/WRAY TW19 ..... 21 J1
  WOKN/KNAP GU21 ..... 78 A2
  WOT/HER KT12 ..... 60 D4
Broadwater Gdns ORP BR6 ..... 71 L3
Broadwater Ri GU GU1 ..... 139 K1
Broadwater Rd North
  WOT/HER KT12 ..... 60 D4
Broadwater Rd South
  WOT/HER KT12 ..... 60 D4
Broad Wy FARN GU14 ..... 112 D1
Broadway SURB KT6 ..... 45 L8
  SUT SM1 ..... 65 M3
  WOKN/KNAP GU21 ..... 95 L1
Broadway Av CROY/NA CR0 ..... 50 A5
  TWK TW1 ..... 17 L8
Broadway Cl SAND/SEL CR2 .. 88 E4
Broadway Gdns MTCM CR4 ..... 48 B4
Broadway Pl CHOB/PIR GU24 .. 55 G7
The Broadway
  ADL/WDHM KT15 ..... 58 D8
  CHEAM SM3 ..... 65 H5
  CRAWE RH10 ..... 212 A3
  STA TW18 ..... 40 F3

THDIT KT7 ..... 44 B8
  WIM/MER SW19 ..... 29 J7
  WOKN/KNAP GU21 ..... 6 C1
Broadwell Rd NFNM GU10 ..... 10 A8
Broadwood Cl HORS RH12 ..... 229 K4
Broadwood Ri CRAWW RH11 .. 211 M8
Brockdene Dr HAYES BR2 ..... 71 G3
Brockenhurst
  E/WMO/HCT KT8 ..... 43 J6
Brockenhurst Av WPK KT4 ..... 46 B8
Brockenhurst Cl
  WOKN/KNAP GU21 ..... 77 J4
Brockenhurst Rd ALDT GU11 .. 134 E1
  ASC SL5 ..... 36 E5
  BRAK RG12 ..... 35 J3
  CROY/NA CR0 ..... 50 E7
Brockenhurst Wy
  STRHM/NOR SW16 ..... 49 G2
Brockham Cl WIM/MER SW19 .. 29 J6
Brockham Crs CROY/NA CR0 .. 70 A6
Brockham Dr BRXS/STRHM SW2 .. 31 J1
Brockham Hill Pk
  KWD/TDW/WH KT20 ..... 123 M5
Brockhamhurst Rd
  BRKHM/BTCW RH3 ..... 145 J7
Brockham La
  BRKHM/BTCW RH3 ..... 123 K8
Brockhurst Cl HORS RH12 ..... 228 C8
Brockhurst Ldg FNM GU9 ..... 10 E6
Brocklebank Rd
  WAND/EARL SW18 ..... 29 M1
Brocklesby Rd SNWD SE25 .. 50 E4
Brockley Combe WEY KT13 ..... 60 A4
Brockley Pk FSTH SE23 ..... 33 H1
Brockley Ri FSTH SE23 ..... 33 H1
Brockley Vw FSTH SE23 ..... 33 H1
Brock Rd CRAWW RH11 ..... 191 L8
Brock's Cl RGODL GU7 ..... 160 D4
Brocks Dr CHEAM SM3 ..... 65 H2
  RGUW GU3 ..... 115 M4
Brockshot Cl BTFD TW8 ..... 18 A1
Brock Wy VW GU25 ..... 38 F5
Brockway Cl GU GU1 ..... 117 K8
Brockwell Park Gdns HNHL SE24.. 31 L1
Brodie Rd GU GU1 ..... 8 E3
Brodrick Gv GT/LBKH KT23 .. 101 K8
Brodrick Rd TOOT SW17 ..... 30 C2
Brograve Gdns BECK BR3 ..... 51 L2
Broke Ct RGUE GU4 ..... 117 M5
Brokes Crs REIG RH2 ..... 125 K6
Brokes Rd REIG RH2 ..... 125 K6
Bromford Ct OXTED RH8 ..... 130 D7
Bromley Cl RGUE GU4 ..... 139 G7
  CAT SE6 ..... 33 L3
Brompton Cl HSLWW TW4 ..... 16 C7
Bronson Rd RYNPK SW20 ..... 47 G2
The Brontes EGRIN RH19 .. 196 A8
Brook Av FNM GU9 ..... 134 C2
Brook Cl DORK RH4 ..... 122 F8
  EGRIN RH19 ..... 196 E8
  HOR/WEW KT19 ..... 64 B7
  RYNPK SW20 ..... 46 E3
  SHST GU47 ..... 52 B8
  STWL/WRAY TW19 ..... 23 J1
Brookdale Rd CAT SE6 ..... 33 L1
Brook Dr BRAK RG12 ..... 35 H4
Brooke Forest RGUW GU3 ..... 115 M4
Brookehowse Rd CAT SE6 ..... 33 L4
Brookers Cl ASHTD KT21 ..... 82 F7
Brook Farm Rd COB KT11 ..... 81 G5
Brookfield RGODL GU7 ..... 160 D1
  WOKN/KNAP GU21 ..... 76 E6
Brookfield Av SUT SM1 ..... 66 B2
Brookfield Cl CHERT KT16 ..... 58 A5
  REDH RH1 ..... 148 D6
Brookfield Gdns
  ESH/CLAY KT10 ..... 62 C5
Brookfield Rd ASHV GU12 ..... 113 H7
Brookfields Av MTCM CR4 ..... 48 B5
Brook Gdns BARN SW13 ..... 19 J5
  FARN GU14 ..... 92 C7
  KUTN/CMB KT2 ..... 45 M1
Brook Hl OXTED RH8 ..... 129 M4
  SHGR GU5 ..... 163 G1
Brookhill Cl CRAWE RH10 ..... 193 K6
Brookhouse Rd FARN GU14 ..... 92 C7
Brookhurst Rd ADL/WDHM KT15.. 58 E5
Brooklands Av
  WAND/EARL SW18 ..... 29 L3
Brooklands Cl COB KT11 ..... 81 H5
  FNM GU9 ..... 134 A2
  NFNM GU10 ..... 154 A4
  SUN TW16 ..... 42 B7
Brooklands La WEY KT13 ..... 59 J5
Brooklands Rd CRAWW RH11 .. 211 M8
  FNM GU9 ..... 134 B2
  THDIT KT7 ..... 44 B8
  WEY KT13 ..... 59 L7
Brooklands Wy EGRIN RH19 .. 216 A1
  FNM GU9 ..... 134 B2
  REDH RH1 ..... 126 B6
Brook La CHOB/PIR GU24 ..... 76 A1
  RPLY/SEND GU23 ..... 98 B4
  SHGR GU5 ..... 141 M8
Brook La North BTFD TW8 ..... 18 A1
Brookley Cl NFNM GU10 ..... 134 E6
Brookleys CHOB/PIR GU24 ..... 56 C8
Brooklyn Av SNWD SE25 ..... 50 E4
Brooklyn Cl CAR SM5 ..... 66 B1
  WOKS/MYFD GU22 ..... 10 E6
Brooklyn Gv SNWD SE25 ..... 50 E4
Brooklyn Rd SNWD SE25 ..... 50 E4
  WOKS/MYFD GU22 ..... 6 C8
Brook Md HOR/WEW KT19 ..... 64 B5
Brookmead MTCM CR4 ..... 48 F6
Brookmead Ct CROY/NA CR0 .. 48 F6
Brook Rd BAGS GU19 ..... 54 B7
  CBLY GU15 ..... 72 E5
  HORS RH12 ..... 229 H3
  MFD/CHID GU8 ..... 200 F1
  REDH RH1 ..... 126 F2
  REDH RH1 ..... 148 C1
  RGUE GU4 ..... 139 M6
  SURB KT6 ..... 63 H1
  THHTH CR7 ..... 49 M4

TWK TW1 ..... 17 K8
Brook Rd South BTFD TW8 ..... 18 B1
Brooks Cl WEY KT13 ..... 59 K8
Brookside CAR SM5 ..... 66 D4
  CHERT KT16 ..... 40 A6
  CRAN GU6 ..... 185 H6
  CRAWE RH10 ..... 193 K6
  CRAWE RH10 ..... 212 C2
  DTCH/LGLY SL3 ..... 12 F2
  FNM GU9 ..... 133 M3
  GDST RH9 ..... 151 G4
  RDKG RH5 ..... 167 J3
  RGUE GU4 ..... 117 G3
Brookside Av ASHF TW15 ..... 22 F6
  STWL/WRAY TW19 ..... 12 A5
Brookside Cl FELT TW13 ..... 24 D4
Brookside Crs WPK KT4 ..... 46 D8
Brookside Wy CROY/NA CR0 .. 51 G6
Brooks La CHSWK W4 ..... 18 D1
Brook St KUT KT1 ..... 2 E7
Brookswood RGUE GU4 ..... 139 M7
Brook Va RDKG RH5 ..... 144 E8
Brookview CRAWE RH10 ..... 193 K6
Brookview Rd
  STRHM/NOR SW16 ..... 30 F6
Brook Wy LHD/OX KT22 ..... 82 D8
Brookwell La SHGR GU5 ..... 161 L7
Brookwood HORL RH6 ..... 170 E5
Brookwood Av BARN SW13 ..... 19 J5
Brookwood Br
  WOKN/KNAP GU21 ..... 95 L2
Brookwood Lye Rd
  WOKS/MYFD GU22 ..... 95 L2
Brookwood Rd FARN GU14 ..... 93 G5
  HSLW TW3 ..... 16 E4
  WAND/EARL SW18 ..... 29 J2
Broom Bank WARL CR6 ..... 109 M1
Broom Cl BLKW GU17 ..... 72 B5
  ESH/CLAY KT10 ..... 61 L4
  TEDD TW11 ..... 2 C2
Broomcroft Dr
  WOKS/MYFD GU22 ..... 78 A5
Broomdashers Rd
  CRAWE RH10 ..... 212 C2
Broome Cl EPSOM KT18 ..... 104 A8
  HORS RH12 ..... 229 G4
Broome Ct BRAK RG12 ..... 34 E3
Broomehall Rd RDKG RH5 ..... 166 A6
Broome Rd HPTN TW12 ..... 43 J1
Broomers La CRAN GU6 ..... 186 B4
Broomfield GUW GU2 ..... 116 B7
Broom Fld LTWR GU18 ..... 74 D2
Broomfield MFD/CHID GU8 ..... 158 B5
  SUN TW16 ..... 42 D1
Broomfield Cl RGUW GU3 ..... 116 B6
  WOKS/MYFD GU22 ..... 78 A6
Broomfield Ct WEY KT13 ..... 59 K5
Broomfield Dr ASC SL5 ..... 37 L6
Broomfield La NFNM GU10 ..... 155 K8
Broomfield Pk ASC SL5 ..... 37 L7
  DORK RH4 ..... 143 M3
Broomfield Ride LHD/OX KT22 .. 82 A2
Broomfield Rd ADL/WDHM KT15 .. 78 E1
  BECK BR3 ..... 51 H4
  BRYLDS KT5 ..... 45 J8
  RCH/KEW TW9 ..... 18 C3
  TEDD TW11 ..... 26 F7
Broomfields ESH/CLAY KT10 .. 61 M4
Broom Gdns CROY/NA CR0 ..... 69 K2
Broom Hall LHD/OX KT22 ..... 81 M4
Broomhall End
  WOKN/KNAP GU21 ..... 6 D3
Broomhall La ASC SL5 ..... 37 J6
  WOKN/KNAP GU21 ..... 6 D4
Broomhall Rd SAND/SEL CR2 .. 68 A7
  WOKN/KNAP GU21 ..... 6 D4
Broomhill NFNM GU10 ..... 133 G1
Broomhill Rd FARN GU14 ..... 92 A4
Broomhurst Ct DORK RH4 ..... 144 E4
Broomlands La OXTED RH8 ..... 131 H1
Broom La CHOB/PIR GU24 ..... 56 B7
Broomleaf Cnr FNM GU9 ..... 134 A7
Broomleaf Rd FNM GU9 ..... 134 A7
Broomloan La SUT SM1 ..... 65 K1
Broom Pk KUT KT1 ..... 2 C2
Broom Rd CROY/NA CR0 ..... 69 K2
  TEDD TW11 ..... 26 E6
Broomsquires Rd BAGS GU19 .. 54 D7
Broom Water TEDD TW11 ..... 26 F7
Broom Water West TEDD TW11.. 26 F6
Broom Wy WEY KT13 ..... 60 A3
Broomwood Cl CROY/NA CR0 .. 51 G5
Broomwood Wy NFNM GU10 .. 11 G7
Broseley Gv SYD SE26 ..... 33 J2
Broster Gdns SNWD SE25 ..... 50 C3
Brougham Pl FNM GU9 ..... 133 J2
Broughton Av
  RCHPK/HAM TW10 ..... 26 F5
Broughton Ms FRIM GU16 ..... 73 J8
Broughton Rd THHTH CR7 ..... 49 K6
Browells La FELT TW13 ..... 24 F3
Brown Cl WLGTN SM6 ..... 67 G6
Browngraves Rd HYS/HAR UB3 .. 14 F4
Brownhill Rd CAT SE6 ..... 33 M1
Browning Av SUT SM1 ..... 66 B3
  WPK KT4 ..... 46 E8
Browning Cl CBLY GU15 ..... 73 M5
  CRAWE RH10 ..... 212 F2
  HPTN TW12 ..... 25 J5
Browning Rd LHD/OX KT22 ..... 102 A7
Brownings EDEN TN8 ..... 183 L4
The Brownings EGRIN RH19 .. 195 M8
Browning Wy HEST TW5 ..... 16 A4
Brownlow Rd CROY/NA CR0 ..... 5 H9
  REDH RH1 ..... 126 B8
Brownrigg Crs BRAK RG12 ..... 35 H1
Brownrigg Rd ASHF TW15 ..... 23 K5
Brown's Hl REDH RH1 ..... 150 A7
Browns La EHSLY KT24 ..... 121 G1
Brown's Rd BRYLDS KT5 ..... 45 J7
Browns Wk NFNM GU10 ..... 155 J4
Browns Wd EGRIN RH19 ..... 196 D5
The Brow REDH RH1 ..... 148 D5
Broxholm Rd WNWD SE27 ..... 31 K4
Brox La ADL/WDHM KT15 ..... 58 A7
Brox Rd CHERT KT16 ..... 57 M6
Broxted Rd FSTH SE23 ..... 33 J3
Bruce Av SHPTN TW17 ..... 41 M6

Bruce Cl BF/WBF KT14 .... 79 G3
Bruce Dr SAND/SEL CR2 .... 69 G7
Bruce Rd MTCM CR4 .... 30 D8
SNWD SE25 .... 50 A4
Brudenell Rd TOOT SW17 .... 30 C4
Brumana Cl WEY KT13 .... 59 L5 1
Brumfield Rd HOR/WEW KT19 .... 63 M4
Brunel Cl HEST TW5 .... 15 L2
NRWD SE19 .... 32 C7
Brunel Pl CRAWE RH10 .... 212 B4
Brunel Wk HSLWW TW4 .... 25 K1 2
Brunner Ct CHERT KT16 .... 57 M4 1
Brunswick BRAK RG12 .... 34 D7
Brunswick Cl CRAWE RH10 .... 212 D5 1
THDIT KT7 .... 44 C8 1
WHTN TW2 .... 26 A4
WOT/HER KT12 .... 60 F1
Brunswick Dr CHOB/PIR GU24 .... 95 G2
Brunswick Gv COB KT11 .... 80 F3 1
Brunswick Ms
STRHM/NOR SW16 .... 31 G7 1
Brunswick Pl NRWD SE19 .... 32 D8 3
Brunswick Rd CHOB/PIR GU24 .... 95 G3
FRIM GU16 .... 93 M3
KUTN/CMB KT2 .... 3 J4
SUT SM1 .... 65 L3
Bruntile Cl FARN GU14 .... 93 G8
Brushwood Rd HORS RH12 .... 229 L3
Bruton Rd MRDN SM4 .... 47 M4
Bruton Wy BRAK RG12 .... 35 H7
Bryan Cl SUN TW16 .... 24 D8
Bryanston Av WHTN TW2 .... 25 L2
Bryanstone Av GUW GU2 .... 116 C4
Bryanstone Cl GUW GU2 .... 116 C5
Bryanstone Gv GUW GU2 .... 116 C4
Bryce Cl HORS RH12 .... 229 K4
Bryce Gdns ALDT GU11 .... 134 F2
Bryden Cl SYD SE26 .... 33 H6
Brympton Cl DORK RH4 .... 144 D4
Brynford Cl WOKN/KNAP GU21 .... 6 D1
Bryn Rd NFNM GU10 .... 10 A6
Bryony Rd GU GU1 .... 117 L5
Bryony Wy SUN TW16 .... 24 D7
Buchans Lawn CRAWW RH11 .... 211 L7
The Buchan CBLY GU15 .... 73 K1
Bucharest Rd WAND/EARL SW18 .. 29 M1
Buckfast Rd MRDN SM4 .... 47 L4
Buckham Thorns Rd
BH/WHM TN16 .... 111 M8
Buckhurst Av CAR SM5 .... 48 B8
Buckhurst Cl EGRIN RH19 .... 195 M6
REDH RH1 .... 126 B6
Buckhurst Hl BRAK RG12 .... 35 J4 2
Buckhurst La ASC SL5 .... 37 K3
Buckhurst Rd ASC SL5 .... 37 J2
BH/WHM TN16 .... 111 L2
FRIM GU16 .... 93 J3
Buckhurst Wy EGRIN RH19 .... 195 M6
Buckingham Av
E/WMO/HCT KT8 .... 43 L2
EBED/NFELT TW14 .... 15 L8
THHTH CR7 .... 49 K1
Buckingham Cl GU GU1 .... 9 M2
HPTN TW12 .... 25 J6
Buckingham Dr EGRIN RH19 .... 216 D2
Buckingham Gdns
THHTH CR7 .... 49 K2 1
Buckingham Ga HORL RH6 .... 192 F1
Buckingham La FSTH SE23 .... 33 H1 1
Buckingham Rd FELT TW13 .... 25 J5
KUT KT1 .... 45 J4
MTCM CR4 .... 49 H5 1
RCHPK/HAM TW10 .... 27 G3
RDKG RH5 .... 166 F2
Buckingham Wy WLGTN SM6 .... 66 F7
Buckland Cl FARN GU14 .... 92 F2
Buckland La
BRKHM/BTCW RH3 .... 124 D4
Buckland Rd BELMT SM2 .... 64 F8
CHSGTN KT9 .... 63 J4
KWD/TDW/WH KT20 .... 125 J3
REIG RH2 .... 125 G7
Bucklands Rd TEDD TW11 .... 26 F7
Buckland Wk MRDN SM4 .... 47 M4 1
Buckland Wy WPK KT4 .... 46 F8
Bucklebury BRAK RG12 .... 34 D7
Buckleigh Av RYNPK SW20 .... 47 J3
Buckleigh Rd STRHM/NOR SW16 .. 31 G7
Buckleigh Wy NRWD SE19 .... 32 C8 1
Bucklers' Wy CAR SM5 .... 66 C2
Buckles Wy BNSTD SM7 .... 85 H6
Buckley Pl CRAWE RH10 .... 214 D1
Buckmans Rd CRAWW RH11 .... 212 A3
Bucknills Cl EPSOM KT18 .... 83 L4
Bucks Cl BF/WBF KT14 .... 78 E4
Buckswood Dr CRAWW RH11 .... 211 K5
Budebury Rd STA TW18 .... 22 C6
Budge La MTCM CR4 .... 48 C7 2
Budgen Cl CRAWE RH10 .... 193 G8
Budgen Dr REDH RH1 .... 126 D5
Budham Wy BRAK RG12 .... 34 E6
Buff Av BNSTD SM7 .... 85 L4
Buffbeards La HASM GU27 .... 219 H2
Buffers La LHD/OX KT22 .... 102 D1
Bug Hl WARL CR6 .... 109 G2
Bugkingham Wy FRIM GU16 .... 93 J1
Bulganak Rd THHTH CR7 .... 49 M4 1
Bulkeley Cl EGH TW20 .... 20 F6
Bullard Rd TEDD TW11 .... 26 C7 2
Bullbeggars La GDST RH9 .... 128 F6
WOKN/KNAP GU21 .... 76 E6
Bullbrook Dr BRAK RG12 .... 35 H1
Buller Ct FARN GU14 .... 92 F8 4
Buller Rd ALDT GU11 .... 112 E5
THHTH CR7 .... 50 A3
Bullers Rd FNM GU9 .... 134 B3
Bullfinch Cl HORL RH6 .... 170 B5 1
HORS RH12 .... 228 F2
SHST GU47 .... 72 B1 2
Bullfinch Rd SAND/SEL CR2 .... 69 G8
Bull Hl LHD/OX KT22 .... 102 D3
Bull La BRAK RG12 .... 34 E1
RGUE GU4 .... 97 J8
Bullrush Cl CROY/NA CR0 .... 50 B6 1
Bulls Aly MORT/ESHN SW14 .... 19 G5 1
Bullswater Common Rd
CHOB/PIR GU24 .... 95 K7
Bulstrode Av HSLW TW3 .... 16 C5
Bulstrode Gdns HSLW TW3 .... 16 D5
Bulstrode Rd HSLW TW3 .... 16 D5
Bunbury Wy EW KT17 .... 84 E6
Bunce Common Rd REIG RH2 .... 146 A7
Bunce Dr CTHM CR3 .... 108 A5
Bunch La HASM GU27 .... 199 M7
Bunch Wy HASM GU27 .... 219 K3
Bundy's Wy STA TW18 .... 22 C7
Bungalow Rd FARN GU14 .... 92 E7
SNWD SE25 .... 50 B4
The Bungalows STRHM/NOR SW16 .. 30 E8 1
Bunting Cl MTCM CR4 .... 48 C5
SWTR RH13 .... 229 J6
The Buntings FNM GU9 .... 10 B5
Bunyan Cl CRAWW RH11 .... 211 H6
Bunyard Dr WOKN/KNAP GU21 .... 77 M4
Burbage Gn BRAK RG12 .... 35 J5 1
Burbeach Cl CRAWW RH11 .... 211 L6 3
Burberry Cl NWMAL KT3 .... 46 B2
Burbidge Rd SHPTN TW17 .... 41 K4 2
Burchets Hollow SHGR GU5 .... 164 A2
Burchetts Wy SHPTN TW17 .... 41 L6
Burcote Rd WAND/EARL SW18 .... 30 A2
Burcott Gdns ADL/WDHM KT15 .... 59 G5
Burcott Rd PUR/KEN CR8 .... 87 K4
Burdenshot Hl RGUW GU3 .... 96 D7
Burdenshott Av
RCHPK/HAM TW10 .... 18 E6
Burdenshott Rd RGUW GU3 .... 96 D7
Burden Wy GUW GU2 .... 116 E3
Burdett Av RYNPK SW20 .... 46 D1
Burdett Cl CRAWE RH10 .... 213 G4 3
Burdett Rd CROY/NA CR0 .... 50 A6
RCH/KEW TW9 .... 18 C4
Burdock Cl CRAWW RH11 .... 211 K7 2
CROY/NA CR0 .... 51 G8
LTWR GU18 .... 74 E1
Burdon La BELMT SM2 .... 65 J7
Burdon Pk BELMT SM2 .... 65 J7
Burfield Cl TOOT SW17 .... 29 M5
Burfield Dr WARL CR6 .... 108 F1
Burfield Rd WDSR SL4 .... 20 D1
Burford La EW KT17 .... 84 F1
Burford Lea MFD/CHID GU8 .... 158 B5
Burford Rd CAT SE6 .... 33 J3
CBLY GU15 .... 72 E5 1
SUT SM1 .... 65 K1
SWTR RH13 .... 229 H7
WPK KT4 .... 46 D7
Burford Wy CROY/NA CR0 .... 69 M6
Burges Gv BARN SW13 .... 19 L2 1
Burges Rd STA TW18 .... 22 D7
Burgess Cl FELT TW13 .... 25 H5 1
Burgess Rd SUT SM1 .... 65 L3
Burgh Cl CRAWE RH10 .... 193 G8
Burghead Cl SHST GU47 .... 72 A2 2
Burgh Heath Rd EW KT17 .... 84 C5
Burghfield EW KT17 .... 84 C5
Burghill Rd SYD SE26 .... 33 G5
Burghley Av NWMAL KT3 .... 46 A1
Burghley Hall Cl
WIM/MER SW19 .... 29 H2 1
Burghley Pl MTCM CR4 .... 48 C5 1
Burghley Rd WIM/MER SW19 .... 29 G5
Burgh Mt BNSTD SM7 .... 85 J5
Burgh Wd BNSTD SM7 .... 85 H5
Burgos Cl CROY/NA CR0 .... 67 K5
Burgoyne Rd CBLY GU15 .... 73 K3
SNWD SE25 .... 50 C4
SUN TW16 .... 24 C7
Burham Cl PGE/AN SE20 .... 32 F8
Burhill Rd WOT/HER KT12 .... 60 F5
Burke Cl PUT/ROE SW15 .... 19 H6
Burlands CRAWW RH11 .... 191 K8
Burlea Cl WOT/HER KT12 .... 60 E4
Burleigh Av WLGTN SM6 .... 66 D2
Burleigh Cl ADL/WDHM KT15 .... 58 E4
CRAWE RH10 .... 214 E1
Burleigh Gdns ASHF TW15 .... 23 M6
WOKN/KNAP GU21 .... 6 F4 1
Burleigh La ASC SL5 .... 36 B1
CRAWE RH10 .... 214 F2
Burleigh Pk COB KT11 .... 81 H2
Burleigh Rd ADL/WDHM KT15 .... 58 E3
ASC SL5 .... 36 B2
CHEAM SM3 .... 47 H8
FRIM GU16 .... 93 G1
Burleigh Wk CAT SE6 .... 33 M2
Burleigh Wy CRAWE RH10 .... 214 E1
Burley Cl BIL RH14 .... 224 D5 1
STRHM/NOR SW16 .... 49 G2
Burleys Rd CRAWE RH10 .... 213 G3
Burlingham Cl RGUE GU4 .... 118 A6 2
The Burlings ASC SL5 .... 36 B2
Burlington Av RCH/KEW TW9 .... 18 D3
Burlington Cl EBED/NFELT TW14 .. 24 A1
ORP BR6 .... 71 L1
Burlington La CHSWK W4 .... 18 F2
Burlington Pl REIG RH2 .... 125 K8
Burlington Rd ISLW TW7 .... 17 G3
NWMAL KT3 .... 46 C4
THHTH CR7 .... 49 M2
Burlsdon Wy BRAK RG12 .... 35 H1 1
Burma Rd CHOB/PIR GU24 .... 56 C1
Burmester Rd TOOT SW17 .... 29 M4
Burnaby Crs CHSWK W4 .... 18 E1
Burnaby Gdns CHSWK W4 .... 18 E1
Burnbury Rd BAL SW12 .... 30 F2
Burn Cl ADL/WDHM KT15 .... 59 G3 2
LHD/OX KT22 .... 81 M5
Burne-jones Dr SHST GU47 .... 72 A3
Burnell Av RCHPK/HAM TW10 .... 26 F6
Burnell Rd SUT SM1 .... 65 L3
Burnet Av GU GU1 .... 117 L5
Burnet Cl CHOB/PIR GU24 .... 75 H3
Burnet Gv HOR/WEW KT19 .... 83 M3
Burney Av BRYLDS KT5 .... 45 J5
Burney Cl GT/LBKH KT23 .... 101 M7
Burney Rd RDKG RH5 .... 122 D5
Burnham Cl WOKN/KNAP GU21 .... 76 A8
Burnham Dr REIG RH2 .... 125 K7
WPK KT4 .... 65 G1
Burnham Gdns CROY/NA CR0 .... 5 K2 1
HEST TW5 .... 15 L3
Burnham Rd MRDN SM4 .... 47 L5
WOKN/KNAP GU21 .... 76 A8
Burnhams Rd GT/LBKH KT23 .... 101 H6
Burnham St KUTN/CMB KT2 .... 3 J5 1
Burnham Wy SYD SE26 .... 33 J6
Burnhill Rd BECK BR3 .... 51 K2
Burn Moor Cha BRAK RG12 .... 35 H7 1
Burnsall Cl FARN GU14 .... 92 E3
Burns Av EBED/NFELT TW14 .... 15 K8
Burns Cl FARN GU14 .... 92 C3
HORS RH12 .... 229 H2
TOOT SW17 .... 30 A7 1
Burns Dr BNSTD SM7 .... 85 H4
Burnside ASHTD KT21 .... 83 J8 1
Burnside Cl TWK TW1 .... 17 K8
Burns Rd CRAWE RH10 .... 212 F1
Burns Wy EGRIN RH19 .... 195 M8
HEST TW5 .... 16 A3
HORS RH12 .... 210 F8
Burntcommon Cl
RPLY/SEND GU23 .... 98 C7 1
Burntcommon La
RPLY/SEND GU23 .... 98 D7
Burnt Hill Rd NFNM GU10 .... 10 D8
Burnt Hill Wy NFNM GU10 .... 155 L4
Burnt House La HORS RH12 .... 210 C2
Burnt Pollard La
CHOB/PIR GU24 .... 55 H8
Burntwood Cl CTHM CR3 .... 108 D3
WAND/EARL SW18 .... 30 B2 1
Burntwood Grange Rd
WAND/EARL SW18 .... 30 A2
Burntwood La CTHM CR3 .... 108 D3
TOOT SW17 .... 30 A3
Burntwood Vw NRWD SE19 .... 32 C6 1
Burnwood Park Rd
WOT/HER KT12 .... 60 E3
Burpham La RGUE GU4 .... 117 K3
Burrell Cl CROY/NA CR0 .... 51 H6
Burrell Rd FRIM GU16 .... 92 F1
Burrell Rw BECK BR3 .... 51 K2
The Burrell DORK RH4 .... 143 M3
Burr Hill La CHOB/PIR GU24 .... 56 B7
Burritt Rd KUT KT1 .... 3 J7
Burrow Hill Gn CHOB/PIR GU24 .... 56 A7
Burrows Cl GT/LBKH KT23 .... 101 J6
GUW GU2 .... 116 C7
Burrows Hill Cl
STWL/WRAY TW19 .... 13 L6
Burrows La SHGR GU5 .... 141 M6
Burr Rd WAND/EARL SW18 .... 29 K2
Burrwood Gdns ASHV GU12 .... 113 K5
Burstead Cl COB KT11 .... 81 G3
Burston Gdns EGRIN RH19 .... 196 A5
Burstow Rd RYNPK SW20 .... 47 H1
Burtenshaw Rd THDIT KT7 .... 44 D7
Burton Cl CHSGTN KT9 .... 63 G6
HORL RH6 .... 170 D7 1
Burton Gdns HEST TW5 .... 16 C3 1
Burton Rd KUTN/CMB KT2 .... 2 F3
Burton's Rd HPTN TW12 .... 25 L5
Burtwell La WNWD SE27 .... 32 A5
Burwash Rd CRAWE RH10 .... 212 D4 1
Burway Crs CHERT KT16 .... 40 D4
Burwood Av HAYES BR2 .... 70 E1
PUR/KEN CR8 .... 87 L4
Burwood Cl GU GU1 .... 117 M7
REIG RH2 .... 126 A8
SURB KT6 .... 45 K8
WOT/HER KT12 .... 60 F5
Burwood Rd WEY KT13 .... 60 A6
WOT/HER KT12 .... 60 C6
Bury Cl WOKN/KNAP GU21 .... 6 A4
Bury Flds GUW GU2 .... 8 F8
Bury Gv MRDN SM4 .... 47 L5
Bury La WOKN/KNAP GU21 .... 76 F6
The Burys RGODL GU7 .... 160 B4
Bury St GUW GU2 .... 8 F8
Busbridge La RGODL GU7 .... 160 B6
Busch Cl ISLW TW7 .... 17 L3
Busdens Cl MFD/CHID GU8 .... 181 J1
Busdens La MFD/CHID GU8 .... 181 J1
Busdens Wy MFD/CHID GU8 .... 181 J1
Bushbury La
BRKHM/BTCW RH3 .... 145 K5
Bush Cl ADL/WDHM KT15 .... 58 F4 1
Bushell Cl BRXS/STRHM SW2 .... 31 J3
Bushetts Gv REIG RH2 .... 126 E3
Bushey Cl PUR/KEN CR8 .... 88 C6
Bushey Cft OXTED RH8 .... 129 M4
Bushey La SUT SM1 .... 65 K2
Bushey Rd CROY/NA CR0 .... 69 K1
RYNPK SW20 .... 46 F2
SUT SM1 .... 65 K3
Bushfield BIL RH14 .... 223 J7
Bushfield Dr REDH RH1 .... 148 D5
Bush La RPLY/SEND GU23 .... 98 A6
Bushnell Rd TOOT SW17 .... 30 E3
Bush Rd RCH/KEW TW9 .... 18 C1
SHPTN TW17 .... 41 J5
Bushwood Rd RCH/KEW TW9 .... 18 D1
Bushy Hill Dr GU GU1 .... 117 M7
Bushy Park Gdns HPTN TW12 .... 26 A6 2
Bushy Park Rd TEDD TW11 .... 26 E8 1
Bushy Rd GT/LBKH KT23 .... 101 L4
TEDD TW11 .... 26 B7
Bushy Shaw ASHTD KT21 .... 82 F7
Busk Crs FARN GU14 .... 92 C6
Butchers Yd ORP BR6 .... 91 K1
Bute Av RCHPK/HAM TW10 .... 27 H3
Bute Gdns WLGTN SM6 .... 66 F4
Bute Gdns West WLGTN SM6 .... 66 F4
Bute Rd CROY/NA CR0 .... 49 K8
WLGTN SM6 .... 66 F3
Butler Rd BAGS GU19 .... 54 C7
Butlers Dene Rd CTHM CR3 .... 109 J2
Butlers Hl EHSLY KT24 .... 119 L4
Butlers Rd SWTR RH13 .... 229 K5
Butt Cl CRAN GU6 .... 185 H5 2
Buttercup Sq
STWL/WRAY TW19 .... 23 G2 1
Butterfield CBLY GU15 .... 72 E5 2
EGRIN RH19 .... 195 L6
Butterfield Cl TWK TW1 .... 17 J8 2
Butterfly Wk WARL CR6 .... 108 F2
Butter Hl DORK RH4 .... 144 D2
WLGTN SM6 .... 66 D2
Buttermer Cl NFNM GU10 .... 155 H2
Buttermere Cl
EBED/NFELT TW14 .... 24 C2 3
FARN GU14 .... 92 B5
HORS RH12 .... 229 L3 1
MRDN SM4 .... 47 G6 1
Buttermere Dr CBLY GU15 .... 74 A5
Buttermere Gdns BRAK RG12 .... 34 F3 1
PUR/KEN CR8 .... 88 A3
Buttermere Wy EGH TW20 .... 21 L8 2
Buttersteep Ri ASC SL5 .... 35 M8
Butts Cl CRAWW RH11 .... 211 L2
Butts Crs FELT TW13 .... 25 K4
Butts Rd WOKN/KNAP GU21 .... 6 C6
The Butts BTFD TW8 .... 18 A1
Buxton Av CTHM CR3 .... 108 B3
Buxton Crs CHEAM SM3 .... 65 H3
Buxton Dr NWMAL KT3 .... 46 A2
Buxton La CTHM CR3 .... 108 B3
Buxton Rd ASHF TW15 .... 23 G6
MORT/ESHN SW14 .... 19 H5
THHTH CR7 .... 49 L5
Byards Cft STRHM/NOR SW16 .... 49 G1
Bychurch End TEDD TW11 .... 26 C6 3
Bycroft St PGE/AN SE20 .... 33 G8 1
Bycroft Wy CRAWE RH10 .... 212 E1
Byerley Wy CRAWE RH10 .... 213 H2
Byers La GDST RH9 .... 150 F8
Bye Ways WHTN TW2 .... 25 L4
The Byeways BRYLDS KT5 .... 45 K5
The Byeway MORT/ESHN SW14 .... 18 F5
Byfeld Gdns BARN SW13 .... 19 K3
Byfield Rd ISLW TW7 .... 17 K5
Byfleet Rd ADL/WDHM KT15 .... 59 G8
COB KT11 .... 79 L2
Byfleets La HORS RH12 .... 228 A4
Bygrove Rd WIM/MER SW19 .... 30 A7
Bylands WOKS/MYFD GU22 .... 7 G9
Byne Rd CAR SM5 .... 66 B1
SYD SE26 .... 32 F7
Bynes Rd SAND/SEL CR2 .... 68 A6
Byrd Rd CRAWW RH11 .... 211 J6
Byrefield Rd GUW GU2 .... 116 C5
Byrne Rd BAL SW12 .... 30 E2
Byron Av COUL/CHIP CR5 .... 87 H5
FRIM GU16 .... 73 L6
HSLWW TW4 .... 15 L4
NWMAL KT3 .... 46 D5
SUT SM1 .... 66 A3
Byron Av East SUT SM1 .... 66 A3
Byron Cl CRAWE RH10 .... 212 E2
HORS RH12 .... 229 H3
HPTN TW12 .... 25 J5
WOKN/KNAP GU21 .... 76 B7
WOT/HER KT12 .... 43 H8
Byron Gdns SUT SM1 .... 66 A3
Byron Gv EGRIN RH19 .... 215 M1
Byron Pl LHD/OX KT22 .... 102 E4
Byron Rd ADL/WDHM KT15 .... 59 G3
SAND/SEL CR2 .... 68 E8
Byton Rd TOOT SW17 .... 30 C7
Byttom Hl RDKG RH5 .... 122 F1
Byward Av
EBED/NFELT TW14 .... 15 M8 1
The Byways HOR/WEW KT19 .... 64 C3
The Byway BELMT SM2 .... 66 A7
Bywood BRAK RG12 .... 34 D7
Bywood Av CROY/NA CR0 .... 50 F6
Bywood Cl PUR/KEN CR8 .... 87 L5
Byworth Cl FNM GU9 .... 133 J7
Byworth Rd FNM GU9 .... 133 J7

C

Cabbell Pl ADL/WDHM KT15 .... 58 F3 1
Cabell Rd GUW GU2 .... 116 B7
Cabin Moss BRAK RG12 .... 35 H7 2
Cabrera Av VW GU25 .... 39 G5
Cabrera Cl VW GU25 .... 38 F6
Cabrol Rd FARN GU14 .... 92 D4
Caburn Hts CRAWW RH11 .... 211 M5
The Cackstones
CRAWE RH10 .... 213 G2 1
Cadbury Cl ISLW TW7 .... 17 K3 1
SUN TW16 .... 24 B8
Cadbury Rd SUN TW16 .... 24 B8
Caddy Cl EGH TW20 .... 21 K6 1
Cadmer Cl NWMAL KT3 .... 46 B4 2
Cadnam Cl ALDT GU11 .... 134 F3
Cadogan Cl TEDD TW11 .... 26 B6 1
Cadogan Ct BELMT SM2 .... 65 L5
Cadogan Rd SURB KT6 .... 45 G5
Cadogen Rd ALDT GU11 .... 113 G2
Caenshill Rd WEY KT13 .... 59 K6
Caenswood Hl WEY KT13 .... 59 K8
Caenwood Cl WEY KT13 .... 59 K5
Caen Wood Rd ASHTD KT21 .... 82 F8
Caerleon Cl GSHT GU26 .... 198 F3 1
Caernarvon FRIM GU16 .... 93 J1
Caernarvon Cl MTCM CR4 .... 49 H3 1
Caesar's Camp Rd CBLY GU15 .... 73 K1
Caesar's Cl CBLY GU15 .... 73 K1 1
Caesars Wk MTCM CR4 .... 48 C5
Caesar's Wy SHPTN TW17 .... 42 A6 1
Caffins Cl CRAWE RH10 .... 212 B1
Caillard Rd BF/WBF KT14 .... 79 G1
Cain Rd BNFD RG42 .... 34 A2
BRAK RG12 .... 34 B2
Cain's La EBED/NFELT TW14 .... 15 G7
Cairn Cl FRIM GU16 .... 73 L6
Cairngorm Pl FARN GU14 .... 92 B2 1
Cairo New Rd CROY/NA CR0 .... 4 B6
Caistor Rd BAL SW12 .... 30 E1
Caithness Dr EPSOM KT18 .... 84 A4 1
Caithness Rd MTCM CR4 .... 30 E8
Calbourne Rd BAL SW12 .... 30 C1
Caldbeck Av WPK KT4 .... 64 E1
Calderdale Cl CRAWW RH11 .... 211 L5 2
Calder Rd MRDN SM4 .... 47 M5 1
Calder Wy DTCH/LGLY SL3 .... 13 H5
Caldwell Rd BFOR GU20 .... 55 G4
Caledonian Wy HORL RH6 .... 192 E2 1
Caledonia Rd STWL/WRAY TW19 .. 23 H2
Caledon Pl GU GU1 .... 117 K5 2
Caledon Rd CAR SM5 .... 66 D3 2
Calfridus Wy BRAK RG12 .... 35 H3
California Rd NWMAL KT3 .... 45 L4
Callander Rd CAT SE6 .... 33 L3
Calley Down Crs CROY/NA CR0 .... 70 A8
Callis Farm Cl STWL/WRAY TW19 .. 14 B8
Callisto Cl CRAWW RH11 .... 211 H6
Callow Fld PUR/KEN CR8 .... 87 K3
Callow Hl VW GU25 .... 38 F2
Calluna Ct WOKS/MYFD GU22 .... 6 E7
Calluna Dr CRAWE RH10 .... 193 K7
Calonne Rd WIM/MER SW19 .... 29 G5
Calshot Rd HTHAIR TW6 .... 14 E4
Calshot Wy FRIM GU16 .... 93 K2
HTHAIR TW6 .... 14 D4 1
Calthorpe Gdns SUT SM1 .... 65 M2
Calton Gdns ALDT GU11 .... 134 F2
Calverley Cl BECK BR3 .... 33 L7
Calverley Rd EW KT17 .... 64 D5
Calvert Cl ASHV GU12 .... 113 G8
Calvert Crs DORK RH4 .... 122 E8
Calvert Rd DORK RH4 .... 122 E8
EHSLY KT24 .... 120 E2
Calvin Cl CBLY GU15 .... 73 L5
Camac Rd WHTN TW2 .... 26 A2
Camber Cl CRAWE RH10 .... 212 F3
Camberley Av RYNPK SW20 .... 46 E2
Camberley Cl CHEAM SM3 .... 65 G2
Camberley Rd HTHAIR TW6 .... 14 D5
Camborne Cl HTHAIR TW6 .... 14 D5
Camborne Rd BELMT SM2 .... 65 K6
CROY/NA CR0 .... 5 L2
MRDN SM4 .... 47 G5
WAND/EARL SW18 .... 29 K1
Camborne Wy HEST TW5 .... 16 D3
Cambray Rd BAL SW12 .... 30 F2
Cambria Cl HSLW TW3 .... 16 D6
Cambria Ct EBED/NFELT TW14 .. 24 E1 1
Cambria Gdns STWL/WRAY TW19 .. 23 H1
Cambrian Cl CBLY GU15 .... 72 E4
WNWD SE27 .... 31 L4
Cambrian Rd FARN GU14 .... 92 A2
RCHPK/HAM TW10 .... 18 C8
Cambridge Av NWMAL KT3 .... 46 B2
Cambridge Cl HSLWW TW4 .... 16 B6
RYNPK SW20 .... 46 E1
WDR/YW UB7 .... 14 A1
WOKN/KNAP GU21 .... 76 C8 2
Cambridge Crs TEDD TW11 .... 26 D6 2
Cambridge Gv PGE/AN SE20 .... 50 E1 3
Cambridge Grove Rd KUT KT1 .... 3 J7 1
Cambridge Pk TWK TW1 .... 27 G1
Cambridge Rd ALDT GU11 .... 112 C7
ASHF TW15 .... 23 M8
BARN SW13 .... 19 J4
CAR SM5 .... 66 B5
E/WMO/HCT KT8 .... 43 J4
HPTN TW12 .... 25 J8
HSLWW TW4 .... 16 B6
KUT KT1 .... 3 J7
MTCM CR4 .... 48 F3
NWMAL KT3 .... 46 A4
RCH/KEW TW9 .... 18 D2 1
RYNPK SW20 .... 46 E1
SHST GU47 .... 52 B8
SNWD SE25 .... 50 D3
SWTR RH13 .... 229 G7
TEDD TW11 .... 26 D5
TWK TW1 .... 18 A8
WOT/HER KT12 .... 42 E6
Cambridge Rd East
FARN GU14 .... 92 F8 3
Cambridge Rd West FARN GU14 .. 92 F8
Camden Av FELT TW13 .... 24 F3
Camden Gdns SUT SM1 .... 65 L4
THHTH CR7 .... 49 L3
Camden Hill Rd NRWD SE19 .... 32 B7
Camden Rd CAR SM5 .... 66 C3 1
LING RH7 .... 174 A6
SUT SM1 .... 65 L4
Camden Wy THHTH CR7 .... 49 L3
Camel Gv KUTN/CMB KT2 .... 27 G6
Camellia Ct CHOB/PIR GU24 .... 75 J3
Camellia Pl WHTN TW2 .... 25 L1
Camelot Cl BH/WHM TN16 .... 90 F6
WIM/MER SW19 .... 29 J5
Camelsdale Rd HASM GU27 .... 219 J4
Camel Wy FARN GU14 .... 112 D1
Cameron Cl CRAN GU6 .... 185 H8 2
Cameron Rd ALDT GU11 .... 113 G2
CAT SE6 .... 33 J3 2
CROY/NA CR0 .... 49 L6
Camilla Cl GT/LBKH KT23 .... 101 L7
SUN TW16 .... 24 C7 2
Camilla Dr RDKG RH5 .... 122 D4
Camille Cl SNWD SE25 .... 50 D3
Camm Gdns KUT KT1 .... 3 H6
THDIT KT7 .... 44 B7
Camomile Av MTCM CR4 .... 48 C1 1
Campbell Av WOKS/MYFD GU22 .... 97 J3
Campbell Cl ALDT GU11 .... 134 E2
STRHM/NOR SW16 .... 31 G5 2
WHTN TW2 .... 26 A2
Campbell Crs EGRIN RH19 .... 195 L8
Campbell Pl FRIM GU16 .... 73 J6
Campbell Rd ALDT GU11 .... 112 D6
CRAWE RH10 .... 212 F5
CROY/NA CR0 .... 4 A1
CTHM CR3 .... 108 A3
WEY KT13 .... 59 K6 1
WHTN TW2 .... 26 A3
Campden Rd SAND/SEL CR2 .... 68 B4
Campen Cl WIM/MER SW19 .... 29 H3
Camp End Rd WEY KT13 .... 79 L2
Camp Farm Rd ALDT GU11 .... 113 G4
Camp Hl NFNM GU10 .... 156 F1
Camphill Ct BF/WBF KT14 .... 78 D2
Camphill Rd BF/WBF KT14 .... 78 D2
Campion Cl BLKW GU17 .... 72 C6 1
SAND/SEL CR2 .... 68 B3
Campion Dr
KWD/TDW/WH KT20 .... 104 E2 1
Campion Rd ISLW TW7 .... 17 J3
PUT/ROE SW15 .... 19 M6
Camp Rd CTHM CR3 .... 109 H3
FARN GU14 .... 112 F1
WIM/MER SW19 .... 28 E6
Camp Vw WIM/MER SW19 .... 28 E6
Camrose Av FELT TW13 .... 24 E5
Camrose Cl CROY/NA CR0 .... 51 H7
MRDN SM4 .... 47 K4
Canada Av REDH RH1 .... 148 D4
Canada Dr REDH RH1 .... 148 D4 1
Canada Rd BF/WBF KT14 .... 79 G1

217 L4
196 C8
Canterbury CI BECK BR3 .... 51 L1
Canterbury Gv WNWD SE27 ..... 31 K4
Canterbury Rd ASHV GU12 ...... 113 K6
  CRAWE RH10 .... 212 B7
  CROY/NA CR0 .... 49 J1
  FARN GU14 .... 93 C7
  FELT TW13 .... 25 H3
  GUW GU2 .... 116 C6
  MRDN SM4 .... 47 M6
The Canter CRAWE RH10 .... 213 H2
Cantley Gdns NRWD SE19 ...... 50 C1
Canvey CI CRAWW RH11 .... 211 M6
Cape Copse HORS RH12 .... 226 A2
Capel Av WLGTN SM6 .... 67 J4
Capel La CRAWW RH11 .... 211 J4
Capel Rd HORS RH12 .... 189 M8
Capern Rd WAND/EARL SW18 ... 29 M2
Capper Rd CBLY GU15 .... 72 D2
Capricorn CI CRAWW RH11 ...... 211 H5
Capri Rd CROY/NA CR0 .... 5 K2
Capsey Rd CRAWW RH11 .... 211 H4
Capstans Whf
  WOKN/KNAP GU21 .... 76 D8
Caradon CI WOKN/KNAP GU21 .. 76 B8
Caraway CI CRAWW RH11 .... 211 L7
Caraway PI GUW GU2 .... 116 D5
  WLGTN SM6 .... 66 E2
Carberry Rd NRWD SE19 .... 32 B7
Carbery La ASC SL5 .... 36 E3
Cardamom CI GUW GU2 .... 116 D4
Card HI FROW RH18 .... 217 J8
Cardigan CI WOKN/KNAP GU21 .. 76 B8
Cardigan Rd BARN SW13 .... 19 K4
  RCHPK/HAM TW10 .... 18 B8
  WIM/MER SW19 .... 29 M7
Cardinal Av KUTN/CMB KT2 ..... 27 H6
  MRDN SM4 .... 47 H6
Cardinal CI MRDN SM4 .... 47 H6
  WPK KT4 .... 64 D1
Cardinal Crs NWMAL KT3 .... 45 M2
Cardinal Dr WOT/HER KT12 ...... 43 G8
Cardinal Rd FELT TW13 .... 24 E2
Cardinal's Wk HPTN TW12 .... 25 M8
  SUN TW16 .... 24 B7
Cardingham WOKN/KNAP GU21 . 76 D7
Cardington Sq HSLWW TW4 ..... 16 A6
Cardwell Rd
Cardwells Keep GUW GU2 ...... 116 D5
Carew CI COUL/CHIP CR5 .... 107 L1
Carew Rd ASHF TW15 .... 23 M7
  MTCM CR4 .... 48 D2
  THHTH CR7 .... 49 L3
  WLGTN SM6 .... 66 F5
Carey's Wd HORL RH6 .... 171 L6
Carfax Av ALDT GU11 .... 112 C8
Cargate Av ALDT GU11 .... 112 C8
Cargate Gv ALDT GU11 .... 112 C8
Cargate HI ALDT GU11 .... 112 C8
Cargate Ter ALDT GU11 .... 112 C8
Cargill Rd WAND/EARL SW18 .... 29 M2
Cargo Forecourt Rd HORL RH6 .. 192 A2
Cargo Rd HORL RH6 .... 192 A1
Cargreen Rd SNWD SE25 .... 50 C4
Carholme Rd FSTH SE23 .... 33 J2
Carisbrooke FRIM GU16 .... 93 J1
Carisbrooke Rd MTCM CR4 ...... 49 H4
Carleton Av WLGTN SM6 .... 67 G7
Carleton CI ESH/CLAY KT10 ..... 44 A8
Carlingford Rd MRDN SM4 ...... 47 G6
Carlinwark Dr CBLY GU15 .... 73 J2
Carlisle CI KUTN/CMB KT2 .... 3 K4
Carlisle Rd HPTN TW12 .... 25 L8
  NFNM GU10 .... 178 D2
  SUT SM1 .... 65 J5
Carlisle Wy TOOT SW17 .... 30 D6
Carlos St RGODL GU7 .... 160 D5
Carlton Av EBED/NFELT TW14 ... 15 M8
  SAND/SEL CR2 .... 68 A4
Carlton CI CHSGTN KT9 .... 63 C5
  FRIM GU16 .... 73 L4
  WOKN/KNAP GU21 .... 77 J4
Carlton Crs CHEAM SM3 .... 65 H3
Carlton Gn REDH RH1 .... 126 B5
Carlton Park Av RYNPK SW20 ... 46 F2

Carlton Rd GDST RH9 .... 150 F7
...PT/ESHN SW14 .... 18 F5
...KT3 .... 46 B2
.... 126 A6
.... 68 A6
.... 24 C8
.... 77 K4
.... 42 E7
Carrington Rd
  RCHPK/HAM TW10 .... 18 D6
Carrinton La ASHV GU12 .... 113 J1
Carroll Av GU 117 L8
Carroll Crs ASC SL5 .... 36 C4
Carrow Rd WOT/HER KT12 ...... 61 C2
Carshalton Gv SUT SM1 .... 66 C4
Carshalton Park Rd CAR SM5 ... 66 C4
Carshalton PI CAR SM5 .... 66 D3
Carshalton Rd BNSTD SM7 ..... 86 C3
  CBLY GU15 .... 53 K8
  MTCM CR4 .... 48 D5
  SUT SM1 .... 65 M4
Carslake Rd PUT/ROE SW15 .... 19 M8
Carson Rd DUL SE21 .... 31 M3
Carstairs Rd CAT SE6 .... 33 M1
Carswell Rd CAT SE6 .... 33 M1
Cartbridge CI
  RPLY/SEND GU23 .... 97 L5
Carter CI WLGTN SM6 .... 67 G6
Carter Rd CRAWE RH10 .... 213 C6
  WIM/MER SW19 .... 30 A7
Carters CI WPK KT4 .... 65 C1
Carters La WOKS/MYFD GU22 ... 97 M2
Cartersmead CI HORL RH6 ..... 170 E5
Carter's Rd EW KT17 .... 84 C5
Carters Wk FNM GU9 .... 134 A1
Carthouse La WOKN/KNAP GU21 . 76 B4
Cartmel CI REDH RH1 .... 126 B7
Cartmel Gdns MRDN SM4 ...... 47 M5
Cartwright Wy BARN SW13 ..... 19 L2
Cascades CROY/NA CR0 .... 69 J8
Caseldon CI ADL/WDHM KT15 .. 58 F4
Casewick Rd WNWD SE27 ...... 31 L6
Casher Rd CRAWE RH10 .... 212 F6
Cassilis Rd TWK TW1 .... 17 L8
Cassino CI ALDT GU11 .... 112 E7
Cassiobury Av
  EBED/NFELT TW14 .... 24 C1
Cassland Rd THHTH CR7 .... 50 A4
Casslee Rd CAT SE6 .... 33 J1
Castello Av PUT/ROE SW15 ..... 19 M7
Castelnau BARN SW13 .... 19 L2
Castlands Rd CAT SE6 .... 33 J3
Castle Av EW KT17 .... 64 D7
Castle CI CBLY GU15 .... 73 J5
  REDH RH1 .... 127 M7
  REIG RH2 .... 147 L4
  WIM/MER SW19 .... 29 G4
Castlecombe Dr 29 G1
Castle Ct SYD SE26 .... 33 H5
Castlecraig Ct SHST GU47 ...... 72 A2
Castledine Rd PGE/AN SE20 .... 32 E8
Castle Dr HORL RH6 .... 170 F8
  REIG RH2 .... 147 K4
Castlefield Rd REIG RH2 .... 125 K7
Castle Gdns DORK RH4 .... 123 J8
Castlegate RCH/KEW TW9 ..... 18 C5
Castle Grove Rd CHOB/PIR GU24 . 76 B2
Castle HI FNM GU9 .... 133 L6
  GU GU1 .... 9 H8
Castle Hill Av CROY/NA CR0 ..... 69 L7
Castle Hill Rd EGH TW20 .... 20 E5
Castlemaine Av EW KT17 .... 64 E7
  SAND/SEL CR2 .... 68 C4
Castle Rd ALDT GU11 .... 112 B5
  CBLY GU15 .... 73 H5
  COUL/CHIP CR5 .... 106 B2
  EPSOM KT18 .... 83 L5
  HORS RH12 .... 228 A6
  ISLW TW7 .... 17 J4
  WEY KT13 .... 60 A2
  WOKN/KNAP GU21 .... 77 J4
Castle Sq REDH RH1 .... 127 M7
Castle St FNM GU9 .... 133 L6
  GU GU1 .... 9 G7
  KUT KT1 .... 2 E6
  REDH RH1 .... 127 L7
The Castle HORS RH12 .... 229 H2
Castleton CI BNSTD SM7 .... 85 K5
  CROY/NA CR0 .... 51 H6
Castleton Dr BNSTD SM7 .... 85 K5
Castleton Rd MTCM CR4 .... 49 G4
Castle View Rd WEY KT13 ...... 59 L3

Castle Wy EW KT17 .... 64 D8
  FELT TW13 .... 24 F5
  WIM/MER SW19 .... 29 G4
Castle Yd RCHPK/HAM TW10 ... 18 A7
Caswell CI FARN GU14 .... 92 C3
Catalina Rd HTHAIR TW6 .... 14 C1
Catena Ri LTWR GU18 .... 54 D8
Caterfield La LING RH7 .... 152 C7
Cater Gdns GUW GU2 .... 116 B6
Caterham By-pass CTHM CR3 .. 108 E5
Caterham Dr COUL/CHIP CR5 .. 107 M1
Caterways HORS RH12 .... 228 D6
Catford Broadway CAT SE6 ..... 33 L1
Catford HI CAT SE6 .... 33 J2
Catford Rd CAT SE6 .... 33 K2
Cathedral Vw GUW GU2 .... 116 C8
Catherine CI BF/WBF KT14 ..... 79 H4
Catherine Gdns HSLW TW3 .... 17 G6
Catherine Rd SURB KT6 .... 45 G5
Catherine Wheel Rd BTFD TW8 . 18 A2
Cathill La RDKG RH5 .... 187 L6
Catlin Crs SHPTN TW17 .... 42 A5
Catlin Gdns GDST RH9 .... 128 E5
Catling CI FSTH SE23 .... 32 F4
Cator CI CROY/NA CR0 .... 90 B1
Cator Crs CROY/NA CR0 .... 90 B1
Cator La BECK BR3 .... 51 J2
Cator Rd CAR SM5 .... 66 C4
  SYD SE26 .... 33 G7
Catteshall Hatch RGODL GU7 .. 160 D3
Catteshall La RGODL GU7 ...... 160 D4
Catteshall Rd RGODL GU7 ...... 160 D3
Causeway EBED/NFELT TW14 .. 15 L6
The Causeway BELMT SM2 .... 65 M7
  CAR SM5 .... 66 D2
  CHSGTN KT9 .... 63 H3
  ESH/CLAY KT10 .... 62 C6
  HORS RH12 .... 228 F8
  STA TW18 .... 21 M5
  TEDD TW11 .... 26 C7
  WIM/MER SW19 .... 28 F6
Cavalier Wy EGRIN RH19 ...... 216 C2
Cavalry Ct ALDT GU11 .... 112 B7
Cavan's Rd ALDT GU11 .... 112 F3
Cavell Wy CRAWE RH10 .... 212 F4
Cavendish Av NWMAL KT3 ..... 46 E5
Cavendish CI HORS RH12 ...... 229 C2
  SUN TW16 .... 24 C7
Cavendish Ct BLKW GU17 ...... 72 A6
Cavendish Dr ESH/CLAY KT10 .. 62 B4
Cavendish Gdns REDH RH1 ... 126 D7
Cavendish Meads ASC SL5 ..... 37 G6
Cavendish Rd ALDT GU11 ...... 112 D8
  BAL SW12 .... 30 F1
  BELMT SM2 .... 65 M6
  CHSWK W4 .... 18 F3
  CROY/NA CR0 .... 4 A3
  NWMAL KT3 .... 46 C5
  REDH RH1 .... 126 D8
  SUN TW16 .... 24 C7
  WEY KT13 .... 59 L7
  WIM/MER SW19 .... 30 B8
  WOKS/MYFD GU22 .... 6 A9
Cavendish Wy WWKM BR4 ..... 51 L8
Cavenham CI WOKS/MYFD GU22 . 6 C9
Caverleigh Wy WPK KT4 .... 46 D8
Cave Rd RCHPK/HAM TW10 .... 26 F5
Caversham Av CHEAM SM3 .... 65 H1
Caversham Rd KUT KT1 .... 3 G6
Cawnpore St NRWD SE19 ...... 32 B6
Cawsey Wy WOKN/KNAP GU21 .. 6 D6
Caxton Av ADL/WDHM KT15 .... 58 D5
Caxton CI CRAWE RH10 .... 212 A6
Caxton La OXTED RH8 .... 131 H5
Caxton Ri REDH RH1 .... 126 D7
Caxton Rd WIM/MER SW19 ..... 29 M6
Cearn Wy COUL/CHIP CR5 ..... 87 J5
Cecil CI ASHF TW15 .... 23 M7
  CHSGTN KT9 .... 63 G3
Cecil PI MTCM CR4 .... 48 C5
Cecil Rd ASHF TW15 .... 23 M8
  CROY/NA CR0 .... 49 H6
  HSLW TW3 .... 16 F5
  SUT SM1 .... 65 J5
  WIM/MER SW19 .... 29 L8
Cedar Av BLKW GU17 .... 72 A4
  COB KT11 .... 80 E4
  WHTN TW2 .... 16 E8
Cedar CI ASHV GU12 .... 135 H1
  BAGS GU19 .... 54 B6
  CAR SM5 .... 66 C5
  CRAWW RH11 .... 191 M8
  DORK RH4 .... 144 C2
  DUL SE21 .... 31 M2
  ESH/CLAY KT10 .... 61 J6
  EW KT17 .... 84 C4
  HAYES BR2 .... 71 H2
  HORS RH12 .... 228 F7
  KUTN/CMB KT2 .... 28 A5
  REIG RH2 .... 147 M2
  STA TW18 .... 40 F3
  WARL CR6 .... 89 H8
Cedar Crs HAYES BR2 .... 71 H2
Cedarcroft Rd CHSGTN KT9 .... 63 J3
Cedar Dr ASC SL5 .... 37 K7
  EDEN TN8 .... 153 L7
  LHD/OX KT22 .... 102 B5
Cedar Gdns BELMT SM2 .... 65 M5
  WOKN/KNAP GU21 .... 76 E8
Cedar Gv CHOB/PIR GU24 ...... 75 K5
  WEY KT13 .... 59 M3
Cedar Hts RCHPK/HAM TW10 .. 27 H2
Cedar HI EPSOM KT18 .... 83 M5
Cedar Rd BELMT SM2 .... 65 M5
  COB KT11 .... 80 E4
  CROY/NA CR0 .... 5 G5
  E/WMO/HCT KT8 .... 44 B4
  EBED/NFELT TW14 .... 24 A2
  FARN GU14 .... 92 F6

HEST TW5 .... 15 M4
  TEDD TW11 .... 26 D6
  WEY KT13 .... 59 K2
  WOKS/MYFD GU22 .... 96 E2
Cedars BNSTD SM7 .... 86 C4
Cedars Av MTCM CR4 .... 48 D4
Cedars Rd BARN SW13 .... 19 K4
  BECK BR3 .... 51 H2
  CROY/NA CR0 .... 67 H2
  E/WMO/HCT KT8 .... 2 A4
  MRDN SM4 .... 47 K4
The Cedars BF/WBF KT14 ...... 79 J7
  GU GU1 .... 117 K5
  LHD/OX KT22 .... 103 G3
  MFD/CHID GU8 .... 181 H1
  REIG RH2 .... 126 A8
  TEDD TW11 .... 26 C7
Cedar Ter RCH/KEW TW9 ...... 18 B6
Cedar Tree Gv WNWD SE27 ... 31 L6
Cedarville Gdns
  STRHM/NOR SW16 .... 31 J7
Cedar Wk ESH/CLAY KT10 ..... 62 C5
  KWD/TDW/WH KT20 ...... 105 J3
  PUR/KEN CR8 .... 87 M6
Cedar Wy GU GU1 .... 116 F5
  SUN TW16 .... 24 B8
Cedarways FNM GU9 .... 10 E6
Celandine CI CRAWW RH11 .... 211 K7
Celandine Rd WOT/HER KT12 .. 61 H3
Celia Crs ASHF TW15 .... 23 G7
Celtic Rd BF/WBF KT14 .... 79 H4
Cemetery La SHPTN TW17 ..... 41 L7
Cemetery Pales CHOB/PIR GU24 . 95 K4
Central Av E/WMO/HCT KT8 .... 43 J5
  HSLW TW3 .... 16 F6
  WLGTN SM6 .... 67 H4
Central HI NRWD SE19 .... 31 M6
Central Pde CROY/NA CR0 ..... 69 M8
Central Rd MRDN SM4 .... 47 L5
  WPK KT4 .... 64 D1
Central Sq E/WMO/HCT KT8 ... 43 J4
  EBED/NFELT TW14 .... 15 L7
  OXTED RH8 .... 130 A1
Central Wy CAR SM5 .... 66 B6
  EBED/NFELT TW14 .... 15 L7
  OXTED RH8 .... 130 A1
Centre Terrace Rd FARN GU14 . 112 D1
The Centre FELT TW13 .... 24 D3
Centurion CI SHST GU47 .... 72 A1
Century Rd EGH TW20 .... 21 M6
Cerne Rd MRDN SM4 .... 47 M6
Cerotus PI CHERT KT16 .... 40 C7
Chadacre Rd EW KT17 .... 64 E4
Chadhurst CI RDKG RH5 ...... 145 G5
Chadwick Av WIM/MER SW19 .. 29 K7
Chadwick CI CRAWW RH11 .... 211 L8
  TEDD TW11 .... 26 D7
Chadworth Wy
  ESH/CLAY KT10 .... 62 A4
Chaffers Md ASHTD KT21 ...... 83 J6
Chaffinch Av CROY/NA CR0 .... 51 G6
Chaffinch CI CRAWW RH11 .... 212 A1
  CROY/NA CR0 .... 51 G6
  HORS RH12 .... 229 C2
  SHST GU47 .... 72 B1
  SURB KT6 .... 63 K2
Chaffinch Rd BECK BR3 .... 51 H1
Chaffinch Wy HORL RH6 ...... 170 B5
Chailey CI CRAWW RH11 ...... 211 K6
  HEST TW5 .... 16 A3
Chailey PI WOT/HER KT12 ..... 61 H3
Chalcot CI BELMT SM2 .... 65 K6
Chalcot Ms STRHM/NOR SW16 . 31 H4
Chalcott Gdns SURB KT6 .... 44 F8
Chaldon CI REDH RH1 .... 148 B2
Chaldon Common Rd
  CTHM CR3 .... 107 M6
Chaldon Rd CRAWW RH11 .... 211 M8
  CTHM CR3 .... 108 A5
Chaldon Wy COUL/CHIP CR5 .. 87 H7
Chalfont Dr FARN GU14 .... 92 F7
Chalfont Rd SNWD SE25 .... 50 C3
Chalford CI E/WMO/HCT KT8 ... 43 K4
Chalford Rd DUL SE21 .... 32 A5
Chalgrove Av MRDN SM4 ...... 47 K5
Chalgrove Rd BELMT SM2 ...... 66 A6
Chalice CI WLGTN SM6 .... 67 G5
Chalkenden CI PGE/AN SE20 ... 32 E8
Chalk La ASHTD KT21 .... 103 K1
  EHSLY KT24 .... 120 C5
  EPSOM KT18 .... 84 B6
  MFD/CHID GU8 .... 159 G1
Chalkley CI MTCM CR4 .... 48 C2
Chalk Paddock EPSOM KT18 ... 84 A5
Chalkpit La DORK RH4 .... 122 D8
  OXTED RH8 .... 129 M1
Chalkpit Ter DORK RH4 .... 122 D8
Chalkpit Wd OXTED RH8 .... 130 A1
Chalk Rd BIL RH14 .... 223 M6
  RGODL GU7 .... 160 B4
Chalky La CHSGTN KT9 .... 63 G7
Challenge Ct LHD/OX KT22 ..... 102 E1
Challenge Rd ASHF TW15 ...... 23 M4
Challice Wy BRXS/STRHM SW2 . 31 J2
Challin St PGE/AN SE20 .... 50 F1
Challis PI BNFD RG42 .... 34 B1
Challock CI BH/WHM TN16 ..... 90 F6
Challoners CI E/WMO/HCT KT8 . 44 A4
Chalmers Ct HORL RH6 .... 191 H5
Chalmers Rd ASHF TW15 ...... 23 L5
  BNSTD SM7 .... 85 M5
Chalmers Rd East ASHF TW15 . 23 L5
Chalmers Wy EBED/NFELT TW14 . 15 L7
Chamberlain Crs WWKM BR4 .. 51 L8
Chamberlain Wy SURB KT6 .... 45 H7
Chamber La NFNM GU10 ...... 154 F1
Chambers Rd ASHV GU12 ..... 113 L3
Champion Crs SYD SE26 .... 33 H5
Champion Rd SYD SE26 .... 33 H5
Champness CI WNWD SE27 ... 32 A5
Champneys CI BELMT SM2 .... 65 J6
Chancellor Gdns SAND/SEL CR2 . 67 L7
Chancellor Gv DUL SE21 .... 31 M3
Chancery La BECK BR3 .... 51 L2
Chanctonbury Cha REDH RH1 . 148 E1
Chanctonbury Dr ASC SL5 ..... 37 H7

Chanctonbury Gdns
  BELMT SM2 .... 65 L6
Chanctonbury Wy
  CRAWW RH11 .... 211 M5
Chandler CI CRAWW RH11 .... 212 A5
  HPTN TW12 .... 43 J1
Chandlers CI EBED/NFELT TW14 . 24 C1
Chandlers Rd ASHV GU12 ..... 113 L5
Chandos Rd STA TW18 .... 22 A6
Channel CI HEST TW5 .... 16 D3
Channings WOKN/KNAP GU21 .. 6 D1
Chantlers CI EGRIN RH19 ...... 195 M7
Chanton Dr BELMT SM2 .... 64 F8
Chantrey CI ASHTD KT21 ...... 102 F1
Chantrey Rd CRAWE RH10 .... 212 B6
Chantry CI FNM GU9 .... 133 K7
  HORL RH6 .... 170 C5
Chantry Hurst EPSOM KT18 .... 84 A5
Chantry La SHGR GU5 .... 141 J8
Chantry Rd BAGS GU19 .... 54 A7
  CHERT KT16 .... 40 E8
  CHSGTN KT9 .... 63 J4
  RGUE GU4 .... 139 L6
The Chantrys FNM GU9 .... 10 B1
Chantry View Rd GU GU1 ...... 139 G3
  RGUE GU4 .... 139 H3
Chantry Wy MTCM CR4 .... 48 A3
Chapel Av ADL/WDHM KT15 ... 58 E3
  CHOB/PIR GU24 .... 95 L3
Chapel CI MFD/CHID GU8 ...... 159 J7
Chapel Ct DORK RH4 .... 144 D2
Chapel Gn PUR/KEN CR8 ...... 87 K3
Chapel Gv ADL/WDHM KT15 .. 58 E3
  KWD/TDW/WH KT20 ...... 104 F1
Chapel HI EHSLY KT24 .... 121 G1
  MFD/CHID GU8 .... 203 J6
Chapelhouse CI GUW GU2 .... 116 B8
Chapel La BAGS GU19 .... 54 A7
  CHOB/PIR GU24 .... 95 K5
  CRAWE RH10 .... 194 C5
  DORK RH4 .... 143 M3
  EGRIN RH19 .... 217 G3
  FARN GU14 .... 92 C1
  FROW RH18 .... 217 J8
  GT/LBKH KT23 .... 121 M2
  MFD/CHID GU8 .... 159 J7
Chapel Park Rd
  ADL/WDHM KT15 .... 58 E3
Chapel Rd CBLY GU15 .... 72 E4
  HORL RH6 .... 171 L6
  HORL RH6 .... 191 H2
  HSLW TW3 .... 16 E5
  KWD/TDW/WH KT20 ...... 104 F5
  NFNM GU10 .... 155 H6
  OXTED RH8 .... 130 F4
  REDH RH1 .... 126 E8
  TWK TW1 .... 26 E1
  WARL CR6 .... 89 G8
  WNWD SE27 .... 31 L5
Chapel Sq CBLY GU15 .... 72 C3
  VW GU25 .... 39 H3
Chapel St FARN GU14 .... 93 G3
  GU GU1 .... 9 G7
  WOKN/KNAP GU21 .... 6 E6
Chapel Vw SAND/SEL CR2 ..... 68 C5
Chapel Wy KWD/TDW/WH KT20 . 104 F1
Chaplain's HI CWTH RG45 ...... 52 A5
Chaplin Crs SUN TW16 .... 24 B7
Chapman Rd CRAWE RH10 .... 212 E7
  CROY/NA CR0 .... 49 K8
Chapman's La EGRIN RH19 .... 196 A8
Chapter Wy HPTN TW12 .... 25 K5
Chara PI CHSWK W4 .... 19 G1
Chargate CI WOT/HER KT12 ... 60 C5
Charlbury CI BRAK RG12 .... 35 J4
Charlecote CI FARN GU14 ...... 93 G4
Charlecote Gv SYD SE26 .... 32 E4
Charlesfield Rd HORL RH6 ..... 170 C5
Charles HI NFNM GU10 .... 157 H5
Charles Rd STA TW18 .... 23 G7
  WIM/MER SW19 .... 47 K1
Charles St BARN SW13 .... 19 H5
  CBLY GU15 .... 72 F4
  CHERT KT16 .... 40 C8
  CROY/NA CR0 .... 4 C7
  HSLW TW3 .... 16 C4
Charleston CI FELT TW13 .... 24 D4
Charleston Ct CRAWE RH10 ... 212 E6
Charleville Circ SYD SE26 ...... 32 E6
Charlmont Rd TOOT SW17 ..... 30 B7
Charlock CI CRAWW RH11 ..... 211 K7
Charlock Wy GU GU1 .... 117 L6
Charlotte CI FNM GU9 .... 134 A1
Charlotte Gv HORL RH6 .... 171 K5
Charlotte Rd BARN SW13 ...... 19 J3
  WLGTN SM6 .... 66 F5
Charlton Av WOT/HER KT12 .... 60 E3
Charlton Ct SHST GU47 .... 52 A8
Charlton Dr BH/WHM TN16 .... 91 G7
Charlton Gdns COUL/CHIP CR5 . 86 F8
Charlton Kings WEY KT13 ...... 60 B2
Charlton La SHPTN TW17 ...... 42 B4
Charlton Rd SHPTN TW17 ..... 41 M2
Charlwood CI GT/LBKH KT23 ... 101 L2
Charlwood Dr LHD/OX KT22 .... 82 A5
Charlwood La RDKG RH5 ...... 190 D4
Charlwood Rd CRAWW RH11 .. 191 J7
  HORL RH6 .... 191 M1
Charlwoods Business Centre
  EGRIN RH19 .... 196 A7
Charlwoods PI EGRIN RH19 .... 196 B6
Charlwoods Rd EGRIN RH19 ... 196 A7
Charman Rd REDH RH1 .... 126 B8
Charm CI HORL RH6 .... 170 B5
Charminster Av WIM/MER SW19 . 47 G2
Charminster Rd WPK KT4 ...... 47 G8
Charnwood ASC SL5 .... 37 J6
Charnwood Av WIM/MER SW19 . 47 K2
Charnwood CI NWMAL KT3 .... 46 B4
Charnwood Rd SNWD SE25 ... 50 A4
Charrington Rd CROY/NA CR0 ... 4 C3
Charrington Wy HORS RH12 ... 227 M6
Charsley Rd CAT SE6 .... 33 L3
Charta Rd EGH TW20 .... 21 M6
Chart CI CROY/NA CR0 .... 50 F6
  MTCM CR4 .... 48 C4
  RDKG RH5 .... 144 F4

Chart Downs RDKG RH5 .... 144 F4
Charter Crs HSLWW TW4 .... 16 B6
Charterhouse Cl BRAK RG12 .... 35 H5
Charterhouse Rd RGODL GU7 .... 160 A3
Charter Rd KUT KT1 .... 3 L8
Charters Cl NRWD SE19 .... 32 B6
Charters La ASC SL5 .... 37 G5
Charter Sq KUT KT1 .... 3 M7
Charters Rd ASC SL5 .... 37 J7
Charters Wy ASC SL5 .... 37 J7
Chartfield Av PUT/ROE SW15 .... 19 L7
Chartfield Rd REIG RH2 .... 147 M1
Chart Gdns RDKG RH5 .... 144 F5
Chartham Gv WNWD SE27 .... 31 L4 2
Chartham Rd SNWD SE25 .... 50 E3
Chart House Rd ASHV GU12 .... 113 K2
Chart La DORK RH4 .... 144 E2
REIG RH2 .... 125 L8
Chart La South RDKG RH5 .... 145 G4
Charts Cl CRAN GU6 .... 185 H7 2
Chartway REIG RH2 .... 125 L8
Chartwell FNM GU9 .... 10 B7
FRIM GU16 .... 93 H4
Chartwell Gdns ALDT GU11 .... 112 F2
Chartwell Pl CHEAM SM3 .... 65 H3
EPSOM KT18 .... 84 B4
Chartwell Wy PGE/AN SE20 .... 50 E1 4
Chase Ct RYNPK SW20 .... 47 H2
Chase End HOR/WEW KT19 .... 84 A2 1
Chasefield Cl GU GU1 .... 117 K5
Chasefield Rd TOOT SW17 .... 30 C5
Chase Gdns WHTN TW2 .... 17 G8
Chase La HASM GU27 .... 220 B5
Chaseley Dr SAND/SEL CR2 .... 68 A8 1
Chasemore Cl MTCM CR4 .... 48 C7 3
Chasemore Gdns
CROY/NA CR0 .... 67 K4 1
Chase Rd HOR/WEW KT19 .... 84 A2
Chaseside Av RYNPK SW20 .... 47 H1
Chaseside Gdns CHERT KT16 .... 40 E7
The Chase ASHTD KT21 .... 82 F8
COUL/CHIP CR5 .... 86 F4
CRAWE RH10 .... 212 D4
EHSLY KT24 .... 100 C8
FARN GU14 .... 93 G3
GUW GU2 .... 8 C6
KWD/TDW/WH KT20 .... 105 M3
LHD/OX KT22 .... 81 M5
REIG RH2 .... 126 A8 2
STRHM/NOR SW16 .... 31 J8
SUN TW16 .... 42 E1 1
WLGTN SM6 .... 67 H4
Chatelet Cl HORL RH6 .... 170 E5
Chatfield Cl FARN GU14 .... 92 F7
Chatfield Ct CTHM CR3 .... 108 A4 1
Chatfield Dr RGUE GU4 .... 117 M6
Chatfield Rd CROY/NA CR0 .... 4 B3
Chatfields CRAWW RH11 .... 211 L5
Chatham Cl CHEAM SM3 .... 47 J7
Chatham Rd KUTN/CMB KT2 .... 3 J6
Chatsfield EW KT17 .... 64 D8 1
Chatsworth Av HASM GU27 .... 219 M1
RYNPK SW20 .... 47 H1
Chatsworth Cl WWKM BR4 .... 70 C1 1
Chatsworth Crs HSLW TW3 .... 17 G6
Chatsworth Gdns NWMAL KT3 .. 46 C5 1
Chatsworth Gv FNM GU9 .... 133 L3 2
Chatsworth Hts CBLY GU15 .... 73 K2
Chatsworth Pl LHD/OX KT22 .... 82 A2
MTCM CR4 .... 48 C3 1
TEDD TW11 .... 26 D5 1
Chatsworth Rd CHEAM SM3 .... 65 G4
CHSWK W4 .... 18 F1
CROY/NA CR0 .... 4 F9
FARN GU14 .... 93 H6
Chatsworth Wy WNWD SE27 .... 31 M3
Chattern Hl ASHF TW15 .... 23 L5 1
Chattern Rd ASHF TW15 .... 23 M5
Chatton Rw CHOB/PIR GU24 .... 75 K7
Chaucer Av EGRIN RH19 .... 215 M1
HSLWW TW4 .... 15 L4
RCH/KEW TW9 .... 18 D4
WEY KT13 .... 59 K6
Chaucer Cl BNSTD SM7 .... 85 H4
Chaucer Gdns SUT SM1 .... 65 K3
Chaucer Gn CROY/NA CR0 .... 50 E7
Chaucer Gv CBLY GU15 .... 73 G4
Chaucer Rd ASHF TW15 .... 23 H5
CRAWE RH10 .... 212 E1
FARN GU14 .... 92 C3
SUT SM1 .... 65 K3 2
Chaucer Wy ADL/WDHM KT15 .... 58 D5
Chaundlers Cft NFNM GU10 .... 132 C4
Chaworth Cl CHERT KT16 .... 57 M5
Chaworth Rd CHERT KT16 .... 57 M5
Cheam Cl BRAK RG12 .... 35 G5
KWD/TDW/WH KT20 .... 104 E3
Cheam Common Rd WPK KT4 .. 64 E1 1
Cheam Park Wy CHEAM SM3 .... 65 G5
Cheam Rd BELMT SM2 .... 65 G7
EW KT17 .... 64 D8
SUT SM1 .... 65 J5
Cheapside WOKN/KNAP GU21 .... 6 A1
Cheapside Rd ASC SL5 .... 36 F3
Cheeseman Cl HPTN TW12 .... 25 H7 2
Cheetah Rd FARN GU14 .... 92 E7
Chellows La LING RH7 .... 152 C7
Chelmsford Cl BELMT SM2 .... 65 K7 1
Chelsea Cl HPTN TW12 .... 25 M7
WPK KT4 .... 46 D7
Chelsea Gdns CHEAM SM3 .... 65 H3
Chelsfield Gdns SYD SE26 .... 32 F4
Chelsham Common Rd
WARL CR6 .... 89 K6
Chelsham Court Rd WARL CR6 .... 90 A8
Chelsham Rd SAND/SEL CR2 .... 68 A6
WARL CR6 .... 89 J7
Cheltenham Av TWK TW1 .... 26 D1 1
Cheltenham Cl NWMAL KT3 .... 45 M3
Chelwood Cl CRAWE RH10 .... 212 C5
EW KT17 .... 84 C2
Chelwood Gdns RCH/KEW TW9 .... 18 D4
Cheniston Cl BF/WBF KT14 .... 78 D3 1
Chennells Wy HORS RH12 .... 229 G4
Chepstow Cl CRAWE RH10 .... 213 H3
Chepstow Ri CROY/NA CR0 .... 5 H7
Chepstow Rd CROY/NA CR0 .... 5 H7
Chequer Gra FROW RH18 .... 217 H8
Chequer Rd EGRIN RH19 .... 196 C8 1
Chequers Cl HORL RH6 .... 170 D5 1
KWD/TDW/WH KT20 .... 104 D7
Chequers Dr HORL RH6 .... 170 D5
Chequers La
KWD/TDW/WH KT20 .... 104 D7
Chequers Pl DORK RH4 .... 144 E2
Chequer Tree Cl
WOKN/KNAP GU21 .... 76 B6
Cherbury Cl BRAK RG12 .... 35 H3
Cherimoya Gdns
E/WMO/HCT KT8 .... 43 L3 1
Cherington Wy ASC SL5 .... 36 B2 1
Cheriton Ct WOT/HER KT12 .... 42 F8 1
Cheriton Sq TOOT SW17 .... 30 D3 1
Cheriton Wy BLKW GU17 .... 72 A4
Cherkley Hl RDKG RH5 .... 102 F8
Cherrimans Orch HASM GU27 .. 219 J3 1
Cherry Cl CAR SM5 .... 66 C1 1
EW KT17 .... 85 G4
MRDN SM4 .... 47 H4 1
Cherrycot Ri ORP BR6 .... 71 M3
Cherry Ct SWTR RH13 .... 229 G8
Cherry Crs BTFD TW8 .... 17 L2
Cherrydale Rd CBLY GU15 .... 74 A4
Cherry Green Cl REDH RH1 .... 148 E2 2
Cherry Hill Gdns CROY/NA CR0 .... 67 J3
Cherry La CRAWW RH11 .... 191 M8
Cherry Orch ASHTD KT21 .... 83 L8
STA TW18 .... 22 D6
Cherry Orchard Gdns
E/WMO/HCT KT8 .... 43 J3
Cherry Orchard Rd CROY/NA CR0 .. 4 F4
E/WMO/HCT KT8 .... 43 K3
HAYES BR2 .... 71 H1
Cherry St WOKN/KNAP GU21 .... 6 C7
Cherry Tree Av GUW GU2 .... 116 C8
HASM GU27 .... 219 J2
STA TW18 .... 22 E7
Cherry Tree Cl CRAWE RH10 .... 213 G1 1
SHST GU47 .... 52 A8 1
Cherry Tree Ct COUL/CHIP CR5 .... 87 J8
Cherry Tree Dr BRAK RG12 .... 35 G3 1
STRHM/NOR SW16 .... 31 H4 3
Cherry Tree Gn SAND/SEL CR2 .... 88 E4
Cherry Tree La RGODL GU7 .... 160 A1
Cherry Tree Rd MFD/CHID GU8 .. 159 H8
NFNM GU10 .... 155 H6
Cherry Tree Wk BECK BR3 .... 51 J4
WWKM BR4 .... 70 C3
Cherry Wy DTCH/LGLY SL3 .... 12 F5
HOR/WEW KT19 .... 64 A5
SHPTN TW17 .... 42 A4
Cherrywood Av EGH TW20 .... 20 E8
Cherrywood Cl KUTN/CMB KT2 .... 3 J3
Cherrywood La MRDN SM4 .... 47 H4
Cherrywood Rd FARN GU14 .... 92 D2
Chertsey Bridge Rd CHERT KT16 .. 41 G7
Chertsey Cl PUR/KEN CR8 .... 87 L5
Chertsey Crs CROY/NA CR0 .... 69 M8
Chertsey Dr CHEAM SM3 .... 65 H1
Chertsey La STA TW18 .... 22 B6
Chertsey Rd ADL/WDHM KT15 .... 58 F2
ASHF TW15 .... 24 A8
BF/WBF KT14 .... 79 G1
BFOR GU20 .... 55 H5
CHOB/PIR GU24 .... 56 D8
FELT TW13 .... 24 B5
SHPTN TW17 .... 41 H7
SUN TW16 .... 24 B7
TWK TW1 .... 17 K8
WHTN TW2 .... 25 M2
WOKN/KNAP GU21 .... 6 F4
Chertsey St GU GU1 .... 9 H5
TOOT SW17 .... 30 D6
Chertsey Wk CHERT KT16 .... 40 D7 3
Chervil Cl FELT TW13 .... 24 D4 2
Cherwell Cl DTCH/LGLY SL3 .... 12 E1 1
Cherwell Ct HOR/WEW KT19 .... 63 M3 2
Cherwell Wk CRAWW RH11 .... 211 J4
Cheselden Rd GU GU1 .... 9 J6
Cheseman St SYD SE26 .... 32 E4
Chesfield Rd KUTN/CMB KT2 .... 2 F2
Chesham Cl BELMT SM2 .... 65 H8
Chesham Crs PGE/AN SE20 .... 50 F1
Chesham Ms GU GU1 .... 9 K6
Chesham Rd GU GU1 .... 9 L6
KUTN/CMB KT2 .... 3 J5
PGE/AN SE20 .... 50 F2
Cheshire Cl CHERT KT16 .... 58 A5 2
MTCM CR4 .... 49 H3
Cheshire Gdns CHSGTN KT9 .... 63 G5
Chesney Crs CROY/NA CR0 .... 69 M6
Chessholme Rd ASHF TW15 .... 23 M7
Chessington Cl HOR/WEW KT19 .... 63 M5
Chessington Hall Gdns
CHSGTN KT9 .... 63 G6
Chessington Hill Pk CHSGTN KT9 .. 63 K5
Chessington Rd CHSGTN KT9 .... 63 K5
HOR/WEW KT19 .... 63 L5
Chessington Wy WWKM BR4 .... 69 L1
Chester Av RCHPK/HAM TW10 .... 18 C8
WHTN TW2 .... 25 J2
Chesterblade La BRAK RG12 .... 35 G7
Chester Cl ASHF TW15 .... 24 A6
ASHV GU12 .... 113 L7
DORK RH4 .... 122 F8
SUT SM1 .... 65 K1
Chesterfield Cl CRAWE RH10 .... 194 F5
Chesterfield Dr ESH/CLAY KT10 .... 62 D1
Chesterfield Rd ASHF TW15 .... 23 G6
CHSWK W4 .... 18 F1
HOR/WEW KT19 .... 64 A6
Chester Gdns MRDN SM4 .... 47 M5 3
Chester Rd ASHV GU12 .... 113 L6
EHSLY KT24 .... 120 E2
HSLWW TW4 .... 15 L5
HTHAIR TW6 .... 14 D5 1
WIM/MER SW19 .... 28 F7
Chesters HORL RH6 .... 170 B4
Chesters Rd CBLY GU15 .... 73 L4
The Chesters NWMAL KT3 .... 46 B1
Chesterton Cl EGRIN RH19 .... 216 C2
Chesterton Dr REDH RH1 .... 127 H2
STWL/WRAY TW19 .... 23 J2 1
Chesterton Ter KUT KT1 .... 3 J7
Chester Wy NFNM GU10 .... 135 J3
Chestnut Av ASHV GU12 .... 135 H2
BH/WHM TN16 .... 111 G4
CBLY GU15 .... 73 K3
E/WMO/HCT KT8 .... 44 C3
ESH/CLAY KT10 .... 44 A7
FNM GU9 .... 10 C4
GUW GU2 .... 138 F4
HASM GU27 .... 219 M2
HOR/WEW KT19 .... 64 B3
HPTN TW12 .... 25 K8
MORT/ESHN SW14 .... 19 G5 2
TEDD TW11 .... 26 C8
VW GU25 .... 38 C4
WEY KT13 .... 59 M6
WOT/HER KT12 .... 60 B7
WWKM BR4 .... 70 B4
Chestnut Cl ADL/WDHM KT15 .... 59 G4 1
ASHF TW15 .... 23 L5
BLKW GU17 .... 72 B4 1
CAR SM5 .... 48 C8 1
CAT SE6 .... 33 M5
EDEN TN8 .... 153 L7 1
EGH TW20 .... 20 F7 1
EGRIN RH19 .... 196 D8
GSHT GU26 .... 198 E6
KWD/TDW/WH KT20 .... 105 K5
LIPH GU30 .... 218 A6
REDH RH1 .... 148 E2 3
RPLY/SEND GU23 .... 98 D7 1
STRHM/NOR SW16 .... 31 K5
SUN TW16 .... 24 C7 4
WDR/YW UB7 .... 14 E2 1
Chestnut Copse OXTED RH8 .... 130 E7
Chestnut Ct ASHV GU12 .... 113 G7
Chestnut Dr EGH TW20 .... 21 G7
Chestnut Gdns HORS RH12 .... 228 F4
Chestnut Gv BAL SW12 .... 30 D1
ISLW TW7 .... 17 K6
MTCM CR4 .... 49 G5
NWMAL KT3 .... 46 A3
SAND/SEL CR2 .... 68 E6
STA TW18 .... 22 F7
WOKS/MYFD GU22 .... 97 H2
Chestnut La CHOB/PIR GU24 .... 55 M5
WEY KT13 .... 59 L4
Chestnut Mnr WLGTN SM6 .... 66 E3
Chestnut Manor Cl STA TW18 .... 22 E6
Chestnut Md REDH RH1 .... 126 B7 1
Chestnut Pl ASHTD KT21 .... 103 H1
Chestnut Rd ASHF TW15 .... 23 K5
FARN GU14 .... 92 D4
GU GU1 .... 9 G3
HORL RH6 .... 170 D4
KUTN/CMB KT2 .... 2 E3
RYNPK SW20 .... 47 G2
WHTN TW2 .... 26 B3
WNWD SE27 .... 31 L4
The Chestnuts WOT/HER KT12 .... 60 D1
Chestnut Wk CRAWW RH11 .... 191 M8
EGRIN RH19 .... 195 M2
SHPTN TW17 .... 42 B5
Chestnut Wy FELT TW13 .... 24 E4 1
RGODL GU7 .... 160 C7
SHGR GU5 .... 161 K5
Cheston Av CROY/NA CR0 .... 51 H8
Chesworth Crs SWTR RH13 .... 228 F8
Chesworth Gdns SWTR RH13 .... 228 F8
Chesworth La SWTR RH13 .... 228 F8
Chetwode Dr
KWD/TDW/WH KT20 .... 85 G8
Chetwode Pl ALDT GU11 .... 134 F2
Chetwode Rd
KWD/TDW/WH KT20 .... 104 F1
TOOT SW17 .... 30 C4
Chetwode Ter ALDT GU11 .... 112 B8
Chetwood Rd HORS RH12 .... 211 G7
Chevening Cl CRAWW RH11 .... 211 M8 1
Chevening Rd NRWD SE19 .... 32 A8
Cheviot Cl BELMT SM2 .... 66 A7
BNSTD SM7 .... 85 L5
CBLY GU15 .... 73 M5
FARN GU14 .... 92 B2
HYS/HAR UB3 .... 15 G2
Cheviot Rd WNWD SE27 .... 31 L6
Chewter La BFOR GU20 .... 54 E3
Cheyham Gdns BELMT SM2 .... 65 G8
Cheyham Wy BELMT SM2 .... 65 H8
Cheylesmore Dr FRIM GU16 .... 74 A6
Cheyne Av WHTN TW2 .... 25 J2
Cheyne Cl HAYES BR2 .... 71 H2
Cheyne Ct BNSTD SM7 .... 85 L5
Cheyne Hl BRYLDS KT5 .... 45 J4
Cheyne Rd ASHF TW15 .... 24 A7 2
Cheyne Wk CROY/NA CR0 .... 5 M6
HORL RH6 .... 170 C8
Cheyne Wy FARN GU14 .... 92 C2
Chichele Gdns CROY/NA CR0 .... 5 H9 1
Chichele Rd OXTED RH8 .... 130 B2
Chichester Cl CRAWE RH10 .... 212 B7 1
DORK RH4 .... 122 E8
HPTN TW12 .... 25 J7 2
MFD/CHID GU8 .... 181 H4
Chichester Ct EW KT17 .... 64 C7 1
Chichester Dr PUR/KEN CR8 .... 87 J2
Chichester Rd ASHV GU12 .... 113 K6
CROY/NA CR0 .... 5 G8
DORK RH4 .... 122 E7
Chichester Ter HORS RH12 .... 229 G7
Chichester Wy
EBED/NFELT TW14 .... 24 F1 1
Chiddingfold Rd
MFD/CHID GU8 .... 202 F6
Chiddingly Cl CRAWE RH10 .... 212 D4
Chiddingstone Cl BELMT SM2 .... 65 K8 1
Chilberton Dr REDH RH1 .... 126 F4
Chilbrook Rd COB KT11 .... 80 D8
Chilcroft La HASM GU27 .... 219 L8
Chilcroft Rd HASM GU27 .... 219 J2
Chilcrofts Rd HASM GU27 .... 219 K8
Childebert Rd TOOT SW17 .... 30 E3
Childs Hall Dr GT/LBKH KT23 .... 101 J7 2
Childs Hall Rd GT/LBKH KT23 .... 101 J7
Childs La NRWD SE19 .... 32 B7 1
Chilham Cl FRIM GU16 .... 93 J1
Chillerton Rd TOOT SW17 .... 30 D6
Chillingham Wy CBLY GU15 .... 72 F5
Chillingworth Gdns TWK TW1 .... 26 C3 1
Chilmans Dr GT/LBKH KT23 .... 101 L7
Chilmark Gdns NWMAL KT3 .... 46 C6
REDH RH1 .... 127 H3
Chilmark Rd STRHM/NOR SW16 .... 49 G2
Chilmead La REDH RH1 .... 127 G6
Chilsey Green Rd CHERT KT16 .... 40 B6
Chiltern WOKS/MYFD GU22 .... 96 F4
Chiltern Av FARN GU14 .... 92 A5
WHTN TW2 .... 25 K2
Chiltern Cl CRAWW RH11 .... 211 L3
CROY/NA CR0 .... 5 H8
HASM GU27 .... 219 L4
STA TW18 .... 22 D6 2
WPK KT4 .... 64 F1 1
Chiltern Dr BRYLDS KT5 .... 45 L5
Chiltern Rd BELMT SM2 .... 65 M8
Chilthorne Cl CAT SE6 .... 33 J1 1
Chiltley La LIPH GU30 .... 218 A7
Chilton Cl CRAN GU6 .... 204 C7
Chilton Rd RCH/KEW TW9 .... 18 D5 1
Chiltons Cl BNSTD SM7 .... 85 L5
Chilworth Gdns SUT SM1 .... 65 M2 1
Chilworth Rd SHGR GU5 .... 140 D5
Chinchilla Dr HSLWW TW4 .... 15 M4
The Chine NFNM GU10 .... 10 B9
Chingford Av FARN GU14 .... 92 F4
Chinthurst La RGUE GU4 .... 139 H7
Chinthurst Pk RGUE GU4 .... 139 H8
Chippendale Rd CRAWW RH11 .... 211 L8
Chipstead Av THHTH CR7 .... 49 L4
Chipstead Cl BELMT SM2 .... 65 L7
COUL/CHIP CR5 .... 86 D7
NRWD SE19 .... 32 C8
REDH RH1 .... 148 D2 2
Chipstead Ct
WOKN/KNAP GU21 .... 76 B7 1
Chipstead La COUL/CHIP CR5 .... 105 L6
Chipstead Rd BNSTD SM7 .... 85 J7
Chipstead Station Pde
COUL/CHIP CR5 .... 86 C8 1
Chipstead Valley Rd
COUL/CHIP CR5 .... 86 E6
Chipstead Wy BNSTD SM7 .... 86 C7 1
COUL/CHIP CR5 .... 86 C7
Chirton Wk WOKN/KNAP GU21 .... 76 D8
Chisbury Cl BRAK RG12 .... 35 H6
Chisholm Rd CROY/NA CR0 .... 5 H5
RCHPK/HAM TW10 .... 18 C8
Chislehurst Rd
RCHPK/HAM TW10 .... 18 B7 1
Chislet Cl BECK BR3 .... 33 K8 1
Chiswick Br MORT/ESHN SW14 .... 18 F4
Chiswick Cl CROY/NA CR0 .... 67 J2
Chiswick La South CHSWK W4 .... 19 J1
Chiswick Ml CHSWK W4 .... 19 J1
Chiswick Quay CHSWK W4 .... 18 F3
Chiswick Sq CHSWK W4 .... 19 H1 3
Chiswick Staithe CHSWK W4 .... 18 E3
Chiswick Village CHSWK W4 .... 18 D1
Chithurst La HORL RH6 .... 194 B2
Chitterfield Ga WDR/YW UB7 .... 14 D2 1
Chitty's Wk RGUW GU3 .... 116 C4
Chivenor Gv KUTN/CMB KT2 .... 27 G6
Chobham Cl CHERT KT16 .... 57 L5 1
Chobham Gdns
WIM/MER SW19 .... 29 G3 1
Chobham La CHERT KT16 .... 38 D8
Chobham Park La CHOB/PIR GU24 .. 56 D8
Chobham Rd CHERT KT16 .... 57 K6
CHOB/PIR GU24 .... 55 M1
CHOB/PIR GU24 .... 76 F3
FRIM GU16 .... 73 H7
WOKN/KNAP GU21 .... 6 D3
WOKN/KNAP GU21 .... 6 E5 1
Choir Gn WOKN/KNAP GU21 .... 76 B7
Cholmley Rd THDIT KT7 .... 44 E6
Chrislaine Cl
STWL/WRAY TW19 .... 14 A8 2
Chrismas Av ASHV GU12 .... 112 F8
Chrismas Pl ASHV GU12 .... 112 F8
Christabel Cl ISLW TW7 .... 17 H5
Christchurch Av TEDD TW11 .... 26 D6 3
Christchurch Cl WIM/MER SW19 .. 30 A8
Christ Church Mt
HOR/WEW KT19 .... 83 L2
Christchurch Pk BELMT SM2 .... 65 M6
Christ Church Rd BECK BR3 .... 51 K2 1
Christchurch Rd
BRXS/STRHM SW2 .... 31 J2
Christ Church Rd BRYLDS KT5 .... 45 J6 2
EPSOM KT18 .... 83 H2
Christchurch Rd
MORT/ESHN SW14 .... 18 E7
PUR/KEN CR8 .... 87 L1 1
VW GU25 .... 39 G4
WIM/MER SW19 .... 30 A8
Christchurch Wy
WOKN/KNAP GU21 .... 6 E5
Christian Flds
STRHM/NOR SW16 .... 31 K8
Christie Cl GT/LBKH KT23 .... 101 J7
LTWR GU18 .... 54 E8
Christie Dr SNWD SE25 .... 50 D5
Christies EGRIN RH19 .... 216 A1 1
Christine Cl ASHV GU12 .... 113 J8
Christmaspie Av RGUW GU3 .... 114 E8
Christopher Rd EGRIN RH19 .... 196 B8
Christy Rd BH/WHM TN16 .... 90 F5
Chrystie La GT/LBKH KT23 .... 101 L8 2
Chuck's La KWD/TDW/WH KT20 .. 104 E6
Chudleigh Gdns SUT SM1 .... 65 M2
Chudleigh Rd WHTN TW2 .... 17 H8 1
Chulsa Rd SYD SE26 .... 32 E6
Chumleigh Wk BRYLDS KT5 .... 45 J4
Church Ap DUL SE21 .... 32 A4
EGH TW20 .... 39 M3
Church Av BECK BR3 .... 51 K1
FARN GU14 .... 92 F7
MORT/ESHN SW14 .... 19 G6
Church Cir FARN GU14 .... 92 F8
Church Cl ADL/WDHM KT15 .... 58 E3 2
CHOB/PIR GU24 .... 95 J2
HASM GU27 .... 200 C7
HSLW TW3 .... 16 C4
KWD/TDW/WH KT20 .... 125 J1
LHD/OX KT22 .... 102 A6
MFD/CHID GU8 .... 159 J8
STA TW18 .... 40 F3
WOKN/KNAP GU21 .... 6 B3
Church Ct REIG RH2 .... 125 L8 1
Churchcroft Cl BAL SW12 .... 30 D1 1
Church Dr WWKM BR4 .... 70 B2
Church Farm La CHEAM SM3 .... 65 H5 1
Churchfield Rd REIG RH2 .... 125 J7
WEY KT13 .... 59 K3 1
WOT/HER KT12 .... 42 D8
Churchfields BOR GU35 .... 176 A8
E/WMO/HCT KT8 .... 43 K4 1
MFD/CHID GU8 .... 181 H5
RGUE GU4 .... 117 K3 1
WOKN/KNAP GU21 .... 6 C3
Churchfields Av FELT TW13 .... 25 J4
WEY KT13 .... 59 L3
Churchfields Rd BECK BR3 .... 51 G2
Church Gn WOT/HER KT12 .... 60 F5
Church Gv KUT KT1 .... 2 B5
Church Hl ALDT GU11 .... 134 E1
BH/WHM TN16 .... 111 G4
CAR SM5 .... 66 C4 3
CBLY GU15 .... 73 H4
CTHM CR3 .... 108 C6
PUR/KEN CR8 .... 67 H8
REDH RH1 .... 106 E8
REDH RH1 .... 127 J7
RSEV TN14 .... 91 M5
SHGR GU5 .... 141 K5
SHGR GU5 .... 162 B6
WIM/MER SW19 .... 29 J6
WOKN/KNAP GU21 .... 6 A4
WOKS/MYFD GU22 .... 78 C7
Church Hill Rd CHEAM SM3 .... 65 G3
SURB KT6 .... 45 H5
Churchill Av ASHV GU12 .... 134 F1
HORS RH12 .... 228 E6
Churchill Cl EBED/NFELT TW14 .. 24 C2 6
LHD/OX KT22 .... 102 B5
WARL CR6 .... 88 F7
Churchill Ct CRAWE RH10 .... 192 C8
Churchill Crs FARN GU14 .... 92 E2
Churchill Dr WEY KT13 .... 59 M2
Churchill Rd ASC SL5 .... 36 C2
GU GU1 .... 9 K5
HOR/WEW KT19 .... 83 K1
HORL RH6 .... 171 L6
SAND/SEL CR2 .... 67 M7
Churchill Wy SUN TW16 .... 24 D6
Church La ASC SL5 .... 37 G4
ASC SL5 .... 37 K3
ASHV GU12 .... 113 L7
CHOB/PIR GU24 .... 75 K5
CHOB/PIR GU24 .... 95 G4
CHSGTN KT9 .... 63 J5
COUL/CHIP CR5 .... 106 D4
CRAN GU6 .... 185 G6
CRAWE RH10 .... 193 K7
CTHM CR3 .... 107 K5
EGRIN RH19 .... 196 C8
EPSOM KT18 .... 103 M7
FARN GU14 .... 92 B5
GDST RH9 .... 129 G6
GSHT GU26 .... 198 F6
HASM GU27 .... 219 M2
HORL RH6 .... 193 H3
HORS RH12 .... 228 A6
MFD/CHID GU8 .... 182 A7
MFD/CHID GU8 .... 200 F1
NFNM GU10 .... 10 B6
NFNM GU10 .... 133 G2
NFNM GU10 .... 155 H6
OXTED RH8 .... 130 A4
RDKG RH5 .... 187 J8
REDH RH1 .... 128 A7
RGUW GU3 .... 116 B1
RPLY/SEND GU23 .... 97 L8
SHGR GU5 .... 140 E5
SHGR GU5 .... 141 K5
TEDD TW11 .... 26 C6
THDIT KT7 .... 44 C6
TWK TW1 .... 26 D2
WARL CR6 .... 89 G7
WARL CR6 .... 89 M6
WEY KT13 .... 59 K3 2
WIM/MER SW19 .... 47 K2
WLGTN SM6 .... 67 G2
Church Lane Av
COUL/CHIP CR5 .... 106 E4
Church Lane Dr
COUL/CHIP CR5 .... 106 E4
Church La East ALDT GU11 .... 134 E1
Church La West ALDT GU11 .... 112 C8
Churchley Rd SYD SE26 .... 32 E5 2
Church Meadow SURB KT6 .... 62 F1 1
Church Ms ADL/WDHM KT15 .... 58 F3
Churchmore Rd
STRHM/NOR SW16 .... 48 F1
Church Pth ASHV GU12 .... 113 K6
CROY/NA CR0 .... 4 C5
MTCM CR4 .... 48 B3
RYNPK SW20 .... 47 J2
WIM/MER SW19 .... 47 J2
Church Pl MTCM CR4 .... 48 B3
Church Ri CHSGTN KT9 .... 63 J5
FSTH SE23 .... 33 G2
Church Rd ADL/WDHM KT15 .... 58 D4
ALDT GU11 .... 134 F1
ASC SL5 .... 35 L1
ASC SL5 .... 36 D4
ASC SL5 .... 37 K6
ASHF TW15 .... 23 J5
ASHTD KT21 .... 83 G8
BAGS GU19 .... 54 A6
BARN SW13 .... 19 K4
BF/WBF KT14 .... 79 H3
BFOR GU20 .... 54 E5
BH/WHM TN16 .... 91 G7
BRAK RG12 .... 34 F2
CBLY GU15 .... 72 C2 1
CHEAM SM3 .... 65 H5 1
CHOB/PIR GU24 .... 75 J2
CRAWE RH10 .... 193 L6
CRAWE RH10 .... 213 H3
CRAWE RH10 .... 214 C6
CROY/NA CR0 .... 4 C8
CTHM CR3 .... 88 C8
CTHM CR3 .... 109 G3
E/WMO/HCT KT8 .... 44 A4
EGH TW20 .... 21 K6
ESH/CLAY KT10 .... 62 C5

EW KT17 .....84 B2
FELT TW13 .....24 F6
FRIM GU16 .....93 C1
GT/LBKH KT23 .....101 J5
GU GU1 .....9 C5
HASM GU27 .....219 M2
HAYES BR2 .....71 C6
HEST TW5 .....16 D2
HOR/WEW KT19 .....64 A6
HORL RH6 .....170 C7
HORL RH6 .....172 C4
HORL RH6 .....192 B4
HORL RH6 .....193 K2
HORS RH12 .....228 A6
HORS RH12 .....229 L4
ISLW TW7 .....17 C3
KUT KT1 .....3 C6
LHD/OX KT22 .....102 E4
LING RH7 .....174 A5
MFD/CHID GU8 .....181 J1
MFD/CHID GU8 .....183 H6
MFD/CHID GU8 .....203 G4
MTCM CR4 .....48 A2
NRWD SE19 .....32 B8
ORP BR6 .....71 M4
PUR/KEN CR8 .....67 H8
PUR/KEN CR8 .....88 E4
RCHPK/HAM TW10 .....18 B7
RCHPK/HAM TW10 .....27 H5
REDH RH1 .....147 K2
REIG RH2 .....41 L7
SHPTN TW17 .....52 A8
SHST GU47 .....44 F8
SURB KT6 .....26 B5
TEDD TW11 .....89 G7
WARL CR6 .....29 H6
WIM/MER SW19 .....66 F2
WOKN/KNAP GU21 .....6 C3
WOKN/KNAP GU21 .....96 D1
WPK KT4 .....46 B8
Church Rd East FARN GU14 .....93 C8
Church Rd West FARN GU14 .....93 C8
Church Side EPSOM KT18 .....83 L3
Churchside CI BH/WHM TN16 .....90 F8
Church Sq SHPTN TW17 .....41 L7
Church St ALDT GU11 .....112 C8
  BRKHM/BTCW RH3 .....146 B1
  CHSWK W4 .....19 H1
  COB KT11 .....80 E5
  CRAWW RH11 .....201 M3
  CROY/NA CR0 .....4 B7
  DORK RH4 .....144 D2
  EHSLY KT24 .....121 C1
  EPSOM KT18 .....84 B3
  ESH/CLAY KT10 .....61 L3
  EW KT17 .....64 D7
  HORS RH12 .....226 B1
  HORS RH12 .....228 C2
  HPTN TW12 .....43 M1
  HSLW TW3 .....16 F7
  ISLW TW7 .....17 L5
  KUT KT1 .....2 D7
  LHD/OX KT22 .....102 E4
  NFNM GU10 .....132 B3
  REIG RH2 .....125 L8
  RGODL GU7 .....160 A5
  STA TW18 .....22 A5
  SUN TW16 .....42 D3
  TWK TW1 .....26 D2
  WEY KT13 .....59 K3
  WOKS/MYFD GU22 .....97 M3
  WOT/HER KT12 .....42 D8
Church St East WOKN/KNAP GU21 .....6 C5
Church St West
  WOKN/KNAP GU21 .....6 C6
Church Ter RCHPK/HAM TW10 .....18 A7
Church V FSTH SE23 .....32 F3
Church Vw ASHV GU12 .....113 K7
Church View CI HORL RH6 .....170 C7
Churchview Rd WHTN TW2 .....26 A2
Church Wk BTFD TW8 .....108 D6
  CTHM CR3 .....108 D6
  HORL RH6 .....170 C7
  LHD/OX KT22 .....102 E4
  REIG RH2 .....125 L8
  REIG RH2 .....125 M8
  RYNPK SW20 .....46 F3
  STRHM/NOR SW16 .....48 F2
  WEY KT13 .....59 K2
  WOT/HER KT12 .....42 D8
Church Wy OXTED RH8 .....130 C6
  SAND/SEL CR2 .....68 C8
Churston Dr MRDN SM4 .....47 C5
Churt Rd NFNM GU10 .....198 C1
Churt Wynde GSHT GU26 .....199 G2
Chuters CI BF/WBF KT14 .....79 J2
Chuters Gv EW KT17 .....84 C2
Cibber Rd FSTH SE23 .....33 C3
Cidermill CI RDKG RH5 .....168 B6
Cinder Pth WOKS/MYFD GU22 .....96 F1
Cinnamon CI CROY/NA CR0 .....49 M7
Cinnamon Gdns GUW GU2 .....116 D3
Cintra Pk NRWD SE19 .....32 C8
Circle Gdns BF/WBF KT14 .....79 J3
  WIM/MER SW19 .....47 K3
Circle Rd WOT/HER KT12 .....60 B8
The Circle RGODL GU7 .....160 C3
Cissbury CI HORS RH12 .....229 K3
Cissbury HI CRAWW RH11 .....211 M5
Clacket La BH/WHM TN16 .....111 H6
  BH/WHM TN16 .....131 J1
Clairvale Rd HEST TW5 .....16 A3
Clairview Rd TOOT SW17 .....30 E6
Clandon Av EGH TW20 .....21 M8
Clandon CI EW KT17 .....84 C2
Clandon Ct FARN GU14 .....93 G6
Clandon Rd GU GU1 .....9 K5
  RPLY/SEND GU23 .....98 D3
Clanfield Ride BLKW GU17 .....72 A4
Clapgate La SWTR RH13 .....227 C5
Clappers Ga CRAWE RH10 .....212 A2
Clappers La CHOB/PIR GU24 .....75 M1
Clappers Meadow CRAN GU6 .....204 D7
Clare CI BF/WBF KT14 .....78 D3
  CRAWE RH10 .....192 F8
Clare Ct CTHM CR3 .....109 K5
Clare Crs LHD/OX KT22 .....82 D8

Claredale WOKS/MYFD GU22 .....97 H1
Clare Gdns EGH TW20 .....21 K6
Clare HI ESH/CLAY KT10 .....61 L4
Clare Hill (No 1)
  ESH/CLAY KT10 .....61 L4
Clare Hill (No 2) ESH/CLAY KT10 .....61 L4
Clare Lawn Av
  MORT/ESHN SW14 .....19 G7
Clare Md NFNM GU10 .....155 J6
Claremont Av CBLY GU15 .....73 J4
  ESH/CLAY KT10 .....61 J5
  NWMAL KT3 .....46 E5
  SUN TW16 .....42 E1
  WOT/HER KT12 .....61 G3
Claremont CI
  BRXS/STRHM SW2 .....31 J2
  ORP BR6 .....71 K3
  SAND/SEL CR2 .....88 E4
  WOT/HER KT12 .....60 F4
Claremont Ct DORK RH4 .....144 E3
Claremont Dr ESH/CLAY KT10 .....61 J6
  SHPTN TW17 .....41 L6
  WOKS/MYFD GU22 .....97 H1
Claremont End
  ESH/CLAY KT10 .....61 L5
Claremont Gdns SURB KT6 .....45 H4
Claremont Gv CHSWK W4 .....19 H2
Claremont La ESH/CLAY KT10 .....61 L4
Claremont Park Rd
  ESH/CLAY KT10 .....61 L5
Claremont Rd BF/WBF KT14 .....78 D2
  CROY/NA CR0 .....5 M3
  ESH/CLAY KT10 .....62 B6
  REDH RH1 .....126 D5
  STA TW18 .....22 A6
  SURB KT6 .....45 H5
  TEDD TW11 .....26 B5
  TWK TW1 .....26 E1
Claremount CI EPSOM KT18 .....84 F7
Claremount Gdns EPSOM KT18 .....84 F7
Clarence Av CLAP SW4 .....31 G1
  NWMAL KT3 .....45 M2
Clarence CI ASHV GU12 .....112 F7
  WOT/HER KT12 .....60 E3
Clarence Dr CBLY GU15 .....73 L2
  EGH TW20 .....20 F5
  EGRIN RH19 .....216 C2
Clarence La PUT/ROE SW15 .....19 J3
Clarence Rd BH/WHM TN16 .....91 J8
  CROY/NA CR0 .....4 E1
  RCH/KEW TW9 .....18 C3
  REDH RH1 .....148 A3
  SUT SM1 .....65 L3
  SWTR RH13 .....229 G8
  TEDD TW11 .....26 C7
  WIM/MER SW19 .....29 L7
  WLGTN SM6 .....66 E4
  WOT/HER KT12 .....60 E3
Clarence St EGH TW20 .....21 J7
  KUT KT1 .....2 D6
  RCH/KEW TW9 .....18 B2
  STA TW18 .....22 A6
Clarence Ter HSLW TW3 .....16 E6
Clarence Wk REDH RH1 .....148 A3
Clarence Wy HORL RH6 .....171 G4
Clarendon Ct BLKW GU17 .....72 A6
Clarendon Crs WHTN TW2 .....26 A4
Clarendon Dr PUT/ROE SW15 .....19 M6
Clarendon Ga CHERT KT16 .....58 A5
Clarendon Gv MTCM CR4 .....48 C3
Clarendon Rd ASHF TW15 .....23 J5
  CROY/NA CR0 .....4 B5
  REDH RH1 .....126 C7
  WIM/MER SW19 .....30 B8
  WLGTN SM6 .....66 F4
Clarens St CAT SE6 .....33 J3
Clare Rd HSLWW TW4 .....16 C5
  STWL/WRAY TW19 .....23 G2
The Clares CTHM CR3 .....108 D6
Claret Gdns SNWD SE25 .....50 B4
Clareville Rd CTHM CR3 .....108 D6
  STMC/STPC BR5 .....71 M1
Clare Wd LHD/OX KT22 .....82 D8
Clarewood Dr CBLY GU15 .....73 K3
Clarice Wy WLGTN SM6 .....67 H7
Claridge Gdns LING RH7 .....174 D7
Claridges Md LING RH7 .....174 D7
Clarke Crs CBLY GU15 .....72 B2
Clarkes Av WPK KT4 .....47 G8
Clark Rd CRAWW RH11 .....211 K8
Clarks HI NFNM GU10 .....132 F7
Clarks La WARL CR6 .....110 E5
Clark Wy HEST TW5 .....16 A2
Claudia PI WIM/MER SW19 .....29 J2
Claverdon BRAK RG12 .....34 D7
Claverdale Rd BRXS/STRHM SW2 .....31 J1
Clavering Av BARN SW13 .....19 L1
Clavering CI TWK TW1 .....26 D5
Clay Av MTCM CR4 .....48 E2
Claycart Rd ALDT GU11 .....112 A6
Claydon Dr CROY/NA CR0 .....67 H1
Claydon Gdns FARN GU14 .....72 D8
Claydon Rd WOKN/KNAP GU21 .....76 D6
Clayford LING RH7 .....174 D7
Claygate Crs CROY/NA CR0 .....69 M5
Claygate La ESH/CLAY KT10 .....62 D1
  THDIT KT7 .....44 D8
Claygate Lodge CI
  ESH/CLAY KT10 .....62 B6
Claygate Rd DORK RH4 .....144 E4
Clay Hall La CRAWE RH10 .....193 M5
Clayhall La REIG RH2 .....147 H3
Clayhanger RGUE GU4 .....117 M6
Clayhill CI BRAK RG12 .....35 J3
Clayhill Rd REIG RH2 .....146 D7
Clayhill Rd REIG RH2 .....146 C8
Clay La EPSOM KT18 .....103 L6
  LING RH7 .....173 G7
  REDH RH1 .....148 F1
  RGUE GU4 .....117 G2
Claymore CI MRDN SM4 .....47 K7
Claypole Dr HEST TW5 .....16 B3
Clays CI EGRIN RH19 .....216 B1
Clayton Barracks ALDT GU11 .....113 G5
Clayton Dr GUW GU2 .....116 C5
Clayton Gv BRAK RG12 .....35 H1
Clayton HI CRAWW RH11 .....211 M5
Clayton Md GDST RH9 .....128 E4

Clayton Rd CHSGTN KT9 .....62 F3
  EW KT17 .....84 B3
  FARN GU14 .....72 C8
  ISLW TW7 .....17 H5
Cleardene DORK RH4 .....144 E2
Cleardown WOKS/MYFD GU22 .....7 J8
Clearsprings LTWR GU18 .....74 C1
The Clears REIG RH2 .....125 H6
Clearwater PI SURB KT6 .....44 F6
Cleaveland Rd SURB KT6 .....45 G5
Cleave Prior COUL/CHIP CR5 .....106 B1
Cleaverholme CI SNWD SE25 .....50 E6
Cleeve HI FSTH SE23 .....32 E2
Cleeve Rd LHD/OX KT22 .....102 D2
The Cleeve GU GU1 .....117 K8
Clement CI PUR/KEN CR8 .....87 L6
Clement Rd BECK BR3 .....51 G2
  WIM/MER SW19 .....29 H6
Clements Md LHD/OX KT22 .....102 D1
Clements Rd WOT/HER KT12 .....60 E1
Clensham La SUT SM1 .....65 K1
Clerks Cft REDH RH1 .....128 A7
Clevedon WEY KT13 .....59 L3
Clevedon Ct FARN GU14 .....93 G6
  FRIM GU16 .....93 K1
Clevedon Gdns HEST TW5 .....15 L4
Clevedon Rd KUT KT1 .....3 J6
  PGE/AN SE20 .....51 G1
  TWK TW1 .....18 A3
Cleveland Av HPTN TW12 .....25 J8
Cleveland CI WOT/HER KT12 .....60 E2
Cleveland Dr STA TW18 .....40 F
Cleveland Gdns BARN SW13 19
  WPK KT4 64
Cleveland Ri MRDN SM4 47
Cleveland Rd BARN SW13 19
  ISLW TW7 .....46 B3
  NWMAL KT3 .....46 B4
  WPK KT4 .....64 B1
Cleves Av EW KT17 .....64 E7
Cleves CI COB KT11 .....80 E4
Cleves Crs CROY/NA CR0 .....89 M1
Cleves Rd RCHPK/HAM TW10 .....26 F4
Cleves Wy HPTN TW12 .....25 J8
  SUN TW16 .....24 C8
Cleves Wd WEY KT13 .....60 B2
Clewborough Dr CBLY GU15 .....73 L3
Clews La CHOB/PIR GU24 .....75 K6
Clifden Rd BTFD TW8 .....18 A1
  TWK TW1 .....26 C2
Cliff End PUR/KEN CR8 .....87 L2
Cliffe Rd RGODL GU7 .....159 M7
Cliffe Rd SAND/SEL CR2 .....68 A4
  RCH/KEW TW9 .....18 E5
  WLGTN SM6 .....66 F3
Clifford Av MORT/ESHN SW14 .....18 F4
Clifford Gv ASHF TW15 .....23 K5
Clifford Manor Rd RGUE GU4 .....139 H4
Clifford Rd HSLWW TW4 .....16 A5
  RCHPK/HAM TW10 .....26 F4
  SNWD SE25 .....50 D4
Clifton Av BELMT SM2 .....85 L1
  FELT TW13 .....24 F4
Clifton CI ADL/WDHM KT15 .....58 E1
  CTHM CR3 .....108 A5
  NFNM GU10 .....155 K5
  ORP BR6 .....71 M4
Clifton Gdns FRIM GU16 .....93 J3
Clifton Ms SNWD SE25 .....50 B4
Clifton Park Av RYNPK SW20 .....46 F2
Clifton PI BNSTD SM7 .....85 K5
Clifton Rd COUL/CHIP CR5 .....86 E5
  CRAWE RH10 .....212 F4
  HTHAIR TW6 .....14 E6
  ISLW TW7 .....17 H4
  KUTN/CMB KT2 .....3 H4
  KUTN/CMB KT2 .....3 J5
  SNWD SE25 .....50 B4
  TEDD TW11 .....26 B5
  WIM/MER SW19 .....29 G7
  WLGTN SM6 .....66 E4
Clifton's La REIG RH2 .....125 C4
Cliftonville DORK RH4 .....144 E3
Clifton Wy WOKN/KNAP GU21 .....76 C7
Climping Rd CRAWW RH11 .....211 L1
Cline Rd GU GU1 .....9 L7
Clinton Av E/WMO/HCT KT8 .....43 M4
Clinton CI WOKN/KNAP GU21 .....76 A8
Clinton HI LING RH7 .....174 D8
Clinton Rd LHD/OX KT22 .....102 F5
Clintons Gn BNFD RG42 .....34 D1
Clippesby CI CHSGTN KT9 .....63 J5
Clipstone Rd HSLW TW3 .....16 D5
Clitherow Gdns CRAWE RH10 .....212 B4
Cliveden PI SHPTN TW17 .....41 M6
Cliveden Rd WIM/MER SW19 .....47 J1
Clive Gn BRAK RG12 .....34 E5
Clive Rd ASHV GU12 .....113 G8
  DUL SE21 .....32 A4
  EBED/NFELT TW14 .....15 K8
  ESH/CLAY KT10 .....61 L3
  TWK TW1 .....26 C5
  WIM/MER SW19 .....30 B7
Clive Wy CRAWE RH10 .....212 F3
Clock Barn La MFD/CHID GU8 .....182 C2
Clock House CI BF/WBF KT14 .....79 J2
Clockhouse CI WIM/MER SW19 .....28 F4
Clock House La ASHF TW15 .....23 L4
  SHGR GU5 .....161 J3
Clockhouse La East EGH TW20 .....21 L8
Clockhouse La West EGH TW20 .....21 K8
Clock House Md COB KT11 .....81 L4
Clock House Rd BECK BR3 .....51 H3
Clockhouse Rd FARN GU14 .....92 E5
Clock Tower Rd ISLW TW7 .....17 J5
Clodhouse HI WOKS/MYFD GU22 .....96 A4
Cloister CI TEDD TW11 .....26 E6
Cloister Gdns SNWD SE25 .....50 E6
The Cloisters FRIM GU16 .....73 L3
  WOKS/MYFD GU22 .....97 L3
Clonmel Rd HPTN TW12 .....26 A5
Clonmore St WAND/EARL SW18 .....29 H1
The Close ASC SL5 .....36 A2
  BECK BR3 .....51 H4
  BF/WBF KT14 .....78 D3
  BIL RH14 .....223 M6
  BRAK RG12 .....34 F4
  BRKHM/BTCW RH3 .....145 L4

CAR SM5 .....66 B7
CHEAM SM3 .....47 J7
EGRIN RH19 .....216 A1
FRIM GU16 .....92 F1
HORL RH6 .....170 F8
ISLW TW7 .....17 G4
LTWR GU18 .....54 D8
MTCM CR4 .....48 C4
NWMAL KT3 .....45 M2
PUR/KEN CR8 .....67 J8
RCH/KEW TW9 .....18 E5
REIG RH2 .....147 L3
RGODL GU7 .....159 L4
SHGR GU5 .....161 J5
SHST GU47 .....52 B7
SURB KT6 .....45 G6
SUT SM1 .....47 J7
VW GU25 .....39 G4
WOKS/MYFD GU22 .....10 A4
Closeworth Rd
Cloudesdale Rd
Clouston CI
Clouston
Clovelly
Clovel
Clo
Clowser CI SUT SM1
Clubhouse Rd ALDT
Club La CWTH RG45
Clump Av KWD/TDW/WH KT20
Clumps Rd NFNM GU10 .....156 B5
The Clumps ASHF TW15 .....24 A5
Clyde Av SAND/SEL CR2 .....88 E5
Clyde CI REDH RH1 .....126 D7
Clyde Rd CROY/NA CR0 .....5 J5
  STWL/WRAY TW19 .....23 G3
  SUT SM1 .....65 K4
  WLGTN SM6 .....66 F4
Clydesdale CI ISLW TW7 .....17 J5
Clydesdale Gdns
  RCHPK/HAM TW10 .....18 E6
Clyde Ter FSTH SE23 .....32 F3
Clyde V FSTH SE23 .....32 F3
Clymping Dene
  EBED/NFELT TW14 .....24 E1
Clyve Wy STA TW18 .....40 B1
Coach House La FRIM GU16 .....73 H6
Coach House Rd BRKHM/BTCW RH3 .....145 K2
Coachlads Av GUW GU2 .....116 C8
Coachmans Dr CRAWW RH11 .....211 L7
Coach Rd BRKHM/BTCW RH3 .....145 J2
  CHERT KT16 .....57 M5
  RDKG RH5 .....123 H8
Coalecroft Rd PUT/ROE SW15 .....19 M6
Coast HI RDKG RH5 .....143 J4
Coast Hill La DORK RH4 .....143 K4
Cobb CI DTCH/LGLY SL3 .....12 A3
Cobbets Wy EDEN TN8 .....175 M1
Cobbett CI CRAWE RH10 .....212 F1
Cobbett Rd GUW GU2 .....116 B7
  WHTN TW2 .....25 K2
Cobbetts CI WOKN/KNAP GU21 .....76 E6
Cobbetts Farm
  CHOB/PIR GU24 .....75 K5
Cobbetts HI WEY KT13 .....59 L6
Cobbetts Wk CHOB/PIR GU24 .....75 K5
Cobbetts Wy NFNM GU10 .....10 B6
Cobbler's Wk TEDD TW11 .....26 B8
Cobbles Crs CRAWE RH10 .....212 B2
Cobblestone PI CROY/NA CR0 .....4 C4
Cobb's Rd HSLWW TW4 .....16 C2
Cob CI CRAWE RH10 .....214 F1
Cobden La HASM GU27 .....220 A2
Cobden Ms SYD SE26 .....32 E6
Cobden Rd SNWD SE25 .....50 D5
Cobham Av NWMAL KT3 .....46 D5
Cobham CI WLGTN SM6 .....67 H5
Cobham Park Rd COB KT11 .....80 E7
Cobham Rd COB KT11 .....81 K8
  HEST TW5 .....15 M2
  KUT KT1 .....3 K6
Cobham Wy CRAWE RH10 .....192 E5
  EHSLY KT24 .....100 B7
Cobnor CI CRAWW RH11 .....211 J5
Cobs Wy ADL/WDHM KT15 .....58 F8
Coburg Crs BRXS/STRHM SW2 .....31 J2
Cob Wk CRAWW RH11 .....211 K4
Cochrane PI BFOR GU20 .....55 G4
Cochrane Rd WIM/MER SW19 .....29 H8
Cock La LHD/OX KT22 .....101 M4
Cocks Crs NWMAL KT3 .....46 C4
Cockshot HI REIG RH2 .....147 L2
Cockshot Rd REIG RH2 .....147 L2
Codrington Ct
  WOKN/KNAP GU21 .....76 C8
Codrington HI FSTH SE23 .....113 J4
Cody CI ASHV GU12 .....113 J7
  WLGTN SM6 .....67 G6
Cody Rd FARN GU14 .....92 C6
Coe Av SNWD SE25 .....50 D6
Coe CI ALDT GU11 .....112 D8
Cokenor Wd NFNM GU10 .....10 A8
Cokers La DUL SE21 .....31 M2
Colborne Wy WPK KT4 .....64 F2
Colburn Av CTHM CR3 .....108 C6
Colburn Crs GU GU1 .....117 K5
Colburn Wy SUT SM1 .....66 A2
Colby Rd NRWD SE19 .....32 B6
  WOT/HER KT12 .....42 D8
Colchester V FROW RH18 .....217 H7
Colcokes Rd BNSTD SM7 .....85 K6
Coldharbour CI EGH TW20 .....39 M3
Coldharbour La CHOB/PIR GU24 .....75 J1
  DORK RH4 .....144 D4
  EGH TW20 .....39 M3

Cold Harbour La FARN GU14 .....92 C1
Coldharbour La PUR/KEN CR8 .....67 K8
  RDKG RH5 .....166 C1
  REDH RH1 .....128 C8
  WOKS/MYFD GU22 .....78 C5
Coldharbour Rd BF/WBF KT14 .....78 C4
  CROY/NA CR0 .....67 K4
  WOKS/MYFD GU22 .....78 C5
Coldharbour Wy CROY/NA CR0 .....67 K4
Coldshott OXTED RH8
Colebrook CHERT
Colebr
  WWKM BR4
Colinette Rd PUT/ROE SW15 .....19 M6
Colin CI CTHM CR3 .....108 D5
Coliston Rd WAND/EARL SW18 .....29 K1
Collamore Av WAND/EARL SW18 .....30 B1
Collards La HASM GU27 .....220 A3
College Av EGH TW20 .....21 L7
  EW KT17 .....84 C4
College CI ADL/WDHM KT15 .....59 G2
  CBLY GU15 .....73 C1
  EGRIN RH19 .....196 C8
  LING RH7 .....174 A5
  WHTN TW2 .....26 A2
College Crs REDH RH1 .....126 D5
  SHST GU47 .....72 B1
College Gdns FNM GU9 .....133 L7
  NWMAL KT3 .....46 C5
  TOOT SW17 .....30 B3
College Gn NRWD SE19 .....32 B8
College HI HASM GU27 .....219 M3
  RGODL GU7 .....159 M6
College Hill Ter HASM GU27 .....219 M3
College La EGRIN RH19 .....196 C8
  WOKS/MYFD GU22 .....96 F1
College Ride BAGS GU19 .....53 M7
  CBLY GU15 .....73 C2
College Rd ASHV GU12 .....113 K6
  BRAK RG12 .....34 F4
  CRAWE RH10 .....212 B3
  CROY/NA CR0 .....4 E6
  DUL SE21 .....32 B1
  EW KT17 .....84 C4
  GU GU1 .....9 C5
  ISLW TW7 .....17 J3
  NRWD SE19 .....32 C6
  SHST GU47 .....72 B2
  WIM/MER SW19 .....30 A7
  WOKS/MYFD GU22 .....7 K4
College Wy ASHF TW15 .....23 J5
Collendean La HORL RH6 .....169 H5
Collens Fld CHOB/PIR GU24 .....95 H6
Colley La REIG RH2 .....125 H5
Colley Manor Dr REIG RH2 .....125 G5
Colley Wy REIG RH2 .....125 H5
Collier CI FARN GU14 .....92 A4
  HOR/WEW KT19 .....63 K5
Collier Rw CRAWE RH10 .....212 A6
Colliers CTHM CR3 .....108 D7
Colliers CI WOKN/KNAP GU21 .....76 A7
Colliers Water La THHTH CR7 .....49 K5
Colliers Wd HAYES BR2 .....71 G4
Collier Wy RGUE GU4 .....118 A6
Collingdon CRAN GU6 .....185 J8
Collingtree Rd SYD SE26 .....32 F5
Collingwood Av BRYLDS KT5 .....45 M8
  EGRIN RH19 .....216 C2
  HORL RH6 .....170 E5
  HSLWW TW4 .....16 B3
Colling Wood CI PGE/AN SE20 .....50 E1
Collingwood Crs GU GU1 .....117 K7
Collingwood Grange CI
  CBLY GU15 .....73 L1
Collingwood Ri CBLY GU15 .....73 K2
Collingwood Rd
  CRAWE RH10 .....213 G4
  HORS RH12 .....228 E4
  MTCM CR4 .....48 B2
  SUT SM1 .....65 K3
Collins Gdns ASHV GU12 .....113 L7
Collins Rd CRAWW RH11 .....211 H5
Collyer Av CROY/NA CR0 .....67 H3
Collyer Rd CROY/NA CR0 .....67 H3
Collyers Crs LIPH GU30 .....218 B5
Colman CI EPSOM KT18 .....84 F7
Colmans HI SHGR GU5 .....164 A2
Colman Wy REDH RH1 .....126 B5
Colmer Rd STRHM/NOR SW16 .....31 H8
Colnbrook By-pass
  DTCH/LGLY SL3 .....12 E1
  WDR/YW UB7 .....13 L2
Colndale Rd DTCH/LGLY SL3 .....13 H1
Colne Bank STWL/WRAY TW19 .....12 F5
Colne Ct HOR/WEW KT19 .....63 M3
Colne Dr WOT/HER KT12 .....61 G2

Colne Rd WHTN TW2 ... 26 B2
Colne Valley Wy
  STWL/WRAY TW19 ... 22 B2
Colne Wy ASHV GU12 ... 113 K8
Colonel's La CHERT KT16 ... 40 D6
Colonial Av WHTN TW2 ... 16 F8
Colonial Rd EBED/NFELT TW14 ... 24 B1
Colonsay Rd CRAWW RH11 ... 211 L6
Colson Crs CROY/NA CR0 ... 4 F5
Colson Rd STRHM/NOR SW16 ... 30 F5
Colston Av CAR SM5 ... 66 B3
Colston Rd MORT/ESHN SW14 ... 18 F6
Coltash Rd CRAWE RH10 ... 212 D4
Coltsfoot Dr GU ... 117 L5
  HORS RH12 ... 229 H4
Coltsfoot La OXTED RH8 ... 130 C7
Columbia Av WPK KT4 ... 46 C7
Columbine Av SAND/SEL CR2 ... 67 L6
Colville Gdns LTWR GU18 ... 74 F1
Colvin Cl SYD SE26 ... 32 F6
Colvin Rd THHTH CR7 ... 49 K5
Colwith Rd HMSMTH W6 ... 19 J1
Colwood Gdns WIM/MER SW19 ... 30 A8
Colworth Rd CROY/NA CR0 ... 5 L3
Colwyn Cl CRAWW RH11 ... 211 H5
  STRHM/NOR SW16 ... 30 F6
Colwyn Crs HSLW TW3 ... 16 F3
Colyton Cl WOKN/KNAP GU21 ... 76 F8
Combe La EHSLY KT24 ... 141 L1
  FARN GU14 ... 92 D3
  MFD/CHID GU8 ... 161 C7
  MFD/CHID GU8 ... 201 J4
  SHGR GU5 ... 141 J3
  WOT/HER KT12 ... 60 C7
Combemartin Rd
  WAND/EARL SW18 ... 29 H1
Combe Ri NFNM GU10 ... 156 A4
Combermere Rd MRDN SM4 ... 47 L6
Combe Rd RGODL GU7 ... 160 B1
Combe Vw MFD/CHID GU8 ... 201 K5
Comeragh Cl WOKS/MYFD GU22 ... 96 D1
Comforts Farm Av OXTED RH8 ... 130 C7
Comet Rd STWL/WRAY TW19 ... 23 G1
Commerce Rd BTFD TW8 ... 17 M1
Commerce Wy CROY/NA CR0 ... 67 J2
Commercial Rd ASHV GU12 ... 134 F1
  GU GU1 ... 9 G6
  STA TW18 ... 22 D7
Commercial Wy
  WOKN/KNAP GU21 ... 6 E5 (2)
Common Cl WOKN/KNAP GU21 ... 77 G4
Commondale PUT/ROE SW15 ... 19 M4
Commonfield Rd BNSTD SM7 ... 85 K4
Commonfields CHOB/PIR GU24 ... 75 J3
Common La ADL/WDHM KT15 ... 58 F7
  ESH/CLAY KT10 ... 62 D6
Common Rd BARN SW13 ... 19 K5
  ESH/CLAY KT10 ... 62 D5
  REDH RH1 ... 148 C2
Common Side EPSOM KT18 ... 83 K5
Commonside GT/LBKH KT23 ... 101 K4
  HAYES BR2 ... 70 F3
Commonside Cl BELMT SM2 ... 85 L1
  COUL/CHIP CR5 ... 107 L2
Commonside East MTCM CR4 ... 48 F4 (1)
Commonwealth Rd CTHM CR3 ... 108 D5
Community Cl HEST TW5 ... 15 L3 (3)
Como Rd FSTH SE23 ... 33 H3
Compass Hl
  RCHPK/HAM TW10 ... 18 A8 (2)
Compassion Cl CRAWW RH11 ... 211 H4 (2)
Comper Cl CRAWW RH11 ... 211 H5 (1)
Comport Gn CROY/NA CR0 ... 90 B2
Compound Rd FARN GU14 ... 92 D7
Compton Cl BRAK RG12 ... 34 B6 (1)
  ESH/CLAY KT10 ... 62 A5 (1)
  CHSWK W4 ...
Compton Crs CHSGTN KT9 ... 63 H5
  CHSWK W4 ...
Compton Rd CROY/NA CR0 ... 50 E8
  WIM/MER SW19 ...
Comptons Brow La SWTR RH13 ... 229 J6
Comptons La SWTR RH13 ... 229 J8
Compton Wy NFNM GU10 ... 134 D7
Comsaye Wk BRAK RG12 ... 34 F5 (1)
Concorde Cl ISLW TW3 ... 16 E4 (1)
Condor Av EW KT17 ... 64 D8
Condor Rd FARN GU14 ... 92 E7
  STA TW18 ... 40 F3
Conduit La SAND/SEL CR2 ... 68 D4
The Conduit REDH RH1 ... 128 A3
Coney Acre DUL SE21 ... 31 M2 (1)
Coneyberry REDH RH1 ... 147 M4
Coneybury REDH RH1 ... 128 B7
Coneybury Cl WARL CR6 ... 108 E1
Coney Cl CRAWW RH11 ... 211 L1
Coney Hill Rd WWKM BR4 ... 70 B1
Coneyhurst La CRAN GU6 ... 185 M2
Conford Dr RGUE GU4 ... 139 H7
Coniers Wy RGUE GU4 ... 117 K3
Conifer Cl REIG RH2 ... 125 K6
Conifer Dr CBLY GU15 ... 73 K5
Conifer Gdns STRHM/NOR SW16 ... 31 J4
  SUT SM1 ... 65 L1 (1)
Conifer La EGH TW20 ... 21 M6
Conifers WEY KT13 ... 60 B3
Conifers Cl HORS RH12 ... 229 L3
Coningsby BRAK RG12 ... 34 C4
Coningsby Rd SAND/SEL CR2 ... 67 M7
Conisborough Crs CAT SE6 ... 33 M5 (1)
Conista Ct WOKN/KNAP GU21 ... 76 C6 (1)
Coniston Cl BARN SW13 ... 19 J2 (1)
  CBLY GU15 ... 73 M6
  CHSWK W4 ... 18 F3
  CRAWW RH11 ... 211 G5 (1)
  FARN GU14 ... 92 B6
  HORS RH12 ... 229 L4
  MRDN SM4 ... 47 G6
Coniston Ct LTWR GU18 ... 54 E8
Coniston Dr FNM GU9 ... 133 K3
Coniston Gdns BELMT SM2 ... 66 A5 (1)
Coniston Rd COUL/CHIP CR5 ... 86 F6
  CROY/NA CR0 ... 5 L2
  WHTN TW2 ... 16 E8
  WOKS/MYFD GU22 ... 97 L2
Coniston Wy CHSGTN KT9 ... 63 H2
  EGH TW20 ... 21 L8 (3)
  REDH RH1 ... 126 B7

Connaught Av ASHF TW15 ... 23 H5 (1)
  HSLWW TW4 ... 16 B7
  MORT/ESHN SW14 ... 18 F5
Connaught Barracks
  ALDT GU11 ... 113 G3
Connaught Cl SUT SM1 ... 66 A1 (1)
Connaught Crs CHOB/PIR GU24 ... 95 J2 (2)
Connaught Dr WEY KT13 ... 79 J1
Connaught Gdns
  CRAWW RH11 ... 212 A1 (1)
  MRDN SM4 ... 47 M5
Connaught Rd ASHV GU12 ... 112 F8
  BAGS GU19 ... 53 M6
  CBLY GU15 ... 73 J4
  CHOB/PIR GU24 ... 95 J2
  HPTN TW12 ... 26 A6
  NWMAL KT3 ... 46 B4
  RCHPK/HAM TW10 ... 18 C7 (2)
  SUT SM1 ... 66 A1
Connop Wy FRIM GU16 ... 73 J6
Conquest Rd ADL/WDHM KT15 ... 58 D7
Conrad Dr WPK KT4 ... 46 F8
Consfield Av NWMAL KT3 ... 46 D4
Consort Dr CBLY GU15 ... 73 M2 (1)
Consort Ms ISLW TW7 ... 17 G8
Consort Wy HORL RH6 ... 170 D6
Consort Wy East HORL RH6 ... 170 D7
Constable Gdns ISLW TW7 ... 17 G7
Constable Rd CRAWE RH10 ... 212 C7
Constable Wy SHST GU47 ... 72 B3
Constance Rd CROY/NA CR0 ... 4 B1
  SUT SM1 ... 65 M3
  WHTN TW2 ... 25 L1
Constitution Hl
  WOKS/MYFD GU22 ... 6 D8
Control Tower Rd HTHAIR TW6 ... 14 D5
Convent Cl BECK BR3 ... 33 M8
Convent Hl NRWD SE19 ... 31 M7
Convent Rd ASHF TW15 ... 23 L6
Conway Dr ASHF TW15 ... 23 M7
  BELMT SM2 ... 65 L5
  FARN GU14 ... 92 A4
Conway Gdns MTCM CR4 ... 49 G4
Conway Rd FELT TW13 ... 25 G6
  HSLW TW3 ... 25 J1
  RYNPK SW20 ... 46 F1
Conyers Cl WOT/HER KT12 ... 61 G4
Conyer's Rd STRHM/NOR SW16 ... 31 G6
Cookes La CHEAM SM3 ... 65 H5
Cookham Rd BRAK RG12 ... 34 B2
  HORS RH12 ... 229 G3
Cooks Hl HORS RH12 ... 205 H8
Cooks Md HORS RH12 ... 210 A2
Coolarne Ri CBLY GU15 ... 73 K3
Coolgardie Rd ASHF TW15 ... 23 M6
Coolhurst La HORS RH12 ... 229 K6
Coombe Av CROY/NA CR0 ... 68 B3
Coombe Bank NWMAL KT3 ... 46 B1
Coombe Cl CRAWW RH11 ... 192 A8
  FRIM GU16 ... 93 G1
  HSLW TW3 ... 16 D6
Coombe Crs HPTN TW12 ... 25 H8
Coombe Dr ADL/WDHM KT15 ... 58 C5
Coombe End KUTN/CMB KT2 ... 27 M8
Coombefield Cl NWMAL KT3 ... 46 B5 (1)
Coombe Gdns NWMAL KT3 ... 46 C4
  RYNPK SW20 ... 46 D2
Coombe Hill Gld KUTN/CMB KT2 ... 28 B8
Coombe Hill Rd EGRIN RH19 ... 215 M3 (1)
  KUTN/CMB KT2 ... 28 B8
Coombe House Cha
  NWMAL KT3 ... 46 A1 (1)
Coombelands La
  ADL/WDHM KT15 ... 58 D5
Coombe La CROY/NA CR0 ... 68 E4
  RGUW GU3 ... 115 M2
  RYNPK SW20 ... 46 D2
Coombe La West KUTN/CMB KT2... 3 M5
  NWMAL KT3 ... 46 C2
Coombe Mnr CHOB/PIR GU24 ... 75 K5 (2)
Coombe Neville KUTN/CMB KT2 ... 27 M8
Coombe Pk KUTN/CMB KT2 ... 27 M6
Coombe Pine BRAK RG12 ... 35 G6
Coombe Ridings KUTN/CMB KT2 ... 27 M6
Coombe Ri KUTN/CMB KT2 ... 45 M1
Coombe Rd CROY/NA CR0 ... 4 E9
  HPTN TW12 ... 25 J7
  KUTN/CMB KT2 ... 3 K5
  NWMAL KT3 ... 46 B3
  SAND/SEL CR2 ... 68 B3
  SYD SE26 ... 32 E5
The Coombes SHGR GU5 ... 161 K4
The Coombe
  BRKHM/BTCW RH3 ... 124 A5
Coombe Wy BF/WBF KT14 ... 79 J2 (3)
Coombe Wood Hl PUR/KEN CR8 ... 87 M2
Coombe Wood Rd
  KUTN/CMB KT2 ... 27 M6
Coomb Fld EDEN TN8 ... 175 M1
Cooper Cl HORL RH6 ... 171 K6
Cooper Crs CAR SM5 ... 66 C2
Cooper Rd BFOR GU20 ... 55 G5
  CROY/NA CR0 ... 67 K4
  GU GU1 ... 9 K7
Cooper Rw CRAWE RH10 ... 212 A6
Coopers Cl STA TW18 ... 22 B6
Coopers Hill Dr CHOB/PIR GU24... 94 F2
Cooper's Hill La EGH TW20 ... 20 F4
Cooper's Hill Rd REDH RH1 ... 127 J7
Coopers Ri RGODL GU7 ... 159 L6
Cooper's Yd NRWD SE19 ... 32 B7
Cootes Av HORS RH12 ... 228 D6
Copelands Cl CBLY GU15 ... 74 A5
Copeman Cl SYD SE26 ... 32 F6
Copenhagen Wy
  WOT/HER KT12 ... 60 E2 (1)
Copers Cope Rd BECK BR3 ... 33 J8
Copleigh Dr
  KWD/TDW/WH KT20 ... 105 H2
Copley Cl REDH RH1 ... 126 B6
  WOKN/KNAP GU21 ... 96 B1
Copley Pk STRHM/NOR SW16 ... 31 J2
Copley Wy KWD/TDW/WH KT20... 105 G2
Copnall Wy HORS RH12 ... 228 F7 (1)
Coppard Gdns CHSGTN KT9 ... 62 F5
Copped Hall Dr CBLY GU15 ... 73 M3
Copped Hall Wy CBLY GU15 ... 73 M3

Copper Beech Cl
  WOKS/MYFD GU22 ... 96 E3
Copper Cl NRWD SE19 ... 32 C8
Copperfield Av SHST GU47 ... 52 B7
Copperfield Pl HORS RH12 ... 228 E6
Copperfield Ri ADL/WDHM KT15... 58 C4
Copperfields LHD/OX KT22 ... 101 M4 (1)
Copper Mill Dr ISLW TW7 ... 17 J4 (1)
Copper Mill La TOOT SW17 ... 29 M5
Coppermill Rd
  STWL/WRAY TW19 ... 12 E8
Coppice Cl FNM GU9 ... 134 B3
  GUW GU2 ... 116 A7
  RYNPK SW20 ... 46 F3 (2)
Coppice Dr PUT/ROE SW15 ... 19 K8
  STWL/WRAY TW19 ... 21 G1
Coppice La REIG RH2 ... 125 J6
Coppice Rd HORS RH12 ... 229 K4 (2)
The Coppice ASHF TW15 ... 23 L7 (1)
  CRAWE RH10 ... 214 E1
Coppice Wk CRAWE RH10 ... 212 D2 (2)
Copping Cl CROY/NA CR0 ... 5 H9
Coppsfield E/WMO/HCT KT8 ... 43 K3 (1)
Copse Av FNM GU9 ... 134 B2
  WWKM BR4 ... 69 L2
Copse Cl CBLY GU15 ... 73 K4
  CRAWE RH10 ... 214 E1 (1)
  EGRIN RH19 ... 196 C6
  HORS RH12 ... 229 J3
  RGUE GU4 ... 139 M6
Copse Crs CRAWW RH11 ... 211 M2
Copse Edge CRAN GU6 ... 185 J5
  MFD/CHID GU8 ... 157 M6
Copse End CBLY GU15 ... 73 J3
Copse Gld SURB KT6 ... 45 G8
Copse Hl BELMT SM2 ... 65 L6
  PUR/KEN CR8 ... 87 H3
  RYNPK SW20 ... 46 D1
Copse La HORL RH6 ... 170 F5
Copsem Dr ESH/CLAY KT10 ... 61 L5
Copsem La ESH/CLAY KT10 ... 61 M7
  LHD/OX KT22 ... 81 M1
Copsem Wy ESH/CLAY KT10 ... 61 M5
Copsen Wd LHD/OX KT22 ... 81 M1
Copse Rd COB KT11 ... 80 E3
  HASM GU27 ... 219 G4
  REIG RH2 ... 147 M2
  WOKN/KNAP GU21 ... 76 C8
Copse Side RGODL GU7 ... 160 A1
The Copse FARN GU14 ... 92 A6
  GT/LBKH KT23 ... 101 L5
  NFNM GU10 ... 155 J5
  REDH RH1 ... 149 H2
Copse Vw SAND/SEL CR2 ... 69 H7
Copse Wy NFNM GU10 ... 10 A8
Copse Wd LHD/OX KT22 ... 81 M1
Copsleigh Av REDH RH1 ... 148 D7
Copsleigh Cl REDH RH1 ... 148 D7
Copsleigh Wy REDH RH1 ... 148 D8
Copthall Gdns TWK TW1 ... 26 D2 (3)
Copthall Wy ADL/WDHM KT15 ... 58 C8
Copt Hill La
  KWD/TDW/WH KT20 ... 105 H2
Copthorne Av BAL SW12 ... 31 G2
  HAYES BR2 ... 71 J1
Copthorne Bank CRAWE RH10... 193 L6
  HORL RH6 ... 193 M3
Copthorne Cl SHPTN TW17 ... 41 M6 (2)
Copthorne Common Rd
  CRAWE RH10 ... 193 M1
Copthorne Dr LTWR GU18 ... 54 E8
Copthorne Ri PUR/KEN CR8 ... 88 A3
Copthorne Rd CRAWE RH10 ... 194 E5
  CRAWE RH10 ... 213 G1
  EGRIN RH19 ... 195 H5
  LHD/OX KT22 ... 102 E2
Copthorne Wy CRAWE RH10... 193 J7
Copyhold Rd EGRIN RH19 ... 216 A1
Corban Rd HSLW TW3 ... 16 D5
Corbet Cl MTCM CR4 ... 48 D8
Corbet Rd EW KT17 ... 64 B8
Corbett Cl CROY/NA CR0 ... 90 A2
Corbett Dr LTWR GU18 ... 74 C2
Corby Cl EGH TW20 ... 20 F7
Corby Dr EGH TW20 ... 20 F7
Cordelia Cft BNFD RG42 ... 35 H1 (2)
Cordelia Gdns ASHV GU12 ... 113 J1 (1)
  STWL/WRAY TW19 ... 23 H1
Cordelia Rd STWL/WRAY TW19... 23 H1
Corderoy Pl CHERT KT16 ... 40 B6
Cordrey Gdns COUL/CHIP CR5 ... 87 H5
Cordwalles Rd CBLY GU15 ... 73 J1
Corfe Cl ASHTD KT21 ... 82 F8
Corfe Gdns FRIM GU16 ... 73 J8
Corfe Wy FARN GU14 ... 93 H8
Coriander Crs GUW GU2 ... 116 D3
Corkran Rd SURB KT6 ... 45 G7
Corkscrew Hl WWKM BR4 ... 69 M1
Cormongers La REDH RH1 ... 127 G7
Cormorant Pl SHST GU47 ... 72 B1
Cornbunting Cl SHST GU47 ... 72 A1 (2)
Cornelia Cl FARN GU14 ... 92 A6 (1)
Corner Farm Cl
  KWD/TDW/WH KT20 ... 104 F4
Cornerside ASHF TW15 ... 23 M8 (2)
Corney Reach Wy CHSWK W4 ... 19 H2
Corney Rd CHSWK W4 ... 19 H1
Cornfield Rd REIG RH2 ... 147 M1
Cornfields RGODL GU7 ... 160 C1 (1)
Cornflower La CROY/NA CR0 ... 51 G8
Cornford Gv BAL SW12 ... 30 E3
Cornhill Cl ADL/WDHM KT15 ... 58 E1
Cornish Gv PGE/AN SE20 ... 50 E1
Cornwall Av BF/WBF KT14 ... 79 J4
  ESH/CLAY KT10 ... 62 C6
Cornwall Cl CBLY GU15 ... 73 J2
Cornwall Gdns EGRIN RH19 ... 216 C1 (1)
Cornwallis Cl CTHM CR3 ... 107 M4
Cornwall Rd BELMT SM2 ... 65 J6
  CROY/NA CR0 ... 4 A5
  TWK TW1 ... 26 D2 (3)
Cornwall Wy STA TW18 ... 22 B7
Coronation Rd ALDT GU11 ... 134 C2
  ASC SL5 ... 36 D8
  EGRIN RH19 ... 216 B2
The Coronet HORL RH6 ... 170 F8 (1)

Corporation Av HSLWW TW4 ... 16 B6
Corrib Dr SUT SM1 ... 66 B4 (1)
Corrie Gdns VW GU25 ... 38 F7
Corrie Rd ADL/WDHM KT15 ... 59 G3
  WOKS/MYFD GU22 ... 97 L2
Corrigan Av COUL/CHIP CR5 ... 86 D5
Corry Rd GSHT GU26 ... 198 F3
Corsair Cl STWL/WRAY TW19 ... 23 G1
Corsair Rd STWL/WRAY TW19 ... 23 H1
Corscombe Cl KUTN/CMB KT2 ... 27 M6
Corsehill St STRHM/NOR SW16... 30 F7
Corsletts Av HORS RH12 ... 228 A6
Cortis Rd PUT/ROE SW15 ... 19 L8
Cortis Ter PUT/ROE SW15 ... 19 L8
Corunna Dr SWTR RH13 ... 229 J7
Cosdach Av WLGTN SM6 ... 67 G6
Cosedge Crs CROY/NA CR0 ... 67 K4
Cosford Rd MFD/CHID GU8 ... 180 B5
Coteford St TOOT SW17 ... 30 C5
Cotelands CROY/NA CR0 ... 5 J6
Cotford Rd THHTH CR7 ... 49 M4
Cotherstone EW/WEW KT19 ... 64 A7 (1)
Cotherstone Rd
  BRXS/STRHM SW2 ... 31 J2
Cotland Acres REDH RH1 ... 148 B2
  REDH RH1 ... 148 A2 (1)
Cotsford Av NWMAL KT3 ... 45 M5
Cotswold Cl CRAWW RH11 ... 211 L3
  ESH/CLAY KT10 ... 62 C1
  FARN GU14 ... 92 B2
  KUTN/CMB KT2 ... 3 M1
  STA TW18 ... 22 D6
Cotswold Rd BELMT SM2 ... 65 L8
  HPTN TW12 ... 25 K7
Cotswold St WNWD SE27 ... 31 L5
Cotswold Wy WPK KT4 ... 64 F1
Cottage Farm Wy EGH TW20 ... 39 M3
Cottage Gdns FARN GU14 ... 92 C5
Cottage Gv SURB KT6 ... 45 G6
Cottage Pl CRAWE RH10 ... 194 B6
Cottenham Dr RYNPK SW20 ... 28 E8
Cottenham Park Rd
  RYNPK SW20 ... 46 D1
Cottenham Pl RYNPK SW20 ... 28 E8
Cottenhams LING RH7 ... 173 H1
Cotterill Rd SURB KT6 ... 63 J1
Cottesbrooke Cl DTCH/LGLY SL3 ... 13 G3
Cottesloe Cl CHOB/PIR GU24 ... 75 J6
Cottesmore BRAK RG12 ... 34 D7
Cottimore Av WOT/HER KT12 ... 42 E8
Cottimore Crs WOT/HER KT12 ... 42 E7
Cottimore La WOT/HER KT12 ... 42 F8 (1)
Cottimore Ter WOT/HER KT12 ... 42 E7 (1)
Cottingham Av HORS RH12 ... 229 G2
Cottingham Rd PGE/AN SE20... 33 G8
Cottington Rd FELT TW13 ... 25 G5
Cottongrass Cl CROY/NA CR0 ... 51 G8 (1)
Cotton Rw RDKG RH5 ... 186 F1
Cotts Wood Dr RGUE GU4 ... 117 K3
Couchmore Av ESH/CLAY KT10... 62 B1
Coulsdon Court Rd
  COUL/CHIP CR5 ... 87 J6
Coulsdon La COUL/CHIP CR5 ... 106 D1
Coulsdon Pl CTHM CR3 ... 108 A4 (2)
Coulsdon Ri COUL/CHIP CR5 ... 87 H7
Coulsdon Rd COUL/CHIP CR5 ... 87 J6
  CTHM CR3 ... 107 M3
Countisbury Gdns
  ADL/WDHM KT15 ... 58 E4
Country Wy FELT TW13 ... 24 F6
County Oak La CRAWW RH11 ... 192 A6
County Oak Wy CRAWW RH11... 192 A7
County Rd THHTH CR7 ... 49 L7
Course Rd ASC SL5 ... 36 D3
Courland Rd ADL/WDHM KT15... 58 E2
Court Av COUL/CHIP CR5 ... 87 K8
Court Bushes Rd CTHM CR3 ... 108 D1
Court Cl EGRIN RH19 ... 196 C6
  FELT TW13 ... 25 L4
Court Close Av FELT TW13 ... 25 L4
Court Crs CHSGTN KT9 ... 63 G5
  EGRIN RH19 ... 196 D8
Court Downs Rd BECK BR3 ... 51 L2
Court Dr CROY/NA CR0 ... 67 J3
  SUT SM1 ... 66 B3
Courtenay Av BELMT SM2 ... 65 J8
Courtenay Ms WOKN/KNAP GU21 ... 7 G3
Courtenay Rd FNM GU9 ... 134 B3
  PGE/AN SE20 ... 33 G7 (1)
  WOKN/KNAP GU21 ... 7 G3
  WPK KT4 ... 64 F2
Court Farm Av HOR/WEW KT19... 64 A4
Court Farm Rd WARL CR6 ... 88 D8
Courtfield Ri WWKM BR4 ... 70 A2
Courtfield Rd ASHF TW15 ... 23 L7
Court Gdns CBLY GU15 ... 73 G4
Court Haw BNSTD SM7 ... 86 B5
Court Hl COUL/CHIP CR5 ... 86 B8
  SAND/SEL CR2 ... 88 B8
Courthope Rd WIM/MER SW19... 29 H6
Courthope Vis WIM/MER SW19... 29 H6 (1)
Courtland Av
  STRHM/NOR SW16 ... 31 J8 (1)
Courtlands RCHPK/HAM TW10... 18 D7
Courtlands Av ESH/CLAY KT10 ... 61 J5
  HPTN TW12 ... 25 J7
  RCH/KEW TW9 ... 18 E4 (1)
Courtlands Cl SAND/SEL CR2 ... 68 C3
Courtlands Crs BNSTD SM7 ... 85 K6
Courtlands Dr HOR/WEW KT19... 64 B5
Courtlands Rd SURB KT6 ... 45 K7
Court Lane Gdns DUL SE21 ... 32 B1
Court Lodge Rd HORL RH6 ... 170 B5
Courtleas COB KT11 ... 81 K3
Court Rd ALDT GU11 ... 112 D7 (1)
  BNSTD SM7 ... 85 K5
  CTHM CR3 ... 108 A5

  GDST RH9 ... 128 F5
  SNWD SE25 ... 50 C2
Courts Hill Rd HASM GU27 ... 219 L3
Courts Mount Rd HASM GU27 ... 219 L3
The Courts STRHM/NOR SW16 ... 31 H8
The Court WARL CR6 ... 89 H8
Court Wy WHTN TW2 ... 26 C1
Court Wood La CROY/NA CR0 ... 69 J8
  EGRIN RH19 ... 196 E8
Coutts Av CHSGTN KT9 ... 63 H4
Coval Gdns MORT/ESHN SW14 ... 18 E6
Coval La MORT/ESHN SW14 ... 18 E6
Coval Rd MORT/ESHN SW14 ... 18 F6
Coveham Crs COB KT11 ... 80 D3
Coventry Rd SNWD SE25 ... 50 D4
Coverack Cl CROY/NA CR0 ... 51 H7
Coverdale Gdns CROY/NA CR0 ... 5 J7
Cove Rd FARN GU14 ... 92 C5
Covert Cl CRAWE RH10 ... 212 B2
Covert La BRAK RG12 ... 34 F4
Coverton Rd TOOT SW17 ... 30 B5
Coverts Cl FNM GU9 ... 134 B5
Coverts Rd ESH/CLAY KT10 ... 62 C6
The Covert ASC SL5 ... 36 E7
  FARN GU14 ... 92 B1
Covey Cl FARN GU14 ... 92 D1
  WIM/MER SW19 ... 47 L2
The Covey CRAWE RH10 ... 213 G1
Covington Gdns
  STRHM/NOR SW16 ... 31 L8
Covington Wy
  STRHM/NOR SW16 ... 31 L8
Cowden St CAT SE6 ... 33 K5
Cowdray Cl CRAWE RH10 ... 212 F4
Cowdrey Rd WIM/MER SW19 ... 29 L7
Cowfold Cl CRAWW RH11 ... 211 J6
Cowick Rd TOOT SW17 ... 30 C5
Cow La RGODL GU7 ... 160 B3
Cowleaze Rd KUTN/CMB KT2 ... 2 F5
Cowley Av CHERT KT16 ... 40 C7
Cowley Cl SAND/SEL CR2 ... 68 F7
Cowley Crs WOT/HER KT12 ... 60 F3
Cowley La CHERT KT16 ... 40 C7
Cowley Rd MORT/ESHN SW14 ... 19 H5
Coworth Cl ASC SL5 ... 37 L5
Coworth Rd ASC SL5 ... 37 K5
Cowper Av SUT SM1 ... 66 A3
Cowper Cl CHERT KT16 ... 40 C5
Cowper Gdns WLGTN SM6 ... 66 F5
Cowper Rd RCHPK/HAM TW10 ... 27 J6
  WIM/MER SW19 ... 29 M7
Cowshot Crs CHOB/PIR GU24 ... 95 G2
Cowslip La RDKG RH5 ... 122 D2
Coxbridge Mdw FNM GU9 ... 10 B1
Coxcombe La MFD/CHID GU8 ... 201 L5
Coxdean KWD/TDW/WH KT20 ... 104 F1
Coxgreen SHST GU47 ... 72 A3
Cox Green Rd HORS RH12 ... 205 L7
Cox La CHSGTN KT9 ... 63 J3
  HOR/WEW KT19 ... 63 L4
Coxley Ri PUR/KEN CR8 ... 87 M3
Coxs Av SHPTN TW17 ... 42 B3
Coxwell Rd NRWD SE19 ... 32 B8
Crabbet Rd CRAWE RH10 ... 212 E2
Crabbs Croft Cl ORP BR6 ... 71 M4
Crab Hill La REDH RH1 ... 149 J4
Crabtree Cl GT/LBKH KT23 ... 101 M8
Crabtree Dr LHD/OX KT22 ... 102 F6
Crabtree La GT/LBKH KT23 ... 101 M8
  LHD/OX KT22 ... 103 M8
  NFNM GU10 ... 178 D7
  RDKG RH5 ... 122 C4
Crabtree Rd CBLY GU15 ... 72 E7
  CRAWW RH11 ... 211 M2
  EGH TW20 ... 39 M2
Craddocks Av ASHTD KT21 ... 83 J6
Cradhurst Cl DORK RH4 ... 143 M3
Craigans CRAWW RH11 ... 211 K3
Craigen Av CROY/NA CR0 ... 50 E8
Craignair Rd BRXS/STRHM SW2... 31 J1
Craignish Av STRHM/NOR SW16... 49 J2
Craig Rd RCHPK/HAM TW10 ... 26 F5
Craigwell Av FELT TW13 ... 24 D4
Craigwell Cl STA TW18 ... 40 B1
Crakell Rd REIG RH2 ... 147 M1
Crake Pl SHST GU47 ... 72 A1
Cramhurst La MFD/CHID GU8 ... 181 H3
Crampshaw La ASHTD KT21 ... 103 J2
Crampton Rd PGE/AN SE20 ... 32 F7
Cranborne Av SURB KT6 ... 63 L1
Cranborne Wk CRAWE RH10 ... 212 C5
Cranbourne Cl HORL RH6 ... 170 E4
  STRHM/NOR SW16 ... 49 H3
Cranbrook Dr ESH/CLAY KT10... 43 L2
  WHTN TW2 ... 25 L2
Cranbrook Rd HSLWW TW4 ... 16 C6
  THHTH CR7 ... 49 M2
  WIM/MER SW19 ... 29 H8
Crane Av ISLW TW7 ... 17 K7
Cranebrook WHTN TW2 ... 25 M3
Crane Ct SHST GU47 ... 72 A1
Craneford Cl WHTN TW2 ... 26 C1
Craneford Wy WHTN TW2 ... 26 B1
Crane Lodge Rd HEST TW5 ... 15 L1
Crane Park Rd WHTN TW2 ... 25 L3
Crane Rd STWL/WRAY TW19 ... 14 D3
  WHTN TW2 ... 26 B2
Cranes Dr BRYLDS KT5 ... 45 H4
Cranes Pk BRYLDS KT5 ... 45 H4
Cranes Park Av SURB KT6 ... 45 H4
Cranes Park Crs BRYLDS KT5 ... 45 J4
Craneswater HYS/HAR UB3 ... 15 G2
Crane Wy WHTN TW2 ... 25 M1
Cranfield Rd East CAR SM5 ... 66 D7
Cranfield Rd West CAR SM5 ... 66 C7 (1)
Cranford Av STWL/WRAY TW19... 23 H1
Cranford Cl PUR/KEN CR8 ... 87 M3 (1)
  RYNPK SW20 ... 46 E1
  STWL/WRAY TW19 ... 23 H1
Cranford La HEST TW5 ... 15 J5
  HTHAIR TW6 ... 15 J3
  HYS/HAR UB3 ... 15 G2
Cranford Ri ESH/CLAY KT10 ... 61 M4
Cranleigh Cl PGE/AN SE20 ... 50 E2
  SAND/SEL CR2 ... 88 D2
Cranleigh Ct FARN GU14 ... 92 C5 (1)
Cranleigh Gdns KUTN/CMB KT2... 27 J7

SAND/SEL CR2 .... 88 D2
SNWD SE25 .... 50 B3 🔢
SUT SM1 .... 65 L1
Cranleigh Md *CRAN* GU6 .... 185 J7 🔢
Cranleigh Rd *CRAN* GU6 .... 186 A5
ESH/CLAY KT10 .... 43 M8
FELT TW13 .... 24 C5
SHGR GU5 .... 161 M2
WIM/MER SW19 .... 47 K3
Cranley Cl *GU* GU1 .... 117 K8
Cranley Gdns *WLGTN* SM6 .... 66 F6
Cranley Rd *GU* GU1 .... 9 M4
WOT/HER KT12 .... 60 C5
Cranmer Cl *MRDN* SM4 .... 47 G6
WARL CR6 .... 89 H7
WEY KT13 .... 59 K6
Cranmer Ct *HPTN* TW12 .... 25 L6
Cranmer Farm Cl *MTCM* CR4 .. 48 C4 🔢
Cranmer Gdns *WARL* CR6 .... 89 H7
Cranmer Rd *CROY/NA* CR0 .... 4 B7
HPTN TW12 .... 25 L6
KUTN/CMB KT2 .... 27 H6
MTCM CR4 .... 48 C4
Cranmer Ter *TOOT* SW17 .... 30 A6
Cranmore Cl *ALDT* GU11 .... 112 B8
Cranmore Gdns *ALDT* GU11 .... 112 B8
Cranmore La *ALDT* GU11 .... 112 B8
EHSLY KT24 .... 119 L3
Cranmore Rd *FRIM* GU16 .... 93 J5
Cranston Cl *HSLW* TW3 .... 16 B4
REIG RH2 .... 147 L1
Cranston Rd *EGRIN* RH19 .... 196 B7
FSTH SE23 .... 33 H2
Cranstoun Cl *RGUW* GU3 .... 116 C4
Crantock Rd *CAT* SE6 .... 33 M3
Cranwell Gv *LTWR* GU18 .... 74 C1
SHPTN TW17 .... 41 J4
Craster Rd *BRXS/STRHM* SW2 .... 31 J1
Cravan Av *FELT* TW13 .... 24 D3
Craven Cl *NFNM* GU10 .... 11 H7
Craven Gdns *WIM/MER* SW19 .... 29 L6
Craven Rd *CRAWE* RH10 .... 212 E4
CROY/NA CR0 .... 50 E8
KUTN/CMB KT2 .... 3 G4
The Cravens *HORL* RH6 .... 171 K6
Crawford Cl *ISLW* TW7 .... 17 H4
Crawford Gdns *CBLY* GU15 .... 72 E4
SWTR RH13 .... 229 H6
Crawford Wy *EGRIN* RH19 .... 196 C6 🔢
CRAWW RH11 .... 211 L6
Crawley Av *CRAWE* RH10 .... 212 B1
Crawley Dr *CBLY* GU15 .... 73 J3
Crawley Hl *CBLY* GU15 .... 73 J4
Crawley La *CRAWE* RH10 .... 212 F2
Crawley Rd *HORS* RH12 .... 229 J5
Crawley Rdg *CBLY* GU15 .... 73 J3
Crawley Wood Cl *CBLY* GU15 .. 73 J4 🔢
Crawshaw Rd *CHERT* KT16 .... 58 A5
Crawters Cl *CRAWE* RH10 .... 212 C2
Cray Av *ASHTD* KT21 .... 83 H6
Crayke Hl *CHSGTN* KT9 .... 63 H6
Credenhill St *STRHM/NOR* SW16 .. 30 F7
Crediton Wy *ESH/CLAY* KT10 .... 62 D4
Credon Cl *FARN* GU14 .... 92 B4
Creek Rd *E/WMO/HCT* KT8 .... 44 B4
The Creek *SUN* TW16 .... 33 J2 🔢
Creeland Gv *CAT* SE6 .... 33 J2
Cree's Meadow *BFOR* GU20 .... 55 G6 🔢
Cremorne Gdns
HOR/WEW KT19 .... 64 A7 🔢
Crerar Cl *FARN* GU14 .... 92 A6
Crescent Gdns *WIM/MER* SW19 .... 29 K4
Crescent Rd *CRNR* CR4 .... 48 B4
Crescent La *ASHV* GU12 .... 113 G1
Crescent Rd *BECK* BR3 .... 51 L2
CTHM CR3 .... 108 D6
EGRIN RH19 .... 196 A8
KUTN/CMB KT2 .... 3 K2
REDH RH1 .... 127 M7
REIG RH2 .... 147 K2
RYNPK SW20 .... 47 G1
SHPTN TW17 .... 41 M5
The Crescent *ASHF* TW15 .... 23 J6
BARN SW13 .... 19 J4
BECK BR3 .... 51 K1
BELMT SM2 .... 85 K1
BRAK RG12 .... 34 F4 🔢
CHERT KT16 .... 40 D3 🔢
CTHM CR3 .... 109 K5
E/WMO/HCT KT8 .... 43 J4
EGH TW20 .... 21 H7
EGRIN RH19 .... 195 M1
EPSOM KT18 .... 83 K4
FARN GU14 .... 92 F6
FNM GU9 .... 134 A1
GUW GU2 .... 8 A1
HORL RH6 .... 170 D8
HORS RH12 .... 228 D7
HYS/HAR UB3 .... 14 F2
LHD/OX KT22 .... 102 E4
NWMAL KT3 .... 45 M2
REIG RH2 .... 125 L8
SHPTN TW17 .... 42 C7
SNWD SE25 .... 50 A6
SURB KT6 .... 45 H5
SUT SM1 .... 66 A4
WEY KT13 .... 59 K2
WIM/MER SW19 .... 29 K4
Crescent Wy *HORL* RH6 .... 170 D8
STRHM/NOR SW16 .... 31 J3
Crescent Wood Rd *DUL* SE21 .. 32 D4
Cressall Cl *LHD/OX* KT22 .... 102 E2
Cressall Md *LHD/OX* KT22 .... 102 E2
Cressingham Gv *SUT* SM1 .... 65 M3
Cresswell Rd *FELT* TW13 .... 25 H4
SNWD SE25 .... 50 D4
TWK TW1 .... 18 A8
Cresta Dr *ADL/WDHM* KT15 .... 58 C8
Crest Hl *SHGR* GU5 .... 142 B8
Creston Av *WOKN/KNAP* GU21 .... 47 G8
Creston Wy *WPK* KT4 .... 47 G8
Crest Rd *SAND/SEL* CR2 .... 68 E6
The Crest *BRYLDS* KT5 .... 45 K5
Crestway *PUT/ROE* SW15 .... 19 K8
Crestwood Wy *HSLWW* TW4 .. 16 C7 🔢
Crewdson Rd *HORL* RH6 .... 170 E6
Crewe's Av *WARL* CR6 .... 88 F6

Crewe's Cl *WARL* CR6 .... 88 F6
Crewe's La *WARL* CR6 .... 89 G6
Crichton Av *WLGTN* SM6 .... 67 G4
Crichton Rd *CAR* SM5 .... 66 C6
Cricket Cl *EGRIN* RH19 .... 196 B6
Cricketers Cl *CHSGTN* KT9 .... 63 G4
RDKG RH5 .... 187 M5
Cricketers La *BFOR* GU20 .... 55 G4
Cricketers Wk *SYD* SE26 .... 32 F6 🔢
Cricket Field Gv *CWTH* RG45 .. 52 A5
Cricket Field Rd *HORS* RH12 .. 228 E8
Cricket Gn *MFD/CHID* GU8 .... 181 M8
MTCM CR4 .... 48 C3
Cricket Hl *REDH* RH1 .... 149 J2
Cricket La *BECK* BR3 .... 33 H7
NFNM GU10 .... 11 K8
Cricket Vw *WEY* KT13 .... 59 L4 🔢
Cricket Wy *WEY* KT13 .... 60 B1
Cricklade Av *BRXS/STRHM* SW2 .. 31 H5
Criffel Av *BRXS/STRHM* SW2 .. 31 G3
Crimea Rd *ALDT* GU11 .... 112 E7 🔢
FRIM GU16 .... 94 A1
Cripley Rd *FARN* GU14 .... 92 B4
Cripplecrutch Hl
MFD/CHID GU8 .... 221 J3
Crispen Rd *FELT* TW13 .... 25 H5
Crispin Crs *WLGTN* SM6 .... 67 G2
Critchmere Hl *HASM* GU27 .... 219 H2
Critchmere La *HASM* GU27 .... 219 H3
Critchmere V *HASM* GU27 .... 219 G3
Critten La *RDKG* RH5 .... 121 G6
Cricket Cl *GSHT* GU26 .... 199 G3
Crocker Cl *ASC* SL5 .... 36 B1
Crockers La *LING* RH7 .... 173 G5
Crockerton Rd *TOOT* SW17 .... 30 C3
Crockford Park Rd
ADL/WDHM KT15 .... 58 F3 🔢
Crockford Park Rd
ADL/WDHM KT15 .... 58 F4
Crockham Cl *CRAWW* RH11 .. 211 M5 🔢
Crocknorth Rd *EHSLY* KT24 .... 120 C6
Crocus Cl *CROY/NA* CR0 .... 51 G8 🔢
Croffets *KWD/TDW/WH* KT20 .... 105 G3
Croft Av *DORK* RH4 .... 122 E8
WWKM BR4 .... 51 M8
Croft Cl *HYS/HAR* UB3 .... 14 F2
Croft Cl *EDEN* TN8 .... 153 M8
Crofters Cl *ISLW* TW7 .... 17 G7
Croft La *EDEN* TN8 .... 153 M8
NFNM GU10 .... 132 B4
Croftleigh Av *PUR/KEN* CR8 .... 87 K6
Crofton *ASHTD* KT21 .... 83 H8
Crofton Av *CHSWK* W4 .... 18 F2
ORP BR6 .... 71 M1
WOT/HER KT12 .... 60 F2
Crofton Cl *BRAK* RG12 .... 35 H5
CHERT KT16 .... 57 M6
Crofton Rd *ORP* BR6 .... 71 K2
Croft Rd *ALDT* GU11 .... 134 E1
BH/WHM TN16 .... 111 L8
CTHM CR3 .... 109 J4
MFD/CHID GU8 .... 181 H4
RGODL GU7 .... 160 A5
STRHM/NOR SW16 .... 31 K8
SUT SM1 .... 66 A4
WIM/MER SW19 .... 29 M8
Crofts Cl *MFD/CHID* GU8 .... 201 L4 🔢
The Crofts *SHPTN* TW17 .... 42 B4
The Croft *CRAWW* RH11 .... 211 K3
HEST TW5 .... 16 B2
Croft Wy *FRIM* GU16 .... 73 J8
HORS RH12 .... 228 D6
RCHPK/HAM TW10 .... 26 K4
Croham Cl *SAND/SEL* CR2 .... 68 B5 🔢
Croham Manor Rd
SAND/SEL CR2 .... 68 B6
Croham Mt *SAND/SEL* CR2 .... 68 B6
Croham Park Av *SAND/SEL* CR2... 68 C4
Croham Rd *SAND/SEL* CR2 .... 68 A4
Croham Valley Rd
SAND/SEL CR2 .... 68 D5
Croindene Rd
STRHM/NOR SW16 .... 49 H1
Cromer Rd *HTHAIR* TW6 .... 14 D5
SNWD SE25 .... 50 E3
TOOT SW17 .... 30 D7
Cromford Wy *NWMAL* KT3 .... 46 A1
Crompton Flds *CRAWE* RH10 .. 192 B8
Crompton Wy *CRAWE* RH10 .. 212 B1
Cromwell Av *NWMAL* KT3 .... 46 C5
Cromwell Cl *WOT/HER* KT12 .. 42 E8
Cromwell Gv *CTHM* CR3 .... 107 M3
Cromwell Pl *CRAN* GU6 .... 185 J8
EGRIN RH19 .... 216 C2 🔢
MORT/ESHN SW14 .... 18 F5 🔢
Cromwell Rd *ASC* SL5 .... 36 E4
BECK BR3 .... 51 H2
CBLY GU15 .... 73 G2
CROY/NA CR0 .... 4 D1
CTHM CR3 .... 107 M3
FELT TW13 .... 24 E2
HSLW TW3 .... 16 D6
KUT KT1 .... 2 F5
KUTN/CMB KT2 .... 3 G5 🔢
REDH RH1 .... 126 C8 🔢
TEDD TW11 .... 26 D7
WIM/MER SW19 .... 29 K6
WPK KT4 .... 64 A2
Cromwell St *HSLW* TW3 .... 16 D6
Cromwell Wy *FARN* GU14 .... 92 E2 🔢
Crondall Cl *CBLY* GU15 .... 72 E5 🔢
Crondall La *NFNM* GU10 .... 132 F7
Crondall Rd *NFNM* GU10 .... 154 D2
Cronks Hl *REIG* RH2 .... 147 M1
Cronks Hill Cl *REDH* RH1 .... 148 A2 🔢
Cronks Hill Rd *REIG* RH2 .... 148 A3
Crooksbury Rd *NFNM* GU10 .. 134 L6
Crosby Cl *FELT* TW13 .... 25 H5 🔢
Crosby Hill Dr *CBLY* GU15 .... 73 J2
Crosby Wy *FNM* GU9 .... 10 D1
Crossacres *WOKS/MYFD* GU22... 78 B6
Cross Deep *TWK* TW1 .... 26 C4
Cross Deep Gdns *TWK* TW1 .. 26 C3
Crossfell Rd *BRAK* RG12 .... 34 D4
Crossfield Pl *WEY* KT13 .... 59 L6
Cross Gdns *FRIM* GU16 .... 93 J3
Cross Gates Cl *BRAK* RG12 .... 35 J3

Cross Keys *CRAWW* RH11 .... 212 A3
Cross Lances Rd *HSLW* TW3 .. 16 E6
Crossland Rd *REDH* RH1 .... 126 D8
THHTH CR7 .... 49 L6
Crosslands *CHERT* KT16 .... 58 B2
Crosslands Rd *HOR/WEW* KT19 .. 64 C5
Cross La *CHERT* KT16 .... 57 L5
FRIM GU16 .... 93 J3
HORL RH6 .... 193 M1
Cross Lanes *GU* GU1 .... 9 M6
Crossley Cl *BH/WHM* TN16 .... 91 G5
Cross Oak La *REDH* RH1 .... 170 F2
Cross Rd *ASC* SL5 .... 37 J8
ASHV GU12 .... 113 L6
BELMT SM2 .... 65 K8
CROY/NA CR0 .... 4 F3
FARN GU14 .... 92 B8
FELT TW13 .... 25 H5
HAYES BR2 .... 71 H1
KUTN/CMB KT2 .... 3 H3
KWD/TDW/WH KT20 .... 104 F4
RDKG RH5 .... 190 A1
SUT SM1 .... 66 A4
WEY KT13 .... 60 A2 🔢
WIM/MER SW19 .... 29 K8
The Crossroads *EHSLY* KT24 .. 121 G2 🔢
Cross St *BARN* SW13 .... 19 H4
FARN GU14 .... 112 F1
WIM/MER SW19 .... 25 M6
Crosswater La *NFNM* GU10 .... 178 B5
Crossway *NWMAL* KT3 .... 46 F4
WOT/HER KT12 .... 60 E1
Crossways *ASHV* GU12 .... 112 F8
BELMT SM2 .... 66 A7
BH/WHM TN16 .... 110 F2
CRAWE RH10 .... 212 D2
EGH TW20 .... 22 A7
EHSLY KT24 .... 121 G1 🔢
NFNM GU10 .... 178 B8
SAND/SEL CR2 .... 69 J6
SUN TW16 .... 42 C1
Crossways Av *EGRIN* RH19 .... 195 M8
Crossways Cl *CRAWE* RH10 .. 212 C2
Crossways La *REIG* RH2 .... 125 M2
Crossways Rd *BECK* BR3 .... 51 K4
MTCM CR4 .... 48 E3
The Crossways *COUL/CHIP* CR5 .. 107 J1
HEST TW5 .... 16 C2
REDH RH1 .... 126 E3
Crosswell Cl *SHPTN* TW17 .... 41 M2 🔢
Crouch Cl *BECK* BR3 .... 33 K7 🔢
Crouch House Rd *EDEN* TN8 .... 153 K6
Crouchmans Cl *DUL* SE21 .... 32 C4
Crouch Oak La *ADL/WDHM* KT15 .. 58 F3
Crowberry Cl *CRAWW* RH11 .. 211 K7 🔢
Crowborough Cl *WARL* CR6 .... 89 H8
Crowborough Dr *WARL* CR6 .... 89 H8
Crowborough Rd *TOOT* SW17 .. 30 D6
Crowhurst *CRAWE* RH10 .... 213 H5
Crowhurst La *LING* RH7 .... 152 A4
Crowhurst Md *GDST* RH9 .... 128 F4
Crowhurst Rd *LING* RH7 .... 174 A3
Crowhurst Village Rd *LING* RH7 .. 152 B7
Crowland Rd *THHTH* CR7 .... 50 A4
Crowland Wk *MRDN* SM4 .... 47 L6
Crowley Crs *CROY/NA* CR0 .... 67 K4
Crown Cl *DTCH/LGLY* SL3 .... 12 F2
WOT/HER KT12 .... 42 F7
Crown Dl *NRWD* SE19 .... 31 M7
Crown Dr *FNM* GU9 .... 134 D4
Crown Hts *GU* GU1 .... 139 H3
Crown Hill Ct *ASC* SL5 .... 36 E5
Crown La *FNM* GU9 .... 134 D4
MRDN SM4 .... 47 K3
STRHM/NOR SW16 .... 31 K6
VW GU25 .... 39 G6
WIM/MER SW19 .... 47 K3
Crown Meadow *DTCH/LGLY* SL3 .. 12 E2
Crownpits La *RGODL* GU7 .... 160 B6
Crown Pl *SHST* GU47 .... 52 B8 🔢
Crown Ri *CHERT* KT16 .... 40 C8
Crown Rd *NWMAL* KT3 .... 45 M1
SUT SM1 .... 65 L3 🔢
TWK TW1 .... 17 L8
VW GU25 .... 38 F6
WIM/MER SW19 .... 47 K4
Crown Rw *BRAK* RG12 .... 35 G6
Crown St *EGH* TW20 .... 21 K6
Crown Ter *RCH/KEW* TW9 .... 18 C6 🔢
Crowntree Cl *ISLW* TW7 .... 17 J1
Crown Yd *HSLW* TW3 .... 16 F5 🔢
Crowther Rd *SNWD* SE25 .... 50 D4
Crowthorne Cl
WAND/EARL SW18 .... 29 J1
Crowthorne Rd *BRAK* RG12 .... 34 D4
Crowthorne Rd North
BRAK RG12 .... 34 E3
Croxden Wk *MRDN* SM4 .... 47 M6 🔢
Croxted Cl *DUL* SE21 .... 31 M1
Croxted Rd *DUL* SE21 .... 32 A3 🔢
Croyde Cl *FARN* GU14 .... 92 D3
Croydonbarn La *GDST* RH9 .. 172 C5
The Croydon F/O *CROY/NA* CR0 .. 4 C3
Croydon Gv *CROY/NA* CR0 .... 4 A3
Croydon La *BNSTD* SM7 .... 86 A3
Croydon La South *BNSTD* SM7 .. 85 L4
Croydon Rd *BECK* BR3 .... 51 H3
BH/WHM TN16 .... 111 L8
CROY/NA CR0 .... 51 G5
CROY/NA CR0 .... 67 H3
CTHM CR3 .... 108 D4
MTCM CR4 .... 48 E5
PGE/AN SE20 .... 50 E2
REIG RH2 .... 125 M8
WARL CR6 .... 110 A4
WLGTN SM6 .... 67 G2
WWKM BR4 .... 70 B2
Croylands Dr *SURB* KT6 .... 45 H7
Croysdale Av *SUN* TW16 .... 42 D3
Crozier Dr *SAND/SEL* CR2 .... 68 E8
Cruikshank Lea *SHST* GU47 .. 72 B3
Crunden Rd *SAND/SEL* CR2 .. 68 A6
Crusader Gdns *CROY/NA* CR0 .. 3 J7
Crusoe Rd *MTCM* CR4 .... 30 C8
Crutchfield La *HORL* RH6 .... 169 K3
WOT/HER KT12 .... 42 E8
Crystal Palace *NRWD* SE19 .... 32 D7
Crystal Palace Pde *NRWD* SE19 .. 32 C7

Crystal Palace Park Rd
NRWD SE19 .... 32 D6
Crystal Palace Rd *SNWD* SE19 .... 32 A7
Cubitt St *CROY/NA* CR0 .... 67 J4
Cubitt Wy *WOKN/KNAP* GU21 .. 76 A8 🔢
Cuckfield Cl *CRAWW* RH11 .... 211 J5
Cuckmere Crs *CRAWW* RH11 .. 211 J4
Cuckoo La *CHOB/PIR* GU24 .... 75 C3
Cuckoo V *CHOB/PIR* GU24 .... 75 C3
Cuda's Cl *HOR/WEW* KT19 .... 64 C3
Cuddington Av *WPK* KT4 .... 64 C2
Cuddington Cl
KWD/TDW/WH KT20 .... 104 F2
Cuddington Gld *HOR/WEW* KT19 .. 83 K2
Cuddington Park Cl *BNSTD* SM7 .. 85 G2
Cuddington Wy *BELMT* SM2 .. 85 C2
Cudham Cl *BELMT* SM2 .... 65 K8 🔢
Cudham Dr *CROY/NA* CR0 .... 69 L8
Cudham La North *RSEV* TN14 .. 91 M4
Cudham La South *RSEV* TN14 .. 91 M5
Cudham Rd *BH/WHM* TN16 .... 111 H1
ORP BR6 .... 91 K1
Cudham St *CAT* SE6 .... 33 M1
Cudworth Rd *RDKG* RH5 .... 190 A1
Cuffs Hl *CRAWE* RH10 .... 213 H7
Cullerne Cl *EW* KT17 .... 64 C8
Cullesden Rd *PUR/KEN* CR8 .. 87 L5
Cull's Rd *RGUW* GU3 .... 114 E8
Culmer La *MFD/CHID* GU8 .... 181 J6
Culmington Rd *SAND/SEL* CR2 .. 67 M6
Culsac Rd *SURB* KT6 .... 63 H1
Culverden Rd *BAL* SW12 .... 30 F4
Culver Dr *OXTED* RH8 .... 130 B4
Culverhay *ASHTD* KT21 .... 83 H6
Culverhouse Gdns
STRHM/NOR SW16 .... 31 J5
Culverlands Crs *ASHV* GU12 .. 113 J6
Culverley Rd *CAT* SE6 .... 33 L2
Culver Rd *SHST* GU47 .... 52 A8
Culvers Av *CAR* SM5 .... 66 C1
Culvers Retreat *CAR* SM5 .... 48 C8
Culvers Wy *CAR* SM5 .... 66 C1
Cumberland Av *GUW* GU2 .... 116 D3
Cumberland Cl *HOR/WEW* KT19 .. 64 B8
RYNPK SW20 .... 29 G8 🔢
TWK TW1 .... 17 L8 🔢
Cumberland Dr *BRAK* RG12 .. 35 H1 🔢
CHSGTN KT9 .... 63 H2
ESH/CLAY KT10 .... 62 D1
Cumberland Pl *SUN* TW16 .... 42 D4
BARN SW13 .... 19 J3
CBLY GU15 .... 73 M5
RCH/KEW TW9 .... 18 D3
SNWD SE25 .... 50 E6
Cumberlands *PUR/KEN* CR8 .... 88 A1
Cumberland St *STA* TW18 .... 22 A6 🔢
Cumberlow Av *SNWD* SE25 .. 50 D3
Cumbernauld Gdns
SUN TW16 .... 24 C6 🔢
Cumbrae Gdns *SURB* KT6 .... 45 G8 🔢
Cumbria Ct *FARN* GU14 .... 93 H8
Cumnor Gdns *EW* KT17 .... 64 D5
Cumnor Ri *PUR/KEN* CR8 .... 87 M7 🔢
Cumnor Rd *BELMT* SM2 .... 65 M5
Cumnor Wy *BRAK* RG12 .... 35 H1
Cunliffe Cl *EPSOM* KT18 .... 103 L6
Cunliffe Rd *HOR/WEW* KT19 .. 64 C3
Cunliffe St *STRHM/NOR* SW16 .. 30 F7
Cunningham Av *GU* GU1 .... 117 K7
Cunningham Cl *WWKM* BR4 .. 69 L1 🔢
Cunningham Rd *BNSTD* SM7 .. 86 A5
Cunnington Rd *FARN* GU14 .. 93 H8
Curfew Bell Rd *CHERT* KT16 .. 40 C7
Curlew Cl *SAND/SEL* CR2 .... 89 C1
Curlew Gdns *RGUE* GU4 .... 118 A6
Curley Hill Rd *LTWR* GU18 .... 74 B2
Curling Cl *COUL/CHIP* CR5 .... 107 J2
Curling V *GUW* GU2 .... 8 A8
Curly Bridge Cl *FARN* GU14 .... 92 C1
Curnick's La *WNWD* SE27 .... 31 M5 🔢
Curran Av *WLGTN* SM6 .... 66 D2
Currie Hill Cl *WIM/MER* SW19 .. 29 J5
Curtis Cl *CBLY* GU15 .... 73 M2 🔢
Curtis Field Rd
STRHM/NOR SW16 .... 31 J5
Curtis Rd *DORK* RH4 .... 144 C1
HOR/WEW KT19 .... 63 M3
HSLWW TW4 .... 25 J1
Curvan Cl *EW* KT17 .... 64 C8 🔢
Curzon Av *HORS* RH12 .... 228 E7
Curzon Br *CHOB/PIR* GU24 .... 94 D4
Curzon Cl *WEY* KT13 .... 59 K3 🔢
Curzon Rd *THHTH* CR7 .... 49 K6
WEY KT13 .... 59 K3
Cusack Cl *TWK* TW1 .... 26 C5 🔢
Cuthbert Gdns *SNWD* SE25 .. 50 B3
Cuthbert Rd *ASHV* GU12 .... 113 K3
CROY/NA CR0 .... 4 B6
Cuttinglye La *CRAWE* RH10 .. 194 D3
Cuttinglye Rd *CRAWE* RH10 .. 194 E7
Cutts Rd *ALDT* GU11 .... 113 G2
Cyclamen Cl *HPTN* TW12 .... 25 K7 🔢
Cyclamen Wy
HOR/WEW KT19 .... 63 M4
Cygnet Av *EBED/NFELT* TW14 .. 24 F1
The Cygnets *FELT* TW13 .... 25 H5
STA TW18 .... 22 C6 🔢
Cypress Av *WHTN* TW2 .... 25 M1
Cypress Gv *ASHV* GU12 .... 113 J2
Cypress Rd *GU* GU1 .... 116 F6
SNWD SE25 .... 50 B2
Cypress Wk *EGH* TW20 .... 20 E7
Cypress Wy *EW* KT17 .... 85 G4
GSHT GU26 .... 199 C7
Cyprians Av *CHOB/PIR* GU24... 95 L3
Cyprus Rd *FRIM* GU16 .... 94 A1

D

D'abernon Cl *ESH/CLAY* KT10 .... 61 K3
D'abernon Dr *COB* KT11 .... 81 H6
Dacre Rd *CROY/NA* CR0 .... 49 H7
Dacres Rd *FSTH* SE23 .... 33 G4
Daffodil Cl *CROY/NA* CR0 .... 51 G8 🔢

HPTN TW12 .... 25 K7 🔢
Daffodil Dr *CHOB/PIR* GU24 .. 75 K6 🔢
Dafforne Rd *TOOT* SW17 .... 30 C4
Dagden Rd *RGUE* GU4 .... 139 H6
Dagley La *RGUE* GU4 .... 139 G6
Dagmar Rd *KUTN/CMB* KT2 .. 3 H1
SNWD SE25 .... 50 B4
Dagnall Pk *SNWD* SE25 .... 50 B5
Dagnall Rd *SNWD* SE25 .... 50 B5
Dagnan Rd *BAL* SW12 .... 30 E1
Dahlia Gdns *MTCM* CR4 .... 48 E5
Dahomey Rd *STRHM/NOR* SW16 .. 30 F7
Daimler Wy *WLGTN* SM6 .... 67 H6
Dairy Cl *THHTH* CR7 .... 49 M2 🔢
Dairyfields *CRAWW* RH11 .... 211 K4 🔢
Dairy Gate Rd *FARN* GU14 .... 112 E1
Dairy La *EDEN* TN8 .... 131 L8
Dairymans Wk *RGUE* GU4 .... 117 L3
Daisy Cl *CROY/NA* CR0 .... 51 C8
Dakin Cl *CRAWE* RH10 .... 212 F7 🔢
The Dakins *EGRIN* RH19 .... 216 B1 🔢
Dalcross *BRAK* RG12 .... 35 H6
Dalcross Rd *HEST* TW5 .... 16 B4
Dale Av *HSLWW* TW4 .... 16 B5
Dalebury Rd *TOOT* SW17 .... 30 C3
Dale Cl *ADL/WDHM* KT15 .... 58 E4
ASC SL5 .... 37 K5
HORS RH12 .... 229 J4
NFNM GU10 .... 10 A6
Dalegarth Gdns *PUR/KEN* CR8.. 88 A3
Daleham Av *EGH* TW20 .... 21 K7
Dale Lodge Rd *ASC* SL5 .... 37 K5
Dale Park Av *CAR* SM5 .... 66 C1
Dale Park Rd *NRWD* SE19 .... 49 M1
Dale Rd *FROW* RH18 .... 217 J8
PUR/KEN CR8 .... 87 K2
SUT SM1 .... 65 J3 🔢
WOT/HER KT12 .... 42 C7
Daleside *HOR/WEW* KT19 .... 64 A5
TOOT SW17 .... 30 E6
The Dale *HAYES* BR2 .... 71 G3
Dale Vw *EPSOM* KT18 .... 103 L5
HASM GU27 .... 219 J4 🔢
WOKN/KNAP GU21 .... 76 D8
WPK KT4 .... 64 E3 🔢
Dalewood Gdns *CRAWE* RH10 .. 212 C1
WPK KT4 .... 64 E1 🔢
Dalkeith Rd *DUL* SE21 .... 31 M2
Dallas Rd *CHEAM* SM3 .... 65 H5 🔢
SYD SE26 .... 32 E5
Dallaway Gdns *EGRIN* RH19 .. 196 A8
Dalley Ct *SHST* GU47 .... 52 A7 🔢
Dallington Cl *WOT/HER* KT12 .. 60 F5 🔢
Dalmain Rd *FSTH* SE23 .... 33 G2
Dalmally Rd *CROY/NA* CR0 .... 5 K2
Dalmeny Av *STRHM/NOR* SW16 .. 49 K2
Dalmeny Crs *HSLW* TW3 .... 17 G6 🔢
Dalmeny Rd *CAR* SM5 .... 66 D6
WPK KT4 .... 64 E2
Dalmore Av *ESH/CLAY* KT10 .. 62 C5
Dalmore Rd *DUL* SE21 .... 31 M3
Dalston Cl *CBLY* GU15 .... 74 A6
Dalton Av *MTCM* CR4 .... 48 B2
Dalton Cl *CRAWW* RH11 .... 211 K8
Dalton St *WNWD* SE27 .... 31 L3
Damask Cl *CHOB/PIR* GU24 .. 75 H3 🔢
Danbrook Rd *STRHM/NOR* SW16 .. 49 H1
Danbury Ms *CAR* SM5 .... 66 E3
Dancer Rd *RCH/KEW* TW9 .... 18 D5
Danebury Av *PUT/ROE* SW15 .. 28 C1
Daneby Rd *CAT* SE6 .... 33 M4
Dane Ct *WOKS/MYFD* GU22 .. 78 C5
Danecourt Gdns *CROY/NA* CR0 .. 5 K7
Danehurst Crs *SWTR* RH13 .. 229 J7
Danemere St *PUT/ROE* SW15 .. 19 M5
Danemore La *GDST* RH9 .... 151 H7
Dane Rd *ASHF* TW15 .... 23 M7
WARL CR6 .... 89 G7
WIM/MER SW19 .... 47 M1
Danesbury Rd *FELT* TW13 .... 24 E2
Danes Cl *LHD/OX* KT22 .... 81 M4
Danescourt Crs *SUT* SM1 .... 65 M1
Danesfield *RPLY/SEND* GU23 .. 98 C5
Danesfield Cl *WOT/HER* KT12 .. 60 E2
Danes Hl *WOKS/MYFD* GU22 .... 7 H8
Daneshill Cl *REDH* RH1 .... 126 B7
Daneshill La *REDH* RH1 .... 126 B7
Danesmead *COB* KT11 .... 81 K1 🔢
Danesrood *GU* GU1 .... 9 L5
Danes Wy *LHD/OX* KT22 .... 82 A4
Daneswood Av *CAT* SE6 .... 33 M4
Daneswood Cl *WEY* KT13 .... 59 L4
Danetree Cl *HOR/WEW* KT19 .. 63 M6
Danetree Rd *HOR/WEW* KT19 .. 63 M6
Daniel Cl *HSLWW* TW4 .... 25 J1 🔢
WIM/MER SW19 .... 30 B7 🔢
Daniell Wy *CROY/NA* CR0 .... 49 J8
Daniels La *WARL* CR6 .... 89 J6
Daniel Wy *BNSTD* SM7 .... 85 K4
Danley La *HASM* GU27 .... 218 D6
Danses Cl *RGUE* GU4 .... 118 A6
Danvers Wy *CTHM* CR3 .... 107 M5
Dapdune Rd *GU* GU1 .... 9 G4
Darby Cl *CTHM* CR3 .... 107 M4
Darby Crs *SUN* TW16 .... 42 F2
Darby Gdns *SUN* TW16 .... 42 F2
Darcy Av *WLGTN* SM6 .... 66 F3
Darcy Cl *COUL/CHIP* CR5 .... 107 L1
Darcy Pl *ASHTD* KT21 .... 83 J7
Darcy Rd *ASHTD* KT21 .... 83 J7
CHEAM SM3 .... 65 G2 🔢
ISLW TW7 .... 17 K3 🔢
STRHM/NOR SW16 .... 49 H2
Darell Rd *RCH/KEW* TW9 .... 18 D5
Darenth Wy *HORL* RH6 .... 170 C4
Darfield Rd *GU* GU1 .... 117 K5
Dargate Cl *NRWD* SE19 .... 32 C8 🔢
Dark La *RGUW* GU3 .... 136 E5
Darlaston Rd *WIM/MER* SW19 .. 29 G8
Darleydale *CRAWW* RH11 .... 211 M6
Darleydale Cl *SHST* GU47 .... 52 A7 🔢
Darley Dr *NWMAL* KT3 .... 46 A2
Darley Gdns *MRDN* SM4 .... 47 M6 🔢
Darlington Rd *WNWD* SE27 .. 31 L6
Darmaine Cl *SAND/SEL* CR2 .. 67 M6

Darnley Pk WEY KT13 ...... 59 L2 [2]
Darracott Cl CBLY GU15 ...... 73 L2 [1]
Dart Cl DTCH/LGLY SL3 ...... 12 E1
Dartmouth Av
  WOKN/KNAP GU21 ...... 77 M4
Dartmouth Cl BRAK RG12 ...... 35 H3 [8]
Dartmouth Pl CHSWK W4 ...... 19 H1
  FSTH SE23 ...... 32 E3
Dartmouth Rd SYD SE26 ...... 32 E4
Dartnell Av BF/WBF KT14 ...... 78 F2
Dartnell Cl BF/WBF KT14 ...... 78 E2
Dartnell Ct BF/WBF KT14 ...... 78 F1 [1]
Dartnell Crs BF/WBF KT14 ...... 78 E2
Dartnell Park Rd BF/WBF KT14 ...... 78 E2
Dartnell Pl BF/WBF KT14 ...... 78 E2
Dartnell Rd CROY/NA CR0 ...... 5 J1
Dart Rd FARN GU14 ...... 92 A3
Darvel Rd WOKN/KNAP GU21 ...... 76 D6
Darvills La FNM GU9 ...... 133 M7
Darwin Cl HORS RH12 ...... 229 J5 [2]
Darwin Gv ALDT GU11 ...... 112 F6
Daryngton Dr GU GU1 ...... 117 L8
  BRAK RG12 ...... 35 G1
Dashwood Cl BF/WBF KT14 ...... 78 F2
Dassett Rd WNWD SE27 ...... 31 L6
Datchet Rd CAT SE6 ...... 33 J4
  DTCH/LGLY SL3 ...... 12 C5
Daux Hl HORS RH12 ...... 228 E3
Davenport Cl TEDD TW11 ...... 26 D7 [3]
Davenport Rd BRAK RG12 ...... 35 H1
Daventry Cl DTCH/LGLY SL3 ...... 13 J3
Daventry Ct BNFD RG42 ...... 34 E1 [2]
David Cl HYS/HAR UB3 ...... 15 G2
David Rd DTCH/LGLY SL3 ...... 13 J4
Davidson Rd CROY/NA CR0 ...... 5 K6
David's Rd FSTH SE23 ...... 32 F2
David Twigg Cl KUTN/CMB KT2 ...... 2 F4 [1]
Davies Cl RGODL GU7 ...... 160 A2 [3]
  SNWD SE25 ...... 50 C6
Davies Wk ISLW TW7 ...... 17 G3 [1]
Davis Cl CRAWW RH11 ...... 211 K8
Davis Gdns SHST GU47 ...... 72 B2
Davis Rd CHSGTN KT9 ...... 63 K3
  WEY KT13 ...... 59 J8
Davos Cl WOKS/MYFD GU22 ...... 97 H1
Dawell Dr BH/WHM TN16 ...... 90 F7
Dawes Av ISLW TW7 ...... 17 K7
Dawes Ct ESH/CLAY KT10 ...... 61 L3
Dawley Ride DTCH/LGLY SL3 ...... 13 H3
Dawlish Av WAND/EARL SW18 ...... 29 L3
Dawnay Cl ASC SL5 ...... 36 C1
Dawnay Gdns
  WAND/EARL SW18 ...... 30 A3 [1]
Dawnay Rd CBLY GU15 ...... 72 D1 [1]
  GT/LBKH KT23 ...... 101 L8
  WAND/EARL SW18 ...... 29 M3
Dawn Cl HSLWW TW4 ...... 16 B5
Dawney Hl CHOB/PIR GU24 ...... 95 H3
Dawneys Rd CHOB/PIR GU24 ...... 95 H4
Dawn Redwood Cl
  DTCH/LGLY SL3 ...... 12 D5
Dawsmere Cl CBLY GU15 ...... 73 M4
Dawson Rd BF/WBF KT14 ...... 79 G1
  KUT KT1 ...... 3 H8
Daybrook Rd WIM/MER SW19 ...... 47 L2
Daylesford Av PUT/ROE SW15 ...... 19 K6
Daymersiea Rdg LHD/OX KT22 ...... 102 F3
Day's Acre SAND/SEL CR2 ...... 68 C8
Daysbrook Rd
  BRXS/STRHM SW2 ...... 31 J2
Dayseys HI REDH RH1 ...... 171 K1
Dayspring GUW GU2 ...... 116 E4
Deacon Cl COB KT11 ...... 100 E1
  CTHM CR3 ...... 107 M5
  PUR/KEN CR8 ...... 67 H7
Deacon Fld GUW GU2 ...... 8 B2
Deacon Rd KUTN/CMB KT2 ...... 3 G5
Deacons Wk HPTN TW12 ...... 25 K5
Deadbrook La ASHV GU12 ...... 113 H6
Deal Rd TOOT SW17 ...... 30 D7
Dealtry Rd PUT/ROE SW15 ...... 19 M6
Dean Cl WOKS/MYFD GU22 ...... 96 E3
Deanery Rd EDEN TN8 ...... 131 M8
  RGODL GU7 ...... 160 B4
Deanhill Rd MORT/ESHN SW14 ...... 18 E6
Dean La CTHM CR3 ...... 88 A8
  REDH RH1 ...... 106 F6
Deanoak La REIG RH2 ...... 169 G2
Dean Rd CROY/NA CR0 ...... 68 A3
  HPTN TW12 ...... 25 K6
  HSLW TW3 ...... 16 E7
  RGODL GU7 ...... 160 A3
Deans Cl CHSWK W4 ...... 18 E1 [1]
  CROY/NA CR0 ...... 5 J7
  KWD/TDW/WH KT20 ...... 104 E6
Deans Ct BFOR GU20 ...... 55 G5 [8]
Deansfield CTHM CR3 ...... 108 C7
Deansgate BRAK RG12 ...... 34 D7
Deans Gate Cl FSTH SE23 ...... 33 G4 [2]
Deans La KWD/TDW/WH KT20 ...... 104 E7
  REDH RH1 ...... 127 K7
Deans Rd REDH RH1 ...... 126 F4
  SUT SM1 ...... 65 K3
Deans Wk COUL/CHIP CR5 ...... 87 K8
De'arn Gdns MTCM CR4 ...... 48 B3
Debden Cl KUTN/CMB KT2 ...... 27 G6 [1]
Deborah Cl ISLW TW7 ...... 17 H3
De Broome Av FELT TW13 ...... 24 F2
De Burgh Pk BNSTD SM7 ...... 85 L6
Deburgh Rd WIM/MER SW19 ...... 29 M8
Dedisham Cl CRAWE RH10 ...... 212 D4 [1]
Dedswell Dr RGUE GU4 ...... 118 D3
Deedman Cl ASHV GU12 ...... 113 K7 [1]
Deepcut Bridge Rd FRIM GU16 ...... 94 A2
Deepdale BRAK RG12 ...... 34 A4
  WIM/MER SW19 ...... 29 G5
Deepdene NFNM GU10 ...... 11 K7
Deepdene Av CROY/NA CR0 ...... 5 K8
  RDKG RH5 ...... 144 F2
Deepdene Avenue Rd
  DORK RH4 ...... 122 F8
Deepdene Dr RDKG RH5 ...... 144 F1
Deepdene Gdns
  BRXS/STRHM SW2 ...... 31 J1
  DORK RH4 ...... 144 E1
Deepdene Park Rd RDKG RH5 ...... 144 F1

Deepdene V DORK RH4 ...... 122 F8
Deepdene Wd RDKG RH5 ...... 145 G2
Deepfield Rd BRAK RG12 ...... 35 G2
Deepfields HORL RH6 ...... 170 C4
Deepfield Wy COUL/CHIP CR5 ...... 87 H6
Deeprose Cl GUW GU2 ...... 116 E4
Deepwell Cl ISLW TW7 ...... 17 K3
Deep Well Dr CBLY GU15 ...... 73 H4
Deerbarn Rd GUW GU2 ...... 8 C1
Deerbrook Rd
  BRXS/STRHM SW2 ...... 31 L2
Deerhurst Cl FELT TW13 ...... 24 D4
Deerhurst Crs HPTN TW12 ...... 25 M6 [3]
Deerhurst Rd
  STRHM/NOR SW16 ...... 31 J6
Deerings Rd REIG RH2 ...... 125 L8
Deer Leap LTWR GU18 ...... 74 D1
Deerleap Rd DORK RH4 ...... 143 L3
Dee Rd RCH/KEW TW9 ...... 18 C6
Deer Park Cl KUTN/CMB KT2 ...... 3 L2
Deer Park Gdns MTCM CR4 ...... 48 A4 [1]
Deer Park Rd WIM/MER SW19 ...... 47 L2
Deer Park Wy WWKM BR4 ...... 70 C1 [1]
Deer Rock Hl BRAK RG12 ...... 34 F6
Deer Rock Rd CBLY GU15 ...... 73 J2
Deers Farm Cl RPLY/SEND GU23 ...... 79 H6
Deerswood Cl CRAWW RH11 ...... 211 L2 [1]
  CTHM CR3 ...... 108 D6
Deerswood Rd CRAWW RH11 ...... 211 L2
Deeside Rd TOOT SW17 ...... 30 A4
Dee Wy HOR/WEW KT19 ...... 64 B8
Defiant Cl FARN GU14 ...... 112 C1
Defiant Wy WLGTN SM6 ...... 67 H6
Defoe Av RCH/KEW TW9 ...... 18 C6
Defoe Cl WIM/MER SW19 ...... 30 B7 [2]
De Frene Rd SYD SE26 ...... 33 G5
De Havilland Dr WEY KT13 ...... 79 H1
De Havilland Rd HEST TW5 ...... 15 M7 [1]
  WLGTN SM6 ...... 67 H6
De Havilland Wy
  STWL/WRAY TW19 ...... 14 A8
Delabole Rd REDH RH1 ...... 127 H3
Delagarde Rd BH/WHM TN16 ...... 111 M8
Delamare Crs CROY/NA CR0 ...... 50 F6
Delamere Rd REIG RH2 ...... 147 L4
  RYNPK SW20 ...... 47 G1 [1]
Delaporte Cl EW KT17 ...... 84 B2 [8]
De Lara Wy WOKN/KNAP GU21 ...... 6 A7
De La Warr Rd EGRIN RH19 ...... 196 C8
Delcombe Av WPK KT4 ...... 46 F8
Delderfield ASHTD KT21 ...... 103 G2
Delfont Cl CRAWE RH10 ...... 213 G5 [3]
Delia St WAND/EARL SW18 ...... 29 L1
Delius Gdns SWTR RH13 ...... 229 L5
Dellbow Rd EBED/NFELT TW14 ...... 15 L7
Dell Cl HASM GU27 ...... 219 K2
  LHD/OX KT22 ...... 102 A5
  RDKG RH5 ...... 122 F1
  WLGTN SM6 ...... 66 F3
Dellfield Cl BECK BR3 ...... 51 M1
Dell Gv FRIM GU16 ...... 73 J7
Dell La EW KT17 ...... 64 D4
Dell Rd EW KT17 ...... 64 D5
The Dell BTFD TW8 ...... 17 M1 [1]
  EBED/NFELT TW14 ...... 24 E1
  EGRIN RH19 ...... 196 E8
  FNM GU9 ...... 133 M2
  HORL RH6 ...... 169 M4
  KWD/TDW/WH KT20 ...... 104 F3
  NRWD SE19 ...... 50 C1
  WOKN/KNAP GU21 ...... 96 F1
Dell Wk NWMAL KT3 ...... 46 B2
Delmey Cl CROY/NA CR0 ...... 5 K7
Delta Cl CHOB/PIR GU24 ...... 56 C8
  WPK KT4 ...... 64 B2
Delta Dr HORL RH6 ...... 170 D8
Delta Rd CHOB/PIR GU24 ...... 56 C8
  WOKN/KNAP GU21 ...... 7 G3
  WPK KT4 ...... 64 B2
Delta Wy EGH TW20 ...... 39 M1
Delves KWD/TDW/WH KT20 ...... 105 G3
Delville Cl FARN GU14 ...... 92 A6
Demesne Rd WLGTN SM6 ...... 67 G3
De Montfort Rd
  STRHM/NOR SW16 ...... 31 G3
Denbigh Cl SUT SM1 ...... 65 J4
Denbigh Gdns
  RCHPK/HAM TW10 ...... 18 C7
Denbigh Rd HASM GU27 ...... 220 A4 [1]
  HSLW TW3 ...... 16 E4
Denby Rd COB KT11 ...... 80 E3
Denchers Plat CRAWW RH11 ...... 192 A8
Dendy St BAL SW12 ...... 30 D2
Dene Av HSLW TW3 ...... 16 C5
Dene Cl BRAK RG12 ...... 34 F1
  COUL/CHIP CR5 ...... 106 B1
  HASM GU27 ...... 219 M3
  HORL RH6 ...... 170 B4
  NFNM GU10 ...... 11 K8
  WPK KT4 ...... 64 C1
Denefield Dr PUR/KEN CR8 ...... 88 A5
Dene Gdns THDIT KT7 ...... 62 D1
Denehurst Gdns
  RCHPK/HAM TW10 ...... 18 D6
  WHTN TW2 ...... 26 A1
Dene La NFNM GU10 ...... 11 K7
Dene La West NFNM GU10 ...... 11 K9
Dene Pl WOKN/KNAP GU21 ...... 76 E8
Dene Rd ASHTD KT21 ...... 103 J1
  FARN GU14 ...... 92 C6
  GU GU1 ...... 9 J5
Dene St DORK RH4 ...... 144 E2
Dene Street Gdns DORK RH4 ...... 144 E2
The Dene BELMT SM2 ...... 85 J1
  CROY/NA CR0 ...... 69 G3
  WOT/HER KT12 ...... 43 J5
Dene Tye CRAWE RH10 ...... 212 F2
Dene Wk NFNM GU10 ...... 11 L8
Denfield DORK RH4 ...... 144 E4
Denham Av MTCM CR4 ...... 48 C4
Denham Gv BRAK RG12 ...... 34 F6 [3]
Denham Rd EBED/NFELT TW14 ...... 24 F1
  EGH TW20 ...... 21 K5
  EW KT17 ...... 84 C2
Denholm Gdns RGUE GU4 ...... 117 K5 [3]
Denison Rd FELT TW13 ...... 24 C5
  WIM/MER SW19 ...... 30 A7
Denleigh Gdns THDIT KT7 ...... 44 B6 [1]

Denly Wy LTWR GU18 ...... 54 F8
Denman Dr ASHF TW15 ...... 23 L7
  ESH/CLAY KT10 ...... 62 D4 [1]
Denmans CRAWE RH10 ...... 213 G2 [3]
Denmark Av WIM/MER SW19 ...... 29 H8
Denmark Gdns CAR SM5 ...... 66 C2
Denmark Rd CAR SM5 ...... 66 C2
  GU GU1 ...... 9 J5
  KUT KT1 ...... 2 F9
  SNWD SE25 ...... 50 D5
  WHTN TW2 ...... 26 A4
  WIM/MER SW19 ...... 29 G7
Denmark Sq ASHV GU12 ...... 113 H7
Denmark St ASHV GU12 ...... 113 G7
Denmead Ct BRAK RG12 ...... 35 H6
Dennan Rd SURB KT6 ...... 45 J8
Denne Pde HORS RH12 ...... 228 F8
Denne Rd CRAWW RH11 ...... 212 A4
  HORS RH12 ...... 228 F8
Dennett Rd CROY/NA CR0 ...... 4 A1
Dennettsland Rd EDEN TN8 ...... 131 M8
Denning Av CROY/NA CR0 ...... 67 K4
Denning Cl HPTN TW12 ...... 25 J6 [1]
Dennis Cl REDH RH1 ...... 126 B6
Dennis Park Crs RYNPK SW20 ...... 47 H1
Dennis Reeve Cl MTCM CR4 ...... 48 C1
Dennistoun Cl CBLY GU15 ...... 73 G4 [1]
Densole Cl BECK BR3 ...... 51 H1 [1]
Denton Cl REDH RH1 ...... 148 D5
Denton Gv WOT/HER KT12 ...... 61 H1
Denton Rd TWK TW1 ...... 18 A8
Denton Wy FRIM GU16 ...... 73 G7
  WOKN/KNAP GU21 ...... 76 D7
Dents Gv KWD/TDW/WH KT20 ...... 126 A2
Denvale Wk WOKN/KNAP GU21 ...... 76 D8
Denzil Rd GUW GU2 ...... 8 D6
Depot Rd CRAWW RH11 ...... 192 A8
  EW KT17 ...... 84 B3
  HSLW TW3 ...... 17 G5
  SWTR RH13 ...... 229 H7
Derby Arms Rd EPSOM KT18 ...... 84 C7
Derby Cl EPSOM KT18 ...... 104 E1
Derby Hl FSTH SE23 ...... 32 F3
Derby Hill Crs FSTH SE23 ...... 32 F3
Derby Rd BRYLDS KT5 ...... 45 K8
  CROY/NA CR0 ...... 4 A4
  GUW GU2 ...... 116 C8
  HASM GU27 ...... 219 L2
  HSLW TW3 ...... 16 E6
  MORT/ESHN SW14 ...... 18 E6
  SUT SM1 ...... 65 H5
  WIM/MER SW19 ...... 29 K8 [2]
Derby Stables Rd EPSOM KT18 ...... 84 B7
Derek Cl HOR/WEW KT19 ...... 63 L4
Deri Dene Cl STWL/WRAY TW19 ...... 14 B8 [3]
Dering Pl CROY/NA CR0 ...... 67 M3 [8]
Dering Rd CROY/NA CR0 ...... 67 M3
Derinton Rd TOOT SW17 ...... 30 D5
Deronda Rd BRXS/STRHM SW2 ...... 31 L2
Deroy Cl CAR SM5 ...... 66 C5
Deroy Ct CAR SM5 ...... 66 C5
Derrick Av SAND/SEL CR2 ...... 67 M8
Derrick Rd BECK BR3 ...... 51 J3
Derry Cl ASHV GU12 ...... 113 J4
Derrydown WOKS/MYFD GU22 ...... 96 E3
Derry Rd FARN GU14 ...... 72 C8
  WLGTN SM6 ...... 67 H2
Derwent Av ASHV GU12 ...... 113 J5
  PUT/ROE SW15 ...... 28 B5
Derwent Cl ADL/WDHM KT15 ...... 59 C4
  CRAWW RH11 ...... 211 J4 [1]
  EBED/NFELT TW14 ...... 24 C2
  ESH/CLAY KT10 ...... 62 B5
  FARN GU14 ...... 92 A5
  FNM GU9 ...... 133 K3
  HORS RH12 ...... 229 L3
Derwent Dr PUR/KEN CR8 ...... 88 A4
Derwent Rd EGH TW20 ...... 21 L7
  LTWR GU18 ...... 74 E1
  MRDN SM4 ...... 47 G6
  PGE/AN SE20 ...... 50 D2
  WHTN TW2 ...... 16 B8
Desborough Cl SHPTN TW17 ...... 41 K7
Desford Wy ASHF TW15 ...... 23 J3
Detillens La OXTED RH8 ...... 130 D3
Detling Rd CRAWW RH11 ...... 211 M8
Dettingen Rd FRIM GU16 ...... 94 B1
Devana End CAR SM5 ...... 66 C2
Devas Rd RYNPK SW20 ...... 46 F1
Devenish La ASC SL5 ...... 37 G8
Devenish Rd ASC SL5 ...... 37 G6
Devereux La BARN SW13 ...... 19 L2
Devey Cl KUTN/CMB KT2 ...... 28 C8
Devil's La EGH TW20 ...... 21 M7
  LIPH GU30 ...... 218 B6
Devitt Cl ASHTD KT21 ...... 83 K6
Devoil Cl RGUE GU4 ...... 117 L4
Devoke Wy WOT/HER KT12 ...... 61 G1
Devon Av WHTN TW2 ...... 25 M2
Devon Bank GUW GU2 ...... 7 G9
Devon Cl PUR/KEN CR8 ...... 88 C6 [1]
  SHST GU47 ...... 72 A2
Devon Crs REIG RH2 ...... 125 A8
Devoncroft Gdns TWK TW1 ...... 26 D1 [1]
Devon Rd ALDT GU11 ...... 112 B2
  BELMT SM2 ...... 65 H7
  REDH RH1 ...... 126 F4
  WOT/HER KT12 ...... 60 F3
Devonshire Av BELMT SM2 ...... 65 M6
  WOKN/KNAP GU21 ...... 77 M4
Devonshire Dr CBLY GU15 ...... 73 J2
  SURB KT6 ...... 45 G8
Devonshire Gdns CHSWK W4 ...... 18 F2
Devonshire Pl ALDT GU11 ...... 112 C8
Devonshire Rd BELMT SM2 ...... 65 M6
  CAR SM5 ...... 66 D3 [1]
  CHSWK W4 ...... 19 H1 [1]
  CROY/NA CR0 ...... 4 E1
  FELT TW13 ...... 25 H4
  FSTH SE23 ...... 33 G1
  SWTR RH13 ...... 229 G7
  WEY KT13 ...... 59 K3 [1]

WIM/MER SW19 ...... 30 B8
Devonshire St CHSWK W4 ...... 69 J1 [1]
Devon Wy CHSGTN KT9 ...... 62 F3
  HOR/WEW KT19 ...... 63 L4 [1]
Devon Waye HEST TW5 ...... 16 C2
Dewar Cl CRAWW RH11 ...... 211 H6 [8]
Dewey St TOOT SW17 ...... 30 C6
Dewlands GDST RH9 ...... 128 F5
Dewlands Cl CRAN GU6 ...... 185 H6 [3]
Dewlands La CRAN GU6 ...... 185 H6
Dewsbury Gdns WPK KT4 ...... 64 D2 [1]
Dexter Dr EGRIN RH19 ...... 216 B1
Diamedes Av
  STWL/WRAY TW19 ...... 23 G1 [1]
Diamond Hl CBLY GU15 ...... 73 G2
Diamond Rdg CBLY GU15 ...... 73 G2
Diamond Wy FARN GU14 ...... 112 B1
Diana Gdns SURB KT6 ...... 63 J1 [1]
Dianthus Cl CHERT KT16 ...... 40 B7 [1]
Dianthus Cl WOKS/MYFD GU22 ...... 6 B8
Dibdin Cl SUT SM1 ...... 65 K2
Dibdin Rd SUT SM1 ...... 65 K2
Diceland Rd BNSTD SM7 ...... 85 J6
Dickens Cl EGRIN RH19 ...... 195 M8
  RCHPK/HAM TW10 ...... 27 H3
Dickens Dr ADL/WDHM KT15 ...... 58 C5
Dickenson Rd FELT TW13 ...... 24 F6
Dickenson's La SNWD SE25 ...... 50 D6
Dickenson's Pl SNWD SE25 ...... 50 D6 [3]
Dickens Rd CRAWE RH10 ...... 212 A6
Dickerage Hl NWMAL KT3 ...... 45 M2
Dickerage La NWMAL KT3 ...... 45 M3
Dickerage Rd KUT KT1 ...... 45 M1
  NWMAL KT3 ...... 45 M2 [1]
Dick Turpin Wy
  EBED/NFELT TW14 ...... 15 J4
Digby Pl CROY/NA CR0 ...... 5 K7
Digby Wy BF/WBF KT14 ...... 79 J2 [3]
Digdens Ri EPSOM KT18 ...... 83 M5
Dilston Rd LHD/OX KT22 ...... 102 C3
Dilton Gdns PUT/ROE SW15 ...... 28 D2
Dingle Rd ASHF TW15 ...... 23 L6
The Dingle CRAWW RH11 ...... 211 L3
Dingley La STRHM/NOR SW16 ...... 31 G3
Dingley Wy FARN GU14 ...... 112 D1
Dingwall Av CROY/NA CR0 ...... 4 D6
Dingwall Rd CAR SM5 ...... 66 C7
  CROY/NA CR0 ...... 4 E4
  WAND/EARL SW18 ...... 29 M1 [1]
Dinsdale Cl WOKS/MYFD GU22 ...... 6 F7
Dinsdale Gdns SNWD SE25 ...... 50 B4
Dinsmore Rd BAL SW12 ...... 30 E1
Dinton Rd KUTN/CMB KT2 ...... 3 H2
  STRHM/NOR SW16 ...... 31 J5
Dippenhall Rd NFNM GU10 ...... 132 C3
Dippenhall St NFNM GU10 ...... 132 C3
Dirdene Cl EW KT17 ...... 84 C2 [1]
Dirdene Gdns EW KT17 ...... 84 C2 [3]
Dirdene Gv EW KT17 ...... 84 C2 [3]
Dirtham La EHSLY KT24 ...... 120 E3
Dirty La EGRIN RH19 ...... 217 H3
Disraeli Ct DTCH/LGLY SL3 ...... 12 E1 [1]
Ditches La COUL/CHIP CR5 ...... 87 G7
Ditchling BRAK RG12 ...... 34 D7
Ditchling Hl CRAWW RH11 ...... 211 M6
Ditton Cl THDIT KT7 ...... 44 D7
Ditton Grange Cl SURB KT6 ...... 45 G8
Ditton Grange Dr SURB KT6 ...... 45 G8
Ditton Hl SURB KT6 ...... 44 F8
Ditton Hill Rd SURB KT6 ...... 44 F8
Ditton Lawn THDIT KT7 ...... 44 D8
Ditton Park Rd DTCH/LGLY SL3 ...... 12 B1
Ditton Reach THDIT KT7 ...... 44 E6
Ditton Rd DTCH/LGLY SL3 ...... 12 A3
  SURB KT6 ...... 63 J1
Dixon Dr WEY KT13 ...... 59 J8
Dixon Pl WWKM BR4 ...... 51 L8
Dixon Rd SNWD SE25 ...... 50 B3
Dobbins Pl CRAWW RH11 ...... 211 H4 [1]
Dobson Rd CRAWW RH11 ...... 192 A8
Dockenfield St WOKN/KNAP GU10 ...... 176 E2
Dockett Eddy La SHPTN TW17 ...... 41 J7
Dock Rd BTFD TW8 ...... 17 M2
Dockwell Cl EBED/NFELT TW14 ...... 15 K6
Doctors Cl SYD SE26 ...... 32 F6
Doctors La CTHM CR3 ...... 107 K6
Dodbrooke Rd WNWD SE27 ...... 31 K4 [1]
Dodd's Crs BF/WBF KT14 ...... 78 E4
Dodd's La BF/WBF KT14 ...... 78 D4
Dodds Pk BRKHM/BTCW RH3 ...... 145 L2 [1]
Doel Cl WIM/MER SW19 ...... 29 M8
Dogflud Wy FNM GU9 ...... 133 G6
Doggets Cl EDEN TN8 ...... 175 M1 [1]
Doggett Rd CAT SE6 ...... 33 K1
Doghurst Av WDR/YW UB7 ...... 14 E2
Doghurst Dr WDR/YW UB7 ...... 14 E2 [1]
Doghurst La COUL/CHIP CR5 ...... 106 C2
Dollis Cl CRAWE RH10 ...... 212 F4 [1]
Dollis Dr FNM GU9 ...... 134 A6 [1]
Dolphin Cl HASM GU27 ...... 219 H3
  SURB KT6 ...... 45 G6
Dolphin Cl STWL/WRAY TW19 ...... 22 D4 [1]
Dolphin Ct North
  STWL/WRAY TW19 ...... 22 D4 [3]
Dolphin St KUT KT1 ...... 2 E6
Doman Rd CBLY GU15 ...... 72 D5
Dome Hl CTHM CR3 ...... 128 B1
Dome Hill Pk SYD SE26 ...... 32 C5
Dome Hill Peak CTHM CR3 ...... 108 B8
Dome Wy REDH RH1 ...... 126 C7
Dominion Rd CROY/NA CR0 ...... 5 J1
Donald Rd CROY/NA CR0 ...... 49 J6
Donald Woods Gdns
  BRYLDS KT5 ...... 63 L1
Doncastle Rd BRAK RG12 ...... 34 C3
Donkey Aly EDUL SE22 ...... 32 D1
Donkey La HORL RH6 ...... 193 G2 [3]
  RDKG RH5 ...... 165 G1
Donnafields CHOB/PIR GU24 ...... 75 K6
Donne Cl CRAWE RH10 ...... 212 E1
Donne Gdns WOKS/MYFD GU22 ...... 78 B5
Donne Pl MTCM CR4 ...... 48 E4
Donnington Cl CBLY GU15 ...... 72 E5 [3]
Donnington Ct CRAWW RH11 ...... 211 J6 [1]
Donnington Rd WPK KT4 ...... 64 D1
Donnybrook BRAK RG12 ...... 34 D7

Donnybrook Rd
  STRHM/NOR SW16 ...... 30 F8
Donovan Cl HOR/WEW KT19 ...... 64 A8
Doods Park Rd REIG RH2 ...... 125 L7
Doods Rd REIG RH2 ...... 125 M7
Doods Wy REIG RH2 ...... 126 A7
Doomsday Gdn SWTR RH13 ...... 229 J8
Doone Cl TEDD TW11 ...... 26 D7
Doral Wy CAR SM5 ...... 66 C4 [3]
Doran Dr REIG RH2 ...... 126 A8
Dora Rd WIM/MER SW19 ...... 29 K6
Dora's Green La NFNM GU10 ...... 132 E3
  NFNM GU10 ...... 132 E7
Dorcas Ct CBLY GU15 ...... 72 E6 [1]
Dorchester Ct WOKS/MYFD GU22 ...... 7 H4
Dorchester Dr
  EBED/NFELT TW14 ...... 15 H8
Dorchester Gv CHSWK W4 ...... 19 H1
Dorchester Ms TWK TW1 ...... 26 F1 [1]
  MRDN SM4 ...... 47 L7
  WEY KT13 ...... 59 L2
  WPK KT4 ...... 46 F8
Doreen Cl FARN GU14 ...... 92 A1
Dore Gdns MRDN SM4 ...... 47 L7 [1]
Dorian Ct WARL CR6 ...... 108 E1 [1]
Dorin Ct ASC SL5 ...... 37 H1
Doric Dr KWD/TDW/WH KT20 ...... 105 J2
Dorien Rd RYNPK SW20 ...... 47 G2
Doris Rd ASHF TW15 ...... 24 A7
Dorking Cl WPK KT4 ...... 65 G1 [3]
Dorking Rd EPSOM KT18 ...... 83 L5
  GT/LBKH KT23 ...... 121 L1
  HORS RH12 ...... 208 D7
  KWD/TDW/WH KT20 ...... 104 E8
  LHD/OX KT22 ...... 102 E4
  RGUE GU4 ...... 140 A6
Dorlcote Rd WAND/EARL SW18 ...... 30 A1
Dorling Dr EW KT17 ...... 84 C2
Dorly Cl SHPTN TW17 ...... 42 B4
Dormans CRAWW RH11 ...... 211 K4
Dormans Av LING RH7 ...... 174 D7
Dorman's Cl LING RH7 ...... 196 D1
Dormans High St LING RH7 ...... 196 D2
Dormans Park Rd EGRIN RH19 ...... 196 A6
Dormans Rd LING RH7 ...... 174 D7
Dormans Station Rd LING RH7 ...... 196 C2
Dormers Cl RGODL GU7 ...... 160 A2 [3]
Dorney Gv WEY KT13 ...... 59 L1
Dorney Wy HSLWW TW4 ...... 16 B7
Dornford Gdns COUL/CHIP CR5 ...... 107 M1
Dornton Rd SAND/SEL CR2 ...... 68 B4
  TOOT SW17 ...... 30 E3
Dorrit Crs RGUW GU3 ...... 116 B6
Dorset Av EGRIN RH19 ...... 195 M6
Dorset Dr WOKS/MYFD GU22 ...... 7 K6
Dorset Gdns EGRIN RH19 ...... 195 M6
  STRHM/NOR SW16 ...... 49 J4 [1]
Dorset Rd ASHF TW15 ...... 23 G4
  ASHV GU12 ...... 113 K4
  BECK BR3 ...... 51 G3
  BELMT SM2 ...... 65 K8
  MTCM CR4 ...... 48 B2
  WIM/MER SW19 ...... 47 K1
Dorset Wy BF/WBF KT14 ...... 79 G1
  WHTN TW2 ...... 25 M2
Dorset Waye HEST TW5 ...... 16 C2
Dorton Wy RPLY/SEND GU23 ...... 98 E3
Douai Cl FARN GU14 ...... 92 F5
Douai Gv HPTN TW12 ...... 43 M1
Douglas Av NWMAL KT3 ...... 46 E4
Douglas Dr CROY/NA CR0 ...... 69 K2 [3]
  RGODL GU7 ...... 160 C4
Douglas Gv NFNM GU10 ...... 155 M4
Douglas La STWL/WRAY TW19 ...... 12 C7
Douglas Ms BNSTD SM7 ...... 85 J6 [1]
Douglas Rd ADL/WDHM KT15 ...... 58 E2 [1]
  ESH/CLAY KT10 ...... 61 L1
  HSLW TW3 ...... 16 E5 [3]
  KUT KT1 ...... 3 L7
  REIG RH2 ...... 125 K7 [3]
  STWL/WRAY TW19 ...... 14 A8 [3]
  SURB KT6 ...... 63 J1
Dounesforth Gdns
  WAND/EARL SW18 ...... 29 L2
Dove Cl CRAWW RH11 ...... 212 A1
  SAND/SEL CR2 ...... 89 C1
Dovecote Cl WEY KT13 ...... 59 L2 [3]
Dovedale Cl GU GU1 ...... 117 K5 [3]
  SHST GU47 ...... 52 A7
Dovedale Crs CRAWW RH11 ...... 211 L5
Dovedale Ri MTCM CR4 ...... 30 C8 [1]
Dover Ct CRAN GU6 ...... 185 K6 [1]
Dovercourt Av THHTH CR7 ...... 49 K4 [1]
Dovercourt La SUT SM1 ...... 65 M2
Doverfield Rd RGUE GU4 ...... 117 K5
Dover Gdns CAR SM5 ...... 66 C2
Dover House Rd PUT/ROE SW15 ...... 19 K6
Dover Park Dr PUT/ROE SW15 ...... 19 L8
Dover Rd NRWD SE19 ...... 32 A7 [1]
Dovers Green Rd REIG RH2 ...... 147 L4
Doversmead
  WOKN/KNAP GU21 ...... 76 B6 [1]
Doves Cl HAYES BR2 ...... 71 H1
Doveton Rd SAND/SEL CR2 ...... 68 A4 [8]
Dowdeswell Cl PUT/ROE SW15 ...... 19 H6
Dowding Rd BH/WHM TN16 ...... 91 G5
Dower Av WLGTN SM6 ...... 67 H5
Dower Wk CRAWW RH11 ...... 211 K4
Dowlands La HORL RH6 ...... 172 A7
Dowlands Ct GT/LBKH KT23 ...... 121 K1
Dowlans Rd GT/LBKH KT23 ...... 121 L1
Dowman Cl WIM/MER SW19 ...... 29 L8 [1]
Downe Av RSEV TN14 ...... 91 M2
Downe Cl HORL RH6 ...... 170 B1
Downer Meadow RGODL GU7 ...... 160 B1
Downe Rd HAYES BR2 ...... 71 H7
  MTCM CR4 ...... 48 C2
Downes Cl TWK TW1 ...... 17 L8 [1]
Downfield WPK KT4 ...... 46 C8
Down Hall Rd KUTN/CMB KT2 ...... 2 D5
Downhurst Rd CRAN GU6 ...... 186 B3
Downing Av GUW GU2 ...... 138 C1
Downing St FNM GU9 ...... 133 L7

Downland Cl *COUL/CHIP* CR5 ...... 86 E4
EPSOM KT18 .... 84 E8
Downland Dr *CRAWW* RH11 ...... 211 M5
Downland Gdns *EPSOM* KT18 ...... 84 E4
Downland Pl *CRAWW* RH11 .... 211 M5
Downlands Rd *PUR/KEN* CR8 .... 87 H3
Downland Wy *EPSOM* KT18 .... 84 E4
Down La *RGUW* GU3 .... 137 L4
TEDD TW11 .... 26 E7
Downs Av *EPSOM* KT18 .... 84 C5
Downs Court Rd *PUR/KEN* CR8 .... 87 M3
Downs Hill Rd *EPSOM* KT18 ...... 84 B5 🔢
Downshire Wy *BNFD* RG42 .... 34 D1
BRAK RG12 .... 34 D3
Downside *EPSOM* KT18 .... 84 B4
GSHT GU26 .... 199 G2 🔢
SUN TW16 .... 42 D1
TWK TW1 .... 26 C4
Downside Bridge Rd *COB* KT11 .... 80 E4
Downside Cl *WIM/MER* SW19 ...... 29 M7
Downside Common *COB* KT11 ...... 80 E8
Downside Common Rd *COB* KT11 .. 80 F8
Downside Orch
WOKS/MYFD GU22 .... 7 G6
Downside Rd *BELMT* SM2 .... 66 A5
COB KT11 .... 80 E8
RGUE GU4 .... 139 L1
Downs La *LHD/OX* KT22 .... 102 E5
Downs Link *CRAN* GU6 .... 184 D5
HORS RH12 .... 225 M1
RGUE GU4 .... 140 B5
SHGR GU5 .... 161 J1
SWTR RH13 .... 226 D5
Downs Rd *BECK* BR3 .... 51 L2
BELMT SM2 .... 85 L1
COUL/CHIP CR5 .... 87 G8
EPSOM KT18 .... 103 M2
PUR/KEN CR8 .... 87 L1
RDKG RH5 .... 122 F2
THHTH CR7 .... 49 M1🔢
Downs Side *BELMT* SM2 .... 85 J1
The Downs *LHD/OX* KT22 .... 102 E7
RYNPK SW20 .... 29 G8
Down St *E/WMO/HCT* KT8 .... 43 K5
Downs Vw *DORK* 122 F8
ISLW TW7 .... 17 K3
KWD/TDW/WH KT20 .... 104 E3
Downsview Av
WOKS/MYFD GU22 .... 97 J3
Downsview Cl *COB* KT11 .... 100 E1
Downsview Gdns *DORK* RH4 ...... 144 E3
NRWD SE19 .... 31 M8 🔢
Downs View Rd *GT/LBKH* KT23 .. 121 M1
NRWD SE19 .... 31 M8
Downs Wy *EPSOM* KT18 .... 84 C6
GT/LBKH KT23 .... 101 M8
KWD/TDW/WH KT20 .... 104 E3
OXTED RH8 .... 130 B1
Downsway *CTHM* CR3 .... 88 C6
GU GU1 .... 118 A3
SAND/SEL CR2 .... 88 B1
Downsway Cl
KWD/TDW/WH KT20 .... 104 D3
The Downsway *BELMT* SM2 .... 65 M7
Downs Wd *EPSOM* KT18 .... 84 E7
Downswood *REDH* RH1 .... 126 A6
Downton Av *BRXS/STRHM* SW2 .... 31 J3
Downview *GSHT* GU26 .... 199 G3
Down Yhonda *MFD/CHID* GU8 .... 157 M6
Doyle Rd *SNWD* SE25 .... 50 D4
Dragon La *WEY* KT13 .... 59 K8
Drake Av *CTHM* CR3 .... 107 M4
FRIM GU16 .... 93 K8
STA TW18 .... 22 C6
Drake Cl *HORS* RH12 .... 229 H3
Drakefield Rd *TOOT* SW17 .... 30 D4
Drake Rd *CHSGTN* KT9 .... 63 K4
CRAWE RH10 .... 212 B6
CROY/NA CR0 .... 49 J7🔢
HORL RH6 .... 170 B6
MTCM CR4 .... 48 D6
Drakes Wy *WOKS/MYFD* GU22 .... 97 G4
Drakewood Rd
STRHM/NOR SW16 .... 31 G8 🔢
Drax Av *RYNPK* SW20 .... 28 D8
Draxmont *WIM/MER* SW19 .... 29 H7🔢
Draycot Rd *SURB* KT6 .... 45 K8
Draycott *BRAK* RG12 .... 35 H5
Drayhorse Dr *BAGS* GU19 .... 54 B7
Draymans Wy *ISLW* TW7 .... 17 J5
Drayton Cl *BRAK* RG12 .... 35 G2 🔢
HSLWW TW4 .... 16 C7
LHD/OX KT22 .... 102 A5
Drayton Rd *CROY/NA* CR0 .... 4 B5
Dresden Wy *WEY* KT13 .... 59 M4
Drew Pl *CTHM* CR3 .... 108 A5
Drewstead Rd
STRHM/NOR SW16 .... 31 G3
The Drift *COB* KT11 .... 100 B6
HAYES BR2 .... 71 G2
Drift Wy *DTCH/LGLY* SL3 .... 12 F3
The Driftway *BNSTD* SM7 .... 84 F5🔢
LHD/OX KT22 .... 102 F5
MTCM CR4 .... 48 D1 🔢
Driftwood Dr *PUR/KEN* CR8 ...... 87 M7
Drill Hall Rd *CHERT* KT16 .... 40 D7
Drive Rd *COUL/CHIP* CR5 .... 107 J2
Drivers Md *LING* RH7 .... 173 M6
The Drive *ASHF* TW15 .... 24 A4
BECK BR3 .... 51 K2
BELMT SM2 .... 85 J2
BIL RH14 .... 224 A7
BNSTD SM7 .... 85 H7
COB KT11 .... 81 H4
COUL/CHIP CR5 .... 87 H4
CRAN GU6 .... 185 H7
CRAWE RH10 .... 193 M6
EBED/NFELT TW14 .... 24 F1
ESH/CLAY KT10 .... 43 M8
FNM GU9 .... 10 F5
GUW GU2 .... 116 C8
GUW GU2 .... 138 C2
HOR/WEW KT19 .... 64 C5
HORL RH6 .... 170 E7
HSLW TW3 .... 17 G4

KUTN/CMB KT2 .... 27 M8
LHD/OX KT22 .... 102 B4
LHD/OX KT22 .... 103 K6
LHD/OX KT22 .... 103 H5
MFD/CHID GU8 .... 159 H5
MRDN SM4 .... 47 M5
RGODL GU7 .... 159 H5
RGODL GU7 .... 160 B7
RGUW GU3 .... 138 E4
RYNPK SW20 .... 161 L3
SHGR GU5 .... 161 L3
STWL/WRAY TW19 .... 12 A7
THHTH CR7 .... 50 A4
WLGTN SM6 .... 66 F8
WOKS/MYFD GU22 .... 96 C2
Dr Johnson Av *TOOT* SW17 .... 30 E4
Drodges Cl *SHGR* GU5 .... 161 J1
Droitwich Cl *BRAK* RG12 .... 35 H3 🔢
SYD SE26 .... 32 D4
Drove Rd *RGUE* GU4 .... 140 D2
Drovers Rd *SAND/SEL* CR2 .... 68 A4
Drovers Wy *ASHV* GU12 .... 113 M8
BRAK RG12 .... 35 J3
FNM GU9 .... 133 K3
Druid's Cl *ASHTD* KT21 .... 103 J2 🔢
Drumaline Rdg *WPK* KT4 .... 64 B1
Drummond Cl *BRAK* RG12 .... 35 J1🔢
Drummond Rd *CRAWW* RH11 .... 211 H4
CROY/NA CR0 .... 4 C6
GU GU1 .... 9 G4
Drummonds Pl
RCH/KEW TW9 .... 18 B6 🔢
Drungewick La *BIL* RH14 .... 225 G8
Drury Cl *CRAWE* RH10 .... 213 G5🔢
Drury Crs *CROY/NA* CR0 .... 67 K1
Dry Arch Rd *ASC* SL5 .... 37 J7
Dryburgh Rd *PUT/ROE* SW15 ...... 19 L5
Dryden *BRAK* RG12 .... 34 D7
Dryden Rd *FARN* GU14 .... 92 C3
WIM/MER SW19 .... 29 M7
Drynham Pk *WEY* KT13 .... 60 B2
Duchess of Kent Barracks
ALDT GU11 .... 112 E6
Dudley Dr *MRDN* SM4 .... 47 G8
Dudley Gv *EPSOM* KT18 .... 83 M4
Dudley Rd *ASHF* TW15 .... 23 J6
EBED/NFELT TW14 .... 24 A2
KUT KT1 .... 3 G7
RCH/KEW TW9 .... 18 C4
WIM/MER SW19 .... 29 K7
WOT/HER KT12 .... 42 D6
Dudset La *HEST* TW5 .... 15 K3
Duffield Rd
KWD/TDW/WH KT20 .... 104 E6
Duffins Orch *CHERT* KT16 .... 57 M6
Duke Cl *CRAWE* RH10 .... 212 F7🔢
Duke of Cambridge Cl
WHTN TW2 .... 17 G8
Duke of Cornwall Av *CBLY* GU15 .. 53 G8🔢
Duke of Edinburgh Cl *SUT* SM1 .... 66 A2
Dukes Av *HSLWW* TW4 .... 16 B6
NWMAL KT3 .... 46 B3
RCHPK/HAM TW10 .... 26 F5
Dukes Cl *ASHF* TW15 .... 23 M5
CRAN GU6 .... 185 K7
FNM GU9 .... 133 K3🔢
HPTN TW12 .... 25 J8
Dukes Covert *BAGS* GU19 .... 54 B3
Duke's Dr *RDKG* RH5 .... 190 A3
RGODL GU7 .... 159 L2
Dukes Hi *BAGS* GU19 .... 54 B4
CTHM CR3 .... 109 H2
Dukeshill Rd *BNFD* RG42 .... 34 E1
Dukes Pk *ALDT* GU11 .... 113 G3
Dukes Ride *RDKG* RH5 .... 145 G5
Dukes Rd *WOT/HER* KT12 .... 61 G4
Dukesthorpe Rd *SYD* SE26 .... 43 L5
Duke St *RCH/KEW* TW9 .... 18 A7 🔢
SUT SM1 .... 65 M3
WOKN/KNAP GU21 .... 6 F5
Dukes Wy *WWKM* BR4 .... 70 B2
Dulverton Rd *SAND/SEL* CR2 ...... 68 F8
Dulwich Common *DUL* SE21 ...... 32 A2
The Dulwich Oaks *DUL* SE21 ...... 32 C4🔢
Dulwich Wood Av *NRWD* SE19 .... 32 B6
Dulwich Wood Pk *NRWD* SE19 .... 32 B5
Dumbleton Cl *KUT* KT1 .... 3 L5
Dump Rd *FARN* GU14 .... 92 B8
Dumville Dr *GDST* RH9 .... 128 E5
Dunally Pk *SHPTN* TW17 .... 42 A7
Dunbar Av *BECK* BR3 .... 51 H4
STRHM/NOR SW16 .... 49 K2
Dunbar Ct *WOT/HER* KT12 .... 60 F1🔢
Dunbar Rd *FRIM* GU16 .... 93 J2
NWMAL KT3 .... 45 M4
Dunbar St *WNWD* SE27 .... 31 M5
Dunboe Pl *SHPTN* TW17 .... 41 M7🔢
Duncan Dr *GU* GU1 .... 117 K7
Duncan Gdns *STA* TW18 .... 22 D7
Duncan Rd *KWD/TDW/WH* KT20 .. 105 H1
RCH/KEW TW9 .... 18 B6🔢
Duncombe Hi *FSTH* SE23 .... 33 H1
Duncombe Rd *RGODL* GU7 .... 160 A7
Duncroft Cl *REIG* RH2 .... 125 J8🔢
Dundaff Cl *CBLY* GU15 .... 73 K4
Dundas Cl *BRAK* RG12 .... 34 E4
Dundas Gdns *E/WMO/HCT* KT8 .... 43 L3
Dundee Rd *SNWD* SE25 .... 50 E5
Dundela Gdns *WPK* KT4 .... 64 E3
Dundonald Rd *WIM/MER* SW19 .... 29 J7
Dundrey Crs *REDH* RH1 .... 127 H3
Dunedin Dr *CTHM* CR3 .... 108 B7
Dunelm Gv *WNWD* SE27 .... 31 M5
Dunfee Wy *BF/WBF* KT14 .... 79 H2🔢
Dunfield Rd *CAT* SE6 .... 33 L6
Dungarvan Av *PUT/ROE* SW15 .... 19 K6
Dungates La
BRKHM/BTCW RH3 .... 124 D7
Dunheved Cl *THHTH* CR7 .... 49 K6🔢
Dunheved Rd North *THHTH* CR7 .. 49 K6
Dunheved Rd South *THHTH* CR7 .. 49 K6
Dunheved Rd West *THHTH* CR7 .. 49 K6🔢
Dunkeld Rd *SNWD* SE25 .... 50 A4🔢
Dunkirk St *WNWD* SE27 .... 31 M5🔢
Dunleary Cl *HSLWW* TW4 .... 25 J1
Dunley Dr *CROY/NA* CR0 .... 69 M5🔢
Dunlin Cl *REDH* RH1 .... 148 B5

Dunlin Ri *RGUE* GU4 .... 118 A6
Dunmail Dr *PUR/KEN* CR8 .... 88 B3
Dunmore *GUW* GU2 .... 116 A7
Dunmore Rd *RYNPK* SW20 .... 46 F1
Dunmow Cl *FELT* TW13 .... 25 H5 🔢
Dunnets *WOKN/KNAP* GU21 .... 76 B3
Dunning's Rd *EGRIN* RH19 .... 216 B2
EGRIN RH19 .... 216 B5
Dunnymans Rd *BNSTD* SM7 .... 85 J5
Dunoon Rd *FSTH* SE23 .... 32 F1
Dunottar Cl *REIG* RH2 .... 148 A2
Dunraven Av *REDH* RH1 .... 148 E8
Dunsbury Cl *BELMT* SM2 .... 65 L7 🔢
Dunsdon Av *GUW* GU2 .... 8 D6
Dunsfold Cl *CRAWW* RH11 .... 211 K4
Dunsfold Common Rd
MFD/CHID GU8 .... 203 J2
Dunsfold Ri *COUL/CHIP* CR5 ...... 87 G3
Dunsfold Rd *BIL* RH14 .... 223 G5
CRAN GU6 .... 204 C5
MFD/CHID GU8 .... 203 L1
MFD/CHID GU8 .... 204 B6
MFD/CHID GU8 .... 222 F2
Dunsfold Wy *CROY/NA* CR0 .... 69 M6 🔢
Dunsmore Rd *WOT/HER* KT12 .... 42 E5
Dunstable Rd *E/WMO/HCT* KT8 .... 43 J4
RCH/KEW TW9 .... 18 B6
Dunstall Pk *FARN* GU14 .... 92 D2
Dunstall Rd *RYNPK* SW20 .... 28 E7
Dunstall Wy *E/WMO/HCT* KT8 .... 43 L3
Dunstan Rd *COUL/CHIP* CR5 ...... 87 G7
Dunstan's Rd *EDUL* SE22 .... 32 D1
Dunster Av *MRDN* SM4 .... 47 G8
Dunsterville Wy *TOOT* SW17 ...... 30 C4
Dunton Cl *SURB* KT6 .... 45 H8🔢
Dunvegan Cl *E/WMO/HCT* KT8 .... 43 L4🔢
Dupont Rd *RYNPK* SW20 .... 47 G2
Duppas Av *CROY/NA* CR0 .... 4 B9
Duppas Cl *SHPTN* TW17 .... 42 A5
Duppas Hill La *CROY/NA* CR0 ...... 67 K3
Duppas Hill Ter *CROY/NA* CR0 ...... 4 B8
Duppas Rd *CROY/NA* CR0 .... 67 K2
Dura Den Cl *BECK* BR3 .... 33 L8
Durban Rd *BECK* BR3 .... 51 J2
WNWD SE27 .... 31 M5
Durbin Rd *CHSGTN* KT9 .... 63 H3
Durfold Dr *REIG* RH2 .... 125 M8
Durfold Rd *HORS* RH12 .... 229 G2
Durfold Wd *BIL* RH14 .... 222 F3
Durford Crs *PUT/ROE* SW15 .... 28 D2
Durham Av *HEST* TW5 .... 16 C1
Durham Cl *CRAWE* RH10 .... 212 B7🔢
GUW GU2 .... 116 C6
Durham Rd *EBED/NFELT* TW14 .... 24 F1🔢
RYNPK SW20 .... 46 E1
SHST GU47 .... 52 B7
Durkins Rd *EGRIN* RH19 .... 196 A6
Durleston Park Dr
GT/LBKH KT23 .... 101 M7
Durley Md *BRAK* RG12 .... 35 J5
Durlston Rd *KUTN/CMB* KT2 .... 2 E1
Durning Rd *NRWD* SE19 .... 32 A6
Durnsford Av *WAND/EARL* SW18 .. 29 K3
Durnsford Rd *WAND/EARL* SW18 .. 29 K3
WIM/MER SW19 .... 29 K4
Durnsford Wy *CRAN* GU6 .... 185 J7🔢
Durrell Wy *SHPTN* TW17 .... 42 A6
Durrington Av *RYNPK* SW20 .... 28 F8🔢
Durrington Park Rd
RYNPK SW20 .... 46 F1
Dutch Barn Cl *STWL/WRAY* TW19.. 14 A8
Dutchells Copse *HORS* RH12 .... 229 H3
Dutch Gdns *KUTN/CMB* KT2 .... 3 L1
Duval Pl *BAGS* GU19 .... 54 B6
Duxhurst La *HORL* RH6 .... 169 L2
Dwelly La *LING* RH7 .... 152 F5
Dyehouse Rd *MFD/CHID* GU8 .... 179 K5
Dyer's Fld *HORL* RH6 .... 171 L6
Dyer's La *PUT/ROE* SW15 .... 19 L5
Dynevor Pl *RGUW* GU3 .... 115 M4
Dynevor Rd *RCHPK/HAM* TW10 .... 18 B7
Dysart Av *KUTN/CMB* KT2 .... 26 F6

E

Eady Cl *SWTR* RH13 .... 229 J7
Eagle Cl *WLGTN* SM6 .... 67 H5🔢
Eagle Hi *NRWD* SE19 .... 32 A7
Eagle Rd *FARN* GU14 .... 92 E7
GU GU1 .... 9 H4
Eagles Dr *BH/WHM* TN16 .... 91 G8
Eardley Rd *STRHM/NOR* SW16 .... 30 F7
Earldom Rd *PUT/ROE* SW15 .... 19 M6
Earle Gdns *KUTN/CMB* KT2 .... 2 F1
Earles Meadow *HORS* RH12 ...... 229 L3
Earleswood *COB* KT11 .... 81 G2
Earleydene *ASC* SL5 .... 36 E8
Earl Rd *MORT/ESHN* SW14 .... 18 F6
Earlsbrook Rd *REDH* RH1 .... 148 C2
Earlsfield Rd *WAND/EARL* SW18 .. 29 M2
Earls Gv *CBLY* GU15 .... 73 H3
Earlsthorpe Rd *SYD* SE26 .... 33 G5
Earlswood *BRAK* RG12 .... 34 E7
Earlswood Av *THHTH* CR7 .... 49 K5🔢
Earlswood Cl *SWTR* RH13 .... 229 J5🔢
Earlswood Rd *REDH* RH1 .... 148 C2
Early Commons
CRAWE RH10 .... 212 C2🔢
CRAWE RH10 .... 212 C2🔢
Easby Crs *MRDN* SM4 .... 47 L6
Eashing La *RGODL* GU7 .... 159 J5
Easington Pl *GU* GU1 .... 9 M5
East Av *CROY/NA* CR0 .... 67 J4
FNM GU9 .... 134 A3
Eastbank Rd *HPTN* TW12 .... 25 M6
Eastbourne Gdns
MORT/ESHN SW14 .... 18 F5🔢
Eastbourne Rd *CHSWK* W4 .... 18 F1
EGRIN RH19 .... 195 J3
FELT TW13 .... 25 G3
GDST RH9 .... 128 F6
TOOT SW17 .... 30 D7
Eastbrook Cl *WOKN/KNAP* GU21 .. 71 H3
Eastbury La *RGUW* GU3 .... 137 K6
Eastbury Rd *KUTN/CMB* KT2 .... 2 E3
Eastchurch Rd *HTHAIR* TW6 ...... 15 H5

Eastcote Av *E/WMO/HCT* KT8 ...... 43 J5
Eastcroft Rd *HOR/WEW* KT19 ...... 64 B6
Eastdean Av *EPSOM* KT18 .... 83 L3
East Dr *CAR* SM5 .... 66 B7
VW GU25 .... 38 E6
Eastern Av *CHERT* KT16 .... 40 D3
CHOB/PIR GU24 .... 95 L3
Eastern La *CWTH* RG45 .... 52 C5
Eastern Perimeter Rd
HTHAIR TW6 .... 15 J5
Eastern Rd *ASHV* GU12 .... 113 H7
BRAK RG12 .... 35 G2
Eastern Vw *BH/WHM* TN16 .... 90 F7
Easter Wy *GDST* RH9 .... 151 J4
Eastfield Rd *REDH* RH1 .... 148 E1
Eastfields *MFD/CHID* GU8 .... 181 J4
Eastfields Rd *MTCM* CR4 .... 48 D2
Eastgate *BNSTD* SM7 .... 85 J4
East Grinstead Rd *LING* RH7 ...... 174 A6
East Hill *BH/WHM* TN16 .... 90 E8
EGRIN RH19 .... 196 B3
OXTED RH8 .... 130 C3
SAND/SEL CR2 .... 68 B8
WOKS/MYFD GU22 .... 7 L4
East Hill La *CRAWE* RH10 .... 194 A3
East Hill Rd *OXTED* RH8 .... 130 B3
Eastlands Cl *OXTED* RH8 .... 130 A1
Eastlands Wy *OXTED* RH8 .... 130 A1
East La *EHSLY* KT24 .... 99 M8
KUT KT1 .... 2 D8
Eastleigh Cl *BELMT* SM2 .... 65 L6🔢
Eastleigh Wy
EBED/NFELT TW14 .... 24 D2🔢
WOKN/KNAP GU21 .... 76 E7
East Meads *GUW* GU2 .... 138 C1
Eastmearn Rd *DUL* SE21 .... 31 M3
Eastmont Rd *ESH/CLAY* KT10 ...... 62 C1
Eastney Rd *CROY/NA* CR0 .... 4 A3
Eastnor Rd *REIG* RH2 .... 147 J2
East Pk *CRAWW* RH11 .... 212 A4
East Park La *LING* RH7 .... 172 F8
East Pl *WNWD* SE27 .... 31 M5
East Rp *HTHAIR* TW6 .... 14 E3
East Rd *EBED/NFELT* TW14 .... 24 A1
KUTN/CMB KT2 .... 2 F4
REIG RH2 .... 125 J7
WEY KT13 .... 60 A6
WIM/MER SW19 .... 29 M7
East Shalford La *RGUE* GU4 ...... 139 J3
East Sheen Av
MORT/ESHN SW14 .... 19 G7
East Station Rd *ASHV* GU12 ...... 112 E8
East Stratton Cl *BRAK* RG12 ...... 35 J5🔢
East St *BTFD* TW8 .... 17 M2
CRAWE RH10 .... 214 E5
EW KT17 .... 84 B2
FNM GU9 .... 133 M7
GT/LBKH KT23 .... 101 L7
HORS RH12 .... 210 B2
HORS RH12 .... 228 F8
East View La *CRAN* GU6 .... 184 F6
East Wk *REIG* RH2 .... 125 L8
East Wy *CROY/NA* CR0 .... 69 H1
Eastway *GUW* GU2 .... 116 C8
HOR/WEW KT19 .... 83 M2
MRDN SM4 .... 47 G5
WLGTN SM6 .... 66 F3🔢
Eastwell Cl *BECK* BR3 .... 51 H1
East Whipley La *SHGR* GU5 ...... 184 C3
Eastwick Dr *GT/LBKH* KT23 ...... 101 L6
Eastwick Park Av
GT/LBKH KT23 .... 101 L6
Eastwick Rd *GT/LBKH* KT23 ...... 101 L7
WOT/HER KT12 .... 60 E7
Eastwood *CRAWE* RH10 .... 212 C3
Eastwood Rd *SHGR* GU5 .... 161 J2
Eastwood St *STRHM/NOR* SW16 .. 30 F7
Eastworth Rd *CHERT* KT16 .... 40 C8
Eaton Ct *KUTN/CMB* KT2 .... 3 K3
Eaton Pk *COB* KT11 .... 81 H4
Eaton Park Rd *COB* KT11 .... 81 H4
Eaton Rd *BELMT* SM2 .... 66 A5
CBLY GU15 .... 72 E5
HSLW TW3 .... 17 G6
Eatonville Rd *TOOT* SW17 .... 30 C3
Eatonville Vls *TOOT* SW17 .... 30 C3🔢
Ebba's Wy *EPSOM* KT18 .... 83 L5
Ebbisham Cl
KWD/TDW/WH KT20 .... 104 C3
Ebbisham Rd *EPSOM* KT18 .... 83 L4
WPK KT4 .... 64 F1
Ebenezer Wk *MTCM* CR4 .... 48 F1
Ebsworth St *FSTH* SE23 .... 33 G1
Ebury Cl *HAYES* BR2 .... 71 H2
Ecclesbourne Rd *THHTH* CR7 .... 49 M5
Eccleshill *RDKG* RH5 .... 144 F6
Echelforde Dr *ASHF* TW15 .... 23 K5
Echo Barn La *NFNM* GU10 .... 155 H4
Echo Pit Rd *RGUE* GU4 .... 139 H4
Ecob Cl *RGUW* GU3 .... 116 C4
Ecton Rd *ADL/WDHM* KT15 .... 58 E3
Eddington Hl *CRAWW* RH11 ...... 211 K8
Eddington Rd *BRAK* RG12 .... 34 B6
Eddy Rd *ASHV* GU12 .... 112 F8
Ede Cl *HSLWW* TW4 .... 16 C5
Eden Cl *ADL/WDHM* KT15 .... 58 E8
Edencourt Rd
STRHM/NOR SW16 .... 30 E7
Edencroft *SHGR* GU5 .... 161 K2🔢
Edenfield Gdns *WPK* KT4 .... 64 C2
Eden Grove Rd *BF/WBF* KT14 ...... 79 H3
Eden Park Av *BECK* BR3 .... 51 H4
Eden Rd *BECK* BR3 .... 51 H4
CRAWW RH11 .... 211 J5
CROY/NA CR0 .... 4 E6
WNWD SE27 .... 31 M6
Edensfield Ct *REDH* RH1 .... 126 C6🔢
Edensor Rd *CHSWK* W4 .... 19 H2
Eden St *KUT* KT1 .... 2 E6
KUT KT1 .... 2 E7
Eden V *EGRIN* RH19 .... 196 B5
Edenvale Rd *MTCM* CR4 .... 30 D8

Eden Valley Wk *EDEN* TN8 .... 175 J3
Eden Wy *BECK* BR3 .... 51 K5
WARL CR6 .... 89 H8
Ederline Av *STRHM/NOR* SW16 .... 49 J3
Edgar Cl *CRAWE* RH10 .... 213 H4
HSLWW TW4 .... 25 J1
SAND/SEL CR2 .... 68 A8
Edge Cl *WEY* KT13 .... 59 K6
Edgecombe Cl *KUTN/CMB* KT2 .... 28 A8
Edgecoombe *SAND/SEL* CR2 ...... 69 G7
Edgefield Cl *CRAN* GU6 .... 184 F5
REDH RH1 .... 148 D5
Edge Hl *WIM/MER* SW19 .... 29 G8
Edgehill Ct *WOT/HER* KT12 .... 42 F8🔢
Edgehill Rd *MTCM* CR4 .... 48 E2
PUR/KEN CR8 .... 67 K8
Edgeley *GT/LBKH* KT23 .... 101 H6
Edgell Cl *VW* GU25 .... 39 J3
Edgell Rd *STA* TW18 .... 22 C7
Edgemoor Rd *FRIM* GU16 .... 73 M6🔢
Edgewood Gn *CROY/NA* CR0 ...... 51 G8
Edgeworth Cl *CTHM* CR3 .... 88 D3
Edgington Rd
STRHM/NOR SW16 .... 31 G7🔢
Edgington Dr *STA* TW18 .... 23 G7
Edinburgh Rd *SUT* SM1 .... 65 M3
Edinburgh Wy *EGRIN* RH19 ...... 216 C2
Edith Gdns *BRYLDS* KT5 .... 45 L7
Edith Rd *SNWD* SE25 .... 50 A5
WIM/MER SW19 .... 29 L7
Edmonds Ct *BRAK* RG12 .... 34 F1🔢
Edmund Gv *FELT* TW13 .... 25 J3🔢
Edmund Rd *MTCM* CR4 .... 48 B3
Edna Rd *RYNPK* SW20 .... 47 G2
Edrich Rd *CRAWW* RH11 .... 211 K8
Edridge Rd *CROY/NA* CR0 .... 4 D8
Edward Av *CBLY* GU15 .... 72 D4
MRDN SM4 .... 48 A4
Edward Cl *HPTN* TW12 .... 25 M6🔢
Edward Ct *STA* TW18 .... 22 F7
Edward Ii Av *BF/WBF* KT14 .... 79 K4🔢
Edward Rd *BFOR* GU20 .... 55 G5
BH/WHM TN16 .... 91 H8
COUL/CHIP CR5 .... 87 G5
CROY/NA CR0 .... 5 H1
EBED/NFELT TW14 .... 15 G7
FNM GU9 .... 11 G5
HPTN TW12 .... 25 M6
PGE/AN SE20 .... 33 H7
Edwards Cl *WPK* KT4 .... 65 G1🔢
Edward St *ALDT* GU11 .... 112 C7
Edward Wy *ASHF* TW15 .... 23 J3
Edwin Cl *EHSLY* KT24 .... 100 A7
Edwin Rd *EHSLY* KT24 .... 99 M7
WHTN TW2 .... 26 B2
Eelmoor Plain Rd *ALDT* GU11 .... 112 A5
Eelmoor Rd *ALDT* GU11 .... 112 A4
FARN GU14 .... 92 C7
Effingham Cl *BELMT* SM2 .... 65 L6
Effingham Common Rd
EHSLY KT24 .... 100 F7
Effingham La *CRAWE* RH10 ...... 194 B4
Effingham Pl *EHSLY* KT24 .... 121 G1
Effingham Rd *CROY/NA* CR0 .... 49 J7
HORL RH6 .... 193 M3
REIG RH2 .... 147 L1
SURB KT6 .... 44 E7
Effort St *TOOT* SW17 .... 30 B6
Effra Rd *WIM/MER* SW19 .... 29 L7
Egerton Pl *WEY* KT13 .... 59 M5
Egerton Rd *CBLY* GU15 .... 72 C3
GUW GU2 .... 116 C8
NWMAL KT3 .... 46 C4
SHST GU47 .... 72 B3
SNWD SE25 .... 50 B3
WEY KT13 .... 59 M5
WHTN TW2 .... 26 B1
Egerton Wy *WDR/YW* UB7 .... 14 E2
Eggars Fld *NFNM* GU10 .... 154 A4
Eggar's Hi *ALDT* GU11 .... 134 D1
Egham By-pass *EGH* TW20 .... 21 J5
Egham Cl *CHEAM* SM3 .... 65 H1🔢
Egham Crs *CHEAM* SM3 .... 65 G2
Egham Hl *EGH* TW20 .... 21 G7
Egleston Rd *MRDN* SM4 .... 47 L6
Eglise Rd *WARL* CR6 .... 89 H7
Eglinton Rd *NFNM* GU10 .... 178 C5
Egliston Ms *PUT/ROE* SW15 .... 19 M5
Egliston Rd *PUT/ROE* SW15 .... 19 M5
Egmont Park Rd
KWD/TDW/WH KT20 .... 104 D7
Egmont Rd *BELMT* SM2 .... 65 M6
NWMAL KT3 .... 46 C4
SURB KT6 .... 45 J8
WOT/HER KT12 .... 42 E7
Egmont Wy
KWD/TDW/WH KT20 .... 105 H1🔢
Egremont Rd *WNWD* SE27 .... 31 K4
Eighteenth Rd *MTCM* CR4 .... 49 H4🔢
Eileen Rd *SNWD* SE25 .... 50 A5
Eindoven Cl *MTCM* CR4 .... 48 D8🔢
Eland Rd *ASHV* GU12 .... 113 G8
CROY/NA CR0 .... 4 A7
Elberon Av *CROY/NA* CR0 .... 48 F6🔢
Elborough Rd *SNWD* SE25 .... 50 D5
Elborough St *WAND/EARL* SW18 .. 29 K2
Elcho Rd *CHOB/PIR* GU24 .... 94 F1
Elder Cl *GU* GU1 .... 117 K5
Eldergrove *FARN* GU14 .... 93 H7🔢
Elder Oak Cl *PGE/AN* SE20 .... 50 E1
Elder Rd *CHOB/PIR* GU24 .... 75 K5
WNWD SE27 .... 31 M6
Eldersley Cl *REDH* RH1 .... 126 C6
Eldersley Gdns *REDH* RH1 .... 126 C6🔢
Elderslie Cl *BECK* BR3 .... 51 K6
Elderton Rd *SYD* SE26 .... 33 H5
Eldertree Wy *MTCM* CR4 .... 48 E1
Elder Wy *RDKG* RH5 .... 144 F6
Eldon Av *CROY/NA* CR0 .... 68 F1
HEST TW5 .... 16 D2
Eldon Dr *NFNM* GU10 .... 11 J3
Eldon Pk *SNWD* SE25 .... 50 E4
Eldon Rd *CTHM* CR3 .... 108 A3
Eldridge Cl *EBED/NFELT* TW14 .... 24 D2

Eleanor Av HOR/WEW KT19 64 A8
Eleanor Gv BARN SW13 19 H5
Elfin Gv TEDD TW11 26 C6
Elfrida Crs CAT SE6 33 K5
Elgal Cl ORP BR6 71 L4
Elgar Av BRYLDS KT5 45 L8
STRHM/NOR SW16 49 H3
Elgar Wy HORS RH12 229 L5
Elger Wy CRAWE RH10 193 K5
Elgin Av ASHF TW15 23 M7
Elgin Crs CTHM CR3 108 D4
HTHAIR TW6 15 H4 1
Elgin Gdns GU GU1 117 K7
Elgin Rd CROY/NA CR0 5 K5
SUT SM1 65 M2
WEY KT13 59 K5
WLGTN SM6 66 F5
Elgin Wy FRIM GU16 93 J2
Eliot Bank FSTH SE23 32 E3
Eliot Cl CBLY GU15 73 L2
Eliot Dr HASM GU27 219 H3
Eliot Gdns PUT/ROE SW15 19 K6
Elizabethan Wy CRAWE RH10 212 F4
STWL/WRAY TW19 23 G1
Elizabeth Av BAGS GU19 54 C7
STA TW18 22 F7
Elizabeth Cl BRAK RG12 34 F4
RGODL GU7 160 B2
SUT SM1 65 J3 2
Elizabeth Cottages
RCH/KEW TW9 18 C3
Elizabeth Ct HORL RH6 170 D6 1
Elizabeth Crs EGRIN RH19 196 C6
Elizabeth Gdns ASC SL5 36 E5
SUN TW16 42 F3
Elizabeth Rd RGODL GU7 160 B2
Elizabeth Wy FELT TW13 24 F5
NRWD SE19 32 A8 1
Elkins Gdns RGUE GU4 117 K5
Elland Rd WOT/HER KT12 61 G1
Ellenborough Cl BRAK RG12 35 G1
Ellenborough Pl
PUT/ROE SW15 19 K6 2
Ellenbridge Wy SAND/SEL CR2 68 B7
Elleray Ct ASHV GU12 113 K4
Elleray Rd TEDD TW11 26 C7 5
Ellerdine Rd HSLW TW3 16 F6
Ellerker Gdns RCHPK/HAM TW10 18 B8
Ellerman Av WHTN TW2 25 J2
Ellerton Rd BARN SW13 19 K3 2
RYNPK SW20 28 D8
SURB KT6 45 J8 1
WAND/EARL SW18 30 A2
Ellery Cl CRAN GU6 185 H8
Ellery Rd NRWD SE19 32 A8
Elles Av GU GU1 117 L8
Elles Cl FARN GU14 92 E6
Ellesfield Av BRAK RG12 34 B4
Ellesmere Av BECK BR3 51 L2 2
Ellesmere Dr SAND/SEL CR2 88 E4
Ellesmere Rd TWK TW1 17 M8
WEY KT13 60 B5
Elles Rd FARN GU14 92 B7
Ellice Rd OXTED RH8 130 C3
Ellies Ms ASHF TW15 23 H3
Ellingham Rd CHSGTN KT9 63 G5
Ellington Rd FELT TW13 24 C5
HSLW TW3 16 E4
Ellington Wy EPSOM KT18 84 E7
Elliot Cl CRAWE RH10 212 F4 2
Elliot Ri ASC SL5 36 A2
Elliott Gdns SHPTN TW17 41 K4
Elliott Rd THHTH CR7 49 L4
Ellis Av GUW GU2 138 C2
Ellis Cl COUL/CHIP CR5 107 J2
Ellis Farm Cl WOKS/MYFD GU22 97 G4
Ellisfield Dr PUT/ROE SW15 28 C1
Ellison Rd BARN SW13 19 J4
STRHM/NOR SW16 31 G8
Ellison Wy NFNM GU10 135 J2
Ellis Rd COUL/CHIP CR5 107 J2
MTCM CR4 48 C6
Ellman Rd CRAWW RH11 211 J5
Ellora Rd STRHM/NOR SW16 31 G6
Ellson Cl CRAWE RH10 212 F5 3
Elmbank Av EGH TW20 20 E8
GUW GU2 8 B6
Elm Bank Gdns BARN SW13 19 H4
Elmbourne Rd TOOT SW17 30 E4
Elmbridge Av BRYLDS KT5 45 M6
Elmbridge La WOKS/MYFD GU22 97 J1
Elmbridge Rd CRAN GU6 184 C7
Elmbrook Cl SUN TW16 42 E1
Elmbrook Rd SUT SM1 65 J3
Elm Cl BRYLDS KT5 45 M7
CAR SM5 48 C8
KWD/TDW/WH KT20 123 M4
LHD/OX KT22 102 E4
RYNPK SW20 46 F4
SAND/SEL CR2 68 A5
STWL/WRAY TW19 23 G2
WARL CR6 89 G7
WHTN TW2 25 L3
WOKN/KNAP GU21 6 A2
Elm Ct WOKN/KNAP GU21 76 A7
Elmcourt Rd WNWD SE27 31 L3
Elm Crs FNM GU9 134 A2
KUTN/CMB KT2 2 F5 1
Elmcroft Cl CHSGTN KT9 63 H2 1
EBED/NFELT TW14 15 J8
FRIM GU16 93 J2 1
Elmcroft Dr ASHF TW15 23 K6 2
CHSGTN KT9 63 H2
Elmdene BRYLDS KT5 45 M8
Elmdene Cl BECK BR3 51 J5 2
Elmdon Rd HEST TW5 16 A4
HTHAIR TW6 15 J5
Elm Dr CHOB/PIR GU24 56 C8
EGRIN RH19 196 D8
LHD/OX KT22 102 E4
SUN TW16 42 F2
Elmer Gdns ISLW TW7 17 G5
Elmer Ms LHD/OX KT22 102 D5
Elmer Rd CAT SE6 33 M1
Elmers Av SURB KT6 45 H5
Elmer's Dr TEDD TW11 26 E7 1
Elmers End Rd BECK BR3 50 F3
PGE/AN SE20 50 F2
Elmerside Rd BECK BR3 51 H4 1
Elmers Rd CROY/NA CR0 5 M1
RDKG RH5 187 M5
Elmfield GT/LBKH KT23 101 K5
Elmfield Av MTCM CR4 48 D1
TEDD TW11 26 C6
Elmfield Rd TOOT SW17 30 E3
Elmfield Wy SAND/SEL CR2 68 C7
Elm Gdns ESH/CLAY KT10 62 C5
KWD/TDW/WH KT20 104 F1
MTCM CR4 49 G4
Elmgate Av FELT TW13 24 E4 2
Elm Gv CHOB/PIR GU24 75 K6
CRAN GU6 184 D6
CTHM CR3 108 B4
EPSOM KT18 83 M4
FNM GU9 133 M2
KUTN/CMB KT2 2 F5
SUT SM1 65 L3
SWTR RH13 229 H8
WIM/MER SW19 29 H8
Elmgrove Cl WOKN/KNAP GU21 96 A1
Elm Grove Pde WLGTN SM6 66 D2 1
Elm Grove Rd BARN SW13 19 K3
COB KT11 81 G6
Elmgrove Rd CROY/NA CR0 50 E7
Elm Grove Rd FARN GU14 92 E5
Elmgrove Rd WEY KT13 59 K3
Elmhurst Av MTCM CR4 30 D8
Elmhurst Ct GU GU1 9 M5
Elmhurst Dr DORK RH4 144 E4
Elm La CAT SE6 33 J3
NFNM GU10 135 J1
RPLY/SEND GU23 99 J1
Elmore Rd COUL/CHIP CR5 106 C3
Elm Pk ASC SL5 37 H8
Elmpark Gdns SAND/SEL CR2 68 F8
Elm Park Rd SNWD SE25 50 C3
Elm Pl ALDT GU11 134 F1
Elm Rd BECK BR3 51 J2
CHSGTN KT9 63 H3
EBED/NFELT TW14 24 A2
ESH/CLAY KT10 62 C5
EW KT17 64 C5
FNM GU9 134 A2
KUTN/CMB KT2 3 H3
LHD/OX KT22 102 E4
MORT/ESHN SW14 18 F5
MTCM CR4 48 D8
NWMAL KT3 46 A3
PUR/KEN CR8 87 L3
REDH RH1 126 B8
RGODL GU7 160 C1
THHTH CR7 49 M4
WARL CR6 89 G7
WOKN/KNAP GU21 6 A8
WOKN/KNAP GU21 6 F1
Elm Rd West MRDN SM4 47 J7
Elmshaw Rd PUT/ROE SW15 19 K7
Elmshorn EW KT17 84 F6 1
Elmside GUW GU2 8 A6
MFD/CHID GU8 159 J8
Elmsleigh Rd FARN GU14 92 D5
STA TW18 22 C6 3
WHTN TW2 26 A3
Elmslie Cl EPSOM KT18 83 M4
Elms Rd ALDT GU11 112 D8
Elmstead Cl HOR/WEW KT19 64 B4 1
Elmstead Gdns WPK KT4 64 D2
Elmstead Rd BF/WBF KT14 78 D3
The Elms BARN SW13 19 J5
NFNM GU10 135 J2
Elmsway ASHF TW15 23 J6 3
Elmswood GT/LBKH KT23 101 J6
Elmsworth Av HSLW TW3 16 E4
Elm Tree Av ESH/CLAY KT10 44 A7
Elm Tree Cl ASHF TW15 23 L6
Elmtree Cl BF/WBF KT14 79 H3
Elm Tree Cl CHERT KT16 58 B1
Elmtree Rd TEDD TW11 26 B6
Elm Vw ASHV GU12 113 L6
Elm Wk ORP BR6 71 J2
RYNPK SW20 46 F4
Elm Wy HOR/WEW KT19 64 A4
WPK KT4 64 F2
Elmwood Av FELT TW13 24 E4
Elmwood Cl EW KT17 64 D6 1
WLGTN SM6 66 E1
Elmwood Ct ASHTD KT21 83 G7
Elmwood Dr EW KT17 64 D6
Elmwood Rd CHSWK W4 18 F1
CROY/NA CR0 4 B1
MTCM CR4 48 C3
REDH RH1 126 D4
WOKN/KNAP GU21 96 A1
Elmworth Gv DUL SE21 32 A3
Elsdon Rd WOKN/KNAP GU21 76 D8
Elsenham St WIM/MER SW19 29 J2
Elsenwood Crs CBLY GU15 73 K3
Elsenwood Dr CBLY GU15 73 K2
Elsinore Av STWL/WRAY TW19 23 H1 2
Elsinore Rd FSTH SE23 33 H2
Elsinore Wy RCH/KEW TW9 18 E5 1
Elsley Cl FRIM GU16 93 J3
Elsrick Av MRDN SM4 47 K5
Elstan Wy CROY/NA CR0 51 H7
Elstead Rd MFD/CHID GU8 159 H3
NFNM GU10 135 K4
Elsted Cl CRAWW RH11 211 L1
Elston Pl ASHV GU12 134 F1
Elston Rd ASHV GU12 134 F1
Elsworth Cl EBED/NFELT TW14 24 B2
Elsworthy THDIT KT7 44 B6
Elthorne Ct FELT TW13 24 F2
Elton Rd KUTN/CMB KT2 3 J4
PUR/KEN CR8 86 F2
Elveden Cl WOKS/MYFD GU22 78 E7
Elveden Rd COB KT11 80 E1
Elvino Rd SYD SE26 33 G6
Elwell Cl EGH TW20 21 K7
Ely Cl CRAWE RH10 212 C7
FRIM GU16 93 K2
NWMAL KT3 46 C2
Ely Rd CROY/NA CR0 50 A5
HSLWW TW4 15 M5
HTHAIR TW6 15 J4 1
Elystan Cl WLGTN SM6 66 F7
The Embankment
STWL/WRAY TW19 20 F1
TWK TW1 26 D2
Ember Cl ADL/WDHM KT15 59 G4
Embercourt Rd THDIT KT7 44 B6
Ember Farm Av
E/WMO/HCT KT8 44 A6
Ember Farm Wy
E/WMO/HCT KT8 44 A5
Ember Gdns ESH/CLAY KT10 44 B7
Ember La ESH/CLAY KT10 44 A8
Emerton Rd LHD/OX KT22 101 M2
Emery Down Cl BRAK RG12 35 K3 1
Emley Rd ADL/WDHM KT15 58 D2
Emlyn La LHD/OX KT22 102 D4
Emlyn Rd HORL RH6 170 B5
REDH RH1 148 D2
Emmanuel Cl GUW GU2 116 D5
Emmanuel Rd BAL SW12 30 F2
Emmetts Cl WOKN/KNAP GU21 6 A5
Empire Vls REDH RH1 170 D2
Empress Av FARN GU14 92 E4
Emsworth Cl CRAWE RH10 212 F6 4
Emsworth St BRXS/STRHM SW2 31 J3
Ena Rd STRHM/NOR SW16 49 H3
Endale Cl CAR SM5 66 C1
Endeavour Wy CROY/NA CR0 49 G7
WIM/MER SW19 29 L5
Endlesham Rd BAL SW12 30 D1
Endsleigh Cl SAND/SEL CR2 68 F8
Endsleigh Gdns SURB KT6 44 F6
WOT/HER KT12 60 F4
Endsleigh Rd REDH RH1 126 F3
Endway BRYLDS KT5 45 K7
Endymion Rd
BRXS/STRHM SW2 31 J1
Enfield Cl LIPH GU30 218 A6 1
Enfield Rd ASHV GU12 113 L4
CRAWW RH11 211 L7
HTHAIR TW6 15 H4 2
Engadine Cl CROY/NA CR0 5 J8
Engadine St WAND/EARL SW18 29 J2
Engalee EGRIN RH19 195 M7
Englefield HORS RH12 228 C7
Englefield Cl CROY/NA CR0 49 M6 2
EGH TW20 20 F7 2
Englefield Rd
WOKN/KNAP GU21 75 M7 1
Engleheart Dr
EBED/NFELT TW14 15 J8
Engleheart Rd CAT SE6 33 L1
Englehurst EGH TW20 20 F7
Englemere Pk ASC SL5 36 A4
COB KT11 81 L4
Englesfield CBLY GU15 74 A4 2
Engliff La WOKS/MYFD GU22 78 C6
English Gdns STWL/WRAY TW19 12 A6
Enmore Av SNWD SE25 50 D5
Enmore Gdns MORT/ESHN SW14 19 G7
Enmore Rd PUT/ROE SW15 19 M6
SNWD SE25 50 D5
Ennerdale BRAK RG12 34 D4
Ennerdale Cl CRAWW RH11 211 L5 3
EBED/NFELT TW14 24 C2 7
SUT SM1 65 J3 3
Ennerdale Gv FNM GU9 133 K3
Ennerdale Rd RCH/KEW TW9 18 C4
Ennismore Av GU GU1 9 L4
Ennismore Gdns THDIT KT7 44 B6
Ensign Cl PUR/KEN CR8 67 K8
STWL/WRAY TW19 23 G2
Ensign Wy STWL/WRAY TW19 23 G2
Enterdent Rd GDST RH9 128 F8
Enterprise Cl CROY/NA CR0 49 K8
Enterprise Wy TEDD TW11 26 C6
Envis Wy RGUW GU3 115 M4
Eothen Cl CTHM CR3 108 D6
Epping Wk CRAWE RH10 212 C5
Epping Wy BRAK RG12 35 J4
Epsom Cl CBLY GU15 72 F1
Epsom La North
KWD/TDW/WH KT20 104 E1
Epsom La South
KWD/TDW/WH KT20 104 F3
Epsom Pl CRAN GU6 185 J6
Epsom Rd ASHTD KT21 83 J8
CRAWE RH10 212 D5
CROY/NA CR0 67 K3
EHSLY KT24 120 A3
EW KT17 64 C8
EW KT17 84 C1 1
GU GU1 9 K6
LHD/OX KT22 102 E3
MRDN SM4 47 J7 1
RGUE GU4 118 A7
Epsom Sq HTHAIR TW6 15 J4 2
Epts Rd FARN GU14 112 D1
Epworth Rd ISLW TW7 17 L2
Eresby Dr BECK BR3 51 K8
Erica Cl CHOB/PIR GU24 75 H3
Erica Ct WOKS/MYFD GU22 6 A8
Erica Gdns CROY/NA CR0 69 L3
Erica Wy CRAWE RH10 193 J6
HORS RH12 229 G4
Eridge Cl CRAWE RH10 212 F3
Eriswell Crs WOT/HER KT12 60 C5
Eriswell Rd WOT/HER KT12 60 C6 1
Erkenwald Cl CHERT KT16 40 B6 1
Ermine Cl HSLWW TW4 15 M4 3
Ermyn Cl LHD/OX KT22 103 G3
Ermyn Wy LHD/OX KT22 103 G3
Erncroft Wy TWK TW1 17 J8
Ernest Av WNWD SE27 31 L5
Ernest Cl BECK BR3 51 K5
NFNM GU10 10 F7
Ernest Gdns CHSWK W4 18 E1
Ernest Gv BECK BR3 51 J5
Ernest Rd KUT KT1 3 L7
Ernest Sq KUT KT1 3 L7
Ernle Rd RYNPK SW20 28 E8
Erpingham Rd PUT/ROE SW15 19 M5
Erridge Rd WIM/MER SW19 47 K2
Errol Gdns NWMAL KT3 46 D4
Erskine Cl CRAWW RH11 211 H7
SUT SM1 66 B2
Erskine Rd SUT SM1 66 A3
Esam Wy STRHM/NOR SW16 31 K6
Escombe Dr GUW GU2 116 E3
Escot Rd SUN TW16 24 B8
Escott Pl CHERT KT16 57 M5
Esher Av CHEAM SM3 65 G2
WOT/HER KT12 42 E8
Esher Cl ESH/CLAY KT10 61 L4
Esher Crs HTHAIR TW6 15 J4
Esher Gn ESH/CLAY KT10 61 L3
Esher Green Dr ESH/CLAY KT10 61 K2
Esher Ms MTCM CR4 48 D3
Esher Park Av ESH/CLAY KT10 61 M4
Esher Place Av ESH/CLAY KT10 61 K3
Esher Rd CBLY GU15 53 K8
E/WMO/HCT KT8 44 A5
WOT/HER KT12 61 H3
Eskdale Gdns PUR/KEN CR8 88 A4
Eskdale Wy CBLY GU15 73 M5
Eskmont Rdg NRWD SE19 32 B8
Esparto St WAND/EARL SW18 29 L1 1
Essendene Cl CTHM CR3 108 B5
Essendene Rd CTHM CR3 108 B5
Essenden Rd SAND/SEL CR2 68 B6
Essex Av ISLW TW7 17 H5
Essex Cl ADL/WDHM KT15 58 F3
FRIM GU16 93 K2
MRDN SM4 47 G7
Essex Ct BARN SW13 19 J4 1
Essex Dr CRAN GU6 184 C7
Essex Gv NRWD SE19 32 A7
Estcots Dr EGRIN RH19 196 E8
Estcourt Rd SNWD SE25 50 E6
Estella Av NWMAL KT3 46 E4
Estoria Cl BRXS/STRHM SW2 31 K1 1
Estreham Rd STRHM/NOR SW16 31 G7
Estridge Cl HSLW TW3 16 D6
Eswyn Rd TOOT SW17 30 C5
Ethelbert Rd RYNPK SW20 47 G1
Ethelbert St BAL SW12 30 E2 1
Ethel Rd ASHF TW15 23 H6
Etherley Hl RDKG RH5 187 K2
Etherstone Rd
STRHM/NOR SW16 31 J5
Eton Av HEST TW5 16 C1
NWMAL KT3 46 A5
Eton Cl WAND/EARL SW18 29 L1
Eton Ct STA TW18 22 C6 4
Eton Pl FNM GU9 133 L2
Eton Rd HYS/HAR UB3 15 J2
Eton St RCHPK/HAM TW10 18 A7
Etps Rd FARN GU14 112 E1
Etton Rd HSLW TW3 16 F7
Etwell Pl BRYLDS KT5 45 J6
Eureka Rd KUT KT1 3 J7
Europa Park Rd GU GU1 8 E1
Eustace Rd RGUE GU4 118 A6
Euston Rd CROY/NA CR0 49 K8
Evans Cl CRAWE RH10 213 G4
Evans Gv FELT TW13 25 K3
Evedon BRAK RG12 34 E7
Evelina Rd PGE/AN SE20 32 F8
Eveline Rd MTCM CR4 48 C1
Evelyn Av ALDT GU11 134 E1
Evelyn Cl WHTN TW2 25 L1
WOKS/MYFD GU22 97 G2
Evelyn Crs SUN TW16 42 C1
Evelyn Gdns GDST RH9 128 F4
RCH/KEW TW9 18 B6
Evelyn Rd RCH/KEW TW9 18 B5
RCHPK/HAM TW10 26 F4
WIM/MER SW19 29 L6
Evelyn Ter RCH/KEW TW9 18 B5
Evelyn Wy COB KT11 81 J6
SUN TW16 42 C1 1
WLGTN SM6 67 G3
Evelyn Woods Rd ALDT GU11 112 F2
Everdon Rd BARN SW13 19 K1
Everest Ct WOKN/KNAP GU21 76 B6
Everest Rd CBLY GU15 73 G1
STWL/WRAY TW19 23 G1
Everglade BH/WHM TN16 91 G8
Evergreen Rd FRIM GU16 73 J7
Evergreen Wy
STWL/WRAY TW19 23 G1 2
Everlands Cl WOKS/MYFD GU22 6 C8
Eve Rd ISLW TW7 17 K6
WOKN/KNAP GU21 7 J2
Eversfield Rd RCH/KEW TW9 18 C4
REIG RH2 125 L8
SWTR RH13 229 H8
Eversley Crs ISLW TW7 17 G3
Eversley Pk WIM/MER SW19 28 E6
Eversley Rd BRYLDS KT5 45 J4
NRWD SE19 32 A8
Eversley Wy CROY/NA CR0 69 K2
EGH TW20 39 M2
Everton Rd CROY/NA CR0 5 L3
Evesham Cl BELMT SM2 65 K6 3
REIG RH2 125 J7
Evesham Gn MRDN SM4 47 L6
Evesham Rd MRDN SM4 47 L6
REIG RH2 125 J7
Evesham Rd North REIG RH2 125 J7 1
Ewart Rd FSTH SE23 33 G1
Ewelands HORL RH6 170 F5
Ewell By-pass EW KT17 64 D6
Ewell Court Av HOR/WEW KT19 64 B4
Ewell Downs Rd EW KT17 84 D1
Ewell House Gv EW KT17 64 C8
Ewell Park Gdns EW KT17 64 D6
Ewell Park Wy EW KT17 64 D5
Ewell Rd CHEAM SM3 65 G5
SURB KT6 45 J6
THDIT KT7 44 E7
Ewelme Rd FSTH SE23 32 F2
Ewen Crs BRXS/STRHM SW2 31 K1
Ewhurst Av SAND/SEL CR2 68 C8 1
Ewhurst Cl BELMT SM2 64 F7
CRAWW RH11 211 M3
Ewhurst Rd CRAN GU6 185 H6
CRAWW RH11 211 L3
SHGR GU5 164 A3
Ewins Cl ASHV GU12 113 K7
Ewood La RDKG RH5 167 J3
Exbury Rd CAT SE6 33 K3
Excalibur Cl CRAWW RH11 211 H4 3
Excelsior Cl KUT KT1 3 J7
Exchange Rd ASC SL5 36 F5
CRAWE RH10 212 B3
Exeforde Av ASHF TW15 23 K5
Exeter Cl CRAWE RH10 212 B7
Exeter Rd ASHV GU12 113 K6
CROY/NA CR0 5 H2
FELT TW13 25 J4
HTHAIR TW6 15 H5
Exeter Wy HTHAIR TW6 15 H4
Exhibition Rd FARN GU14 112 D1
Explorer Av STWL/WRAY TW19 23 H2
Eyhurst Cl KWD/TDW/WH KT20 105 J6
Eyhurst Sp KWD/TDW/WH KT20 105 J6
Eyles Cl HORS RH12 228 E5
Eylewood Rd WNWD SE27 31 M6
Eynella Rd DUL SE21 32 C1
Eyston Dr WEY KT13 59 K8

F

Factory La CROY/NA CR0 4 A5
Faggs Rd EBED/NFELT TW14 15 J6
EBED/NFELT TW14 15 K6
Fairacre NWMAL KT3 46 B3
Fairacres COB KT11 81 G2
KWD/TDW/WH KT20 104 F3
Fairbairn Cl PUR/KEN CR8 87 K3 1
Fairbank Av ORP BR6 71 L1
Fairborne Wy GUW GU2 116 D5
Fairbourne COB KT11 81 G3
Fairbourne Cl WOKN/KNAP GU21 76 D7
Fairbourne La CTHM CR3 107 M4
Fairchildes Av CROY/NA CR0 90 A2
Fairchildes Rd WARL CR6 90 A5
Faircross BRAK RG12 34 E3
Fairdale Gdns PUT/ROE SW15 19 L6 1
Fairdene Rd COUL/CHIP CR5 87 G8
Fairfax BNFD RG42 34 D1
Fairfax Av EW KT17 64 E7
REDH RH1 126 C7
Fairfax Cl WOT/HER KT12 42 E8
Fairfax Ms FARN GU14 93 G7 1
Fairfax Rd FARN GU14 92 E2
TEDD TW11 26 D8
WOKS/MYFD GU22 97 L2
Fairfield Ap STWL/WRAY TW19 12 A8
Fairfield Av HORL RH6 170 D8
STA TW18 22 C5
WHTN TW2 25 L2
Fairfield Cl GT/LBKH KT23 101 L7
HOR/WEW KT19 64 B4
WIM/MER SW19 30 B8
Fairfield Dr DORK RH4 122 E8
FRIM GU16 73 H6
Fairfield East KUT KT1 2 F6
Fairfield La CHOB/PIR GU24 75 J2
Fairfield North KUT KT1 2 F6
Fairfield Pk COB KT11 81 G4
Fairfield Pth CROY/NA CR0 4 F7
Fairfield Pl KUT KT1 2 F8
Fairfield Ri GUW GU2 116 C7
Fairfield Rd BECK BR3 51 K2
CROY/NA CR0 4 F7
EGRIN RH19 216 C1
KUT KT1 2 F7
LHD/OX KT22 102 E3
STWL/WRAY TW19 12 A8
Fairfield South KUT KT1 2 F8
The Fairfield FNM GU9 133 M7
Fairfield Wy COUL/CHIP CR5 87 G4
HOR/WEW KT19 64 B4
Fairfield West KUT KT1 2 F7
Fairford Av CROY/NA CR0 51 G5
Fairford Cl BF/WBF KT14 78 C3
CROY/NA CR0 51 G5
REIG RH2 125 M6
Fairford Gdns WPK KT4 64 C2
Fairgreen Rd THHTH CR7 49 L5 1
Fairhaven EGH TW20 21 J6 2
Fairhaven Av CROY/NA CR0 51 G6
Fairhaven Rd REDH RH1 126 D4
Fairholme EBED/NFELT TW14 24 A1 1
Fairholme Crs ASHTD KT21 82 F7
Fairholme Gdns FNM GU9 11 H2
Fairholme Rd ASHF TW15 23 H6
CROY/NA CR0 49 K7
SUT SM1 65 J5
Fairlands Av RGUW GU3 115 M4
SUT SM1 65 K1
THHTH CR7 49 J4
Fairlands Rd RGUW GU3 115 M3
Fair La COUL/CHIP CR5 105 M7
Fairlawn GT/LBKH KT23 101 J6
Fairlawn Cl ESH/CLAY KT10 62 C5 2
FELT TW13 25 J5
KUTN/CMB KT2 27 M7
Fairlawn Crs EGRIN RH19 195 L7
Fairlawn Dr EGRIN RH19 195 L7
REDH RH1 148 B2
Fairlawn Gv BNSTD SM7 86 A3
Fairlawn Pk SYD SE26 33 H6
WOKN/KNAP GU21 77 H4
Fairlawn Rd BELMT SM2 85 M1
WIM/MER SW19 29 J8
Fairlawns ADL/WDHM KT15 78 C1 1
HORL RH6 170 E7
SUN TW16 42 D3
TWK TW1 18 A8 3
Fairlawns Cl STA TW18 22 E7 1
Fairlie Gdns FSTH SE23 32 F1
Fairlight Cl WPK KT4 64 F3
Fairlight Rd TOOT SW17 30 A5
Fairmead BRYLDS KT5 45 L8
WOKN/KNAP GU21 76 F8
Fairmead Cl HEST TW5 16 A2
NWMAL KT3 46 A3 1
SHST GU47 72 B2
Fairmead Rd CROY/NA CR0 49 J7 2
EDEN TN8 153 L4
Fairmeads COB KT11 81 H3
Fairmile Av COB KT11 81 H4
STRHM/NOR SW16 31 G6
Fairmile Ct COB KT11 81 H2
Fairmile Hts COB KT11 81 K3
Fairmile La COB KT11 81 G2
Fairmile Park Copse COB KT11 81 J2
Fairmile Park Rd COB KT11 81 J3
Fair Oak Cl LHD/OX KT22 82 A1
Fairoak Cl PUR/KEN CR8 87 L5

Fairoak La *LHD/OX* KT22 .... 82 B1
Fairs Rd *LHD/OX* KT22 .... 102 D1
Fairstone Ct *HORL* RH6 .... 170 E5 🔢
Fair St *HSLW* TW3 .... 16 F5 🔢
Fairview *EW* KT17 .... 84 F1
Fair Vw *HORS* RH12 .... 228 D6
Fairview Av *WOKS/MYFD* GU22 .... 6 D8
Fairview Cl *WOKS/MYFD* GU22 ...... 6 E8
Fairview Dr *SHPTN* TW17 .... 41 J5
Fairview Gdns *FNM* GU9 .... 134 A3
Fairview Pl *BRXS/STRHM* SW2 .... 31 J1
Fairview Rd *ASHV* GU12 .... 113 L6
        EW KT17 .... 84 C1 🔢
        STRHM/NOR SW16 .... 49 J1
        SUT SM1 .... 66 A4
Fairwater Dr
        ADL/WDHM KT15 .... 59 G7 🔢
Fairway *CAR* SM5 .... 85 M1
        CHERT KT16 .... 40 E8
        CRAWE RH10 .... 193 L7
        CRAWW RH11 .... 211 G4
        GU GU1 .... 118 A8
        RYNPK SW20 .... 46 F3
Fairway Cl *CRAWE* RH10 .... 193 L7
        CROY/NA CR0 .... 51 H5
        HOR/WEW KT19 .... 63 M3 🔢
        WOKS/MYFD GU22 .... 96 E1
Fairway Hts *CBLY* GU15 .... 73 L3
Fairways *ASHF* TW15 .... 23 K7
        GSHT GU26 .... 198 E3
        PUR/KEN CR8 .... 87 M7
        TEDD TW11 .... 2 C2
The Fairways *REDH* RH1 .... 148 A3 🔢
The Fairway *CHOB/PIR* GU24 .... 95 M6
        E/WMO/HCT KT8 .... 43 L3
        FNM GU9 .... 134 A2 🔢
        FRIM GU16 .... 73 K6
        LHD/OX KT22 .... 82 D8
        NWMAL KT3 .... 46 A1
        RGODL GU7 .... 160 C7
        WEY KT13 .... 79 K1
Fairwell La *EHSLY* KT24 .... 119 L2
Fairwyn Rd *SYD* SE26 .... 33 H4
Fakenham Wy *SHST* GU47 .... 52 A8
Falaise *EGH* TW20 .... 21 H6 🔢
Falaise Cl *ALDT* GU11 .... 112 E6
Falcon Cl *CHSWK* W4 .... 18 E1
        CRAWW RH11 .... 212 A1
        LTWR GU18 .... 74 C1
Falcon Dr *STWL/WRAY* TW19 .... 14 A8
Falconhurst *LHD/OX* KT22 .... 82 A5
Falcon Rd *GU* GU1 .... 9 H4
        HPTN TW12 .... 25 J8
Falcons Cl *BH/WHM* TN16 .... 91 G7
Falcon Wy *SUN* TW16 .... 42 B2
Falconwood *EGH* TW20 .... 21 H6 🔢
        EHSLY KT24 .... 100 C6
Falcon Wd *LHD/OX* KT22 .... 102 C2
Falconwood Rd *CROY/NA* CR0 .... 69 J7
Falcourt Cl *SUT* SM1 .... 65 L4
Falkland Gv *DORK* RH4 .... 144 D3
Falkland Park Av *SNWD* SE25 .... 50 B3
Falkland Rd *DORK* RH4 .... 144 D3
Falklands Dr *SWTR* RH13 .... 229 L5
Falkner Rd *FNM* GU9 .... 133 K7
Fallow Deer Cl *SWTR* RH13 .... 229 L6
Fallowfield Wy *HORL* RH6 ...... 170 E5 🔢
Fallsbrook Rd
        STRHM/NOR SW16 .... 30 E7
Falmer Cl *CRAWW* RH11 .... 212 A5 🔢
Falmouth Cl *CBLY* GU15 .... 73 K5
Falmouth Rd *WOT/HER* KT12 .... 60 F3 🔢
Falstone *WOKN/KNAP* GU21 .... 76 E8
Fambridge Cl *SYD* SE26 .... 33 J5
Famet Av *PUR/KEN* CR8 .... 87 M7
Famet Cl *PUR/KEN* CR8 .... 87 M7
Famet Wk *PUR/KEN* CR8 .... 87 M7
Fanes Cl *BNFD* RG42 .... 34 C1
Fanshawe Rd
        RCHPK/HAM TW10 .... 26 F5 🔢
Fanthorpe St *PUT/ROE* SW15 .... 19 M5
Faraday Av *EGRIN* RH19 .... 216 C3
Faraday Rd *CRAWE* RH10 .... 192 C7
        E/WMO/HCT KT8 .... 43 K4
        FARN GU14 .... 92 F3
        WIM/MER SW19 .... 29 L7
Fareham Rd *EBED/NFELT* TW14 ... 24 F1
Farewell Pl *MTCM* CR4 .... 48 A1
Farhalls Crs *HORS* RH12 .... 229 J3
Faringdon Dr *BRAK* RG12 .... 35 G5
Faris Barn Dr *ADL/WDHM* KT15 .. 78 C7
Faris La *ADL/WDHM* KT15 .... 78 C1
Farleigh Court Rd *WARL* CR6 ..... 89 J4
Farleigh Dean Crs *CROY/NA* CR0 .. 89 L1
Farleigh Rd *ADL/WDHM* KT15 ... 78 D1
        WARL CR6 .... 89 H7
Farleton Cl *WEY* KT13 .... 60 A5
Farley Copse *BNFD* RG42 .... 34 B1
Farleycroft *BH/WHM* TN16 .... 111 L8
Farley Heath Rd *SHGR* GU5 ... 162 E5
Farley La *BH/WHM* TN16 ...... 131 L1
Farley Nursery *BH/WHM* TN16 .. 131 M1
Farley Pk *OXTED* RH8 .... 130 D4
Farley Pl *SNWD* SE25 .... 50 D4
Farley Rd *CAT* SE6 .... 33 M1
        SAND/SEL CR2 .... 68 C6
Farleys Cl *EHSLY* KT24 .... 99 M8
Farlington Pl *PUT/ROE* SW15 .... 28 E1
Farlton Rd *WAND/EARL* SW18 ... 29 L1 🔢
Farm Av *HORS* RH12 .... 228 E6
        STRHM/NOR SW16 .... 31 H5
Farm Cl *ASC* SL5 .... 36 F5
        BELMT SM2 .... 66 A6
        BF/WBF KT14 .... 79 J2
        BIL RH14 .... 224 D6
        BNFD RG42 .... 34 C1
        CHERT KT16 .... 39 K6
        CRAWE RH10 .... 212 C2
        EGRIN RH19 .... 216 E1
        EHSLY KT24 .... 120 C2
        HORS RH12 .... 228 C2
        LHD/OX KT22 .... 102 A6
        RGUW GU3 .... 115 M3
        SHPTN TW17 .... 41 J7
        STA TW18 .... 22 B6
        WLGTN SM6 .... 66 F8
        WWKM BR4 .... 70 C2
Farmdale Rd *CAR* SM5 .... 66 B6

Farm Dr *CROY/NA* CR0 .... 69 J1
        PUR/KEN CR8 .... 87 G2
Farmer's Rd *STA* TW18 .... 22 B6 🔢
Farm Flds *SAND/SEL* CR2 .... 88 C1
Farmhouse Cl
        WOKS/MYFD GU22 .... 78 A5 🔢
Farmhouse Rd
        STRHM/NOR SW16 .... 30 F8
Farmington Av *SUT* SM1 .... 66 A2
Farm La *ADL/WDHM* KT15 .... 58 D5
        ASHTD KT21 .... 83 L8
        CROY/NA CR0 .... 69 J1
        EHSLY KT24 .... 120 C2
        NFNM GU10 .... 132 B4
        PUR/KEN CR8 .... 66 F8
        RPLY/SEND GU23 .... 97 M5
Farmleigh Cl *CRAWE* RH10 .... 212 F1 🔢
Farmleigh Gv *WOT/HER* KT12 .... 60 C4
Farm Pl *BIL* RH14 .... 224 C6
Farm Rd *ASHV* GU12 .... 113 H6
        BELMT SM2 .... 66 A6
        ESH/CLAY KT10 .... 43 K8
        FRIM GU16 .... 73 H7
        HSLWW TW4 .... 25 H2
        MRDN SM4 .... 47 L5
        STA TW18 .... 22 E7
        WARL CR6 .... 109 H1
        WOKS/MYFD GU22 .... 97 L2
Farmstead Dr *EDEN* TN8 ...... 153 M6
Farmstead Rd *CAT* SE6 .... 33 L5
Farmview *COB* KT11 .... 81 G6
Farm Wk *ASHV* GU12 .... 135 M1
        WPK KT4 .... 64 F2
Farnan Rd *STRHM/NOR* SW16 .. 31 H6
Farnborough Av *SAND/SEL* CR2 .. 69 H6
Farnborough Common
        ORP BR6 .... 71 J2
Farnborough Crs *SAND/SEL* CR2 .. 69 H7
Farnborough Rd *ALDT* GU11 .. 112 A8
        FARN GU14 .... 92 F4
        FARN GU14 .... 134 A1
Farnborough St *FARN* GU14 .... 93 G4
Farncombe Hl *RGODL* GU7 .... 160 A2
Farncombe St *RGODL* GU7 .... 160 B2
Farnell Rd *ISLW* TW7 .... 17 G5
        STA TW18 .... 22 D4
Farnham By-pass *FNM* GU9 .... 10 B3
Farnham Cl *BRAK* RG12 .... 35 G2 🔢
Farnham Gdns *RYNPK* SW20 .... 46 E2 🔢
Farnham La *HASM* GU27 ...... 199 K8
Farnham Park Cl *FNM* GU9 .... 133 L3
Farnham Rd *GUW* GU2 .... 8 E7
        GUW GU2 .... 138 A3
        MFD/CHID GU8 .... 157 M5
        NFNM GU10 .... 157 L4
Farnhurst La *CRAN* GU6 ...... 204 C5
Farningham *BRAK* RG12 .... 35 H6
Farningham Crs *CTHM* CR3 .... 108 D5
Farningham Rd *CTHM* CR3 .... 108 D5
Farnley *WOKN/KNAP* GU21 .... 76 C7
Farnley Rd *THHTH* CR7 .... 50 A4
Farquhar Rd *NRWD* SE19 .... 32 C6
        WIM/MER SW19 .... 29 K4 🔢
Farquharson Rd *CROY/NA* CR0 ... 4 C7
Farrell Cl *CBLY* GU15 .... 72 F6
Farren Rd *FSTH* SE23 .... 33 H3
Farriers Cl *EW* KT17 .... 84 B2 🔢
Farriers Rd *EW* KT17 .... 84 B1
The Farriers *SHGR* GU5 ...... 161 K4 🔢
Farthingham La *CRAN* GU6 .... 186 B3 🔢
Farthings *WOKN/KNAP* GU21 .... 76 B6
Farthing St *ORP* BR6 .... 71 J6
Fassett Rd *KUT* KT1 .... 45 H4
Fauconberg Rd *CHSWK* W4 .... 18 F1
Faulkner Pl *BAGS* GU19 .... 54 B5
Faulkner's Rd *WOT/HER* KT12 ... 60 F4
Faversham Rd *BECK* BR3 .... 51 J2 🔢
        CAT SE6 .... 33 J1
        MRDN SM4 .... 47 L6
        SHST GU47 .... 52 A8 🔢
Fawcett Cl *STRHM/NOR* SW16 .. 31 K5 🔢
Fawcett Rd *CROY/NA* CR0 .... 4 C8
Fawcus Cl *ESH/CLAY* KT10 .... 62 B5
Fawler Md *BRAK* RG12 .... 35 J4 🔢
Fawns Manor Rd
        EBED/NFELT TW14 .... 24 A2
Fawsley Cl *DTCH/LGLY* SL3 .... 13 H2
Faygate La *GDST* RH9 ...... 151 H6
        HORS RH12 .... 210 B2
Faygate Rd *BRXS/STRHM* SW2 .. 31 J3
Fayland Av *STRHM/NOR* SW16 .. 30 F6
Fay Rd *HORS* RH12 .... 228 F5
Fearn Cl *EHSLY* KT24 .... 120 B3
Fearnley *RGUW* KT13 .... 22 F6 🔢
Feathercombe La
        MFD/CHID GU8 .... 182 A5
Feathers La *STWL/WRAY* TW19 ... 21 K3
Featherstone *LING* RH7 ...... 151 L8
Featherstone Av *FSTH* SE23 .... 32 F3 🔢
Fee Farm Rd *ESH/CLAY* KT10 ... 62 C6
Felbridge Av *CRAWE* RH10 .... 213 G2
Felbridge Cl *BELMT* SM2 .... 65 L7
        EGRIN RH19 .... 195 M6
        FRIM GU16 .... 73 J7
        STRHM/NOR SW16 .... 31 K5
Felbridge Ct *EGRIN* RH19 .... 195 K6
Felbridge Rd *EGRIN* RH19 .... 195 G6
Felcot Rd *CRAWE* RH10 ...... 194 F6
Felcott Cl *WOT/HER* KT12 .... 60 F2
Felcott Rd *WOT/HER* KT12 .... 60 F2
Felcourt La *LING* RH7 ...... 173 L8
Felcourt Rd *EGRIN* RH19 ...... 195 M2
Felday Gld *RDKG* RH5 .... 164 E4
Felday Rd *RDKG* RH5 .... 142 C6
Felix La *SHPTN* TW17 .... 42 B6
Felix Rd *WOT/HER* KT12 .... 42 D6
Felland Wy *REDH* RH1 .... 148 A4
Fellbrook *RCHPK/HAM* TW10 ... 26 E4
Fellcott Wy *HORS* RH12 ...... 228 C8
Fellmongers Yd *CROY/NA* CR0 ... 4 C7
Fellowes Rd *CAR* SM5 .... 66 B2
Fellow Gn *CHOB/PIR* GU24 .... 75 J3
Fellow Green Rd
        CHOB/PIR GU24 .... 75 J3
Fellows Rd *FARN* GU14 .... 93 G8

Fell Rd *CROY/NA* CR0 .... 4 D7
Felmingham Rd *PGE/AN* SE20 .. 50 F2
Felsham Rd *PUT/ROE* SW15 .... 19 M5
Felstead Rd *HOR/WEW* KT19 ... 84 A1
Feltham Av *E/WMO/HCT* KT8 ... 44 B4
Felthambrook Wy *FELT* TW13 ... 24 E4
Feltham Hill Rd *ASHF* TW15 ... 23 K6
Felthamhill Rd *FELT* TW13 ...... 24 D5
Felton Av *ASHF* TW15 .... 23 L5
        MTCM CR4 .... 48 C2
        REDH RH1 .... 148 C5
Fenby Cl *SWTR* RH13 .... 229 L5
Fenchurch Rd *CRAWE* RH10 .. 212 E5
Fencote *BRAK* RG12 .... 35 G7
Fendall Rd *HOR/WEW* KT19 ... 63 M4
Fengates Rd *REDH* RH1 ...... 126 B8
Fenhurst Cl *HORS* RH12 ...... 228 C8
Fennel Cl *CROY/NA* CR0 .... 51 G8 🔢
        GU GU1 .... 117 L5
Fennel Crs *CRAWW* RH11 ...... 211 L6
Fennells Md *HOR/WEW* KT19 ... 64 C7
Fennscombe Ct *CHOB/PIR* GU24 .. 75 H3
Fenns La *CHOB/PIR* GU24 .... 75 H3
Fenn's Wy *WOKN/KNAP* GU21 ... 6 D2
Fenton Av *STA* TW18 .... 22 F7
Fenton Cl *REDH* RH1 .... 126 D8
Fenton Rd *REDH* RH1 .... 126 D8
Fentum Rd *GUW* GU2 .... 116 D6
Fenwick Cl *WOKN/KNAP* GU21 ... 76 E8
Fenwick Pl *SAND/SEL* CR2 .... 67 L6 🔢
Ferguson Av *BRYLDS* KT5 .... 45 J5
Ferguson Cl *BECK* BR3 .... 51 M3
Fermandy La *CRAWE* RH10 .... 194 D8
Fermor Rd *FSTH* SE23 .... 33 H2
Fern Av *MTCM* CR4 .... 49 G4
Fernbank Av *WOT/HER* KT12 ... 43 H7
Fernbank Crs *ASC* SL5 .... 36 A1
Fernbank Pl *ASC* SL5 .... 35 M1
Fernbank Rd *ADL/WDHM* KT15 .. 58 D4
        ASC SL5 .... 36 A2
Fernbrae Cl *NFNM* GU10 ...... 155 L7
Fern Cl *FRIM* GU16 .... 73 M6
        WARL CR6 .... 89 H8
Ferndale *GUW* GU2 .... 116 B6
Ferndale Av *CHERT* KT16 .... 58 B2
        HSLWW TW4 .... 16 B5
Ferndale Rd *ASHF* TW15 .... 23 G6
        BNSTD SM7 .... 85 J6
        SNWD SE25 .... 50 E5
        WOKN/KNAP GU21 .... 6 E4
Fernden La *HASM* GU27 ...... 219 L6
Ferndown *CRAWE* RH10 ...... 193 G7
        HORL RH6 .... 170 D4 🔢
        GU GU1 .... 139 K1
Ferndown Cl *BELMT* SM2 .... 66 A5
Ferndown Gdns *COB* KT11 .... 80 F4
Fernery *STA* TW18 .... 22 B5 🔢
The Fernery *STA* TW18 .... 22 B6 🔢
Ferney Ct *BF/WBF* KT14 .... 78 D3
Ferney Meade Wy *ISLW* TW7 ... 17 K4 🔢
Fern Gv *EBED/NFELT* TW14 ...... 24 E1
Fernham Rd *THHTH* CR7 .... 49 M3
Fernhill *LHD/OX* KT22 .... 82 A4
Fernhill Cl *CRAWE* RH10 ...... 194 E8 🔢
        FARN GU14 .... 72 B8
        FNM GU9 .... 133 L3
        WOKS/MYFD GU22 .... 96 F2
Fernhill Dr *FNM* GU9 .... 133 L3
Fernhill Gdns *KUTN/CMB* KT2 .. 27 G6
Fernhill La *FARN* GU14 .... 72 C8
        FNM GU9 .... 133 L2
        WOKS/MYFD GU22 .... 96 F2
Fernhill Pk *WOKS/MYFD* GU22 ... 96 F2
Fernhill Rd *BLKW* GU17 .... 72 B7
        FARN GU14 .... 92 B2
        HORL RH6 .... 193 G2
Fernhill Wk *FARN* GU14 .... 72 C8 🔢
Fernhurst Cl *CRAWW* RH11 .... 211 L1
Fernhurst Rd *ASHF* TW15 ...... 23 M5
Ferniehurst *CBLY* GU15 .... 73 J5
Ferniehough Cl *WEY* KT13 ...... 79 K1 🔢
Fernlands Cl *CHERT* KT16 .... 58 B2
Fernlea *GT/LBKH* KT23 ...... 101 L6
Fernlea Rd *BAL* SW12 .... 30 E2
        MTCM CR4 .... 48 D2
Fernleigh Cl *CROY/NA* CR0 .... 67 K3 🔢
        WOT/HER KT12 .... 60 C1
Fernleigh Ri *FRIM* GU16 .... 93 M2
Ferns Cl *SAND/SEL* CR2 .... 68 D3
Fernside Av *FELT* TW13 .... 24 E5
Fernside Rd *BAL* SW12 .... 30 C2
Fernthorpe Rd
        STRHM/NOR SW16 .... 30 F7
Fern Towers *CTHM* CR3 ...... 108 D7
Fern Wk *ASHF* TW15 .... 23 G6
Fern Wy *HORS* RH12 .... 229 G4
Fernwood *CROY/NA* CR0 .... 69 H7
Fernwood Av *STRHM/NOR* SW16 .. 31 G5
Feroners Cl *CRAWE* RH10 .... 212 D5 🔢
Ferrard Cl *ASC* SL5 .... 36 A1
Ferraro Cl *HEST* TW5 .... 16 D1
Ferrers Av *WLGTN* SM6 .... 67 G3
Ferrers Rd *STRHM/NOR* SW16 .. 31 G6
Ferriers Wy
        KWD/TDW/WH KT20 ...... 104 F1
Ferrings *DUL* SE21 .... 32 B3
Ferris Av *CROY/NA* CR0 .... 69 J2
Ferry Av *STA* TW18 .... 22 B8
Ferry La *BARN* SW13 .... 19 J1
        BTFD TW8 .... 18 B1
        CHERT KT16 .... 40 D6
        GUW GU2 .... 138 C4
        RCH/KEW TW9 .... 18 D1
        SHPTN TW17 .... 41 K8
        STA TW18 .... 40 F3
        STWL/WRAY TW19 .... 21 L3
Ferrymoor *RCHPK/HAM* TW10 .. 26 E4 🔢
Ferry Rd *BARN* SW13 .... 19 K2
        E/WMO/HCT KT8 .... 43 K3 🔢
        TEDD TW11 .... 26 E6
        THDIT KT7 .... 44 E6
Ferry Sq *BTFD* TW8 .... 18 B1 🔢
Fetcham Common La
        LHD/OX KT22 .... 101 L3 🔢
Fetcham Park Dr *LHD/OX* KT22 .. 102 B5
Fettes Rd *CRAN* GU6 ...... 185 K6

Fiddicroft Av *BNSTD* SM7 .... 85 L5 🔢
Field Cl *CHSGTN* KT9 .... 62 F4
        E/WMO/HCT KT8 .... 43 L5 🔢
        HSLWW TW4 .... 15 L3
        HYS/HAR UB3 .... 14 F2
        RGUE GU4 .... 118 A6
        SAND/SEL CR2 .... 88 E4
Fieldcommon La *WOT/HER* KT12 .. 43 H8
Field Ct *OXTED* RH8 .... 130 B2
Field End *CHOB/PIR* GU24 .... 75 J3
        COUL/CHIP CR5 .... 87 G4
        FNM GU9 .... 134 C5
Fieldend *HORS* RH12 .... 229 L4 🔢
        TEDD TW11 .... 26 C5
Fieldend Rd *STRHM/NOR* SW16 .. 48 F1
Fielden Pl *BRAK* RG12 .... 35 G2
Fielders Gn *GU* GU1 .... 117 K8 🔢
Field House Cl *ASC* SL5 .... 36 D8
Fieldhouse Rd *BAL* SW12 .... 30 F2
Fieldhurst Cl *ADL/WDHM* KT15 .. 58 E4
Fielding Av *WHTN* TW2 .... 25 M4
Fielding Rd *SHST* GU47 .... 72 B3
The Fieldings *FSTH* SE23 .... 32 F2
        HORL RH6 .... 170 E5
        WOKN/KNAP GU21 .... 76 D6
Field La *BTFD* TW8 .... 17 M2
        FRIM GU16 .... 73 H8
        RGODL GU7 .... 160 C2
        TEDD TW11 .... 26 D6
Field Pk *BRAK* RG12 .... 35 G1
Field Pl *NWMAL* KT3 .... 46 C6 🔢
Field Rd *EBED/NFELT* TW14 ...... 15 L8
        FARN GU14 .... 92 E2
Fieldsend Rd *CHEAM* SM3 .... 65 H4 🔢
Fieldside Cl *ORP* BR6 .... 71 M3
Field Stores Ap *ALDT* GU11 .. 112 F6
Field Vw *EGH* TW20 .... 21 M6
        FELT TW13 .... 24 A5
Fieldview *HORL* RH6 .... 170 E5 🔢
        WAND/EARL SW18 .... 30 A2
Field Wk *HORL* RH6 .... 171 M5
Field Wy *ASHV* GU12 .... 113 H7
        CROY/NA CR0 .... 69 L6
        NFNM GU10 .... 135 J2
        RPLY/SEND GU23 .... 98 C7
Fieldway *HASM* GU27 ...... 219 M2
Fie Yard Rd *FARN* GU14 .... 92 D7
Fifehead Cl *ASHF* TW15 .... 23 H7
Fife Rd *KUT* KT1 .... 2 E6
        MORT/ESHN SW14 .... 18 F7
Fife Wy *GT/LBKH* KT23 ...... 101 K7
Fifield La *NFNM* GU10 ...... 155 M7
Fifth Cross Rd *WHTN* TW2 ...... 26 A3
Figge's Rd *MTCM* CR4 .... 30 D8
Filbert Crs *CRAWW* RH11 .... 211 K3
Filby Rd *CHSGTN* KT9 .... 63 J5
Filey Cl *BELMT* SM2 .... 65 M6 🔢
        BH/WHM TN16 .... 110 E1
        CRAWW RH11 .... 211 J5
Filmer Gv *RGODL* GU7 ...... 160 B4
Finborough Rd *TOOT* SW17 .... 30 C8
Finch Av *WNWD* SE27 .... 32 A5
Finch Cl *WOKN/KNAP* GU21 ... 75 M7
Finch Dr *EBED/NFELT* TW14 ... 25 G1
Finches Ri *GU* GU1 .... 117 L6
Finch Rd *GU* GU1 .... 117 L6
Findhorn Cl *SHST* GU47 .... 72 A2 🔢
The Findings *FARN* GU14 .... 92 B1
Findlay Dr *RGUW* GU3 ...... 116 C4
Findon Cl *CRAWW* RH11 .... 211 L1
Findon Wy *HORS* RH12 ...... 228 B5
Finlay Gdns *ADL/WDHM* KT15 .. 58 F3
Finlays Cl *CHSGTN* KT9 .... 63 K4 🔢
Finmere *BRAK* RG12 .... 34 F6
Finnart Cl *WEY* KT13 .... 59 M3 🔢
Finney Dr *BFOR* GU20 .... 55 G5
Finsbury Cl *CRAWW* RH11 ...... 211 M7
Finstock Gn *BRAK* RG12 .... 35 J4 🔢
Fintry Pl *FARN* GU14 .... 92 B2 🔢
Fiona Cl *GT/LBKH* KT23 ...... 101 K6
Fir Acre Rd *ASHV* GU12 .... 113 K5
Firbank Dr *WOKN/KNAP* GU21 .. 96 D1
Firbank La *WOKN/KNAP* GU21 ... 96 E1
Firbank Pl *EGH* TW20 .... 20 E7
Fir Cl *WOT/HER* KT12 .... 42 D7
Fircroft Cl *WOKS/MYFD* GU22 .... 6 E5
Fircroft Rd *CHSGTN* KT9 .... 63 J3
        TOOT SW17 .... 30 C4
Fircroft Wy *EDEN* TN8 ...... 153 M6
Firdene *BRYLDS* KT5 .... 45 M8
Fir Dene *ORP* BR6 .... 71 J2
Fir Dr *BLKW* GU17 .... 72 A6
Fireball Hl *ASC* SL5 .... 37 G7
Fire Bell Aly *SURB* KT6 .... 45 H6 🔢
Firebell Ms *SURB* KT6 .... 45 H6 🔢
Fire Station Rd *ALDT* GU11 .. 112 E6
Firfield Rd *ADL/WDHM* KT15 ... 58 D3
        FNM GU9 .... 10 D6
Firfields *WEY* KT13 .... 59 L6
Fir Grange Av *WEY* KT13 .... 59 L4
Fir Gv *NWMAL* KT3 .... 46 C6
Firgrove *WOKN/KNAP* GU21 ... 96 D1
Firgrove Ct *FNM* GU9 .... 11 G1
Firgrove Hl *FNM* GU9 .... 11 G2
Firgrove Pde *FARN* GU14 .... 92 E5 🔢
Firgrove Rd *FARN* GU14 .... 92 E5
Firhill Rd *CAT* SE6 .... 33 K4
Firlands *BRAK* RG12 .... 34 F5
        HORL RH6 .... 170 E5
        WEY KT13 .... 60 B5
Firlands Av *CBLY* GU15 .... 73 G4 🔢
Firle Cl *CRAWE* RH10 .... 212 B1
Fir Rd *CHEAM* SM3 .... 47 J8
        FELT TW13 .... 25 G6
Firsby Av *CROY/NA* CR0 .... 51 G8
Firs Cl *DORK* RH4 .... 144 D4
        ESH/CLAY KT10 .... 62 B5
        FARN GU14 .... 92 E5
        FSTH SE23 .... 33 G1
        MTCM CR4 .... 48 E2
Firsdene Cl *CHERT* KT16 .... 58 A5
Firs Dr *HEST* TW5 .... 15 L2
Firs La *SHGR* GU5 ...... 162 A5
Firs Rd *PUR/KEN* CR8 .... 87 L5
First Av *ADL/WDHM* KT15 .... 58 E7

E/WMO/HCT* KT8 .... 43 J4
        HOR/WEW KT19 .... 64 B7
        MORT/ESHN SW14 .... 19 H4
        WOT/HER KT12 .... 42 E6
First Cl *E/WMO/HCT* KT8 .... 43 M4 🔢
First Cross Rd *WHTN* TW2 ...... 26 B3
The Firs *RGUW* GU3 .... 138 E4
Firstway *RYNPK* SW20 .... 46 F2
Firsway *GUW* GU2 .... 116 C7
Firswood Av *HOR/WEW* KT19 ... 64 B4
Fir Tree Av *HASM* GU27 ...... 219 G3
Firtree Av *MTCM* CR4 .... 48 D2
Fir Tree Cl *ASC* SL5 .... 36 D7
        CRAWW RH11 .... 191 L8
        ESH/CLAY KT10 .... 61 M4
        EW KT17 .... 84 F5
        HOR/WEW KT19 .... 64 C3
        LHD/OX KT22 .... 102 F5
        STRHM/NOR SW16 .... 30 F6
Fir Tree Gdns *CROY/NA* CR0 ... 69 K3 🔢
Fir Tree Gv *CAR* SM5 .... 66 C6
Fir Tree Rd *BNSTD* SM7 .... 85 G4
        EW KT17 .... 84 E6
        GU GU1 .... 116 F5
        HSLWW TW4 .... 16 B5
        LHD/OX KT22 .... 102 F5
Fir Tree Wk *REIG* RH2 ...... 126 A8
Fir Wk *EW* KT17 .... 65 G5
Firway *GSHT* GU26 ...... 198 B4
Firwood Cl *WOKN/KNAP* GU21 .. 96 B2
Firwood Dr *CBLY* GU15 .... 72 F4
Firwood Rd *VW* GU25 .... 38 B6
Fisher Cl *CRAWE* RH10 ...... 212 B5
        CROY/NA CR0 .... 5 J4
        WOT/HER KT12 .... 60 C1
Fisherdene *ESH/CLAY* KT10 ... 62 D6 🔢
Fisher La *MFD/CHID* GU8 ...... 222 D2
Fisherman Cl
        RCHPK/HAM TW10 .... 26 F5 🔢
Fishermen's Cl *ALDT* GU11 .. 113 H4
Fisher Rowe Cl *SHGR* GU5 .... 161 K3
Fishers Ct *HORS* RH12 ...... 228 F5
Fishers Wd *ASC* SL5 .... 37 M8
Fishponds Rd *HAYES* BR2 .... 71 G4
        TOOT SW17 .... 30 B5
Fitchet Cl *CRAWW* RH11 ...... 211 L1
Fitzalan Rd *ESH/CLAY* KT10 .... 62 B6
        HORS RH12 .... 229 K5
Fitzgeorge Av *NWMAL* KT3 .... 46 A1
Fitzgerald Av *MORT/ESHN* SW14 .. 19 H5
Fitzgerald Rd
        MORT/ESHN SW14 .... 19 G5 🔢
        THDIT KT7 .... 44 D4
Fitzjames Av *CROY/NA* CR0 ...... 5 M6
Fitzjohn Cl *RGUE* GU4 ...... 117 M5
Fitzrobert Pl *EGH* TW20 .... 21 K7
Fitzroy Crs *CHSWK* W4 .... 19 G3 🔢
Fitzroy Gdns *NRWD* SE19 ...... 32 B8
Fitzwilliam Av *RCH/KEW* TW9 ... 18 C4
Fitz Wygram Cl *HPTN* TW12 ... 25 M6 🔢
Fiveacre Cl *THHTH* CR7 .... 49 K6
Five Acres *CRAWE* RH10 ...... 212 B1
Five Elms Rd *HAYES* BR2 .... 70 F2
Five Oaks Cl *WOKN/KNAP* GU21 .. 96 A1
Five Oaks Rd *SWTR* RH13 ...... 227 K8
Flag Cl *CROY/NA* CR0 .... 51 G8
Flambard Wy *RGODL* GU7 .... 160 A5
Flamborough Cl
        BH/WHM TN16 .... 110 E1
Flanchford Rd *REIG* RH2 ...... 125 G6
Flanders Crs *TOOT* SW17 .... 30 C8
Flaxley Rd *MRDN* SM4 .... 47 L6
Fleece Rd *SURB* KT6 .... 44 F8
Fleet Cl *E/WMO/HCT* KT8 .... 43 J5
Fleetside *E/WMO/HCT* KT8 .... 43 J5
Fleetway *EGH* TW20 .... 39 M3 🔢
Fleetwood Cl *CHSGTN* KT9 .... 63 G6 🔢
        CROY/NA CR0 .... 3 J7
        KWD/TDW/WH KT20 .... 105 G3 🔢
Fleetwood Ct *BF/WBF* KT14 ... 78 D3 🔢
Fleetwood Rd *NWMAL* KT3 .... 3 M8
Fleetwood Sq *NWMAL* KT3 .... 3 M8
Fleming Cl *FARN* GU14 .... 93 G3
Fleming Ct *CROY/NA* CR0 .... 67 K4 🔢
Fleming Md *WIM/MER* SW19 .... 30 A8
Fleming Wy *CRAWE* RH10 .... 192 B7
        ISLW TW7 .... 17 J5
Flemish Flds *CHERT* KT16 .... 40 D7
Fletcher Cl *CHERT* KT16 .... 58 A5
        CRAWE RH10 .... 212 B5 🔢
Fletcher Gdns *BNFD* RG42 ...... 34 A1
Fletcher Rd *CHERT* KT16 .... 58 A5
Fletchers Cl *SWTR* RH13 ...... 229 H8
Flexford Gn *BRAK* RG12 .... 34 B6 🔢
Flexford Rd *RGUW* GU3 ...... 136 C1
Flint Cl *BNSTD* SM7 .... 85 L4
        CRAWE RH10 .... 212 E6
        GT/LBKH KT23 ...... 101 K6
        REDH RH1 .... 126 C7
Flintgrove *BRAK* RG12 .... 35 G1
Flint Hl *DORK* RH4 .... 144 E4
Flint Hill Cl *DORK* RH4 .... 144 E4
Flintlock Cl *STWL/WRAY* TW19 ... 13 K1
Flitwick Gra *MFD/CHID* GU8 .... 159 J8
Flock Mill Pl *WAND/EARL* SW18 .. 29 L2
Flood La *TWK* TW1 .... 26 D2 🔢
Flora Gdns *CROY/NA* CR0 .... 89 M1
Florence Av *ADL/WDHM* KT15 .. 78 D1
        MRDN SM4 .... 47 M5
Florence Cl *WOT/HER* KT12 ... 42 E7
Florence Gdns *CHSWK* W4 .... 18 F1 🔢
        STA TW18 .... 22 E8
Florence Rd *BECK* BR3 .... 51 G2
        FELT TW13 .... 24 E2
        KUTN/CMB KT2 .... 3 H3
        SAND/SEL CR2 .... 68 A7
        SHST GU47 .... 72 B2
        WIM/MER SW19 .... 29 L7
        WOT/HER KT12 .... 42 E7
Florence Wy *BAL* SW12 .... 30 C2
Florian Av *SUT* SM1 .... 66 A3
Florida Rd *RGUE* GU4 ...... 139 H6 🔢
        THHTH CR7 .... 49 L1
Floss St *PUT/ROE* SW15 ...... 19 M4
Flower Crs *CHERT* KT16 .... 57 L6
Flower La *GDST* RH9 ...... 129 G3
Flower Wk *GUW* GU2 .... 8 F9
Floyds La *WOKS/MYFD* GU22 ... 78 D6

Foden Rd *ALDT* GU11 .... 112 D8
Foley Ms *ESH/CLAY* KT10 ... 62 B5
Foley Rd *BH/WHM* TN16 ... 91 G8
  ESH/CLAY KT10 ... 62 B6
Follyfield Rd *BNSTD* SM7 ... 85 K4
Folly Hl *FNM* GU9 ... 133 K4
Folly La *RDKG* RH5 ... 166 E2
Folly La North *FNM* GU9 ... 133 L2
Folly La South *FNM* GU9 ... 133 K3 ▣
Fontaine Rd *STRHM/NOR* SW16 ... 31 J7
Fontenoy Rd *TOOT* SW17 ... 30 E3
Fontley Wy *PUT/ROE* SW15 ... 28 D1
Fontmell Cl *ASHF* TW15 ... 23 K6
Fontmell Pk *ASHF* TW15 ... 23 K6 ▣
Fontwell Rd *CRAWE* RH10 ... 212 D6 ▣
The Footpath *PUT/ROE* SW15 ... 19 H7 ▣
Forbes Cha *SHST* GU47 ... 72 A2
Forbes Cl *CRAWE* RH10 ... 212 E7 ▣
Fordbridge Rd *ASHF* TW15 ... 23 H7
  SHPTN TW17 ... 42 B6
  SUN TW16 ... 42 D5
Ford Cl *ASHF* TW15 ... 23 H7
  SHPTN TW17 ... 41 K4 ▣
  THHTH CR7 ... 49 L6
Fordingbridge Cl *CHERT* KT16 ... 40 E8 ▣
  HORS RH12 ... 228 F8
Ford La *NFNM* GU10 ... 10 E7
Ford Manor Rd *LING* RH7 ... 174 E7
Fordmill Rd *CAT* SE6 ... 33 K3
Ford Rd *ASHF* TW15 ... 23 J5
  CHOB/PIR GU24 ... 55 M8
  WOKS/MYFD GU22 ... 97 L2
Fordwater Rd *CHERT* KT16 ... 40 C8
Fordwells Dr *BRAK* RG12 ... 35 J4
Foreman Pk *ASHV* GU12 ... 113 L7
Foreman Rd *ASHV* GU12 ... 113 L8
Forest Cl *ASC* SL5 ... 35 M3
  CRAWE RH10 ... 214 E1
  EHSLY KT24 ... 100 C7
  SWTR RH13 ... 229 L5
  WOKS/MYFD GU22 ... 78 A5
Forest Crs *ASHTD* KT21 ... 83 K6
Forestdale *GSHT* GU26 ... 199 G6
Forest Dr *HAYES* BR2 ... 71 H2 ▣
  KWD/TDW/WH KT20 ... 105 K3
  NFNM GU10 ... 155 M5
  SUN TW16 ... 24 C8
Forester Rd *CRAWE* RH10 ... 212 B5
Foresters Cl *WLGTN* SM6 ... 67 G6
  WOKN/KNAP GU21 ... 76 C8
Foresters Dr *WLGTN* SM6 ... 67 G6
Foresters Sq *BRAK* RG12 ... 35 H3 ▣
Foresters Wy *CWTH* RG45 ... 52 C2
Forestfield *CRAWE* RH10 ... 212 E5
  SWTR RH13 ... 229 K6
Forest Gld *NFNM* GU10 ... 155 C6
Forest Gn *BRAK* RG12 ... 35 G2 ▣
Forest Hills *CBLY* GU15 ... 72 E5
Forest La *EHSLY* KT24 ... 100 C6
Forest Oaks *SWTR* RH13 ... 229 L5 ▣
Forest Rdg *BECK* BR3 ... 51 K3
  HAYES BR2 ... 71 H3
Forest Rd *CHEAM* SM3 ... 47 K8
  EHSLY KT24 ... 100 D5
  FELT TW13 ... 24 F4
  FROW RH18 ... 217 L8
  HORS RH12 ... 229 L5
  RCH/KEW TW9 ... 18 D2
  WOKS/MYFD GU22 ... 78 A5
Forest Side *WPK* KT4 ... 46 C8
Forest Vw *CRAWE* RH10 ... 212 C6
Forest View Rd *EGRIN* RH19 ... 216 B3
Forest Wy *ASHTD* KT21 ... 83 K7
  EGRIN RH19 ... 216 E4
Forge Av *COUL/CHIP* CR5 ... 107 K2
Forge Cl *FNM* GU9 ... 134 A6
  HORS RH12 ... 228 B5
Forge Cft *EDEN* TN8 ... 153 M8
Forge Dr *ESH/CLAY* KT10 ... 62 D6
Forge End *WOKN/KNAP* GU21 ... 91 G6
Forgefield *BH/WHM* TN16 ... 91 G6
Forge La *ALDT* GU11 ... 112 C3
  BELMT SM2 ... 65 H6
  CRAWE RH10 ... 212 B2 ▣
  FELT TW13 ... 25 H6
  HORS RH12 ... 228 A5
  SUN TW16 ... 42 D3
Forge Rd *BOR* GU35 ... 176 D8
  CRAWE RH10 ... 212 D2
Forge Wd *CRAWE* RH10 ... 193 G6
The Forge *HORS* RH12 ... 228 B2
Forrester Pth *SYD* SE26 ... 32 F5 ▣
Forrest Gdns *STRHM/NOR* SW16 ... 49 J3
  BRXS/STRHM SW2 ... 31 H1
  CROY/NA CR0 ... 4 D1
Forsyte Crs *NRWD* SE19 ... 50 B1
Forsyth Rd *WOKN/KNAP* GU21 ... 7 M1
Fortescue Av *WHTN* TW2 ... 25 H4
Fortescue Rd *WEY* KT13 ... 59 J3
  WIM/MER SW19 ... 30 B5
Forth Cl *FARN* GU14 ... 92 A3
Fort La *REIG* RH2 ... 125 L4
Fort Rd *GU* GU1 ... 9 J9
  KWD/TDW/WH KT20 ... 123 L5
Fortrose Cl *SHST* GU47 ... 72 A2 ▣
Fortrose Gdns
  BRXS/STRHM SW2 ... 31 H2
Fortune Dr *CRAN* GU6 ... 185 H8
Fortyfoot Rd *LHD/OX* KT22 ... 103 G4 ▣
The Forum *E/WMO/HCT* KT8 ... 43 L4 ▣
Forval Cl *MTCM* CR4 ... 48 C5
Foss Av *CROY/NA* CR0 ... 67 K4
Fosse Wy *BF/WBF* KT14 ... 78 B3
Fossewood Dr *CBLY* GU15 ... 73 G1
Foss Rd *TOOT* SW17 ... 30 A5
Fosterdown *GDST* RH9 ... 128 E3
Fosters La *WOKN/KNAP* GU21 ... 75 M7
Foulser Rd *TOOT* SW17 ... 30 C4
Foulsham Rd *THHTH* CR7 ... 49 M3
Founders Gdns *NRWD* SE19 ... 31 M8 ▣
Foundry Ct *CHERT* KT16 ... 40 D7 ▣
  HASM GU27 ... 219 K3
  SWTR RH13 ... 229 H6
Fountain Dr *CAR* SM5 ... 66 C6

NRWD SE19 ... 32 C5
Fountain Rd *REDH* RH1 ... 148 B2
  THHTH CR7 ... 49 M2
  TOOT SW17 ... 30 A6
Fountains Av *FELT* TW13 ... 25 J4
Fountains Cl *CRAWW* RH11 ... 211 K5 ▣
  FELT TW13 ... 25 J3
Fountains Garth *BRAK* RG12 ... 34 D3
Four Acres *COB* KT11 ... 81 H3
  GU GU1 ... 117 M6
Four Seasons Crs *CHEAM* SM3 ... 65 J1
Fourth Cross Rd *WHTN* TW2 ... 26 A3
Fourth Dr *COUL/CHIP* CR5 ... 87 G6
Four Wents *COB* KT11 ... 80 E3
Fowler Av *FARN* GU14 ... 92 E7
Fowler Cl *CRAWE* RH10 ... 212 F5
Fowler Rd *FARN* GU14 ... 92 C7
Fowlers La *BNFD* RG42 ... 34 E1 ▣
Fowlers Md *CHOB/PIR* GU24 ... 56 B7
Fowler's Rd *ALDT* GU11 ... 112 F4
Foxacre *CTHM* CR3 ... 108 B4
Foxborough Hill Rd
  MFD/CHID GU8 ... 160 F6
  SHGR GU5 ... 161 H1
Foxbourne Rd *TOOT* SW17 ... 30 D3
Foxbridge La *BIL* RH14 ... 223 M8
Foxburrows Av *GUW* GU2 ... 116 C8
Fox Cl *CRAWW* RH11 ... 211 L1
  WEY KT13 ... 60 A4
  WOKS/MYFD GU22 ... 78 A5
  LTWR GU18 ... 74 D1
Fox Covert Cl *ASC* SL5 ... 36 F5
Fox Dene *RGODL* GU7 ... 159 M7
Foxdown Cl *CBLY* GU15 ... 72 F4
Foxearth Cl *BH/WHM* TN16 ... 91 H8
Foxearth Rd *SAND/SEL* CR2 ... 68 E8
Foxearth Sp *SAND/SEL* CR2 ... 68 E7
Foxenden Rd *GU* GU1 ... 9 J5
Foxes Pth *RGUE* GU4 ... 97 J8
Foxglove Av *HORS* RH12 ... 229 H3
Foxglove Cl *STWL/WRAY* TW19 ... 23 G2
Foxglove Gdns *PUR/KEN* CR8 ... 87 L1
  RGUE GU4 ... 117 M6
Foxglove La *CHSGTN* KT9 ... 63 K3
Foxglove Wy *MTCM* CR4 ... 48 D7 ▣
Foxgrove Av *BECK* BR3 ... 33 L8
Foxgrove Dr *WOKN/KNAP* GU21 ... 7 G1
Foxgrove Rd *BECK* BR3 ... 33 L8
Foxhanger Gdns
  WOKS/MYFD GU22 ... 7 H4
Fox Hl *NRWD* SE19 ... 32 C8
Foxhill Crs *CBLY* GU15 ... 73 L1
Fox Hill Gdns *NRWD* SE19 ... 32 B8 ▣
Foxhills *WOKN/KNAP* GU21 ... 76 F7 ▣
Foxhills Cl *CHERT* KT16 ... 57 L5
Fox Hills La *ASHV* GU12 ... 113 M6
Fox Hills Rd *CHERT* KT16 ... 57 K4
Foxholes *HORS* RH12 ... 226 A1
  WEY KT13 ... 60 A4
Foxhurst Rd *ASHV* GU12 ... 113 K4
Foxlake Rd *BF/WBF* KT14 ... 79 J2 ▣
Fox La *GT/LBKH* KT23 ... 101 J6
  HAYES BR2 ... 70 E4
Fox La North *CHERT* KT16 ... 40 C7
Fox La South *CHERT* KT16 ... 40 C8 ▣
Foxleigh Cha *HORS* RH12 ... 229 J4 ▣
Foxley Cl *REDH* RH1 ... 148 D5 ▣
Foxley Gdns *PUR/KEN* CR8 ... 87 L3
Foxley Hill Rd *PUR/KEN* CR8 ... 87 K2
Foxley La *PUR/KEN* CR8 ... 67 H8
Foxley Rd *PUR/KEN* CR8 ... 87 L5
  THHTH CR7 ... 49 L4
Foxoak Hl *WEY* KT13 ... 60 B8
Foxon Cl *CTHM* CR3 ... 108 B3
Foxon La *CTHM* CR3 ... 108 A3
Foxon Lane Gdns *CTHM* CR3 ... 108 B3
Fox Rd *BRAK* RG12 ... 34 F4
  HASM GU27 ... 219 H3
  NFNM GU10 ... 11 H6
Foxton Gv *MTCM* CR4 ... 48 A2
Foxwarren *ESH/CLAY* KT10 ... 62 C7
Fox Wy *NFNM* GU10 ... 133 G1
Foxwood Cl *FELT* TW13 ... 24 E4
Fox Yd *FNM* GU9 ... 133 L7 ▣
Frailey Cl *WOKS/MYFD* GU22 ... 7 K4
Frailey Hl *WOKS/MYFD* GU22 ... 7 K3
Framfield Cl *CRAWW* RH11 ... 211 K1
Framfield Rd *MTCM* CR4 ... 30 D8
Frampton Cl *BELMT* SM2 ... 65 K6
Frampton Rd *HSLWW* TW4 ... 16 B7
France Hill Dr *CBLY* GU15 ... 72 F4
Franche Court Rd *TOOT* SW17 ... 29 M4
Francis Av *FELT* TW13 ... 24 D4
Francis Barber Cl
  STRHM/NOR SW16 ... 31 J5 ▣
Franciscan Rd *TOOT* SW17 ... 30 D5
Francis Chichester Cl *ASC* SL5 ... 36 E5
Francis Cl *HOR/WEW* KT19 ... 64 A3
  SHPTN TW17 ... 41 K4
Francis Edwards Wy
  CRAWW RH11 ... 211 H7 ▣
Francis Gv *WIM/MER* SW19 ... 29 J7 ▣
Francis Rd *CROY/NA* CR0 ... 4 B1
  CTHM CR3 ... 108 A4
  HSLWW TW4 ... 16 A4
  WLGTN SM6 ... 66 F5

Fraser Md *SHST* GU47 ... 72 B3
Fraser Rd *BNFD* RG42 ... 34 E1
Frederick Cl *SUT* SM1 ... 65 J3 ▣
Frederick Gdns *SUT* SM1 ... 65 J4
Frederick Sanger Rd
  GUW GU2 ... 138 A1 ▣
Frederick St *ALDT* GU11 ... 112 D7
Freeborn Wy *BRAK* RG12 ... 35 H2 ▣
Freelands Av *SAND/SEL* CR2 ... 69 G7
Freelands Rd *COB* KT11 ... 80 E4
Freeman Cl *SHPTN* TW17 ... 42 B4
Freeman Dr *E/WMO/HCT* KT8 ... 43 J4
Freeman Rd *HORS* RH12 ... 228 B1
  MRDN SM4 ... 48 A5
Freemantle Rd *BAGS* GU19 ... 54 C6
Freemason's Rd *CROY/NA* CR0 ... 5 G3
Free Prae Rd *CHERT* KT16 ... 40 D8
Freesia Dr *CHOB/PIR* GU24 ... 75 K6
Freethorpe Cl *NRWD* SE19 ... 50 B1
Frenchaye *ADL/WDHM* KT15 ... 58 F4 ▣
Frenches Rd *REDH* RH1 ... 126 D6
The Frenches *REDH* RH1 ... 126 D6
Frenches Ct *REDH* RH1 ... 126 D6 ▣
Frenchlands Hatch *EHSLY* KT24... 120 B1
French La *MFD/CHID* GU8 ... 180 B7
French St *SUN* TW16 ... 42 F2
French's Wls *WOKN/KNAP* GU21 ... 76 E7
Frensham *BRAK* RG12 ... 35 G6
Frensham Ct *NFNM* GU10 ... 155 L5
Frensham Dr *CROY/NA* CR0 ... 69 M6
  PUT/ROE SW15 ... 28 D4
Frensham Heights Rd
  NFNM GU10 ... 155 K7
Frensham Rd *FNM* GU9 ... 11 H5
  NFNM GU10 ... 156 A5
  PUR/KEN CR8 ... 87 L4 ▣
Frensham V *NFNM* GU10 ... 155 M5
Frensham Wy *EW* KT17 ... 84 F6 ▣
Freshborough Ct *GU* GU1 ... 9 L5 ▣
Freshfield Bank *FROW* RH18 ... 217 H7
Freshfield Cl *CRAWE* RH10 ... 212 D4 ▣
Freshfields *CROY/NA* CR0 ... 51 J7
Freshford St *TOOT* SW17 ... 29 M4
Freshmount Gdns
  HOR/WEW KT19 ... 63 M4
Freshwater Cl *TOOT* SW17 ... 30 D7 ▣
Freshwater Rd *TOOT* SW17 ... 30 D7
Freshwood Cl *BECK* BR3 ... 51 L1
Freshwood Wy *WLGTN* SM6 ... 66 F7 ▣
Frewin Rd *WAND/EARL* SW18 ... 30 A2
Friar Ms *WNWD* SE27 ... 31 L4 ▣
Friars Av *PUT/ROE* SW15 ... 28 C4
Friars Cft *RGUE* GU4 ... 117 M5
Friar's Ga *GUW* GU2 ... 8 A8
Friars Keep *BRAK* RG12 ... 34 E4
Friars La *RCH/KEW* TW9 ... 18 A7
Friars Orch *LHD/OX* KT22 ... 102 A3
Friars Ri *WOKS/MYFD* GU22 ... 7 H8
Friars Rd *VW* GU25 ... 39 G4
Friars Rookery *CRAWE* RH10 ... 212 B3
Friars Stile Rd
  RCHPK/HAM TW10 ... 18 B8
Friars Wy *CHERT* KT16 ... 40 D6
Friary Br *GU* GU1 ... 8 C7
Friary Ct *WOKN/KNAP* GU21 ... 76 C8
Friary Pas *GU* GU1 ... 8 C7
Friary Rd *ASC* SL5 ... 36 E6
Friary St *GU* GU1 ... 8 C7
Friary Wy *CRAWE* RH10 ... 212 B4 ▣
Friday Rd *MTCM* CR4 ... 30 C8
Friday St *HORS* RH12 ... 209 H4
  HORS RH12 ... 228 B2
  RDKG RH5 ... 188 A5
Friday Street Rd *RDKG* RH5 ... 165 H1
Friend Av *ASHV* GU12 ... 113 G8
Friends Cl *CRAWW* RH11 ... 192 A8 ▣
Friendship Wy *BRAK* RG12 ... 34 E3 ▣
Friends' Rd *CROY/NA* CR0 ... 4 E7
  PUR/KEN CR8 ... 87 L2 ▣
Frimley Av *WLGTN* SM6 ... 67 H4
Frimley Cl *CROY/NA* CR0 ... 69 M6
  WIM/MER SW19 ... 29 H3
Frimley Crs *CROY/NA* CR0 ... 69 M6
Frimley Gdns *MTCM* CR4 ... 48 B3
Frimley Green Rd *FRIM* GU16 ... 93 G8
Frimley Grove Gdns *FRIM* GU16 ... 73 G8
Frimley Hall Dr *CBLY* GU15 ... 73 J5
Frimley High St *FRIM* GU16 ... 73 F8 ▣
  FRIM GU16 ... 93 G1 ▣
Frimley Rd *ASHV* GU12 ... 113 K1
  CBLY GU15 ... 72 E5
  CHSGTN KT9 ... 63 G4
  FRIM GU16 ... 72 F8
Frinton Rd *TOOT* SW17 ... 30 D7
Friston Wk *CRAWW* RH11 ... 211 K2
Fritham Cl *NWMAL* KT3 ... 46 B6
Frith End Rd *ALTN* GU34 ... 176 C1
  BOR GU35 ... 176 C5
Frith Hill Rd *FRIM* GU16 ... 73 K8
  RGODL GU7 ... 160 A3
Frith Knowle *WOT/HER* KT12 ... 60 E4
Frith Pk *EGRIN* RH19 ... 196 B6
Frith Rd *CROY/NA* CR0 ... 4 C6
Friths Dr *REIG* RH2 ... 125 L3
Frithwald Rd *CHERT* KT16 ... 40 C7
Frobisher *BRAK* RG12 ... 34 F7
Frobisher Cl *PUR/KEN* CR8 ... 87 M7
Frobisher Crs *STWL/WRAY* TW19 ... 23 H1
Frobisher Gdns *GU* GU1 ... 117 K7
Frodsham Wy *SHST* GU47 ... 52 B7 ▣
Froggetts La *CRAN* GU6 ... 186 F8
Frog Grove La *RGUW* GU3 ... 115 J4
Frog La *BRAK* RG12 ... 34 D3
  RGUE GU4 ... 97 H7
Frogmore Cl *CHEAM* SM3 ... 65 G2
Frogmore Gdns *CHEAM* SM3 ... 65 H3 ▣
Frogmore Park Dr *BLKW* GU17 ... 72 A5
Frome Cl *FARN* GU14 ... 92 A3
Fromondes Rd *CHEAM* SM3 ... 65 H4
Fromow Gdns *BFOR* GU20 ... 55 G3 ▣
Froxfield Down *BRAK* RG12 ... 35 J5 ▣
Fruen Rd *EBED/NFELT* TW14... 24 C1
Fry Cl *CRAWW* RH11 ... 211 L8
Fryern Wd *CTHM* CR3 ... 107 M6
Fryston Av *COUL/CHIP* CR5... 86 E5

CROY/NA CR0 ... 5 M6
Fuchsia Wy *CHOB/PIR* GU24 ... 75 H3
Fulbourne Cl *REDH* RH1 ... 126 B6
Fulbrook La *MFD/CHID* GU8 ... 158 A3
Fulford Rd *CTHM* CR3 ... 108 A3
  HOR/WEW KT19 ... 64 A6
Fulham Cl *CRAWW* RH11 ... 211 L7
Fullbrook Av *ADL/WDHM* KT15... 78 D1
Fullbrooks Av *WPK* KT4 ... 46 C8
Fullers Av *SURB* KT6 ... 63 J1
Fullers Farm Rd *EHSLY* KT24... 119 L7
Fullers Rd *NFNM* GU10 ... 155 G5
Fullers Wy North *SURB* KT6 ... 63 J3
Fullers Wy South *CHSGTN* KT9 ... 63 H3
Fuller's Wd *CROY/NA* CR0 ... 69 K4
Fullers Wood La *REDH* RH1 ... 126 F8
Fullerton Cl *BF/WBF* KT14 ... 79 J4
Fullerton Dr *BF/WBF* KT14 ... 79 H4 ▣
Fullerton Rd *BF/WBF* KT14 ... 79 H4
  CAR SM5 ... 66 B7
  CROY/NA CR0 ... 5 J2
Fullerton Wy *BF/WBF* KT14... 79 H4
Fullmer Wy *ADL/WDHM* KT15... 58 C8
Fulmar Cl *CRAWW* RH11 ... 211 G4 ▣
Fulmar Dr *EGRIN* RH19 ... 196 D6
Fulmer Cl *HPTN* TW12 ... 25 H6
Fulstone Cl *HSLWW* TW4 ... 16 C6 ▣
Fulvens *SHGR* GU5 ... 164 B1
Fulwell Park Av *WHTN* TW2 ... 25 J5
Fulwell Rd *HPTN* TW12 ... 26 A5
Fulwood Gdns *TWK* TW1 ... 17 L8
Fulwood Wk *WIM/MER* SW19 ... 29 H2
Furlong Cl *MTCM* CR4 ... 48 E8 ▣
Furlong Rd *DORK* RH4 ... 143 M5
The Furlough *WOKS/MYFD* GU22... 7 H4
Furmage St *WAND/EARL* SW18... 29 L1
Furnace Dr *CRAWE* RH10 ... 212 C5
Furnace Farm Rd
  CRAWE RH10 ... 212 D5 ▣
Furnace Pde *CRAWE* RH10 ... 212 D5
Furnace Pl *CRAWE* RH10 ... 212 D5
Furnace Rd *CRAWE* RH10 ... 194 F6
Furneaux Av *WNWD* SE27 ... 31 L6
Furness Rd *MRDN* SM4 ... 47 L6
Furnival Cl *VW* GU25 ... 39 G6
Furrows Pl *CTHM* CR3 ... 108 C5
The Furrows *WOT/HER* KT12 ... 60 F1
Furse Cl *CBLY* GU15 ... 73 L5
Furtherfield Cl *CROY/NA* CR0 ... 49 K6 ▣
Furzebank *ASC* SL5 ... 37 G4 ▣
Furze Cl *ASHV* GU12 ... 113 K2
  REDH RH1 ... 126 C7
Furzedown Cl *EGH* TW20 ... 21 H7 ▣
Furzedown Dr *TOOT* SW17 ... 30 E6
Furzedown Rd *BELMT* SM2 ... 65 M6
  TOOT SW17 ... 30 E6
Furzefield *CRAWW* RH11 ... 211 L2
Furzefield Cha *EGRIN* RH19 ... 196 E5
Furzefield Crs *REIG* RH2 ... 147 M2
Furzefield Rd *EGRIN* RH19 ... 196 A5
  HORS RH12 ... 229 L4
  REIG RH2 ... 147 M2
Furze Gv *KWD/TDW/WH* KT20 ... 105 J3
Furze Hl *KWD/TDW/WH* KT20 ... 105 J3
  PUR/KEN CR8 ... 87 H1
Furzehill *REDH* RH1 ... 126 B7
Furze La *EGRIN* RH19 ... 195 L6
  PUR/KEN CR8 ... 87 H1
  RGODL GU7 ... 160 C1
Furzen La *HORS* RH12 ... 206 D6
Furze Rd *ADL/WDHM* KT15 ... 58 C5
  HORS RH12 ... 226 A1
  THHTH CR7 ... 49 M3 ▣
Furzewood *SUN* TW16 ... 42 D1
Fyfield Cl *BLKW* GU17 ... 72 A4

G

Gable Ct *SYD* SE26 ... 32 E5 ▣
Gables Av *ASHF* TW15 ... 23 J6
Gables Cl *ASHV* GU12 ... 113 K4
  FARN GU14 ... 92 D5
  WOKS/MYFD GU22 ... 97 J2 ▣
The Gables *BNSTD* SM7 ... 85 J7
  HORS RH12 ... 229 G5 ▣
  LHD/OX KT22 ... 81 M2
  WEY KT13 ... 59 M4
Gabriel Cl *FELT* TW13 ... 25 H5 ▣
Gabriel Dr *CBLY* GU15 ... 73 L5
Gabriel Rd *CRAWE* RH10 ... 212 F7
Gabriel St *FSTH* SE23 ... 33 G1
Gadbridge La *CRAN* GU6 ... 186 B5
Gadbrook Rd
  BRKHM/BTCW RH3 ... 146 A5
Gadesden Rd *HOR/WEW* KT19... 63 M5
Gaffney Cl *ALDT* GU11 ... 113 G2 ▣
Gage Cl *CRAWE* RH10 ... 194 F8
Gage Rdg *FROW* RH18 ... 217 H8
Gainsborough *BRAK* RG12 ... 34 F6
Gainsborough Cl *BECK* BR3 ... 33 K8 ▣
  CBLY GU15 ... 73 J2 ▣
  ESH/CLAY KT10 ... 44 B8 ▣
  FARN GU14 ... 93 G7 ▣
Gainsborough Ct
  WOT/HER KT12 ... 60 D3
Gainsborough Dr *ASC* SL5 ... 36 A3
  SAND/SEL CR2 ... 88 D3 ▣
Gainsborough Gdns *ISLW* TW7 ... 17 G7
Gainsborough Rd *CRAWE* RH10... 212 C7
  HOR/WEW KT19 ... 63 M8
  NWMAL KT3 ... 46 A6
  RCH/KEW TW9 ... 18 C4
Gaist Av *CTHM* CR3 ... 108 C4
Galahad Rd *CRAWW* RH11 ... 211 H3 ▣
Galata Rd *BARN* SW13 ... 19 K2
Gale Cl *HPTN* TW12 ... 25 H7 ▣
  MTCM CR4 ... 48 A3 ▣
Gale Crs *BNSTD* SM7 ... 85 K7 ▣
Gale Dr *LTWR* GU18 ... 54 D8
Galen Cl *HOR/WEW* KT19 ... 83 K1 ▣
Gales Cl *RGUE* GU4 ... 118 A5 ▣
Gales Dr *CRAWE* RH10 ... 212 C3
Gales Pl *CRAWE* RH10 ... 212 C3
Galgate Cl *WIM/MER* SW19 ... 29 H2 ▣
Gallery Rd *DUL* SE21 ... 32 A2

Galleymead Rd *DTCH/LGLY* SL3 .... 13 J3
The Gallop *BELMT* SM2 ... 66 A7
  SAND/SEL CR2 ... 68 E6
Galloway Pth *CROY/NA* CR0 ... 68 A3
Gallwey Rd *ALDT* GU11 ... 112 E6
Galpin's Rd *THHTH* CR7 ... 49 H4
Galsworthy Rd *CHERT* KT16 ... 40 D7 ▣
  KUTN/CMB KT2 ... 3 L3
Galton Rd *ASC* SL5 ... 37 J6
Gambles La *RPLY/SEND* GU23 ... 98 F7
Gambole Rd *TOOT* SW17 ... 30 B5
Gander Green Crs *HPTN* TW12 ... 43 K1
Gander Green La *CHEAM* SM3 ... 65 H3
  SUT SM1 ... 65 K5
Gangers Hl *GDST* RH9 ... 129 J1
Ganghill *GU* GU1 ... 117 K6
Gapemouth Rd *CHOB/PIR* GU24 ... 94 D4
  FRIM GU16 ... 94 B4
Gap Rd *WIM/MER* SW19 ... 29 K6
Garbetts Wy *NFNM* GU10 ... 135 H3
Garbrand Wk *EW* KT17 ... 64 C7
Garden Av *MTCM* CR4 ... 30 E8
Garden Cl *ADL/WDHM* KT15 ... 59 G3
  ASHF TW15 ... 23 M7
  BNSTD SM7 ... 85 K5
  EGRIN RH19 ... 216 C2
  FARN GU14 ... 92 B7
  HPTN TW12 ... 25 J6
  LHD/OX KT22 ... 102 F6
  PUT/ROE SW15 ... 28 E1
  SHGR GU5 ... 162 A5
  WLGTN SM6 ... 67 H4
Gardeners Cl *HORS* RH12 ... 228 B1
Gardeners Gn *HORS* RH12 ... 209 M3
Gardener's Hill Rd *NFNM* GU10 ... 155 L5
Gardeners Rd *CROY/NA* CR0 ... 4 B4
Gardener's Wk
  GT/LBKH KT23 ... 101 L8 ▣
Garden House La *EGRIN* RH19 ... 216 B2
Gardenia Ct *CHOB/PIR* GU24 ... 75 J3 ▣
Garden La *BRXS/STRHM* SW2 ... 31 J2
Garden Rd *PGE/AN* SE20 ... 50 F1
  RCH/KEW TW9 ... 18 D5
  WOT/HER KT12 ... 42 E6
The Gardens *BECK* BR3 ... 51 M2
  CHOB/PIR GU24 ... 95 J4
  EBED/NFELT TW14 ... 15 G8
  ESH/CLAY KT10 ... 61 K3
  NFNM GU10 ... 135 J2
Garden Wk *BECK* BR3 ... 51 J1
  COUL/CHIP CR5 ... 106 E5
Garden Wood Rd *EGRIN* RH19 ... 195 M8
Gardner La *CRAWE* RH10 ... 214 D1
Gardner Pl *EBED/NFELT* TW14 ... 15 L8 ▣
Gardner Rd *GU* GU1 ... 117 J6
Garendon Gdns *MRDN* SM4 ... 47 L7 ▣
Garendon Rd *MRDN* SM4 ... 47 L7
Gareth Cl *WPK* KT4 ... 65 G1 ▣
Garfield Rd *ADL/WDHM* KT15 ... 58 F4 ▣
  ADL/WDHM KT15 ... 58 F4 ▣
  CBLY GU15 ... 72 F4
  TWK TW1 ... 26 D2
  WIM/MER SW19 ... 29 M7
Garibaldi Rd *REDH* RH1 ... 148 C1
Garland Rd *EGRIN* RH19 ... 196 A8
Garlands Rd *LHD/OX* KT22 ... 102 E3
  REDH RH1 ... 126 C8
Garland Wy *CTHM* CR3 ... 108 A4
Garlichill Rd *EPSOM* KT18 ... 84 F7
Garlies Rd *FSTH* SE23 ... 33 H4
Garnet Rd *THHTH* CR7 ... 49 M4
Garrad's Rd *STRHM/NOR* SW16 ... 31 G4
Garrard Rd *BNSTD* SM7 ... 85 K6
Garratt Cl *CROY/NA* CR0 ... 67 H3
Garratt La *TOOT* SW17 ... 30 A4
  WAND/EARL SW18 ... 29 L1
Garratts La *BNSTD* SM7 ... 85 J6
Garratt Ter *TOOT* SW17 ... 30 B5
Garrett Cl *CRAWE* RH10 ... 212 F5 ▣
Garrick Cl *RCH/KEW* TW9 ... 17 M7
  STA TW18 ... 22 D8
  WOT/HER KT12 ... 60 E3
Garrick Crs *CROY/NA* CR0 ... 5 G6
Garrick Gdns *E/WMO/HCT* KT8 ... 43 K3
Garrick Rd *RCH/KEW* TW9 ... 18 D4 ▣
Garrick Wy *FRIM* GU16 ... 93 H3
Garrison Cl *HSLWW* TW4 ... 16 C7
Garrison La *CHSGTN* KT9 ... 63 H6
The Garrones *CRAWE* RH10 ... 213 H2 ▣
Garside Cl *HPTN* TW12 ... 25 L8
Garson La *STWL/WRAY* TW19 ... 21 G1
Garson Rd *ESH/CLAY* KT10 ... 61 J4
Garston La *PUR/KEN* CR8 ... 88 A5
The Garstons *GT/LBKH* KT23 ... 101 J7
Garswood *BRAK* RG12 ... 35 G6
Garth Cl *FNM* GU9 ... 10 D5
  KUTN/CMB KT2 ... 27 J6
  MRDN SM4 ... 47 G7
Garthorne Rd *FSTH* SE23 ... 33 G1
Garth Rd *KUTN/CMB* KT2 ... 27 J6
  MRDN SM4 ... 47 G8
Garthside *RCHPK/HAM* TW10 ... 27 J8
The Garth *ASHV* GU12 ... 113 J8
  COB KT11 ... 81 H3
  FARN GU14 ... 93 G5
  HPTN TW12 ... 25 L7
Gartmoor Gdns *WIM/MER* SW19 ... 29 J2
Garton Cl *CRAWW* RH11 ... 211 H4 ▣
Gascoigne Rd *CROY/NA* CR0 ... 69 M8
  WEY KT13 ... 59 L2 ▣
Gasden Copse *MFD/CHID* GU8 ... 181 G4
Gasden Dr *MFD/CHID* GU8 ... 181 G3
Gasden La *MFD/CHID* GU8 ... 181 G3
Gaskyns Cl *HORS* RH12 ... 226 A2
Gassiot Rd *TOOT* SW17 ... 30 C5
Gassiot Wy *SUT* SM1 ... 66 A2
Gasson Wood Rd *CRAWW* RH11 ... 211 H5
Gaston Bell Cl *RCH/KEW* TW9 ... 18 C5 ▣
Gaston Bridge Rd
  SHPTN TW17 ... 42 B5 ▣
Gaston Rd *MTCM* CR4 ... 48 D3
Gaston Wy *SHPTN* TW17 ... 42 A5
Gateford Dr *HORS* RH12 ... 229 J3
Gatehouse Cl *KUTN/CMB* KT2 ... 27 M8
Gates Cl *CRAWE* RH10 ... 212 F7 ▣
Gatesden Rd *LHD/OX* KT22 ... 101 M5
Gates Green Rd *WWKM* BR4 ... 70 D3
Gateside Rd *TOOT* SW17 ... 30 C4

Gatestone Rd *NRWD* SE19 .... 32 B7
Gateways *GU* CU1 .... 139 L1
The Gateway *WOKN/KNAP* GU21 ... 77 L4
Gatfield Gv *FELT* TW13 .... 25 K3
Gatley Av *HOR/WEW* KT19 .... 63 L4
Gatley Dr *GU* GU1 .... 117 J5
Gatton Bottom *REIG* RH2 .... 126 C2
Gatton Cl *BELMT* SM2 .... 65 L7 🔲
    REIG RH2 .... 125 M5
Gatton Park Rd *REDH* RH1 .... 126 A5
Gatton Rd *REIG* RH2 .... 125 M5
    TOOT SW17 .... 30 B5
Gatwick Rd *CRAWE* RH10 .... 192 D7
    HORL RH6 .... 192 D5
    WAND/EARL SW18 .... 29 J1
Gatwick Wy *HORL* RH6 .... 192 C1
Gauntlet Crs *PUR/KEN* CR8 .... 108 A1
Gauntlett Rd *SUT* SM1 .... 66 A4
Gavell Rd *COB* KT11 .... 80 D5 🔲
Gaveston Cl *BF/WBF* KT14 .... 79 J3
Gaveston Rd *LHD/OX* KT22 .... 102 D2
Gavina Cl *MRDN* SM4 .... 48 B5
Gayfere Rd *EW* KT17 .... 64 D4
Gayhouse La *REDH* RH1 .... 172 B2
Gayler Cl *REDH* RH1 .... 128 C8
Gaynesford Rd *CAR* SM5 .... 66 C6
    FSTH SE23 .... 33 G3
Gayton Cl *ASHTD* KT21 .... 83 H8
Gaywood Cl *BRXS/STRHM* SW2 .... 31 J2
Gaywood Rd *ASHTD* KT21 .... 83 J8
Geary Cl *HORL* RH6 .... 171 L8
Geffers Ride *ASC* SL5 .... 36 B3
Gemini Cl *CRAWW* RH11 .... 211 G5
Genesis Cl *STWL/WRAY* TW19 ...... 23 J2
Geneva Cl *SHPTN* TW17 .... 42 B2 🔲
Geneva Rd *KUT* KT1 .... 45 H4
    THHTH CR7 .... 49 M5
Genoa Av *PUT/ROE* SW15 .... 19 M7
Genoa Rd *PGE/AN* SE20 .... 50 F7
Genyn Rd *GUW* GU2 .... 8 D7
George Denyer Cl
    HASM GU27 .... 219 M2 🔲
George Eliot Cl
    MFD/CHID GU8 .... 181 J5 🔲
George Gdns *ALDT* GU11 .... 134 F2 🔲
George Groves Rd *PGE/AN* SE20 ... 50 F7
Georgeham Rd *SHST* GU47 .... 52 A7 🔲
George Rd *GU* GU1 .... 9 C4
    KUTN/CMB KT2 .... 3 M2
    MFD/CHID GU8 .... 159 J7
    NWMAL KT3 .... 46 C4
    RGODL GU7 .... 160 B2
George's Rd *BH/WHM* TN16 .... 111 C2
Georges Ter *CTHM* CR3 .... 108 A4 🔲
George St *CHOB/PIR* GU24 .... 94 D3
    CROY/NA CR0 .... 4 D6
    HSLW TW3 .... 16 C4
    RCHPK/HAM TW10 .... 18 A7
    STA TW18 .... 22 C3
Georgetown Cl *NRWD* SE19 ...... 32 A6 🔲
George Wyver Cl
    WIM/MER SW19 .... 29 H1 🔲
Georgian Cl *CBLY* GU15 .... 73 H2
    CRAWE RH10 .... 213 G4
    STA TW18 .... 22 E5
Georgia Rd *NWMAL* KT3 .... 45 M4
    THHTH CR7 .... 49 L1
Geraldine Rd *CHSWK* W4 .... 18 D1
Gerald's Gv *BNSTD* SM7 .... 85 G4
Gerard Av *HSLWW* TW4 .... 25 K1
Gerard Rd *BARN* SW13 .... 19 J3
Germander Dr *RGUE* GU4 .... 75 K6
Gerrards Md *BNSTD* SM7 .... 85 J6
Ghent St *CAT* SE6 .... 33 K3
Giant Arches Rd *HNHL* SE24 ...... 31 M1
Gibbet La *CBLY* GU15 .... 73 K2
Gibbon Rd *KUTN/CMB* KT2 .... 2 F4
Gibbons Cl *CRAWE* RH10 .... 212 F6 🔲
Gibbon Wk *PUT/ROE* SW15 .... 19 K6 🔲
Gibb's Acre *CHOB/PIR* GU24 .... 95 J5
Gibbs Av *NRWD* SE19 .... 32 A7
Gibbs Cl *NRWD* SE19 .... 130 A8
Gibbs Sq *NRWD* SE19 .... 32 A6 🔲
Giblets La *HORS* RH12 .... 229 J2
Giblets Wy *HORS* RH12 .... 229 H2
Gibraltar Crs *HOR/WEW* KT19 ..... 64 B8
Gibson Cl *CHSGTN* KT9 .... 62 F4 🔲
    ISLW TW7 .... 17 C5
Gibson Pl *STWL/WRAY* TW19 ..... 13 M1
Gibson Rd *SUT* SM1 .... 65 L4
Gibson's HI *STRHM/NOR* SW16 .... 31 K7
Gidd HI *COUL/CHIP* CR5 .... 86 D6
Giffard Dr *FARN* GU14 .... 92 C3
Giffards Md *EGRIN* RH19 .... 196 C8 🔲
Giffards Meadow *FNM* GU9 .... 11 L1
Giffard Wy *GUW* GU2 .... 116 D5
Giggs Hill Gdns *THDIT* KT7 .... 44 D8
Giggs Hill Rd *THDIT* KT7 .... 44 D7
Gilbert Dr *FRIM* GU16 .... 72 F4
    WIM/MER SW19 .... 29 M8
Gilbert St *HSLW* TW3 .... 16 F5 🔲
Gilbey Rd *TOOT* SW17 .... 30 B5
Gilders Rd *CHSGTN* KT9 .... 63 J5
Giles Coppice *NRWD* SE19 .... 32 C5
Giles Travers Cl *ECH* TW20 .... 39 M3 🔲
Gilham La *FROW* RH18 .... 217 H7
Gilham's Av *BNSTD* SM7 .... 85 G2
Gill Av *GUW* GU2 .... 138 B1
Gillett Ct *SWTR* RH13 .... 229 L5 🔲
Gillett Rd *THHTH* CR7 .... 50 A4
Gillham's La *HASM* GU27 .... 218 D5
Gilliam Gv *PUR/KEN* CR8 .... 67 K8
Gillian Av *ASHV* GU12 .... 134 F1
Gillian Cl *ASHV* GU12 .... 135 C1
Gillian Park Rd *CHEAM* SM3 .... 47 J8
Gilliat Dr *RGUE* GU4 .... 118 A4
Gilligan Cl *HORS* RH12 .... 228 E7
Gilmais *GT/LBKH* KT23 .... 101 M7
Gilmore Crs *ASHF* TW15 .... 23 K6
Gilpin Av *MORT/ESHN* SW14 .... 19 C6
Gilpin Cl *MTCM* CR4 .... 48 B2 🔲
Gilpin Crs *WHTN* TW2 .... 25 L1
Gilpin Wy *HYS/HAR* UB3 .... 15 C2
Gilsland Rd *THHTH* CR7 .... 50 A4
Gilson Ct *STWL/WRAY* TW19 .... 20 F1 🔲
Gimcrack HI *LHD/OX* KT22 .... 102 E4
Ginhams Rd *CRAWW* RH11 .... 211 L3 🔲

Gipsy HI *NRWD* SE19 .... 32 B6
Gipsy La *BARN* SW13 .... 19 K5
    BRAK RG12 .... 35 G3
Gipsy Rd *WNWD* SE27 .... 32 A5
Gipsy Road Gdns *WNWD* SE27 .... 31 M5
Girdwood Rd
    WAND/EARL SW18 .... 29 H1 🔲
Girling Wy *EBED/NFELT* TW14 ..... 15 K5
Girton Cl *SHST* GU47 .... 52 B8
Girton Gdns *CROY/NA* CR0 .... 69 K2
Girton Rd *SYD* SE26 .... 33 G6
Gisbourne Cl *WLGTN* SM6 .... 67 C2 🔲
Glade Cl *SURB* KT6 .... 63 C1 🔲
Glade Gdns *CROY/NA* CR0 .... 51 H7
Gladeside *CROY/NA* CR0 .... 51 G6
Glade Sp *KWD/TDW/WH* KT20 .... 105 L3
The Glades *ASC* SL5 .... 36 F5
    BELMT SM2 .... 65 H7
    BF/WBF KT14 .... 78 B3
    COUL/CHIP CR5 .... 107 K1
    CRAWE RH10 .... 212 D5
    CROY/NA CR0 .... 51 G5
    EW KT17 .... 64 D5
    FNM GU9 .... 134 A2
    FRIM GU16 .... 93 J7
    KWD/TDW/WH KT20 .... 105 L3
    LHD/OX KT22 .... 101 K4
    NFNM GU10 .... 154 E8
    STA TW18 .... 22 E8
    SWTR RH13 .... 229 K6
    WWKM BR4 .... 69 L2
Gladiator Wy *FARN* GU14 .... 112 D1
Gladioli Cl *HPTN* TW12 .... 25 K7 🔲
Gladsmuir Cl *WOT/HER* KT12 ...... 60 F1
Gladstone Av *EBED/NFELT* TW14 . 15 K8
    WHTN TW2 .... 26 A1
Gladstone Gdns *HSLW* TW3 .... 16 F3 🔲
Gladstone Ms *PGE/AN* SE20 .... 32 F8 🔲
Gladstone Rd *ASHTD* KT21 .... 83 C8
    CROY/NA CR0 .... 4 F2
    HORS RH12 .... 229 G6
    KUT KT1 .... 3 K8
    ORP BR6 .... 71 M4
    SURB KT6 .... 63 G1
    WIM/MER SW19 .... 29 K8 🔲
Glamis Cl *FRIM* GU16 .... 93 J2
Glamorgan Cl *MTCM* CR4 .... 49 H3 🔲
Glamorgan Rd *KUT* KT1 .... 2 B3
Glanfield Rd *BECK* BR3 .... 51 J4
The Glanty *ECH* TW20 .... 21 M5
Glasbrook Av *WHTN* TW2 .... 25 J2
Glasford St *TOOT* SW17 .... 30 C7
Glastonbury Rd *MRDN* SM4 .... 47 K6 🔲
    MRDN SM4 .... 47 K6 🔲
Glazebrook Cl *DUL* SE21 .... 32 A3
Glazebrook Rd *TEDD* TW11 .... 26 C8
Glaziers La *RGUW* GU3 .... 114 E6
Cleave Cl *EGRIN* RH19 .... 196 D7
Glebe Av *MTCM* CR4 .... 48 B2
Glebe Cl *CRAWE* RH10 .... 212 A2
    GT/LBKH KT23 .... 101 K8
    LTWR GU18 .... 54 F8
    SAND/SEL CR2 .... 88 C2
Glebe Cottages *RGUE* GU4 .... 118 E6
Glebe Gdns *BF/WBF* KT14 .... 79 C4
    NWMAL KT3 .... 46 B7
Glebe Hyrst *SAND/SEL* CR2 .... 88 C2
Glebeland Gdns *SHPTN* TW17 .... 41 M6
Glebeland Rd *CBLY* GU15 .... 72 C5
Glebelands *BIL* RH14 .... 224 C5
    CRAWE RH10 .... 214 D1
    E/WMO/HCT KT8 .... 43 L5
    ESH/CLAY KT10 .... 62 C7
Glebelands Rd
    EBED/NFELT TW14 .... 24 D1 🔲
Glebe La *NFNM* GU10 .... 178 F4
    RDKG RH5 .... 165 G1
Glebe Pth *MTCM* CR4 .... 48 C3
Glebe Rd *ASHTD* KT21 .... 83 C8
    BARN SW13 .... 19 K4
    BELMT SM2 .... 65 H7
    CAR SM5 .... 66 C5
    COUL/CHIP CR5 .... 106 D6
    CRAN GU6 .... 185 H5
    DORK RH4 .... 144 C2
    ECH TW20 .... 21 M7
    FARN GU14 .... 92 C4
    NFNM GU10 .... 132 C3
    STA TW18 .... 22 E6
    WARL CR6 .... 89 C7
Glebe Side *TWK* TW1 .... 17 J8
The Glebe *BLKW* GU17 .... 72 B5
    CRAN GU6 .... 186 B3
    CRAWE RH10 .... 193 L6
    EGRIN RH19 .... 195 K5
    HORL RH6 .... 170 C6 🔲
    REIG RH2 .... 146 D7
    WPK KT4 .... 46 C8
Glebe Wy *FELT* TW13 .... 25 K4
    SAND/SEL CR2 .... 88 C2
    WWKM BR4 .... 69 M1
Glebewood *BRAK* RG12 .... 34 F5
Gledhow Wd
    KWD/TDW/WH KT20 .... 105 L4
Glen Albyn Rd *WIM/MER* SW19 ... 29 C3 🔲
Glena Mt *SUT* SM1 .... 65 M3
Glen Av *ASHF* TW15 .... 23 K5
Glenavon Cl *ESH/CLAY* KT10 .... 62 D5
Glenbuck Rd *SURB* KT6 .... 45 G6
Glenburnie Rd *TOOT* SW17 .... 30 C4
Glencairn Rd *STRHM/NOR* SW16 . 31 H8
Glen Cl *GSHT* GU26 .... 198 F3
    KWD/TDW/WH KT20 .... 105 H5
    SHPTN TW17 .... 41 K4
Glencoe Cl *FRIM* GU16 .... 93 J1
Glencoe Rd *WEY* KT13 .... 59 K2 🔲
Glendale Cl *HORS* RH12 .... 229 K3
Glendale Dr *RGUE* GU4 .... 117 M4
Glen Dale Ms *BECK* BR3 .... 51 L1
Glendale Ri *PUR/KEN* CR8 .... 87 L5
Glendene Av *EHSLY* KT24 .... 100 B8
Glendower Gdns
    MORT/ESHN SW14 .... 19 G5 🔲
Glendower Rd
    MORT/ESHN SW14 .... 19 G5 🔲
Glendyne Cl *EGRIN* RH19 .... 216 D1

Glendyne Wy *EGRIN* RH19 .... 216 D1
Gleneagle Ms
    STRHM/NOR SW16 .... 31 G6 🔲
Gleneagle Rd
    STRHM/NOR SW16 .... 31 G6 🔲
Gleneagles Cl *HTHAIR* TW6 .... 13 M7
Gieneldon Ms
    STRHM/NOR SW16 .... 31 H5 🔲
Gleneldon Rd *STRHM/NOR* SW16 . 31 H5
Glenfield Cl *BRKHM/BTCW* RH3 . 145 L3
Glenfield Rd *ASHF* TW15 .... 23 L7
    BAL SW12 .... 30 F2
    BNSTD SM7 .... 85 L5
    BRKHM/BTCW RH3 .... 145 L4
Glen Gdns *CROY/NA* CR0 .... 67 K2
Glenheadon Cl *LHD/OX* KT22 .... 103 G5
Glenheadon Ri *LHD/OX* KT22 .... 103 G5
Glenhurst *BFOR* GU20 .... 54 D3
Glenhurst Cl *BLKW* GU17 .... 72 B5 🔲
Glenhurst Ri *NRWD* SE19 .... 31 M8
Glenhurst Rd *BTFD* TW8 .... 17 M1
Glen Innes *SHST* GU47 .... 52 C3
Glenister Park Rd
    STRHM/NOR SW16 .... 31 C8
Glenlea *GSHT* GU26 .... 199 H8
Glenlea Hollow *GSHT* GU26 ...... 219 H1
Glenmore Cl *ADL/WDHM* KT15 .... 58 E2
Glenmount Rd *FRIM* GU16 .... 93 K7
Glenn Av *PUR/KEN* CR8 .... 87 L1
Glennie Rd *WNWD* SE27 .... 31 K4
Glen Rd *CHSGTN* KT9 .... 63 H2
    GSHT GU26 .... 198 F3
Glentanner Wy *TOOT* SW17 .... 30 A4 🔲
Glentham Rd *BARN* SW13 .... 19 K1
The Glen *ADL/WDHM* KT15 .... 58 C4
    CROY/NA CR0 .... 69 G2
    ORP BR6 .... 71 J2
Glenthorne Av *CROY/NA* CR0 ...... 50 F8
Glenthorne Cl *CHEAM* SM3 .... 47 K8
Glenthorne Gdns *CHEAM* SM3 .... 47 K8
Glenthorne Rd *KUT* KT1 .... 45 J4 🔲
Glenthorpe Rd *MRDN* SM4 .... 47 C5
Glenview Cl *CRAWE* RH10 .... 212 C1
Glenville Gdns *GSHT* GU26 .... 199 J5
Glenville Ri *LHD/OX* KT22 .... 3 J4
Glen Vue *EGRIN* RH19 .... 196 B8
Glenwood *BRAK* RG12 .... 35 G4
    RDKG RH5 .... 144 F4
Glenwood Rd *CAT* SE6 .... 33 J2
    EW KT17 .... 64 D5
    HSLW TW3 .... 17 C5
Glenwood Wy *CROY/NA* CR0 .... 51 C6
Glorney Md *FNM* GU9 .... 134 D3
Glory Md *DORK* RH4 .... 144 F5
Glossop Rd *SAND/SEL* CR2 .... 68 A7
Gloster Rd *NWMAL* KT3 .... 46 B4 🔲
    WOKS/MYFD GU22 .... 97 K2
Gloucester Cl *FRIM* GU16 .... 93 H3
    THDIT KT7 .... 44 D8 🔲
Gloucester Ct *RCH/KEW* TW9 ...... 18 D2 🔲
Gloucester Crs *STA* TW18 .... 23 G7
Gloucester Dr *STWL/WRAY* TW19 . 21 M4
Gloucester Gdns *SUT* SM1 .... 65 L1
Gloucester Rd *ALDT* GU11 .... 134 F2
    BACS GU19 .... 54 B6
    CRAWE RH10 .... 212 B6
    CROY/NA CR0 .... 4 F3
    FELT TW13 .... 24 F2
    GUW GU2 .... 116 C6
    HPTN TW12 .... 25 L8
    HTHAIR TW6 .... 16 B6
    KUT KT1 .... 3 K7
    RCH/KEW TW9 .... 18 D2
    REDH RH1 .... 126 C7
    TEDD TW11 .... 26 B6
    WHTN TW2 .... 25 M2
Glover's Rd *HORL* RH6 .... 191 C7
    REIG RH2 .... 147 L1
Glyn Cl *EW* KT17 .... 64 D7
    SNWD SE25 .... 50 B2
Glyndebourne Pk *ORP* BR6 .... 71 L2
Glynde Pl *HORS* RH12 .... 228 F7 🔲
Glyn Rd *WPK* KT4 .... 65 G1
Glynswood *CBLY* GU15 .... 73 J6
    NFNM GU10 .... 155 K5
Goaters Rd *ASC* SL5 .... 35 M2
Goat Rd *MTCM* CR4 .... 48 D7
Goatsfield Rd *BH/WHM* TN16 .... 110 F2
Goat Whf *BTFD* TW8 .... 18 B1
Godalming Av *WLGTN* SM6 .... 67 H4
Godalming Rd *MFD/CHID* GU8 .. 183 G5
    RGODL GU7 .... 160 C6
Goddard Cl *CRAWE* RH10 .... 212 E6
    SHPTN TW17 .... 41 J3 🔲
Goddard Rd *BECK* BR3 .... 51 G4
Goddards La *CBLY* GU15 .... 72 E6
Godfrey Av *WHTN* TW2 .... 26 A1
Godfrey Wy *HSLWW* TW4 .... 25 H1
Godley Rd *BF/WBF* KT14 .... 79 J3
    WAND/EARL SW18 .... 30 A2
Godolphin Cl *BELMT* SM2 .... 85 J1
Godolphin Rd *WEY* KT13 .... 60 A5
Godric Crs *CROY/NA* CR0 .... 70 A7
Godson Rd *CROY/NA* CR0 .... 67 K2
Godstone Green Rd *GDST* RH9 .. 128 E5
Godstone HI *GDST* RH9 .... 128 F4
Godstone Rd *CTHM* CR3 .... 108 D6
    GDST RH9 .... 129 L5
    LING RH7 .... 173 M4
    OXTED RH8 .... 129 M4
    PUR/KEN CR8 .... 88 B5
    REDH RH1 .... 128 B7
    SUT SM1 .... 65 M3
    TWK TW1 .... 17 K8
Godwin Cl *HOR/WEW* KT19 .... 63 M5
Goffs Cl *CRAWW* RH11 .... 211 M4
Goffs La *CRAWW* RH11 .... 211 L3
Goffs Park Rd *CRAWW* RH11 .... 211 M4
Goffs Rd *ASHF* TW15 .... 24 A7
Cogmore Farm Cl *CHERT* KT16 .. 40 B7
Cogmore La *CHERT* KT16 .... 40 D7 🔲
Goidel Cl *WLGTN* SM6 .... 67 G3 🔲
Goidcliff Cl *MRDN* SM4 .... 47 K7
Goldcrest Wy *CROY/NA* CR0 .... 70 A7
    PUR/KEN CR8 .... 67 C8
Gold Cup La *ASC* SL5 .... 36 A1
Golden Flds *LIPH* GU30 .... 218 A6

Golden Orb Wd *BNFD* RG42 .... 34 A1
Goldfinch Cl *CRAWW* RH11 .... 212 A1
    HORS RH12 .... 228 F2
Goldfinch Gdns *RGUE* GU4 .... 118 A7
Goldfinch Rd *SAND/SEL* CR2 .... 69 G8
Goldhill *NFNM* GU10 .... 11 H8
Golding Cl *CRAWE* RH10 .... 212 F4 🔲
The Goldings *WOKN/KNAP* GU21 . 76 C6
Gold La *ALDT* GU11 .... 113 H5
Goldney Rd *CBLY* GU15 .... 73 L5
Goldsmiths Cl
    WOKN/KNAP GU21 .... 76 F8 🔲
Goldsworth Orch
    WOKN/KNAP GU21 .... 76 D8 🔲
Goldsworth Rd
    WOKN/KNAP GU21 .... 6 A7
Goldwell Rd *THHTH* CR7 .... 49 J4
Gole Rd *CHOB/PIR* GU24 .... 95 C3
Golf Cl *STRHM/NOR* SW16 .... 49 K1
    WOKS/MYFD GU22 .... 78 B4
Golf Club Dr *KUTN/CMB* KT2 ...... 28 A8
Golf Club Rd *WEY* KT13 .... 59 L8
    WOKS/MYFD GU22 .... 96 F7
Golf Dr *CBLY* GU15 .... 73 J5
Golf Links Av *GSHT* GU26 .... 198 E3
Golf Rd *PUR/KEN* CR8 .... 88 A8
Golf Side *BELMT* SM2 .... 85 H1
    WHTN TW2 .... 26 A4 🔲
Gomer Gdns *TEDD* TW11 .... 26 D7 🔲
Gomer Pl *TEDD* TW11 .... 26 D7
Gomshall Av *WLGTN* SM6 .... 67 H4
Gomshall Gdns *PUR/KEN* CR8 .... 88 B5
Gomshall La *SHGR* GU5 .... 141 K5
Gomshall Rd *BELMT* SM2 .... 64 F8 🔲
Gong HI *NFNM* GU10 .... 156 A6
Gong Hill Dr *NFNM* GU10 .... 156 A5
Gonston Cl *WIM/MER* SW19 .... 29 H3 🔲
Gonville Rd *THHTH* CR7 .... 49 J5
Goodden Crs *FARN* GU14 .... 92 C7
Goodenough Cl
    COUL/CHIP CR5 .... 107 K2
Goodenough Rd
    WIM/MER SW19 .... 29 J8
Goodenough Wy
    COUL/CHIP CR5 .... 107 J2
Goodhew Rd *SNWD* SE25 .... 50 D6
Gooding Cl *NWMAL* KT3 .... 45 K3
Goodley Stock Rd *EDEN* TN8 ... 131 L3
Goodman Crs
    BRXS/STRHM SW2 .... 31 G3 🔲
    BRXS/STRHM SW2 .... 31 H3 🔲
Goodways Dr *BRAK* RG12 .... 34 F2
Goodwin Cl *CRAWW* RH11 .... 211 H6
    MTCM CR4 .... 48 A3
Goodwin Gdns *CROY/NA* CR0 ...... 67 L5
    SAND/SEL CR2 .... 67 L5
Goodwin Rd *CROY/NA* CR0 .... 67 L5
Goodwins Cl *EGRIN* RH19 .... 196 A6
Goodwood Cl *CBLY* GU15 .... 72 F1
    CRAWE RH10 .... 212 D6 🔲
    MRDN SM4 .... 47 K4 🔲
Goodwood Pl *FARN* GU14 .... 93 H6 🔲
Goodwood Rd *REDH* RH1 .... 126 C6
Goodwyns Rd *DORK* RH4 .... 144 E5
Goose Gn *SHGR* GU5 .... 141 M5
Goose Green Cl *HORS* RH12 ...... 229 C4
Goose La *WOKS/MYFD* GU22 ...... 96 E4
Goose Rye Rd *RGUW* GU3 .... 96 A8
Goossens Cl *SUT* SM1 .... 65 M3 🔲
Gordon Av *CBLY* GU15 .... 72 F1
    MORT/ESHN SW14 .... 19 H6
    PUR/KEN CR8 .... 67 K8
    TWK TW1 .... 17 K7
Gordon Cl *CHERT* KT16 .... 58 B2
    STA TW18 .... 22 E7
Gordon Crs *CBLY* GU15 .... 72 F5
    CROY/NA CR0 .... 5 H3
Gordondale Rd
    WIM/MER SW19 .... 29 K3 🔲
Gordon Dr *CHERT* KT16 .... 58 B2
    SHPTN TW17 .... 42 A2 🔲
Gordon Rd *ALDT* GU11 .... 112 D8
    ASHF TW15 .... 23 H4
    BECK BR3 .... 51 J3
    BRYLDS KT5 .... 45 J7
    CAR SM5 .... 66 C5
    CBLY GU15 .... 72 F5
    CHSWK W4 .... 18 E1
    CTHM CR3 .... 108 A3
    CWTH RG45 .... 52 A6
    ESH/CLAY KT10 .... 62 B6
    FARN GU14 .... 113 C1
    HORS RH12 .... 229 H3
    HSLW TW3 .... 16 F6
    KUTN/CMB KT2 .... 3 C5
    RCH/KEW TW9 .... 18 C4
    REDH RH1 .... 126 D5
    SHPTN TW17 .... 42 A6
Gordons Wy *OXTED* RH8 .... 130 A2
Gore Rd *RYNPK* SW20 .... 46 F2
Goring Rd *STA* TW18 .... 22 A6
Goring's Md *SWTR* RH13 .... 229 C8
Gorling Cl *CRAWW* RH11 .... 211 H4 🔲
Gorringe Park Av *MTCM* CR4 ...... 30 C8
Gorringes Brook *HORS* RH12 .... 229 C3
Gorse Bank *LTWR* GU18 .... 74 D1 🔲
Gorse Cl *CRAWE* RH10 .... 193 L7
    KWD/TDW/WH KT20 .... 104 E2
    NFNM GU10 .... 10 D7
Gorse Ct *RGUE* GU4 .... 117 M6
Gorse Dr *HORL* RH6 .... 171 L5
Gorse End *HORS* RH12 .... 229 C4
Gorse Hill La *VW* GU25 .... 39 C4
Gorse Hill Rd *VW* GU25 .... 39 C4
Gorselands *ASHV* GU12 .... 113 K4
    BF/WBF KT14 .... 78 D1 🔲
Gorse La *CHOB/PIR* GU24 .... 56 B6
    NFNM GU10 .... 10 D7
Gorse Ri *TOOT* SW17 .... 30 D6
Gorse Rd *CROY/NA* CR0 .... 69 K2
    FRIM GU16 .... 73 H7
Gorsewood Rd
    WOKN/KNAP GU21 .... 96 A1 🔲
Gort Cl *ALDT* GU11 .... 113 H2
Gosberton Rd *BAL* SW12 .... 30 C2

Gosbury HI *CHSGTN* KT9 .... 63 H3
Gosden Cl *CRAWE* RH10 .... 212 D3 🔲
    SHGR GU5 .... 161 J1
Gosden Hill Rd *RGUE* GU4 .... 117 M4
Gosden Rd *CHOB/PIR* GU24 .... 75 J3
Gosfield Rd *HOR/WEW* KT19 ...... 84 A2
Gosnell Cl *FRIM* GU16 .... 74 A6 🔲
Gossops Dr *CRAWW* RH11 .... 211 K4
Gossops Green La
    CRAWW RH11 .... 211 K4
Gostling Rd *WHTN* TW2 .... 25 K2
Goston Gdns *THHTH* CR7 .... 49 K3
Gostrode La *MFD/CHID* GU8 .... 221 C3
Gothic Ct *HYS/HAR* UB3 .... 15 C1 🔲
Gothic Rd *WHTN* TW2 .... 26 A3
Goudhurst Cl *CRAWE* RH10 ...... 213 H3
Gough's La *BRAK* RG12 .... 34 F1
Gould Ct *RGUE* GU4 .... 118 A6
Goulding Gdns *THHTH* CR7 .... 49 M2 🔲
Gould Rd *EBED/NFELT* TW14 ...... 24 B1
    WHTN TW2 .... 26 B2
Government House Rd
    ALDT GU11 .... 112 D2
Government Rd *ALDT* GU11 ...... 113 H5
Governor's Rd *CBLY* GU15 .... 72 C3
Govett Av *SHPTN* TW17 .... 41 M5 🔲
Govett Gv *BFOR* GU20 .... 55 G4
Gower Pk *SHST* GU47 .... 72 A2
Gower Rd *HORL* RH6 .... 170 B6
    ISLW TW7 .... 17 J1 🔲
    WEY KT13 .... 60 A5
The Gower *ECH* TW20 .... 39 L3
Gowland Pl *BECK* BR3 .... 51 J2 🔲
Graburn Wy *E/WMO/HCT* KT8 .... 44 A3
Grace Bennett Cl *FARN* GU14 .... 92 D2 🔲
Gracedale Rd *TOOT* SW17 .... 30 E6
Gracefield Gdns
    STRHM/NOR SW16 .... 31 H4
Grace Rd *CRAWW* RH11 .... 211 K8
    CROY/NA CR0 .... 49 M6
Gracious Pond Rd *CHOB/PIR* GU24 56 C4
The Gradient *SYD* SE26 .... 32 D5
Graemesdyke Av
    MORT/ESHN SW14 .... 18 E5
Graffham Cl *CRAWW* RH11 .... 211 L1
Grafton Cl *BF/WBF* KT14 .... 78 D1
    HSLWW TW4 .... 25 H2
    WPK KT4 .... 64 B2
Grafton Park Rd *WPK* KT4 .... 64 B1
Grafton Rd *CROY/NA* CR0 .... 49 K8
    NWMAL KT3 .... 46 B4
    WPK KT4 .... 64 A2
Grafton Wy *E/WMO/HCT* KT8 ..... 43 J4
Graham Av *MTCM* CR4 .... 48 D1
Graham Cl *CROY/NA* CR0 .... 69 K1
Graham Gdns *SURB* KT6 .... 45 H8
Graham Rd *BFOR* GU20 .... 54 F5
    HPTN TW12 .... 25 K5
    MTCM CR4 .... 48 D1
    PUR/KEN CR8 .... 87 K3
    WIM/MER SW19 .... 29 J8
Grainger Rd *ISLW* TW7 .... 17 J4
Grampian Cl *HYS/HAR* UB3 .... 15 C1 🔲
Granada St *TOOT* SW17 .... 30 C6 🔲
Granard Av *PUT/ROE* SW15 .... 19 L7
Granard Rd *BAL* SW12 .... 30 C1
Granary Cl *HORL* RH6 .... 170 D4 🔲
Granary Wy *HORS* RH12 .... 228 C8
Grand Av *BRYLDS* KT5 .... 45 L6
    CBLY GU15 .... 72 F3
Grand Dr *RYNPK* SW20 .... 46 F3
Granden Rd
    STRHM/NOR SW16 .... 49 H2 🔲
Grandison Rd *WPK* KT4 .... 64 F1
Grand Stand Rd *EPSOM* KT18 ..... 84 C7
Grand View Av *BH/WHM* TN16 .... 90 F7
Grange Av *SNWD* SE25 .... 50 B2
    WHTN TW2 .... 26 B3
Grangecliffe Gdns *SNWD* SE25 ... 50 B2
Grange Cl *CRAWE* RH10 .... 212 A2
    E/WMO/HCT KT8 .... 43 L4
    EDEN TN8 .... 153 M3 🔲
    GUW GU2 .... 116 A4
    LHD/OX KT22 .... 103 G2
    REDH RH1 .... 128 A3
    REIG RH2 .... 126 E2
    RGODL GU7 .... 160 D4
    STWL/WRAY TW19 .... 12 B8
Grange Ct *GDST* RH9 .... 151 H4
    WOT/HER KT12 .... 60 D1
Grange Crs *CRAWE* RH10 .... 214 E2
Grange Dr *REDH* RH1 .... 126 E2
    WOKN/KNAP GU21 .... 6 D1
Grange End *HORL* RH6 .... 171 K6
Grange Farm Rd *ASHV* GU12 .... 113 K6
Grangefields Rd *RGUE* GU4 ...... 117 G2
Grange Gdns *BNSTD* SM7 .... 85 L3
    SNWD SE25 .... 50 B2
Grange HI *SNWD* SE25 .... 50 B2
Grange La *DUL* SE21 .... 32 C3
Grange Meadow *BNSTD* SM7 ..... 85 L3
Grangemill Rd *CAT* SE6 .... 33 K4
Grangemill Wy *CAT* SE6 .... 33 K3
Grangemount *LHD/OX* KT22 ..... 103 G2
Grange Pk *CRAN* GU6 .... 185 J6
    WOKN/KNAP GU21 .... 6 D1
Grange Park Pl *RYNPK* SW20 ...... 28 E8
Grange Park Rd *THHTH* CR7 .... 50 A4
Grange Pl *STA* TW18 .... 40 F2
Grange Rd *ADL/WDHM* KT15 ...... 58 D2
    ASHV GU12 .... 113 L8
    BARN SW13 .... 19 J3
    BELMT SM2 .... 65 K6
    BRAK RG12 .... 34 F1
    CBLY GU15 .... 73 H4
    CHOB/PIR GU24 .... 95 G4
    CHSGTN KT9 .... 63 H3
    CRAWE RH10 .... 214 E4
    CTHM CR3 .... 108 D7
    E/WMO/HCT KT8 .... 43 L4
    ECH TW20 .... 21 J6
    FARN GU14 .... 92 D3
    KUT KT1 .... 2 E8
    LHD/OX KT22 .... 103 G2
    NFNM GU10 .... 135 H3
    NFNM GU10 .... 178 E1
    ORP BR6 .... 71 M1

RGUW GU3 116 E3
SAND/SEL CR2 67 M8
SNWD SE25 50 A3
WOT/HER KT12 61 H3
The Grange CHOB/PIR GU24 56 B8
CROY/NA CR0 69 J1
HOR/WEW KT19 64 A3
WIM/MER SW19 29 G7
WOT/HER KT12 60 E1
Grange V BELMT SM2 65 L6
Grangeway HORL RH6 171 K6
Grangewood La BECK BR3 33 J7
Granston Wy CRAWE RH10 214 F1
Grant Cl SHPTN TW17 41 L6
Grantham Cl SHST GU47 52 B8
Grantham Rd CHSWK W4 19 H2
Grantley Av SHGR GU5 161 L3
Grantley Cl RGUE GU4 139 H7
Grantley Gdns GUW GU2 8 B1
Grantley Rd GUW GU2 8 A1
HSLWW TW4 15 M4
Granton Rd STRHM/NOR SW16 48 F1
Grant Rd CROY/NA CR0 5 J3
Grants La OXTED RH8 130 F7
OXTED RH8 153 G3
Grant Wk ASC SL5 37 H8
Grant Wy ISLW TW7 17 K1
Grantwood Cl REDH RH1 148 D5
Granville Av FELT TW13 24 D3
HSLWW TW4 16 D7
Granville Cl BF/WBF KT14 79 J3
CROY/NA CR0 5 G7
WEY KT13 59 M5
Granville Gdns
STRHM/NOR SW16 49 J1
Granville Rd BH/WHM TN16 111 M8
OXTED RH8 130 C3
WAND/EARL SW18 29 J1
WEY KT13 59 M6
WIM/MER SW19 29 K8
WOKS/MYFD GU22 97 J2
Grasmere Av HSLW TW3 16 E8
ORP BR6 71 L2
PUT/ROE SW15 28 A5
WIM/MER SW19 47 K3
Grasmere Cl
EBED/NFELT TW14 24 C2
EGH TW20 21 L8
GU GU1 117 L7
Grasmere Gdns HORS RH12 229 L3
ORP BR6 71 L2
Grasmere Rd FARN GU14 92 B6
FNM GU9 133 K3
LTWR GU18 54 E8
ORP BR6 71 L2
PUR/KEN CR8 87 L1
SNWD SE25 50 E6
STRHM/NOR SW16 31 J6
Grasmere Wy BF/WBF KT14 79 J2
Grasslands HORL RH6 171 K6
Grassmere HORL RH6 170 E5
Grassmount FSTH SE23 32 E3
WLGTN SM6 66 F8
Grassway WLGTN SM6 66 F3
Grattons Dr CRAWE RH10 192 F8
The Grattons SWTR RH13 227 H6
Gravel Hl CROY/NA CR0 69 G5
LHD/OX KT22 102 E3
SAND/SEL CR2 69 H5
Gravel Hill Rd NFNM GU10 154 C5
Gravelly Hl REDH RH1 128 C2
Gravel Pits La SHGR GU5 141 M5
Gravel Rd FARN GU14 113 G1
FNM GU9 133 L2
HAYES BR2 71 H1
WHTN TW2 26 B2
Graveney Gv PGE/AN SE20 32 F8
Graveney Rd CRAWE RH10 212 F4
TOOT SW17 30 B5
Gravetts La RGUW GU3 116 B5
Gravetye Cl CRAWE RH10 212 D5
Grayham Crs NWMAL KT3 46 A4
Grayham Rd NWMAL KT3 46 A4
Graylands Cl WOKN/KNAP GU21 6 C4
Gray Pl CHERT KT16 58 A5
Grays Cl HASM GU27 220 B1
Grayscroft Rd
STRHM/NOR SW16 31 G8
Grays La ASHF TW15 23 L5
ASHTD KT21 103 J1
Grays Rd BH/WHM TN16 111 L3
RGODL GU7 160 C2
Grays Wd HORL RH6 170 F6
Grayswood Dr FRIM GU16 93 K8
Grayswood Gdns
RYNPK SW20 46 E2
Grayswood Rd HASM GU27 220 A1
Great Austins FNM GU9 11 J4
Great Brownings DUL SE21 32 C5
Great Chertsey Rd CHSWK W4 19 G3
FELT TW13 25 J4
Great Elshams BNSTD SM7 85 K6
Greatfield Cl FARN GU14 92 E1
Greatfield Rd FARN GU14 92 D1
Greatford Dr GU GU1 118 A8
Great George St RGODL GU7 160 B5
Great Goodwin Dr GU GU1 117 L6
Greatham Rd CRAWE RH10 212 F6
Great Hollands Rd BRAK RG12 34 C6
Great Hollands Sq BRAK RG12 34 C6
Greatlake Ct HORL RH6 170 E5
Great Oaks Pk RGUE GU4 117 L4
Great Quarry GU GU1 9 H9
Great Tattenhams EPSOM KT18 84 F8
Great West Rd CHSWK W4 18 F1
HEST TW5 16 B4
ISLW TW7 17 H2
Great West Road Chiswick
CHSWK W4 19 J1
Great West Road Ellesmere Rd
CHSWK W4 18 F1
Great West Road Hogarth La
CHSWK W4 19 G1
Greatwood Cl CHERT KT16 57 M7
Great Woodcote Dr
PUR/KEN CR8 67 G8
Great Woodcote Pk
PUR/KEN CR8 67 H8
Greaves Pl TOOT SW17 30 B5
Grebe Crs SWTR RH13 229 K8
Grecian Crs NRWD SE19 31 L7
Green Acre ALDT GU11 112 C8
Greenacre Ct EGH TW20 20 F7
Greenacre Pl WLGTN SM6 66 E1
Greenacres CRAWE RH10 212 E4
Green Acres CROY/NA CR0 5 J7
Greenacres GT/LBKH KT23 101 K6
HORS RH12 228 F5
NFNM GU10 134 F7
OXTED RH8 130 B1
Greenacres Cl ORP BR6 71 M3
Greenbush La CRAN GU6 185 J8
Green Chain Wk BECK BR3 33 M8
SYD SE26 33 G7
Green Cl CAR SM5 66 C1
FELT TW13 25 H6
Green Court Av CROY/NA CR0 68 E1
Green Court Gdns CROY/NA CR0 68 E1
Greencroft FARN GU14 92 E5
GU GU1 117 L8
Greencroft Rd HEST TW5 16 C3
Green Cross La NFNM GU10 178 D8
Green Curve BNSTD SM7 85 J5
Green Dene EHSLY KT24 120 A7
Green Dr RPLY/SEND GU23 98 C5
Greene Fielde End STA TW18 23 G8
Green End CHSGTN KT9 63 G3
Green Farm Rd BAGS GU19 54 C6
Greenfield Av BRYLDS KT5 45 L7
Greenfield Link COUL/CHIP CR5 87 H5
Greenfield Rd FNM GU9 10 B6
SWTR RH13 227 G6
Greenfields Cl HORL RH6 170 B4
HORS RH12 229 K3
Greenfields Pl RDKG RH5 167 G5
Greenfields Rd HORL RH6 170 B4
HORS RH12 229 K4
Greenfields Wy HORS RH12 229 K3
Greenfinch Wy HORS RH12 229 G2
Greenford Rd SUT SM1 65 L3
Green Gdns ORP BR6 71 M4
Greenham Wk
WOKN/KNAP GU21 76 F8
Greenham Wd BRAK RG12 34 F7
Greenhanger NFNM GU10 198 C1
Greenhayes Av BNSTD SM7 85 K4
Greenhayes Cl REIG RH2 125 M8
Greenhayes Gdns BNSTD SM7 85 K5
Green Hedges Av
EGRIN RH19 196 A7
Green Hedges Cl EGRIN RH19 196 A7
Green Heights Ct
WOKS/MYFD GU22 96 F2
Greenheys Pl WOKS/MYFD GU22 6 F6
Green Hl ORP BR6 91 H2
Greenhill SUT SM1 65 M1
Greenhill Av CTHM CR3 108 E3
Green Hill Cl CBLY GU15 73 M3
Greenhill Cl FNM GU9 10 C6
RGODL GU7 160 A6
Greenhill Gdns RGUE GU4 117 M5
Greenhill La WARL CR6 89 H7
Green Hill Rd CBLY GU15 73 M3
Greenhill Rd FNM GU9 11 K4
Greenhill Wy FNM GU9 10 C6
Greenholme CBLY GU15 74 A4
Greenhow BRAK RG12 34 D3
Greenhurst La OXTED RH8 130 C6
Greenhurst Rd WNWD SE27 31 K6
Greenlands CHERT KT16 57 M2
HOR/WEW KT19 63 L4
Greenlands Rd CBLY GU15 72 E8
STA TW18 22 D5
WEY KT13 59 L2
Green La ASC SL5 37 H1
ASHTD KT21 82 F7
BAGS GU19 54 C7
BF/WBF KT14 79 J2
BLKW GU17 72 B5
CHERT KT16 58 B1
CHOB/PIR GU24 56 C8
CHSGTN KT9 63 H7
COB KT11 81 H2
CRAN GU6 204 C5
CRAWE RH10 194 C5
CRAWE RH10 212 B1
CRAWE RH10 213 G3
CTHM CR3 107 M5
E/WMO/HCT KT8 43 L5
EGH TW20 21 L5
EGH TW20 39 M2
EHSLY KT24 99 L6
FELT TW13 25 H6
FNM GU9 10 D4
FNM GU9 134 C3
GU GU1 117 L8
HASM GU27 219 L5
HORL RH6 193 J3
HORS RH12 209 H5
HSLWW TW4 15 M6
KWD/TDW/WH KT20 105 J8
LHD/OX KT22 103 G3
LING RH7 173 M6
MFD/CHID GU8 181 H1
MRDN SM4 47 L7
NFNM GU10 157 G3
NFNM GU10 177 H3
NFNM GU10 198 C1
NWMAL KT3 45 M5
PGE/AN SE20 33 G8
PUR/KEN CR8 86 F5
RDKG RH5 190 A1
REDH RH1 126 B6
REDH RH1 148 D5
REDH RH1 149 J8
REIG RH2 125 J8
REIG RH2 168 B1
RGODL GU7 138 B8
RGUE GU4 118 D1
RGUW GU3 115 K6
SHGR GU5 162 C3
SHPTN TW17 41 M5
STA TW18 40 B1
SUN TW16 24 C8
THHTH CR7 49 L1
WOT/HER KT12 60 E4
WPK KT4 46 D8
Green Lane Av WOT/HER KT12 60 E4
Green Lane Cl BF/WBF KT14 79 J2
CBLY GU15 72 F2
CHERT KT16 58 B1
Green La East RGUW GU3 136 D1
Green Lane Gdns THHTH CR7 49 M2
Green La HOR/WEW KT19 64 B7
Green La West ASHV GU12 136 B1
EHSLY KT24 99 K7
Greenlaw Gdns NWMAL KT3 46 C7
Green Leaf Av WLGTN SM6 67 G3
Greenleas FRIM GU16 73 H7
Green Leas SUN TW16 24 C8
Green Leas Cl SUN TW16 24 C7
Green Man La EBED/NFELT TW14 15 K6
Green Md ESH/CLAY KT10 61 J5
Greenmead Cl SNWD SE25 50 D5
Greenmeads WOKS/MYFD GU22 97 H4
Greenoak Ri BH/WHM TN16 90 F8
Greenoak Wy WIM/MER SW19 29 G5
Greenock Rd STRHM/NOR SW16 49 G1
Greeno Crs SHPTN TW17 41 K5
Green Pk STA TW18 22 B4
Green Rd CHERT KT16 39 L4
EGH TW20 39 K4
Greensand Cl REDH RH1 127 G2
Greensand Rd REDH RH1 126 D7
Greensand Wy
BRKHM/BTCW RH3 124 D8
DORK RH4 144 B3
EDEN TN8 131 M5
FNM GU9 134 B7
GDST RH9 129 G8
GSHT GU26 199 K7
HASM GU27 219 M2
MFD/CHID GU8 179 M6
NFNM GU10 157 G7
OXTED RH8 110 B8
RDKG RH5 122 A8
REDH RH1 127 L8
REIG RH2 125 H6
SHGR GU5 183 K3
Greenside Cl RGUE GU4 117 M6
Greenside Rd CROY/NA CR0 49 K7
Green Springs NFNM GU10 132 C2
Greenstead Gdns
PUT/ROE SW15 19 L7
Greenstede Av EGRIN RH19 196 C6
Green St SUN TW16 42 D1
The Green BRAK RG12 34 E4
CRAN GU6 186 B5
CRAWE RH10 193 L6
CROY/NA CR0 69 J7
CTHM CR3 109 K5
EW KT17 84 D2
FELT TW13 24 E3
FNM GU9 133 M3
FNM GU9 134 D4
FRIM GU16 93 J3
GDST RH9 128 E6
HEST TW5 16 D1
KWD/TDW/WH KT20 105 G5
LHD/OX KT22 102 A6
MFD/CHID GU8 201 M6
MRDN SM4 47 H4
NFNM GU10 135 H8
NWMAL KT3 45 M3
RCH/KEW TW9 18 A7
STWL/WRAY TW19 12 B8
SUT SM1 65 L2
WHTN TW2 26 B2
Greenvale Rd WOKN/KNAP GU21 96 A1
Green Vw CHSGTN KT9 63 J6
Greenview Av BECK BR3 51 H6
CROY/NA CR0 51 H6
Green Wk CRAWE RH10 212 B1
Green Wy ASHV GU12 113 H6
REDH RH1 126 B6
SUN TW16 42 D4
Greenway BH/WHM TN16 110 F2
GT/LBKH KT23 101 L5
HORS RH12 228 D6
RYNPK SW20 46 F4
WLGTN SM6 66 F3
Greenway Cl BF/WBF KT14 78 D3
Greenway Dr STA TW18 40 F1
Greenway Gdns CROY/NA CR0 69 J2
Greenways BECK BR3 51 K2
EGH TW20 21 H7
ESH/CLAY KT10 62 B3
KWD/TDW/WH KT20 104 D7
Greenways Dr ASC SL5 37 H8
The Greenway EPSOM KT18 83 K5
HSLWW TW4 16 C6
OXTED RH8 130 D7
Greenwell Cl GDST RH9 128 E4
Greenwich Cl CRAWW RH11 211 M7
Green Wd ASC SL5 35 M1
Greenwood Cl ADL/WDHM KT15 78 C1
MRDN SM4 47 H4
THDIT KT7 44 D8
Greenwood Dr REDH RH1 148 D5
Greenwood Gdns CTHM CR3 108 D7
Greenwood La HPTN TW12 25 L6
Greenwood Pk KUTN/CMB KT2 28 B8
Greenwood Rd CHOB/PIR GU24 94 E3
CROY/NA CR0 4 B1
ISLW TW7 17 J5
MTCM CR4 49 G3
THDIT KT7 44 D8
WOKN/KNAP GU21 96 B2
The Greenwood GU GU1 117 K8
Green Wrythe Crs CAR SM5 48 B8
Green Wrythe La CAR SM5 48 B8
MRDN SM4 48 A6
Gregory Cl CRAWE RH10 212 F7
Gregsons HORS RH12 228 B1
Grenaby Av CROY/NA CR0 4 E2
Grenaby Rd CROY/NA CR0 4 E2
Grenadier Rd ASHV GU12 113 L5
Grena Gdns RCH/KEW TW9 18 C6
Grena Rd RCH/KEW TW9 18 C6
Grendon Cl HORL RH6 170 C4
Grenfell Rd TOOT SW17 30 C7
Grennell Cl SUT SM1 66 A1
Grennell Rd SUT SM1 65 M1
Grenside Rd WEY KT13 59 L2
Grenville Cl BRYLDS KT5 45 M8
COB KT11 81 G3
Grenville Gdns FRIM GU16 93 H3
Grenville Ms HPTN TW12 25 L6
Grenville Rd CROY/NA CR0 69 M8
Gresham Av WARL CR6 89 H8
Gresham Cl OXTED RH8 130 C3
Gresham Rd BECK BR3 51 H2
HEST TW5 16 F3
HPTN TW12 25 K7
OXTED RH8 130 C3
SNWD SE25 50 D4
STA TW18 22 C6
Gresham Wk CRAWE RH10 212 B6
Gresham Wy FRIM GU16 93 H3
WIM/MER SW19 29 K4
Gressenhall Rd
WAND/EARL SW18 29 J1
Greta Bank EHSLY KT24 99 M8
Greville Av SAND/SEL CR2 69 G8
Greville Cl ASHTD KT21 103 H1
GUW GU2 116 B8
TWK TW1 26 E1
Greville Ct GT/LBKH KT23 101 L7
Greville Park Av ASHTD KT21 83 H8
Greville Park Rd ASHTD KT21 83 H8
Greville Rd RCHPK/HAM TW10 18 C8
Grey Alders EW KT17 84 F4
Greybury La EDEN TN8 175 L6
Greycot Rd BECK BR3 33 K6
Greyfields Cl PUR/KEN CR8 87 L3
Greyfriars Dr ASC SL5 36 E6
CHOB/PIR GU24 75 K5
Greyfriars Rd RPLY/SEND GU23 98 D6
Greyhound Cl ASHV GU12 113 J8
Greyhound La
STRHM/NOR SW16 31 H7
Greyhound Rd SUT SM1 65 M4
Greyhound Slip CRAWE RH10 213 G2
Greyhound Ter
STRHM/NOR SW16 48 F1
Greys Ct ALDT GU11 112 B7
Greys Park Cl HAYES BR2 70 F4
Greystead Pk NFNM GU10 155 H3
Greystead Rd FSTH SE23 32 F1
Greystone Cl SAND/SEL CR2 88 F1
Greystones Cl REDH RH1 148 A2
Greystones Dr REIG RH2 125 M6
Greyswood St
STRHM/NOR SW16 30 E7
Greythorne Rd
WOKN/KNAP GU21 76 D8
Greywaters SHGR GU5 161 K3
Grice Av BH/WHM TN16 90 E3
Grier Cl CRAWW RH11 211 H4
Grieve Cl NFNM GU10 135 H2
Griffin Wy GT/LBKH KT23 101 K8
SUN TW16 42 D2
Griffiths Rd WIM/MER SW19 29 K8
Griffon Cl FARN GU14 92 A6
Griggs Meadow MFD/CHID GU8 203 J2
Grimwade Av CROY/NA CR0 5 M8
Grimwood Rd TWK TW1 26 C1
Grindall Cl CROY/NA CR0 67 L3
Grindley Gdns CROY/NA CR0 50 C6
Grindstone Crs
WOKN/KNAP GU21 75 L8
Grisedale Cl CRAWW RH11 211 M5
PUR/KEN CR8 88 B4
Grisedale Gdns PUR/KEN CR8 88 B4
Grobars Av WOKN/KNAP GU21 76 F5
Groombridge Cl
WOT/HER KT12 60 E4
Groombridge Wy HORS RH12 228 C8
Groom Crs WAND/EARL SW18 30 A1
Groomfield Cl TOOT SW17 30 D5
The Grooms CRAWE RH10 213 G1
Grosse Wy PUT/ROE SW15 19 L8
Grosvenor Av CAR SM5 66 C5
MORT/ESHN SW14 19 H5
Grosvenor Ct BLKW GU17 72 A6
Grosvenor Gdns
KUTN/CMB KT2 27 G7
MORT/ESHN SW14 19 H5
WLGTN SM6 66 F6
Grosvenor Hl WIM/MER SW19 29 H7
Grosvenor Pl WEY KT13 60 A2
Grosvenor Rd ALDT GU11 112 D7
BTFD TW8 18 A1
CHOB/PIR GU24 76 A3
EGRIN RH19 196 A8
EPSOM KT18 104 B1
HSLWW TW4 16 C5
RCHPK/HAM TW10 18 B7
RGODL GU7 160 B6
SNWD SE25 50 D4
STA TW18 22 D8
TWK TW1 26 D1
WLGTN SM6 66 E5
WWKM BR4 69 L1
Groton Rd WAND/EARL SW18 29 L3
Grotto Rd TWK TW1 26 C3
WEY KT13 59 M3
Grove Av EW KT17 84 B3
SUT SM1 65 K5
TWK TW1 26 C2
Grove Cl CRAN GU6 185 J8
FSTH SE23 33 G2
HAYES BR2 70 D1
KUT KT1 45 H4
WDSR SL4 20 E1
Grove Ct E/WMO/HCT KT8 44 A5
EGH TW20 21 K6
Grove Crs FELT TW13 25 H5
KUT KT1 2 E9
WOT/HER KT12 42 E7
Grove Cross Rd FRIM GU16 73 G8
Grove End BAGS GU19 54 C5
Grove End La ESH/CLAY KT10 44 A8
Grove End Rd FNM GU9 10 E5
Grovefields Av FRIM GU16 73 G8
Grove Gdns TEDD TW11 26 D5
Grove Heath La
RPLY/SEND GU23 98 F6
Grove Heath North
RPLY/SEND GU23 98 E4
Grovehill Rd REDH RH1 126 B8
Groveland Av STRHM/NOR SW16 31 J8
Groveland Rd BECK BR3 51 J3
Grovelands E/WMO/HCT KT8 43 K4
NFNM GU10 11 L6
Grovelands Rd PUR/KEN CR8 87 J2
Groveland Wy NWMAL KT3 45 M5
Grove La COUL/CHIP CR5 86 E5
KUT KT1 45 H4
Groveley Rd SUN TW16 24 C6
Grove Park Br CHSWK W4 18 F2
Grove Park Gdns CHSWK W4 18 E2
Grove Park Rd CHSWK W4 18 E2
Grove Park Ter CHSWK W4 18 E2
Grove Pl WEY KT13 59 M4
Grove Rd ASHTD KT21 83 J8
ASHV GU12 113 K5
BARN SW13 19 J4
BELMT SM2 65 K5
BH/WHM TN16 110 F2
CBLY GU15 73 H4
CHERT KT16 40 C6
CRAN GU6 185 J8
E/WMO/HCT KT8 44 A4
EPSOM KT18 84 B3
GSHT GU26 198 F3
GU GU1 117 M8
HORL RH6 170 B5
HSLW TW3 16 D6
ISLW TW7 17 H3
LING RH7 174 B4
MTCM CR4 48 E2
RCHPK/HAM TW10 18 C8
RGODL GU7 159 M6
SHPTN TW17 41 M6
SURB KT6 45 G5
SUT SM1 65 L5
THHTH CR7 49 K4
WHTN TW2 26 A4
WIM/MER SW19 29 M8
WOKN/KNAP GU21 6 F4
Groveside GT/LBKH KT23 121 K1
Groveside Cl CAR SM5 66 B1
GT/LBKH KT23 121 K1
Grovestile Waye
EBED/NFELT TW14 24 A1
Grove Ter TEDD TW11 26 D5
The Grove ADL/WDHM KT15 58 E4
ALDT GU11 112 D8
ASC SL5 35 M1
BH/WHM TN16 91 G8
COUL/CHIP CR5 87 G5
CRAWW RH11 211 M3
CTHM CR3 107 L3
EGH TW20 21 K6
EW KT17 84 B3
FARN GU14 93 G8
FRIM GU16 73 G8
HORL RH6 170 E7
ISLW TW7 17 H3
TEDD TW11 26 D5
WOKN/KNAP GU21 6 E4
WOT/HER KT12 42 E7
WWKM BR4 69 M2
Grove Wy ESH/CLAY KT10 43 M8
Grove Wood Hl COUL/CHIP CR5 87 G4
Grub St OXTED RH8 130 F3
Guardian Ct MFD/CHID GU8 157 M6
Guards Ct ASC SL5 37 L7
Guerdon Pl BRAK RG12 35 G7
Guernsey Cl CRAWW RH11 211 K7
HEST TW5 16 D3
RGUE GU4 117 K3
Guernsey Farm Dr
WOKN/KNAP GU21 6 B1
Guernsey Gv HNHL SE24 31 M1
Guildables La EDEN TN8 153 H2
OXTED RH8 131 H8
Guildcroft GU GU1 117 K8
Guildersfield Rd
STRHM/NOR SW16 31 H8
Guildford Av FELT TW13 24 D3
Guildford Business Park Rd
GUW GU2 8 C2
Guildford La SHGR GU5 140 D4
Guildford Park Av GUW GU2 8 D5
Guildford Park Rd GUW GU2 8 D6
Guildford Rd ALDT GU11 135 G2
ASHV GU12 114 A6
BAGS GU19 54 C7
CHERT KT16 40 C8
CHERT KT16 58 A2
CHOB/PIR GU24 75 H2
CRAN GU6 184 E5
CROY/NA CR0 50 A6
DORK RH4 143 L4
FNM GU9 134 A6
FRIM GU16 93 K4
GT/LBKH KT23 121 J2
HORS RH12 225 J1
LHD/OX KT22 102 D4
LTWR GU18 54 D8
NFNM GU10 134 D5
RDKG RH5 142 D6
RGODL GU7 160 D3
RGUE GU4 96 F7
RGUW GU3 95 M7
SHGR GU5 162 C7
WOKS/MYFD GU22 6 D6
Guildford Rd East FARN GU14 92 F8
Guildford Rd West FARN GU14 92 F8
Guildford St CHERT KT16 40 D7
STA TW18 22 D7
Guildford Wy WLGTN SM6 67 H4
Guildown Av GUW GU2 138 E3
Guildown Rd GUW GU2 138 E3
Guileshill La RPLY/SEND GU23 99 H4
Guilford Av BRYLDS KT5 45 J5
Guillemont Flds FARN GU14 92 A4
Guinevere Rd CRAWW RH11 211 H3
Gull Cl WLGTN SM6 67 H6
Gulley Rd FARN GU14 112 D1
Gumbrells Cl RGUW GU3 115 M4
Gumley Gdns ISLW TW7 17 K5
Gumping Rd STMC/STPC BR5 71 M1
Gun Hl ALDT GU11 112 E6
Gunnell Cl SNWD SE25 50 C6
Gunners Rd WAND/EARL SW18 30 A3
Gunning Cl CRAWW RH11 211 K6
Gun Pit Rd LING RH7 173 M5

Gunton Rd TOOT SW17 30 D7
Gurdon's La MFD/CHID GU8 181 J7
Gurney Crs CROY/NA CR0 49 J8
Gurney Rd CAR SM5 66 D3
Gurney's Cl REDH RH1 148 C1 1
Guyatt Gdns MTCM CR4 48 D2
Guy Rd WLGTN SM6 67 G2
Gwydor Rd BECK BR3 51 G4
Gwynne Av CROY/NA CR0 51 G7
Gwynne Gdns EGRIN RH19 195 M7
Gwynne Rd CTHM CR3 108 A5
Gwynne Vaughan Av GUW GU2 116 D4
Gwynne Whf CHSWK W4 19 J1 1

H

Habershon Dr FRIM GU16 74 A7
Haccombe Rd WIM/MER SW19 29 M7
Hackbridge Park Gdns
CAR SM5 66 D1 1
Hackbridge Rd CAR SM5 66 D1
Hackenden Cl EGRIN RH19 196 B6
Hackenden La EGRIN RH19 196 B6
Hacketts La WOKS/MYFD GU22 78 C4
Hackhurst La RDKG RH5 142 C5
Hackington Crs BECK BR3 33 K7
Haddon Cl NWMAL KT3 46 C5
WEY KT13 60 A3 1
Haddon Rd SUT SM1 65 L3 5
Hadfield Rd STWL/WRAY TW19 14 A8
Hadleigh Cl RYNPK SW20 47 J2
Hadleigh Dr BELMT SM2 65 K7
Hadley Pl WEY KT13 59 K6
Hadley Rd MTCM CR4 49 G4
Hadleys NFNM GU10 155 H6
Hadley Wood Ri PUR/KEN CR8 87 L5
Hadmans Cl HORS RH12 228 F8
Hadrian Cl STWL/WRAY TW19 23 H1 3
Hadrian Wy
STWL/WRAY TW19 23 H1 4
Haggard Rd TWK TW1 26 E1
Haigh Crs REDH RH1 148 E2
Haig Rd ASHV GU12 112 F8
BH/WHM TN16 91 H7
CBLY GU15 72 C3
Hailes Cl WIM/MER SW19 29 M7
Hailsham Av BRXS/STRHM SW2 31 J3
Hailsham Cl SHST GU47 52 A8 3
SURB KT6 45 G7
Hailsham Rd TOOT SW17 30 D7
Haines Ct WEY KT13 60 A4
Haines Wk MRDN SM4 47 L7
Haining Gdns FRIM GU16 93 K6
Hainthorpe Rd WNWD SE27 31 L4
Haldane Pl WAND/EARL SW18 29 L2
Halebourne La CHOB/PIR GU24 55 K8
Hale Cl ORP BR6 71 M3
Hale End BRAK RG12 35 J4
Hale Ends WOKS/MYFD GU22 96 E3
Hale House La NFNM GU10 178 D8
Hale Pit Rd GT/LBKH KT23 101 M8
Hale Pl FNM GU9 134 B4
Hale Reeds FNM GU9 134 A3
Hale Rd FNM GU9 134 A6
Hales Fld HASM GU27 219 M3
Hales Oak GT/LBKH KT23 101 M8
Halesowen Rd MRDN SM4 47 L7
Hale St STA TW18 22 B5
Haleswood COB KT11 80 E4
Hale Wy FRIM GU16 73 G8
Halewood BRAK RG12 34 C6
Half Acre BTFD TW8 18 A1
Half Acre Ms BTFD TW8 18 A1 6
Half Moon Hl HASM GU27 219 M3
Halford Rd RCHPK/HAM TW10 18 B7
Halfpenny Cl RGUE GU4 140 A6
Halfpenny La ASC SL5 37 K7
RGUE GU4 139 M3
Halfway Gn WOT/HER KT12 60 E2
Halfway La RGODL GU7 159 M5
Haliburton Rd TWK TW1 17 K7
Halifax Cl CRAWE RH10 193 H8
FARN GU14 92 C6
Halifax St SYD SE26 32 E4
Halifax Wy FARN GU14 112 C2
Halimote Rd ALDT GU11 112 D8
Haling Gv SAND/SEL CR2 67 M6
Haling Park Gdns
SAND/SEL CR2 67 L5 1
Haling Park Rd SAND/SEL CR2 67 L5
Haling Rd SAND/SEL CR2 68 A5
Hallam Rd RGODL GU7 160 C3
Halland Cl CRAWE RH10 212 D2 4
Hall Cl CBLY GU15 73 H3
RGODL GU7 160 B2
Hall Ct TEDD TW11 26 C6 4
Hall Dene Cl GU GU1 117 M7
Hall Dr SYD SE26 32 F6
Halley Cl CRAWW RH11 211 L8
Halley Dr ASC SL5 36 A2
Halley's Ap WOKN/KNAP GU21 76 D8
Halley's Ct WOKN/KNAP GU21 76 D8 3
Halley's Wk ADL/WDHM KT15 58 F6 1
Hall Farm Dr WHTN TW2 26 A1
Hall Hl OXTED RH8 130 A6
The Halliards WOT/HER KT12 42 D6 2
Halliford Cl SHPTN TW17 42 B3
Halliford Rd SHPTN TW17 42 B5
SUN TW16 42 D4
Hallington Cl WOKN/KNAP GU21 76 E7
Hall La HYS/HAR UB3 15 G2
Hallmark Cl SHST GU47 72 B1
Hallmead Rd SUT SM1 65 L2
Hallowell Av CROY/NA CR0 67 H3
Hallowell Cl MTCM CR4 48 D3
Hallowfield Wy MTCM CR4 48 A3
Hall Pl WOKN/KNAP GU21 7 G4
Hall Place Dr WEY KT13 60 B4
Hall Rd FARN GU14 92 E7
ISLW TW7 17 G7
SHGR GU5 161 J2
WLGTN SM6 66 E7
Halls Farm Cl WOKN/KNAP GU21 76 A7
Hallsland CRAWE RH10 214 F1
Hallsland Wy OXTED RH8 130 C7
Halsford La EGRIN RH19 195 L7
Halsford Park Rd EGRIN RH19 195 M7
Halstead Cl CROY/NA CR0 4 C7
Halters End GSHT GU26 198 D6
Hamble Av BLKW GU17 72 A4
Hamble Cl WOKN/KNAP GU21 76 D7
Hambledon Gdns SNWD SE25 50 C3 1
Hambledon Hl EPSOM KT18 83 M6
Hambledon Pk MFD/CHID GU8 181 L8
Hambledon Pl DUL SE21 32 C2
GT/LBKH KT23 101 K5
Hambledon Rd CTHM CR3 108 A5
MFD/CHID GU8 182 A5
WAND/EARL SW18 29 J1
Hambledon V EPSOM KT18 83 M6
Hambleton Cl CBLY GU15 73 L6
WPK KT4 64 F1 2
Hambleton Hl CRAWW RH11 211 M5
Hambrook Rd SNWD SE25 50 E3
Hambro Rd STRHM/NOR SW16 31 G7
Ham Common
RCHPK/HAM TW10 27 G4
Hamesmoor Rd FRIM GU16 93 H5
Hamesmoor Wy FRIM GU16 93 J5
Ham Farm Rd
RCHPK/HAM TW10 27 G5
Hamfield Cl OXTED RH8 129 M1
Ham Gate Av RCHPK/HAM TW10 27 H5
Hamilton Av CHEAM SM3 65 H1
COB KT11 80 D3
SURB KT6 63 K1
WOKS/MYFD GU22 78 B6
Hamilton Cl CHERT KT16 40 C8
FELT TW13 24 C6
GUW GU2 116 D3 3
HOR/WEW KT19 83 M2
PUR/KEN CR8 87 L2 2
Hamilton Crs HSLW TW3 16 E7
Hamilton Dr ASC SL5 37 H7
GUW GU2 116 D3
Hamilton Pl GUW GU2 116 D3
KWD/TDW/WH KT20 105 J5
SUN TW16 24 E8
Hamilton Rd BTFD TW8 18 A1 7
FELT TW13 24 B6
HORS RH12 228 E6
THHTH CR7 50 A3
WHTN TW2 26 B2 1
WIM/MER SW19 29 L8
WNWD SE27 32 A5
Hamilton Road Ms
WIM/MER SW19 29 L8 2
Hamilton Wy WLGTN SM6 67 G7
Ham La EGH TW20 20 E5
MFD/CHID GU8 158 B5
Hamlash La NFNM GU10 155 M8
Hamlet Rd NRWD SE19 32 C8
Hamlet St BNFD RG42 35 H1
Hamlyn Gdns NRWD SE19 32 B8
Hammerfield Dr RDKG RH5 142 C7
Hammer Hl HASM GU27 218 F5
Hammer La GSHT GU26 198 B2
GSHT GU26 218 F1
HASM GU27 218 F4
LIPH GU30 218 D3
Hammersley Rd ALDT GU11 112 E2
Hammersmith Bridge Rd
BARN SW13 19 L1
Hammerwood Copse
HASM GU27 219 G4 1
Hammerwood Rd EGRIN RH19 217 H3
Hamm Moor La
ADL/WDHM KT15 59 H4
Hammond Av MTCM CR4 48 E2
Hammond Cl HPTN TW12 43 K1
WOKN/KNAP GU21 76 F5
Hammond Rd
WOKN/KNAP GU21 76 F5
Hammond Wy LTWR GU18 54 E8 1
Hamond Cl SAND/SEL CR2 67 L7
Hampden Av BECK BR3 51 H2
Hampden Cl CRAWE RH10 193 H8 2
Hampden Rd BECK BR3 51 H2
KUT KT1 3 K8
Hamper's La SWTR RH13 229 K7
Hampshire Cl ASHV GU12 135 G2 1
Hampshire Rd CBLY GU15 73 J1
Hampstead La DORK RH4 144 C3
Hampstead Rd DORK RH4 144 D3
Hampton Cl RYNPK SW20 28 F8 2
Hampton Court Av
E/WMO/HCT KT8 44 B5 1
Hampton Court Rd
E/WMO/HCT KT8 44 D3
HPTN TW12 44 A2
Hampton Court Wy
E/WMO/HCT KT8 44 B4
ESH/CLAY KT10 62 B1
THDIT KT7 44 B7
Hampton Gv EW KT17 84 C1
Hampton La FELT TW13 25 H5
Hampton Rd CROY/NA CR0 49 M6
FNM GU9 133 K4
HPTN TW12 26 A6
REDH RH1 148 C5
WHTN TW2 26 A4
WPK KT4 64 D1
Hampton Rd East FELT TW13 25 J5 1
Hampton Rd West FELT TW13 25 H3
Hampton Wy EGRIN RH19 216 C2
Ham Ridings RCHPK/HAM TW10 27 J6
Hamsey Green Gdns WARL CR6 88 E6
Hamsey Wy SAND/SEL CR2 88 E5
Ham St RCHPK/HAM TW10 26 F3
The Ham BTFD TW8 17 M2
Ham Vw CROY/NA CR0 51 H6
Hanbury Dr BH/WHM TN16 90 E3
Hanbury Rd CRAWW RH11 211 H4
Hanbury Wy CBLY GU15 72 F6
Hancock Rd NRWD SE19 32 A7
Hancocks Mt ASC SL5 37 G6
Handcroft Cl NFNM GU10 132 C1
Handcroft Rd CROY/NA CR0 4 A2
Handside Cl WPK KT4 47 G8 1
Hanford Cl WAND/EARL SW18 29 K2
Hanger Hl WEY KT13 59 L4
Hang Grove Hl ORP BR6 91 L3
Hanley Pl BECK BR3 33 K8
Hannah Cl BECK BR3 51 L3
Hannam's Farm NFNM GU10 132 B3 1
Hannen Rd WNWD SE27 31 L4 4
Hannibal Rd STWL/WRAY TW19 23 H1
Hannibal Wy CROY/NA CR0 67 J4
Hanover Av FELT TW13 24 D2
Hanover Cl CHEAM SM3 65 H3
CRAWE RH10 212 C5
EGH TW20 20 E7 1
FRIM GU16 73 H8
RCH/KEW TW9 18 D2 3
REDH RH1 126 F2
Hanover Ct DORK RH4 144 C2
WOKS/MYFD GU22 6 B9
Hanover Gdns BRAK RG12 34 C7 1
FARN GU14 92 B3
Hanover Rd WIM/MER SW19 29 M8
Hanover St CROY/NA CR0 4 B7
Hanover Wk WEY KT13 60 A2
Hansler Gv E/WMO/HCT KT8 44 A5
Hanson Cl BAL SW12 30 E1
BECK BR3 33 L7 1
CBLY GU15 73 L2
GU GU1 117 J5
MORT/ESHN SW14 18 F5 4
Hanworth Cl BRAK RG12 34 F6 4
Hanworth La CHERT KT16 40 C8
Hanworth Rd BRAK RG12 34 D7
FELT TW13 24 E2
HPTN TW12 25 J5
HSLW TW3 16 E5 3
HSLWW TW4 25 J1
REDH RH1 148 C5
SUN TW16 24 D8
Hanworth Ter HSLW TW3 16 E6
Harberson Rd BAL SW12 30 E2
Harbledown Rd SAND/SEL CR2 88 D1
Harborough Rd
STRHM/NOR SW16 31 J5
Harbour Cl FARN GU14 92 D1
Harbourfield Rd BNSTD SM7 85 L5
Harbridge Av PUT/ROE SW15 28 C1
Harbury Rd CAR SM5 66 B7
Harcourt STWL/WRAY TW19 12 B8
Harcourt Av WLGTN SM6 66 E3
Harcourt Cl EGH TW20 21 M7
ISLW TW7 17 K5 3
Harcourt Fld WLGTN SM6 66 E3
Harcourt Rd BRAK RG12 34 E6
CBLY GU15 72 E4
THHTH CR7 49 J6
WIM/MER SW19 29 K8 5
WLGTN SM6 66 E3 1
Harcourt Wy GDST RH9 151 H3
Hardcastle Cl SNWD SE25 50 D6 3
Hardcourts Cl WWKM BR4 69 L3
Hardell Cl EGH TW20 21 K6 4
Hardel Wk BRXS/STRHM SW2 31 K1
Hardham Cl CRAWW RH11 211 K1
Harding Cl CROY/NA CR0 5 K7
KUTN/CMB KT2 3 G4
Harding Rd EPSOM KT18 104 B1
Hardings La PGE/AN SE20 33 G7 2
Hardman Rd KUTN/CMB KT2 2 F6
Hardwell Wy BRAK RG12 35 H4
Hardwick Cl LHD/OX KT22 81 M5
Hardwicke Av HEST TW5 16 D3 1
Hardwicke Rd
RCHPK/HAM TW10 26 F5
REIG RH2 125 K7
Hardwick La CHERT KT16 39 M7
Hardwick Rd REDH RH1 148 A2
Hardy Cl CRAWE RH10 212 F2 1
HORL RH6 170 B6 1
HORS RH12 228 E5 1
RDKG RH5 144 E6
Hardy Rd WIM/MER SW19 29 L8
Harebell Hl COB KT11 81 G4
Harecroft DORK RH4 144 F5
GT/LBKH KT23 101 L5
Haredon Cl FSTH SE23 32 F1
Harefield ESH/CLAY KT10 62 B2
Harefield Av BELMT SM2 65 H7
Harefield Rd STRHM/NOR SW16 31 J8
Hare Hl ADL/WDHM KT15 58 C5
Hare Hill Cl WOKS/MYFD GU22 78 D5
Harelands Cl WOKN/KNAP GU21 76 F7
Hare La CRAWW RH11 191 L8
ESH/CLAY KT10 62 B5
LING RH7 173 G4
RGODL GU7 160 C3
Harendon KWD/TDW/WH KT20 104 F3
Hares Bank CROY/NA CR0 70 A8
Harestone Dr CTHM CR3 108 C6
Harestone Hl CTHM CR3 108 C8
Harestone La CTHM CR3 108 B7
Harestone Valley Rd CTHM CR3 108 C7
Harewood Cl CRAWE RH10 192 D8
REIG RH2 125 M6
Harewood Gdns SAND/SEL CR2 88 E5
Harewood Rd ISLW TW7 17 J2
RGUE GU4 117 M5
SAND/SEL CR2 68 B5
WIM/MER SW19 30 B7
Harfield Rd SUN TW16 43 G2
Harington Pl REIG RH2 125 K6
Harkness Cl EW KT17 84 F6 3
Harland Av CROY/NA CR0 5 K7
Harland Cl WIM/MER SW19 47 L3 1
Harlands Gv ORP BR6 71 L3 3
Harlech Gdns HEST TW5 15 M1
Harlech Rd BLKW GU17 72 A5 1
Harlequin Av BTFD TW8 17 K1
Harlequin Cl ISLW TW7 17 H7
Harlequin Rd TEDD TW11 26 E8 2
Harlington Cl HYS/HAR UB3 14 F2 1
Harlington High St
HYS/HAR UB3 15 G2
Harlington Rd East
EBED/NFELT TW14 24 E1
Harlington Rd West
EBED/NFELT TW14 15 L8
Harman Pl PUR/KEN CR8 87 L1
Harmans Md EGRIN RH19 196 D8
Harmans Water Rd BRAK RG12 35 G5
Harmondsworth La
WDR/YW UB7 14 B1
Harmony Cl CRAWW RH11 211 H5 2
WLGTN SM6 67 H7 1
Harms Gv RGUE GU4 117 M5
Harold Rd CRAWE RH10 213 H4
NRWD SE19 32 A8
SUT SM1 66 A3
Haroldslea HORL RH6 171 H7
Haroldslea Cl HORL RH6 170 F8
Haroldslea Dr HORL RH6 170 F8
Harpenden Rd WNWD SE27 31 L3
Harper Dr CRAWE RH10 212 F7
Harper's Rd ASHV GU12 113 M7
Harpesford Av VW GU25 38 F5
Harps Oak La REDH RH1 106 C7
Harpurs KWD/TDW/WH KT20 105 G3
Harrier Cl CRAN GU6 185 H5 3
Harriet Cl BRXS/STRHM SW2 31 K1
Harriet Gdns CROY/NA CR0 5 M5
Harrington Cl CROY/NA CR0 67 H1
REIG RH2 146 D7
Harrington Rd SNWD SE25 50 D4
Harriotts Cl ASHTD KT21 103 G2
LHD/OX KT22 103 G2
Harriotts La ASHTD KT21 102 F1
Harris Cl CRAWW RH11 211 L6 4
HEST TW5 16 D3
Harrison Cl REIG RH2 147 L1
Harrison Ct SHPTN TW17 41 L5 1
Harrison's Ri CROY/NA CR0 4 A7
Harris Wy SUN TW16 42 B1
Harrow Cl ADL/WDHM KT15 58 E1
CHSGTN KT9 63 G6 2
DORK RH4 144 D3
Harrowdene CRAN GU6 185 H5 4
Harrowdene Gdns TEDD TW11 26 D8
Harrow Gdns WARL CR6 89 J6
Harrowlands Pk DORK RH4 144 E3
Harrow La RGODL GU7 160 B2
Harrow Rd ASHF TW15 23 K2
CAR SM5 66 B5
WARL CR6 89 J5
Harrow Rd East DORK RH4 144 E4
Harrow Rd West DORK RH4 144 D4
Harrowsley Ct HORL RH6 170 E5 10
Harrow Wy SHPTN TW17 41 M2 2
Hart Cl FARN GU14 92 B1
REDH RH1 128 C7
Hart Dene Ct BAGS GU19 54 B6
Harte Rd HSLW TW3 16 C4
Hartfield Crs WIM/MER SW19 29 J8
WWKM BR4 70 D2
Hartfield Gv PGE/AN SE20 50 E1
Hartfield Rd CHSGTN KT9 63 G4
FROW RH18 217 K7
WIM/MER SW19 29 J8
WWKM BR4 70 D3
Hartford Ri CBLY GU15 73 G3
Hartford Rd HOR/WEW KT19 63 K5
Hart Gdns DORK RH4 144 E1 1
Hartham Cl ISLW TW7 17 K3 4
Hartham Rd ISLW TW7 17 J3
Harting Ct CRAWW RH11 211 J6
Hartington Cl ORP BR6 71 M4
Hartington Rd CHSWK W4 18 E2
TWK TW1 26 E1 3
Hartland Cl ADL/WDHM KT15 58 F8
Hartland Pl FARN GU14 92 D3 2
Hartland Rd ADL/WDHM KT15 58 D6
HPTN TW12 25 L5 1
ISLW TW7 17 K5 4
MRDN SM4 47 K7
The Hartlands HEST TW5 15 L1
Hartland Wy CROY/NA CR0 69 H1
MRDN SM4 47 J7
Hartley Down COUL/CHIP CR5 87 J5
Hartley Farm PUR/KEN CR8 87 J5
Hartley Hl PUR/KEN CR8 87 J5
Hartley Old Rd PUR/KEN CR8 87 J5
Hartley Rd CROY/NA CR0 4 C1
Hartley Wy PUR/KEN CR8 87 J5
Hart Rd BF/WBF KT14 79 H3
DORK RH4 144 E1
Harts Gdns GUW GU2 116 E5
Hartsgrove MFD/CHID GU8 201 L4
Hartshill GUW GU2 116 A7
Hart's La GDST RH9 151 G2
Hartspiece Rd REDH RH1 148 D2
Hartswood RDKG RH5 145 G5 2
Hartswood Av REIG RH2 147 K4
The Hart FNM GU9 133 L7
Harvard Hl CHSWK W4 18 E1 2
Harvard Rd ISLW TW7 17 H3
SHST GU47 52 C8
Harvest Bank Rd WWKM BR4 70 D2
Harvester Rd HOR/WEW KT19 64 A8
Harvesters HORS RH12 229 G5
Harvesters Cl ISLW TW7 17 G7
Harvest Hl EGRIN RH19 216 B1
RGODL GU7 160 A5
Harvest La THDIT KT7 44 D6
Harvest Ride BNFD RG42 35 J1
Harvest Rd CRAWE RH10 212 F5
EGH TW20 21 G6
FELT TW13 24 D5
Harvestside HORL RH6 170 F5
Harvey Cl CRAWW RH11 211 K8
Harvey Dr HPTN TW12 43 L1
Harvey Rd GU GU1 9 J7
HSLWW TW4 25 J1
WOT/HER KT12 42 D7 1
Harwarden Cl CRAWE RH10 214 F1
Harwood Av MTCM CR4 48 B3
Harwood Gdns WDSR SL4 20 E1
Harwood Pk REDH RH1 170 D1
Harwood Rd SWTR RH13 229 H6
Harwoods Cl EGRIN RH19 216 C2 3
Harwood's La EGRIN RH19 216 C1
EGRIN RH19 216 C3
Haseltine Rd SYD SE26 33 J5
Haslam Av CHEAM SM3 47 H8
Hasle Dr HASM GU27 219 L4
Haslemere Av HEST TW5 15 M4
MTCM CR4 48 A2
WAND/EARL SW18 29 L3
Haslemere Cl FRIM GU16 73 M6 2
HPTN TW12 25 J6 2
WLGTN SM6 67 H4 3
Haslemere Rd HASM GU27 219 L7
LIPH GU30 218 A5
MFD/CHID GU8 180 F7
THHTH CR7 49 L5
Haslett Av East CRAWE RH10 212 C3
Haslett Av West CRAWE RH10 212 A4
CRAWW RH11 212 A3
Haslett Rd SHPTN TW17 42 B2 2
Hassocks Cl SYD SE26 32 E4 2
Hassocks Ct CRAWW RH11 211 J6 2
Hassocks Rd STRHM/NOR SW16 49 G1
Hassock Wd HAYES BR2 71 G3
Haste Hl HASM GU27 220 A4
Hastings Cl FRIM GU16 93 K2
Hastings Dr SURB KT6 44 F6
Hastings Rd CRAWE RH10 212 E3
CROY/NA CR0 5 J3
Hatch Cl ADL/WDHM KT15 58 E2
CRAN GU6 204 D6
Hatch End BFOR GU20 54 F5
FROW RH18 217 J7
The Hatches FNM GU9 10 B4
FRIM GU16 93 J3
Hatchett Rd EBED/NFELT TW14 23 M2
Hatchetts Dr HASM GU27 218 F3
Hatch Gdns
KWD/TDW/WH KT20 105 G2
Hatchgate HORL RH6 170 C7
Hatchgate Copse BRAK RG12 34 B6
Hatch Hl HASM GU27 219 L8
Hatchlands HORS RH12 229 K2
Hatchlands Rd REDH RH1 126 B8
Hatch La HASM GU27 219 L7
MFD/CHID GU8 201 G1
REDH RH1 149 J7
RPLY/SEND GU23 99 L2
WDR/YW UB7 14 A2
Hatch Pl RCHPK/HAM TW10 27 J6
Hatch Rd STRHM/NOR SW16 49 H2
Hatfield Cl BELMT SM2 65 L7 3
BF/WBF KT14 78 E2 1
MTCM CR4 48 A4 2
Hatfield Ct CBLY GU15 72 E4 1
Hatfield Gdns FARN GU14 93 H6 2
Hatfield Rd ASHTD KT21 103 J1
Hathaway Rd CROY/NA CR0 4 B2
Hatherleigh Cl CHSGTN KT9 63 G4 2
MRDN SM4 47 K4 2
Hatherley Rd RCH/KEW TW9 18 C3
Hatherop Rd HPTN TW12 25 J8
Hathersham Cl HORL RH6 171 K5
Hathersham La HORL RH6 171 J3
Hatherwood ASHTD KT21 103 G2 1
Hatton Gdns MTCM CR4 48 C5
Hatton Gn EBED/NFELT TW14 15 K6
Hatton Hl BFOR GU20 54 F4
Hatton Rd CROY/NA CR0 49 K8
EBED/NFELT TW14 23 M1
HTHAIR TW6 15 J6
Havana Rd WIM/MER SW19 29 K3
Havelock Rd CROY/NA CR0 5 K5
WIM/MER SW19 29 M6
Havelock Wk FSTH SE23 32 F2
Haven Cl WIM/MER SW19 29 G4
Haven Gdns CRAWE RH10 194 D8
Havengate HORS RH12 229 J4
Haven Rd ASHF TW15 23 L5
BIL RH14 226 A6
The Haven RCH/KEW TW9 18 D5
SUN TW16 24 D8
Haven Wy FNM GU9 134 A5
Haverfield Gdns
RCH/KEW TW9 18 D2 4
Haverhill Rd BAL SW12 30 F2
Havers Av WOT/HER KT12 61 G4
Haversham Cl CRAWE RH10 212 C3 1
TWK TW1 18 A8 4
Haversham Dr BRAK RG12 34 E6
Havisham Pl STRHM/NOR SW16 31 L7
Hawarden Gv HNHL SE24 31 M1
Hawarden Rd CTHM CR3 107 M3
Hawes La WWKM BR4 51 M8
Hawes Rd
KWD/TDW/WH KT20 105 G2 1
Hawke Rd NRWD SE19 32 A7
Hawker Rd ASHV GU12 113 J4
Hawkesbourne Rd HORS RH12 229 J4
Hawkesbury Rd PUT/ROE SW15 19 L7
Hawkesfield Rd FSTH SE23 33 H3
Hawkes Leap BFOR GU20 54 E3
Hawkesley Cl TWK TW1 26 D5 3
Hawkesmoore Dr RDKG RH5 166 F5
Hawkesmoor Rd CRAWW RH11 211 H5
Hawkes Rd EBED/NFELT TW14 24 D1
MTCM CR4 48 B1
Hawkesworth Dr BAGS GU19 54 A8
Hawkewood Rd SUN TW16 42 E3
Hawkhirst Rd PUR/KEN CR8 88 A6
Hawkhurst COB KT11 81 K4
Hawkhurst Rd
STRHM/NOR SW16 31 G8
Hawkhurst Wk CRAWE RH10 212 E5 2
Hawkhurst Wy NWMAL KT3 46 A5 2
WWKM BR4 69 L1
Hawkins Cl BRAK RG12 35 K2
Hawkins Rd CRAWE RH10 212 B5
TEDD TW11 26 E7 2
Hawkins Wy CAT SE6 33 K6
Hawk La BRAK RG12 35 G4
Hawkley Gdns WNWD SE27 31 L3
Hawksbrook La BECK BR3 51 L6
Hawkshaw Cl LIPH GU30 218 A5 1
Hawk's Hl LHD/OX KT22 102 C5
Hawkshill Cl ESH/CLAY KT10 61 K5
Hawks Hill Cl LHD/OX KT22 102 C5
Hawks Hill Ct LHD/OX KT22 102 C5
Hawkshill Wy ESH/CLAY KT10 61 J5
Hawks Rd KUT KT1 3 H7
Hawksview COB KT11 81 J3 1
Hawksway STA TW18 22 C4 1
Hawkswell Cl WOKN/KNAP GU21 76 C7
Hawkswood Av FRIM GU16 73 J7
Hawkwood Dell GT/LBKH KT23 101 K8
Hawkwood Ri GT/LBKH KT23 101 K8
Hawley Cl HPTN TW12 25 J7 3
Hawley Gn BLKW GU17 72 B6
Hawley La FARN GU14 92 E1
Hawley Rd BLKW GU17 72 B6
Hawley Wy ASHF TW15 23 L6 1
Hawmead CRAWE RH10 214 F1
Haworth Rd CRAWE RH10 212 E4

Hawth Av CRAWE RH10 .... 212 D3 ▣
Hawth Cl CRAWE RH10 .... 212 B5
Hawthorn Av THHTH CR7 .... 49 L1
Hawthorn Cl ASHV GU12 .... 135 H1 ▣
  BNFD RG42 .... 34 D1
  BNSTD SM7 .... 85 H4 ▣
  CRAWW RH11 .... 191 M8 ▣
  EDEN TN8 .... 153 M7 ▣
  HEST TW5 .... 15 L2
  HORS RH12 .... 228 F5 ▣
  HPTN TW12 .... 25 K6 ▣
  REDH RH1 .... 148 D5
  WOKS/MYFD GU22 .... 97 H2
Hawthorn Crs SAND/SEL CR2 .... 88 F1 ▣
Hawthorndene Cl HAYES BR2 ... 70 C1 ▣
Hawthorndene Rd
  HAYES BR2 .... 70 D1 ▣
Hawthorn Dr WWKM BR4 .... 70 B3
Hawthorne Av BH/WHM TN16 ..... 91 C5
  CAR SM5 .... 66 D6
  MTCM CR4 .... 48 A2
Hawthorne Crs BLKW GU17 ...... 72 B5
Hawthorne Pl EW KT17 .... 84 B2
Hawthorne Rd ECH TW20 .... 21 M6
Hawthorne Wy RGUE GU4 .... 117 L4 ▣
Hawthorn Gv PGE/AN SE20 ...... 50 E1
Hawthorn Hatch BTFD TW8 ...... 17 L2
Hawthorn La NFNM GU10 .... 155 J6
Hawthorn Rd BTFD TW8 .... 17 L2 ▣
  FRIM GU16 .... 73 J7
  RGODL GU7 .... 159 L7
  RPLY/SEND GU23 .... 98 C6
  SUT SM1 .... 66 E4
  WLGTN SM6 .... 66 E6
  WOKS/MYFD GU22 .... 97 G2
The Hawthorns DTCH/LGLY SL3 .. 13 J3
  EW KT17 .... 64 C5
  OXTED RH8 .... 130 D7 ▣
Hawthorn Wy ADL/WDHM KT15 ... 58 E8
  CHOB/PIR GU24 .... 75 K6
  REDH RH1 .... 148 E2
  SHPTN TW17 .... 42 A4
Haxted Rd LING RH7 .... 174 B2
Haybarn Dr HORS RH12 .... 229 H2
Haycroft Cl PUR/KEN CR8 ...... 107 L1
Haycroft Rd SURB KT6 .... 63 C1
Hayden Ct ADL/WDHM KT15 ...... 58 E8
Haydn Av PUR/KEN CR8 .... 87 K5
Haydon Park Rd
  WIM/MER SW19 .... 29 K6
Haydon Pl GU GU1 .... 9 C5
Haydon's Rd WIM/MER SW19 ..... 29 M7
Hayes Barton
  WOKS/MYFD GU22 .... 78 A6
Hayes Cl HAYES BR2 .... 70 D1
Hayes Crs CHEAM SM3 .... 65 G3
Hayes Gdn HAYES BR2 .... 70 D1
Hayes La PUR/KEN CR8 .... 87 L6
  SWTR RH13 .... 226 F8
The Hayes EPSOM KT18 .... 104 A1
Hayes Wk HORL RH6 .... 170 F5 ▣
Hayes Wy BECK BR3 .... 51 M4
Hayfields HORL RH6 .... 170 F5 ▣
Haygarth Pl WIM/MER SW19 ..... 29 L8
Haygreen Cl KUTN/CMB KT2 ..... 3 L1
Hayling Av FELT TW13 .... 24 D4
Haymeads Dr ESH/CLAY KT10 .... 61 M5
Haymer Gdns WPK KT4 .... 64 D2 ▣
Hayne Rd BECK BR3 .... 51 J2
Haynes Cl RPLY/SEND GU23 ..... 98 C6
Haynes La NRWD SE19 .... 32 B7
Haynt Wk RYNPK SW20 .... 47 H3
Haysleigh Gdns PGE/AN SE20 ... 50 D1 ▣
Hays Wk BELMT SM2 .... 65 G8
The Haywain OXTED RH8 .... 130 A4
Hayward Cl WIM/MER SW19 ...... 29 L8
Haywardens LING RH7 .... 174 A4
Hayward Gdns PUT/ROE SW15 ... 19 M8
Hayward Rd THDIT KT7 .... 44 C8
Haywards CRAWE RH10 .... 193 G8
Haywood BRAK RG12 .... 34 F7
Hazel Av FARN GU14 .... 92 C7
  GU GU1 .... 116 F4
Hazel Bank BRYLDS KT5 .... 45 M8
Hazelbank Cl LIPH GU30 .... 218 A5
Hazelbank Rd CHERT KT16 ...... 40 F7
Hazelbury Cl WIM/MER SW19 .... 47 K2
Hazel Cl BTFD TW8 .... 17 L2 ▣
  CRAWE RH10 .... 214 F1
  CRAWW RH11 .... 191 M8
  CROY/NA CR0 .... 51 G7
  EGH TW20 .... 20 E7
  MTCM CR4 .... 49 G4
  REIG RH2 .... 147 M2
  WHTN TW2 .... 25 M1
Hazeldene ADL/WDHM KT15 ...... 58 F4 ▣
Hazeldene Ct PUR/KEN CR8 ..... 88 A5
Hazel Dr RPLY/SEND GU23 ...... 98 C7
Hazel Gv GSHT GU26 .... 199 H8
  ORP BR6 .... 71 L1
  STA TW18 .... 22 E7
  SYD SE26 .... 33 C5
Hazelhurst HORL RH6 .... 170 F5 ▣
Hazelhurst Cl RGUE GU4 .... 117 L3
Hazelhurst Crs HORS RH12 ..... 228 C8
Hazelhurst Dr CRAWE RH10 ..... 213 H3
Hazelhurst Rd TOOT SW17 ...... 29 M5
Hazell Hl BRAK RG12 .... 34 F3
Hazell Rd FNM GU9 .... 133 J7
Hazel Md EW KT17 .... 84 B2
Hazelmere Cl EBED/NFELT TW14 . 15 G8
  LHD/OX KT22 .... 102 E4
Hazel Rd ASHV GU12 .... 135 M2
  BF/WBF KT14 .... 78 D4
  FRIM GU16 .... 93 K7
  REIG RH2 .... 147 M2
Hazel Wy COUL/CHIP CR5 .... 106 C1
  CRAWE RH10 .... 214 E1
  LHD/OX KT22 .... 101 M4
Hazelwick Av CRAWE RH10 ...... 212 D1
Hazelwick Mill La
  CRAWE RH10 .... 212 D1 ▣
Hazelwick Rd CRAWE RH10 ...... 212 D2 ▣
Hazelwood CRAWW RH11 .... 211 K3
Hazelwood Av MRDN SM4 .... 47 L4
Hazelwood Cl CRAWE RH10 ...... 214 C1
Hazelwood Ct SURB KT6 .... 45 H6 ▣
Hazelwood Gv SAND/SEL CR2 .... 88 E4

Hazelwood Hts OXTED RH8 ...... 130 D5
Hazelwood La COUL/CHIP CR5 ... 106 C1
Hazelwood Rd OXTED RH8 .... 130 E6
  WOKN/KNAP GU21 .... 76 B8 ▣
Hazledean Rd CROY/NA CR0 ..... 4 F6
Hazledene Rd CHSWK W4 .... 18 F1
Hazlemere Gdns WPK KT4 .... 46 E8 ▣
Hazlewell Rd PUT/ROE SW15 .... 19 M7
Hazlewood MFD/CHID GU8 .... 158 B5
Hazlitt Cl FELT TW13 .... 25 H5 ▣
Hazon Wy HOR/WEW KT19 .... 84 A2
Headcorn Rd THHTH CR7 .... 49 J4
Headington Rd
  WAND/EARL SW18 .... 29 M2
Headland Wy LING RH7 .... 173 M5
Headley Av WLGTN SM6 .... 67 J4
Headley Cl CHSGTN KT9 .... 63 K5
  CRAWE RH10 .... 193 G8
Headley Common Rd
  EPSOM KT18 .... 124 A1
Headley Dr CROY/NA CR0 .... 69 M6
  KWD/TDW/WH KT20 .... 104 E1
Headley Gv
  KWD/TDW/WH KT20 .... 104 E2
  KWD/TDW/WH KT20 .... 124 A2
Headley Heath Ap
  KWD/TDW/WH KT20 .... 123 L4
Headley Rd ASHTD KT21 .... 83 M8
  EPSOM KT18 .... 103 M2
  GSHT GU26 .... 198 C5
  LHD/OX KT22 .... 102 F4
  RDKG RH5 .... 122 F3
Headway Cl
  RCHPK/HAM TW10 .... 26 F5 ▣
The Headway EW KT17 .... 64 C7
Hearnville Rd BAL SW12 .... 30 D2
Hearn Wk BRAK RG12 .... 35 H1 ▣
Heatham Pk WHTN TW2 .... 26 C1
Heathbridge WEY KT13 .... 59 K6 ▣
Heath Cl BNSTD SM7 .... 85 L4
  FNM GU9 .... 133 M2 ▣
  GSHT GU26 .... 198 F2
  HORS RH12 .... 228 B6 ▣
  HYS/HAR UB3 .... 15 G2
  STWL/WRAY TW19 .... 13 M8
  VW GU25 .... 39 G4
Heathcote KWD/TDW/WH KT20 .... 105 G4
Heathcote Dr EGRIN RH19 ...... 195 L7
Heathcote Rd ASHV GU12 .... 113 L6
  CBLY GU15 .... 73 G4
  EPSOM KT18 .... 84 A4
  TWK TW1 .... 17 L8
Heathcroft KWD/TDW/WH KT20 ... 105 H1
Heathdale Av HSLWW TW4 .... 16 B5
Heathdene
  KWD/TDW/WH KT20 .... 105 H1
Heathdene Rd
  STRHM/NOR SW16 .... 31 J8
  WLGTN SM6 .... 66 E6
Heathdown Rd
  WOKS/MYFD GU22 .... 78 A5
Heath Dr BELMT SM2 .... 65 M7
  CHOB/PIR GU24 .... 95 K2
  KWD/TDW/WH KT20 .... 104 D7
  RPLY/SEND GU23 .... 97 L5
  RYNPK SW20 .... 46 F4
Heathedge FSTH SE23 .... 32 E3 ▣
Heather Cl ADL/WDHM KT15 ..... 58 F4 ▣
  ALDT GU11 .... 112 B8 ▣
  ASHV GU12 .... 113 L4 ▣
  CRAWE RH10 .... 193 L4 ▣
  FNM GU9 .... 10 B8
  GUW GU2 .... 116 E6
  HORS RH12 .... 229 C4
  HPTN TW12 .... 43 J1
  ISLW TW7 .... 17 G7 ▣
  KWD/TDW/WH KT20 .... 105 H4
  REDH RH1 .... 126 E5
  WOKN/KNAP GU21 .... 76 F5
Heatherdale Cl KUTN/CMB KT2 .. 3 K1
Heatherdale Rd CBLY GU15 ..... 72 F5
Heatherdeane EHSLY KT24 ...... 100 A7
Heatherdene Cl MTCM CR4 ...... 48 A4
Heatherset Gdns
  STRHM/NOR SW16 .... 31 J8
Heatherside Dr VW GU25 .... 38 D6
Heatherside Rd HOR/WEW KT19 .. 64 A6
Heathers Land RDKG RH5 .... 144 F5 ▣
The Heathers
  STWL/WRAY TW19 .... 23 J1 ▣
Heathervale Rd
  ADL/WDHM KT15 .... 58 E8
Heather Wk CHOB/PIR GU24 ..... 95 C3
  HORL RH6 .... 171 M6
Heather Wy CHOB/PIR GU24 ..... 56 B6
  GSHT GU26 .... 199 J5
  SAND/SEL CR2 .... 69 C7
Heatherway LING RH7 .... 195 J2
Heathfield COB KT11 .... 81 K4
  CRAWE RH10 .... 193 C8 ▣
Heathfield Av ASC SL5 .... 37 H5
  WAND/EARL SW18 .... 30 A1 ▣
Heathfield Cl HAYES BR2 ...... 70 F4 ▣
  RGODL GU7 .... 160 A7
  WOKS/MYFD GU22 .... 7 H7 ▣
Heathfield Dr MTCM CR4 .... 48 B1
  REDH RH1 .... 148 B5
  WIM/MER SW19 .... 30 B8
Heathfield North WHTN TW2 .... 26 B1
Heathfield Rd CROY/NA CR0 .... 68 A4 ▣
  HAYES BR2 .... 70 F4
  WOKS/MYFD GU22 .... 7 H7 ▣
  WOT/HER KT12 .... 61 H3
Heathfield South WHTN TW2 .... 26 B1
Heathfield Sq WAND/EARL SW18 . 30 A1
Heathfield V SAND/SEL CR2 .... 69 G7
Heath Gdns TWK TW1 .... 26 C2

Heath Gv PGE/AN SE20 .... 32 F8 ▣
  SUN TW16 .... 24 C8
Heath Hl DORK RH4 .... 144 E2
Heath Mill La RGUW GU3 .... 100 E7
Heathpark Dr BFOR GU20 .... 55 H5
Heath Ridge Gn COB KT11 ...... 81 K3
Heath Ri CBLY GU15 .... 73 G4
  DORK RH4 .... 143 M4
Heathrise RPLY/SEND GU23 ..... 98 E5
Heath Ri VW GU25 .... 39 G4
Heath Rd BAGS GU19 .... 54 B6
  CTHM CR3 .... 108 A5
  HASM GU27 .... 219 C4
  HSLW TW3 .... 16 F6
  LHD/OX KT22 .... 81 M2
  THHTH CR7 .... 49 M3
  TWK TW1 .... 26 C2
  WEY KT13 .... 59 K4
  WOKS/MYFD GU22 .... 6 C1
Heathrow SHGR GU5 .... 141 M5
Heathrow Cl WDR/YW UB7 .... 13 L3
Heathside ESH/CLAY KT10 ...... 62 B2
  HSLWW TW4 .... 25 J1
  WHTN TW2 .... 26 C2
  WOKS/MYFD GU22 .... 6 C1
Heathside Cl ESH/CLAY KT10 ... 62 B2
Heathside Ct
  KWD/TDW/WH KT20 .... 104 D5
Heathside Crs WOKS/MYFD GU22 . 6 E6
Heathside Gdns
  WOKS/MYFD GU22 .... 7 G6
Heathside La GSHT GU26 .... 199 C1 ▣
Heathside Pk CBLY GU15 .... 73 M2
Heathside Park Rd
  WOKS/MYFD GU22 .... 6 F7
Heathside Pl
  KWD/TDW/WH KT20 .... 85 G8
Heathside Rd WOKS/MYFD GU22 .. 6 E7
The Heath CTHM CR3 .... 107 M6
Heathvale Bridge Rd
  ASHV GU12 .... 113 K3
Heath Vw EHSLY KT24 .... 100 C7
Heathview Gdns PUT/ROE SW15 .. 28 F1
Heathview Rd MFD/CHID GU8 .... 181 H2
  THHTH CR7 .... 49 K4
Heath Wy HORS RH12 .... 229 C4
Heathway ASC SL5 .... 36 B1
  CBLY GU15 .... 73 G4
  CROY/NA CR0 .... 69 J2
  CTHM CR3 .... 107 M7
  EHSLY KT24 .... 100 C6
Heathway Cl CBLY GU15 .... 73 G4
Heathyfields Rd FNM GU9 ...... 133 J3
Heaton Rd MTCM CR4 .... 30 D8
Hebdon Rd TOOT SW17 .... 30 B5
Heddon Cl ISLW TW7 .... 17 K6 ▣
Heddon Wk FARN GU14 .... 92 D2 ▣
Hedgehog La HASM GU27 .... 219 L4
Hedgerley Ct WOKN/KNAP GU21 .. 76 F7
Hedgeside CRAWW RH11 .... 211 M8 ▣
Hedgeway GUW GU2 .... 8 A7
Hedingham Cl HORL RH6 .... 170 F5 ▣
Hedley Rd HSLWW TW4 .... 25 K1 ▣
Heenan Cl FRIM GU16 .... 93 H2
Heidegger Crs BARN SW13 ...... 19 L2
Heighton Gdns CROY/NA CR0 .... 67 L4
Heights Cl BNSTD SM7 .... 85 H6
  RYNPK SW20 .... 28 E8
Helder St SAND/SEL CR2 .... 68 A5
Heldmann Cl ISLW TW7 .... 17 G6
Helen Av EBED/NFELT TW14 ..... 24 E1
Helen Cl E/WMO/HCT KT8 .... 43 L4
Helen Ct FARN GU14 .... 92 E5 ▣
Helford Wk
  WOKN/KNAP GU21 .... 76 D8 ▣
Helgiford Gdns SUN TW16 ...... 24 B8 ▣
Helksham Cl SHST GU47 .... 52 A8 ▣
Helme Cl WIM/MER SW19 .... 29 J6 ▣
Helmsdale BRAK RG12 .... 35 H5
  WOKN/KNAP GU21 .... 76 E8
Helmsdale Rd
  STRHM/NOR SW16 .... 48 F1
Helvellyn Cl EGH TW20 .... 21 M8 ▣
Helvetia St CAT SE6 .... 33 J3
Hemingford Rd CHEAM SM3 ...... 64 F4
Hemlock Cl
  KWD/TDW/WH KT20 .... 105 H5 ▣
Hemming Cl HPTN TW12 .... 43 K1 ▣
Hempshaw Av BNSTD SM7 .... 86 C6
Hemsby Rd CHSGTN KT9 .... 63 J5
Henbit Cl
  KWD/TDW/WH KT20 .... 104 E1 ▣
Henchley Dene RGUE GU4 .... 118 A5
Henderson Av GUW GU2 .... 116 E3
Henderson Rd BH/WHM TN16 ..... 90 F2
  CRAWW RH11 .... 211 L8
  CROY/NA CR0 .... 50 A6
  WAND/EARL SW18 .... 30 B1
Hendham Rd TOOT SW17 .... 30 B3
Hendon Wy STWL/WRAY TW19 ..... 14 A7
Heneage Crs CROY/NA CR0 ...... 69 M8
Henfield Rd WIM/MER SW19 ..... 47 J1
Henfold Dr RDKG RH5 .... 167 H2
Henfold La RDKG RH5 .... 167 H2
Hengelo Gdns MTCM CR4 .... 48 A4
Hengist Cl HORS RH12 .... 228 D8
Hengrave Rd FSTH SE23 .... 32 F1
Hengrove Crs ASHF TW15 .... 23 G4
Henhurst Cross La RDKG RH5 ... 166 D6
Henley Av CHEAM SM3 .... 65 H2
Henley Bank GUW GU2 .... 8 A8
Henley Cl CRAWE RH10 .... 213 G6 ▣
  FARN GU14 .... 92 B1 ▣

  ISLW TW7 .... 17 J3 ▣
Henley Ct WOKS/MYFD GU22 ..... 97 K2 ▣
Henley Dr FRIM GU16 .... 93 H2
  KUTN/CMB KT2 .... 3 M1
Henley Ga CHOB/PIR GU24 ...... 114 F1
Henley Wy FELT TW13 .... 25 C6 ▣
Hennel Cl FSTH SE23 .... 32 F4
Hennessy Ct WOKN/KNAP GU21 ... 77 M3
Henry Doulton Dr TOOT SW17 ... 30 D5
Henry Peters Dr TEDD TW11 .... 26 B6 ▣
Hensford Gdns SYD SE26 .... 32 E5 ▣
Henshaw Cl CRAWW RH11 .... 211 J5 ▣
Henslow Wy WOKN/KNAP GU21 .... 78 A4
Henson Cl ORP BR6 .... 71 L1
Henson Rd CRAWE RH10 .... 212 E2
Hensworth Rd ASHF TW15 .... 23 G7
Henty Cl CRAWW RH11 .... 211 H6
Henty Wk PUT/ROE SW15 .... 19 L7
Hepple Cl ISLW TW7 .... 17 L4
Hepplewhite Cl CRAWW RH11 .... 211 L8
Hepworth Cft SHST GU47 .... 72 B3 ▣
Hepworth Rd
  STRHM/NOR SW16 .... 31 H8
Hepworth Wy WOT/HER KT12 ..... 42 C8
Herald Gdns WLGTN SM6 .... 66 E2
Herbert Cl BRAK RG12 .... 34 E5
Herbert Crs WOKN/KNAP GU21 ... 76 B8
Herbert Gdns CHSWK W4 .... 18 E1
Herbert Rd KUT KT1 .... 3 C9
  WIM/MER SW19 .... 29 J8
Hereford Cl CRAWE RH10 .... 212 B7
  EPSOM KT18 .... 84 A3
  GUW GU2 .... 116 C6
  STA TW18 .... 40 E1
Hereford Copse
  WOKS/MYFD GU22 .... 96 E1
Hereford Gdns WHTN TW2 .... 25 M2 ▣
Hereford La FNM GU9 .... 133 L3
Hereford Rd FELT TW13 .... 24 F2
Hereford Wy CHSGTN KT9 .... 62 F4
Hereward Av PUR/KEN CR8 ...... 67 K8
Hereward Rd TOOT SW17 .... 30 B5
Heriot Rd CHERT KT16 .... 40 D7
Heritage Hl HAYES BR2 .... 70 F4
Heritage Lawn HORL RH6 .... 170 F5
Herlwyn Gdns TOOT SW17 .... 30 C5
Herm Cl CRAWW RH11 .... 211 K7 ▣
  ISLW TW7 .... 16 F2
Hermes Wy WLGTN SM6 .... 67 G6
Hermitage Cl ESH/CLAY KT10 ... 62 D5
  FARN GU14 .... 93 C8 ▣
  FRIM GU16 .... 73 J8
  SHPTN TW17 .... 41 K4
Hermitage Dr ASC SL5 .... 36 B2
Hermitage Gdns NRWD SE19 ..... 31 M8 ▣
Hermitage La CROY/NA CR0 ..... 5 K1
  EGRIN RH19 .... 216 C1
  STRHM/NOR SW16 .... 31 J8 ▣
Hermitage Rd EGRIN RH19 ...... 196 A6
  NRWD SE19 .... 32 A7
  PUR/KEN CR8 .... 87 M6
  WOKN/KNAP GU21 .... 96 A1
The Hermitage BARN SW13 ...... 19 J3 ▣
  FSTH SE23 .... 32 F2
  RCHPK/HAM TW10 .... 18 B7
Hermitage Woods Crs
  WOKN/KNAP GU21 .... 96 A2
Hermits Rd CRAWE RH10 .... 212 C1
Hermonger La HORS RH12 .... 206 C7
Herndon Cl EGH TW20 .... 21 K5
Herne Rd SURB KT6 .... 63 C1
Heron Cl ASC SL5 .... 36 A1
  CRAWW RH11 .... 211 M1 ▣
  FRIM GU16 .... 93 J5
  GUW GU2 .... 116 E5
Heron Dl ADL/WDHM KT15 .... 59 G4
Herondale BRAK RG12 .... 34 F7
  HASM GU27 .... 219 H3
  SAND/SEL CR2 .... 69 G7
Herondale Av WAND/EARL SW18 .. 30 A2
Heron Pl EGRIN RH19 .... 216 C1
Heron Rd CROY/NA CR0 .... 5 H5
  TWK TW1 .... 17 K6
The Heronry WOT/HER KT12 ..... 60 D5
Herons Cl CRAWE RH10 .... 194 D4
Heronscourt LTWR GU18 .... 74 F1
Heronsfield LTWR GU18 .... 74 F1
Herons Cft WEY KT13 .... 59 M5
Heron Shaw CRAN GU6 .... 185 H8 ▣
Herons Lea CRAWE RH10 .... 194 D4
Herons Pl ISLW TW7 .... 17 L5
Herons Wy CHOB/PIR GU24 ...... 95 C3
Herons Wood Ct HORL RH6 ...... 170 C5 ▣
Herontye Dr EGRIN RH19 .... 216 C1
Heron Wy SWTR RH13 .... 229 K7
Heron Wood Rd ASHV GU12 ...... 135 C5
Herretts Gdns ASHV GU12 ...... 113 C8
Herrett St ASHV GU12 .... 135 C5
Herrick Cl CRAWE RH10 .... 212 F1
  FRIM GU16 .... 73 M6
Herrings La BFOR GU20 .... 55 C5
Herschell Rd FSTH SE23 .... 33 C1
Herschel Pk PUT/ROE SW15 ..... 28 D1
Hersham Gdns
  WOT/HER KT12 .... 60 F3 ▣
Hersham Rd WOT/HER KT12 ...... 60 F3
Hertford Av MORT/ESHN SW14 ... 19 C7
Hertford Wy MTCM CR4 .... 49 H4 ▣
Hesiers Hl WARL CR6 .... 90 B7
Hesiers Rd WARL CR6 .... 90 B7
Hesketh Cl CRAN GU6 .... 185 H6 ▣
Heslop Rd BAL SW12 .... 30 C2
Hessle Gv EW KT17 .... 84 C1
Hesterman Wy CROY/NA CR0 ..... 49 H8
Hester Ter RCH/KEW TW9 .... 18 D5
Heston Av HEST TW5 .... 16 B2
Heston Grange La HEST TW5 .... 16 C1
Heston Rd HEST TW5 .... 16 C2
  REDH RH1 .... 148 C5
Hethersett Cl REIG RH2 .... 125 M5 ▣
Hetherington Rd SHPTN TW17 ... 41 M2 ▣
Hewers Wy
  KWD/TDW/WH KT20 .... 104 E2
Hewitt Cl CROY/NA CR0 .... 69 K2 ▣
Hewlett Pl BAGS GU19 .... 54 B6
Hewshott Gv LIPH GU30 .... 218 B4

Hewshott La LIPH GU30 .... 218 A4
Hexham Cl CRAWE RH10 .... 213 H3
  SHST GU47 .... 52 A7
Hexham Gdns ISLW TW7 .... 17 K2
Hexham Rd MRDN SM4 .... 47 L8
  WNWD SE27 .... 31 M3
Hextalls La REDH RH1 .... 128 A3
Heybridge Av STRHM/NOR SW16 .. 31 J7
Heyford Av RYNPK SW20 .... 47 J3
Heyford Rd MTCM CR4 .... 48 B2
Heymede LHD/OX KT22 .... 102 F5
Heythorpe Cl
  WOKN/KNAP GU21 .... 76 C7 ▣
Heythorp St WAND/EARL SW18 ... 29 J2
Heywood Dr BAGS GU19 .... 53 M7
Hibernia Gdns HSLW TW3 .... 16 D7
Hibernia Rd HSLW TW3 .... 16 D6
Hickmans Cl GDST RH9 .... 128 F6
Hidcote Cl WOKS/MYFD GU22 .... 7 K4
Hidcote Gdns RYNPK SW20 ...... 46 E3 ▣
Higgs La BAGS GU19 .... 54 A7
Highacre DORK RH4 .... 144 E5
Highams Hl CRAWW RH11 .... 211 J4
Highams La CHOB/PIR GU24 ..... 55 K5
High Barn Rd EHSLY KT24 ...... 121 G3
Highbarrow Rd CROY/NA CR0 .... 5 L3
High Beech BRAK RG12 .... 35 J4 ▣
  SAND/SEL CR2 .... 68 B6
High Beeches EW KT17 .... 85 G4
  FRIM GU16 .... 73 G7
High Beeches Cl
  PUR/KEN CR8 .... 67 G8 ▣
High Broom Crs WWKM BR4 ...... 51 L7
Highbury Av THHTH CR7 .... 49 K2
Highbury Cl NWMAL KT3 .... 45 M4
  WWKM BR4 .... 69 L1 ▣
Highbury Crs CBLY GU15 .... 73 K2
Highbury Gv HASM GU27 .... 219 M1 ▣
Highbury Rd WIM/MER SW19 ..... 29 H6
High Cedar Dr RYNPK SW20 ..... 28 E8
Highclere ASC SL5 .... 37 C5
  GU GU1 .... 117 K5
Highclere Cl PUR/KEN CR8 ..... 87 M5
Highclere Ct WOKN/KNAP GU21 .. 75 M7 ▣
Highclere Dr CBLY GU15 .... 73 K2
Highclere Gdns
  WOKN/KNAP GU21 .... 75 M7 ▣
Highclere Rd ASHV GU12 .... 135 G1
  NWMAL KT3 .... 46 A3
  WOKN/KNAP GU21 .... 75 M7 ▣
Highclere St SYD SE26 .... 33 H5
Highcliffe Dr PUT/ROE SW15 ... 19 J8
High Coombe Pl KUTN/CMB KT2 .. 28 A8
Highcotts La RGUE GU4 .... 98 D8
Highcroft MFD/CHID GU8 .... 181 J1
  SHGR GU5 .... 162 B5
Highcroft Ct GT/LBKH KT23 .... 101 K5 ▣
Highcroft Dr HORS RH12 .... 206 B8
Highdaun Dr STRHM/NOR SW16 ... 49 J4
Highdown WPK KT4 .... 64 B1
Highdown Ct CRAWE RH10 .... 212 G6
High Down Rd BELMT SM2 .... 85 L1
Highdown Rd PUT/ROE SW15 ..... 19 L8
  WOKN/KNAP GU21 .... 229 J2
High Dr CTHM CR3 .... 109 J4
  LHD/OX KT22 .... 82 A4
  NWMAL KT3 .... 45 M1
High Elms Rd ORP BR6 .... 71 M7
Higher Alham BRAK RG12 .... 35 H7 ▣
  BRAK RG12 .... 35 H7 ▣
  BRAK RG12 .... 35 H7 ▣
Highercombe Rd HASM GU27 ..... 220 B1
Higher Dr BNSTD SM7 .... 85 G3
  EHSLY KT24 .... 120 F1
  PUR/KEN CR8 .... 87 K3
Higher Gn EW KT17 .... 84 D3
Highfield BNSTD SM7 .... 86 B7
  BRAK RG12 .... 34 C6
  RGUE GU4 .... 139 J8
Highfield Av ALDT GU11 .... 134 D1
Highfield Cl ALDT GU11 .... 134 E1
  FARN GU14 .... 92 C5
  FNM GU9 .... 10 E6
  LHD/OX KT22 .... 82 A7
  SURB KT6 .... 44 F8
Highfield Crs GSHT GU26 ...... 199 H5
Highfield Dr HOR/WEW KT19 .... 64 C6
  WWKM BR4 .... 69 L2
Highfield Gdns ALDT GU11 ..... 134 D1
Highfield Hl NRWD SE19 .... 32 A8
Highfield La LIPH GU30 .... 218 A7
  MFD/CHID GU8 .... 179 L8
  RGUW GU3 .... 136 D6
Highfield Pth FARN GU14 ...... 92 C5
Highfield Rd BF/WBF KT14 ..... 78 D3
  BH/WHM TN16 .... 91 H7
  BRYLDS KT5 .... 45 M7
  CHERT KT16 .... 40 D8 ▣
  CTHM CR3 .... 108 D4
  EGH TW20 .... 21 G7
  EGRIN RH19 .... 196 A6
  FARN GU14 .... 92 C5
  FELT TW13 .... 24 D2
  ISLW TW7 .... 17 J3
  PUR/KEN CR8 .... 67 J8
  SUN TW16 .... 42 C5
  SUT SM1 .... 66 B4
  WOT/HER KT12 .... 42 B8
High Flds ASC SL5 .... 37 J5
Highfields ASHTD KT21 .... 103 G1
  EHSLY KT24 .... 120 C2
  FROW RH18 .... 217 J7
  LHD/OX KT22 .... 102 A6
Highfields Rd EDEN TN8 .... 153 M4
High Foleys ESH/CLAY KT10 .... 62 E6 ▣
Highgate La FARN GU14 .... 92 F4
Highgate Rd FROW RH18 .... 217 J8
Highgrove FARN GU14 .... 92 E2 ▣
Highgrove Ms CAR SM5 .... 66 C2 ▣
Highland Cft BECK BR3 .... 33 L6
Highland Pk FELT TW13 .... 24 C5
Highland Rd ASHV GU12 .... 113 G7
  CBLY GU15 .... 73 H1
  NRWD SE19 .... 32 B7
  PUR/KEN CR8 .... 87 K5
  RDKG RH5 .... 166 F6
Highlands Av LHD/OX KT22 ..... 102 F4

SWTR RH13 .... 229 H7
Highlands Cl *FNM* GU9 .... 10 E6
  HSLW TW3 .... 16 E3
  LHD/OX KT22 .... 102 E4
Highlands Crs *SWTR* RH13 .... 229 H7
Highlands La *WOKS/MYFD* GU22 .. 97 H3
Highlands Pk *LHD/OX* KT22 ...... 103 C5
Highlands Rd *FNM* GU9 .... 133 M2
  LHD/OX KT22 .... 102 F4
  REDH RH1 .... 126 A7
  SWTR RH13 .... 229 J7
The Highlands *EHSLY* KT24 ...... 100 B7
High La *CTHM* CR3 .... 109 J1
  HASM GU27 .... 219 M1
  WARL CR6 .... 89 J8
High Level Dr *SYD* SE26 .... 32 D5
High Loxley Rd *MFD/CHID* GU8 .. 203 L3
High Md *WWKM* BR4 .... 70 A1
High Meadow Cl *DORK* RH4 ..... 144 E3
High Meadow Pl *CHERT* KT16 .... 40 C6
High Oaks *CRAWW* RH11 .... 211 L5
High Park Av *EHSLY* KT24 .... 100 A5
High Park Rd *FNM* GU9 .... 133 L6
  RCH/KEW TW9 .... 18 D3
High Pth *WIM/MER* SW19 .... 47 L1
High Path Rd *GU* GU1 .... 117 M8
High Pewley *GU* GU1 .... 9 J8
High Pine Cl *WEY* KT13 .... 59 M4
High Pines *WARL* CR6 .... 108 F1
High Pitfold *GSHT* GU26 .... 59 K4
Highpoint *WEY* KT13 .... 160 A7
High Rdg *RGODL* GU7 .... 84 B5
Highridge Cl *EPSOM* KT18 .... 79 J2
High Rd *BF/WBF* KT14 .... 106 B6
  COUL/CHIP CR5 ....
High Standing *CTHM* CR3 .... 107 M7
High St *ADL/WDHM* KT15 .... 58 E3
  ALDT GU11 .... 112 E7
  ASC SL5 .... 36 C3
  ASC SL5 .... 37 G5
  ASC SL5 .... 37 C5
  ASHV GU12 .... 112 E8
  BAGS GU19 .... 54 B6
  BECK BR3 .... 51 K2
  BH/WHM TN16 .... 131 M1
  BNSTD SM7 .... 34 E2
  BRAK RG12 .... 18 C1
  BTFD TW8 .... 66 C4
  CAR SM5 .... 73 G3
  CBLY GU15 .... 65 H5
  CHEAM SM3 .... 75 H2
  CHOB/PIR GU24 .... 76 B1
  CHOB/PIR GU24 .... 80 E4
  COB KT11 .... 185 C6
  CRAN GU6 .... 212 A3
  CRAWW RH11 ....
  CROY/NA CR0 .... 108 B5
  CTHM CR3 .... 144 E2
  DORK RH4 .... 12 F2
  DTCH/LGLY SL3 .... 43 K4
  E/WMO/HCT KT8 .... 153 M8
  EDEN TN8 .... 21 J6
  EGH TW20 .... 216 C1
  EGRIN RH19 .... 61 L3
  ESH/CLAY KT10 .... 62 C5
  ESH/CLAY KT10 .... 64 C8
  EW KT17 .... 112 F1
  FARN GU14 .... 24 C4
  FELT TW13 .... 101 L7
  GDST RH9 .... 9 G7
  GT/LBKH KT23 .... 8 F7
  GU GU1 .... 220 A3
  GUW GU2 .... 15 L2
  HASM GU27 .... 170 E6
  HEST TW5 .... 209 M1
  HORL RH6 .... 43 L1
  HORS RH12 .... 16 E5
  HPTN TW12 .... 15 G1
  HSLW TW3 .... 2 D7
  HYS/HAR UB3 .... 104 F5
  KUT KT1 .... 82 A3
  KWD/TDW/WH KT20 .... 102 E4
  LHD/OX KT22 .... 174 A5
  LING RH7 .... 155 H6
  NFNM GU10 .... 46 B4
  NWMAL KT3 .... 71 M4
  ORP BR6 .... 91 K1
  ORP BR6 .... 130 A4
  OXTED RH8 .... 130 E2
  OXTED RH8 .... 32 F8
  PGE/AN SE20 .... 87 K1
  PUR/KEN CR8 .... 126 E2
  REDH RH1 .... 126 C8
  REDH RH1 .... 127 J8
  REDH RH1 .... 128 A7
  REDH RH1 .... 125 K8
  REIG RH2 .... 160 A6
  RGODL GU7 .... 98 F3
  RPLY/SEND GU23 .... 161 J3
  SHGR GU5 .... 41 M6
  SHPTN TW17 .... 50 C4
  SNWD SE25 .... 22 C5
  STA TW18 .... 12 B8
  STWL/WRAY TW19 .... 14 A8
  STWL/WRAY TW19 .... 65 L3
  SUT SM1 .... 26 D6
  TEDD TW11 .... 44 D6
  THDIT KT7 .... 49 M4
  THHTH CR7 .... 14 A1
  WDR/YW UB7 .... 29 C6
  WEY KT13 .... 6 E6
  WHTN TW2 .... 25 M1
  WIM/MER SW19 .... 29 C6
  WOKN/KNAP GU21 .... 6 E6
  WOKN/KNAP GU21 .... 75 M8
  WOKS/MYFD GU22 .... 97 K3
  WOT/HER KT12 .... 42 D8
  WWKM BR4 .... 51 J8
High Street Collier's Wd
  WIM/MER SW19 .... 30 A8
High Street Gn *WIM/MER* GU8... 202 B8
High Street Ms *WIM/MER* SW19... 29 H6
The High St *CRAWW* RH11 .... 212 A3
High Thicket Rd *NFNM* GU10 ... 177 C5
High Tree Cl *ADL/WDHM* KT15 .. 58 D4
High Trees *BRXS/STRHM* SW2... 31 K2

  CROY/NA CR0 .... 51 H8
High Trees Cl *CTHM* CR3 .... 108 C4
High Trees Rd *REIG* RH2 .... 148 A1
High Vw *BELMT* SM2 .... 85 J1
  SHGR GU5 .... 141 M5
Highview *CTHM* CR3 .... 108 B6
High View Av *WLGTN* SM6 .... 67 J4
High View Cl *FARN* GU14 .... 92 D5
  SNWD SE25 .... 50 C2
Highview Crs *CBLY* GU15 .... 53 J8
High View Rd *FARN* GU14 .... 92 D5
  GUW GU2 .... 138 A3
  LTWR GU18 .... 74 B1
  NRWD SE19 .... 32 A7
Highwayman's Rdg *BFOR* GU20 .. 54 E3
The Highway *BELMT* SM2 .... 85 M7
High Weald Landscape Trail
  EGRIN RH19 .... 216 A2
Highwold *COUL/CHIP* CR5 .... 86 D8
Highwood Cl *ORP* BR6 .... 71 M1
  PUR/KEN CR8 .... 87 M7
Highwood Dr *ORP* BR6 .... 71 M1
Highwoods *CTHM* CR3 .... 108 B7
  LHD/OX KT22 .... 102 F3
Hilary Av *MTCM* CR4 .... 48 D3
Hilbert Rd *CHEAM* SM3 .... 65 G3
Hilborough Cl *WIM/MER* SW19 .. 29 M8
Hilda Vale Rd *ORP* BR6 .... 71 K3
Hildenley Cl *REDH* RH1 .... 127 G2
Hilder Gdns *FARN* GU14 .... 93 G6
Hilders Cl *EDEN* TN8 .... 153 L5
Hilders La *EDEN* TN8 .... 153 J5
The Hilders *ASHTD* KT21 .... 83 L7
Hildreth St *BAL* SW12 .... 30 E2
Hilgay *GU* GU1 .... 9 L4
Hilgay Cl *GU* GU1 .... 9 L4
Hillars Heath Rd *COUL/CHIP* CR5.. 87 H5
Hillary Cl *EGRIN* RH19 .... 196 D7
  FNM GU9 .... 10 F5
Hillary Crs *WOT/HER* KT12 ...... 42 F8
Hillary Rd *FNM* GU9 .... 10 E5
Hillbarn *SAND/SEL* CR2 .... 88 B3
Hillberry *BRAK* RG12 .... 34 F7
Hillbrook Gdns *WEY* KT13 .... 59 K6
Hillbrook Ri *FNM* GU9 .... 133 K3
Hillbrook Rd *TOOT* SW17 .... 30 C4
Hillbrow *NWMAL* KT3 .... 46 C3
Hillbrow Cl *RGUW* GU3 .... 115 J1
Hillbrow Rd *ESH/CLAY* KT10 .... 61 M3
Hillbury Cl *WARL* CR6 .... 88 E8
Hillbury Gdns *WARL* CR6 .... 88 F8
Hillbury Rd *TOOT* SW17 .... 30 E4
  WARL CR6 .... 88 D7
Hill Cl *PUR/KEN* CR8 .... 87 M2
  SHGR GU5 .... 161 L3
  WOKN/KNAP GU21 .... 6 A2
Hill Copse Vw *BRAK* RG12 .... 35 H1
Hillcote Av *STRHM/NOR* SW16 .. 31 K8
Hill Ct *FARN* GU14 .... 72 C8
Hill Crs *BRYLDS* KT5 .... 45 J5
  WPK KT4 .... 64 F1
Hill Crest *EGRIN* RH19 .... 196 B3
  MFD/CHID GU8 .... 158 A6
Hillcrest *WEY* KT13 .... 59 L3
Hillcrest Av *CHERT* KT16 .... 58 B2
Hillcrest Cl *BECK* BR3 .... 51 J6
  CRAWE RH10 .... 213 C3
  EPSOM KT18 .... 84 C5
  SYD SE26 .... 32 D5
Hill Crest Dr *NFNM* GU10 .... 10 B8
Hillcrest Gdns *ESH/CLAY* KT10 .. 62 C2
Hillcrest Rd *BH/WHM* TN16 ...... 91 C6
  CBLY GU15 .... 73 L2
  CTHM CR3 .... 88 C7
  EDEN TN8 .... 153 M5
  GUW GU2 .... 116 C7
  PUR/KEN CR8 .... 67 J8
Hillcrest Vw *BECK* BR3 .... 51 J6
Hillcroft Av *PUR/KEN* CR8 .... 86 F3
Hillcroome Rd *BELMT* SM2 ...... 66 A5
Hillcross Av *MRDN* SM4 .... 47 H6
Hilldale Rd *SUT* SM1 .... 65 J3
Hilldeane Rd *PUR/KEN* CR8 ..... 67 K8
Hilldown Rd *STRHM/NOR* SW16 .. 31 H8
Hill Dr *STRHM/NOR* SW16 .... 49 J3
Hillersdon Av *BARN* SW13 .... 19 K4
Hilley Field La *LHD/OX* KT22 ... 101 M4
Hill Farm Cl *HASM* GU27 .... 219 J4
Hillfield Av *MRDN* SM4 .... 48 B6
Hillfield Cl *GU* GU1 .... 117 M6
  REDH RH1 .... 126 D8
Hill Field Rd *HPTN* TW12 .... 25 J8
Hillfield Rd *REDH* RH1 .... 126 D8
Hillford Pl *REDH* RH1 .... 148 D6
Hillgarth *GSHT* GU26 .... 199 G4
Hill Gv *FELT* TW13 .... 25 J3
Hillhampton *ASC* SL5 .... 37 J7
Hill House Cl *CRAWE* RH10 ..... 214 D5
Hill House Dr *REIG* RH2 .... 147 L2
  WEY KT13 .... 79 K1
Hill House Drive *HPTN* TW12.... 43 K1
Hillhouse La *HORS* RH12 .... 205 H8
Hill House Rd *STRHM/NOR* SW16.. 31 K8
Hillhurst Gdns *CTHM* CR3 .... 108 B2
Hillier Gdns *CROY/NA* CR0 ...... 67 K4
Hillier Pl *CHSGTN* KT9 .... 63 C5
Hillier Rd *GU* GU1 .... 117 K8
Hillier's La *CROY/NA* CR0 .... 67 H2
Hillingdale *BH/WHM* TN16 .... 90 E8
  CRAWW RH11 .... 211 M8
Hillingdon Av *STWL/WRAY* TW19 .. 13 K7
Hill La *KWD/TDW/WH* KT20 ... 105 H3
Hillmead *CRAWW* RH11 .... 211 J3
Hill Md *HORS* RH12 .... 228 D6
Hillmont Rd *ESH/CLAY* KT10 .... 62 B2
Hillmore Gv *SYD* SE26 .... 32 E6
Hill Pl *CRAWW* RH11 .... 211 M4
Hill Ri *DORK* RH4 .... 122 D8
Hillrise *DTCH/LGLY* SL3 .... 12 D1
Hill Ri *ESH/CLAY* KT10 .... 62 E1
  RCHPK/HAM TW10 .... 18 A7
Hill Rd *CAR* SM5 .... 66 B5
  CAR SM5 .... 134 A2
  GSHT GU26 .... 198 F3
  GT/LBKH KT23 .... 101 L4
  HASM GU27 .... 219 M3
  MTCM CR4 .... 48 E1

PUR/KEN CR8 .... 87 J2
  SUT SM1 .... 65 L4
Hillsborough Ct *FARN* GU14 .... 92 B1
Hillsborough Pk *CBLY* GU15 .... 73 M4
Hill School *WOKN/KNAP* GU21 .. 10 A6
Hills Farm La *HORS* RH12 ...... 228 C8
Hillside *BNSTD* SM7 .... 85 H5
  CBLY GU15 .... 72 C2
  CRAWE RH10 .... 214 E1
  HORS RH12 .... 228 D7
  VW GU25 .... 38 F6
  WIM/MER SW19 .... 29 G7
  WOKS/MYFD GU22 .... 97 C2
Hillside Av *PUR/KEN* CR8 .... 87 L3
Hillside Cl *BNSTD* SM7 .... 85 H6
  CRAWW RH11 .... 211 L5
  EGRIN RH19 .... 196 B6
  MRDN SM4 .... 47 H4
  RDKG RH5 .... 145 K1
  WOKN/KNAP GU21 .... 76 A7
Hillside Crs *FRIM* GU16 .... 93 J2
Hillside Gdns
  ADL/WDHM KT15 .... 58 C4
  BRKHM/BTCW RH3 .... 123 K8
  BELMT SM2 .... 66 F6
  WIM/MER SW6 ....
Hillside La *FNM* GU9 .... 134 A2
  HAYES BR2 .... 70 D1
Hillside Pk *ASC* SL5 .... 37 J8
Hillside Rd *ALDT* GU11 .... 134 C1
  ASHTD KT21 .... 83 J7
  ASHV GU12 .... 113 L6
  BELMT SM2 .... 65 J6
  BH/WHM TN16 .... 111 H1
  BRXS/STRHM SW2 .... 31 J3
  COUL/CHIP CR5 .... 87 H8
  CROY/NA CR0 .... 67 L4
  DTCH/LGLY SL3 .... 31 H3
  EDEN TN8 .... 88 D8
  EW KT17 .... 64 F8
  FNM GU9 .... 134 B2
  HASM GU27 .... 219 J4
  NFNM GU10 .... 155 L6
Hillside Wy *RGODL* GU7 .... 160 A2
Hillsmead Wy *SAND/SEL* CR2 .. 88 D3
Hills Pl *HORS* RH12 .... 228 D7
Hillspur Cl *GUW* GU2 .... 116 C7
Hillspur Rd *GUW* GU2 .... 116 C7
Hillswood Dr *CHERT* KT16 ...... 57 M3
The Hill *CTHM* CR3 .... 108 C6
Hill Top *MRDN* SM4 .... 47 H7
Hilltop Cl *ASC* SL5 .... 37 H2
  LHD/OX KT22 .... 102 F5
  RGUW GU3 .... 116 C4
Hilltop La *CTHM* CR3 .... 107 K8
Hilltop Ri *GT/LBKH* KT23 .... 101 M8
Hilltop Rd *CTHM* CR3 .... 88 B7
  REIG RH2 .... 147 L2
Hilltop Wk *CTHM* CR3 .... 109 H2
Hillview *CTHM* CR3 .... 88 C7
  RYNPK SW20 .... 28 E8
Hill View Cl
  KWD/TDW/WH KT20 .... 104 F3
  PUR/KEN CR8 .... 87 L1
Hill View Crs *GUW* GU2 .... 116 C6
Hillview Dr *REDH* RH1 .... 148 D1
Hill View Rd *ESH/CLAY* KT10 .. 62 C7
  FNM GU9 .... 133 J7
  STWL/WRAY TW19 .... 12 A8
Hillview Rd *SUT* SM1 .... 65 M2
Hill View Rd *TWK* TW1 .... 17 K8
Hillworth Rd *BRXS/STRHM* SW2.. 31 K1
Hillybarn Rd *CRAWW* RH11 .... 190 F8
Hilton Wy *SAND/SEL* CR2 .... 88 E5
Himley Rd *TOOT* SW17 .... 30 B6
Hinaidi Wy *FARN* GU14 .... 112 C1
Hinchley Cl *ESH/CLAY* KT10 .... 62 C2
Hinchley Dr *ESH/CLAY* KT10 ... 62 C2
Hinchley Wy *ESH/CLAY* KT10 .. 62 D2
Hindell Cl *FARN* GU14 .... 92 D1
Hindhead Cl *CRAWW* RH11 .... 211 M5
Hindhead Rd *HASM* GU27 ...... 219 J3
Hindhead Wy *WLGTN* SM6 .... 67 H4
Hindsley's Pl *FSTH* SE23 .... 32 F3
Hinstock Cl *FARN* GU14 .... 92 D6
Hinton Av *HSLWW* TW4 .... 16 A6
Hinton Rd *WLGTN* SM6 .... 66 F5
Hipley St *WOKS/MYFD* GU22 .. 97 L2
Hitchcock Cl *SHPTN* TW17 ..... 41 J3
Hitchings Wy *REIG* RH2 .... 147 K4
Hitherbury Cl *GUW* GU2 .... 138 C3
Hitherfield Rd
  STRHM/NOR SW16 .... 31 J3
Hithermoor Rd
  STWL/WRAY TW19 .... 13 K8
Hitherwood *CRAN* GU6 .... 185 H7
Hitherwood Cl *REDH* RH1 ...... 126 B6
Hitherwood Dr *DUL* SE21 ...... 32 C5
H Jones Crs *ALDT* GU11 .... 112 F6
Hoadly Rd *STRHM/NOR* SW16 .. 31 G4
Hobart Gdns *THHTH* CR7 ...... 50 A3
Hobart Pl *RCHPK/HAM* TW10 .. 27 L1
Hobart Rd *WPK* KT4 .... 64 E2
Hobbes Wk *PUT/ROE* SW15 ... 19 L7
Hobbs Cl *BF/WBF* KT14 .... 78 E3
Hobbs Rd *CRAWW* RH11 ...... 211 K8
  SNWD SE27 .... 31 M5
Hockering Rd
  WOKS/MYFD GU22 .... 7 J7
Hockering Rd *WOKS/MYFD* GU22 .. 7 H7
Hockford Cl *RGUW* GU3 .... 95 L8
Hodgkin Cl *CRAWE* RH10 ...... 212 E4
Hodgson Gdns *GU* GU1 .... 117 K5
Hoebrook Cl *WOKS/MYFD* GU22... 97 G3
Hoe La *MFD/CHID* GU8 .... 183 G5
  SHGR GU5 .... 164 B1
Hogarth Av *ASHF* TW15 .... 23 M7
Hogarth Cl *SHST* GU47 .... 72 B3
Hogarth Crs *CROY/NA* CR0 ..... 4 D2
  WIM/MER SW19 .... 48 A1
Hogarth Gdns *HEST* TW5 .... 16 D2
Hogarth Rd *CRAWE* RH10 ...... 212 C6
Hogarth Wy *HPTN* TW12 .... 43 M1
Hogback Wd *BFOR* GU20 ....
Hogden La *RDKG* RH5 ....
Hogdens La *CHSGTN* KT9 ....
Hog's Back *RGUW* GU3 ....
Hogscross La *COUL/CHIP* CR5 ... 106 C4
Hogshill La *COB* KT11 .... 80 F4
Hogsmill Wy *HOR/WEW* KT19 .. 63 M4
Hogspudding La *RDKG* RH5 .... 167 M7

Hogtrough La *OXTED* RH8 ...... 129 L2
  REDH RH1 .... 149 G1
Hogwood Rd *BIL* RH14 .... 223 M6
Holbeach Rd *CAT* SE6 .... 33 K1
Holbeck *BRAK* RG12 .... 34 C6
Holbein Rd *CRAWE* RH10 ...... 212 C6
Holborn Wy *MTCM* CR4 .... 48 C2
Holbreck Pl *WOKS/MYFD* GU22 .. 6 E7
Holbrook Cl *FNM* GU9 .... 134 C1
Holbrook Meadow *EGH* TW20 .. 21 M7
Holbrook School La
  HORS RH12 .... 229 C2
Holbrook Wy *ALDT* GU11 ...... 134 E2
Holcon Ct *REDH* RH1 .... 126 D5
Holdernesse Rd *ISLW* TW7 ..... 17 K3
  TOOT SW17 .... 30 C4
Holderness Wy *WNWD* SE27 ... 31 L6
Holder Rd *ASHV* GU12 .... 113 H8
  CRAWE RH10 .... 212 E6
Holdfast La *HASM* GU27 .... 220 C1
Hole Hi *DORK* RH4 .... 143 L2
Hole La *EDEN* TN8 .... 153 K3
Holford Rd *GU* GU1 .... 117 M8
Holland Av *BELMT* SM2 .... 65 K6
  RYNPK SW20 .... 46 C1
Holland Cl *FNM* GU9 .... 11 L2
  HAYES BR2 .... 70 C1
  REDH RH1 .... 126 C8
Holland Crs *OXTED* RH8 .... 130 D7
Holland Dr *FSTH* SE23 .... 33 H4
Holland Gdns *FNM* GU20 .... 40 C2
Holland La *OXTED* RH8 .... 130 D7
Holland Pines *BRAK* RG12 ...... 34 C7
Holland Rd *OXTED* RH8 .... 130 D7
  SNWD SE25 .... 50 D5
Hollands Fld *HORS* RH12 .... 228 B5
The Hollands *WPK* KT4 .... 64 D1
Hollands Wy *EGRIN* RH19 ...... 196 D5
  HORS RH12 .... 228 C1
Holland Wy *HAYES* BR2 .... 70 C1
Holles Cl *HPTN* TW12 .... 25 K7
Hollies Av *BF/WBF* KT14 .... 78 C3
Hollies Cl *STRHM/NOR* SW16 .. 31 K7
  TWK TW1 .... 26 C3
Hollies Ct *ADL/WDHM* KT15 ... 58 F4
Hollin Ct *CRAWW* RH11 .... 192 B8
Hollingsworth Rd
  SAND/SEL CR2 .... 68 B4
Hollington Crs *NWMAL* KT3 .... 46 C6
Hollingworth Cl
  E/WMO/HCT KT8 .... 43 J4
Hollis Wood Dr *NFNM* GU10 ... 155 H4
Hollman Gdns
  STRHM/NOR SW16 .... 31 L7
Holloway Dr *VW* GU25 .... 39 H4
Holloway Hl *CHERT* KT16 ...... 57 M2
  RGODL GU7 .... 160 A5
Holloway St *HSLW* TW3 .... 16 E5
Hollow Cl *GUW* GU2 .... 8 C5
Hollow La *LING* RH7 .... 196 E1
  RDKG RH5 .... 143 G7
  VW GU25 .... 38 F3
The Hollow *CRAWW* RH11 .... 211 J4
  RGODL GU7 .... 159 J5
Holly Av *ADL/WDHM* KT15 .... 58 D8
  FRIM GU16 .... 73 L6
  WOT/HER KT12 .... 43 G8
Hollybank *CHOB/PIR* GU24 .... 75 J3
Hollybank Cl *HPTN* TW12 ...... 25 K3
Hollybank Rd *BF/WBF* KT14 ... 78 C4
Holly Bank Rd
  WOKS/MYFD GU22 .... 96 E3
Hollybush Cl *ALDT* GU11 ...... 113 H2
Holly Bush La *HPTN* TW12 ..... 25 J8
Hollybush Ride *BFOR* GU20 .... 54 C2
Hollybush Rd *CRAWE* RH10 ... 212 B2
  KUTN/CMB KT2 .... 27 H6
Holly Cl *ASHV* GU12 .... 112 F7
  CHERT KT16 .... 56 D2
  CRAWE RH10 .... 212 D1
  EGH TW20 .... 20 E7
  FARN GU14 .... 92 D5
  FELT TW13 .... 25 H6
  HORS RH12 .... 229 L4
  WOKN/KNAP GU21 .... 96 E1
Hollycombe *EGH* TW20 .... 21 G5
Holly Crs *BECK* BR3 .... 51 J5
Hollycroft Cl *SAND/SEL* CR2 ... 68 B4
  WDR/YW UB7 .... 14 D1
Hollycroft Gdns *WDR/YW* UB7 .. 14 D1
Hollydale Dr *HAYES* BR2 .... 71 J2
Hollyfield Rd *BRYLDS* KT5 ..... 45 J7
Hollyfields Cl *CBLY* GU15 ...... 72 E4
Hollygrove Cl *HSLWW* TW4 .... 16 C6
Holly Hedge Cl *FRIM* GU16 .... 73 H7
Holly Hedge La *COB* KT11 ..... 80 E4
  FRIM GU16 .... 73 H7
Holly Hill Dr *BNSTD* SM7 ...... 85 K7
Holly Hock *CHOB/PIR* GU24 ... 75 K5
Holly Hough
  KWD/TDW/WH KT20 .... 123 L4
Holly La *BNSTD* SM7 .... 86 A8
  RGODL GU7 .... 159 M5
  RGUW GU3 .... 116 A3
Holly La East *BNSTD* SM7 ...... 85 L6
Holly La West *BNSTD* SM7 ..... 85 L7
Holly Lea *RGUE* GU4 .... 117 C2
Hollymead *CAR* SM5 .... 66 C2
Hollymead Rd *COUL/CHIP* CR5... 86 D8
Hollymoor La *HOR/WEW* KT19 .. 64 A8
Hollyridge *HASM* GU27 .... 219 M3
Holly Rd *ASHV* GU12 .... 112 F8
  FARN GU14 .... 92 C5
  HPTN TW12 .... 25 M7
  HSLW TW3 .... 16 E5
  REIG RH2 .... 147 L2
  TWK TW1 .... 26 C2
Holly Spring La *BRAK* RG12 .... 35 G1
Hollytree Cl *WIM/MER* SW19 ... 29 G2
Hollytree Gdns *FRIM* GU16 ..... 93 G1
Holly Tree Rd *CTHM* CR3 ...... 108 B4
Holly Wy *BLKW* GU17 .... 72 A5
  MTCM CR4 .... 49 G4

Holmbury Hill Rd *RDKG* RH5 .. 164 F4
Holmbury Rd *RDKG* RH5 .... 165 H8
Holm Cl *ADL/WDHM* KT15 .... 78 B2
Holmcroft *CRAWE* RH10 ...... 212 B4
  KWD/TDW/WH KT20 .... 104 E7
Holmdene Cl *BECK* BR3 .... 51 M2
Holmes Cl *ASC* SL5 .... 36 F6
  WOKS/MYFD GU22 .... 97 J3
Holmesdale Av
  MORT/ESHN SW14 .... 18 E5
Holmesdale Cl *GU* GU1 .... 117 L7
  SNWD SE25 .... 50 C3
Holmesdale Rd *CROY/NA* CR0 .. 50 A5
  RCH/KEW TW9 .... 18 C3
  RDKG RH5 .... 144 E6
  REDH RH1 .... 149 J2
  REIG RH2 .... 125 L7
  SNWD SE25 .... 50 B4
  TEDD TW11 .... 2 A2
Holmes Rd *TWK* TW1 .... 26 C3
  WIM/MER SW19 .... 29 M8
Holmethorpe Av *REDH* RH1 ... 126 E5
Holmewood Gdns
  BRXS/STRHM SW2 .... 31 J1
Holmewood Rd
  BRXS/STRHM SW2 .... 31 H1
  SNWD SE25 .... 50 B3
Holming End *HORS* RH12 ...... 229 L4
Holmlea Rd *DTCH/LGLY* SL3 ... 12 A3
Holmshaw Cl *SYD* SE26 .... 33 H5
Holmsley Cl *NWMAL* KT3 ...... 46 C6
Holmsley Av *SAND/SEL* CR2 ... 88 C3
Holmwood Cl
  ADL/WDHM KT15 .... 58 D4
  BELMT SM2 .... 65 G7
  EHSLY KT24 .... 120 B2
Holmwood Gdns *WLGTN* SM6... 66 E5
Holmwood Rd *BELMT* SM2 .... 64 F7
  CHSGTN KT9 .... 63 H4
Holmwood View Rd *RDKG* RH5 .. 144 E8
Holne Cha *MORT* SM4 .... 47 K6
Holroyd Rd *ESH/CLAY* KT10 ... 62 C7
  PUT/ROE SW15 .... 19 M6
Holstein Av *WEY* KT13 .... 59 K3
Holsworthy Wy *CHSGTN* KT9 .. 62 F4
Holt Cl *FARN* GU14 .... 92 F2
Holton Heath *BRAK* RG12 ...... 35 J4
Holt Pound La *NFNM* GU10 ... 154 F4
The Holt *WLGTN* SM6 .... 66 F3
Holtwood Rd *LHD/OX* KT22 .... 81 M3
Holtye Av *EGRIN* RH19 .... 196 C6
Holtye Rd *EGRIN* RH19 .... 196 C7
Holwood Cl *WOT/HER* KT12 ... 60 F1
Holwood Park Av *ORP* BR6 .... 71 J3
Holyoake Av *WOKN/KNAP* GU21... 76 F7
Holyoake Crs *WOKN/KNAP* GU21 .. 76 F7
Holyport Rd *FUL/PGN* SW6 .... 19 M2
Holyrood Pl *CRAWW* RH11 .... 211 L7
Holywell Cl *FARN* GU14 .... 92 D2
  STWL/WRAY TW19 .... 23 H2
Holywell Wy *STWL/WRAY* TW19.. 23 H2
Hombrook Dr *BNFD* RG42 ..... 34 B1
Home Cl *CAR* SM5 .... 66 C1
  CRAWE RH10 .... 212 F1
  LHD/OX KT22 .... 102 A3
  VW GU25 .... 39 G6
Homecroft Rd *SYD* SE26 .... 32 F6
Home Farm Cl
  BRKHM/BTCW RH3 .... 146 B1
  CHERT KT16 .... 57 K6
  EPSOM KT18 .... 85 G7
  ESH/CLAY KT10 .... 61 L5
  FARN GU14 .... 93 G5
  SHPTN TW17 .... 42 B4
  THDIT KT7 .... 44 C7
Home Farm Gdns
  WOT/HER KT12 .... 60 F1
Home Farm Rd *RGODL* GU7 .... 160 B3
Homefield *ADL/WDHM* KT15 ... 78 B2
  HORL RH6 .... 170 E5
  LHD/OX KT22 .... 102 F3
Homefield Gdns
  KWD/TDW/WH KT20 .... 104 F2
  WIM/MER SW19 .... 47 M3
Homefield Pk *SUT* SM1 .... 65 L5
Homefield Rd *COUL/CHIP* CR5 .. 107 L2
  WARL CR6 .... 108 A4
  WIM/MER SW19 .... 29 G7
  WOT/HER KT12 .... 43 J7
Homeland Dr *BELMT* SM2 ..... 65 L7
Homelands *LHD/OX* KT22 ...... 102 F2
Homelands Dr *NRWD* SE19 .... 32 B8
Homelea Cl *FARN* GU14 .... 92 F1
Homeleigh Crs *ASHV* GU12 .... 113 K1
Home Meadow *BNSTD* SM7 ... 85 K6
Homemead Rd *CROY/NA* CR0 .. 48 F6
Home Pk *OXTED* RH8 .... 130 C8
Home Park Cl *SHGR* GU5 ...... 161 J3
Home Park Rd *WIM/MER* SW19.. 29 J5
Home Park Ter *KUT* KT1 ...... 2 C6
Home Park Wk *KUT* KT1 ...... 45 G4
Homer Rd *CROY/NA* CR0 ...... 51 G6
Homersham Rd *KUT* KT1 ...... 3 K6
Homestall *GUW* GU2 .... 116 A8
Homestall Rd *EGRIN* RH19 .... 217 H1
Homestead *CRAN* GU6 .... 185 K6
Homestead Gdns
  ESH/CLAY KT10 .... 62 B4
  EDEN TN8 .... 153 L4
  STA TW18 .... 22 E7
Homestead Rd *CTHM* CR3 ..... 108 A5
Homestead Wy *CROY/NA* CR0 .. 89 M1
Homewaters Av *SUN* TW16 .... 42 C1
Homewood *CRAN* GU6 .... 185 K6
Homewood Cl *HPTN* TW12 .... 25 J7
Honeybrook Rd *BAL* SW12 ..... 30 F1
Honeyhill Rd *BNFD* RG42 ...... 34 D1
Honeypot La *LING* RH7 .... 153 C5
Honeypots Rd
  WOKS/MYFD GU22 .... 97 C5
Honeysuckle Bottom
  EHSLY KT24 .... 120 B8
Honeysuckle Cl *HORL* RH6 .... 170 F5
Honeysuckle Gdns
  CROY/NA CR0 .... 51 G7

Honeysuckle La CRAWW RH11 .... 191 M8
Honeysuckle Wk HORS RH12 ...... 229 K4
Honeywood La RDKG RH5 .... 207 H4
Honeywood Rd ISLW TW7 .... 17 K6 🖪
SWTR RH13 .... 229 K5
Honeywood Wk CAR SM5 .... 66 C3 🖪
Honister Hts PUR/KEN CR8......... 88 A4
Honley Rd CAT SE6 .... 33 L1
Honnor Rd STA TW18 .... 23 G8
Honor Oak Rd FSTH SE23 .... 32 F2
Hood Av MORT/ESHN SW14 .... 18 F7
Hood Rd RYNPK SW20 .... 28 C8
Hooke Rd EHSLY KT24 .... 100 C7
Hookfield HOR/WEW KT19 .... 83 M3
Hook Heath Av
WOKS/MYFD GU22................... 96 E1
Hook Heath Gdns
WOKS/MYFD GU22................... 96 C3
Hook Heath Rd
WOKS/MYFD GU22................... 96 F3
Hook HI SAND/SEL CR2 .... 68 B8
Hook Hill La WOKS/MYFD GU22 ... 96 E3
Hook Hill Pk WOKS/MYFD GU22 ... 96 E3
Hookhouse Rd MFD/CHID GU8 .... 203 G2
Hook La CHOB/PIR GU24 .... 74 F3
RGUW GU3 .... 137 G7
SHGR GU5 .... 141 L7
Hookley Cl MFD/CHID GU8 .... 158 B6
Hookley La MFD/CHID GU8 .... 158 B6
Hook Mill La CHOB/PIR GU24 ...... 55 C7
Hook Ri North SURB KT6 .... 63 J2
Hook Ri South CHSGTN KT9 .... 63 J3
Hook Rd CHSGTN KT9 .... 63 G3 🖪
HOR/WEW KT19 .... 63 M8
SURB KT6 .... 63 H1
Hookstile La FNM GU9 .... 11 C2
Hookstone La CHOB/PIR GU24..... 75 J1
Hook Underpass
(Kingston By-pass) SURB KT6.... 63 G2 🖪
Hookwood Cnr OXTED RH8 .... 130 E2
Hooley La REDH RH1 .... 148 C1
Hope Av BRAK RG12 .... 35 H7
Hope Cl BRAK RG12 .... 35 H7
Hope Fountain CBLY GU15 .... 73 J5
Hope Grant's Rd ALDT GU11 .... 112 D5
Hope La FNM GU9 .... 133 L3
Hopeman Cl SHST GU47 .... 72 A2 🖪
Hopes Cl HEST TW5 .... 16 D1 🖪
Hope St MFD/CHID GU8 .... 158 A5
Hopfield WOKN/KNAP GU21 .... 6 C3
Hopfield Av BF/WBF KT14 .... 79 H2
Hophurst Cl CRAWE RH10 .... 214 C1 🖪
Hophurst Dr CRAWE RH10 .... 214 E1
Hophurst HI CRAWE RH10 .... 195 C7
Hophurst La CRAWE RH10 .... 194 E8
The Hoppety
KWD/TDW/WH KT20 .... 105 G4
Hoppingwood Av NWMAL KT3 .... 46 B3
Hopton Gdns NWMAL KT3 .... 46 D6
Hopton Rd STRHM/NOR SW16 ..... 31 H1
Hopwood Cl TOOT SW17 .... 29 M4
Horace Rd KUT KT1 .... 3 G7
Horatio Av BNFD RG42 .... 35 H1
Horatius Wy CROY/NA CR0 .... 67 J5
Horewood Rd BRAK RG12 .... 34 E6
Horley Lodge La REDH RH1 .... 170 C1
Horley Rd HORL RH6 .... 191 K2
REDH RH1 .... 148 C5
Horley Rw HORL RH6 .... 170 C5
Hormer Cl SHST GU47 .... 52 A8 🖪
Hornbeam Cl SHST GU47 .... 52 A8 🖪
SWTR RH13 .... 229 J8
Hornbeam Crs BTFD TW8 .... 17 L2
Hornbeam Rd GU GU1 .... 116 F5
REIG RH2................................ 147 M3
Hornby Av BRAK RG12 .... 35 C7
Hornchurch Cl
KUTN/CMB KT2 .... 27 G6 🖪
Hornchurch HI CTHM CR3 .... 88 C7
Horndean Cl CRAWE RH10 .... 193 C7 🖪
PUT/ROE SW15 .... 28 D2 🖪
Horndean Rd BRAK RG12 .... 35 K6 🖪
Hornecourt HI GDST RH9 .... 172 C2
Horner La MTCM CR4 .... 48 A2 🖪
Horne Rd SHPTN TW17 .... 41 J4
Horne Wy PUT/ROE SW15 .... 19 M4
Hornhatch RGUE GU4 .... 139 L7
Hornhatch Cl RGUE GU4 .... 139 L6 🖪
Hornhatch La RGUE GU4 .... 139 K6
Horniman Dr FSTH SE23 .... 32 E2
Horn Rd FARN GU14 .... 92 B4
Hornshill La HORS RH12 .... 225 J2
Horsebrass Dr BAGS GU19 .... 54 B7 🖪
Horsecroft BNSTD SM7 .... 85 J7 🖪
Horse Fair KUT KT1 .... 2 D6
Horse Gate Ride ASC SL5 .... 36 D6
Horse HI HORL RH6 .... 169 L5
Horsell Birch WOKN/KNAP GU21 ... 76 D5
Horsell Common Rd
WOKN/KNAP GU21................... 76 F4
Horsell Ct CHERT KT16 .... 40 E7
Horsell Moor
WOKN/KNAP GU21..................... 6 B5 🖪
Horsell Pk WOKN/KNAP GU21 .... 6 B5
Horsell Ri WOKN/KNAP GU21 .... 6 B1
Horsell Rise Cl WOKN/KNAP GU21 ... 6 B1
Horsell V WOKN/KNAP GU21 .... 6 C3
Horsell Wy WOKN/KNAP GU21 ..... 76 F6
Horseshoe Bend GSHT GU26 ...... 198 D6
Horseshoe Cl CBLY GU15 .... 73 J1 🖪
CRAWE RH10 .... 213 H2 🖪
Horseshoe Crs CBLY GU15 .... 73 J1
Horseshoe La ASHV GU12 .... 113 K3
CRAN GU6 .... 184 F5
Horseshoe La West GU GU1 .... 117 L7
Horseshoe Rdg WEY KT13 .... 79 M1
The Horseshoe BNSTD SM7 .... 85 J5
COUL/CHIP CR5 .... 87 C3
RGODL GU7 .... 159 M6
Horsham Rd BIL RH14 .... 205 G8
CRAN GU6 .... 184 A6
CRAWW RH11 .... 211 H7
DORK RH4 .... 144 D3
EBED/NFELT TW14 .... 14 F8
HORS RH12 .... 209 K5
RDKG RH5 .... 164 F7
RDKG RH5 .... 167 C8

RDKG RH5 .... 187 G8
RDKG RH5 .... 188 F7
RDKG RH5 .... 207 G3
SHGR GU5 .... 142 C8
SHST GU47 .... 52 A8
Horshoe La East GU GU1 .... 117 L7
Horsley Cl HOR/WEW KT19 .... 84 A3
Horsley Dr CROY/NA CR0 .... 69 M6
KUTN/CMB KT2 .... 27 G6 🖪
Horsley Rd COB KT11 .... 100 E1
Horsneile La BNFD RG42 .... 34 E1
Horton Gdns HOR/WEW KT19 .... 83 M1
Horton HI HOR/WEW KT19 .... 83 M1
Horton Rd DTCH/LGLY SL3 .... 12 E3
STWL/WRAY TW19 .... 13 K6
Horton Wy CROY/NA CR0 .... 51 G5
Horvath Cl WEY KT13 .... 60 A3 🖪
Hosack Rd BAL SW12 .... 30 C3
Hoskins Pl EGRIN RH19 .... 196 C5
Hoskins Rd OXTED RH8 .... 130 B3
Hospital Bridge Rd WHTN TW2 ...... 25 L2
Hospital HI ALDT GU11 .... 112 D6
Hospital Rd ALDT GU11 .... 112 D6
HSLW TW3 .... 16 D5
Hostel Rd FARN GU14 .... 112 E1
Hotham Cl E/WMO/HCT KT8 .... 43 K3 🖪
Hotham Rd PUT/ROE SW15 .... 19 M5
WIM/MER SW19 .... 29 M8
Houblon Rd
RCHPK/HAM TW10 .... 18 B7 🖪
Houghton Cl HPTN TW12 .... 25 H7
Houghton Rd CRAWE RH10 .... 212 F6 🖪
Houlder Crs CROY/NA CR0 .... 67 L5
Houlton Ct BAGS GU19 .... 54 B7
Hound House Rd SHGR GU5 .... 141 K7
Hounslow Av HSLW TW3 .... 16 E7
Hounslow Gdns HSLW TW3 .... 16 E7
Hounslow Rd EBED/NFELT TW14 ... 24 E1
FELT TW13................................ 25 G4
HSLW TW3 .... 16 B8
WHTN TW2 .... 16 F8
Houseman Rd FARN GU14 .... 92 C3
Houston Rd FSTH SE23 .... 33 H3
Hove Gdns SUT SM1 .... 47 L8 🖪
Howard Av EW KT17 .... 64 D8
Howard Cl ASHTD KT21 .... 83 J8
EHSLY KT24 .... 100 A1
HPTN TW12 .... 25 M8
KWD/TDW/WH KT20 .... 104 C7
LHD/OX KT22 .... 102 F5
SUN TW16 .... 24 C7
Howard Cole Wy ALDT GU11 .... 112 B7
Howard Gdns GU GU1 .... 117 K7
Howard Rdg RGUE GU4 .... 117 K4
Howard Rd BRYLDS KT5 .... 45 J6
COUL/CHIP CR5 .... 86 F5
CRAWW RH11 .... 211 G7
DORK RH4 .... 144 D2
EHSLY KT24 .... 100 D4
GT/LBKH KT23 .... 121 L1
ISLW TW7 .... 17 J5
NWMAL KT3 .... 46 B3
PGE/AN SE20 .... 50 F1
RDKG RH5 .... 144 F6 🖪
REIG RH2................................ 147 L1
SNWD SE25 .... 50 D5
SWTR RH13 .... 229 K5
Howards Cl WOKS/MYFD GU22 .... 97 K2
Howards Crest Cl BECK BR3 .... 51 M2 🖪
Howards La ADL/WDHM KT15 .... 58 B5
PUT/ROE SW15 .... 19 M6
Howard St THDIT KT7 .... 44 E7
Howberry Rd THHTH CR7 .... 50 A1
Howden Rd SNWD SE25 .... 50 C2
Howe Dr CTHM CR3 .... 108 A4
Howell Hill Cl EW KT17 .... 84 F1 🖪
Howell Hill Gv EW KT17 .... 84 F1
Howgate Rd MORT/ESHN SW14 ... 19 G5
Howitts Cl ESH/CLAY KT10 .... 61 K5
How La COUL/CHIP CR5 .... 86 D8
Howley Rd CROY/NA CR0 .... 4 B7
Howsman Rd BARN SW13 .... 19 K1
Hoylake Cl CRAWW RH11 .... 211 G4
Hoylake Gdns MTCM CR4 .... 48 F3
Hoyle HI RDKG RH5 .... 167 G8
Hoyle Rd TOOT SW17 .... 30 B6
Hubbard Dr CHSGTN KT9 .... 62 F5 🖪
Hubbard Rd WNWD SE27 .... 31 M5
Hubberholme BRAK RG12 .... 34 D3 🖪
Huddleston Crs REDH RH1 .... 127 G2
Hudson Rd CRAWE RH10 .... 212 B5
HYS/HAR UB3 .... 15 G1
Hudsons KWD/TDW/WH KT20 .... 105 G3
Huggins Pl BRXS/STRHM SW2 ...... 31 J2 🖪
Hughenden Rd WPK KT4 .... 46 D7 🖪
Hughes Rd ASHF TW15 .... 23 M8
Hughes Wk CROY/NA CR0 .... 4 C1
Hullbrook La SHGR GU5 .... 162 A5
Hullmead SHGR GU5 .... 162 B5
Hulton Cl LHD/OX KT22 .... 102 F5
Hulverston Cl BELMT SM2 .... 65 L8
Humber Wy SHST GU47 .... 72 A1
Humbolt Cl GUW GU2 .... 116 B8
Hummer Rd EGH TW20 .... 21 K5
Humphrey Cl LHD/OX KT22 .... 101 M4
Hungry Hill La RPLY/SEND GU23 .... 98 F8
Hunstanton Cl CRAWW RH11 ..... 211 G4 🖪
DTCH/LGLY SL3 .... 12 F2
Hunston Rd MRDN SM4 .... 47 L8
Hunter Cl BAL SW12 .... 30 D2
Hunter Rd CRAWW RH11 .... 212 A6
FARN GU14 .... 92 C6
GU GU1 .... 9 K6
RYNPK SW20 .... 46 F1
THHTH CR7 .... 50 A3
Hunters Cha GDST RH9 .... 151 J3
Hunters Cl HOR/WEW KT19 .... 83 M3
Hunters Ct RCH/KEW TW9 .... 18 A7 🖪
Huntersfield Cl REIG RH2 .... 125 M5
Hunter's Gv ORP BR6 .... 71 M3 🖪
Hunters Meadow NRWD SE19 ...... 32 B5 🖪
Hunters Rd CHSGTN KT9 .... 63 H2
Hunters Wy CROY/NA CR0 .... 5 H9
CROY/NA CR0 .... 68 B3 🖪
Hunting Cl ESH/CLAY KT10 .... 61 K3
Huntingdon Cl MTCM CR4 .... 49 H3 🖪

Huntingdon Gdns CHSWK W4 .... 18 F2 🖪
WPK KT4 .... 64 F2 🖪
Huntingdon House Dr
GSHT GU26 .... 199 H5
Huntingdon Rd REDH RH1 .... 126 D8 🖪
WOKN/KNAP GU21 .... 76 B7
Huntingfield CROY/NA CR0 .... 69 J6
Huntingfield Rd PUT/ROE SW15 ... 19 K8
Huntingford Cl EGH TW20 .... 22 A8
Huntingford Cl GSHT GU26 .... 198 F2 🖪
Hunting Gate Dr CHSGTN KT9 ...... 63 H6
Hunting Gate Ms WHTN TW2 .... 26 B2 🖪
Huntley Wy RYNPK SW20 .... 46 D2 🖪
Huntly Rd SNWD SE25 .... 50 B4
Hunts Cl GUW GU2 .... 116 A7
Hunts Hill Rd RGUW GU3 .... 114 D4
Huntsman Cl FELT TW13 .... 24 E5 🖪
Huntsman Cl WARL CR6 .... 89 C1
Huntsmans Meadow ASC SL5 .... 36 C1
Huntsman's Ms FRIM GU16 .... 93 J6 🖪
Huntsmoor Rd HOR/WEW KT19 .... 64 A4
Huntspill St TOOT SW17 .... 29 M4
Hunts Slip Rd DUL SE21 .... 32 B4
Hurlands Cl FNM GU9 .... 134 C5
Hurlands La MFD/CHID GU8 .... 203 J8
Hurlands Pl FNM GU9 .... 134 C5 🖪
Hurley Cl WOT/HER KT12 .... 60 E1
Hurley Gdns RGUE GU4 .... 117 K5
Hurlford WOKN/KNAP GU21 .... 76 D7
Hurlstone Rd SNWD SE25 .... 50 A5
Hurn Court Rd HEST TW5 .... 16 A4 🖪
Hurnford Cl SAND/SEL CR2 .... 68 B8
Huron Rd TOOT SW17 .... 30 D3
Hurricane Wy FARN GU14 .... 112 C2
Hurst Av HORS RH12 .... 229 G6
Hurst Cl CHSGTN KT9 .... 63 K4
CRAWW RH11 .... 211 J5
EPSOM KT18 .... 103 M6
WOKS/MYFD GU22 .... 96 F2
Hurst Ct HORS RH12 .... 229 G6
Hurstcourt Rd CHEAM SM3 .... 47 L8
Hurst Cft GU GU1 .... 9 K9
Hurstdene Av STA TW18 .... 22 E7
Hurst Dr KWD/TDW/WH KT20 ..... 104 D8
Hurst Farm Cl MFD/CHID GU8 ..... 159 J7
Hurst Farm Rd EGRIN RH19 .... 216 A1
Hurstfield Rd E/WMO/HCT KT8 ..... 43 K3
Hurst Green Cl OXTED RH8 .... 130 D6
Hurst Green Rd OXTED RH8 .... 130 D6
Hurst Gv WOT/HER KT12 .... 42 C8
Hurstlands OXTED RH8 .... 130 D6
Hurst La E/WMO/HCT KT8 .... 43 M4
EGH TW20 .... 39 J3
EPSOM KT18 .... 104 A4
Hurstleigh Cl REDH RH1 .... 126 C6
Hurstleigh Dr REDH RH1 .... 126 C6
Hurstmere Cl GSHT GU26 .... 199 G6
Hurst Rd ALDT GU11 .... 112 F6
CROY/NA CR0 .... 68 A4
E/WMO/HCT KT8 .... 43 M3
EPSOM KT18 .... 104 B5
FARN GU14 .... 92 E1
HOR/WEW KT19 .... 84 A1
HORL RH6................................ 170 B5
HORS RH12 .... 229 G6
WOT/HER KT12 .... 43 G4
Hurst View Rd SAND/SEL CR2 .... 68 B6
Hurst Wy SAND/SEL CR2 .... 68 B5
WOKS/MYFD GU22 .... 78 B4
Hurstwood ASC SL5 .... 36 C6
Hurtmore Cha RGODL GU7 .... 159 L1
Hurtmore Rd MFD/CHID GU8 ...... 159 L3
RGODL GU7 .... 159 L1
Hurtwood Rd WOT/HER KT12 .... 43 J7
Hussar Ct ALDT GU11 .... 112 B7 🖪
Hussars Cl HSLWW TW4 .... 16 B5 🖪
Hutchinson's Rd
CROY/NA CR0 .... 89 M1 🖪
Hutchins Wy HORL RH6 .... 170 C4
Hutton Cl BFOR GU20 .... 55 G6
Hutton Rd ASHV GU12 .... 113 K3
Huxley Cl RGODL GU7 .... 160 A2
Hyacinth Cl HPTN TW12 .... 25 K7 🖪
Hyacinth Rd PUT/ROE SW15 .... 28 D2 🖪
Hyde Dr CRAWW RH11 .... 211 H4
Hyde La MFD/CHID GU8 .... 179 K7
NFNM GU10 .... 132 A2
RGUW GU3 .... 109 G8
Hyde Rd RCHPK/HAM TW10 .... 18 C7 🖪
SAND/SEL CR2 .... 88 B3
Hyde Ter SUN TW16 .... 24 B7
Hydethorpe Rd BAL SW12 .... 30 F2
Hyde Wk MRDN SM4 .... 47 K7
Hylands Cl CRAWE RH10 .... 212 D4
Hylands Ms EPSOM KT18 .... 83 M5
Hylands Rd EPSOM KT18 .... 83 M5
Hyperion Ct CRAWW RH11 .... 211 H5 🖪
Hyperion Pl HOR/WEW KT19 .... 64 A7
Hythe Cl BRAK RG12 .... 35 H5
Hythe End Rd STWL/WRAY TW19 ... 21 K3
Hythe Field Av EGH TW20 .... 22 A7
Hythe Park Rd EGH TW20 .... 21 M6
Hythe Rd STA TW18 .... 22 A6
THHTH CR7 .... 50 A2
The Hythe STA TW18 .... 22 B6

Iberian Av WLGTN SM6................... 67 G3
Iberian Wy CBLY GU15 .... 73 K3
Ibis La CHSWK W4 .... 18 F3
Ibsley Gdns PUT/ROE SW15 .... 28 D2
Icehouse Wd OXTED RH8 .... 130 B5
Icklingham Rd COB KT11 .... 80 F2
Idlecombe Rd TOOT SW17 .... 30 D7
Idmiston Rd WNWD SE27 .... 31 M4
WPK KT4 .... 46 C7
Idmiston Sq WPK KT4 .... 46 C7
Ifield Av CRAWW RH11 .... 211 M2
Ifield Cl REDH RH1 .... 148 B3
Ifield Dr CRAWW RH11 .... 211 K2
Ifield Gn CRAWW RH11 .... 191 K8
Ifield Rd CRAWW RH11 .... 211 M3
HORL RH6................................ 191 H4
Ifield St CRAWW RH11 .... 211 J1

Ifield Wd CRAWW RH11 .... 191 G8
Ifold Bridge La BIL RH14 .... 223 M5
Ifoldhurst BIL RH14 .... 223 M7
Ifold Rd REDH RH1 .... 148 D2
Ildersly Gv DUL SE21 .... 32 A3
Ilex Cl EGH TW20 .... 20 E8
SUN TW16 .... 42 F2 🖪
Ilex Wy STRHM/NOR SW16 .... 31 K6
Ilkley Cl NRWD SE19 .... 32 A7 🖪
Illingworth Cl MTCM CR4 .... 48 A3
Illingworth Gv BRAK RG12 .... 35 J1
Imber Gv ESH/CLAY KT10 .... 44 A7
Imberhorne La EGRIN RH19 .... 195 G6
Imberhorne Wy EGRIN RH19 .... 195 L6
Imber Park Rd ESH/CLAY KT10 ..... 44 A8
Imjin Cl ALDT GU11 .... 112 E6
Imperial Gdns MTCM CR4 .... 48 E3
Imperial Rd EBED/NFELT TW14 ..... 24 B1
Imperial Wy CROY/NA CR0 .... 67 J5
Imran Cl GUW GU2 .... 134 F1
Ince Rd WOT/HER KT12 .... 60 B4
Inchmery Rd CAT SE6 .... 33 L3
Inchwood BRAK RG12 .... 34 F8
CROY/NA CR0 .... 69 L3
Ingatestone Rd SNWD SE25 .... 50 E4 🖪
Ingham Cl SAND/SEL CR2 .... 69 G7
Ingham Rd SAND/SEL CR2 .... 68 F7
Ingleboro Dr PUR/KEN CR8 .... 88 A3
Ingleby Wy WLGTN SM6 .... 67 G7
Ingle Dell CBLY GU15 .... 73 G5
Ingleheath ADL/WDHM KT15 .... 58 E8
Inglemere Rd FSTH SE23 .... 33 G4
TOOT SW17............................... 30 C3
Ingleside DTCH/LGLY SL3 .... 13 J1 🖪
Ingleside Cl BECK BR3 .... 33 K8
Ingleton BRAK RG12 .... 34 D3
Ingleton Rd CAR SM5 .... 66 B7
Inglewood CHERT KT16 .... 58 C2 🖪
WOKN/KNAP GU21 .... 76 B8
Inglewood Av CBLY GU15 .... 73 M5
Inglis Rd CROY/NA CR0 .... 5 K3
Ingram Cl HORS RH12 .... 228 D7
Ingram Rd THHTH CR7 .... 49 M1
Ingrams Cl WOT/HER KT12 .... 60 F4
Inholms La RDKG RH5 .... 144 F6
Inkerman Rd WOKN/KNAP GU21 ... 76 B8
Inkerman Wy WOKN/KNAP GU21 ... 76 B8
Inkpen La FROW RH18 .... 217 J8
Inman Rd WAND/EARL SW18 .... 29 M1
Inner Park Rd WIM/MER SW19 ...... 29 G3
Innes Cl RYNPK SW20 .... 47 H2
Innes Gdns PUT/ROE SW15 .... 19 L8
Innes Rd HORS RH12 .... 229 J5
Innes Yd CROY/NA CR0 .... 4 D8
Innings La BNFD RG42 .... 35 G1
Institute Rd ASHV GU12 .... 113 G8
DORK RH4............................... 143 M3
Instow Gdns FARN GU14 .... 92 D3
Inval HI HASM GU27 .... 219 M1
Inveresk Gdns WPK KT4 .... 64 C2
Inverness Rd HSLW TW3 .... 16 C6
WPK KT4 .... 47 G8
Inverness Wy SHST GU47 .... 72 A2
Invicta Cl EBED/NFELT TW14 .... 24 C2 🖪
Invincible Rd FARN GU14 .... 92 D7
Inwood Av COUL/CHIP CR5 .... 107 K2
HSLW TW3 .... 16 F5
Inwood Cl CROY/NA CR0 .... 69 H1
Inwood Rd HSLW TW3 .... 16 F6
Iona Cl CAT SE6 .... 33 K1
Ipswich Rd TOOT SW17 .... 30 D7
Iron La SHGR GU5 .... 161 G4
Irons Bottom Rd REIG RH2 .... 169 J1
Irvine Dr FARN GU14 .... 92 B1
Irvine Pl GUW GU2 .... 95 H5
Irving Wk CRAWE RH10 .... 212 B6
Irwin Dr HORS RH12 .... 228 D7
Irwin Rd GUW GU2 .... 8 B7
Isabella Dr ORP BR6 .... 71 M3
Isbells Dr REIG RH2 .... 147 L2
Isham Rd STRHM/NOR SW16 .... 49 H1
Isis St WAND/EARL SW18 .... 29 M3
Isis Wy SHST GU47 .... 72 A1
Island Cl STA TW18 .... 22 B5
Island Farm Av E/WMO/HCT KT8 .. 43 J5
Island Farm Rd E/WMO/HCT KT8 .. 43 J5
Islay Gdns HSLWW TW4 .... 16 A7
Itchel La NFNM GU10 .... 132 A2
Itchingwood Common Rd
OXTED RH8 .... 130 F7
Ivanhoe Cl CRAWW RH11 .... 192 A8
Ivanhoe Rd HSLWW TW4 .... 16 A5
Iveagh Cl CRAWW RH11 .... 211 M8
Iveagh Rd GUW GU2 .... 8 C6
Ively Rd FARN GU14 .... 92 A7
Iverna Gdns EBED/NFELT TW14 ... 15 G7
Ivers Wy CROY/NA CR0 .... 69 L6
Ivor Cl GU GU1 .... 9 M5
Ivory Ct FELT TW13 .... 24 D3 🖪
Ivory Wk CRAWW RH11 .... 211 H6 🖪
Ivybank RGODL GU7 .... 160 B3
Ivybridge Cl TWK TW1 .... 17 K8
Ivychurch Cl PGE/AN SE20 .... 32 F8
Ivy Cl SUN TW16 .... 42 F2
Ivydale Rd CAR SM5 .... 66 C1 🖪
Ivyday Gv STRHM/NOR SW16 .... 31 J4
Ivydene WOKN/KNAP GU21 .... 75 J7 🖪
WOT/HER KT12 .... 43 J5
Ivydene Cl REDH RH1 .... 148 E5
SUT SM1 .... 65 M3
Ivy Dene La EGRIN RH19 .... 217 G3
Ivy Dr LTWR GU18 .... 74 D2
Ivy Gdns MTCM CR4 .... 49 G3 🖪
Ivy La FNM GU9 .... 133 L7
HSLWW TW4 .... 16 C6
WOKS/MYFD GU22 .... 7 J7 🖪
Ivy Mill Cl GDST RH9 .... 128 E6
Ivy Mill La REDH RH1 .... 128 D6
Ivymount Rd WNWD SE27 .... 31 K4

Ivy Rd ASHV GU12 .... 113 H7
HSLW TW3 .... 16 E6 🖪
SURB KT6 .... 45 K8 🖪
TOOT SW17 .... 30 B6 🖪

Jacaranda Cl NWMAL KT3 .... 46 B3 🖪
Jackass La GDST RH9 .... 129 J5
HAYES BR2 .... 70 E5
Jackdaw Cl CRAWW RH11 .... 211 M1
Jackdaw La HORS RH12 .... 229 H4
Jackman's La WOKN/KNAP GU21 ... 96 D1
Jackson Cl BRAK RG12 .... 34 E5 🖪
EPSOM KT18 .... 84 A4
Jackson's Pl CROY/NA CR0 .... 4 F4
Jackson's Wy CROY/NA CR0 .... 69 K2
Jacob Cl BNFD RG42 .... 34 A2 🖪
Jacobean Cl CRAWE RH10 .... 212 F4
Jacob Rd CBLY GU15 .... 72 D2
Jacobs Well Rd RGUE GU4 .... 117 G3
Jaggard Wy BAL SW12 .... 30 C1 🖪
Jaguar Rd FARN GU14 .... 92 E7
James Rd ALDT GU11 .... 113 G2
CBLY GU15 .... 72 E7
RGUW GU3 .... 138 F8
James St HSLW TW3 .... 17 G5
Jameston BRAK RG12 .... 34 F8
James Watt Wy CRAWE RH10 ...... 192 D5
James Wy CBLY GU15 .... 72 E7
Jamnagar Cl STA TW18 .... 22 C7
Janoway Hill La
WOKN/KNAP GU21................... 96 F1
Japonica Cl WOKN/KNAP GU21 ..... 96 F1
Jarrett Cl BRXS/STRHM SW2 .... 31 L2 🖪
Jarrow Cl MRDN SM4 .... 47 L5
Jarvis Rd SAND/SEL CR2 .... 68 A5
Jasmine Cl HAYES BR2 .... 71 L1
REDH RH1................................ 148 D5 🖪
WOKN/KNAP GU21 .... 76 C6
Jasmine Gdns CROY/NA CR0......... 69 L2
Jasmine Gv PGE/AN SE20 .... 50 E1
Jasmin Rd HOR/WEW KT19 .... 63 M6
Jason Cl REDH RH1 .... 148 B5
WEY KT13 .... 59 M4
Jasons Dr RGUE GU4 .... 117 M5
Jasper Rd NRWD SE19 .... 32 C7
Jay Av ADL/WDHM KT15 .... 59 H2 🖪
Jay's La HASM GU27 .... 220 E6
Jays Nest Cl BLKW GU17 .... 72 A5 🖪
Jeffries Rd EHSLY KT24 .... 119 L5
Jeffs Cl HPTN TW12 .... 25 L7 🖪
Jeffs Rd SUT SM1 .... 65 J3
Jemmett Cl KUTN/CMB KT2 .... 27 M1
Jengar Cl SUT SM1 .... 65 L3
Jenkins' Hill London Rd
BAGS GU19 .... 53 M8
Jenner Dr CHOB/PIR GU24 .... 75 K3
Jenner Rd CRAWE RH10 .... 192 C6
GU GU1 .... 9 J6
Jenners Cl LING RH7 .... 174 A5
Jennett Rd CROY/NA CR0 .... 67 K2
Jennings Cl ADL/WDHM KT15 .... 58 F7 🖪
Jenny La LING RH7 .... 173 M5
Jenson Wy NRWD SE19 .... 32 C8
Jeppo's La MTCM CR4 .... 48 C4
Jeremiah Ct REDH RH1 .... 127 J1 🖪
Jerome Cl HOR/WEW KT19 .... 64 A7
Jersey Brow Rd FARN GU14 .... 92 D7
Jersey Cl CHERT KT16 .... 58 C2 🖪
RGUE GU4 .... 117 L3 🖪
Jersey Rd CRAWW RH11 .... 211 K7
HEST TW5 .... 16 E3
ISLW TW7 .... 16 F2
TOOT SW17 .... 30 E8
Jerviston Gdns
SW16 .... 31 K7
Jesmond Cl MTCM CR4 .... 48 E3
Jesmond Rd CROY/NA CR0 .... 5 K1
Jessamy Rd WEY KT13 .... 59 K1
Jesses La SHGR GU5 .... 163 M1
Jessiman Ter SHPTN TW17 .... 41 K5
Jessops Wy MTCM CR4 .... 48 F6
Jevington BRAK RG12 .... 34 D3
Jewels Hi WARL CR6 .... 90 D2
Jeypore Rd WAND/EARL SW18 ..... 29 M1
Jig's La South BNFD RG42 .... 35 H1
Jillian Cl HPTN TW12 .... 25 K8
Jocelyn Rd RCH/KEW TW9 .... 18 B5
Jock's La BNFD RG42 .... 34 B1
Jodrell Cl ISLW TW7 .... 17 K3 🖪
John Austin Cl KUTN/CMB KT2 ...... 3 G5 🖪
John Cl ALDT GU11 .... 134 B1
John Cobb Rd WEY KT13 .... 59 K6 🖪
John Russell Cl GUW GU2 .... 116 D5
John's Cl ASHF TW15 .... 23 M5 🖪
Johnsdale OXTED RH8 .... 130 C3
Johns La MRDN SM4 .... 47 M5
Johnson Rd CROY/NA CR0 .... 4 E1
HEST TW5 .... 15 M2
Johnson's Cl CAR SM5 .... 66 C2
Johnsons Dr HPTN TW12 .... 43 M1
Johnson Wk CRAWE RH10 .... 212 A6
John's Rd BH/WHM TN16 .... 111 C2
John's Ter CROY/NA CR0 .... 5 G4
Johnston Wk GUW GU2 .... 116 D4
John St HSLW TW3 .... 16 B4
SNWD SE25 .... 50 D4
Johns Wk CTHM CR3 .... 108 D1
John Wiskar Dr CRAN GU6 .... 185 G7
Joinville Pl ADL/WDHM KT15 .... 59 G3 🖪
Jolesfield CRAWW RH11 .... 211 J6
Jolliffe Rd REDH RH1 .... 106 F8
Jones Cnr ASC SL5 .... 36 B1
Jonson Cl MTCM CR4 .... 48 E4
Jordan Cl SAND/SEL CR2 .... 88 C1
Jordans Cl CRAWW RH11 .... 212 A1
GU GU1 .... 9 L7
REDH RH1................................ 148 D5
STWL/WRAY TW19 .... 22 F1
Jordans Crs CRAWW RH11 .... 192 A8
Jordans Ms WHTN TW2 .... 26 B3 🖪
The Jordans EGRIN RH19 .... 216 B1

Josephine Av
  KWD/TDW/WH KT20 .... 125 J1
Josephine Cl
  KWD/TDW/WH KT20 .... 125 J1
Joseph Locke Wy
  ESH/CLAY KT10 .... 61 K1
Joseph's Rd GU GU1 .... 8 F1
Jubilee Av ASC SL5 .... 36 B1
  WHTN TW2 .... 25 M2
Jubilee Cl ASC SL5 .... 36 B1
  STWL/WRAY TW19 .... 22 F1
Jubilee Crs ADL/WDHM KT15 ... 59 G4
Jubilee Dr ASHV GU12 ...... 113 K3
Jubilee Hall Rd FARN GU14 ... 92 F5
Jubilee La GSHT GU26 ...... 198 F6 [2]
  NFNM GU10 .... 155 K4
Jubilee Rd ALDT GU11 ...... 134 E2
  CHEAM SM3 .... 65 G6
  FRIM GU16 .... 93 K7
  HORS RH12 .... 226 A1
Jubilee Ter BRKHM/BTCW RH3 ... 145 M4
  DORK RH4 .... 144 E1
Jubilee Wk CRAWE RH10 ..... 212 D5 [2]
Jubilee Wy CHSGTN KT9 ..... 63 L2
  EBED/NFELT TW14 .... 24 D2
  WIM/MER SW19 .... 47 L1
Judge's Ter EGRIN RH19 .... 216 B1 [2]
Judge Wk ESH/CLAY KT10 .... 62 B5
Julian Cl WOKN/KNAP GU21 ... 76 F2
Julian HI WEY KT13 .... 59 K6 [2]
Julien Rd COUL/CHIP CR5 ... 86 F5
Julius HI BNFD RG42 .... 35 J1
Jumps Rd NFNM GU10 .... 178 B6
Junction Rd ASHF TW15 ..... 23 M6
  DORK RH4 .... 144 D2
  LTWR GU18 .... 54 E8
  SAND/SEL CR2 .... 68 A5
June Cl COUL/CHIP CR5 ..... 86 E4 [1]
June La REDH RH1 .... 148 E7
Junewood Cl
  ADL/WDHM KT15 .... 78 C1 [3]
Juniper BRAK RG12 .... 34 F8
Juniper Cl BH/WHM TN16 .... 91 H7
  CHSGTN KT9 .... 63 J5
  GU GU1 .... 116 E3
  REIG RH2 .... 147 M2
Juniper Dr CHOB/PIR GU24 ... 75 K5
  SUN TW16 .... 24 C1
Juniper Gdns MTCM CR4 ..... 48 F1 [1]
  SUN TW16 .... 24 C1
Juniper Rd CRAWW RH11 ..... 191 M8
  REIG RH2 .... 147 M2
Jura Cl CRAWW RH11 .... 211 L6
Justin Cl BTFD TW8 .... 18 A2
Jutland Pl EGH TW20 .... 21 M6 [3]
Jutland Rd CAT SE6 .... 33 M1
Juxon Cl CRAWW RH11 .... 211 J5

K

Kangley Bridge Rd SYD SE26 ... 33 J6
Kashmir Cl ADL/WDHM KT15 ... 59 G7
Katharine St CROY/NA CR0 ... 4 D7
Katherine Cl ADL/WDHM KT15 ... 58 D5
Katherine Rd EDEN TN8 ..... 175 M1
Kay Av ADL/WDHM KT15 ...... 59 H2
Kaye Don Wy WEY KT13 ...... 59 K8
Kayemoor Rd BELMT SM2 ..... 66 B6
Kaynes Pk ASC SL5 .... 36 B1
Keable Rd NFNM GU10 .... 10 A6
Kearton Cl PUR/KEN CR8 .... 87 M7
Keates Av REDH RH1 .... 126 D6
Keats Av REDH RH1 .... 126 D6
Keats Cl HORS RH12 .... 229 H2
  WIM/MER SW19 .... 30 A7 [2]
Keats Pl EGRIN RH19 .... 196 A8 [1]
Keats Wy CROY/NA CR0 ...... 50 F6
Keble Cl CRAWE RH10 .... 193 G8
  WPK KT4 .... 46 C8 [1]
Keble Pl BARN SW13 .... 19 L1 [1]
Keble St TOOT SW17 .... 29 M5
Keble Wy SHST GU47 .... 52 B7
Keeley Rd CROY/NA CR0 ..... 4 C4
Keens Cl STRHM/NOR SW16 ... 31 G6 [3]
Keens La RGUW GU5 .... 116 C4
Keens Park Rd RGUW GU3 .... 116 C4
Keen's Rd CROY/NA CR0 ..... 4 D9
Keepers Cl RGUE GU4 .... 118 A5
Keepers Combe BRAK RG12 ... 35 G6
Keepers Ms TEDD TW11 ...... 26 F7
Keepers Wk VW GU25 .... 39 G5
The Keep KUTN/CMB KT2 ..... 3 G2
Keevil Dr WIM/MER SW19 .... 29 G1
Keith Lucas Rd FARN GU14 ... 92 C7
Keith Park Crs BH/WHM TN16 ... 90 F7
Keldholme BRAK RG12 .... 34 D3
Kelling Gdns CROY/NA CR0 ... 4 A1
Kellino St TOOT SW17 ...... 30 B5
Kelly Cl SHPTN TW17 .... 42 B2 [3]
Kelsey Cl HORL RH6 .... 170 C6 [2]
Kelsey La BECK BR3 .... 51 K3
Kelsey Park Av BECK BR3 ... 51 L3
Kelsey Park Rd BECK BR3 ... 51 K3
Kelsey Sq BECK BR3 .... 51 K3
Kelsey Wy BECK BR3 .... 51 K3
Kelso Cl CRAWE RH10 .... 213 H2
Kelso Rd CAR SM5 .... 47 M7
Kelvedon Av WOT/HER KT12 ... 60 B6
Kelvedon Cl KUTN/CMB KT2 ... 27 K7
Kelvin Av LHD/OX KT22 ..... 102 C2
Kelvinbrook E/WMO/HCT KT8 ... 43 K3 [3]
Kelvin Cl HOR/WEW KT19 .... 63 K5 [1]
Kelvin Dr TWK TW1 .... 17 M8 [1]
Kelvin Gdns CROY/NA CR0 ... 49 H7
Kelvin Gv SURB KT6 .... 63 H2
  SYD SE26 .... 32 E4
Kelvington Cl CROY/NA CR0 ... 51 H7 [2]
Kelvin La CRAWE RH10 ...... 192 C1
Kelvin Wy CRAWE RH10 ...... 192 C1
Kemble Cl WEY KT13 .... 60 A3
Kemble Dr HAYES BR2 .... 71 H2
Kemble Rd CROY/NA CR0 ..... 4 A7
  FSTH SE23 .... 33 G2
Kembleside Rd
  BH/WHM TN16 .... 90 F8 [3]
Kemerton Rd BECK BR3 ...... 51 L2
  CROY/NA CR0 .... 5 J2

Kemishford WOKS/MYFD GU22 ... 96 D5
Kemnal Pk HASM GU27 .... 220 A1
Kemp Ct BAGS GU19 .... 54 C7
Kemp Gdns CROY/NA CR0 ..... 49 M6 [3]
Kempshott Rd HORS RH12 .... 228 E5
  STRHM/NOR SW16 .... 31 H8
Kempton Av SUN TW16 .... 42 C1
Kempton Ct FARN GU14 ...... 92 C7
  SUN TW16 .... 42 C1
Kempton Rd HPTN TW12 ...... 43 J2
Kempton Wk CROY/NA CR0 .... 51 H6
Kemsing Cl THHTH CR7 ...... 49 M4 [2]
Kemsley Rd BH/WHM TN16 .... 111 G1
Kendal Cl EBED/NFELT TW14 ... 24 C2 [10]
  FARN GU14 .... 92 B5 [2]
  REDH RH1 .... 126 A7
Kendale Cl CRAWE RH10 ..... 212 F7 [2]
Kendal Gdns SUT SM1 .... 65 M1
Kendal Gv CBLY GU15 .... 74 A5
Kendall Av BECK BR3 .... 51 H2
  SAND/SEL CR2 .... 68 A7
Kendall Av South SAND/SEL CR2 ... 67 M8
Kendall Rd BECK BR3 .... 51 H2
  ISLW TW7 .... 17 K4
Kendor Av HOR/WEW KT19 .... 83 M1
Kendra Hall Rd SAND/SEL CR2 ... 67 L6
Kendrey Gdns WHTN TW2 ..... 17 H8
Kenilford Rd BAL SW12 ..... 30 E1 [1]
Kenilworth Av BRAK RG12 ... 34 F1
  COB KT11 .... 81 L4
  WIM/MER SW19 .... 29 K6
Kenilworth Cl BNSTD SM7 ... 85 L6
  CRAWW RH11 .... 211 L7 [2]
Kenilworth Dr WOT/HER KT12 ... 61 G2
Kenilworth Gdns STA TW18 ... 22 F6
Kenilworth Rd ASHF TW15 ... 23 G4
  EW KT17 .... 64 D5
  PGE/AN SE20 .... 51 G1
Kenley Gdns THHTH CR7 ..... 49 L4
Kenley La PUR/KEN CR8 ..... 87 M4
Kenley Rd KUT KT1 .... 3 M6
  TWK TW1 .... 17 K8
  WIM/MER SW19 .... 47 K3
Kenley Wk CHEAM SM3 .... 65 G3
Kenlor Rd TOOT SW17 .... 30 A6
Kenmara Cl CRAWE RH10 ..... 192 E8
Kenmara Ct CRAWE RH10 ..... 192 E7
Kenmare Dr MTCM CR4 .... 30 C8 [2]
Kenmare Rd THHTH CR7 ...... 49 K6 [3]
Kenmore Cl FRIM GU16 ...... 93 G1 [2]
Kenmore Rd PUR/KEN CR8 .... 87 L4
Kennedy Av EGRIN RH19 ..... 196 A6
Kennedy Cl MTCM CR4 .... 48 D1 [3]
  MTCM CR4 .... 48 D2 [3]
Kennedy Rd SWTR RH13 ...... 229 G8
Kennel Av ASC SL5 .... 36 C1
Kennel Cl GT/LBKH KT23 .... 101 M6
Kennel Gn ASC SL5 .... 36 B1
Kennel La BFOR GU20 .... 54 F4
  HORL RH6 .... 170 A7
  LHD/OX KT22 .... 101 M5
  NFNM GU10 .... 155 M7
Kennel Wk ASC SL5 .... 36 C1
Kennel Wood Crs CROY/NA CR0 ... 90 A1
Kennet Cl ASHV GU12 .... 113 K8
  CRAWW RH11 .... 211 J4
  FARN GU14 .... 92 A3
Kenneth Rd BNSTD SM7 ...... 86 A5
Kennet Rd ISLW TW7 .... 17 J5
Kennington Gdns KUT KT1 ... 2 D9
Kenrick Sq REDH RH1 .... 128 B8
Kensington Av THHTH CR7 ... 49 K1
Kensington Rd CRAWW RH11 ... 211 L7
Kensington Ter
  SAND/SEL CR2 .... 68 A6 [1]
Kent Cl MTCM CR4 .... 49 H4 [3]
  STA TW18 .... 23 G7
Kent Dr TEDD TW11 .... 26 B6
Kent Gate Wy CROY/NA CR0 ... 69 J5
Kent Hatch Rd OXTED RH8 ... 130 F4
Kent House La BECK BR3 .... 33 H7
Kent House Rd BECK BR3 .... 33 G8
Kentigern Dr CWTH RG45 .... 52 B4
Kenton Av SUN TW16 .... 43 G2
Kenton Cl BRAK RG12 .... 35 G2 [3]
  FRIM GU16 .... 73 J7
Kenton Wy WOKN/KNAP GU21 ... 76 C7
Kent Rd BFOR GU20 .... 55 G4
  E/WMO/HCT KT8 .... 43 M4
  RCH/KEW TW9 .... 18 D2 [3]
  WOKS/MYFD GU22 .... 7 K3
  WWKM BR4 .... 51 L8
Kent Wy SURB KT6 .... 63 H2 [1]
Kentwode Gn BARN SW13 ..... 19 K2 [1]
Kentwyns Ri REDH RH1 ...... 148 J1
Kenwood Cl WDR/YW UB7 ..... 14 D1 [3]
Kenwood Dr BECK BR3 .... 51 M3
  WOT/HER KT12 .... 60 E5
Kenwood Pk WEY KT13 .... 60 A5 [2]
Kenwood Rdg PUR/KEN CR8 ... 87 L7 [2]
Kenworth Gv LTWR GU18 ..... 54 D8
Kenwyn Rd RYNPK SW20 ...... 46 F1
Kenyngton Dr SUN TW16 ..... 24 D6
Kenyons EHSLY KT24 .... 119 L2
Keogh Barracks FRIM GU16 ... 93 M8 [3]
Keogh Cl FRIM GU16 .... 93 L8
Keppel Rd DORK RH4 .... 122 E8
Keppel Sp WDSR SL4 .... 20 L1
Kepple Pl BAGS GU19 .... 54 B6
Kerria Wy CHOB/PIR GU24 ... 75 H3 [3]
Kerrill Av COUL/CHIP CR5 ... 107 K1
Kerry Ter WOKN/KNAP GU21 ... 7 J3
Kersey Dr SAND/SEL CR2 .... 88 F2
Keston Av ADL/WDHM KT15 ... 78 D1
  COUL/CHIP CR5 .... 107 K1
  HAYES BR2 .... 70 F4
Keston Gdns HAYES BR2 ..... 70 F4
Keston Park Cl HAYES BR2 ... 71 J3
Keston Rd THHTH CR7 .... 49 J6
Kestrel Av STA TW18 .... 22 C4
Kestrel Cl CRAWW RH11 ..... 211 M1 [3]
  HORS RH12 .... 229 H4
  KUTN/CMB KT2 .... 27 G5
  NFNM GU10 .... 133 G2
  RGUE GU4 .... 118 A6
Kestrel Rd FARN GU14 ...... 92 A3
Kestrel Wy CROY/NA CR0 .... 70 A7
Keswick Av KUTN/CMB KT2 ... 28 B6

SHPTN TW17 .... 42 B3 [2]
  WIM/MER SW19 .... 47 K2
Keswick Cl CBLY GU15 ...... 73 M5
  CRAWW RH11 .... 211 G5
  SUT SM1 .... 65 M3
Keswick Dr LTWR GU18 ...... 74 E1
Keswick Rd ECH TW20 .... 21 L8
  GT/LBKH KT23 .... 101 M7
  MFD/CHID GU8 .... 181 G3
  WHTN TW2 .... 16 F8
  WWKM BR4 .... 70 B1
Kettering St STRHM/NOR SW16 ... 30 F7
Kettlewell Cl WOKN/KNAP GU21 ... 6 C1
Kettlewell HI WOKN/KNAP GU21 ... 6 C1
Kevan Dr RPLY/SEND GU23 ... 98 B7
Kevin Cl HSLWW TW4 .... 16 A4
Kew Br RCH/KEW TW9 .... 18 D1
Kew Bridge Rd BTFD TW8 .... 18 C1
Kew Crs CHEAM SM3 .... 65 J2
Kew Foot Rd RCH/KEW TW9 ... 18 B6
Kew Gardens Rd
  RCH/KEW TW9 .... 18 C2 [1]
Kew Gn RCH/KEW TW9 .... 18 C1
Kew Meadow Pth
  RCH/KEW TW9 .... 18 E3
Kew Rd RCH/KEW TW9 .... 18 B6
Keymer Cl BH/WHM TN16 ..... 90 F6
Keymer Rd BRXS/STRHM SW2 ... 31 J3
  CRAWW RH11 .... 212 A5
Keynsham Rd MRDN SM4 ...... 47 L8
Keynsham Wy SHST GU47 ..... 52 A7
Keysham Av HEST TW5 .... 15 K3
Keywood Dr SUN TW16 .... 24 D7
Khama Rd TOOT SW17 .... 30 B5
Khartoum Rd MFD/CHID GU8 ... 181 H3
  TOOT SW17 .... 30 A5
Kibble Gn BRAK RG12 .... 34 F6
Kidborough Down
  GT/LBKH KT23 .... 121 K1
Kidborough Rd CRAWW RH11 ... 211 J5
Kidderminster Rd CROY/NA CR0 ... 4 A2
Kidmans Cl HORS RH12 ...... 229 J3 [3]
Kidworth Cl HORL RH6 ...... 170 C4
Kier Pk ASC SL5 .... 36 F3
Kilberry Cl ISLW TW7 ...... 17 G3
Kilcorral Cl EW KT17 ...... 84 D4
Killester Gdns EW KT17 .... 64 E3
Killicks CRAN GU6 .... 185 J5
Killieser Av BRXS/STRHM SW2 ... 31 H3
Killinghurst La HASM GU27 ... 220 F3
Kilmarnock Pk REIG RH2 .... 125 L7 [1]
Kilmartin Av STRHM/NOR SW16 ... 49 G1
Kilmartin Gdns FRIM GU16 ... 73 J8 [2]
Kilmington Cl BRAK RG12 ... 35 H7 [4]
Kilmington Rd BARN SW13 ... 19 K1
Kilmiston Av SHPTN TW17 ... 41 M6
Kilmorey Gdns TWK TW1 ..... 17 L7
Kilmorey Rd TWK TW1 .... 17 L6
Kilmorie Rd FSTH SE23 ..... 33 H2
Kilmuir Cl SHST GU47 ...... 72 A2
Kiln Cl HYS/HAR UB3 .... 15 G1
Kiln Copse CRAN GU6 .... 185 H5
Kilnfield Rd HORS RH12 .... 226 A1
Kiln Flds HASM GU27 .... 219 M1
Kiln La ASC SL5 .... 37 K5
  BRAK RG12 .... 34 D2
  BRKHM/BTCW RH3 .... 123 M8
  EW KT17 .... 84 B1
  HORL RH6 .... 170 C4
  NFNM GU10 .... 11 G7
  RPLY/SEND GU23 .... 98 G3
Kilnmead CRAWE RH10 .... 212 B2
Kilnmead Cl CRAWE RH10 .... 212 B2
Kiln Mdw RGUW GU3 .... 115 M4
Kiln Ms TOOT SW17 .... 30 A6
Kiln Rd CRAWE RH10 .... 214 E2
Kilnside ESH/CLAY KT10 .... 62 D6
Kiln Wy ALDT GU11 .... 134 E2
  GSHT GU26 .... 198 B4
Kilnwood La HORS RH12 ..... 210 D6
Kilross Rd EBED/NFELT TW14 ... 24 A2
Kilrue La WOT/HER KT12 .... 60 C3
Kilrush Ter WOKN/KNAP GU21 ... 7 H3
Kilsha Rd WOT/HER KT12 .... 42 E6
Kimber Ct RGUE GU4 .... 118 A6 [3]
Kimberley BRAK RG12 .... 34 F8
Kimberley Cl HORL RH6 ..... 170 B6 [2]
Kimberley Pl PUR/KEN CR8 ... 87 K1 [1]
Kimberley Ride COB KT11 ... 81 L3
Kimberley Rd BECK BR3 ..... 51 G2
  CRAWE RH10 .... 212 E2 [2]
  CROY/NA CR0 .... 49 L6
Kimber Rd WAND/EARL SW18 ... 29 L1
Kimbers La FNM GU9 .... 134 A6
Kimble Rd TOOT SW17 .... 30 A7
Kimmeridge BRAK RG12 ...... 35 H6 [1]
Kimpton Rd CHEAM SM3 ...... 65 J2
  SUN TW16 .... 24 C2
  SURB KT6 .... 63 K1
Kinburn Dr EGH TW20 .... 21 H6
Kindersley Cl EGRIN RH19 ... 196 E6 [1]
Kinfauns Rd BRXS/STRHM SW2 ... 31 K3
King Alfred Av CAT SE6 .... 33 K4
King Charles' Rd BRYLDS KT5 ... 45 J7
King Charles Crs BRYLDS KT5 ... 45 J6
King Charles Wk
  WIM/MER SW19 .... 29 H2 [1]
Kingcup Cl CROY/NA CR0 .... 51 G8 [3]
Kingcup Dr CHOB/PIR GU24 ... 75 K5
King Edward Dr SURB KT6 ... 63 H8 [1]
King Edward's Gv TEDD TW11 ... 26 E7
King Edwards Ri ASC SL5 ... 36 B1
King Edwards Rd ASC SL5 ... 36 B1
Kingfield Cl WOKS/MYFD GU22 ... 97 J2
Kingfield Dr WOKS/MYFD GU22 ... 97 J2
Kingfield Gdns
  WOKS/MYFD GU22 .... 97 J2
Kingfield Rd WOKS/MYFD GU22 ... 97 J2
Kingfisher Cl CRAWE RH10 ... 192 D8 [1]
  ESH/CLAY KT10 .... 61 H4 [1]
Kingfisher Dr
  RCHPK/HAM TW10 .... 26 F5
  REDH RH1 .... 126 D5
  RGUE GU4 .... 117 M6
  STA TW18 .... 22 C5
Kingfisher Gdns SAND/SEL CR2 ... 69 G8
Kingfisher Ri EGRIN RH19 ... 216 C1 [1]
Kingfisher Wk ASHV GU12 ... 113 J6

Kingfisher Wy CROY/NA CR0 ... 51 G5
  REDH RH1 .... 228 F4
King Gdns CROY/NA CR0 ..... 67 L4 [3]
King Garth Ms FSTH SE23 ... 32 F3
King George Av EGRIN RH19 ... 195 M6
  WOT/HER KT12 .... 43 G8
King George VI Av MTCM CR4 ... 48 C4
King George's Dr
  ADL/WDHM KT15 .... 58 D8
King George Sq
  RCHPK/HAM TW10 .... 18 C8
King George Vi Av MTCM CR4 ... 48 C4
Kingham Cl WAND/EARL SW18 ... 29 M1
King Henry's Dr CROY/NA CR0 ... 69 M7
King Henry's Rd KUT KT1 ... 3 M8
Kings Av BAL SW12 .... 31 G2
  BF/WBF KT14 .... 79 G2
  CAR SM5 .... 66 B6
  CHOB/PIR GU24 .... 95 G1
  HSLW TW3 .... 16 E3 [3]
  NFNM GU10 .... 135 H1
  NWMAL KT3 .... 46 C4
  REDH RH1 .... 148 B2
  SUN TW16 .... 24 C6
Kingsbridge Rd LHD/OX KT22 ... 82 D8
  WOT/HER KT12 .... 42 E7 [3]
Kingsbrook LHD/OX KT22 .... 82 D8
Kingsbury Crs STA TW18 .... 22 A5
Kingsbury Dr WDSR SL4 ..... 20 D1
Kings Cha E/WMO/HCT KT8 ... 43 K3
Kingsclear Pk CBLY GU15 ... 73 G5
Kingsclere Cl PUT/ROE SW15 ... 28 D1 [1]
Kingscliffe Gdns
  WIM/MER SW19 .... 29 J2
Kings Cl STA TW18 .... 23 G8 [1]
  THDIT KT7 .... 44 D6
  WOT/HER KT12 .... 42 E8 [3]
Kings Copse EGRIN RH19 .... 216 C1 [3]
Kingscote HI CRAWW RH11 ... 211 L5
Kingscote Rd CROY/NA CR0 ... 50 E7
  NWMAL KT3 .... 46 A3
Kings Ct KWD/TDW/WH KT20 ... 104 F4
Kingscourt Rd
  STRHM/NOR SW16 .... 31 G4
King's Crs CBLY GU15 ...... 72 F1
Kingscroft Rd BNSTD SM7 ... 86 A5
  LHD/OX KT22 .... 102 E2
Kings Cross La REDH RH1 ... 149 J3
Kingsdale Rd PGE/AN SE20 ... 33 G8 [2]
Kingsdene KWD/TDW/WH KT20 ... 104 E3
Kingsdown Av SAND/SEL CR2 ... 67 M7
Kingsdowne Rd SURB KT6 .... 45 H7
Kingsdown Rd CHEAM SM3 .... 65 H4
  EW KT17 .... 84 D3
Kings Dr BRYLDS KT5 .... 45 K7
  THDIT KT7 .... 44 E6
The Kings Dr WOT/HER KT12 ... 60 C7
Kings Farm Av
  RCHPK/HAM TW10 .... 18 D6
Kingsford Av WLGTN SM6 .... 67 H6
Kingsgate Rd KUT KT1 ...... 2 E5
Kings Hall Rd BECK BR3 .... 33 J8
King's Head La BF/WBF KT14 ... 79 G1
Kingshill Av WPK KT4 ...... 46 D7
Kingsland RDKG RH5 .... 167 K8
Kings La BFOR GU20 .... 55 H4
  ECH TW20 .... 20 D6
  NFNM GU10 .... 10 B8
  SUT SM1 .... 66 A4
Kingslawn Cl PUT/ROE SW15 ... 19 L7 [3]
Kingslea LHD/OX KT22 ...... 102 E2
Kingsleigh Pl MTCM CR4 .... 48 C3
Kingsley Av BNSTD SM7 ..... 85 K5
  CBLY GU15 .... 72 F5
  ECH TW20 .... 20 E7
  HSLW TW3 .... 16 F4
  SUT SM1 .... 66 A3
Kingsley Cl HORL RH6 ...... 170 C4
Kingsley Dr WPK KT4 .... 64 C1 [1]
Kingsley Gv REIG RH2 ...... 147 K3
Kingsley Rd CRAWW RH11 .... 211 K6
  CROY/NA CR0 .... 49 K8
  FARN GU14 .... 92 C3
  HORL RH6 .... 170 C4
  HSLW TW3 .... 16 F4
  WIM/MER SW19 .... 29 L6
Kingslyn Crs NRWD SE19 .... 50 B1
Kings Md HORL RH6 .... 171 L6
  REDH RH1 .... 149 H2
Kingsmead BH/WHM TN16 ..... 91 G6
  CRAN GU6 .... 185 H6 [3]
  FARN GU14 .... 92 E5
  FRIM GU16 .... 93 H2
  RCHPK/HAM TW10 .... 18 C8
  WOKN/KNAP GU21 .... 7 H3 [3]
Kingsmead Av MTCM CR4 ..... 48 F3
  SUN TW16 .... 43 G2
  SURB KT6 .... 63 K1
  WPK KT4 .... 64 E2
Kingsmead Cl HOR/WEW KT19 ... 64 A6
  TEDD TW11 .... 26 E7
Kings Mead Pk ESH/CLAY KT10 ... 62 B6
Kingsmead Pl HORS RH12 .... 228 A6 [1]
Kingsmead Rd
  BRXS/STRHM SW2 .... 31 K3
  HORS RH12 .... 227 M6
Kingsmere Rd BNFD RG42 .... 34 C1
  WIM/MER SW19 .... 29 G3
Kings Mill La REDH RH1 .... 149 G4
Kingsnympton Pk
  KUTN/CMB KT2 .... 3 L1
King's Paddock HPTN TW12 ... 43 M1
King's Pas KUTN/CMB KT2 ... 2 D4
King's Ride ASC SL5 .... 35 M4
  CBLY GU15 .... 53 G8
Kings Rd ADL/WDHM KT15 .... 58 B8
  ALDT GU11 .... 112 B8
  ASC SL5 .... 37 G5
  BELMT SM2 .... 65 K8
  BH/WHM TN16 .... 90 F7
  CHOB/PIR GU24 .... 75 K4
  CRAN GU6 .... 185 J7
  EGH TW20 .... 21 K5
  FELT TW13 .... 24 E3
  HASM GU27 .... 219 K3
  HORL RH6 .... 170 D6

  KUTN/CMB KT2 .... 2 E4
  MORT/ESHN SW14 .... 19 G5
  MTCM CR4 .... 48 D3
  RCHPK/HAM TW10 .... 18 C7
  RGODL GU7 .... 160 C3
  RGUE GU4 .... 139 H6 [3]
  SHGR GU5 .... 161 L1
  SNWD SE25 .... 50 D3
  SURB KT6 .... 44 F8
  SWTR RH13 .... 229 H6
  TEDD TW11 .... 26 A6
  TWK TW1 .... 17 L8 [3]
  WIM/MER SW19 .... 29 K7
  WOKN/KNAP GU21 .... 7 H3
  WOT/HER KT12 .... 60 E1
Kings's Rd GU GU1 .... 9 H4
Kingsthorpe Rd SYD SE26 ... 33 G5
Kingston Av CHEAM SM3 ..... 65 H2
  EBED/NFELT TW14 .... 15 H8
  EHSLY KT24 .... 100 B8
  LHD/OX KT22 .... 102 E3
Kingston By-pass BRYLDS KT5 ... 45 M7
  CHSGTN KT9 .... 63 J2
  ESH/CLAY KT10 .... 62 B1
Kingston Crs ASHF TW15 .... 22 F6
  BECK BR3 .... 51 H2
Kingston Gdns CROY/NA CR0 ... 67 H2
Kingston Hall Rd KUT KT1 ... 2 D8
Kingston HI KUTN/CMB KT2 ... 3 K4
Kingston Hill Pl KUTN/CMB KT2 ... 27 M5
Kingston House Gdns
  LHD/OX KT22 .... 102 E3 [2]
Kingston La EHSLY KT24 .... 119 K1
  TEDD TW11 .... 26 E7 [3]
Kingston Ldg NWMAL KT3 .... 46 B4 [1]
Kingston Ri ADL/WDHM KT15 ... 58 D8
Kingston Rd ASHF TW15 ..... 23 H7
  BRYLDS KT5 .... 63 L1
  CBLY GU15 .... 53 K8
  EW KT17 .... 64 C6
  HOR/WEW KT19 .... 64 B4
  LHD/OX KT22 .... 82 D8
  NWMAL KT3 .... 46 C4
  PUT/ROE SW15 .... 28 E2
  RYNPK SW20 .... 28 E2
  SHPTN TW17 .... 23 J7
  STA TW18 .... 22 D5
  TEDD TW11 .... 26 F7
  WIM/MER SW19 .... 29 K8
Kingston Sq NRWD SE19 ..... 32 A6
Kingston V PUT/ROE SW15 ... 28 A5
King St CHERT KT16 .... 40 D8
  RCH/KEW TW9 .... 18 A7 [3]
  TWK TW1 .... 17 L8
Kings Wk SAND/SEL CR2 ..... 88 E4
Kings Wy CROY/NA CR0 ...... 67 J4
Kingsway ALDT GU11 .... 112 C8
  BLKW GU17 .... 72 B5
  MORT/ESHN SW14 .... 18 E5
  NWMAL KT3 .... 46 F4
  STWL/WRAY TW19 .... 23 G2
  WOKN/KNAP GU21 .... 6 A8
  WWKM BR4 .... 70 C2
Kingsway Av SAND/SEL CR2 ... 68 F7
  WOKN/KNAP GU21 .... 6 B7
Kingsway Rd CHEAM SM3 ..... 65 H6 [3]
Kingsway WEY KT13 .... 59 K6
The Kingsway EW KT17 ...... 64 C8
Kingswick Cl ASC SL5 ...... 37 H4
Kingswick Dr ASC SL5 ...... 37 G4
Kingswood Av HEST TW5 ..... 16 C4
  HPTN TW12 .... 25 L7 [3]
  SAND/SEL CR2 .... 88 E5
  THHTH CR7 .... 49 K5
Kingswood Cl EGH TW20 ..... 21 G5
  GU GU1 .... 117 M7 [3]
  NWMAL KT3 .... 46 C6 [2]
  SURB KT6 .... 45 H7 [2]
  WEY KT13 .... 59 L6
Kingswood Creek
  STWL/WRAY TW19 .... 12 A7
Kingswood Dr BELMT SM2 .... 65 L7 [3]
  CAR SM5 .... 48 C8
  NRWD SE19 .... 32 B5
Kingswood Firs GSHT GU26 ... 198 F6
Kingswood La GSHT GU26 .... 198 F7
  WARL CR6 .... 88 F5
Kingswood Rd EGH TW20 ..... 21 G6
Kingswood Rd KWD/TDW/WH KT20 ... 104 G3
  PGE/AN SE20 .... 32 F7
  WIM/MER SW19 .... 47 J1
Kingswood Wy SAND/SEL CR2 ... 89 G2
  WLGTN SM6 .... 67 H4 [3]
Kingsworth Cl BECK BR3 .... 51 H5 [1]
Kingsworthy Cl KUT KT1 .... 3 H8 [3]
Kinloss Rd CAR SM5 .... 47 M7
Kinnaird Av CHSWK W4 ...... 18 F2
Kinnersley Ms REIG RH2 .... 147 K5
Kinnibrugh Dr LING RH7 .... 174 D8
Kinross Av ASC SL5 .... 36 C5
  WPK KT4 .... 64 D1
Kinross Cl SUN TW16 .... 24 C6
Kinross Ct ASC SL5 .... 36 C5
Kinross Dr SUN TW16 .... 24 C6
Kintyre Cl STRHM/NOR SW16 ... 49 J3
Kinver Rd SYD SE26 .... 32 F5
Kipings KWD/TDW/WH KT20 ... 105 G4
Kipling Cl CRAWE RH10 ..... 212 F1 [3]
Kipling Ct SWTR RH13 ...... 229 K5
Kipling Dr TOOT SW17 ...... 30 A7
Kipling Wy EGRIN RH19 ..... 195 M4
Kirby Cl HOR/WEW KT19 ..... 64 C4
Kirby Rd WOKN/KNAP GU21 ... 6 A5
Kirdford Cl CRAWW RH11 .... 211 K1
Kirkdale SYD SE26 .... 32 E5
Kirkfields GUW GU2 .... 116 D5 [3]
Kirkham Cl SHST GU47 ...... 52 A7 [3]
Kirkland Av WOKN/KNAP GU21 ... 76 B4 [3]
Kirkleas Rd SURB KT6 ...... 45 H8
Kirklees Rd THHTH CR7 ..... 49 K5
Kirkley Rd WIM/MER SW19 ... 47 K1
Kirkly Cl SAND/SEL CR2 .... 68 B7
Kirkstall Gdns BRXS/STRHM SW2 ... 31 G2
Kirksted Rd MRDN SM4 ...... 47 L8
Kirkstone Cl CBLY GU15 .... 74 A5
Kirrane Cl NWMAL KT3 ...... 46 C5

Kirriemuir Gdns *ASHV* GU12 .... 114 A6
Kirtley Rd *SYD* SE26 .... 33 H5
Kitchener Rd *ALDT* GU11 .... 113 C3
  THHTH CR7 .... 50 A3
Kites Cl *CRAWW* RH11 .... 211 M8
Kithurst Cl *CRAWW* RH11 .... 212 A5
Kitley Gdns *NRWD* SE19 .... 50 C1
Kitsmead *CRAWE* RH10 .... 193 K2
Kitsmead La *CHERT* KT16 .... 38 F8
Kitson Rd *BARN* SW13 .... 19 K3
Kittiwake Cl *CRAWW* RH11 .... 211 C5
  SAND/SEL CR2 .... 69 H8
Kitts La *NFNM* GU10 .... 198 C1
Knapdale Cl *FSTH* SE23 .... 32 E3
Knapmill Rd *CAT* SE6 .... 33 K3
Knapmill Wy *CAT* SE6 .... 33 K3
Knapp Rd *ASHF* TW15 .... 23 J5
Knapton Ms *TOOT* SW17 .... 30 D7
Knaresborough Dr
  WAND/EARL SW18 .... 29 L2
Kneller Gdns *ISLW* TW7 .... 17 G8
Kneller HI *NWMAL* KT3 .... 46 B7
  WHTN TW2 .... 16 F8
Knepp Cl *CRAWE* RH10 .... 212 F3
Knighton Cl *CRAWE* RH10 .... 193 C7
  SAND/SEL CR2 .... 67 L7
Knighton Park Rd *SYD* SE26 .... 33 G6
Knighton Rd *REDH* RH1 .... 148 D2
Knightons La *MFD/CHID* GU8 .... 203 J5
Knightsbridge Crs *STA* TW18 .... 22 E7
Knightsbridge Rd *CBLY* GU15 .... 73 H2
Knights Cl *EGH* TW20 .... 22 A7
Knight's HI *WNWD* SE27 .... 31 L6
Knight's Hill Sq *WNWD* SE27 .... 31 L5
Knight's Pk *KUT* KT1 .... 8 C7
Knights Pl *REDH* RH1 .... 126 D7
Knights Rd *FNM* GU9 .... 134 B2
Knights Wy *CBLY* GU15 .... 73 M5
Knightswood *BRAK* RG12 .... 34 E8
  WOKN/KNAP GU21 .... 76 C7
Knightwood Cl *REIG* RH2 .... 147 K2
Knightwood Crs *NWMAL* KT3 .... 46 B6
Knipp HI *COB* KT11 .... 81 J3
Knobfield *SHGR* GU5 .... 164 C1
Knob HI *HORS* RH12 .... 208 D8
Knockhundred La *CSHT* GU26 .... 218 E1
Knole Cl *CRAWE* RH10 .... 213 C2
  CROY/NA CR0 .... 50 F6
Knole Gv *EGRIN* RH19 .... 195 M6
Knollmead *BRYLDS* KT5 .... 45 M8
Knoll Park Rd *CHERT* KT16 .... 40 C8
Knoll Quarry *RGODL* GU7 .... 160 B3
Knoll Rd *CBLY* GU15 .... 73 G3
  DORK RH4 .... 144 E1
  RGODL GU7 .... 160 A3
Knolls Cl *WPK* KT4 .... 64 E2
The Knolls *EW* KT17 .... 84 F6
The Knoll *BECK* BR3 .... 51 L1
  CHERT KT16 .... 40 C8
  COB KT11 .... 81 K3
  HAYES BR2 .... 70 D1
  LHD/OX KT22 .... 102 F3
Knoll Wd *RGODL* GU7 .... 160 B3
Knolly's Cl *WNWD* SE27 .... 31 K4
Knollys' Rd *ALDT* GU11 .... 112 C6
  STRHM/NOR SW16 .... 31 K4
Knowle Cl *CRAWE* RH10 .... 193 L6
Knowle Dr *CRAWE* RH10 .... 193 L6
Knowle Gdns *BF/WBF* KT14 .... 78 C3
Knowle Gn *STA* TW18 .... 22 D6
Knowle Gv *VW* GU25 .... 38 F7
Knowle Grove Cl *VW* GU25 .... 38 F7
Knowle HI *VW* GU25 .... 38 E7
Knowle La *CRAN* GU6 .... 205 G1
Knowle Pk *COB* KT11 .... 81 H5
Knowle Park Av *STA* TW18 .... 22 E7
Knowle Rd *HAYES* BR2 .... 71 H1
  WHTN TW2 .... 26 B2
Knowl HI *WOKS/MYFD* GU22 .... 7 K8
Knox Rd *GUW* GU2 .... 116 E4
Kohat Ct *ALDT* GU11 .... 112 C7
Kohat Rd *WIM/MER* SW19 .... 29 L6
Kohima Cl *ALDT* GU11 .... 112 E7
Koonowla Cl *BH/WHM* TN16 .... 91 G5
Kooringa *WARL* CR6 .... 108 C1
Korda Cl *SHPTN* TW17 .... 41 J3
Krooner Rd *CBLY* GU15 .... 72 E6
Kuala Gdns *STRHM/NOR* SW16 .... 49 J1
Kyle Cl *BRAK* RG12 .... 34 E3
Kynaston Av *THHTH* CR7 .... 49 M5
Kynaston Crs *THHTH* CR7 .... 49 M5
Kynaston Rd *THHTH* CR7 .... 49 M5
Kynersley Cl *CAR* SM5 .... 66 C2

L

Laburnum Av *SUT* SM1 .... 66 B2
Laburnum Cl *GU* GU1 .... 116 F5
Laburnum Crs *SUN* TW16 .... 42 E1
Laburnum Gdns *CROY/NA* CR0 .... 51 G7
Laburnum Gv *DTCH/LGLY* SL3 .... 12 D1
  HSLW TW3 .... 16 C6
  NWMAL KT3 .... 46 A2
Laburnum Pl *EGH* TW20 .... 20 E7
Laburnum Rd *ALDT* GU11 .... 112 D8
  CHERT KT16 .... 40 D8
  EPSOM KT18 .... 84 B3
  FNM GU9 .... 134 B2
  MTCM CR4 .... 48 D2
  WIM/MER SW19 .... 29 M8
  WOKS/MYFD GU22 .... 97 G2
Laburnum Wy
  STWL/WRAY TW19 .... 23 J2
Lacey Av *COUL/CHIP* CR5 .... 107 K2
Lacey Cl *EGH* TW20 .... 22 A8
Lacey Dr *COUL/CHIP* CR5 .... 107 K2
  HPTN TW12 .... 43 J1
Lackford Rd *COUL/CHIP* CR5 .... 86 C3
Lacock Cl *WIM/MER* SW19 .... 29 M7
Lacy Gn *COUL/CHIP* CR5 .... 107 K2
Ladas Rd *WNWD* SE27 .... 31 M6
  REDH RH1 .... 126 D7
Ladbrook Rd *SNWD* SE25 .... 50 A3
Ladderstile Ride
  RCHPK/HAM TW10 .... 27 L6
Ladybank *BRAK* RG12 .... 34 E8
Lady Booth Rd *KUT* KT1 .... 2 D7
Ladycroft Gdns *ORP* BR6 .... 71 M4
Ladycroft Wy *ORP* BR6 .... 71 M4
Ladycross *MFD/CHID* GU8 .... 181 H1
Ladygate Cl *RDKG* RH5 .... 145 G1
Ladygate Rd *RDKG* RH5 .... 144 F2
Ladygrove Dr *GSHT* GU26 .... 198 D6
Ladygrove Dr *RGUE* GU4 .... 117 L3
Lady Hay *WPK* KT4 .... 64 C1
Lady Margaret Rd *ASC* SL5 .... 37 J8
  CRAWW RH11 .... 211 K2
Ladymead *GU* GU1 .... 8 F1
Ladymead Cl *CRAWE* RH10 .... 212 F6
Ladymount *WLGTN* SM6 .... 67 G3
Ladythorpe Cl
  ADL/WDHM KT15 .... 58 E3
Ladywood Rd *SURB* KT6 .... 63 K1
Laffan's Rd *ALDT* GU11 .... 112 C4
Lafone Av *FELT* TW13 .... 24 F3
Lagham Pk *GDST* RH9 .... 151 H3
Lagham Rd *GDST* RH9 .... 151 H4
Laglands Cl *REIG* RH2 .... 125 M6
Laings Av *MTCM* CR4 .... 48 C2
Lainlock Pl *HSLW* TW3 .... 5 L3
Lainson St *WAND/EARL* SW18 .... 29 K1
Lairdale Cl *DUL* SE21 .... 31 M2
Laird Ct *BAGS* GU19 .... 54 B8
Laitwood Rd *BAL* SW12 .... 30 E2
Lake Cl *BF/WBF* KT14 .... 79 C2
  WLGTN SM6 .... 66 E2
Lake Gdns *RCHPK/HAM* TW10 .... 26 E4
  WLGTN SM6 .... 66 E2
Lakehall Gdns *THHTH* CR7 .... 49 L5
Lakehall Rd *THHTH* CR7 .... 49 L5
Lakehurst Rd *HOR/WEW* KT19 .... 64 B4
Lakeland Cl *FRIM* GU16 .... 73 H8
Lake La *HORL* RH6 .... 170 F4
  NFNM GU10 .... 177 H3
Lake Rd *CROY/NA* CR0 .... 69 J1
  FRIM GU16 .... 93 K3
  RDKG RH5 .... 187 M3
  VW GU25 .... 38 E4
  WIM/MER SW19 .... 29 J5
Lakers Ri *BNSTD* SM7 .... 86 B6
Lakes Cl *RGUE* GU4 .... 139 L6
Lakeside *BECK* BR3 .... 51 L3
  HOR/WEW KT19 .... 64 B5
  HORS RH12 .... 228 E4
  REDH RH1 .... 126 D6
  WEY KT13 .... 60 B1
  WLGTN SM6 .... 66 E3
  WOKN/KNAP GU21 .... 96 B1
Lakeside Cl *ASHV* GU12 .... 113 J5
  SNWD SE25 .... 50 D2
  WOKN/KNAP GU21 .... 96 B1
Lakeside Dr *ESH/CLAY* KT10 .... 61 M5
  HAYES BR2 .... 71 H2
Lakeside Gdns *FARN* GU14 .... 92 A4
Lakeside Gra *WEY* KT13 .... 59 M2
Lakeside Rd *ALDT* GU11 .... 112 C2
  ASHV GU12 .... 113 J5
  DTCH/LGLY SL3 .... 13 J2
The Lake Side *BLKW* GU17 .... 72 A5
Lakes Rd *HAYES* BR2 .... 70 F4
Lake Vw *RDKG* RH5 .... 144 F5
Lake View Rd *CRAWE* RH10 .... 194 E6
  EGRIN RH19 .... 196 C4
Lakeview Rd *WNWD* SE27 .... 31 K6
Laleham Cl *STA* TW18 .... 40 E1
Laleham Rd *CAT* SE6 .... 33 M1
  SHPTN TW17 .... 41 J4
  STA TW18 .... 22 C7
Lamberhurst Rd *WNWD* SE27 .... 31 K5
Lambert Av *RCH/KEW* TW9 .... 18 D5
Lambert Cl *BH/WHM* TN16 .... 91 G6
Lambert Rd *BNSTD* SM7 .... 85 K4
Lambert's Pl *CROY/NA* CR0 .... 4 F3
Lambert's Rd *SURB* KT6 .... 45 H5
Lambeth Cl *CRAWW* RH11 .... 211 K1
Lambeth Rd *CROY/NA* CR0 .... 49 K7
Lambly HI *VW* GU25 .... 39 H3
Lambourn Cl *EGRIN* RH19 .... 196 B6
Lambourne Av *WIM/MER* SW19 .... 29 J5
Lambourne Cl *CRAWE* RH10 .... 212 C5
Lambourne Crs
  WOKN/KNAP GU21 .... 78 A3
Lambourne Dr *BAGS* GU19 .... 54 A7
  COB KT11 .... 80 F5
Lambourne Gv *BRAK* RG12 .... 35 H2
  KUT KT1 .... 3 L6
Lambourne Wy *NFNM* GU10 .... 135 H2
Lambs Crs *HORS* RH12 .... 229 J4
Lambs Farm Cl *HORS* RH12 .... 229 K4
Lambs Farm Rd *HORS* RH12 .... 229 J4
Lambs Green Rd *HORS* RH12 .... 210 C4
Lambton Rd *RYNPK* SW20 .... 46 F3
Lambyn Cft *HORL* RH6 .... 170 F5
Lammas Av *MTCM* CR4 .... 48 C2
Lammas Cl *RGODL* GU7 .... 160 D3
  STA TW18 .... 22 B4
Lammas Dr *STA* TW18 .... 22 A5
Lammas La *ESH/CLAY* KT10 .... 61 K3
Lammas Rd *RCHPK/HAM* TW10 .... 26 F5
  RGODL GU7 .... 160 D4
Lammermoor Rd *BAL* SW12 .... 30 E1
Lampard La *NFNM* GU10 .... 178 A7
Lampeter Cl *WOKS/MYFD* GU22 .... 6 C8
Lampton Av *HSLW* TW5 .... 16 D3
Lampton House Cl
  WIM/MER SW19 .... 29 G5
Lampton Park Rd *HSLW* TW3 .... 16 E4
Lampton Rd *HSLW* TW3 .... 16 E4
Lanark Cl *FRIM* GU16 .... 73 H7
Lancaster Av *FNM* GU9 .... 11 H5
  MTCM CR4 .... 49 H5
  WIM/MER SW19 .... 29 G6
  WNWD SE27 .... 31 L3
Lancaster Cl *ASHV* GU12 .... 113 G8
  CRAWE RH10 .... 193 G8
  EGH TW20 .... 21 G6
  STWL/WRAY TW19 .... 14 B8
  WOKN/KNAP GU21 .... 7 G4
Lancaster Ct *WOT/HER* KT12 .... 42 D7
Lancaster Dr *CBLY* GU15 .... 73 G3
  EGRIN RH19 .... 196 D6
Lancaster Gdn *KUTN/CMB* KT2 .... 27 G6
Lancaster Gdns *WIM/MER* SW19 .... 29 H6
Lancaster Ms
  RCHPK/HAM TW10 .... 18 B8
Lancaster Pk *RCHPK/HAM* TW10 .... 18 B7
Lancaster Pl *TWK* TW1 .... 26 D1
  WIM/MER SW19 .... 29 G6
Lancaster Rd *FARN* GU14 .... 92 E8
  SNWD SE25 .... 50 C2
  WIM/MER SW19 .... 29 G6
Lancaster Wy *FARN* GU14 .... 92 F2
Lancelot Cl *CRAWW* RH11 .... 211 H3
Lancer Ct *ALDT* GU11 .... 112 B7
Lancing Cl *CRAWW* RH11 .... 211 K2
Lancing Rd *CROY/NA* CR0 .... 49 J6
  FELT TW13 .... 24 C3
Landen Pk *HORL* RH6 .... 170 B4
Landford Rd *PUT/ROE* SW15 .... 19 M6
Landgrove Rd *WIM/MER* SW19 .... 29 K6
Landon Wy *ASHF* TW15 .... 23 L7
Landscape Rd *WARL* CR6 .... 108 E1
Landseer Cl *SHST* GU47 .... 72 B3
  WIM/MER SW19 .... 48 A1
Landseer Rd *NWMAL* KT3 .... 46 A7
  SUT SM1 .... 65 K5
Lane Cl *ADL/WDHM* KT15 .... 58 D4
Lane End *EPSOM* KT18 .... 83 L4
  MFD/CHID GU8 .... 201 L1
Lane End Dr *WOKN/KNAP* GU21 .... 75 M7
Lanercost Rd *BRXS/STRHM* SW2 .... 31 K3
  CRAWW RH11 .... 211 M4
The Lane *BIL* RH14 .... 223 M5
  CHERT KT16 .... 40 D3
  MFD/CHID GU8 .... 179 L5
  VW GU25 .... 39 H3
Laneway *PUT/ROE* SW15 .... 19 L7
Langbourne Wy *ESH/CLAY* KT10 .... 62 C5
Lang Cl *GT/LBKH* KT23 .... 101 L5
Langcroft Cl *CAR* SM5 .... 66 C2
Langdale Av *MTCM* CR4 .... 48 C3
Langdale Cl *FARN* GU14 .... 92 B5
  MORT/ESHN SW14 .... 18 E6
  ORP BR6 .... 71 L2
  WOKN/KNAP GU21 .... 76 F6
Langdale Dr *ASC* SL5 .... 36 C3
Langdale Rd *CRAWW* RH11 .... 211 G5
  THHTH CR7 .... 49 K4
Langdon Cl *CBLY* GU15 .... 73 M5
Langdon Pl *MORT/ESHN* SW14 .... 18 F7
Langdon Wk *MRDN* SM4 .... 47 M5
Langham Cl *RGODL* GU7 .... 160 C5
Langham Dene *PUR/KEN* CR8 .... 87 L5
Langham Gdns
  RCHPK/HAM TW10 .... 26 F5
Langham House Cl
  RCHPK/HAM TW10 .... 27 G5
Langham Pk *RGODL* GU7 .... 160 C4
Langham Pl *CHSWK* W4 .... 19 H1
  EGH TW20 .... 21 J6
Langham Rd *RYNPK* SW20 .... 46 F1
  TEDD TW11 .... 26 E6
Langholm Cl *BAL* SW12 .... 31 G1
Langhorn Dr *WHTN* TW2 .... 26 B1
Langhurst Cl *HORS* RH12 .... 209 C5
Langhurst La *HORS* RH12 .... 210 D1
Langhurstwood Rd *HORS* RH12 .... 209 C5
Langland Gdns *CROY/NA* CR0 .... 69 J1
Langlands Ri *HOR/WEW* KT19 .... 83 M3
Langley Av *SURB* KT6 .... 45 G8
  FRIM GU16 .... 73 H7
  WPK KT4 .... 65 G1
Langley Cl *EPSOM* KT18 .... 104 A1
  GU GU1 .... 8 F1
Langley Crs *HYS/HAR* UB3 .... 15 J2
Langley Dr *CBLY* GU15 .... 73 C3
  CRAWW RH11 .... 211 M1
Langley Gv *NWMAL* KT3 .... 46 A2
Langley La *CRAWW* RH11 .... 211 K1
Langley Oaks Av *SAND/SEL* CR2 .... 68 D8
Langley Pde *CRAWW* RH11 .... 191 M8
Langley Park Rd *BELMT* SM2 .... 65 M5
Langley Pl *CRAWW* RH11 .... 191 M8
Langley Rd *BECK* BR3 .... 51 C4
  ISLW TW7 .... 17 J4
  SAND/SEL CR2 .... 69 G7
  STA TW18 .... 22 C7
  SURB KT6 .... 45 H7
  WIM/MER SW19 .... 29 J7
Langley Vale Rd *EPSOM* KT18 .... 84 A8
Langley Wk *CRAWW* RH11 .... 191 L8
  WOKS/MYFD GU22 .... 6 C8
Langmans Wy
  WOKN/KNAP GU21 .... 76 B6
Langmead St *WNWD* SE27 .... 31 M5
Langport Ct *WOT/HER* KT12 .... 42 F8
Langridge Dr *EGRIN* RH19 .... 216 B1
Langridge Ms *HPTN* TW12 .... 25 J7
Langroyd Rd *TOOT* SW17 .... 30 C3
Langshott *HORL* RH6 .... 171 G4
Langshott Cl *ADL/WDHM* KT15 .... 78 B1
Langshott La *HORL* RH6 .... 170 F5
Langside Av *PUT/ROE* SW15 .... 19 K6
Langsmead *LING* RH7 .... 173 H1
Langstone Cl *CRAWE* RH10 .... 212 F6
Langton Av *EW* KT17 .... 84 C1
Langton Cl *ADL/WDHM* KT15 .... 58 E2
  WOKN/KNAP GU21 .... 76 C7
Langton Ri *EDUL* SE22 .... 32 E1
Langton Wy *CROY/NA* CR0 .... 5 H9
  EGH TW20 .... 21 M7
Langwood Cha *TEDD* TW11 .... 2 B1
Lanigan Dr *HSLW* TW3 .... 16 E7
Lankton Cl *BECK* BR3 .... 51 M1
Lansbury Av *EBED/NFELT* TW14 .... 15 L8
Lansbury Rd *CRAWW* RH11 .... 211 L8
Lansdell Rd *MTCM* CR4 .... 48 C1
Lansdown Cl *GU* GU1 .... 117 K8
  WOKN/KNAP GU21 .... 77 M3
  WOT/HER KT12 .... 42 F8
Lansdowne Cl *BRYLDS* KT5 .... 63 L1
  RYNPK SW20 .... 29 G8
  TWK TW1 .... 26 C2
Lansdowne HI *WNWD* SE27 .... 31 L4
Lansdowne Pl *NRWD* SE19 .... 32 C8
Lansdowne Rd *ALDT* GU11 .... 112 D8
  CROY/NA CR0 .... 4 D5
  FRIM GU16 .... 93 K1
  HOR/WEW KT19 .... 63 H6
  HSLW TW3 .... 16 E5
  PUR/KEN CR8 .... 87 K2
  RYNPK SW20 .... 28 E3
  STA TW18 .... 22 E8
Lansdowne Wood Cl
  WNWD SE27 .... 31 L4
Lantern Cl *PUT/ROE* SW15 .... 19 K6
Lanyon Cl *HORS* RH12 .... 229 K3
Lapse Wood Wk *DUL* SE21 .... 32 E2
Lapwing Cl *CROY/NA* CR0 .... 69 H8
  SWTR RH13 .... 229 J6
Lapwing Gv *RGUE* GU4 .... 118 A6
Lara Cl *CHSGTN* KT9 .... 63 H6
Larbert Rd *STRHM/NOR* SW16 .... 48 F1
Larby Pl *EW* KT17 .... 64 B8
Larch Av *ASC* SL5 .... 37 H5
  GU GU1 .... 116 F6
Larch Cl *BAL* SW12 .... 30 E3
  CBLY GU15 .... 53 H8
  KWD/TDW/WH KT20 .... 105 M3
  REIG RH2 .... 147 M2
  WARL CR6 .... 109 H1
Larch Dene *ORP* BR6 .... 71 K1
Larch End *HORS* RH12 .... 228 F4
Larches Av *MORT/ESHN* SW14 .... 19 G6
  WOKN/KNAP GU21 .... 6 D3
The Larches *HORS* RH12 .... 229 M3
  WOKN/KNAP GU21 .... 6 D3
Larch Tree Wy *CROY/NA* CR0 .... 69 K2
Larchwood Dr *EGH* TW20 .... 20 E7
Larchwood Gld *CBLY* GU15 .... 73 K2
Larchwood Rd
  WOKN/KNAP GU21 .... 96 A2
Larcombe Cl *CROY/NA* CR0 .... 68 C3
Larges Bridge Dr *BRAK* RG12 .... 34 F3
Larges La *BRAK* RG12 .... 34 F2
Largewood Av *SURB* KT6 .... 63 K1
Lark Av *STA* TW18 .... 22 C4
Larkbere Rd *SYD* SE26 .... 33 H5
Larkfield *COB* KT11 .... 80 D3
  CRAN GU6 .... 186 B5
Larkfield Cl *FNM* GU9 .... 133 J6
  RCH/KEW TW9 .... 18 B6
Larkfield Ct *HORL* RH6 .... 171 K6
Larkham Cl *FELT* TW13 .... 24 B4
Larkin Cl *COUL/CHIP* CR5 .... 87 J7
Larkins Rd *HORL* RH6 .... 192 A2
Lark Ri *CRAWW* RH11 .... 211 M1
  EHSLY KT24 .... 120 B5
Larksfield *EGH* TW20 .... 20 E8
  HORL RH6 .... 170 E5
Larkspur Cl *ALDT* GU11 .... 112 C8
  RDKG RH5 .... 145 G5
Larkspur Wy *HOR/WEW* KT19 .... 63 M4
Larks Wy *WOKN/KNAP* GU21 .... 75 M6
Lark Wy *CAR* SM5 .... 48 B7
Larpent Av *PUT/ROE* SW15 .... 19 M7
Lascombe La *RGUA* GU3 .... 136 D5
Lashmere *CRAN* GU6 .... 184 D6
  CRAWE RH10 .... 194 A6
Lasswade Rd *CHERT* KT16 .... 40 C7
Latchmere Cl *RCHPK/HAM* TW10 .... 27 H6
Latchmere La *KUTN/CMB* KT2 .... 27 J7
Latchmere Rd *KUTN/CMB* KT2 .... 2 F2
Latchwood La *NFNM* GU10 .... 156 A4
Lateward Rd *BTFD* TW8 .... 18 A1
Latham Av *FRIM* GU16 .... 73 H7
Latham Cl *BH/WHM* TN16 .... 90 F6
Latham Rd *TWK* TW1 .... 26 C1
Latham's Wy *CROY/NA* CR0 .... 49 J8
Latimer *BRAK* RG12 .... 34 E8
Latimer Cl *CRAWW* RH11 .... 192 A8
  WOKS/MYFD GU22 .... 7 K3
  WPK KT4 .... 64 E2
Latimer Rd *CROY/NA* CR0 .... 4 B7
  RGODL GU7 .... 160 B5
  TEDD TW11 .... 26 C6
  WIM/MER SW19 .... 29 L7
La Tourne Gdns *ORP* BR6 .... 71 M2
Lattimer Pl *CHSWK* W4 .... 19 H2
Latton Cl *ESH/CLAY* KT10 .... 61 L3
  WOT/HER KT12 .... 43 J7
Latymer Cl *WEY* KT13 .... 59 M3
Laud Dr *CRAWE* RH10 .... 213 G4
Lauder Cl *FRIM* GU16 .... 73 H7
Lauderdale *FARN* GU14 .... 92 A6
Lauderdale Dr
  RCHPK/HAM TW10 .... 27 G4
Laud St *CROY/NA* CR0 .... 4 C8
Laughton Rd *HORS* RH12 .... 229 J4
Laundry La *CBLY* GU15 .... 72 B4
Laundry Rd *GU* GU1 .... 8 F5
Laundry Wy *RDKG* RH5 .... 188 F4
Lauradale *BRAK* RG12 .... 34 D4
Laurel Av *EGH* TW20 .... 20 E6
  TWK TW1 .... 26 C2
Laurel Cl *CBLY* GU15 .... 73 G5
  CRAWE RH10 .... 212 D6
  DTCH/LGLY SL3 .... 13 H2
  TOOT SW17 .... 30 B6
Laurel Crs *CROY/NA* CR0 .... 69 K2
  WOKN/KNAP GU21 .... 77 M3
Laurel Dene *EGRIN* RH19 .... 196 C8
Laurel Gdns *ALDT* GU11 .... 134 D2
  HSLW TW4 .... 16 B6
Laurel Gv *NFNM* GU10 .... 10 B9
  PGE/AN SE20 .... 32 E8
  SYD SE26 .... 33 G6
Laurel Rd *BARN* SW13 .... 19 K4
  HPTN TW12 .... 25 K6
  RYNPK SW20 .... 46 E1
The Laurels *BNSTD* SM7 .... 85 J7
  COB KT11 .... 81 H5
  FNM GU9 .... 134 C2
Lauriston Rd *WIM/MER* SW19 .... 29 G7
Lauser Rd *STWL/WRAY* TW19 .... 22 F1
Laustan Cl *GU* GU1 .... 117 M8
Lavant Cl *CRAWW* RH11 .... 211 J4
Lavender Av *MTCM* CR4 .... 48 B1
  WPK KT4 .... 64 F2
Lavender Cl *CAR* SM5 .... 66 D3
  COUL/CHIP CR5 .... 106 F1
  CTHM CR3 .... 107 M7
  REDH RH1 .... 148 E3
Lavender Ct *E/WMO/HCT* KT8 .... 43 L3
Lavender Gv *MTCM* CR4 .... 48 B1
Lavender La *NFNM* GU10 .... 155 J5
Lavender Park Rd
  BF/WBF KT14 .... 78 D3
Lavender Rd *CAR* SM5 .... 66 D4
  CROY/NA CR0 .... 49 J6
  HOR/WEW KT19 .... 63 L4
  SUT SM1 .... 66 A3
  WOKS/MYFD GU22 .... 7 K4
Lavender Wy *WLGTN* SM6 .... 67 G5
Lavender Wy *CROY/NA* CR0 .... 51 G6
Lavengro Rd *WNWD* SE27 .... 31 M3
Lavenham Rd *WAND/EARL* SW18 .... 29 J3
Laverstoke Gdns *PUT/ROE* SW15 .... 28 C1
Lavington Cl *CRAWW* RH11 .... 211 J2
Lavington Rd *CROY/NA* CR0 .... 67 J2
Lawbrook La *SHGR* GU5 .... 163 M1
Lawday Link *FNM* GU9 .... 133 K2
Lawday Pl *FNM* GU9 .... 133 K2
Lawday Place La *FNM* GU9 .... 133 K2
Lawdon Gdns *CROY/NA* CR0 .... 67 L3
Lawford Cl *WLGTN* SM6 .... 67 H7
Lawford Gdns *PUR/KEN* CR8 .... 87 M6
Lawford Rd *CHSWK* W4 .... 18 F2
Lawn Cl *NWMAL* KT3 .... 46 B2
Lawn Crs *RCH/KEW* TW9 .... 18 D4
Lawn Rd *BECK* BR3 .... 33 J8
  GUW GU2 .... 8 F9
Lawns Rd *HORS* RH12 .... 205 K6
The Lawns *BELMT* SM2 .... 65 H6
  FARN GU14 .... 92 B6
  MFD/CHID GU8 .... 159 J8
  NRWD SE19 .... 50 A1
Lawrence Cl *RGUE* GU4 .... 117 L3
Lawrence Crs *BFOR* GU20 .... 55 C5
Lawrence Gv *BNFD* RG42 .... 34 A1
Lawrence La
  BRKHM/BTCW RH3 .... 124 E6
Lawrence Rd *HPTN* TW12 .... 25 J3
  HSLWW TW4 .... 15 M6
  RCHPK/HAM TW10 .... 26 F5
  SNWD SE25 .... 50 C4
  WWKM BR4 .... 70 D3
Lawrence Wy *CBLY* GU15 .... 72 C5
Lawrie Park Av *SYD* SE26 .... 32 E6
Lawrie Park Crs *SYD* SE26 .... 32 E6
Lawrie Park Gdns *SYD* SE26 .... 32 E6
Lawrie Park Rd *SYD* SE26 .... 32 F7
Laws Cl *CRAWW* RH11 .... 211 H4
Lawson Cl *WIM/MER* SW19 .... 29 G3
Lawson Wy *ASC* SL5 .... 37 L6
Laws Ter *ALDT* GU11 .... 112 F6
Laxton Gdns *REDH* RH1 .... 127 G2
Layard Rd *THHTH* CR7 .... 50 A2
Layburn Crs *DTCH/LGLY* SL3 .... 12 E1
Layhams Rd *HAYES* BR2 .... 70 D6
  WWKM BR4 .... 70 B3
Layton Ct *WEY* KT13 .... 59 L3
Layton Crs *CROY/NA* CR0 .... 67 K4
Layton Pl *RCH/KEW* TW9 .... 18 D3
Layton Rd *HSLW* TW3 .... 16 E6
Layton's La *SUN* TW16 .... 42 C2
Leach Gv *LHD/OX* KT22 .... 102 F4
Lea Cl *ASHV* GU12 .... 113 K8
  CRAWW RH11 .... 211 J4
  FNM GU9 .... 134 D3
Lea Ct *FNM* GU9 .... 134 C2
Leacroft *ASC* SL5 .... 37 K5
  STA TW18 .... 22 E5
Leacroft Av *BAL* SW12 .... 30 C1
Leacroft Cl *PUR/KEN* CR8 .... 87 M6
  STA TW18 .... 22 E5
Leaf Cl *THDIT* KT7 .... 44 B5
Leaf Gv *STRHM/NOR* SW16 .... 31 K6
Leafield Cl *STRHM/NOR* SW16 .... 31 L7
  WOKN/KNAP GU21 .... 76 D8
Leafield Copse *BRAK* RG12 .... 35 J4
Leafield Rd *RYNPK* SW20 .... 47 J3
  SUT SM1 .... 65 K1
Leafy Gv *HAYES* BR2 .... 70 F4
Leafy Wy *CROY/NA* CR0 .... 5 J6
Leamington Av *MRDN* SM4 .... 47 J4
Leamington Cl *HSLW* TW3 .... 16 F7
Leander Rd *THHTH* CR7 .... 49 J4
Leapale La *GU* GU1 .... 9 G6
Leapale Rd *GU* GU1 .... 9 G6
Lea Rd *BECK* BR3 .... 51 K2
  CBLY GU15 .... 72 E7
Leas Cl *CHSGTN* KT9 .... 63 J6
Leaside *GT/LBKH* KT23 .... 101 K5
Leas La *WARL* CR6 .... 89 G8
Leas Rd *GU* GU1 .... 8 F5
  WARL CR6 .... 89 G8
The Lea *EGH* TW20 .... 21 L8
Leather Cl *EDEN* TN8 .... 175 M1
  MTCM CR4 .... 48 D2
Leatherhead By Pass Rd
  LHD/OX KT22 .... 102 E2
Leatherhead By-pass Rd
  LHD/OX KT22 .... 103 C3
Leatherhead Rd *ASHTD* KT21 .... 103 G2
  CHSGTN KT9 .... 82 E4
  GT/LBKH KT23 .... 101 M8
  LHD/OX KT22 .... 82 A4
Leaveland Cl *BECK* BR3 .... 51 K4
Leavesden Rd *WEY* KT13 .... 59 L4
Leaves Gn *BRAK* RG12 .... 35 G6
Leaves Green Crs *HAYES* BR2 .... 90 F5
Leaves Green Rd *HAYES* BR2 .... 91 G1
Lea Wy *ASHV* GU12 .... 113 K6
Leazes Av *CTHM* CR3 .... 107 K5
Lebanon Av *FELT* TW13 .... 25 G6
Lebanon Dr *COB* KT11 .... 81 K3
Lebanon Gdns *BH/WHM* TN16 .... 91 G7
Lebanon Pk *TWK* TW1 .... 26 E1
Lebanon Rd *CROY/NA* CR0 .... 5 H4

Lechford Rd HORL RH6 ....170 C8
Leckford Rd WAND/EARL SW18 ...29 M3
Leconfield Av PUT/ROE SW15 ...19 J5 ²
Ledbury Rd CROY/NA CRO....67 M4
  REIG RH2 ....125 K7 ²
Ledger Cl GU GU1 ....117 L6
Ledger Dr ADL/WDHM KT15 ...58 C5
Ledgers Rd WARL CR6 ....109 L1
Ledrington Rd NRWD SE19 ...32 C7
Leechcroft Rd WLGTN SM6 ...66 D2
Leech La LHD/OX KT22....103 M8
Leechpool La BF/WBF RH13 ....134 F1
Lee Ct ALDT GU11....112 B7
Leehurst MFD/CHID GU8 ....159 H8
Lee Rd ALDT GU11 ....112 B7
  WIM/MER SW19....47 L1
The Lees CROY/NA CRO 69 J1
Lee St HORL RH6....170 C8
Leeward Gdns WIM/MER SW19 ...29 H7
Leewood Wy LHD/OX KT24 ...120 F1 ¹
Lefroy's Fld NFNM GU10....132 C1
Legge Crs ALDT GU11....112 B8
Legrace Av HSLWW TW4....16 A4
Leicester BRAK RG12....35 G7
Leicester Av MTCM CR4....49 H4 ²
Leicester Cl WPK KT4 ....64 F3
Leicester Rd CROY/NA CRO....5 H2
Leigham Av STRHM/NOR SW16 ...31 H4
Leigham Court Rd
  STRHM/NOR SW16....31 J4
Leigham Dr ISLW TW7....17 H2 ²
Leigham V STRHM/NOR SW16 ...31 K4
Leigh Cl ADL/WDHM KT15....58 C6
  NWMAL KT3....46 A4
Leigh Court Cl COB KT11....80 F4
Leigh Crs CROY/NA CRO....69 L6
Leigh Hill Rd COB KT11....80 F4
Leighlands CRAWE RH10....212 F1
Leigh La FNM GU9....11 L4
Leigh Orchard Cl
  STRHM/NOR SW16....31 J4 ³
Leigh Pl COB KT11....80 F5
Leigh Place La GDST RH9....129 C6
Leigh Place Rd REIG RH2....146 D6
Leigh Rd BRKHM/BTCW RH3 ...145 M6
  COB KT11....80 E3
  HSLW TW3....17 G6 ²
Leighton Gdns SAND/SEL CR2 ...88 E3
Leighton St CROY/NA CRO....4 A4
Leighton Wy EPSOM KT18....84 A4
Leinster Av MORT/ESHN SW14 ...18 F5
Leisure La BF/WBF KT14....78 E2 ²
Leithcote Gdns
  STRHM/NOR SW16....31 J5
Leithcote Pth
  STRHM/NOR SW16....31 J4
Leith Gv RDKG RH5....167 C5
Leith Hill Rd RDKG RH5....165 H2
Leith Rd EW KT17....84 B2
  RDKG RH5....166 F5
Leith Vw RDKG RH5....144 F6
Leith View Rd HORS RH12....229 K4
Lela Av HSLWW TW4....15 M4
Le Marchant Rd FRIM GU16....73 J6
Le May Cl HORL RH6....170 D5
Lemington Gv BRAK RG12....34 E6 ¹
Lemmington Wy HORS RH12 ...229 J2
Lemon's Farm Rd RDKG RH5 ...165 J3
Lendore Rd FRIM GU16....93 G1
Lenelby Rd SURB KT6....45 K8
Lenham Rd SUT SM1....65 L3
  THHTH CR7....50 A2
Lennard Av WWKM BR4....70 B1
Lennard Cl WWKM BR4....70 B1
Lennard Rd CROY/NA CRO....4 C3
  PGE/AN SE20....32 F7
  SYD SE26....32 F7
Lennox Gdns CROY/NA CRO ...67 L3 ⁴
Lenten Cl SHGR GU5....142 A8
Lenton Ri RCH/KEW TW9....18 B5
Leof Crs CAT SE6....33 L6
Leominster Rd MRDN SM4....47 M6
Leominster Wk MRDN SM4 ...47 M6 ³
Leonard Av MRDN SM4....47 M5
Leonard Cl FRIM GU16....93 G1
Leonard Rd MTCM CR4....48 E7
Leonardslee Ct CRAWE RH10 ...212 E6 ³
Leonard Wy SWTR RH13....229 J7
Leopold Av FARN GU14....92 E4
  WIM/MER SW19....29 J5
Leopold Rd CRAWW RH11 ...211 M3 ¹
  WIM/MER SW19....29 J5
Le Personne Rd CTHM CR3 ...108 A4
Leppington BRAK RG12....34 E8
Leret Wy LHD/OX KT22....102 D3
Lesbourne Rd REIG RH2....147 L1
Lescombe Cl FSTH SE23....33 H4
Lescombe Rd FSTH SE23....33 H4
Leslie Gdns BELMT SM2....65 K6
Leslie Gv CROY/NA CRO....4 F3
Leslie Park Rd CROY/NA CRO ...5 G4
Leslie Rd CHOB/PIR GU24....56 A8
  DORK RH4....123 G8
Lessingham Av TOOT SW17 ...30 C5
Lessing St FSTH SE23....33 H1
Lessness Rd MRDN SM4....47 M6
Letchworth Av
  EBED/NFELT TW14....24 C1
Letchworth St TOOT SW17 ...30 C5
Letcombe Sq BRAK RG12....35 J4
Levana Cl WIM/MER SW19 ...29 H2 ²
Levendale Rd FSTH SE23....33 H3
Leveret Cl CROY/NA CRO....90 A1
Leveret La CRAWW RH11 ...211 L1 ⁴
Leverkusen Rd BRAK RG12 ...34 E3 ³
Levern Dr FNM GU9....133 M3 ³
Leverson St STRHM/NOR SW16 ...30 F7
Levett Rd LHD/OX KT22....102 E2
Levylsdene GU GU1....118 A3
Lewes Cl CRAWE RH10....212 F3
Lewesdon Cl WIM/MER SW19 ...29 G2 ¹
  FROW RH18....217 H6
Lewes Rd EGRIN RH19....216 C1
Lewin Rd MORT/ESHN SW14 ...19 G5
  STRHM/NOR SW16....31 G7
Lewins Rd EPSOM KT18....83 L4
Lewis Cl ADL/WDHM KT15 ...58 C5
Lewisham Cl CRAWW RH11 ...211 M7 ³

Lewisham Wy SHST GU47....52 A8
Lewis Rd MTCM CR4....48 B2
  RCHPK/HAM TW10....18 A7 ³
  SUT SM1....65 L3
Lexden Rd MTCM CR4....49 G4
Lexington Ct PUR/KEN CR8 ...67 M8
Lexton Gdns BAL SW12....31 G2
Leyborne Pk RCH/KEW TW9 ...18 D3
Leybourne Av BF/WBF KT14 ...79 J3 ⁴
Leybourne Cl BF/WBF KT14 ...79 J3 ⁴
  CRAWW RH11....211 M8 ³
Leyburn Gdns CROY/NA CRO....5 H6
Leycester Cl BFOR GU20....54 E3
Leyfield WPK KT4....64 B1
Leylands La STWL/WRAY TW19 ...13 J6
Ley Rd FARN GU14....92 D1
Leys Rd LHD/OX KT22....82 A2
Leyton Rd WIM/MER SW19....29 M8
Liberty Av WIM/MER SW19....48 A1
Liberty Hall Rd ADL/WDHM KT15 ...58 D4
Liberty La ADL/WDHM KT15 ...58 E4
Liberty Ri ADL/WDHM KT15....58 D5
Library Rd FARN GU14....92 E7
Lichfield Gdns
  RCHPK/HAM TW10....18 B7 ³
Lichfield Rd HSLWW TW4....15 M5
  RCH/KEW TW9....18 C3
Lichfields BRAK RG12....35 H2 ³
Lichfield Wy SAND/SEL CR2 ...69 G8
Lickfolds Rd NFNM GU10....155 H7
Liddell Wy ASC SL5....36 C5
Liddington Hall Dr RGUW GU3 ...116 B5
Liddington New Rd RGUW GU3 ...116 B5
Lidiard Rd WAND/EARL SW18 ...29 M3
Lido Rd GU GU1....9 H2
Lidsey Cl CRAWE RH10....212 F5
Lidstone Cl WOKN/KNAP GU21 ...76 E7
Lightwater Meadow LTWR GU18 ...74 E1
Lightwater Rd LTWR GU18....74 E1
Lightwood BRAK RG12....35 G6
Lilac Av WOKS/MYFD GU22....97 G2
Lilac Cl GU GU1....116 F4
Lilac Gdns CROY/NA CRO....69 K2
Lilian Rd MTCM CR4....48 F1
Lille Barracks ALDT GU11....113 G1
Lilleshall Rd MRDN SM4....48 A6
Lilley Dr KWD/TDW/WH KT20 ...105 L4
Lilian Rd BARN SW13....19 K1
Lillie Rd BH/WHM TN16....91 G8
Lillyfields Cha CRAN GU6....186 B5
Lily Av CBLY GU15....73 K3
  HORS RH12....229 K5
Lily Hill Dr BRAK RG12....35 J2
Lily Hill Rd BRAK RG12....35 J2
Lime Av CBLY GU15....73 K3
  HORS RH12....229 K5
Limebush Cl ADL/WDHM KT15 ...58 F7
Lime Cl CRAWE RH10....193 L6
  CRAWW RH11....191 M8
  REIG RH2....147 L3
  RGUE GU4....118 C2
Lime Crs ASHF TW15....24 A6
Limecroft Cl HOR/WEW KT19 ...64 A6
Lime Gv ADL/WDHM KT15....58 D3
  GU GU1....116 E4
  NWMAL KT3....46 A3
  ORP BR6....71 L1
  RGUE GU4....118 C2
  TWK TW1....17 J8
  WARL CR6....109 H1
  WOKS/MYFD GU22....97 H3
Lime Meadow Av SAND/SEL CR2 ...88 E3
Limerick Cl BAL SW12....30 F1 ³
  BNFD RG42....34 D1
Limes Av BARN SW13....19 J4
  CAR SM5....48 C8
  CROY/NA CRO....67 J2
  HORL RH6....170 E8
  PGE/AN SE20....32 E8 ³
Limes Cl ASHF TW15....23 K6
  CAR SM5....66 C1
Limes Field Rd BARN SW13 ...19 H5 ³
Limes Rd BECK BR3....51 L2
  CROY/NA CRO....50 A6
  EGH TW20....21 J6
  WEY KT13....59 K3
Limes Rw ORP BR6....71 L4
The Limes EDEN TN8....153 M8
  EGRIN RH19....216 A2
  LHD/OX KT22....102 E5 ¹
  WOKN/KNAP GU21....6 A2
Lime St ALDT GU11....112 C7
Lime Tree Av THDIT KT7....44 B8
Lime Tree Cl GT/LBKH KT23 ...101 K6
Lime Tree Gv CROY/NA CRO....69 J2
Limetree Pl MTCM CR4....48 E1 ⁴
Lime Tree Rd HEST TW5....16 E3
Lime Tree Wk VW GU25....39 H4
  WWKM BR4....70 C3
Lime Wk BRAK RG12....34 F4
Limeway Ter DORK RH4....122 D8
Limewood Cl WOKN/KNAP GU21 ...96 A2
  WIM/MER SW19....29 G3
Limpsfield Av THHTH CR7....49 J5
  WIM/MER SW19....29 G3
Limpsfield Rd SAND/SEL CR2 ...88 E4
  WARL CR6....109 K1
Linacre Dr CRAN GU6....205 M3
  HORS RH12....205 M6
Lince La DORK RH4....144 A2
Linchmere Pl CRAWW RH11 ...211 K2 ⁵
Linchmere Rd HASM GU27....218 F6
Lincoln Av WHTN TW2....25 M3
  WIM/MER SW19....29 G4
Lincoln Cl ASHV GU12....113 K4
  CBLY GU15....73 L5
  CRAWE RH10....212 B6
Lincoln Dr WOKS/MYFD GU22 ...78 B5
Lincoln Rd DORK RH4....122 F8
  FARN GU14....92 D8
  FELT TW13....25 J4
  GUW GU2....116 C6
  MTCM CR4....48 F5
  NWMAL KT3....45 M3 ³
  SNWD SE25....50 E3
  WPK KT4....64 E8
Lincolns Md LING RH7....173 M6
Lincoln Wy SUN TW16....42 B1
Lindale Cl VW GU25....38 C4

Lindbergh Rd WLGTN SM6....67 H7
Linden Av COUL/CHIP CR5....86 E6
  EGRIN RH19....195 M7
  HSLW TW3....16 F7
  THHTH CR7....49 L4
Linden Cl ADL/WDHM KT15 ...78 D1
  CRAWE RH10....212 D6
  HORS RH12....229 H5
  KWD/TDW/WH KT20....105 G2
  THDIT KT7....44 D7 ³
Linden Ct CBLY GU15....73 J3
  EGH TW20....20 E7 ³
  LHD/OX KT22....102 E5
Linden Crs KUT KT1....3 H7
Linden Dr CTHM CR3....107 M6
Linden Gdns LHD/OX KT22....102 F5
  PGE/AN SE20....32 F7
  WARL CR6....89 H8
  WOT/HER KT12....60 C1
Lindenhill Rd BNFD RG42....34 C1
Linden Leas WWKM BR4....70 A1
Linden Pit Pth LHD/OX KT22 ...102 E5
Linden Pl EW KT17....84 B2 ¹
  MTCM CR4....48 B4
Linden Rd GU GU1....9 G3
  HPTN TW12....43 K1
  LHD/OX KT22....102 E5
  WEY KT13....59 M7
Lindens EHSLY KT24....121 H2
The Lindens CHSWK W4....18 F5 ¹
  CRAWE RH10....193 L6 ³
Linden Wy RPLY/SEND GU23 ...98 C7
  SHPTN TW17....41 M5
  WLGTN SM6....66 F8
  WOKS/MYFD GU22....97 J3
Lindfield Gdns GU GU1....9 M2
Lindfield Rd CROY/NA CRO....50 C6
Lindisfarne Rd RYNPK SW20 ...28 D8
Lindley Pl RCH/KEW TW9....18 D3
Lindley Rd GDST RH9....128 F4
  WOT/HER KT12....61 H2
Lindores Rd CAR SM5....47 M7
Lind Rd SUT SM1....65 M4
Lindsay Cl CHSGTN KT9....63 H6 ²
  HOR/WEW KT19....83 M3
  STWL/WRAY TW19....14 A3
Lindsay Dr SHPTN TW17....42 A6
Lindsay Rd ADL/WDHM KT15 ...78 D1
  HPTN TW12....25 L5
  WPK KT4....64 E2
Lindsey Cl MTCM CR4....49 H4 ³
Lindsey Gdns
  EBED/NFELT TW14....24 A1 ²
Lindum Dene ALDT GU11....112 D8
Lindum Rd TEDD TW11....2 A3
Lindway WNWD SE27....31 L6
Linersh Dr SHGR GU5....161 K3
Linersh Wood Cl SHGR GU5 ...161 K4
Linersh Wood Rd SHGR GU5 ...161 K3
Linfield Cl WOT/HER KT12....60 E4 ³
Ling Dr LTWR GU18....74 C2
Lingfield Av BRYLDS KT5....45 H4
Lingfield Common Rd
  LING RH7....173 M4
Lingfield Dr CRAWE RH10....213 H2
Lingfield Gdns COUL/CHIP CR5 ...107 L1
Lingfield Rd EDEN TN8....196 A6 ¹
  EGRIN RH19....196 A6 ¹
  WIM/MER SW19....29 H5
  WPK KT4....64 F2
Lingwell Rd TOOT SW17....30 B4
Lingwood BRAK RG12....34 F6
Lingwood Gdns ISLW TW7....17 H2
Linkfield E/WMO/HCT KT8....43 K3
Linkfield Gdns REDH RH1....126 B8 ¹
Linkfield La REDH RH1....126 C7
Linkfield Rd ISLW TW7....17 J4
Linkfield St REDH RH1....126 B8
Link La WLGTN SM6....67 G5
Link Rd ADL/WDHM KT15....59 H3 ³
  EBED/NFELT TW14....24 C1
  FARN GU14....112 A1
  MTCM CR4....48 D8
Links Av MRDN SM4....47 K4
Links Brow LHD/OX KT22....102 B5
Links Cl ASHTD KT21....82 F7
  CRAN GU6....186 B3
Linkscroft Av ASHF TW15....23 L7
Links Gdns STRHM/NOR SW16 ...31 K8
Links Green Wy COB KT11....81 K4
Linkside NWMAL KT3....46 B3
Linkside East GSHT GU26....198 E2
Linkside North GSHT GU26 ...198 E2
Linkside South GSHT GU26 ...198 E3
Linkside West GSHT GU26....198 E2
Links Pl ASHTD KT21....83 G7
Links Rd ASHF TW15....23 H6 ¹
  ASHTD KT21....82 F7
  EW KT17....84 D3
  SHGR GU5....161 H2
  TOOT SW17....30 D7
  WWKM BR4....51 M8
The Links ASC SL5....36 B2
  WOT/HER KT12....60 D1
Links View Av RDKG RH5....123 K8
Links View Rd CROY/NA CRO ...69 K2
  HPTN TW12....25 M6
Links Wy BECK BR3....51 K6
  EHSLY KT24....121 H2
The Link CRAWW RH11....212 A3
  TEDD TW11....26 C7
Link Wy RCHPK/HAM TW10....26 E3
  STA TW18....22 E7
Linkway CBLY GU15....72 F5
  GU GU1....116 C8
  RYNPK SW20....46 E3
  WOKS/MYFD GU22....7 M5
The Linkway BELMT SM2....65 M4
Linnell Rd REDH RH1....148 D1
Linnet Cl SAND/SEL CR2....69 G8
Linnet Gv RGUE GU4....118 A6 ³
Linnet Ms BAL SW12....30 D1
Linsford La FRIM GU16....93 J6
Linslade Cl HSLWW TW4....16 B7 ³
Linstead Rd FARN GU14....92 B1
Linstead Wy WAND/EARL SW18 ...29 H1

Linton Cl CAR SM5....48 C7 ⁴
Linton Gld CROY/NA CRO....69 H8
Linton Gv WNWD SE27....31 L6
Linton's La EW KT17....84 B2
Lintott Gdns SWTR RH13....229 H6 ²
Lion Av TWK TW1....26 C2
Lion Cl SHPTN TW17....41 J7
Lion Gate Gdns RCH/KEW TW9 ...18 C5
Lion Green Rd COUL/CHIP CR5 ...87 G5
Lion La CRAWE RH10....214 D5
  GSHT GU26....199 J8
Lion Md HASM GU27....219 J3
Lion Park Av CHSGTN KT9....63 K3
Lion Rd CROY/NA CRO....49 M5
  FARN GU14....92 E7
  WHTN TW2....26 C2
Lion Wy BTFD TW8....18 A2
Lion Wharf Rd ISLW TW7....17 L5
Liphook Crs FSTH SE23....32 F1
Liphook Rd HASM GU27....218 D5
  HASM GU27....219 H3
Lipscomb Cl REIG RH2....147 L1
Lisbon Av WHTN TW2....25 M3
Liscombe BRAK RG12....34 E7
Liskeard Dr FARN GU14....92 D3 ³
Lisle Cl TOOT SW17....30 E5
Lismore Cl ISLW TW7....17 K4
Lismore Crs CRAWW RH11....211 L6
Lismore Rd SAND/SEL CR2....68 B5
Lissoms Rd COUL/CHIP CR5 ...86 D8
Lister Av EGRIN RH19....216 B3
Lister Cl WIM/MER SW19....48 B1 ¹
Litchfield Rd SUT SM1....65 M5
Litchfield Wy GUW GU2....138 C2
Lithgow's Rd HTHAIR TW6....15 H6
Little Acre BECK BR3....51 K3
Little Aly EDEN TN8....175 L4
Little Austins Rd FNM GU9....11 K3
Little Birch Cl
  ADL/WDHM KT15....59 G7 ³
Little Bookham St
  GT/LBKH KT23....101 J8
Little Bornes DUL SE21....32 B5
Little Borough
  BRKHM/BTCW RH3....145 K1
Littlebrook Cl CROY/NA CRO....51 C6 ²
Little Browns La EDEN TN8 ...153 H5
Little Common La REDH RH1 ...127 L6
Little Comptons SWTR RH13 ...229 J7
Littlecote Cl WIM/MER SW19 ...29 G1 ¹
Little Ct WWKM BR4....70 C2
Little Crabtree CRAWW RH11 ...211 M2
Little Cranmore La EHSLY KT24 ...119 J2
Littlecroft Rd EGH TW20....21 J6
Littledale Cl BRAK RG12....35 H3
Little Dimocks BAL SW12....30 E3
Little Elms HYS/HAR UB3....15 G2
Little Ferry Rd TWK TW1....26 E2 ¹
Littlefield Cl ASHV GU12....113 K8
  KUT KT1....2 F7 ¹
  RGUW GU3....116 A4
Littlefield Gdns ASHV GU12 ...113 K8
Littlefield Wy RGUW GU3....115 M4
Littleford La RGUE GU4....140 B8
  SHGR GU5....162 C3
Little Grebe HORS RH12....228 F4
Little Green La CHERT KT16....58 B2
  FNM GU9....10 B6
Little Hatch HORS RH12....229 J5
Little Haven La HORS RH12....229 J4
Littleheath La COB KT11....81 K4
Little Heath Rd CHOB/PIR GU24 ...56 B7
Littleheath Rd SAND/SEL CR2 ...68 F7
Little Hide GU GU1....117 L6
Little Kiln RGODL GU7....160 B1
Little King St EGRIN RH19....196 B8 ¹
Little London MFD/CHID GU8 ...181 H4
Little Manor Gdns CRAN GU6 ...185 H7 ³
Littlemead ESH/CLAY KT10....62 A3
Little Md WOKN/KNAP GU21 ...76 C6
Little Moreton Cl
  BF/WBF KT14....78 E2 ³
Little Orch ADL/WDHM KT15 ...78 D1
  WOKN/KNAP GU21....6 A2
Little Orchards EPSOM KT18 ...84 B4 ¹
Little Orchard Wy RGUE GU4 ...118 B8
Little Paddock CBLY GU15....73 K1
Little Park Dr FELT TW13....25 G3
Little Platt GUW GU2....116 A7
Little Queens Rd TEDD TW11 ...26 C7
Little Ringdale BRAK RG12....35 H4
Little Roke Av PUR/KEN CR8 ...87 L4
Little Roke Rd PUR/KEN CR8 ...87 M4
Little Rownings FSTH SE23....32 E3
Littlers Cl WIM/MER SW19....48 A1 ³
Little St Leonards
  MORT/ESHN SW14....18 F5
Littlestone Cl BECK BR3....33 K7 ²
Little St GUW GU2....116 E4
Little Sutton La DTCH/LGLY SL3 ...12 E1
Little Thatch RGODL GU7....160 C3 ³
Little Thurbans Cl FNM GU9 ...10 C7
Littleton La REIG RH2....147 H2
  RGUW GU3....138 D6
  STA TW18....41 H5
Littleton St WAND/EARL SW18 ...29 M3
Little Tumners Ct RGODL GU7 ...160 B3
Little Warren Cl RGUE GU4....139 L2
Little Wellington St ALDT GU11 ...112 D7
Littlewick Rd WOKN/KNAP GU21 ...76 B6
  WOKN/KNAP GU21....76 B5
Littlewood CRAN GU6....185 J6
Littlewood Cl CAR SM5....86 E2
Littlewoodcote Av ESH/CLAY KT10 ...62 A4
Littleworth Common Rd
  ESH/CLAY KT10....62 A3
Littleworth La ESH/CLAY KT10 ...62 A3
Littleworth Pl ESH/CLAY KT10 ...62 A3
Littleworth Rd ESH/CLAY KT10 ...62 B2
  MFD/CHID GU8....158 B2
  NFNM GU10....135 J8

Littit Halliards WOT/HER KT12 ...42 D6 ³
Liverpool Rd KUTN/CMB KT2 ...3 K2
  THHTH CR7....49 M5
Livesey Cl KUT KT1....3 G5
Livingstone Rd CRAWE RH10 ...212 B5
  CTHM CR3....108 A4
  HSLW TW3....16 F6
  SWTR RH13....229 G3
  THHTH CR7....50 A2
Llanaway Cl RGODL GU7....160 C3 ³
Llanaway Rd RGODL GU7....160 C3
Llanthony Rd MRDN SM4....48 A6
Llanvair Cl ASC SL5....36 C6
Llanvair Dr ASC SL5....36 C7
Lloyd Av COUL/CHIP CR5....86 C4
  STRHM/NOR SW16....49 H1
Lloyd Park Av CROY/NA CRO ...68 C3
Lloyd Rd WPK KT4....64 F3
Lloyds Wy BECK BR3....51 H5
Lobelia Rd CHOB/PIR GU24 ...75 K5
Lochaline St HMSMTH W6....19 M1
Lochinvar St BAL SW12....30 E1
Lochinver BRAK RG12....34 E7
Lock Cl WOKN/KNAP GU21 ...78 B2
Locke King Cl WEY KT13....59 K6
Locke King Rd WEY KT13....59 K6
Locke Rd LIPH GU30....218 A5
Locke Wy WOKN/KNAP GU21....6 F5
Lockfield Dr WOKN/KNAP GU21 ...76 B3
Lockhart Rd COB KT11....80 F3
Lockhursthatch La SHGR GU5 ...163 H5
Lock La WOKS/MYFD GU22....78 E6
Lock Rd ALDT GU11....113 G4
  GU GU1....117 G4
  RCHPK/HAM TW10....26 F5
Lock's La MTCM CR4....48 D1
Locksley Dr
  WOKN/KNAP GU21....76 C8 ⁴
Locksmeade Rd
  RCHPK/HAM TW10....26 E5
Locks Meadow LING RH7....174 D8 ²
Lockswood CHOB/PIR GU24 ...95 L2
Lockton Cha ASC SL5....36 A3
Lockwood Cl FARN GU14....92 B1
  HORS RH12....229 K4 ³
  SYD SE26....33 G5 ¹
Lockwood Pth
  WOKN/KNAP GU21....78 A3
Lockwood Wy CHSGTN KT9 ...63 K4
Loddon Cl CBLY GU15....73 K3
Loddon Rd FARN GU14....92 A3
Loddon Wy ASHV GU12....113 K8
Loder Cl WOKN/KNAP GU21 ...78 A3
Lodge Av CROY/NA CRO....67 J2
Lodgebottom Rd RDKG RH5 ...123 K1
Lodge Cl COB KT11....81 J6
  CRAWW RH11....211 M3 ²
  EGH TW20....21 G6
  EGRIN RH19....195 M8
  EW KT17....64 F8 ³
  ISLW TW7....17 L3
  LHD/OX KT22....102 A4
  MTCM CR4....48 C8
  RDKG RH5....144 F6
Lodge Gdns BECK BR3....51 J5
Lodge Hl PUR/KEN CR8....87 K5
Lodge Hill Cl NFNM GU10....11 K7
Lodge Hill Rd NFNM GU10....11 K7
Lodge La BH/WHM TN16....131 M7 ³
  CROY/NA CRO....69 L6
  RDKG RH5....167 J2
  REDH RH1....148 B8
Lodge Pl SUT SM1....65 L4
Lodge Rd CROY/NA CRO....49 L6
  LHD/OX KT22....101 M4
  SUT SM1....65 L3 ³
  WLGTN SM6....66 E4
Lodge Wy ASHF TW15....23 H3
  SHPTN TW17....41 M2 ³
Lodsworth FARN GU14....92 A6 ³
Lofthouse Pl CHSGTN KT9....62 F5
Logan Cl HSLWW TW4....16 C5
Logmore La DORK RH4....144 B7
Lois Dr SHPTN TW17....41 L5
Lollesworth La EHSLY KT24....99 M8 ³
Loman Rd FRIM GU16....93 K6
Lomas Cl CROY/NA CRO....69 M6
Lombard Av WIM/MER SW19 ...47 L2
Lombard St MFD/CHID GU8 ...158 C3
Lombardy Cl
  WOKN/KNAP GU21....76 C7 ²
Lomond Gdns SAND/SEL CR2 ...69 H6
Loncin Mead Av
  ADL/WDHM KT15....58 F7
London La SHGR GU5....141 K5
London Loop BNSTD SM7....85 J3
  COUL/CHIP CR5....107 H1
  CROY/NA CRO....69 G2
  PUR/KEN CR8....88 B5
  SAND/SEL CR2....88 D5
  WARL CR6....70 A2
London Rd ASC SL5....35 K3
  BFOR GU20....54 F2
  BH/WHM TN16....111 M5
  BLKW GU17....72 B5
  BRAK RG12....35 G2
  CBLY GU15....72 C4
  CHEAM SM3....65 G1
  CRAWE RH10....213 K8
  CRAWW RH11....212 A2
  CROY/NA CRO....4 B3
  CTHM CR3....108 A5
  DORK RH4....122 F6
  EGH TW20....20 F8
  EGRIN RH19....196 B4
  FROW RH18....217 H5
  FSTH SE23....32 F2
  GU GU1....117 L5 ³
  HORL RH6....192 D1
  HORS RH12....228 F7
  ISLW TW7....17 H4
  KUT KT1....3 H5
  KUTN/CMB KT2....2 F6
  MTCM CR4....48 C2
  REDH RH1....126 D7
  REIG RH2....125 K3
  RPLY/SEND GU23....98 B8

STA TW18 ... 22 C5
STRHM/NOR SW16 ... 49 J2
STWL/WRAY TW19 ... 23 G3
THHTH CR7 ... 49 K6
TWK TW1 ... 26 D1
WLGTN SM6 ... 66 E6
London Rd North
  COUL/CHIP CR5 ... 106 E6
  REDH RH1 ... 106 E7
London Rd South REDH RH1 ... 126 E4
London St CHERT KT16 ... 40 D7
Loneacre BFOR GU20 ... 55 H5
Lone Oak HORL RH6 ... 171 L8
Lonesome La REIG RH2 ... 147 M4
Lonesome Wy MTCM CR4 ... 48 E1
Longacre ASHV GU12 ... 113 K7
Long Acre CRAWE RH10 ... 214 D1
Longacre Pl CAR SM5 ... 66 D5
Longbourne Wy CHERT KT16 ... 40 C6
Longboyds COB KT11 ... 80 E5
Long Br FNM GU9 ... 133 M7
Longbridge Rd HORL RH6 ... 170 C8
Longbridge Wk HORL RH6 ... 170 C8
Long Copse Ct GT/LBKH KT23 ... 101 L5
Longcroft Av BNSTD SM7 ... 85 M4
Longcross Rd CHERT KT16 ... 56 B6
Longdene Rd HASM GU27 ... 219 L3
Longdon Wd HAYES BR2 ... 71 H3
Longdown Cl NFNM GU10 ... 11 H8
Longdown La North EW KT17 ... 84 D3
Longdown La South EW KT17 ... 84 D5
Longdown Rd CAT SE6 ... 33 K5
  EW KT17 ... 84 D4
  NFNM GU10 ... 155 L4
  RGUE GU4 ... 139 L3
Long Dyke GU GU1 ... 117 L6
Longfellow Rd WPK KT4 ... 46 D8
Longfield Av WLGTN SM6 ... 48 D8
Longfield Cl FARN GU14 ... 92 D1
Longfield Crs
  KWD/TDW/WH KT20 ... 104 F2
  SYD SE26 ... 32 F4
Longfield Dr MORT/ESHN SW14 ... 18 E7
  WIM/MER SW19 ... 48 B1
Longfield Rd ASHV GU12 ... 113 K7
  DORK RH4 ... 144 C3
Longfield St WAND/EARL SW18 ... 29 K1
Longford Av EBED/NFELT TW14 ... 15 H6
  STWL/WRAY TW19 ... 23 H2
Longford Cl CBLY GU15 ... 73 G5
  HPTN TW12 ... 25 K5
Longford Ct HOR/WEW KT19 ... 63 M3
Longford Gdns SUT SM1 ... 65 M2
Longford Rd WHTN TW2 ... 25 K2
Longford Wy STWL/WRAY TW19 ... 23 H2
Long Garden Wk FNM GU9 ... 133 L7
Long Garden Wk East
  FNM GU9 ... 133 L7
Long Garden Wk West
  FNM GU9 ... 133 L7
Long Garden Wy FNM GU9 ... 133 L7
Long Gore RGODL GU7 ... 160 B1
Long Grove Rd HOR/WEW KT19 ... 63 L8
Longheath Dr GT/LBKH KT23 ... 101 H6
Longheath Gdns CROY/NA CR0 ... 50 F5
Long Hl CTHM CR3 ... 109 H3
  NFNM GU10 ... 135 H8
Long Hill Rd ASC SL5 ... 35 L1
  BRAK RG12 ... 35 K2
Longhope Dr NFNM GU10 ... 10 D8
Longhurst Rd CRAWW RH11 ... 211 K8
  CROY/NA CR0 ... 50 E6
  EHSLY KT24 ... 120 B3
Longlands Av COUL/CHIP CR5 ... 86 E4
Long La CROY/NA CR0 ... 50 E6
  STWL/WRAY TW19 ... 23 J1
Longleat Sq FARN GU14 ... 93 H6
Longleat Wy EBED/NFELT TW14 ... 23 M1
Longley Rd CROY/NA CR0 ... 4 A2
  FNM GU9 ... 11 J1
  TOOT SW17 ... 30 B7
Long Lodge Dr WOT/HER KT12 ... 60 F2
Longmead GU GU1 ... 117 M8
Longmead Cl CTHM CR3 ... 108 B6
Longmeadow FRIM GU16 ... 73 J6
  GT/LBKH KT23 ... 101 J7
Long Meadow Cl BECK BR3 ... 51 M7
Longmead Rd HOR/WEW KT19 ... 64 B8
  THDIT KT7 ... 44 B7
  TOOT SW17 ... 30 C6
Longmere Gdns
  KWD/TDW/WH KT20 ... 104 F1
Longmere Rd CRAWW RH11 ... 212 A1
Longmore Rd WOT/HER KT12 ... 61 H3
Longpoles Rd CRAN GU6 ... 185 J7
Long Reach EHSLY KT24 ... 99 L6
Longridge Gv
  WOKS/MYFD GU22 ... 78 C4
Longs Cl WOKS/MYFD GU22 ... 78 D6
Longsdon Wy CTHM CR3 ... 108 D6
Long Shaw LHD/OX KT22 ... 102 D1
Longshot La BRAK RG12 ... 34 B2
Longside Cl EGH TW20 ... 39 M1
Longstone Rd TOOT SW17 ... 30 E6
Longthornton Rd
  STRHM/NOR SW16 ... 48 F2
Longton Av SYD SE26 ... 32 D5
Longton Gv SYD SE26 ... 32 D5
Long Wk KWD/TDW/WH KT20 ... 105 G1
  NWMAL KT3 ... 45 M3
The Long Wk WDSR SL4 ... 20 A2
Longwater Rd BRAK RG12 ... 34 F6
Longwood Ct WPK KT4 ... 64 D1
Longwood Dr PUT/ROE SW15 ... 19 K8
Longwood Rd PUR/KEN CR8 ... 88 A6
Longwood Vw CRAWE RH10 ... 212 D6
Lonsdale Gdns
  STRHM/NOR SW16 ... 49 J4
Lonsdale Ms RCH/KEW TW9 ... 18 D3
Lonsdale Rd BARN SW13 ... 19 J2
  DORK RH4 ... 144 E1
  SNWD SE25 ... 50 E4
  SWTR KT13 ... 59 K6
Loop Rd EPSOM KT18 ... 83 M6

WOKS/MYFD GU22 ... 97 J2
Loppets Rd CRAWE RH10 ... 212 C5
Loraine Gdns ASHTD KT21 ... 83 H7
Loraine Rd CHSWK W4 ... 18 E1
Lord Chancellor Wk
  KUTN/CMB KT2 ... 45 M1
Lord Knyvett Cl
  STWL/WRAY TW19 ... 14 A8
Lord Knyvetts Ct
  STWL/WRAY TW19 ... 14 B8
Lordsbury Fld WLGTN SM6 ... 66 F8
Lords Cl DUL SE21 ... 31 M3
  FELT TW13 ... 25 H3
Lordsgrove Cl
  KWD/TDW/WH KT20 ... 104 E2
Lordshill Rd SHGR GU5 ... 162 A6
Lordship La DUL SE21 ... 32 D2
Loretto Cl CRAN GU6 ... 185 K6
Lorian Dr REIG RH2 ... 125 M7
Loriners CRAWE RH10 ... 212 A6
Loring Rd ISLW TW7 ... 17 J4
Lorne Av CROY/NA CR0 ... 51 G7
Lorne Gdns CROY/NA CR0 ... 51 G7
  WOKN/KNAP GU21 ... 96 A1
Lorne Rd RCHPK/HAM TW10 ... 18 C2
The Lorne GT/LBKH KT23 ... 101 K8
Lorraine Rd CBLY GU15 ... 73 J1
Lory Rdg BAGS GU19 ... 54 B5
Loseberry Rd ESH/CLAY KT10 ... 62 A4
Loseley Rd RGODL GU7 ... 160 B1
Lothian Cl CHOB/PIR GU24 ... 94 D3
Lothian Wd
  KWD/TDW/WH KT20 ... 104 E4
  KUTN/CMB KT2 ... 3 H4
Lotus Rd BH/WHM TN16 ... 91 M8
Loubet St TOOT SW17 ... 30 C7
Loudwater Cl SUN TW16 ... 42 D4
Loughborough BRAK RG12 ... 35 H6
Louise Margaret Rd ALDT GU11 ... 112 E7
Louis Flds RGUW GU3 ... 115 M4
Louisville Rd TOOT SW17 ... 30 D4
Lovedean Ct BRAK RG12 ... 35 H6
Lovekyn Cl KUTN/CMB KT2 ... 2 F6
Lovelace Cl EHSLY KT24 ... 100 D5
Lovelace Dr WOKS/MYFD GU22 ... 78 B6
Lovelace Gdns SURB KT6 ... 45 G7
  WOT/HER KT12 ... 60 F4
Lovelace Rd BRAK RG12 ... 34 B4
  DUL SE21 ... 31 M3
  SURB KT6 ... 44 F7
Loveletts CRAWW RH11 ... 211 K4
Lovell Rd RCHPK/HAM TW10 ... 26 F4
Lovells Cl LTWR GU18 ... 54 E8
Lovelock Cl PUR/KEN CR8 ... 87 M7
Lovers La NFNM GU10 ... 177 M2
Lovibonds Av ORP BR6 ... 71 L2
Lowbury BRAK RG12 ... 35 H4
Lowburys DORK RH4 ... 144 D5
Lowdells Cl EGRIN RH19 ... 195 M5
Lowdells Dr EGRIN RH19 ... 196 A5
Lowdells La EGRIN RH19 ... 195 M6
Lower Addiscombe Rd
  CROY/NA CR0 ... 4 F3
Lower Barn Rd PUR/KEN CR8 ... 229 J4
Lower Barn Rd PUR/KEN CR8 ... 87 M2
Lower Breache Rd CRAN GU6 ... 186 D5
Lower Bridge Rd REDH RH1 ... 126 C8
Lower Broadmoor Rd
  CWTH RG45 ... 52 A5
Lower Church La FNM GU9 ... 133 L7
Lower Church St CROY/NA CR0 ... 4 B6
Lower Common South
  PUT/ROE SW15 ... 19 L5
Lower Coombe St CROY/NA CR0 ... 4 C9
Lower Ct HOR/WEW KT19 ... 84 A1
Lower Court Rd HOR/WEW KT19 ... 83 M1
Lower Dene EGRIN RH19 ... 196 D8
Lower Downs Rd RYNPK SW20 ... 47 G1
Lower Dunnymans
  BNSTD SM7 ... 85 J4
Lower Eashing RGODL GU7 ... 159 H5
Lower Edgeborough Rd GU GU1 ... 9 L5
Lower Farm Rd EHSLY KT24 ... 100 E6
Lower Farnham Rd ALDT GU11 ... 134 F2
Lower Green Rd ESH/CLAY KT10 ... 61 L1
Lower Gn West MTCM CR4 ... 48 B3
Lower Grove Rd
  RCHPK/HAM TW10 ... 18 C8
Lower Guildford Rd
  WOKN/KNAP GU21 ... 76 A7
Lower Ham La MFD/CHID GU8 ... 158 B5
Lower Hampton Rd SUN TW16 ... 43 G2
Lower Ham Rd KUTN/CMB KT2 ... 27 G7
Lower Hanger HASM GU27 ... 218 F3
Lower Hill Rd HOR/WEW KT19 ... 83 L2
Lower House Rd
  MFD/CHID GU8 ... 180 C8
Lower Manor Rd
  MFD/CHID GU8 ... 159 H8
  RGODL GU7 ... 160 B3
Lower Marsh La KUT KT1 ... 45 J4
Lower Mere EGRIN RH19 ... 216 C1
Lower Mill Fld BAGS GU19 ... 54 A7
Lower Morden La MRDN SM4 ... 47 H6
Lower Mortlake Rd
  RCH/KEW TW9 ... 18 B6
Lower Moushill La
  MFD/CHID GU8 ... 159 G8
Lower Newport Rd ASHV GU12 ... 113 G8
Lower Northfield BNSTD SM7 ... 85 J4
Lower Park Rd BNSTD SM7 ... 86 B8
Lower Peryers EHSLY KT24 ... 120 B2
Lower Pillory Down CAR SM5 ... 86 D3
Lower Richmond Rd
  MORT/ESHN SW14 ... 18 F5
  PUT/ROE SW15 ... 19 M5
  RCH/KEW TW9 ... 18 D5
Lower Rd GT/LBKH KT23 ... 101 J8
  HASM GU27 ... 200 C7

LHD/OX KT22 ... 102 A5
PUR/KEN CR8 ... 87 L3
REDH RH2 ... 148 A2
SUT SM1 ... 66 A4
Lower Sandfields
  RPLY/SEND GU23 ... 98 A5
Lower Sawleywood
  BNSTD SM7 ... 85 J4
Lower Shott GT/LBKH KT23 ... 101 L8
Lower South St RGODL GU7 ... 160 A5
Lower South Vw FNM GU9 ... 133 M6
Lower St HASM GU27 ... 219 L3
  SHGR GU5 ... 141 K5
Lower Sunbury Rd HPTN TW12 ... 43 J2
Lower Tanbridge Wy
  HORS RH12 ... 228 E7
Lower Teddington Rd KUT KT1 ... 2 C5
Lower Terrace Rd FARN GU14 ... 112 D1
Lower Village Rd ASC SL5 ... 36 F5
Lower Weybourne La FNM GU9 ... 134 C3
Lower Wood Rd ESH/CLAY KT10 ... 62 D5
Lowfield Cl LTWR GU18 ... 74 D1
Lowfield Heath Rd HORL RH6 ... 191 J3
Lowfield Rd SWTR RH13 ... 227 G6
Lowfield Wy HORL RH6 ... 192 B4
Lowicks Rd RFNM GU10 ... 178 E3
Lowlands Rd STWL/WRAY TW19 ... 14 A7
Low La FNM GU9 ... 134 E3
Lowry Cl SHST GU47 ... 72 A3
Lowry Crs MTCM CR4 ... 48 B2
Lowther Hl FSTH SE23 ... 33 H1
Lowther Rd BARN SW13 ... 19 J3
  KUTN/CMB KT2 ... 3 H3
Loxford Rd CTHM CR3 ... 108 C7
Loxford Wy CTHM CR3 ... 108 C7
Loxley Cl SYD SE26 ... 33 G6
Loxley Rd HPTN TW12 ... 25 J3
  WAND/EARL SW18 ... 30 A2
Loxton Rd FSTH SE23 ... 33 G2
Loxwood Cl EBED/NFELT TW14 ... 24 A2
Loxwood Rd BIL RH14 ... 223 K7
  BIL RH14 ... 225 G5
  CRAN GU6 ... 224 C2
Loxwood Wk CRAWW RH11 ... 211 J2
Lucan Dr STA TW18 ... 23 C8
Lucas Cl EGRIN RH19 ... 196 C8
Lucas Fld HASM GU27 ... 219 H3
Lucas Green Rd CHOB/PIR GU24 ... 75 G5
Lucas Rd HORS RH12 ... 228 B1
  PGE/AN SE20 ... 32 F7
Lucerne Cl WOKS/MYFD GU22 ... 97 H1
Lucerne Dr CRAWE RH10 ... 213 G5
Lucerne Rd THHTH CR7 ... 49 L5
Lucie Av ASHF TW15 ... 23 L7
Lucien Rd TOOT SW17 ... 30 D5
  WAND/EARL SW18 ... 29 M2
Lucilina Dr EDEN TN8 ... 175 M1
Luddington Av EGH TW20 ... 39 J2
Ludford Cl CROY/NA CR0 ... 4 A9
Ludlow BRAK RG12 ... 34 E7
Ludlow Cl FRIM GU16 ... 93 K2
Ludlow Rd FELT TW13 ... 24 D4
  GUW GU2 ... 8 D6
Ludovick Wk PUT/ROE SW15 ... 19 H6
Luke Rd ALDT GU11 ... 134 B1
Luke Rd East FNM GU9 ... 134 B1
Lullarook Cl BH/WHM TN16 ... 90 F6
Lullington Rd PGE/AN SE20 ... 32 D8
Lulworth Av HEST TW5 ... 16 E4
Lulworth Cl CRAWW RH11 ... 211 K6
  FARN GU14 ... 92 C6
Lulworth Crs MTCM CR4 ... 48 B2
Lumley Gdns CHEAM SM3 ... 65 H4
Lumley Rd CHEAM SM3 ... 65 H5
  HORL RH6 ... 170 D6
Lunar Cl BH/WHM TN16 ... 91 G6
Luna Rd THHTH CR7 ... 49 M3
Lundy Cl CRAWW RH11 ... 211 M6
Lunghurst Rd CTHM CR3 ... 109 K3
Lunham Rd NRWD SE19 ... 32 B7
Lupin Cl BAGS GU19 ... 53 M8
  BRXS/STRHM SW2 ... 31 L3
  CROY/NA CR0 ... 51 G8
Lushington Dr COB KT11 ... 80 E4
Lushington Rd CAT SE6 ... 33 L6
Lusted Hall La BH/WHM TN16 ... 110 F2
Lusteds Cl DORK RH4 ... 144 F5
Luttrell Av PUT/ROE SW15 ... 19 L7
Lutwyche Rd FSTH SE23 ... 33 J3
Lutyens Cl CRAWW RH11 ... 211 H5
Luxford Cl HORS RH12 ... 229 J4
Luxfords La EGRIN RH19 ... 216 E4
  EGRIN RH19 ... 216 E3
Luxted Rd ORP BR6 ... 91 K2
Lyall Av DUL SE21 ... 32 B5
Lyall Pl FNM GU9 ... 133 L2
Lych Wy WOKN/KNAP GU21 ... 6 B4
Lyconby Gdns CROY/NA CR0 ... 51 H7
Lydbury BRAK RG12 ... 35 J5
Lydden Gv WAND/EARL SW18 ... 29 L1
Lydden Rd WAND/EARL SW18 ... 29 L1
Lydele Cl WOKN/KNAP GU21 ... 6 F1
Lydford Cl FARN GU14 ... 92 D2
  FRIM GU16 ... 93 K2
Lydhurst Av BRXS/STRHM SW2 ... 31 J3
Lydney BRAK RG12 ... 34 F7
Lydney Cl WIM/MER SW19 ... 29 H5
Lye Copse Av FARN GU14 ... 92 E1
Lyefield La CRAN GU6 ... 186 F3
The Lye KWD/TDW/WH KT20 ... 104 F4
Lyfield COB KT11 ... 81 L4
Lyford Rd WAND/EARL SW18 ... 30 A1
Lyle Cl MTCM CR4 ... 48 D7
Lymbourne Cl BELMT SM2 ... 65 K8
Lymden Gdns REIG RH2 ... 147 L2
Lymer Av NRWD SE19 ... 32 C6
Lyme Regis Rd BNSTD SM7 ... 85 J7
Lymescote Gdns SUT SM1 ... 65 K1
Lyminge Gdns
  WAND/EARL SW18 ... 30 B2
Lymington Cl STRHM/NOR SW16 ... 49 G2
Lymington Gdns
  HOR/WEW KT19 ... 64 C4
Lynchen Cl HEST TW5 ... 15 L3
Lynchford La FARN GU14 ... 93 H8
Lynchford Rd ALDT GU11 ... 112 F7
  FARN GU14 ... 112 F1
Lynch Rd FNM GU9 ... 134 A7

Lyncroft Gdns EW KT17 ... 64 C7
  HSLW TW3 ... 16 F7
Lyndale Hampton Court Wy
  ESH/CLAY KT10 ... 44 B7
Lyndale Rd REDH RH1 ... 126 C5
Lyndhurst Av BRYLDS KT5 ... 45 L8
  FNM GU9 ... 134 F3
  STRHM/NOR SW16 ... 49 G2
  SUN TW16 ... 42 D3
  WHTN TW2 ... 25 J2
Lyndhurst Cl BRAK RG12 ... 35 K3
  CRAWW RH11 ... 212 A4
  CROY/NA CR0 ... 5 J8
  ORP BR6 ... 71 L3
Lyndhurst Dr NWMAL KT3 ... 46 B6
Lyndhurst Farm Cl EGRIN RH19 ... 195 G5
Lyndhurst Rd ASC SL5 ... 36 D4
  COUL/CHIP CR5 ... 86 D6
  REIG RH2 ... 147 K3
  THHTH CR7 ... 49 K4
Lyndhurst Wy BELMT SM2 ... 65 K6
  CHERT KT16 ... 58 B1
Lyndon Av WLGTN SM6 ... 66 D2
Lyndon Yd TOOT SW17 ... 29 L5
Lyne Cl VW GU25 ... 39 J6
Lyne Crossing Rd CHERT KT16 ... 39 K6
Lynegrove Av ASHF TW15 ... 23 M6
Lyne La CHERT KT16 ... 39 J6
  VW GU25 ... 39 G6
Lyne Rd VW GU25 ... 39 G6
Lynmead Cl EDEN TN8 ... 153 L5
Lynmouth Av MRDN SM4 ... 47 G7
Lynmouth Gdns HEST TW5 ... 16 A3
Lynn Cl ASHF TW15 ... 24 A6
Lynne Cl SAND/SEL CR2 ... 88 F1
Lynne Wk ESH/CLAY KT10 ... 61 M4
Lynn Rd BAL SW12 ... 30 E1
Lynn Wk REIG RH2 ... 147 L4
Lynn Wy FARN GU14 ... 92 C2
Lynscott Wy SAND/SEL CR2 ... 67 L7
Lynsted Ct BECK BR3 ... 51 H2
Lynton Cl CHSGTN KT9 ... 63 H3
  FNM GU9 ... 10 C5
  ISLW TW7 ... 17 J6
Lynton Park Av EGRIN RH19 ... 196 D7
Lynton Rd CROY/NA CR0 ... 49 K6
  NWMAL KT3 ... 46 A5
Lynwick St HORS RH12 ... 206 A8
Lynwood GUW GU2 ... 8 C5
Lynwood Av COUL/CHIP CR5 ... 86 E6
  EGH TW20 ... 21 H7
  EW KT17 ... 84 B4
Lynwood Cl WOKN/KNAP GU21 ... 78 A3
Lynwood Ct HORS RH12 ... 228 F6
Lynwood Crs ASC SL5 ... 37 H6
Lynwood Dr FRIM GU16 ... 93 K6
  WPK KT4 ... 64 D1
Lynwood Gdns CROY/NA CR0 ... 67 J3
Lynwood Rd EW KT17 ... 84 C4
  REDH RH1 ... 126 D6
  THDIT KT7 ... 62 C1
  TOOT SW17 ... 30 C4

M

Mabbotts
  KWD/TDW/WH KT20 ... 105 G3
Mabel St WOKN/KNAP GU21 ... 6 A7
Maberley Crs NRWD SE19 ... 32 D6
Maberley Rd BECK BR3 ... 51 G3
  NRWD SE19 ... 50 C1
Macaulay Av ESH/CLAY KT10 ... 62 B1
Macaulay Rd CTHM CR3 ... 108 B4
Macbeth Ct BNFD RG42 ... 35 H1
Macclesfield Rd SNWD SE25 ... 50 E5
Macdonald Rd FNM GU9 ... 133 L2
  LTWR GU18 ... 74 C1
Macfarlane La ISLW TW7 ... 17 J1
Mackenzie Rd BECK BR3 ... 51 H1
Mackie Rd BRXS/STRHM SW2 ... 31 K1
Mackies Hl SHGR GU5 ... 164 A2
Macleod Rd SWTR RH13 ... 229 H8
Mada Rd ORP BR6 ... 71 L2
Maddison Rd TEDD TW11 ... 26 C7
Maddox La GT/LBKH KT23 ... 101 H6
Maddox Pk GT/LBKH KT23 ... 101 H6
Madehurst Ct CRAWW RH11 ... 211 J6
Madeira Av HORS RH12 ... 228 F7
Madeira Crs BF/WBF KT14 ... 78 C3
Madeira Rd BF/WBF KT14 ... 78 C3
  MTCM CR4 ... 48 C4
  STRHM/NOR SW16 ... 31 H6
Madeira Wk EPSOM KT18 ... 84 H6
  REIG RH2 ... 126 A7
Madeline Rd PGE/AN SE20 ... 32 D8

Madgehole La SHGR GU5 ... 162 E5
Madingley BRAK RG12 ... 34 E8
Madox Brown End SHST GU47 ... 72 E5
Madrid Rd BARN SW13 ... 19 K3
  GUW GU2 ... 8 C6
Maesmaur Rd BH/WHM TN16 ... 111 G3
Mafeking Av BTFD TW8 ... 18 A1
Mafeking Rd STWL/WRAY TW19 ... 21 L3
Magazine Pl LHD/OX KT22 ... 102 E4
Magazine Rd CTHM CR3 ... 107 L4
  FARN GU14 ... 112 A1
Magdala Rd ISLW TW7 ... 17 K5
  SAND/SEL CR2 ... 68 A6
Magdalen Cl BF/WBF KT14 ... 79 H4
Magdalen Crs BF/WBF KT14 ... 79 H4
Magdalene Cl CRAWE RH10 ... 192 F8
Magdalene Rd SHPTN TW17 ... 41 J3
  SHST GU47 ... 52 C7
Magdalen Rd WAND/EARL SW18 ... 29 M2
Magna Carta La
  STWL/WRAY TW19 ... 21 G2
Magna Rd EGH TW20 ... 20 E7
Magnolia Cl KUTN/CMB KT2 ... 3 M1
  SHST GU47 ... 52 A8
Magnolia Dr BH/WHM TN16 ... 91 G6
Magnolia Rd CHSWK W4 ... 18 E1
Magnolia Wy HOR/WEW KT19 ... 63 M4
  RDKG RH5 ... 145 G5
Magpie Cl COUL/CHIP CR5 ... 86 F8
  NFNM GU10 ... 133 G1
Maguire Dr FRIM GU16 ... 73 M6
  RCHPK/HAM TW10 ... 26 F5
Mahonia Cl CHOB/PIR GU24 ... 75 J3
Maida Rd ALDT GU11 ... 112 E5
Maidenbower Dr CRAWE RH10 ... 212 F5
Maidenbower La
  CRAWE RH10 ... 212 F5
Maidenbower Pl
  CRAWE RH10 ... 212 F5
Maiden La CRAWW RH11 ... 211 M1
Maidenshaw Rd HOR/WEW KT19 ... 84 A2
Main Gate Rd FARN GU14 ... 92 E7
Mainprize Rd BRAK RG12 ... 35 H1
Main Rd BH/WHM TN16 ... 90 F5
  EDEN TN8 ... 131 M8
  EDEN TN8 ... 153 L4
Mainstone Cl FRIM GU16 ... 93 M2
Mainstone Crs CHOB/PIR GU24 ... 95 G3
Mainstone Rd CHOB/PIR GU24 ... 75 J6
Main St ADL/WDHM KT15 ... 59 H2
  FELT TW13 ... 25 G6
Maise Webster Cl
  STWL/WRAY TW19 ... 23 G1
Maitland Cl BF/WBF KT14 ... 78 D3
  HSLWW TW4 ... 16 C5
  WOT/HER KT12 ... 61 H1
Maitland Rd FARN GU14 ... 112 C1
  SYD SE26 ... 33 G7
Maitlands Cl NFNM GU10 ... 135 H3
Maizecroft HORL RH6 ... 170 F5
Major's Farm Rd DTCH/LGLY SL3 ... 12 A2
Major's Hl CRAWE RH10 ... 214 A5
Malacca Farm RGUE GU4 ... 118 E2
Malan Cl BH/WHM TN16 ... 91 H7
Malbrook Rd PUT/ROE SW15 ... 19 L6
Malcolm Dr SURB KT6 ... 45 G8
Malcolm Gdns HORL RH6 ... 170 A8
Malcolm Rd COUL/CHIP CR5 ... 87 G5
  PGE/AN SE20 ... 32 F8
  SNWD SE25 ... 50 D6
  WIM/MER SW19 ... 29 H7
Malden Av SNWD SE25 ... 50 E4
Malden Green Av WPK KT4 ... 46 C8
Malden Hl NWMAL KT3 ... 46 C4
Malden Hill Gdns NWMAL KT3 ... 46 C3
Malden Pk NWMAL KT3 ... 46 C6
Malden Rd CHEAM SM3 ... 65 G3
  NWMAL KT3 ... 46 C7
  WPK KT4 ... 46 C7
Malden Wy NWMAL KT3 ... 46 C5
Malden Way (Kingston by Pass)
  NWMAL KT3 ... 46 B6
Maldon Rd WLGTN SM6 ... 66 E4
Malet Cl EGH TW20 ... 22 A7
Maley Av WNWD SE27 ... 31 L3
Malham Cl CRAWE RH10 ... 212 F6
Malham Fell BRAK RG12 ... 34 D4
Malham Rd FSTH SE23 ... 33 G2
Mallard Cl ASHV GU12 ... 113 J7
  HASM GU27 ... 219 H3
  HORL RH6 ... 170 D4
  HORS RH12 ... 228 F4
  HSLWW TW4 ... 25 K1
  REDH RH1 ... 126 D5
  TWK TW1 ... 26 D4
Mallard Rd SAND/SEL CR2 ... 69 G8
Mallard's Reach WEY KT13 ... 60 L3
The Mallards STA TW18 ... 40 E2
Mallards Wy LTWR GU18 ... 74 D1
Mallard Wk CROY/NA CR0 ... 51 G5
Mallard Wy WLGTN SM6 ... 66 F7
Malling Cl CROY/NA CR0 ... 50 F6
Malling Gdns MRDN SM4 ... 47 M6
Mallow Cl CROY/NA CR0 ... 51 G8
  HORS RH12 ... 229 H3
  KWD/TDW/WH KT20 ... 104 E1
Mallow Crs RGUE GU4 ... 117 L5
Mallowdale Rd BRAK RG12 ... 35 H7
The Mall MORT/ESHN SW14 ... 18 F7
  SURB KT6 ... 45 G5
Malmains Wy BECK BR3 ... 51 M4
Malmesbury Rd MRDN SM4 ... 47 M7
Malmstone Av REDH RH1 ... 126 C4
Malta Rd FRIM GU16 ... 94 A1
Maltby Rd CHSGTN KT9 ... 63 K5
Malt Hl EGH TW20 ... 21 H6
Malt House Cl WDSR SL4 ... 20 C1
Malthouse Dr FELT TW13 ... 25 G6
Malthouse La CHOB/PIR GU24 ... 75 J2
  RGUW GU3 ... 95 M6
Malthouse Md MFD/CHID GU8 ... 181 J4
The Maltings BF/WBF KT14 ... 79 H3
  LIPH GU30 ... 218 A5
  OXTED RH8 ... 130 C5
  STA TW18 ... 22 B5

Malting Wy ISLW TW7 ... 17 J5
Maltlhouse La MFD/CHID GU8 ... 181 M8
Malus Cl ADL/WDHM KT15 ... 58 C6
Malus Dr ADL/WDHM KT15 ... 58 C6
Malvern Cl CHERT KT16 ... 57 M5 2
MTCM CR4 ... 48 F3
SURB KT6 ... 45 H8
Malvern Dr FELT TW13 ... 25 G6 2
Malvern Rd CRAWW RH11 ... 211 M5
FARN GU14 ... 92 A2
HPTN TW12 ... 43 K1
HYS/HAR UB3 ... 15 H2
SURB KT6 ... 63 H1
THHTH CR7 ... 49 K4
The Malyons SHPTN TW17 ... 42 A6 3
Manbre Rd HMSMTH W6 ... 19 M1
Manchester Rd THHTH CR7 ... 49 M3
Mandeville Cl GUW GU2 ... 116 D5
WIM/MER SW19 ... 29 H8
Mandeville Dr SURB KT6 ... 45 G8
Mandeville Rd ISLW TW7 ... 17 K4
SHPTN TW17 ... 41 K5
Mandora Rd ALDT GU11 ... 112 E5
Mandrake Rd TOOT SW17 ... 30 C4
Manfield Pk CRAN GU6 ... 184 E4
Manfield Rd ASHV GU12 ... 113 K7
Mangles Rd GU GU1 ... 117 G6
Manley Bridge Rd NFNM GU10 ... 155 H5
Mannamead EPSOM KT18 ... 104 B1
Mannamead Cl EPSOM KT18 ... 104 B1 1
Mann Cl CROY/NA CR0 ... 4 C7
Manning Cl EGRIN RH19 ... 196 A7
Manning Pl
RCHPK/HAM TW10 ... 18 C8 2
Mannings Cl CRAWE RH10 ... 193 G8
Manningtree Cl WIM/MER SW19 ... 29 H2
Mann's Cl ISLW TW7 ... 17 J7
Manoel Rd WHTN TW2 ... 25 M3
Manor Av CTHM CR3 ... 108 B6
HSLWW TW4 ... 16 A5
Manor Cha WEY KT13 ... 59 L4
Manor Cl EHSLY KT24 ... 120 B2
GDST RH9 ... 151 J4
HASM GU27 ... 219 H3
HORL RH6 ... 170 C6
NFNM GU10 ... 135 J2
WARL CR6 ... 89 H7
WOKS/MYFD GU22 ... 78 C6
WPK KT4 ... 46 B8
Manor Ct WEY KT13 ... 59 L3
Manor Crs BF/WBF KT14 ... 79 J3
BRYLDS KT5 ... 45 K6
CHOB/PIR GU24 ... 95 C2
GUW GU2 ... 116 E6
Manorcrofts Rd EGH TW20 ... 21 K7
Manordene Cl THDIT KT7 ... 44 D8 4
Manor Dr ADL/WDHM KT15 ... 58 D8
BRYLDS KT5 ... 45 K6
ESH/CLAY KT10 ... 62 C2
FELT TW13 ... 25 G6 3
HOR/WEW KT19 ... 64 B5
HORL RH6 ... 170 C6
SUN TW16 ... 42 D2
Manor Dr North NWMAL KT3 ... 46 A7
WPK KT4 ... 46 B8
The Manor Dr WPK KT4 ... 46 B8
Manor Farm Av SHPTN TW17 ... 41 L6
Manor Farm Cl ASHV GU12 ... 113 J8 1
Manor Farm La EGH TW20 ... 21 K6
Manor Farm Rd
STRHM/NOR SW16 ... 49 K2 2
Manorfields CRAWW RH11 ... 211 G7
Manor Flds LIPH GU30 ... 218 A5
SWTR RH13 ... 229 K5
Manor Gdns EHSLY KT24 ... 121 G2
GUW GU2 ... 116 E6
HPTN TW12 ... 25 L8
NFNM GU10 ... 156 A4
RCH/KEW TW9 ... 18 C6
RGODL GU7 ... 160 B2 1
RYNPK SW20 ... 47 J2
SAND/SEL CR2 ... 68 C5
SUN TW16 ... 42 D1
Manorgate Rd KUTN/CMB KT2 ... 3 J5
Manor Green Rd
HOR/WEW KT19 ... 83 M2
Manor Gv BECK BR3 ... 51 L2
RCH/KEW TW9 ... 18 D6
Manor Hl BNSTD SM7 ... 86 C5
Manor House Ct EPSOM KT18 ... 83 M3 2
Manor House Gdns EDEN TN8 ... 153 M8
Manorhouse La GT/LBKH KT23 ... 101 H8
Manor House Wy ISLW TW7 ... 17 L5 1
Manor La FELT TW13 ... 24 D3
HYS/HAR UB3 ... 15 G1
KWD/TDW/WH KT20 ... 125 K3
SHGR GU5 ... 162 B6
SUN TW16 ... 42 D2
SUT SM1 ... 65 M4
Manor Lea Rd MFD/CHID GU8 ... 159 H7
Manor Leaze EGH TW20 ... 21 L6
Manor Mt FSTH SE23 ... 32 F2
Manor Pk RCH/KEW TW9 ... 18 C6
STA TW18 ... 22 A4
Manor Park Cl WWKM BR4 ... 51 L8
Manor Park Rd SUT SM1 ... 65 M4
WWKM BR4 ... 51 L8
Manor Pl EBED/NFELT TW14 ... 24 D2
GT/LBKH KT23 ... 101 K8
MTCM CR4 ... 48 F3 1
STA TW18 ... 22 E6
SUT SM1 ... 65 L4
Manor Rd ALDT GU11 ... 134 D1
ASHF TW15 ... 23 J6
ASHV GU12 ... 113 J8
BECK BR3 ... 51 K2
BELMT SM2 ... 65 J6
BH/WHM TN16 ... 111 H2
E/WMO/HCT KT8 ... 44 A4
EDEN TN8 ... 153 L8
EGRIN RH19 ... 195 M7
FARN GU14 ... 93 C6
FNM GU9 ... 134 B5
GUW GU2 ... 116 E6
HORS RH12 ... 229 J4
MTCM CR4 ... 48 F3
NFNM GU10 ... 135 J1
RCH/KEW TW9 ... 18 C5
REDH RH1 ... 126 F3
REIG RH2 ... 125 J6
RPLY/SEND GU23 ... 98 C5
RYNPK SW20 ... 47 J2
SNWD SE25 ... 50 D3
TEDD TW11 ... 26 D6
WHTN TW2 ... 25 M3
WLGTN SM6 ... 66 E4
WOT/HER KT12 ... 42 C7
WWKM BR4 ... 69 L1
Manor Rd North ESH/CLAY KT10 ... 62 C2
WLGTN SM6 ... 66 E3
Manor Rd South ESH/CLAY KT10 ... 62 B3
Manor Royal CRAWE RH10 ... 192 B8
Manorside Cl NFNM GU10 ... 135 J1 1
The Manor MFD/CHID GU8 ... 159 J8
Manor Wk ASHV GU12 ... 112 E8
WEY KT13 ... 59 L4
Manor Wy BAGS GU19 ... 54 B7
BECK BR3 ... 51 K3
BNSTD SM7 ... 86 C6
EGH TW20 ... 21 J7
GUW GU2 ... 138 B3
LHD/OX KT22 ... 81 M6
MTCM CR4 ... 48 F3
PUR/KEN CR8 ... 87 H2
SAND/SEL CR2 ... 68 B5
WOKS/MYFD GU22 ... 97 L2
WPK KT4 ... 46 B8
The Manor Wy WLGTN SM6 ... 66 E3
Manor Wood Rd PUR/KEN CR8 ... 87 H3
Mansard Beeches TOOT SW17 ... 30 D6
Manse Cl HYS/HAR UB3 ... 15 G1
Mansel Cl GUW GU2 ... 116 E3
Mansell Wy CTHM CR3 ... 108 A4
Mansel Rd WIM/MER SW19 ... 29 H7
Mansfield Cl ASC SL5 ... 36 A2 1
Mansfield Crs BRAK RG12 ... 34 E6
Mansfield Dr REDH RH1 ... 127 G2
Mansfield Pl ASC SL5 ... 36 A2
SAND/SEL CR2 ... 68 A5 1
Mansfield Rd CHSGTN KT9 ... 62 F4
SAND/SEL CR2 ... 68 A5
Manship Rd MTCM CR4 ... 48 D1
Manston Cl PGE/AN SE20 ... 50 F1
Manston Dr BRAK RG12 ... 34 E6
Manston Gv KUTN/CMB KT2 ... 27 G6
Manston Rd RGUE GU4 ... 117 K4
Mantilla Rd TOOT SW17 ... 30 D5
Mantlet Cl STRHM/NOR SW16 ... 30 F8
Manville Gdns TOOT SW17 ... 30 E4 1
Manville Rd TOOT SW17 ... 30 D3
Manygate La SHPTN TW17 ... 41 M6
Many Gates BAL SW12 ... 30 E3
Maori Rd GU GU1 ... 9 M4
Maple Cl ASHV GU12 ... 113 J2
CRAWW RH11 ... 191 M8
CTHM CR3 ... 88 C7 2
HORS RH12 ... 229 K4
HPTN TW12 ... 25 J7
MTCM CR4 ... 48 E1
Maple Ct EGH TW20 ... 20 E7 2
NWMAL KT3 ... 46 A3
Mapledale Av CROY/NA CR0 ... 5 M7
Mapledrakes Cl CRAN GU6 ... 186 B4
Mapledrakes Rd CRAN GU6 ... 186 B4
Maple Dr EGRIN RH19 ... 196 D8
LTWR GU18 ... 74 C1
Maple Gdns ASHF TW15 ... 23 H3 1
Maple Gv BTFD TW8 ... 17 L2
GU GU1 ... 117 G6
WOKS/MYFD GU22 ... 97 H3
Maplehatch Cl RGODL GU7 ... 160 B7
Maplehurst LHD/OX KT22 ... 102 A5
Maplehurst Cl KUT KT1 ... 45 H4 2
Maple Leaf Cl FARN GU14 ... 92 C6 1
Maple Ms STRHM/NOR SW16 ... 31 J6
Maple Pl EW KT17 ... 85 G4 3
Maple Rd ASHTD KT21 ... 103 G1
CTHM CR3 ... 88 C7
PGE/AN SE20 ... 50 E1
REDH RH1 ... 148 C4
RPLY/SEND GU23 ... 98 D6
SURB KT6 ... 45 H5
Maplestead Rd
BRXS/STRHM SW2 ... 31 J1
The Maples BNSTD SM7 ... 85 L3
CHERT KT16 ... 57 L5
Maplethorpe Rd THHTH CR7 ... 49 K4
Maple Wk ASHV GU12 ... 113 M3 1
Maple Wy COUL/CHIP CR5 ... 106 E3
FELT TW13 ... 24 D4
Marble Hill Cl TWK TW1 ... 26 E1 1
Marble Hill Gdns TWK TW1 ... 26 E1
Marbles Wy
KWD/TDW/WH KT20 ... 105 G1
Marcheria Cl BRAK RG12 ... 34 E6 2
Marches Rd HORS RH12 ... 208 A5
The Marches HORS RH12 ... 208 E4
Marchmont Rd
RCHPK/HAM TW10 ... 18 C7 7
WLGTN SM6 ... 66 F7
March Rd TWK TW1 ... 26 D1 3
WEY KT13 ... 59 K4
Marchside Cl HEST TW5 ... 16 A3 2
Marcus Ct WOKS/MYFD GU22 ... 6 E7 3
Marcuse Rd CTHM CR3 ... 107 M5
Mardale CBLY GU15 ... 73 M5
Mardell Rd CROY/NA CR0 ... 51 G5
Marden Crs CROY/NA CR0 ... 49 J6
Marden Rd CROY/NA CR0 ... 49 J6
The Mardens CRAWW RH11 ... 211 L2
Mare Hl MFD/CHID GU8 ... 181 H4
Mare La MFD/CHID GU8 ... 182 E5
Mareschal Rd GUW GU2 ... 8 E8
Mareth Cl ALDT GU11 ... 112 E7
Marfleet Cl CAR SM5 ... 66 B1 2
Margaret Cl STA TW18 ... 23 G8
Margaret Lockwood Cl
KUT KT1 ... 45 J4 2
Margaret Rd GU GU1 ... 8 F5
Margaret Wy PUR/KEN CR8 ... 107 L1
Margery Gv
KWD/TDW/WH KT20 ... 125 H3
Margery La
KWD/TDW/WH KT20 ... 125 J3
Margin Dr WIM/MER SW19 ... 29 G6
Marham Gdns MRDN SM4 ... 47 M6 5
WAND/EARL SW18 ... 30 B2 3
Marian Rd STRHM/NOR SW16 ... 48 F1
Maria Theresa Cl NWMAL KT3 ... 46 A5 3
Mariette Wy WLGTN SM6 ... 67 H7
Marigold Ct GU GU1 ... 117 H5
Marigold Dr CHOB/PIR GU24 ... 75 K5 3
Marigold Wy CROY/NA CR0 ... 51 G8
Marina Av NWMAL KT3 ... 46 E6
Marina Cl CHERT KT16 ... 40 E8
Marina Wy TEDD TW11 ... 2 C2
Mariner Gdns RCHPK/HAM TW10 ... 26 E4
Mariners Dr RGUW GU3 ... 114 E6
Marion Av SHPTN TW17 ... 41 L5
Marion Rd CRAWE RH10 ... 212 E6
CROY/NA CR0 ... 49 M5
Marius Rd TOOT SW17 ... 30 D3
Marjoram Cl GUW GU2 ... 116 D4 1
Mark Cl HAYES BR2 ... 71 H3
Markedge La COUL/CHIP CR5 ... 106 C6
Markenfield Rd GU GU1 ... 9 G4
Markenhorn RGODL GU7 ... 160 A2 4
Market Field Rd REDH RH1 ... 126 C7 3
Marketfield Wy REDH RH1 ... 126 C8
Market Pl BTFD TW8 ... 17 M2
Market Rd RCH/KEW TW9 ... 18 D5
Market Sq BH/WHM TN16 ... 131 M1
HORS RH12 ... 228 F8 1
Market St BRAK RG12 ... 34 E2
GU GU1 ... 9 G6
Markfield Rd CTHM CR3 ... 108 E7
Markham Ct CBLY GU15 ... 73 G3 2
Markham Rd RDKG RH5 ... 188 F4
Markhole Cl HPTN TW12 ... 25 J8 1
Mark Oak La LHD/OX KT22 ... 101 K3
Marksbury Av RCH/KEW TW9 ... 18 D5
Marks Rd WARL CR6 ... 89 H8
Mark St REIG RH2 ... 125 L7 2
Markville Gdns CTHM CR3 ... 108 D7
Mark Wy RGODL GU7 ... 159 L1
The Markway SUN TW16 ... 42 F2
Markwell Cl SYD SE26 ... 32 E5 3
Markwick La MFD/CHID GU8 ... 182 E6
Marlborogh Rd ISLW TW7 ... 17 L2
Marlborough Cl
CRAWW RH11 ... 211 M7 4
HORS RH12 ... 229 G4 1
WIM/MER SW19 ... 30 B7 3
WOT/HER KT12 ... 61 G2 2
Marlborough Dr WEY KT13 ... 59 M2
Marlborough Ri CBLY GU15 ... 73 H3
Marlborough Rd ASHF TW15 ... 23 H6
DORK RH4 ... 144 E2
FELT TW13 ... 25 G3
HPTN TW12 ... 25 K7 5
RCHPK/HAM TW10 ... 18 B8
SAND/SEL CR2 ... 67 M6 1
SUT SM1 ... 65 K2
WIM/MER SW19 ... 30 B7
WOKN/KNAP GU21 ... 7 G4
The Marld ASHTD KT21 ... 83 J8
Marler Rd FSTH SE23 ... 33 J2
Marles La BIL RH14 ... 225 M8
Marley Cl ADL/WDHM KT15 ... 58 C5
Marley Combe Rd HASM GU27 ... 219 J4
Marley Hanger HASM GU27 ... 219 K6
Marley La HASM GU27 ... 219 H4
Marley Ri DORK RH4 ... 144 D5
Marlhurst EDEN TN8 ... 153 L5
Marlin Cl SUN TW16 ... 24 B7 2
Marlingdene Cl HPTN TW12 ... 25 K7
Marlings Cl CTHM CR3 ... 88 B7
Marlins Cl SUT SM1 ... 65 M4 1
Marlow Cl PGE/AN SE20 ... 50 E3
Marlow Ct CRAWW RH11 ... 212 A2 3
Marlow Crs TWK TW1 ... 17 J8
Marlow Dr CHEAM SM3 ... 65 G2
Marlowe Wy CROY/NA CR0 ... 67 H1
Marlow Rd PGE/AN SE20 ... 50 E3
Marlpit Av COUL/CHIP CR5 ... 87 H7
Marlpit Cl EDEN TN8 ... 153 M5
EGRIN RH19 ... 196 B6
Marlpit La COUL/CHIP CR5 ... 87 G6
Marlyns Cl RGUE GU4 ... 117 K4
Marlyns Dr RGUE GU4 ... 117 K5
Marmot Rd HSLWW TW4 ... 16 A5
Marnell Wy HSLWW TW4 ... 16 A5
Marneys Cl EPSOM KT18 ... 103 M1
Marnfield Crs BRXS/STRHM SW2 ... 31 J2
Marnham Pl ADL/WDHM KT15 ... 58 F3
Maroons Wy CAT SE6 ... 33 K6
Marrick Cl PUT/ROE SW15 ... 19 K6
Marriott Cl EBED/NFELT TW14 ... 15 G8
Marriott Lodge Cl
ADL/WDHM KT15 ... 58 F3
Marrowbrook Cl FARN GU14 ... 92 D6
Marrowbrook La FARN GU14 ... 92 C7
Marrowells WEY KT13 ... 60 B2
Marryat Pl WIM/MER SW19 ... 29 H5
Marryat Rd WIM/MER SW19 ... 29 G6
Marshall Cl FARN GU14 ... 92 C2
FRIM GU16 ... 74 A7 1
HSLWW TW4 ... 16 C7
SAND/SEL CR2 ... 88 D3
Marshall Pl ADL/WDHM KT15 ... 58 F7
Marshall Rd CRAWE RH10 ... 212 F5
RGODL GU7 ... 160 B3
SHST GU47 ... 72 A2
Marshalls Cl HOR/WEW KT19 ... 83 M3
Marshall's Rd SUT SM1 ... 65 L3 2
Marsh Av HOR/WEW KT19 ... 64 B8
MTCM CR4 ... 48 C2
Marsh Farm Rd WHTN TW2 ... 26 C2
Marsh Green Rd EDEN TN8 ... 175 L5
Marsh La ADL/WDHM KT15 ... 58 E3
Marshwood Rd LTWR GU18 ... 75 G1
Marston HOR/WEW KT19 ... 83 M1
Marston Av CHSGTN KT9 ... 63 H5
Marston Ct WOT/HER KT12 ... 42 F8 5
Marston Dr FARN GU14 ... 92 E2
WARL CR6 ... 89 H8
Marston Rd FNM GU9 ... 10 B1
TEDD TW11 ... 26 E6
WOKN/KNAP GU21 ... 76 E7
Marston Wy ASC SL5 ... 36 B2 2
NRWD SE19 ... 31 L8
Martel Cl CBLY GU15 ... 73 M2
Martell Rd DUL SE21 ... 32 A4
Martens Pl RGODL GU7 ... 160 B3 1
Martin Cl CRAWW RH11 ... 212 A1 3
SAND/SEL CR2 ... 89 G1
WARL CR6 ... 88 E6
Martin Crs CROY/NA CR0 ... 49 J8
Martindale MORT/ESHN SW14 ... 18 F7 1
Martindale Av CBLY GU15 ... 73 M6
Martindale Cl RGUE GU4 ... 118 A6 3
Martindale Rd BAL SW12 ... 30 E1
HSLWW TW4 ... 16 B5
WOKN/KNAP GU21 ... 76 C8
Martineau Cl ESH/CLAY KT10 ... 62 A3
Martineau Dr DORK RH4 ... 144 E4
Martingale Cl SUN TW16 ... 42 D4
Martingale Ct ALDT GU11 ... 112 B7
Martingales Cl
RCHPK/HAM TW10 ... 27 G4
Martin Gv WIM/MER SW19 ... 47 K3
Martin Rd GUW GU2 ... 116 D6
Martins Cl BLKW GU17 ... 72 A5
GU GU1 ... 117 M7
WWKM BR4 ... 70 A1
Martins La BRAK RG12 ... 35 H3
The Martins CRAWE RH10 ... 214 F1
SYD SE26 ... 32 E6 2
Martins Wd MFD/CHID GU8 ... 181 H2
Martinsyde WOKS/MYFD GU22 ... 7 M5 1
Martin Wy FRIM GU16 ... 73 H8
RYNPK SW20 ... 47 H3
WOKN/KNAP GU21 ... 76 D8
Martlets Cl HORS RH12 ... 228 F4
The Martlets CRAWE RH10 ... 212 B3
Marton Cl CAT SE6 ... 33 K4
The Marts HORS RH12 ... 226 A2
Martyns Pl EGRIN RH19 ... 216 D1
Martyr Rd GU GU1 ... 9 G6
Martyrs Av CRAWW RH11 ... 191 M8 3
Martyrs La WOKN/KNAP GU21 ... 77 L2
Marvell Cl CRAWE RH10 ... 212 F1
Marwell BH/WHM TN16 ... 111 L8
Marwell Cl WWKM BR4 ... 70 C1 1
Mary Adelaide Cl
PUT/ROE SW15 ... 28 B5 1
Maryhill Cl PUR/KEN CR8 ... 87 M7
Maryland Rd THHTH CR7 ... 49 L1
Maryland Wy SUN TW16 ... 42 D2
Mary Rd GU GU1 ... 8 F5
Mary Rose Cl HPTN TW12 ... 43 K1 2
Mary Rose Gdns CHSGTN KT9 ... 63 H3
Mary's Ter TWK TW1 ... 26 D1 1
Mary V RGODL GU7 ... 160 A7
Masefield Rd CRAWW RH11 ... 211 H6
FELT TW13 ... 25 J5 3
Masefield Vw ORP BR6 ... 71 M2
Masefield Wy STWL/WRAY TW19 ... 23 J2
Maskell Rd TOOT SW17 ... 29 M4
Mason Cl EGRIN RH19 ... 196 B7
HPTN TW12 ... 43 J1
RYNPK SW20 ... 47 G1 2
Masonic Hall Rd CHERT KT16 ... 40 C6
Mason Rd CRAWE RH10 ... 212 B5
FARN GU14 ... 92 B3
Mason's Av CROY/NA CR0 ... 4 D8
Mason's Bridge Rd REDH RH1 ... 148 E5
Masons Paddock DORK RH4 ... 122 D8 1
Mason's Pl MTCM CR4 ... 48 C1 2
Mason Wy ALDT GU11 ... 134 E2 3
Massetts Rd HORL RH6 ... 170 C7
Massingberd Wy TOOT SW17 ... 30 E5
Master Cl OXTED RH8 ... 130 B3
Maswell Park Crs HSLW TW3 ... 16 F7
Maswell Park Rd HSLW TW3 ... 16 E7 3
Matham Rd E/WMO/HCT KT8 ... 44 A5
Mathias Cl EPSOM KT18 ... 83 M3 3
Mathisen Wy DTCH/LGLY SL3 ... 13 H3
Matilda Cl NRWD SE19 ... 32 A8
Matlock Crs CHEAM SM3 ... 65 H3
Matlock Gdns CHEAM SM3 ... 65 H3
Matlock Pl SUT SM1 ... 65 H3 2
Matlock Rd CTHM CR3 ... 108 B4
Matlock Wy NWMAL KT3 ... 46 A1
Matthew Arnold Cl COB KT11 ... 80 D4
STA TW18 ... 22 F7 1
Matthew Ct MTCM CR4 ... 49 G5 1
Matthew Rd FNM GU9 ... 134 B1
Matthews Dr CRAWE RH10 ... 212 F7
Matthew's Gdns
CROY/NA CR0 ... 90 A1 1
Matthews La STA TW18 ... 22 C5 1
Matthews Rd CBLY GU15 ... 72 F1
Matthew's St REIG RH2 ... 147 K4
Matthey Pl CRAWE RH10 ... 193 G8
Maultway Cl CBLY GU15 ... 73 L1 1
Maultway Crs CBLY GU15 ... 73 L1
Maultway North CBLY GU15 ... 53 L8
The Maultway CBLY GU15 ... 73 M1
Maunsell Pk CRAWE RH10 ... 212 E3 1
Maurice Av CTHM CR3 ... 108 A4
Mavins Rd FNM GU9 ... 11 J3
Mavis Av HOR/WEW KT19 ... 64 B4
Mavis Cl HOR/WEW KT19 ... 64 B4
Mawbey Rd CHERT KT16 ... 58 A5 4
Mawson Cl RYNPK SW20 ... 47 H2
Mawson La CHSWK W4 ... 19 J1
Maxwell Cl CROY/NA CR0 ... 49 H8
Maxwell Dr BF/WBF KT14 ... 78 F1
Maxwell Rd ASHF TW15 ... 23 M7
Maxwell Wy CRAWE RH10 ... 192 D8
May Bate Av KUTN/CMB KT2 ... 2 D4
Maybelle Cl RDKG RH5 ... 167 G6 1
Mayberry Pl BRYLDS KT5 ... 45 J7 3
Maybourne Ri
WOKS/MYFD GU22 ... 97 G6
Maybury Cl FRIM GU16 ... 93 G1
KWD/TDW/WH KT20 ... 105 H1 1
Maybury Hl WOKN/KNAP GU21 ... 7 J3
WOKS/MYFD GU22 ... 7 K4
Maybury Rd WOKN/KNAP GU21 ... 7 G5
Maybury St TOOT SW17 ... 30 B6
May Cl CHSGTN KT9 ... 63 J5
RGODL GU7 ... 159 L7
SHST GU47 ... 72 A1
May Crs ASHV GU12 ... 113 H8
Maycross Av MRDN SM4 ... 47 J4
Mayday Rd THHTH CR7 ... 49 L6
Maydwell Av SWTR RH13 ... 226 E7
Mayefield Rd THHTH CR7 ... 49 J4
Mayell Cl LHD/OX KT22 ... 102 F5
Mayes Cl CRAWE RH10 ... 212 F4
WARL CR6 ... 89 G8
Mayes La HORS RH12 ... 208 B8
Mayfair Av WHTN TW2 ... 25 M1
WPK KT4 ... 46 D8
Mayfair Cl BECK BR3 ... 51 L1 2
SURB KT6 ... 45 H8
Mayfield CRAWE RH10 ... 213 G3
LING RH7 ... 174 D8
NFNM GU10 ... 155 J6
Mayfield Av ADL/WDHM KT15 ... 58 E8
Mayfield Cl ADL/WDHM KT15 ... 58 F8
ASHF TW15 ... 23 L7
FNM GU9 ... 134 E3 1
REDH RH1 ... 148 D6 1
THDIT KT7 ... 44 E8
WOT/HER KT12 ... 60 D3
Mayfield Crs THHTH CR7 ... 49 J4
Mayfield Gdns STA TW18 ... 22 C8
WOT/HER KT12 ... 60 D3
Mayfield Gn GT/LBKH KT23 ... 121 K1 1
Mayfield Rd BELMT SM2 ... 66 A5
CBLY GU15 ... 72 E8 1
FARN GU14 ... 92 C2
SAND/SEL CR2 ... 68 A7
WEY KT13 ... 59 J4
WIM/MER SW19 ... 47 J1
WOT/HER KT12 ... 60 D3
Mayflower Cl CRAWE RH10 ... 213 G4 3
Mayford Cl BAL SW12 ... 30 C1 2
BECK BR3 ... 51 G3 1
WOKS/MYFD GU22 ... 97 G4
Mayford Rd BAL SW12 ... 30 C1
Mayhurst Av WOKS/MYFD GU22 ... 7 L4
Mayhurst Cl WOKS/MYFD GU22 ... 7 L4
Mayhurst Crs WOKS/MYFD GU22 ... 7 L4
Maynooth Gdns MTCM CR4 ... 48 C7
Mayo Rd CROY/NA CR0 ... 50 A5
WOT/HER KT12 ... 42 D7
Mayow Rd SYD SE26 ... 33 G5
Maypole Rd EGRIN RH19 ... 196 A7
EGRIN RH19 ... 217 H3
May Rd WHTN TW2 ... 26 B2
Mayroyd Av SURB KT6 ... 63 K1 1
Mays Cl WEY KT13 ... 59 J8 1
Maysfield Rd RPLY/SEND GU23 ... 98 A5
Mays Gv RPLY/SEND GU23 ... 98 A5
Mays Rd HPTN TW12 ... 26 A6
Maytree Cl GU GU1 ... 116 E5
Maytree Ct MTCM CR4 ... 48 D3
Maytrees WOKN/KNAP GU21 ... 75 M7 2
Maywater Cl SAND/SEL CR2 ... 88 A1
Maywood Dr CBLY GU15 ... 73 L2
Maze Rd RCH/KEW TW9 ... 18 D2
Mcalmont Rdg RGODL GU7 ... 160 A2
Mccarthy Rd FELT TW13 ... 25 G6 1
Mcdonough Cl CHSGTN KT9 ... 63 H3 1
Mcdougall Ct RCH/KEW TW9 ... 18 D4
Mcgrigor Barracks ALDT GU11 ... 112 E6
Mcindoe Rd EGRIN RH19 ... 196 A6
Mcintosh Cl WLGTN SM6 ... 67 H6
Mciver Cl EGRIN RH19 ... 195 J5
Mckay Cl ALDT GU11 ... 112 F6
Mckay Rd RYNPK SW20 ... 28 E8
Mcrae La MTCM CR4 ... 48 C7 3
Mead Av REDH RH1 ... 148 D8
Mead Cl CRAN GU6 ... 185 H7 4
EGH TW20 ... 21 L7
REDH RH1 ... 126 D5
STWL/WRAY TW19 ... 21 G2
Mead Ct EGH TW20 ... 21 M7 2
WOKN/KNAP GU21 ... 76 B7
Mead Crs GT/LBKH KT23 ... 101 K7
SUT SM1 ... 66 B3
Mead Dr COUL/CHIP CR5 ... 87 H4 2
Meade Cl CHSWK W4 ... 18 D1
Mead End ASHTD KT21 ... 83 J7
Meades Cl LING RH7 ... 174 D8 3
The Meades LING RH7 ... 174 E8
Meadfoot Rd STRHM/NOR SW16 ... 48 F1
Meadhurst Rd CHERT KT16 ... 40 E8 2
Meadlands Dr
RCHPK/HAM TW10 ... 27 G3
Mead La CHERT KT16 ... 40 E8
Meadow Ap CRAWE RH10 ... 193 K6
Meadow Av CROY/NA CR0 ... 51 G6 3
Meadowbank BRYLDS KT5 ... 45 J6
Meadow Bank EHSLY KT24 ... 120 C1
Meadowbank Cl FUL/PGN SW6 ... 19 M2
Meadowbank Gdns HEST TW5 ... 15 L3 1
Meadowbank Rd LTWR GU18 ... 54 F8
Meadowbrook OXTED RH8 ... 129 M4
Meadowbrook Cl
DTCH/LGLY SL3 ... 13 H4
Meadowbrook Rd
DORK RH4 ... 144 D1 1
Meadow Cl ASHV GU12 ... 93 J8
BLKW GU17 ... 72 A5
CAT SE6 ... 33 K6
CRAWE RH10 ... 193 K6
ESH/CLAY KT10 ... 62 C2 1
HORS RH12 ... 229 K4 1
HSLWW TW4 ... 16 D8
MFD/CHID GU8 ... 159 K8
PUR/KEN CR8 ... 87 G3
RCHPK/HAM TW10 ... 27 H2
RGODL GU7 ... 160 B2 2
RYNPK SW20 ... 46 F4
WOT/HER KT12 ... 61 J3
Meadow Ct EPSOM KT18 ... 83 M3 4
STA TW18 ... 22 B4 1
Meadowcroft Cl
CRAWW RH11 ... 211 J4 2
EGRIN RH19 ... 195 M7
Meadow Croft Cl HORL RH6 ... 192 F1 1
Meadow Dr RPLY/SEND GU23 ... 98 C5
Meadow Farm La HORS RH12 ... 229 J2
Meadow Gdns STA TW18 ... 22 A6
Meadow Gate Rd FARN GU14 ... 92 C8
Meadow Hl COUL/CHIP CR5 ... 86 F3
NWMAL KT3 ... 46 B6
Meadowlands COB KT11 ... 80 D3 2
CRAWW RH11 ... 211 M3
OXTED RH8 ... 130 D8
RGUE GU4 ... 118 E4
Meadow La EDEN TN8 ... 153 L5
LHD/OX KT22 ... 101 M4
Meadowlea Cl WDR/YW UB7 ... 14 A1
Meadow Ri COUL/CHIP CR5 ... 87 G3

WOKN/KNAP GU21 75 M7
Meadow Rd *ASHF* TW15 24 A6
ASHTD KT21 83 H7
ESH/CLAY KT10 62 B4
FARN GU14 92 E2
FELT TW13 25 H3
RGUE GU4 117 K4
SUT SM1 66 B3
VW GU25 38 B5
WIM/MER SW19 29 M8
Meadows End *SUN* TW16 42 D1
Meadowside *GT/LBKH* KT23 101 K5
HORL RH6 170 E5 14
TWK TW1 27 G1
WOT/HER KT12 60 F1
Meadowside Rd *BELMT* SM2 65 H7
Meadows Leigh Cl *WEY* KT13 59 M2 1
The Meadows *GUW* GU2 138 F3
NFNM GU10 178 C8
WARL CR6 89 G7
Meadow Stile *CROY/NA* CR0 4 D8
Meadowsweet Cl *NWMAL* KT3 46 F5
The Meadow *CRAWE* RH10 193 K6
Meadow V *HASM* GU27 219 K3
Meadow Vw *HORL* RH6 171 M6
STWL/WRAY TW19 13 J7
Meadowview Rd *CAT* SE6 33 K5
HOR/WEW KT19 64 B7
Meadow View Rd *THHTH* CR7 49 L5
Meadow Wk *EW* KT17 64 C6
HOR/WEW KT19 64 B5
KWD/TDW/WH KT20 104 E6
WLGTN SM6 66 E2
Meadow Wy *ADL/WDHM* KT15 58 E3
ASHV GU12 113 J6
CHOB/PIR GU24 75 J3
CHSGTN KT9 63 H4
EHSLY KT24 100 A7
GT/LBKH KT23 101 L5
KWD/TDW/WH KT20 85 H7
NFNM GU10 155 J6
ORP BR6 71 K2
REIG RH2 147 L3 1
Meadow Waye *HEST* TW5 16 B2
Mead Pth *TOOT* SW17 30 A7
Mead Pl *CROY/NA* CR0 4 B4
Mead Rd *CRAN* GU6 185 H6
CRAWE RH10 212 C2
CTHM CR3 108 C5
GSHT GU26 199 J5
RCHPK/HAM TW10 26 F4
WOT/HER KT12 61 H3
Meadrow *RGODL* GU7 160 C3
Meadside Cl *BECK* BR3 51 H1
Meads Rd *GU* GU1 117 L8
The Meads *CHEAM* SM3 65 G2
EGRIN RH19 216 B2
HASM GU27 219 J3
WEY KT13 59 M5
The Mead *ASHTD* KT21 103 H1
BECK BR3 51 M2
WLGTN SM6 67 G5
Meadvale *HORS* RH12 228 C7
Meadvale Rd *CROY/NA* CR0 5 K1
Mead Wy *COUL/CHIP* CR5 87 H8
CROY/NA CR0 69 H1
RGUE GU4 117 M3
Meadway *ASHF* TW15 23 K5
BECK BR3 51 M1
BRYLDS KT5 45 M8
EHSLY KT24 121 H2
ESH/CLAY KT10 61 L7
FRIM GU16 73 J7
HASM GU27 219 J3
HOR/WEW KT19 83 M3
LHD/OX KT22 82 A4
RYNPK SW20 46 F4
STA TW18 22 D8
WARL CR6 88 F6
WHTN TW2 26 A2
Meadway Cl *STA* TW18 22 C8
Meadway Dr *ADL/WDHM* KT15 58 F6
WOKN/KNAP GU21 76 F6
The Meadway *HORL* RH6 170 F6
Meaford Wy *PGE/AN* SE20 32 E8
Meare Cl *KWD/TDW/WH* KT20 104 F5
Meath Green Av *HORL* RH6 170 C4
Meath Green La *REDH* RH1 170 B1
Medcroft Gdns
MORT/ESHN SW14 18 F6 1
Mede Fld *LHD/OX* KT22 102 A6
Medfield St *PUT/ROE* SW15 28 D1
Medhurst Cl *CHOB/PIR* GU24 56 C7
Medina Av *ESH/CLAY* KT10 62 B2
Medlake Rd *EGH* TW20 21 M7
Medland Cl *MTCM* CR4 48 D8
Medlar Cl *CRAWW* RH11 191 M8
GU GU1 116 F6
Medlar Dr *BLKW* GU17 72 C6
Medway *CRAWE* RH10 214 D4
Medway Cl *CROY/NA* CR0 50 F6 4
Medway Dr *EGRIN* RH19 216 A3
FARN GU14 92 B2
FROW RH18 217 K7
Medway Rd *CRAWW* RH11 211 J4
Medwin Wy *HORS* RH12 228 F7
Melbourne Cl *WLGTN* SM6 66 F4 1
Melbourne Ms *CAT* SE6 33 M1 1
Melbourne Rd *TEDD* TW11 26 F7
WIM/MER SW19 47 K1
WLGTN SM6 66 E4
Melbury Cl *BF/WBF* KT14 78 D4
CHERT KT16 40 D7
ESH/CLAY KT10 62 E5
Melbury Gdns *RYNPK* SW20 46 E1
Meldone Cl *BRYLDS* KT5 45 L6
Meldrum Cl *OXTED* RH8 130 C6
Melfield Gdns *CAT* SE6 33 L5
Melfont Av *THHTH* CR7 49 L3
Melford Cl *CHSGTN* KT9 63 J4 1
Melford Rd *DUL* SE21 32 D2
Melfort Rd *THHTH* CR7 49 L3
Melksham Cl *SWTR* RH13 229 H7
Meller Cl *WLGTN* SM6 67 H2
Mellersh Hill Rd *SHGR* GU5 161 L3
Mellison Rd *TOOT* SW17 30 B6
Mellor Cl *WOT/HER* KT12 43 J7
Mellow Cl *BNSTD* SM7 85 M4
Mellows Rd *WLGTN* SM6 67 G4
Melody Rd *BH/WHM* TN16 90 F8
Melrose *BRAK* RG12 34 E8
Melrose Av *MTCM* CR4 30 E8
STRHM/NOR SW16 49 J3
WHTN TW2 25 L1
WIM/MER SW19 29 J3
Melrose Gdns *NWMAL* KT3 46 A3
WOT/HER KT12 60 F4
Melrose Rd *BARN* SW13 19 J4 2
BH/WHM TN16 90 F6
COUL/CHIP CR5 86 E5
WEY KT13 59 K4
WIM/MER SW19 47 K2
Melsa Rd *MRDN* SM4 47 M6
Melton Flds *HOR/WEW* KT19 64 A7 3
Melton Pl *HOR/WEW* KT19 64 A7
Melton Rd *REDH* RH1 126 F4
Melville Av *FRIM* GU16 73 J8
RYNPK SW20 28 D8
SAND/SEL CR2 68 C4
Melville Rd *BARN* SW13 19 K3
Melvin Rd *PGE/AN* SE20 50 F1
Melvinshaw *LHD/OX* KT22 102 F3
Membury Cl *FRIM* GU16 93 K2 3
Membury Wk *BRAK* RG12 35 J4 8
Memorial Cl *HEST* TW5 16 C1
Mendip Cl *HYS/HAR* UB3 15 G2 2
SYD SE26 32 F5
WPK KT4 64 F1
Mendip Rd *BRAK* RG12 35 H5
FARN GU14 92 B2
Menin Wy *FNM* GU9 11 K2
Menlo Gdns *NRWD* SE19 32 A8
Meon Cl *FARN* GU14 92 A3
KWD/TDW/WH KT20 104 E4
Meopham Rd *MTCM* CR4 48 F1
Merantum Wy *WIM/MER* SW19 47 L1
Mercer Cl *CRAWE* RH10 212 F6
Mercer Rd *HORS* RH12 228 F1
Mercury Cl *CRAWW* RH11 211 H6
Merebank *RDKG* RH5 167 G5
Merebank La *WLGTN* SM6 67 J4
Mere Cl *ORP* BR6 71 L1
WIM/MER SW19 29 G1
Meredyth Rd *BARN* SW13 19 K4
Mere End *CROY/NA* CR0 51 G7
Merefield Gdns
KWD/TDW/WH KT20 105 G1
Mere Rd *KWD/TDW/WH* KT20 104 E6
SHPTN TW17 41 L6 2
WEY KT13 60 A2 4
Mereside *ORP* BR6 71 K1
Merevale Crs *MRDN* SM4 47 M6
Mereway Rd *WHTN* TW2 26 A2
Mereworth Dr *CRAWE* RH10 213 G1
Meridian Gv *HORL* RH6 170 F5 9
Meridian Wy *EGRIN* RH19 196 C6
Merland Cl *KWD/TDW/WH* KT20 104 F2
Merland Gn
KWD/TDW/WH KT20 104 F2
Merland Ri *KWD/TDW/WH* KT20 104 F1
Merle Common Rd *OXTED* RH8 152 D2
Merlewood *BRAK* RG12 35 G5 1
Merlewood Cl *CTHM* CR3 108 A2
Merlin Cl *CRAWW* RH11 211 H3 4
CROY/NA CR0 5 G9
DTCH/LGLY SL3 12 E1 4
MTCM CR4 48 B3
Merlin Gv *BECK* BR3 51 J4
Merlin Rd *FARN* GU14 92 E7
Merlins Cl *FNM* GU9 11 G2
Merlin Wy *EGRIN* RH19 196 D6
FARN GU14 92 A6
Merrilands Rd *WPK* KT4 46 F8
Merrilyn Cl *ESH/CLAY* KT10 62 D5
Merritt Gdns *CHSGTN* KT9 63 G5 1
Merrivale Gdns
WOKN/KNAP GU21 76 F7
Merrow Cha *GU* GU1 117 M8
Merrow Common Rd
RGUE GU4 118 A5
Merrow Copse *GU* GU1 117 L7
Merrow Cft *GU* GU1 117 M7
Merrow La *RGUE* GU4 117 M3
Merrow Rd *BELMT* SM2 65 G7
Merrow St *RGUE* GU4 118 A6
Merrow Wy *CROY/NA* CR0 69 M5
Merrow Woods *GU* GU1 117 L6
Merryacres *MFD/CHID* GU8 181 H2
Merryfield Dr *HORS* RH12 228 D6
Merryhill Rd *BNFD* RG42 34 D1
Merryhills Cl *BH/WHM* TN16 91 G6
Merryhills La *BIL* RH14 224 D4
Merrylands *CHERT* KT16 58 B2
Merrylands Farm
GT/LBKH KT23 101 J6
Merrylands Rd *GT/LBKH* KT23 101 J5
Merrymeet *BNSTD* SM7 86 C4
Merrywood Gv
KWD/TDW/WH KT20 125 G4
Merrywood Pk *CBLY* GU15 73 J5
REIG RH2 125 L6
Mersham Pl *PGE/AN* SE20 50 E1 3
THHTH CR7 50 A2 2
Mersham Rd *THHTH* CR7 50 A3
Merstham Rd *REDH* RH1 127 K4
Merthyr Ter *BARN* SW13 19 L1
Merton Cl *SHST* GU47 52 C7
Merton Gdns
KWD/TDW/WH KT20 105 G1 1
Merton Hall Gdns *RYNPK* SW20 47 H1
Merton Hall Rd *WIM/MER* SW19 47 H1
Merton High St *WIM/MER* SW19 29 M8
Merton Rd *SNWD* SE25 50 C5
WIM/MER SW19 29 L8
Merton Wy *E/WMO/HCT* KT8 43 M4
LHD/OX KT22 102 D1
Mervyn Rd *SHPTN* TW17 41 M7
Metcalf Rd *ASHF* TW15 23 L6
Metcalf Wy *CRAWW* RH11 192 A7
Meteor Wy *FARN* GU14 92 D8
WLGTN SM6 67 H6 3
Meudon Av *FARN* GU14 92 E6
Mews Ct *EGRIN* RH19 216 C3
Mewsend *BH/WHM* TN16 91 G8
The Mews *MFD/CHID* GU8 203 J4
Meyrick Cl *WOKN/KNAP* GU21 76 B6
Michael Crs *HORL* RH6 170 D8
Michael Flds *FROW* RH18 217 H7
Michaelmas Cl *RYNPK* SW20 46 F3 3
Michael Rd *SNWD* SE25 50 B3
Micheldever Wy *BRAK* RG12 35 J6
Michelet Cl *LTWR* GU18 54 E8
Michelham Gdns
KWD/TDW/WH KT20 104 F2 1
TWK TW1 26 C4
Michell Cl *HORS* RH12 228 D7 1
Mickleham Dr *LHD/OX* KT22 102 F8
Mickleham Gdns *CHEAM* SM3 65 H5
Mickleham Wy *CROY/NA* CR0 70 A6
Middle Av *FNM* GU9 11 J4
Middle Bourne La *NFNM* GU10 10 F7
Middle Church La *FNM* GU9 133 L7 7
Middle Cl *CBLY* GU15 73 M3
COUL/CHIP CR5 107 K2
EW KT17 84 B2 5
Middle Farm Pl *EHSLY* KT24 121 G1
Middlefield *FNM* GU9 10 C5
HORL RH6 170 F5
Middle Gordon Rd *CBLY* GU15 72 F4
Middle Green Cl *BRYLDS* KT5 45 J6 4
Middle Hl *ALDT* GU11 112 D7
EGH TW20 20 F6
Middle La *EW* KT17 84 B2
TEDD TW11 26 C7 6
Middlemarch *MFD/CHID* GU8 181 H4
Middlemead Cl *GT/LBKH* KT23 101 K7
Middlemead Rd *GT/LBKH* KT23 101 J7
Middlemoor Rd *FRIM* GU16 93 H1
Middle Old Pk *FNM* GU9 133 J5
Middle Rd *LHD/OX* KT22 102 E3
STRHM/NOR SW16 48 F2
Middlesex Rd *MTCM* CR4 49 H5
Middle St *BRKHM/BTCW* RH3 145 L2
CROY/NA CR0 4 D6
HORS RH12 228 F7 3
SHGR GU5 141 K5
Middleton Gdns *FARN* GU14 92 B3
Middleton Rd *CAR* SM5 48 A7
CBLY GU15 73 H3
COB KT11 100 E1
HOR/WEW KT19 64 A8 2
HORS RH12 228 D7
MRDN SM4 47 M6
NWMAL KT3 45 M3
Middleton Wy *CRAWW* RH11 211 H4
Middle Wy *STRHM/NOR* SW16 49 G2
Midgley Rd *CRAWE* RH10 212 C1 1
Midholm Rd *CROY/NA* CR0 69 H2
Mid Holmwood La *RDKG* RH5 144 E8
Midhope Cl *WOKS/MYFD* GU22 97 H1
Midhope Gdns
WOKS/MYFD GU22 6 C9 1
Midhope Rd *WOKS/MYFD* GU22 6 C9
Midhurst Av *CROY/NA* CR0 49 K7
Midhurst Cl *CRAWW* RH11 211 K2 1
Midhurst Rd *HASM* GU27 219 L4
Midleton Cl *MFD/CHID* GU8 159 J7
Midleton Industrial Estate Rd
GUW GU2 8 D1
Midleton Rd *GUW* GU2 8 C2
GUW GU2 8 A4
Midmoor Rd *BAL* SW12 30 F2
WIM/MER SW19 47 G1
Mid St *REDH* RH1 127 J8
Midsummer Av *HSLWW* TW4 16 C6
Midsummer Wk
WOKN/KNAP GU21 6 A3
Midway *CHEAM* SM3 47 J7
WOT/HER KT12 60 E1
Midway Av *CHERT* KT16 40 D3
EGH TW20 39 L3
Midway Cl *STA* TW18 22 E4
Miena Wy *ASHTD* KT21 83 G7
Mike Hawthorn Dr *FNM* GU9 133 M6 1
Milbanke Ct *BRAK* RG12 34 C2 1
Milbanke Wy *BRAK* RG12 34 C2
Milborne Rd *CRAWE* RH10 212 F7
Milbourne La *ESH/CLAY* KT10 61 M5
Milbrook *ESH/CLAY* KT10 61 M5
Milburn Wk *EPSOM* KT18 84 B5
Milden Cl *FRIM* GU16 93 K3
Milden Gdns *FRIM* GU16 93 K3
Mile Pth *WOKS/MYFD* GU22 96 E2
Mile Rd *WLGTN* SM6 48 D8
Miles La *COB* KT11 81 H3
GDST RH9 151 K2
Miles Pl *LTWR* GU18 74 C2
Miles Rd *ASHV* GU12 113 L6
HOR/WEW KT19 84 A2
MTCM CR4 48 B3
Miles's Hl *RDKG* RH5 164 F6
Milestone Cl *BELMT* SM2 66 A5
RPLY/SEND GU23 98 D4
Milestone Rd *NRWD* SE19 32 C7
Milford by Pass Rd
MFD/CHID GU8 181 G1
Milford Gv *SUT* SM1 65 M3
Milford Ldg *MFD/CHID* GU8 181 J1
Milford Ms *STRHM/NOR* SW16 31 J4
Milford Rd *MFD/CHID* GU8 158 B5
Milking La *ORP* BR6 91 H2
Millais *SWTR* RH13 229 K6
Millais Cl *CRAWW* RH11 211 J7 1
Millais Ct *SWTR* RH13 229 K5 1
Millais Rd *NWMAL* KT3 46 B7
Millais Wy *HOR/WEW* KT19 63 M3
Millan Cl *ADL/WDHM* KT15 58 E8 1
The Millbank *CRAWW* RH11 211 J3
Mill Bay La *HORS* RH12 228 E8
Millbourne Rd *FELT* TW13 25 H5
Millbrook *GUW* GU2 9 G7
WEY KT13 60 B3 3
Millbrook Wy *DTCH/LGLY* SL3 13 H4
Mill Cl *BAGS* GU19 54 A6
CAR SM5 66 D1 2
EGRIN RH19 216 B2
GT/LBKH KT23 101 K6
HASM GU27 219 H3 3
HORL RH6 170 B5
Millcombe Cl
WOKN/KNAP GU21 76 E8 1
Mill Copse Rd *HASM* GU27 219 L5
Miller Cl *MTCM* CR4 48 C7
Miller Rd *CROY/NA* CR0 49 J8 1
RGUE GU4 117 M5
WIM/MER SW19 30 A7
Millers Cl *STA* TW18 22 E6
Millers Copse *EPSOM* KT18 104 A1
REDH RH1 171 L2
Millers Ga *HORS* RH12 229 G3
Miller's La *REDH* RH1 171 L2
Mill Farm Av *SUN* TW16 24 B8
Mill Farm Crs *HSLWW* TW4 25 H2
Mill Farm Rd *SWTR* RH13 229 K5
Mill Fld *BAGS* GU19 54 A6
Millfield *SUN* TW16 42 A1
Millfield La *KWD/TDW/WH* KT20 105 K7
Millfield Rd *HSLWW* TW4 25 H2
Millford *WOKN/KNAP* GU21 76 E7 2
Mill Gdns *SYD* SE26 32 E5
Mill Green Rd *MTCM* CR4 48 D7
Millhedge Cl *COB* KT11 81 H6
Mill Hl *BARN* SW13 19 K5
BRKHM/BTCW RH3 145 L1
Mill Hill La *BRKHM/BTCW* RH3 123 L8
Mill Hill Rd *BARN* SW13 19 L5
Mill House La *CHERT* KT16 39 L4
Millhouse Pl *WNWD* SE27 31 L5 4
Millins Cl *SHST* GU47 52 A8
Mill La *ASC* SL5 37 L2
BF/WBF KT14 79 J3
BH/WHM TN16 131 M1
BRAK RG12 34 D5
CAR SM5 66 D3
CHOB/PIR GU24 95 G6
CRAWE RH10 194 B6
CRAWW RH11 211 K1
CROY/NA CR0 67 K2
DORK RH4 144 E1
DTCH/LGLY SL3 12 E5
EGH TW20 39 M4
EGRIN RH19 195 G4
EW KT17 64 C7
GUW GU2 9 G7
HASM GU27 219 M5
HORL RH6 170 A6
LHD/OX KT22 102 D4
LING RH7 174 C6
MFD/CHID GU8 181 J4
MFD/CHID GU8 201 K6
MFD/CHID GU8 203 H5
NFNM GU10 177 L2
ORP BR6 71 K8
OXTED RH8 130 C6
OXTED RH8 131 J5
RDKG RH5 168 A4
RDKG RH5 187 G2
REDH RH1 126 F5
RGODL GU7 160 A5
RGUE GU4 140 C5
RGUW GU3 138 F8
RPLY/SEND GU23 99 G1
SHGR GU5 161 J3
Millmead *BF/WBF* KT14 79 J2
GUW GU2 8 F7
Mill Md *STA* TW18 22 C5
Millmead Ter *GUW* GU2 8 F8
Mill Pl *DTCH/LGLY* SL3 12 A4
KUT KT1 3 G8
Mill Plat *ISLW* TW7 17 K4
Mill Plat Av *ISLW* TW7 17 K4
Millpond Ct *ADL/WDHM* KT15 59 H4
Mill Pond Rd *BFOR* GU20 54 E3
Mill Ride *ASC* SL5 36 A1 1
Mill Rd *COB* KT11 80 F5
CRAWE RH10 212 E2
ESH/CLAY KT10 61 K1
EW KT17 84 C2
KWD/TDW/WH KT20 105 G5
RDKG RH5 166 F2
WHTN TW2 25 M3
WIM/MER SW19 29 M8
Mill Shaw *OXTED* RH8 130 C6
Millshot Cl *FUL/PGN* SW6 19 M3
Millside *CAR* SM5 66 C1
Millside Pl *ISLW* TW7 17 L4
Mills Rd *WOT/HER* KT12 60 F4
Mills Sp *WDSR* SL4 20 E1
Millstead Cl
KWD/TDW/WH KT20 104 E5
Mill Stream *FNM* GU9 134 B3
The Millstream *HASM* GU27 219 H4
Mill St *DTCH/LGLY* SL3 13 G2
KUT KT1 2 F8
REDH RH1 148 B1
Millthorpe Rd *HORS* RH12 229 J5
Mill View Cl *EW* KT17 64 C6
Millview Cl *REDH* RH1 126 A6
Mill View Gdns *CROY/NA* CR0 69 G2
Mill Wy *EBED/NFELT* TW14 15 L7
EGRIN RH19 216 B2
LHD/OX KT22 103 J7
Millway *REIG* RH2 126 A8
Millwood *EGRIN* RH19 215 H4
Millwood Rd *HSLW* TW3 16 F7
Milman Cl *BRAK* RG12 35 K2 1
Milne Cl *CRAWW* RH11 211 H6 3
Milne Pk East *CROY/NA* CR0 90 A1
Milne Pk West *CROY/NA* CR0 90 A1
Milner Ap *CTHM* CR3 108 D3
Milner Cl *CTHM* CR3 108 D4
Milner Dr *COB* KT11 81 J2
WHTN TW2 26 A1
Milner Rd *CTHM* CR3 108 D4
KUT KT1 2 D9
MRDN SM4 48 A5
THHTH CR7 50 A3
WIM/MER SW19 47 L1
Milnthorpe Rd *CHSWK* W4 19 G1
Milnwood Rd *HORS* RH12 228 F6
Milton Av *CROY/NA* CR0 4 F2
DORK RH4 144 A3
SUT SM1 66 A2
Milton Cl *BRAK* RG12 34 E6
DTCH/LGLY SL3 12 D5
SUT SM1 66 A2
Miltoncourt La *DORK* RH4 144 B2
Milton Crs *EGRIN* RH19 195 M8
Milton Dr *SHPTN* TW17 41 H4
Milton Gdns *EPSOM* KT18 84 B4
STWL/WRAY TW19 23 J2 3
Milton Mount Av
CRAWE RH10 193 G8 6
CRAWE RH10 212 F1 3
Milton Rd *ADL/WDHM* KT15 58 D5
CRAWE RH10 212 F2
CROY/NA CR0 4 F2
CTHM CR3 108 A3
EGH TW20 21 J6
HORS RH12 228 F6
HPTN TW12 25 K8
MORT/ESHN SW14 19 G5
MTCM CR4 30 D8
SUT SM1 65 K2
WIM/MER SW19 29 M7
WLGTN SM6 66 F5
WOT/HER KT12 61 G2
Miltons Crs *RGODL* GU7 159 L7
Milton St *DORK* RH4 144 A3
Milton Wy *GT/LBKH* KT23 101 M7
Mina Rd *WIM/MER* SW19 47 K1
Minchin Cl *LHD/OX* KT22 102 D4
Mincing La *CHOB/PIR* GU24 56 C7
Minden Rd *CHEAM* SM3 65 H1
PGE/AN SE20 50 E1 7
Mindleheim Av *EGRIN* RH19 196 E7
Minehead Rd *STRHM/NOR* SW16 31 J6
Minehurst Rd *FRIM* GU16 93 J5
Minerva Rd *FARN* GU14 92 E8
KUT KT1 3 G7
Minimax Cl *EBED/NFELT* TW14 15 K8
Mink Ct *HSLWW* TW4 15 M4
Minley Cl *FARN* GU14 92 B5
Minniedale *BRYLDS* KT5 45 J5
Minorca Av *FRIM* GU16 74 B7
Minorca Rd *FRIM* GU16 74 B8
WEY KT13 59 K3 5
Minstead Cl *BRAK* RG12 35 J3
Minstead Gdns *PUT/ROE* SW15 28 C1
Minstead Wy *NWMAL* KT3 46 B6
Minster Av *SUT* SM1 65 K1 2
Minster Dr *CROY/NA* CR0 5 G9
Minster Gdns
E/WMO/HCT KT8 43 J4 3
Minsterley Av *SHPTN* TW17 42 B4
Minster Rd *RGODL* GU7 160 A7
Minstrel Gdns *BRYLDS* KT5 45 J4 3
Mint Gdns *DORK* RH4 144 D1
Mint La *KWD/TDW/WH* KT20 125 K3
Mint Rd *BNSTD* SM7 85 M6
WLGTN SM6 66 E4
Mint St *RGODL* GU7 160 A5
The Mint *RGODL* GU7 160 A5
Mint Wk *CROY/NA* CR0 4 D7
WARL CR6 89 G7
WOKN/KNAP GU21 76 B7
Misbrooks Green Rd *RDKG* RH5 189 H2
Missenden Cl
EBED/NFELT TW14 24 C2 11
Missenden Gdns *MRDN* SM4 47 M6 6
Mistletoe Cl *CROY/NA* CR0 51 G8 12
Misty's Fld *WOT/HER* KT12 42 F8
Mitcham La *STRHM/NOR* SW16 30 F6
Mitcham Pk *MTCM* CR4 48 B4
Mitcham Rd *CBLY* GU15 53 K8
CROY/NA CR0 49 G6
TOOT SW17 30 C6
Mitchell Gdns *SWTR* RH13 227 H6
Mitchells Cl *RGUE* GU4 139 H6 4
Mitchells Rd *CRAWE* RH10 212 C3
Mitchley Av *PUR/KEN* CR8 88 A3
Mitchley Gv *SAND/SEL* CR2 88 D3
Mitchley Hl *SAND/SEL* CR2 88 C3
Mitchley Vw *SAND/SEL* CR2 88 D3
Mitre Cl *BELMT* SM2 65 M6
SHPTN TW17 42 A6
Mixbury Gv *WEY* KT13 60 A5 2
Mixnams La *CHERT* KT16 40 D3
Mizen Cl *COB* KT11 81 G4
Mizen Wy *COB* KT11 80 F5 2
Moat Ct *ASHTD* KT21 83 H7
Moated Farm Dr
ADL/WDHM KT15 58 F6
Moat Rd *EGRIN* RH19 196 B8 2
Moat Side *FELT* TW13 24 F5
Moats La *REDH* RH1 149 H6
The Moat *NWMAL* KT3 46 B1
Moat Wk *CRAWE* RH10 212 F2
Moberly Rd *CLAP* SW4 31 G1
Moffat Rd *THHTH* CR7 49 M2
TOOT SW17 30 B5
Mogador Rd
KWD/TDW/WH KT20 125 H2
Mogden La *ISLW* TW7 17 J7
Moir Cl *SAND/SEL* CR2 68 D7
Mole Abbey Gdns
E/WMO/HCT KT8 43 K3
Mole Cl *CRAWW* RH11 211 L1 4
FARN GU14 92 A3
Mole Ct *HOR/WEW* KT19 63 M3
Molember Rd *E/WMO/HCT* KT8 44 B5
Mole Rd *LHD/OX* KT22 102 A3
WOT/HER KT12 61 G4
Molesey Av *E/WMO/HCT* KT8 43 J4
Molesey Cl *WOT/HER* KT12 61 G3
Molesey Dr *CHEAM* SM3 65 H1
Molesey Park Av
E/WMO/HCT KT8 43 L5
Molesey Park Cl
E/WMO/HCT KT8 43 M5
Molesey Park Rd
E/WMO/HCT KT8 44 A5 2
Molesey Rd *WOT/HER* KT12 43 H5
WOT/HER KT12 61 G4
Molesham Cl *E/WMO/HCT* KT8 43 L3 3
Molesham Wy *E/WMO/HCT* KT8 43 L4
Moles Hl *LHD/OX* KT22 82 A1
Moles Md *EDEN* TN8 153 M7
Mole St *RDKG* RH5 187 L5
RDKG RH5 187 K2
Mole Valley Pl *ASHTD* KT21 103 G1
Mollison Dr *WLGTN* SM6 67 H6
Molly Huggins Cl *BAL* SW12 30 F1
Molyneux Dr *TOOT* SW17 30 E5 1
Molyneux Rd *BFOR* GU20 55 G5 4
RGODL GU7 160 C2
WEY KT13 59 K3
Monahan Av *PUR/KEN* CR8 87 J2
Monarch Cl *CRAWW* RH11 211 K6

EBED/NFELT TW14 .... 24 B1
WWKM BR4 .... 70 C3
Monarch Ms WNND SE27 .... 31 K6 ⑥
Monaveen Cl
E/WMO/HCT KT8 .... 43 L3 ⑥
Mondial Wy WDR/YW UB7 .... 14 F2
Money Av CTHM CR3 .... 108 A4
Money Rd CTHM CR3 .... 108 A4
Mongers La EW KT17 .... 64 D8 ⑥
Monivea Rd BECK BR3 .... 33 J8
Monkleigh Rd MRDN SM4 .... 47 H3
Monks Av E/WMO/HCT KT8 .... 43 L5
Monks Cl ASC SL5 .... 36 E6
FARN GU14 .... 92 F5
Monks Crs ADL/WDHM KT15 .... 58 E4
WOT/HER KT12 .... 42 E8
Monksdene Gdns SUT SM1 .... 65 L2 ⑥
Monks Dr ASC SL5 .... 36 E6
Monksfield CRAWE RH10 .... 212 C3
Monks Gn LHD/OX KT22 .... 101 M3
Monkshanger FNM GU9 .... 134 B7
Monks La OXTED RH8 .... 153 G3
RDKG RH5 .... 207 J4
Monks Orchard Rd BECK BR3 .... 51 K8
Monks Rd BNSTD SM7 .... 85 K7
VW GU25 .... 39 G4
Monks Wk ASC SL5 .... 36 E6
NFNM GU10 .... 156 C2
REIG RH2 .... 125 L8
Monks Wy BECK BR3 .... 51 K6
STA TW18 .... 23 G8
Monks' Well NFNM GU10 .... 156 F1
Monkswell La COUL/CHIP CR5 .... 105 L6
Monkton La FNM GU9 .... 134 B4
Monmouth Av KUT KT1 .... 2 B3
Monmouth Cl MTCM CR4 .... 49 H4 ⑥
Monro Dr GUW GU2 .... 116 E5
Monroe Dr MORT/ESHN SW14 .... 18 E7
Mons Barracks ALDT GU11 .... 112 F4
Mons Cl ALDT GU11 .... 113 H2
Monson Rd REDH RH1 .... 126 C5
Mons Wk EGH TW20 .... 21 M6 ⑥
Montacute Cl FARN GU14 .... 93 G5 ⑥
Montacute Rd CAT SE6 .... 33 J1
CROY/NA CR0 .... 69 M7
MRDN SM4 .... 48 A6
Montague Av SAND/SEL CR2 .... 88 B2
Montague Cl CBLY GU15 .... 72 E4 ⑥
LTWR GU18 .... 54 D8
WOT/HER KT12 .... 42 D7 ⑥
Montague Dr CTHM CR3 .... 107 M4 ⑥
Montague Rd CROY/NA CR0 .... 4 B3
HSLW TW3 .... 16 E5
RCHPK/HAM TW10 .... 18 B8 ⑥
WIM/MER SW19 .... 29 L8
Montagu Gdns WLGTN SM6 .... 66 F3
Montana Cl SAND/SEL CR2 .... 68 A8
Montana Gdns CAT SE6 .... 33 J6 ⑥
SUT SM1 .... 65 M4 ⑥
Montana Rd RYNPK SW20 .... 46 F1
TOOT SW17 .... 30 D4
Montem Rd FSTH SE23 .... 33 J1
NWMAL KT3 .... 46 B4
Montford Rd SUN TW16 .... 42 D4
Montfort Pl WIM/MER SW19 .... 29 G2 ⑥
Montfort Ri REDH RH1 .... 148 C8
Montgomerie Dr GUW GU2 .... 116 D3
Montgomery Av ESH/CLAY KT10 .... 62 B1
Montgomery Cl MTCM CR4 .... 49 H4 ⑥
Montgomery Rd FARN GU14 .... 92 C6
WOKS/MYFD GU22 .... 6 D7
Montolieu Gdns
PUT/ROE SW15 .... 19 L7 ⑥
Montpelier Rd PUR/KEN CR8 .... 67 L8
SUT SM1 .... 65 M3 ⑥
Montpelier Rw TWK TW1 .... 26 E1
Montrave Rd PGE/AN SE20 .... 32 F8 ⑥
Montrell Rd BRXS/STRHM SW2 .... 31 H2
Montrose Av WHTN TW2 .... 25 L1
Montrose Cl ASHF TW15 .... 23 M7
FRIM GU16 .... 73 H7 ⑥
Montrose Gdns LHD/OX KT22 .... 82 A2
MTCM CR4 .... 48 C2 ⑥
SUT SM1 .... 65 L1
Montrose Rd EBED/NFELT TW14 .... 15 L2
Montrose Wk WEY KT13 .... 59 L2
Montrose Wy DTCH/LGLY SL3 .... 12 A3
FSTH SE23 .... 33 G2 ⑥
Montrouge Crs EW KT17 .... 84 F6
Mont St Aignan Wy EDEN TN8 .... 153 M8
Montserrat Cl NRWD SE19 .... 32 A6 ⑥
Monument HI WEY KT13 .... 59 L3
Monument Rd WEY KT13 .... 59 L3
Monument Wy East
WOKN/KNAP GU21 .... 7 J2
Monument Wy West
WOKN/KNAP GU21 .... 7 H2
Moons HI NFNM GU10 .... 155 L9
Moon's La EGRIN RH19 .... 197 G2
SWTR RH13 .... 229 H8 ⑥
Moor Cl SHST GU47 .... 52 B8
Moorcroft Cl CRAWW RH11 .... 211 L2
Moorcroft Rd
STRHM/NOR SW16 .... 31 H4 ⑥
Moordale Av BNFD RG42 .... 34 B1
Moore Cl ADL/WDHM KT15 .... 58 E4
MORT/ESHN SW14 .... 18 F5 ⑥
MTCM CR4 .... 48 E2 ⑥
NFNM GU10 .... 135 J1 ⑥
WLGTN SM6 .... 67 H6
Moore Grove Crs EGH TW20 .... 21 H8
Moore Rd CHOB/PIR GU24 .... 94 E3
NRWD SE19 .... 31 M7
Moore's Rd DORK RH4 .... 144 E1
Moore Wy BELMT SM2 .... 65 K7
Moorfield HASM GU27 .... 219 J4
Moorfield Rd CHSGTN KT9 .... 63 H4
GU GU1 .... 117 G4
Moorfields Cl STA TW18 .... 40 B1
Moorhayes Dr STA TW18 .... 40 F3
Moorhead Rd HORS RH12 .... 229 L4
Moorhouse Rd OXTED RH8 .... 131 J4
Moorhurst La RDKG RH5 .... 166 D5
The Moorings BF/WBF KT14 .... 78 F2
EGRIN RH19 .... 195 K6
STWL/WRAY TW19 .... 20 F1 ⑥
Moorland Cl HSLWW TW4 .... 25 K1 ⑥
Moorland Rd CRAWE RH10 .... 212 F2

WDR/YW UB7 .... 13 M2
Moorlands Cl GSHT GU26 .... 199 H5
Moorlands Rd CBLY GU15 .... 72 D5
The Moorlands
WOKS/MYFD GU22 .... 97 J3
Moor La CHSGTN KT9 .... 63 J4
STWL/WRAY TW19 .... 21 M2
WDR/YW UB7 .... 13 M1
WOKS/MYFD GU22 .... 97 H4
Moormead Dr HOR/WEW KT19 .... 64 B4
Moor Mead Rd TWK TW1 .... 17 K8
Moormede Crs STA TW18 .... 22 C5
Moor Park Crs CRAWW RH11 .... 211 C4 ⑥
Moor Park Gdns KUTN/CMB KT2 .... 28 B8
Moor Park La NFNM GU10 .... 134 C6
Moor Park Wy FNM GU9 .... 134 C7
Moor Pl BFOR GU20 .... 54 E4
EGRIN RH19 .... 196 A7
Moor Rd FARN GU14 .... 92 D1
FRIM GU16 .... 93 J1
HASM GU27 .... 218 F4
Moorside Cl FARN GU14 .... 72 D8
Moors La MFD/CHID GU8 .... 157 M6
Moorsom Wy COUL/CHIP CR5 .... 87 G7
The Moors NFNM GU10 .... 135 J2 ⑥
Moray Av SHST GU47 .... 72 A2
Morden Cl BRAK RG12 .... 35 J4 ⑥
KWD/TDW/WH KT20 .... 105 G2 ⑥
Morden Ct MRDN SM4 .... 47 L4
Morden Gdns MTCM CR4 .... 48 A4
Morden Hall Rd MRDN SM4 .... 47 L3
Morden Wy CHEAM SM3 .... 47 K7
Morecambe Cl CRAWW RH11 .... 211 J5 ⑥
More Cir PUR/KEN CR8 .... 87 J1
Morecoombe Cl KUTN/CMB KT2 .... 3 M2
Morecote Cl RGUE GU4 .... 139 H7
Moreland Cl DTCH/LGLY SL3 .... 12 F2 ⑥
More La ESH/CLAY KT10 .... 61 L2
Morella Cl VW GU25 .... 38 F4
Morella Rd BAL SW12 .... 30 C1
Moremead Rd CAT SE6 .... 33 J5
Morena St CAT SE6 .... 33 L1
Moresby Av BRYLDS KT5 .... 45 L7
Moreton Av ISLW TW7 .... 17 H3 ⑥
Moreton Cl NFNM GU10 .... 178 B8
Moreton Rd SAND/SEL CR2 .... 68 A4
WPK KT4 .... 64 D1
Moring Rd TOOT SW17 .... 30 D5
Morland Av CROY/NA CR0 .... 5 H3
Morland Cl HPTN TW12 .... 25 H8 ⑥
MTCM CR4 .... 48 B3 ⑥
Morland Rd ALDT GU11 .... 134 F2
CROY/NA CR0 .... 5 J2
PGE/AN SE20 .... 33 G8
SUT SM1 .... 65 M4
Morland's Rd ALDT GU11 .... 113 C4
Morley Cl ORP BR6 .... 71 L1
Morley Rd CHEAM SM3 .... 47 J8
FNM GU9 .... 11 H2
SAND/SEL CR2 .... 68 C3
TWK TW1 .... 18 A8
Morningside Rd WPK KT4 .... 64 E1
Mornington Crs HEST TW5 .... 15 L3
Mornington Rd ASHF TW15 .... 23 M6
Mornington Wk
RCHPK/HAM TW10 .... 26 F5
Morrell Av HORS RH12 .... 229 J4
Morris Cl CROY/NA CR0 .... 51 H6
Morris Gdns WAND/EARL SW18 .... 29 K1
Morrish Rd BRXS/STRHM SW2 .... 31 H1
Morston Cl KWD/TDW/WH KT20 .... 104 E2
Mortaine Rd ASHF TW15 .... 23 G4 ⑥
Mortimer Cl BAL SW12 .... 31 G3
Mortimer Crs WPK KT4 .... 64 A2
Mortimer Rd BH/WHM TN16 .... 90 F2
MTCM CR4 .... 48 C1
RDKG RH5 .... 189 C3
Mortlake Cl CROY/NA CR0 .... 67 J2
ISLW TW7 .... 17 J5
REDH RH1 .... 149 H2
Mortlake High St
MORT/ESHN SW14 .... 19 G5
Mortlake Rd RCH/KEW TW9 .... 18 E4
Morton KWD/TDW/WH KT20 .... 105 G3
Morton Cl FRIM GU16 .... 93 J2
WOKN/KNAP GU21 .... 76 F5
Morton Gdns WLGTN SM6 .... 66 F4
Morton Rd EGRIN RH19 .... 216 B2
MRDN SM4 .... 48 A5
WOKN/KNAP GU21 .... 76 F5
Morval Cl FARN GU14 .... 92 B5
Morven Rd TOOT SW17 .... 30 C4 ⑥
Moselle Cl FARN GU14 .... 92 A4
Moselle Rd BH/WHM TN16 .... 91 H8
Mosford Cl HORL RH6 .... 170 C4
Mospey Crs EW KT17 .... 84 C5
Mossfield COB KT11 .... 80 D3
Moss Gdns SAND/SEL CR2 .... 69 G6 ⑥
Moss La RGODL GU7 .... 160 A5
Mosslea Rd CTHM CR3 .... 88 C3
ORP BR6 .... 71 M2
PGE/AN SE20 .... 32 F8
Mossville Gdns MRDN SM4 .... 47 J3
Mostyn Rd WIM/MER SW19 .... 47 J2
Mostyn Ter REDH RH1 .... 148 D1
Motspur Pk NWMAL KT3 .... 46 E6
Motts Hill La
KWD/TDW/WH KT20 .... 104 D5
Mouchotte Cl BH/WHM TN16 .... 90 E4
Moulton Av HEST TW5 .... 16 B4
Mountacre Pk SYD SE26 .... 32 C5
Mount Adon Pk DUL SE21 .... 32 D1
Mount Angelus Rd
PUT/ROE SW15 .... 28 C1 ⑥
Mount Ararat Rd
RCHPK/HAM TW10 .... 18 B7 ⑥
Mount Ash Rd SYD SE26 .... 32 E4
Mount Av CTHM CR3 .... 107 M6
Mountbatten Cl
CRAWW RH11 .... 211 M7 ⑥
NRWD SE19 .... 32 B6
Mount Cl CAR SM5 .... 66 D7
CRAN GU6 .... 186 B4
CRAWE RH10 .... 212 F2

LHD/OX KT22 .... 102 C5
PUR/KEN CR8 .... 87 M6
WOKS/MYFD GU22 .... 96 E3
The Mount Cl VW GU25 .... 39 G6 ⑥
Mountcombe Cl SURB KT6 .... 45 H7 ⑥
Mount Ct WWKM BR4 .... 70 B1
Mount Dr REIG RH2 .... 125 M6
Mountearl Gdns
STRHM/NOR SW16 .... 31 J4
Mount Ephraim La
STRHM/NOR SW16 .... 31 G4
Mount Ephraim Rd
STRHM/NOR SW16 .... 31 G4
Mount Felix WOT/HER KT12 .... 42 C8
Mount Gdns SYD SE26 .... 32 E4
Mount Hermon Cl
WOKS/MYFD GU22 .... 6 C8
Mount Hermon Rd
WOKS/MYFD GU22 .... 6 B9
Mount La BRAK RG12 .... 34 F3
CRAWE RH10 .... 214 D5
Mount Lee EGH TW20 .... 21 H6
Mount Nod Rd
STRHM/NOR SW16 .... 31 J4
Mount Pk CAR SM5 .... 66 D7
Mount Park Av SAND/SEL CR2 .... 67 L7
Mount Pleasant BH/WHM TN16 .... 91 G7
BRAK RG12 .... 34 F3
EHSLY KT24 .... 119 L3
EHSLY KT24 .... 121 H2
EW KT17 .... 64 C8
FNM GU9 .... 133 K7
WEY KT13 .... 59 K2
WNWD SE27 .... 31 M5
Mount Pleasant Cl LTWR GU18 .... 54 D8
Mount Pleasant Rd ASHV GU12 .... 112 F7
CTHM CR3 .... 108 D5
LING RH7 .... 173 M5
NWMAL KT3 .... 45 M3
Mount Ri FSTH SE23 .... 32 F3
REDH RH1 .... 148 A2
Mount Rd CHOB/PIR GU24 .... 76 E2
CHSGTN KT9 .... 63 J4
CRAN GU6 .... 185 H7
FELT TW13 .... 25 H4
HSLW TW3 .... 16 F4
MTCM CR4 .... 48 A2
NRWD SE19 .... 32 A7 ⑥
NWMAL KT3 .... 46 A3
WAND/EARL SW18 .... 29 K3
WOKS/MYFD GU22 .... 96 E3
Mountsfield Cl
STWL/WRAY TW19 .... 13 K7 ⑥
Mountside GUW GU2 .... 8 D8
Mount St DORK RH4 .... 144 D2 ⑥
The Mount COUL/CHIP CR5 .... 86 D5
CRAN GU6 .... 185 H7
CRAN GU6 .... 186 B4
ESH/CLAY KT10 .... 61 K5
EW KT17 .... 64 C8
GUW GU2 .... 8 D9
HASM GU27 .... 200 D3
HORS RH12 .... 190 E8
KWD/TDW/WH KT20 .... 105 J8
LHD/OX KT22 .... 102 B5
NWMAL KT3 .... 46 C3
VW GU25 .... 39 G6 ⑥
WARL CR6 .... 108 D1
WEY KT13 .... 60 B1
WOKN/KNAP GU21 .... 6 A8
WPK KT4 .... 64 E3
Mount Vw ALDT GU11 .... 112 D8
Mountview Cl REDH RH1 .... 148 B2 ⑥
Mountview Dr REDH RH1 .... 148 B2
Mount View Rd ESH/CLAY KT10 .... 62 E6
Mount Vis WNWD SE27 .... 31 L4
Mount Wy CAR SM5 .... 66 D7
Mountwood E/WMO/HCT KT8 .... 43 L3
Mountwood Cl SAND/SEL CR2 .... 68 E8
Moushill La MFD/CHID GU8 .... 181 H1
Mowbray Av BF/WBF KT14 .... 79 H3
Mowbray Crs EGH TW20 .... 21 K6
Mowbray Dr CRAWW RH11 .... 211 J5
Mowbray Gdns DORK RH4 .... 122 E8
Mowbray Rd NRWD SE19 .... 50 C1
RCHPK/HAM TW10 .... 26 F4
Mower Pl CRAN GU6 .... 185 H5 ⑥
Moyne Rd CRAWW RH11 .... 211 M7
Moys Cl CROY/NA CR0 .... 49 H6
Moyser Rd TOOT SW17 .... 30 E6
Mucheleney Rd MRDN SM4 .... 47 M6
Muckhatch La EGH TW20 .... 39 L3
Muggeridge Cl SAND/SEL CR2 .... 68 A4
Muggeridge's HI RDKG RH5 .... 209 H1
Muirdown Av MORT/ESHN SW14 .... 18 F6
Muirfield Cl CRAWW RH11 .... 211 G4
Muirfield Rd WOKN/KNAP GU21 .... 76 D8
Muirkirk Rd CAT SE6 .... 33 M2
Mulberry Av STWL/WRAY TW19 .... 23 H2
Mulberry Cl ASHV GU12 .... 113 K5
HORS RH12 .... 228 F4 ⑥
SHST GU47 .... 72 A1 ⑥
STRHM/NOR SW16 .... 30 F5
WEY KT13 .... 59 L2
WOKN/KNAP GU21 .... 77 H4 ⑥
Mulberry La CROY/NA CR0 .... 5 K4
Mulberry Rd CRAWW RH11 .... 191 L8 ⑥
Mulberry Trees SHPTN TW17 .... 42 A7 ⑥
Mulgrave Rd BELMT SM2 .... 65 J6
CROY/NA CR0 .... 2 E9
FRIM GU16 .... 73 J7 ⑥
Mulgrave Wy WOKN/KNAP GU21 .... 76 B8
Mulholland Cl MTCM CR4 .... 48 E2
Mullards Cl MTCM CR4 .... 48 C8
Mullens Rd EGH TW20 .... 21 M6
Mullins Pth MORT/ESHN SW14 .... 19 G5
Multon Rd WAND/EARL SW18 .... 30 A1
Muncaster Cl ASHF TW15 .... 23 K5
Muncaster Rd ASHF TW15 .... 23 L6
Muncies Ms CAT SE6 .... 33 M3 ⑥
Munday's Boro RGUW GU3 .... 136 D5
Munday's Boro Rd
RGUW GU3 .... 136 D5 ⑥
Munnery Wy ORP BR6 .... 71 K2
Munnings Dr SHST GU47 .... 72 A3
Munnings Gdns ISLW TW7 .... 17 G7

Munstead Heath Rd
MFD/CHID GU8 .... 160 F5
Munstead Pk MFD/CHID GU8 .... 160 F6
Munstead Vw RGUW GU3 .... 138 E5
Munstead View Rd SHGR GU5 .... 161 G4
Munster Av HSLWW TW4 .... 16 B6
Munster Rd TEDD TW11 .... 26 E5
Murdoch Cl STA TW18 .... 22 D6
Murfett Cl WIM/MER SW19 .... 29 H3
Murray Av HSLW TW3 .... 16 E7
Murray Ct ASC SL5 .... 36 F6
SWTR RH13 .... 229 L5
Murray Rd CHERT KT16 .... 58 A5
FARN GU14 .... 92 C6
RCHPK/HAM TW10 .... 26 E3
WIM/MER SW19 .... 29 G7
Murray's La BF/WBF KT14 .... 79 C4
Murray's Rd ASHV GU12 .... 113 C4
Murrell Rd ASHV GU12 .... 113 K6
Murrells La CBLY GU15 .... 72 E6
Murrells Wk GT/LBKH KT23 .... 101 K5
The Murreys ASHTD KT21 .... 83 G8
Muschamp Rd CAR SM5 .... 66 B1
Museum HI HASM GU27 .... 220 D1
Musgrave Av EGRIN RH19 .... 216 B2
Musgrave Rd ISLW TW7 .... 17 J3
Musquash Wy HSLWW TW4 .... 15 M4 ⑥
Mustard Mill Rd STA TW18 .... 22 C5
Mutton HI LING RH7 .... 196 D2
Mutton Oaks BNFD RG42 .... 34 A1
Muybridge Rd NWMAL KT3 .... 45 M2
Myers Wy FRIM GU16 .... 74 A7 ⑥
Mylis Cl SYD SE26 .... 32 E5
Mylor Cl WOKN/KNAP GU21 .... 77 H4
Mynn's Cl EPSOM KT18 .... 83 L4 ⑥
Myrna Cl WIM/MER SW19 .... 30 B8
Myrtle Av EBED/NFELT TW14 .... 15 H6
Myrtle Cl DTCH/LGLY SL3 .... 13 H3 ⑥
LTWR GU18 .... 74 E1
Myrtle Dr BLKW GU17 .... 72 A5
Myrtle Gv CROY/NA CR0 .... 69 K2
DORK RH4 .... 144 D1
HPTN TW12 .... 25 M7
HSLW TW3 .... 16 F4
SUT SM1 .... 65 M4
Mytchett Heath FRIM GU16 .... 93 K6
Mytchett Lake Rd FRIM GU16 .... 93 K8
Mytchett Place Rd FRIM GU16 .... 93 K6
Mytchett Rd FRIM GU16 .... 93 J5
Myton Rd DUL SE21 .... 32 C2

N

Nailsworth Crs REDH RH1 .... 127 G3
Nairn Cl FRIM GU16 .... 73 H7 ⑥
Naldrett Cl HORS RH12 .... 229 J5
Naldretts La HORS RH12 .... 225 M4
Nallhead Rd FELT TW13 .... 24 F6
Namba Roy Cl
STRHM/NOR SW16 .... 31 J5
Namton Dr STRHM/NOR SW16 .... 49 J4 ⑥
Napier Cl ALDT GU11 .... 113 H2 ⑥
Napier Ct CTHM CR3 .... 108 B4
Napier Dr CBLY GU15 .... 73 K2
Napier Gdns GU GU1 .... 117 L7
Napier Rd ASHF TW15 .... 24 A8
ISLW TW7 .... 17 K6
SAND/SEL CR2 .... 68 A5
SNWD SE25 .... 50 E4 ⑥
WDR/YW UB7 .... 14 A3
Napier Wk ASHF TW15 .... 24 A8
Napier Wy CRAWE RH10 .... 192 C8
Napoleon Av FARN GU14 .... 92 E3
Napoleon Rd TWK TW1 .... 26 E1 ⑥
Napper Cl ASC SL5 .... 35 M2
Napper Pl CRAN GU6 .... 185 H8
Narrow La WARL CR6 .... 108 E1
Naseby BRAK RG12 .... 34 E8
Naseby Cl ISLW TW7 .... 17 H3
Naseby Rd NRWD SE19 .... 32 A7
Nash Cl FARN GU14 .... 92 C5
REDH RH1 .... 126 C6
Nash La HAYES BR2 .... 70 D5
Nash Rd CRAWE RH10 .... 212 B6
Nassau Rd BARN SW13 .... 19 J3
Nasturtium Dr
CHOB/PIR GU24 .... 75 K5 ⑥
Natalie Cl EBED/NFELT TW14 .... 24 A1
Natal Rd STRHM/NOR SW16 .... 31 G7
THHTH CR7 .... 50 A3
Neale Cl EGRIN RH19 .... 195 L6
Neath Gdns MRDN SM4 .... 47 M6
Neb La OXTED RH8 .... 129 M5
Needles Bank GDST RH9 .... 128 E5
Needles Cl HORS RH12 .... 228 E8 ⑥
Neil Cl ASHF TW15 .... 23 M6
Neigarde Rd CAT SE6 .... 33 K1
Nell Ball BIL RH14 .... 223 H7
Nell Gwynn Av SHPTN TW17 .... 42 A6
Nell Gwynne Av ASC SL5 .... 37 G4
Nell Gwynne Cl
HOR/WEW KT19 .... 83 K1 ⑥
Nello James Gdns WNWD SE27 .... 32 A5
Nelson Cl ASHV GU12 .... 112 F8
BH/WHM TN16 .... 91 H7
BRAK RG12 .... 35 H2
CRAWE RH10 .... 212 F4
EBED/NFELT TW14 .... 24 C2 ⑥
FNM GU9 .... 134 A1
WOT/HER KT12 .... 42 E8
Nelson Gdns GU GU1 .... 117 K7
HSLWW TW4 .... 16 D8
Nelson Grove Rd
WIM/MER SW19 .... 47 L1
Nelson Rd ASHF TW15 .... 23 H6
CTHM CR3 .... 108 A5
FNM GU9 .... 134 A1
HORS RH12 .... 228 E6
HSLWW TW4 .... 16 D8
NWMAL KT3 .... 46 A5
WDR/YW UB7 .... 14 C3
WHTN TW2 .... 25 L1
WIM/MER SW19 .... 29 L8
Nelson St ALDT GU11 .... 112 D7

Nelson Wy CBLY GU15 .... 72 C5
Nene Gdns FELT TW13 .... 25 J3
Nene Rd HTHAIR TW6 .... 14 E3
Nepean St PUT/ROE SW15 .... 19 K8
Neptune Cl CRAWW RH11 .... 211 H5 ⑥
Neptune Rd HTHAIR TW6 .... 14 E3 ⑥
Netheravon Rd South
CHSWK W4 .... 19 J1
Netherby Pk WEY KT13 .... 60 B4
Netherby Rd FSTH SE23 .... 32 F1
Nethercote Av
WOKN/KNAP GU21 .... 76 C7
Netherfield Rd TOOT SW17 .... 30 D4 ⑥
The Netherlands
COUL/CHIP CR5 .... 106 F1
Netherleigh Pk REDH RH1 .... 149 H3
Nether Mt GUW GU2 .... 8 D8
Nethern Court Rd CTHM CR3 .... 109 K5
Netherton BRAK RG12 .... 34 D4
Netherton Rd TWK TW1 .... 17 K7
Netherwood CRAWW RH11 .... 211 K6
Netley Cl CHEAM SM3 .... 65 G4
CROY/NA CR0 .... 69 M6
Netley Dr WOT/HER KT12 .... 43 J7
Netley Gdns MRDN SM4 .... 47 M7 ⑥
Netley Rd BTFD TW8 .... 18 B1
MRDN SM4 .... 47 M7
Netley St FARN GU14 .... 112 F1
Nettlecombe BRAK RG12 .... 35 G5
Nettlecombe Cl BELMT SM2 .... 65 L7 ⑥
Nettlefold Pl WNWD SE27 .... 31 L4 ⑥
Nettlestead Cl BECK BR3 .... 33 J8 ⑥
Nettles Ter GU GU1 .... 9 G3
Nettleton Rd HTHAIR TW6 .... 14 E3
Nettlewood Rd
STRHM/NOR SW16 .... 31 G8 ⑥
Neuchatel Rd CAT SE6 .... 33 J5
Nevada Cl FARN GU14 .... 92 A6 ⑥
NWMAL KT3 .... 45 M4 ⑥
Nevelle Cl BNFD RG42 .... 34 A1
Neville Av NWMAL KT3 .... 46 A1
Neville Cl BNSTD SM7 .... 85 L6 ⑥
ESH/CLAY KT10 .... 61 J5
HSLW TW3 .... 16 D4
Neville Duke Rd FARN GU14 .... 92 C1
Neville Rd CROY/NA CR0 .... 4 F1
KUT KT1 .... 3 K6
RCHPK/HAM TW10 .... 26 F4
Neville Wk CAR SM5 .... 48 B7 ⑥
Nevil Wk CAR SM5 .... 48 B7 ⑥
Nevis Rd TOOT SW17 .... 30 D5
Newall Rd HTHAIR TW6 .... 14 F3
Newark Cl RGUE GU4 .... 117 L3 ⑥
RPLY/SEND GU23 .... 98 C3
Newark Ct WOT/HER KT12 .... 42 F8 ⑥
Newark La RPLY/SEND GU23 .... 98 C2
Newark Rd BFOR GU20 .... 54 E3
CRAWE RH10 .... 212 C1
SAND/SEL CR2 .... 68 A5
RDKG RH5 .... 187 K6
New Barn Av CTHM CR3 .... 88 B7
New Barns Av MTCM CR4 .... 49 G4
New Battlebridge La REDH RH1 .... 126 E4
New Berry La WOT/HER KT12 .... 61 G5
Newbolt Av CHEAM SM3 .... 64 F4
Newborough Gn NWMAL KT3 .... 46 A4
Newbridge Cl HORS RH12 .... 227 M6 ⑥
Newbury Gdns HOR/WEW KT19 .... 64 C3
Newbury Rd CRAWE RH10 .... 213 G3
WDR/YW UB7 .... 14 C3
New Cswy REIG RH2 .... 147 L3
Newchapel Rd LING RH7 .... 173 K7
New Cl FELT TW13 .... 25 H6
WIM/MER SW19 .... 47 M3
Newcome Gdns
STRHM/NOR SW16 .... 31 H5 ⑥
Newcome Pl ASHV GU12 .... 135 G2
Newcome Rd FNM GU9 .... 134 B2
New Coppice WOKN/KNAP GU21 .... 96 B1
New Cross Rd GUW GU2 .... 116 D6
New Dawn Cl FARN GU14 .... 92 A4
Newdigate Rd HORS RH12 .... 210 A1
RDKG RH5 .... 167 G2
Newenham Rd GT/LBKH KT23 .... 101 K8
Newent Cl CAR SM5 .... 48 C8
New Farthingdale LING RH7 .... 196 D1
Newfield Av FARN GU14 .... 92 B3
Newfield Cl HPTN TW12 .... 43 K1 ⑥
Newfield Rd ASHV GU12 .... 113 K3
New Forest Ride BRAK RG12 .... 35 H7
Newfoundland Rd FRIM GU16 .... 94 A1
Newgate CROY/NA CR0 .... 4 D3
Newgate Cl FELT TW13 .... 25 H3 ⑥
New Green Pl NRWD SE19 .... 32 B7 ⑥
Newhache LING RH7 .... 174 D8
Newhall Gdns WOT/HER KT12 .... 60 F1
Newhaven Crs ASHF TW15 .... 24 A6
Newhaven Rd SNWD SE25 .... 50 A5
New Haw Rd ADL/WDHM KT15 .... 58 F5
New Heston Rd HEST TW5 .... 16 C2
Newhouse Cl NWMAL KT3 .... 46 B7
New House Farm La
RGUW GU3 .... 115 M7
New House La REDH RH1 .... 149 G3
Newhouse Wk MRDN SM4 .... 47 M3
New Inn La RGUE GU4 .... 117 L5
New Kelvin Av TEDD TW11 .... 26 B7
Newland Rd THDIT KT7 .... 44 B8
WOKS/MYFD GU22 .... 97 J3
Newlands Cl HORL RH6 .... 170 C4
WOT/HER KT12 .... 61 H3 ⑥
Newlands Crs EGRIN RH19 .... 196 A7
Newlands Dr ASHV GU12 .... 113 L5
DTCH/LGLY SL3 .... 13 H5
Newlands Pk CRAWE RH10 .... 194 B6
SYD SE26 .... 32 F6
Newlands Rd CRAWW RH11 .... 211 M4
FRIM GU16 .... 72 E8
HORS RH12 .... 228 F5
STRHM/NOR SW16 .... 49 H2
The Newlands WLGTN SM6 .... 66 F6
Newlands Wy CHSGTN KT9 .... 62 F4
New La RGUE GU4 .... 97 J6
New Lodge Dr OXTED RH8 .... 130 C2
Newman Cl CRAWE RH10 .... 212 F5 ⑥
Newman Rd CROY/NA CR0 .... 49 J7 ⑥

Newmans Ct FNM GU9 133 K3
Newmarket Rd CRAWE RH10 212 D6
New Meadow ASC SL5 36 A1
New Mile Rd ASC SL5 36 E2
Newminster Rd MRDN SM4 47 M6
New Moorhead Dr HORS RH12 229 M3
Newnham Cl THHTH CR7 49 M2 4
New North Rd REIG RH2 147 J3
New Park Rd ASHF TW15 23 M6
BAL SW12 31 H2
BRXS/STRHM SW2 31 H1
CRAN GU6 185 H6
New Pond Rd RGUW GU3 138 B8
Newport Rd ASHV GU12 112 F8
BARN SW13 19 K3
HTHAIR TW6 14 D3 1
Newquay Rd CAT SE6 33 L3
New Rd BAGS GU19 54 C6
BLKW GU17 72 B5
BRAK RG12 35 G2
DTCH/LGLY SL3 12 A3
E/WMO/HCT KT8 43 K3
EBED/NFELT TW14 15 G8
EBED/NFELT TW14 24 E2
ESH/CLAY KT10 61 M3
FELT TW13 25 H6
GDST RH9 151 K2
HASM GU27 219 J4
HORL RH6 171 L6
HSLW TW3 16 E6
HYS/HAR UB3 14 F2
KUTN/CMB KT2 3 J2
KWD/TDW/WH KT20 104 F5
MFD/CHID GU8 181 H1
MFD/CHID GU8 182 B4
MFD/CHID GU8 201 K1
MTCM CR4 48 D8
NFNM GU10 135 J3
OXTED RH8 130 E4
RCHPK/HAM TW10 26 F5
RDKG RH5 187 H3
RGUE GU4 119 H5
RGUE GU4 139 L7
SHGR GU5 141 M5
SHGR GU5 141 G5
SHGR GU5 161 L1
SHPTN TW17 41 K3
STA TW18 21 M6
WEY KT13 59 M4
New Road Hl HAYES BR2 71 H7
Newry Rd TWK TW1 17 K6
Newsham Rd WOKN/KNAP GU21 76 C7
Newstead Hall HORL RH6 171 G7
Newstead Ri CTHM CR3 108 E8
Newstead Wk MRDN SM4 47 M7
Newstead Wy WIM/MER SW19 29 G5
New St BH/WHM TN16 131 M1
CRAWE RH10 212 D2
STA TW18 22 D5
SWTR RH13 229 G7
Newton Av EGRIN RH19 216 C3
Newton Rd CRAWE RH10 192 C7
FARN GU14 93 G3
ISLW TW7 17 J4
PUR/KEN CR8 86 F2
WDR/YW UB7 14 B3
WIM/MER SW19 29 H8
Newton Wy NFNM GU10 135 H2
Newton Wood Rd ASHTD KT21 83 J6
New Town CRAWE RH10 193 L6
New Wy RGODL GU7 159 M5
New Wickham La EGH TW20 21 K8
New Zealand Av WOT/HER KT12 42 C8
Nicholas Gdns
WOKS/MYFD GU22 78 B6
Nicholas Rd CROY/NA CR0 67 H3
Nicholes Rd HSLW TW3 16 D6 1
Nicholsfield BIL RH14 224 C5
Nicholson Rd CROY/NA CR0 5 K3
Nicholson Wk EGH TW20 21 K6 3
Nicola Cl SAND/SEL CR2 67 M5
Nicosia Rd WAND/EARL SW18 30 B1
Niederwald Rd SYD SE26 33 H5 2
Nigel Fisher Wy CHSGTN KT9 63 G6
Nightingale Av EHSLY KT24 100 A7
Nightingale Cl BH/WHM TN16 90 F5
CAR SM5 66 D1 3
CHSWK W4 18 F1 2
COB KT11 81 G1
CRAWW RH11 211 M1
EGRIN RH19 216 A2 1
HOR/WEW KT19 83 K2 1
Nightingale Crs BRAK RG12 34 F5
EHSLY KT24 100 A7
Nightingale Dr FRIM GU16 93 K6 1
HOR/WEW KT19 63 L5
Nightingale La BAL SW12 30 C1
RCHPK/HAM TW10 27 H1
Nightingale Rd ASHV GU12 113 M6
CAR SM5 66 C2
E/WMO/HCT KT8 43 L5
EHSLY KT24 100 C7
ESH/CLAY KT10 61 J4
GU GU1 9 H3
HORS RH12 229 G6
HPTN TW12 25 K7
RGODL GU7 160 B3
SAND/SEL CR2 89 G1
WOT/HER KT12 42 F7 1
Nightingales CRAN GU6 185 H8
Nightingale Shott EGH TW20 21 J7
Nightingale Sq BAL SW12 30 D1
The Nightingales
STWL/WRAY TW19 23 J2 4
Nightingale Wy REDH RH1 128 B8
Nightjar Cl NFNM GU10 133 G1
Nimbus Rd HOR/WEW KT19 64 A8
Nimrod Rd STRHM/NOR SW16 30 E7
Nineacres Wy COUL/CHIP CR5 87 H6
Nine Elms Cl
EBED/NFELT TW14 24 C2 13
Ninehams Cl CTHM CR3 108 A2
Ninehams Gdns CTHM CR3 108 A2
Ninehams Rd BH/WHM TN16 111 G3
CTHM CR3 108 A3
Nine Mile Ride CWTH RG45 34 D8
Nineteenth Rd MTCM CR4 49 H4
Ninhams Wd ORP BR6 71 K3
Niton Rd RCH/KEW TW9 18 D5 3
Niven Cl CRAWE RH10 213 G4 3
Nobel Dr HYS/HAR UB3 15 H2
Nobles Wy EGH TW20 21 H8
Noke Dr REDH RH1 126 D7
Nonsuch Court Av EW KT17 64 E8
Nonsuch Wk BELMT SM2 65 G8
Noons Corner Rd RDKG RH5 165 J1
Norbiton Av KUT KT1 3 K6
Norbiton Common Rd
NWMAL KT3 3 M8
Norbury Av HSLW TW3 17 G7
STRHM/NOR SW16 49 J1
Norbury Cl STRHM/NOR SW16 49 K1
Norbury Court Rd
STRHM/NOR SW16 49 H2
Norbury Crs STRHM/NOR SW16 49 K2
Norbury Cross
STRHM/NOR SW16 49 H3
Norbury Hl STRHM/NOR SW16 31 K8
Norbury Ri STRHM/NOR SW16 49 H3
Norbury Rd REIG RH2 125 J8
THHTH CR7 49 M2
Norbury Wy GT/LBKH KT23 101 M7
Norcroft Gdns EDUL SE22 32 D1
Norcutt Rd WHTN TW2 26 B2
Norfolk Av SAND/SEL CR2 68 D8
Norfolk Cl CRAWW RH11 211 H7 3
HORL RH6 170 D7
TWK TW1 17 L8 3
Norfolk Farm Cl
WOKS/MYFD GU22 7 M3
Norfolk Farm Rd
WOKS/MYFD GU22 78 A5
Norfolk House Rd
STRHM/NOR SW16 31 G4
Norfolk La RDKG RH5 144 E8
Norfolk Rd DORK RH4 144 D2
ESH/CLAY KT10 62 B4 2
FELT TW13 24 F2
HORS RH12 229 G7
RDKG RH5 166 F3
THHTH CR7 49 M3
WIM/MER SW19 30 B8
Norgrove St BAL SW12 30 D2
Norheads La BH/WHM TN16 90 F6
Norhyrst Av SNWD SE25 50 C3
Nork Gdns BNSTD SM7 85 H4
Nork Ri BNSTD SM7 85 G6
Nork Wy BNSTD SM7 85 G5
Norlands La EGH TW20 40 B2
Norley V PUT/ROE SW15 28 D2 4
Norman Av EW KT17 84 C2
FELT TW13 25 H3
SAND/SEL CR2 67 M8
TWK TW1 26 E1
Norman Cl ORP BR6 71 M2
Norman Crs HEST TW5 16 A2
Normandy HORS RH12 228 F8 2
Normandy Cl CRAWE RH10 212 E5 3
EGRIN RH19 216 C1 4
FRIM GU16 94 B1
SYD SE26 33 H4 2
Normandy Gdns HORS RH12 228 F8
Normanhurst Cl CRAWE RH10 212 C3
Normanhurst Dr TWK TW1 17 L7 1
Normanhurst Rd
BRXS/STRHM SW2 31 J3 1
WOT/HER KT12 61 G1
Norman Keep BNFD RG42 35 J1
Norman Rd ASHF TW15 24 A7
SUT SM1 65 K4
THHTH CR7 49 L5
WIM/MER SW19 29 M8 1
Normansfield Av KUT KT1 2 B3
Normans La EDEN TN8 175 H1
Norman's Rd HORL RH6 171 M4
Normanton Av WIM/MER SW19 29 K3
Normanton Rd SAND/SEL CR2 68 B5
Normanton St FSTH SE23 33 G3
Normington Cl
STRHM/NOR SW16 31 K6 2
Norrels Dr EHSLY KT24 100 C8
Norrels Ride EHSLY KT24 100 C8
Norris Rd STA TW18 22 C5 2
Norstead Pl PUT/ROE SW15 28 D3
North Acre BNSTD SM7 85 J6
Northampton Cl BRAK RG12 35 H3 4
Northampton Rd CROY/NA CR0 5 L5
Northanger Rd
STRHM/NOR SW16 31 H7
North Av CAR SM5 66 D6 1
FNM GU9 134 A2
RCH/KEW TW9 18 D3 2
WOT/HER KT12 60 B7
North Beta Rd FARN GU14 92 E7
Northborough Rd
STRHM/NOR SW16 49 H2
Northbourne RGODL GU7 160 C1
Northbrook Copse BRAK RG12 35 J6 2
Northbrook Rd ALDT GU11 134 E1
CROY/NA CR0 50 A5
Northcliffe Cl WPK KT4 64 B2
North Cl ASHV GU12 113 H8
CRAWE RH10 212 C2
EBED/NFELT TW14 15 G8
FARN GU14 92 D1
MRDN SM4 47 H4
RDKG RH5 144 F6
North Common WEY KT13 59 M3 3
Northcote ADL/WDHM KT15 59 G3
Northcote Av BRYLDS KT5 45 K7
ISLW TW7 17 K7
Northcote Crs EHSLY KT24 99 M7
Northcote La SHGR GU5 162 B4
Northcote Rd ASHV GU12 113 K2
CROY/NA CR0 50 A6
EHSLY KT24 99 M7
FARN GU14 92 B3
NWMAL KT3 45 M3
TWK TW1 17 K7
Northcott BRAK RG12 34 D8
Northcroft Cl EGH TW20 20 E6
Northcroft Gdns EGH TW20 20 E6
Northcroft Rd EGH TW20 20 E6
HOR/WEW KT19 64 B6
Northcroft Vls EGH TW20 20 E6
North Dene HEST TW5 16 E3
North Down SAND/SEL CR2 88 B1
Northdown Cl HORS RH12 229 J5
Northdown La GU GU1 9 K9
Northdown Rd BELMT SM2 65 K8 4
GDST RH9 109 K7
Northdowns CRAN GU6 185 H8
North Downs Crs CROY/NA CR0 69 L8
North Downs Rd CROY/NA CR0 69 L8
North Downs Wy
BRKHM/BTCW RH3 124 B4
NFNM GU10 134 D7
OXTED RH8 110 D5
RDKG RH5 121 K8
REDH RH1 128 A1
RGUE GU4 139 K4
RGUW GU3 136 C6
North Dr CHOB/PIR GU24 94 F3
HSLW TW3 16 F4
STRHM/NOR SW16 30 F5
VW GU25 38 B5
North End CROY/NA CR0 4 C4
North End La ASC SL5 37 K7
ORP BR6 71 L7
Northernhay Wk MRDN SM4 47 H4 3
Northern Perimeter Road (West)
HTHAIR TW6 14 B3
Northey Av BELMT SM2 65 G8
North Farm Rd FARN GU14 92 B1
Northfield LTWR GU18 74 E1 2
MFD/CHID GU8 181 J5 2
RGUE GU4 139 H8
Northfield Cl ASHV GU12 113 G8 1
Northfield Ct STA TW18 40 E1
Northfield Crs CHEAM SM3 65 H3 3
Northfield Pl WEY KT13 59 L6
Northfield Rd COB KT11 80 D3
North Field Rd HEST TW5 16 A1
Northfield Rd STA TW18 40 E1
Northfields ASHTD KT21 103 H1 1
EW KT17 84 B1
North Gdns WIM/MER SW19 30 A8
Northgate Av CRAWE RH10 212 C2
Northgate Dr CBLY GU15 73 K2
Northgate Pl CRAWE RH10 212 B2 2
Northgate Rd CRAWW RH11 212 A3
North Gate Rd FARN GU14 92 F7
North Gn BRAK RG12 35 G1
North Gv CHERT KT16 40 C6
North Hatton Rd HTHAIR TW6 15 G3
North Heath Cl HORS RH12 229 G4
North Heath La HORS RH12 229 G4
North Holmes Cl HORS RH12 229 L4
Northington Cl BRAK RG12 35 J6 3
Northlands Rd HORS RH12 208 A8
HORS RH12 229 H2
North La ALDT GU11 113 G6
TEDD TW11 26 C7
North Lodge Dr ASC SL5 35 M2
North Md CRAWE RH10 212 B1
Northmead FARN GU14 92 E5
North Md REDH RH1 126 C5
North Munstead La RGODL GU7 160 D8
Northolt Rd WDR/YW UB7 14 A3
North Pde CHSGTN KT9 63 J4
HORS RH12 228 F5
North Park La REDH RH1 128 D3
North Pl TEDD TW11 26 C7
WIM/MER SW19 30 C8 3
North Pole La HAYES BR2 70 D5
North Rd ALDT GU11 113 G2
ASC SL5 35 L1
ASHV GU12 113 J5
BTFD TW8 18 B1
CRAWE RH10 212 D2
EBED/NFELT TW14 15 G8
GUW GU2 116 E5
HEST TW5 15 M1
RCH/KEW TW9 18 D4
REIG RH2 147 J3
SURB KT6 45 G6
TOOT SW17 30 A7 3
WIM/MER SW19 29 M7
WOKN/KNAP GU21 7 G3
WOT/HER KT12 60 F4
WWKM BR4 51 L8 1
Northrop Rd HTHAIR TW6 15 H3
Northspur Rd SUT SM1 65 K2
North Station Ap REDH RH1 149 J2 1
Northstead Rd
BRXS/STRHM SW2 31 K3
North St CAR SM5 66 C3
CRAWE RH10 214 D5
DORK RH4 144 D2
EGH TW20 21 J6
GU GU1 9 G6
HORS RH12 229 G7
ISLW TW7 17 K5
LHD/OX KT22 102 D4
REDH RH1 126 C7
RGODL GU7 160 B2
Northumberland Av ISLW TW7 17 J3
Northumberland Cl
STWL/WRAY TW19 14 B8
Northumberland Crs
EBED/NFELT TW14 15 H8
Northumberland Gdns
MTCM CR4 49 G5 2
North Vw WIM/MER SW19 28 E6
North View Crs EPSOM KT18 84 F7
Northway GUW GU2 116 D6
RGODL GU7 159 L2
RYNPK SW20 47 H3
WLGTN SM6 66 F3
Northway Rd CROY/NA CR0 50 C6
North Weald La KUTN/CMB KT2 26 F6
Northwood Av PUR/KEN CR8 87 K3
WOKN/KNAP GU21 76 A8
Northwood Rd CAR SM5 66 D5
FSTH SE23 33 J2
HTHAIR TW6 14 A3 1
THHTH CR7 49 M2
North Worple Wy
MORT/ESHN SW14 19 G5
Norton Av BRYLDS KT5 45 L7
Norton Cl RGUW GU3 96 A8
Norton Gdns STRHM/NOR SW16 49 H2
Norton Pk ASC SL5 36 F5
Norton Rd CBLY GU15 73 M5
Norwich Av CBLY GU15 73 H6
Norwich Rd CRAWE RH10 212 D5
THHTH CR7 49 M3
Norwood Cl EHSLY KT24 121 H2
WHTN TW2 26 A3
Norwood Crs HTHAIR TW6 14 F3
Norwood Farm La COB KT11 80 D1
Norwood High St WNWD SE27 31 M5
Norwood Hl HORL RH6 169 G6
Norwoodhill Rd HORL RH6 169 J8
Norwood Park Rd WNWD SE27 31 M6
Norwood Rd EHSLY KT24 121 H2
HNHL SE24 31 L2
Notley End EGH TW20 20 F8 1
Notson Rd SNWD SE25 50 E4
Nottingham Cl
WOKN/KNAP GU21 76 C8
Nottingham Rd ISLW TW7 17 J4 2
SAND/SEL CR2 67 M3
TOOT SW17 30 C2
Nova Ms MRDN SM4 47 H7 2
Nova Rd CROY/NA CR0 4 B3
Nowell Rd BARN SW13 19 K1
Nower Rd DORK RH4 144 D2
Nowhurst La HORS RH12 227 K4
Noyna Rd TOOT SW17 30 C4
Nuffield Dr SHST GU47 52 C8
Nugent Cl MFD/CHID GU8 203 J3
Nugent Rd SNWD SE25 50 C3
Nunappleton Wy
OXTED RH8 130 D6 1
Nuneaton BRAK RG12 35 H6
Nuns Wk VW GU25 39 G5
Nursery Av CROY/NA CR0 69 G1
Nursery Cl ADL/WDHM KT15 58 C8
CROY/NA CR0 69 G1
EBED/NFELT TW14 24 E1 2
EW KT17 64 B8
FRIM GU16 93 J2
KWD/TDW/WH KT20 104 E7
RDKG RH5 188 F4
WOKN/KNAP GU21 76 F6
Nursery Gdns HSLWW TW4 16 C7 4
RGUE GU4 139 L6
STA TW18 22 E8
SUN TW16 42 C2
Nursery Hl SHGR GU5 162 A5
Nurserylands CRAWW RH11 211 K3
Nursery La HORL RH6 170 A7
Nursery Rd
KWD/TDW/WH KT20 104 E7
MTCM CR4 48 B4
RGODL GU7 160 C2
SUN TW16 42 B2
SUT SM1 65 M3 3
THHTH CR7 50 A4
WIM/MER SW19 29 H8
WOKN/KNAP GU21 76 A7
Nursery Wy STWL/WRAY TW19 12 A8
Nutbourne FNM GU9 134 B2
Nutcombe La DORK RH4 144 C1
GSHT GU26 199 H8
Nutcroft Gv LHD/OX KT22 102 B4
Nutfield Cl CAR SM5 66 B2
Nutfield Marsh Rd REDH RH1 127 G5
Nutfield Rd COUL/CHIP CR5 86 D6
REDH RH1 126 E8
THHTH CR7 49 L4
Nutfield Wy ORP BR6 71 K1
Nuthatch Cl NFNM GU10 133 G2
Nuthatch Gdns REIG RH2 147 M4
Nuthurst BRAK RG12 35 H5
Nuthurst Av BRXS/STRHM SW2 31 J3
CRAN GU6 185 H6 3
Nuthurst Cl CRAWW RH11 211 K2
Nutley BRAK RG12 34 D8
Nutley La REIG RH2 125 J7
Nutshell La FNM GU9 133 M3
Nutty La SHPTN TW17 41 M4
Nutwell St TOOT SW17 30 B6
Nutwood Av
BRKHM/BTCW RH3 145 M1
Nutwood Cl BRKHM/BTCW RH3 145 M1
Nyefield Pk
KWD/TDW/WH KT20 104 D8
Nylands Av RCH/KEW TW9 18 D4
Nymans Cl HORS RH12 229 K2
Nymans Ct CRAWE RH10 212 E6 4
Nymans Gdns RYNPK SW20 46 E3 2
Nyon Gv FSTH SE23 33 J3

O

Oakapple Cl CRAWW RH11 211 L8 1
SAND/SEL CR2 88 E4 1
Oak Av CHOB/PIR GU24 95 K3
CROY/NA CR0 69 K1
EGH TW20 21 M8
HEST TW5 16 A2
HPTN TW12 25 H6
SHST GU47 52 A8
Oakbank LHD/OX KT22 101 M5
WOKS/MYFD GU22 6 D9
Oakbank Av WOT/HER KT12 43 J7
Oak Cl CRAWE RH10 193 J6
KWD/TDW/WH KT20 123 L4
MFD/CHID GU8 201 K5
RGODL GU7 160 B1
Oakcombe Cl NWMAL KT3 46 B1
Oak Cnr RDKG RH5 166 F6
Oak Cottage Cl RGUW GU3 115 M7
Oak Ct FNM GU9 10 F2
Oak Cft EGRIN RH19 216 D1
Oakcroft Cl BF/WBF KT14 78 C4 2
Oakcroft Rd BF/WBF KT14 78 C4
CHSGTN KT9 63 J3
Oakcroft Vls CHSGTN KT9 63 J3
Oakdale BRAK RG12 35 G6
Oakdale La EDEN TN8 131 M7
Oakdale Rd HOR/WEW KT19 64 A7
STRHM/NOR SW16 31 H6
WEY KT13 59 K2 2
Oakdale Wy MTCM CR4 48 D7 2
Oak Dell CRAWE RH10 212 F2
Oakdene ASC SL5 37 J6
CHOB/PIR GU24 56 C8
KWD/TDW/WH KT20 105 H2
Oakdene Av THDIT KT7 44 D8 5
Oakdene Cl BRKHM/BTCW RH3 145 M2
GT/LBKH KT23 121 M1
Oakdene Dr BRYLDS KT5 45 M8
Oakdene Ms CHEAM SM3 47 J8
Oakdene Rd
BRKHM/BTCW RH3 145 M3
COB KT11 80 E4
GT/LBKH KT23 101 J6 2
REDH RH1 126 C8
RGODL GU7 160 A6
RGUW GU3 138 F8
Oak Dr KWD/TDW/WH KT20 123 L4
Oaken Coppice ASHTD KT21 103 K1
Oaken Copse CBLY GU15 73 M2
Oaken Copse Crs FARN GU14 92 E2
Oak End RDKG RH5 166 F6
Oaken Dr ESH/CLAY KT10 62 C5
Oak End Wy ADL/WDHM KT15 78 B2
Oakengates BRAK RG12 34 D8
Oaken La ESH/CLAY KT10 62 B3
Oakenshaw Cl SURB KT6 45 H7 4
Oakfield BIL RH14 223 H7
WOKN/KNAP GU21 76 B6
Oakfield Cl NWMAL KT3 46 C5
WEY KT13 59 M3
Oakfield Dr REIG RH2 125 K6
Oakfield Gdns BECK BR3 51 K5
CAR SM5 48 B8
Oakfield Gld WEY KT13 59 M3
Oakfield La HAYES BR2 70 F3
Oakfield Rd ASHF TW15 23 L6
ASHTD KT21 83 H8
BLKW GU17 72 B5
COB KT11 80 E3
CROY/NA CR0 4 C3
EDEN TN8 153 L5
PGE/AN SE20 32 E8
WIM/MER SW19 29 G4
Oakfields BF/WBF KT14 78 E4
CRAWE RH10 213 G2
GUW GU2 116 B6
RDKG RH5 207 H1
WOT/HER KT12 42 D8
Oakfield Wy EGRIN RH19 196 C6
Oak Gdns CROY/NA CR0 69 K1
Oak Grange Rd RGUE GU4 118 E3
Oak Gv BIL RH14 224 D5 2
CRAN GU6 185 J8 3
SUN TW16 24 E8
WWKM BR4 69 M1
Oak Grove Crs CBLY GU15 72 C3
Oak Grove Rd PGE/AN SE20 50 F1
Oakhall Dr SUN TW16 24 C6
Oakham Cl CAT SE6 33 J3 3
Oakhaven CRAWE RH10 212 A5 3
Oak Hl EPSOM KT18 84 A6
Oakhill ESH/CLAY KT10 62 D5
Oak Hl RGUE GU4 117 M4
RGUW GU3 115 K6
SURB KT6 45 H7
Oakhill Cl ASHTD KT21 82 F8
Oak Hill Crs SURB KT6 45 H7 5
Oakhill Gdns WEY KT13 60 B1
Oak Hill Gv SURB KT6 45 H6
Oakhill Rd ADL/WDHM KT15 58 C5
ASHTD KT21 82 F8
BECK BR3 51 M2
REIG RH2 147 L1
STRHM/NOR SW16 49 H1
Oak Hill Rd SURB KT6 45 H6 3
Oakhill Rd SUT SM1 65 L2
SWTR RH13 229 H7
Oakhurst CHOB/PIR GU24 56 B7
GSHT GU26 199 G6
Oakhurst Cl TEDD TW11 26 B6 3
Oakhurst Gdns EGRIN RH19 195 M7
Oakhurst La BIL RH14 224 B3
Oakhurst Ri CAR SM5 66 B8
Oakhurst Rd HOR/WEW KT19 63 M5
Oakington Dr SUN TW16 42 F2
Oakland Av FNM GU9 134 B2
Oaklands GDST RH9 151 H4
HASM GU27 219 M2 2
HORL RH6 170 F6
LHD/OX KT22 102 A6
PUR/KEN CR8 87 M4
Oaklands Av ESH/CLAY KT10 44 A8
ISLW TW7 17 J1
THHTH CR7 49 K4
WWKM BR4 69 L2
Oaklands Cl CHSGTN KT9 62 F3
RGUE GU4 139 H8
Oaklands Ct ADL/WDHM KT15 58 E2
Oaklands Dr REDH RH1 148 E2
Oaklands Gdns PUR/KEN CR8 87 M4 1
Oaklands La BH/WHM TN16 90 F5
Oaklands Rd MORT/ESHN SW14 19 G5
Oaklands Wy
KWD/TDW/WH KT20 104 F4
WLGTN SM6 66 F6
Oakland Wy HOR/WEW KT19 64 A5
Oak La EGH TW20 20 F4
HORS RH12 228 B6
ISLW TW7 17 H6
TWK TW1 26 D1 5
WOKS/MYFD GU22 7 K4
Oaklawn Rd LHD/OX KT22 82 C6
Oaklea ASHV GU12 113 K4
Oak Leaf Cl HOR/WEW KT19 83 M2 1
Oakleigh Av SURB KT6 45 K8
Oakleigh Rd HORS RH12 229 J5 4
Oakleigh Wy MTCM CR4 48 E1
SURB KT6 45 L8 2
Oakley Av CROY/NA CR0 67 H3
Oakley Cl ADL/WDHM KT15 59 G3
EGRIN RH19 216 E2
ISLW TW7 17 G3
Oakley Dell RGUE GU4 117 M6
Oakley Dr HAYES BR2 71 H2
Oakley Gdns BNSTD SM7 85 L5
Oakley Rd CBLY GU15 72 E5
HAYES BR2 71 H2
SNWD SE25 50 E5
WARL CR6 88 D8
Oak Lodge Cl WOT/HER KT12 60 F4
Oak Lodge Dr REDH RH1 148 D8

WWKM BR4 .... 51 L7
Oak Md RGODL GU7 .... 160 A1
Oakmead Gn EPSOM KT18 ...... 83 M5
Oakmead Pl MTCM CR4 .... 48 B1
Oakmead Rd BAL SW12 .... 30 C2
CROY/NA CR0 .... 49 G6
Oak Pk BF/WBF KT14 .... 78 B3
Oak Park Gdns WIM/MER SW19 ... 29 G3
Oakridge CHOB/PIR GU24 .... 75 J3
Oak Rdg DORK RH4 .... 144 E6
Oak Rd COB KT11 .... 81 C5
CRAWW RH11 .... 211 M4
CTHM CR3 .... 108 B4
FARN GU14 .... 92 F6
LHD/OX KT22 .... 102 D1
NWMAL KT3 .... 46 A2
REIG RH2 .... 125 L7
Oak Rw MTCM CR4 .... 48 F2
Oaks Av FELT TW13 .... 25 H3
NRWD SE19 .... 32 B6
WPK KT4 .... 64 E3
Oaks Cl HORS RH12 .... 229 L3
LHD/OX KT22 .... 102 D3
Oaksford Av SYD SE26 .... 32 E4
Oakshade Rd LHD/OX KT22 ...... 81 M4
Oakshaw Rd WAND/EARL SW18 ... 29 L1
Oakshaw OXTED RH8 .... 130 A1
Oakside Ct HORL RH6 .... 170 F5 [10]
Oakside La HORL RH6 .... 170 F5
Oaks La CROY/NA CR0 .... 68 F2
RDKG RH5 .... 144 E8
Oaks Rd CROY/NA CR0 .... 68 E4
PUR/KEN CR8 .... 87 L4
REIG RH2 .... 126 A7
STWL/WRAY TW19 .... 14 A7
WOKN/KNAP GU21 .... 6 C6
The Oaks BF/WBF KT14 .... 78 D4
BRAK RG12 .... 35 G2
EGRIN RH19 .... 216 D1
EPSOM KT18 .... 84 B4
SURB KT6 .... 62 F2 [1]
Oaks Tr CAR SM5 .... 66 D8
Oaks Wy CAR SM5 .... 66 C6
EPSOM KT18 .... 104 E1
PUR/KEN CR8 .... 87 M4
SURB KT6 .... 63 G1
Oak Tree Cl ASHV GU12 .... 93 J8 [2]
ASHV GU12 .... 135 H1
RGUE GU4 .... 116 F2
RGUE GU4 .... 117 M3
VW GU25 .... 39 G6
WOKN/KNAP GU21 .... 75 L8
Oak Tree Dr EGH TW20 .... 20 F6
GU GU1 .... 116 F4
Oak Tree La HASM GU27 .... 219 G3
MFD/CHID GU8 .... 203 J4
Oak Tree Rd MFD/CHID GU8 ...... 159 J8
WOKN/KNAP GU21 .... 75 L8
Oaktrees ASHV GU12 .... 113 J8
FNM GU9 .... 133 L3 [3]
Oak Tree Vw FNM GU9 .... 134 A3
Oak Tree Wy SWTR RH13 ...... 229 J5
Oak Vw EDEN TN8 .... 153 L7
Oakview Gv CROY/NA CR0 ...... 51 H8
Oakview Rd CAT SE6 .... 33 L6
Oak Wk HORS RH12 .... 210 C8
Oak Wy ASHTD KT21 .... 83 K6
Oakway ASHV GU12 .... 135 H1
Oak Wy CRAWE RH10 .... 212 B1
CROY/NA CR0 .... 51 G6
EBED/NFELT TW14 .... 24 B2
REIG RH2 .... 148 A1
Oakway RYNPK SW20 .... 46 F4
WOKN/KNAP GU21 .... 96 B1
Oakway Dr FRIM GU16 .... 73 H8
Oakwood GU2 .... 116 D3 [4]
WLGTN SM6 .... 66 E7
Oakwood Av BECK BR3 .... 51 M2
MTCM CR4 .... 48 A2
PUR/KEN CR8 .... 87 L2
Oakwood Cl EHSLY KT24 ...... 120 B1
REDH RH1 .... 126 D8
REDH RH1 .... 149 J2 [5]
Oakwood Ct CHOB/PIR GU24 ... 75 K6
Oakwood Dr EHSLY KT24 ...... 120 B1
NRWD SE19 .... 32 A7
Oakwood Gdns ORP BR6 ...... 71 M1
SUT SM1 .... 65 K1 [5]
WOKN/KNAP GU21 .... 75 K8
Oakwood Pl CROY/NA CR0 ...... 49 K6
Oakwood Rd CTHM CR3 .... 108 B7
Oakwood Rd BFOR GU20 ...... 55 H5
BRAK RG12 .... 35 H2
CROY/NA CR0 .... 49 K6 [4]
HORL RH6 .... 170 E5
ORP BR6 .... 71 M1
REDH RH1 .... 127 K3
RYNPK SW20 .... 46 D1
VW GU25 .... 38 F5
WOKN/KNAP GU21 .... 96 B1
Oareborough BRAK RG12 ...... 35 H4
Oarsman Pl E/WMO/HCT KT8 ... 44 B4 [1]
Oast House Cl STWL/WRAY TW19 ... 21 H1
Oast House La FNM GU9 .... 134 A4
Oast La ALDT GU11 .... 134 E2
Oast Rd OXTED RH8 .... 130 C5
Oatfield Rd
KWD/TDW/WH KT20 .... 104 E3
Oatlands CRAWH RH11 .... 211 K4
HORL RH6 .... 170 E5 [11]
Oatlands Av WEY KT13 .... 60 A4
Oatlands Cha WEY KT13 .... 60 B2
Oatlands Cl WEY KT13 .... 59 M3
Oatlands Dr WEY KT13 .... 60 A2
Oatlands Gn WEY KT13 .... 60 A2 [3]
Oatlands Mere WEY KT13 ...... 60 A2
Oatlands Rd
KWD/TDW/WH KT20 .... 105 H1
Oban Rd SNWD SE25 .... 50 A4 [3]
Obelisk Wy CBLY GU15 .... 72 F3
Oberon Wy CRAWW RH11 ...... 211 H6 [5]
SHPTN TW17 .... 41 H3
Observatory Rd
MORT/ESHN SW14 .... 18 F6
Occam Rd GUW GU2 .... 116 A8
Ockenden Cl
WOKS/MYFD GU22 .... 6 F8 [3]

Ockenden Gdns
WOKS/MYFD GU22 .... 6 E8
Ockenden Rd WOKS/MYFD GU22 .. 6 E8
Ockfields MFD/CHID GU8 .... 159 J8
Ockford Dr RGODL GU7 .... 159 M6
Ockford Rdg RGODL GU7 .... 159 L7
Ockford Rd RGODL GU7 .... 159 M6
Ockham La COB KT11 .... 80 D8
RPLY/SEND 99 M2
Ockham Rd North
RPLY/SEND 99 L4
Ockham Rd South
.... 120 B3 [3]
Ockley Ct RGUE GU4 .... 117 L3 [3]
Ockley Rd CRAN GU6 .... 186 B3
CROY/NA CR0 .... 49 J7
RDKG RH5 .... 187 L2
STRHM/NOR SW16 .... 31 H4
Ockleys Md GDST RH9 .... 128 F3 [3]
O'connor Rd ALDT GU11 .... 113 G2
Octagon Rd WOT/HER KT12 ...... 60 B8
Octavia BRAK RG12 .... 34 D8
Octavia Cl MTCM CR4 .... 48 B5
Octavia Rd ISLW TW7 .... 17 J5
Octavia Wy STA TW18 .... 22 D7
Odard Rd E/WMO/HCT KT8 ...... 43 K4
WEY KT13 .... 59 M6
Odiham Rd NFNM GU10 .... 132 E1
Off Upper Manor Rd
RGODL GU7 .... 160 B2
O'gorman Av FARN GU14 .... 92 E7
Okeburn Rd TOOT SW17 .... 30 D6 [2]
Okehurst Rd BIL RH14 .... 225 M8
Okingham Cl SHST GU47 .... 52 A8 [3]
Old Acre BF/WBF KT14 .... 78 D4
Oldacre CHOB/PIR GU24 .... 75 J2
Old Av BF/WBF KT14 .... 78 A4
WEY KT13 .... 59 M6
Old Avenue Cl
WOKN/KNAP GU21 .... 78 B3
Old Barn Cl BELMT SM2 .... 65 H6
Old Barn Dr RDKG RH5 .... 189 C3
Old Barn La CTHM CR3 .... 88 C6
NFNM GU10 .... 178 E7
Old Barn Rd EPSOM KT18 ...... 83 M7
Old Barn Vw RGODL GU7 ...... 159 M7 [2]
Old Bisley Rd FRIM GU16 ...... 73 K7
Old Bracknell Cl BRAK RG12 ... 34 E3 [1]
Old Bracknell La East
BRAK RG12 .... 34 E3
Old Bracknell La West
BRAK RG12 .... 34 D3
Old Brickfield Rd ALDT GU11 ... 134 E2
Old Bridge St KUT KT1 .... 2 C6
Old Brighton Rd South
CRAWE RH10 .... 192 B5
Oldbury BRAK RG12 .... 34 C3
Oldbury Cl FRIM GU16 .... 93 J1 [1]
HORS RH12 .... 229 K2
Oldbury Rd CHERT KT16 .... 40 B7
Old Charlton Rd SHPTN TW17 ... 41 M5
Old Chertsey Rd CHOB/PIR GU24 .. 56 E8
Old Chestnut Av ESH/CLAY KT10 .. 61 K5
Old Church La FNM GU9 .... 11 J5
Old Church Pth
ESH/CLAY KT10 .... 61 L3 [3]
Old Claygate La ESH/CLAY KT10 .. 62 D5
Old Common Rd COB KT11 ...... 80 E2
Old Cote Dr HEST TW5 .... 16 D1
Old Ct ASHTD KT21 .... 103 H1
Old Court Rd GUW GU2 .... 8 B5
Old Crawley Rd HORS RH12 ... 229 M3
Old Cross Tree Wy ASHV GU12 . 135 M1
Old Dean Rd CBLY GU15 .... 73 G2
Old Deer Park Gdns
RCH/KEW TW9 .... 18 B5
Old Denne Gdns HORS RH12 ... 228 F8 [3]
Old Devonshire Rd BAL SW12 ... 30 E1
Old Dock Cl RCH/KEW TW9 ...... 18 D1 [1]
Old Elstead Rd MFD/CHID GU8 .. 159 H7
Olden La PUR/KEN CR8 .... 87 K2
Old Esher Cl WOT/HER KT12 .... 61 G4 [1]
Old Esher Rd WOT/HER KT12 .... 61 G4 [3]
Old Farleigh Rd SAND/SEL CR2 .. 68 F8
WARL CR6 .... 89 J3
Old Farm Cl HSLWW TW4 ...... 16 C6
Old Farmhouse Dr LHD/OX KT22 .. 82 A5
Old Farm Pl ASHV GU12 ...... 113 J5
Old Farm Rd GU GU1 .... 117 G5
HPTN TW12 .... 25 J7
Old Farnham La FNM GU9 ...... 11 H3
NFNM GU10 .... 132 D8
Oldfield Gdns ASHTD KT21 ...... 103 G1
Oldfield Rd HORL RH6 .... 170 C8
HPTN TW12 .... 43 K1
WIM/MER SW19 .... 29 H7
Oldfields RD CHEAM SM3 ...... 65 K1
Oldfieldwood WOKS/MYFD GU22 .. 7 K5
Old Forge Crs SHPTN TW17 ...... 41 L6 [3]
Old Fox Cl CTHM CR3 .... 107 L3
Old Frensham Rd NFNM GU10 ... 11 K8
Old Green La CBLY GU15 .... 72 F2
Old Guildford Rd FRIM GU16 ...... 93 L4
HORS RH12 .... 228 B6
Old Haslemere Rd HASM GU27 .. 219 M4
Old Heath Wy FNM GU9 .... 133 M2 [3]
Old HI WOKS/MYFD GU22 ...... 97 G2
Old Holbrook HORS RH12 ...... 229 H1
Old Hollow CRAWE RH10 ...... 213 J1
Old Horsham Rd CRAWW RH11 .. 191 L5
Old Hospital Cl TOOT SW17 ...... 30 C2 [3]
Old House Cl EW KT17 .... 84 A2
WIM/MER SW19 .... 29 H6 [3]
Oldhouse La CHOB/PIR GU24 .... 54 F7
CHOB/PIR GU24 .... 75 K4
Old Kiln Cl NFNM GU10 .... 178 C7
Old Kiln La BRKHM/BTCW RH3 .. 123 M8
NFNM GU10 .... 178 C7
Old Kingston Rd WPK KT4 ...... 63 M3
Old Lands HI BRAK RG12 ...... 35 G1
Old La ALDT GU11 .... 134 D2
ASHV GU12 .... 113 H6
BH/WHM TN16 .... 111 G3
COB KT11 .... 100 A1
NFNM GU10 .... 177 H5
OXTED RH8 .... 130 C4
Old Lane Gdns COB KT11 ...... 100 C4
Old Lodge La PUR/KEN CR8 .... 159 L6 [3]

Old Lodge La PUR/KEN CR8 ...... 87 J3
Old London Rd EPSOM KT18 .... 84 D8
RDKG RH5 .... 122 F2
Old Malden La WPK KT4 .... 64 B1
Old Malt Wy WOKN/KNAP GU21 .. 6 B5
Old Manor Cl CRAWW RH11 .... 211 K1
Old Manor Dr ISLW TW7 .... 16 F8
Old Manor Gdns RGUE GU4 .... 139 M6
Old Martyrs CRAWW RH11 ...... 192 A8 [3]
Old Merrow St RGUE GU4 ...... 117 M5
Old Mill La REDH RH1 .... 126 E2
Old Millmeads HORS RH12 ...... 228 F4
Old Mill Pl HASM GU27 .... 219 J2
Old Nursery Pl ASHF TW15 ...... 23 L6
Old Oak Av COUL/CHIP CR5 .... 106 B1
Old Orch BF/WBF KT14 .... 79 J2
SUN TW16 .... 42 F2
Old Orchards CRAWE RH10 ...... 213 H3
The Old Orch FNM GU9 .... 10 C5
Old Palace Rd CROY/NA CR0 .... 4 B7
GUW GU2 .... 8 B6
WEY KT13 .... 59 L2
Old Palace Yd RCH/KEW TW9 ... 17 M7
Old Park Cl FNM GU9 .... 133 K3
Old Park La FNM GU9 .... 133 K3
Old Park Ms HEST TW5 .... 16 C2
Old Parvis Rd BF/WBF KT14 .... 78 F2
Old Pasture Rd FRIM GU16 ...... 73 J6
Old Pond Cl FRIM GU16 .... 72 E8
Old Portsmouth Rd CBLY GU15 .. 73 K5
PGE/AN SE20 .... 32 D8
Old Pottery Cl REIG RH2 ...... 147 L2
Old Pound Cl ISLW TW7 .... 17 K3
The Old Quarry HASM GU27 .... 219 J3
Old Rectory Cl
KWD/TDW/WH KT20 .... 104 D6
Old Rectory Dr ASHV GU12 .... 113 L7
Old Rectory Gdns FARN GU14 ... 93 G5 [3]
RGODL GU7 .... 160 C7
Old Rectory La EHSLY KT24 .... 100 B8
Old Redstone Dr REDH RH1 .... 148 D1 [3]
Old Reigate Rd
BRKHM/BTCW RH3 .... 123 M8
DORK RH4 .... 123 H8
Oldridge Rd BAL SW12 .... 30 D1
Old Rd ADL/WDHM KT15 ...... 58 C6
BRKHM/BTCW RH3 .... 124 C7
EGRIN RH19 .... 216 C1
Old School Cl ASHV GU12 ...... 113 K6
BECK BR3 .... 51 G2
Old School Ct STWL/WRAY TW19 .. 21 H1
Old School La
BRKHM/BTCW RH3 .... 145 K3
RDKG RH5 .... 167 L8
Old School Ms WEY KT13 ...... 60 A3
Old School Pl LING RH7 .... 174 A5
WOKS/MYFD GU22 .... 97 H3
Old Schools La EW KT17 ...... 64 C7
Old Station Ap LHD/OX KT22 .... 102 D3
Old Station Cl CRAWE RH10 .... 214 E2
Old Station La STWL/WRAY TW19 .. 12 C8
Old Station Wy RGODL GU7 .... 160 B3
Oldstead BRAK RG12 .... 35 G5
Old Swan Yd CAR SM5 .... 66 C3
Old Town CROY/NA CR0 .... 4 B7
Old Tye Av BH/WHM TN16 ...... 91 H6
Old Westhall Cl WARL CR6 ...... 108 F1
Old Wickhurst La HORS RH12 ... 228 A8
Old Woking Rd BF/WBF KT14 ... 78 D3
WOKS/MYFD GU22 .... 7 K9
Oliver Av SNWD SE25 .... 50 C3
Oliver Cl ADL/WDHM KT15 ...... 58 E3
CHSWK W4 .... 18 E1
Oliver Gv SNWD SE25 .... 50 C4
Olive Rd WIM/MER SW19 ...... 29 M8 [3]
Olivier Rd CRAWE RH10 ...... 213 G4
Ollerton BRAK RG12 .... 34 D8
Olley Cl WLGTN SM6 .... 67 H6
Olveston Wk MRDN SM4 ...... 48 A6 [3]
Olyffe Dr BECK BR3 .... 51 M1
Omega Rd WOKN/KNAP GU21 .... 7 H2
Omega Wy EGH TW20 .... 39 M1
One Tree Hill Rd RGUE GU4 .... 139 L2
Ongar Cl ADL/WDHM KT15 ...... 58 C5
Ongar HI ADL/WDHM KT15 ...... 58 D5
Ongar Pl ADL/WDHM KT15 ...... 58 D5
Ongar Rd ADL/WDHM KT15 ...... 58 D5
Onslow Av BELMT SM2 .... 65 J8
RCHPK/HAM TW10 .... 18 B7
Onslow Cl WOKS/MYFD GU22 .... 7 H5
THDIT KT7 .... 44 B8 [2]
WLGTN SM6 .... 66 F6
Onslow Crs WOKS/MYFD GU22 .. 7 H5
Onslow Gdns SAND/SEL CR2 .... 88 D2
THDIT KT7 .... 44 B8 [3]
WLGTN SM6 .... 66 F6
Onslow Ms CHERT KT16 .... 40 C6
Onslow Rd ASC SL5 .... 37 L7
CROY/NA CR0 .... 49 K7
GU GU1 .... 9 H4
NWMAL KT3 .... 46 D4
RCHPK/HAM TW10 .... 18 B8
WOT/HER KT12 .... 60 D3
Onslow St GU GU1 .... 6 F7
Onslow Wy THDIT KT7 .... 44 B8
WOKS/MYFD 78 C5
Ontario Cl HORL RH6 .... 171 K7
Openview WAND/EARL SW18 .... 29 M2
Opladen Wy BRAK RG12 ...... 35 G7
Opossum Wy HSLWW TW4 ...... 15 M5
Orange Court La ORP BR6 ...... 71 K7
The Orangery
RCHPK/HAM TW10 .... 26 C3
Orchard Av ADL/WDHM KT15 .... 78 C1
ASHF TW15 .... 23 M7
CROY/NA CR0 .... 69 H1
EBED/NFELT TW14 .... 15 G7
HEST TW5 .... 16 B2
MTCM CR4 .... 48 D8
NWMAL KT3 .... 46 B2
THDIT KT7 .... 44 D8

CHOB/PIR GU24 .... 75 G3
EDEN TN8 .... 153 L7
FARN GU14 .... 72 C8
FNM GU9 .... 134 D3
GU GU1 .... 117 L8
HOR/WEW KT19 .... 63 L5 [3]
HORL RH6 .... 170 C5
LHD/OX KT22 .... 102 A4
RGUW GU3 .... 114 E8
RYNPK SW20 .... 46 F4
WOKS/MYFD GU22 .... 7 K4
WOT/HER KT12 .... 42 E7
Orchard Ct BRAK RG12 .... 34 F2 [3]
Orchard Dr EDEN TN8 .... 153 L7
SHPTN TW17 .... 42 B3
WOKN/KNAP GU21 .... 6 E2
Orchard End CTHM CR3 .... 108 B4
GT/LBKH KT23 .... 101 M6
NFNM GU10 .... 155 J6
WEY KT13 .... 60 B1
Orchardfield Rd RGODL GU7 .... 160 C2
CHSGTN KT9 .... 63 H3
CRAN GU6 .... 185 J7
EHSLY KT24 .... 121 H2
EPSOM KT18 .... 83 M5 [3]
Orchard Ga ESH/CLAY KT10 .... 44 A8
Orchard Gdns ALDT GU11 ...... 134 F1
CHSGTN KT9 .... 63 H3
CRAN GU6 .... 185 J7
EHSLY KT24 .... 121 H2
EPSOM KT18 .... 83 M5 [3]
Orchard Gv CROY/NA CR0 ...... 51 H7
PGE/AN SE20 .... 32 D8
Orchard HI BFOR GU20 .... 55 G6
HORS RH12 .... 225 M2
Orchard Lea Cl
WOKS/MYFD GU22 .... 78 B5
Orchardleigh LHD/OX KT22 ...... 102 E4 [3]
Orchard Mains
WOKS/MYFD GU22 .... 96 F2
Orchard Ri CROY/NA CR0 ...... 51 H8
KUTN/CMB KT2 .... 45 M1
RCHPK/HAM TW10 .... 18 E6
Orchard Rd BTFD TW8 .... 17 M1
CHSGTN KT9 .... 63 H3
DORK RH4 .... 144 E3
FARN GU14 .... 92 D5
FNM GU9 .... 134 D3
GUW GU2 .... 138 C2
HORL RH6 .... 171 L6
HPTN TW12 .... 25 J8
HSLWW TW4 .... 16 C7
KUT KT1 .... 2 E7
ORP BR6 .... 71 L4
RCH/KEW TW9 .... 18 D5
REIG RH2 .... 125 L8
RGUE GU4 .... 117 L4
RGUE GU4 .... 139 H6
SAND/SEL CR2 .... 88 E4
SHGR GU5 .... 141 K5
SUN TW16 .... 24 D8
SUT SM1 .... 65 K4
SWTR RH13 .... 229 H8
TWK TW1 .... 17 K7
WDSR SL4 .... 20 E1
Old Swan Yd CAR SM5 .... 66 C3
The Orchards CRAWW RH11 .... 211 G4 [3]
Orchard St CRAWW RH11 ...... 212 A3
THDIT KT7 .... 44 B8
The Orchard EW KT17 .... 64 C6
HASM GU27 .... 219 J4
LTWR GU18 .... 74 E1 [3]
RDKG RH5 .... 144 F6
VW GU25 .... 39 H5
WOKS/MYFD GU22 .... 97 H4
Orchard Wy ADL/WDHM KT15 .. 58 E4
ALDT GU11 .... 134 F1
ASHF TW15 .... 23 J3
CBLY GU15 .... 72 E7
CROY/NA CR0 .... 51 H7
DORK RH4 .... 144 E3
EGRIN RH19 .... 196 B8
ESH/CLAY KT10 .... 61 M5
KWD/TDW/WH KT20 .... 105 H8
OXTED RH8 .... 130 D7
REIG RH2 .... 147 L3
RGUW GU3 .... 114 E8
RPLY/SEND GU23 .... 97 M7
SUT SM1 .... 66 A3
Orchid Dr CHOB/PIR GU24 ...... 75 K5
Orde Cl CRAWE RH10 .... 193 G8
Ordnance Cl FELT TW13 .... 24 D3 [3]
Ordnance Rd ALDT GU11 ...... 113 G6
Oregano Wy GUW GU2 .... 116 D3
Oregon Cl NWMAL KT3 .... 45 M4 [3]
Orestan La EHSLY KT24 ...... 120 F1
Orford Gdns TWK TW1 .... 26 C3
Orford Rd CAT SE6 .... 33 L4
Oriel Cl CRAWE RH10 .... 192 F8 [3]
MTCM CR4 .... 49 G4
Oriel Dr BARN SW13 .... 19 M1
Oriel HI CBLY GU15 .... 73 G5
Oriental Cl WOKS/MYFD GU22 .. 6 F5
Oriental Rd ASC SL5 .... 37 G4
WOKS/MYFD GU22 .... 6 F6
Orion BRAK RG12 .... 34 C3
Orlando Gdns HOR/WEW KT19 .. 64 A8 [3]
Orleans Rd NRWD SE19 .... 32 A7
TWK TW1 .... 26 E1
Oritons La HORS RH12 .... 190 C7
Ormanton Rd SYD SE26 ...... 32 D5
Ormeley Rd BAL SW12 .... 30 E1
Orme Rd KUT KT1 .... 3 M6
Ormerod Gdns MTCM CR4 ...... 48 D2
Ormond Av HPTN TW12 .... 43 L1
ORP BR6 .... 71 M1
Ormond Crs HPTN TW12 .... 25 L8
Ormond Dr HPTN TW12 .... 25 L8
Ormonde Av HOR/WEW KT19 .. 64 A8
Ormonde Rd MORT/ESHN SW14 .. 18 E5
RGODL GU7 .... 160 B3
WOKN/KNAP GU21 .... 76 C3
Ormond Rd RCHPK/HAM TW10 .. 18 A7
Ormside Wy REDH RH1 .... 126 E4
Orpin Rd REDH RH1 .... 126 F6
Orpwood Cl HPTN TW12 ...... 25 J7 [3]
Orwell Cl FARN GU14 .... 92 B2
Orwell Gdns REIG RH2 .... 147 L2 [3]
Osborne Av STWL/WRAY TW19 .. 23 H2

Osborne Cl BECK BR3 .... 51 H4
FELT TW13 .... 42 D1
Osborne Dr LTWR GU18 .... 74 D1
Osborne Gdns THHTH CR7 ...... 49 M2 [3]
Osborne Rd EGH TW20 .... 21 J7
FARN GU14 .... 112 F1
HSLWW TW4 .... 16 C5
KUTN/CMB KT2 .... 2 E2
REDH RH1 .... 126 D5
THHTH CR7 .... 49 M2
WOT/HER KT12 .... 42 D8 [3]
Osborn La FSTH SE23 .... 33 H1
Osborn Rd FNM GU9 .... 134 A5
Osier Pl EGH TW20 .... 21 M7
Osier Wy BNSTD SM7 .... 85 H4
Oslac Rd CAT SE6 .... 33 L6
Osmond Gdns WLGTN SM6 .... 66 F4
Osmunda Bank EGRIN RH19 .... 196 B3
Osmund Cl CRAWE RH10 ...... 213 H3
Osnaburgh HI CBLY GU15 ...... 72 E4
Osney Cl CRAWW RH11 ...... 211 M4
Osney Wk MRDN SM4 .... 48 A6
Osprey Gdns SAND/SEL CR2 .... 69 G8
Ospringe Cl PGE/AN SE20 ...... 32 F8 [3]
Ostade Rd BRXS/STRHM SW2 .. 31 J1
Osterley Av ISLW TW7 .... 17 G2
Osterley Crs ISLW TW7 .... 17 H3
Osterley Gdns THHTH CR7 ...... 49 M2
Osterley Rd ISLW TW7 .... 17 H2
Oswald Cl LHD/OX KT22 ...... 101 M4
Oswald Rd LHD/OX KT22 ...... 101 M4
Osward CROY/NA CR0 .... 69 J8
Osward Rd BAL SW12 .... 30 C3
Otford Cl PGE/AN SE20 .... 50 F1
Othello Gv BNFD RG42 .... 35 H1 [3]
Otterbourne Rd CROY/NA CR0 .. 4 C5 [3]
Otterburn Gdns ISLW TW7 ...... 17 K2
Otterburn St TOOT SW17 ...... 30 C7 [3]
Otter Cl CHERT KT16 .... 57 L5
Otterden St CAT SE6 .... 33 K5
Ottermead La CHERT KT16 ...... 57 M5
Ottways Av ASHTD KT21 ...... 103 G1
Ottways La ASHTD KT21 ...... 103 H1
Otway Cl CRAWW RH11 ...... 211 J5 [3]
Ouseley Rd BAL SW12 .... 30 C2
STWL/WRAY TW19 .... 20 F1
Outdowns EHSLY KT24 .... 120 E4
Outram Pl WEY KT13 .... 59 M4 [3]
Outram Rd CROY/NA CR0 ...... 5 K5
Outwood La
KWD/TDW/WH KT20 .... 105 L4
REDH RH1 .... 128 A8
REDH RH1 .... 172 A1
Oval Rd CROY/NA CR0 .... 4 F5
The Oval BNSTD SM7 .... 85 K4
GUW GU2 .... 8 B5
RGODL GU7 .... 160 C2
RGUW GU3 .... 115 L7
Overbrae BECK BR3 .... 33 K7
Overbrook EHSLY KT24 .... 119 L3
RGODL GU7 .... 160 D4
Overbury Av BECK BR3 .... 51 L3
Overbury Crs CROY/NA CR0 .... 69 M8
Overdale ASHTD KT21 .... 83 H6
RDKG RH5 .... 144 F1
REDH RH1 .... 127 M7
Overdale Av NWMAL KT3 ...... 45 M2
Overdale Ri FRIM GU16 .... 73 H6
Overdene Dr CRAWW RH11 .... 211 K3
Overdown Rd CAT SE6 .... 33 K5
Overford Cl CRAN GU6 .... 185 H7 [3]
Overford Dr CRAN GU6 .... 185 H7
Overhill WARL CR6 .... 108 F1
Overhill Rd EDUL SE22 .... 32 C1
PUR/KEN CR8 .... 67 K7
Overlord Cl CBLY GU15 .... 72 F1
Overstand Cl BECK BR3 .... 51 K5
Overstone Gdns CROY/NA CR0 .. 51 J7
Overthorpe Cl
WOKN/KNAP GU21 .... 76 B7
Overton Cl ALDT GU11 .... 134 F3
ISLW TW7 .... 17 J3 [3]
Overton Rd BELMT SM2 .... 65 K5
Overton Shaw EGRIN RH19 .... 196 B6
Overton's Yd CROY/NA CR0 .... 4 C7
Oveton Wy GT/LBKH KT23 .... 101 K8
Ovett Cl NRWD SE19 .... 32 B7
Ovington Ct
WOKN/KNAP GU21 .... 76 C6 [3]
Owen Cl CROY/NA CR0 .... 50 A6
Owen Pl LHD/OX KT22 .... 102 E4 [3]
Owen Rd BFOR GU20 .... 55 G4
RGODL GU7 .... 160 C3
Owens Wy FSTH SE23 .... 33 H1
Owlbeech Wy SWTR RH13 ...... 229 L5
Owl Cl SAND/SEL CR2 .... 69 G8 [3]
Owlets CRAWE RH10 .... 213 G2 [3]
Owlscastle Cl HORS RH12 ...... 229 G4
Owlsmoor Rd SHST GU47 ...... 72 A1
Ownstead Gdns SAND/SEL CR2 .. 88 C1
Ownsted HI CROY/NA CR0 ...... 69 M8
Oxdowne Cl COB KT11 .... 81 L4
Oxenden Ct NFNM GU10 ...... 135 H1 [3]
Oxenden Rd NFNM GU10 ...... 135 H1
Oxenhope BRAK RG12 .... 34 D4
Oxford Av HYS/HAR UB3 ...... 15 J2
RYNPK SW20 .... 47 H2
Oxford Cl ASHF TW15 .... 23 M8 [3]
MTCM CR4 .... 48 F3
Oxford Crs NWMAL KT3 ...... 46 A6
Oxford Rd CAR SM5 .... 66 B5
CRAWE RH10 .... 212 B7
FARN GU14 .... 92 F8
GU GU1 .... 9 H7
HPTN TW12 .... 26 A6
NRWD SE19 .... 32 A7
REDH RH1 .... 126 B7
SHST GU47 .... 52 B7
SWTR RH13 .... 229 G7
WLGTN SM6 .... 66 F4 [3]
Oxford Ter GU GU1 .... 9 H7
Oxford Wy FELT TW13 .... 25 G5
Oxleigh Cl NWMAL KT3 .... 46 B5 [3]
Oxshott Ri COB KT11 .... 81 K4
Oxshott Rd LHD/OX KT22 ...... 82 D8
Oxshott Wy COB KT11 .... 81 H5
Oxted Cl MTCM CR4 .... 48 A3
Oxted Gn MFD/CHID GU8 ...... 181 H2
Oxted Rd GDST RH9 .... 129 J5

Oxtoby Wy *STRHM/NOR* SW16 ..... 49 G1
Oyster La *BF/WBF* KT14 ..... 79 H2

P

Pacific Cl *EBED/NFELT* TW14 ..... 24 C2
Packway *FNM* GU9 ..... 11 L5
Padbrook *OXTED* RH8 ..... 130 D3
Padbury Cl *EBED/NFELT* TW14 ..... 24 A2
Paddock Cl *CBLY* GU15 ..... 73 K3
  LING RH7 ..... 173 M5
  ORP BR6 ..... 71 L3 ⬚
  OXTED RH8 ..... 130 C5
  RDKG RH5 ..... 167 G5 ⬚
  SYD SE26 ..... 33 G5
  WPK KT4 ..... 46 B8
Paddock Gdns *EGRIN* RH19 ..... 216 B2
  NRWD SE19 ..... 32 B7 ⬚
Paddock Gv *RDKG* RH5 ..... 167 G5
Paddockhurst Rd *CRAWE* RH10 ..... 213 M7
  CRAWW RH11 ..... 211 K4
Paddocks Cl *COB* KT11 ..... 80 F4
Paddocks Md *WOKN/KNAP* GU21 ..... 76 E6
Paddocks Rd *RGUE* GU4 ..... 117 M8
The Paddocks *GT/LBKH* KT23 ..... 101 L8 ⬚
  RGUW GU3 ..... 114 F8
  WEY KT13 ..... 60 B2
Paddocks Wy *ASHTD* KT21 ..... 83 H8
  CHERT KT16 ..... 40 E8
The Paddock *BH/WHM* TN16 ..... 111 M8
  BRAK RG12 ..... 34 F3
  CRAN GU6 ..... 186 B5
  CRAWE RH10 ..... 213 G2 ⬚
  DORK RH4 ..... 143 L3
  GSHT GU26 ..... 198 D5 ⬚
  GU GU1 ..... 118 A7
  HASM GU27 ..... 219 K1
  RGODL GU7 ..... 160 C6
Paddock Wk *WARL* CR6 ..... 108 E1
Paddock Wy *HASM* GU27 ..... 200 D7
  OXTED RH8 ..... 130 C5
  WOKN/KNAP GU21 ..... 77 L3
Padstow Wk *EBED/NFELT* TW14 ..... 24 C3
Padua Rd *PGE/AN* SE20 ..... 50 F1
Padwick Rd *SWTR* RH13 ..... 229 J7
Pageant Wk *CROY/NA* CR0 ..... 5 C7
Page Cl *FELT* TW13 ..... 25 H7
Page Crs *CROY/NA* CR0 ..... 67 L4 ⬚
Pagehurst Rd *CROY/NA* CR0 ..... 5 M1
Page Rd *EBED/NFELT* TW14 ..... 15 G8
Paget Av *SUT* SM1 ..... 66 A2
Paget Cl *CBLY* GU15 ..... 73 L2
  HPTN TW12 ..... 26 A5 ⬚
Paget La *ISLW* TW7 ..... 17 G5
Paget Pl *THDIT* KT7 ..... 44 C8
Pagewood Cl *CRAWE* RH10 ..... 213 G5
Pagoda Av *RCH/KEW* TW9 ..... 18 C5
Pain's Cl *MTCM* CR4 ..... 48 E2 ⬚
Pains Hl *OXTED* RH8 ..... 130 F6
Paisley Rd *CAR* SM5 ..... 48 A8
Pakenham Cl *BAL* SW12 ..... 30 D2 ⬚
Pakenham Rd *BRAK* RG12 ..... 35 G7
Palace Dr *WEY* KT13 ..... 59 L2
Palace Gdns West *WEY* KT13 ..... 59 L2 ⬚
Palace Gdns *CROY/NA* CR0 ..... 69 J6
Palace Gv *NRWD* SE19 ..... 32 C8
Palace Rd *ADL/WDHM* KT15 ..... 58 E7 ⬚
  BH/WHM TN16 ..... 111 K3
  BRXS/STRHM SW2 ..... 31 J2
  E/WMO/HCT KT8 ..... 43 M3
  KUT KT1 ..... 45 G4
  NRWD SE19 ..... 32 C8
Palace Sq *NRWD* SE19 ..... 32 C8
Palace Vw *CROY/NA* CR0 ..... 69 J3
Palestine Gv *WIM/MER* SW19 ..... 48 A1
Palewell Common Dr
  MORT/ESHN SW14 ..... 19 G7
Palewell Pk *MORT/ESHN* SW14 ..... 19 G7
Pallant Wy *ORP* BR6 ..... 71 K2
Pallingham Dr *CRAWE* RH10 ..... 212 F6
Palmer Av *CHEAM* SM3 ..... 64 F3
Palmer Cl *HEST* TW5 ..... 16 D3 ⬚
  HORL RH6 ..... 170 C4
  REDH RH1 ..... 148 D1
  WWKM BR4 ..... 70 A1
Palmer Crs *CHERT* KT16 ..... 58 A5
  KUT KT1 ..... 2 E8
Palmer Rd *CRAWE* RH10 ..... 212 F6
Palmers Gv *E/WMO/HCT* KT8 ..... 43 K4
Palmer's Ldg *GUW* GU2 ..... 8 B6
Palmers Rd *MORT/ESHN* SW14 ..... 18 F5
  STRHM/NOR SW16 ..... 49 J2 ⬚
Palmerston Cl *FARN* GU14 ..... 92 A6 ⬚
  WOKN/KNAP GU21 ..... 77 K4 ⬚
Palmerston Gv
  WIM/MER SW19 ..... 29 K8 ⬚
Palmerston Rd *CAR* SM5 ..... 66 C3 ⬚
  CROY/NA CR0 ..... 50 A5 ⬚
  HSLW TW3 ..... 16 F3
  MORT/ESHN SW14 ..... 18 F6
  ORP BR6 ..... 71 M3
  SUT SM1 ..... 65 M4 ⬚
  WHTN TW2 ..... 17 H8 ⬚
  WHTN TW2 ..... 17 J8 ⬚
  WIM/MER SW19 ..... 29 K8 ⬚
Palm Gv *GU* GU1 ..... 116 F3
Pampisford Rd *PUR/KEN* CR8 ..... 87 K1
Pams Wy *HOR/WEW* KT19 ..... 64 A4
Pankhurst Cl *ISLW* TW7 ..... 17 J5 ⬚
Pankhurst Dr *BRAK* RG12 ..... 35 G5
Pankhurst Rd *WOT/HER* KT12 ..... 42 F7
Pankridge St *NFNM* GU10 ..... 132 C2
Panmuir Rd *RYNPK* SW20 ..... 46 E1
Panmure Rd *SYD* SE26 ..... 32 E4
Pannell Cl *EGRIN* RH19 ..... 196 A8
Pannells *NFNM* GU10 ..... 11 K9
Pannells Cl *CHERT* KT16 ..... 40 C8 ⬚
Pan's Gdns *CBLY* GU15 ..... 73 J5
Pantile Rd *WEY* KT13 ..... 60 A3
Pantiles Cl *WOKN/KNAP* GU21 ..... 76 E8 ⬚
Papercourt La *RPLY/SEND* GU23 ..... 98 C4
Paper Ms *DORK* RH4 ..... 144 E1 ⬚
Papermill Cl *CAR* SM5 ..... 66 D3
Papworth Wy *BRXS/STRHM* SW2 ..... 31 K1
Parade Cl *RPLY/SEND* GU23 ..... 97 M5
Parade Ms *BRXS/STRHM* SW2 ..... 31 L3 ⬚

The Parade *BIL* RH14 ..... 224 C5
  CRAWE RH10 ..... 212 B2 ⬚
  EPSOM KT18 ..... 84 A3
  ESH/CLAY KT10 ..... 62 B5
  SUN TW16 ..... 42 B3 ⬚
Paradise Rd *RCHPK/HAM* TW10 ..... 18 B7
Paragon Gv *BRYLDS* KT5 ..... 45 J6
Parbury Ri *CHSGTN* KT9 ..... 63 H5
Parchmore Rd *THHTH* CR7 ..... 49 L2
Parchmore Wy *THHTH* CR7 ..... 49 L1 ⬚
Pares Cl *WOKN/KNAP* GU21 ..... 6 A3
Parfitts Cl *FNM* GU9 ..... 133 K7
Parfour Dr *PUR/KEN* CR8 ..... 87 M6
Parfrey St *HMSMTH* W6 ..... 19 M1
Parham Rd *CRAWW* RH11 ..... 211 J2
Parish Cl *ASHV* GU12 ..... 113 L8
  FNM GU9 ..... 133 K3
Parish La *PGE/AN* SE20 ..... 33 G8
Parish Rd *FARN* GU14 ..... 112 E1
Park Av *CAR* SM5 ..... 66 D5
  CBLY GU15 ..... 72 F5
  CTHM CR3 ..... 108 B6
  EDEN TN8 ..... 153 L7
  EGH TW20 ..... 21 M8
  HSLW TW3 ..... 16 E8
  MFD/CHID GU8 ..... 158 F4
  MORT/ESHN SW14 ..... 19 G6
  MTCM CR4 ..... 30 E8
  ORP BR6 ..... 71 J1
  REDH RH1 ..... 148 C8
  SHPTN TW17 ..... 42 B3
  STA TW18 ..... 22 C7
  STWL/WRAY TW19 ..... 12 A7
  WWKM BR4 ..... 69 M1
Park Av East *EW* KT17 ..... 64 D5
Park Av West *EW* KT17 ..... 64 D5
Park Barn Dr *GUW* GU2 ..... 116 B7
Park Barn East *GUW* GU2 ..... 116 C7
Park Cha *GU* GU1 ..... 9 J4
  RGODL GU7 ..... 160 B7
Park Cl *ADL/WDHM* KT15 ..... 58 E8
  BOR SM5 ..... 176 B8
  BRKHM/BTCW RH3 ..... 145 L5
  CAR SM5 ..... 66 C5
  ESH/CLAY KT10 ..... 61 J5
  HASM GU27 ..... 200 C8
  HPTN TW12 ..... 43 M1
  ISLW TW7 ..... 16 F7 ⬚
  KUTN/CMB KT2 ..... 3 J3
  LHD/OX KT22 ..... 102 A6
  NFNM GU10 ..... 154 D7
  WEY KT13 ..... 60 C1
Park Copse *RDKG* RH5 ..... 145 G2
Park Corner Dr *EHSLY* KT24 ..... 120 B2
Park Ct *NWMAL* KT3 ..... 46 A4
  WOKS/MYFD GU22 ..... 6 E8
Park Crs *ASC* SL5 ..... 37 J5
  FROW RH18 ..... 217 K7
  WHTN TW2 ..... 26 A2
Parkdale Crs *WPK* KT4 ..... 64 A2
Park Dr *ASC* SL5 ..... 37 J6
  CRAN GU6 ..... 185 J5
  MORT/ESHN SW14 ..... 19 G7
  SHGR GU5 ..... 161 J3
  WEY KT13 ..... 59 L4
  WOKS/MYFD GU22 ..... 6 E8
Parker Cl *CRAWE* RH10 ..... 213 G5
Parke Rd *BARN* SW13 ..... 19 K3
  SUN TW16 ..... 42 D4
Parker Rd *CROY/NA* CR0 ..... 4 D9
Parker's Cl *ASHTD* KT21 ..... 103 H1
Parker's Hl *ASHTD* KT21 ..... 103 H1
Parker's La *ASHTD* KT21 ..... 103 J1
Park Farm Cl *HORS* RH12 ..... 229 G2
Park Farm Rd *KUTN/CMB* KT2 ..... 2 F2
Parkfield *HORS* RH12 ..... 228 F6
  RGODL GU7 ..... 160 B7
Parkfield Av *FELT* TW13 ..... 24 D4 ⬚
  MORT/ESHN SW14 ..... 19 H6
Parkfield Cl *CRAWW* RH11 ..... 211 J3
Parkfield Crs *FELT* TW13 ..... 24 D4
Parkfield Rd *FELT* TW13 ..... 24 D4
Parkfields *CROY/NA* CR0 ..... 51 J8
  LHD/OX KT22 ..... 82 A1
  PUT/ROE SW15 ..... 19 M6
Parkfields Av *RYNPK* SW20 ..... 46 E1
Parkfields Cl *CAR* SM5 ..... 66 D3 ⬚
Parkfields Rd *KUTN/CMB* KT2 ..... 27 J6
Park Gdns *KUTN/CMB* KT2 ..... 27 J6
Parkgate Cl *KUTN/CMB* KT2 ..... 27 L7 ⬚
Parkgate Gdns
  MORT/ESHN SW14 ..... 19 G7
Parkgate Rd *CAR* SM5 ..... 66 D4
  RDKG RH5 ..... 167 L7
  REIG RH2 ..... 147 L1
Park Gn *GT/LBKH* KT23 ..... 101 K6
  REIG RH2 ..... 125 K6
Park Hall Rd *DUL* SE21 ..... 32 A3
  FSTH SE23 ..... 32 E3
Park Hl *CAR* SM5 ..... 66 B4 ⬚
  RCHPK/HAM TW10 ..... 18 C8
Parkhill Cl *BLKW* GU17 ..... 72 A5
Park Hill Cl *CAR* SM5 ..... 66 B4 ⬚
Parkhill Rd *BLKW* GU17 ..... 72 A5
Park Hill Rd *CROY/NA* CR0 ..... 5 G6
  EW KT17 ..... 84 C1
  WLGTN SM6 ..... 66 E6
Park Horsley *EHSLY* KT24 ..... 120 D3
Park House Dr *REIG* RH2 ..... 147 J2
Park House Gdns *TWK* TW1 ..... 17 M7
Parkhurst *HOR/WEW* KT19 ..... 63 M8 ⬚
Parkhurst Flds *NFNM* GU10 ..... 178 C8
Parkhurst Gv *HORL* RH6 ..... 170 B5 ⬚
Parkhurst Rd *GUW* GU2 ..... 8 C1
  HORL RH6 ..... 170 B5
  SUT SM1 ..... 66 A3
Parkland Dr *BRAK* RG12 ..... 35 H1
Parkland Gv *ASHF* TW15 ..... 23 K5
  FNM GU9 ..... 134 C1
Parkland Rd *ASHF* TW15 ..... 23 K5
Parklands *ADL/WDHM* KT15 ..... 58 F4
  BRYLDS KT5 ..... 45 J5
  GT/LBKH KT23 ..... 101 K5
  OXTED RH8 ..... 130 B5
  RDKG RH5 ..... 144 E6
Parklands Cl *MORT/ESHN* SW14 ..... 18 F7
Parklands Pl *GU* GU1 ..... 117 L8

Parklands Rd *TOOT* SW17 ..... 30 E6
Parklands Wy *WPK* KT4 ..... 64 B1 ⬚
Park La *ASHTD* KT21 ..... 83 J8
  CAR SM5 ..... 66 D3
  CBLY GU15 ..... 72 F4 ⬚
  CHEAM SM3 ..... 65 H5
  COUL/CHIP CR5 ..... 107 G3
  CROY/NA CR0 ..... 4 E8
  DORK RH4 ..... 144 D1
  GU GU1 ..... 9 M1
  GU GU1 ..... 9 H1
  RYNPK SW20 ..... 47 G4
  WEY KT13 ..... 60 A3 ⬚
Parkland Rd *TOOT* ...
Parkwood *BECK* BR3 ..... 33 K8
Park La East *REIG* RH2 ..... 147 J3
Park La West ...
Parklawn Av *EPSOM* KT18 ..... 83 L3
  HORL RH6 ..... 170 C4
Park Lawn Rd *WEY* KT13 ..... 59 M3
Parkleigh Rd *WIM/MER* SW19 ..... 47 L2 ⬚
Park Ley Rd *CTHM* CR3 ..... 109 G2
Parkleys *KUTN/CMB* KT2 ..... 27 G5
Parkmead *PUT/ROE* SW15 ..... 19 L8
Park Ms *STWL/WRAY* TW19 ..... 23 J1
Parkpale La *BRKHM/BTCW* RH3 ..... 145 K5
Park Pl *HPTN* TW12 ..... 25 M7
Park Ri *HORS* RH12 ..... 228 E5
  LHD/OX KT22 ..... 102 D3
Park Rise Cl *LHD/OX* KT22 ..... 102 E3
Park Rise Rd *FSTH* SE23 ..... 33 H2
Park Rd *ALDT* GU11 ..... 134 E2
  ASHF TW15 ..... 23 L6
  ASHTD KT21 ..... 83 H8
  BECK BR3 ..... 33 J8
  BNSTD SM7 ..... 85 M6
  BRAK RG12 ..... 35 G1
  BRYLDS KT5 ..... 45 J6
  CBLY GU15 ..... 72 F6
  CHEAM SM3 ..... 65 H5
  CHSWK W4 ..... 19 G1
  CTHM CR3 ..... 108 B5
  E/WMO/HCT KT8 ..... 2 A5
  E/WMO/HCT KT8 ..... 43 M4
  EGH TW20 ..... 21 K5
  EGRIN RH19 ..... 196 A8
  EGRIN RH19 ..... 196 B3
  ESH/CLAY KT10 ..... 61 L3
  FARN GU14 ..... 93 H8
  FELT TW13 ..... 25 G5
  FNM GU9 ..... 134 A5
  FROW RH18 ..... 217 K7
  GU GU1 ..... 9 G4
  HASM GU27 ..... 219 M3
  HORL RH6 ..... 171 M8
  HORS RH12 ..... 210 C8
  HPTN TW12 ..... 25 M6
  HSLW TW3 ..... 16 F7
  ISLW TW7 ..... 17 L3
  KUT KT1 ..... 2 B5
  LING RH7 ..... 152 B6
  NWMAL KT3 ..... 46 A4
  OXTED RH8 ..... 130 C2
  PUR/KEN CR8 ..... 87 M5
  RCHPK/HAM TW10 ..... 18 C8
  REDH RH1 ..... 126 C6
  RGODL GU7 ..... 160 A7
  SHGR GU5 ..... 141 H7
  SHPTN TW17 ..... 41 K8
  SNWD SE25 ..... 50 B4
  STWL/WRAY TW19 ..... 13 L8
  SUN TW16 ..... 24 E8
  SWTR RH13 ..... 227 C6
  TEDD TW11 ..... 26 C8
  TWK TW1 ..... 17 M8
  WARL CR6 ..... 90 B4
  WIM/MER SW19 ..... 30 A8
  WLGTN SM6 ..... 66 E4
  WOKS/MYFD GU22 ..... 7 G6
Park Rd North *CHSWK* W4 ..... 19 C1
Park Rw *FNM* GU9 ..... 133 L6
Parkshot *RCH/KEW* TW9 ..... 18 A6
Park Side *ADL/WDHM* KT15 ..... 58 E8
Parkside *CHEAM* SM3 ..... 65 H5
  CRAWE RH10 ..... 212 B3 ⬚
  EGRIN RH19 ..... 195 M8
  FNM GU9 ..... 133 M3
  HPTN TW12 ..... 26 A6
  WIM/MER SW19 ..... 29 G5
Parkside Av *WIM/MER* SW19 ..... 29 G6
Parkside Cl *EHSLY* KT24 ..... 100 C7
  PGE/AN SE20 ..... 32 F8
Parkside Crs *BRYLDS* KT5 ..... 45 M6
Parkside Gdns *COUL/CHIP* CR5 ..... 86 E7
  WIM/MER SW19 ..... 29 G5
Parkside Ms *HORS* RH12 ..... 229 G6 ⬚
Parkside Pl *EHSLY* KT24 ..... 100 B7
Parkside Rd *ASC* SL5 ..... 37 K6
  HSLW TW3 ..... 16 F7
Parkstead Rd *PUT/ROE* SW15 ..... 19 K7
Parkstone Dr *CBLY* GU15 ..... 72 F5
Park St *BAGS* GU19 ..... 54 B6
  CBLY GU15 ..... 72 F5
  CROY/NA CR0 ..... 4 D6
  DTCH/LGLY SL3 ..... 13 G3
  HORS RH12 ..... 229 G7
  SWTR RH13 ..... 226 F6
  TEDD TW11 ..... 26 B7
Park Ter *WPK* KT4 ..... 46 D8
Park Ter East *SWTR* RH13 ..... 229 G8
Park Ter West *SWTR* RH13 ..... 229 G8
The Park *CAR* SM5 ..... 66 C4
  GT/LBKH KT23 ..... 101 K6
Parkthorne Rd *BAL* SW12 ..... 31 G1
Park Vw *BAGS* GU19 ..... 54 A6
  CRAWW RH11 ..... 211 M4
  GT/LBKH KT23 ..... 101 K7
  HORL RH6 ..... 170 D6
  NWMAL KT3 ..... 46 C3
Park View Cl *EDEN* TN8 ..... 153 L7
Park View Dr *MTCM* CR4 ..... 48 A2
Parkview Rd *CROY/NA* CR0 ..... 5 M3
Park View Rd *CTHM* CR3 ..... 109 J4
  REDH RH1 ..... 148 D7
Parkview V *RGUE* GU4 ..... 117 M5
Park Wy *CRAWE* RH10 ..... 212 F1
  E/WMO/HCT KT8 ..... 43 L3

EBED/NFELT TW14 ..... 24 E1
GT/LBKH KT23 ..... 101 K5
HORS RH12 ..... 228 F2 ⬚
Parkway *CBLY* GU15 ..... 72 F6
  CROY/NA CR0 ..... 69 M7
  DORK RH4 ..... 144 D1
  GU GU1 ..... 9 M1
  GU GU1 ..... 9 H1
  RYNPK SW20 ..... 47 G4
  WEY KT13 ..... 60 A3 ⬚
Parkwood *BECK* BR3 ..... 33 K8
Park Wood Cl *BNSTD* SM7 ..... 85 G5 ⬚
Parkwood Gv *SUN* TW16 ..... 42 D3 ⬚
Parkwood Rd *BH/WHM* TN16 ..... 111 H3
Park Wood Rd *BNSTD* SM7 ..... 85 G5
Parkwood Rd *ISLW* TW7 ..... 17 J3
  REDH RH1 ..... 127 H7
  WIM/MER SW19 ..... 29 J6
Park Wood Vw *BNSTD* SM7 ..... 84 F6
Park Works Rd *REDH* RH1 ..... 127 H8
Parley Dr *WOKN/KNAP* GU21 ..... 76 F3
Parliamentary Rd
  CHOB/PIR GU24 ..... 94 D3
Parnell Gdns *WEY* KT13 ..... 79 J1
Parnham Av *LTWR* GU18 ..... 75 G1 ⬚
Parr Av *EW* KT17 ..... 64 E7
Parr Cl *LHD/OX* KT22 ..... 102 C2
Parris Cft *RDKG* RH5 ..... 144 F5
Parr's Cl *SAND/SEL* CR2 ..... 68 A7
Parr's Pl *HPTN* TW12 ..... 25 K8
Parry Cl *EW* KT17 ..... 64 D6
  SWTR RH13 ..... 229 M5
Parry Dr *WEY* KT13 ..... 59 K8
Parry Rd *SNWD* SE25 ..... 50 B3
Parsonage Cl *WARL* CR6 ..... 89 H6
Parsonage La *DORK* RH4 ..... 143 M3
Parsonage Rd *CRAN* GU6 ..... 185 G6
  EGH TW20 ..... 21 G6
  HORS RH12 ..... 229 G5
Parsonage Sq *DORK* RH4 ..... 144 D1 ⬚
Parsonage Wy *FRIM* GU16 ..... 73 H8
  HORS RH12 ..... 229 H5
Parsons Cl *HASM* GU27 ..... 219 M1
  HORL RH6 ..... 170 B5 ⬚
Parsonsfield Cl *BNSTD* SM7 ..... 85 G5
Parsonsfield Rd *BNSTD* SM7 ..... 85 G6
Parsons Gn *HASM* GU27 ..... 219 M1
Parsons La *GSHT* GU26 ..... 198 F3
Parson's Md *CROY/NA* CR0 ..... 4 B4
  E/WMO/HCT KT8 ..... 43 M3
Parthia Cl *KWD/TDW/WH* KT20 ..... 104 E1
Partridge Cl *FRIM* GU16 ..... 73 H8
  NFNM GU10 ..... 133 G2 ⬚
Partridge Dr *ORP* BR6 ..... 71 M2
Partridge Knoll *PUR/KEN* CR8 ..... 87 L2
Partridge La *HORS* RH12 ..... 190 B7
  RDKG RH5 ..... 168 A5
Partridge Md *HPTN* TW12 ..... 25 J7
Partridge Pl *ESH/CLAY* KT10 ..... 61 M2 ⬚
Pates Manor Dr
  EBED/NFELT TW14 ..... 24 A1
Pathfield *MFD/CHID* GU8 ..... 201 L5
Pathfield Cl *HORS* RH12 ..... 226 A2 ⬚
Pathfield Rd *HORS* RH12 ..... 226 A2 ⬚
  STRHM/NOR SW16 ..... 31 G7
Pathfields *SHGR* GU5 ..... 141 K6
Pathfields Cl *HASM* GU27 ..... 220 A2
Path Link *CRAWE* RH10 ..... 212 B2
The Path *WIM/MER* SW19 ..... 47 L1
The Pathway *RPLY/SEND* GU23 ..... 98 C7
Patmore La *WOT/HER* KT12 ..... 60 C5
Patrington Cl *CRAWW* RH11 ..... 211 K6
Pattenden Rd *FSTH* SE23 ..... 33 J2
Patten Rd *WAND/EARL* SW18 ..... 30 B1
Patterdale Cl *CRAWW* RH11 ..... 211 M5 ⬚
Patterson Rd *NRWD* SE19 ..... 32 C7
Paul Cl *ALDT* GU11 ..... 134 B1
Paul Gdns *CROY/NA* CR0 ..... 5 J6
Pauline Crs *WHTN* TW2 ..... 25 M2
Pauls Md *LING* RH7 ..... 174 B4
Paul's Pl *ASHTD* KT21 ..... 83 L8
Pavilion Gdns *STA* TW18 ..... 22 E8
Pavilion Rd *ALDT* GU11 ..... 112 B8
The Pavilions End *CBLY* GU15 ..... 73 G6 ⬚
Pavilion Wy *EGRIN* RH19 ..... 216 B1 ⬚
Pawley Cl *NFNM* GU10 ..... 135 J2
Pawleyne Cl *PGE/AN* SE20 ..... 32 F8
Pawson's Rd *CROY/NA* CR0 ..... 49 M6
Pax Cl *CRAWW* RH11 ..... 211 H5
Paxton Cl *RCH/KEW* TW9 ..... 18 C4 ⬚
  WOT/HER KT12 ..... 42 F7 ⬚
Paxton Gdns *WOKN/KNAP* GU21 ..... 78 B3
Paxton Pl *WNWD* SE27 ..... 32 B5
Paxton Rd *FSTH* SE23 ..... 33 H4
Payne Cl *CROY/NA* CR0 ..... 213 G1
Paynesfield Av
  MORT/ESHN SW14 ..... 19 G5
Paynesfield Rd *BH/WHM* TN16 ..... 110 F2
Peabody Cl *CROY/NA* CR0 ..... 50 B7
Peabody Est *HNHL* SE24 ..... 31 L1
Peabody Hl *DUL* SE21 ..... 31 L2
Peabody Rd *FARN* GU14 ..... 93 G8
Peace Cl *SNWD* SE25 ..... 50 B4
Peacemaker Cl
  CRAWW RH11 ..... 211 H5 ⬚
Peaches Cl *BELMT* SM2 ..... 65 H6
Peach Tree Cl *FARN* GU14 ..... 92 D2
Peacock Av *EBED/NFELT* TW14 ..... 24 B2
Peacock Gdns *CROY/NA* CR0 ..... 69 H8
Peacocks La *BRAK* RG12 ..... 34 A4
Peakfield *NFNM* GU10 ..... 177 M2
Peak Hill Av *SYD* SE26 ..... 32 F5
Peak Hill Gdns *SYD* SE26 ..... 32 F5
Peak Hill *SYD* SE26 ..... 32 F5
Peak Rd *GUW* GU2 ..... 116 D5
Peaks Hl *PUR/KEN* CR8 ..... 67 H8
Peaks Hill Ri *PUR/KEN* CR8 ..... 67 H8

The Peak *SYD* SE26 ..... 32 F4
Peall Rd *CROY/NA* CR0 ..... 49 J6
Pear Av *SHPTN* TW17 ..... 42 B3
Pearce Av *MTCM* CR4 ..... 48 D2
Pearcefield Av *FSTH* SE23 ..... 32 F2 ⬚
Pearfield Rd *FSTH* SE23 ..... 33 H4
Pearmain Cl *SHPTN* TW17 ..... 41 L5 ⬚
Pearson Rd *CRAWE* RH10 ..... 212 E3
Pears Rd *HSLW* TW3 ..... 16 F5
Pear Tree Cl *ADL/WDHM* KT15 ..... 58 D4 ⬚
  MTCM CR4 ..... 48 C3 ⬚
Peartree Cl *SAND/SEL* CR2 ..... 88 E4 ⬚
Pear Tree La *NFNM* GU10 ..... 155 J6
Pear Tree Rd
  ADL/WDHM KT15 ..... 58 D4 ⬚
  ASHF TW15 ..... 23 M6
Peary Cl *HORS* RH12 ..... 229 G3
Peaslake La *SHGR* GU5 ..... 164 A3
Peat Common *MFD/CHID* GU8 ..... 157 M7
Peatmore Av *WOKS/MYFD* GU22 ..... 78 D6
Peatmore Cl *WOKS/MYFD* GU22 ..... 78 D6
Peatmore Dr *CHOB/PIR* GU24 ..... 94 F3
Pebble Cl *KWD/TDW/WH* KT20 ..... 124 D2
Pebble Hl *EHSLY* KT24 ..... 119 M7
Pebblehill Rd
  BRKHM/BTCW RH3 ..... 124 D4
Pebble La *EPSOM* KT18 ..... 103 K4
Peckarmans Wd *DUL* SE21 ..... 32 D4
Peek Crs *WIM/MER* SW19 ..... 29 G6
Peeks Brook La *HORL* RH6 ..... 171 J7
Peel Av *FRIM* GU16 ..... 93 K2
Peel Rd *ORP* BR6 ..... 71 M3
Pegasus Av *ASHV* GU12 ..... 113 H6
Pegasus Cl *HASM* GU27 ..... 219 G4
Pegasus Rd *CROY/NA* CR0 ..... 67 K5
  FARN GU14 ..... 92 C2 ⬚
Pegasus Wy *EGRIN* RH19 ..... 196 D6
Peggotty Pl *SHST* GU47 ..... 52 B7 ⬚
Pegg Rd *HEST* TW5 ..... 16 A2
Pegler Wy *CRAWW* RH11 ..... 212 A3
Pegwell Cl *CRAWW* RH11 ..... 211 J5
Peket Cl *STA* TW18 ..... 40 B1
Pelham Ct *CRAWW* RH11 ..... 211 L7
Pelham Dr *CRAWW* RH11 ..... 211 K7
Pelham Pl *CRAWW* RH11 ..... 211 K7
  NFNM GU10 ..... 155 K5 ⬚
Pelham Rd *PGE/AN* SE20 ..... 50 F2
  WIM/MER SW19 ..... 29 K8
Pelhams Cl *ESH/CLAY* KT10 ..... 61 K3 ⬚
Pelhams Wk *ESH/CLAY* KT10 ..... 61 K2
Pelham Wy *GT/LBKH* KT23 ..... 101 L8
Pelling Hl *WDSR* SL4 ..... 20 E1
Pelton Av *BELMT* SM2 ..... 65 L8
Pemberley Cha *HOR/WEW* KT19 ..... 63 L4 ⬚
Pemberley Cl *HOR/WEW* KT19 ..... 63 L4 ⬚
Pemberton Pl *ESH/CLAY* KT10 ..... 61 M2 ⬚
Pemberton Rd *E/WMO/HCT* KT8 ..... 43 M4
Pembley Gn *CRAWE* RH10 ..... 194 B6
Pembridge Av *HSLWW* TW4 ..... 25 J2
Pembroke *BRAK* RG12 ..... 34 C7
Pembroke Av *BRYLDS* KT5 ..... 45 L5
  WOT/HER KT12 ..... 61 G3
Pembroke Broadway
  CBLY GU15 ..... 72 F4
Pembroke Cl *ASC* SL5 ..... 37 G5 ⬚
  BNSTD SM7 ..... 85 L7
Pembroke Gdns
  WOKS/MYFD GU22 ..... 7 H7
Pembroke Pl *ISLW* TW7 ..... 17 H4 ⬚
Pembroke Rd *CRAWE* RH10 ..... 192 F8
  MTCM CR4 ..... 48 C2 ⬚
  SNWD SE25 ..... 50 B4
  WOKS/MYFD GU22 ..... 7 H6
Pembury Av *WPK* KT4 ..... 46 D7
Pembury Cl *COUL/CHIP* CR5 ..... 86 D4
Pembury Ct *HYS/HAR* UB3 ..... 15 G1 ⬚
Pembury Rd *SNWD* SE25 ..... 50 D4
Pemdevon Rd *CROY/NA* CR0 ..... 49 K7
Penates *ESH/CLAY* KT10 ..... 62 A3
Penberth Rd *CAT* SE6 ..... 33 M5
Pendarves Rd *RYNPK* SW20 ..... 46 F1
Pendell Av *HYS/HAR* UB3 ..... 15 J2
Pendell Rd *REDH* RH1 ..... 127 L6 ⬚
Pendennis Cl *BF/WBF* KT14 ..... 78 D4
Pendennis Rd
  STRHM/NOR SW16 ..... 31 H5
Penderel Rd *HSLW* TW3 ..... 16 D7
Pendine Pl *BRAK* RG12 ..... 34 E3 ⬚
Pendlebury *BRAK* RG12 ..... 34 D7
Pendle Rd *STRHM/NOR* SW16 ..... 30 E7
Pendleton Cl *REDH* RH1 ..... 148 D3
Pendleton Rd *REDH* RH1 ..... 148 A3
Pendragon Wy *CBLY* GU15 ..... 74 A5
Penerley Rd *CAT* SE6 ..... 33 L2
Penfold Cl *CROY/NA* CR0 ..... 67 K2 ⬚
Penfold Cft *FNM* GU9 ..... 134 C5
Penfold Rd *CRAWE* RH10 ..... 212 E2
Penge La *PGE/AN* SE20 ..... 32 F8
Penge Rd *SNWD* SE25 ..... 50 D3
Pengilly Rd *FNM* GU9 ..... 133 L7
Penhurst *WOKN/KNAP* GU21 ..... 77 J4
Peninsular Cl *EBED/NFELT* TW14 ..... 15 G8
Penistone Rd *STRHM/NOR* SW16 ..... 31 H8
Penlee Cl *EDEN* TN8 ..... 153 M7
The Pennards *SUN* TW16 ..... 42 F3 ⬚
Penn Cl *CRAWW* RH11 ..... 192 A8 ⬚
Pennefather's Rd *ALDT* GU11 ..... 112 C6
Penner Cl *WIM/MER* SW19 ..... 29 H3
Penners Gdns *SURB* KT6 ..... 45 H7
Pennine Cl *CRAWW* RH11 ..... 211 L3 ⬚
Pennine Wy *FARN* GU14 ..... 92 A2
  HYS/HAR UB3 ..... 15 G2
Pennings Av *GUW* GU2 ..... 116 C5
Pennington Dr *WEY* KT13 ..... 60 B2
Penn Rd *DTCH/LGLY* SL3 ..... 12 A3
Penns Wd *FARN* GU14 ..... 93 G8
Penns Yd *FNM* GU9 ..... 133 L7 ⬚
Penny Dr *RGUW* GU3 ..... 115 L7
Pennyfield *COB* KT11 ..... 80 D3
Penny La *SHPTN* TW17 ..... 42 B7
Pennymead Dr *EHSLY* KT24 ..... 120 C1
Pennypot La *CHOB/PIR* GU24 ..... 75 L3
Penrhyn Cl *ALDT* GU11 ..... 112 E8 ⬚
Penrhyn Crs
  MORT/ESHN SW14 ..... 18 F6 ⬚
Penrhyn Rd *KUT* KT1 ..... 45 H4
Penrith Cl *BECK* BR3 ..... 51 L1 ⬚

REDH RH1.............................126 B7
Penrith Pl *STRHM/NOR* SW16......31 L3
Penrith Rd *NWMAL* KT3..............46 A4
THHTH CR7...............................49 M2
Penrith St *STRHM/NOR* SW16......30 F7 ☐
Penrose Ct *EGH* TW20................20 F7
Penrose Rd *LHD/OX* KT22...........101 M4
Pensfold La *HORS* RH12.............226 B4
Pensford Av *RCH/KEW* TW9..........18 D4
Penshurst Cl *CRAWE* RH10..........213 G2 ☐
Penshurst Ri *FRIM* GU16.............93 J1
Penshurst Rd *THHTH* CR7............49 L5
Penshurst Wy *BELMT* SM2............65 K6 ☐
Pentelow Gdns
    EBED/NFELT TW14..................15 K8
Pentland Av *SHPTN* TW17............41 K5
Pentlands Cl *MTCM* CR4.............48 E5
Pentlow St *PUT/ROE* SW15...........19 M4
Pentney Rd *BAL* SW12................30 F2
    RYNPK SW20........................47 H1 ☐
Penton Av *STA* TW18..................22 C8
Penton Hall Dr *STA* TW18............40 D1
Penton Hook Rd *STA* TW18...........22 C8
Penton Rd *STA* TW18..................22 C8
Pentreath Av *GUW* GU2..............138 C1
Penwerris Av *ISLW* TW7..............16 F7
Penwith Dr *HASM* GU27..............219 G5
Penwith Rd *WAND/EARL* SW18.......29 L3
Penwood End
    WOKS/MYFD GU22....................96 E3
Penwood Gdns *EWKG* RG40...........34 A6
Penwortham Rd *SAND/SEL* CR2.....68 A8
    STRHM/NOR SW16....................30 E7
Peperham Rd *HASM* GU27............219 M1
Peper Harow La
    MFD/CHID GU8.......................158 F3
Peperharow Rd *RGODL* GU7..........159 M3
Peppard Rd *CRAWE* RH10............213 G5
Pepperbox La *SHGR* GU5.............184 B5
Pepper Cl *CTHM* CR3.................108 B7
Peppermint Cl *CROY/NA* CR0........49 H7 ☐
Pepys Cl *ASHTD* KT21................83 K7
    DTCH/LGLY SL3.......................12 E1
Pepys Rd *RYNPK* SW20...............46 F1
Percheron Dr *WOKN/KNAP* GU21....95 L1
Percival Rd *FELT* TW13...............24 C3
    MORT/ESHN SW14....................18 F7
    ORP BR6.............................71 L1
Percival Wy *HOR/WEW* KT19..........63 M3
Percy Av *ASHF* TW15..................23 K6
Percy Bryant Rd *SUN* TW16..........24 B8 ☐
Percy Gdns *WPK* KT4..................46 A8
Percy Rd *GUW* GU2...................116 E6
    HORS RH12..........................228 E6
    HPTN TW12............................25 K8
    ISLW TW7.............................17 K6
    MTCM CR4.............................48 D7
    PGE/AN SE20..........................51 C1
    SNWD SE25............................50 D5 ☐
    WHTN TW2.............................25 L2
Percy Wy *WHTN* TW2....................25 M2 ☐
Peregrine Cl *BRAK* RG12..............34 E5 ☐
    CRAN GU6...........................185 H5 ☐
Peregrine Gdns *CROY/NA* CR0........69 H1 ☐
Peregrine Rd *SUN* TW16..............42 B2
Peregrine Wy
    WIM/MER SW19......................28 F8 ☐
Perifield *DUL* SE21.....................31 M2
Perimeter Rd East *HORL* RH6.......192 E2
Perimeter Rd North *HORL* RH6.......170 B8
Perimeter Rd South *HORL* RH6......192 C4
Perleybrooke La
    WOKN/KNAP GU21....................76 D7
Perowne St *ALDT* GU11..............112 C7
Perran Av *BRXS/STRHM* SW2........31 L3
Perrin Cl *ASHF* TW15..................23 K6 ☐
Perrin Ct *WOKN/KNAP* GU21..........7 K1
Perring Av *FARN* GU14.................92 B1
Perring Rd *FARN* GU14.................92 D7
Perrior Rd *RGODL* GU7...............160 B2
Perry Av *EGRIN* RH19.................196 B6
Perry Cl *RGODL* GU7..................160 D4
Perryfield Rd *CRAWW* RH11..........212 A4
Perryfield Wy *RCHPK/HAM* TW10....26 E3
Perry Hl *CAT* SE6.......................33 J3
Perry How *WPK* KT4....................46 C8
Perrylands *HORL* RH6.................191 J2
Perrylands La *HORL* RH6.............171 J7
Perry Oak Dr *HTHAIR* TW6............14 A4
Perry Oaks *BRAK* RG12................35 H2
Perry Oaks Dr *WDR/YW* UB7..........13 L4
Perry Ri *FSTH* SE23....................33 H4
Perry V *FSTH* SE23......................33 G3 ☐
Perry Wy *BRAK* RG12...................35 H2 ☐
    FNM GU9.............................133 L2
    LTWR GU18...........................74 C2
Persfield Rd *EW* KT17..................64 D8 ☐
Pershore Gv *CAR* SM5..................48 A6
Perth Cl *CRAWW* RH11................192 A8
    RYNPK SW20.........................46 C2
Perth Rd *BECK* BR3....................51 M2
Perth Wy *HORS* RH12.................229 J5
Petauel Rd *TEDD* TW11................26 B6
Petavel Rd *TEDD* TW11.................26 B7
Peter Av *OXTED* RH8..................130 A3
Peterborough Rd *CAR* SM5...........48 B6
    CRAWE RH10.........................212 B2
    GUW GU2............................116 C6
Peterhouse Cl *SHST* GU47............52 C7
Petersfield Av *STA* TW18.............22 E2
Petersfield Crs *COUL/CHIP* CR5.....87 H5
Petersfield Ri *PUT/ROE* SW15........28 E2
Petersfield Rd *STA* TW18..............22 F6
Petersham Av *BF/WBF* KT14..........79 H2 ☐
Petersham Cl *BF/WBF* KT14...........79 H2 ☐
    RCHPK/HAM TW10...................27 G3 ☐
    SUT SM1.............................65 J4
Petersham Rd
    RCHPK/HAM TW10....................18 B8
Petersmead Cl
    KWD/TDW/WH KT20.................104 F5 ☐
Peterstow Cl *WIM/MER* SW19.........29 H3
Peterwood Wy *CROY/NA* CR0.........67 J1
Petley Rd *HMSMTH* W6................19 M1
Petridge Rd *REDH* RH1...............148 C5 ☐
Petters Rd *ASHTD* KT21...............83 J8
Pettiward Cl *PUT/ROE* SW15.........19 M6 ☐
Petts La *SHPTN* TW17.................41 K4

Petworth Cl *COUL/CHIP* CR5.........106 F1 ☐
    FRIM GU16...........................93 J1 ☐
Petworth Ct *CRAWW* RH11...........211 A6 ☐
Petworth Dr *HORS* RH12.............229 J2
Petworth Gdns *RYNPK* SW20.........46 E3 ☐
Petworth Rd *HASM* GU27.............220 A4
    MFD/CHID GU8......................181 H2
    MFD/CHID GU8......................201 M5
Pevensey Cl *CRAWE* RH10...........212 F4 ☐
    ISLW TW7.............................16 F2
Pevensey Rd *FELT* TW13..............25 H2
    TOOT SW17............................30 A5
Pevensey Wy *FRIM* GU16..............93 K1
Peverel Rd *CRAWW* RH11............211 H4
Peveril Dr *TEDD* TW11.................26 A6
Pewley Bank *GU* GU1....................9 K7
Pewley Hl *GU* GU1.......................9 H7
Pewley Point *GU* GU1...................9 K8
Pewley Wy *GU* GU1.......................9 K7
Pewsey V *BRAK* RG12...................35 J5
Pharaoh Cl *MTCM* CR4.................48 C7 ☐
Pheasant Cl *PUR/KEN* CR8.............87 L3
Philanthropic Rd *REDH* RH1.........148 E1
Philip Gdns *CROY/NA* CR0..............69 J1
Philip Rd *STA* TW18....................23 G7
Philips Cl *MTCM* CR4..................48 D8
Phillips Cl *CRAWE* RH10..............212 E7 ☐
    NFNM GU10..........................135 H1
    RGODL GU7..........................159 M7
Phillips Hatch *SHGR* GU5.............161 M1
Philpot La *CHOB/PIR* GU24............76 F2
Phipp's Bridge Rd *MTCM* CR4........48 A3 ☐
    WIM/MER SW19......................47 M2
Phoenix Cl *WWKM* BR4................70 A1
Phoenix Dr *HAYES* BR2.................71 G3
Phoenix La *EGRIN* RH19...............217 H3
Phoenix Rd *PGE/AN* SE20..............32 F7
Phoenix Wy *HEST* TW5..................16 A1
Phyllis Av *NWMAL* KT3................46 E5
Pickering Gdns *CROY/NA* CR0.........50 C6
Pickering Rd *SNWD* SE25..............50 C6
Picket Post Cl *BRAK* RG12............35 K3 ☐
Pickets St *BAL* SW12...................30 D1
Picketts Hl *BOR* GU35................176 F8
Picketts La *REDH* RH1.................170 F1
Pickford St *ALDT* GU11................112 E7 ☐
Pickhurst Rd *MFD/CHID* GU8.........201 M6
Pickins Piece *DTCH/LGLY* SL3.........12 D4
Pickwick Cl *HSLWW* TW4................16 B7 ☐
Pickwick Rd *DUL* SE21.................32 A1
Picquets Wy *BNSTD* SM7...............85 H6
Picton Cl *CBLY* GU15...................73 M2
Pierrefondes Av *FARN* GU14...........92 D4
Pier Rd *EBED/NFELT* TW14.............15 L7
Pigbush La *BIL* RH14..................224 C2
Pigeonhouse La
    COUL/CHIP CR5.....................105 H7
Pigeon La *HPTN* TW12..................25 K5
Pike Cl *ALDT* GU11....................112 F7
Pikes Hl *EW* KT17.......................84 B3
Pikes La *LING* RH7....................152 B8
Pilgrim Cl *MRDN* SM4....................47 L7
Pilgrim Hl *WNWD* SE27.................31 M5
Pilgrims Cl *FNM* GU9....................10 D3
    RDKG RH5............................122 D6
    SHGR GU5............................141 K5
Pilgrims' La *CTHM* CR3................107 J8
    OXTED RH8............................110 F6
Pilgrims Pl *REIG* RH2..................125 K6
Pilgrims Vw *ASHV* GU12...............135 M1
Pilgrims Wy *CHOB/PIR* GU24...........75 K6
    RDKG RH5............................122 E5
    REIG RH2............................125 J6
    RGUE GU4............................139 G4
    SAND/SEL CR2.........................68 C5
    SHGR GU5............................141 K5
Pilkington Rd *ORP* BR6.................71 M2
Pilsden Cl *WIM/MER* SW19.............29 G2 ☐
Pimms Cl *RGUE* GU4....................117 K4
Pinckards *MFD/CHID* GU8.............201 K4 ☐
Pincott La *EHSLY* KT24................119 L3
Pincott Rd *WIM/MER* SW19............29 M8 ☐
Pine Av *CBLY* GU15......................73 G5
    WWKM BR4.............................51 L8
Pine Bank *GSHT* GU26.................199 H5
Pine Cl *ADL/WDHM* KT15...............78 E1
    ASHV GU12...........................113 K3
    CBLY GU15.............................72 B2
    CRAWW RH11..........................191 M8
    PGE/AN SE20...........................50 F1
    PUR/KEN CR8..........................87 M7
    WOKN/KNAP GU21......................76 F7
Pine Coombe *CROY/NA* CR0............69 G3
Pinecote Dr *ASC* SL5....................37 J7
Pine Crs *CAR* SM5.......................86 A1
Pinecrest Gdns *ORP* BR6...............71 L3
Pine Dean *GT/LBKH* KT23.............101 L7
Pine Dr *BLKW* GU17.....................72 B6
Pine Gdns *BRYLDS* KT5.................45 K6
    HORL RH6............................170 D7 ☐
Pine Gld *ORP* BR6......................71 J3
Pine Gv *BFOR* GU20.....................55 C5
    EDEN TN8............................153 L7
    EGRIN RH19..........................195 L6
    NFNM GU10............................11 L7
    WEY KT13..............................59 L4
    WIM/MER SW19.........................29 J6
Pine Hl *EPSOM* KT18.....................84 A6
Pinehurst Av *FARN* GU14...............92 E7
Pinehurst Cl
    KWD/TDW/WH KT20.................105 K4
Pinel Cl *VW* GU25.......................39 H4
Pine Mount Rd *CBLY* GU15.............73 G5
Pine Pl *EW* KT17........................85 L4 ☐
Pine Rdg *CAR* SM5.......................66 D7
Pine Ridge Dr *NFNM* GU10.............10 F9
Pine Rd *WOKS/MYFD* GU22............96 F3
Pine Shaw *CRAWE* RH10..............212 F2
The Pines *CBLY* GU15...................73 J2
    HORS RH12..........................229 M4
    PUR/KEN CR8...........................87 L3
    SUN TW16.............................42 D3
    WOKN/KNAP GU21......................77 J4
Pine Tree Cl *HEST* TW5.................15 L3
Pine Tree Hl *WOKS/MYFD* GU22......78 A6
Pinetrees Cl *CRAWE* RH10............193 L6

Pine View Cl *FNM* GU9................134 D4
    HASM GU27.........................219 M1
    RGUE GU4............................140 C6
Pine Wk *BELMT* SM2....................66 A8
    BNSTD SM7...........................86 C6
    BRYLDS KT5...........................45 K6
    CAR SM5.............................66 A8
    COB KT11.............................81 G4
    CTHM CR3............................108 B4
    EHSLY KT24..........................120 C2
    GT/LBKH KT23........................101 L7
Pine Wy *EGH* TW20......................20 D7
Pine Way Cl *EGRIN* RH19..............216 B2
Pine Wd *SUN* TW16......................42 D1
Pinewood Av *ADL/WDHM* KT15.......58 F7
Pinewood Cl *CROY/NA* CR0.............69 H2
    HORS RH12...........................228 A6
    WOKN/KNAP GU21......................7 G1
Pinewood Crs *FARN* GU14.............92 A4
Pinewood Dr *STA* TW18.................22 D6 ☐
Pinewood Gdns *BAGS* GU19............53 M6
Pinewood Gv *ADL/WDHM* KT15........58 E8
Pinewood Ms
    STWL/WRAY TW19....................14 A8 ☐
Pinewood Pk *ADL/WDHM* KT15.......78 E1
Pinewood Rd *ASHV* GU12.............114 A6
    FELT TW13............................24 E4
    VW GU25..............................38 D5
Pinfold Rd *STRHM/NOR* SW16........31 H5
Pinglestone Cl *WDR/YW* UB7..........14 B2
Pinkcoat Cl *FELT* TW13.................24 E3 ☐
Pinkhurst La *SWTR* RH13.............227 K7
Piper Rd *KUT* KT1........................3 J8
Pipers End *SWTR* RH13................227 H6
    VW GU25..............................39 G3
Pipers Gdns *CROY/NA* CR0............51 H7
Pipewell Rd *CAR* SM5...................48 B6
Pippbrook Gdns *DORK* RH4...........144 E1 ☐
Pippin Cl *CROY/NA* CR0..................51 J8
Pippins Ct *ASHF* TW15..................23 L7
Piquet Rd *PGE/AN* SE20................50 F2
Pirbright Crs *CROY/NA* CR0............69 M5
Pirbright Rd *FARN* GU14................92 F6
    WAND/EARL SW18.....................29 J2
Pisley La *RDKG* RH5...................187 K4
Pitcairn Rd *MTCM* CR4.................30 C8
Pitchfont La *OXTED* RH8..............110 D8
Pit Farm Rd *GU* GU1...................117 K8
Pitfold Av *HASM* GU27................219 G3
Pitfold Cl *HASM* GU27................219 H3 ☐
Pitlake *CROY/NA* CR0.....................4 B5
Pitland St *RDKG* RH5..................164 F4
Pit La *EDEN* TN8......................153 M5
Pitson Cl *ADL/WDHM* KT15.............59 G3 ☐
Pitt Crs *WIM/MER* SW19................29 L5
Pitt La *NFNM* GU10....................177 K3
Pitt Rd *EW* KT17.........................84 B4
    ORP BR6.............................71 M3
    THHTH CR7............................49 M5
Pittville Gdns *SNWD* SE25.............50 D3
Pitt Wy *FARN* GU14.....................92 C4
Pit Wood Gn
    KWD/TDW/WH KT20.................104 F2
Pixham La *DORK* RH4..................122 F7
Pixholme Gv *DORK* RH4...............122 F8
Pixton Wy *CROY/NA* CR0................69 H7
Place Farm Rd *REDH* RH1.............128 A4
Placehouse La *COUL/CHIP* CR5.......107 J1
Plaistow Rd *BIL* RH14.................224 B8
    MFD/CHID GU8......................203 H6
Plaistow St *LING* RH7.................173 M5
The Planes *CHERT* KT16................40 F7
Plane St *SYD* SE26......................32 E4 ☐
Plane Tree Crs *FELT* TW13............24 E4
Plantagenet Cl
    HOR/WEW KT19.......................64 A3 ☐
Plantagenet Pk *BNFD* RG42...........35 J1 ☐
Plantain Crs *CRAWW* RH11...........211 K7
Plantation La *WARL* CR6..............109 H1
Plassy Rd *CAT* SE6......................33 L1
The Plat *HORS* RH12..................228 D7
Platt Meadow *RGUE* GU4..............118 A6 ☐
The Platt *LING* RH7....................196 D1
Plawsfield Rd *BECK* BR3................51 G1 ☐
Plaws Hl *SHGR* GU5...................164 A3
Playgreen Wy *CAT* SE6..................33 K5
Playground Cl *BECK* BR3................51 G1 ☐
Pleasance Rd *PUT/ROE* SW15..........19 L7
The Pleasance *PUT/ROE* SW15........19 L6 ☐
Pleasant Gv *CROY/NA* CR0..............69 J2
Pleasant Mt *GUW* GU2....................8 E8
Pleasant Pl *WOT/HER* KT12............61 G5
Pleasant Vw *ORP* BR6..................71 M4
Pleasure Pit Rd *ASHTD* KT21..........83 L8
Plesman Wy *WLGTN* SM6...............67 H7 ☐
Plevna Rd *HPTN* TW12..................43 L1
Pleydell Av *NRWD* SE19................32 C8
Plough Cl *CRAWW* RH11..............211 J1 ☐
Ploughlands *BNFD* RG42...............34 C1 ☐
Plough La *COB* KT11....................80 D6
    CRAN GU6............................186 C5
    CROY/NA CR0..........................67 H3 ☐
    HORS RH12...........................229 H4
    PUR/KEN CR8..........................67 J8
    WIM/MER SW19.........................29 L6
    WLGTN SM6............................67 H7
Plough Lane Cl *WLGTN* SM6...........67 H4
Ploughmans End *ISLW* TW7............17 G7 ☐
Plough Rd *HOR/WEW* KT19.............64 A6
    HORL RH6............................171 M6
    LING RH7............................174 D7
Plover Cl *CRAWW* RH11...............211 M1
    STA TW18............................22 C4 ☐
Plovers Ri *CHOB/PIR* GU24.............95 H2
Plovers Rd *SWTR* RH13................229 J5
Plummer La *MTCM* CR4..................48 C1
Plummer Rd *CLAP* SW4..................31 G1
Plumpton Wy *CAR* SM5..................66 B2
Pocket Cl *BRAK* RG12...................34 A2 ☐
Pockford Rd *MFD/CHID* GU8...........202 A5
Pointers Hl *DORK* RH4................143 M4
The Pointers *ASHTD* KT21.............103 H2
Polden Cl *FARN* GU14...................92 B2
Polecroft La *CAT* SE6...................33 J3

Polesden Gdns *RYNPK* SW20..........46 E3
Polesden La *RPLY/SEND* GU23.........98 C5
Polesden Rd *GT/LBKH* KT23..........121 K1
Polesden Vw *GT/LBKH* KT23..........121 L1
Poles La *CRAWW* RH11................191 M5
Polesteeple Hl *BH/WHM* TN16........91 G7
Police Station Rd
    WOT/HER KT12........................60 F5
Pollard Gv *CBLY* GU15..................73 M5 ☐
Pollard Rd *MRDN* SM4..................48 A5
    WOKS/MYFD GU22.....................7 K3
Pollardrow Av *BNFD* RG42.............34 C1
Pollards *CRAWW* RH11................211 K4
Pollards Crs *STRHM/NOR* SW16.......49 H3
Pollards Dr *SWTR* RH13..............229 J7
Pollards Hl East
    STRHM/NOR SW16....................49 J3
Pollards Hl North
    STRHM/NOR SW16....................49 J3
Pollards Hl South
    STRHM/NOR SW16....................49 J3
Pollards Hl West
    STRHM/NOR SW16....................49 J3
Pollards Oak Crs *OXTED* RH8........130 D6
Pollards Oak Rd *OXTED* RH8.........130 D6
Pollards Wood Hl *OXTED* RH8........130 D5
Pollards Wood Rd *OXTED* RH8........130 D5
    STRHM/NOR SW16....................49 H2
Polsted La *RGUW* GU3.................138 A6
Polsted Rd *CAT* SE6.....................33 J1
Poltimore Rd *GUW* GU2..................8 B7
Polworth Rd *STRHM/NOR* SW16.......31 H6
Pond Cl *BIL* RH14......................224 C5
    WOT/HER KT12........................60 D5
Pond Copse La *BIL* RH14..............224 C4
Pond Cottage La *BECK* BR3............51 K8
Pond Farm Cl
    KWD/TDW/WH KT20.................104 E6 ☐
    ORP BR6..............................71 L2
    PUR/KEN CR8..........................87 L6
    RGODL GU7...........................160 C3
Pond Head La *RDKG* RH5..............187 C6
Pond Hill Gdns *CHEAM* SM3...........65 H5 ☐
Pond La *NFNM* GU10...................177 M5 ☐
    SHGR GU5...........................163 M2
Pond Meadow *GUW* GU2................116 B8
Pond Moor Rd *BRAK* RG12..............34 E5
Pond Piece *LHD/OX* KT22...............81 L4
Pond Rd *EGH* TW20.....................21 M7
    FARN GU14............................92 E7
    WOKS/MYFD GU22......................96 D2
Pondside Cl *HYS/HAR* UB3.............15 G2 ☐
Ponds La *SHGR* GU5...................141 H8
The Ponds *WEY* KT13....................60 A5
Pondtail Cl *HORS* RH12...............229 G4
Pondtail Copse *HORS* RH12............229 G3
Pondtail Dr *HORS* RH12...............229 G3
Pondtail Rd *HORS* RH12...............228 F4
Pond Wy *EGRIN* RH19.................196 B8
    TEDD TW11............................26 B1
Pond Wood Rd *CRAWE* RH10...........212 D1
Ponsonby Rd *PUT/ROE* SW15..........28 E1 ☐
Pony Cha *COB* KT11......................81 J3
Pook Hl *MFD/CHID* GU8...............201 H6
Pool Cl *BECK* BR3........................33 K6
    E/WMO/HCT KT8.......................43 J5
Pool Ct *CAT* SE6.........................33 K3
Poole Court Rd *HEST* TW5..............16 A5
Pool End Cl *SHPTN* TW17...............41 K5 ☐
Poole Rd *HOR/WEW* KT19...............64 A5
    WOKN/KNAP GU21......................6 C6
Pooley Av *EGH* TW20....................21 L6
Pooley Green Rd *EGH* TW20...........21 L6
Pool Rd *ALDT* GU11...................134 F2
    E/WMO/HCT KT8.......................43 J5
Pope Cl *EBED/NFELT* TW14.............24 C2 ☐
    WIM/MER SW19........................30 A7 ☐
Pope's Av *WHTN* TW2.....................26 B3
Popes Cl *DTCH/LGLY* SL3................12 F2
Popes Gv *CROY/NA* CR0...................69 J2
    WHTN TW2.............................26 B3
Popes La *OXTED* RH8..................152 C1
Popes Md *HASM* GU27.................219 M2
Popeswood Rd *BNFD* RG42.............34 A1
Popham Cl *BRAK* RG12..................35 J5 ☐
    FELT TW13.............................25 H4
Poplar Av *BFOR* GU20...................54 D3
    LHD/OX KT22..........................102 E4
    MTCM CR4.............................48 C1
    ORP BR6..............................71 L1
Poplar Crs *HOR/WEW* KT19............63 M5
Poplar Dr *BNSTD* SM7...................85 G4 ☐
Poplar Farm Cl *HOR/WEW* KT19......63 M5
Poplar Gdns *NWMAL* KT3...............46 A2
Poplar Gv *WOKS/MYFD* GU22..........96 E4
Poplar Rd *ASHF* TW15.................23 M6
    CHEAM SM3............................47 J8
    LHD/OX KT22..........................102 E4
    RGUE GU4............................139 H7
    WIM/MER SW19.........................47 K2
Poplar Rd South
    WIM/MER SW19.......................47 K3
The Poplars *ASC* SL5...................36 D5
    SWTR RH13...........................229 H6 ☐
Poplar Wk *CROY/NA* CR0.................4 C4
    CTHM CR3............................108 B5
    FNM GU9.............................134 A2
Poplar Wy *FELT* TW13...................24 D4
Poppy Cl *MTCM* CR4....................48 D8
Poppyhills Rd *CBLY* GU15...............73 J1
Poppy La *CROY/NA* CR0.................50 F7
Popular Gv *WIM/MER* SW19.............46 A3
Porchester *ASC* SL5......................36 D4
Porchester Md *BECK* BR3................33 L7
Porchester Rd *KUT* KT1..................3 L6
Porchfield Cl *BELMT* SM2...............65 L8 ☐
Porridge Pot Aly *GUW* GU2..............8 F8
Portal Cl *WNWD* SE27...................31 K4
Portesbery Rd *CBLY* GU15...............73 G3
Portesbery Hill Dr *CBLY* GU15........73 G3
Porthcawe Rd *SYD* SE26................33 H5
Portia Gv *BNFD* RG42...................35 H1
Portland Av *NWMAL* KT3................46 C7
Portland Crs *ASHF* TW15................24 A5

Portland Dr *REDH* RH1.................126 F3
Portland Pl *EW* KT17....................84 B2 ☐
    SNWD SE25............................50 D4 ☐
Portland Rd *ASHF* TW15.................23 H4
    DORK RH4............................144 D1
    EGRIN RH19..........................216 B1
    KUT KT1................................2 F7
    MTCM CR4.............................48 B2
    SNWD SE25............................50 E4
Portley La *CTHM* CR3..................108 B3
Portley Wood Rd *CTHM* CR3..........108 C3
Portman Av *MORT/ESHN* SW14........19 G5
Portman Cl *BNFD* RG42.................34 D1 ☐
Portman Rd *KUT* KT1.....................3 H7
Portmore Park Rd *WEY* KT13..........59 J3 ☐
Portmore Quays *WEY* KT13............59 J3 ☐
Portmore Wy *WEY* KT13.................59 K2 ☐
Portnall Dr *VW* GU25....................38 C5
Portnall Ri *VW* GU25....................38 C5
Portnall Rd *VW* GU25...................38 C5
Portnalls Cl *COUL/CHIP* CR5..........86 E6
Portnalls Ri *COUL/CHIP* CR5..........86 F6
Portnalls Rd *COUL/CHIP* CR5..........86 E7
Portsmouth Av *THDIT* KT7.............44 D7
Portsmouth Rd *CBLY* GU15............73 K3
    COB KT11..............................80 C3
    ESH/CLAY KT10.......................61 M2
    FRIM GU16............................73 H6
    GUW GU2...............................8 F9
    LIPH GU30............................218 D2
    MFD/CHID GU8.......................180 A7
    PUT/ROE SW15........................28 E1
    RGODL GU7...........................159 K8
    RPLY/SEND GU23......................99 C3
Portugal Gdns *WHTN* TW2..............25 M3 ☐
Portugal Rd *WOKN/KNAP* GU21........6 F1
Port Wy *CHOB/PIR* GU24................75 K7
Portway *EW* KT17........................64 D8
Portway Crs *EW* KT17...................64 D7
Post Horn La *FROW* RH18..............217 K8
Post House La *GT/LBKH* KT23.........101 K7
Post La *WHTN* TW2.......................26 A2
Postmill Cl *CROY/NA* CR0...............68 F2
Potter Cl *MTCM* CR4....................48 E3 ☐
Potteries La *FRIM* GU16.................93 J6
The Potteries *CHERT* KT16.............58 B5 ☐
    FARN GU14.............................92 A3
Potterne Cl *WIM/MER* SW19............29 G3 ☐
Potters Cl *CROY/NA* CR0................51 H8
    MFD/CHID GU8.......................159 J7
Potters Crs *ASHV* GU12................113 L6
Potters Cft *SWTR* RH13................229 H7
Potters Ga *FNM* GU9...................133 K7
Potters Gv *NWMAL* KT3.................45 M4
Potters Hl *MFD/CHID* GU8.............181 M5
Potters La *RPLY/SEND* GU23............97 L7
    STRHM/NOR SW16....................31 G7 ☐
Potters Wy *REIG* RH2..................147 M4
Pottery Ct *NFNM* GU10.................10 A8
Pottery La *NFNM* GU10..................10 A8
Pottery Rd *BTFD* TW8....................18 B1
Poulcott *STWL/WRAY* TW19............12 B8 ☐
Poulett Gdns *TWK* TW1..................26 C3
Poulters Wd *HAYES* BR2.................71 G4
Poulton Av *SUT* SM1.....................66 A2
Pound Cl *BIL* RH14....................224 C4
    RGODL GU7...........................160 B5 ☐
    SURB KT6..............................44 F8
Pound Ct *ASHTD* KT21....................83 J8
    RGUW GU3............................115 L6
Pound Crs *LHD/OX* KT22...............102 A3
Pound Farm La *ASHV* GU12............114 A4
Pound Fld *GU* GU1........................9 G2
Poundfield Gdns
    WOKS/MYFD GU22.....................97 M2
Poundfield La *BIL* RH14................223 L6
Pound Hl *RGUW* GU3...................115 L7
Pound Hill Pl *CRAWE* RH10............212 F3
Pound La *BFOR* GU20....................54 F5
    HOR/WEW KT19........................84 A1
    RGODL GU7...........................160 B5
    RGUW GU3............................115 L7
Pound Pl *RGUE* GU4....................139 J7
Pound Place Cl *RGUE* GU4............139 J6 ☐
Pound Rd *ASHV* GU12..................112 F8
    BNSTD SM7.............................85 K7
    CHERT KT16............................40 E7
Pound St *CAR* SM5.......................66 C4
Povey Cross Rd *HORL* RH6............170 B4
Powderham Ct
    WOKN/KNAP GU21....................76 A8 ☐
Powder Mill La *WHTN* TW2.............25 J2
Powell Cl *GUW* GU2....................138 C2
    HORL RH6............................170 B5
Powers Ct *TWK* TW1......................27 J1
Pownall Gdns *HSLW* TW3.................16 E6
Pownall Rd *HSLW* TW3..................16 E6
Poyle Gdns *BRAK* RG12..................35 G1
Poyle Rd *DTCH/LGLY* SL3...............13 H4
    GU GU1..................................9 J8
    NFNM GU10..........................135 K2
Poynders Rd *CLAP* SW4..................30 F1
Poynes Rd *HORL* RH6..................170 B4
Poynings Rd *CRAWW* RH11............211 G4
Prairie Cl *ADL/WDHM* KT15............58 E2
Prairie Rd *ADL/WDHM* KT15...........58 E2
Pratts La *WOT/HER* KT12...............61 K3
The Precinct *CRAN* GU6...............185 H5 ☐
Prentice Cl *FARN* GU14.................92 E1 ☐
Prentis Rd *STRHM/NOR* SW16.........31 G5
Presburg Rd *NWMAL* KT3...............46 B5
Prescott *BRAK* RG12....................34 C7
Prescott Rd *DTCH/LGLY* SL3...........13 H4
Presentation Ms
    BRXS/STRHM SW2....................31 J2 ☐
Prestbury Crs *BNSTD* SM7..............86 C6
Preston Cl *WHTN* TW2...................26 B4
Preston Dr *HOR/WEW* KT19............64 B5
Preston Gv *ASHTD* KT21.................82 F1
Preston La *KWD/TDW/WH* KT20......104 C2
Preston Pl *RCHPK/HAM* TW10.........18 B7 ☐
Preston Rd *NRWD* SE19.................31 L7
    RYNPK SW20..........................28 D8
    SHPTN TW17...........................41 K5
Prestons Rd *HAYES* BR2.................70 D2
Prestwick Cl *CRAWW* RH11............211 G4 ☐
Prestwick La *HASM* GU27..............200 D7

Prestwood Cl CRAWW RH11 .... 191 L8
Prestwood Gdns CROY/NA CR0 ...... 4 D1
Prestwood La CRAWW RH11 .... 190 F7
Pretoria Rd CHERT KT16 .... 40 C8
STRHM/NOR SW16 .... 30 E7
Pretty La COUL/CHIP CR5 .... 106 F3
Prey Heath Cl
WOKS/MYFD GU22 .... 96 F6
Prey Heath Rd
WOKS/MYFD GU22 .... 96 E6
Price Cl TOOT SW17 .... 30 C4
Price Rd CROY/NA CR0 .... 67 L4
Prices La REIG RH2 .... 147 K3
Pridham Rd THHTH CR7 .... 50 A4
Priest Croft Cl CRAWW RH11 ...... 211 L8
Priestfield Rd FSTH SE23 .... 33 H4
Priest Hl EGH TW20 .... 20 F3
OXTED RH8 .... 130 E3
Priest La CHOB/PIR GU24 .... 74 F4
Priestley Gdns
WOKS/MYFD GU22 .... 97 K2
Priestley Rd GUW GU2 .... 138 A1
MTCM CR4 .... 48 D2
Priestley Wy CRAWE RH10 .... 192 D6 ▣
Priests Br MORT/ESHN SW14 ...... 19 H5
Priestwood Court Rd
BNFD RG42 .... 34 D1 ▣
Primrose Av HORL RH6 .... 170 E8
Primrose Cl CAT SE6 .... 33 M6
CRAWW RH11 .... 211 L6 ▣
MTCM CR4 .... 48 E8
Primrose Copse HORS RH12 ...... 229 G2
Primrose Dr CHOB/PIR GU24 ...... 75 K5 ▣
Primrose La FARN GU14 .... 92 B6 ▣
Primrose La CROY/NA CR0 .... 50 F8
FROW RH18 .... 217 K8
Primrose Rdg RGODL GU7 .... 159 L7
Primrose Rd WOT/HER KT12 ...... 60 F4
Primrose Wk BRAK RG12 .... 34 F5
EW KT17 .... 64 C6
Primrose Wy SHGR GU5 .... 161 G4
Prince Albert Dr ASC SL5 .... 36 A4
Prince Albert Sq REDH RH1 ...... 148 C5
Prince Andrew Wy ASC SL5 ...... 36 A2
Prince Charles Crs FARN GU14 .... 92 E1
Prince Charles Wy WLGTN SM6 .. 66 E4
Prince Consort Dr ASC SL5 ...... 36 A4
Prince George's Rd RYNPK SW20 .. 46 F2
WIM/MER SW19 .... 48 A1
Prince of Wales Rd REDH RH1 .... 149 K8
SUT SM1 .... 66 A1
Prince Regent Rd HSLW TW3 ...... 16 F5
Prince Rd SNWD SE25 .... 50 B5
Prince's Av ALDT GU11 .... 112 F4
CAR SM5 .... 66 C6
SAND/SEL CR2 .... 88 E5
SURB KT6 .... 63 K1
Princes Cl BAGS GU19 .... 54 B8
HPTN TW12 .... 26 A5
SAND/SEL CR2 .... 87 L8
Prince's Dr LHD/OX KT22 .... 82 B2
Princes Rd ASHF TW15 .... 23 J6
EGH TW20 .... 21 J7
FELT TW13 .... 24 C4
HPTN TW12 .... 26 A5
KUTN/CMB KT2 .... 3 J4
MORT/ESHN SW14 .... 19 G5
PGE/AN SE20 .... 33 G7
RCH/KEW TW9 .... 18 C3
RCHPK/HAM TW10 .... 18 C7
REDH RH1 .... 148 C2
WEY KT13 .... 59 L4
WIM/MER SW19 .... 29 K7
Princess Anne Rd
HORS RH12 .... 226 A2 ▣
Princess Gdns WOKS/MYFD GU22 .. 7 K3
Princess Margaret Rd
HORS RH12 .... 226 A2 ▣
Princess Mary's Rd
ADL/WDHM KT15 .... 58 F3
Princess Rd CRAWW RH11 .... 211 M3
CROY/NA CR0 .... 49 M6
WOKS/MYFD GU22 .... 7 K3
Prince's St RCHPK/HAM TW10 .. 18 B7 ▣
SUT SM1 .... 66 A3
Princess Wy CBLY GU15 .... 72 F4
REDH RH1 .... 126 D7
Princes Wy ALDT GU11 .... 112 D7
CROY/NA CR0 .... 67 J4
WIM/MER SW19 .... 29 G1
WWKM BR4 .... 70 C3
Princethorpe Rd SYD SE26 ...... 33 G3
Pringle Gdns PUR/KEN CR8 ...... 67 J8
STRHM/NOR SW16 .... 30 F5 ▣
Prior Av BELMT SM2 .... 66 B6
Prior Croft Cl CBLY GU15 .... 73 K5
Prior End CBLY GU15 .... 73 K4
Prior Rd CBLY GU15 .... 73 K4
Prioress Rd WNWD SE27 .... 31 L4
Priors Cl FARN GU14 .... 92 E1
Priors Ct WOKN/KNAP GU21 ...... 76 D8
Priors Cft WOKS/MYFD GU22 .... 97 K2
Priorsfield Rd RGODL GU7 .... 159 K1
Priors Hatch La RGODL GU7 ...... 137 J8
Priors Md GT/LBKH KT23 .... 101 M7
The Priors ASHTD KT21 .... 103 G1
Priors Wk CRAWE RH10 .... 212 C3
Priors Wd HASM GU27 .... 219 J3
Priorswood RGUW GU3 .... 137 J7
Priory Av CHEAM SM3 .... 65 G3
Priory Cl ASC SL5 .... 37 K7
BECK BR3 .... 51 H3
DORK RH4 .... 144 D4
HORL RH6 .... 170 C5
HPTN TW12 .... 43 J1
SUN TW16 .... 24 D8
WOKN/KNAP GU21 .... 78 A3
WOT/HER KT12 .... 60 F3
Priory Crs CHEAM SM3 .... 65 G3
NRWD SE19 .... 31 M8
Priory Dr REIG RH2 .... 147 K2
Priory Gdns ASHF TW15 .... 24 A6
BARN SW13 .... 19 J5 ▣
HPTN TW12 .... 25 J8
SNWD SE25 .... 50 C4
Priory Gn STA TW18 .... 22 E6
Priory La E/WMO/HCT KT8 ...... 43 K4

NFNM GU10 .... 178 A1
PUT/ROE SW15 .... 19 J7
Priory Ms STA TW18 .... 22 E6 ▣
Priory Rd ASC SL5 .... 35 L1
ASC SL5 .... 37 K7
CHEAM SM3 .... 65 G3
CHSGTN KT9 .... 63 H7
CROY/NA CR0 .... 49 K7
HPTN TW12 .... 25 J8
HSLW TW3 .... 16 F7
RCH/KEW TW9 .... 18 D1
REIG RH2 .... 147 K2
WIM/MER SW19 .... 30 A8
Priory St FARN GU14 .... 93 G5
The Priory GDST RH9 .... 128 E5
Priory Wk BRAK RG12 .... 35 J4 ▣
Priory Wy WDR/YW UB7 .... 14 B1
Probyn Rd BRXS/STRHM SW2 .. 31 L3
Proctor Cl CRAWE RH10 .... 212 F5
MTCM CR4 .... 48 D1 ▣
Proctor Gdns GT/LBKH KT23 .... 101 L7
Proctors Cl EBED/NFELT TW14 .. 24 D2
Profumo Rd WOT/HER KT12 ...... 61 G4 ▣
Progress Wy CROY/NA CR0 ...... 67 J1
Promenade Approach Rd
CHSWK W4 .... 19 H2
Promenade De Verdun
PUR/KEN CR8 .... 87 G1
The Promenade CHSWK W4 ...... 19 H3
Propeller Rd FARN GU14 .... 92 E7
Prospect Av FARN GU14 .... 92 E3
Prospect Cl HEST TW5 .... 16 C3
SYD SE26 .... 32 E5
Prospect Crs WHTN TW2 .... 16 F8
Prospect La EGH TW20 .... 20 D6
Prospect Pl CRAWW RH11 .... 211 M3 ▣
EW KT17 .... 84 B5 ▣
RYNPK SW20 .... 28 E8
STA TW18 .... 22 C6
Prospect Rd ASHV GU12 .... 113 K4
FARN GU14 .... 92 D5
NFNM GU10 .... 155 H6
SURB KT6 .... 44 F6
Prossers KWD/TDW/WH KT20 .. 105 G3
Providence La HYS/HAR UB3 .... 15 G2
Prune Hl EGH TW20 .... 21 G8
Prunus Cl CHOB/PIR GU24 .... 75 H3
Puckeridge Gate Rd ALDT GU11 .. 112 A3
Puckeridge Hill Rd ALDT GU11 .. 112 B4
Puckshill WOKN/KNAP GU21 .... 76 A7
Puckshott Wy HASM GU27 ...... 220 A1
Pudding La HORL RH6 .... 191 H1
Puffin Cl CROY/NA CR0 .... 51 G5
Puffin Rd CRAWW RH11 .... 211 G4 ▣
Pulborough Wy HSLWW TW4 .... 15 M6
Pullman Gdns PUT/ROE SW15 .. 19 M8 ▣
Pullman La RGODL GU7 .... 159 M7
Pullmans Pl STA TW18 .... 22 D6 ▣
Pump Aly BTFD TW8 .... 18 B1
Pumping Station Rd CHSWK W4 .. 19 H2
Pump La ASC SL5 .... 37 H1
Punchbowl La RDKG RH5 .... 145 L1
Punch Copse Rd CRAWE RH10 .. 212 C2
Purbeck Av NWMAL KT3 .... 46 C6
Purbeck Cl REDH RH1 .... 126 F3
Purbeck Dr WOKN/KNAP GU21 .. 77 J4
Purberry Gv EW KT17 .... 64 C8
Purbrook Ct BRAK RG12 .... 35 H5
Purcell Cl PUR/KEN CR8 .... 87 M4 ▣
Purcell Rd CRAWW RH11 .... 211 J6
Purley Bury Av PUR/KEN CR8 .. 87 M1
Purley Bury Cl PUR/KEN CR8 .... 87 M1
Purley La CRAWE RH10 .... 213 G6 ▣
Purley Downs Rd PUR/KEN CR8 .. 67 M8
Purley Knoll PUR/KEN CR8 ...... 87 L2
Purley Knoll PUR/KEN CR8 ...... 87 J1
Purley Oaks Rd SAND/SEL CR2 .. 68 A3
Purley Park Rd PUR/KEN CR8 .. 67 L8
Purley Ri PUR/KEN CR8 .... 87 J2
Purley Rd SAND/SEL CR2 .... 68 A6
Purley V PUR/KEN CR8 .... 87 J2
Purley Wy CROY/NA CR0 .... 49 J7
FRIM GU16 .... 93 H1
PUR/KEN CR8 .... 87 K1
Pursers Hollow SHGR GU5 ...... 164 A2
Pursers La SHGR GU5 .... 142 A8
Purton Rd HORS RH12 .... 228 E5
Putney Common
PUT/ROE SW15 .... 19 M5
Putney Heath PUT/ROE SW15 .. 19 L8
Putney Park Av PUT/ROE SW15 .. 19 K6
Putney Park La PUT/ROE SW15 .. 19 L6
Puttenham Heath Rd
RGUW GU3 .... 137 G5
Puttenham Hl RGUW GU3 .... 136 F4
Puttenham La MFD/CHID GU8 .. 136 F8
Puttenham Rd NFNM GU10 ...... 135 L5
Puttock Cl HASM GU27 .... 219 G4 ▣
Pye Cl CTHM CR3 .... 108 A5
Pyecombe Ct CRAWW RH11 .... 211 K6 ▣
Pyegrove Cha BRAK RG12 ...... 35 H7 ▣
Pyle Hl WOKS/MYFD GU22 ...... 97 G6
Pymers Md DUL SE21 .... 31 M2
Pyne Rd SURB KT6 .... 45 K8 ▣
Pyrcroft La WEY KT13 .... 59 L4
Pyrcroft Rd CHERT KT16 .... 40 C7
Pyrford Common Rd
WOKS/MYFD GU22 .... 78 B6
Pyrford Heath
WOKS/MYFD GU22 .... 78 C6
Pyrford Rd BF/WBF KT14 .... 78 D4
WOKS/MYFD GU22 .... 78 E6
Pyrford Woods Cl
WOKS/MYFD GU22 .... 78 C5 ▣
Pyrford Woods Rd
WOKS/MYFD GU22 .... 78 C5 ▣
Pyrland Rd RCHPK/HAM TW10 .. 18 C8 ▣
Pyrmont Gv WNWD SE27 .... 31 L4 ▣
Pyrmont Rd CHSWK W4 .... 18 D1
Pytchley Crs NRWD SE19 .... 31 M7

Q

The Quadrangle GUW GU2 .... 8 B6
Quadrant Ct BRAK RG12 .... 35 H3 ▣
Quadrant Rd RCH/KEW TW9 .... 18 A6 ▣
THHTH CR7 .... 49 L4
The Quadrant ASHV GU12 .... 113 K5
BELMT SM2 .... 65 M5 ▣
RCH/KEW TW9 .... 18 B6 ▣
RYNPK SW20 .... 47 H1
Quadrant Wy WEY KT13 .... 59 J3
Quail Cl HORS RH12 .... 229 G2
Quail Gdns CROY/NA CR0 .... 69 H8
Quakers Wy RGUW GU3 .... 115 M4
Qualitas BRAK RG12 .... 34 C8
Quality St REDH RH1 .... 126 E5
Quantock Cl CRAWW RH11 ...... 211 L3 ▣
HYS/HAR UB3 .... 15 G2 ▣
Quarr Rd CAR SM5 .... 48 A6
Quarry Bank LTWR GU18 .... 74 C1
Quarry Cl HORS RH12 .... 229 J3 ▣
LHD/OX KT22 .... 103 G3
OXTED RH8 .... 130 B4
Quarry Hl RGODL GU7 .... 159 L6
Quarry Hill Pk REIG RH2 .... 125 M5
Quarry Park Rd SUT SM1 .... 65 J5
SUT SM1 .... 65 J5
Quarry Rd GDST RH9 .... 128 F2
OXTED RH8 .... 130 B4
RGODL GU7 .... 159 K2
Quarry St GU GU1 .... 9 G7
The Quarry BRKHM/BTCW RH3 .. 124 A6
Quarterbrass Farm Rd
HORS RH12 .... 229 G2 ▣
Quartermaine Av
WOKS/MYFD GU22 .... 97 J4
Quarter Mile Rd RGODL GU7 .... 160 B7
Quarters Rd FARN GU14 .... 92 F7
Quebec Cl HORL RH6 .... 171 K6
Quebec Gdns BLKW GU17 .... 72 A5 ▣
Queen Adelaide Rd
PGE/AN SE20 .... 32 F7
Queen Anne Dr ESH/CLAY KT10 .. 62 B6
Queen Annes Cl WHTN TW2 .... 26 A4 ▣
Queen Anne's Gdns
MTCM CR4 .... 48 C3 ▣
Queen Anne's Ga FNM GU9 .... 134 A2
Queen Anne's Ter
LHD/OX KT22 .... 102 E3 ▣
Queendale Ct
WOKN/KNAP GU21 .... 76 C6 ▣
Queen Eleanor's Rd GUW GU2 .. 138 C1
Queen Elizabeth Dr ALDT GU11 .. 112 C7
Queen Elizabeth Gdns
MRDN SM4 .... 47 K4 ▣
Queen Elizabeth Rd CBLY GU15 .. 53 G8
HORS RH12 .... 226 A2
KUTN/CMB KT2 .... 3 G5 ▣
Queen Elizabeth's Dr
CROY/NA CR0 .... 70 A8
Queen Elizabeth's Wk
WLGTN SM6 .... 67 G3
Queen Elizabeth Wk
BARN SW13 .... 19 K3
Queen Elizabeth Wy
WOKS/MYFD GU22 .... 97 J1
Queenhill Rd SAND/SEL CR2 .... 68 E8
Queenhythe Rd RGUE GU4 ...... 117 G2
Queen Mary Av CBLY GU15 ...... 72 D4
MRDN SM4 .... 47 G5
Queen Mary Cl CHSGTN KT9 .... 63 K2 ▣
WOKS/MYFD GU22 .... 7 L3
Queen Mary Rd NRWD SE19 .... 31 L7 ▣
SHPTN TW17 .... 41 M2 ▣
Queen Mary's Av CAR SM5 ...... 66 C6
Queen Mary's Dr
ADL/WDHM KT15 .... 58 C8
Queens Acre CHEAM SM3 .... 65 G6
Queen's Av ALDT GU11 .... 112 E4
BF/WBF KT14 .... 79 G2
FELT TW13 .... 24 F5
Queensbridge Pk ISLW TW7 .... 17 G8
Queens Cl CHOB/PIR GU24 ...... 75 K7
FARN GU14 .... 112 E1 ▣
KWD/TDW/WH KT20 .... 104 D6
WLGTN SM6 .... 66 E4 ▣
Queens Ct WEY KT13 .... 60 B5 ▣
Queens Court Ride COB KT11 .. 80 D5
Queens Crs RCHPK/HAM TW10 .. 18 C7
Queens Dr BRYLDS KT5 .... 45 K7
GUW GU2 .... 116 D5
LHD/OX KT22 .... 81 M1
RGODL GU7 .... 159 L2
THDIT KT7 .... 44 D6
Queen's Gdns HEST TW5 .... 16 B3
Queensgate COB KT11 .... 81 G2
Queens Ga HORL RH6 .... 192 D1
Queensgate Gdns
PUT/ROE SW15 .... 19 L6 ▣
Queen's Gate Rd FARN GU14 .. 112 E1
Queenshill Ldg ASC SL5 .... 36 E3
Queens Hill Ri ASC SL5 .... 36 F3
Queensland Av
WIM/MER SW19 .... 47 L1 ▣
Queens La FNM GU9 .... 133 L2
Queen's Md MFD/CHID GU8 .... 201 L6
Queensmead Av EW KT17 ...... 64 E8
Queensmere Cl
WIM/MER SW19 .... 29 G3 ▣
Queensmere Rd
WIM/MER SW19 .... 29 G3
Queens Park Gdns FELT TW13 .. 24 C4 ▣
Queens Pine BRAK RG12 .... 35 H6
Queen's Pl ASC SL5 .... 36 D3
MRDN SM4 .... 47 K4 ▣
WOT/HER KT12 .... 60 B4
Queen's Ride BARN SW13 ...... 19 L5
Queens Ri RCHPK/HAM TW10 .. 18 C6
Queens Rd ALDT GU11 .... 112 C7
ASC SL5 .... 37 G5
BECK BR3 .... 51 H2
BELMT SM2 .... 65 M8
CBLY GU15 .... 72 E5
CHOB/PIR GU24 .... 95 H2
CROY/NA CR0 .... 49 L6
EGH TW20 .... 21 J7
EGRIN RH19 .... 216 B1 ▣
FARN GU14 .... 113 G1
FELT TW13 .... 24 E2 ▣
FNM GU9 .... 133 M3 ▣

GU GU1 .... 9 H4
HORL RH6 .... 170 D6
HPTN TW12 .... 25 L5
HSLW TW3 .... 16 E5
KUTN/CMB KT2 .... 3 K3
MORT/ESHN SW14 .... 19 G5
MRDN SM4 .... 47 K4 ▣
NWMAL KT3 .... 46 C5
RCHPK/HAM TW10 .... 18 C8
TEDD TW11 .... 26 C7
THDIT KT7 .... 44 C5
TWK TW1 .... 26 C2
WEY KT13 .... 60 A4
WIM/MER SW19 .... 29 L6
WLGTN SM6 .... 66 E4
WOKN/KNAP GU21 .... 75 M8
WOT/HER KT12 .... 60 B4
Queens Sq CRAWE RH10 .... 212 A3
Queen's Ter ISLW TW7 .... 17 K6
Queen St ASHV GU12 .... 113 G7
CHERT KT16 .... 40 D8
CROY/NA CR0 .... 4 C9
RGODL GU7 .... 160 B5
SHGR GU5 .... 141 M5
SWTR RH13 .... 229 G8
Queensville Rd CLAP SW4 .... 31 G1
Queens Wk ASHF TW15 .... 23 G5
WLGTN SM6 .... 66 E4
WOKN/KNAP GU21 .... 75 M8
WOT/HER KT12 .... 60 B4
Queensway CRAN GU6 .... 185 J7
CRAWE RH10 .... 212 B3
CROY/NA CR0 .... 67 J4
EGRIN RH19 .... 216 B1 ▣
FRIM GU16 .... 93 K2
REDH RH1 .... 126 C7
SUN TW16 .... 42 E2
SWTR RH13 .... 228 F8
WOT/HER KT12 .... 60 E4
WWKM BR4 .... 70 D3
Queensway North
WOT/HER KT12 .... 60 F3
Queensway South
WOT/HER KT12 .... 60 F4
Queenswood Av HEST TW5 ...... 16 C2
HPTN TW12 .... 25 L7
THHTH CR7 .... 49 K5
WLGTN SM6 .... 67 G3
Queenswood Rd FSTH SE23 .... 33 H4
WOKS/MYFD GU22 .... 96 A1
Quennell Cl ASHTD KT21 .... 103 J1 ▣
Quennells Hl NFNM GU10 .... 155 H5
Quentin Wy VW GU25 .... 38 E4
Quicks Rd WIM/MER SW19 ...... 29 L8
Quiet Cl ADL/WDHM KT15 ...... 58 D3
Quiet Nook HAYES BR2 .... 71 G2
The Quillot WOT/HER KT12 ...... 60 C4
Quince Cl ASC SL5 .... 37 G4 ▣
Quince Dr CHOB/PIR GU24 ...... 75 L5
Quincy Rd EGH TW20 .... 21 K6 ▣
Quintilis BRAK RG12 .... 34 C8
Quintin Av RYNPK SW20 .... 47 H1
Quinton Cl BECK BR3 .... 51 M3
HEST TW5 .... 15 L2
WLGTN SM6 .... 66 E3
Quinton Rd THDIT KT7 .... 44 D8
Quinton St WAND/EARL SW18 .. 29 M3
Quintrell Cl WOKN/KNAP GU21 .. 76 E7

R

Rabies Heath Rd REDH RH1 ...... 128 D8
Raby Rd NWMAL KT3 .... 46 A4
Raccoon Wy HSLWW TW4 .... 15 M4
Racecourse Rd LING RH7 .... 174 C6
Racecourse Wy HORL RH6 ...... 192 C2
Rackfield HASM GU27 .... 219 G2
Rackham Cl CRAWW RH11 ...... 212 A5
Rackham Ms
STRHM/NOR SW16 .... 30 F7 ▣
Rackstraw Rd SHST GU47 ...... 52 A8
Racquets Court Hl RGODL GU7 .. 159 M3
Radar Rd FARN GU14 .... 92 A8
Radbourne Rd BAL SW12 .... 30 F1
Radcliffe Cl FRIM GU16 .... 93 J2
Radcliffe Gdns CAR SM5 .... 66 B6
Radcliffe Rd CROY/NA CR0 ...... 5 K6
Radcliff Ms HPTN TW12 .... 25 M6 ▣
Radford Cl FNM GU9 .... 134 B4
Radford Rd CRAWE RH10 .... 192 F5
Rad La SHGR GU5 .... 142 A8
Radlet Av FSTH SE23 .... 32 E4
Radley Cl EBED/NFELT TW14 .. 24 C3 ▣▣
Radnor Cl MTCM CR4 .... 49 H5
Radnor Gdns TWK TW1 .... 26 C3
Radnor La CRAN GU6 .... 164 D7
SHGR GU5 .... 164 D2
Radnor Rd BRAK RG12 .... 35 J3
SHGR GU5 .... 164 A3
TWK TW1 .... 26 C3
WEY KT13 .... 59 K2
Radnor Wk CROY/NA CR0 ...... 51 H7
Radolphs KWD/TDW/WH KT20 .. 105 G4
Radstock Wy REDH RH1 .... 127 G2
Raeburn Av BRYLDS KT5 .... 45 L6
Raeburn Cl KUT KT1 .... 2 C3
Raeburn Ct WOKN/KNAP GU21 .. 76 B8
Rae Rd FARN GU14 .... 92 E8
Raf Gate Rd FARN GU14 .... 92 E8 ▣
Rag Hill Rd BH/WHM TN16 ...... 111 L3
Raglan Cl ASHV GU12 .... 112 F8
FRIM GU16 .... 93 J1
HSLWW TW4 .... 16 B7
REIG RH2 .... 125 M6
Raglan Ct CROY/NA CR0 .... 67 L4
Raglan Rd REIG RH2 .... 125 L6
WOKN/KNAP GU21 .... 76 B8
Raikes La RDKG RH5 .... 142 E8
Railey Rd CRAWE RH10 .... 212 B3
Railshead Rd ISLW TW7 .... 17 L6
Railton Rd GUW GU2 .... 116 E4
Railway Ap CHERT KT16 .... 40 C7 ▣
EGRIN RH19 .... 196 A8
TWK TW1 .... 26 D1 ▣
WLGTN SM6 .... 66 E4 ▣
Railway Rd TEDD TW11 .... 26 B5

Railway Side BARN SW13 .... 19 H5 ▣
Railway Ter FELT TW13 .... 24 D2
STA TW18 .... 22 A6
Rainbow Ct WOKN/KNAP GU21 .. 76 B6
Rainville Rd HMSMTH W6 .... 19 M1
Rake La MFD/CHID GU8 .... 181 J2
Rakers Rdg HORS RH12 .... 229 G4
Raleigh Av WLGTN SM6 .... 67 G3
Raleigh Ct STA TW18 .... 22 D5
Raleigh Dr BRYLDS KT5 .... 45 M8
ESH/CLAY KT10 .... 62 A4
HORL RH6 .... 171 K6
Raleigh Gdns MTCM CR4 .... 48 C3
Raleigh Rd FELT TW13 .... 24 C3
PGE/AN SE20 .... 33 G8
RCH/KEW TW9 .... 18 C5
Raleigh Wk CRAWE RH10 ...... 212 B5 ▣
Raleigh Wy CBLY GU15 .... 73 J6
FELT TW13 .... 24 F6
Ralliwood Rd ASHTD KT21 ...... 103 K1
Ralph Perring Ct BECK BR3 .... 51 K4
Ralphs Ride BRAK RG12 .... 35 H3
Rama Cl STRHM/NOR SW16 .... 31 H8
Rambler Cl STRHM/NOR SW16 .. 30 F5
Ramblers Wy CRAWW RH11 .... 211 L8
Rame Cl TOOT SW17 .... 30 D6
Ramillies Cl ALDT GU11 .... 113 H2
Ramornie Cl WOT/HER KT12 .... 61 J3
Ramsay Cl CBLY GU15 .... 73 L1 ▣
Ramsay Rd BFOR GU20 .... 55 H4
Ramsbury Cl BRAK RG12 .... 34 B6 ▣
Ramsdale Rd TOOT SW17 ...... 30 D6
Ramsden Rd BAL SW12 .... 30 D1
RGODL GU7 .... 160 A6
Ramsey Cl HORL RH6 .... 170 C6
HORS RH12 .... 229 G4
Ramsey Pl CTHM CR3 .... 107 M4
Ramsey Rd THHTH CR7 .... 49 J6
Ramslade Rd BRAK RG12 ...... 34 F5
Rams La MFD/CHID GU8 .... 203 K7
Randal Crs REIG RH2 .... 147 K2
Randalls Crs LHD/OX KT22 ...... 102 D2
Randalls Park Av LHD/OX KT22 .. 102 D2
Randalls Park Dr LHD/OX KT22 .. 102 D3
Randalls Rd LHD/OX KT22 ...... 102 B2
Randalls Wy LHD/OX KT22 ...... 102 D3
Randle Rd RCHPK/HAM TW10 .. 26 F5
Randlesdown Rd CAT SE6 ...... 33 K5
Randolph Cl COB KT11 .... 81 K6
KUTN/CMB KT2 .... 27 M6 ▣
WOKN/KNAP GU21 .... 76 B7 ▣
Randolph Rd EW KT17 .... 84 C4
Ranelagh Av BARN SW13 .... 19 K4
Ranelagh Crs ASC SL5 .... 35 M1
Ranelagh Dr BRAK RG12 .... 34 F3
TWK TW1 .... 17 L6
Ranelagh Gdns CHSWK W4 .... 18 F2 ▣
Ranelagh Pl NWMAL KT3 .... 46 B5 ▣
Ranelagh Rd REDH RH1 .... 126 B8
Ranfurly Rd SUT SM1 .... 65 K1
Range Ride CBLY GU15 .... 72 C2
Range Rd FARN GU14 .... 92 A7
The Range SHGR GU5 .... 161 G5
Range Vw SHST GU47 .... 72 B1
Range Wy SHPTN TW17 .... 41 K7
Rankine Cl FNM GU9 .... 134 D3
Ranmere St BAL SW12 .... 30 E2 ▣
Ranmore Av CROY/NA CR0 ...... 5 K8
Ranmore Cl REDH RH1 .... 126 D5
Ranmore Common Rd
RDKG RH5 .... 122 A7
Ranmore Rd BELMT SM2 .... 65 G2
DORK RH4 .... 144 D1
RDKG RH5 .... 122 B8
Rannoch Rd HMSMTH W6 ...... 19 M1
Ransome Cl CRAWW RH11 ...... 211 G6
Ranyard Cl CHSGTN KT9 .... 63 J2
Rapallo Cl FARN GU14 .... 92 F5 ▣
Raphael Dr THDIT KT7 .... 44 C7
Rapley Cl CBLY GU15 .... 73 J1
Rapley Gn BRAK RG12 .... 34 F6
Rapley's Fld CHOB/PIR GU24 .. 95 H5
Rapsley La WOKN/KNAP GU21 .. 75 L8
Rastell Av BAL SW12 .... 31 G3
Ratcliffe Rd FARN GU14 .... 92 C1
Rathfern Rd FSTH SE23 .... 33 J2
Rathgar Cl REDH RH1 .... 148 D5
Rathlin Rd CRAWW RH11 .... 211 L6
Ravelin Cl NFNM GU10 .... 132 C4 ▣
Ravendale Rd SUN TW16 .... 42 C2
Ravenfield Rd TOOT SW17 ...... 30 C4
Raven La CRAWW RH11 .... 211 M1
Ravensbourne Av
STWL/WRAY TW19 .... 23 H2
Ravensbourne Pk BROCKY SE4 .. 33 K1
Ravensbourne Park Crs CAT SE6 .. 33 J1
Ravensbourne Rd FSTH SE23 .. 33 J1
TWK TW1 .... 17 M8
Ravensbury Av MRDN SM4 .... 47 M5
Ravensbury Gv MTCM CR4 .... 48 A4
Ravensbury La MTCM CR4 ...... 48 A4
Ravensbury Rd
WAND/EARL SW18 .... 29 L3
Ravensbury Ter
WAND/EARL SW18 .... 29 L2
Ravenscar Rd SURB KT6 .... 63 J1
Ravens Cl REDH RH1 .... 126 C6
WOKN/KNAP GU21 .... 75 M6
Ravenscourt SUN TW16 .... 42 C1
Ravenscroft Cl ASHV GU12 .... 113 M6
Ravenscroft Rd BECK BR3 ...... 50 F2
WEY KT13 .... 79 M1
Ravensdale Gdns NRWD SE19 .. 32 A8
Ravensdale Ms STA TW18 ...... 22 E7 ▣
Ravensdale Rd ASC SL5 .... 36 D5
HSLWW TW4 .... 16 B5
Ravenstone Rd EGH TW20 ...... 20 E7
Ravensfield Gdns
HOR/WEW KT19 .... 64 B4
Ravenshead Cl SAND/SEL CR2 .. 88 F1
Ravenslea Rd BAL SW12 .... 30 C1
Ravensroyd Cl CBLY GU15 ...... 54 B8
Ravenstone St BAL SW12 ...... 30 D2
Ravens Wold PUR/KEN CR8 .... 87 M5
Ravenswood Av SURB KT6 ...... 63 J1
WWKM BR4 .... 51 M8
Ravenswood Cl COB KT11 ...... 81 G5
Ravenswood Crs WWKM BR4 .. 51 M8

Ravenswood Dr CBLY GU15 .... 73 K4
Ravenswood Gdns ISLW TW7 .. 17 H3 ☐
Ravenswood Rd BAL SW12 ...... 30 E1
  CROY/NA CR0 .... 4 A8
Rawlins Cl SAND/SEL CR2 .... 69 J6
Rawlinson Rd CBLY GU15 .... 72 C3
Rawnsley Av MTCM CR4 .... 48 A4 ☐
Raworth Cl CRAWE RH10 .... 212 F5 ☐
Ray La LING RH7 .... 173 K2
Rayleigh Av TEDD TW11 .... 26 B7
Rayleigh Ct KUT KT1 .... 3 J6
Rayleigh Ri SAND/SEL CR2 ...... 68 B5
Rayleigh Rd WIM/MER SW19 .... 47 J1
Raymead Av THHTH CR7 .... 49 K5
Raymead Cl LHD/OX KT22 ...... 102 B4
Raymead Wy LHD/OX KT22 .... 102 B4
Raymer Wk HORL RH6 .... 170 F5
Raymond Cl DTCH/LGLY SL3 .... 13 H3
  SYD SE26 .... 32 F6 ☐
Raymond Crs GUW GU2 .... 138 C1
Raymond Rd BECK BR3 .... 51 H4
  WIM/MER SW19 .... 29 J7 ☐
Raymond Wy ESH/CLAY KT10 .. 62 D5 ☐
Rayners Cl DTCH/LGLY SL3 ...... 12 F2
Ray Rd E/WMO/HCT KT8 .... 43 L5
Rays Rd WWKM BR4 .... 51 M7
Raywood Cl WDR/YW UB7 ...... 14 A2
Rdffye Ct HORS RH12 .... 229 K5
The Readens BNSTD SM7 .... 86 B6
Reading Arch Rd REDH RH1 .... 126 C8
Reading Rd FARN GU14 .... 92 F8
  SUT SM1 .... 65 M4
Read Rd ASHTD KT21 .... 83 G7
Reads Rest La
  KWD/TDW/WH KT20 .... 105 J1
Reapers Cl HORS RH12 .... 229 G4
Reapers Wy ISLW TW7 .... 17 G7
Recovery St TOOT SW17 .... 30 B6 ☐
Recreation Cl FARN GU14 .... 72 C8 ☐
Recreation Rd GU GU1 .... 8 F3
  NFNM GU10 .... 155 H6
  SYD SE26 .... 33 G5
Recreation Wy MTCM CR4 ...... 49 H3
Rectory Cl ASHTD KT21 .... 103 J1
  BF/WBF KT14 .... 79 H3
  BRAK RG12 .... 34 F4
  CRAN GU6 .... 186 B3
  RDKG RH5 .... 187 M6
  RGODL GU7 .... 160 C7
  RGUE GU4 .... 118 A6
  RYNPK SW20 .... 46 F2
  SHGR GU5 .... 161 J3
  SHPTN TW17 .... 41 K5
  SURB KT6 .... 44 F8
Rectory Gn BECK BR3 .... 51 J1
Rectory Gv CROY/NA CR0 .... 4 A6
  FELT TW13 .... 25 J5
Rectory La ASHTD KT21 .... 83 J8
  BF/WBF KT14 .... 79 H3
  BFOR GU20 .... 54 F6
  BH/WHM TN16 .... 111 H5
  BNSTD SM7 .... 86 C5
  BRAK RG12 .... 34 E4
  BRKHM/BTCW RH3 .... 124 C6
  CRAWW RH11 .... 211 J1
  GT/LBKH KT23 .... 101 J8
  HORL RH6 .... 218 A2
  LIPH GU30 .... 154 A5
  NFNM GU10 .... 141 J5
  SHGR GU5 .... 141 J5
  SURB KT6 .... 44 F8
  TOOT SW17 .... 30 D6
  WLGTN SM6 .... 66 F3
Rectory Orch WIM/MER SW19 .. 29 H5
Rectory Pk SAND/SEL CR2 ...... 88 B3
Rectory Rd BARN SW13 .... 19 K4
  BECK BR3 .... 51 K2
  COUL/CHIP CR5 .... 106 A7
  FARN GU14 .... 92 F5
  HAYES BR2 .... 71 G6
  HEST TW5 .... 15 L4
  SUT SM1 .... 65 K2
Red Admiral St HORS RH12 .... 229 H4
Redan Gdns ASHV GU12 .... 112 F7
Redan Rd ASHV GU12 .... 112 F7
Redbarn PUR/KEN CR8 .... 87 L1 ☐
Redberry Gv SYD SE26 .... 32 F4
Redclose Av MRDN SM4 .... 47 K5
Redcote Pl DORK RH4 .... 144 C8
Redcourt WOKS/MYFD GU22 .... 78 A5
Redcrest Gdns CBLY GU15 ...... 73 J4
Redcroft Wk CRAN GU6 .... 185 H1
Red Deer Cl SWTR RH13 .... 229 L6
Reddington Cl SAND/SEL CR2 .. 68 A7 ☐
Redding Wy WOKN/KNAP GU21 .. 76 A8
Redditch BRAK RG12 .... 35 G7
Redditch Cl CRAWW RH11 ..... 211 H7
Reddons Rd BECK BR3 .... 33 H8
Reddown Rd COUL/CHIP CR5 .... 87 G8
Redehall Rd HORL RH6 .... 171 L8
Redesdale Gdns ISLW TW7 ...... 17 K2
Redfern Av HSLWW TW4 .... 25 K1
Redfern Rd CAT SE6 .... 33 M1
Redford Av COUL/CHIP CR5 ...... 86 E5
  HORS RH12 .... 228 A5
  THHTH CR7 .... 49 J4
  WLGTN SM6 .... 67 H5
Redford Cl FELT TW13 .... 24 C3
Redgarth Ct EGRIN RH19 .... 195 L6
Redgate Dr HAYES BR2 .... 70 E1
Redgrave Cl SNWD SE25 .... 50 C6 ☐
Redgrave Dr CRAWE RH10 ..... 213 G4
Redhearne Flds NFNM GU10 .. 178 B7
Redhill Cl COB KT11 .... 79 L3
Red House La MFD/CHID GU8.. 157 M6
  WOT/HER KT12 .... 60 D1
Redhouse Rd BH/WHM TN16 .. 110 F5
Red House Rd CROY/NA CR0 .... 49 G6
Redkiln Cl SWTR RH13 .... 229 L6
Redkiln Wy SWTR RH13 .... 229 L6
Redland Gdns
  E/WMO/HCT KT8 .... 43 J4 ☐
Redlands COUL/CHIP CR5 .... 87 H6
Redlands La NFNM GU10 .... 132 C2
  RDKG RH5 .... 144 E7 ☐
Redlands Wy BRXS/STRHM SW2 .. 31 H1
Red La ESH/CLAY KT10 .... 62 D5
  OXTED RH8 .... 130 E7

RDKG RH5 .... 145 K7
Redleaves Av ASHF TW15 .... 23 L7
Redlees Cl ISLW TW7 .... 17 K6
Red Lion La CHOB/PIR GU24 .... 56 B7
  FNM GU9 .... 10 F2
Red Lion Rd CHOB/PIR GU24 .... 56 B7
  SURB KT6 .... 63 J1
Red Lion St RCHPK/HAM TW10.. 18 A7
Red Lodge Rd WWKM BR4 .... 51 M8
Redmayne CBLY GU15 .... 73 M5 ☐
Red Oak Cl ORP BR6 .... 71 L2
Red Rd LTWR GU18 .... 74 D2
Redroofs Cl BECK BR3 .... 51 L1
Redstart Cl CROY/NA CR0 .... 70 A8
Redstone Hl REDH RH1 .... 126 D8
Redstone Hollow REDH RH1 .. 148 D1
Redstone Mnr REDH RH1 ...... 126 D8 ☐
Redstone Pk REDH RH1 .... 126 D8
Redstone Rd REDH RH1 .... 148 D1
Redvers Buller Rd ALDT GU11 .. 112 F2
Redvers Rd BRAK RG12 .... 34 E5
  WARL CR6 .... 89 G8
Redway Dr WHTN TW2 .... 25 M1
Redwing Av RGODL GU7 .... 138 A8
Redwing Cl SAND/SEL CR2 ...... 89 G1
  SWTR RH13 .... 229 J6 ☐
Redwing Gdns BF/WBF KT14 .... 78 E2
Redwing Ri RGUE GU4 .... 118 A6 ☐
Redwood EGH TW20 .... 40 B2
  PUR/KEN CR8 .... 87 M4 ☐
Redwood Cl CRAWE RH10 ..... 212 B1
  PUR/KEN CR8 .... 87 M4 ☐
Redwood Dr ASC SL5 .... 37 L6
  CBLY GU15 .... 74 A5
Redwood Gv RGUE GU4 .... 139 M6
Redwood Mt REIG RH2 .... 125 K5
Redwoods ADL/WDHM KT15 .... 58 D5
Reed Cl ALDT GU11 .... 113 G3
Reedham Dr PUR/KEN CR8 ...... 87 J3
Reedham Park Av PUR/KEN CR8.. 87 K6
Reedings CRAWW RH11 .... 211 C5
Reed Pl WOKN/KNAP GU21 ...... 78 B3
Reedsfield Cl ASHF TW15 .... 23 L4 ☐
Reedsfield Rd ASHF TW15 ...... 23 L5 ☐
Reed's Hl BRAK RG12 .... 34 E5
The Reeds NFNM GU10 .... 156 A8
Rees Gdns CROY/NA CR0 .... 50 C6
Reeve Rd REDH RH1 .... 147 M4
Reeves Cnr CROY/NA CR0 .... 4 B6 ☐
Reeves Rd ASHV GU12 .... 112 F8
Regal Ct MTCM CR4 .... 48 C3 ☐
Regal Crs WLGTN SM6 .... 66 E2 ☐
Regal Dr EGRIN RH19 .... 216 C1
Regalfield Cl GUW GU2 .... 116 D4
Regan Cl GUW GU2 .... 116 E3
Regency Cl HPTN TW12 .... 25 J6 ☐
Regency Dr BF/WBF KT14 .... 78 C3 ☐
Regency Gdns WOT/HER KT12 .. 42 F8 ☐
Regency Ms BECK BR3 .... 51 M1 ☐
Regency Wk CROY/NA CR0 ...... 51 H6
Regent Cl ADL/WDHM KT15 ..... 58 F7 ☐
  HEST TW5 .... 15 L3
  REDH RH1 .... 126 F3
Regent Ct BAGS GU19 .... 54 C7 ☐
Regent Crs REDH RH1 .... 126 C6
Regent Pl WIM/MER SW19 ...... 29 M6
Regent Rd BRYLDS KT5 .... 45 J5
Regents Cl CRAWW RH11 ...... 211 M7
  CTHM CR3 .... 88 B3
  SAND/SEL CR2 .... 68 B5
Regents Dr HAYES BR2 .... 71 G4
Regents Wk ASC SL5 .... 36 F6
Regent Wy FRIM GU16 .... 73 J8
Regina Rd SNWD SE25 .... 50 D3
Reid Av CTHM CR3 .... 108 A3
Reid Cl COUL/CHIP CR5 .... 86 E6
Reigate Av SUT SM1 .... 47 L8
Reigate Cl CRAWE RH10 .... 193 G8
Reigate Hl REIG RH2 .... 125 L6
Reigate Hill Cl REIG RH2 ...... 125 K5
Reigate Rd BRKHM/BTCW RH3.. 123 M7
  DORK RH4 .... 123 H8
  EW KT17 .... 64 C8
  HORL RH6 .... 170 A4
  LHD/OX KT22 .... 102 F5
  REIG RH2 .... 125 M8
Reigate Wy WLGTN SM6 .... 67 H4
Reindorp Cl GUW GU2 .... 8 B5
Rembrandt Ct
  HOR/WEW KT19 .... 64 C5 ☐
Rendle Cl CROY/NA CR0 .... 50 C5
Renfree Wy SHPTN TW17 .... 41 K7
Renfrew Rd HEST TW5 .... 16 A4
  KUTN/CMB KT2 .... 3 M2
The Renmans ASHTD KT21 ...... 83 J6
Renmuir St TOOT SW17 .... 30 C7
Rennie Cl ASHF TW15 .... 23 G4
Rennie Ter REDH RH1 .... 148 D1
Renown Cl CROY/NA CR0 .... 4 B4
Replingham Rd
  WAND/EARL SW18 .... 29 J2
Repton Cl SUT SM1 .... 66 B4
Repton Ct BECK BR3 .... 51 L1 ☐
Reservoir Rd FARN GU14 .... 92 A8
Restmor Wy WLGTN SM6 .... 66 D1
Restwell Av CRAN GU6 .... 184 E3
Retreat Rd RCH/KEW TW9 ...... 18 A7 ☐
The Retreat BARN SW13 .... 19 H5 ☐
  BRYLDS KT5 .... 45 J6
  EGH TW20 .... 21 H8
  THHTH CR7 .... 50 A4
  WPK KT4 .... 64 E1 ☐
Revell Cl LHD/OX KT22 .... 101 L4
Revell Dr LHD/OX KT22 .... 101 L4
Revell Rd KUT KT1 .... 3 M5
  SUT SM1 .... 65 J5
Revelstoke Av FARN GU14 .... 92 E3
Revelstoke Rd WIM/MER SW19 .. 29 K3
Revesby Cl CHOB/PIR GU24 ..... 75 G3
Revesby Rd CAR SM5 .... 48 B6
Rewley Rd CAR SM5 .... 48 A6
Rex Av ASHF TW15 .... 23 K7
Reynard Dr NRWD SE19 .... 32 C8 ☐
Reynolds Av CHSGTN KT9 .... 63 H6
Reynolds Cl CAR SM5 .... 48 C8
  WIM/MER SW19 .... 48 A1
Reynolds Gn SHST GU47 .... 72 A3 ☐

Reynolds Pl CRAWW RH11 .... 211 M2 ☐
  RCHPK/HAM TW10 .... 18 C8 ☐
Reynolds Rd CRAWW RH11 ... 211 M2
  NWMAL KT3 .... 46 A7
Reynolds Wy CROY/NA CR0 ...... 5 H9
Rheingold Wy WLGTN SM6 ...... 67 H7 ☐
Rhine Banks FARN GU14 .... 92 A4
Rhodes Cl EGH TW20 .... 21 M6 ☐
Rhodes Wy CRAWE RH10 ...... 212 C5
Rhododendron Ride EGH TW20.. 20 C6
Rhododendron Rd FRIM GU16.. 93 L1
Rhodrons Av CHSGTN KT9 ...... 63 H4
Rialto Rd MTCM CR4 .... 48 D2
Ribble Pl FARN GU14 .... 92 B3
Ribblesdale Rd
  STRHM/NOR SW16 .... 30 E6
Ricardo Ct SHGR GU5 .... 161 J4
Ricards Rd WIM/MER SW19 ..... 29 J3
Rices Hl EGRIN RH19 .... 196 B8
Richards Cl ASHV GU12 .... 113 K4 ☐
  HYS/HAR UB3 .... 15 G1
Richards Fld HOR/WEW KT19 .. 64 A7
Richards Rd COB KT11 .... 81 L4
Richbell Cl ASHTD KT21 .... 83 G8
Richens Cl HSLW TW3 .... 17 G4
Richland Av COUL/CHIP CR5 .... 86 D5 ☐
Richlands Av EW KT17 .... 64 D3
Richmond Av EBED/NFELT TW14.. 15 H8
  RYNPK SW20 .... 47 H1
Richmond Cl BH/WHM TN16 .. 110 E1 ☐
  EPSOM KT18 .... 84 B4 ☐
  FARN GU14 .... 92 A6
  FRIM GU16 .... 73 J8
  GT/LBKH KT23 .... 101 M6
Richmond Ct CRAWE RH10 .... 212 B4 ☐
Richmond Crs STA TW18 .... 22 C6 ☐
Richmond Dr SHPTN TW17 ..... 41 M6
Richmond Gn CROY/NA CR0 .... 67 H2
Richmond Hl
  RCHPK/HAM TW10 .... 18 B8 ☐
Richmond Park Rd
  KUTN/CMB KT2 .... 2 F4
  MORT/ESHN SW14 .... 18 F7
Richmond Rd COUL/CHIP CR5 .. 86 E5
  CROY/NA CR0 .... 67 H2
  HORS RH12 .... 228 F5
  ISLW TW7 .... 17 K5 ☐
  RGODL GU7 .... 160 B3 ☐
  RYNPK SW20 .... 46 E1
  SHST GU47 .... 72 B1
  STA TW18 .... 22 C6
  THHTH CR7 .... 49 L4
  TWK TW1 .... 26 E1
Richmondwood ASC SL5 .... 37 L8
Rickard Cl BRXS/STRHM SW2 ... 31 K2 ☐
Rickards Cl SURB KT6 .... 63 H1
Ricketts Hill Rd BH/WHM TN16 .. 91 G8
Rickfield CRAWW RH11 .... 211 K4 ☐
Rickford Hl RGUE GU3 .... 96 A8
Rickman Cl BRAK RG12 .... 34 F6 ☐
Rickman Crs ADL/WDHM KT15 .. 58 E2
Rickman Hl COUL/CHIP CR5 .... 86 E7
Rickman Hill Rd COUL/CHIP CR5.. 86 E8
Rickman's La BIL RH14 .... 223 J7
Ricksons La EHSLY KT24 .... 119 L1
Rickwood HORL RH6 .... 170 E5
Rickyard GUW GU2 .... 116 A8
The Riddings CTHM CR3 .... 108 C7
Riddlesdown Av PUR/KEN CR8 .. 87 M2
Riddlesdown Rd
  PUR/KEN CR8 .... 67 M8 ☐
Ride La SHGR GU5 .... 163 G2
Riders Wy GDST RH9 .... 128 F5
The Ride BIL RH14 .... 223 M7
Ride Wy CRAN GU6 .... 163 L7
Rideway Cl CBLY GU15 .... 72 E5
Ridge Cl BRKHM/BTCW RH5 ... 145 L4
  WOKS/MYFD GU22 .... 96 E3
Ridgegate Cl REIG RH2 .... 126 A6
Ridge Gn REDH RH1 .... 149 H3
Ridge Green Cl REDH RH1 ..... 149 H3
Ridgehurst Dr HORS RH12 .... 228 C8
Ridgelands LHD/OX KT22 ...... 102 A6
Ridge Langley SAND/SEL CR2 .. 68 D8
Ridgemead Rd EGH TW20 ...... 20 E4
Ridge Moor Cl GSHT GU26 .... 199 H4
Ridgemount GUW GU2 .... 8 C5
  WEY KT13 .... 60 B1
Ridgemount Av COUL/CHIP CR5.. 86 E7
  CROY/NA CR0 .... 69 G1
Ridge Mount Rd ASC SL5 .... 37 K8
Ridgemount Wy REDH RH1 ... 148 A2
Ridge Pk WLGTN SM6 .... 67 G8
Ridge Rd CHEAM SM3 .... 47 J8
  MTCM CR4 .... 30 E8
Ridgeside CRAWE RH10 .... 212 C3 ☐
The Ridges RGUW GU3 .... 138 F5
The Ridge BRYLDS KT5 .... 45 K5
  COUL/CHIP CR5 .... 87 H4
  CTHM CR3 .... 110 B7
  EPSOM KT18 .... 83 M8
  HORS RH12 .... 226 B1
  LHD/OX KT22 .... 102 A6
  PUR/KEN CR8 .... 67 G8
  WHTN TW2 .... 26 A1
  WOKS/MYFD GU22 .... 97 J5
Ridge Wy EDEN TN8 .... 153 M5
  FELT TW13 .... 25 H4 ☐
  VW GU25 .... 39 H5
Ridgeway EGRIN RH19 .... 216 B2 ☐
  HAYES BR2 .... 70 D1
  HOR/WEW KT19 .... 83 M2
  WOKN/KNAP GU21 .... 6 B2
  WOT/HER KT12 .... 42 C8
Ridgeway Cl CRAN GU6 .... 185 K6
  DORK RH4 .... 144 D4
  LTWR GU18 .... 74 D1
  WOKN/KNAP GU21 .... 6 A3
Ridgeway Dr DORK RH4 .... 144 D5
Ridgeway Gdns
  WOKN/KNAP GU21 .... 6 B2
Ridgeway Hill Rd FNM GU9..... 11 G4
Ridgeway Rd DORK RH4 .... 144 D4
  FNM GU9 .... 11 H4
  ISLW TW7 .... 17 H2

  REDH RH1 .... 126 C8
Rivernook Cl WOT/HER KT12 .. 42 F5
River Park Av STA TW18 .... 22 A5
River Reach TEDD TW11 .... 26 F7
River Rd STA TW18 .... 40 C1
Rivers Cl FARN GU14 .... 93 H8
Riversdale Rd THDIT KT7 .... 44 D5
Riversdell Cl CHERT KT16 .... 40 C7
Riverside DORK RH4 .... 123 G3 ☐
  EDEN TN8 .... 153 M8
  FROW RH18 .... 217 H6
  GU GU1 .... 117 G6
  HORL RH6 .... 170 D8
  HORS RH12 .... 228 D7
  SHPTN TW17 .... 42 B7
  STWL/WRAY TW19 .... 20 F1
  TWK TW1 .... 26 E2
Riverside Av E/WMO/HCT KT8 .. 44 A5
  LTWR GU18 .... 74 F1
Riverside Cl CHOB/PIR GU24 ... 95 J2
  FARN GU14 .... 92 C4
  KUT KT1 .... 45 G4
  STA TW18 .... 40 C1
  WLGTN SM6 .... 66 E1
Riverside Dr CHSWK W4 .... 19 G2 ☐
  ESH/CLAY KT10 .... 61 K3
  MTCM CR4 .... 48 B5
  RCHPK/HAM TW10 .... 26 E4
  SHGR GU5 .... 161 K3
  STA TW18 .... 40 C1
Riverside Gdns
  WOKS/MYFD GU22 .... 97 L3
Riverside Pl STWL/WRAY TW19 .. 14 A8
Riverside Rd STA TW18 .... 22 C8
  STWL/WRAY TW19 .... 14 A7
  TOOT SW17 .... 29 L5
  WOT/HER KT12 .... 61 G3
Riverside Wk ISLW TW7 .... 17 H5
Riverside Wy CBLY GU15 .... 72 D6
Riverview Gdns BARN SW13 .... 19 L1
  COB KT11 .... 80 D3 ☐
River View Gdns TWK TW1 ..... 26 C3
Riverview Pk CAT SE6 .... 33 K3
Riverview Rd CHSWK W4 .... 18 E2
  HOR/WEW KT19 .... 64 A4
River Wk SUN TW16 .... 43 G2
  WOT/HER KT12 .... 42 D6
River Wy FELT TW13 .... 25 L3
  HOR/WEW KT19 .... 64 A4
Riverway STA TW18 .... 40 E1
Rivett-drake Rd GUW GU2 .... 116 D4
Rivey Cl BF/WBF KT14 .... 78 C4
Roakes Av ADL/WDHM KT15 ... 58 E1
Robert Cl WOT/HER KT12 ...... 60 E4
Robertsbridge Rd CAR SM5 .... 47 M7
Roberts Cl CHEAM SM3 .... 65 G6 ☐
  STWL/WRAY TW19 .... 13 M8
Robertson Wy ASHV GU12 ..... 113 J8
  CBLY GU15 .... 72 D3
Roberts Rd ASHV GU12 .... 113 G8
  CBLY GU15 .... 72 D3
Robert St CROY/NA CR0 .... 4 D7 ☐
Roberts Wy EGH TW20 .... 20 F8
Robert Wy FRIM GU16 .... 93 J6
  HORS RH12 .... 229 J2
Robin Cl ADL/WDHM KT15 ..... 59 G4
  ASHV GU12 .... 113 J3
  CRAWW RH11 .... 211 M1
  EGRIN RH19 .... 196 B7
  HPTN TW12 .... 25 H6
Robin Gdns REDH RH1 .... 126 D6 ☐
Robin Gv BTFD TW8 .... 17 M1
Robin Hl RGODL GU7 .... 160 A2
Robin Hill Dr CBLY GU15 .... 73 K6
Robin Hood Cl FARN GU14 ..... 92 D2
Robinhood Cl MTCM CR4 .... 48 F4
Robin Hood Cl
  WOKN/KNAP GU21 .... 76 C8
Robin Hood Crs
  WOKN/KNAP GU21 .... 76 B7
Robin Hood La HORS RH12 ... 228 B4
Robinhood La MTCM CR4 .... 48 F3
Robin Hood La PUR/ROE SW15 .. 28 B4
  RGUE GU4 .... 97 J6
  SUT SM1 .... 65 K4
Robin Hood Rd PUR/ROE SW15 .. 28 B5
  WOKN/KNAP GU21 .... 76 C8
Robin Hood Way (Kingston by Pass)
  PUT/ROE SW15 .... 28 B5
Robins Dl WOKN/KNAP GU21 .. 75 M7
Robins Gv WWKM BR4 .... 70 D2
Robinson Rd CRAWW RH11 ... 212 A4
  WIM/MER SW19 .... 30 A1
Robinsway WOT/HER KT12 ..... 60 F3
Robin Wy GUW GU2 .... 116 E4
  STA TW18 .... 22 B6
Robinwood Pl RCHPK/HAM TW10.. 28 A5
Robson Rd WNWD SE27 .... 31 L4
Roby Dr BRAK RG12 .... 35 G7
Roche Rd STRHM/NOR SW16 .. 49 J1 ☐
Rochester Av FELT TW13 .... 24 C3
Rochester Cl
  STRHM/NOR SW16 .... 31 H8 ☐
Rochester Gdns CROY/NA CR0 .. 5 H7
  CTHM CR3 .... 108 B4
Rochester Rd CAR SM5 .... 66 C3 ☐
  EGH TW20 .... 22 A6
Rochford Wy CROY/NA CR0 .... 49 H6
Rock Av MORT/ESHN SW14 .... 19 G5
Rockbourne Rd FSTH SE23 .... 33 G2
Rockdale Dr GSHT GU26 .... 199 G6 ☐
The Rockery FARN GU14 .... 92 A6
Rocket Rd FARN GU14 .... 92 B1
Rockfield Cl OXTED RH8 .... 130 C5
Rockfield Rd OXTED RH8 ...... 130 C4
Rockfield Wy SHST GU47 .... 72 A1 ☐
Rock Gdns ALDT GU11 .... 112 C4
Rockhampton Rd
  SAND/SEL CR2 .... 68 A3
  STRHM/NOR SW16 .... 31 K5
Rock Hl NRWD SE19 .... 32 C5
Rockingham Cl
  PUT/ROE SW15 .... 19 J6 ☐
Rock La NFNM GU10 .... 155 K4
Rockmount Rd NRWD SE19 .... 32 A7
Rockshaw Rd REDH RH1 .... 126 F1
Rocks La BARN SW13 .... 19 K5
The Rocks EGRIN RH19 .... 216 F3

Rockwell Gdns NRWD SE19 ...... 32 B5 ⓸
Rocky La REIG RH2 ...... 126 D3
Rocombe Crs FSTH SE23 ...... 32 F1 ⓫
Roden Gdns CROY/NA CR0 ...... 50 B6 ⓶
Rodenhurst Rd CLAP SW4 ...... 30 F1
Rodmel Ct FARN GU14 ...... 93 H8
Rodney Cl NWMAL KT3 ...... 46 B5
   WOT/HER KT12 ...... 42 F8 ⓭
Rodney Gdns WWKM BR4 ...... 70 D3
Rodney Pl WIM/MER SW19 ...... 47 M1 ⓵
Rodney Rd HSLWW TW4 ...... 16 B8 ⓫
   HSLWW TW4 ...... 25 K1 ⓫
   MTCM CR4 ...... 48 B2
   NWMAL KT3 ...... 46 B5
   WOT/HER KT12 ...... 60 E1
Rodney Wy DTCH/LGLY SL3 ...... 13 H3
   GU GU1 ...... 117 K7
Rodona Rd WEY KT13 ...... 80 A1
Rodway Rd PUT/ROE SW15 ...... 28 D1
Roebuck Cl ASHTD KT21 ...... 103 H2
   FELT TW13 ...... 24 E5
   REIG RH2 ...... 125 K8
   SWTR RH13 ...... 229 L5
Roebuck Rd CHSGTN KT9 ...... 63 K4
Roedean Crs PUT/ROE SW15 ...... 19 H8
Roedeer Copse HASM GU27 ...... 219 H3
Roehampton Cl
   PUT/ROE SW15 ...... 19 K6 ⓫
Roehampton Ga
   PUT/ROE SW15 ...... 19 H8
Roehampton High St
   PUT/ROE SW15 ...... 28 D1
Roehampton La PUT/ROE SW15 .. 19 K7
Roehampton V PUT/ROE SW15 ... 28 C4
Roe Wy WLGTN SM6 ...... 67 H5
Roffes La CTHM CR3 ...... 108 A7
Roffey Cl HORL RH6 ...... 170 C6
   PUR/KEN CR8 ...... 87 L6
Roffey's Cl CRAWW RH10 ...... 193 K5
Roffords WOKN/KNAP GU21 ...... 76 E7
Rogers Cl COUL/CHIP CR5 ...... 87 L8
Rogers La WARL CR6 ...... 89 J8
Rogers Md GDST RH9 ...... 128 C6
Rogers Rd TOOT SW17 ...... 30 A5
Rojack Rd FSTH SE23 ...... 33 G2
Rokeby Cl BRAK RG12 ...... 35 G2
Rokeby Pl RYNPK SW20 ...... 28 E8
Roke Cl MFD/CHID GU8 ...... 181 H4
   PUR/KEN CR8 ...... 87 M4
Roke La MFD/CHID GU8 ...... 181 H4
Roke Lodge Rd PUR/KEN CR8 ... 87 L3
Roke Rd PUR/KEN CR8 ...... 87 M5
Rokers La MFD/CHID GU8 ...... 159 G2
Roland Wy WPK KT4 ...... 64 C1
Rolinsden Wy HAYES BR2 ...... 71 G3
Rollesby Rd CHSGTN KT9 ...... 63 K5
Rolleston Rd SAND/SEL CR2 ...... 68 A6 ⓭
Rollit Crs HSLW TW3 ...... 16 D7
Roman Cl EBED/NFELT TW14 ...... 15 M7
Romanfield Rd
   BRXS/STRHM SW2 ...... 31 J1
Roman Ri NRWD SE19 ...... 32 A7
Roman Rd DORK RH4 ...... 144 D4
Romans Wy WOKS/MYFD GU22 .. 78 D5
Roman Wy BNFD RG42 ...... 35 J1
   CROY/NA CR0 ...... 4 B5
   FNM GU9 ...... 134 B5
Romany Gdns CHEAM SM3 ...... 47 K7
Romayne Cl FARN GU14 ...... 92 D4
Romberg Rd TOOT SW17 ...... 30 D4
Romeyn Rd STRHM/NOR SW16 ... 31 J4
Rommany Rd WNWD SE27 ...... 32 A5
Romney Cl ASHF TW15 ...... 23 M6 ⓫
   CHSGTN KT9 ...... 63 H3
Romney Rd FARN GU14 ...... 92 B8
   NWMAL KT3 ...... 46 A6
Romola Rd BRXS/STRHM SW2 ... 31 L2
   ORP BR6 ...... 71 M3 ⓭
Romsey Cl ALDT GU11 ...... 134 F3
Rona Cl CRAWW RH11 ...... 211 L6
Ronald Ct BECK BR3 ...... 51 J5
Ronelean Rd SURB KT6 ...... 63 J1
Ronneby Cl WEY KT13 ...... 60 B2
Rookeries Cl FELT TW13 ...... 24 E4
Rookery Cl LHD/OX KT22 ...... 102 B6
Rookery Dr DORK RH4 ...... 143 K4
Rookery Hl ASHTD KT21 ...... 83 K8
   REDH RH1 ...... 171 L3
   STA TW18 ...... 22 E6
Rookery Wy
   KWD/TDW/WH KT20 ...... 125 J1
Rook La CTHM CR3 ...... 107 K6
Rookley Cl BELMT SM2 ...... 65 L7 ⓭
   BELMT SM2 ...... 65 L8 ⓸
Rooks Hl SHGR GU5 ...... 161 M7
Rookstone Rd TOOT SW17 ...... 30 C6
Rook Wy HORS RH12 ...... 229 H3
Rookwood Av NWMAL KT3 ...... 46 D4
   SHST GU47 ...... 52 B8
   WLGTN SM6 ...... 67 G3
Rookwood Cl REDH RH1 ...... 126 E3
Rookwood Ct GUW GU2 ...... 8 E9
Rookwood Pk HORS RH12 ...... 228 D6
Roothill La BRKHM/BTCW RH3 .. 145 K6
Ropeland Wy HORS RH12 ...... 229 H2
Roper Wy MTCM CR4 ...... 48 D2 ⓭
Rorkes Drift FRIM GU16 ...... 93 J3
Rosa Av ASHF TW15 ...... 23 K5
Rosamond St SYD SE26 ...... 32 E4
Rosamund Cl SAND/SEL CR2 ... 68 A3 ⓫
Rosamund Rd CRAWE RH10 ...... 212 F5
Rosary Cl HSLW TW3 ...... 16 B4
Rosary Gdns ASHF TW15 ...... 23 L5
Roseacre OXTED RH8 ...... 130 D7
Roseacre Cl SHPTN TW17 ...... 41 K5 ⓶
Roseacre Gdns RGUE GU4 ...... 140 C6
Rose Av MRDN SM4 ...... 47 M5
   MTCM CR4 ...... 48 C1
Rosebank EPSOM KT18 ...... 83 M4
   PGE/AN SE20 ...... 32 E8
Rosebank Cl TEDD TW11 ...... 26 D7 ⓸
Rosebery Av EW KT17 ...... 84 C3
   NWMAL KT3 ...... 46 C2
   THHTH CR7 ...... 49 M2

Rosebery Cl MRDN SM4 ...... 47 G6 ⓶
Rosebery Crs WOKS/MYFD GU22 .. 97 J2
Rosebery Gdns SUT SM1 ...... 65 L3 ⓶
Rosebery Rd ISLW TW7 ...... 16 F7
   KUT KT1 ...... 3 L7
   SUT SM1 ...... 65 J5
Rosebery Sq KUT KT1 ...... 3 L7
Rosebine Av WHTN TW2 ...... 26 A1 ⓫
Rosebriar Cl
   WOKS/MYFD GU22 ...... 78 D6 ⓫
Rosebriars CTHM CR3 ...... 108 B2 ⓶
   ESH/CLAY KT10 ...... 61 M4 ⓶
Rosebury Dr CHOB/PIR GU24 ... 75 K5
Rose Bushes EW KT17 ...... 84 F6
Rosecourt Rd CROY/NA CR0 ...... 49 J6
Rosecroft Cl BH/WHM TN16 ...... 91 J8 ⓫
Rosecroft Gdns WHTN TW2 ...... 26 A2
Rosedale ASHTD KT21 ...... 82 F8
   ASHV GU12 ...... 112 F7
Rose Dl ORP BR6 ...... 71 L1
Rosedale Cl CRAWW RH11 ...... 211 K5 ⓶
   MRDN SM4 ...... 47 K5
   STRHM/NOR SW16 ...... 31 J4
Rosedene Av CROY/NA CR0 ...... 49 J7 ⓶
   MRDN SM4 ...... 47 K5
   STRHM/NOR SW16 ...... 31 J4
Rosedene La SHST GU47 ...... 72 B2 ⓫
Rose End WPK KT4 ...... 47 G8
Rosefield Cl CAR SM5 ...... 66 B4
Rosefield Gdns CHERT KT16 ...... 58 A5
Rosefield Rd STA TW18 ...... 22 D5
Rose Gdns FARN GU14 ...... 92 A6
   FELT TW13 ...... 24 D3
   STWL/WRAY TW19 ...... 23 G1
Roseheath Rd HSLWW TW4 ...... 16 C7
Rosehill ESH/CLAY KT10 ...... 62 D5
   HPTN TW12 ...... 43 K1
Rose Hl SUT SM1 ...... 65 L1
Rosehill Av SUT SM1 ...... 47 M8
   WOKN/KNAP GU21 ...... 76 F6
Rosehill Farm Meadow
   BNSTD SM7 ...... 85 L5
Rose Hill Pk West SUT SM1 ...... 47 M8
Rosehill Rd BH/WHM TN16 ...... 90 F7
Rose La RPLY/SEND GU23 ...... 99 G4
Roseleigh Cl TWK TW1 ...... 18 A8 ⓶
Rosemary Av ASHV GU12 ...... 113 K1
   E/WMO/HCT KT8 ...... 43 K3
   HSLWW TW4 ...... 16 A4
Rosemary Cl CROY/NA CR0 ...... 49 H7
   FARN GU14 ...... 92 A4
   OXTED RH8 ...... 130 D7 ⓶
Rosemary Crs RGUW GU3 ...... 116 C4
Rosemary La BLKW GU17 ...... 72 A5
   CRAN GU6 ...... 224 A1
   EGH TW20 ...... 39 L3
   HORL RH6 ...... 170 E7
   HORL RH6 ...... 191 H2
   MORT/ESHN SW14 ...... 18 F5
   NFNM GU10 ...... 155 H5
Rosemary Rd TOOT SW17 ...... 29 M4 ⓶
Rosemead CHERT KT16 ...... 40 E7
   MTCM CR4 ...... 48 F3
Rosemead Cl REDH RH1 ...... 148 A2 ⓶
Rosemead Rd FELT TW13 ...... 24 C3 ⓫
Rosemont Rd NWMAL KT3 ...... 45 M3 ⓶
   RCHPK/HAM TW10 ...... 18 B8
Rosemount Av BF/WBF KT14 ... 78 B3 ⓫
Rosendale Rd DUL SE21 ...... 31 M3
   HNHL SE24 ...... 31 M1
Rosenheath Ct CTHM CR3 ...... 108 D7 ⓸
The Rosery CROY/NA CR0 ...... 51 G6
Rosethorn Cl BAL SW12 ...... 30 F1
Rosetrees GU GU1 ...... 139 K1
Roseville Av HSLWW TW4 ...... 16 D7
Rosevine Rd RYNPK SW20 ...... 46 F1
Rose Wk BRYLDS KT5 ...... 45 L5
   PUR/KEN CR8 ...... 87 G1
   WWKM BR4 ...... 70 A1
Rosewarne Cl
   WOKN/KNAP GU21 ...... 76 D8
Rosewell Cl PGE/AN SE20 ...... 32 E8
Rose Wd WOKS/MYFD GU22 ...... 7 G9
Rosewood Ct KUTN/CMB KT2 ...... 3 J3
Rosewood Dr SHPTN TW17 ...... 41 J5
Rosewood Gv SUT SM1 ...... 65 M1
Rosewood Wy CHOB/PIR GU24 .. 75 H3
Roslyn Cl MTCM CR4 ...... 48 A2
Ross Cl CRAWE RH10 ...... 212 C6
Rossdale SUT SM1 ...... 66 B4
Rossdale Rd PUT/ROE SW15 ...... 19 M6
Rosset Cl BRAK RG12 ...... 34 E4
Rossetti Gdns COUL/CHIP CR5 .. 87 J7
Rossignol Gdns CAR SM5 ...... 66 D1 ⓫
Rossindel Rd HSLW TW3 ...... 16 D7
Rossiter Rd BAL SW12 ...... 30 E2
Rosslea BFOR GU20 ...... 54 D3
Rosslyn Av BARN SW13 ...... 19 H5
   EBED/NFELT TW14 ...... 15 K8
Rosslyn Cl SUN TW16 ...... 24 B7
   WWKM BR4 ...... 70 C2 ⓶
Rosslyn Pk WEY KT13 ...... 60 A3
Rosslyn Rd TWK TW1 ...... 17 M8
Rossmore Cl CRAWE RH10 ...... 193 G2 ⓶
Ross Pde WLGTN SM6 ...... 66 E5
Ross Rd COB KT11 ...... 80 F3
   SNWD SE25 ...... 50 B3
   WHTN TW2 ...... 25 M2
   WLGTN SM6 ...... 66 E4
Rosswood Gdns WLGTN SM6 ... 66 F5 ⓫
Rostella Rd TOOT SW17 ...... 30 A5
Rostrevor Rd WIM/MER SW19 .. 29 K6 ⓭
Rothbury Gdns ISLW TW7 ...... 17 K2
Rother Crs CRAWW RH11 ...... 211 H5
Rotherfield Rd CAR SM5 ...... 66 D3
Rotherhill Av
   STRHM/NOR SW16 ...... 31 G7 ⓸
Rothermere Rd CROY/NA CR0 .. 67 J4 ⓫
Rother Rd FARN GU14 ...... 92 B3
Rothervale HORL RH6 ...... 170 C4 ⓫
Rotherwood Cl RYNPK SW20 ... 47 H1
Rothesay Av RCHPK/HAM TW10 .. 18 E6
   RYNPK SW20 ...... 47 H2
Rothesay Rd SNWD SE25 ...... 50 A4
Rothes Rd DORK RH4 ...... 144 E1

Rothschild St WNWD SE27 ...... 31 L5
Rougemont Av MRDN SM4 ...... 47 K6
Roughets La REDH RH1 ...... 128 B3
Rough Fld EGRIN RH19 ...... 196 A5 ⓸
Roughlands WOKS/MYFD GU22 .. 78 B5
Rough Rew RDKG RH5 ...... 144 E5
Rough Rd WOKS/MYFD GU22 ... 95 M4
Rough Wy HORS RH12 ...... 229 J4
Rounce La CHOB/PIR GU24 ...... 75 G3
Roundals La MFD/CHID GU8 .... 202 B1
Round Gv CROY/NA CR0 ...... 51 G7
Roundhay Cl FSTH SE23 ...... 33 G3
Round Hl FSTH SE23 ...... 32 E3
Roundhill Dr WOKS/MYFD GU22 .. 7 K9
Roundhill Wy COB KT11 ...... 81 L1
   GUW GU2 ...... 116 C8
Round Oak Rd WEY KT13 ...... 59 J3
Roundthorn Wy
   WOKN/KNAP GU21 ...... 76 C6
Roundway CBLY GU15 ...... 73 M3
   EGH TW20 ...... 21 M6
The Roundway ESH/CLAY KT10 .. 62 C5
Roundwood Vw BNSTD SM7 ...... 85 G5
Roundwood Wy BNSTD SM7 ...... 85 G5
Roupell Rd BRXS/STRHM SW2 ... 31 J2
Rouse Gdns DUL SE21 ...... 32 B5
Routh Rd WAND/EARL SW18 ...... 30 B1
Rowan Av EGH TW20 ...... 21 M6
Rowan Cha NFNM GU10 ...... 10 D9
Rowan Cl CBLY GU15 ...... 73 J1
   CRAWE RH10 ...... 212 C3 ⓸
   GU GU1 ...... 116 E5
   HORS RH12 ...... 229 L4
   NWMAL KT3 ...... 46 B2
   REIG RH2 ...... 147 M2
   STRHM/NOR SW16 ...... 48 F1 ⓶
Rowan Crs STRHM/NOR SW16 .. 48 F1
Rowan Gdns CROY/NA CR0 ...... 5 K7
Rowan Gv COUL/CHIP CR5 ...... 106 E3
Rowan Md KWD/TDW/WH KT20 .. 104 E1
Rowan Rd BTFD TW8 ...... 17 L2
   STRHM/NOR SW16 ...... 48 F2
Rowans Cl FARN GU14 ...... 72 B8
The Rowans GSHT GU26 ...... 199 G7 ⓸
   SUN TW16 ...... 24 C6
Rowan Wk HAYES BR2 ...... 71 J2
Rowan Wy HORS RH12 ...... 229 M4
Rowans Wy EHSLY KT24 ...... 120 C4
Rowberry Cl FUL/PGN SW6 ...... 19 M2 ⓫
Rowbury RGODL GU7 ...... 160 C1
Rowcroft Cl ASHV GU12 ...... 113 K3
Rowden Rd BECK BR3 ...... 51 H1
   E/WMO/HCT KT8 ...... 43 M3
Rowdown Crs CROY/NA CR0 ...... 70 A7
Rowe La CHOB/PIR GU24 ...... 95 K6
Rowfant Cl CRAWE RH10 ...... 213 H3
Rowfant Rd TOOT SW17 ...... 30 D3
Row Hl ADL/WDHM KT15 ...... 58 C5
Rowhill Av ALDT GU11 ...... 134 C1
Rowhill Crs ALDT GU11 ...... 134 C1 ⓶
Rowhills Cl FNM GU9 ...... 134 C1
Rowhills Cl FNM GU9 ...... 134 C1
Rowhook Rd HORS RH12 ...... 207 J8
Rowhurst Av ADL/WDHM KT15 .. 58 E5
Rowland Cl CRAWE RH10 ...... 194 B4
Rowland Gv SYD SE26 ...... 32 E4 ⓶
   SYD SE26 ...... 32 E4
Rowland Rd CRAN GU6 ...... 185 G6
Rowlands Rd HORS RH12 ...... 229 K3
Rowland Wy ASHF TW15 ...... 24 A8 ⓶
   WIM/MER SW19 ...... 47 L1 ⓫
Row La SHGR GU5 ...... 163 H4
Rowley Cl BRAK RG12 ...... 35 H3
   WOKS/MYFD GU22 ...... 78 D6
Rowley Ct CTHM CR3 ...... 107 M4
Rowlls Rd KUT KT1 ...... 3 H8
Rowly Dr CRAN GU6 ...... 184 D4
Rowly Edge CRAN GU6 ...... 184 D3
Rowntree Rd WHTN TW2 ...... 26 B2
Rowplatt La EGRIN RH19 ...... 195 H6
Row Town ADL/WDHM KT15 ...... 58 C6
Roxborough Av ISLW TW7 ...... 17 J2
Roxburgh Cl CBLY GU15 ...... 73 M5
Roxburgh Rd WNWD SE27 ...... 31 L6
Roxford Cl SHPTN TW17 ...... 42 B5
Roxton Gdns CROY/NA CR0 ...... 69 J5
Royal Av WPK KT4 ...... 64 B1
Royal Circ WNWD SE27 ...... 31 K4
Royal Cl WPK KT4 ...... 64 B1
Royal Dr EPSOM KT18 ...... 84 E3
Royale Cl ALDT GU11 ...... 134 F2
Royal Ms BAL SW12 ...... 30 E1 ⓸
Royal Oak Rd WOKN/KNAP GU21 .. 76 F8
Royal Orchard Cl
   WAND/EARL SW18 ...... 29 H1
Royal Rd TEDD TW11 ...... 26 A6
Royce Rd CRAWE RH10 ...... 192 D6
Roydon Ct WOT/HER KT12 ...... 60 D3
Roy Gv HPTN TW12 ...... 25 L7
Royston Av BF/WBF KT14 ...... 79 H2
   SUT SM1 ...... 66 A2
   WLGTN SM6 ...... 66 E4
Royston Cl CRAWE RH10 ...... 192 D7 ⓫
   HEST TW5 ...... 15 L3
   WOT/HER KT12 ...... 42 D8
Royston Rd BF/WBF KT14 ...... 79 H2
   PGE/AN SE20 ...... 51 G1
   RCHPK/HAM TW10 ...... 18 B7 ⓸
The Roystons BRYLDS KT5 ...... 45 L5
Rubens St CAT SE6 ...... 33 J3
Rubus Cl CHOB/PIR GU24 ...... 75 H3
Ruckmans La RDKG RH5 ...... 207 K3
Rudd Hall Ri CBLY GU15 ...... 73 G6
Ruden Wy EW KT17 ...... 84 E5
Rudge Ri ADL/WDHM KT15 ...... 58 B5
Rudgwick Rd CRAWW RH11 .... 211 J2 ⓫
Rudloe Rd BAL SW12 ...... 30 F1
Rudsworth Cl DTCH/LGLY SL3 .. 13 G3 ⓫
Ruffetts Cl SAND/SEL CR2 ...... 68 E6
The Ruffetts SAND/SEL CR2 ...... 68 E6
Ruffetts Wy
   KWD/TDW/WH KT20 ...... 85 H8
Rufwood CRAWE RH10 ...... 214 C1 ⓫
Rugby Cl SHST GU47 ...... 52 B8 ⓶
Rugby La BELMT SM2 ...... 65 G7 ⓫
Rugby Rd WHTN TW2 ...... 17 H8

Ruggles-brise Rd ASHF TW15 ... 23 G6
Rugosa Rd CHOB/PIR GU24 ...... 75 H3
Ruislip St TOOT SW17 ...... 30 C5
Rumsey Cl HPTN TW12 ...... 25 J7
Runcorn Cl CRAWW RH11 ...... 211 H7
Runes Cl MTCM CR4 ...... 48 A4
Runnemede Rd EGH TW20 ...... 21 K6
Runnymede WIM/MER SW19 .... 48 A1
Runnymede Cl WHTN TW2 ...... 16 E8
Runnymede Ct EGH TW20 ...... 21 K5 ⓸
Runnymede Crs
   STRHM/NOR SW16 ...... 49 G1
Runnymede Gdns WHTN TW2 ... 16 E8
Runnymede Rd WHTN TW2 ...... 16 E8
Runtley Wood La RGUE GU4 ...... 97 J3
Runwick La NFNM GU10 ...... 133 G8
Rupert Rd GUW GU2 ...... 8 D6
   STRHM/NOR SW16 ...... 30 E8
Rural Wy REDH RH1 ...... 126 D8
Ruscoe Dr WOKS/MYFD GU22 ... 7 H5
Ruscombe Wy
   EBED/NFELT TW14 ...... 24 C1 ⓫
Rusham Park Av EGH TW20 ...... 21 J7
Rusham Rd EGH TW20 ...... 21 J7
Rushams Rd HORS RH12 ...... 228 E7
Rush Cft RGODL GU7 ...... 160 D1
Rushden Cl NRWD SE19 ...... 32 A8 ⓶
Rushdene Wk BH/WHM TN16 ... 91 G7
Rushen Wk CAR SM5 ...... 66 A1 ⓫
Rushett Cl THDIT KT7 ...... 44 E8
Rushett Dr DORK RH4 ...... 144 E5
Rushett La CHSGTN KT9 ...... 83 G2
Rushett Rd THDIT KT7 ...... 44 E7
Rushetts Pl CRAWW RH11 ...... 191 M8
Rushetts Rd CRAWW RH11 ...... 191 L8
   REIG RH2 ...... 147 M4
Rushey Cl NWMAL KT3 ...... 46 A4
Rushey Gn CAT SE6 ...... 33 L1
Rushfords LING RH7 ...... 174 B3
Rushley Cl HAYES BR2 ...... 71 J5
Rushmead RCHPK/HAM TW10 .. 26 E4 ⓶
Rushmead Cl CROY/NA CR0 ...... 5 J9
Rushmere Ct WPK KT4 ...... 64 D1 ⓫
Rushmere Pl EGH TW20 ...... 21 H6
   WIM/MER SW19 ...... 29 G6 ⓶
Rushmoor Cl GUW GU2 ...... 116 C5
Rushmoor Rd ALDT GU11 ...... 112 B6
Rusholme Gv NRWD SE19 ...... 32 B6
Rushton Av GDST RH9 ...... 150 F4
Rushworth Rd REIG RH2 ...... 125 K7
Rushy Meadow La CAR SM5 ...... 66 B2
Ruskin Av EBED/NFELT TW14 ... 24 C1
   RCH/KEW TW9 ...... 18 D2
Ruskin Cl CRAWE RH10 ...... 192 F8 ⓫
Ruskin Dr WPK KT4 ...... 64 E1
Ruskin Rd CAR SM5 ...... 66 C4
   CROY/NA CR0 ...... 4 B5
   ISLW TW7 ...... 17 J5
   STA TW18 ...... 22 C7
Ruskin Wy WIM/MER SW19 ...... 48 A2
Rusper Rd CRAWW RH11 ...... 211 J3
   HORS RH12 ...... 190 A8
   HORS RH12 ...... 229 K1
   RDKG RH5 ...... 189 G6
Ruspers Keep CRAWW RH11 .... 211 J2 ⓸
Russel Cl BECK BR3 ...... 51 L3
Russell Cl BRAK RG12 ...... 35 G8
   KWD/TDW/WH KT20 ...... 104 D7
   WOKN/KNAP GU21 ...... 76 F5
   LHD/OX KT22 ...... 102 E4 ⓸
Russell Dr STWL/WRAY TW19 ... 14 A8
Russell Gdns RCHPK/HAM TW10 .. 26 F3
Russell Green Cl PUR/KEN CR8 .. 67 K8
Russell Hl PUR/KEN CR8 ...... 67 J8
Russell Hill Pl PUR/KEN CR8 ... 87 K1
Russell Hill Rd PUR/KEN CR8 ... 67 K8
Russell Kerr Cl CHSWK W4 ...... 18 F2 ⓫
Russell Rd MTCM CR4 ...... 48 B3
   SHPTN TW17 ...... 41 M7
   WHTN TW2 ...... 17 J8 ⓶
   WIM/MER SW19 ...... 29 K8
   WOKN/KNAP GU21 ...... 76 F5
   WOT/HER KT12 ...... 42 D6
Russells KWD/TDW/WH KT20 ... 105 G4
Russells Crs HORL RH6 ...... 170 D7
Russell Wy CRAWE RH10 ...... 212 D4
   SUT SM1 ...... 65 L4 ⓸
Russet Av SUN TW16 ...... 42 B3
Russet Dr CROY/NA CR0 ...... 51 H8
Russet Gdns CBLY GU15 ...... 73 G6
Russet Gld FNM GU9 ...... 134 A1
Russetts Cl WOKN/KNAP GU21 .. 6 D2
Russet Wy RDKG RH5 ...... 145 G5
Russ Hl HORL RH6 ...... 190 F3
   RDKG RH5 ...... 190 D5
Russington Rd SHPTN TW17 ...... 42 A6
Rusthall Cl CROY/NA CR0 ...... 50 F6
Rustic Av STRHM/NOR SW16 ... 30 E8
Rustington Wk MRDN SM4 ...... 47 J3
Ruston Av BRYLDS KT5 ...... 45 L7
Ruston Cl CRAWE RH10 ...... 212 F6 ⓸
Ruston Wy ASC SL5 ...... 36 B2
Rutford Rd STRHM/NOR SW16 .. 31 H4
Ruthen Cl EPSOM KT18 ...... 83 L4 ⓸
Rutherford Cl BELMT SM2 ...... 66 A5
Rutherford Wy CRAWE RH10 .... 192 D6
Rutherwick Cl HORL RH6 ...... 170 C6
Rutherwick Ri COUL/CHIP CR5.. 87 H7
Rutherwyke Cl EW KT17 ...... 64 D5
Rutherwyk Rd CHERT KT16 ...... 57 K6
Rutland Cl ALDT GU11 ...... 112 D6
   ASHTD KT21 ...... 83 H7
   HOR/WEW KT19 ...... 64 A7
   MORT/ESHN SW14 ...... 18 E5
   REDH RH1 ...... 126 C7
Rutland Dr MRDN SM4 ...... 47 K7
   RCHPK/HAM TW10 ...... 27 G2
Rutland Gdns CROY/NA CR0 ...... 68 B3
Rutland Pk CAT SE6 ...... 33 J3
Rutland Rd WHTN TW2 ...... 26 A3
   WIM/MER SW19 ...... 30 B8 ⓭
Rutland Wk CAT SE6 ...... 33 J3
Rutlish Rd WIM/MER SW19 ...... 47 K1

Rutson Rd BF/WBF KT14 ...... 79 J4
Rutter Gdns MTCM CR4 ...... 48 A4
Rutton Hill Rd MFD/CHID GU8 .. 200 B1
Ruxbury Rd CHERT KT16 ...... 40 A6
Ruxley Cl HOR/WEW KT19 ...... 63 L4
Ruxley Crs ESH/CLAY KT10 ...... 62 E6
Ruxley La HOR/WEW KT19 ...... 63 L5
Ruxley Ms HOR/WEW KT19 ...... 63 L4 ⓸
Ruxley Rdg ESH/CLAY KT10 ...... 62 D6
Ryan Dr BTFD TW8 ...... 17 K1
Rydal Cl CBLY GU15 ...... 74 A4
   CRAWW RH11 ...... 211 G5
   FARN GU14 ...... 92 A6 ⓭
   PUR/KEN CR8 ...... 88 A3 ⓶
Rydal Dr WWKM BR4 ...... 70 B1
Rydal Gdns HSLW TW3 ...... 16 E8
   PUT/ROE SW15 ...... 28 B6
Rydal Pl LTWR GU18 ...... 74 E1
Rydal Rd STRHM/NOR SW16 ... 31 G6
Rydal Wy EGH TW20 ...... 21 L8
Ryde Cl RPLY/SEND GU23 ...... 98 F3
Ryde Heron WOKN/KNAP GU21 .. 76 B7
Ryde Lands CRAN GU6 ...... 185 J5
Rydens Av WOT/HER KT12 ...... 60 F1
Rydens Cl WOT/HER KT12 ...... 60 F1
Rydens Gv WOT/HER KT12 ...... 61 G3
Rydens Pk WOT/HER KT12 ...... 61 G1
Rydens Rd WOT/HER KT12 ...... 60 E2
Rydens Wy WOKS/MYFD GU22 .. 97 K2
Ryde Pl TWK TW1 ...... 17 M8
Ryders Wy HORS RH12 ...... 229 J2 ⓫
Rydes Av GUW GU2 ...... 116 C5
Ryde's Hill Crs RGUW GU3 ...... 116 C4
Ryde's Hill Rd GUW GU2 ...... 116 C6
The Ryde STA TW18 ...... 40 E1
Ryde Vale Rd BAL SW12 ...... 30 E3
Rydon's La COUL/CHIP CR5 ...... 107 M2
Rydon's Wood Cl
   COUL/CHIP CR5 ...... 107 M2
Rye Ash CRAWE RH10 ...... 212 D2
Rye Cl FARN GU14 ...... 92 B3
   GUW GU2 ...... 116 B7
Ryecotes Md DUL SE21 ...... 32 B2
Ryecroft WHTN TW2 ...... 25 L2
Ryecroft Dr HORS RH12 ...... 228 D6
Ryecroft Gdns BLKW GU17 ...... 72 B5 ⓫
Ryecroft Rd STRHM/NOR SW16 .. 31 K7
Ryefield Rd NRWD SE19 ...... 31 M7
Rye Gv CHOB/PIR GU24 ...... 55 H8
Ryelands CRAWW RH11 ...... 211 K6 ⓸
   HORL RH6 ...... 170 F5 ⓫
Ryelands Ct CTHM CR3 ...... 108 B3
Ryelands Ct LHD/OX KT22 ...... 82 D8 ⓶
Ryelands Pl WEY KT13 ...... 60 B2
Ryersh La RDKG RH5 ...... 188 F2
Ryfold Rd WIM/MER SW19 ...... 29 K4
Ryland Cl FELT TW13 ...... 24 C5
Rylandes Rd SAND/SEL CR2 ...... 68 E7
Ryle Rd FNM GU9 ...... 5 F3
Rymer Rd CROY/NA CR0 ...... 10 F3
Rysted La BH/WHM TN16 ...... 111 M8
Ryst Wood Rd FROW RH18 ...... 217 L7
Rythe Ct THDIT KT7 ...... 44 D7
Rythe Rd ESH/CLAY KT10 ...... 62 A4
The Rythe LHD/OX KT22 ...... 61 L8

S

Sable Cl HSLWW TW4 ...... 15 M5
Sabre Ct ALDT GU11 ...... 112 B7 ⓶
Sackville Cl EGRIN RH19 ...... 195 M6
Sackville La EGRIN RH19 ...... 195 L6
Sackville Rd BELMT SM2 ...... 65 K6
Saddleback Rd CBLY GU15 ...... 73 H1
Saddlebrook Pk SUN TW16 ...... 24 B3
Saddler Rw CRAWE RH10 ...... 212 A6 ⓭
Saddlers Scarp GSHT GU26 ...... 198 D5
Saddlers Wy EPSOM KT18 ...... 104 A1
Saddlewood CBLY GU15 ...... 72 F5
Sadler Cl MTCM CR4 ...... 48 C2
Sadlers Rd RGUE GU4 ...... 118 A7
Sadlers Ride E/WMO/HCT KT8 .. 43 L3 ⓸
Saffron Cl CRAWW RH11 ...... 211 K6 ⓸
   CROY/NA CR0 ...... 49 H6
Saffron Platt GUW GU2 ...... 116 D4
Saffron Rd BRAK RG12 ...... 34 E4
Saffron Wy SURB KT6 ...... 45 G8
Sailors La MFD/CHID GU8 ...... 179 J3
Sainfoin Rd TOOT SW17 ...... 30 D3
Sainsbury Rd NRWD SE19 ...... 32 B6
St Agatha's Dr KUTN/CMB KT2 .. 3 H1
St Agatha's Gv CAR SM5 ...... 48 C8 ⓭
St Agnes Rd EGRIN RH19 ...... 195 M3
St Albans Av FELT TW13 ...... 25 G6
   WEY KT13 ...... 59 K2
St Albans Cl RGUW GU3 ...... 115 L7
St Alban's Gdns TEDD TW11 ...... 26 C6
St Alban's Gv CAR SM5 ...... 48 B7
St Albans Rd KUTN/CMB KT2 ...... 2 E1
   REIG RH2 ...... 125 K8
   SUT SM1 ...... 65 J3
St Amunds Cl CAT SE6 ...... 33 K5 ⓫
St Andrew Av CHOB/PIR GU24 .. 95 L3
St Andrews BRAK RG12 ...... 34 B6
St Andrew's Cl REIG RH2 ...... 147 L1 ⓫
   SHPTN TW17 ...... 42 B6
   STWL/WRAY TW19 ...... 12 B8
   WOKN/KNAP GU21 ...... 76 F7
St Andrew's Ct
   WAND/EARL SW18 ...... 29 M3 ⓸
St Andrews Gdns COB KT11 ...... 80 F3
St Andrews Rd CAR SM5 ...... 66 B2
   COUL/CHIP CR5 ...... 86 E6
   CRAWW RH11 ...... 211 G4
   CROY/NA CR0 ...... 4 C9
   SURB KT6 ...... 45 G6
St Andrew's Wk COB KT11 ...... 80 E5 ⓫
St Andrew's Wy FRIM GU16 ...... 93 J2
   OXTED RH8 ...... 131 H5
St Anne's Av STWL/WRAY TW19 .. 23 G1
St Anne's Dr REDH RH1 ...... 126 D7
St Annes Gld BAGS GU19 ...... 54 A6
St Annes Mt REDH RH1 ...... 126 D7 ⓸
St Annes Ri REDH RH1 ...... 126 D7 ⓫
St Annes Rd CRAWE RH10 ...... 192 F7

RGODL GU7 .... 160 D4
St Annes Wy *REDH RH1* .... 126 D7 ⑥
St Ann's Cl *CHERT KT16* 40 C5
St Ann's Hill Rd *CHERT KT16* 39 M6
St Anns Rd *BARN SW13* .... 19 J3 ⑥
CHERT KT16 .... 40 C6
St Ann's Wy *CROY/NA CR0* 67 L5
St Anthonys Cl *BNFD RG42* 34 D1
TOOT SW17 .... 30 B3 ④
St Anthony's Wy
EBED/NFELT TW14 .... 15 J6
St Arvans Cl *CROY/NA CR0* 5 H7
St Aubin Cl *CRAWW RH11* .... 211 J7 ⑥
St Aubyn's Av *HSLWW TW4* ... 16 D7
WIM/MER SW19 .... 29 J6
St Aubyn's Rd *NRWD SE19* .... 32 C7 ⑥
St Augustine's Av *SAND/SEL CR2* 67 M6
St Augustine's Cl *ASHV GU12* ... 113 G8
St Barnabas Av *CHOB/PIR GU24*.. 95 K4
St Barnabas Cl *BECK BR3* .... 51 M2 ③
St Barnabas Gdns
E/WMO/HCT KT8 .... 43 K5
St Barnabas Rd *MTCM CR4* 30 D8
SUT SM1 .... 66 A4
St Bartholomew's Cl *SYD SE26* .. 32 F5
St Bartholomew's Ct *GU GU1* 9 L7
St Benedict's Cl *ALDT GU11* 112 D8
TOOT SW17 .... 30 D6 ④
St Benets Cl *CROY/NA CR0* 4 C1
St Benet's Gv *MRDN SM4* ..... 47 M7 ④
St Bernards *CROY/NA CR0* 3 J8
St Bernards Cl *WNWD SE27* .... 32 A5 ⑥
St Brelades Cl *DORK RH4*....... 144 D8
St Brelades Rd *CRAWW RH11* .. 211 J7 ⑥
St Catherines *WOKS/MYFD GU22*.. 96 F1
St Catherines Cl *TOOT SW17* ... 30 B3 ④
St Catherines Ct *FELT TW13* .... 24 D2 ⑥
St Catherine's Cross *REDH RH1* . 128 B8
St Catherine's Dr *GUW GU2* 138 E4
St Catherine's Pk *GU GU1* 9 L7
St Catherines Rd *CRAWE RH10*.. 192 F8 ⑥
FRIM GU16 .... 73 K8
St Chad Av *WOKS/MYFD GU22*.. 95 M4
St Chads Cl *SURB KT6*......... 44 F7
St Charles Pl *WEY KT13* 59 K4
St Christophers Cl
HORS RH12 .... 228 F5 ⑦
ISLW TW7 .... 17 H3 ⑥
St Christophers Gdns *ASC SL5* .. 36 A1
St Christopher's Ms
WLGTN SM6 .... 66 F4 ③
St Christophers Pl *FARN GU14*... 92 C6 ⑥
St Christopher's Rd *FARN GU14*.. 92 D6
HASM GU27 .... 219 K3
St Clair Cl *OXTED RH8* 129 M4
REIG RH2............ 125 M8
St Clair Dr *WPK KT4* 64 C2
St Clair's Rd *CROY/NA CR0* 5 G6
St Clement Rd *CRAWW RH11* .. 211 J7 ⑥
CROY/NA CR0 .... 4 B7
St Cloud Rd *WNWD SE27* 31 M5
St Crispins Wy *CHERT KT16* 57 M7
St Cross Rd *FNM GU9* .... 133 M6 ④
FRIM GU16 .... 93 K2
GU GU10 .... 132 C4
St Cuthbert's Cl *EGH TW20* 21 G7
St Cyprian's St *TOOT SW17* .... 30 C5 ⑥
St David's *COUL/CHIP CR5* 87 J7
St David's Cl *FARN GU14* 92 C1
FNM GU9 .... 134 B2
REIG RH2............ 125 M7
WWKM BR4............ 51 L7
St David's Dr *EGH TW20* 20 F8
St Denis Rd *WNWD SE27* 32 A5
St Deny's Cl
WOKN/KNAP GU21 .... 76 A8 ④
St Dunstan's Hl *SUT SM1* 65 H3
St Dunstan's La *BECK BR3* 51 M6
St Dunstan's Rd *FELT TW13* 24 C4
HEST TW5 .... 15 M4 ⑥
HSLWW TW4 .... 15 L4 ⑥
SNWD SE25 .... 50 C4
St Edmund Cl *CRAWW RH11* .. 192 A4 ⑥
St Edmunds Cl *TOOT SW17* .... 30 B3 ⑥
St Edmund's La *WHTN TW2* .... 25 L1 ⑥
St Edwards Cl *CROY/NA CR0* ... 90 A1
EGRIN RH19 .... 195 M8
St Elizabeth Dr *EPSOM KT18* ... 83 M4
St Faith's Rd *HNHL SE24* 31 L2
St Fillans Rd *CAT SE6* 33 M2
St Francis Gdns *CRAWE RH10*... 193 M5
St George Av *CHOB/PIR GU24*... 95 L4
St George's Av *WEY KT13* 59 M5
St George's Cl *FNM GU9* ...... 134 E3 ④
HORL RH6 .... 170 E6
WEY KT13 .... 59 M4 ⑥
St Georges Ct *CRAWW RH11* .. 212 A2
St George's Gdns *EW KT17* 84 C4
SURB KT6 .... 63 L1 ⑥
SWTR RH13 .... 229 H5
St George's Gv *TOOT SW17* ... 30 A4
St George's La *ASC SL5* 36 E3
St Georges Rd *ADL/WDHM KT15* .. 58 F3
ASHV GU12 .... 112 E8
BECK BR3 .... 51 L1
CBLY GU15 .... 73 G3
FELT TW13............ 11 J1
FNM GU9 .... 9 J1
FNM GU9 .... 134 E3
KUTN/CMB KT2 .... 3 J3
MTCM CR4 .... 48 E3
NFNM GU10 .... 134 E5
RCH/KEW TW9 .... 18 C5
REDH RH1 .... 149 G8
TWK TW1............. 17 L7
WEY KT13............ 60 A5
WIM/MER SW19 .... 29 J7
St George's Wk *CROY/NA CR0* .. 4 D6
St German's Rd *FSTH SE23* 33 H2
St Gothard Rd *WNWD SE27*.... 32 A4
St Helen's Crs
STRHM/NOR SW16 ...... 49 J1 ⑥
St Helen Av *MRDN SM4* 47 M7
St Helier Cl *CRAWW RH11* .... 211 K7 ⑥
St Heliers Av *HSLWW TW3* 16 D7
St Hilda's Av *ASHF TW15* 23 H6
St Hilda's Cl *CRAWE RH10* .... 192 F8 ⑥

HORL RH6 .... 170 E6
TOOT SW17........... 30 B3
WOKN/KNAP GU21 .... 76 A7
Saint Hill Rd *EGRIN RH19* 215 L3
St Hilda's Rd *BARN SW13* 19 L1
St Hughes Cl *TOOT SW17* .... 30 B3 ⑥
St Hugh's Cl *CRAWE RH10* .... 192 F8 ⑥
St Hugh's Rd *PGE/AN SE20* ... 32 E8 ⑥
St James Av *EW KT17* 84 C1
FNM GU9 .... 134 A5
SUT SM1............. 65 K4
St James Cl *EPSOM KT18* 84 B4
NWMAL KT3 .... 46 C5
WOKN/KNAP GU21 ...... 96 B1
St James Ga *CTHM CR3* .... 108 D4 ⑥
St James Ms *WEY KT13* 59 L3
St James Rd *CAR SM5* 66 B2
MTCM CR4 .... 30 D8
PUR/KEN CR8 .... 87 L3
SURB KT6 .... 45 G6
SUT SM1............. 65 K5
St James's Av *BECK BR3* 51 H3
HPTN TW12 .... 25 M6
St James's Cl *TOOT SW17* .... 30 C3 ⑥
St James's Cottages
RCHPK/HAM TW10 .... 18 A7 ③
St James's Dr *BAL SW12* 30 C2
TOOT SW17........... 30 C2
St James's Pk *CROY/NA CR0* ... 4 C1
St James's Pl *CRAN GU6* 184 F6
St James Sq *SURB KT6* 44 F7
St James's Rd *CROY/NA CR0* ... 4 B2
CROY/NA CR0 .... 4 E2
EGRIN RH19 .... 196 A8
HPTN TW12 .... 25 L6
KUT KT1............. 2 D7
St James' Ter *FNM GU9* 133 M6
St Joan Cl *CRAWW RH11* 192 A8
St John Cl *SWTR RH13* 229 H8
St John's *RDKG RH5* 144 F6
St Johns Av *EW KT17* 84 C2
LHD/OX KT22 .... 102 E3
St John's Cl *EGRIN RH19* 196 B7
GUW GU2 .... 8 A5
LHD/OX KT22 .... 102 F3
St Johns Ct *EGH TW20* 21 G7
ISLW TW7............ 17 J4 ⑥
St John's Crs *HORS RH12* .... 228 B6 ⑦
St John's Dr *WAND/EARL SW18* .. 29 L2
WOT/HER KT12 .... 42 F8
St John's Gv *BARN SW13* .... 19 J4 ⑥
FNM GU9............. 5 J8
RCH/KEW TW9 .... 18 B6 ⑥
St John's Hl *PUR/KEN CR8* 87 K7
St John's Hill Rd
WOKN/KNAP GU21 ...... 96 D1
St John's Lye *WOKN/KNAP GU21* .. 96 C1
St John's Lye (Festival Path)
WOKN/KNAP GU21 ...... 96 C1
St John's Meadow *LING RH7* .. 173 G1
St Johns Ms *WOKN/KNAP GU21* .. 76 D8
St John's Ri *WOKN/KNAP GU21* .. 96 E1
St John's Rd *CAR SM5* 66 B2
CRAWW RH11 .... 211 M3 ⑥
CROY/NA CR0 .... 4 B7
DORK RH4 .... 143 M3
E/WMO/HCT KT8 .... 44 A4
EGRIN RH19 .... 196 B7
FARN GU14 .... 92 B5
FELT TW13........... 25 J5
FNM GU9 .... 10 F4
GUW GU2 .... 138 C1
ISLW TW7............ 17 J4
KUT KT1............. 2 B6
LHD/OX KT22......... 102 F3
NWMAL KT3.......... 45 M3
PGE/AN SE20 .... 32 F8
RCH/KEW TW9 .... 18 B6 ⑥
REDH RH1 .... 148 C2
SUT SM1............. 65 L1 ⑥
WIM/MER SW19 .... 29 H8
WOKN/KNAP GU21 ...... 96 D1
St John's Road Rd
WOKN/KNAP GU21 ...... 76 E8
St John's St *RGODL GU7* 160 D3
St John's Terrace Rd *REDH RH1*.. 148 C2
St John's Wy *ADL/WDHM KT15*.. 58 D1
St Joseph's Rd *ALDT GU11*.... 112 D8
St Jude's Cl *EGH TW20* 20 F6
St Jude's Rd *EGH TW20* 20 F5
St Julian's Cl
STRHM/NOR SW16 ...... 31 K5 ②
St Julian's Farm Rd *WNWD SE27*.. 31 K5
St Katharines Rd *CTHM CR3*... 108 D7
St Kitts Ter *NRWD SE19* 32 B6
St Lawrences Wy *REIG RH2* ... 125 K8
St Lawrence Wy *CTHM CR3*.... 108 A5
St Leonards Dr *CRAWE RH10*... 212 D6
St Leonard's Gdns *HEST TW5*... 16 B2
St Leonard's Rd *CROY/NA CR0*.. 4 A8
ESH/CLAY KT10......... 62 C5
KWD/TDW/WH KT20 .... 104 F1
MORT/ESHN SW14 .... 18 F5
SURB KT6 .... 45 G5
SWTR RH13 .... 229 J8
THDIT KT7............ 44 D6
St Leonard's Wk
STRHM/NOR SW16 ...... 31 J8
St Louis Rd *WNWD SE27* 31 M5
St Luke's Cl *SNWD SE25* 50 E6
St Lukes Ct
WOKN/KNAP GU21 ...... 77 M4 ⑥
St Luke's Rd *CTHM CR3* 88 C8
St Luke's Sq *GU GU1* 9 L6
St Margarets *GU GU1* 9 L6
St Margarets Av *ASHF TW15* ... 23 L6
CHEAM SM3........... 65 H4
EGRIN RH19 .... 196 B3
St Margaret's Crs
PUT/ROE SW15 .... 19 L7 ⑥
St Margarets Dr *EPSOM KT18* .. 84 A4 ⑥
TWK TW1............. 17 L7
St Margaret's Gv *TWK TW1* ... 17 K8 ⑥
St Margaret's Rd
COUL/CHIP CR5 .... 106 C3 ⑥
EGRIN RH19 .... 196 C6 ②
TWK TW1............. 17 L6
St Mark Av *CHOB/PIR GU24* ... 95 L5

St Marks Cl *FARN GU14* ..... 92 F8 ⑥
St Mark's Hl *SURB KT6* 45 H6
St Mark's La *HORS RH12* .... 229 H3 ⑦
St Marks Pl *FNM GU9* ...... 133 L2 ⑥
WIM/MER SW19 .... 29 J7 ③
St Marks Rd *EPSOM KT18* 84 F8
MTCM CR4 .... 48 C2
SNWD SE25 .... 50 D4 ⑥
TEDD TW11 .... 26 E8
St Martha's Av
WOKS/MYFD GU22 ...... 97 J3
St Martin's Av *EPSOM KT18* ... 84 B4
St Martins Cl *EHSLY KT24* 120 B3
EW KT17............. 84 C3 ⑥
St Martins Ct *ASHF TW15* 22 F6
St Martin's Dr *WOT/HER KT12* .. 60 F2
St Martins Ms *DORK RH4* .... 144 D2 ⑥
WOKS/MYFD GU22 ...... 78 D6
St Martin's Wy *TOOT SW17* ... 29 M4
St Mary Av *WLGTN SM6* 66 D2
St Mary's Av *STWL/WRAY TW19* . 23 G1
TEDD TW11 .... 26 C7 ⑥
St Mary's Cl *CHSGTN KT9* 63 J6
EW KT17 .... 64 C6
LHD/OX KT22 .... 102 A5
OXTED RH8 .... 130 B3
SUN TW16 .... 42 D4 ⑥
St Mary's Crs *ISLW TW7* 17 G2
STWL/WRAY TW19 ...... 23 G1
St Mary's Dr *CRAWE RH10* ... 212 E1
EBED/NFELT TW14 ...... 23 M1
St Mary's Gdns *BAGS GU19* ... 54 B6 ⑥
HORS RH12 .... 228 F8
St Mary's Gn *BH/WHM TN16* .. 90 F8
St Mary's Gv *BARN SW13* 19 L5
BH/WHM TN16 .... 90 F8
CHSWK W4 .... 18 E1
RCH/KEW TW9 .... 18 C6
St Mary's Hl *ASC SL5* 36 F6
St Mary's Mt *CTHM CR3* 108 C6
St Mary's Rd *ASC SL5* 36 E7
ASHV GU12........... 113 K4
CBLY GU15........... 72 F3 ⑥
E/WMO/HCT KT8 .... 44 A5
LHD/OX KT22......... 102 A4
REIG RH2............ 147 L1
SAND/SEL CR2 .... 68 A8
SNWD SE25 .... 50 B3
SURB KT6 .... 44 F7
WEY KT13............ 60 A3
WIM/MER SW19 .... 29 H6
WOKN/KNAP GU21 ...... 76 F7
WPK KT4............ 64 B1 ⑥
St Matthew's Av *SURB KT6* ... 45 H8
St Matthew's Rd *REDH RH1*... 126 C7 ⑥
St Michael's Av *RGUW GU3* ... 115 M3
St Michael's Cl *WOT/HER KT12* .. 60 F1 ⑥
WPK KT4............ 64 C1
St Michael's Rd *ALDT GU11* ... 112 E8
ASHF TW15........... 23 K6
CBLY GU15........... 72 E4 ⑥
CROY/NA CR0.......... 4 D4 ⑥
CTHM CR3 .... 108 A4
EGRIN RH19 .... 196 B7
FARN GU14........... 92 E3
WLGTN SM6........... 66 F5
WOKN/KNAP GU21 ...... 78 A4
St Mildred's Rd *GU GU1* 9 M1
St Monica's Rd
KWD/TDW/WH KT20 .... 105 J3
St Nazaire Cl *EGH TW20* ..... 21 M6 ⑥
St Nicholas Av *GT/LBKH KT23* .. 101 L7
St Nicholas Crs
WOKS/MYFD GU22 ...... 78 D6
St Nicholas Dr *SHPTN TW17* ... 41 K7
St Nicholas Glebe *TOOT SW17* .. 30 D7 ⑥
St Nicholas Hl *LHD/OX KT22* .. 102 A4
St Nicholas Rd *SUT SM1* ..... 65 L4 ⑥
THDIT KT7........... 44 C6
St Nicholas Wy *SUT SM1* 65 L3
St Nicolas Av *CRAN GU6* 185 H6
St Nicolas Cl *CRAN GU6* ..... 185 H6 ⑥
St Normans Wy *EW KT17* 64 D8
St Olave's Cl *STA TW18* 22 C8
St Olave's Wk *STRHM/NOR SW16*. 48 F7
St Omer Barracks *ALDT GU11*.. 113 G4
St Omer Rdg *GU GU1* 139 K1
St Omer Rd *GU GU1* 139 K1
St Oswald's Rd
STRHM/NOR SW16....... 49 L1
St Paul's Cl *ADL/WDHM KT15* .. 58 D7
ASHF TW15........... 23 M6 ⑥
CAR SM5 .... 48 B7
CHSGTN KT9.......... 63 G3 ⑥
HSLW TW3........... 16 B4 ②
NFNM GU10 .... 135 J2 ⑥
St Paul's Rd *BTFD TW8*...... 18 A1
RCH/KEW TW9 .... 18 C5
STA TW18............ 22 A6
THHTH CR7........... 49 M3
WOKS/MYFD GU22 ...... 7 J5
St Paul's Rd East *DORK RH4*... 144 E3
St Paul's Rd West *DORK RH4*... 144 D3
St Peter's Cl *STA TW18* ..... 22 C7 ⑥
TOOT SW17........... 30 B3 ⑥
WOKS/MYFD GU22 ...... 97 M2
St Peters Ct *E/WMO/HCT KT8*... 43 K4 ②
St Peter's Gdns *NFNM GU10* ... 10 A7
WNWD SE27 .... 31 K4 ⑥
St Peters Md *ASHV GU12* 113 L7
St Peters Pk *FNM GU9* 134 B1
St Peter's Rd *CRAWW RH11* .. 211 M3 ⑥
E/WMO/HCT KT8 .... 43 K4
KUT KT1............. 3 J7
TWK TW1............ 17 L7
WOKS/MYFD GU22 ...... 97 L3
St Peter's St *SAND/SEL CR2*... 68 A4
St Peter's Wy *CHERT KT16* ... 58 B3
FRIM GU16........... 93 J2
St Philip's Av *WPK KT4* 64 E1
St Philip's Rd *SURB KT6*..... 45 G6
St Pier's La *LING RH7* 174 C6
St Pinnock Av *STA TW18* 40 D1
St Sampson Rd *CRAWW RH11* . 211 J7 ⑥
St Saviour Rd *CROY/NA CR0* .. 49 M6
St Saviour's Rd *CROY/NA CR0*.. 49 M6
Saints Cl *WNWD SE27* ...... 31 L5 ⑥
St Simon's Av *PUT/ROE SW15*.. 19 M7

St Stephens Av *ASHTD KT21* ... 83 H7
St Stephens Cl *HASM GU27* ... 219 M2
St Stephens Ct *GDST RH9* .... 151 H4 ⑥
St Stephen's Crs *THHTH CR7* ... 49 K3 ⑥
St Stephen's Gdns *HSLW TW3* .. 16 D8
St Stephen's Rd *HSLW TW3* ... 16 D8
St Swithun's Cl *EGRIN RH19* ... 196 E8 ⑥
St Theresa Cl *EPSOM KT18* ... 83 M4 ⑥
St Theresa's Rd
EBED/NFELT TW14 ...... 15 J6
St Thomas Cl *SURB KT6* ..... 45 J8 ⑥
WOKN/KNAP GU21 ...... 76 F7
St Thomas' Rd *CHSWK W4* ... 18 F2
St Thomas's Dr *RGUE GU4* ... 119 H5 ⑥
St Thomas Wk *DTCH/LGLY SL3* . 13 G2 ⑥
St Vincent Cl *CRAWE RH10* ... 213 G4 ⑦
WNWD SE27 .... 31 L6 ⑥
St Vincent Rd *WHTN TW2* 16 B1
WOT/HER KT12 .... 60 E2
St Winifred's Rd *BH/WHM TN16*.. 91 J1 ⑥
TEDD TW11 .... 26 E7
Salamander Cl *KUTN/CMB KT2* .. 26 F6 ⑥
Salcombe Dr *MRDN SM4* 47 G8
Salcombe Rd *ASHF TW15* 23 G8
Salcot Crs *CROY/NA CR0* 69 M8
Salcott Rd *CROY/NA CR0* 67 H2
Salehurst Rd *CRAWE RH10* ... 213 H3
Salem Pl *CROY/NA CR0* 4 B8
Salerno Cl *ALDT GU11* 112 D7
Salesian Vw *FARN GU14* 113 H1
Salford Rd *BAL SW12* 31 G2
Salisbury Av *BELMT SM2* 65 J5
Salisbury Cl *WPK KT4* ...... 64 C2 ⑥
Salisbury Gdns
WIM/MER SW19 .... 29 H8 ⑥
Salisbury Gv *FRIM GU16* 93 K6
Salisbury Pl *BF/WBF KT14* ... 78 F1 ⑥
Salisbury Rd *ASHV GU12*.... 113 K7
BNSTD SM7........... 85 L5
CAR SM5 .... 66 C5
CRAWE RH10......... 212 B7
CROY/NA CR0......... 50 D6
FARN GU14........... 92 F5
FELT TW13........... 24 F2
GDST RH9........... 128 F5
HOR/WEW KT19........ 64 A3
HSLWW TW4 .... 15 M5
NWMAL KT3.......... 46 A3
RCH/KEW TW9 .... 18 B6 ⑥
WIM/MER SW19 .... 29 H8
WOKS/MYFD GU22 ...... 97 H1
Salisbury Ter *FRIM GU16* 93 K6
Salix Cl *SUN TW16* .... 24 E8 ②
Salmons Cl *CTHM CR3* 108 B2
Salmons La *CTHM CR3* 108 B2
Salmons Rd *CHSGTN KT9* 63 H5
EHSLY KT24.......... 120 F3
Saltash Cl *SUT SM1* 65 J3
Saltbox Hl *BH/WHM TN16* ... 90 E8
Salt Box Rd *RGUW GU3* 116 D3
Saltdean Cl *CRAWW RH11* ... 211 J4 ⑥
Salterford Rd *TOOT SW17* 30 D7
Salterns Rd *CRAWE RH10* ... 212 F6
Salter's Hl *NRWD SE19* 32 A6
Saltram Rd *FARN GU14* 93 H7
Salvador *TOOT SW17* 30 B6
Salvation Pl *LHD/OX KT22* ... 102 D6
Salvington Rd *CRAWW RH11* . 211 J6
Salwey Cl *BRAK RG12* ...... 34 E6 ⑥
Samaritan Cl *CRAWW RH11* .. 211 H5 ⑦
Samarkand Cl *CBLY GU15* ... 73 L5
Samos Rd *PGE/AN SE20* 50 E2
Samphire Cl *CRAWW RH11* .. 211 K6 ⑥
Sampleoak La *RGUE GU4* 140 B7
Sampson Pk *BNFD RG42* 34 A1
San Carlos Ap *ALDT GU11* ... 112 F7
Sanctuary Rd *STWL/WRAY TW19* .. 14 D8
Sandal Rd *NWMAL KT3* 46 B4
Sandalwood *GUW GU2* 8 C5
Sandalwood Av *CHERT KT16* .. 58 A2
Sandalwood Rd *FELT TW13* ... 24 E4
Sandbourne Av *WIM/MER SW19*. 47 L3
Sandcross La *REIG RH2* 147 J3
Sandell's Av *ASHF TW15*..... 23 M5
Sanders Cl *HPTN TW12* ..... 25 M6 ③
Sandersfield Rd *BNSTD SM7*... 85 K5
Sanderstead Cl *BAL SW12* ... 30 F1
Sanderstead Court Av
SAND/SEL CR2 .... 88 D3
Sanderstead Hl *SAND/SEL CR2*.. 88 B1
Sanderstead Rd *SAND/SEL CR2* .. 68 A6
Sandes Pl *LHD/OX KT22* 82 D8
Sandfield Gdns *THHTH CR7* ... 49 L3 ③
Sandfield Pl *THHTH CR7* .... 49 M3 ③
Sandfield Rd *THHTH CR7* 49 L3
Sandfields *RPLY/SEND GU23*... 98 A6
Sandfield Ter *GU GU1* 9 G5
Sandford Ct *ALDT GU11* ..... 112 C8 ⑥
Sandford Down *BRAK RG12* ... 35 J5 ③
Sandford Rd *ALDT GU11* 112 C8
FNM GU9 .... 133 L2
Sandgate La *WAND/EARL SW18* . 30 B2
Sandhawes Hl *EGRIN RH19* ... 196 D5 ⑥
Sandheath Rd *GSHT GU26*.... 198 F2
Sand Hl *FARN GU14* 92 E2
Sandhill La *CRAWE RH10* 214 E2
Sandhills *WLGTN SM6*....... 67 G3
Sandhills Ct *VW GU25* 39 H5
Sandhills La *VW GU25* 39 H5
Sandhills Rd *REIG RH2* 147 K2
Sandhurst Av *BRYLDS KT5* ... 45 L7
Sandhurst Cl *SAND/SEL CR2*... 68 B7
Sandhurst Wy *SAND/SEL CR2*.. 68 B6
Sandiford Rd *CHEAM SM3* ... 65 J1
Sandiland Crs *HAYES BR2* ... 70 C1
Sandilands *CROY/NA CR0*..... 5 L7
Sandlands Gv
KWD/TDW/WH KT20 .... 104 D5
Sandlands Rd
KWD/TDW/WH KT20 .... 104 D5
Sandon Cl *ESH/CLAY KT10* ... 44 A7
Sandown Av *ESH/CLAY KT10*.... 61 M4 ⑥
Sandown Cl *BLKW GU17* 72 A6
HEST TW5 .... 15 K3
Sandown Crs *ALDT GU11* 134 E2
Sandown Dr *CAR SM5* ..... 66 D7 ②
FRIM GU16........... 73 G7
Sandown Ga *ESH/CLAY KT10*... 62 A1

Sandown Rd *COUL/CHIP CR5* .. 86 D6
ESH/CLAY KT10........ 61 M3 ⑥
SNWD SE25 .... 50 E5
Sandpiper Cl *CRAWW RH11* .. 211 G5 ⑥
Sandpiper Rd *SAND/SEL CR2*... 89 G1
Sandpit Hall Rd *CHOB/PIR GU24*. 76 D2
Sandpit Heath *RGUW GU3* ... 116 A4
Sandpit Rd *REDH RH1* 148 B1
Sandpits Rd *CROY/NA CR0* ... 69 G3
RCHPK/HAM TW10 ...... 27 G3
Sandra Cl *HSLW TW3* ...... 16 E7 ⑥
Sandringham Av *RYNPK SW20*.. 47 H1
Sandringham Cl
WIM/MER SW19 .... 29 G2 ⑥
WOKS/MYFD GU22 ...... 78 D6
Sandringham Gdns *HEST TW5* .. 15 K3 ⑥
Sandringham Pk *COB KT11* ... 81 J2
Sandringham Rd *CRAWW RH11* . 211 L7
CROY/NA CR0.......... 49 M5
WPK KT4............ 64 D2
Sandringham Wy *FRIM GU16*.. 93 J1 ⑦
Sandrock *HASM GU27* 219 M3
Sandrock Hill Rd *NFNM GU10*.. 10 B9
Sandrock Pl *CROY/NA CR0* ... 69 G3
Sandrock Rd *DORK RH4* 143 L4
Sandroyd Wy *COB KT11* ..... 81 K3 ⑥
Sands Cl *NFNM GU10* 135 G7
Sands Rd *NFNM GU10* 134 F7
Sandy Cl *WOKS/MYFD GU22* ... 7 L6
Sandycombe Rd
EBED/NFELT TW14 ...... 24 D2
RCH/KEW TW9 .... 18 D4
Sandycoombe Rd *TWK TW1* ... 17 M8
Sandy Ct *COB KT11* 81 J3
Sandy Cft *EW KT17* 64 F8
Sandy Dr *COB KT11* 81 K1
EBED/NFELT TW14 ...... 24 B2
Sandy Hill Rd *FNM GU9* .... 133 K2 ⑥
WLGTN SM6 .... 66 F7 ③
Sandy Holt *COB KT11* 81 J3
Sandy La *ASC SL5* 35 M1
ASC SL5 .... 37 K5
BELMT SM2 .... 65 H7
BRAK RG12 .... 34 F1
BRKHM/BTCW RH3..... 124 B8
CBLY GU15........... 73 H3
CHOB/PIR GU24 .... 56 B7
COB KT11........... 81 J2
CRAWE RH10 .... 214 D1
E/WMO/HCT KT8 .... 44 A1
EGRIN RH19 .... 196 B8
GSHT GU26.......... 199 J7
HASM GU27.......... 200 B8
HASM GU27.......... 218 F2
KWD/TDW/WH KT20 .... 105 J6
MFD/CHID GU8 .... 181 G1
MTCM CR4 .... 48 D1
NFNM GU10 .... 155 M8
NFNM GU10 .... 178 D3
OXTED RH8 .... 129 M3
OXTED RH8 .... 130 E1
RCHPK/HAM TW10 ...... 26 F3
REDH RH1 .... 127 H8
REDH RH1 .... 127 L6
REIG RH2............ 146 E1
RGODL GU7 .... 160 A3
RGUW GU3........... 115 G5
RGUW GU3........... 138 D5
RPLY/SEND GU23 ...... 97 M3
SHGR GU5........... 141 G7
SHGR GU5........... 141 K6
TEDD TW11 .... 26 D8
VW GU25............ 39 H5
WOKS/MYFD GU22 ...... 7 L6
WOKS/MYFD GU22 ...... 78 D6
WOT/HER KT12........ 42 E6
Sandy La North *WLGTN SM6* ... 67 G4
Sandy Rd *ADL/WDHM KT15*.... 58 D5
Sandy Wy *COB KT11* 81 K2
CROY/NA CR0.......... 69 J2
WOKS/MYFD GU22 ...... 7 L5
WOT/HER KT12........ 42 C4
San Feliu Ct *EGRIN RH19* 196 E7
Sanger Av *CHSGTN KT9* 63 J4
Sanger Dr *RPLY/SEND GU23*... 97 M4
Sangers Dr *HORL RH6* 170 C7
Sangley Rd *CAT SE6* 33 L1
SNWD SE25 .... 50 B4
Santina Cl *FNM GU9* 134 A1
Sanway Cl *BF/WBF KT14* 79 H4
Sanway Rd *BF/WBF KT14* 79 H4
Sappho Cl *WOKN/KNAP GU21* .. 76 B8 ②
Sapte Cl *CRAN GU6* 185 K6
Saracen Cl *CROY/NA CR0* 50 A6
Sarah Wy *FARN GU14* 92 F5
Sarel Wy *HORL RH6* 170 E4
Sargent Cl *CRAWE RH10* .... 212 C7 ⑥
Sark Cl *CRAWW RH11* ...... 211 K7 ⑥
HEST TW5 .... 16 D2
Sarsby Dr *STWL/WRAY TW19* .. 21 K3
Sarsen Av *HSLW TW3* 16 C4
Sarsfeld Rd *BAL SW12* 30 C2
Sarum *BRAK RG12*.......... 34 B8
Sarum Gn *WEY KT13* 60 B2
Saturn Cl *CRAWW RH11* .... 211 H5 ⑥
Saunders Cl *CRAWE RH10* ... 212 E3
Saunders Copse
WOKS/MYFD GU22 ...... 96 E4
Saunders La *WOKS/MYFD GU22*. 96 C4
Saunton Av *HYS/HAR UB3* ... 15 J2
Saunton Gdns *FARN GU14* ... 92 D3 ③
Savernake Wk *CRAWE RH10*... 212 C6 ⑥
Savernake Wy *BRAK RG12* ... 35 J6
Savile Cl *NWMAL KT3* 46 B5
THDIT KT7........... 44 C8
Savile Gdns *CROY/NA CR0*.... 5 K6
Saville Crs *ASHF TW15* ..... 24 A7 ⑥
Saville Gdns *CBLY GU15* 73 L4
Saville Rd *TWK TW1* 26 C2
Savill Gdns *RYNPK SW20* 46 D3
Savona Cl *WIM/MER SW19* ... 29 G8
Savoy Gv *BLKW GU17* 72 A6
Sawkins Cl *WIM/MER SW19* .. 29 G3
Sawtry Cl *CAR SM5* 48 A7
Saxby Rd *BRXS/STRHM SW2* .. 31 H1
Saxby's La *LING RH7* 174 B4
Saxley *HORL RH6* 170 F5

Saxon Av FELT TW13 25 J3
Saxonbury Av SUN TW16 42 E3
Saxonbury Cl MTCM CR4 48 A3 4
Saxonbury Gdns SURB KT6 44 F8
Saxon Cl SURB KT6 45 G6
Saxon Crs HORS RH12 228 E5
Saxon Cft FNM GU9 11 G1
Saxon Dr BNFD RG42 35 J1
Saxonfield Cl
BRXS/STRHM SW2 31 J1 1
Saxon Rd ASHF TW15 24 A7
CRAWE RH10 213 H4
CROY/NA CR0 50 A5
WOT/HER KT12 61 G2
Saxons KWD/TDW/WH KT20 105 G3
Saxon Wy REIG RH2 125 J7
WDR/YW UB7 13 M1
Sayers Cl FRIM GU16 93 H2
LHD/OX KT22 101 M6
SWTR RH13 229 H7
The Sayers EGRIN RH19 195 M8
Sayes Ct ADL/WDHM KT15 58 E4
Sayes Court Farm Dr
ADL/WDHM KT15 58 E4
Sbac Tr ALDT GU11 112 B3
Scallows Cl CRAWE RH10 212 D2
Scallows Rd CRAWE RH10 212 D2
Scarborough Cl BELMT SM2 65 J8
BH/WHM TN16 90 F8
Scarbrook Rd CROY/NA CR0 4 C8
Scarlet Oaks CBLY GU15 73 H6
Scarlett Cl WOKN/KNAP GU21 76 C8
Scarlett's Rd ALDT GU11 112 D6
Scarth Rd BARN SW13 19 J5
Scawen Cl CAR SM5 66 D3
Scholars Rd BAL SW12 30 F2
School Cl CHOB/PIR GU24 75 J5
GU GU1 117 G6
HORS RH12 229 K3 1
School Fld EDEN TN8 153 M7
School Flds BOR GU35 176 A8
School Hl CWTH RG45 52 A5
HORS RH12 228 C1
NFNM GU10 10 A7
NFNM GU10 135 L5
REDH RH1 126 F2
School House La TEDD TW11 26 E8 3
School La ADL/WDHM KT15 58 D3
BAGS GU19 54 A7
BFOR GU20 55 G5
CHOB/PIR GU24 95 H4
DORK RH4 144 A3
EGH TW20 21 K6
EGRIN RH19 217 G3
EHSLY KT24 119 L3
FROW RH18 217 J7
KUT KT1 2 B5
LHD/OX KT22 102 A4
MFD/CHID GU8 159 H3
MFD/CHID GU8 201 L5
NFNM GU10 11 J7
NFNM GU10 154 A4
RDKG RH5 122 F1
RGUE GU4 119 H5
RGUW GU3 136 F5
RPLY/SEND GU23 99 L4
SHPTN TW17 41 L6 5
SURB KT6 45 J8
School Pas KUT KT1 3 H7
School Rd ASC SL5 37 G5
ASHF TW15 23 L7
BFOR GU20 54 D3
E/WMO/HCT KT8 44 A4
GSHT GU26 198 E6
HASM GU27 219 J4
HPTN TW12 25 M7
HSLW TW3 16 F5
KUT KT1 2 B5 1
NFNM GU10 155 H6
WDR/YW UB7 14 A1
School Road Av HPTN TW12 25 M7 1
Schroder Ct EGH TW20 20 E6
Scillonian Rd GUW GU2 8 B7
Scizdons Climb RGODL GU7 160 C5
Scoles Crs BRXS/STRHM SW2 31 K2
Scory Cl CRAWW RH11 211 K6
Scotia Rd BRXS/STRHM SW2 31 K1 2
Scotland Bridge Rd
ADL/WDHM KT15 78 D1
Scotland Cl ASHV GU12 113 K4
Scotland Farm Rd ASHV GU12 113 K4
Scotland La HASM GU27 219 L4
Scotlands Cl HASM GU27 219 L4
Scotlands Dr HASM GU27 219 L4 1
Scots Cl STWL/WRAY TW19 23 G2
Scotsdale Cl BELMT SM2 65 H6
Scotshall La WARL CR6 89 M5
Scott Cl GUW GU2 116 D6
HOR/WEW KT19 63 M4
STRHM/NOR SW16 49 J1
Scott Farm Cl THDIT KT7 44 E8
Scott Gdns HEST TW5 16 A2 1
Scott Rd CRAWE RH10 212 C6
Scotts Av SUN TW16 24 B8
Scott's Ct FARN GU14 92 E2
Scotts Dr HPTN TW12 25 L8
Scotts Farm Rd HOR/WEW KT19 63 M5
Scott's Grove Cl CHOB/PIR GU24 76 A3
Scott's Grove Rd
CHOB/PIR GU24 75 L4
Scott's Hl HORL RH6 172 A5
Scotts Wy SUN TW16 24 B8
Scott Ter BNFD RG42 35 H1
Scott Trimmer Wy HEST TW5 16 B4 2
Scylla Crs HTHAIR TW6 23 L1
Scylla Rd HTHAIR TW6 14 E8
Seabrook Dr WWKM BR4 70 B1
Seafire Wy FARN GU14 112 B2
Seaford Rd CRAWW RH11 211 K8
Seaforth Av NWMAL KT3 46 E5
Seaforth Gdns HOR/WEW KT19 64 C3
Sealand Rd HTHAIR TW6 14 D8
Seale La NFNM GU10 135 G5
RGUW GU3 136 C5
Seale Rd MFD/CHID GU8 157 L1
Seaman's Gn RDKG RH5 189 G1
Searchwood Rd WARL CR6 88 E8
Searle Hl REIG RH2 147 K2
Searle Rd FNM GU9 11 G3
Searle's Vw HORS RH12 229 J4 3
Seaton Cl PUT/ROE SW15 28 E1
WHTN TW2 17 G8
Seaton Dr ASHF TW15 23 H3
Seaton Rd CBLY GU15 72 E4
MTCM CR4 48 B2
WHTN TW2 16 F8
Sebastopol Rd ALDT GU11 112 E7
Second Av ADL/WDHM KT15 58 E7
MORT/ESHN SW14 19 H5
WOT/HER KT12 42 E6
Second Cl E/WMO/HCT KT8 43 L4
Second Cross Rd WHTN TW2 26 A3
Seddon Rd MRDN SM4 48 A5
Sedgefield Cl CRAWE RH10 213 H2
Sedgehill Rd CAT SE6 33 K6
Sedgemoor FARN GU14 92 E2
Sedgewick Cl CRAWE RH10 212 F3 1
Seebys Oak SHST GU47 72 B3 3
Seeley Dr DUL SE21 32 B5
Seely Rd TOOT SW17 30 D7
Seething Wells La SURB KT6 44 F6
Sefton Cl CHOB/PIR GU24 75 J3
Sefton Rd CROY/NA CR0 5 M4
HOR/WEW KT19 64 A8
Sefton St PUT/ROE SW15 19 M4
Segrave Cl WEY KT13 59 K6
Segsbury Gv BRAK RG12 35 H4
Sekhon Ter FELT TW13 25 K4 1
Selborne Av ALDT GU11 134 F2
Selborne Gdns FNM GU9 10 C5
Selborne Rd CROY/NA CR0 5 H8
NWMAL KT3 46 B2 1
Selbourne Av ADL/WDHM KT15 58 E8
SURB KT6 63 J1
Selbourne Cl ADL/WDHM KT15 58 E8 2
CRAWE RH10 193 G7
Selbourne Rd GU GU1 117 K5
Selbourne Sq GDST RH9 128 F4
Selby Cl CHSGTN KT9 63 H6
Selby Gn CAR SM5 48 B7
Selby Rd ASHF TW15 23 M7
CAR SM5 48 B7
PGE/AN SE20 50 D2
Selbys LING RH7 174 B4
Selby Wk WOKN/KNAP GU21 76 E8 2
Selham Cl CRAWW RH11 211 K2
Selhurst Cl WIM/MER SW19 29 G2
WOKN/KNAP GU21 6 F1
Selhurst New Rd SNWD SE25 50 B6
Selhurst Pl CROY/NA CR0 50 B6
Selhurst Rd SNWD SE25 50 B5
Selkirk Rd TOOT SW17 30 B5
WHTN TW2 25 M3
Sellar's Hl RGODL GU7 160 A2 2
Sellincourt Rd TOOT SW17 30 B6
Sellindge Cl BECK BR3 33 J8 3
Selsdon Av SAND/SEL CR2 68 A5 2
Selsdon Cl SURB KT6 45 H5
Selsdon Crs SAND/SEL CR2 68 F8 1
Selsdon Park Rd SAND/SEL CR2 69 H7
Selsdon Rd ADL/WDHM KT15 78 D1
SAND/SEL CR2 68 B6 1
WNWD SE27 31 L4
Selsey Rd CRAWW RH11 211 K7
Selsfield Rd CRAWE RH10 214 D6
Seltops Cl CRAN GU6 185 J7 3
Selwood Cl STWL/WRAY TW19 13 M8 1
Selwood Gdns
STWL/WRAY TW19 13 M8
Selwood Rd CHEAM SM3 47 J8
CHSGTN KT9 63 G3
CROY/NA CR0 68 E1
WOKS/MYFD GU22 97 L2
Selworthy Rd CAT SE6 33 J4
Selwyn Av RCH/KEW TW9 18 C5
Selwyn Cl CRAWE RH10 192 F8
HSLWW TW4 16 B6 1
Selwyn Rd NWMAL KT3 46 A5
Semaphore Rd GU GU1 9 J8
Semley Rd STRHM/NOR SW16 49 H2
Semper Cl WOKN/KNAP GU21 76 B7
Send Barns La RPLY/SEND GU23 98 B6
Send Cl RPLY/SEND GU23 97 M5
Send Hl RPLY/SEND GU23 97 M7
Send Marsh Rd
RPLY/SEND GU23 98 B5
Send Rd RPLY/SEND GU23 97 M5
Seneca Rd THHTH CR7 49 M4
Senga Rd MTCM CR4 48 D8
Senhouse Rd CHEAM SM3 65 G2
Serrin Wy HORS RH12 229 H4
Service Rd HORL RH6 192 C1
Setley Wy BRAK RG12 35 J3
Seven Acres CAR SM5 66 B1 3
Seven Arches Ap WEY KT13 59 J6
Seven Hills Cl WEY KT13 60 B7
Seven Hills Rd WOT/HER KT12 60 B6
Seven Hills Road (South)
COB KT11 80 B3
Sevenoaks Cl BELMT SM2 65 K8
Severn Dr ESH/CLAY KT10 62 D1
WOT/HER KT12 61 G1 1
Severn Rd CRAWE RH10 212 F4
FARN GU14 92 B3
Seward Rd BECK BR3 51 G2
Sewer's Farm Rd RDKG RH5 165 J3
Sewill Cl HORL RH6 191 J2
Seymour Av CTHM CR3 107 M5
EW KT17 64 E7
MRDN SM4 47 G7
Seymour Cl E/WMO/HCT KT8 43 M5
Seymour Dr CBLY GU15 73 L1
Seymour Gdns BRYLDS KT5 45 J5
FELT TW13 24 E5
TWK TW1 26 E1
Seymour Ms EW KT17 64 D8 4
Seymour Pl SNWD SE25 50 E4 3
WOKS/MYFD GU22 96 E2
Seymour Rd CAR SM5 66 D4 1
CRAWW RH11 211 K7
E/WMO/HCT KT8 43 M5
HPTN TW12 25 M6
KUT KT1 2 C4
MTCM CR4 48 D7
RGODL GU7 159 L6
WAND/EARL SW18 29 J1
WIM/MER SW19 29 G4
Seymour Ter PGE/AN SE20 50 E1
Seymour Vls PGE/AN SE20 50 E1
Seymour Wy SUN TW16 24 B7
Shackleford Rd MFD/CHID GU8 159 G2
WOKS/MYFD GU22 97 K2
Shacklegate La TEDD TW11 26 B5
Shackleton Cl FSTH SE23 32 E3
Shackleton Rd CRAWE RH10 212 B6
Shackstead La RGODL GU7 159 M6
Shackster La RGODL GU7 159 M6
Shadbolt Cl WPK KT4 64 C1
Shadyhanger RGODL GU7 160 B3
Shady Nook FNM GU9 133 L3
Shaef Wy TEDD TW11 26 D8
Shaftesbury Av
EBED/NFELT TW14 15 K8
Shaftesbury Cl BRAK RG12 35 G5
Shaftesbury Crs STA TW18 23 G8
Shaftesbury Rd BECK BR3 51 J2
CAR SM5 48 A7
CHOB/PIR GU24 75 J6
CRAWE RH10 213 G5
RCH/KEW TW9 18 B5
WOKS/MYFD GU22 7 J6
Shaftesbury Wy WHTN TW2 26 A4
Shakespeare Av
EBED/NFELT TW14 15 K8
Shakespeare Gdns
FARN GU14 92 A4 1
Shakespeare Rd
ADL/WDHM KT15 59 G3
Shakespeare Wy BNFD RG42 35 H1
FELT TW13 24 F5
Shalbourne Ri CBLY GU15 73 G4
Shalden Rd ASHV GU12 135 G1
Shaldon Dr MRDN SM4 47 H5
Shaldon Wy WOT/HER KT12 60 F2
Shalesbrook La FROW RH18 217 J8
Shalford Cl ORP BR6 71 M3
Shalford La RGUE GU4 139 H5
Shalford Rd GU GU1 139 G3
Shalstone Rd MORT/ESHN SW14 18 E5
Shalston Vls SURB KT6 45 J6 5
The Shambles GU GU1 9 G7
Shamrock Cl FRIM GU16 93 G1 3
LHD/OX KT22 102 A3
Shamrock Rd CROY/NA CR0 49 J6
Shandys Cl HORS RH12 228 D8
Shanklin Ct ASHV GU12 112 F8
Shannon Wy BECK BR3 33 L7
Shap Crs CAR SM5 48 C8
Sharland Cl THHTH CR7 49 K6 5
Sharon Cl CRAWE RH10 212 D6
GT/LBKH KT23 101 K6
HOR/WEW KT19 83 M3
SURB KT6 44 F8
Sharpthorne Cl CRAWW RH11 211 J3 1
Shaw Cl CHERT KT16 57 M5
EW KT17 84 C1
SAND/SEL CR2 88 C2
Shaw Crs SAND/SEL CR2 88 B2
Shaw Dr WOT/HER KT12 42 F7
Shawfield La ASHV GU12 113 J7
Shawfield Rd ASHV GU12 113 J8
Shawford Rd HOR/WEW KT19 64 A5
Shaw Gv KWD/TDW/WH KT20 105 H6
Shawley Crs EPSOM KT18 84 F8
Shawley Wy EPSOM KT18 84 F8
Shaw Rd BH/WHM TN16 110 F2
Shaw's Cottages FSTH SE23 33 H4 3
Shaws Rd CRAWE RH10 212 B2
Shaw Wy WLGTN SM6 67 H6
Shaxton Crs CROY/NA CR0 69 M7
Shearing Dr MRDN SM4 47 M7
Shearwater Rd SUT SM1 65 J4
Sheath La LHD/OX KT22 81 L3
Sheen Common Dr
RCHPK/HAM TW10 18 D6
Sheen Court Rd
RCHPK/HAM TW10 18 D6
Sheendale Rd RCH/KEW TW9 18 C6
Sheenewood SYD SE26 32 E6
Sheen Gate Gdns
MORT/ESHN SW14 18 F6
Sheen La MORT/ESHN SW14 18 F6
Sheen Pk RCH/KEW TW9 18 B6
Sheen Rd RCHPK/HAM TW10 18 B6
Sheen Wy WLGTN SM6 67 J4
Sheen Wd MORT/ESHN SW14 18 F7
Sheepbarn La WARL CR6 90 D2
Sheepcote Cl HEST TW5 15 K2
Sheepfold Rd GUW GU2 116 C5
Sheephatch La NFNM GU10 156 E4
Sheephouse FNM GU9 11 G3
Sheephouse Gn RDKG RH5 143 J5
Sheephouse La RDKG RH5 143 J5
RDKG RH5 165 K2
Sheephouse Wy NWMAL KT3 46 A8
Sheeplands Av GU GU1 117 M6
Sheep Wk REIG RH2 125 J5
Sheepwalk SHPTN TW17 41 J6
Sheep Walk Ms WIM/MER SW19 29 G7
Sheerwater Av ADL/WDHM KT15 78 B2
Sheerwater Rd
ADL/WDHM KT15 78 B2
WOKN/KNAP GU21 78 B2 1
Sheet's Heath La
CHOB/PIR GU24 95 K1
Sheffield Cl CRAWE RH10 212 E5 5
FARN GU14 92 C5
Sheffield Rd EBED/NFELT TW14 14 F8
Sheffield Wy HTHAIR TW6 15 G7 1
Sheldon Cl CRAWE RH10 213 G4
PGE/AN SE20 50 E1 3
REIG RH2 147 L1
Sheldon Ct GU GU1 9 L5
Sheldon St CROY/NA CR0 4 C8
Sheldrick Cl MTCM CR4 48 A2
Shelford Ri NRWD SE19 32 B8
Shelley Av BRAK RG12 35 H2
Shelley Cl COUL/CHIP CR5 87 J7
CRAWE RH10 212 F1 3
Shelley Ct CBLY GU15 72 F4
Shelley Crs HEST TW5 16 A3
Shelley Dr HORS RH12 227 M6
Shelley Rd EGRIN RH19 196 A8 4
HORS RH12 228 E6
Shelley Wy TOOT SW17 30 A7 5
Shellwood Dr RDKG RH5 144 F6
Shellwood Rd REIG RH2 146 A7
Shelly Cl BNSTD SM7 85 G5
Shelly Ri FARN GU14 92 C3
Shellys Ct SWTR RH13 229 K6 2
Shelson Av FELT TW13 24 C4
Shelton Av WARL CR6 88 F7
Shelton Cl GUW GU2 116 D3
WARL CR6 88 F7
Shelton Rd WIM/MER SW19 47 K1
Shelvers Gn
KWD/TDW/WH KT20 104 F3
Shelvers Hl
KWD/TDW/WH KT20 104 F3 1
Shelvers Sp
KWD/TDW/WH KT20 104 F3
Shelvers Wy
KWD/TDW/WH KT20 104 F3
Shenfield Cl COUL/CHIP CR5 106 E1
Shenley Rd HEST TW5 16 B3
Shenstone Pk ASC SL5 37 H4
Shepherd Cl CRAWE RH10 212 A6
Shepherds Cha BAGS GU19 54 B7 2
Shepherds Cl SHPTN TW17 41 L6
Shepherdsgrove La
EGRIN RH19 197 J4
Shepherds Hl BRAK RG12 34 F1
GUW GU2 116 D6
HASM GU27 219 M3
REDH RH1 106 F8
Shepherds La BFOR GU20 55 K4
GUW GU2 116 C5
Shepherds' Wk EPSOM KT18 103 L3
FARN GU14 92 B2
Shepherds Wy HORS RH12 229 K4
LIPH GU30 218 A6
NFNM GU10 156 F5
RGUE GU4 139 H4
SAND/SEL CR2 69 G6
Shepley Cl CAR SM5 66 D2
Shepley Dr ASC SL5 38 A6
Shepley End ASC SL5 37 M5
Sheppard Cl SURB KT6 45 H4 3
Shepperton Court Dr
SHPTN TW17 41 L5 3
Shepperton Rd STA TW18 41 G4
Sheppey Cl CRAWW RH11 211 L6
Sheraton Cl BLKW GU17 72 B5
Sheraton Dr HOR/WEW KT19 83 M3
Sherborne Cl DTCH/LGLY SL3 13 H3
EPSOM KT18 84 F7
Sherborne Crs CAR SM5 48 B7
Sherborne Rd CHEAM SM3 65 K1
CHSGTN KT9 63 H4
EBED/NFELT TW14 24 A1 3
FARN GU14 113 G1
Sherbourne SHGR GU5 141 G5
Sherbourne Dr VW GU25 38 A5
Sherbourne Gdns
SHPTN TW17 42 B7 1
Shere Av BELMT SM2 64 F8
Shere Cl CHSGTN KT9 63 G4
RDKG RH5 144 F6
Shere La SHGR GU5 141 K5
Shere Rd CRAN GU6 186 A2
EHSLY KT24 119 M8
RGUE GU4 140 E2
SHGR GU5 141 J4
Sherfield Gdns PUT/ROE SW15 19 J8
Sheridan Cl EGRIN RH19 195 M8
Sheridan Ct HSLWW TW4 16 B7
Sheridan Dr REIG RH2 125 L6
Sheridan Pl HPTN TW12 43 L1 1
Sheridan Rd FRIM GU16 93 G1
RCHPK/HAM TW10 26 F4
WIM/MER SW19 47 J1
Sheridans Rd GT/LBKH KT23 101 M8
Sheridan Wy BECK BR3 51 J1 2
Sheringham Av WHTN TW2 25 J2
Sheringham Rd PGE/AN SE20 50 E2
Sherland Rd TWK TW1 26 C2
Sherrden La EDEN TN8 175 M4
Sherringham Av FELT TW13 24 D4 1
Sherrydon CRAN GU6 185 J5
Sherwin Crs FARN GU14 92 E1
Sherwood SURB KT6 63 G1 2
Sherwood Av STRHM/NOR SW16 49 H1
Sherwood Cl BRAK RG12 35 K2 2
LHD/OX KT22 101 M5
WOKN/KNAP GU21 76 B7
Sherwood Crs REIG RH2 147 L4
Sherwood Park Rd MTCM CR4 48 F4
SUT SM1 65 K4
Sherwood Rd COUL/CHIP CR5 86 F6
CROY/NA CR0 50 E7
HPTN TW12 25 M6
WIM/MER SW19 29 J8 1
Sherwood Wk CRAWE RH10 212 C6 1
Sherwood Wy WWKM BR4 69 M1
Shetland Cl CRAWE RH10 213 H2 3
RGUE GU4 117 L3 4
Shewens Rd WEY KT13 60 A3 4
Shey Copse WOKS/MYFD GU22 7 L6
Shield Dr BTFD TW8 17 L1
Shield Rd ASHF TW15 23 M5
Shilburn Wy WOKN/KNAP GU21 76 D8
Shildon Cl CBLY GU15 74 A6
Shillinglee Rd BIL RH14 223 G6
MFD/CHID GU8 221 L4
The Shimmings GU GU1 117 K7
Shinners Cl SNWD SE25 50 D5
Ship Aly FARN GU14 92 F3
Ship Field Cl BH/WHM TN16 110 F3
Ship Hl BH/WHM TN16 111 G3
Shipka Rd BAL SW12 30 E2
Ship La FARN GU14 92 F3
MORT/ESHN SW14 18 F5
Shipleybridge La HORL RH6 193 J4
Shipley Rd CRAWW RH11 211 K3
Shipman Rd FSTH SE23 33 G3
Ship St EGRIN RH19 216 B1
Ship Yd WEY KT13 59 K2
Shirburn Cl FSTH SE23 32 F1
Shire Cl BAGS GU19 54 B7
Shire Ct EW KT17 64 C6 1
Shire Horse Wy ISLW TW7 17 J5
Shire Pde CRAWE RH10 213 G2 3
The Shires RCHPK/HAM TW10 27 H5
Shirley Av BELMT SM2 65 J8
COUL/CHIP CR5 107 L1
CROY/NA CR0 50 F8
REDH RH1 148 C5
SUT SM1 66 B3
Shirley Church Rd
CROY/NA CR0 69 G2
Shirley Cl HSLW TW3 16 F7
Shirley Crs BECK BR3 51 H4
Shirley Dr HSLW TW3 16 F7
Shirley Hills Rd CROY/NA CR0 69 G4
Shirley Oaks Rd CROY/NA CR0 51 G8
Shirley Park Rd CROY/NA CR0 50 E8
Shirley Pl WOKN/KNAP GU21 75 M7
Shirley Rd CROY/NA CR0 50 E8
WLGTN SM6 66 F7
Shirley Wy CROY/NA CR0 69 J2
Shoe La ALDT GU11 112 D3
Shophouse La SHGR GU5 163 G2
Shord Hl PUR/KEN CR8 88 A6
Shore Cl EBED/NFELT TW14 24 D1
HPTN TW12 25 H6
Shore Gv FELT TW13 25 K3
Shoreham Cl CROY/NA CR0 50 F6
Shoreham Rd CRAWE RH10 212 F6
Shore's Rd WOKN/KNAP GU21 77 J4
Shorndean St CAT SE6 33 M2
Shortacres REDH RH1 127 J7
Short Cl CRAWW RH11 212 A1 4
Shortcroft Rd EW KT17 64 C6
Short Dale Rd ALDT GU11 134 F3
Shortfield Rd NFNM GU10 155 M8
Short Gallop CRAWE RH10 213 G2 3
Shortheath Crest FNM GU9 10 B7
Shortheath Rd FNM GU9 10 D7
Shortlands HYS/HAR UB3 15 G1
Shortlands Rd KUTN/CMB KT2 3 H3
Short La OXTED RH8 130 E6
STWL/WRAY TW19 23 J1
Short Rd CHSWK W4 19 H1
Shortsfield Cl HORS RH12 228 F4 2
Shorts Rd CAR SM5 66 B3
Short St ALDT GU11 112 D7
Short Wy WHTN TW2 25 M1
Shortwood Av STA TW18 22 E4
Shotfield WLGTN SM6 66 E5
Shott Cl SUT SM1 65 M4 3
Shottermill HORS RH12 229 K2
Shottfield Av MORT/ESHN SW14 19 H6
Shovelstrode La EGRIN RH19 197 H7
Shrewsbury Av
MORT/ESHN SW14 18 F6
Shrewsbury Cl SURB KT6 63 H1
Shrewsbury Rd BECK BR3 51 H3
CAR SM5 48 B7
EBED/NFELT TW14 14 F8
HTHAIR TW6 14 F8
REDH RH1 126 B8
Shrewton Rd TOOT SW17 30 C8 4
Shrivenham Cl SHST GU47 72 A1 3
Shropshire Cl MTCM CR4 49 H4 3
Shrubbery Rd
STRHM/NOR SW16 31 H5
The Shrubbery FARN GU14 92 A6
Shrubbs Hl CHOB/PIR GU24 55 M7
Shrubbs Hill La ASC SL5 37 M6
Shrubbs La NFNM GU10 155 J5
Shrubland Gv WPK KT4 64 F2 2
Shrubland Rd BNSTD SM7 85 J6
Shrublands Av CROY/NA CR0 69 K3
Shrublands Cl SYD SE26 32 F4 2
Shrublands Dr LTWR GU18 74 E1
Shurlock Dr ORP BR6 71 M3 3
Sibthorp Rd MTCM CR4 48 C2 2
Sibton Rd CAR SM5 48 B7
Sickle Rd HASM GU27 219 J4
Sickles Rd BOR GU35 176 A7
Sidbury Cl ASC SL5 37 K5
Siddeley Dr HSLWW TW4 16 B5
Siddons Rd CROY/NA CR0 67 K2
FSTH SE23 33 H3
Sidestrand Rd ALDT GU11 112 B2
Sideways La HORL RH6 169 M8
The Sidings ALDT GU11 112 F6 3
STA TW18 22 E5
Sidlaws Rd FARN GU14 92 A2
Sidmouth Av ISLW TW7 17 H4
Sidney Gdns BTFD TW8 18 A1 3
Sidney Rd BECK BR3 51 H2
SNWD SE25 50 D5 3
STA TW18 22 D5
TWK TW1 17 K8
WOT/HER KT12 60 E2
Signal Ct LING RH7 174 B4
Silbury Av MTCM CR4 48 B1
Silchester Dr CRAWW RH11 211 K6
Silkham Rd OXTED RH8 130 A1
Silkmore La EHSLY KT24 119 L1
RPLY/SEND GU23 99 J8
Silo Cl RGODL GU7 160 C1
Silo Dr RGODL GU7 160 C1
Silo Rd RGODL GU7 160 C1
Silver Birch Cl ADL/WDHM KT15 78 B2
Silver Birches Wy
MFD/CHID GU8 158 B6
Silver Cl KWD/TDW/WH KT20 105 H6 1
Silverdale SYD SE26 32 F5
Silverdale Av LHD/OX KT22 81 M4
WEY KT13 60 C1
Silverdale Cl
BRKHM/BTCW RH3 145 L4
SUT SM1 65 J3
Silverdale Dr SUN TW16 42 E2
Silver Dr FRIM GU16 73 M6
Silverglade CHSGTN KT9 82 F2
Silverhall St ISLW TW7 17 K5
Silver Hl SHST GU47 72 B1
Silverlands Cl CHERT KT16 58 A2 1
Silver La PUR/KEN CR8 87 G2
WWKM BR4 70 A1
Silverlea Gdns HORL RH6 170 F7
Silverleigh Rd THHTH CR7 49 J4
Silversmiths Wy
WOKN/KNAP GU21 76 F8
Silverstone Cl REDH RH1 126 C6 2
Silver Tree Cl WOT/HER KT12 60 D3 1

Silverwood Cl BECK BR3 ...... 33 K8
  CROY/NA CR0 ...... 69 J7
Silverwood Dr CBLY GU15 ...... 73 K2
Silwood BRAK RG12 ...... 34 B8
Silwood Rd ASC SL5 ...... 37 C2
Silwood Rd ASC SL5 ...... 37 J4
Simmil Rd ESH/CLAY KT10 ...... 62 B4
Simmonds Cl BNFD RG42 ...... 34 B1
Simmondstone La NFNM GU10 .. 178 A7
Simmons Pl STA TW18 ...... 22 B6
Simms Cl CAR SM5 ...... 66 B1
Simone Dr PUR/KEN CR8 ...... 87 M6
Simon Gray Gdns KUTN/CMB KT2 .. 2 D4
Simons Cl CHERT KT16 ...... 57 M5
Simons Wk EGH TW20 ...... 20 F8
Simplemarsh Cl
  ADL/WDHM KT15 ...... 58 D3
Simpson Rd HSLWW TW4 ...... 16 C8
  RCHPK/HAM TW10 ...... 26 F5
Simpson Wy SURB KT6 ...... 44 F6
Sinclair Cl CRAWE RH10 ...... 212 F5
Sinclair Dr BELMT SM2 ...... 65 L7
Sincots Rd REDH RH1 ...... 126 C8
Sine Cl FARN GU14 ...... 92 E1
Single St BH/WHM TN16 ...... 91 L5
Singleton Cl CROY/NA CR0 ...... 4 C1
  WIM/MER SW19 ...... 30 C8
Singleton Rd HORS RH12 ...... 228 A6
Sinhurst Rd CBLY GU15 ...... 72 E5
Sion Rd TWK TW1 ...... 26 E2
Sipson Cl WDR/YW UB7 ...... 14 D1
Sipson La WDR/YW UB7 ...... 14 E1
Sipson Rd WDR/YW UB7 ...... 14 D2
Sir Cyril Black Wy
  WIM/MER SW19 ...... 29 K8
Sirdar Rd MTCM CR4 ...... 30 D7
Siskin Cl HORS RH12 ...... 229 H4
Sissinghurst Cl CRAWE RH10.. 213 G2
Sissinghurst Rd CROY/NA CR0 .. 5 M1
Sistova Rd BAL SW12 ...... 30 E2
Siward Rd TOOT SW17 ...... 29 M4
Six Penny Cl EDEN TN8 ...... 175 M1
Sixth Cross Rd WHTN TW2 ...... 25 M4
Skeena Hl WIM/MER SW19 ...... 29 H1
Skelbrook St WAND/EARL SW18 .. 29 L3
Skelwith Rd HMSMTH W6 ...... 19 M1
Skerne Rd KUTN/CMB KT2 ...... 2 D4
Skeynes Rd EDEN TN8 ...... 153 L8
Skid Hill La WARL CR6 ...... 90 C5
Skiffington Cl
  BRXS/STRHM SW2 ...... 31 K2
Skiff La BIL RH14 ...... 224 D8
Skimpedhill La BRAK RG12 ...... 34 D2
Skinners La ASHTD KT21 ...... 83 C8
  HEST TW5 ...... 16 E3
  MFD/CHID GU8 ...... 202 A4
Skipton Wy HORL RH6 ...... 170 E4
Skyes Dr STA TW18 ...... 22 E6
Skylark Vw HORS RH12 ...... 229 G2
Skyport Dr WDR/YW UB7 ...... 14 A2
Slade Ct CHERT KT16 ...... 58 A5
Slade Rd CHERT KT16 ...... 58 A5
  CHOB/PIR GU24 ...... 95 G2
Slaidburn Gn BRAK RG12 ...... 35 H7
Slattery Rd FELT TW13 ...... 24 F2
Slaugham Ct CRAWW RH11 .. 211 J6
Sleets Rd HORS RH12 ...... 228 B6
Slim Cl ALDT GU11 ...... 113 H2
Slim Rd CBLY GU15 ...... 72 E2
Slines New Rd CTHM CR3 ...... 109 G2
Slines Oak Rd CTHM CR3 ...... 109 K5
Slinfold Wk CRAWW RH11 ...... 211 K2
Slip of Wd CRAN GU6 ...... 185 H3
Slipshatch Rd REIG RH2 ...... 147 J4
Slipshoe St REIG RH2 ...... 125 J8
The Slip BH/WHM TN16 ...... 111 M8
Sloane Gdns ORP BR6 ...... 71 M2
Sloane Wk CROY/NA CR0 ...... 51 J6
Slocock Hl WOKN/KNAP GU21 .. 76 F7
Sloughbrook Cl HORS RH12 .. 229 J3
Slough La BRKHM/BTCW RH3 .. 124 C7
  EPSOM KT18 ...... 103 M7
Slyfield Gn GU GU1 ...... 117 H4
Smallberry Av ISLW TW7 ...... 17 J4
Smallfield Rd HORL RH6 ...... 170 E6
Smallmead HORL RH6 ...... 170 E6
Smalls Hill Rd REIG RH2 ...... 168 F2
Smalls Md CRAWW RH11 ...... 211 M3
Smallwood Rd TOOT SW17 ...... 30 A5
Smart's Heath La
  WOKS/MYFD GU22 ...... 96 D5
Smart's Heath Rd
  WOKS/MYFD GU22 ...... 96 D5
Smeaton Rd WAND/EARL SW18 .. 29 K1
Smitham Bottom La
  PUR/KEN CR8 ...... 87 G2
Smitham Downs Rd
  COUL/CHIP CR5 ...... 87 H2
Smithbarn SWTR RH13 ...... 229 K6
Smithbarn Cl HORL RH6 ...... 170 E5
Smith Cl CRAWE RH10 ...... 212 A6
The Smithers
  BRKHM/BTCW RH3 ...... 145 L2
Smithfield La BOR GU35 ...... 177 K8
Smith Rd REIG RH2 ...... 147 J3
Smiths La EDEN TN8 ...... 131 M7
Smith Sq BRAK RG12 ...... 35 G1
Smith St BYFLS KT5 ...... 45 J6
Smithwood Av CRAN GU6 ...... 184 D2
Smithwood Cl WIM/MER SW19 .. 29 H3
Smithwood Common Rd
  CRAN GU6 ...... 184 E1
Smithy Cl KWD/TDW/WH KT20 .. 105 J8
Smithy La BOR GU35 ...... 177 H7
  KWD/TDW/WH KT20 ...... 105 J8
Smithy's Gn BFOR GU20 ...... 55 G5
Smoke La REIG RH2 ...... 147 L2
Smolletts EGRIN RH19 ...... 215 M1
Smugglers' La HASM GU27 .. 208 B2
Smugglers' Wy NFNM GU10 .. 157 H1
Snailslynch FNM GU9 ...... 134 A7
Snatts Hl OXTED RH8 ...... 130 C3
Snell Hatch CRAWW RH11 ...... 211 L3
Snellings Rd WOT/HER KT12 .. 60 F4
Snipe La HASM GU27 ...... 219 K8
Snowdenham La SHGR GU5 .. 161 G5
Snowdenham Links Rd
  SHGR GU5 ...... 161 G4

Snowdon Rd FARN GU14 ...... 92 B2
Snowdon Rd West HTHAIR TW6.. 14 F8
Snowdown Cl PGE/AN SE20 ...... 50 F1
Snowdrop Cl CRAWW RH11.. 211 K7
  HPTN TW12 ...... 25 K7
Snowdrop Wy CHOB/PIR GU24 .. 75 K7
Snowerhill Rd
  BRKHM/BTCW RH3 ...... 146 C4
Snow Hl CRAWE RH10 ...... 194 C6
Snowhill La CRAWE RH10 ...... 194 C4
Snows Paddock BFOR GU20 ...... 54 E2
Snows Ride BFOR GU20 ...... 54 E2
Snowy Fielder Waye ISLW TW7 .. 17 L4
Snoxhall Fld CRAN GU6 ...... 185 G7
Soames Wk NWMAL KT3 ...... 46 B1
Soane Cl CRAWW RH11 ...... 211 H5
Solartron Rd FARN GU14 ...... 92 D6
Solecote GT/LBKH KT23 ...... 101 K7
Sole Farm Av GT/LBKH KT23 .. 101 J7
Sole Farm Cl GT/LBKH KT23 .. 101 J6
Sole Farm Rd GT/LBKH KT23 .. 101 J7
Solna Av PUT/ROE SW15 ...... 19 M7
Solomons Court BNSTD SM7 .. 86 A7
  COUL/CHIP CR5 ...... 86 C7
Solway Cl HSLWW TW4 ...... 16 B5
Somerfield Cl
  KWD/TDW/WH KT20 ...... 105 H1
Somergate HORS RH12 ...... 228 C7
Somersbury La CRAN GU6.. 186 C7
Somers Ct REIG RH2 ...... 125 K7
Somerset Av CHSGTN KT9 ...... 63 G3
  RYNPK SW20 ...... 46 E2
Somerset Cl HOR/WEW KT19 .. 64 B7
  NWMAL KT3 ...... 46 B6
Somerset Gdns
  STRHM/NOR SW16 ...... 49 J3
  TEDD TW11 ...... 26 B6
Somerset Waye HEST TW5 ...... 16 B1
Somers Pl BRXS/STRHM SW2 .. 31 J1
Somers Rd REIG RH2 ...... 125 K7
Somerswey RGUE GU4 ...... 139 H8
Somerton Av RCH/KEW TW9 .. 18 E5
Somerton Rd PUR/KEN CR8.. 87 K6
Somertons Cl GUW GU2 ...... 116 D4
Somerville Dr CRAWE RH10 .. 192 F8
Somerville Rd COB KT11 ...... 81 K4
  PGE/AN SE20 ...... 33 G8
Sondes Place Dr DORK RH4 .. 144 C2
Sonia Gdns HEST TW5 ...... 16 C2
Sonning Cl SHST GU47 ...... 72 A1
Sonning Gdns HPTN TW12 ...... 25 H7
Sonning Rd CROY/NA CR0...... 50 D6
Soper Dr CTHM CR3 ...... 108 A5
Sopwith Av CHSGTN KT9 ...... 63 H4
Sopwith Cl BH/WHM TN16 ...... 91 C6
  RCHPK/HAM TW10 ...... 27 J6
Sopwith Dr WEY KT13 ...... 79 H1
Sopwith Rd HEST TW5 ...... 15 M2
Sopwith Wy KUTN/CMB KT2.. 2 E5
Sorbie Cl WEY KT13 ...... 59 M5
Sorrel Cl CRAWW RH11 ...... 211 K7
Sorrel Dr LTWR GU18 ...... 74 C2
Sorrel Rd HORS RH12 ...... 229 H4
Sorrento Rd SUT SM1 ...... 65 L2
South Albert Rd REIG RH2 ...... 125 J7
Southampton Gdns
  MTCM CR4 ...... 49 H5
Southampton St FARN GU14 .. 112 E1
South Atlantic Dr ALDT GU11 .. 112 F6
South Av CAR SM5 ...... 66 D6
  EGH TW20 ...... 21 M7
  FNM GU9 ...... 134 A3
  RCH/KEW TW9 ...... 18 D4
  WOT/HER KT12 ...... 60 B8
South Bank SURB KT6 ...... 45 H6
Southbank THDIT KT7 ...... 44 E7
South Bank Ter SURB KT6 .. 45 H6
South Beta Rd FARN GU14 ...... 92 E7
The South Border PUR/KEN CR8.. 87 G1
Southborough Cl SURB KT6 .. 45 G8
Southborough Rd SURB KT6 .. 45 H8
Southborough Road (The Lane)
  SURB KT6 ...... 45 H8
Southbridge Pl CROY/NA CR0.. 4 C9
Southbridge Rd CROY/NA CR0.. 4 C9
Southbrook CRAWW RH11 .. 211 M8
Southbrook Rd
  STRHM/NOR SW16...... 49 H1
South Cl CRAWE RH10 ...... 212 C2
  FELT TW13 ...... 25 K4
  WOKN/KNAP GU21 ...... 76 F6
South Close Gn REIG RH2 .. 126 E3
Southcote WOKN/KNAP GU21 .. 6 B2
Southcote Av BRYLDS KT5 ...... 45 L7
  FELT TW13 ...... 24 D3
Southcote Dr CBLY GU15 ...... 73 K4
Southcote Rd REDH RH1 ...... 126 F4
  SAND/SEL CR2 ...... 68 B8
  SNWD SE25 ...... 50 E5
Southcroft EGH TW20 ...... 20 E6
Southcroft Av WWKM BR4 ...... 69 M1
Southcroft Rd TOOT SW17 ...... 30 A5
South Croxted Rd DUL SE21...... 32 A4
Southdean Gdns
  WIM/MER SW19 ...... 29 J3
Southdown Cl HORS RH12 .. 229 K4
Southdown Dr RYNPK SW20 .. 29 G8
Southdown Rd CAR SM5 ...... 66 D7
  CTHM CR3 ...... 109 J4
  RYNPK SW20 ...... 47 G1
  WOT/HER KT12 ...... 61 H3
South Downs Wy
  BRKHM/BTCW RH3 ...... 124 C4
  DORK RH4 ...... 122 F6
  KWD/TDW/WH KT20 ...... 123 J6
South Dr BELMT SM2 ...... 65 H8
  BNSTD SM7 ...... 86 B3
  CHOB/PIR GU24 ...... 94 F3
  COUL/CHIP CR5 ...... 87 G3
  RDKG RH5 ...... 144 F2
  VW GU25 ...... 38 D7
South Eden Park Rd BECK BR3 .. 51 L5

South End CROY/NA CR0...... 4 D9
  GT/LBKH KT23 ...... 101 L8
Southend La CAT SE6...... 33 J5
Southend Rd BECK BR3...... 33 K8
Southerland Ct WEY KT13 ...... 59 M3
Southern Av EBED/NFELT TW14.. 24 D2
  REDH RH1 ...... 148 B7
  SNWD SE25 ...... 50 C3
Southern Rd CBLY GU15 ...... 72 F3
Southerns La COUL/CHIP CR5 .. 105 M6
Southern Wy FARN GU14 ...... 92 A6
  FNM GU9 ...... 11 H1
Southey Rd WIM/MER SW19 .. 29 K8
Southey St PGE/AN SE20...... 33 G8
South Farm La BAGS GU19 ...... 54 D7
Southfield Pl WEY KT13...... 59 L6
Southfields E/WMO/HCT KT8 .. 44 B6
Southfields Av ASHF TW15 ...... 23 L7
Southfields Rd CTHM CR3...... 109 L5
  GDST RH9 ...... 109 L7
South Gdns WIM/MER SW19 .. 30 A8
South Gate Av FELT TW13 .. 24 A5
Southgate Dr CRAWE RH10.. 212 A5
Southgate Rd CRAWW RH11.. 212 A5
South Gv CHERT KT16 ...... 40 C6
  SWTR RH13 ...... 229 G8
South Hl GU GU1 ...... 9 H7
  RGODL GU7 ...... 160 C5
South Hill Rd BRAK RG12 ...... 34 E6
South Holmes Rd SWTR RH13 .. 229 L5
Southlands EGRIN RH19 ...... 216 B2
Southlands Av HORL RH6 ...... 170 C5
  COUL/CHIP CR5 ...... 87 J7
Southlands Dr WIM/MER SW19 .. 29 G3
Southlands La OXTED RH8 ...... 129 L8
Southlands Rd ASHV GU12 .. 113 K8
South La ASHV GU12 ...... 113 L8
  KUT KT1 ...... 2 D9
  NWMAL KT3 ...... 46 A4
South La West NWMAL KT3 .. 46 A4
South Lodge Av MTCM CR4 .. 49 H4
South Lodge Rd WOT/HER KT12 .. 60 D7
South Lynn Crs BRAK RG12 .. 34 E5
South Md HOR/WEW KT19 .. 64 C6
  REDH RH1 ...... 126 C5
South Meadow CWTH RG45 .. 52 A6
Southmead Rd ALDT GU11 .. 134 E1
  WIM/MER SW19 ...... 29 H2
Southmont Rd ESH/CLAY KT10.. 62 B1
South Munstead La
  MFD/CHID GU8...... 182 E2
South Norwood Hl SNWD SE25 .. 50 B2
South Oak Rd
  STRHM/NOR SW16 ...... 31 K5
South Park Gv NWMAL KT3 .. 45 M4
South Park Hill Rd
  SAND/SEL CR2 ...... 68 A4
South Park La REDH RH1 .. 150 D3
South Park Rd WIM/MER SW19 .. 29 K7
South Pier Rd HORL RH6 ...... 192 D2
South Pl BRYLDS KT5 ...... 45 J7
South Rdg WEY KT13 ...... 59 L8
Southridge Pl RYNPK SW20 .. 29 G8
South Ri CAR SM5 ...... 66 B7
South Rd ASHV GU12 ...... 113 J5
  CHOB/PIR GU24 ...... 75 J6
  CWTH RG45 ...... 52 B6
  ECH TW20 ...... 20 F7
  EWKG RG40 ...... 34 B8
  FELT TW13 ...... 25 G6
  FSTH SE23 ...... 33 G3
  GUW GU2 ...... 116 E6
  HPTN TW12 ...... 25 G7
  REIG RH2 ...... 147 L1
  WEY KT13 ...... 59 M4
  WHTN TW2 ...... 26 A4
  WIM/MER SW19 ...... 30 A7
  WOKN/KNAP GU21 ...... 77 G4
Southsea Rd KUT KT1 ...... 45 H4
Southside Common
  WIM/MER SW19 ...... 29 G7
South Station Ap REDH RH1 .. 149 J2
South St DORK RH4 ...... 144 D3
  EPSOM KT18 ...... 84 A3
  FARN GU14 ...... 93 H4
  FNM GU9 ...... 133 M7
  HORS RH12 ...... 228 F7
  ISLW TW7 ...... 17 K5
  RGODL GU7 ...... 160 A5
  STA TW18 ...... 22 C6
South Ter DORK RH4 ...... 144 E3
  SURB KT6 ...... 45 H6
South V NRWD SE19 ...... 32 B7
South Vale Rd SURB KT6 ...... 63 H1
South View Cl CRAWE RH10 .. 194 B6
South View Rd ASHTD KT21 .. 103 G1
Southview Cl TOOT SW17 ...... 30 D6
Southview Gdns WLGTN SM6.. 66 F6
South View Rd ASHTD KT21 .. 103 G1
Southview Rd CTHM CR3 ...... 108 D1
  WARL CR6 ...... 108 D1
Southviews SAND/SEL CR2 .. 69 G7
Southville Cl EBED/NFELT TW14.. 24 B1
  HOR/WEW KT19 ...... 64 A7
Southville Crs
  EBED/NFELT TW14...... 24 B2
Southville Rd EBED/NFELT TW14.. 24 B2
  THDIT KT7 ...... 44 D7
South Wk ASHV GU12 ...... 113 G7
  WWKM BR4 ...... 70 B2
Southwark Cl CRAWW RH11 .. 211 L7
Southwater Cl BECK BR3 ...... 33 L8
South Wy CAR SM5 ...... 66 A8
Southway CBLY GU15 ...... 72 E5
South Wy CROY/NA CR0 ...... 69 H2
Southway GUW GU2 ...... 8 A1
  RYNPK SW20 ...... 47 G4
  WLGTN SM6 ...... 66 F3
Southwell Park Rd CBLY GU15 .. 72 E4
Southwell Rd CROY/NA CR0 .. 49 K6
South Western Rd TWK TW1 .. 17 L8
Southwick BAGS GU19 ...... 54 B8
Southwick Cl EGRIN RH19 .. 196 A7
Southwick Ct BRAK RG12 ...... 35 H6

Southwold BRAK RG12 ...... 34 B8
  COUL/CHIP CR5 ...... 86 F5
  KUTN/CMB KT2 ...... 45 M1
  WOKN/KNAP GU21 ...... 76 A8
Southwood Av CHERT KT16 .. 57 M6
  COUL/CHIP CR5 ...... 86 F5
  KUTN/CMB KT2 ...... 45 M1
  WOKN/KNAP GU21 ...... 76 A8
Southwood Cha CRAN GU6 .. 185 J8
Southwood Cl WORPK KT4 .. 47 G8
Southwood Dr BRYLDS KT5 .. 45 M7
Southwood Gdns
  ESH/CLAY KT10...... 62 D2
Southwood La FARN GU14 ...... 92 A6
Southwood Rd FARN GU14 .. 92 B5
South Worple Wy
  MORT/ESHN SW14 ...... 19 G5
Sovereign Cl PUR/KEN CR8.. 67 J8
Sovereign Ct E/WMO/HCT KT8 .. 43 J4
Sovereign Dr CBLY GU15 ...... 73 L2
Space Waye EBED/NFELT TW14 .. 15 K7
Spa Cl NRWD SE19 ...... 50 B1
Spa Dr EPSOM KT18 ...... 83 K4
Spa Hl THHTH CR7 ...... 50 A1
Spalding Rd TOOT SW17 ...... 30 E6
Sparks Cl HPTN TW12 ...... 25 H7
Sparrow Cl FELT TW13 ...... 25 H7
Sparrow Farm Dr
  EBED/NFELT TW14 ...... 24 F1
Sparrow Farm Rd EW KT17 .. 64 D3
Sparrowhawk Cl NFNM GU10 .. 133 G1
Sparrow Rw CHOB/PIR GU24 .. 55 L5
Sparrows Md REDH RH1 .. 126 D5
Sparvell Rd WOKN/KNAP GU21.. 95 L1
Speart La HEST TW5 ...... 16 B2
Speedbird Wy WDR/YW UB7 .. 13 L2
Speedwell Cl RGUE GU4 ...... 117 M5
Speedwell Wy HORS RH12 .. 229 H4
Speer Rd THDIT KT7 ...... 44 C6
Speirs Cl NWMAL KT3 ...... 46 C6
Speke Rd THHTH CR7 ...... 50 A2
Spelthorne Gv SUN TW16 ...... 24 C8
Spelthorne La ASHF TW15 ...... 23 M8
Spence Av BF/WBF KT14 ...... 79 H4
Spencer Cl EPSOM KT18 ...... 104 B1
  FRIM GU16 ...... 93 H3
  WOKN/KNAP GU21 ...... 77 M4
Spencer Gdns EGH TW20 ...... 21 G6
  MORT/ESHN SW14 ...... 18 F7
Spencer Hl WIM/MER SW19 .. 29 H7
Spencer Hill Rd WIM/MER SW19.. 29 H8
Spencer Ms DUL SE21 ...... 32 A2
Spencer Pl CROY/NA CR0 ...... 4 F1
Spencer Rd BNFD RG42 ...... 34 C1
  CHSWK W4 ...... 18 F2
  COB KT11 ...... 80 E5
  CTHM CR3 ...... 108 A3
  E/WMO/HCT KT8 ...... 43 M4
  ISLW TW7 ...... 17 G3
  MTCM CR4 ...... 48 D3
  RYNPK SW20 ...... 46 E1
  SAND/SEL CR2 ...... 68 B4
  WHTN TW2 ...... 26 B4
Spenser Av WEY KT13 ...... 59 K7
Spiceall RGUW GU3 ...... 137 L6
Spicer Cl WOT/HER KT12 ...... 42 F6
Spicers Fld LHD/OX KT22 ...... 82 A3
Spices Yd CROY/NA CR0 ...... 4 D9
Spiers Wy HORL RH6 ...... 170 E8
Spindle Wy CRAWE RH10 .. 212 B4
Spindlewood Gdns
  CROY/NA CR0 ...... 4 F9
Spindlewoods
  KWD/TDW/WH KT20 ...... 104 E4
Spinis BRAK RG12 ...... 34 D5
Spinner Gn BRAK RG12 ...... 34 D5
Spinney Cl COB KT11 ...... 81 K1
  CRAWE RH10 ...... 214 F1
  HORS RH12 ...... 229 L3
  NWMAL KT3 ...... 46 B5
  WPK KT4 ...... 64 C2
Spinneycroft LHD/OX KT22 .. 82 A5
Spinney Dr EBED/NFELT TW14 .. 23 M1
Spinney Gdns NRWD SE19 .. 32 C6
Spinney Hl ADL/WDHM KT15 .. 58 A5
Spinney Oak CHERT KT16 .. 58 A5
The Spinney ASC SL5 ...... 37 H5
  CBLY GU15 ...... 73 M3
  CHEAM SM3 ...... 64 F3
  CRAWW RH11 ...... 211 L5
  EPSOM KT18 ...... 104 E1
  GSHT GU26 ...... 198 D5
  GT/LBKH KT23 ...... 101 L6
  HASM GU27 ...... 219 M1
  HORL RH6 ...... 170 D4
  LHD/OX KT22 ...... 81 M1
  PUR/KEN CR8 ...... 87 L3
  STRHM/NOR SW16 ...... 31 G4
  SUN TW16 ...... 42 D1
The Spinning Wk SHGR GU5 .. 141 H3
Spital Heath RDKG RH5 ...... 144 F1
Spitfire Wy FARN GU14 ...... 112 B1
Spoil La NFNM GU10 ...... 135 J2
Spokane Cl ALDT GU11 ...... 134 C1
Spook Hl RDKG RH5 ...... 144 F1
Spooners Rd HORS RH12 .. 229 K5
Spooner Wk WLGTN SM6 ...... 67 G4
Sportsbank St CAT SE6 ...... 33 M1
Spout Hl CROY/NA CR0 ...... 69 K4
Spout La EDEN TN8 ...... 131 M8
  STWL/WRAY TW19 ...... 13 K7
Spout La North
  STWL/WRAY TW19 ...... 13 L6
Spratts La ADL/WDHM KT15 .. 58 F5
Spreighton Rd E/WMO/HCT KT8.. 43 J4
Spring Bottom La REDH RH1 .. 127 M1
Springbourne Ct BECK BR3 .. 51 M1
Springclose La CHEAM SM3 .. 65 H5
Spring Copse CRAWE RH10 .. 193 M6
Spring Copse Rd REIG RH2 .. 147 M3
Springcross Av BLKW GU17 .. 72 A5
Springfarm Rd HASM GU27 .. 219 H4
Springfield EGRIN RH19 ...... 196 A5
  LTWR GU18 ...... 74 F1
  OXTED RH8 ...... 130 A4
Springfield Av HPTN TW12 .. 25 L7

RYNPK SW20 ...... 47 J3
Springfield Cl WOKN/KNAP GU21.. 76 A8
Springfield Crs HORS RH12 .. 228 E7
Springfield Gdns WWKM BR4.. 69 L1
Springfield Gv SUN TW16 ...... 42 D7
Springfield La WEY KT13 ...... 59 L3
Springfield Mdw WEY KT13 ...... 59 L3
Springfield Park Rd
  HORS RH12 ...... 228 E7
Springfield Pl NWMAL KT3 ...... 45 M4
Springfield Ri SYD SE26 ...... 32 E5
Springfield Rd ASHF TW15 ...... 23 J6
  ASHV GU12 ...... 113 K4
  CBLY GU15 ...... 73 K4
  CRAWW RH11 ...... 211 M4
  DORK RH4 ...... 143 L3
  DTCH/LGLY SL3 ...... 12 E2
  EDEN TN8 ...... 153 L8
  EW KT17 ...... 64 F8
  GU GU1 ...... 9 J5
  HORS RH12 ...... 228 E7
  KUT KT1 ...... 2 F9
  SYD SE26 ...... 32 E6
  TEDD TW11 ...... 26 D6
  THHTH CR7 ...... 49 M1
  WHTN TW2 ...... 25 K2
  WIM/MER SW19 ...... 29 J6
  WLGTN SM6 ...... 66 E4
Springfields Ct CHERT KT16 .. 40 E8
Springfields Wy MFD/CHID GU8 .. 158 B6
Spring Gdns ASC SL5 ...... 36 E4
  BH/WHM TN16 ...... 90 F8
  CBLY GU15 ...... 73 K4
  CRAWE RH10 ...... 193 M6
  E/WMO/HCT KT8 ...... 43 M1
  FARN GU14 ...... 92 D2
  WLGTN SM6 ...... 66 F4
Spring Gv GT/LBKH KT23 ...... 101 L5
  HPTN TW12 ...... 43 L1
  MTCM CR4 ...... 48 D1
  RGODL GU7 ...... 160 B1
Spring Grove Crs HEST TW5 .. 16 F3
Spring Grove Rd HSLW TW5 .. 16 F3
  HSLW TW3 ...... 18 C7
Springhaven Cl GU GU1 ...... 117 K8
Springhill MFD/CHID GU8 ...... 158 B6
Spring Hl SYD SE26 ...... 32 F5
Springholm Cl BH/WHM TN16 .. 90 F8
Springhurst Cl CROY/NA CR0 .. 69 J3
Spring La FNM GU9 ...... 133 K2
  OXTED RH8 ...... 130 A1
  SNWD SE25 ...... 50 E6
  SWTR RH13 ...... 226 F6
Spring La West FNM GU9 ...... 133 K3
Spring Meadow BRAK RG12 .. 35 G1
  FROW RH18 ...... 217 J8
Spring Park Av CROY/NA CR0.. 69 G1
Springpark Dr BECK BR3 ...... 51 M3
Spring Park Rd CROY/NA CR0.. 69 G1
Spring Plat CRAWE RH10 ...... 212 F3
Spring Ri EGH TW20 ...... 21 H7
Spring Rd FELT TW13 ...... 24 C4
Spring St EW KT17 ...... 64 C7
Spring Wy EGRIN RH19 ...... 196 B5
Springwell Rd HEST TW5 ...... 16 A3
  RDKG RH5 ...... 167 G6
  STRHM/NOR SW16 ...... 31 K5
Springwood MFD/CHID GU8 .. 159 K8
Spring Woods VW GU25 ...... 38 E4
Sprucedale Gdns CROY/NA CR0.. 69 G3
  PUR/KEN CR8 ...... 67 H7
Spruce Dr LTWR GU18 ...... 74 D2
Spruce Rd BH/WHM TN16 ...... 91 G6
Spur Dr KWD/TDW/WH KT20.. 105 L3
Spurfield E/WMO/HCT KT8 .. 43 L3
Spurgeon Av NRWD SE19 ...... 50 A1
Spurgeon Cl CRAWW RH11 .. 211 M2
Spurgeon Rd NRWD SE19 ...... 32 A8
Spur Rd EBED/NFELT TW14 .. 15 L7
  ISLW TW7 ...... 17 K2
Spurs Ct ALDT GU11 ...... 112 B7
The Spur WOKN/KNAP GU21 .. 75 L8
Spy La BIL RH14 ...... 224 D5
Square Dr HASM GU27 ...... 219 L8
The Square BH/WHM TN16 .. 110 F2
  CAR SM5 ...... 66 D4
  CRAWW RH11 ...... 212 A2
  GU GU2 ...... 138 C2
  LING RH7 ...... 173 M5
  RCHPK/HAM TW10 ...... 18 B7
  WDR/YW UB7 ...... 13 L3
Squeary St TOOT SW17 ...... 29 M4
Squerryes Mede
  BH/WHM TN16 ...... 131 M1
Squire's Bridge Rd SHPTN TW17 .. 41 J4
Squires Cl CRAWE RH10 ...... 214 D1
Squires Ct WIM/MER SW19 .. 29 K5
Squires Hill La NFNM GU10 .. 156 F4
Squire's Rd SHPTN TW17 ...... 41 J4
Squires Wk ASHF TW15 ...... 24 A8
Squirrel Cl CRAWW RH11 .. 191 L8
  HSLWW TW4 ...... 15 M5
Squirrel La FARN GU14 ...... 92 D4
Squirrels Cl RGODL GU7 ...... 138 A3
Squirrels Gn GT/LBKH KT23 .. 101 K5
  WPK KT4 ...... 64 C1
Squirrel's Wy EPSOM KT18 .. 84 A5
Squirrel Wd BF/WBF KT14 .. 78 E2
Stable Cl CRAWE RH10 ...... 213 G6
Stable Cft BAGS GU19 ...... 54 A7
Stable Ms REIG RH2 ...... 125 K8
  WNWD SE27 ...... 31 M6
Stables End ORP BR6 ...... 71 M2
The Stables COB KT11 ...... 81 J4
Stacey's Farm Rd
  MFD/CHID GU8 ...... 158 A6
Stackfield Rd CRAWW RH11 .. 211 H4
Staff College Rd CBLY GU15 .. 72 E3
Staffhurst Wood Rd
  OXTED RH8 ...... 152 F3
Stafford Cl CHEAM SM3 ...... 65 H5
  CTHM CR3 ...... 108 C5
Stafford Gdns CROY/NA CR0 .. 67 J4
Stafford Pl RCHPK/HAM TW10 .. 27 J1
Stafford Rd CRAWW RH11 .. 191 K8
  CROY/NA CR0 ...... 67 K3
  CTHM CR3 ...... 108 C5

NWMAL KT3 45 M3
WLGTN SM6 66 F5
Staffords Pl HORL RH6 170 E7
Staff Rd ASHV GU12 112 F7
Stagbury Av COUL/CHIP CR5 86 B8
Stagbury Cl COUL/CHIP CR5 106 B1 1
Stagelands CRAWW RH11 211 L1
Stag Hl GUW GU2 8 B5
Stag La PUT/ROE SW15 28 C4
Stag Leys ASHTD KT21 103 H2
Stag Leys Cl BNSTD SM7 86 B5
Stags Wy ISLW TW7 17 J1
Stainash Crs STA TW18 22 E6
Stainbank Rd MTCM CR4 48 E3
Staines Av CHEAM SM3 65 G1
Staines By-pass
STWL/WRAY TW19 22 B4
Staines La CHERT KT16 40 D6 3
Staines Lane Cl CHERT KT16 40 C5 1
Staines Rd CHERT KT16 40 D4
EBED/NFELT TW14 24 A1
HSLWW TW4 16 A7
STA TW18 40 E1
STWL/WRAY TW19 21 J2
WHTN TW2 25 M4
Staines Rd East SUN TW16 42 F1
Staines Rd West ASHF TW15 23 M8
Stainford Cl ASHF TW15 24 A6
Staiths Wy
KWD/TDW/WH KT20 104 E2 3
Stake La FARN GU14 92 D5
Stakescorner Rd RGUW GU3 138 D8
Stambourne Wy NRWD SE19 32 B8
WWKM BR4 69 M2
Stamford Av FRIM GU16 73 J8 3
Stamford Green Rd
EPSOM KT18 83 L3
Stamford Rd WOT/HER KT12 61 G2 3
Stanborough Cl HPTN TW12 25 J7 7
Stanborough Rd ISLW TW7 17 G5 1
Stanbridge Cl CRAWW RH11 211 H3 5
Stanbridge Rd EDEN TN8 153 L7
PUT/ROE SW15 19 M5 2
Standard Rd HSLWW TW4 16 B5
ORP BR6 71 K8
Standen Cl EGRIN RH19 195 K6
Standen Pl HORS RH12 229 K2
Standen Rd WAND/EARL SW18 29 K1
Standinghall La CRAWE RH10 213 K7
Standon La RDKG RH5 187 H7
Stane Cl WIM/MER SW19 29 L8 3
Stane St RDKG RH5 187 M7
SWTR RH13 226 E8
Stane Wy EW KT17 64 D8
Stanford Cl HPTN TW12 25 J7 8
Stanford Orch HORS RH12 228 C1 1
Stanford Rd STRHM/NOR SW16 49 H2
Stanfords Pl LING RH7 174 A6
The Stanfords EW KT17 84 C2 4
Stanford Wy HORS RH12 228 A6
STRHM/NOR SW16 49 G2
Stanger Rd SNWD SE25 50 D4
Stangrove Rd EDEN TN8 153 M8
Stan Hl HORL RH6 190 F1
Stanhope Gv BECK BR3 51 J5
Stanhope Heath
STWL/WRAY TW19 13 M8 2
Stanhope Rd CAR SM5 66 D6
CBLY GU15 72 C5
CROY/NA CR0 5 G8
Stanhopes OXTED RH8 130 E2
Stanhope Wy
STWL/WRAY TW19 13 M8 3
Stanier Cl CRAWE RH10 212 E4 1
Staniland Dr WEY KT13 79 J1
Stanley Av BECK BR3 51 M3
NWMAL KT3 46 D5
Stanley Cl COUL/CHIP CR5 87 J7
CRAWE RH10 212 B5
Stanleycroft Cl ISLW TW7 17 H3 4
Stanley Gdns MTCM CR4 30 D7 5
SAND/SEL CR2 88 D2 1
WLGTN SM6 66 F5
WOT/HER KT12 60 F4
Stanley Gardens Rd TEDD TW11 26 B6
Stanley Gv THHTH CR7 49 K6
Stanley Hl CHOB/PIR GU24 94 F4
Stanley Park Rd CAR SM5 66 C6
WLGTN SM6 66 E6
Stanley Rd ASHF TW15 23 H6
BELMT SM2 65 L5
CAR SM5 66 D6
CROY/NA CR0 49 K7
HSLW TW3 16 F6
MORT/ESHN SW14 18 E6
MRDN SM4 47 K4
MTCM CR4 30 D8
TEDD TW11 26 B6
WHTN TW2 26 A4
WIM/MER SW19 29 K8
WOKN/KNAP GU21 6 F4
Stanley Sq CAR SM5 66 C7
Stanley St CTHM CR3 107 M4
Stanmore Cl ASC SL5 36 D4 1
Stanmore Gdns
RCH/KEW TW9 18 C5 3
SUT SM1 65 M2 2
Stanmore Rd RCH/KEW TW9 18 C5
Stanmore Ter BECK BR3 51 K2 3
Stannet Wy WLGTN SM6 66 F3
Stansfield Rd HSLWW TW4 15 L4
Stanstead Gv FSTH SE23 33 J2 2
Stanstead Rd CTHM CR3 108 B6
FSTH SE23 33 G2
Stanthorpe Rd
STRHM/NOR SW16 31 H6
Stanton Av TEDD TW11 26 B7
Stanton Cl CRAN GU6 184 E6
HOR/WEW KT19 63 L4
WPK KT4 47 G8 2
Stanton Rd BARN SW13 19 J4
CROY/NA CR0 4 C2
RYNPK SW20 47 G2
Stantons Whf SHGR GU5 161 K2
Stanton Wy SYD SE26 33 J5
Stanwell Cl STWL/WRAY TW19 14 A8 3
Stanwell Gdns
STWL/WRAY TW19 14 A8
Stanwell Moor Rd
STWL/WRAY TW19 22 E3
WDR/YW UB7 13 L3
Stanwell New Rd STA TW18 22 E5
Stanwell Rd ASHF TW15 23 H4
DTCH/LGLY SL3 12 E5
EBED/NFELT TW14 23 L1
Staplecross Ct CRAWW RH11 211 J7
Stapleford Cl KUT KT1 3 K7
WIM/MER SW19 29 H1
Staple Hl CHOB/PIR GU24 56 A5
Staplehurst BRAK RG12 34 B7
Staplehurst Cl REDH RH1 147 M4
Staplehurst Rd CAR SM5 66 B6
REDH RH1 147 M4
Staple La RGUE GU4 141 J1
Stapleton Gdns CROY/NA CR0 67 K4
Stapleton Rd TOOT SW17 30 D4
Star And Garter Hl
RCHPK/HAM TW10 27 H2
Starborough Rd EDEN TN8 175 H5
Star Hl NFNM GU10 178 A7
WOKS/MYFD GU22 96 F1
Star Hill Dr NFNM GU10 178 A6
Star La ASHV GU12 113 J7
COUL/CHIP CR5 106 D4
Star Post Rd CBLY GU15 73 H1
Star Rd ISLW TW7 17 G4
Starrock La COUL/CHIP CR5 106 D2
Starrock Rd COUL/CHIP CR5 106 E1
Starts Cl ORP BR6 71 K2
Starts Hill Av ORP BR6 71 M4 3
Starts Hill Rd ORP BR6 71 L2
Starwood Cl BF/WBF KT14 78 F1 3
State Farm Av ORP BR6 71 L3
Staten Gdns TWK TW1 26 C2
Statham Ct BNFD RG42 34 B1
Station Ap ASHF TW15 23 J5 5
ASHV GU12 113 K2
BECK BR3 33 H8 1
BELMT SM2 65 H6 3
BELMT SM2 65 L8 5
BF/WBF KT14 78 D2
CAT SE6 33 J6
COUL/CHIP CR5 86 C8
COUL/CHIP CR5 87 G6
CTHM CR3 88 D7
DORK RH4 122 F8
EDEN TN8 153 M8
EHSLY KT24 100 B8
ESH/CLAY KT10 62 C2
EW KT17 64 E8 1
GU GU1 9 J5
HOR/WEW KT19 64 D4 1
HOR/WEW KT19 84 A3
HORL RH6 170 E6
HPTN TW12 43 K1
KUTN/CMB KT2 3 K5
LHD/OX KT22 102 D3 1
MFD/CHID GU8 201 J1
OXTED RH8 130 B3
PUR/KEN CR8 87 K1 2
RCH/KEW TW9 18 D3 3
RGODL GU7 160 A5 3
SAND/SEL CR2 68 A7 2
SHPTN TW17 41 M5 3
STA TW18 22 D5 1
STRHM/NOR SW16 31 G6
SUN TW16 42 D1
SURB KT6 45 H6 5
VW GU25 39 G4
WEY KT13 59 K5
WOKS/MYFD GU22 6 E6
WPK KT4 46 D8 3
Station Ap East REDH RH1 148 C2 2
Station Approach Rd
CHSWK W4 18 F2
COUL/CHIP CR5 87 G5
HORL RH6 192 E1 1
KWD/TDW/WH KT20 104 F4
Station Ap West REDH RH1 148 C2 3
Station Av CTHM CR3 108 D6
HOR/WEW KT19 64 B7
NWMAL KT3 46 B3 2
WOT/HER KT12 60 C3
Station Cl HPTN TW12 43 L1
SWTR RH13 229 G7
Station Crs ASHF TW15 23 G5
Station Est BECK BR3 51 G4 1
Station Estate Rd
EBED/NFELT TW14 24 E2
Station Gdns CHSWK W4 18 F2 4
Station Hl ASC SL5 36 D3
CRAWE RH10 212 E2
FNM GU9 133 M7
HAYES BR2 70 D1
Station La MFD/CHID GU8 181 L3
MFD/CHID GU8 201 H1
Station Pde RCH/KEW TW9 18 D3
VW GU25 39 G4
Station Ri WNWD SE27 31 L3 3
Station Rd ADL/WDHM KT15 58 F3
ADL/WDHM KT15 59 G3 5
ALDT GU11 112 E7
ASC SL5 37 K6
ASHF TW15 23 J5
BAGS GU19 54 B5
BELMT SM2 65 K8
BF/WBF KT14 78 D2
BIL RH14 224 C6
BRAK RG12 34 E3
BRKHM/BTCW RH3 124 B5
CAR SM5 66 C3
CHERT KT16 40 C8
CHOB/PIR GU24 76 C2
CHSGTN KT9 63 H4
COB KT11 81 H7
CRAWE RH10 212 A4 1
CRAWE RH10 214 E1
CROY/NA CR0 4 C4
CTHM CR3 88 C8
CTHM CR3 109 H4
DORK RH4 144 C1
EDEN TN8 153 M6
EDEN TN8 153 L1
EGH TW20 21 K6
EGRIN RH19 196 A8
ESH/CLAY KT10 62 A4
FARN GU14 92 E5
FRIM GU16 72 F8
FROW RH18 217 J6
GDST RH9 151 H4
HORL RH6 170 E6
HORS RH12 205 L7
HORS RH12 226 A2
HORS RH12 228 E1
HPTN TW12 43 L1
HSLW TW3 16 E6
KUT KT1 2 C4
KUTN/CMB KT2 3 J5
LHD/OX KT22 102 D3
LING RH7 174 B4
NRWD SE19 32 D7 2
NWMAL KT3 46 E5
PGE/AN SE20 32 F7
PUR/KEN CR8 87 M4
REDH RH1 126 C7
REDH RH1 126 F2
RGODL GU7 160 C2
RGODL GU7 160 A5
RGUE GU4 139 H6
SHGR GU5 142 A5
SHGR GU5 161 J2
SHPTN TW17 41 M5
SNWD SE25 50 C4
STWL/WRAY TW19 12 C8
SUN TW16 24 D8 1
SWTR RH13 229 H7
TEDD TW11 26 D7
THDIT KT7 44 C7
TWK TW1 26 C2
WIM/MER SW19 47 M1
WWKM BR4 51 M8
Station Rd East ASHV GU12 113 J2
OXTED RH8 130 B3
Station Rd North REDH RH1 126 F2
Station Rd South REDH RH1 126 F2
Station Rd West OXTED RH8 130 B3
Station Rw RGUE GU4 139 H6
Station Vw ASHV GU12 113 K1
GU GU1 8 E5
Station Wy CHEAM SM3 65 H5
CRAWE RH10 212 A4
Station Yd TWK TW1 26 D1 7
Staunton Rd KUTN/CMB KT2 2 F1
Staveley Gdns CHSWK W4 19 G3
Staveley Rd ASHF TW15 24 A7 4
CHSWK W4 19 G2
Staveley Wy WOKN/KNAP GU21 76 B7
Stavordale Rd CAR SM5 47 M7
Stayne End VW GU25 38 D4
Stayton Rd SUT SM1 65 K2
Steadfast Rd KUT KT1 2 D5
Steam Farm La
EBED/NFELT TW14 15 J6 1
Steele Rd ISLW TW7 17 K6
Steeles Rd ALDT GU11 112 E5
Steel's La LHD/OX KT22 81 L4
Steep Hl CHOB/PIR GU24 55 M6
CROY/NA CR0 5 G9
STRHM/NOR SW16 31 G4
Steeple Cl WIM/MER SW19 29 H5
Steeple Heights Dr
BH/WHM TN16 91 G7
Steepways GSHT GU26 198 E3
Steeres Hl HORS RH12 209 M2
Steerforth Copse SHST GU47 52 B7 4
Steerforth St WAND/EARL SW18 29 L3
Steers La CRAWE RH10 192 F5
Steers Md MTCM CR4 48 C1
Stella Rd TOOT SW17 30 C7
Stembridge Rd PGE/AN SE20 50 E2
The Stennings EGRIN RH19 195 M6
Stepgates CHERT KT16 40 E7
Stepgates Cl CHERT KT16 40 E7 1
Stephen Cl CRAWW RH11 192 A8 9
EGH TW20 21 M7
Stephendale Rd FNM GU9 134 A5
Stephenson Dr EGRIN RH19 216 C3
Stephenson Pl CRAWE RH10 212 E3
Stephenson Rd HSLWW TW4 25 K1 7
Stephenson Wy CRAWE RH10 212 E3
Stepney Cl CRAWE RH10 212 F5 10
Sterling Av SHPTN TW17 42 B3
Sternhold Av BRXS/STRHM SW2 31 H3
Sterry Dr HOR/WEW KT19 64 B3
THDIT KT7 44 B6
Steucers La FSTH SE23 33 H2 1
Steve Biko La CAT SE6 33 K5
Steve Biko Wy HSLW TW3 16 D5
Stevenage Rd CRAWW RH11 211 H7
Stevens Cl BECK BR3 33 K7 3
EW KT17 84 B2 7
HPTN TW12 25 J7
Stevens' La ESH/CLAY KT10 62 D6
Stevens Pl PUR/KEN CR8 87 L3 1
Stewart KWD/TDW/WH KT20 105 G3
Stewart Av SHPTN TW17 41 K4
Stewart Cl HPTN TW12 25 H7
WOKN/KNAP GU21 76 C7 3
Steyning Cl CRAWE RH10 212 B1
PUR/KEN CR8 87 L6
Steyning Wy HSLWW TW4 15 M6
Sthrathbrook Rd
STRHM/NOR SW16 31 J8
Stile Gdns HASM GU27 219 J3
Stile Pth SUN TW16 42 D3 2
Stillingfleet Rd BARN SW13 19 K2
Stirling Cl BNSTD SM7 85 J7
CRAWE RH10 212 E4
FARN GU14 92 D6
FRIM GU16 73 H7 4
STRHM/NOR SW16 48 F1
Stirling Gv HSLW TW3 16 F4
Stirling Rd WHTN TW2 25 K1
Stirling Wy EGRIN RH19 196 E6
FARN GU14 112 A2
SWTR RH13 229 H7
Stirrup Wy CRAWE RH10 213 G2
Stites Hill Rd CTHM CR3 107 L2
Stoatley Hollow HASM GU27 219 K1
Stoatley Ri HASM GU27 219 K1
Stoats Nest Rd COUL/CHIP CR5 87 H5
Stockbridge Dr ALDT GU11 134 F3
Stockbury Rd CROY/NA CR0 50 F6
Stockers La WOKS/MYFD GU22 97 J2
Stockfield HORL RH6 170 E5 17
Stockfield Rd ESH/CLAY KT10 62 B4 3
STRHM/NOR SW16 31 J4
Stockhams Cl SAND/SEL CR2 68 A8 2
Stock Hl BH/WHM TN16 91 G6
Stockhurst Cl PUT/ROE SW15 19 M4 1
Stockport Rd STRHM/NOR SW16 49 G1
Stocks Cl HORL RH6 170 E7
Stockton Rd REIG RH2 147 K3
Stockwell Rd EGRIN RH19 216 B3
Stockwood Ri CBLY GU15 73 J4
Stockwood Wy FNM GU9 134 C2 1
Stocton Cl GU GU1 8 F2
Stocton Rd GU GU1 9 G2
Stodart Rd PGE/AN SE20 50 F1
Stoford Cl WIM/MER SW19 29 H2 6
Stoke Cl COB KT11 81 J6
Stoke Flds GU GU1 9 H4
Stokeford Cl BRAK RG12 35 J5 7
Stoke Gv GU GU1 9 H4
Stoke Hills FNM GU9 133 M6
Stoke Ms GU GU1 9 H4
Stoke Rd COB KT11 81 H6
GU GU1 9 H3
KUTN/CMB KT2 27 M8
WOT/HER KT12 60 F2
Stokesby Rd CHSGTN KT9 63 J5
Stokes Cl CRAWE RH10 212 F5 11
Stokesheath Rd LHD/OX KT22 81 M1
Stokes Ridings
KWD/TDW/WH KT20 105 G5 1
Stokes Rd CROY/NA CR0 51 G6 4
Stompond La WOT/HER KT12 60 D1
Stonards Brow SHGR GU5 162 A5
Stondon Pk FSTH SE23 33 H1
Stonebanks WOT/HER KT12 42 D7
Stonebridge Flds RGUE GU4 139 G7
Stonebridge Whf RGUE GU4 139 G7
Stonecot Cl MRDN SM4 47 H8
Stonecot Hl CHEAM SM3 47 H8 1
MRDN SM4 47 J7 2
Stonecourt Cl HORL RH6 170 F6
Stone Crs EBED/NFELT TW14 24 C1
Stonecroft Wy CROY/NA CR0 49 H7
Stonecrop Cl CRAWW RH11 211 L6 6
Stonecrop Rd GU GU1 117 M6
Stonedene Cl FROW RH18 217 L7
Stonefield Cl CRAWE RH10 212 A4
Stonegate CBLY GU15 73 M3
Stone Hatch CRAN GU6 204 D6
Stonehill Cl GT/LBKH KT23 101 K7
MORT/ESHN SW14 19 G7
Stonehill Crs CHERT KT16 57 H5
Stonehill Rd CHERT KT16 57 H5
CHOB/PIR GU24 57 G6
LTWR GU18 54 D8
MORT/ESHN SW14 18 F7
Stonehills Ct DUL SE21 32 B4
Stone House Gdns CTHM CR3 108 B7
Stonehouse Ri FRIM GU16 73 H8
Stonehouse Rd LIPH GU30 218 A5
Stoneleigh Av WPK KT4 64 D2
Stoneleigh Broadway
EW KT17 64 D4 2
Stoneleigh Cl EGRIN RH19 196 C7 1
Stoneleigh Ct FRIM GU16 73 J8
Stoneleigh Crs HOR/WEW KT19 64 D4
Stoneleigh Pk WEY KT13 59 M5 2
Stoneleigh Park Av
CROY/NA CR0 51 G6
Stoneleigh Park Rd
HOR/WEW KT19 64 C5
Stoneleigh Rd CAR SM5 48 B7
OXTED RH8 131 H4
Stone Park Av BECK BR3 51 K4
Stonepark Dr FROW RH18 217 K7
Stonepit Cl RGODL GU7 159 L5
Stone Pl WPK KT4 64 D1
Stoners Cl HORL RH6 192 A1
Stones La DORK RH4 143 M3
Stone's Rd EW KT17 84 B1
Stone St ASHV GU12 135 G1
CROY/NA CR0 67 K4
Stoneswood Rd OXTED RH8 130 E4
Stoney Bottom GSHT GU26 198 F6
Stoney Brook GUW GU2 116 B7
Stoneybrook HORS RH12 228 C8
Stoneyfield Rd COUL/CHIP CR5 87 J7
Stoneyfields FNM GU9 11 L2
Stoneyland Ct EGH TW20 21 J6 4
Stoneylands Rd EGH TW20 21 J6
Stoney La NRWD SE19 32 C7 4
Stoney Rd BNFD RG42 34 D1
Stonny Cft ASHTD KT21 83 J7
Stony Hl ESH/CLAY KT10 61 J6
Stopham Rd CRAWE RH10 212 F6
Stormont Wy CHSGTN KT9 62 F4
Storrington Rd CROY/NA CR0 5 K3
Storr's La RGUW GU3 95 M6
Stoughton Av CHEAM SM3 65 G4
Stoughton Cl PUT/ROE SW15 28 D2 6
Stoughton Rd GUW GU2 116 D5
Stour Cl HAYES BR2 70 F3
Stourhead Cl FARN GU14 93 G5
WIM/MER SW19 29 G1 3
Stourhead Gdns RYNPK SW20 46 D3 1
Stourton Av FELT TW13 25 J5
Stovolds Hl CRAN GU6 184 A8
Stovold's Wy ALDT GU11 134 C1
Stowell Av CROY/NA CR0 70 A8
Strachan Pl RYNPK SW20 28 F7
Strafford Rd HSLW TW3 16 C5
TWK TW1 26 D1 3
Strand Cl CRAWE RH10 213 G5 6
EPSOM KT18 104 A1
Strand-on-the-green
CHSWK W4 18 D1
Stratfield BRAK RG12 34 B8
Stratford Ct NWMAL KT3 46 A4 2
Stratford Rd ASHV GU12 113 J1
THHTH CR7 49 K4
Strathavon Cl CRAN GU6 184 E2
Strathcona Av EHSLY KT24 121 H2
Strathcona Gdns
WOKN/KNAP GU21 96 A1
Strathdale STRHM/NOR SW16 31 J6
Strathdon Dr TOOT SW17 30 A4
Strathearn Av HYS/HAR UB3 15 J2 1
WHTN TW2 25 M2
Strathearn Rd SUT SM1 65 K4
WIM/MER SW19 29 K6
Strathmore Cl CTHM CR3 108 B3
Strathmore Rd CRAWW RH11 191 K8
CROY/NA CR0 4 D2
TEDD TW11 26 B5
WIM/MER SW19 29 K4 2
Strathville Rd WAND/EARL SW18 29 L3
Strathyre Av STRHM/NOR SW16 49 K3
Stratton Av WLGTN SM6 67 G7
Stratton Cl HEST TW5 16 C3
WIM/MER SW19 47 J2
WOT/HER KT12 42 F8 9
Stratton Rd SUN TW16 42 C2
WIM/MER SW19 47 K2
Stratton Ter BH/WHM TN16 131 M1 3
Stratton Wk FARN GU14 92 D2 3
Strawberry Cl CHOB/PIR GU24 95 G3
Strawberry Flds CHOB/PIR GU24 75 K5
Strawberry Hill Rd TWK TW1 26 C4
Strawberry La CAR SM5 66 C2
Strawberry Ri
CHOB/PIR GU24 75 K5 6
Strawberry V TWK TW1 26 C4
Straw Cl CTHM CR3 107 M5
Stream Cl BF/WBF KT14 79 H2
Stream Farm Cl NFNM GU10 11 J6
Stream Pk EGRIN RH19 195 K6
Stream Valley Rd NFNM GU10 11 G7
Streatham Common North
STRHM/NOR SW16 31 J6
Streatham Common South
STRHM/NOR SW16 31 H7
Streatham Ct STRHM/NOR SW16 31 H4
Streatham High Rd
STRHM/NOR SW16 31 H5
Streatham Hl BRXS/STRHM SW2 31 H2
Streatham Pl BRXS/STRHM SW2 31 H1
Streatham Rd MTCM CR4 48 C1
Streatham V STRHM/NOR SW16 30 F8
Streathbourne Rd TOOT SW17 30 D3
Streeters Cl RGODL GU7 160 D3
Streeters La WLGTN SM6 67 G2
Streetfield Rd SWTR RH13 227 G6
Street Hl CRAWE RH10 213 H4
Streets Heath CHOB/PIR GU24 75 J1
The Street ASHTD KT21 83 J8
BIL RH14 223 H7
BRKHM/BTCW RH3 124 A8
CRAN GU6 186 A3
EHSLY KT24 119 L2
EHSLY KT24 121 G2
HORL RH6 191 H2
LHD/OX KT22 102 A4
MFD/CHID GU8 159 G2
MFD/CHID GU8 179 M5
NFNM GU10 10 A7
NFNM GU10 135 J4
NFNM GU10 177 H3
NFNM GU10 177 M2
RDKG RH5 189 G3
RGUE GU4 118 D4
RGUE GU4 119 G5
RGUE GU4 139 G5
RGUW GU3 136 E5
RGUW GU3 137 L7
SHGR GU5 161 K2
SWTR RH13 227 G5
Stretton Rd CROY/NA CR0 5 H1
RCHPK/HAM TW10 26 F3
Strickland Cl CRAWW RH11 211 H4 12
Strickland Rw WAND/EARL SW18 30 A1
Stringer's Av RGUE GU4 117 G2
Stringhams Copse
RPLY/SEND GU23 98 C6
Strodes College La EGH TW20 21 J6 5
Strode St EGH TW20 21 K5
Strood La HORS RH12 227 M2
Stroud Crs PUT/ROE SW15 28 C4
Stroude Rd EGH TW20 21 K7
VW GU25 39 H3
Stroudes Cl WPK KT4 46 C7 2
Stroud Green Wy
CROY/NA CR0 50 F6 5
Stroud La SHGR GU5 162 D7
Stroudley Cl CRAWE RH10 212 E4 2
Stroud Rd SNWD SE25 50 D6
WIM/MER SW19 29 K4
Stroudwater Pk WEY KT13 59 L5
Stroud Wy ASHF TW15 23 L7
Strudgate Cl CRAWE RH10 212 E5 5
Strudwicks Fld CRAN GU6 185 J5 2
Stuart Av WOT/HER KT12 42 F8
Stuart Cl CRAWE RH10 213 G4 3
FARN GU14 92 D4
Stuart Crs CROY/NA CR0 69 J2
REIG RH2 147 K3
Stuart Gv TEDD TW11 26 B6
Stuart Pl MTCM CR4 48 C1
Stuart Rd RCHPK/HAM TW10 26 E3
REIG RH2 147 K3
THHTH CR7 49 M4
WARL CR6 108 E2
WIM/MER SW19 29 K4
Stuart Wy EGRIN RH19 216 C1
STA TW18 22 E7
VW GU25 38 D4
Stubbs Folly SHST GU47 72 A2
Stubbs La KWD/TDW/WH KT20 125 J2
Stubbs Moor Rd FARN GU14 92 C4
Stubbs Wy WIM/MER SW19 48 A1 3
Stubfield HORS RH12 228 D6
Stubpond La LING RH7 195 G2
Stubs Cl DORK RH4 144 F4
Stubs Hl DORK RH4 144 F4
Stucley Rd ISLW TW7 16 F2
Studios Rd SHPTN TW17 41 J3
Studland Rd BF/WBF KT14 79 J3 5
KUTN/CMB KT2 2 F1
SYD SE26 33 G6
Stumblets CRAWE RH10 212 F2 2
Stumps Hill La BECK BR3 33 K7
Sturdee Cl FRIM GU16 73 H8
Sturt Av HASM GU27 219 J4
Sturt Ct GU GU1 117 L6
Sturt Rd FNM GU9 133 L2
FRIM GU16 93 J4

HASM GU27 .... 219 K5
Sturt's La KWD/TDW/WH KT20 .. 124 C1
Stychens Cl REDH RH1 .... 127 M7
Stychens La REDH RH1 .... 127 M7
Styles End GT/LBKH KT23 .... 121 L1 🇯
Styles Wy BECK BR3 .... 51 M4
Styventon Pl CHERT KT16 .... 40 C7 🇯
Succomb's HI CTHM CR3 .... 108 E2
Succombs Pl WARL CR6 .... 108 E1
Sudbrook Gdns
    RCHPK/HAM TW10 .... 27 H4
Sudbrook La RCHPK/HAM TW10 .... 27 H2
Sudbury Gdns CROY/NA CR0 .... 5 H9
Suffield Cl SAND/SEL CR2 .... 89 G2
Suffield La RGUW GU3 .... 158 C1
Suffield Rd PGE/AN SE20 .... 50 F2
Suffolk Cl BAGS GU19 .... 54 B7 🇯
    HORL RH6 .... 170 D7 🇯
Suffolk Dr RGUE GU4 .... 117 L3
Suffolk Rd BARN SW13 .... 19 J2
    SNWD SE25 .... 50 C4
    WPK KT4 .... 64 C1
Sugden Rd THDIT KT7 .... 44 E8
Sulina Rd BRXS/STRHM SW2 .... 31 H1
Sullington HI CRAWW RH11 .... 212 A5 🇯
Sullington Md HORS RH12 .... 228 B6
Sullivan Cl E/WMO/HCT KT8 .... 43 K3
    FARN GU14 .... 92 E5 🇯
Sullivan Dr CRAWW RH11 .... 211 H6
Sullivan Rd CBLY GU15 .... 72 D4
Sullivans Reach
    WOT/HER KT12 .... 42 C7 🇯
    WOT/HER KT12 .... 42 D7 🇯
Sultan St BECK BR3 .... 51 G2
Summer Cl E/WMO/HCT KT8 .... 44 B5
Summerene Cl
    STRHM/NOR SW16 .... 30 F8 🇯
Summerfield ASHTD KT21 .... 103 G1 🇯
Summerfield La NFNM GU10 .... 155 K7
    SURB KT6 .... 63 G1
Summerfields Cl
    ADL/WDHM KT15 .... 58 D4 🇯
Summer Gdns CBLY GU15 .... 73 M4
    E/WMO/HCT KT8 .... 44 B5
Summerhayes Cl
    WOKN/KNAP GU21 .... 77 H4
Summerhays COB KT11 .... 81 G3
Summerhill Wy MTCM CR4 .... 48 D1 🇯
Summerhouse Av HEST TW5 .... 16 B3
Summerhouse Cl RGODL GU7 .... 160 A6
Summerhouse La WDR/YW UB7 .... 14 A1
Summerhouse Rd RGODL GU7 ...... 160 A6
Summerlands CRAN GU6 .... 185 H5
Summerlay Cl
    KWD/TDW/WH KT20 .... 105 H3
Summerley St
    WAND/EARL SW18 .... 29 L3
Summerly Av REIG RH2 .... 125 K7
Summer Rd E/WMO/HCT KT8 .... 44 A5 🇯
    THDIT KT7 .... 44 C5
Summersbury Dr RGUE GU4 .... 139 H8
Summers Cl BELMT SM2 .... 65 K6
    WEY KT13 .... 79 K1
Summers La RGODL GU7 .... 159 K1
Summer's Rd RGODL GU7 .... 160 C2 🇯
Summerstown TOOT SW17 .... 29 M4
Summersvere Cl CRAWE RH10 ...... 192 D8
Summerswood Cl PUR/KEN CR8 .... 88 A6
Summer Trees SUN TW16 .... 42 E1 🇯
Summerville Gdns SUT SM1 .... 65 J5
Summerwood Rd TWK TW1 .... 17 J8
Summit Wy NRWD SE19 .... 32 B8
Sumner Cl LHD/OX KT22 .... 102 A6
    ORP BR6 .... 71 M7 🇯
Sumner Gdns CROY/NA CR0 .... 49 K8
Sumner Pl ADL/WDHM KT15 .... 58 D4
Sumner Rd CROY/NA CR0 .... 4 A3
    FNM GU9 .... 133 M6
Sumner Rd South CROY/NA CR0 .... 49 K8
Summnit Pl WEY KT13 .... 59 K6 🇯
Sun Brow HASM GU27 .... 219 J4
Sunbury Av MORT/ESHN SW14 ..... 19 G6
Sunbury Cl SUN TW16 .... 43 G2
Sunbury Court Rd SUN TW16 .... 42 F2
Sunbury La WOT/HER KT12 .... 42 D6
Sunbury Rd CHEAM SM3 .... 65 G2
    FELT TW13 .... 24 C4
Sunbury Wy FELT TW13 .... 24 F6
Suncroft Pl SYD SE26 .... 32 F4
Sundale Av SAND/SEL CR2 .... 68 F8
Sunderland Rd FSTH SE23 .... 33 G2
Sundew Cl CRAWW RH11 .... 211 K7 🇯
    LTWR GU18 .... 75 C1
Sundial Av SNWD SE25 .... 50 C2
Sundon Crs VW GU25 .... 38 E5
Sundown Av SAND/SEL CR2 .... 88 C1
Sundown Rd ASHF TW15 .... 23 M6 🇯
Sundridge Rd CROY/NA CR0 .... 5 K3
    WOKS/MYFD GU22 .... 97 K1
Sun HI WOKS/MYFD GU22 .... 96 C3
Sun Inn Rd MFD/CHID GU8 .... 203 J4
Sunkist Wy WLGTN SM6 .... 67 H7
Sunlight Cl WIM/MER SW19 .... 29 M7 🇯
Sunmead Cl LHD/OX KT22 .... 102 C4
Sunmead Rd SUN TW16 .... 42 D3
Sunna Gdns SUN TW16 .... 42 E2
Sunning Av ASC SL5 .... 37 H7
Sunningdale Av FELT TW13 .... 25 H3
Sunningdale Cl SURB KT6 .... 63 H1 🇯
Sunningdale Ct
    CRAWW RH11 .... 212 A5 🇯
Sunningdale Rd SUT SM1 .... 65 J2
Sunninghill Cl ASC SL5 .... 37 G5
Sunninghill Rd ASC SL5 .... 37 G5
    BFOR GU20 .... 54 D2
Sunningvale Av BH/WHM TN16 ..... 90 F7
Sunningvale Cl BH/WHM TN16 ...... 91 G7
Sunny Av CRAWE RH10 .... 214 D1
Sunnybank ASC SL5 .... 36 D4 🇯
Sunny Bank EPSOM KT18 .... 83 M6
    SNWD SE25 .... 50 D3
    WARL CR6 .... 89 H7
Sunnybank Rd FARN GU14 .... 92 A3
Sunnycroft Rd HSLW TW3 .... 16 F4
    SNWD SE25 .... 50 D5
Sunnydale ORP BR6 .... 71 K1
Sunnydell La FNM GU9 .... 10 C8
Sunnydene Rd PUR/KEN CR8 .... 87 L1

Sunnydene St SYD SE26 .... 33 H5
Sunny Down MFD/CHID GU8 .... 181 H5
Sunny HI MFD/CHID GU8 .... 181 H4
Sunnyhill Cl CRAWE RH10 .... 214 D1 🇯
Sunny Hill Rd ALDT GU11 .... 112 A7
Sunnyhill Rd STRHM/NOR SW16 .... 31 H5
Sunnyhurst Cl SUT SM1 .... 65 K2 🇯
Sunnymead CRAWW RH11 .... 212 A3
Sunnymead Av MTCM CR4 .... 49 G3 🇯
Sunnymead Rd PUT/ROE SW15 ..... 19 L7
Sunnymede Av CAR SM5 .... 86 A1
    HOR/WEW KT19 .... 64 B7
Sunny Nook Gdns
    SAND/SEL CR2 .... 68 A5 🇯
Sunny Ri CTHM CR3 .... 108 A6
Sunnyside WIM/MER SW19 .... 29 H7
    WOT/HER KT12 .... 42 F5
Sunnyside Rd TEDD TW11 .... 26 A5
Sunray Av BRYLDS KT5 .... 63 L1
Sunrise Cl FELT TW13 .... 25 J4 🇯
Sunset Gdns SNWD SE25 .... 50 C2 🇯
Sunshine Wy MTCM CR4 .... 48 C2
Sunvale Av HASM GU27 .... 219 G3
Sunvale Cl HASM GU27 .... 219 G3 🇯
Surbiton Crs SURB KT6 .... 45 H4
Surbiton Hall Cl KUT KT1 .... 45 H4 🇯
Surbiton Hill Pk BRYLDS KT5 .... 45 J3
Surbiton Hill Rd SURB KT6 .... 45 H4
Surbiton Rd CBLY GU15 .... 53 K8
    KUT KT1 .... 45 G4
Surrey Av CBLY GU15 .... 72 D5
Surrey Gdns COB KT11 .... 100 C5
Surrey Gv SUT SM1 .... 66 A2
Surrey Hills Av
    KWD/TDW/WH KT20 .... 123 M5 🇯
Surrey Hills Wy
    KWD/TDW/WH KT20 .... 123 M4
Surrey Ms WNWD SE27 .... 32 B5 🇯
Surrey Rd WWKM BR4 .... 51 L8
Surrey St CROY/NA CR0 .... 4 C6
Surridge Ct BAGS GU19 .... 54 B7 🇯
Surridge Gdns NRWD SE19 .... 32 A7 🇯
Sussex Av ISLW TW7 .... 17 H5
Sussex Border Pth
    CRAWE RH10 .... 194 A7
    EDEN TN8 .... 197 M1
    EGRIN RH19 .... 196 D8
    HASM GU27 .... 220 C8
    HORL RH6 .... 191 M1
    HORS RH12 .... 209 M2
    MFD/CHID GU8 .... 221 J4
    RDKG RH5 .... 207 H4
Sussex Cl NWMAL KT3 .... 46 B4
    REIG RH2 .... 142 A1
    TWK TW1 .... 17 L8 🇯
    WOKN/KNAP GU21 .... 75 M8 🇯
Sussex Ct WOKN/KNAP GU21 .... 75 M7
Sussex Gdns CHSGTN KT9 .... 63 G5
Sussex Pl NWMAL KT3 .... 46 B4
Sussex Rd CAR SM5 .... 66 C5
    MTCM CR4 .... 49 H5 🇯
    NWMAL KT3 .... 46 B4 🇯
    SAND/SEL CR2 .... 68 A5
    WOKN/KNAP GU21 .... 75 M8
    WWKM BR4 .... 51 L8 🇯
Sutherland Av BH/WHM TN16 ...... 91 G7
    RGUE GU4 .... 117 G2
    SUN TW16 .... 42 C2
Sutherland Cha ASC SL5 .... 36 B2
Sutherland Dr GU GU1 .... 117 K5
    WIM/MER SW19 .... 48 A1
Sutherland Gdns
    MORT/ESHN SW14 .... 19 H5 🇯
    SUN TW16 .... 42 C2 🇯
    WPK KT4 .... 46 E8 🇯
Sutherland Gv TEDD TW11 .... 26 B6
    WAND/EARL SW18 .... 29 J1
Sutherland Rd CHSWK W4 .... 19 H1
    CROY/NA CR0 .... 49 K7
Sutton Av WOKN/KNAP GU21 .... 96 B1
Sutton Cl BECK BR3 .... 51 L1 🇯
Sutton Common Rd CHEAM SM3 ... 47 J7
Sutton Ct BELMT SM2 .... 65 M6
Sutton Court Rd BELMT SM2 .... 65 M5
    CHSWK W4 .... 18 F1
    SUT SM1 .... 65 M5 🇯
Sutton Dene HSLW TW3 .... 16 E3
Sutton Gdns CROY/NA CR0 .... 50 C5 🇯
    REDH RH1 .... 127 G3
Sutton Green Rd RGUE GU4 .... 97 H8
Sutton Gv SUT SM1 .... 66 A4
Sutton Hall HEST TW5 .... 16 D2
Sutton La BELMT SM2 .... 85 L2
    BNSTD SM7 .... 85 L5
    DTCH/LGLY SL3 .... 12 E1
    HSLW TW3 .... 16 C4
    RDKG RH5 .... 164 E1
Sutton La South CHSWK W4 .... 18 F1
Sutton Park Rd SUT SM1 .... 65 L5
Sutton Pl DTCH/LGLY SL3 .... 12 E1
    SHGR GU5 .... 164 C1
Sutton Rd CBLY GU15 .... 53 K8
    HEST TW5 .... 16 D3
Sutton Sq HEST TW5 .... 16 C3
Sutton Wy HEST TW5 .... 16 C3
Swaby Rd WAND/EARL SW18 .... 29 M3
Swaffield Rd WAND/EARL SW18 .... 29 M1
Swain Cl TOOT SW17 .... 30 E7
Swain Rd THHTH CR7 .... 49 M5
Swains Rd MTCM CR4 .... 30 C8
Swaledale BRAK RG12 .... 34 D5
Swaledale Cl CRAWW RH11 .... 211 M6 🇯
Swale Rd FARN GU14 .... 92 A3
Swallands Rd CAT SE6 .... 33 K4
Swallow Cl MFD/CHID GU8 .... 181 H2 🇯
    STA TW18 .... 22 C5
Swallowdale SAND/SEL CR2 .... 69 G7
Swallowfield EGH TW20 .... 20 E7 🇯
    LING RH7 .... 174 D7 🇯
Swallow Gdns
    STRHM/NOR SW16 .... 31 G6 🇯
Swallow La RDKG RH5 .... 144 E8
Swallow Ri WOKN/KNAP GU21 ...... 76 C6 🇯
Swallowtail Rd HORS RH12 .... 229 H3
Swan Cl FELT TW13 .... 25 H5
Swancote Gn BRAK RG12 .... 34 E5 🇯

Swan Ct GU GU1 .... 117 G6
Swan La EDEN TN8 .... 153 M5
    GU GU1 .... 9 G6
    HORL RH6 .... 191 J2
Swan Mill Gdns DORK RH4 .... 122 F6
Swanns Meadow
    GT/LBKH KT23 .... 101 K8
    CAR SM5 .... 66 D4
    FNM GU9 .... 10 E3
    ISLW TW7 .... 17 K6
    LING RH7 .... 174 A6
    WHTN TW2 .... 26 C2 🇯
Swan Wk HORS RH12 .... 228 B6
Swan Wk SHPTN TW17 .... 42 B7
Swanwick Cl PUT/ROE SW15 .... 28 C1
Swanwick La RDKG RH5 .... 122 E2
Swaynesland Rd OXTED RH8 .... 131 J8
Swayne's La GU GU1 .... 118 B8
Sweeps Ditch Cl STA TW18 .... 40 D1
Sweeps La EGH TW20 .... 21 J6
Sweet La SHGR GU5 .... 164 A1
Sweetwater Cl SHGR GU5 .... 162 A5
Sweetwater La MFD/CHID GU8 .... 181 K6
    SHGR GU5 .... 162 A5
Swievelands Rd BH/WHM TN16 ... 110 E1
Swift La BAGS GU19 .... 54 C6
    CRAWW RH11 .... 212 A1
Swift Rd FELT TW13 .... 25 G5
    FNM GU9 .... 133 L2
Swift's Cl NFNM GU10 .... 134 E8
Swinburne Crs CROY/NA CR0 .... 50 E6
Swinburne Rd PUT/ROE SW15 ...... 19 K6
Swindon Rd HORS RH12 .... 228 E5
    HTHAIR TW6 .... 14 F8 🇯
Swinfield Cl FELT TW13 .... 25 H5 🇯
Swingate Rd FNM GU9 .... 11 J4
Swinley Rd ASC SL5 .... 35 M4
Swires Shaw HAYES BR2 .... 71 J3
Swiss Cl NFNM GU10 .... 155 J5
Swissland HI EGRIN RH19 .... 196 B3
Switchback La NFNM GU10 .... 155 J5 🇯
Swordfish Wy FARN GU14 .... 112 B2
Sycamore Av HORS RH12 .... 229 M4
    RCHPK/HAM TW10 .... 18 E5 🇯
Sycamore Cl CAR SM5 .... 66 C3
    CRAWW RH11 .... 191 M8
    FELT TW13 .... 24 D4
    FRIM GU16 .... 73 H8
    LHD/OX KT22 .... 102 C4
Sycamore Ct WEY KT13 .... 60 C2 🇯
Sycamore Dr ASHV GU12 .... 113 J2
    EGRIN RH19 .... 196 D8
    FRIM GU16 .... 73 H7
    NFNM GU10 .... 10 D8
Sycamore Gdns MTCM CR4 .... 48 A2 🇯
Sycamore Gv NWMAL KT3 .... 46 B3
    PGE/AN SE20 .... 50 D1 🇯
Sycamore Ri BNSTD SM7 .... 85 G4 🇯
    BRAK RG12 .... 35 G3
Sycamore Rd FARN GU14 .... 92 F7
    GU GU1 .... 9 G3
    WIM/MER SW19 .... 28 F7
The Sycamores FARN GU14 .... 93 G6
Sycamore Wk EGH TW20 .... 20 E7
    REIG RH2 .... 147 M3
Sycamore Wy TEDD TW11 .... 26 E7
Sydenham Av SYD SE26 .... 32 E6
Sydenham HI EDUL SE22 .... 32 D4
    SYD SE26 .... 32 D4
Sydenham Pk SYD SE26 .... 32 F3
Sydenham Park Rd SYD SE26 .... 32 F4
Sydenham Ri FSTH SE23 .... 32 F3
Sydenham Rd CROY/NA CR0 .... 4 D5
    SYD SE26 .... 33 G6
Sydenham Station Ap
    SYD SE26 .... 32 F5 🇯
Sydney Av PUR/KEN CR8 .... 87 J2 🇯
Sydney Crs ASHF TW15 .... 23 L7
Sydney Pl GU GU1 .... 9 L6
Sydney Rd EBED/NFELT TW14 ..... 24 D2 🇯
    GU GU1 .... 9 L6
    RCH/KEW TW9 .... 18 B6 🇯
    RYNPK SW20 .... 47 G2
    SUT SM1 .... 65 K3
    TEDD TW11 .... 26 C6 🇯
Sydney Smith Av FARN GU14 .... 92 E8
Sylvan Cl OXTED RH8 .... 130 E3
    SAND/SEL CR2 .... 68 E8
    WOKS/MYFD GU22 .... 7 K7
Sylvan Gdns SURB KT6 .... 45 G7
Sylvan HI NRWD SE19 .... 50 B1
Sylvan Rd CRAWE RH10 .... 212 D5
    NRWD SE19 .... 50 C1
Sylvanus BRAK RG12 .... 34 C7
Sylvan Wy REDH RH1 .... 148 E1
    WWKM BR4 .... 70 B3
Sylvaways Cl CRAN GU6 .... 185 K6
Sylverdale Rd CROY/NA CR0 .... 4 A7
    PUR/KEN CR8 .... 87 L3
Sylvia Cl CHOB/PIR GU24 .... 75 K5
Syon Gate Wy BTFD TW8 .... 17 K2
Syon La BTFD TW8 .... 17 L2
    ISLW TW7 .... 17 L2
Syon Park Gdns ISLW TW7 .... 17 J2
Syon Pl FARN GU14 .... 93 G5 🇯
Sythwood WOKN/KNAP GU21 .... 76 E7
Szabo Crs RGUW GU3 .... 114 E8

T

Tabarin Wy EW KT17 .... 84 F6
Tabor Gdns CHEAM SM3 .... 65 H5
Tabor Gv WIM/MER SW19 .... 29 H8
Tachbrook Rd
    EBED/NFELT TW14 .... 24 C1
Tadmor Cl SUN TW16 .... 42 C4
Tadorne Rd
    KWD/TDW/WH KT20 .... 104 F3
Tadworth Av NWMAL KT3 .... 46 C5 🇯
Tadworth Cl
    KWD/TDW/WH KT20 .... 105 G4 🇯
Tadworth St
    KWD/TDW/WH KT20 .... 104 F5
Taffy's How MTCM CR4 .... 48 B3 🇯

Tait Rd CROY/NA CR0 .... 5 G1
Talbot Cl FRIM GU16 .... 93 K5
    REIG RH2 .... 147 L1
Talbot La HORS RH12 .... 228 F8 🇯
Talbot Pl BAGS GU19 .... 54 B6
Talbot Rd ASHF TW15 .... 23 G6
    CAR SM5 .... 66 D4
    FNM GU9 .... 10 E3
    ISLW TW7 .... 17 K6
    LING RH7 .... 174 A6
    WHTN TW2 .... 26 C2 🇯
Taleworth Cl ASHTD KT21 .... 103 G2
Taleworth Pk ASHTD KT21 .... 103 G2
Taleworth Rd ASHTD KT21 .... 103 G1
Talgarth Dr FARN GU14 .... 93 G7
Talisman Sq SYD SE26 .... 32 D5 🇯
Talisman Wy EW KT17 .... 84 F6
Tallis Cl CRAWW RH11 .... 211 J6
    STRHM/NOR SW16 .... 49 J3
Tally Rd OXTED RH8 .... 131 H5
Talma Gdns WHTN TW2 .... 26 B1
Talmage Cl FSTH SE23 .... 32 F1 🇯
Talman Cl CRAWW RH11 .... 211 H4 🇯🇯
Tamar Cl CRAWE RH10 .... 212 F4 🇯
Tamarind Cl GUW GU2 .... 116 D3
Tamerton Sq WOKS/MYFD GU22 .... 6 C9
Tamesis Gdns WPK KT4 .... 64 B1 🇯
Tamian Wy HSLWW TW4 .... 15 M6
Tamworth BRAK RG12 .... 35 G7
Tamworth La MTCM CR4 .... 48 E3
Tamworth Pk MTCM CR4 .... 48 E4
Tamworth Pl CROY/NA CR0 .... 4 C6 🇯
Tamworth Rd CROY/NA CR0 .... 4 C5
Tanbridge Pk HORS RH12 .... 228 D8
Tanbridge Pl HORS RH12 .... 228 E8
Tandridge Gdns SAND/SEL CR2 .... 88 C3
Tandridgehill La GDST RH9 .... 129 J2
Tandridge La LING RH7 .... 173 J1
    OXTED RH8 .... 129 K7
Tandridge Rd WARL CR6 .... 109 G1
Tanfield Rd CROY/NA CR0 .... 4 C9
Tangier Rd GU GU1 .... 139 K1
    RCHPK/HAM TW10 .... 18 E5 🇯
Tangier Wy KWD/TDW/WH KT20 .. 85 H7
Tangier Wd KWD/TDW/WH KT20 .. 85 H8
Tangle Oak EGRIN RH19 .... 195 H5
Tanglewood Cl CHERT KT16 .... 56 E2
    CROY/NA CR0 .... 68 F2
    WOKS/MYFD GU22 .... 78 A6
Tanglewood Ride
    CHOB/PIR GU24 .... 75 G2
Tanglewood Wy FELT TW13 .... 24 E4 🇯
Tangley La PUT/ROE SW15 .... 28 E1
Tangley La RGUW GU3 .... 116 A8
Tangley Park Rd HPTN TW12 .... 25 J6 🇯
Tanglyn Av SHPTN TW17 .... 41 K5
Tangmere Gv KUTN/CMB KT2 ...... 27 G6 🇯
Tangmere Rd CRAWW RH11 .... 211 J3
Tanhouse Rd OXTED RH8 .... 130 A6
Tanhurst La RDKG RH5 .... 165 J7
Tanker Rd FARN GU14 .... 92 E8
Tankerton Rd SURB KT6 .... 63 J1
Tankerville Rd
    STRHM/NOR SW16 .... 31 G8
Tank Rd CBLY GU15 .... 72 C4
Tanners Cl WOT/HER KT12 .... 42 E6
Tanners Dean LHD/OX KT22 .... 103 G4
Tannersfield SHGR GU5 .... 139 H8
Tanner's HI BRKHM/BTCW RH3 ... 145 L2
Tanners La HASM GU27 .... 219 M2
Tanners Md EDEN TN8 .... 153 M8
Tanners Meadow
    BRKHM/BTCW RH3 .... 145 L4
Tannery Cl CROY/NA CR0 .... 51 G5
    SWTR RH13 .... 226 F6
Tannery La RPLY/SEND GU23 .... 98 B4
The Tannery REDH RH1 .... 126 B8
Tannsfeld Rd SYD SE26 .... 33 G6
Tansy Cl RGUE GU4 .... 117 M6
Tantallon Rd BAL SW12 .... 30 D2
Tanyard Av EGRIN RH19 .... 216 D1
Tanyard Cl CRAWE RH10 .... 212 F6
    SWTR RH13 .... 229 H8
Tanyard La SHGR GU5 .... 161 J2
Tanyard Wy HORL RH6 .... 170 E5
Tapestry Cl BELMT SM2 .... 65 L6
Taplow Ct MTCM CR4 .... 48 B4
Tapner's Rd REIG RH2 .... 146 C6
Tapping Cl KUTN/CMB KT2 .... 3 J3
Tara Pk COUL/CHIP CR5 .... 106 C2
Tarbat Ct SHST GU47 .... 72 A1 🇯
Target Cl EBED/NFELT TW14 .... 15 H8
Tarham Cl HORL RH6 .... 170 B4
Tarleton Gdns FSTH SE23 .... 32 E2 🇯
Tarmac Wy WDR/YW UB7 .... 13 L2
Tarnbrook Wy BRAK RG12 .... 35 H7
Tarn Cl FARN GU14 .... 92 B7
Tarn Rd GSHT GU26 .... 199 C6
Tarragon Dr GUW GU2 .... 116 D3
Tarragon Gv SYD SE26 .... 33 G7
Tarrington Cl
    STRHM/NOR SW16 .... 31 G4 🇯
Tartar HI COB KT11 .... 80 E3
Tartar Rd COB KT11 .... 80 F3
Tasker Cl HYS/HAR UB3 .... 14 F2
Tate Cl LHD/OX KT22 .... 102 F5
Tate Rd SUT SM1 .... 65 K4
Tates Wy HORS RH12 .... 226 A2
Tatsfield La BH/WHM TN16 .... 111 J3
Tattenham Corner Rd
    EPSOM KT18 .... 84 D8
Tattenham Crs EPSOM KT18 .... 84 D8
Tattenham Gv EPSOM KT18 .... 84 E8
    KWD/TDW/WH KT20 .... 104 E1
Tattenham Wy
    KWD/TDW/WH KT20 .... 85 H7
Taunton Av CTHM CR3 .... 108 C5
    HSLW TW3 .... 16 F4
    RYNPK SW20 .... 46 E2
Taunton Cl CHEAM SM3 .... 47 K8
Taunton La COUL/CHIP CR5 .... 107 L1
Tavern Cl CAR SM5 .... 48 C8
Tavistock Cl STA TW18 .... 23 G8 🇯
Tavistock Crs MTCM CR4 .... 49 H4
Tavistock Gdns FARN GU14 .... 92 E2
Tavistock Gv CROY/NA CR0 .... 4 E2

Tavistock Rd CAR SM5 .... 48 A8
    CROY/NA CR0 .... 4 E4
Tawfield BRAK RG12 .... 34 B7
Tawny Cl FELT TW13 .... 24 D4
Tawny Av WHTN TW2 .... 17 H8 🇯
Tay Cl FARN GU14 .... 92 B3
Tayles Hill Dr EW KT17 .... 84 C8
Taylor Av RCH/KEW TW9 .... 18 E4
Taylor Cl HPTN TW12 .... 25 M6
    HSLW TW3 .... 16 F3
Taylor Rd ASHTD KT21 .... 83 G7
    WIM/MER SW19 .... 30 B8
    WLGTN SM6 .... 66 E4
Taylors Ct FELT TW13 .... 24 E3 🇯
Taylors Crs CRAN GU6 .... 185 J6
Taylor's La SYD SE26 .... 32 E5
Taymount Ri FSTH SE23 .... 32 F3
Taynton Dr REDH RH1 .... 127 G4
Teal Cl HORS RH12 .... 228 F4
    SAND/SEL CR2 .... 89 G1
Tealing Dr HOR/WEW KT19 .... 64 A3
Teasel Cl CRAWW RH11 .... 211 L6
    CROY/NA CR0 .... 51 G8
Teazlewood Pk LHD/OX KT22 .... 82 D7
Tebbit Cl BRAK RG12 .... 35 G2 🇯
Teck Cl ISLW TW7 .... 17 K4
Tedder Cl CHSGTN KT9 .... 62 F4 🇯
Tedder Rd SAND/SEL CR2 .... 69 G6
Teddington Cl HOR/WEW KT19 .... 64 A8
Teddington Pk TEDD TW11 .... 26 C6
Teddington Park Rd TEDD TW11 ... 26 C5
Tedham La GDST RH9 .... 172 E2
Tees Cl FARN GU14 .... 92 B3
Teesdale CRAWW RH11 .... 211 M6
Teesdale Av ISLW TW7 .... 17 K3
Teesdale Gdns ISLW TW7 .... 17 K3
    SNWD SE25 .... 50 B2 🇯
Teevan Cl CROY/NA CR0 .... 5 M1
Teevan Rd CROY/NA CR0 .... 5 M2
Tegg's La WOKS/MYFD GU22 .... 78 C6
Tekels Av CBLY GU15 .... 73 G5
Tekels Wy CBLY GU15 .... 73 J6
Telegraph La ESH/CLAY KT10 .... 62 C3
Telegraph Rd PUT/ROE SW15 .... 28 F1 🇯
Telegraph Tr WLGTN SM6 .... 86 D1
Telferscot Rd BAL SW12 .... 31 G2
Telford Av BAL SW12 .... 31 G2
    BRXS/STRHM SW2 .... 31 H2
Telford Cl NRWD SE19 .... 32 C7 🇯
Telford Dr WOT/HER KT12 .... 42 F7
Telford Pl CRAWE RH10 .... 212 B4
Telford Rd HSLWW TW4 .... 25 K1 🇯
Telham Ct CRAWW RH11 .... 211 J6 🇯
Tellisford ESH/CLAY KT10 .... 61 L3
Temperley Rd BAL SW12 .... 30 D1
Tempest Rd EGH TW20 .... 21 M7
Templar Pl HPTN TW12 .... 25 K8
Temple Av CROY/NA CR0 .... 69 J2
Temple Bar Rd
    WOKN/KNAP GU21 .... 96 C1
Temple Cl CRAWE RH10 .... 213 G4
Templecombe Ms
    WOKS/MYFD GU22 .... 7 H4 🇯
Templecombe Wy MRDN SM4 ..... 47 H5
Templecroft ASHF TW15 .... 24 A7 🇯
Templedene Av STA TW18 .... 22 E8
Temple Field Cl
    ADL/WDHM KT15 .... 58 E5
Temple Gdns STA TW18 .... 40 C1
Temple La RDKG RH5 .... 189 H3
Templeman Cl PUR/KEN CR8 .... 87 K6
Temple Rd HOR/WEW KT19 .... 84 A2
    HSLW TW3 .... 16 E6
    RCH/KEW TW9 .... 18 C4
Temple's Cl NFNM GU10 .... 134 F8
Temple Sheen Rd
    MORT/ESHN SW14 .... 18 F6
Templeton Cl THHTH CR7 .... 50 A1
Temple Wy BNFD RG42 .... 34 B1
    SUT SM1 .... 66 A2
Ten Acre WOKN/KNAP GU21 .... 76 D8 🇯
Ten Acre La EGH TW20 .... 39 M2
Ten Acres LHD/OX KT22 .... 102 A6
Tenbury Ct BAL SW12 .... 31 G2
Tenby Dr ASC SL5 .... 37 G5
Tenby Rd FRIM GU16 .... 93 K1
Tenchley's La OXTED RH8 .... 131 G5
Tenham Av BRXS/STRHM SW2 ...... 31 G3
Tenniel Cl GUW GU2 .... 116 E6
Tennison Cl COUL/CHIP CR5 ...... 107 L2
Tennison Rd SNWD SE25 .... 50 C4
Tennyson Av NWMAL KT3 .... 46 E5
    TWK TW1 .... 26 C2
Tennyson Cl CRAWE RH10 .... 212 E1
    EBED/NFELT TW14 .... 15 K8 🇯
    HORS RH12 .... 229 H3
Tennyson Ri EGRIN RH19 .... 195 M8
Tennyson Rd ADL/WDHM KT15 ... 59 H3
    ASHF TW15 .... 23 H6
    HSLW TW3 .... 16 F4
    PGE/AN SE20 .... 33 G8
    WIM/MER SW19 .... 29 M7
Tennyson's La HASM GU27 .... 220 B5
Tenterden Gdns CROY/NA CR0 .... 5 M1
Tenterden Rd CROY/NA CR0 .... 5 M1
Tern Rd CRAWW RH11 .... 211 G4
Terrace Gdns BARN SW13 .... 19 J4 🇯
Terrace La RCHPK/HAM TW10 ...... 18 B8
Terrace Rd WOT/HER KT12 .... 42 E7
The Terrace ADL/WDHM KT15 ..... 59 H4 🇯
    ASC SL5 .... 37 G3 🇯
    BARN SW13 .... 19 H4
    CBLY GU15 .... 72 C4
    CWTH RG45 .... 52 A4
Terra Cotta Rd GDST RH9 .... 150 F4
Terrapin Rd TOOT SW17 .... 30 E4
Terry Rd CRAWW RH11 .... 211 L8
Testard Rd GUW GU2 .... 8 E7
Testers Cl OXTED RH8 .... 130 C5
Teviot Cl GUW GU2 .... 116 D5
Tewkesbury Av FSTH SE23 .... 32 E2
Tewkesbury Cl BF/WBF KT14 .... 79 G1
Tewkesbury Rd CAR SM5 .... 48 A8
Thackeray Cl ISLW TW7 .... 17 K4 🇯
    WIM/MER SW19 .... 29 G8 🇯
Thakeham Cl SYD SE26 .... 32 E6 🇯
Thames Av CHERT KT16 .... 40 D4
Thames Bank MORT/ESHN SW14 .. 18 F4

Thames CI *CHERT* KT16 .... 40 E7
HPTN TW12 .... 43 L2
Thames Down Link *ASHTD* KT21 .. 83 K6
CHSGTN KT9 .... 63 M3
EPSOM KT18 .... 83 J4
WPK KT4 .... 64 A2
Thamesfield Ct *SHPTN* TW17 .. 41 M7 🄳
Thamesgate *STA* TW18 .... 40 E2 🄳
Thamesgate CI
RCHPK/HAM TW10 .... 26 E5 🄳
Thameside *TEDD* TW11 .... 2 C2
Thames Md *WOT/HER* KT12 .. 42 D7 🄳
Thames Meadow
E/WMO/HCT KT8 .... 43 K2
WOT/HER KT12 .... 42 A8
Thames Pth *CHSWK* W4 .... 19 J3
EGH TW20 .... 21 H3
RCH/KEW TW9 .... 17 M4
STA TW18 .... 22 C8
WEY KT13 .... 59 L1
WOT/HER KT12 .... 42 F3
Thames Rd *CHSWK* W4 .... 18 E1
RCH/KEW TW9 .... 17 M4
Thames Side *KUTN/CMB* KT2 .... 2 D5
STA TW18 .... 40 F5
THDIT KT7 .... 44 E6 🄳
Thames St *HPTN* TW12 .... 43 L2
KUT KT1 .... 2 D6
STA TW18 .... 22 C6 🄳
SUN TW16 .... 42 E3
WEY KT13 .... 59 L2 🄳
WOT/HER KT12 .... 42 C7
Thamesvale CI *HSLW* TW3 .... 16 D4
Thames Village *CHSWK* W4 .... 18 F3
Thanescroft Gdns *CROY/NA* CR0 .. 5 H8
Thanet Dr *HAYES* BR2 .... 71 G2 🄳
Thanet PI *CROY/NA* CR0 .... 4 D9
Tharp Rd *WLGTN* SM6 .... 67 G4
Thatcher CI *CRAWE* RH10 .... 212 A6
Thatchers CI *HORL* RH6 .... 170 E4 🄳
HORS RH12 .... 229 H5
Thatchers La *RGUW* GU3 .... 116 A1
Thatchers Wy *ISLW* TW7 .... 17 G7
Thaxted PI *RYNPK* SW20 .... 29 G8 🄳
Thayers Farm Rd *BECK* BR3 .... 51 H1
Theal CI *SHST* GU47 .... 72 A1
Theatre Rd *FARN* GU14 .... 112 E1
Thelma Gv *TEDD* TW11 .... 26 D7 🄳
Thelton Av *HORS* RH12 .... 228 A6
Theobald Rd *CROY/NA* CR0 .... 4 A5
Theobalds Wy *FRIM* GU16 .... 73 M6
Thepps CI *REDH* RH1 .... 149 J3
Therapia La *CROY/NA* CR0 .... 49 C7
Theresa's Wk *SAND/SEL* CR2 .... 68 A7
Thesiger Rd *PGE/AN* SE20 .... 33 G8
Thetford Rd *ASHF* TW15 .... 23 H5
NWMAL KT3 .... 46 A6
Theydon CI *CRAWE* RH10 .... 212 D5
Thicket Crs *SUT* SM1 .... 65 M3
Thicket Gv *PGE/AN* SE20 .... 32 D8 🄳
Thicket Rd *PGE/AN* SE20 .... 32 E8
SUT SM1 .... 65 M3
Thickthorne La *STA* TW18 .... 22 F8 🄳
Third Cl *E/WMO/HCT* KT8 .... 43 L4
Third Cross Rd *WHTN* TW2 .... 26 A3
Thirlmere CI *EGH* TW20 .... 21 L8 🄳
FARN GU14 .... 92 B5
Thirlmere Rd *CRAWW* RH11 .... 211 C5
STRHM/NOR SW16 .... 31 G5
Thirsk Ct *ASHV* GU12 .... 113 G7 🄳
Thirsk Rd *MTCM* CR4 .... 30 D8
SNWD SE25 .... 50 A4
Thistlecroft Rd *WOT/HER* KT12 .. 60 F3
Thistledene *BF/WBF* KT14 .... 78 C3 🄳
THDIT KT7 .... 44 B6
Thistle Wy *HORL* RH6 .... 171 M6 🄳
Thistlewood Crs
CROY/NA CR0 .... 90 A2 🄳
Thistleworth CI *ISLW* TW7 .... 17 G2
Thistley La *CRAN* GU6 .... 185 H5
Thistledown V *BIL* RH14 .... 224 A5
Thomas Av *CTHM* CR3 .... 107 M3
Thomas Dean Rd *SYD* SE26 .. 33 J5 🄳
Thomas Wall CI *SUT* SM1 .... 65 L4 🄳
Thomas' La *CAT* SE6 .... 33 L1
Thompson Av *RCH/KEW* TW9 .. 18 E5
Thompsons CI *CROY/NA* CR0 .. 95 C5
Thompson's La *CHOB/PIR* GU24 .. 56 A7
Thomson Crs *CROY/NA* CR0 .... 49 K8
Thorburn Cha *SHST* GU47 .... 72 B3 🄳
Thorburn Wy *WIM/MER* SW19 .. 48 A1 🄳
Thorkhill Gdns *THDIT* KT7 .... 44 D8
Thorkhill Rd *THDIT* KT7 .... 44 E8
Thorley CI *BF/WBF* KT14 .... 78 D4
Thorley Gdns *BF/WBF* KT14 .... 78 D4
Thornash CI *WOKN/KNAP* GU21 .. 76 F5
Thornash Rd *WOKN/KNAP* GU21 .. 76 F5
Thornash Wy *WOKN/KNAP* GU21 .. 76 F5
Thorn Bank *GUW* GU4 .... 8 A8
Thornbank CI
STWL/WRAY TW19 .... 13 K7 🄳
Thornbury Av *ISLW* TW7 .... 17 G2
Thornbury Rd *ISLW* TW7 .... 17 G2
Thorn CI *NFNM* GU10 .... 155 J5 🄳
Thorncombe St *MFD/CHID* GU8 .. 183 G1
SHGR GU5 .... 161 G6
Thorncroft *EGH* TW20 .... 20 F8 🄳
Thorncroft CI
COUL/CHIP CR5 .... 107 K1 🄳
Thorncroft Rd *SUT* SM1 .... 65 L3
Thorndean St
WAND/EARL SW18 .... 29 M3 🄳
Thorndon Gdns *HOR/WEW* KT19 .. 64 B3 🄳
Thorndown La *BFOR* GU20 .... 55 C6
Thorndyke CI *CRAWE* RH10 .. 213 C4 🄳
Thorne CI *ASHF* TW15 .... 23 M8 🄳
Thorneloe Gdns *CROY/NA* CR0 .. 49 H1 🄳
Thorne's CI *BECK* BR3 .... 51 M3
Thorne St *BARN* SW13 .... 19 H5
Thorneycroft CI
WOT/HER KT12 .... 42 F6 🄳
Thornfield Gn *BLKW* GU17 .... 72 C6
Thornfield Rd *BNSTD* SM7 .... 85 K7
Thornhill *BRAK* RG12 .... 35 H4
Thornhill Av *SURB* KT6 .... 63 H1
Thornhill Rd *ALDT* GU11 .... 113 C5
CROY/NA CR0 .... 4 D1
SURB KT6 .... 63 H1
Thornhill Wy *SHPTN* TW17 .. 41 K5 🄳

Thornlaw Rd *WNWD* SE27 .... 31 K5
Thornleas PI *EHSLY* KT24 .... 100 B8
Thorn Rd *NFNM* GU10 .... 155 J4
Thornsbeach Rd *CAT* SE6 .... 33 M2
Thornsett Ct *SHPTN* TW17 .. 41 M7 🄳
Thornsett PI *PGE/AN* SE20 .... 50 E2
Thornsett Rd *PGE/AN* SE20 .... 50 E2
WAND/EARL SW18 .... 29 L2 🄳
Thornton Av *BAL* SW12 .... 31 G2
CROY/NA CR0 .... 49 J6
Thornton CI *GUW* GU2 .... 116 D5 🄳
HORL RH6 .... 170 B6
Thornton Crs *COUL/CHIP* CR5 .. 107 K1
Thornton Dene *BECK* BR3 .... 51 K2
Thornton Gdns *BAL* SW12 .... 31 G2
Thornton HI *WIM/MER* SW19 .. 29 H8
Thornton PI *HORL* RH6 .... 170 C6 🄳
Thornton Rd *BAL* SW12 .... 31 G1
CAR SM5 .... 48 B7 🄳
MORT/ESHN SW14 .... 19 C5
THHTH CR7 .... 49 K5
WIM/MER SW19 .... 29 C7
Thornton Rw *THHTH* CR7 .... 49 K5
Thornville Gv *MTCM* CR4 .... 47 M2
Thornyhurst Rd *FRIM* GU16 .... 93 K5
Thorold CI *SAND/SEL* CR2 .... 69 G8
Thorold Rd *FNM* GU9 .... 133 M6 🄳
Thorpe By-pass *EGH* TW20 .... 39 L3
Thorpe CI *CROY/NA* CR0 .... 89 M1
Thorpe Lea Rd *EGH* TW20 .... 21 L8
Thorpe Rd *CHERT* KT16 .... 40 A5
EGH TW20 .... 22 A7
KUTN/CMB KT2 .... 2 F2
Thorpes CI *GUW* GU2 .... 116 D5 🄳
Thorpeside CI *EGH* TW20 .... 40 B2
Thorpewood Av *SYD* SE23 .... 32 E3
Thorsden CI *WOKS/MYFD* GU22 .. 6 D9
Thorsden Wy *NRWD* SE19 .. 32 B6 🄳
Thrale Rd *STRHM/NOR* SW16 .. 30 F6
Three Acres *HORS* RH12 .... 228 D8
Three Arch Rd *REDH* RH1 .... 148 D4
Three Bridges Rd
CRAWE RH10 .... 212 E3 🄳
Three Castles Pth *ASC* SL5 .... 35 M3
Three Gates *GU* GU1 .... 117 M7
Three Gates La *HASM* GU27 .... 220 A2
Three Mile Rd *CRAN* GU6 .... 186 D1
Three Pears Rd *GU* GU1 .... 118 B8
Threestile Rd *HORS* RH12 .... 208 C8
Three Stiles Rd *FNM* GU9 .... 133 J6
Threshfield *BRAK* RG12 .... 34 E6
Thriftwood *FSTH* SE23 .... 32 F4 🄳
Thrift V *RGUE* GU4 .... 118 A5
Thrigby Rd *CHSGTN* KT9 .... 63 J5
Throwley Rd *SUT* SM1 .... 65 L4 🄳
Throwley Wy *SUT* SM1 .... 65 L4 🄳
Thrupp CI *MTCM* CR4 .... 48 E2 🄳
Thrupps Av *WOT/HER* KT12 .. 61 G4
Thrupps La *WOT/HER* KT12 .. 61 G4
Thundery HI *NFNM* GU10 .... 135 J5
Thurbans Rd *FNM* GU9 .... 10 C6
Thurbarn Rd *CAT* SE6 .... 33 L6
Thurbarns HI *RDKG* RH5 .... 167 H8
Thurlby Rd *WNWD* SE27 .... 31 K5
Thurleston Av *MRDN* SM4 .... 47 H5
Thurlestone CI *SHPTN* TW17 .. 41 M6 🄳
Thurlestone Rd *WNWD* SE27 .. 31 K4
Thurlow HI *DUL* SE21 .... 31 M2
Thurlow Park Rd *DUL* SE21 .. 31 L3
Thurlow Wk *CRAN* GU6 .... 185 H8
Thurlton Ct *WOKN/KNAP* GU21 .. 6 D3 🄳
Thurne Wy *HORS* RH12 .... 226 A2
Thurnham Wy
KWD/TDW/WH KT20 .... 105 G2
Thursby Rd *WOKN/KNAP* GU21 .. 76 D8
Thursley Crs *CROY/NA* CR0 .... 70 A6
Thursley Gdns *WIM/MER* SW19 .. 29 C3
Thursley Rd *MFD/CHID* GU8 .. 157 M7
NFNM GU10 .... 178 F6
Thurso St *TOOT* SW17 .... 30 A5
Thurstan Rd *RYNPK* SW20 .... 28 E8
Thyer CI *ORP* BR6 .... 71 M3
Thyme Ct *GU* GU1 .... 117 L5 🄳
Tibbets CI *WIM/MER* SW19 .... 29 G2
Tibbet's Ride *PUT/ROE* SW15 .. 29 G1
Ticehurst CI *CRAWE* RH10 .... 213 H3
Ticehurst Rd *FSTH* SE23 .... 33 H3
Tichborne CI *BLKW* GU17 .... 72 A4
Tichborne PI *ASHV* GU12 .... 135 G1 🄳
Tichbourne CI *FRIM* GU16 .... 73 J5
Tichmarsh *HOR/WEW* KT19 .. 63 M8 🄳
Tidenham Gdns *CROY/NA* CR0 .. 5 H7
Tideswell Rd *CROY/NA* CR0 .... 69 K2
PUT/ROE SW15 .... 19 M6
Tideway CI *RCHPK/HAM* TW10 .. 26 E5
Tidwells Lea *BNFD* RG42 .... 35 H1 🄳
Tiepigs La *WWKM* BR4 .... 70 B1
Tierney Rd *BRXS/STRHM* SW2 .. 31 H2
Tilburstow Hill Rd *GDST* RH9 .. 128 F6 🄳
Tildesley Rd *PUT/ROE* SW15 .. 19 M8
Tile Barn CI *FARN* GU14 .... 92 D5
Tilehouse Rd *RGUE* GU4 .... 139 H4
Tilehurst La *RDKG* RH5 .... 145 H3
Tilehurst Rd *CHEAM* SM3 .... 65 H4
WAND/EARL SW18 .... 30 A2
Tiler's Wy *REDH* RH1 .... 147 M4
Tilford Av *CROY/NA* CR0 .... 69 M6
Tilford Gdns *WIM/MER* SW19 .. 29 C2
Tilford Rd *FNM* GU9 .... 11 J1
GSHT GU26 .... 199 J4
NFNM GU10 .... 156 F6
NFNM GU10 .... 178 C5
Tilford St *NFNM* GU10 .... 156 F6
Tilgate Common *REDH* RH1 .. 127 M7
Tilgate Dr *CRAWE* RH10 .... 212 B8
Tilgate Pde *CRAWE* RH10 .... 212 B6
Tilgate PI *CRAWE* RH10 .... 212 B6
Tilgate Wy *CRAWE* RH10 .... 212 B6
Tilletts La *HORS* RH12 .... 228 B1
Tilley La *EPSOM* KT18 .... 103 M5 🄳
Tillingbourne Rd *RGUE* GU4 .. 139 H6
Tillingdown HI *CTHM* CR3 .... 108 E4
Tillingdown La *CTHM* CR3 .... 108 C6
Tillotson CI *CRAWE* RH10 .... 213 G4
Tilson Gdns *CLAP* SW4 .... 31 H1
Tilt CI *COB* KT11 .... 81 H6
Tilthams Corner Rd *RGODL* GU7 .. 160 E1 🄳
Tilthams Gn *RGODL* GU7 .... 160 E2
Tilt Meadow *COB* KT11 .... 81 H6

Tilt Rd *COB* KT11 .... 81 G6
Tiltwood Dr *CRAWE* RH10 .. 194 F8
Timber Bank *FRIM* GU16 .... 93 K4
Timber CI *GT/LBKH* KT23 .... 121 M1
WOKS/MYFD GU22 .... 78 C5
Timbercroft *HOR/WEW* KT19 .. 64 B3
Timberham Farm Rd
HORL RH6 .... 192 A1
Timber HI *ASHTD* KT21 .... 103 H1 🄳
Timber Hill Rd *CTHM* CR3 .... 108 D6
Timberlands *CRAWW* RH11 .. 211 L8 🄳
Timberling Gdns
SAND/SEL CR2 .... 68 A8 🄳
Timbermill Ct *HASM* GU27 .... 219 J3 🄳
Timberslip Dr *WLGTN* SM6 .. 67 G7 🄳
Timbertop Rd *BH/WHM* TN16 .. 90 F8
Timline Gn *BRAK* RG12 .... 35 J2
Timperley Gdns *REDH* RH1 .... 126 B6
Timsway *STA* TW18 .... 22 C6
Tindale CI *SAND/SEL* CR2 .... 88 A1
Tinsey CI *EGH* TW20 .... 21 L6
Tinsley Gn *CRAWE* RH10 .... 192 E6
Tinsley La *CRAWE* RH10 .... 192 D8
Tinsley La North *CRAWE* RH10 .. 192 E6
Tinsley La South
CRAWE RH10 .... 212 D1 🄳
Tintagel CI *EW* KT17 .... 84 C4
Tintagel Dr *FRIM* GU16 .... 73 J8
Tintagel Wy *WOKS/MYFD* GU22 .. 7 H4
Tintells La *EHSLY* KT24 .... 119 L2
Tintern CI *WIM/MER* SW19 .. 29 M7 🄳
Tintern Rd *CAR* SM5 .... 48 A8
CRAWW RH11 .... 211 K5
Tippits Md *BNFD* RG42 .... 34 A3
Tipton Dr *CROY/NA* CR0 .... 5 H9
CROY/NA CR0 .... 68 B3 🄳
Tirlemont Rd *SAND/SEL* CR2 .. 67 M6
Tirrell Rd *CROY/NA* CR0 .... 49 M2
Tisbury Rd *STRHM/NOR* SW16 .. 49 H2
Titchfield Rd *CAR* SM5 .... 48 A8
Titchfield Wk *CAR* SM5 .... 48 A7
Tite HI *EGH* TW20 .... 21 G6
Tithe Barn CI *KUTN/CMB* KT2 .. 3 C5
Tithe CI *VW* GU25 .... 39 G6
WOT/HER KT12 .... 42 E6
Tithe La *STWL/WRAY* TW19 .. 12 C8
Tithe Orch *EGRIN* RH19 .... 195 H5
Tithepit Shaw La *SAND/SEL* CR2 .. 88 E5
WARL CR6 .... 88 E7
Titlarks Hill Rd *ASC* SL5 .... 37 L8
Titmus Dr *CRAWE* RH10 .... 212 C6
Titsey HI *OXTED* RH8 .... 110 E6
WARL CR6 .... 110 C6
Titsey Rd *OXTED* RH8 .... 130 E1
Tiverton CI *HSLW* TW3 .... 16 E4
Tiverton Wy *CHSGTN* KT9 .. 62 F4
Tivoli Rd *HSLWW* TW4 .... 16 B6
WNWD SE27 .... 31 M6
Toad La *BLKW* GU17 .... 72 B5
HSLWW TW4 .... 16 C6
Toby Wy *SURB* KT6 .... 63 L1
Todds CI *HORL* RH6 .... 170 B4
Toftwood CI *CRAWE* RH10 .. 212 F4
Toland Sq *PUT/ROE* SW15 .. 19 K7
Toll dene CI *WOKN/KNAP* GU21 .. 76 B7 🄳
Tollers La *COUL/CHIP* CR5 .... 107 J1
Toll Gdns *BRAK* RG12 .... 35 H3
Tollgate *GU* GU1 .... 118 A7
Tollgate Av *REDH* RH1 .... 148 C5
Tollgate Dr *DUL* SE21 .... 32 B3
Tollgate Rd *DORK* RH4 .... 144 E5
Tollhouse La *WLGTN* SM6 .. 66 F7 🄳
Tolson Rd *ISLW* TW7 .... 17 K5
Tolvaddon *WOKN/KNAP* GU21 .. 76 D7 🄳
Tolverne Rd *RYNPK* SW20 .. 46 F1
Tolworth CI *SURB* KT6 .... 45 L8
Tolworth Park Rd *SURB* KT6 .. 63 L1
Tolworth Ri North *BRYLDS* KT5 .. 45 M7
Tolworth Ri South *BRYLDS* KT5 .. 45 L8
Tolworth Rd *SURB* KT6 .... 63 H1
Tomlin CI *HOR/WEW* KT19 .. 84 A1 🄳
Tomlins Av *FRIM* GU16 .... 73 J7
Tomlinscote Wy *FRIM* GU16 .. 73 K7
Tomtits La *FROW* RH18 .... 217 H8
Tonbridge Rd
E/WMO/HCT KT8 .... 43 J4 🄳
Tonbridge St *BNSTD* SM7 .... 86 C4 🄳
Tonfield Rd *CHEAM* SM3 .... 47 J8
Tongham Mdw *NFNM* GU10 .. 135 J2 🄳
Tongham Rd *ASHV* GU12 .... 135 G2
NFNM GU10 .... 134 F5
Tonstall Rd *HOR/WEW* KT19 .. 64 A8
MTCM CR4 .... 48 D2
Tooting Bec Gdns
STRHM/NOR SW16 .... 31 G5
Tooting Bec Rd *TOOT* SW17 .. 30 D4
Tooting Gv *TOOT* SW17 .... 30 B6
Tooting High St *TOOT* SW17 .. 30 B6
Topiary Sq *RCH/KEW* TW9 .. 18 C5 🄳
The Topiary *ASHTD* KT21 .... 103 H2
FARN GU14 .... 112 D1
Toplady PI *FNM* GU9 .... 133 M2 🄳
Topsham Rd *TOOT* SW17 .... 30 C4
Top Terrace *FARN* GU14 .... 112 D1
Torcross Dr *FSTH* SE23 .... 32 F3
Torin Ct *EGH* TW20 .... 20 F6
Torland Dr *LHD/OX* KT22 .... 82 A4
Tor La *WEY* KT13 .... 80 A1
Tormead CI *SUT* SM1 .... 65 K5
Tormead Rd *GU* GU1 .... 9 M3
Toronto Dr *HORL* RH6 .... 171 K7
Torridge Rd *DTCH/LGLY* SL3 .. 12 E1
THHTH CR7 .... 49 L5
Torridon CI *WOKN/KNAP* GU21 .. 76 D7
Torrington CI *ESH/CLAY* KT10 .. 62 B5 🄳
Torrington Rd *ESH/CLAY* KT10 .. 62 B5
Torrington Wy *MRDN* SM4 .. 47 K7
Tor Rd *FNM* GU9 .... 133 J7
Torr Rd *PGE/AN* SE20 .... 33 G8
Torwood La *CTHM* CR3 .... 108 C2
Torwood Rd *PUT/ROE* SW15 .. 19 K7
Totford La *NFNM* GU10 .... 136 B6
Totland CI *FARN* GU14 .... 92 D3
Tottenham Rd *RGODL* GU7 .. 160 B3
Tottenham Wk *SHST* GU47 .. 52 A8
Totton Rd *THHTH* CR7 .... 49 K3
Tournai CI *ALDT* GU11 .... 113 H2

Tovil CI *PGE/AN* SE20 .... 50 D2
Tower CI *EGRIN* RH19 .... 196 B7
HORL RH6 .... 170 C6 🄳
PGE/AN SE20 .... 32 E8 🄳
WOKN/KNAP GU21 .... 6 A5
Tower Gdns *ESH/CLAY* KT10 .. 62 D6 🄳
ESH/CLAY KT10 .... 62 D6 🄳
Tower Gv *WEY* KT13 .... 60 B1
Tower HI *DORK* RH4 .... 144 E4
FARN GU14 .... 92 D6
Towerhill *SHGR* GU5 .... 141 M6
Tower Hill Ri *SHGR* GU5 .... 141 M6
Tower Hill Rd *DORK* RH4 .... 144 E4
Tower Ri *RCH/KEW* TW9 .... 18 B5
Tower Rd *GSHT* GU26 .... 199 H5
KWD/TDW/WH KT20 .... 104 F5
WHTN TW2 .... 26 B4
Towers PI *RCHPK/HAM* TW10 .. 18 B7 🄳
The Towers *PUR/KEN* CR8 .. 87 M5
Towers Wk *WEY* KT13 .... 59 L5
Tower Vw *CROY/NA* CR0 .... 51 H8
Towfield Rd *FELT* TW13 .... 25 J3
Town Barn Rd *CRAWW* RH11 .. 211 M3
Townend *CTHM* CR3 .... 108 B4
Town End CI *CTHM* CR3 .... 108 B4
RGODL GU7 .... 160 B5 🄳
Town End St *RGODL* GU7 .... 160 B5
Town Farm Wy
STWL/WRAY TW19 .... 23 G1 🄳
Townfield Rd *DORK* RH4 .... 144 E4
Town Field Wy *ISLW* TW7 .... 17 K4
Towngate *COB* KT11 .... 81 H5
Town HI *LING* RH7 .... 174 B5
Town Md *CRAWW* RH11 .... 212 A2
REDH RH1 .... 128 A7
Town Meadow *BTFD* TW8 .. 18 A2 🄳
Townmead Rd *RCH/KEW* TW9 .. 18 E4
Town Quay *STA* TW18 .... 40 F3 🄳
Townsend CI *BRAK* RG12 .... 35 H5 🄳
Townsend La
WOKS/MYFD GU22 .... 97 J3 🄳
Townsend Rd *ASHF* TW15 .... 23 H6
Townshend Rd *RCH/KEW* TW9 .. 18 C6
Townshend Ter *RCH/KEW* TW9 .. 18 C6
Townshott CI *GT/LBKH* KT23 .. 101 K8
Townside PI *CBLY* GU15 .... 73 G3 🄳
Town Tree Rd *ASHF* TW15 .... 23 K6
Towpath *SHPTN* TW17 .... 41 J8
Towpath Wy *CROY/NA* CR0 .. 50 C6
Towton Rd *WNWD* SE27 .... 31 M3
Toynbee Rd *RYNPK* SW20 .. 47 H1
The Tracery *BNSTD* SM7 .... 85 L5
Tracious CI *WOKN/KNAP* GU21 .. 76 E6
Trafalgar Av *WPK* KT4 .... 47 G8
FNM GU9 .... 10 F1
Trafalgar Ct *COB* KT11 .... 80 D3 🄳
Trafalgar Dr *WOT/HER* KT12 .. 60 E2
Trafalgar Rd *HORS* RH12 .... 228 F5
WHTN TW2 .... 26 A3
WIM/MER SW19 .... 29 L8
Trafalgar Wy *CBLY* GU15 .... 72 C5
CROY/NA CR0 .... 67 J1
Trafford Rd *FRIM* GU16 .... 93 C1
THHTH CR7 .... 49 J5
Tramway Pth *MTCM* CR4 .... 48 B4
Tranmere Rd *WAND/EARL* SW18 .. 29 M3 🄳
WHTN TW2 .... 25 L1
Tranquil DI *BRKHM/BTCW* RH3 .. 124 C6
Transport Av *BTFD* TW8 .... 17 L1
Transport Rd *FARN* GU14 .... 92 E8
Trap La *RDKG* RH5 .... 187 J7
Traps La *NWMAL* KT3 .... 46 B2
Trasher Md *RDKG* RH5 .... 144 F5
Travellers Wy *HEST* TW5 .... 15 M4
Travis La *SHST* GU47 .... 72 A2
Treadcroft Dr *HORS* RH12 .. 229 H4
Treadwell Rd *EPSOM* KT18 .. 84 C5
Trebor Av *FNM* GU9 .... 11 J2
Tredenham CI *FARN* GU14 .. 112 F1 🄳
Tredown Rd *SYD* SE26 .... 32 F6
Tredwell Rd *WNWD* SE27 .. 31 L5 🄳
Treebourne Rd *BH/WHM* TN16 .. 90 F7
Treebys Av *RGUE* GU4 .... 117 G2
Tree CI *RCHPK/HAM* TW10 .. 27 G2 🄳
Treelands *RDKG* RH5 .... 144 F5
Treen Av *BARN* SW13 .... 19 H5
Treeside Dr *FNM* GU9 .... 134 B2
Tree Tops Av *CBLY* GU15 .... 73 K1
Tree Tops *WARL* CR6 .... 88 D8
Treetops *GDST* RH9 .... 151 H3
Treeview *CRAWW* RH11 .... 211 M8
Tree View CI *NRWD* SE19 .... 50 B1
Treeway *REIG* RH2 .... 125 L5
Trefoil CI *HORS* RH12 .... 229 H4
Trefoil Crs *CRAWW* RH11 .... 211 K7
Tregaron Gdns *NWMAL* KT3 .. 46 B4 🄳
Tregarthen PI *LHD/OX* KT22 .. 102 F3
Tregarth PI *WOKN/KNAP* GU21 .. 76 C7 🄳
Tregolls Dr *FARN* GU14 .... 92 F6
Trehaven Pde *REIG* RH2 .... 147 L3 🄳
Trehern Rd *MORT/ESHN* SW14 .. 19 C5 🄳
Trelawn CI *CHERT* KT16 .... 57 M4
Trelawn Dr *CRAN* GU6 .... 185 H7
Trelawney Gv *WEY* KT13 .... 59 K5
Treloar Gdns *NRWD* SE19 .. 32 A7 🄳
Tremaine Rd *PGE/AN* SE20 .. 50 E2
Tremayne Wk *CBLY* GU15 .... 73 M5
Trenance *WOKN/KNAP* GU21 .. 76 D7
Trenchard CI *WOT/HER* KT12 .. 60 F4
Trenear CI *SWTR* RH13 .... 229 H7
Trenham Dr *WARL* CR6 .... 88 F6
Trenholme Rd *PGE/AN* SE20 .. 32 E8
Trenholme Ter *PGE/AN* SE20 .. 32 E8 🄳
Trent CI *CRAWW* RH11 .... 211 J5
Trentham Crs *WOKS/MYFD* GU22 .. 97 K3
Trentham Rd *REDH* RH1 .... 148 C2
Trentham St *WAND/EARL* SW18 .. 29 K2
Trenton CI *FRIM* GU16 .... 73 K7
Trent Rd *DTCH/LGLY* SL3 .... 12 E1
Trent Wy *WPK* KT4 .... 64 F2
Treport St *WAND/EARL* SW18 .. 29 L1
Tresillian Wy *WOKN/KNAP* GU21 .. 76 D5
Tresta Wk *WOKN/KNAP* GU21 .. 76 B5
Trevanne Plat *CRAWE* RH10 .. 213 G2 🄳
Trevelyan *BRAK* RG12 .... 34 B7

Trevelyan Rd *TOOT* SW17 .... 30 B7
Trevereux HI *OXTED* RH8 .... 131 K6
Treville St *PUT/ROE* SW15 .... 28 E1
Treviso Rd *FSTH* SE23 .... 33 G3
Trevithick CI *EBED/NFELT* TW14 .. 24 C7
Trevor CI *ISLW* TW7 .... 17 J7 🄳
Trevor Rd *WIM/MER* SW19 .. 29 H8
Trevose Av *BF/WBF* KT14 .... 78 C4
Trewenna Dr *CHSGTN* KT9 .. 63 G4 🄳
Trewince Rd *RYNPK* SW20 .... 46 F1
Trewint St *WAND/EARL* SW18 .. 29 M3
Trewsbury Rd *SYD* SE26 .... 33 G6
Treyford CI *CRAWW* RH11 .... 211 J3
The Triangle *NWMAL* KT3 .... 45 M2 🄳
WOKN/KNAP GU21 .... 76 F8
Trigg's CI *WOKS/MYFD* GU22 .. 6 A9
Trigg's La *WOKN/KNAP* GU21 .. 96 F1
Trig St *RDKG* RH5 .... 189 H1
Trilby Rd *FSTH* SE23 .... 33 G3
Trimmers CI *FNM* GU9 .... 133 M2 🄳
Trimmers Wd *GSHT* GU26 .. 199 G3
Trindles Rd *REDH* RH1 .... 149 J2
Tringham Ct *CHERT* KT16 .... 57 L4
Trinity *SHST* GU47 .... 52 B7
Trinity CI *CRAWE* RH10 .... 212 F1
HSLWW TW4 .... 16 B5
SAND/SEL CR2 .... 68 B7
STWL/WRAY TW19 .... 13 M8
Trinity Crs *ASC* SL5 .... 37 K5
TOOT SW17 .... 30 C3
Trinity Flds *FNM* GU9 .... 133 K3 🄳
Trinity Gn *FNM* GU9 .... 133 K3
Trinity Ri *NHNL* SE24 .... 31 L1
Trinity Rd *RCH/KEW* TW9 .... 18 C5 🄳
TOOT SW17 .... 30 C3
WIM/MER SW19 .... 29 K7
WOKN/KNAP GU21 .... 75 L8
Tritton Av *CROY/NA* CR0 .... 67 H3
Tritton Rd *WNWD* SE27 .... 32 A4
Trittons *KWD/TDW/WH* KT20 .. 104 F5
Triumph CI *HYS/HAR* UB3 .... 14 F3
Trodd's La *RGUE* GU4 .... 140 C1
Trojan Wy *CROY/NA* CR0 .... 67 J2
Troon CI *CRAWW* RH11 .... 211 C4 🄳
Trotsworth Av *VW* GU25 .... 39 C4
Trotters La *CHOB/PIR* GU24 .. 76 E2
Trotton CI *CRAWE* RH10 .... 212 F6 🄳
Trotts La *BH/WHM* TN16 .... 131 M1
Trotwood CI *SHST* GU47 .... 52 B7 🄳
Trout Rd *HASM* GU27 .... 219 H3
Trowers Wy *REDH* RH1 .... 126 E5
Trowlock Av *TEDD* TW11 .... 26 F7
Trowlock Wy *TEDD* TW11 .... 2 C1
Troy La *EDEN* TN8 .... 153 J5
Troy Rd *NRWD* SE19 .... 32 A7
Trumpetshill Rd *REIG* RH2 .... 146 D1
Trumpsgreen Av *VW* GU25 .. 39 G6
Trumps Green CI *VW* GU25 .... 39 H5 🄳
Trumpsgreen Rd *VW* GU25 .. 38 F8
Trumps Mill La *VW* GU25 .... 39 J6
Trundle Md *HORS* RH12 .... 228 F4
Trunley Heath Rd *SHGR* GU5 .. 160 F1
Truslove Rd *WNWD* SE27 .. 31 K6
Truss Hill Rd *ASC* SL5 .... 36 F3
Trys Hill Longcross Rd
CHERT KT16 .... 57 H2
Trystings CI *ESH/CLAY* KT10 .. 62 D5
Tucker Rd *CHERT* KT16 .... 58 A5
Tuckers Dr *CRAN* GU6 .... 184 E6
Tuckey Gv *RPLY/SEND* GU23 .. 98 C6
Tudor Av *HPTN* TW12 .... 25 K7
WPK KT4 .... 64 E2
Tudor Cir *RGODL* GU7 .... 160 B2
Tudor CI *ASHF* TW15 .... 23 H5
BNSTD SM7 .... 85 H5
CHEAM SM3 .... 65 G4
CHSGTN KT9 .... 63 H4
COB KT11 .... 81 J3
COUL/CHIP CR5 .... 87 K4
CRAWE RH10 .... 213 G4
EGRIN RH19 .... 216 C2 🄳
GSHT GU26 .... 199 G7
GT/LBKH KT23 .... 101 J6
HORL RH6 .... 171 L6
HPTN TW12 .... 25 M6 🄳
SAND/SEL CR2 .... 88 E5
WLGTN SM6 .... 66 F6
WOKS/MYFD GU22 .... 7 C5
Tudor Dr *KUTN/CMB* KT2 .. 27 H6
MRDN SM4 .... 47 J7 🄳
WOT/HER KT12 .... 43 G8
Tudor Gdns *BARN* SW13 .... 19 H5 🄳
TWK TW1 .... 26 C2 🄳
WWKM BR4 .... 69 M2
Tudor La *WDSR* SL4 .... 20 F1
Tudor PI *WIM/MER* SW19 .. 30 B8 🄳
Tudor Rd *ASHF* TW15 .... 24 A7
BECK BR3 .... 51 M3
HPTN TW12 .... 25 K8
HSLW TW3 .... 17 G6
KUTN/CMB KT2 .... 3 J3
NRWD SE19 .... 32 C8
RGODL GU7 .... 160 B2
SNWD SE25 .... 50 E5
Tudor Wk *LHD/OX* KT22 .... 102 D2
Tuesley Cnr *RGODL* GU7 .. 160 A6 🄳
Tuesley La *RGODL* GU7 .... 160 A6
Tufton Gdns *E/WMO/HCT* KT8 .. 43 L2
Tugela Rd *CROY/NA* CR0 .... 50 A6
Tugela St *CAT* SE6 .... 33 J3
Tuggles Plat *HORS* RH12 .... 228 B2
Tugmutton CI *ORP* BR6 .... 71 L3 🄳
Tulip CI *CROY/NA* CR0 .... 51 G8
HPTN TW12 .... 25 J7 🄳
Tullett Rd *CRAWE* RH10 .... 212 E2
Tull St *MTCM* CR4 .... 48 C6
Tulse CI *BECK* BR3 .... 51 M3
Tulse Hill *BRXS/STRHM* SW2 .. 31 K1
Tulsemere Rd *WNWD* SE27 .. 31 M3
Tulyar CI *KWD/TDW/WH* KT20 .. 104 E1
Tumber St *EPSOM* KT18 .... 103 M7
Tumblewood Rd *BNSTD* SM7 .. 85 H6
Tumbling Bay *WOT/HER* KT12 .. 42 D6
Tummons Gdns *SNWD* SE25 .. 50 B2
Tunley Rd *BAL* SW12 .... 30 D3
Tunnel Link Rd *HTHAIR* TW6 .. 14 D7
Tunnel Rd *FARN* GU14 .... 92 B8

Tunnel Rd East *HTHAIR* TW6 ...... 14 E3
Tunnel Rd West *HTHAIR* TW6 ...... 14 D4
Tunnmeade *CRAWW* RH11 ...... 211 H3
Tunsgate *GU* GU1 ...... 9 H7
Tunstall Rd *CROY/NA* CR0 ...... 5 H4
Tunworth Crs *PUT/ROE* SW15 ...... 19 J8
Tupwood La *CTHM* CR3 ...... 108 D8
Tupwood Scrubbs Rd
GDST RH9 ...... 128 D2
Turf Hill Rd *CBLY* GU15 ...... 73 J1
Turfhouse La *CHOB/PIR* GU24 ...... 56 B7
Turkey Oak Cl *NRWD* SE19 ...... 50 B1
Turle Rd *STRHM/NOR* SW16 ...... 49 H2
Turnberry *BRAK* RG12 ...... 34 B6
Turner Av *MTCM* CR4 ...... 48 C1
WHTN TW2 ...... 25 M4
Turner Cl *GU* GU1 ...... 117 J5
Turner Ct *EGRIN* RH19 ...... 196 B6
Turner Pl *SHST* GU47 ...... 72 A3
Turner Rd *BH/WHM* TN16 ...... 90 F2
NWMAL KT3 ...... 46 A7
Turners Cl *STA* TW18 ...... 22 E6
Turners Hill Rd *CRAWE* RH10...... 194 C6
CRAWE RH10 ...... 213 H3
EGRIN RH19 ...... 215 K4
Turners La *WOT/HER* KT12 ...... 60 E5
Turners Md *MFD/CHID* GU8 ...... 201 M6
Turners Meadow Wy *BECK* BR3.. 51 J1
Turners Wy *CROY/NA* CR0 ...... 67 L4
Turney Rd *DUL* SE21 ...... 31 M1
Turnham Cl *GUW* GU2 ...... 138 F4
Turnoak Av *WOKS/MYFD* GU22.. 97 H2
Turnoak La *WOKS/MYFD* GU22 ...... 97 H2
Turnpike La *SUT* SM1 ...... 65 M4
Turnpike Link *CROY/NA* CR0 ...... 5 H6
Turnpike Pl *CRAWW* RH11 ...... 212 A1
Turnpike Rd *BNFD* RG42 ...... 34 A2
Turnpike Wy *ISLW* TW7 ...... 17 K3
Turnstone Cl *SAND/SEL* CR2 ...... 69 H8
Turnville Cl *LTWR* GU18 ...... 54 B8
Turpin Rd *EBED/NFELT* TW14 ...... 15 J8
Turpins Ri *BFOR* GU20 ...... 54 E3
Turpin Wy *WLGTN* SM6 ...... 66 E6
Tuscany Gdns *CRAWE* RH10 ...... 192 B8
Tushmore Av *CRAWW* RH11 ...... 192 B8
Tushmore Crs *CRAWW* RH11 ...... 192 B8
Tushmore La *CRAWE* RH10 ...... 212 B1
Tussock Cl *CRAWW* RH11 ...... 211 K5
Tuxford Cl *CRAWE* RH10 ...... 212 F5
Tweed Cl *FARN* GU14 ...... 92 B3
Tweeddale Rd *CAR* SM5 ...... 48 A8
Tweed La *BRKHM/BTCW* RH3 ...... 145 L5
CRAWW RH11 ...... 191 J8
Tweed Rd *DTCH/LGLY* SL3 ...... 12 E1
Tweedsmuir Cl *FARN* GU14 ...... 92 A6
Twelve Acre Cl *GT/LBKH* KT23.... 101 L6
Twelve Acre Crs *FARN* GU14 ...... 92 A4
Twickenham Cl *CROY/NA* CR0 ... 67 J2
Twickenham Rd *FELT* TW13 ...... 25 J4
ISLW TW7 ...... 17 K6
RCH/KEW TW9 ...... 17 M7
TEDD TW11 ...... 26 D5
Twilley St *WAND/EARL* SW18..... 29 L1
Twining Av *WHTN* TW2 ...... 25 M4
Twinoaks *COB* KT11 ...... 81 K3
Twitten La *EGRIN* RH19 ...... 195 H5
Two Ways *BIL* RH14 ...... 224 D5
Twycross Rd *RGODL* GU7 ...... 160 A2
Twyford La *NFNM* GU10 ...... 10 E8
Twyford Rd *CAR* SM5 ...... 48 A8
Twyhurst Ct *EGRIN* RH19 ...... 196 A6
Twyne Cl *CRAWW* RH11 ...... 211 J5
Twyner Cl *HORL* RH6 ...... 170 F5
Twynersh Av *CHERT* KT16 ...... 40 C6
Tybenham Rd *WIM/MER* SW19 ... 47 K3
Tychbourne Dr *RGUE* GU4 ...... 117 M5
Tydcombe Rd *WARL* CR6 ...... 108 F1
Tye La *ORP* BR6 ...... 71 M4
Tylden Wy *HORS* RH12 ...... 229 J3
Tylecroft Rd
STRHM/NOR SW16 ...... 49 H2
Tylehost *GU* GU2 ...... 116 D4
Tyler Gdns *ADL/WDHM* KT15..... 58 F3
Tyler Rd *CRAWE* RH10 ...... 212 A6
Tylers Cl *GDST* RH9 ...... 128 C4
Tylney Av *NRWD* SE19 ...... 32 C6
Tynan Cl *EBED/NFELT* TW14 ...... 24 D2
Tyne Cl *CRAWE* RH10 ...... 212 F4
FARN GU14 ...... 92 B3
Tynedale Rd
BRKHM/BTCW RH3 ...... 145 L4
Tynemouth Rd *MTCM* CR4 ...... 30 D8
Tynley Gv *RGUE* GU4 ...... 117 G2
Tyrwhitt Av *GUW* GU2 ...... 116 E4
Tyson Rd *FSTH* SE23 ...... 32 F1
Tythebarn Cl *RGUE* GU4 ...... 117 L3
Tythebarns La *RPLY/SEND* GU23 .. 98 D3
Tytherton *BRAK* RG12 ...... 34 F2

U

Uckfield Gv *MTCM* CR4 ...... 48 D1
Udney Park Rd *TEDD* TW11 ...... 26 D6
Uffington Dr *BRAK* RG12 ...... 35 H4
Uffington Rd *WNWD* SE27 ...... 31 K5
Ullathorne Rd *STRHM/NOR* SW16.. 30 F5
Ullswater *BRAK* RG12 ...... 34 B7
Ullswater Av *FARN* GU14 ...... 92 B6
Ullswater Cl *FNM* GU9 ...... 133 K3
LTWR GU18 ...... 54 E8
PUT/ROE SW15 ...... 28 A5
Ullswater Crs *COUL/CHIP* CR5 ...... 87 H6
PUT/ROE SW15 ...... 28 A5
Ullswater Rd *BARN* SW13 ...... 19 K2
LTWR GU18 ...... 54 E8
WNWD SE27 ...... 31 L4
Ulstan Cl *CTHM* CR3 ...... 109 K5
Ulwyn Av *BF/WBF* KT14 ...... 79 H3
Umbria St *PUT/ROE* SW15 ...... 19 K8
Underhill Cl *RGODL* GU7 ...... 160 B6
Underhill La *FNM* GU9 ...... 10 F6
Underhill Park Rd *REIG* RH2 ...... 125 K3
Underhill Rd *RDKG* RH5 ...... 167 L8
DUL SE22 ...... 32 B6
Underwood Av *ASHV* GU12 ...... 113 H4
Underwood Cl *CRAWE* RH10 ...... 214 E1

Underwood Ct *CTHM* CR3 ...... 108 C6
Underwood Rd *CTHM* CR3 ...... 108 B7
HASM GU27 ...... 219 J2
Undine St *TOOT* SW17 ...... 30 C6
Union Cl *SHST* GU47 ...... 52 B7
Union Rd *CROY/NA* CR0 ...... 4 D1
FNM GU9 ...... 133 M7
FRIM GU16 ...... 94 A1
Union St *CHOB/PIR* GU24 ...... 94 D3
FARN GU14 ...... 92 D5
KUT KT1 ...... 2 D6
Union Ter *ALDT* GU11 ...... 112 D7
Unity Cl *CROY/NA* CR0 ...... 69 L7
WNWD SE27 ...... 31 M6
University Rd *WIM/MER* SW19 ...... 30 A7
Unstead La *SHGR* GU5 ...... 160 F2
Unwin Av *EBED/NFELT* TW14 ...... 15 G7
Unwin Rd *ISLW* TW7 ...... 17 H5
Upavon Gdns *BRAK* RG12 ...... 35 J5
Updown Hl *BFOR* GU20 ...... 55 G5
Upfield *CROY/NA* CR0 ...... 68 E1
HORL RH6 ...... 170 D7
Upfield Cl *HORL* RH6 ...... 170 D8
Upfold Cl *CRAN* GU6 ...... 184 E3
Upfold La *CRAN* GU6 ...... 184 E4
Upfolds Gn *RGUE* GU4 ...... 117 M4
Upland Rd *BELMT* SM2 ...... 66 A6
CBLY GU15 ...... 73 G2
CTHM CR3 ...... 109 K2
EDUL SE22 ...... 32 D1
SAND/SEL CR2 ...... 68 A4
Uplands *ASHTD* KT21 ...... 103 G2
BECK BR3 ...... 51 K2
Uplands Cl *HASM* GU27 ...... 220 A1
MORT/ESHN SW14 ...... 18 E7
Uplands Dr *LHD/OX* KT22 ...... 82 A4
Uplands Rd *FNM* GU9 ...... 11 M1
PUR/KEN CR8 ...... 87 M7
Upland Wy *EPSOM* KT18 ...... 84 F8
Uppark Gdns *HORS* RH12 ...... 229 J3
Upper Beulah Hl *NRWD* SE19 ...... 50 B1
Upper Bourne La *NFNM* GU10 ...... 10 D9
Upper Bourne V *NFNM* GU10 ...... 10 D9
Upper Bridge Rd *REDH* RH1 ...... 126 B8
Upper Brighton Rd *SURB* KT6 ...... 45 G6
Upper Broadmoor Rd
CWTH RG45 ...... 52 A4
Upper Butts *BTFD* TW8 ...... 17 M1
Upper Charles St *CBLY* GU15 ...... 72 E3
Upper Chobham Rd *CBLY* GU15 .. 73 L5
FRIM GU16 ...... 73 K6
Upper Church La *FNM* GU9 ...... 133 L7
Upper College Ride *CBLY* GU15 .. 73 H1
Upper Court Rd *CTHM* CR3 ...... 109 K5
HOR/WEW KT19 ...... 83 M1
Upper Dr *BH/WHM* TN16 ...... 90 F8
Upper Dunnymans
BNSTD SM7 ...... 85 J4
Upper Edgeborough Rd *GU* GU1.. 9 M5
Upper Elmers End Rd
BECK BR3 ...... 51 H4
BECK BR3 ...... 51 K6
Upper Elms Rd *ALDT* GU11 ...... 112 D8
Upper Fairfield Rd
LHD/OX KT22 ...... 102 F3
Upper Farm Rd
E/WMO/HCT KT8 ...... 43 J4
Upper Gordon Rd *CBLY* GU15 ...... 73 G4
Upper Gn East *MTCM* CR4 ...... 48 C2
Upper Gn West *MTCM* CR4 ...... 48 C2
Upper Grotto Rd *TWK* TW1 ...... 26 C3
Upper Guildown Rd *GUW* GU2 .... 138 E3
Upper Hale Rd *FNM* GU9 ...... 133 L2
Upper Halliford Rd *SHPTN* TW17 .. 42 B2
Upper Ham Rd
RCHPK/HAM TW10 ...... 27 G5
Upper Harestone *CTHM* CR3 ...... 128 D1
Upper High St *EW* KT17 ...... 84 B3
Upper House La *SHGR* GU5 ...... 162 C8
Upper Manor Rd
MFD/CHID GU8 ...... 159 H8
RGODL GU7 ...... 160 B2
Upper Mnt *HASM* GU27 ...... 200 D8
Upper Mulgrave Rd *BELMT* SM2 .. 65 H6
Upper Old Park La *FNM* GU9 ...... 133 J4
Upper Park Rd *CBLY* GU15 ...... 73 G4
KUTN/CMB KT2 ...... 3 J1
Upper Pillory Down *CAR* SM5..... 86 D3
Upper Pines *BNSTD* SM7 ...... 86 C7
Upper Pinewood Rd
ASHV GU12 ...... 113 M6
Upper Queen St *RGODL* GU7 ...... 160 B5
Upper Richmond Rd
PUT/ROE SW15 ...... 19 L6
Upper Richmond Rd West
RCHPK/HAM TW10 ...... 18 D6
Upper Rd *WLGTN* SM6 ...... 67 G4
Upper Rose Hl *DORK* RH4 ...... 144 E3
Upper St Michael's Rd
ALDT GU11 ...... 134 E1
Upper Sawleywood
BNSTD SM7 ...... 85 J4
Upper Selsdon Rd
SAND/SEL CR2 ...... 68 C7
Upper Shirley Rd *CROY/NA* CR0... 68 C7
Upper South Vw *FNM* GU9 ...... 133 M6
Upper Springfield
MFD/CHID GU8 ...... 158 A5
Upper Sq *ISLW* TW7 ...... 17 K5
Upper Stanford Rd
CHOB/PIR GU24 ...... 95 J7
Upper St *SHGR* GU5 ...... 141 J4
Upper Sunbury Rd *HPTN* TW12 .. 43 J1
Upper Sutton La *HEST* TW5 ...... 16 D3
Upper Teddington Rd
TEDD TW11 ...... 2 A3
Upper Terrace Rd *FARN* GU14..... 112 D1
Upperton Rd *GUW* GU2 ...... 8 E7
Upper Tooting Pk *TOOT* SW17 .... 30 C5
Upper Tooting Rd *TOOT* SW17 .... 30 C5
Upper Tulse Hl
BRXS/STRHM SW2 ...... 31 J1
Upper Union St *ALDT* GU11 ...... 112 C7
Upper Union Ter *ALDT* GU11 ...... 112 D7
Upper Vann La *MFD/CHID* GU8.... 182 D8
Upper Vernon Rd *SUT* SM1 ...... 66 A4

Upper Verran Rd *CBLY* GU15 ...... 73 G6
Upper Village Rd *ASC* SL5 ...... 36 F5
Upper Vw *VW* GU25 ...... 39 H4
Upper Wy *FNM* GU9 ...... 10 D4
Upper West St *REIG* RH2 ...... 125 J8
Upper Weybourne La *FNM* GU9.. 134 A1
Upper Woodcote Village
PUR/KEN CR8 ...... 87 G3
Upshire Gdns *BRAK* RG12 ...... 35 J4
Upshott La *WOKS/MYFD* GU22 .... 78 C7
Upton *WOKN/KNAP* GU21 ...... 76 D7
Upton Cl *FARN* GU14 ...... 93 G6
Upton Dene *BELMT* SM2 ...... 65 L6
Upton Rd *HSLW* TW3 ...... 16 D5
THHTH CR7 ...... 50 A2
Upwood Rd *STRHM/NOR* SW16 .. 49 H1
Urmston Dr *WIM/MER* SW19 ...... 29 H2
Usherwood Cl
KWD/TDW/WH KT20 ...... 123 M5
Uvedale Cl *CROY/NA* CR0 ...... 90 A1
Uvedale Crs *CROY/NA* CR0 ...... 90 A1
Uvedale Rd *OXTED* RH8 ...... 130 C3
Veryan *WOKN/KNAP* GU21 ...... 76 D7
Uxbridge Rd *FELT* TW13 ...... 25 G3
HPTN TW12 ...... 25 K5
SURB KT6 ...... 45 G4

V

Vachery La *CRAN* GU6 ...... 205 J1
Vaillant Rd *WEY* KT13 ...... 59 M3
Vale Cl *COUL/CHIP* CR5 ...... 87 H4
NFNM GU10 ...... 155 M5
ORP BR6 ...... 71 K3
WEY KT13 ...... 60 A2
WOKN/KNAP GU21 ...... 6 C3
Vale Ct *WEY* KT13 ...... 60 A2
Vale Crs *PUT/ROE* SW15 ...... 28 B5
Vale Cft *ESH/CLAY* KT10 ...... 62 C6
Vale Dr *HORS* RH12 ...... 228 E7
Vale Rd *ASHV* GU12 ...... 113 K4
CBLY GU15 ...... 72 D5
ESH/CLAY KT10 ...... 62 B7
HOR/WEW KT19 ...... 64 C3
MTCM CR4 ...... 49 G3
SUT SM1 ...... 65 L3
WEY KT13 ...... 60 A2
WPK KT4 ...... 64 C2
Vale Rd North *SURB* KT6 ...... 63 H1
The Vale *COUL/CHIP* CR5 ...... 87 H4
CROY/NA CR0 ...... 69 G1
EBED/NFELT TW14 ...... 15 L8
HEST TW5 ...... 16 B1
SUN TW16 ...... 24 D7
Vale Wood Dr *NFNM* GU10 ...... 156 A5
Vale Wood La *GSHT* GU26 ...... 198 F5
Valewood La *HASM* GU27 ...... 219 M5
Valiant Wy *FRIM* GU16 ...... 93 L1
Valley End Rd *CHOB/PIR* GU24 .... 55 L5
Valleyfield Rd
STRHM/NOR SW16 ...... 31 J6
Valley Gdns *WIM/MER* SW19 ...... 30 A8
Valley La *FNM* GU9 ...... 11 G6
Valley Rd *FRIM* GU16 ...... 93 L1
PUR/KEN CR8 ...... 88 A1
STRHM/NOR SW16 ...... 31 J5
Valley Vw *BH/WHM* TN16 ...... 90 F8
RGODL GU7 ...... 160 A5
Valley View Gdns *PUR/KEN* CR8 .. 88 B5
Valley Wk *CROY/NA* CR0 ...... 68 F1
Vallis Wy *CHSGTN* KT9 ...... 63 G3
Valnay St *TOOT* SW17 ...... 30 C6
Valroy Cl *CBLY* GU15 ...... 73 G3
Vampire Wy *FARN* GU14 ...... 112 B1
Vanbrugh Cl *CRAWW* RH11 ...... 211 H6
Vanbrugh Dr *WOT/HER* KT12 ...... 42 F7
Vancouver Cl *HOR/WEW* KT19 .... 83 M1
Vancouver Ct *HORL* RH6 ...... 171 K6
Vancouver Dr *CRAWW* RH11...... 192 A8
Vancouver Rd *FSTH* SE23 ...... 33 H3
RCHPK/HAM TW10 ...... 26 F5
Vanderbilt Rd *WAND/EARL* SW18.. 29 L2
Van Dyck Av *NWMAL* KT3 ...... 46 A7
Vandyke *BRAK* RG12 ...... 34 B6
Vandyke Cl *REDH* RH1 ...... 126 C6
Vanguard Cl *CROY/NA* CR0 ...... 4 A4
Vanguard Wy *CROY/NA* CR0...... 5 J9
EDEN TN8 ...... 131 K8
EDEN TN8 ...... 175 H3
EGRIN RH19 ...... 197 K6
LING RH7 ...... 197 K1
OXTED RH8 ...... 110 C7
WARL CR6 ...... 89 J3
WLGTN SM6 ...... 67 H6
Vanneck Sq *PUT/ROE* SW15 ...... 19 K7
Vanners *CRAWE* RH10 ...... 212 B2
Vann Farm Rd *RDKG* RH5 ...... 188 B5
Vann Lake *RDKG* RH5 ...... 188 C5
Vann Lake Rd *RDKG* RH5 ...... 188 C6
Vann La *MFD/CHID* GU8 ...... 182 A8
Vant Rd *TOOT* SW17 ...... 30 C6
Vapery La *CHOB/PIR* GU24 ...... 95 G3
Varley Wy *MTCM* CR4 ...... 48 A2
Varna Rd *HPTN* TW12 ...... 43 L1
Varney Cl *FARN* GU14 ...... 92 B4
Varsity Dr *ISLW* TW7 ...... 17 J7
Varsity Rw *MORT/ESHN* SW14 .... 18 F4
Vaughan Rd *THDIT* KT7 ...... 44 E7
Vaughan Wy *DORK* RH4 ...... 144 D2
Vaux Crs *WOT/HER* KT12 ...... 60 E5
Vauxhall Gdns *SAND/SEL* CR2..... 67 M5
Veals Md *MTCM* CR4 ...... 48 B1
Vectis Gdns *TOOT* SW17 ...... 30 E7
Vectis Rd *TOOT* SW17 ...... 30 E7
Vegal Crs *EGH* TW20 ...... 20 F6
Vellum Dr *CAR* SM5 ...... 66 D2
Venner Rd *SYD* SE26 ...... 32 F7
Ventnor Rd *BELMT* SM2 ...... 65 L6
Ventnor Ter *ASHV* GU12 ...... 112 F8
Venton Cl *WOKN/KNAP* GU21 .... 76 E7
Verbania Wy *EGRIN* RH19 ...... 196 B6
Verdayne Av *CROY/NA* CR0 ...... 51 G8
Verdayne Gdns *WARL* CR6 ...... 88 F6
Verdun Rd *BARN* SW13 ...... 19 K1
Vereker Dr *SUN* TW16 ...... 42 D3

Vermont Rd *NRWD* SE19 ...... 32 A7
SUT SM1 ...... 65 L2
Vernon Av *RYNPK* SW20 ...... 47 G2
Vernon Cl *CHERT* KT16 ...... 58 A5
HOR/WEW KT19 ...... 63 M5
HORS RH12 ...... 229 K5
Vernon Dr *ASC* SL5 ...... 36 A2
CTHM CR3 ...... 107 M4
Vernon Rd *FELT* TW13 ...... 24 D4
MORT/ESHN SW14 ...... 19 G5
SUT SM1 ...... 65 M4
Vernon Wk
KWD/TDW/WH KT20 ...... 105 G2
Vernon Wy *GUW* GU2 ...... 116 C7
Verona Dr *SURB* KT6 ...... 63 H1
Veronica Gdns *MTCM* CR4 ...... 48 F1
Veronica Rd *TOOT* SW17 ...... 30 E4
Verralls *WOKS/MYFD* GU22 ...... 7 K5
Verran Rd *BAL* SW12 ...... 30 E1
CBLY GU15 ...... 73 G6
Versailles Rd *PGE/AN* SE20 ...... 32 D8
Verulam Av *PUR/KEN* CR8 ...... 86 F2
Veryan *WOKN/KNAP* GU21 ...... 76 D7
Vesey Cl *FARN* GU14 ...... 92 D4
Vestris Rd *FSTH* SE23 ...... 33 G3
Vevers Rd *REIG* RH2 ...... 147 L3
Vevey St *FSTH* SE23 ...... 33 J3
Vibart Gdns *BRXS/STRHM* SW2 .. 31 J1
Vibia Cl *STWL/WRAY* TW19 ...... 23 G1
Viburnum Ct *CHOB/PIR* GU24 .... 75 H3
Vicarage Av *EGH* TW20 ...... 21 L7
Vicarage Cl *FNM* GU9 ...... 11 K5
GT/LBKH KT23 ...... 101 K7
KWD/TDW/WH KT20 ...... 105 H6
LING RH7 ...... 174 A5
WPK KT4 ...... 46 B8
Vicarage Ct *EGH* TW20 ...... 21 L7
Vicarage Crs *EGH* TW20 ...... 21 L6
Vicarage Dr *BECK* BR3 ...... 51 K1
MORT/ESHN SW14 ...... 19 G7
Vicarage Farm Rd *HEST* TW5 ...... 16 B3
HSLWW TW4 ...... 16 B4
Vicarage Flds *WOT/HER* KT12..... 42 F6
Vicarage Gdns *ASC* SL5 ...... 36 D5
GSHT GU26 ...... 198 F6
MTCM CR4 ...... 48 B3
Vicarage Ga *GUW* GU2 ...... 8 A8
Vicarage Hl *FNM* GU9 ...... 11 J5
Vicarage La *FNM* GU9 ...... 11 K5
FNM GU9 ...... 133 L7
FNM GU9 ...... 133 M2
HASM GU27 ...... 219 J3
HORL RH6 ...... 170 C5
LHD/OX KT22 ...... 102 E4
RDKG RH5 ...... 189 G3
RPLY/SEND GU23 ...... 97 M8
STA TW18 ...... 40 E3
STWL/WRAY TW19 ...... 21 H2
WHTN TW2 ...... 16 F8
WOKS/MYFD GU22 ...... 97 J3
Vicarage Rd *BFOR* GU20 ...... 53 M6
BLKW GU17 ...... 72 B5
CHOB/PIR GU24 ...... 76 A1
CRAWE RH10 ...... 214 D2
CROY/NA CR0 ...... 67 G2
E/WMO/HCT KT8 ...... 2 A4
EGH TW20 ...... 21 L6
KUT KT1 ...... 2 D6
LING RH7 ...... 174 A5
MORT/ESHN SW14 ...... 18 F7
STA TW18 ...... 22 A4
SUN TW16 ...... 24 C6
SUT SM1 ...... 65 K3
TEDD TW11 ...... 26 D6
WHTN TW2 ...... 16 F8
WOKS/MYFD GU22 ...... 97 J3
Vicarage Wy *DTCH/LGLY* SL3 ...... 13 G2
Vicars Oak Rd *NRWD* SE19 ...... 32 B7
Vickers Dr North *WEY* KT13 ...... 59 H8
Vickers Dr South *WEY* KT13 ...... 79 H1
Vickers Rd *ASHV* GU12 ...... 113 J4
Victoria Av *CAR* SM5 ...... 66 D2
CBLY GU15 ...... 72 D4
E/WMO/HCT KT8 ...... 43 J3
HSLWW TW4 ...... 16 D7
SAND/SEL CR2 ...... 67 M8
SURB KT6 ...... 45 G6
Victoria Cl *E/WMO/HCT* KT8 ...... 43 K3
HORL RH6 ...... 170 D6
WEY KT13 ...... 60 A2
Victoria Cottages
RCH/KEW TW9 ...... 18 C3
Victoria Ct *BAGS* GU19 ...... 54 B8
Victoria Crs *NRWD* SE19 ...... 32 B6
WIM/MER SW19 ...... 29 J8
Victoria Dr *WIM/MER* SW19 ...... 29 G1
Victoria Gdns *BH/WHM* TN16 ...... 90 F5
HEST TW5 ...... 16 B3
Victoria Ms *WAND/EARL* SW18 .... 29 M2
Victoria Pl *EW* KT17 ...... 84 B2
RCHPK/HAM TW10 ...... 18 A7
Victoria Rd *ADL/WDHM* KT15..... 59 G3
ALDT GU11 ...... 112 D7
ASC SL5 ...... 36 E5
COUL/CHIP CR5 ...... 87 G5
CRAN GU6 ...... 185 G6
CRAWW RH11 ...... 211 M3
EDEN TN8 ...... 175 M1
FARN GU14 ...... 92 E5
FELT TW13 ...... 24 E2
FNM GU9 ...... 133 M2
GU GU1 ...... 9 J5
HORL RH6 ...... 170 D6
KUT KT1 ...... 3 H7
MORT/ESHN SW14 ...... 19 G5
REDH RH1 ...... 148 D1
RGODL GU7 ...... 160 B5
SHST GU47 ...... 52 C8
STA TW18 ...... 22 B4
SURB KT6 ...... 45 G6
SUT SM1 ...... 66 A4
TEDD TW11 ...... 26 D6
TWK TW1 ...... 26 E1
WEY KT13 ...... 60 A2
WOKN/KNAP GU21 ...... 76 A7
Victoria Ter *DORK* RH4 ...... 144 D2

Victoria Tr *ALDT* GU11 ...... 112 A2
Victoria Vls *RCH/KEW* TW9 ...... 18 C5
Victoria Wy *EGRIN* RH19 ...... 216 C2
WEY KT13 ...... 60 A2
WOKN/KNAP GU21 ...... 6 D6
Victor Rd *PGE/AN* SE20 ...... 33 G8
TEDD TW11 ...... 25 M7
Victory Av *MRDN* SM4 ...... 47 M5
Victory Park Rd *ADL/WDHM* KT15.. 58 F2
Victory Pl *NRWD* SE19 ...... 32 B7
Victory Rd *CHERT* KT16 ...... 40 D7
HORS RH12 ...... 228 E6
WIM/MER SW19 ...... 29 M8
View Cl *BH/WHM* TN16 ...... 90 F6
View Ter *LING* RH7 ...... 196 D1
Viggory La *WOKN/KNAP* GU21 .... 76 B5
Vigilant Cl *SYD* SE26 ...... 32 D5
Viking *BRAK* RG12 ...... 34 B5
Village Cl *WEY* KT13 ...... 60 A2
Village Green Av *BH/WHM* TN16 .. 91 H7
Village Green Wy *BH/WHM* TN16 .. 91 H7
Village Rd *EGH* TW20 ...... 39 M3
Village Rw *BELMT* SM2 ...... 65 K6
Village St *RDKG* RH5 ...... 167 L8
Village Wy *ASHF* TW15 ...... 23 J5
BECK BR3 ...... 51 K3
SAND/SEL CR2 ...... 88 D3
Villiers Av *BRYLDS* KT5 ...... 45 J5
WHTN TW2 ...... 25 J2
Villiers Cl *BRYLDS* KT5 ...... 45 J4
Villiers Gv *BELMT* SM2 ...... 65 G7
Villiers Rd *BECK* BR3 ...... 51 G2
ISLW TW7 ...... 17 H4
KUT KT1 ...... 3 G7
Vinall Gdns *HORS* RH12 ...... 228 A5
Vincam Cl *WHTN* TW2 ...... 25 K1
Vincent Av *BRYLDS* KT5 ...... 45 L8
CAR SM5 ...... 86 A1
Vincent Cl *CHERT* KT16 ...... 40 B7
ESH/CLAY KT10 ...... 61 L2
GT/LBKH KT23 ...... 101 L5
SWTR RH13 ...... 229 H7
WDR/YW UB7 ...... 14 D1
Vincent Dr *DORK* RH4 ...... 144 D3
SHPTN TW17 ...... 42 B3
Vincent La *DORK* RH4 ...... 144 D2
Vincent Ri *BRAK* RG12 ...... 35 H3
Vincent Rd *CHERT* KT16 ...... 40 B7
COB KT11 ...... 81 H6
COUL/CHIP CR5 ...... 86 F6
CROY/NA CR0 ...... 5 H2
DORK RH4 ...... 144 D2
HSLWW TW4 ...... 16 A5
ISLW TW7 ...... 17 G3
KUT KT1 ...... 3 K8
Vincent Rw *HPTN* TW12 ...... 25 M6
Vincents Cl *COUL/CHIP* CR5 ...... 106 C2
Vincent Sq *BH/WHM* TN16 ...... 90 F3
Vine Cl *ALDT* GU11 ...... 112 D3
BRYLDS KT5 ...... 45 J5
NFNM GU10 ...... 155 K5
RGUW GU3 ...... 96 A3
STWL/WRAY TW19 ...... 13 K7
SUT SM1 ...... 65 M2
Vine House Cl *FRIM* GU16 ...... 93 K6
Vine Pl *HSLW* TW3 ...... 16 E6
Vineries Cl *WDR/YW* UB7 ...... 14 D1
Vine Rd *BARN* SW13 ...... 19 J5
E/WMO/HCT KT8 ...... 43 K3
Viners Cl *WOT/HER* KT12 ...... 42 F6
Vine St *ALDT* GU11 ...... 112 D8
Vine Wy *NFNM* GU10 ...... 155 K4
Vineyard Cl *CAT* SE6 ...... 33 K2
KUT KT1 ...... 3 G8
Vineyard Hill Rd *WIM/MER* SW19.. 29 K5
Vineyard Pth *MORT/ESHN* SW14 .. 19 G5
Vineyard Rd *FELT* TW13 ...... 24 D4
Vineyard Rw *E/WMO/HCT* KT8 .... 2 A2
The Vineyard *RCHPK/HAM* TW10.. 18 A7
Viola Av *EBED/NFELT* TW14 ...... 15 M8
STWL/WRAY TW19 ...... 23 H2
Viola Cft *BNFD* RG42 ...... 35 J1
Violet Cl *MTCM* CR4 ...... 48 B8
Violet Gdns *CROY/NA* CR0 ...... 67 L4
Violet La *CROY/NA* CR0 ...... 67 L4
Virginia Av *VW* GU25 ...... 38 F5
Virginia Cl *ASHTD* KT21 ...... 83 G8
NWMAL KT3 ...... 45 M4
STA TW18 ...... 22 F7
WEY KT13 ...... 59 M5
Virginia Dr *VW* GU25 ...... 38 F4
Virginia Gdns *FARN* GU14 ...... 92 F4
Virginia Rd *THHTH* CR7 ...... 49 L1
Viscount Gdns *BF/WBF* KT14 ...... 79 H2
Viscount Rd *STWL/WRAY* TW19 .. 23 G1
Viscount Wy *HTHAIR* TW6 ...... 15 H4
Vivien Cl *CHSGTN* KT9 ...... 63 H6
Vivienne Cl *CRAWW* RH11 ...... 192 A6
TWK TW1 ...... 18 A8
Voewood Cl *NWMAL* KT3 ...... 46 C6
Vogan Cl *REIG* RH2 ...... 147 L3
Volta Wy *CROY/NA* CR0 ...... 49 J8
Vowels La *EGRIN* RH19 ...... 215 G2
Vulcan Cl *CRAWW* RH11 ...... 211 M7
Vulcan Wy *CROY/NA* CR0 ...... 70 B8

W

Waddington Av *COUL/CHIP* CR5 .. 107 K1
Waddington Cl *COUL/CHIP* CR5 .. 107 L1
CRAWW RH11 ...... 211 K6
Waddington Wy *NRWD* SE19 ...... 49 M1
Waddon Cl *CROY/NA* CR0 ...... 67 K2
Waddon Court Rd *CROY/NA* CR0.. 67 K3
Waddon Marsh Wy *CROY/NA* CR0 49 J8
Waddon New Rd *CROY/NA* CR0 .. 4 A7
Waddon Park Av *CROY/NA* CR0 .. 67 K3
Waddon Rd *CROY/NA* CR0 ...... 67 K5
Wade's La *TEDD* TW11 ...... 26 D6
Wadham *SHST* GU47 ...... 52 C8
Wadham Cl *CRAWE* RH10 ...... 192 B6
SHPTN TW17 ...... 41 M7
Wadhurst Cl *PGE/AN* SE20 ...... 50 E2

Wadlands Brook Rd *EGRIN*
RH19 .... 196 A4
Wagbullock Ri *BRAK* RG12 .... 34 F6 ⑤
Wagg Cl *EGRIN* RH19 .... 196 D8
Waggon Cl *GUW* GU2 .... 116 B2
Waggoners Hollow *BAGS* GU19 .. 54 B7 ⑤
Waggoners Wy *GSHT* GU26 .... 198 D5
Waggoners Wells Rd
GSHT 198 D7
Wagtail Cl *HORS* RH12 .... 228 F2
Wagtail Gdns *SAND/SEL* CR2 .... 69 C8
Waights Ct *KUTN/CMB* KT2 .... 2 F4
Wain End *HORS* RH12............ 229 G4
Wainford Cl *WIM/MER* SW19 .... 29 G2 ⑧
Wainwright Gv *ISLW* TW7 ...... 17 C6
Wainwrights *CRAWW* RH11 .... 212 A6 ⑧
Wakefield Cl *BF/WBF* KT14 .... 79 H2 ④
Wakefield Gdns *NRWD* SE19 .... 32 B8
Wakefield Rd
RCHPK/HAM TW10 .... 18 A7 ⑨
Wakehams Green Dr
CRAWE RH10 .... 193 C8
Wakehurst Dr *CRAWE* RH10 .... 212 A6
Wakehurst Ms *HORS* RH12 .... 228 C8
Wakely Cl *BH/WHM* TN16 .... 90 F8
Walbury *BRAK* RG12 .... 35 H4
Walburton Rd *PUR/KEN* CR8 .... 86 F3
Waldeck Gv *WNWD* SE27 .... 31 L4
Waldeck Rd *CHSWK* W4 .... 18 D1
MORT/ESHN SW14 .... 18 F5 ⑦
Waldegrave Gdns *TWK* TW1 .... 26 C3
Waldegrave Pk *TWK* TW1 ...... 26 C5
Waldegrave Rd *NRWD* SE19 .... 32 C8
TWK TW1 .... 26 C5
Waldegrove *CROY/NA* CR0 .... 5 J8
Waldemar Av *WIM/MER* SW19 .. 29 K6
Walden Cottages *FRIM* GU16 .. 114 D6
Walden Gdns *THHTH* CR7 .... 49 J4
Waldenshaw Rd *FSTH* SE23 .... 32 F2
Waldens Park Rd
WOKN/KNAP GU21 .... 76 F7
Waldens Rd *WOKN/KNAP* GU21 .. 6 A5
Waldorf Cl *SAND/SEL* CR2 ...... 67 L7
Waldorf Hts *BLKW* GU17 .... 72 A5
Waldram Crs *FSTH* SE23 .... 32 F2
Waldram Park Rd *FSTH* SE23 .... 33 C2
Waldron Hl *BRAK* RG12 .... 35 J1
Waldronhyrst *CROY/NA* CR0 .... 67 L3
Waldron Rd *WAND/EARL* SW18.. 29 M4
The Waldrons *CROY/NA* CR0 ...... 4 C9
OXTED RH8 .... 130 C5
Waldy Ri *CRAN* GU6 .... 185 H5
Wales Av *CAR* SM5 .... 66 C4
Walesbeech *CRAWE* RH10 .... 212 D4 ⑧
Waley's La *RDKG* RH5 .... 188 A8
Walford Rd *RDKG* RH5 .... 144 E6
Walham Ri *WIM/MER* SW19 .... 29 H7 ②
Walker Cl *EBED/NFELT* TW14 .... 24 F1 ⑧
HPTN TW12 .... 25 J7 ⑦
Walker Rd *CRAWE* RH10 ...... 212 E5
Walkerscroft Md *DUL* SE21 .... 31 M2
Walker's Rdg *GU15 .... 73 H4
Walkfield Dr *EPSOM* KT18 .... 84 E7
Walking Bottom *SHGR* GU5 .... 163 M3
The Walk *OXTED* RH8 .... 129 K7
Wallace Cl *RGUW* GU3 .... 115 M4
SHPTN TW17 .... 42 A4 ⑪
Wallace Crs *CAR* SM5 .... 66 C4 ⑧
Wallace Flds *EW* KT17 .... 84 C2
Wallace Wk *ADL/WDHM* KT15.... 58 F3
Wallage La *CRAWE* RH10 .... 214 A3
The Walled Gdn *BIL* RH14 .... 224 C2
BRKHM/BTCW RH3 .... 146 A1
Wall Hill Rd *FROW* RH18........ 217 C4
Wallingford Cl *BRAK* RG12...... 35 H4
Wallington Rd *CBLY* GU15 ...... 73 K3
Wallis Wy *SWTR* RH13 .... 229 K5
Wallorton Gdns *MORT/ESHN* SW14.. 19 C6
Walmer Cl *FRIM* GU16 .... 93 J2
Walnut Cl *ALDT* GU11 .... 134 D1 ⑪
CAR SM5 .... 66 C4
EPSOM KT18 .... 84 C5
Walnut Dr
KWD/TDW/WH KT20 .... 105 H6 ③
Walnut Gv *BNSTD* SM7 .... 85 G4
Walnut La *CRAWW* RH11 ...... 191 L8
Walnut Ms *CRAWW* RH11 ...... 65 M6
Walnut Tree Av *MTCM* CR4 .... 48 B3 ⑤
Walnut Tree Cl *BARN* SW13 ...... 19 J3
BNSTD SM7 .... 85 H2
GU GU1 .... 8 E5
Walnut Tree Gdns *RGODL* GU7 .. 160 B2 ⑧
Walnut Tree La *BF/WBF* KT14 .. 79 C2 ④
Walnut Tree Rd *BTFD* TW8 .... 18 B1 ③
HEST TW5 .... 16 C1 ⑤
SHPTN TW17 .... 41 M3
Walpole Av *COUL/CHIP* CR5 .... 106 C1
RCH/KEW TW9 .... 18 C4
Walpole Crs *TEDD* TW11 .... 26 C6 ④
Walpole Gdns *WHTN* TW2 ...... 26 B5
Walpole Pl *TEDD* TW11 .... 26 C6 ⑤
Walpole Rd *CROY/NA* CR0 .... 4 E5
SURB KT6 .... 45 H7
TEDD TW11 .... 26 C6
WDSR SL4 .... 20 E1
WHTN TW2 .... 26 B3
WIM/MER SW19 ...... 30 A7
Walrus Rd *FARN* GU14 .... 112 A4
Walsham Rd *EBED/NFELT* TW14.. 24 E1
Walsh Crs *CROY/NA* CR0 .... 90 B2
Walsingham Gdns *HOR/WEW* KT19 .. 64 B3
Walsingham Rd *CROY/NA* CR0 .. 69 M8
MTCM CR4 .... 48 C5
Walter's Md *ASHTD* KT21 ...... 83 H7
Walter's Rd *SNWD* SE25 ...... 50 B4 ⑧
Walter St *KUTN/CMB* KT2 .... 2 E5
Waltham Av *GUW* GU2 .... 116 E5
Waltham Cl *SHST* GU47 ...... 52 A8 ⑧
Waltham Rd *CAR* SM5 .... 48 A8
CTHM CR3 .... 108 E4
WALTON CHEAM SM3 ...... 65 J2
NWMAL KT3 .... 46 C4 ⑧
Walton Bridge Rd
SHPTN TW17 .... 42 B7 ⑧
Walton Dr *ASC* SL5 .... 36 C1
SWTR RH13 .... 229 M5

Walton Gdns *FELT* TW13 ...... 24 C5
Walton Gn *CROY/NA* CR0 ...... 69 L7
Walton Heath *CRAWE* RH10 .. 213 C5 ⑪
Walton La *SHPTN* TW17 .... 42 A7
WEY KT13 .... 59 M1
WOT/HER KT12 .... 41 M8
Walton Pk *WOT/HER* KT12 .... 61 G1 ⑧
Walton Park La *WOT/HER* KT12 .. 61 G1
Walton Rd *EPSOM* KT18 ...... 103 M3
WOKN/KNAP GU21 .... 7 G4
WOT/HER KT12 .... 43 G5
Walton St *KWD/TDW/WH* KT20.. 104 D6
Walton Ter *WOKN/KNAP* GU21 .... 7 J2
Walton Wy *MTCM* CR4 .... 48 F4
Wanborough Dr *PUT/ROE* SW15 .. 28 E2
Wanborough Hl *RGUW* GU3 .... 136 F3
Wanborough La *CRAN* GU6 .... 185 K5
Wandle Bank *CROY/NA* CR0 .... 67 H2
WIM/MER SW19 ...... 30 A7
Wandle Cl *ASHV* GU12 .... 113 K8
CRAWE RH10 .... 212 F4 ⑦
Wandle Ct *HOR/WEW* KT19 .... 63 M3
Wandle Court Gdns
CROY/NA CR0 .... 67 H2 ⑨
Wandle Rd *CROY/NA* CR0 .... 4 C8
CROY/NA CR0 .... 67 H2
MRDN SM4 .... 48 A5
TOOT SW17 .... 30 B3
WLGTN SM6 .... 66 E2
Wandle Side *CROY/NA* CR0 .... 67 J2 ②
WLGTN SM6 .... 66 E2 ⑧
Wandle Wy *MTCM* CR4 .... 48 C5
WAND/EARL SW18 ...... 29 L2
Wandsdyke Cl *FRIM* GU16 .... 93 J1
Wansford Gn
WOKN/KNAP GU21 ...... 76 C7 ⑧
Wanstraw Gv *BRAK* RG12 ...... 35 H7 ⑧
Wantage Cl *BRAK* RG12 .... 35 H5 ⑧
CRAWE RH10 .... 212 F6
Wantage Rd *SHST* GU47 .... 72 A1
Wapiti Wy *FARN* GU14 .... 112 A1
Wapshott Rd *STA* TW18 .... 22 B7
Warbank Cl *CROY/NA* CR0........ 70 D5
Warbank Crs *CROY/NA* CR0 .... 70 B8
Warbank La *KUTN/CMB* KT2 .... 28 C8
Warblers Gn *COB* KT11 .... 81 J4
Warboys Ap *KUTN/CMB* KT2 .... 27 L7 ⑧
Warboys Rd *KUTN/CMB* KT2 .... 27 L7 ⑧
Warburton Cl *EGRIN* RH19 .... 196 D8 ⑧
Warburton Rd *WHTN* TW2 ...... 25 L2
Warbury La *WOKN/KNAP* GU21 .. 75 M5
War Coppice Rd *REDH* RH1 .... 128 A1
Ward Cl *SAND/SEL* CR2 .... 68 B4
Ward La *WARL* CR6 .... 88 F6
Wardle Cl *BAGS* GU19 .... 54 B6
Wardley St *WAND/EARL* SW18 .. 29 L1 ⑧
The Wardrobe
RCH/KEW TW9 .... 18 A7 ⑪
Wards Hl *EGH* TW20 .... 21 M7
Wards Stone Pk *BRAK* RG12 .... 35 H7 ⑧
Ward St *GU* GU1 .... 9 H6
Wareham Cl *HSLW* TW3 .... 16 E6
Wareham Rd *BRAK* RG12........ 35 J5
Warenne Hts *REDH* RH1 ...... 148 A2
Warenne Rd *LHD/OX* KT22 .... 101 M4
Warfield Rd *BRAK* RG12 .... 34 F1
EBED/NFELT TW14 .... 24 B1
HPTN TW12 .... 43 L1
Wargrove Dr *SHST* GU47 ...... 72 A1
Warham Rd *SAND/SEL* CR2 ...... 67 M4
SAND/SEL CR2 .... 68 A4
Waring St *WNWD* SE27 .... 31 M5 ⑧
Warkworth Gdns *ISLW* TW7 .... 17 K2
Warlingham Rd *THHTH* CR7 .... 49 L4
Warltersville Wy *HORL* RH6 .. 170 F8
Warminster Rd *SNWD* SE25 .... 50 D2
Warminster Sq *SNWD* SE25 .... 50 D2 ③
Warminster Wy *MTCM* CR4 .... 48 E1
Warner Av *CHEAM* SM3 .... 65 H1
Warner Cl *CRAWE* RH10 ...... 212 F7
HPTN TW12 .... 25 J6 ③
HYS/HAR UB3 .... 15 C2 ③
Warners La *SHGR* GU5 .... 141 H7
Warnham Court Rd *CAR* SM5 .. 66 C6
Warnham Rd *CRAWE* RH10 .... 212 D5
HORS RH12 .... 228 A5
Warpole Pk *WEY* KT13 .... 59 K6 ⑦
Warramill Rd *RGODL* GU7 .... 160 D4
Warren Av *BELMT* SM2 .... 65 J8
RCHPK/HAM TW10 .... 18 E6
SAND/SEL CR2 .... 69 C6
Warren Cl *EGRIN* RH19 ...... 195 H6
ESH/CLAY KT10 .... 61 L3
Warren Cnr *NFNM* GU10 ...... 132 F2
Warren Cutting *KUTN/CMB* KT2.. 28 A3
Warren Down *BNFD* RG42 ...... 34 B1 ③
Warren Dr *CRAWW* RH11 ...... 211 K2
KWD/TDW/WH KT20 .... 105 J4
Warren Dr North *SURB* KT6 .... 45 L8
Warren Dr South *BRYLDS* KT5 .. 45 M8
Warreners La *WEY* KT13 .... 60 A7
Warren Hl *EPSOM* KT18 .... 84 A6
Warren La *LHD/OX* KT22 .... 84 A6
OXTED RH8 .... 130 D8
WOKS/MYFD GU22 .... 78 D8
Warren Lodge Dr
KWD/TDW/WH KT20 .... 105 H6
Warren Md *BNSTD* SM7 .... 84 F5 ②
Warrenne Rd
BRKHM/BTCW RH3 .... 145 L2
Warrenne Wy *REIG* RH2 ...... 125 K8
Warren Pk *KUTN/CMB* KT2 .... 27 M7
WARL CR6 .... 89 C8
Warren Park Rd *SUT* SM1 ...... 66 A5
Warren Ri *FRIM* GU16 .... 73 H6
NWMAL KT3 .... 46 A1
Warren Rd *ADL/WDHM* KT15 .... 58 D8
ASHF TW15 .... 24 B8
BNSTD SM7 .... 85 C5
CROY/NA CR0 .... 5 H3
GU GU1 .... 9 L6
HAYES BR2 .... 71 H1
KUTN/CMB KT2 .... 27 M7
PUR/KEN CR8 .... 87 L2
REIG RH2 .... 125 L7
RGODL GU7 .... 160 B2
WHTN TW2 .... 17 C8
WIM/MER SW19 .... 30 B7
Warren Rw *ASC* SL5 .... 36 A2

The Warren *ALDT* GU11 ...... 112 C8 ②
ASHTD KT21 .... 103 J2
CHSGTN KT9 .... 66 A4
EHSLY KT24 .... 120 C4
FNM GU9 .... 134 B1
HEST TW5 .... 16 C2
HOR/WEW KT19 .... 64 A3
KWD/TDW/WH KT20 .... 105 H5
LHD/OX KT22 .... 81 M2
Warren Wy *WEY* KT13 .... 59 M4 ⑧
Warren Wood Cl *HAYES* BR2 .... 70 D1
Warrington Ms *ALDT* GU11 .... 134 B1 ③
Warrington Rd *CROY/NA* CR0 ...... 4 A8
RCHPK/HAM TW10 ...... 18 A7 ⑪
Warrington Sp *WDSR* SL4 ...... 20 E1
Warwick *BRAK* RG12 .... 35 H7
STA TW18 .... 22 F7
Warwick Cl *ALDT* GU11 .... 134 F1 ⑧
CBLY GU15 .... 73 L6
HPTN TW12 .... 25 M8
RDKG RH5 .... 166 E2
Warwick Deeping
CHERT KT16 .... 57 M4 ②
Warwick Dr *BARN* SW13 .... 19 L5
Warwick Gdns *ASHTD* KT21...... 82 F7
THDIT KT7 .... 44 C5
Warwick Gv *BRYLDS* KT5 .... 45 J7
Warwick La *WOKN/KNAP* GU21.. 96 D1
Warwick Rd *ASHF* TW15 .... 23 H6
ASHV GU12 .... 93 J8
COUL/CHIP CR5 ...... 86 F4
FARN GU14 .... 112 A1
HSLWW TW4 .... 15 L5
KUT KT1 .... 2 B4
NWMAL KT3 .... 45 M3 ⑧
PGE/AN SE20 .... 50 E3
RDKG RH5 .... 166 F3
REDH RH1 .... 126 C7
SUT SM1 .... 65 M4 ⑩
THDIT KT7 .... 44 C5
THHTH CR7 .... 49 K3
WHTN TW2 .... 26 B2
Warwick's Bench *GU* GU1 ...... 9 H8
Warwick's Bench Rd *GU* GU1 .... 9 J9
Warwick Wold Rd *REDH* RH1 .. 127 K3
Wasdale Cl *SHST* GU47 .... 52 A7
Washington Cl *REIG* RH2 ...... 125 K6
Washington Rd *BARN* SW13 .... 19 K2
CRAWW RH11 .... 211 H6
KUT KT1 .... 3 J7
WPK KT4 .... 64 E1
Washpond La *WARL* CR6 .... 89 M8
Wasp Green La *REDH* RH1 .... 171 L1
Wassand Cl *CRAWE* RH10 .... 212 D3
Wastdale Rd *FSTH* SE23 .... 33 C2
Watchetts Dr *CBLY* GU15 ...... 72 F7
Watchetts Lake Cl *CBLY* GU15 .. 73 C6 ⑧
Watchetts Rd *CBLY* GU15 ...... 72 E6
Watchmoor Rd *CBLY* GU15 .... 72 D5
Watcombe Rd *SNWD* SE25 .... 50 E5
Waterbank Rd *CAT* SE6 .... 33 L4
Watercress Wy
WOKN/KNAP GU21 ...... 76 E7
Waterden Rd *GU* GU1 .... 9 K5
Waterer Gdns
KWD/TDW/WH KT20 .... 85 H8
Waterer Ri *WLGTN* SM6 .... 67 C5
Waterers Ri *WOKN/KNAP* GU21 .. 76 A7
Waterfall Cl *VW* GU25 .... 38 C3
Waterfall Cottages
WIM/MER SW19 .... 30 A7
Waterfall Rd *WIM/MER* SW19 .. 30 A7 ⑧
Waterfall Ter *TOOT* SW17 ...... 30 B7 ⑧
Waterfield *KWD/TDW/WH* KT20.. 104 E2
Waterfield Cl *SWTR* RH13 .... 229 H6 ⑧
Waterfield Dr *WARL* CR6 ...... 108 E1
Waterfield Gdns *CRAWW* RH11.. 211 H5
SNWD SE25 .... 50 B4 ③
Waterfield Gn
KWD/TDW/WH KT20 .... 104 E2
Waterfields *LHD/OX* KT22 .... 102 E1
Waterford Cl *COB* KT11 .... 81 H1
Waterham Rd *BRAK* RG12 ...... 34 E6
Waterhouse La
KWD/TDW/WH KT20 .... 105 J3
PUR/KEN CR8 .... 107 M1
REDH RH1 .... 127 C8
Waterhouse Md *SHST* GU47 .... 72 A2 ⑦
Waterlakes *EDEN* TN8 .... 175 M1
Waterlands La *HORS* RH12 .... 227 H1
Water La *CHOB/PIR* GU24 ...... 95 H1
COB KT11 .... 81 J4
EDEN TN8 .... 175 G2
FARN GU14 .... 92 D2
FNM GU9 .... 134 C5
GDST RH9 .... 151 G4
GT/LBKH KT23 .... 101 H8
KUT KT1 .... 2 D5
MFD/CHID GU8 .... 181 L5
OXTED RH8 .... 110 D8
RCH/KEW TW9 .... 18 A7
RDKG RH5 .... 164 E1
SHGR GU5 .... 140 E4
TWK TW1 .... 26 D2
Water Lea *CRAWE* RH10 ...... 212 D6
Waterloo Cl *CBLY* GU15 .... 73 L2
EBED/NFELT TW14 .... 24 C2
Waterloo Pl *RCH/KEW* TW9 .... 18 D1 ③
Waterloo Rd *ASHV* GU12 ...... 112 F8
HOR/WEW KT19 .... 84 A2
SUT SM1 .... 66 A4
Waterlow Rd *REIG* RH2 ...... 147 M1
Watermead *EBED/NFELT* TW14.. 24 B2
KWD/TDW/WH KT20 .... 104 E3
WOKN/KNAP GU21 .... 76 E8
Watermead La *MTCM* CR4 ...... 48 C6
Watermead Rd *CAT* SE6 ...... 33 M5
Watermill Cl *RCHPK/HAM* TW10.. 26 F4
Water Mill Wy *FELT* TW13 ...... 25 J3
Watermill Wy *WIM/MER* SW19.. 47 M1
Waterperry La *CHOB/PIR* GU24 .. 56 C8
Waters Dr *STA* TW18............ 22 C5
Watersedge *HOR/WEW* KT19 .. 63 M3
Waterside *EGRIN* RH19 ...... 196 E8
HORL RH6 .... 170 D4 ⑧
Waterside Cl *CRAWW* RH11 .... 211 H5

Waterside Dr *WOT/HER* KT12 .. 42 E5
Waterside La *RGODL* GU7 .... 159 M6
Waterside Ms *GU* GU1 .... 116 F6
Waterside Rd *GU* GU1 .... 117 G5
Waterside Wy *TOOT* SW17 .... 29 M5
WOKN/KNAP GU21 ...... 76 E8
Waterslade *REDH* RH1 ...... 126 B8
Watersmeet Cl *RGUE* GU4 .... 117 K3 ③
Watersplash Cl *KUT* KT1 .... 2 E8 ③
Water Splash La *ASC* SL5 ...... 37 H1
Watersplash Rd *SHPTN* TW17 .. 41 K4
Waters Rd *KUT* KT1 .... 3 L7
Waters Sq *KUT* KT1 .... 3 L8
Water Tower Hl *CROY/NA* CR0 .... 4 F9
Waterway Rd *LHD/OX* KT22 .... 102 D3
Watery La *CHOB/PIR* GU24 .... 56 A8
RYNPK SW20 .... 47 J2
Wates Wy *MTCM* CR4 .... 48 C6
Watford Cl *GU* GU1 .... 9 M4
Wathen Rd *DORK* RH4 .... 144 E1
Watlings Cl *CROY/NA* CR0 ...... 51 H6
Watlington Gv *SYD* SE26 ...... 33 H6 ⑧
Watney Rd *MORT/ESHN* SW14 .. 18 F5
Watneys Rd *MTCM* CR4 .... 49 C5
Watson Av *CHEAM* SM3 .... 65 H1
Watson Cl *CRAWE* RH10 ...... 212 F6
WIM/MER SW19 ...... 30 B7 ③
Watson Rd *DORK* RH4 ...... 143 M3
Wattendon Rd *PUR/KEN* CR8 .. 87 L6
Watts Common Rd *ALDT* GU11.. 112 B2
Watt's La *KWD/TDW/WH* KT20 .. 105 G4
TEDD TW11 .... 26 C6
Watts Lea *WOKN/KNAP* GU21 .. 76 D6
Watt's Md *KWD/TDW/WH* KT20 .. 105 G4
Watts Rd *GU* GU14 .... 92 C4
THDIT KT7 .... 44 D7
Wavel Pl *NRWD* SE19 .... 32 C5
Wavendene Av *EGH* TW20 .... 21 M8
Waverleigh Rd *CRAN* GU6 .... 185 H8
Waverley *BRAK* RG12 .... 34 B5 ⑧
PUR/KEN CR8 .... 88 B6
SUT SM1 .... 65 L1
WHTN TW2 .... 25 J2
Waverley Av *BRYLDS* KT5 ...... 45 L6
PUR/KEN CR8 .... 88 B6
SUT SM1 .... 65 L1
WHTN TW2 .... 25 J2
Waverley Cl *CBLY* GU15 .... 73 J5
E/WMO/HCT KT8 ...... 43 K5
Waverley Dr *ASHV* GU12 ...... 113 K3
CBLY GU15 .... 73 H4
CHERT KT16 .... 58 A2
VW GU25 .... 38 D4
Waverley Gdns *ASHV* GU12 .. 113 K3 ③
CROY/NA CR0 ....
CTHM CR3 .... 107 M4
EBED/NFELT TW14 .... 15 H7
HORS RH12 .... 229 G7
HPTN TW12 .... 26 A5
WIM/MER SW19 ...... 29 K3
Wellington Rd North
HSLWW TW4 .... 16 C5
Wellington Rd South
HSLWW TW4 .... 16 C6
Wellington St *ALDT* GU11 .... 112 D7
Wellington Town Rd
EGRIN RH19 .... 196 A6
Wellington Wy *FARN* GU14 .... 112 A2
HORL RH6 .... 170 C4
WEY KT13 .... 59 J8
Well La *HASM* GU27 .... 220 A3
MORT/ESHN SW14 .... 18 F7
WOKN/KNAP GU21 ...... 76 F7
Well Pth *WOKN/KNAP* GU21 .... 76 F7
Well Rd *NFNM* GU10 .... 132 B3
Wells Cl *GT/LBKH* KT23 ...... 101 L6
HORS RH12 .... 228 C7
Wells Cottages *FNM* GU9 ...... 10 C6
Wellside Gdns
MORT/ESHN SW14 .... 18 F6 ③
Wells La *ASC* SL5 .... 36 E4
Wells Lea *EGRIN* RH19 ...... 196 A6
Wells Meadow *EGRIN* RH19 .. 196 A6 ⑧
Wells Park Rd *SYD* SE26 ...... 32 D4
Wells Pl *REDH* RH1 .... 126 E4
Wells Rd *CRAWE* RH10 ...... 212 B7 ⑧
EPSOM KT18 .... 83 L5
RGUE GU4 .... 117 M5
Well Wy *EPSOM* KT18 .... 83 K4
Wellwood Cl *COUL/CHIP* CR5 .. 87 H4
SWTR RH13 .... 229 L5 ③
Wellwynds Rd *CRAN* GU6 .... 185 H7
Welwyn Av *EBED/NFELT* TW14 .. 15 J8 ③
Welwyn Cl *CRAWW* RH11 ...... 211 H6
Wembley Rd *HPTN* TW12 ...... 43 K1 ③
Wembury Pk *LING* RH7 ...... 173 J8
Wendela Cl *WOKS/MYFD* GU22 .. 6 F8
Wendley Dr *ADL/WDHM* KT15 .. 58 E3
Wendling Rd *CAR* SM5 .... 48 A8
Wendover Dr *FRIM* GU16 ...... 73 M6
NWMAL KT3 .... 46 C6
Wendover Pl *STA* TW18 .... 22 A6 ②
Wendover Rd *STA* TW18 .... 22 A6
Wendron Cl
WOKN/KNAP GU21 ...... 76 D8 ③
The Wend *COUL/CHIP* CR5 .... 87 G4
Wendy Crs *GUW* GU2 .... 116 D6
Wenlock Cl *CRAWW* RH11 .... 211 K5
Wensleydale *CRAWW* RH11 .. 211 M6
Wensleydale Dr *CBLY* GU15 .... 74 A4
Wensleydale Gdns *HPTN* TW12.. 25 L8
Wensleydale Rd *HPTN* TW12 .. 25 L8
Wentworth Av *ASHF* TW15 .... 23 L5 ⑧
Wentworth Cl *ASHF* TW15 .... 23 L5 ⑧
ASHV GU12 .... 113 K2
FNM GU9 .... 134 C3
HAYES BR2 .... 70 D1 ③
MRDN SM4 .... 47 K7 ②
RPLY/SEND GU23 ...... 98 E3
SURB KT6 .... 63 G1
Wentworth Crs *ASHV* GU12 .. 113 K3
VW GU25 .... 38 C4
Wentworth Dr *CRAWE* RH10 .. 213 G2
VW GU25 .... 38 C4
Wentworth Rd *CROY/NA* CR0 .. 49 K7
Wentworth Wy *ASC* SL5 ...... 35 M2
SAND/SEL CR2 .... 88 D5
Werndee Rd *SNWD* SE25 ...... 50 D4
Wesley Av *HSLW* TW3 .... 16 B4
Wesley Cl *CRAWW* RH11 ...... 211 H6
HORL RH6 .... 170 D4
REIG RH2 .... 147 J1
Wesley Dr *EGH* TW20 .... 21 M8
Wessels *KWD/TDW/WH* KT20 .. 105 C3
Wessex Av *WIM/MER* SW19 .. 47 K2
Wessex Cl *KUTN/CMB* KT2 ...... 3 L5
Wessex Pl *FNM* GU9 .... 11 H1

Wessex Rd *FARN* GU14............ 92 C7
HTHAIR TW6........................... 13 M6
Westacres *ESH/CLAY* KT10..... 61 J6 🔟
West Av *CRAWE* RH10........... 212 C1
FNM GU9.............................. 134 A3
REDH RH1............................ 148 C6
WLGTN SM6.......................... 67 H4
WOT/HER KT12...................... 60 B8
West Bank *DORK* RH4........... 144 C3
Westbank Rd *HPTN* TW12....... 25 M7
West Barnes La *NWMAL* KT3.. 46 D5
RYNPK SW20........................ 46 E3
Westbourne Av *CHEAM* SM3... 65 H1 🔟
Westbourne Dr *FSTH* SE23..... 33 G2
Westbourne Rd *CROY/NA* CR0. 50 C6
FELT TW13........................... 24 C4
SHST GU47........................... 72 B2
STA TW18............................. 22 E8 🔟
SYD SE26............................. 33 G7
Westbrook Av *HPTN* TW12..... 25 J8
Westbrook Gdns *BRAK* RG12. 35 G1 🔟
Westbrook HI *MFD/CHID* GU8. 157 L5
Westbrook Rd *HEST* TW5...... 16 C2
RGODL GU7.......................... 159 M4
STA TW18............................. 22 C6
THHTH CR7........................... 50 A1
Westbury Av *ESH/CLAY* KT10. 62 C5 🔟
SHPTN TW17.......................... 41 L6 🔟
Westbury Gdns *FNM* GU9....... 134 B5 🔟
Westbury PI *BTFD* TW8.......... 18 A1 🔟
Westbury Rd *BECK* BR3......... 51 H3
CROY/NA CR0........................ 50 A6
FELT TW13........................... 25 G2
NWMAL KT3.......................... 46 A4
PGE/AN SE20........................ 51 G1
Westbury Ter *BH/WHM* TN16.. 111 M8
Westbury Wy *ASHV* GU12...... 113 G7
Westcar La *WOT/HER* KT12.... 60 E5
West CI *ASHF* TW15.............. 23 H5
FNM GU9.............................. 134 A2
Westcombe Av *CROY/NA* CR0. 49 H6
Westcombe CI *BRAK* RG12.... 35 G7
West Common Rd *HAYES* BR2. 70 D1
Westcoombe Av *RYNPK* SW20. 46 C1
Westcote Rd *STRHM/NOR* SW16. 30 F6
Westcott CI *CROY/NA* CR0..... 69 L7 🔟
Westcott Rd *DORK* RH4......... 144 C2
Westcott St *DORK* RH4......... 143 L3
Westcott Wy *BELMT* SM2....... 64 F8
Westcroft Gdns *MRDN* SM4.... 47 J3
Westcroft Rd *CAR* SM5.......... 66 D3
West Cross Wy *BTFD* TW8...... 17 L1
Westdene Mdw *CRAN* GU6..... 184 D6
Westdene Wy *WEY* KT13........ 60 B2
Westdown Rd *CAT* SE6........... 33 K1
West Dr *ADL/WDHM* KT15...... 58 E8 🔟
ASC SL5............................... 38 A5
BELMT SM2.......................... 65 G7
CAR SM5.............................. 66 A8
KWD/TDW/WH KT20............... 85 G8
TOOT SW17.......................... 30 E5
VW GU25.............................. 38 A6
West End Gdns *ESH/CLAY* KT10. 61 J4
West End Gv *FNM* GU9.......... 133 K7
West End La *ESH/CLAY* KT10.. 61 J6
HASM GU27........................... 221 G1
HYS/HAR UB3........................ 14 F2
NFNM GU10........................... 155 H8
Westerdale Dr *FRIM* GU16..... 73 L6
Westerfolds CI *WOKS/MYFD* GU22. 7 L4
Westerham CI *ADL/WDHM* KT15. 58 F5
BELMT SM2........................... 65 K8 🔟
Westerham HI *BH/WHM* TN16. 111 L4
Westerham Rd *HAYES* BR2..... 71 C5
OXTED RH8............................ 130 D3
Westerley Crs *SYD* SE26........ 33 J6 🔟
Westermain *ADL/WDHM* KT15. 58 F8 🔟
Western Av *CHERT* KT16......... 40 D3
CHOB/PIR GU24...................... 95 K3
EGH TW20............................. 39 L3
Western Dr *SHPTN* TW17........ 42 A5
Western La *BAL* SW12............ 30 D1
Western Perimeter Rd
STWL/WRAY TW19................... 13 L6
Western Rd *ALDT* GU11......... 112 B8
BNFD RG42........................... 34 B1
BRAK RG12........................... 34 C2
MTCM CR4............................ 48 B1
SUT SM1............................... 65 K4
West Farm Av *ASHTD* KT21... 82 F8
West Farm CI *ASHTD* KT21.... 102 F1
West Farm Dr *ASHTD* KT21.... 103 G1
Westfield *REIG* RH2.............. 125 L5
SHGR GU5............................. 164 B1
Westfield Av *SAND/SEL* CR2... 88 A3
WOKS/MYFD GU22................. 97 H3
Westfield CI *SUT* SM1........... 65 J3 🔟
Westfield Common
WOKS/MYFD GU22................. 97 H4
Westfield Dr *GT/LBKH* KT23.. 101 L3
Westfield Gv
WOKS/MYFD GU22................. 97 H2 🔟
Westfield La *NFNM* GU10...... 155 H8
Westfield Rd *BECK* BR3......... 51 J2
CBLY GU15........................... 72 E4
CRAWW RH11......................... 211 L3
CROY/NA CR0........................ 4 A5
GU GU1................................ 117 H4
MTCM CR4............................ 48 B2
SURB KT6............................. 45 G5
SUT SM1............................... 65 J3
WOKS/MYFD GU22................. 97 G5
WOT/HER KT12...................... 43 H7
Westfields *BARN* SW13......... 19 J5
Westfields Av *BARN* SW13..... 19 H6
Westfield Wy *WOKS/MYFD* GU22. 97 H4
West Flexford La *RGUW* GU3. 137 H1
West Gdns *EW* KT17.............. 64 B8
WIM/MER SW19..................... 30 B7
Westgate Rd *BECK* BR3......... 51 M1
SNWD SE25.......................... 50 C4
Westglade *FARN* GU14......... 92 A5 🔟
West Green Dr *CRAWW* RH11. 211 M3
West Hall Rd *RCH/KEW* TW9.. 18 E3

Westhall Rd *WARL* CR6.......... 88 D8
Westhay Gdns
MORT/ESHN SW14................. 18 E7
West Heath *CHOB/PIR* GU24.. 95 G5 🔟
West Heath Rd *FARN* GU14.... 92 C5
West HI *EGRIN* RH19............. 196 B3
EGRIN RH19.......................... 216 A1
HOR/WEW KT19...................... 83 M3
MFD/CHID GU8....................... 157 M6
ORP BR6............................... 91 J2
OXTED RH8........................... 130 A4
PUT/ROE SW15...................... 29 C1
SAND/SEL CR2....................... 68 B7
West Hill Av *HOR/WEW* KT19. 83 M2
West Hill Bank *OXTED* RH8.... 130 A4
West Hill CI *CHOB/PIR* GU24.. 95 L2
MFD/CHID GU8....................... 157 M6
West Hill Rd *WOKS/MYFD* GU22. 6 B9
West Hoathly Rd *EGRIN* RH19. 215 M6
Westhorpe Rd *PUT/ROE* SW15. 19 M5
West House CI *WIM/MER* SW19. 29 H2
Westhumble St *RDKG* RH5..... 122 E5
Westland CI
STWL/WRAY TW19.................. 14 B8 🔟
Westland Dr *HAYES* BR2........ 70 C1
Westlands Ct *EPSOM* KT18.... 83 M5
Westlands Wy *OXTED* RH8..... 130 A1
West La *EGRIN* RH19............. 216 A1
RDKG RH5............................. 143 G5
Westleas *HORL* RH6.............. 170 B4
Westlees CI *RDKG* RH5......... 144 F5
West Leigh *EGRIN* RH19........ 216 C2
Westleigh Av *COUL/CHIP* CR5. 86 D6
PUT/ROE SW15...................... 19 M7
Westmacott Dr
EBED/NFELT TW14.................. 24 D2 🔟
Westmead *FARN* GU14........... 92 E6
West Md *PUT/ROE* SW15....... 64 B5
Westmead Dr *REDH* RH1....... 148 D8 🔟
Westmead Rd *SUT* SM1......... 66 A3
West Meads *GUW* GU2........... 138 C1
Westminster Av *THHTH* CR7... 49 L2
Westminster CI
EBED/NFELT TW14.................. 24 B6
TEDD TW11............................ 26 D6 🔟
Westminster Dr *CRAWE* RH10. 212 F4
SUT SM1............................... 66 A1
Westmoat CI *BECK* BR3......... 33 M8 🔟
Westmont Rd *ESH/CLAY* KT10. 62 B1
Westmoreland Dr *BELMT* SM2. 65 L6 🔟
Westmoreland Rd *BARN* SW13. 19 J3
Westmore Rd *BH/WHM* TN16. 110 F3
Westmorland CI
HOR/WEW KT19...................... 64 B7 🔟
TWK TW1.............................. 17 L8 🔟
Westmorland Dr *CBLY* GU15.. 73 L6
Westmorland Wy *MTCM* CR4.. 49 G4
Weston Av *ADL/WDHM* KT15.. 58 D3
E/WMO/HCT KT8.................... 43 H4
ESH/CLAY KT10...................... 44 B7
Weston CI *COUL/CHIP* CR5.... 107 J2
Weston Ct *RGODL* GU7.......... 160 B3
Weston Flds *SHGR* GU5......... 140 F5
Weston Gdns *ISLW* TW7........ 17 H3 🔟
WOKS/MYFD GU22................. 78 B6
Weston Gn *THDIT* KT7............ 44 B8
Weston Green Rd
ESH/CLAY KT10...................... 44 A8
THDIT KT7............................ 44 B8
Weston Gv *BAGS* GU19.......... 54 C7 🔟
Weston Lea *EHSLY* KT24........ 100 A7
Weston Pk *KUT* KT1.............. 2 E6
THDIT KT7............................ 44 B8
Weston Park CI *THDIT* KT7.... 44 B8 🔟
Weston Rd *EW* KT17............. 84 B1
GUW GU2.............................. 8 A1
THDIT KT7............................ 44 B8
Weston Wy *WOKS/MYFD* GU22. 78 B6
Westover CI *BELMT* SM2........ 65 L7 🔟
Westow HI *NRWD* SE19.......... 32 B7
Westow St *NRWD* SE19......... 32 B7
West Pde *HORS* RH12............ 228 T5
West Park Av *RCH/KEW* TW9.. 18 D3
West Park CI *HEST* TW5......... 16 C1
West Park Rd *CRAWE* RH10... 194 C6
HOR/WEW KT19...................... 83 J2
LING RH7.............................. 194 D3
RCH/KEW TW9...................... 18 D3
West PI *WIM/MER* SW19........ 28 F6
West Rp *HTHAIR* TW6........... 14 D3
West Rd *CBLY* GU15.............. 73 G4
CHSGTN KT9.......................... 82 F1
EBED/NFELT TW14.................. 24 A1
FARN GU14........................... 92 D1
GU GU1................................ 9 K5
KUTN/CMB KT2...................... 45 M1
REIG RH2.............................. 147 L1
WEY KT13............................. 59 L7
West Sheen V *RCH/KEW* TW9. 18 C6
West Side Common
WIM/MER SW19..................... 28 F6
West St *CAR* SM5.................. 66 C2
CRAWW RH11......................... 212 A4
CROY/NA CR0........................ 4 D9
DORK RH4............................. 144 D2
EGRIN RH19.......................... 216 B1
EPSOM KT18.......................... 83 M3
EW KT17............................... 64 B8
HASM GU27........................... 219 M3
HOR/WEW KT19...................... 83 M3
HORS RH12........................... 228 E7
LING RH7.............................. 174 D8
REIG RH2.............................. 125 J8
SUT SM1............................... 65 L4
WOKN/KNAP GU21................. 6 E5
West Street La *CAR* SM5....... 66 C3
West Street PI *CROY/NA* CR0. 4 D9
West Temple Sheen
MORT/ESHN SW14................. 18 E7
West Vw *EBED/NFELT* TW14.. 23 M2
West View Av *CTHM* CR3....... 88 C8
Westview CI *REDH* RH1......... 148 B3
West View Gdns *EGRIN* RH19. 216 B1
West View Rd *WARL* CR6....... 108 E1
Westville Rd *THDIT* KT7........ 44 D7
Westward Ho *GU* GU1........... 117 J6

Westwates CI *BRAK* RG12..... 35 G1 🔟
West Wy *CAR* SM5................. 66 A8
Westway *CRAWE* RH10.......... 193 K6
West Wy *CRAWE* RH10.......... 212 D2
CROY/NA CR0........................ 69 H1
Westway *CTHM* CR3............. 108 A4
GUW GU2.............................. 116 C6
West Wy *HEST* TW5.............. 16 C3
Westway *RYNPK* SW20.......... 46 A6
West Wy *SHPTN* TW17.......... 42 A6
SWTR RH13........................... 227 G6
Westway CI *RYNPK* SW20...... 46 A6
West Way Gdns *CROY/NA* CR0. 69 G1
Westway Gdns *REDH* RH1..... 126 D5
Westways *BH/WHM* TN16...... 111 M8
EDEN TN8.............................. 153 M7
HOR/WEW KT19...................... 64 C3
Westway *STRHM/NOR* SW16. 31 H7
Westwell Road Ap
STRHM/NOR SW16................. 31 H7 🔟
Westwick Gdns *HEST* TW5.... 15 L4
Westwood Av *ADL/WDHM* KT15. 78 C2
NRWD SE19........................... 49 M1 🔟
Westwood CI *ESH/CLAY* KT10. 61 M2 🔟
Westwood Gdns *BARN* SW13. 19 J5 🔟
Westwood HI *SYD* SE26......... 32 D6
Westwood La *RGUW* GU3....... 114 D6
RGUW GU3............................ 136 E2
Westwood Pk *FSTH* SE23...... 32 E1
Westwood Rd *BARN* SW13..... 19 J5
BFOR GU20........................... 55 H1
COUL/CHIP CR5...................... 87 G8
Wetherby Gdns *FARN* GU14... 112 F1
Wetherby Wy *CHSGTN* KT9.... 63 H6 🔟
Wettern CI *SAND/SEL* CR2..... 68 B8
Wetton PI *EGH* TW20............. 21 J6 🔟
Wexfenne Gdns
WOKS/MYFD GU22................. 78 E6
Wexford Rd *BAL* SW12.......... 30 C1
Wey Av *CHERT* KT16............. 40 D3
Wey Bank *ALTN* GU34........... 154 B6
Weybank *RPLY/SEND* GU23... 79 H6
Weybank CI *FNM* GU9............ 133 M6 🔟
Weybarton *BF/WBF* KT14....... 79 J3
Weybourne PI *SAND/SEL* CR2. 68 A8
Weybourne Rd *FNM* GU9....... 134 B4
Weybourne St
WAND/EARL SW18.................. 29 M3
Weybridge Pk *WEY* KT13....... 59 L4 🔟
Weybridge Rd *ADL/WDHM* KT15. 59 H3
THHTH CR7........................... 49 K4
Wey CI *ASHV* GU12............... 113 K8
BF/WBF KT14......................... 78 E3
CBLY GU15........................... 72 E4
Weycombe Rd *HASM* GU27.... 219 M1
Wey Ct *ADL/WDHM* KT15...... 59 G7
HOR/WEW KT19...................... 63 M3
RGODL GU7........................... 160 D3
Weydon Hill CI *FNM* GU9....... 10 F3
Weydon Hill Rd *FNM* GU9...... 10 F3
Weydon La *FNM* GU9............. 10 B5
Weydon Mill La *FNM* GU9...... 10 E2
Weydown CI *GUW* GU2........... 116 C3
WIM/MER SW19..................... 29 H2
Weydown La *GUW* GU2.......... 116 D3
Weydown Rd *HASM* GU27...... 219 L2
Wey HI *HASM* GU27............... 219 K3
Weylands CI *WOT/HER* KT12.. 60 A5
Weylea Av *RGUE* GU4........... 117 K5
Wey Lodge CI *LIPH* GU30....... 218 A5 🔟
Wey Manor Rd *ADL/WDHM* KT15. 59 G7
Weymead CI *CHERT* KT16...... 40 F7
Wey Rd *RGODL* GU7.............. 160 D4
WEY KT13............................. 59 J2
Weyside *BF/WBF* KT14.......... 79 J2
Weyside Gdns *GU* GU1.......... 116 E6
Wey South Pth *CRAN* GU6..... 184 C5
Wey - South Pth *GUW* GU2.... 9 G8
Wey South Pth *MFD/CHID* GU8. 203 M7
Wey - South Pth *RGUE* GU4... 139 H8
SHGR GU5............................. 184 B1
Weysprings *HASM* GU27........ 219 J2
Weyview CI *GU* GU1.............. 116 F6
Wey View Ct *GU* GU1............. 8 E5
Weywood CI *FNM* GU9........... 134 C2
Weywood La *FNM* GU9.......... 134 B2
Wharf Bridge Rd *ISLW* TW7... 17 L5
Wharfedale Gdns
STRHM/NOR SW16................. 49 J4
Wharfenden Wy *FRIM* GU16... 93 J3
Wharf La *RPLY/SEND* GU23.... 97 M5
TWK TW1.............................. 26 D2
Wharf Rd *ASHV* GU12........... 113 K5
FRIM GU16............................ 93 J3
GU GU1................................ 8 F4
STWL/WRAY TW19.................. 20 F1
Wharf St *RGODL* GU7............ 160 B5 🔟
Wharf Wy *FNM* GU16............ 93 J3
Wharncliffe Gdns *SNWD* SE25. 50 B2
Wharncliffe Rd *SNWD* SE25.. 50 A2
Wharton Rd *GUW* GU2........... 116 D3
PGE/AN SE20......................... 33 G8
Whatley Av *RYNPK* SW20...... 47 G3
Whatley Gn *BRAK* RG12........ 34 E6 🔟
Whatman Rd *FSTH* SE23....... 33 G1
Whatmore CI
STWL/WRAY TW19.................. 13 K8 🔟
Wheatash Rd *ADL/WDHM* KT15. 58 E1
Wheatfield Wy *HORL* RH6..... 170 E5
KUT KT1............................... 2 E8
Wheathill Rd *PGE/AN* SE20... 50 F2
Whitlet CI *FNM* GU9.............. 10 E1
Whitley CI *STWL/WRAY* TW19. 14 A8
Wheat Knoll *PUR/KEN* CR8.... 87 M6
Wheatlands *HEST* TW5......... 16 D1
Wheatlands Rd *TOOT* SW17... 30 D4 🔟
Wheatley *BRAK* RG12............ 34 B5
Wheatley Rd *ISLW* TW7......... 17 J5
Wheatsheaf CI *CHERT* KT16... 58 A5
HORS RH12........................... 229 H4
WOKN/KNAP GU21................. 6 D3
Wheatsheaf La *FUL/PGN* SW6. 19 M2 🔟
STA TW18............................. 22 C8
Wheatstone CI *CRAWE* RH10. 192 E6
WIM/MER SW19..................... 48 A1
Wheeler Av *OXTED* RH8........ 130 A3
Wheeler La *MFD/CHID* GU8.... 181 H3
Wheeler Rd *CRAWE* RH10..... 212 E5

Wheelers La
BRKHM/BTCW RH3................ 145 L2
EPSOM KT18.......................... 83 M4
HORL RH6............................. 171 K7
Wheelers Wy *EGRIN* RH19.... 195 M8
Wheelwrights La *GSHT* GU26. 198 D5
Whelan Wy *WLGTN* SM6........ 67 G2
Wherwell Rd *GUW* GU2.......... 8 E7
Whimbrel CI *PUR/KEN* CR8.... 88 A1
Whinfell CI *STRHM/NOR* SW16. 31 G6
Whins CI *CBLY* GU15............. 72 E5
Whins Dr *CBLY* GU15............ 72 E5
Whinshill Ct *ASC* SL5............ 37 K8
Whipley CI *RGUE* GU4........... 117 L3 🔟
Whistler CI *CRAWE* RH10...... 212 C6
Whistler Gv *SHST* GU47........ 72 A3
Whistley CI *BRAK* RG12........ 35 H3
Whitby CI *BH/WHM* TN16...... 110 E1
FARN GU14........................... 93 H8 🔟
Whitby Gdns *SUT* SM1.......... 66 A1 🔟
Whitby Rd *SUT* SM1.............. 66 A1
Whitchurch CI *ALDT* GU11..... 135 G3
White Acres Rd *FRIM* GU16... 93 J5
Whitebeam Dr *REIG* RH2...... 147 M3
White Beam Wy
KWD/TDW/WH KT20............... 104 D3
Whiteberry Rd *RDKG* RH5..... 165 L2
White Bridge Av *MTCM* CR4... 48 A4
White Bridge CI
EBED/NFELT TW14.................. 15 J8
White Bushes *REDH* RH1...... 148 D4
White City *CWTH* RG45......... 52 A4
White Cottage CI *FNM* GU9.... 134 A1
Whitecroft Wy *BECK* BR3...... 51 M4
Whitefield Av *PUR/KEN* CR8.. 87 K1
Whitefoot La *BMLY* BR1........ 33 M5
Whitegates *WOKS/MYFD* GU22. 97 J2 🔟
Whitegate Wy
KWD/TDW/WH KT20............... 104 C2
Whitehall Crs *CHSGTN* KT9... 63 G4
Whitehall Dr *CRAWW* RH11... 211 H3
Whitehall Farm La *VW* GU25.. 39 H3
Whitehall Gdns *CHSWK* W4... 18 E1
Whitehall La *EGH* TW20......... 21 J8
REIG RH2.............................. 147 J4
STWL/WRAY TW19.................. 14 A7
Whitehall Park Rd *CHSWK* W4. 18 E1
Whitehall PI *CAR* SM5........... 66 E3 🔟
Whitehall Rd *THHTH* CR7...... 49 K5
White Hart Ct *HORS* RH12..... 228 F5
White Hart La *BARN* SW13.... 19 H4
RGUW GU3............................ 115 K7
White Hart Mdw
RPLY/SEND GU23.................. 98 F3
White Hart Rw *CHERT* KT16... 40 D7 🔟
Whitehead
WAND/EARL SW18.................. 29 M1 🔟
White Heron Ms *TEDD* TW11. 26 C7 🔟
White HI *BFOR* GU20............. 54 E3
COUL/CHIP CR5...................... 106 A5
SAND/SEL CR2....................... 68 A8 🔟
Whitehill CI *CBLY* GU15......... 73 G2
Whitehill La *REDH* RH1......... 128 A1
RPLY/SEND GU23.................. 99 M5
Whitehill PI *VW* GU25........... 39 G6
White Horse Dr *EPSOM* KT18. 83 M5 🔟
White Horse La
RPLY/SEND GU23.................. 98 F3
Whitehorse La *SNWD* SE25... 50 B4
Whitehorse Rd *CROY/NA* CR0. 4 E1
HORS RH12........................... 229 L3
Whitehouse Dr *GU* GU1......... 117 L8 🔟
White House La *RGUE* GU4.... 117 K8
White House Wk *FNM* GU9.... 134 A2 🔟
White Knights Rd *WEY* KT13.. 59 M6
White Knobs Wy *CTHM* CR3.. 108 D7
Whitelands Dr *ASC* SL5......... 36 A1
White La *ASHV* GU12............. 113 M8
BH/WHM TN16...................... 110 C5
NFNM GU10........................... 135 M2
RGUE GU4............................. 139 M2
Whiteley Rd *NRWD* SE19...... 32 A6
Whiteleys Wy *FELT* TW13...... 25 K4
White Ldg *NRWD* SE19.......... 31 L8
White Lodge CI *BELMT* SM2.. 65 M6
White Lodge Gdns
REDH RH1............................. 148 D8 🔟
Whitemore Rd *GU* GU1.......... 117 G4
White Oak Dr *BECK* BR3....... 51 M2
Whiteoaks *BNSTD* SM7......... 85 L3
Whitepost HI *REDH* RH1........ 126 B8
White Post La *NFNM* GU10.... 155 K5
White Rd *CBLY* GU15............ 72 C3
White Rose La *FNM* GU9........ 10 F6
WOKS/MYFD GU22................. 6 E6
Whites Rd *FARN* GU14.......... 93 H8
Whitethorn Av *COUL/CHIP* CR5. 86 D5
Whitethorn CI *ASHV* GU12..... 113 L8
Whitethorn Gdns *CROY/NA* CR0. 68 E1
White Wy *GT/LBKH* KT23...... 101 L8
Whitewood Cottages
BH/WHM TN16...................... 110 F2
Whitewood La *GDST* RH9...... 172 E5
Whitewood La *CROY/NA* CR0. 116 D5
HASM GU27........................... 199 M8 🔟
Whitford Gdns *MTCM* CR4..... 48 C3
Whitgift Av *SAND/SEL* CR2.... 67 M4
Whitgift St *CROY/NA* CR0...... 4 C8
Whitland Rd *CAR* SM5........... 48 A4
Whitley CI *STWL/WRAY* TW19. 14 A8
Whitley HI *CRAWE* RH10....... 213 J8
Whitley Wy *FARN* GU14........ 92 B8
Whitlock Dr *WIM/MER* SW19.. 29 H1
Whitmead CI *SAND/SEL* CR2.. 68 A3
Whitmead La *NFNM* GU10..... 157 C5
Whitmoor La *RGUE* GU4........ 97 G8
Whitmoor Vale Rd *BAGS* GU19. 54 B7
Whitmore CI *SHST* GU47........ 72 A1
Whitmore Gn *FNM* GU9......... 134 B3
Whitmore La *ASC* SL5........... 37 K5
Whitmore Rd *BECK* BR3........ 51 J3
Whitmores CI *EPSOM* KT18... 83 M5 🔟
Whitmore V *GSHT* GU26........ 198 C3
Whitmore Vale Rd *GSHT* GU26. 198 C5
Whitmore Wy *HORL* RH6....... 170 A5

Whitnell Wy *PUT/ROE* SW15.. 19 M7 🔟
Whitstable CI *BECK* BR3........ 51 J1 🔟
Whitstable PI *CROY/NA* CR0.. 67 M3
Whittaker Av *RCH/KEW* TW9.. 18 A7 🔟
Whittaker Rd *CHEAM* SM3..... 65 J2
Whittell Gdns *SYD* SE26........ 32 F4
Whittington Rd *CRAWE* RH10. 212 A6
Whittle Crs *FARN* GU14......... 92 C2
Whittle Rd *HEST* TW5............ 15 M2
Whittle Wy *CRAWE* RH10...... 192 D5
Whitton Dene *HSLW* TW3...... 16 E7
WHTN TW2............................ 17 G8
Whitton Manor Rd *ISLW* TW7. 16 F8
Whitton Rd *BRAK* RG12........ 35 J3
HSLW TW3............................ 16 E6
WHTN TW2............................ 17 H8
Whitton Waye *HSLW* TW3...... 16 D8
Whitworth Rd *CRAWW* RH11. 192 A6
SNWD SE25.......................... 50 B3
Whopshott Av
WOKN/KNAP GU21................. 76 F6
Whopshott CI
WOKN/KNAP GU21................. 76 E6
Whopshott Dr
WOKN/KNAP GU21................. 76 F6 🔟
Whynstones Rd *ASC* SL5....... 36 D5
Whyte Av *ASHV* GU12........... 135 G2
Whytebeam Vw *CTHM* CR3.... 88 C8
Whytecliffe Rd North
PUR/KEN CR8........................ 87 L1
Whytecliffe Rd South
PUR/KEN CR8........................ 87 L1 🔟
Whytecroft *HEST* TW5.......... 16 A2
Whyteleafe HI *CTHM* CR3...... 108 B1
Whyteleafe Rd *CTHM* CR3..... 108 B3
Wicket HI *NFNM* GU10.......... 10 C8
The Wickets *ASHF* TW15....... 23 H5
The Wicket *CROY/NA* CR0..... 69 K4
Wickham Av *CHEAM* SM3...... 64 F4
CROY/NA CR0........................ 69 H1
Wickham CI *HORL* RH6......... 170 C5
NWMAL KT3.......................... 46 C5 🔟
Wickham Court Rd *WWKM* BR4. 69 M1
Wickham Crs *WWKM* BR4...... 69 M1
Wickham La *EGH* TW20......... 21 K8
Wickham Rd *BECK* BR3......... 51 L3
CBLY GU15........................... 73 H1
CROY/NA CR0........................ 68 F7
Wickham V *BRAK* RG12......... 34 B6 🔟
Wickham Wy *BECK* BR3........ 51 M4
Wickhurst La *HORS* RH12..... 228 B6
Wick La *EGH* TW20............... 20 C7
Wick Rd *EGH* TW20............... 20 E8
TEDD TW11........................... 26 E8
Wide Wy *STRHM/NOR* SW16. 49 G3
Widgeon Wy *HORS* RH12...... 228 T1
Wigan Rd *FARN* GU14........... 112 A1
Wiggie La *REDH* RH1............ 126 D6
Wigley Rd *FELT* TW13........... 25 G3
Wigmore La *RDKG* RH5......... 166 F8
Wigmore Rd *CAR* SM5.......... 66 A1
Wilberforce Wy *BRAK* RG12.. 35 G5 🔟
WIM/MER SW19..................... 29 G7
Wilbury Av *BELMT* SM2........ 65 J8
Wilbury Rd *WOKN/KNAP* GU21. 6 B6
Wilcot CI *CHOB/PIR* GU24..... 75 K6
Wilcot Gdns *CHOB/PIR* GU24. 75 J6
Wilcox Gdns *SHPTN* TW17.... 41 J3
Wilcox Rd *SUT* SM1.............. 65 L3 🔟
TEDD TW11........................... 26 A5
Wildacre CI *BIL* RH14............ 224 D4
Wild Acres *BF/WBF* KT14...... 78 F1
Wildcroft Dr *RDKG* RH5......... 145 G3
Wildcroft Rd *PUT/ROE* SW15. 28 F1
Wildcroft Wd *MFD/CHID* GU8. 181 G3
Wilderness Ri *EGRIN* RH19.... 196 D4
Wilderness Rd *FRIM* GU16..... 73 H7
GUW GU2.............................. 138 C2
OXTED RH8........................... 130 C3
The Wilderness *E/WMO/HCT* KT8. 43 M7
HPTN TW12........................... 25 L3
Wilders CI *FRIM* GU16........... 73 H6
WOKN/KNAP GU21................. 76 F8
Wilderwick Rd *EGRIN* RH19... 196 M6
Wildfell Rd *CAT* SE6.............. 33 L1
Wildgoose Dr *HORS* RH12..... 228 A6
Wildridings Rd *BRAK* RG12... 34 D3 🔟
Wildwood CI *CRAN* GU6........ 185 J8 🔟
EHSLY KT24.......................... 100 C7
WOKS/MYFD GU22................. 78 C5
Wildwood Ct *PUR/KEN* CR8... 88 A5
Wildwood La *CRAN* GU6........ 204 D4
Wilford Rd *CROY/NA* CR0...... 4 D1
Wilfred St *WOKN/KNAP* GU21. 6 A6
Wilhelmina Av *COUL/CHIP* CR5. 106 F1
Wilkes Rd *BTFD* TW8............ 18 B1 🔟
Wilkins CI *MTCM* CR4............ 48 B1
Wilks Gdns *CROY/NA* CR0..... 51 H8
Willats CI *CHERT* KT16.......... 40 C6 🔟
Willcocks CI *CHSGTN* KT9..... 63 H2
Willems Av *ALDT* GU11......... 112 C7
Willett Rd *THHTH* CR7........... 49 K5
Willey Broom La *CTHM* CR3... 107 K7
Willey Farm La *CTHM* CR3.... 107 M8
Willey La *CTHM* CR3............. 108 A7
William Booth Rd *PGE/AN* SE20. 50 D1
William Farthing CI
ALDT GU11........................... 112 D7 🔟
William Gdns *PUT/ROE* SW15. 19 L7
William Rd *CTHM* CR3........... 108 A4
GU GU1................................ 8 E4
SUT SM1............................... 65 M4
WIM/MER SW19..................... 29 H7
Williams CI *CROY/NA* CR0..... 186 B4
Williams La *MORT/ESHN* SW14. 18 F5
MRDN SM4............................ 47 M5
Williams Ter *CROY/NA* CR0... 67 K5
William St *CAR* SM5.............. 66 B2
Williams Wy *CRAWE* RH10.... 212 E3 🔟
Willingham Wy *KUT* KT1....... 3 J7
Willington CI *CBLY* GU15....... 72 E3 🔟
Willis Av *BELMT* SM2............ 66 B5
Willis CI *EPSOM* KT18........... 83 L3
Willis Rd *CROY/NA* CR0......... 4 D1
Willmore End *WIM/MER* SW19. 47 L1

Willoughby Av *CROY/NA* CR0 ...... **67** J3
Willoughby Rd *BRAK* RG12 ...... **34** C3
  KUTN/CMB KT2 ...... **3** H4
  TWK TW1 ...... **17** M7 🖪
Willow Av *BARN* SW13 ...... **19** J4
Willow Bank *WOKS/MYFD* GU22.. **97** H4
Willowbank Gdns
  KWD/TDW/WH KT20 ...... **104** E4
Willow Brean *HORL* RH6 ...... **170** B5
Willowbrook Rd
  STWL/WRAY TW19 ...... **23** H2
The Willow Centre *MTCM* CR4 ...... **48** C5
Willow Cl *ADL/WDHM* KT15 ...... **78** C1
  BTFD TW8 ...... **17** M1
  CRAWE RH10 ...... **212** B1
  DTCH/LGLY SL3 ...... **12** F2 🖪
  EGRIN RH19 ...... **196** A6
  FRIM GU16 ...... **93** J1
  LIPH GU30 ...... **218** A6 🖪
  RDKG RH5 ...... **166** F5
Willow Cnr *HORL* RH6 ...... **191** J2
Willow Ct *FRIM* GU16 ...... **73** C8
Willow Crs *FARN* GU14 ...... **92** E2
Willowdene *WHTN* TW2 ...... **25** M1 🖪
Willow Dr *BRAK* RG12 ...... **34** F1
  RGUW GU3 ...... **114** F8
  RPLY/SEND GU23 ...... **98** D6
Willow Gdns *HEST* TW5 ...... **16** D3 🖪
  LIPH GU30 ...... **218** A6
Willow Gn *CHOB/PIR* GU24 ...... **75** K3
Willowhayne Dr *WOT/HER* KT12 .. **42** E7
Willowhayne Gdns *WPK* KT4 ...... **64** F3 🖪
Willow La *BLKW* GU17 ...... **72** A5
  GU GU1 ...... **117** K7
  MTCM CR4 ...... **48** C5
Willow Md *DORK* RH4 ...... **144** D1 🖪
  EGRIN RH19 ...... **216** C1
  MFD/CHID GU8.. ...... **181** H4
Willowmead *STA* TW18 ...... **40** E1 🖪
Willowmead Cl
  WOKN/KNAP GU21 ...... **76** D6
Willowmere *ESH/CLAY* KT10 ...... **61** M3
Willow Mt *CROY/NA* CR0 ...... **5** H8 🖪
Willow Pk *ASHV* GU12 ...... **113** J7
Willow Rdg *CRAWE* RH10 ...... **214** D6
Willow Rd *DTCH/LGLY* SL3 ...... **13** H4
  HORS RH12 ...... **229** L4
  NWMAL KT3 ...... **45** M4
  REIG RH2.. ...... **147** M2
  RGODL GU7 ...... **160** C1
  WLGTN SM6 ...... **66** E6
Willows Av *MRDN* SM4 ...... **47** L5
Willows Pth *EPSOM* KT18 ...... **83** L4
The Willows *BF/WBF* KT14 ...... **79** H3 🖪
  ESH/CLAY KT10 ...... **62** B5 🖪
  LTWR GU18 ...... **74** F1
  NFNM GU10 ...... **134** F5
  WEY KT13 ...... **59** K2
Willow Tree Cl
  WAND/EARL SW18 ...... **29** L2 🖪
Willowtree Wy
  STRHM/NOR SW16.. ...... **49** K1
Willow V *GT/LBKH* KT23 ...... **101** L5
Willow Vw *WIM/MER* SW19 ...... **48** A1
Willow Wk *CHEAM* SM3 ...... **65** J2
  EGH TW20 ...... **20** F6
  KWD/TDW/WH KT20 ...... **123** L4
  ORP BR6 ...... **71** L2
  REDH RH1 ...... **148** E2
  SHGR GU5 ...... **141** K5
Willow Wy *ASHV* GU12 ...... **135** H1
  BF/WBF KT14 ...... **78** F1
  FNM GU9 ...... **134** A3
  GDST RH9 ...... **128** E6
  GU GU1 ...... **116** E4
  HOR/WEW KT19 ...... **64** A5
  SUN TW16 ...... **42** D4
  SYD SE26 ...... **32** E4
  WHTN TW2 ...... **25** L3
  WOKS/MYFD GU22.. ...... **97** H2
Willow Wood Crs *SNWD* SE25.. ...... **50** B6
Wills Crs *HSLW* TW3 ...... **16** E8
Willson Rd *EGH* TW20 ...... **20** E6
Wilmar Gdns *WWKM* BR4 ...... **51** L8
Wilmer Cl *RCHPK/HAM* TW10 ...... **27** J6
Wilmer Crs *RCHPK/HAM* TW10 ...... **27** J6
Wilmerhatch La *EPSOM* KT18.. ...... **83** L7
Wilmington Av *CHSWK* W4 ...... **19** J2
Wilmington Cl *CRAWW* RH11 .. **211** M8 🖪
Wilmot Rd *CAR* SM5 ...... **66** C4 🖪
  PUR/KEN CR8.. ...... **87** K2
Wilmots Cl *REIG* RH2 ...... **125** M7
Wilmot's La *HORL* RH6 ...... **172** B5
  REDH RH1 ...... **172** A2
Wilmot Wy *BNSTD* SM7 ...... **85** K4
  CBLY GU15 ...... **73** J8
Wilna Rd *WAND/EARL* SW18 ...... **29** M1
Wilson Av *MTCM* CR4 ...... **30** B8
Wilson Cl *CRAWE* RH10 ...... **213** G6 🖪
  SAND/SEL CR2 ...... **68** A4 🖪
Wilson Dr *CHERT* KT16 ...... **57** L4
Wilson Rd *ASHV* GU12 ...... **113** C8
  CHSGTN KT9 ...... **63** G5
  FARN GU14 ...... **92** C6 🖪
Wilsons *KWD/TDW/WH* KT20 ...... **105** C3
Wilson Wy *WOKN/KNAP* GU21 ...... **6** A4
Wilton Av *WDR/YW* UB7 ...... **14** A1 🖪
Wilton Cl *FARN* GU14 ...... **93** C6
Wilton Ct *FARN* GU14 ...... **93** C6
Wilton Crs *WIM/MER* SW19 ...... **47** J1
Wilton Gdns *E/WMO/HCT* KT8 ...... **43** C8 🖪
  WOT/HER KT12 ...... **43** C8 🖪
Wilton Gv *NWMAL* KT3 ...... **46** C6
  WIM/MER SW19 ...... **29** J8
Wilton Pl *ADL/WDHM* KT15 ...... **59** G7
Wilton Rd *CBLY* GU15 ...... **72** E6
  HSLWW TW4 ...... **16** A5
  REDH RH1 ...... **148** C1
  WIM/MER SW19 ...... **30** B8
Wiltshire Gdns *WHTN* TW2 ...... **25** M2
Wiltshire Rd *THHTH* CR7 ...... **49** K3
Wilverley Crs *NWMAL* KT3 ...... **46** B6
Wilwood Rd *BNFD* RG42 ...... **34** B1
Wimbart Rd
  BRXS/STRHM SW2 ...... **31** J1 🖪
Wimbledon Br
  WIM/MER SW19 ...... **29** J7 🖪
Wimbledon Cl *CBLY* GU15 ...... **53** J8

Wimbledon Hill Rd
  WIM/MER SW19.. ...... **29** H7
Wimbledon Park Rd
  WIM/MER SW19 ...... **29** H4
Wimbledon Park Side
  WIM/MER SW19.. ...... **29** G3
  TOOT SW17 ...... **29** M5
Wimblehurst Rd *HORS* RH12 ...... **228** F5
Wimborne Av *REDH* RH1 ...... **148** C5
Wimborne Cl *EW* KT17 ...... **84** B3
  WPK KT4 ...... **46** F8 🖪
Wimborne Wy *BECK* BR3.. ...... **51** G3
Wimland Hl *HORS* RH12 ...... **210** A7
Wimland Rd *HORS* RH12 ...... **209** L4
Wimlands La *HORS* RH12 ...... **210** A6
Wimpole Cl *KUT* KT1 ...... **3** H7
Wimshurst Cl *CROY/NA* CR0 ...... **49** H8
Wincanton Cl *CRAWE* RH10 ...... **213** G3 🖪
Wincanton Rd
  WAND/EARL SW18 ...... **29** J1
Winchcombe Rd *CAR* SM5.. ...... **48** A7
Winchelsey Ri *SAND/SEL* CR2 ...... **68** C5
Winchendon Rd *TEDD* TW11.. ...... **26** A5
Winchester Av *HEST* TW5 ...... **16** C1
Winchester Cl *DTCH/LGLY* SL3 ...... **13** H3
  ESH/CLAY KT10.. ...... **61** K3
  KUTN/CMB KT2 ...... **3** M2
Winchester Rd *ASHV* GU12 ...... **113** K6
  CRAWE RH10 ...... **212** B7
  FELT TW13.. ...... **25** J4
  HYS/HAR UB3.. ...... **15** H2
  NFNM GU10 ...... **178** E2
  TWK TW1 ...... **17** L8
  WOT/HER KT12.. ...... **42** D8
Winchester St *FARN* GU14.. ...... **112** F1
Winchfield Rd *SYD* SE26 ...... **33** H6
Winchilsea Crs *E/WMO/HCT* KT8 .. **43** M2
Winchstone Cl *SHPTN* TW17 ...... **41** J4
Windall Cl *NRWD* SE19 ...... **50** D1 🖪
Windborough Rd *CAR* SM5.. ...... **66** D6
Windermere Av *WIM/MER* SW19 .. **47** L3
Windermere Cl
  EBED/NFELT TW14 ...... **24** C2 🖪🖪
  EGH TW20 ...... **21** L8 🖪
  FARN GU14 ...... **92** B6 🖪
  ORP BR6 ...... **71** L2
  STWL/WRAY TW19 ...... **23** G2 🖪
Windermere Rd *COUL/CHIP* CR5 .. **87** H5
  CROY/NA CR0 ...... **5** K3
  LTWR GU18 ...... **54** E8
  PUT/ROE SW15 ...... **28** B5
  STRHM/NOR SW16 ...... **48** F1
  WWKM BR4 ...... **70** B1
Windermere Wy *FNM* GU9 ...... **133** K3 🖪
  REDH RH1 ...... **126** B7
Windfield *LHD/OX* KT22 ...... **102** F3 🖪
Windfield Cl *SYD* SE26 ...... **33** G5 🖪
Windgates *RGUE* GU4 ...... **117** M5 🖪
Windham Av *CROY/NA* CR0 ...... **70** A8
Windham Rd *RCH/KEW* TW9 ...... **18** C5 🖪
The Windings *SAND/SEL* CR2 ...... **88** C1
Winding Wood Dr *CBLY* GU15.. ...... **73** L5
Windlebrook Gn *BNFD* RG42 ...... **34** D1 🖪
Windle Cl *BFOR* GU20 ...... **55** G5
Windlesham Ct *BFOR* GU20.. ...... **54** F3
Windlesham Gv *WIM/MER* SW19.. **29** G2
Windlesham Rd *BNFD* RG42 ...... **34** C1
  CHOB/PIR GU24 ...... **55** K6
Windley Cl *FSTH* SE23 ...... **32** E3 🖪
Windmill Av *EW* KT17 ...... **84** C1
Windmill Cl *CTHM* CR3 ...... **107** M3 🖪
  EW KT17 ...... **84** C2
  HORL RH6 ...... **170** E6 🖪
  SUN TW16 ...... **24** B8
  SURB KT6 ...... **44** F8
  SWTR RH13 ...... **229** K6
Windmill Cl *CRAWW* RH11 ...... **212** A1
Windmill Dr *HAYES* BR2 ...... **70** F3
  LHD/OX KT22 ...... **102** E5
  REDH RH1 ...... **126** A6
Windmill End *EW* KT17 ...... **84** C2 🖪
Windmill Fld *BFOR* GU20 ...... **55** G5
Windmill Gv *CROY/NA* CR0 ...... **4** C1
Windmill La *EGRIN* RH19 ...... **196** A6
  EGRIN RH19 ...... **216** F2
  EW KT17 ...... **84** C2
  THDIT KT7 ...... **44** E7
Windmill Ri *KUTN/CMB* KT2 ...... **3** L2
Windmill Rd *ASHV* GU12 ...... **112** F8
  BNFD RG42 ...... **34** C1
  CROY/NA CR0 ...... **4** C1
  HPTN TW12 ...... **25** L6
  MTCM CR4 ...... **48** D5
  SUN TW16 ...... **42** B1
  WIM/MER SW19 ...... **28** E6
Windmill Rd West *SUN* TW16 ...... **42** B7 🖪
Windmill Shott *EGH* TW20 ...... **21** J7 🖪
Windmill Wy *REDH* RH1 ...... **126** A6
Windrush Cl *CHSWK* W4 ...... **18** F2 🖪
  CRAWW RH11 ...... **211** J5
  SHGR GU5 ...... **161** J3
Windrush La *FSTH* SE23 ...... **33** G4
Windsor Av *CHEAM* SM3 ...... **65** H2
  E/WMO/HCT KT8 ...... **43** K3
  NWMAL KT3 ...... **45** M5
  WIM/MER SW19 ...... **47** M1
Windsor Cl *CRAWW* RH11 ...... **211** M7
  GUW GU2 ...... **138** C2
  WNWD SE27 ...... **31** M5 🖪
Windsor Court Rd
  CHOB/PIR GU24 ...... **56** B7
Windsor Crs *FNM* GU9 ...... **133** L3
Windsor Dr *ASHF* TW15 ...... **23** G7
Windsor Gdns *ASHV* GU12 ...... **113** J8 🖪
  CROY/NA CR0 ...... **67** J2
Windsor Gv *WNWD* SE27 ...... **31** M5 🖪
Windsor Ms *CAT* SE6 ...... **33** M2 🖪
Windsor Park Rd *HYS/HAR* UB3.. ...... **15** J2
Windsor Pl *EGRIN* RH19 ...... **216** D1 🖪
Windsor Ride *ASC* SL5 ...... **35** L5
  BFOR GU20 ...... **35** H8
  CBLY GU15 ...... **72** D1
Windsor Rd *ASC* SL5 ...... **36** C2
  CHOB/PIR GU24 ...... **56** B7
  EGH TW20 ...... **21** J4
  FARN GU14 ...... **93** G8
  HSLWW TW4 ...... **15** L4

Wolf's Rd *OXTED* RH8.. ...... **130** E4
Wolfs Wd *OXTED* RH8.. ...... **130** D6
Wolseley Av *WAND/EARL* SW18 .. **29** K3
Wolseley Gdns *CHSWK* W4 ...... **18** E1
Wolseley Rd *ALDT* GU11 ...... **112** D8 🖪
  MTCM CR4 ...... **48** D7
  RGODL GU7 ...... **160** B3
Wolsey Cl *HSLW* TW3 ...... **16** F6
  KUTN/CMB KT2 ...... **3** M5
  RYNPK SW20 ...... **28** E8
  WPK KT4 ...... **64** D5
Wolsey Crs *CROY/NA* CR0 ...... **69** M7
  MRDN SM4 ...... **47** J7
Wolsey Dr *KUTN/CMB* KT2 ...... **27** H6
  WOT/HER KT12 ...... **43** G8
Wolsey Gv *ESH/CLAY* KT10 ...... **61** L3 🖪
Wolsey Rd *ASHF* TW15 ...... **23** H5
  E/WMO/HCT KT8 ...... **44** A4
  ESH/CLAY KT10 ...... **61** L3
  HPTN TW12 ...... **25** L7
  SUN TW16 ...... **24** D7
Wolsey Wy *CHSGTN* KT9 ...... **63** K4
Wolstonbury Cl *CRAWW* RH11 .. **211** M5
Wolvens La *DORK* RH4.. ...... **143** K6
  RDKG RH5 ...... **166** B4
Wolverton Av *KUTN/CMB* KT2 ...... **3** K4
Wolverton Cl *HORL* RH6 ...... **170** C8
Wolverton Gdns *HORL* RH6.. ...... **170** C7
Wolves Hl *RDKG* RH5 ...... **188** F5
Wonersh Wy *BELMT* SM2 ...... **65** G7
Wonford Cl
  KWD/TDW/WH KT20 ...... **104** D8
  NWMAL KT3 ...... **46** B1
Wonham La *BRKHM/BTCW* RH3.. **146** C1
Wonham Wy *SHGR* GU5.. ...... **142** A8
Wontford Rd *PUR/KEN* CR8 ...... **87** K5
Wontner Rd *BAL* SW12 ...... **30** C3
Woodbastwick Rd *SYD* SE26 ...... **33** G7
Woodberry Cl *MFD/CHID* GU8 ...... **201** M4
  SUN TW16 ...... **24** D7
Woodbine Cl *WHTN* TW2 ...... **26** A3 🖪
Woodbine Gv *PGE/AN* SE20 ...... **32** E8
Woodbine La *WPK* KT4 ...... **64** E2
Woodbines Av *KUT* KT1 ...... **2** D9
Woodborough Rd
  PUT/ROE SW15 ...... **19** L6
Woodbourne *FNM* GU9 ...... **134** B2
Woodbourne Av
  STRHM/NOR SW16.. ...... **31** G4
Woodbourne Dr *ESH/CLAY* KT10 .. **62** C5
Woodbourne Gdns
  WLGTN SM6 ...... **66** E6 🖪
Woodbridge Av *LHD/OX* KT22 ...... **82** D8
Woodbridge Dr *CBLY* GU15 ...... **73** C2
Woodbridge Gv *LHD/OX* KT22 ...... **82** D8
Woodbridge Hl *GUW* GU2 ...... **8** C1
Woodbridge Hill Gdns *GUW* GU2 .. **8** B1
Woodbridge Mdw *GU* GU1 ...... **8** D2
Woodbridge Rd *GU* GU1 ...... **8** F2
Woodbury Av *EGRIN* RH19 ...... **216** E1
Woodbury Cl *BH/WHM* TN16 ...... **91** J8
  CROY/NA CR0 ...... **5** K6
  EGRIN RH19 ...... **216** E1
Woodbury Dr *BELMT* SM2.. ...... **65** M8
Woodbury St *TOOT* SW17 ...... **30** B6
Woodby Dr *ASC* SL5 ...... **37** J7
Wood Cl *REDH* RH1.. ...... **170** D1
Woodcock Dr *CHOB/PIR* GU24 ...... **55** M6
Woodcock Hl *LING* RH7 ...... **195** G5
Woodcock La *CHOB/PIR* GU24 ...... **55** L6
Woodcombe Crs *FSTH* SE23 ...... **32** F2
Woodcote *CRAN* GU6 ...... **184** E5
  HORL RH6 ...... **170** E5
  RGUW GU3 ...... **138** E4
Woodcote Av *THHTH* CR7 ...... **49** L4
  WLGTN SM6 ...... **66** C6
Woodcote Cl *EPSOM* KT18 ...... **84** A4
  KUTN/CMB KT2 ...... **27** J6
Woodcote End *EPSOM* KT18.. ...... **84** A5
Woodcote Gn *WLGTN* SM6 ...... **66** F7
Woodcote Green Rd
  EPSOM KT18 ...... **83** M6
Woodcote Grove Rd
  COUL/CHIP CR5 ...... **87** G5
Woodcote Hurst *EPSOM* KT18 ...... **83** M6
Woodcote La *PUR/KEN* CR8 ...... **87** G1
Woodcote Ms *WLGTN* SM6 ...... **66** E5
Woodcote Park Av
  PUR/KEN CR8 ...... **86** F1
Woodcote Park Rd *EPSOM* KT18.. **83** M6
Woodcote Pl *ASC* SL5.. ...... **36** C1
  WNWD SE27 ...... **31** L6 🖪
Woodcote Rd *FROW* RH18 ...... **217** H7
  WLGTN SM6 ...... **66** E5
Woodcote Side *EPSOM* KT18 ...... **83** L5
Woodcote Valley Rd
  PUR/KEN CR8 ...... **87** G3
Woodcot Gdns *FARN* GU14 ...... **92** A5 🖪
Woodcott Ter *ASHV* GU12 ...... **135** G1
Woodcourt *CRAWW* RH11 ...... **211** M8 🖪
Woodcrest Rd *PUR/KEN* CR8 ...... **87** H3
Woodcrest Wk *REDH* RH1 ...... **126** B6
Woodcroft Rd *CRAWW* RH11 ...... **211** G5 🖪
  THHTH CR7 ...... **49** L5
Woodcut Rd *NFNM* GU10 ...... **10** A9
Woodend *ESH/CLAY* KT10 ...... **61** M1
  FARN GU14 ...... **93** G6 🖪
Wood End *HORS* RH12 ...... **229** M4
Woodend *LHD/OX* KT22 ...... **102** F7
  NRWD SE19.. ...... **31** M7
  SUT SM1 ...... **65** M1
Woodend Cl *CRAWE* RH10 ...... **212** D1 🖪
  WOKN/KNAP GU21.. ...... **96** D1
Wood End Cl *WOKS/MYFD* GU22 .. **78** C6
Woodend Dr *ASC* SL5.. ...... **36** E5
Woodend Pk *COB* KT11 ...... **81** G5
Woodend Rd *FRIM* GU16 ...... **93** M2
The Wood End *WLGTN* SM6 ...... **66** E7 🖪
Woodenhill *BRAK* RG12 ...... **34** B7
Wooderson Cl *SNWD* SE25 ...... **50** B4
Woodfield *ASHTD* KT21 ...... **83** G7
  BOR GU35.. ...... **176** A8
Woodfield Av *CAR* SM5 ...... **66** D5
  STRHM/NOR SW16.. ...... **31** G4
Woodfield Cl *ASHTD* KT21 ...... **83** G7
  COUL/CHIP CR5 ...... **106** F1
  CRAWE RH10 ...... **212** B2
  NRWD SE19.. ...... **31** M8

  REDH RH1 ...... **126** B7
Woodfield Gdns *NWMAL* KT3 ...... **46** C5
Woodfield Gv
  STRHM/NOR SW16 ...... **31** G4 🖪
Woodfield Hl *COUL/CHIP* CR5.. ...... **106** E1
Woodfield La *ASHTD* KT21 ...... **83** G7
Woodfield Rd *ASHTD* KT21 ...... **83** G7
  CRAWE RH10 ...... **212** C1
  ESH/CLAY KT10 ...... **62** C1 🖪
  HORS RH12 ...... **226** A2
  HSLWW TW4 ...... **15** L3 🖪
The Woodfields *SAND/SEL* CR2 ...... **88** C1
Woodfield Wy *REDH* RH1 ...... **126** B7
Woodford Gn *BRAK* RG12 ...... **35** J4
Woodgate Av *CHSGTN* KT9 ...... **63** G4
Woodgate Dr
  STRHM/NOR SW16.. ...... **31** G8
Woodgates Cl *SWTR* RH13 ...... **229** J6
Woodgavil *BNSTD* SM7 ...... **85** J6
Woodger Cl *GU* GU1 ...... **117** M6
Woodhall Cl *SHST* GU47 ...... **52** C8
Woodhall Dr *DUL* SE21 ...... **32** C4
Woodhall Gn *GU* GU2.. ...... **55** H1
Woodham La *ADL/WDHM* KT15 ...... **58** E8
  WOKN/KNAP GU21 ...... **77** L3
Woodham Park Rd
  ADL/WDHM KT15 ...... **58** C8
Woodham Park Wy
  ADL/WDHM KT15 ...... **78** C1
Woodham Rd *CAT* SE6 ...... **33** M4
  WOKN/KNAP GU21 ...... **6** D1
Woodham Waye
  WOKN/KNAP GU21 ...... **77** L3
Woodhatch Rd *REDH* RH1 ...... **148** C5 🖪
Woodhatch Spinney
  COUL/CHIP CR5 ...... **87** H6
Woodhaw *EGH* TW20 ...... **21** L5
Woodhayes *HORL* RH6 ...... **170** E5 🖪🖪
Woodhayes Rd *RYNPK* SW20 ...... **28** F8
  WIM/MER SW19 ...... **28** F7 🖪
Woodhill *RPLY/SEND* GU23 ...... **98** A7
Woodhill La *SHGR* GU5 ...... **162** B5
Woodhouse La *SHGR* GU5 ...... **164** D1
Woodhurst La *OXTED* RH8 ...... **130** B5
Woodhurst Pk *OXTED* RH8 ...... **130** B4
Woodhyrst Gdns *PUR/KEN* CR8 ...... **87** L5
Wooding Gv *CRAWW* RH11 ...... **211** L8 🖪
Woodland Av *CRAN* GU6 ...... **185** J6
Woodland Cl *EHSLY* KT24 ...... **120** C1 🖪
  HOR/WEW KT19 ...... **64** B5 🖪
  NRWD SE19 ...... **32** B7 🖪
  SWTR RH13 ...... **229** L5
Woodland Ct *OXTED* RH8 ...... **130** A2
Woodland Dr *CRAWE* RH10 ...... **214** E1
  EHSLY KT24 ...... **120** C1
  NFNM GU10 ...... **10** E7
  RDKG RH5 ...... **188** D4
Woodland Gdns *ISLW* TW7 ...... **17** H5
  SAND/SEL CR2 ...... **88** F1
Woodland Gv *WEY* KT13 ...... **60** A3
Woodland Hl *NRWD* SE19 ...... **32** B7
Woodland Ri *OXTED* RH8 ...... **130** B4
Woodland Rd *NRWD* SE19.. ...... **32** B6
  THHTH CR7 ...... **49** K4
Woodlands *ADL/WDHM* KT15 ...... **59** H2
  CRAWE RH10 ...... **213** G1
  RPLY/SEND GU23 ...... **98** C7 🖪
  RYNPK SW20 ...... **47** G4 🖪
  WOKS/MYFD GU22 ...... **6** D8
Woodlands Av *BF/WBF* KT14 ...... **78** C3
  FNM GU9 ...... **134** C2
  NWMAL KT3 ...... **46** A1
  REDH RH1 ...... **148** C1
  WPK KT4 ...... **64** C1
Woodlands Cl *ASC* SL5 ...... **36** C6
  ASHV GU12 ...... **113** K4 🖪
  CHERT KT16 ...... **57** L8
  CRAN GU6 ...... **185** J6
  CRAWE RH10 ...... **214** E2
  ESH/CLAY KT10 ...... **62** C6 🖪
  FARN GU14 ...... **72** B8
Woodlands Ct *SHST* GU47 ...... **52** C8
Woodlands Dr *GDST* RH9.. ...... **151** H3
  SUN TW16 ...... **42** F2
Woodlands Gv *COUL/CHIP* CR5 ...... **86** E7
  ISLW TW7 ...... **17** H4
Woodlands La *CHOB/PIR* GU24 ...... **55** J6
  COB KT11 ...... **81** K7
  HASM GU27 ...... **219** J2
Woodlands Pde *ASHF* TW15 ...... **23** M7 🖪
Woodlands Pk *ADL/WDHM* KT15 .. **58** C4
  GU GU1 ...... **117** L7
  KWD/TDW/WH KT20 ...... **123** L5
  WOKN/KNAP GU21 ...... **77** M3
Woodlands Ride *ASC* SL5.. ...... **36** C6
Woodlands Rd *BARN* SW13 ...... **19** J5
  BF/WBF KT14 ...... **78** C4
  CBLY GU15 ...... **72** E4
  EGRIN RH19 ...... **196** D5
  EHSLY KT24 ...... **121** J2
  EPSOM KT18 ...... **83** K5
  FARN GU14 ...... **92** A3
  GU GU1 ...... **117** G4
  ISLW TW7 ...... **17** H5
  LHD/OX KT22 ...... **82** A8
  MFD/CHID GU8.. ...... **182** A8
  REDH RH1 ...... **148** C2
  SURB KT6 ...... **45** G7
  VW GU25 ...... **38** F4
Woodlands Rd East *VW* GU25.. ...... **38** F4
Woodlands Rd West *VW* GU25.. ...... **38** F3
The Woodlands *ESH/CLAY* KT10.. **61** M1
  HORL RH6 ...... **171** L6
  ISLW TW7 ...... **17** J4
  NRWD SE19.. ...... **31** M8
  WLGTN SM6 ...... **66** E7 🖪
Woodlands Wk *FARN* GU14.. ...... **72** B8
Woodlands Wy *ASHTD* KT21 ...... **83** K6
  KWD/TDW/WH KT20 ...... **123** H4
Woodland Vw *RGODL* GU7 ...... **138** E8
Woodland Wk *HOR/WEW* KT19 ...... **63** K5
Woodland Wy *BRYLDS* KT5 ...... **45** J7
  CROY/NA CR0 ...... **51** L8
  KWD/TDW/WH KT20 ...... **105** H4
  MRDN SM4 ...... **47** J4
  MTCM CR4 ...... **30** D8
  PUR/KEN CR8.. ...... **87** K3

REDH RH1 .... 128 B2
SWTR RH13 .... 229 K5
WEY KT13 .... 60 A4
WWKM BR4 .... 69 M2
Wood La CTHM CR3 .... 108 A6
FARN GU14 .... 92 D6
ISLW TW7 .... 17 H1
KWD/TDW/WH KT20 .... 85 J7
NFNM GU10 .... 135 L5
WEY KT13 .... 59 M7
WOKN/KNAP GU21 .... 76 A8
Woodlawn Crs WHTN TW2 ... 25 L3
Woodlawn Dr FELT TW13 ..... 25 G3
Woodlawn Gv WOKN/KNAP GU21 .. 6 F1
Woodleigh Gdns
STRHM/NOR SW16 .... 31 H4
Woodley Cl TOOT SW17 ...... 30 C8 🖫
Woodley La SUT SM1 .... 66 B2
Wood Lodge La WWKM BR4 ... 69 M2
Woodmancote Gdns
BF/WBF KT14 .... 78 D3
Woodmancott Cl BRAK RG12 ... 35 J5
Woodmancourt RGODL GU7 .. 159 M1
Woodman Rd COUL/CHIP CR5 .. 86 F6
Woodmans HI CRAWW RH11 .. 211 M8
Woodmansterne La BNSTD SM7 .. 85 L5
CAR SM5 .... 86 C2
WLGTN SM6 .... 86 E1
Woodmansterne Rd CAR SM5 .. 86 E1
COUL/CHIP CR5 .... 86 F5
STRHM/NOR SW16 .... 49 H1
Woodmansterne St BNSTD SM7 .. 86 B5
Woodmere BRAK RG12 .... 35 H4
Woodmere Av CROY/NA CR0 .. 51 G7
Woodmere Cl CROY/NA CR0 ... 51 G7
Woodmere Gdns CROY/NA CR0 .. 51 G7
Woodnook Rd
STRHM/NOR SW16 .... 30 E6
Wood Peckarmans DUL SE21 .. 32 D4
Woodpecker Cl COB KT11 ..... 74 A3
NFNM GU10 .... 133 G1 🖫
Woodpecker La RDKG RH5 .... 167 M7
Woodpeckers MFD/CHID GU8 .. 181 K7
Woodpecker Wy
WOKS/MYFD GU22 .... 97 G5
Woodplace Cl COUL/CHIP CR5 .. 106 F1
Woodplace La COUL/CHIP CR5 .. 106 F1
Woodridge Cl BRAK RG12 ...... 34 F3
Wood Riding WOKS/MYFD GU22 .. 78 B5
Wood Ri GUW GU2 .... 116 B6
Wood Rd BH/WHM TN16 .... 90 F8
CBLY GU15 .... 72 E8
FNM GU9 .... 133 M2
GSHT GU26 .... 199 G3
RGODL GU7 .... 160 C2
SHPTN TW17 .... 41 K4
Woodrough Copse SHGR GU5 .. 161 K4
Woodroyd Av HORL RH6 .... 170 C7
Woodroyd Gdns HORL RH6 .... 170 C8
Woodruff Av GU GU1 .... 117 K5
Woods Hill Cl EGRIN RH19 .... 217 G3
Woods Hill La EGRIN RH19 .... 217 G3
Woodshore Cl VW GU25 .... 38 G6
Woodside CBLY GU15 .... 99 M8
EHSLY KT24 ....
KWD/TDW/WH KT20 .... 125 J2
LHD/OX KT22 .... 101 L4
SWTR RH13 .... 229 L5
WIM/MER SW19 .... 29 J6
WOT/HER KT12 .... 42 D8
Woodside Av ESH/CLAY KT10 .. 44 B7
SNWD SE25 .... 50 E6
WOT/HER KT12 .... 60 E3
Woodside Cl BRYLDS KT5 ...... 45 M7
CTHM CR3 .... 108 B6
WOKN/KNAP GU21 .... 76 A7
Woodside Court Rd
CROY/NA CR0 .... 5 M2
Woodside Crs HORL RH6 ...... 171 K6
Woodside Gn SNWD SE25 ..... 50 D6
Woodside Pk SNWD SE25 ..... 50 D6
Woodside Rd ALDT GU11 ...... 112 C2
COB KT11 .... 81 K3
CRAWE RH10 .... 212 C1
FNM GU9 .... 134 B2
GUW GU2 .... 116 C7
KUTN/CMB KT2 .... 2 E3

MFD/CHID GU8 .... 201 J4
NWMAL KT3 .... 46 A2
PUR/KEN CR8 .... 87 H3
RDKG RH5 .... 167 G6
SNWD SE25 .... 50 E6
SUT SM1 .... 65 M2
Woodside Wy CROY/NA CR0 .. 50 F6 🖫
MTCM CR4 .... 48 F1
REDH RH1 .... 148 D1
VW GU25 .... 38 E3
Woodslands HORL RH6 .... 171 G5
Woodspring Rd WIM/MER SW19 .. 29 H3
Woodstock EGRIN RH19 .... 195 M7
RGUE GU4 .... 118 E2
Woodstock Av CHEAM SM3 ... 47 J8
ISLW TW7 .... 17 K7
Woodstock Cl CRAN GU6 ...... 185 J8 🖫
HORS RH12 .... 229 C4
WOKN/KNAP GU21 .... 6 C4
Woodstock Gdns BECK BR3 ... 51 L1
Woodstock Gv RGODL GU7 .... 160 B2 🖫
Woodstock La North SURB KT6 .. 62 F1
Woodstock La South
ESH/CLAY KT10 .... 62 E4
Woodstock Ri CHEAM SM3 .... 47 J8
Woodstock Rd CAR SM5 .... 66 D4
COUL/CHIP CR5 .... 86 E6 🖫
CROY/NA CR0 .... 4 E8
Woodstocks FARN GU14 .... 92 F3
Woodstock Wy MTCM CR4 .... 48 F2
Woodstone Av EW KT17 .... 64 D4
Wood St ASHV GU12 .... 113 K3
EGRIN RH19 .... 196 A8
KUT KT1 .... 2 E5
MTCM CR4 .... 48 D7
REDH RH1 .... 126 F5
Woodsway LHD/OX KT22 ...... 82 B4
Woodsyre NRWD SE19 .... 32 C5
Woodthorpe Rd ASHF TW15 .. 23 G6
PUT/ROE SW15 .... 19 L6
Wood V EDUL SE22 .... 32 E2
Woodvale Av SNWD SE25 ..... 50 C3
Woodview CHSGTN KT9 .... 82 F2
Woodview Cl KUTN/CMB KT2 .. 28 A5
SAND/SEL CR2 .... 88 E4
Woodville Cl TEDD TW11 ...... 26 D5 🖫
Woodville Rd LHD/OX KT22 ... 102 E2
MRDN SM4 .... 47 K4
RCHPK/HAM TW10 .... 26 E4
THHTH CR7 .... 49 M4 🖫
Woodward Cl ESH/CLAY KT10 .. 62 C5
Woodwards CRAWW RH11 .... 211 L8
Woodway CBLY GU15 .... 72 E4 🖫
GU GU1 .... 117 L7
Wood Wy ORP BR6 .... 71 K1
Woodyard La DUL SE21 .... 32 B1
Woodyers Cl SHGR GU5 .... 161 L2
Woolborough Cl
CRAWE RH10 .... 212 B2 🖫
Woolborough La
CRAWE RH10 .... 212 D1 🖫
REDH RH1 .... 171 J1
Woolborough Rd CRAWE RH10 .. 212 A2
Woolfords La MFD/CHID GU8 .. 157 L8
Woolhampton Wy BRAK RG12 .. 35 G5
Woolhams CTHM CR3 .... 108 C8
Woollards Rd ASHV GU12 ..... 113 K5
Woolmead Rd FNM GU9 .... 133 M1
Woolmer Hill Rd HASM GU27 .. 218 F2
Wool Rd RYNPK SW20 .... 28 E7
Woolsack Wy RGODL GU7 .... 160 C5
Woolstone Rd FSTH SE23 ...... 33 H3
Wootton Cl EPSOM KT18 ...... 84 B6
Worbeck Rd PGE/AN SE20 ..... 50 E2
Worcester Cl CROY/NA CR0 ... 69 J1
FARN GU14 .... 92 E3 🖫
MTCM CR4 .... 48 D2
Worcester Ct WOT/HER KT12 .. 60 F1
Worcester Dr ASHF TW15 ..... 23 L6 🖫
Worcester Gdns WPK KT4 ..... 64 B2
Worcester Park Rd WPK KT4 .. 63 M2
Worcester Rd BELMT SM2 ..... 65 K6
CRAWE RH10 .... 212 B7
GUW GU2 .... 116 C6
REIG RH2 .... 125 K7 🖫
WIM/MER SW19 .... 29 J6
Wordsworth BRAK RG12 .... 34 C5

Wordsworth Av PUR/KEN CR8 .. 88 A5
Wordsworth Cl CRAWE RH10 .. 212 E1 🖫
Wordsworth Dr CHEAM SM3 .. 64 F3
Wordsworth Md REDH RH1 .... 126 E6
Wordsworth Pl HORS RH12 .... 229 H2 🖫
Wordsworth Ri EGRIN RH19 ... 195 M8 🖫
Wordsworth Rd
ADL/WDHM KT15 .... 59 G3
FELT TW13 .... 25 J3
HPTN TW12 .... 25 J5
PGE/AN SE20 .... 33 G8
WLGTN SM6 .... 66 F5
Works Rd ADL/WDHM KT15 ... 58 E7
Worlds End HI BRAK RG12 ..... 35 J6
Wormley La MFD/CHID GU8 ... 181 K8
Worple Av ISLW TW7 .... 17 K7
STA TW18 .... 22 E7
WIM/MER SW19 .... 29 G8
Worple Rd EPSOM KT18 .... 84 A5
ISLW TW7 .... 17 K6
LHD/OX KT22 .... 102 E5
RYNPK SW20 .... 47 G1
STA TW18 .... 22 E8
WIM/MER SW19 .... 29 H8
Worple Road Ms
WIM/MER SW19 .... 29 J7 🖫
Worplesdon Hill House Rd
WOKS/MYFD GU22 .... 95 M4
Worplesdon Rd RGUW GU3 .... 116 C3
Worple St MORT/ESHN SW14 .. 19 G5
The Worple STWL/WRAY TW19 .. 12 C8 🖫
Worple Wy RCHPK/HAM TW10 .. 18 B7
Worslade Rd TOOT SW17 ...... 30 A5
Worsley Bridge Rd CAT SE6 .. 33 J4
Worsley Rd FRIM GU16 .... 93 J2
Worsted Gn REDH RH1 .... 127 G3
Worsted La EGRIN RH19 .... 216 E2
Worthfield Cl HOR/WEW KT19 .. 64 A6
Worthing Rd HEST TW5 .... 16 C1
HORS RH12 .... 228 E8
Worthington Cl MTCM CR4 .... 48 E4
Worthington Rd SURB KT6 ..... 45 J8
Worth Park Av CRAWE RH10 .. 212 F2
Worth Rd CRAWE RH10 .... 212 F3
Worth Wy CRAWE RH10 .... 213 G4 🖫
Wortley Rd CROY/NA CR0 ...... 49 K7
Worton Gdns ISLW TW7 .... 17 G4
Worton Rd ISLW TW7 .... 17 J5
Worton Wy ISLW TW7 .... 17 G4
Wotton Dr RDKG RH5 .... 143 H6
Wotton Wy BELMT SM2 .... 64 F8
Wrabness Wy STA TW18 .... 40 E1
Wray Cl EGRIN RH19 .... 217 G3
Wray Common Rd REIG RH2 .. 125 M7
Wrayfield Av REIG RH2 .... 125 M7
Wrayfield Rd CHEAM SM3 ..... 65 G2
Wraylands Dr REIG RH2 .... 126 A6
Wray La REIG RH2 .... 125 M4
Wray Mill Pk REDH RH1 .... 126 A6
Wray Park Rd REIG RH2 .... 125 L7
Wraysbury Cl HSLWW TW4 .... 16 B7
Wraysbury Rd
STWL/WRAY TW19 .... 21 M4
Wrecclesham HI WFNM GU10 .. 155 H4
Wrecclesham Rd FNM GU9 .... 10 A5
The Wrekin FARN GU14 .... 93 H8
Wren Cl HORS RH12 .... 229 C2
SAND/SEL CR2 .... 69 G7 🖫
Wren Ct ASHV GU12 .... 113 L6
Wren Crs ADL/WDHM KT15 ... 59 G4
Wren's Av ASHF TW15 .... 23 M6
Wren's HI LHD/OX KT22 .... 81 M5
Wren Wy FARN GU14 .... 92 F2
Wright Cl CRAWE RH10 .... 212 E7 🖫
Wright Gdns SHPTN TW17 ..... 41 K5
Wright Rd HEST TW5 .... 15 M2
Wrights Rd SNWD SE25 .... 50 B3
Wright's Rw CAR SM5 .... 66 E3
Wrotham HI MFD/CHID GU8 ... 203 H6
Wroxham BRAK RG12 .... 34 C5
Wrythe Gn CAR SM5 .... 66 C2 🖫
Wrythe Green Rd CAR SM5 .... 66 C2
Wrythe La CAR SM5 .... 48 A8
Wyatt Cl FELT TW13 .... 25 G2
Wyatt Dr BARN SW13 .... 19 L1

Wyatt Park Rd
BRXS/STRHM SW2 .... 31 J3
Wyatt Rd STA TW18 .... 22 D6
Wyatt's Cl RGODL GU7 .... 160 D3
Wyche Gv SAND/SEL CR2 ...... 67 M6
Wychelm Rd LTWR GU18 .... 74 F1
Wych HI La WOKS/MYFD GU22 .. 96 F1
Wych HI Ri WOKS/MYFD GU22 .. 97 G1
Wych HI Pk WOKS/MYFD GU22.. 6 A9
Wych HI Ri WOKS/MYFD GU22 .. 96 F1
Wychwood BIL RH14 .... 224 A6
Wychwood Av BRAK RG12 ..... 35 J4
THHTH CR7 .... 49 L3
Wychwood Cl ASHV GU12 ..... 113 J7
SUN TW16 .... 24 D7
Wychwood Pl CBLY GU15 ...... 53 L8
Wycliffe Rd WIM/MER SW19 .. 29 L7
Wydell Cl MRDN SM4 .... 46 F6
Wydenhurst Rd CROY/NA CR0 .. 5 M1
Wyecliffe Gdns REDH RH1 ..... 126 F4
Wye Cl ASHF TW15 .... 23 L5
Wyeth's Rd EW KT17 .... 84 C3
Wyke Av ASHV GU12 .... 114 A6
Wyke Cl ISLW TW7 .... 17 J1
Wykeham Cl WDR/YW UB7 .... 14 D1 🖫
Wykeham Rd FNM GU9 .... 133 M6 🖫
GU GU1 .... 118 A7
Wyke La ASHV GU12 .... 114 A6
Wyke Rd RYNPK SW20 .... 46 F2
Wykwood LIPH GU30 .... 218 A5 🖫
Wylam BRAK RG12 .... 34 C5
Wyleu St FSTH SE23 .... 33 H1
Wymering Ct FARN GU14 ...... 93 G6
Wymond St PUT/ROE SW15 ... 19 M5
Wyncote Wy SAND/SEL CR2 ... 69 G7
Wyndham Av COB KT11 .... 80 D3
Wyndham Cl BELMT SM2 .... 65 K6
Wyndham Crs CRAN GU6 .... 184 D6
HSLWW TW4 .... 16 C8
Wyndham Rd KUTN/CMB KT2 .. 3 H2
WOKN/KNAP GU21 .... 76 E8
Wyndham St ASHV GU12 ...... 112 F8
Wynell Rd FSTH SE23 .... 33 G4
Wynfields FRIM GU16 .... 93 J6
Wynlea Cl CRAWE RH10 .... 214 D1
Wynnstow Pk OXTED RH8 ..... 130 C5
Wynsham Wy BFOR GU20 ..... 54 L4
Wynton Gdns SNWD SE25 ..... 50 B5
Wynton Gv WOT/HER KT12 ... 60 D2
Wyphurst Rd CRAN GU6 .... 185 C5
Wyresdale BRAK RG12 .... 35 J7 🖫
Wysemead HORL RH6 .... 170 F5
Wyvern Cl ASHV GU12 .... 113 J4 🖫
BRAK RG12 .... 34 D4 🖫
Wyvern Rd PUR/KEN CR8 ..... 67 K8

Y

Yaffle Rd WEY KT13 .... 59 M8
Yale Cl HSLWW TW4 .... 16 C7
SHST GU47 .... 52 C7
Yarborough Rd
WIM/MER SW19 .... 48 A1 🖫
Yarbridge Cl BELMT SM2 ...... 65 L8 🖫
Yardley BRAK RG12 .... 34 C5
Yardley Cl REIG RH2 .... 125 L6
Yard Md EGH TW20 .... 21 K4
Yarm Cl LHD/OX KT22 .... 102 F5
Yarm Court Rd LHD/OX KT22 .. 102 F5
Yarmouth Cl CRAWE RH10 .... 212 D5
Yarm Wy LHD/OX KT22 .... 102 F5
Yarrow Cl HORS RH12 .... 229 H4
Yatesbury Cl FNM GU9 .... 10 A5
Yattendon Rd HORL RH6........ 170 E6
Yaverland Dr BAGS GU19 ...... 54 A7
Yeats Cl REDH RH1 .... 147 M3
Yeend Cl E/WMO/HCT KT8 .... 43 K4
Yellowcress Dr
CHOB/PIR GU24 .... 75 K6 🖫
Yenston Cl MRDN SM4 .... 47 K6
Yeomanry Cl EW KT17 .... 84 C3 🖫
Yeomans Cl FARN GU14 .... 92 D4
NFNM GU10 .... 135 J1

Yeomans Wy CBLY GU15 ...... 73 H4
Yeoman Wy REDH RH1 .... 148 E5
Yeoveney Cl STWL/WRAY TW19 .. 22 A3
Yeovil Cl FARN GU14 .... 93 G8
Yeovil Rd SHST GU47 .... 52 C7
Yetminster Rd FARN GU14 .... 93 G8
Yewbank Cl PUR/KEN CR8 ..... 88 A5
Yew La EGRIN RH19 .... 195 L6
Yew Tree Bottom Rd EW KT17 .. 84 E7
Yew Tree Cl COUL/CHIP CR5 .. 106 C1
HORL RH6 .... 170 D4
WPK KT4 .... 46 B8 🖫
Yew Tree Dr CTHM CR3 .... 108 C7
GU GU1 .... 116 E3
Yew Tree Gdns EPSOM KT18 .. 83 M5
Yew Tree La REIG RH2 .... 125 L5
Yew Tree Rd DORK RH4 .... 122 D8
HORL RH6 .... 191 H2
MFD/CHID GU8 .... 181 G3
Yewtree Rd BECK BR3 .... 51 J3 🖫
Yewtrees EGH TW20 .... 39 M3
Yew Tree Wk EHSLY KT24 ..... 121 C1
FRIM GU16 .... 73 H8
HSLWW TW4 .... 16 C7
PUR/KEN CR8 .... 67 M8
Yockley Cl CBLY GU15 .... 74 A5
Yolland Cl FNM GU9 .... 133 M2
York Av EGRIN RH19 .... 216 D1
MORT/ESHN SW14 .... 18 F7
York Cl BF/WBF KT14 .... 79 H2
MRDN SM4 .... 47 L4
SWTR RH13 .... 229 J6
York Crs ALDT GU11 .... 112 C8
Yorke Gdns REIG RH2 .... 125 K7
Yorke Gate Rd CTHM CR3 ..... 108 A4
Yorke Rd REIG RH2 .... 125 K7
York Gdns WOT/HER KT12 ..... 61 G3
York HI STRHM/NOR SW16 .... 31 L4
York Pl CBLY GU15 .... 73 G2
York Rd ALDT GU11 .... 112 C8
ASHV GU12 .... 113 K6
BELMT SM2 .... 65 K5
BF/WBF KT14 .... 79 G2
BH/WHM TN16 .... 110 E1
CBLY GU15 .... 73 G2
CRAWE RH10 .... 212 B7
CROY/NA CR0 .... 49 K7
FARN GU14 .... 92 C4
FNM GU9 .... 11 H3
GU GU1 .... 9 H5
HSLW TW3 .... 16 E5
KUTN/CMB KT2 .... 3 H3
RCHPK/HAM TW10 .... 18 C7 🖫
SAND/SEL CR2 .... 69 G8
TEDD TW11 .... 26 B5
WEY KT13 .... 59 M4
WIM/MER SW19 .... 29 L7
WOKS/MYFD GU22 .... 6 D7
Yorkshire Rd MTCM CR4 .... 49 H5
York St MTCM CR4 .... 48 D7
TWK TW1 .... 26 D2
Yorktown Rd SHST GU47 ...... 72 B2
York Wy CHSGTN KT9 .... 63 G6 🖫
FELT TW13 .... 25 J4
Youlden Cl CBLY GU15 .... 73 K4
Youlden Dr CBLY GU15 .... 73 K4
Youngs Dr ASHV GU12 .... 113 J7
Young St LHD/OX KT22 .... 102 C6
Youngstroat La CHOB/PIR GU24 .. 57 H8
Yukon Rd BAL SW12 .... 30 E1

Z

Zealand Av WDR/YW UB7 ...... 14 A2
Zennor Rd BAL SW12 .... 30 F2 🖫
Zermatt Rd THHTH CR7 .... 49 M4
Zig Zag Rd PUR/KEN CR8 ...... 87 M6
RDKG RH5 .... 122 F4
Zinnia Dr CHOB/PIR GU24 ..... 75 K6
Zion Pl THHTH CR7 .... 50 A4 🖫
Zion Rd THHTH CR7 .... 50 A4

Index - featured places

Abbey Business Park
FNM GU9 .... 156 D1
Abbey Industrial Estate
MTCM CR4 .... 48 C5
Abbeylands School
ADL/WDHM KT15 .... 58 D4
The Abbey School
FNM GU9 .... 11 K2
Abbey Trading Estate
SYD SE26 .... 33 H6
Abbotsbury Primary First School
MRDN SM4 .... 47 K5
Abbots Hospital
GU GU1 .... 9 H6
A B C Cinema
CAT SE6 .... 33 L2
A B C Cinema
ESH/CLAY KT10 .... 61 G4
A B C Cinema
STA TW18 .... 22 B6
A B C Cinema
STRHM/NOR SW16 .... 31 H3
A B C Cinema
BECK BR3 .... 51 K2
Aberdour School
KWD/TDW/WH KT20 .... 85 J8
**Abinger Common
Primary School**
RDKG RH5 .... 143 G8
Abinger Hammer School
RDKG RH5 .... 142 C5
Abro Industrial Estate
ALDT GU11 .... 113 G6

**Aches & Pains Osteopathic
Clinic**
HOR/WEW KT19 .... 64 A4
The Acorn Group Practise
TWK TW1 .... 26 D1
Acre Road Health Clinic
KUTN/CMB KT2 .... 3 G3
Adamsrill Primary School
SYD SE26 .... 33 H4
Addington Business Centre
CROY/NA CR0 .... 70 B8
Addiscombe Cricket Club
CROY/NA CR0 .... 5 L8
The Adrian Ross Gallery
REIG RH2 .... 125 K7
Adult Education Centre
GU GU1 .... 9 J6
Ailsa Gallery
TWK TW1 .... 17 L4
Airborne Forces Museum
ALDT GU11 .... 112 D4
Airport Industrial Estate
BH/WHM TN16 .... 91 G5
Alan Carter Gallery
OXTED RH8 .... 130 B3
Albany Clinic
WIM/MER SW19 .... 29 L8
Albemarle Primary School
WIM/MER SW19 .... 29 H3
Alderbrook Primary School
BAL SW12 .... 30 E1

**Aldershot & Farnham
County Court**
ALDT GU11 .... 112 E7
Aldershot Health Centre
ALDT GU11 .... 112 C7
**Aldershot Military Historical
Trust & Museum**
ALDT GU11 .... 112 E7
Aldershot School
NRWD SE19 .... 50 B1
Aldershot Town Football Club
ALDT GU11 .... 112 E7
Aldro School
MFD/CHID GU8 .... 158 C2
Alexander Barracks
CHOB/PIR GU24 .... 94 E3
Alexandra Infant School
PGE/AN SE20 .... 33 G8
Alexandra Junior School
HSLW TW3 .... 16 E4
Alexandra Junior School
SYD SE26 .... 33 G7
Alexandra Surgery
ALDT GU11 .... 112 C7
Alfred Mizen First School
MTCM CR4 .... 49 G3
**The All England Lawn Tennis
& Croquet Club**
WIM/MER SW19 .... 29 H4
All Hallows RC Secondary School
FNM GU9 .... 134 C2
All Saints Benhilton School
SUT SM1 .... 65 L2
All Saints C of E First School
NFNM GU10 .... 156 F6

All Saints C of E First School
WIM/MER SW19 .... 29 M8
All Saints C of E School
LHD/OX KT22 .... 102 D1
All Saints C of E School
PUT/ROE SW15 .... 19 M5
All Saints School
NRWD SE19 .... 50 B1
Alton Medical Practice
PUT/ROE SW15 .... 28 D1
The Alton School
PUT/ROE SW15 .... 28 C1
Ambleside Junior School
WOT/HER KT12 .... 42 F8
**The American Community
School**
COB KT11 .... 61 G8
Amesbury School
GSHT GU26 .... 199 H8
A M F Bowling
CRAWW RH11 .... 212 A3
Amy Johnson Primary School
WLGTN SM6 .... 67 H6
**Andrew Ewing Junior &
Infant School**
HEST TW5 .... 16 C2
Anerley Primary School
PGE/AN SE20 .... 50 D1
**Anerley Secondary
Boarding School**
NRWD SE19 .... 50 D1
Anerley Surgery
PGE/AN SE20 .... 50 D1

All Saints C of E First School
WIM/MER SW19 .... 29 M8

Animal Care College
ASC SL5 .... 36 D3
The Antiques Gallery
BELMT SM2 .... 65 K8
Apex Retail Park
FELT TW13 .... 25 J4
Apostolic Nuncio
WIM/MER SW19 .... 28 F4
Applegarth Infant School
CROY/NA CR0 .... 69 L5
Arbormar Tree Surgery
ADL/WDHM KT15 .... 58 B8
**Archbishop Tenisons C of E
School**
CROY/NA CR0 .... 5 J8
Archdeacon Cambridges School
WHTN TW2 .... 26 B3
Architon Group Practice
EPSOM KT18 .... 83 M3
Archway Theatre
HORL RH6 .... 170 E7
Arena Leisure Centre
CBLY GU15 .... 72 E6
Arlington Business Park
BRAK RG12 .... 34 E2
Army Golf Club
ALDT GU11 .... 112 B3
Army Training Regiment
CHOB/PIR GU24 .... 94 F3
Arnhem Barracks
ALDT GU11 .... 112 D6
Arrow Industrial Estate
FARN GU14 .... 92 C7

The Art Gallery
RCH/KEW TW9 ...... 18 B6
Art School
BECK BR3 ...... 51 H1
Arunside CP School
HORS RH12 ...... 228 D7
Ashburton Primary School
CROY/NA CR0 ...... 50 E6
The Ashcombe School
DORK RH4 ...... 122 H6
Ashdown Forest Health Centre
FROW RH18 ...... 217 H6
Ashford Clinic
ASHF TW15 ...... 23 H4
Ashford C of E School
ASHF TW15 ...... 23 L7
Ashford High School
ASHF TW15 ...... 23 H4
Ashford Hospital A & E
STWL/WRAY TW19 ...... 23 H3
The Ashford & St Peters
Hospitals NHS Trust
CHERT KT16 ...... 58 A2
Ashford Sports Club
ASHF TW15 ...... 23 G5
Ashford Sports Club
STWL/WRAY TW19 ...... 23 J2
Ash Grange CP School
ASHV GU12 ...... 113 L7
Ashley Centre Surgery
EPSOM KT18 ...... 84 A3
Ashley Gallery
HPTN TW12 ...... 43 K1
Ashley Infant School
WOT/HER KT12 ...... 42 D8
Ash Manor School
ASHV GU12 ...... 135 J1
Ashtead Clinic
ASHTD KT21 ...... 83 H7
Ashtead Cricket Club
ASHTD KT21 ...... 83 H7
Ashtead Hospital
ASHTD KT21 ...... 103 H2
Ashton House School
ISLW TW7 ...... 17 G3
Ash Vale Health Centre
ASHV GU12 ...... 113 L5
Ashvale Medical Centre
TOOT SW17 ...... 30 C6
Aspen House Secondary &
Primary School
BRXS/STRHM SW2 ...... 31 H1
Aston Clinic
NWMAL KT3 ...... 46 B4
Astra Business Centre
REDH RH1 ...... 170 D2
Athelney Primary School
CAT SE6 ...... 33 K4
Athelstan House School
HPTN TW12 ...... 43 K1
Atkinson Morley Hospital
RYNPK SW20 ...... 28 E8
Atlas Medical Centre
HORL RH6 ...... 192 D2
Atwood Primary School
SAND/SEL CR2 ...... 88 D3
Audley CP School
CTHM CR3 ...... 108 B2
Aultone Yard
CAR SM5 ...... 66 C2
Auriol Junior School
HOR/WEW KT19 ...... 64 C3
Avalon Chinese Medicine Clinic
CHSWK W4 ...... 18 F2
The Avenue Primary School
BELMT SM2 ...... 65 K8
Avicenna Medical Practice
REIG RH2 ...... 147 L3
BAA Visitor Centre
HTHAIR TW6 ...... 14 F3
Back Care Clinic
WPK KT4 ...... 46 D8
Badshot Lea County
First School
FNM GU9 ...... 134 D3
Baldwins Hill CP School
EGRIN RH19 ...... 195 M6
Balgowan Primary School
BECK BR3 ...... 51 H2
Balham Health Centre
BAL SW12 ...... 30 E3
Balham Mosque
BAL SW12 ...... 30 E1
Bandon Hill School
WLGTN SM6 ...... 67 G5
Bank Gallery
CHOB/PIR GU24 ...... 76 B1
Banstead Athletic
Football Club
KWD/TDW/WH KT20 ...... 104 F2
Banstead Clinic
BNSTD SM7 ...... 85 K5
Banstead County
Infants School
BNSTD SM7 ...... 85 J5
Banstead Sports Centre
KWD/TDW/WH KT20 ...... 104 F2
Banstead Village Clinic
BNSTD SM7 ...... 85 L5
Barn Elms Water Sports Centre
BARN SW13 ...... 19 M4
Barnes Hospital
MORT/ESHN SW14 ...... 19 H5
Barnes Sports Club
BARN SW13 ...... 19 J3
Barnett Wood County School
ASHTD KT21 ...... 83 G7
Barnsbury County
Infant School
WOKS/MYFD GU22 ...... 97 G3
The Barn Theatre Club
WOT/HER KT12 ...... 60 E3
Barnwood County
First School
GUW GU2 ...... 116 A7
Barrow Hedges School
CAR SM5 ...... 66 B6
Barrow Hills School
MFD/CHID GU8 ...... 181 H5

Barry Jackson Practice
RPLY/SEND GU23 ...... 97 M6
Barwell Business Park
CHSGTN KT9 ...... 63 G6
Battersea Tutorial College
TOOT SW17 ...... 30 D3
Beacon Hill County Primary
School
GSHT GU26 ...... 198 F3
Beacon School
BNSTD SM7 ...... 85 H7
Beatrix Potter Primary School
WAND/EARL SW18 ...... 29 M2
Beauclerc County Infant School
SUN TW16 ...... 42 F7
Beaufort County Primary
School
WOKN/KNAP GU21 ...... 76 C6
Beaumont County
Junior School
ALDT GU11 ...... 112 C7
Beaumont Primary School
PUR/KEN CR8 ...... 87 J4
Beavers Primary School
HSLWW TW4 ...... 15 M5
Beckenham Business Centre
BECK BR3 ...... 33 H7
Beckenham Cricket Club
BECK BR3 ...... 33 L8
Beckenham Hospital
BECK BR3 ...... 51 J2
Beckenham Leisure Centre
BECK BR3 ...... 51 H1
Beckenham Rugby
Football Club
BECK BR3 ...... 51 H4
Beckenham Town Football Club
BECK BR3 ...... 51 K5
Beckmead School
BECK BR3 ...... 51 K8
Beddington Infant School
WLGTN SM6 ...... 66 F3
Beddington Infants School
WLGTN SM6 ...... 66 F2
Beddington Medical Centre
CROY/NA CR0 ...... 67 H3
Beddington Park
Primary School
WLGTN SM6 ...... 67 H2
Beddington Trading Estate
CROY/NA CR0 ...... 49 H8
Bedelsford School
KUT KT1 ...... 2 E9
Bedfont Health Clinic
EBED/NFELT TW14 ...... 24 B1
Bedfont Junior & Infant School
EBED/NFELT TW14 ...... 15 H4
Beech House School
SAND/SEL CR2 ...... 68 C8
Beechnut Industrial Estate
ASHV GU12 ...... 112 E8
Beecholme Primary School
MTCM CR4 ...... 48 C1
Bellerby Theatre
GU GU1 ...... 9 G5
Belle Vue County Infant School
ASHV GU12 ...... 113 G4
Bell Farm County
Middle School
WOT/HER KT12 ...... 60 F3
Bellingham Trading Estate
CAT SE6 ...... 33 L4
Belmont School
RDKG RH5 ...... 164 F3
Bensham Manor School
THHTH CR7 ...... 49 M5
Benson Primary School
CROY/NA CR0 ...... 69 H2
Bentalls Shopping Centre
KUT KT1 ...... 2 D6
Berkeley School
HEST TW5 ...... 16 A1
The Berkshire Golf Club
ASC SL5 ...... 35 H4
Bertrum House & Little
Wandsworth School
TOOT SW17 ...... 30 D3
Betchworth Park Golf Club
RDKG RH5 ...... 145 H1
Bethel Temple
STRHM/NOR SW16 ...... 31 G5
Bethlem Royal Hospital
BECK BR3 ...... 51 K7
Beulah Junior & Infant School
THHTH CR7 ...... 49 M2
Beverley County
Secondary School for Boys
NWMAL KT3 ...... 46 C5
Beverley Trading Estate
MRDN SM4 ...... 47 G7
Bewbush Community
Middle School
CRAWW RH11 ...... 211 H6
Bewbush Leisure Centre
CRAWW RH11 ...... 211 J7
Bewbush Medical Centre
CRAWW RH11 ...... 211 H6
Bewhurst County First School
CRAWW RH11 ...... 211 J6
Biggin Hill Business Park
BH/WHM TN16 ...... 91 G5
Biggin Hill Junior School
BH/WHM TN16 ...... 91 H6
Bilton Industrial Estate
BRAK RG12 ...... 34 B4
Binscombe Medical Centre
RGODL GU7 ...... 160 A1
Birch Hill Medical Centre
BRAK RG12 ...... 34 E7
Birch Hill Primary School
BRAK RG12 ...... 34 F8
Bishop David Brown School
WOKN/KNAP GU21 ...... 78 A3
Bishop Gilpin Primary School
WIM/MER SW19 ...... 29 J6
Bishop Perrin School
WHTN TW2 ...... 25 L1
Bishop Reindorp C of E School
GU GU1 ...... 116 F5

Bishopsgate School
EGH TW20 ...... 20 D4
Bishop Thomas Grant
RC School
STRHM/NOR SW16 ...... 31 J6
Bishop Wand C of E School
SUN TW16 ...... 42 C2
Blackburn Trading Estate
STWL/WRAY TW19 ...... 14 C8
Blackdown Primary School
FRIM GU16 ...... 94 B1
Blackwater & Hawley
Leisure Centre
BLKW GU17 ...... 72 A6
Blackwater Industrial Estate
BLKW GU17 ...... 72 B5
Blackwater Trading Estate
ASHV GU12 ...... 135 H1
Blackwell CP School
EGRIN RH19 ...... 196 B6
Blenheim Business Centre
MTCM CR4 ...... 48 C1
Blenheim High School
HOR/WEW KT19 ...... 64 A8
Blenheim Shopping Centre
PGE/AN SE20 ...... 32 F8
Bletchingley Golf Club
REDH RH1 ...... 128 A7
The Blue C of E School
ISLW TW7 ...... 17 K5
Boathouse Gallery
SHPTN TW17 ...... 42 C7
Bond First School
MTCM CR4 ...... 48 C2
Bond Road School
MTCM CR4 ...... 48 C2
Bookham Galleries
GT/LBKH KT23 ...... 101 M7
Borers Business Park
CRAWE RH10 ...... 193 M6
Boundary Business Centre
WOKN/KNAP GU21 ...... 7 H2
Boundary House Surgery
BRAK RG12 ...... 34 F2
Bourne County First School
NFNM GU10 ...... 11 J6
Bourne Gallery
REIG RH2 ...... 147 L1
Bourne Hall Health Centre
EW KT17 ...... 64 C7
Bourne Mill Industrial Estate
FNM GU9 ...... 134 B6
Bourne Tennis Club
FNM GU9 ...... 11 H4
Bournewood Community
& Mental Health NHS Trust
WOKN/KNAP GU21 ...... 76 D7
Bournewood Community
& Mental NHS Trust
EGH TW20 ...... 21 K6
Box Hill School
RDKG RH5 ...... 122 E1
Bracknell Business Centre
BRAK RG12 ...... 34 C2
Bracknell College
BRAK RG12 ...... 34 F2
Bracknell Forest
Borough Council
BRAK RG12 ...... 34 C2
Bracknell Rugby Football Club
BRAK RG12 ...... 35 H2
Bracknell Sports Centre
BRAK RG12 ...... 34 F5
Bracknell Town Council
BRAK RG12 ...... 34 C2
Bracknell Town Football Club
BRAK RG12 ...... 34 F2
Brakenhale School
BRAK RG12 ...... 34 E4
Brambletye County
Middle School
REDH RH1 ...... 148 D2
Brambletye School
EGRIN RH19 ...... 216 M4
Bramley C of E First School
SHGR GU5 ...... 161 K3
Bramley Golf Club
SHGR GU5 ...... 161 H2
Brentford Business Centre
BTFD TW8 ...... 17 M2
The Brentford Clinic
BTFD TW8 ...... 18 B1
Brentford County Court
BTFD TW8 ...... 18 A2
Brentford Health Centre
BTFD TW8 ...... 17 M1
Brentford Medical Centre
BTFD TW8 ...... 18 A2
Brentford School for Girls
BTFD TW8 ...... 18 A1
Brent Knoll School
SYD SE26 ...... 33 G4
Brentwaters Business Park
BTFD TW8 ...... 17 M2
Brickfields Industrial Park
BRAK RG12 ...... 34 C2
Bridge Industrial Estate
HORL RH6 ...... 170 E6
Bridge Medical Centre
CRAWE RH10 ...... 212 D2
Brigstock Medical Centre
THHTH CR7 ...... 49 L5
Bristow County First School
GU GU15 ...... 72 E7
Britannia Industrial Estate
DTCH/LGLY SL3 ...... 13 H4
Brit Performing Arts &
Technology School
SNWD SE25 ...... 50 A6
Broadbridge Heath
Leisure Centre
HORS RH12 ...... 228 B7
Broadfield East First School
CRAWW RH11 ...... 211 M4
Broadfield Health Centre
CRAWW RH11 ...... 211 L7
Broadford Park
Business Centre
RGUE GU4 ...... 139 H7

Broadmead Junior School
CROY/NA CR0 ...... 50 A6
Broadmere County
Middle School
WOKN/KNAP GU21 ...... 78 A3
Broadmoor County
Primary School
CWTH RG45 ...... 52 A5
Broadmoor Hospital
CWTH RG45 ...... 52 A5
Broadwater Junior &
Infant School
TOOT SW17 ...... 30 B5
Broadwater Park Golf Club
RGODL GU7 ...... 160 E1
Broadwater School
RGODL GU7 ...... 160 D1
Brockham School
BRKHM/BTCW RH3 ...... 145 L2
Brocklebank Health Centre
WAND/EARL SW18 ...... 29 L1
Bromley Hospitals NHS Trust
ORP BR6 ...... 71 K3
Bromley Road Infant School
BECK BR3 ...... 51 L1
Brookfield Primary School
CHEAM SM3 ...... 47 H8
Brookham School
LIPH GU30 ...... 218 B7
Brooklands College
WEY KT13 ...... 59 J5
Brooklands Museum
WEY KT13 ...... 59 K7
Brooklands School
REIG RH2 ...... 125 L6
Brookmead Industrial Estate
MTCM CR4 ...... 48 F6
The Brook Trading Estate
ASHV GU12 ...... 113 H6
Brookwood County
Primary School
CHOB/PIR GU24 ...... 95 K2
Broomfield House School
RCH/KEW TW9 ...... 18 C3
Broomsleigh Business Park
CAT SE6 ...... 33 J6
Broomwood Hall School
BAL SW12 ...... 30 D1
Browning Barracks
ALDT GU11 ...... 112 D4
Brunel University
ISLW TW7 ...... 17 H2
Brunel University
TWK TW1 ...... 17 L6
Buckingham Primary School
HPTN TW12 ...... 25 J6
Buckland County Junior
& Infant School
STA TW18 ...... 22 F8
Buckland Infant School
CHSGTN KT9 ...... 63 J4
Buddhapadipa Temple
WIM/MER SW19 ...... 29 G5
Burghwood Clinic
BNSTD SM7 ...... 85 J6
Burhill County Infant School
WOT/HER KT12 ...... 61 G4
Burhill Golf Club
WOT/HER KT12 ...... 60 D7
Burlington Road School
NWMAL KT3 ...... 46 C4
Burnhill Business Centre
BECK BR3 ...... 51 K2
Burntwood School
TOOT SW17 ...... 30 A3
Burpham Primary School
RGUE GU4 ...... 117 K4
Burstow Business Centre
HORL RH6 ...... 171 L4
Burstow First & Middle
School
HORL RH6 ...... 171 L6
Burwood Park School &
College
WOT/HER KT12 ...... 60 C5
Burys Court School
REIG RH2 ...... 147 G6
Busbridge C of E
Middle School
RGODL GU7 ...... 160 C6
Busbridge County
Infant School
RGODL GU7 ...... 160 C7
Bushey Middle School
RYNPK SW20 ...... 46 E3
Bushy Hill Junior School
GU GU1 ...... 118 A6
Business Park 5
LHD/OX KT22 ...... 102 D2
Byfleet Business Centre
BF/WBF KT14 ...... 79 G1
Byfleet CP School
BF/WBF KT14 ...... 79 G1
Byron Junior School
COUL/CHIP CR5 ...... 87 H7
Cable House School
WOKN/KNAP GU21 ...... 6 C2
Camberley County Infant
School
CBLY GU15 ...... 72 E4
Camberley Cricket Club
CBLY GU15 ...... 73 G6
Camberley Health Centre
CBLY GU15 ...... 72 E6
Camberley Heath Golf Club
CBLY GU15 ...... 73 K5
Camberley Magistrates Court
CBLY GU15 ...... 73 G3
Camberley Rugby
Football Club
CBLY GU15 ...... 72 F6
Camberley Town Football Club
CBLY GU15 ...... 72 E6
Cambridge Military Hospital
ALDT GU11 ...... 112 E4
Cambridge Park Bowling &
Sports Club
TWK TW1 ...... 17 M8
Camden Junior School
CAR SM5 ...... 66 B3

Camelsdale County
First School
HASM GU27 ...... 219 J4
Camphill Industrial Estate
ADL/WDHM KT15 ...... 78 E1
Camphill Road First School
BF/WBF KT14 ...... 78 E2
Campion House College
ISLW TW7 ...... 17 G2
Camp Road Industrial Estate
FARN GU14 ...... 112 F1
Canbury Business Centre
KUTN/CMB KT2 ...... 2 F5
Canbury 2000 Business Park
KUTN/CMB KT2 ...... 2 F5
Canbury Medical Centre
KUTN/CMB KT2 ...... 3 G4
Canbury School
RCHPK/HAM TW10 ...... 27 L7
Capefield Surgery
ESH/CLAY KT10 ...... 62 C5
Capital Business Centre
MTCM CR4 ...... 48 C5
Caplan Estate
MTCM CR4 ...... 48 F1
Cardinal Newman RC School
WOT/HER KT12 ...... 61 G2
Cardinal Road School
FELT TW13 ...... 24 E2
Carew Manor Special School
WLGTN SM6 ...... 67 G2
Carlisle Primary School
HPTN TW12 ...... 25 L7
Carlyle Business Centre
CHERT KT16 ...... 40 D7
Carshalton College
CAR SM5 ...... 66 C5
Carshalton High School
for Boys
CAR SM5 ...... 66 A1
Carshalton High School
for Girls
CAR SM5 ...... 66 B2
Carshalton War
Memorial Hospital
CAR SM5 ...... 66 C4
Carwarden House School
CBLY GU15 ...... 73 K6
The Cassel Hospital
RCHPK/HAM TW10 ...... 27 C5
The Caterham Dene Hospital
CTHM CR3 ...... 108 C5
Caterham Preparatory School
CTHM CR3 ...... 108 C8
Caterham School
CTHM CR3 ...... 108 C8
Catford & Bromley Synagogue
CAT SE6 ...... 33 L3
Catford Cricket & Sports Club
CAT SE6 ...... 33 L2
Catford Cyphers Cricket Club
CAT SE6 ...... 33 J5
Catford Synagogue
CAT SE6 ...... 33 L3
Catford Trading Estate
CAT SE6 ...... 33 L3
Catford Wanderers
Sports Club
CAT SE6 ...... 33 M5
Catherington School
CRAWW RH11 ...... 192 A7
Cator Park School for Girls
BECK BR3 ...... 33 H8
Cavendish Primary School
CHSWK W4 ...... 19 G2
The Cedar House Gallery
RPLY/SEND GU23 ...... 98 F3
The Cedars Primary School
HEST TW5 ...... 15 K2
Centaurs Business Centre
BTFD TW8 ...... 17 K1
Centaurs Rugby Football Club
ISLW TW7 ...... 17 J1
Central Estate
ALDT GU11 ...... 112 E7
Central Estate
E/WMO/HCT KT8 ...... 43 J5
Central Medical Centre
MRDN SM4 ...... 47 M4
Central Road Surgery
MRDN SM4 ...... 47 M4
Chambers Business Park
WDR/YW UB7 ...... 14 D1
The Chandler C of E
Junior School
MFD/CHID GU8 ...... 181 J4
Chandlers Field Primary School
E/WMO/HCT KT8 ...... 43 K5
Chandos Business Centre
WLGTN SM6 ...... 66 F5
Charles Darwin School
BH/WHM TN16 ...... 91 J5
Charlwoods Industrial Estate
EGRIN RH19 ...... 196 B6
Charlwood Village School
HORL RH6 ...... 191 J2
Charrington Bowl
SURB KT6 ...... 63 L1
Charterhouse School
RGODL GU7 ...... 159 M2
Charterhouse School Students
Residences
RGODL GU7 ...... 159 L2
Charters
Comprehensive School
ASC SL5 ...... 37 G7
Chatfield School
PUT/ROE SW15 ...... 19 L7
Chatham Park Golf Club
EGRIN RH19 ...... 195 M3
Chase Bridge School
WHTN TW2 ...... 17 H8
Chatsworth Junior &
Infant School
HSLW TW3 ...... 16 F6
Cheam Common County
Junior School
WPK KT4 ...... 64 E1
Cheam Common Infant School
WPK KT4 ...... 64 E1

Cheam Family Practice
CHEAM SM3 .... 65 H5
Cheam Family Practice
SUT SM1 .... 65 J2
Cheam High School
CHEAM SM3 .... 65 H3
Cheam Leisure Centre
CHEAM SM3 .... 65 G3
Cheam Park Farm
Junior School
CHEAM SM3 .... 65 H2
Cheam Sports Club
BELMT SM2 .... 65 G6
Cheapside C of E School
ASC SL5 .... 37 H1
Chelsea Fields Industrial Estate
WIM/MER SW19 .... 48 A1
Chennestone County
Middle School
SUN TW16 .... 42 E2
Chertsey Business Centre
CHERT KT16 .... 40 D7
Chertsey Museum
CHERT KT16 .... 40 D7
Chertsey Recreation Centre
CHERT KT16 .... 40 C8
Chertsey Town Football Club
CHERT KT16 .... 40 C6
Chessington
Community College
CHSGTN KT9 .... 63 G6
Chessington Cricket Club
CHSGTN KT9 .... 62 F6
Chesworth Junior School
SWTR RH13 .... 229 H6
Cheswycks School
FRIM GU16 .... 93 L4
Cheyne Galleries
TWK TW1 .... 17 L8
Chiddingford Golf Club
MFD/CHID GU8 .... 201 L8
Childrens Hospital Trust Fund
WIM/MER SW19 .... 29 J5
Chilworth C of E School
RGUE GU4 .... 140 A6
Chinese Health Centre
BECK BR3 .... 51 H3
Chinese Health Centre
PGE/AN SE20 .... 33 G8
Chinese Medicine Clinic
STRHM/NOR SW16 .... 31 H5
Chinthurst School
KWD/TDW/WH KT20 .... 104 F5
Chipstead Rugby Football Club
COUL/CHIP CR5 .... 106 C3
Chipstead Valley Schools
COUL/CHIP CR5 .... 86 D6
Chipstead Vp School
COUL/CHIP CR5 .... 86 D6
Chiropodist Podiatrist Surgery
WPK KT4 .... 46 D8
Chiropractic Surgery
COUL/CHIP CR5 .... 86 F4
Chiswick Community School
CHSWK W4 .... 19 G2
Chiswick House
CHSWK W4 .... 19 G1
Chobham Football Club
CHOB/PIR GU24 .... 76 C1
Chobham Parish Council
CHOB/PIR GU24 .... 76 B1
Chobham St Lawrence
C of E First & Middle School
CHOB/PIR GU24 .... 76 B1
Christchurch C of E
Infant School
VW GU25 .... 38 D3
Christ Church C of E
Junior School
NWMAL KT3 .... 46 A3
Christ Church C of E
Primary School
BRXS/STRHM SW2 .... 31 J2
Christ Church C of E
Primary School
BRYLDS KT5 .... 45 K6
Christ Church C of E School
CHERT KT16 .... 58 A5
Christ Church C of E School
FSTH SE23 .... 33 G3
Christ Church Primary School
NWMAL KT3 .... 46 B3
Christ Church Primary School
PUR/KEN CR8 .... 67 L8
Christchurch School
FSTH SE23 .... 33 G3
Christs School
RCHPK/HAM TW10 .... 18 C7
Christ the King RC First School
STWL/WRAY TW19 .... 14 A8
Chrysalis Theatre
BAL SW12 .... 30 D2
Chrysanthemum Clinic
CHSWK W4 .... 18 F2
Churchfields Primary School
BECK BR3 .... 51 G3
Church Hill House Hospital
BRAK RG12 .... 34 D5
Churchill College
RYNPK SW20 .... 46 F2
Churchill College
TOOT SW17 .... 30 C3
Churchill Gallery
BH/WHM TN16 .... 131 M1
The Churchill Medical Centre
KUTN/CMB KT2 .... 3 J5
Churchill School
BH/WHM TN16 .... 111 M7
Church Lane Practice
WIM/MER SW19 .... 47 J1
Church of England School
COUL/CHIP CR5 .... 87 J8
The Church School
BTFD TW8 .... 18 B1
City Business Centre
SWTR RH13 .... 229 G8
The City Business Centre
CRAWW RH11 .... 192 A7

City of London Freemans
School
ASHTD KT21 .... 103 L1
Civic Hall
GU GU1 .... 9 J5
Civil Service College
ASC SL5 .... 37 J5
Clandon C of E First School
RGUE GU4 .... 118 D5
Clandon Regis Golf Club
RGUE GU4 .... 118 E5
Clare House Primary School
BECK BR3 .... 51 M2
Claremont Fan Court School
ESH/CLAY KT10 .... 61 L5
Clarence Road School
SWTR RH13 .... 229 G8
Clarendon County
Primary School
ASHF TW15 .... 23 J4
Clarendon School
HPTN TW12 .... 25 L7
Claygate Junior School
ESH/CLAY KT10 .... 62 B6
Clayton Barracks
ALDT GU11 .... 113 G5
Clerklands Surgery
HORL RH6 .... 170 C6
Cleves County Junior School
WEY KT13 .... 60 C3
Clewborough House
Preparatory School
CBLY GU15 .... 73 K3
Clifton School
CTHM CR3 .... 108 A6
Clockhouse Industrial Estate
EBED/NFELT TW14 .... 23 L2
Club House
BRAK RG12 .... 35 G8
Club House
RDKG RH5 .... 187 M5
Cobham Bus Museum
COB KT11 .... 79 M2
Cobham Galleries Antiques
& Fines Arts
COB KT11 .... 80 D4
The Cobham Health Centre
COB KT11 .... 80 E5
Coliseum Business Centre
CBLY GU15 .... 72 D6
College Fields Business Centre
WIM/MER SW19 .... 48 B1
The College of St Barnabas
LING RH7 .... 196 C1
Colliers Wood Surgery
WIM/MER SW19 .... 30 B7
Collingwood College
CBLY GU15 .... 73 K1
Collingwood School
WLGTN SM6 .... 66 E4
Collis Primary School
TEDD TW11 .... 26 E7
Collyers Sixth Form College
HORS RH12 .... 229 G5
Colnbrook C of E
Combined School
DTCH/LGLY SL3 .... 12 F2
Colnbrook Sports Club
DTCH/LGLY SL3 .... 13 J3
Coln Industrial Estate
DTCH/LGLY SL3 .... 13 J3
Colours Sports Club
SUT SM1 .... 65 M4
Coltwood Business Centre
ALDT GU11 .... 112 E7
Commonwealth Lodge School
PUR/KEN CR8 .... 87 G2
Coney Hill School
HAYES BR2 .... 70 C1
Connaught Business Centre
CROY/NA CR0 .... 67 J5
Connaught County
Junior School
BAGS GU19 .... 54 B7
The Connaught School
ASHV GU12 .... 135 H2
Coombe Girls School
NWMAL KT3 .... 46 A2
Coombe Hill Junior &
Infant School
NWMAL KT3 .... 46 A1
The Copthorne
Business Centre
CRAWE RH10 .... 193 L6
Copthorne Fairway
Infant School
CRAWE RH10 .... 193 L6
Copthorne Golf Club
CRAWE RH10 .... 193 M6
Copthorne Junior School
CRAWE RH10 .... 193 L6
Copthorne Squash Club
CRAWE RH10 .... 193 K7
Cordwalles County
Middle School
CBLY GU15 .... 73 J1
Corinthian Casuals
Football Club
CHSGTN KT9 .... 63 K2
Cornhill Sports Club
BECK BR3 .... 33 K6
Cottenham Park C of E
Primary School
RYNPK SW20 .... 46 D1
Coulsdon College
COUL/CHIP CR5 .... 107 K1
The Coulsdon Eye Clinic
COUL/CHIP CR5 .... 86 F5
Coulsdon High School
COUL/CHIP CR5 .... 107 L2
Council Offices
LTWR GU18 .... 54 D8
Country Club
GU GU1 .... 9 H7
Country Gardens Estate
BFOR GU20 .... 54 F1
County Hall
KUT KT1 .... 2 D9
County Oak Retail Park
CRAWW RH11 .... 192 A7

Court Lodge First School
HORL RH6 .... 170 C6
Courtwood Primary School
CROY/NA CR0 .... 69 J8
The Courtyard Surgery
HORS RH12 .... 228 F7
Cove County Infant School
FARN GU14 .... 92 B3
Cove County Junior School
FARN GU14 .... 92 B4
Cove County Secondary
School
FARN GU14 .... 92 B4
Cove Cricket Club
FARN GU14 .... 92 B3
Cove Manor County
Junior & Infant School
FARN GU14 .... 92 C3
Cowarth Park School
CHOB/PIR GU22 .... 55 L3
The Coworth Gallery
ASC SL5 .... 37 J5
Crane School
FELT TW13 .... 25 J3
Cranford Community School
HEST TW5 .... 15 L1
Cranford Infant School
HSLWW TW4 .... 15 K4
Cranford School
HSLWW TW4 .... 15 L4
Cranleigh Health Centre
CRAN GU6 .... 185 G7
Cranleigh Leisure Centre
CRAN GU6 .... 185 G7
Cranleigh Preparatory School
CRAN GU6 .... 185 G5
Cranleigh School
CRAN GU6 .... 184 F4
Cranleigh Village Hospital
CRAN GU6 .... 185 H6
Cranmer Middle School
MTCM CR4 .... 48 C5
Cranmore School
EHSLY KT24 .... 119 M3
Crawley College
CRAWE RH10 .... 212 B3
Crawley College
HORS RH12 .... 229 G6
Crawley College Annexe
CRAWW RH11 .... 211 M2
Crawley Down C of E
Infant School
CRAWE RH10 .... 214 E1
Crawley Down C of E School
CRAWE RH10 .... 214 E1
Crawley Down Health Centre
CRAWE RH10 .... 214 D1
Crawley Health Clinic
CRAWE RH10 .... 212 B3
Crawley Hospital
CRAWW RH11 .... 211 M3
The Crawley Lawn Tennis Club
CRAWE RH10 .... 212 E2
Crawley Leisure Centre
CRAWE RH10 .... 212 C4
Crawley Ridge First School
CBLY GU15 .... 73 J3
Crawley Rugby Club
CRAWW RH11 .... 191 K7
Crawley Town Football Club
CRAWW RH11 .... 211 M7
Crockham Hill C of E
Primary School
EDEN TN8 .... 131 M7
Croham Hurst School
SAND/SEL CR2 .... 68 C4
Crondall CP School
NFNM GU10 .... 132 C3
Cross Deep Surgery
TWK TW1 .... 26 D2
Crouch Industrial Estate
LHD/OX KT22 .... 102 D1
Crown Court
GU GU1 .... 8 E5
Crown Court
ISLW TW7 .... 17 H3
Crown Lane CP School
WNWD SE27 .... 31 L6
Crown Prosecution Service
GU GU1 .... 8 F6
Crown Road Doctors Surgery
TWK TW1 .... 26 E1
Crown Wood CP School
BRAK RG12 .... 35 G6
Crow Place Doctors Surgery
CRAWW RH11 .... 212 A4
Croydon Council
CROY/NA CR0 .... 50 E7
Croydon Football Club
SNWD SE25 .... 50 F5
Croydon Health Authority
CROY/NA CR0 .... 4 C3
Croydon Health Authority
CROY/NA CR0 .... 68 D3
Croydon High School for Girls
SAND/SEL CR2 .... 88 F1
Croydon Mosque & Islamic
Centre
THHTH CR7 .... 49 K6
Croydon Road Industrial
Estate
SNWD SE25 .... 50 F4
Crystal Palace Football
Club 1986
SNWD SE25 .... 50 B4
Crystal Palace Museum
NRWD SE19 .... 32 C7
Crystal Palace National
Sports Centre
NRWD SE19 .... 32 D7
Cuaco Sports Ground
BECK BR3 .... 33 K7
Cuddington CP School
HOR/WEW KT19 .... 64 C2
Cudham School
BH/WHM TN16 .... 91 K6
Culvers House Primary School
MTCM CR4 .... 48 D8
Cumnor House School
SAND/SEL CR2 .... 67 L7

Cygnets Galleries
WOKN/KNAP GU21 .... 6 D5
Cypress Infant School
SNWD SE25 .... 50 B2
Cypress Junior School
SNWD SE25 .... 50 B2
Cyprus College of Art
WNWD SE27 .... 31 L5
Dalmain Primary School
FSTH SE23 .... 33 H2
Danesfield Preparatory School
WOT/HER KT12 .... 60 E1
Danes Hill Preparatory School
LHD/OX KT22 .... 81 M4
Danetree School
HOR/WEW KT19 .... 63 M6
Darell Junior & Infant School
RCH/KEW TW9 .... 18 D5
Darley Dene CP School
ADL/WDHM KT15 .... 58 F4
Darrick Wood Junior &
Primary School
ORP BR6 .... 71 L3
Darrick Wood Swimming Pool
ORP BR6 .... 71 L2
David Curzon Gallery
WIM/MER SW19 .... 29 H6
David Livingstone School
THHTH CR7 .... 49 M1
Davidson Infant &
Junior School
CROY/NA CR0 .... 5 J1
Day Hospital
PUR/KEN CR8 .... 87 K1
Deerswood School
CRAWW RH11 .... 211 K1
Denmead School
HPTN TW12 .... 25 K8
The Dental Health Centre
TWK TW1 .... 18 A8
Desmond Anderson School
CRAWE RH10 .... 212 A7
De Stafford School
CTHM CR3 .... 108 C3
Deutsche Schule
RCHPK/HAM TW10 .... 27 G2
Devonshire School
BELMT SM2 .... 65 M6
Doctors Group Practice
BELMT SM2 .... 65 L8
Donyngs Recreation Centre
REDH RH1 .... 126 B7
Doods Brow School
REDH RH1 .... 127 J7
Dorchester Primary School
WPK KT4 .... 46 F8
The Dorking Business Park
DORK RH4 .... 144 D1
Dorking Football Club
RDKG RH5 .... 122 F3
Dorking General Hospital
DORK RH4 .... 144 D3
Dorking Golf Club
RDKG RH5 .... 144 F3
Dorking Lawn Tennis &
Squash Club
DORK RH4 .... 144 D4
Dorking Museum
DORK RH4 .... 144 D2
Dorking Rugby Football Club
BRKHM/BTCW RH3 .... 123 L8
Dorking Swimming &
Sports Centre
DORK RH4 .... 144 F1
Douglas Bader Foundation
PUT/ROE SW15 .... 19 K8
Dovers Green First School
REIG RH2 .... 147 M4
Downe Primary School
ORP BR6 .... 91 K1
Down House
ORP BR6 .... 91 K2
Downland Surgery
COUL/CHIP CR5 .... 107 J1
Downs Way School
OXTED RH8 .... 130 B1
Duke of Kent School
CRAN GU6 .... 164 A7
Dulwich College
DUL SE21 .... 32 B2
Dulwich College Picture
Gallery
DUL SE21 .... 32 A1
Dulwich College
Preparatory School
DUL SE21 .... 32 B4
Dundonald Primary School
WIM/MER SW19 .... 29 J8
Dunnings Squash Club
EGRIN RH19 .... 216 B3
Dunottar School
REIG RH2 .... 148 A1
Dunraven Lower School
STRHM/NOR SW16 .... 31 J4
Dunraven Upper School
STRHM/NOR SW16 .... 31 J4
Duppas Primary School
CROY/NA CR0 .... 67 L4
Dysart School
KUTN/CMB KT2 .... 27 G5
Eagle Trading Estate
MTCM CR4 .... 48 C6
Eardley Primary School
STRHM/NOR SW16 .... 30 F7
Earlsfield Primary School
WAND/EARL SW18 .... 29 M4
Earlswood First School
REDH RH1 .... 148 D1
Earlswood Mosque
REDH RH1 .... 148 D1
East Court
EGRIN RH19 .... 196 C7
Eastern Business Centre
BRAK RG12 .... 35 G2
Eastfields Secondary
Modern Boys School
MTCM CR4 .... 48 E2
East Grinstead Health Clinic
EGRIN RH19 .... 196 B7

East Grinstead Sports Club
EGRIN RH19 .... 215 M4
Easthampstead Park School
EWKG RG40 .... 34 A6
East Molesey Cricket Club
E/WMO/HCT KT8 .... 43 M3
East Molesey Infants School
E/WMO/HCT KT8 .... 44 A5
East Sheen CP Junior School
MORT/ESHN SW14 .... 19 H6
East Surrey College
REDH RH1 .... 126 D4
East Surrey Hospital
REDH RH1 .... 148 E4
East Surrey Museum
CTHM CR3 .... 108 C6
Eastwick County
Junior School
GT/LBKH KT23 .... 101 L6
Ebbisham County Infants
School
EPSOM KT18 .... 83 M4
Ebbisham Sports Club
HOR/WEW KT19 .... 83 M2
Ecclesbourne Junior &
Infants School
THHTH CR7 .... 49 M5
Echelford Primary School
ASHF TW15 .... 23 L6
Eclipse Estate
HOR/WEW KT19 .... 83 M3
Edenbridge CP School
EDEN TN8 .... 153 M8
Edenbridge & District War
Memorial Hospital
EDEN TN8 .... 175 M2
Edenbridge Golf &
Country Club
EDEN TN8 .... 153 K7
Edenbridge Leisure Centre
EDEN TN8 .... 153 L7
The Edenbridge Medical
Centre
EDEN TN8 .... 153 M8
Edenham High School
CROY/NA CR0 .... 51 J7
Edenvale Child Health Clinic
TOOT SW17 .... 30 D8
Eden Valley School
EDEN TN8 .... 153 M7
Edes Business Park
WLGTN SM6 .... 66 D1
Edgeborough School
NFNM GU10 .... 155 M6
Edward Ash Gallery
ORP BR6 .... 71 K2
Edward Cross Gallery
WEY KT13 .... 60 A2
Edward Pauling School
FELT TW13 .... 24 B3
Effingham Cricket Club
EHSLY KT24 .... 100 E6
Effingham Golf Club
EHSLY KT24 .... 121 G2
Effingham Park Golf Club
CRAWE RH10 .... 194 C5
Egham Cricket Club
EGH TW20 .... 21 L7
Egham Sports Centre
EGH TW20 .... 21 L7
Egham Town Football Club
EGH TW20 .... 21 M7
Electrical Trades Union College
ESH/CLAY KT10 .... 61 K3
The Electric Theatre
GU GU1 .... 8 E6
Elfrida Primary School
CAT SE6 .... 33 L5
Elica Gallery
NRWD SE19 .... 32 B7
Eliot Bank Primary School
FSTH SE23 .... 32 E3
Elizabeth Barracks
CHOB/PIR GU24 .... 94 D3
Ellingham Primary School
CHSGTN KT9 .... 63 G6
Elliott Gm School
PUT/ROE SW15 .... 19 M8
Elliott Industrial Park
ASHV GU12 .... 113 H7
Elmbridge Borough Council
COB KT11 .... 81 H6
Elmbridge Borough Council
WOT/HER KT12 .... 42 D7
Elmbridge Leisure Centre
WOT/HER KT12 .... 42 E5
Elmbridge Museum
WEY KT13 .... 59 K3
Elmcourt School
WNWD SE27 .... 31 L3
Elm House Business Centre
MFD/CHID GU8 .... 158 C5
Elm House Surgery
BECK BR3 .... 51 J2
Elmhurst Preparatory School
BECK BR3 .... 51 G4
Elmhurst School
CROY/NA CR0 .... 68 A3
Elmwood Junior & Infant School
CROY/NA CR0 .... 4 B1
Elm Wood Primary School
WNWD SE27 .... 32 A4
Ember Sports Club
ESH/CLAY KT10 .... 43 M8
Emerson College
FROW RH18 .... 217 L6
Empson & Ewell Bo Co
EW KT17 .... 84 A3
Englefield Green School
EGH TW20 .... 20 F6
Ensham Secondary School
TOOT SW17 .... 30 C6
Enterprise Industrial Estate
ASHV GU12 .... 113 J2
Epsom Business Park
EW KT17 .... 84 B1
Epsom College
EW KT17 .... 84 D4
Epsom County Court
EPSOM KT18 .... 84 A3

Epsom CP School
HOR/WEW KT19 .... 84 A1
Epsom Downs County
Infant School
EPSOM KT18 .... 104 A1
Epsom & Ewell Borough Council
EPSOM KT18 .... 84 B6
Epsom & Ewell High School
HOR/WEW KT19 .... 63 M4
Epsom Ewell & St Hellier
NHS Trust
EPSOM KT18 .... 83 M5
Epsom Ewell & St Helliers
NHS Trust
HOR/WEW KT19 .... 83 J2
Epsom Golf Club
EW KT17 .... 84 D5
Epsom Health Clinic
EPSOM KT18 .... 84 B3
Epsom School of Art & Design
EW KT17 .... 84 B2
Epsom Sports Club
EPSOM KT18 .... 83 M5
Ernest Bevin School
TOOT SW17 .... 30 B4
Escotts Country Primary School
EGRIN RH19 .... 196 D8
Esher Church School
ESH/CLAY KT10 .... 61 M5
Esher College
THDIT KT7 .... 44 B7
Esher Green Surgery
ESH/CLAY KT10 .... 61 K2
Esher Rugby Club
WOT/HER KT12 .... 61 H1
Essex House Surgery
BARN SW13 .... 19 J4
Evendine College
WIM/MER SW19 .... 29 H7
Eversley Medical Centre
THHTH CR7 .... 49 K6
Ewell Castle School
EW KT17 .... 64 D7
Ewell Grove Infant School
EW KT17 .... 64 C7
Ewhurst C of E First School
CRAN GU6 .... 186 A4
Fairfax Industrial Estate
ASHV GU12 .... 113 H7
Fairfield Industrial Estate
KUT KT1 .... 3 H9
Fairfield Medical Centre
GT/LBKH KT23 .... 101 L8
Fairhill Medical Practice
KUTN/CMB KT2 .... 3 K3
Fairholme Junior &
Infant School
EBED/NFELT TW14 .... 24 A2
Fairlands Practice
RGUW GU3 .... 115 M4
Fairlawn Primary School
FSTH SE23 .... 32 F1
Fairview Industrial Estate
OXTED RH8 .... 130 D7
Fairview Medical Centre
STRHM/NOR SW16 .... 49 H1
Family Doctor Unit Surgery
HSLW TW3 .... 16 D5
Farleigh Rovers F C
WARL CR6 .... 89 J5
Farley Road Surgery
SAND/SEL CR2 .... 68 E7
Farlington School
HORS RH12 .... 227 L3
Farnborough Business Centre
FARN GU14 .... 92 C7
Farnborough
College of Technology
ASHV GU12 .... 112 E8
Farnborough
College of Technology
FARN GU14 .... 92 F7
Farnborough
College of Technology
FARN GU14 .... 112 E9
Farnborough Grange
County Junior School
FARN GU14 .... 92 C1
Farnborough Hill School
FARN GU14 .... 92 F4
Farnborough Recreation
Centre
FARN GU14 .... 92 E6
Farnborough Rugby
Football Club
FARN GU14 .... 92 D3
Farnborough Town
Football Club
FARN GU14 .... 92 D1
Farncombe C of E
Infant School
RGODL GU7 .... 160 B2
Farncombe Cricket Club
RGODL GU7 .... 160 C2
Farnell House Medical Centre
HSLW TW3 .... 16 E3
Farnham Business Centre
FNM GU9 .... 10 D3
Farnham Business Centre
FNM GU9 .... 133 M6
Farnham Business Park
FNM GU9 .... 10 E2
Farnham Business Park
FNM GU9 .... 133 M6
Farnham College
FNM GU9 .... 11 H2
Farnham Golf Club
NFNM GU10 .... 135 G7
Farnham Hospital
FNM GU9 .... 134 B6
Farnham Museum
FNM GU9 .... 133 L7
Farnham Retail Park
FNM GU9 .... 134 B6
Farnham Road Hospital
GUW GU2 .... 8 D7
Fashion Gallery
MORT/ESHN SW14 .... 18 F5
Faygate Business Centre
HORS RH12 .... 210 C8

Felbridge CP School
EGRIN RH19 .... 195 J5
Felnex Trading Estate
WLGTN SM6 .... 66 D1
Feltham Airparcs Leisure
Centre
FELT TW13 .... 25 G3
Feltham Hill Junior School
FELT TW13 .... 24 C4
Feltham & Hounslow
Boro Football Club
EBED/NFELT TW14 .... 24 D1
The Feltham School
FELT TW13 .... 24 F3
Feltham Superbowl
FELT TW13 .... 24 E3
Fenstanton Junior &
Infant School
BRXS/STRHM SW2 .... 31 K2
Fernfell Golf & Country Club
CRAN GU6 .... 185 K3
Fernhill Comprehensive School
FARN GU14 .... 72 C8
Fernhill Primary School
FARN GU14 .... 72 C8
Fern Hill Primary School
KUTN/CMB KT2 .... 27 H7
Fetcham County First School
LHD/OX KT22 .... 102 A2
Fetcham Village Surgery
GT/LBKH KT23 .... 101 L7
Finton House School
TOOT SW17 .... 30 C3
Fircroft Primary School
TOOT SW17 .... 30 C3
Fir Road Surgery
CRAN GU6 .... 25 H6
Fitznells Manor Surgery
EW KT17 .... 64 C7
Five Ways Business Centre
FELT TW13 .... 24 E4
Floral Gallery
CTHM CR3 .... 108 D6
Folly Hill County Infant School
FNM GU9 .... 133 K3
Follys End Christian
High School
SNWD SE25 .... 50 B6
Fonthill Lodge School
EGRIN RH19 .... 215 M3
Fontigarry Farm
Business Park
REIG RH2 .... 169 M1
The Foot Clinic
WIM/MER SW19 .... 29 H6
The Foot Health Centre
COUL/CHIP CR5 .... 87 G5
Fordbridge Medical Centre
ASHF TW15 .... 23 J5
Fordwater Trading Estate
ADL/WDHM KT15 .... 40 F8
Forest Community School
SWTR RH13 .... 229 J8
Forestdale Primary School
CROY/NA CR0 .... 69 H7
Forest End Medical Centre
BRAK RG12 .... 34 E4
Foresters Primary School
WLGTN SM6 .... 67 G5
Forest Gallery Fine Art
GU GU1 .... 9 H4
Forest Hill Business Centre
FSTH SE23 .... 32 F3
Forest Hill Industrial Estate
FSTH SE23 .... 32 F3
Forest Hill Secondary School
FSTH SE23 .... 33 C4
Forest Row Business Park
FROW RH18 .... 217 J6
Forest Row C of E
Infant School
FROW RH18 .... 217 J7
Forge Lane Junior School
FELT TW13 .... 25 H6
Forge Wood Industrial Estate
CRAWE RH10 .... 192 E7
The Fort House Surgery
WOT/HER KT12 .... 60 D1
Foxbridge Golf Club
BIL RH14 .... 223 M8
Foxhill Primary School
BRAK RG12 .... 34 E5
France Hill School
CBLY GU15 .... 72 F7
Franciscan Primary School
TOOT SW17 .... 30 D5
The Franciscan Surgery
TOOT SW17 .... 30 C5
Franklin Industrial Estate
PGE/AN SE20 .... 50 F1
Freehold Industrial Centre
HSLWW TW4 .... 15 M7
Freemantles School
CHERT KT16 .... 40 B7
Frensham C of E First School
NFNM GU10 .... 178 A1
Frensham Heights School
NFNM GU10 .... 155 K7
Frensham Pond Sailing Club
NFNM GU10 .... 177 M4
The Friary Centre
GU GU1 .... 8 F6
Frimley C of E First &
Middle School
FRIM GU16 .... 93 H2
Frimley Green Medical Centre
FRIM GU16 .... 93 J3
Frimley Park Hospital
FRIM GU16 .... 73 G7
Froebel College
PUT/ROE SW15 .... 19 K8
Fullbrook County Secondary
School
ADL/WDHM KT15 .... 78 D1
Fuller Smith & Turner Sports Club
CHSWK W4 .... 19 H3
Furnace Green Surgery
CRAWE RH10 .... 212 C5
Furzedown Primary School
TOOT SW17 .... 30 E7

Furzefield Primary School
REDH RH1 .... 127 G2
Gaflac Sports Ground Pavilion
SUN TW16 .... 42 D1
The Gallery
CRAN GU6 .... 184 F6
The Gallery
SNWD SE25 .... 50 C4
The Gallery
WOKN/KNAP GU21 .... 75 M7
Gardener Industrial Estate
BECK BR3 .... 33 H6
Garfield First School
WIM/MER SW19 .... 29 M7
The Garratt Lane Surgery
WIM/MER SW19 .... 29 L4
Garratt Park School
WAND/EARL SW18 .... 29 M4
The Garth Hill School
BRAK RG12 .... 34 F1
Garth Primary School
MRDN SM4 .... 48 A5
Gatton Park Business Centre
REDH RH18 .... 126 A4
Gatwick Medical Centre
HORL RH6 .... 192 E2
Gatwick Park Hospital
HORL RH6 .... 170 B7
Genesis Business Centre
SWTR RH13 .... 229 J6
Genesis Business Park
WOKN/KNAP GU21 .... 7 L1
Genevieve the Gallery
EGH TW20 .... 20 F7
George Abbot School
GU GU1 .... 117 K6
Giggs Hill Surgery
THDIT KT7 .... 44 D4
Gilbert Scotts Primary School
SAND/SEL CR2 .... 69 H5
Glebelands School
CRAN GU6 .... 185 G6
Glenesk House
Preparatory School
EHSLY KT24 .... 100 A7
Glenlyn Medical Centre
E/WMO/HCT KT8 .... 43 M5
Glenthorne High School
CHEAM SM3 .... 47 K8
Global Adventure Sailing Club
FNM GU9 .... 133 L7
Glyn A D T Technology School
EW KT17 .... 84 C1
Goal Farm Golf Club
CHOB/PIR GU24 .... 95 G3
The Godalming
Badminton Club
RGODL GU7 .... 160 A7
Godalming Business Centre
RGODL GU7 .... 160 C5
Godalming County
Junior School
RGODL GU7 .... 160 C4
Godalming & Guildford
Football Club
RGODL GU7 .... 160 D3
Godalming Leisure Centre
RGODL GU7 .... 160 D2
Godalming Museum
RGODL GU7 .... 160 A5
Godalming 6th Form College
RGODL GU7 .... 160 A7
Goldsworth CP School
WOKN/KNAP GU21 .... 76 F7
Goldsworth Park Trading Estate
WOKN/KNAP GU21 .... 76 D6
Goldsworth Rd Industrial Estate
WOKN/KNAP GU21 .... 6 A6
Golf Club Club House
BF/WBF KT14 .... 78 C3
Golf Club House
REIG RH2 .... 124 F8
The Gomshall Gallery
SHGR GU5 .... 142 A5
Gonville School
THHTH CR7 .... 49 J5
The Gooday Gallery
RCHPK/HAM TW10 .... 18 A8
Gorringe Park Middle School
MTCM CR4 .... 48 D1
Gosbury Hill Health Centre
CHSGTN KT9 .... 63 H3
Gosden House Special School
SHGR GU5 .... 161 H1
Gossops Green Clinic
CRAWW RH11 .... 211 J5
Gossops Green First &
Middle School
CRAWW RH11 .... 211 K4
Grace Business Centre
MTCM CR4 .... 48 C6
Granard Primary School
PUT/ROE SW15 .... 19 L8
Grand Avenue Infant &
Primary School
BRYLDS KT5 .... 45 M6
Grand Drive Surgery
RYNPK SW20 .... 46 F3
Grange CP School
ADL/WDHM KT15 .... 58 D8
Granton Primary School
STRHM/NOR SW16 .... 30 F8
Granville House Practice
REDH RH1 .... 126 B7
The Grapevine Gallery
REDH RH1 .... 126 C7
Grasshoppers Rugby
Football Club
ISLW TW7 .... 17 J1
Graveney School
TOOT SW17 .... 30 E7
Grayshott Clinic
GSHT GU26 .... 198 E5
Grayshott Council Office
GSHT GU26 .... 199 G6
Grayshott Primary School
GSHT GU26 .... 198 E6
Grayshott Surgery
GSHT GU26 .... 199 G6

Grayswood C of E School
HASM GU27 .... 200 C7
Great Bookham County
Infant School
GT/LBKH KT23 .... 101 K8
Great Bookham Middle School
GT/LBKH KT23 .... 101 K8
Great Hollands County
Infant School
BRAK RG12 .... 34 B5
Great Hollands County
Junior School
BRAK RG12 .... 34 B5
Great Hollands Health Centre
BRAK RG12 .... 34 C6
Great Hollands Recreation
Centre
BRAK RG12 .... 34 B8
Green Business Centre
EGH TW20 .... 21 M5
Green Croft School
FARN GU14 .... 93 G3
Greenfield School
FROW RH18 .... 216 F8
Greenfield School
WOKS/MYFD GU22 .... 6 C9
Green Lane Primary School
WPK KT4 .... 46 E7
Greenmead Primary School
PUT/ROE SW15 .... 19 L7
The Green School for Girls
ISLW TW7 .... 17 K2
Greenshaw High School
SUT SM1 .... 65 M1
The Green Surgery
WHTN TW2 .... 26 B3
Greenvale Primary School
SAND/SEL CR2 .... 89 G1
Greenway School
HORS RH12 .... 228 E6
Greenwood First School
MTCM CR4 .... 49 G3
Green Wrythe Primary School
CAR SM5 .... 48 A6
Gresham Industrial Estate
ASHV GU12 .... 113 H7
Gresham School
SAND/SEL CR2 .... 88 C2
Gresham Way Industrial Estate
WIM/MER SW19 .... 29 L4
The Greville CP School
ASHTD KT21 .... 83 J7
Grey Court School
RCHPK/HAM TW10 .... 26 F4
Greystone House Practice
REDH RH1 .... 126 B7
Grist Memorial Sports Club
E/WMO/HCT KT8 .... 44 B5
Grovebell Industrial Estate
FNM GU9 .... 10 B5
Grove County Primary School
FRIM GU16 .... 73 H7
Grove House Primary School
WNWD SE27 .... 31 L3
Grovelands School
WOT/HER KT12 .... 42 E6
Grove Park Primary School
CHSWK W4 .... 18 F1
Grove Road Primary School
HSLW TW3 .... 16 D6
The Groves Medical Centre
NWMAL KT3 .... 46 B3
Grove Village Medical Centre
EBED/NFELT TW14 .... 24 B2
Guildford Borough Council
GUW GU2 .... 117 H4
Guildford Borough Council
GUW GU2 .... 8 F9
Guildford Castle
GU GU1 .... 9 H7
Guildford Cathedral
GUW GU2 .... 8 C4
Guildford County College of
Further & Higher Education
GU GU1 .... 9 H2
Guildford County School
GU GU1 .... 8 D7
Guildford & District Synagogue
GU GU1 .... 9 G5
Guildford Golf Club
GU GU1 .... 117 M8
Guildford High School for Girls
GU GU1 .... 9 K4
Guildford Hockey & Cricket Club
GU GU1 .... 8 F4
Guildford Industrial Estate
GUW GU2 .... 8 A2
Guildford Natural Health
Centre
GU GU1 .... 9 G7
The Guildford
Nuffield Hospital
GUW GU2 .... 116 B8
Guildford Road Industrial
Estate
FNM GU9 .... 134 A6
Guildford Rowing Club
GU GU1 .... 9 G9
Gumley House Convent
School for Girls
ISLW TW7 .... 17 K5
Hackbridge Junior School
WLGTN SM6 .... 48 D8
Hale County First &
Middle School
FNM GU9 .... 133 L2
Haling Manor High School
CROY/NA CR0 .... 67 L6
Hall Grove School
BAGS GU19 .... 54 D4
Halliford Health Clinic
SHPTN TW17 .... 42 B4
Halliford School
SHPTN TW17 .... 41 M7
Hall School Wimbledon
PUT/ROE SW15 .... 28 D4
Halsford Park Primary School
EGRIN RH19 .... 195 J2
Ham Health Clinic
RCHPK/HAM TW10 .... 26 F4

Hammel House Surgery
TOOT SW17 .... 30 B5
Hammersmith Industrial Estate
HMSMTH W6 .... 19 M1
Hammerwood Park
EGRIN RH19 .... 197 M7
Hammond Middle School
LTWR GU18 .... 54 D8
Ham & Petersham Cricket Club
RCHPK/HAM TW10 .... 27 G5
Hampton Community College
HPTN TW12 .... 25 K6
Hampton Court Palace
E/WMO/HCT KT8 .... 44 C3
Hampton Farm Industrial Estate
FELT TW13 .... 25 H4
Hampton Football Club
HPTN TW12 .... 43 L1
The Hampton Hill Gallery
HPTN TW12 .... 25 M6
Hampton Hill Junior
Mixed School
HPTN TW12 .... 25 M6
Hampton Infants School
HPTN TW12 .... 25 J8
Hampton Junior School
HPTN TW12 .... 43 K1
The Hampton Medical Centre
HPTN TW12 .... 25 K8
Hampton School
HPTN TW12 .... 25 K6
Hampton Swimming Baths
HPTN TW12 .... 25 M8
Hampton Wick Infants School
KUT KT1 .... 2 B3
Hampton Wick Surgery
KUT KT1 .... 2 B4
Hamshere Gallery
BARN SW13 .... 19 J4
Ham Surgery
RCHPK/HAM TW10 .... 26 F4
Hankley Common Golf Club
NFNM GU10 .... 157 G8
Hanworth Trading Estate
FELT TW13 .... 25 H4
Harland First School
WIM/MER SW19 .... 47 M2
Harlequin Football Club
WHTN TW2 .... 26 B1
Harlequin Theatre & Cinema
REDH RH1 .... 126 D7
Harmans Water Infant &
Junior School
BRAK RG12 .... 35 H5
Harris City Technology College
NRWD SE19 .... 50 C1
Harrodian School
BARN SW13 .... 19 J2
Harven School
WOKS/MYFD GU22 .... 7 G6
Haslemere District Hospital
HASM GU27 .... 220 A2
Haslemere Health Centre
HASM GU27 .... 220 A2
Haslemere Industrial Estate
WAND/EARL SW18 .... 29 L3
Haslemere Museum
HASM GU27 .... 220 A2
Haslemere Preparatory School
HASM GU27 .... 220 A4
Hatton Medical Practice
EBED/NFELT TW14 .... 15 H8
Hawes Down Clinic
WWKM BR4 .... 70 A1
Hawkedale Gm School
SUN TW16 .... 42 C3
Hawkins Clinic
EW KT17 .... 84 F5
Hawkins Clinic
RYNPK SW20 .... 46 C1
Hawley CP School
BLKW GU17 .... 72 B6
Hawley Lane Industrial Estate
FARN GU14 .... 92 E1
Hawley Place School
BLKW GU17 .... 72 A8
The Hawth Theatre &
Conference Complex
CRAWE RH10 .... 212 C4
Haydons Medical Practice
WIM/MER SW19 .... 29 L7
Hayes Grove Priory Hospital
HAYES BR2 .... 70 D1
The Hayes Primary School
PUR/KEN CR8 .... 87 L6
Hayes School
HAYES BR2 .... 70 E1
Haysbridge Business Centre
GDST RH9 .... 172 F3
Hazelhurst School
RYNPK SW20 .... 47 G1
Hazelwick School
CRAWE RH10 .... 212 D1
Hazelwood School
OXTED RH8 .... 130 D5
Headley Park Country Club
BOR GU35 .... 177 G8
Hearnville Primary School
BAL SW12 .... 30 D2
Heath Business Centre
HSLW TW3 .... 16 F6
Heath Business Centre
REDH RH1 .... 170 D1
Heathcote Medical Centre
KWD/TDW/WH KT20 .... 105 G4
Heath End County
Secondary School
FNM GU9 .... 134 B3
Heathermount School
ASC SL5 .... 37 G6
Heather Ridge County
Infants School
CBLY GU15 .... 74 A5
Heathside Surgery
CBLY GU15 .... 73 M5
Heatherwood Hospital
ASC SL5 .... 36 B3
Heathfield College
HAYES BR2 .... 70 F5

Heathfield Junior School
WHTN TW2 ...... 25 K2
Heathfield School
ASC SL5 ...... 35 L2
Heathland School
HSLWW TW4 ...... 16 C8
Heathmere Primary School
PUT/ROE SW15 ...... 28 D2
Heathrow Airport
WDR/YW UB7 ...... 13 M3
Heathrow International
Trading Estate
HSLWW TW4 ...... 15 L5
Heathrow School
WDR/YW UB7 ...... 14 C1
Heathside School
WEY KT13 ...... 59 J4
Heavers Farm Primary School
SNWD SE25 ...... 50 C5
Henderson Hospital
BELMT SM2 ...... 65 K7
Hengrove CP School
ASHF TW15 ...... 23 C8
Henry Cavendish Junior School
BAL SW12 ...... 30 F2
Hermitage County First School
WOKN/KNAP GU21 ...... 96 B1
Hermitage County
Primary School
WOKN/KNAP GU21 ...... 96 B1
The Herons Swimming and
Fitness Centre
HASM GU27 ...... 219 J3
Heron Way CP School
SWTR RH13 ...... 229 K8
Hersham Surgery
WOT/HER KT12 ...... 61 K7
Heston Community School
HEST TW5 ...... 16 D2
Heston Infants School
HEST TW5 ...... 16 D2
Heston Junior School
HEST TW5 ...... 16 D1
Heston Park Cricket Club
HEST TW5 ...... 16 C1
Heston Swimming Baths
HEST TW5 ...... 16 C1
Hewitts Industrial Estate
CRAN GU6 ...... 184 E6
Hibernia House Surgery
HSLW TW3 ...... 16 D6
High Elms Golf Course
ORP BR6 ...... 71 M6
Highfield School
LIPH GU30 ...... 218 B7
Highview Primary School
WLGTN SM6 ...... 67 H4
Hillbrook Primary School
TOOT SW17 ...... 30 C5
Hillcroft College
SURB KT6 ...... 45 H6
Hillcroft Primary School
CTHM CR3 ...... 108 B5
Hill School
BH/WHM TN16 ...... 111 L5
Hinchley Wood Practice
NWMAL KT3 ...... 46 C6
Hinchley Wood
Secondary School
ESH/CLAY KT10 ...... 62 D1
Hindhead Golf Club
GSHT GU26 ...... 198 E3
Hitherfield Junior School
STRHM/NOR SW16 ...... 31 K3
HM Young
Offender Institution
FELT TW13 ...... 24 A4
Hoe Bridge School
WOKS/MYFD GU22 ...... 97 L1
Hogan Business Centre
WOKN/KNAP GU21 ...... 6 C6
Hogarth Business Park
CHSWK W4 ...... 19 H1
Hogarth's Ho
CHSWK W4 ...... 19 G1
Holbeach Primary School
CAT SE6 ...... 33 K1
Holbrook CP School
HORS RH12 ...... 229 H2
Holbrook Recreation Centre
HORS RH12 ...... 229 H2
Hollyfield Secondary School
SURB KT6 ...... 45 H5
Holly Lodge CP School
ASHV GU12 ...... 113 J1
Hollymount Primary School
RYNPK SW20 ...... 46 F1
Hollyspring Junior &
Infants School
BRAK RG12 ...... 35 H2
Holly Tree Surgery
NFNM GU10 ...... 155 K5
Hollywood Bowl
BRAK RG12 ...... 34 E2
Hollywood Bowl
CRAWW RH11 ...... 212 A2
Holmesdale Cf School
REIG RH2 ...... 125 L6
Holmwood Corner Surgery
NWMAL KT3 ...... 46 B5
Holy Cross Convent School
NWMAL KT3 ...... 46 A4
Holy Cross Hospital
HASM GU27 ...... 219 J2
Holy Cross Preparatory School
KUTN/CMB KT2 ...... 27 M8
Holy Cross RC School
CAT SE6 ...... 33 M2
Holy Family RC Primary School
ADL/WDHM KT15 ...... 58 D4
Holy Ghost RC Primary School
BAL SW12 ...... 30 C1
Holy Trinity C of E First School
WIM/MER SW19 ...... 29 K7
Holy Trinity C of E Middle School
GU GU1 ...... 9 M7
Holy Trinity C of E
Primary School
BRXS/STRHM SW2 ...... 31 J1

Holy Trinity C of E School
CRAWW RH11 ...... 211 K5
Holy Trinity C of E School
RCHPK/HAM TW10 ...... 18 D6
Holy Trinity School
CHOB/PIR GU24 ...... 75 K2
Holy Trinity School
FSTH SE23 ...... 32 F3
Holy Trinity School
WLGTN SM6 ...... 66 F3
Hong Kong & Shanghai
Sports Club
BECK BR3 ...... 33 H7
Hook Rise South Industrial
Park
CHSGTN KT9 ...... 63 K2
Hook Road Surgery
SURB KT6 ...... 63 H2
The Hop Kiln
FNM GU9 ...... 10 F2
Horley Health Centre
HORL RH6 ...... 170 D6
The Horniman Museum &
Gardens
FSTH SE23 ...... 32 E2
Horniman School
FSTH SE23 ...... 32 E2
Horsell C of E School
WOKN/KNAP GU21 ...... 76 F6
Horsell High School
WOKN/KNAP GU21 ...... 6 A1
Horsell Village County
Infants School
WOKN/KNAP GU21 ...... 6 A4
Horsham Cricket &
Sports Club
HORS RH12 ...... 228 E8
Horsham District Council
HORS RH12 ...... 229 G7
Horsham Football Club
SWTR RH13 ...... 229 G8
Horsham Hospital
HORS RH12 ...... 228 F6
Horsham Museum
HORS RH12 ...... 228 F8
Horsham Trading Estate
HORS RH12 ...... 229 H5
Horsham Ymca Football Club
SWTR RH13 ...... 229 G8
Horsley Sports Club
EHSLY KT24 ...... 120 C1
Horton Hospital
HOR/WEW KT19 ...... 83 M1
Horton Trading Estate
DTCH/LGLY SL3 ...... 12 E5
The Hospital
CBLY GU15 ...... 72 D1
Hotham Primary School
PUT/ROE SW15 ...... 19 M6
Hounslow Business Park
HSLW TW3 ...... 16 D6
Hounslow College
Independent School
FELT TW13 ...... 25 G5
Hounslow Cricket Club
HSLW TW3 ...... 16 C4
Hounslow Heath Junior School
HSLWW TW4 ...... 16 B5
Hounslow Manor School
HSLW TW3 ...... 16 E5
Hounslow & Spelthorne
Community & Mental
Health NHS Trust
STA TW18 ...... 22 D6
Hounslow Town Primary School
HSLW TW3 ...... 16 F5
Howard of Effingham School
EHSLY KT24 ...... 121 H1
Howard School
CROY/NA CR0 ...... 67 M3
H & S Community & NHS Trust
STWL/WRAY TW19 ...... 23 H3
Hubbard School
EGRIN RH19 ...... 196 B8
Humphries Industrial Estate
BRAK RG12 ...... 34 E4
Hunt Gallery
RGODL GU7 ...... 160 A5
Hurst Farm Surgery
MFD/CHID GU8 ...... 159 J8
Hurst Lodge School
ASC SL5 ...... 36 E8
Hurst Park Primary School
HPTN TW12 ...... 43 K2
Hurtmore Golf Club
RGODL GU7 ...... 159 J2
Hurtwood House School
CRAN GU6 ...... 164 D7
Hydeburn School
BAL SW12 ...... 30 D2
Hyland Business Centre
REDH RH1 ...... 126 C8
The Hythe School
STA TW18 ...... 22 A6
Ibstock Place School
PUT/ROE SW15 ...... 19 H8
Ifield Community College
CRAWW RH11 ...... 211 K2
Ifield First School
CRAWW RH11 ...... 211 J1
Ifield Golf & Country Club
CRAWW RH11 ...... 211 H3
Ifield Golf & Country Club
RDKG RH5 ...... 189 M5
Ifield Middle School
CRAWW RH11 ...... 211 K3
Imber Court Trading Estate
E/WMO/HCT KT8 ...... 44 A6
Imberhorne School
EGRIN RH19 ...... 195 L7
The Imber Sports Centre
EGRIN RH19 ...... 196 A6
Immanuel & St Andrew
C of E Primary School
STRHM/NOR SW16 ...... 31 H7
Imperial College Athletic
Ground
HYS/HAR UB3 ...... 14 F1

Imperial College of
Science Technology &
Medicine
ASC SL5 ...... 37 J3
Independent Business Park
EGRIN RH19 ...... 195 K6
The Industrial Estate
EDEN TN8 ...... 153 L6
Inwood Business Centre
HSLW TW3 ...... 16 E6
The Islamic Grammar School
WAND/EARL SW18 ...... 29 J1
Isleworth Baths
ISLW TW7 ...... 17 J6
Isleworth Centre Practice
ISLW TW7 ...... 17 K5
Isleworth & Syon School
for Boys
ISLW TW7 ...... 17 H2
Isleworth Town Primary School
ISLW TW7 ...... 17 J4
Ivybridge Primary School
TWK TW1 ...... 17 J8
Jack & Jill School
HPTN TW12 ...... 25 K7
James Dixon Primary School
PGE/AN SE20 ...... 32 D8
James Searle Industrial Estate
HORS RH12 ...... 229 H5
Jamia Mosque
HSLW TW3 ...... 16 C6
Jenner Health Centre
FSTH SE23 ...... 33 H2
Jenner House Surgery
FARN GU14 ...... 92 B5
The Jigsaw School
FRIM GU16 ...... 93 H6
JMI School
SURB KT6 ...... 45 G5
John Busch School
ISLW TW7 ...... 17 L3
The John Deal Practice
RPLY/SEND SG23 ...... 98 F3
John Fisher School
PUR/KEN CR8 ...... 67 H8
John Fisher Sports Club
WARL CR6 ...... 89 H8
John Nightingale School
E/WMO/HCT KT8 ...... 43 J3
John Paul Ii School
WIM/MER SW19 ...... 29 G1
John Ruskin Sixth Form
College
SAND/SEL CR2 ...... 69 H6
John the Baptist C of E
Junior School
KUT KT1 ...... 2 C3
Joseph Hood Primary &
Middle School
RYNPK SW20 ...... 47 H2
Jubilee Hall Clinic
CRAWE RH10 ...... 212 D3
Julians Primary School
STRHM/NOR SW16 ...... 31 K5
Junior School
KWD/TDW/WH KT20 ...... 104 F1
Junior School
SAND/SEL CR2 ...... 68 A7
Kangley Business Centre
SYD SE26 ...... 33 J6
Kelsey Park School
BECK BR3 ...... 51 K3
Kelvin Business Centre
CRAWE RH10 ...... 192 C8
Kenley Primary School
PUR/KEN CR8 ...... 88 B6
Kenley Sports Club
PUR/KEN CR8 ...... 87 M4
Kensington Avenue
Junior & Infant School
THHTH CR7 ...... 49 K1
Kenyngton Manor CP School
SUN TW16 ...... 24 D7
Keston Ave Infant
Primary School
COUL/CHIP CR5 ...... 107 K1
Keston C of E Primary School
HAYES BR2 ...... 71 C4
Keston County Junior School
COUL/CHIP CR5 ...... 107 K1
Keston House Medical Practice
PUR/KEN CR8 ...... 87 J2
Kew College
RCH/KEW TW9 ...... 18 D2
Kew Palace
RCH/KEW TW9 ...... 18 B2
Kilmorie Primary School
FSTH SE23 ...... 33 H3
King Athelstan Primary School
KUT KT1 ...... 3 H9
King Edwards School
MFD/CHID GU8 ...... 181 J8
Kingfield School
WOKS/MYFD GU22 ...... 97 K2
The Kings Centre
ALDT GU11 ...... 112 D7
Kings College
GUW GU2 ...... 116 B8
King's College School
WIM/MER SW19 ...... 28 F7
Kings Corner Surgery
ASC SL5 ...... 37 H5
Kings Court Primary School
WDSR SL4 ...... 20 D1
Kingscroft School
STA TW18 ...... 22 D7
Kingsdale Secondary School
DUL SE21 ...... 32 B4
Kingsdowne Surgery
SURB KT6 ...... 45 J3
Kingsfield Business Centre
REDH RH1 ...... 148 D1
Kingsgate Business Centre
KUTN/CMB KT2 ...... 2 E5
Kingsgrove Industrial Estate
FARN GU14 ...... 92 D6
Kings House School
RCHPK/HAM TW10 ...... 18 C7
Kingsley Business Park
BOR GU35 ...... 176 B8

Kingsley Primary School
CROY/NA CR0 ...... 49 J8
Kingston Business Centre
CHSGTN KT9 ...... 63 H2
Kingston College
KUT KT1 ...... 2 D8
Kingston Council for
Voluntary Service
KUT KT1 ...... 2 E6
Kingston Crown Court
KUT KT1 ...... 2 D8
Kingston & District
Community NHS Trust
SURB KT6 ...... 63 K1
Kingston Grammar School
KUT KT1 ...... 3 G6
Kingston Hospital NHS Trust
KUTN/CMB KT2 ...... 3 L4
Kingston Hospital NHS Trust
KUTN/CMB KT2 ...... 3 K4
Kingstonian Football Club
KUT KT1 ...... 3 L8
Kingston Liberal Synagogue
THDIT KT7 ...... 44 E7
Kingston Magistrates Court
KUT KT1 ...... 2 C7
Kingston Museum &
Heritage Service
KUTN/CMB KT2 ...... 27 G7
Kingston & Richmond
Health Authority
BRYLDS KT5 ...... 45 J7
Kingstons Industrial Estate
ASHV GU12 ...... 113 H7
Kingston Sport &
Recreation Centre
NWMAL KT3 ...... 46 C4
Kingston University
KUT KT1 ...... 3 G5
Kingston University
KUTN/CMB KT2 ...... 46 A1
Kingsway Business Park
HPTN TW12 ...... 43 J1
Kingswey Business Park
WOKN/KNAP GU21 ...... 77 M4
Kingswood CP School
KWD/TDW/WH KT20 ...... 125 J2
Kingswood House School
HOR/WEW KT19 ...... 83 L3
Kingswood Primary School
WNWD SE27 ...... 32 A5
Knaphill County Junior School
WOKN/KNAP GU21 ...... 75 M8
Knaphill Lower School
WOKN/KNAP GU21 ...... 75 L8
Knaphill Surgery
WOKN/KNAP GU21 ...... 75 M8
Knollmead Primary School
WPK KT4 ...... 63 M1
Knowle Park County School
STA TW18 ...... 22 D6
Knowl Hill School
CHOB/PIR GU24 ...... 95 H4
The Lady Eleanor Holles School
HPTN TW12 ...... 25 L6
Laine Theatre Arts
EW KT17 ...... 84 B3
Laker Industrial Estate
BECK BR3 ...... 33 H6
Lakeside Country Club
FRIM GU16 ...... 93 K3
Lakeside County Primary School
FRIM GU16 ...... 73 J8
Lakeside Industrial Estate
DTCH/LGLY SL3 ...... 13 H2
Laleham C of E Primary School
STA TW18 ...... 40 F7
Lambs Business Park
GDST RH9 ...... 150 B4
Lamont Business Centre
CROY/NA CR0 ...... 49 H7
Lampton School
HEST TW5 ...... 16 D3
Lanfranc Secondary
School for Boys
CROY/NA CR0 ...... 49 L4
Langbourne Primary School
DUL SE21 ...... 32 B4
Langley Corner Surgery
CRAWW RH11 ...... 211 J1
Langley Green First School
CRAWW RH11 ...... 192 A7
Langley Park School for Boys
BECK BR3 ...... 51 L6
Langley Park School for Girls
BECK BR3 ...... 51 L6
Langshott County
Infant School
HORL RH6 ...... 170 E6
The Lansbury Estate
WOKN/KNAP GU21 ...... 76 A8
La Retraite RC Girls School
BAL SW12 ...... 30 F1
Latchmere Junior School
KUTN/CMB KT2 ...... 3 G1
Lavender Golf Club
ASC SL5 ...... 35 M3
Lavenders Fields Surgery
MTCM CR4 ...... 48 B1
Lawn Tennis Club
HORL RH6 ...... 170 C6
Lawn Tennis Club
REDH RH1 ...... 126 C6
Lawson Hunt Industrial Park
HORS RH12 ...... 228 A5
Lazards Sports Club
SUN TW16 ...... 42 E1
Leacroft Medical Practice
CRAWW RH11 ...... 211 M1
Leacroft Medical Practice
CRAWW RH11 ...... 211 L3
Leatherhead Clinic
LHD/OX KT22 ...... 102 F3
Leatherhead Cricket Club
LHD/OX KT22 ...... 102 D5
Leatherhead Football Club
LHD/OX KT22 ...... 102 D4
Leatherhead Hospital
LHD/OX KT22 ...... 102 F4

Leatherhead Industrial Estate
LHD/OX KT22 ...... 102 D3
Leatherhead Leisure
Centre & Water Park
LHD/OX KT22 ...... 102 D5
Leechpool Lane County
Primary School
SWTR RH13 ...... 229 K5
Leigh Close Industrial Estate
NWMAL KT3 ...... 46 A4
Leigh Primary School
REIG RH2 ...... 146 D6
Leisure Centre
KUT KT1 ...... 2 F7
The Leith Hill Practice
RDKG RH5 ...... 188 A4
Lewin Mead Community
Mental Health Centre
STRHM/NOR SW16 ...... 31 G7
Lewis Clinic
CAR SM5 ...... 66 D3
Lewisham Council
CAT SE6 ...... 33 L4
Liberty Middle School
MTCM CR4 ...... 48 B2
The Licensed Victuallers School
ASC SL5 ...... 35 M2
Lifecare NHS Trust
CTHM CR3 ...... 108 B5
Lightwater First School
LTWR GU18 ...... 54 D8
Limes Business Centre
HORL RH6 ...... 191 J3
Limpsfield Chart Golf Club
OXTED RH8 ...... 130 F3
Limpsfield C of E School
OXTED RH8 ...... 130 E3
Limpsfield Grange School
OXTED RH8 ...... 130 D1
Limpsfield Lawn Tennis Club
OXTED RH8 ...... 130 D2
Linden Bridge School
WPK KT4 ...... 64 B2
Linden Lodge School
WIM/MER SW19 ...... 29 H2
Lindon Bennett School
FELT TW13 ...... 25 G6
Lingfield Primary School
LING RH7 ...... 174 A5
Lingfield Squash & Leisure Club
LING RH7 ...... 174 C6
The Link Primary School
CROY/NA CR0 ...... 67 H3
Links Primary School
TOOT SW17 ...... 30 D7
Linsford Business Park
FRIM GU16 ...... 93 J6
Littlefield School
LIPH GU30 ...... 218 A7
Littlehaven School
HORS RH12 ...... 229 J4
Little Mead Industrial Estate
CRAN GU6 ...... 184 E6
Littleton C of E Infant School
SHPTN TW17 ...... 41 K3
Lloyds Register Cricket Club
DUL SE21 ...... 32 A2
Lombard Business Park
CROY/NA CR0 ...... 49 J7
Lombard Business Park
WIM/MER SW19 ...... 47 M2
London Borough of Croydon
Council
CROY/NA CR0 ...... 49 M6
The London Executive College
TOOT SW17 ...... 30 D4
London Gatwick Airport
HORL RH6 ...... 192 D2
London Irish Rugby
Football Club
SUN TW16 ...... 42 D1
London Ladies &
Girls Football Club
CAT SE6 ...... 33 L5
London Living Theatre
SYD SE26 ...... 33 G5
London Road Medical Centre
THHTH CR7 ...... 49 K6
London Welsh Football Club
RCH/KEW TW9 ...... 18 B5
Lonesome First School
MTCM CR4 ...... 48 E2
Longacre School
SHGR GU5 ...... 162 A5
The Longcroft Clinic
BNSTD SM7 ...... 85 M5
Long Ditton County Infant
School
SURB KT6 ...... 44 F8
Longford School
EBED/NFELT TW14 ...... 24 C1
Longley Trading Estate
CRAWE RH10 ...... 212 B4
Longmead Business Centre
HOR/WEW KT19 ...... 84 A1
Longmead Industrial Estate
HOR/WEW KT19 ...... 84 A1
Longshot Industrial Estate
BRAK RG12 ...... 34 B3
Lorraine County First School
CBLY GU15 ...... 73 K1
Loseley House
RGUW GU3 ...... 138 C6
Lovelace Primary School
CHSGTN KT9 ...... 62 F4
Lower Sydenham Industrial
Estate
CAT SE6 ...... 33 J6
Lowther CP School
BARN SW13 ...... 19 K2
Loxwood Primary School
BIL RH14 ...... 224 D5
L S E Sports Club
NWMAL KT3 ...... 45 M6
Lyndhurst School
CBLY GU15 ...... 72 E4
Lyne & Longcross C of E School
CHERT KT16 ...... 57 L1
Lynton Preparatory School
EW KT17 ...... 84 C1

Lyons Farm Estate
SWTR RH13 .... **227** K7
Magna Carta Secondary School
EGH TW20 .... **22** A4
Magnolia House Surgery
ASC SL5 .... **37** J5
Maidenbower First School
CRAWE RH10 .... **212** F5
Malcolm Primary School
PGE/AN SE20 .... **32** F8
Malden Manor Junior School
NWMAL KT3 .... **46** B7
Malden Parochial School
WPK KT4 .... **46** B8
Malden Road Baths
CHEAM SM3 .... **65** G3
Malham Road Industrial Estate
FSTH SE23 .... **33** G2
The Mall School
WHTN TW2 .... **26** A4
Malmesbury Middle School
MRDN SM4 .... **47** M6
Malmesbury Primary School
MRDN SM4 .... **47** M7
Manby Lodge Infant School
WEY KT13 .... **59** M4
Manorcroft School
EGH TW20 .... **21** K7
Manor Drive Health Centre
WPK KT4 .... **46** C8
Manor Farm Business Centre
NFNM GU10 .... **135** J4
Manor House School
EHSLY KT24 .... **121** H1
Manor Mead School
SHPTN TW17 .... **41** L5
Manor Park Primary School
SUT SM1 .... **65** M4
Manor Practice
WLGTN SM6 .... **66** E4
Manor Practice
WLGTN SM6 .... **67** H6
The Manor School
BF/WBF KT14 .... **79** M4
Maple Grove Business Centre
HSLWW TW4 .... **15** M6
Maple Industrial Estate
FELT TW13 .... **24** D3
Marden Lodge School
CTHM CR3 .... **108** E3
Margaret Roper RC Primary School
PUR/KEN CR8 .... **67** J8
Marion Vian Primary School
BECK BR3 .... **51** G5
Marist RC Primary School
BF/WBF KT14 .... **78** C3
Marist Senior School
ASC SL5 .... **37** C4
The Marjory Kinnon School
EBED/NFELT TW14 .... **15** H7
Marlborough County Infant School
ALDT GU11 .... **112** F2
Marlborough Cricket Club
DUL SE21 .... **32** D2
Marlborough School
ISLW TW7 .... **17** K3
Marshfield C of E School
ADL/WDHM KT15 .... **58** B5
Martin Hewitt Practice
TOOT SW17 .... **30** B2
Marymount International School
KUTN/CMB KT2 .... **27** M8
Mary Wallace Theatre
TWK TW1 .... **26** D2
Maswell Park Health Centre
HSLW TW3 .... **16** F7
Matthew Arnold County Secondary School
STA TW18 .... **22** F7
Maybury County First School
WOKN/KNAP GU21 .... **6** F4
The Maybury Surgery
WOKS/MYFD GU22 .... **7** J4
Mayday Healthcare NHS Trust
THHTH CR7 .... **49** L6
Mayfield County Junior & Infant School
FARN GU14 .... **92** D3
Mayfield Surgery
PUT/ROE SW15 .... **28** E1
Mckay Trading Estate
DTCH/LGLY SL3 .... **13** H4
The Mead County First School
HOR/WEW KT19 .... **64** C3
Meadlands School
RCHPK/HAM TW10 .... **26** F5
Meadowcroft County First School
CHERT KT16 .... **58** C2
Meads School
EGRIN RH19 .... **216** B2
Meath Green County Junior School
HORL RH6 .... **170** C4
Meath Green First School
HORL RH6 .... **170** C4
Meath School
CHERT KT16 .... **58** A6
Medwyn Doctors Surgery
DORK RH4 .... **144** E1
Megabowl
BRXS/STRHM SW2 .... **31** H3
Melrose School
MTCM CR4 .... **48** B3
Merland Rise County First School
KWD/TDW/WH KT20 .... **104** F1
Merrist Wood College
RGUW GU3 .... **115** M2
Merrow Clinic
GU GU1 .... **117** L7
Merrow C of E First School
RGUE GU4 .... **118** A6
Merrow Park Surgery
RGUE GU4 .... **118** A6
Merstham County Primary School
REDH RH1 .... **126** F2

Merton Abbey Primary School
WIM/MER SW19 .... **47** L1
Merton Adult College
RYNPK SW20 .... **47** H3
Merton College
MRDN SM4 .... **47** J5
Merton Industrial Park
WIM/MER SW19 .... **47** M1
Merton Park Primary School
WIM/MER SW19 .... **47** J2
Merton Surgery
WIM/MER SW19 .... **29** L8
Merton Sutton & Wandsworth Health Authority
MTCM CR4 .... **48** C4
Merton Sutton & Wandsworth Health Authority
WIM/MER SW19 .... **47** M1
Metro Business Centre
SYD SE26 .... **33** J7
Metropolitan Police Football Club
E/WMO/HCT KT8 .... **44** A6
Metropolitan Police Hayes Sports Club
HAYES BR2 .... **70** C2
Michael Hall School
FROW RH18 .... **217** G8
Middle Hill Health Clinic
ALDT GU11 .... **112** D6
Milford Golf Club
MFD/CHID GU8 .... **159** K8
Milford Hospital
RGODL GU7 .... **181** M1
Milford School
MFD/CHID GU8 .... **159** J8
Millais School
SWTR RH13 .... **229** J7
Millbourne Lodge Junior School
ESH/CLAY KT10 .... **61** M4
Millbourne Lodge Senior School
ESH/CLAY KT10 .... **62** A5
Mill Farm Business Park
HSLWW TW4 .... **25** H1
Mill Green Business Park
MTCM CR4 .... **48** C1
Mill Lane Trading Estate
CROY/NA CR0 .... **67** J2
Mill Ride Golf Club Plc
ASC SL5 .... **36** A1
Milo Hawkins Clinic
GU GU1 .... **9** H6
Milton Mount School
CRAWE RH10 .... **212** F1
Mitcham Cricket Club
MTCM CR4 .... **48** B4
Mitcham Industrial Estate
MTCM CR4 .... **48** D1
Mitcham Parochial Church Council
MTCM CR4 .... **48** B3
Mitcham Road Surgery
TOOT SW17 .... **30** D7
Moatfield Surgery
EGRIN RH19 .... **196** B7
Mole Business Park
LHD/OX KT22 .... **102** D3
Molesey Hospital
E/WMO/HCT KT8 .... **43** K5
Mole Valley District Council
LHD/OX KT22 .... **102** D3
Mole Valley District Council
LHD/OX KT22 .... **102** E1
Mollison Drive Health Centre
WLGTN SM6 .... **67** H6
Monks Orchard School
CROY/NA CR0 .... **51** G5
Monument Hill County Primary School
WOKS/MYFD GU22 .... **7** M2
Moor House School
OXTED RH8 .... **130** C8
Moor Lane Junior School
CHSGTN KT9 .... **63** J4
Moor Park College
NFNM GU10 .... **134** D8
Morden First School
MRDN SM4 .... **47** K5
Morden Hall Medical Centre
WIM/MER SW19 .... **47** L3
Morden Road Clinic
WIM/MER SW19 .... **47** L3
Morehouse School
ISLW TW7 .... **17** H3
More House School
NFNM GU10 .... **155** M7
Mortimer School
STRHM/NOR SW16 .... **31** G3
Moss Lane CP School
RGODL GU7 .... **160** A5
Mount Alvernia Hospital
GU GU1 .... **9** K7
The Mount Infant & Junior Schools
NWMAL KT3 .... **3** M9
Mount Medical Centre
FELT TW13 .... **25** H4
Murky Puddle Theatre Co/magic Fox/panic
NWMAL KT3 .... **46** C3
Muschamp Junior & Infant School
CAR SM5 .... **66** B1
The Musical Museum
BTFD TW8 .... **18** B1
Mytchett County First School
FRIM GU16 .... **93** J5
Natural Therapy Clinic
TOOT SW17 .... **30** E6
Natwest Sports Club
BECK BR3 .... **33** J7
Nelson Hospital
WIM/MER SW19 .... **47** J2
Nelson Primary School
WHTN TW2 .... **26** A4
Nelson Trading Estate
WIM/MER SW19 .... **47** L1
New Addington Swimming Pools
CROY/NA CR0 .... **69** M8

New Ashgate Gallery
FNM GU9 .... **133** L7
New Chiswick Swimming Pool
CHSWK W4 .... **19** H2
Newdigate School
RDKG RH5 .... **167** L8
New Grafton Gallery
BARN SW13 .... **19** J4
New Haw Therapy Clinic
ADL/WDHM KT15 .... **58** E8
Newhouse Farm Business Centre
HORS RH12 .... **229** M2
New House Surgery
DORK RH4 .... **144** D3
New Inn Surgery
GU GU1 .... **117** L5
Newland House School
TWK TW1 .... **26** C5
New Life School
EGRIN RH19 .... **196** A7
Newport County Junior & Infant School
ASHV GU12 .... **113** G8
New Surgery
BH/WHM TN16 .... **110** F3
New Victoria Hospital
KUTN/CMB KT2 .... **28** B8
New Zealand Golf Club House
WOKN/KNAP GU21 .... **78** B2
Nightingale School
TOOT SW17 .... **30** B3
Nomad Theatre
EHSLY KT24 .... **120** C3
Nonsuch High School for Girls
EW KT17 .... **65** G6
Nonsuch Industrial Estate
EW KT17 .... **84** B1
Nonsuch Primary School
EW KT17 .... **64** E4
Norbury Complementary Therapy Clinic
STRHM/NOR SW16 .... **49** J1
Norbury Health Centre
STRHM/NOR SW16 .... **49** J2
Norbury Manor Primary School
STRHM/NOR SW16 .... **49** H1
Norbury Manor Secondary Girls School
STRHM/NOR SW16 .... **49** J1
Norbury Trading Estate
STRHM/NOR SW16 .... **49** J2
North Croydon Medical Centre
THHTH CR7 .... **49** L6
North Downs Golf Club
GDST RH9 .... **109** K7
North East Surrey College of Technology
EW KT17 .... **84** D1
North Farnborough County Infant School
FARN GU14 .... **93** G4
Northgate First & Middle School
CRAWE RH10 .... **212** B1
Northgate Surgery
CRAWE RH10 .... **212** B2
North Heath CP School
HORS RH12 .... **229** G4
North Holmwood Cricket Club
RDKG RH5 .... **144** F7
Northlands Business Park
HORS RH12 .... **207** M5
North Lane Practice
ASHV GU12 .... **113** H8
Northlmes County Junior School
HORS RH12 .... **229** K4
Northtown Trading Estate
ASHV GU12 .... **113** H8
North Weylands Industrial Estate
WOT/HER KT12 .... **61** H1
Norwood Park Primary School
WNWD SE27 .... **31** M5
Norwood School
WNWD SE27 .... **31** M6
Norwood Surgery
WNWD SE27 .... **31** L4
Notre Dame School
LING RH7 .... **174** C6
Notre Dame Senior School
WOT/HER KT12 .... **80** C1
Novello Theatre
ASC SL5 .... **37** G5
Nower Lodge School
DORK RH4 .... **144** D3
Nuffield Hospital Midland Regional Office
SURB KT6 .... **45** G5
Nutfield Church Primary School
REDH RH1 .... **149** J1
Nutley Dean Business Park
HORL RH6 .... **169** H3
Oak Farm Community School
FARN GU14 .... **92** D3
Oakfield Junior School
LHD/OX KT22 .... **101** M5
Oakfield Preparatory School
DUL SE21 .... **32** A3
Oakfield School
WOKS/MYFD GU22 .... **78** C5
Oak Hill Health Centre
SURB KT6 .... **45** H6
Oakhurst Grange School
CTHM CR3 .... **108** A8
Oakland Primary School
BH/WHM TN16 .... **90** F6
Oakland School
BNSTD SM7 .... **85** K4
Oaklands Junior School
BH/WHM TN16 .... **90** F6
Oaklands School
ISLW TW7 .... **17** G5
Oak Lane Medical Centre
TWK TW1 .... **26** E1
Oak Lodge JMI School
WWKM BR4 .... **51** L7
Oak Park Golf Club
NFNM GU10 .... **132** D3

The Oaks First & Middle School
CRAWE RH10 .... **212** C6
Oaks Sports Centre
CAR SM5 .... **86** C1
Oak Tree Clinic
WOKN/KNAP GU21 .... **76** A3
Oakwood Independent School
PUR/KEN CR8 .... **87** L3
Oakwood Industrial Park
CRAWE RH10 .... **192** D8
Oatlands Infant School
WEY KT13 .... **60** A3
Occupational Health Centre
CROY/NA CR0 .... **4** E8
Odeon Cinema
RCH/KEW TW9 .... **18** A7
Odeon Cinema
STRHM/NOR SW16 .... **31** H4
Odeon Cinema
WIM/MER SW19 .... **29** K8
Odeon Multiplex
GU GU1 .... **8** F6
Old Barn Theatre
CRAWW RH11 .... **211** J1
Old Beckehamian Rugby Football Club
WWKM BR4 .... **70** A2
Old Club House
CRAWE RH10 .... **214** C5
The Old Cottage Hospital
EW KT17 .... **84** C3
Oldfield House School
HPTN TW12 .... **43** J1
Old Guildfordians Rugby Football Club
GU GU1 .... **9** L1
Old Palace School
CROY/NA CR0 .... **4** B7
Old Tiffinians Sports Ground
E/WMO/HCT KT8 .... **44** B5
Ongar Place Infant School
ADL/WDHM KT15 .... **58** D5
Onslow County Infant School
GUW GU2 .... **138** C2
The Open University
EGRIN RH19 .... **196** B8
The Optical Gallery
CHSGTN KT9 .... **63** G4
The Optical Gallery
TWK TW1 .... **26** D2
Optimum Health Services NHS Trust
FSTH SE23 .... **33** H2
Orange Tree Theatre
RCH/KEW TW9 .... **18** B6
Orchard Business Centre
REDH RH1 .... **170** D1
Orchard Business Centre
SYD SE26 .... **33** J6
Orchard Infant School
REIG RH2 .... **147** K3
Orchard School
HSLW TW3 .... **16** D6
Orchard Way Primary School
CROY/NA CR0 .... **51** H7
Oriel Junior & Infant School
FELT TW13 .... **25** H4
Orleans House Gallery
TWK TW1 .... **26** E2
Orleans Infant School
TWK TW1 .... **26** E1
Orleans Park School
TWK TW1 .... **26** E1
Our Lady Immaculate RC Primary School
SURB KT6 .... **45** K8
Our Lady of the Rosary School
STA TW18 .... **22** D7
Our Lady Queen of Heaven RC Primary School
WIM/MER SW19 .... **29** G1
Our Lady & St Philip Neri RC Primary School
FSTH SE23 .... **33** G4
Oval Primary School
CROY/NA CR0 .... **5** G4
Overton Grange School
BELMT SM2 .... **65** L6
Owlsmoor Primary School
SHST GU47 .... **52** B8
Oxshott Medical Practice
LHD/OX KT22 .... **81** M3
Oxted County School
OXTED RH8 .... **130** C2
Oxted Gallery
OXTED RH8 .... **130** B3
Oxted Health Centre
OXTED RH8 .... **130** C3
Oxted & Limpsfield Hospital
OXTED RH8 .... **130** A1
Paddock School
PUT/ROE SW15 .... **19** J6
Palace Road Surgery
BRXS/STRHM SW2 .... **31** J2
Palmer Galleries
RCH/KEW TW9 .... **18** A7
Palmerston Business Centre
SUT SM1 .... **65** M4
Papplewick School
ASC SL5 .... **36** C1
Paradise Road Practice
RCHPK/HAM TW10 .... **18** B7
Parchmore Medical Centre
THHTH CR7 .... **49** M3
Park Gallery
KUTN/CMB KT2 .... **3** J5
Park Hall Trading Estate
WNWD SE27 .... **31** M4
Park Hill Junior School
CROY/NA CR0 .... **5** G8
Parkhouse Middle School
WIM/MER SW19 .... **29** J5
Park House Rugby Football Club
HAYES BR2 .... **70** F1
Parkmead County First School
CRAN GU6 .... **185** J6
Parkmead County Middle School
CRAN GU6 .... **185** K6

The Park Practice
PGE/AN SE20 .... **32** D8
Park Primary School
ALDT GU11 .... **134** F2
Park Road Surgery
WLGTN SM6 .... **66** E5
Park School
WOKS/MYFD GU22 .... **7** G6
Parks Golf Courses & Sports Grounds
STA TW18 .... **22** E4
Parkside Group Practice
SAND/SEL CR2 .... **68** A7
Parkside Hospital
WIM/MER SW19 .... **29** G4
Parkside School
COB KT11 .... **81** K8
Park Surgery
HORS RH12 .... **228** F7
Parkway Trading Estate
HEST TW5 .... **15** M1
Parsons Mead School
ASHTD KT21 .... **103** H1
The Patrick Doody Clinic & Health Centre
WIM/MER SW19 .... **29** K8
Pattinson Clinic
RCHPK/HAM TW10 .... **18** A7
The Paul Robeson Theatre
HSLW TW3 .... **16** E5
Paxton Green Group Practice
DUL SE21 .... **32** B5
Paxton Primary School
NRWD SE19 .... **32** C7
Payne Clinic
EW KT17 .... **84** D3
Peall Road Industrial Estate
CROY/NA CR0 .... **49** J6
Peaslake School
SHGR GU5 .... **164** B2
Peaslake Surgery
SHGR GU5 .... **164** A3
Pelham CP School
WIM/MER SW19 .... **29** K8
Pennthorpe School
HORS RH12 .... **225** M2
Penwortham Primary School
STRHM/NOR SW16 .... **30** E7
Perrymount Primary School
FSTH SE23 .... **33** G3
Perrywood Business Park
REDH RH1 .... **148** E8
Pewley Down Infant School
GU GU1 .... **9** J7
Phoenix College
MRDN SM4 .... **47** L5
Phoenix College
TOOT SW17 .... **30** B3
Phoenix Leisure Centre
CAT SE6 .... **33** L1
Pierreponte School
NFNM GU10 .... **156** B8
Pilgrims Way Infants School
FNM GU9 .... **10** E3
Pilton Estate
CROY/NA CR0 .... **4** B5
Pineridge County First School
CBLY GU15 .... **53** K8
The Pines Junior & Infant School
BRAK RG12 .... **34** D7
The Pines Trading Estate
RGUW GU3 .... **116** A6
Pinewood Infants School
FARN GU14 .... **92** A2
Pioneers Industrial Park
CROY/NA CR0 .... **49** H8
Pippins School
DTCH/LGLY SL3 .... **13** H3
Pirbright Camp
CHOB/PIR GU24 .... **94** E2
Pirbright County First & Middle School
CHOB/PIR GU24 .... **95** H4
Pitwood Park Industrial Estate
KWD/TDW/WH KT20 .... **105** G2
Pixham School
DORK RH4 .... **122** F8
Plaistow Primary School
BIL RH14 .... **223** J6
Plough Industrial Estate
LHD/OX KT22 .... **102** D2
Polka Theatre for Children
WIM/MER SW19 .... **29** L7
Polygon Business Centre
DTCH/LGLY SL3 .... **13** J4
Poplar First School
WIM/MER SW19 .... **47** K3
Portesbery School
CBLY GU15 .... **73** G3
Portland Medical Centre
SNWD SE25 .... **50** E5
The Portrait Gallery
CTHM CR3 .... **108** D6
Potters Gate Primary School
FNM GU9 .... **133** K7
Pound Hill First & Middle School
CRAWE RH10 .... **212** F2
Pound Hill Surgery
CRAWE RH10 .... **212** F2
The Pountney Clinic
HSLW TW3 .... **16** D5
Powell Corderoy CP School
DORK RH4 .... **144** C3
The Practice
SAND/SEL CR2 .... **68** A6
Preston Cross Hotel & Country Club
GT/LBKH KT23 .... **101** J8
P R for Schools
SYD SE26 .... **32** F4
Princes Hall
ALDT GU11 .... **112** D7
Prior Heath School
CBLY GU15 .... **73** K4
Priory C of E Middle School
WIM/MER SW19 .... **29** L6
Priory Hospital Group
KWD/TDW/WH KT20 .... **125** K2
Priory House School
CAT SE6 .... **33** L2

Priory School
BNSTD SM7 .... 85 J5
Priory School
SNWD SE25 .... 50 C4
The Priory School
DORK RH4 .... 144 C3
Progress Business Park
CROY/NA CR0 .... 67 J1
Prospect House School
PUT/ROE SW15 .... 29 G1
Public Baths
FSTH SE23 .... 32 F3
Purley Community Health Clinic
PUR/KEN CR8 .... 87 K1
Purley & District War
Memorial Hospital
PUR/KEN CR8 .... 67 K8
Purley Gallery
PUR/KEN CR8 .... 87 K1
Purley Oaks Primary School
SAND/SEL CR2 .... 68 A6
Purley Sports Club
WLGTN SM6 .... 67 G8
Purley Swimming Pool &
Recreation Centre
PUR/KEN CR8 .... 87 L1
The Purple Picture Gallery
RGODL GU7 .... 160 A4
Putney Hospital
PUT/ROE SW15 .... 19 M5
Putney Leisure Centre
PUT/ROE SW15 .... 19 M6
Putneymead Medical Centre
PUT/ROE SW15 .... 19 M6
Puttenham C of E School
RGUW GU3 .... 136 E5
Puttenham Golf Club
RGUW GU3 .... 137 G5
Pyrcroft Grange Primary School
CHERT KT16 .... 40 B7
Pyrford County Middle School
WOKS/MYFD GU22 .... 78 C6
Quarryside Business Park
REDH RH1 .... 126 E4
Queen Eleanors C of E
Junior School
GUW GU2 .... 8 A6
Queen Elizabeth Hospital
BNSTD SM7 .... 85 M8
Queen Elizabeth Ii Silver
Jubilee School
SWTR RH13 .... 229 J8
Queen Marys Hospital for
Children
CAR SM5 .... 66 C7
The Queens C of E Primary
School
RCH/KEW TW9 .... 18 D2
Queens Manor Primary School
FUL/PGN SW6 .... 19 M2
Queens Medical Centre
RCHPK/HAM TW10 .... 18 C7
Queens Road Surgery
WIM/MER SW19 .... 29 K7
Queens Sports Centre
RGODL GU7 .... 159 L2
Queen Victoria Hospital NHS Trust
EGRIN RH19 .... 196 C6
Rachor House Surgery
ASC SL5 .... 36 E3
Radha Krishna Temple
BAL SW12 .... 30 E1
Rainbow Industrial Estate
RYNPK SW20 .... 46 E2
Rainbow Natural Health Centre
REDH RH1 .... 148 C1
The Raleigh School
EHSLY KT24 .... 99 M7
Ranelagh School
BRAK RG12 .... 34 F3
Rathfern Primary School
FSTH SE23 .... 33 J2
Ravensbourne Galleries
BECK BR3 .... 51 M3
Ravensbourne Trust
COUL/CHIP CR5 .... 86 F7
Ravenstone Primary School
BAL SW12 .... 30 D2
Ravenswood School for Boys
HAYES BR2 .... 71 G2
Ravin Galleries
FSTH SE23 .... 32 F3
Raynes Park High School
NWMAL KT3 .... 46 E3
Raynes Park Sports Ground
RYNPK SW20 .... 46 D2
Raynes Park Vale Football Club
RYNPK SW20 .... 47 G5
Redhill Business Centre
REDH RH1 .... 126 C7
Redhill Football Club
REDH RH1 .... 148 C4
Redhill & Reigate Golf Club
REDH RH1 .... 148 A3
Redlands Junior School
RDKC RH5 .... 144 E5
Red Lion Business Park
SURB KT6 .... 63 J1
Reedham Park School
PUR/KEN CR8 .... 87 K4
Reeds School
COB KT11 .... 81 K2
Refuge Temple
STRHM/NOR SW16 .... 31 H5
Regal Gallery
ECH TW20 .... 21 J6
The Regina Codi School
CROY/NA CR0 .... 67 L6
Reigate & Banstead
Borough Council
BNSTD SM7 .... 85 J7
Reigate College
REIG RH2 .... 125 L7
Reigate Day Hospital
REIG RH2 .... 126 A8
Reigate Grammar School
REIG RH2 .... 125 M8
Reigate Priory Middle School
REIG RH2 .... 125 K8

Reigate St Marys
Preparatory & Choir School
REIG RH2 .... 125 L8
Reigate School
REIG RH2 .... 147 M3
Replingham Clinic
WAND/EARL SW18 .... 29 K2
The Retail Business Centre
EW KT17 .... 64 D8
Ricards Lodge High School
WIM/MER SW19 .... 29 J6
Richard Atkins School
BRXS/STRHM SW2 .... 31 H1
Richards Osteopathic
Clinic & Natural Health
Centre
CRAWE RH10 .... 212 B3
Richmond Adult &
Community College
RCH/KEW TW9 .... 18 A6
Richmond Adult &
Community College
TWK TW1 .... 26 C2
The Richmond Clinic
RCHPK/HAM TW10 .... 18 C6
Richmond College
RCHPK/HAM TW10 .... 18 B8
Richmond Football Club
RCH/KEW TW9 .... 18 A6
The Richmond Green
Medical Centre
RCH/KEW TW9 .... 18 A7
Richmond House School
HPTN TW12 .... 25 J6
Richmond Magistrates Court
RCH/KEW TW9 .... 18 A6
Richmond Road Medical Centre
KUTN/CMB KT2 .... 2 E3
Richmond Synagogue
RCH/KEW TW9 .... 18 B6
Richmond Theatre
RCH/KEW TW9 .... 18 A6
Richmond Twickenham &
Roehampton NHS Trust
HPTN TW12 .... 25 J7
Richmond-upon-Thames College
WHTN TW2 .... 26 B1
Riddlesdown School
SAND/SEL CR2 .... 88 B4
Ridgeway Infant School
SAND/SEL CR2 .... 68 B7
Ridgeway School
FNM GU9 .... 11 H5
Rikkyo School
BIL RH14 .... 225 G1
Ripley C of E School
RPLY/SEND GU23 .... 98 E3
Ripley Court School
RPLY/SEND GU23 .... 98 F3
Ripley Cricket Club
RPLY/SEND GU23 .... 98 F2
Riverdene Industrial Estate
WOT/HER KT12 .... 61 G4
River Gardens Business Centre
EBED/NFELT TW14 .... 15 L6
Riversdale Primary School
WAND/EARL SW18 .... 29 K2
Riverside Business Centre
WAND/EARL SW18 .... 29 L2
The Riverside Business Centre
GU GU9 .... 8 E4
Riverside Business Park
FNM GU9 .... 133 M6
Riverside Business Park
WIM/MER SW19 .... 47 M1
Riverside Park Industrial Estate
FNM GU9 .... 134 A6
Riverside Wandle
Trading Estate
MTCM CR4 .... 48 C7
Riverview CP School
HOR/WEW KT19 .... 63 M3
Riverway Industrial Estate
RGODL GU7 .... 160 F1
Robin Hood Junior School
SUT SM1 .... 65 L4
Robin Hood Lane Health Centre
SUT SM1 .... 65 K4
Robin Hood Primary School
KUTN/CMB KT2 .... 28 A6
Rock & Bowl Bowling Alley
EGRIN RH19 .... 196 B8
Rockmount School
NRWD SE19 .... 31 M7
Rodborough County
Secondary School
MFD/CHID GU8 .... 181 J2
Rodd Estate
SHPTN TW17 .... 41 M5
Roehampton Church School
PUT/ROE SW15 .... 28 E1
Roehampton Community
Council
PUT/ROE SW15 .... 19 J3
Roehampton Institute
PUT/ROE SW15 .... 19 K7
The Roehampton Priory
Hospital
PUT/ROE SW15 .... 19 J4
Roehampton Recreation Centre
PUT/ROE SW15 .... 28 D1
The Roehampton Surgery
PUT/ROE SW15 .... 28 D1
Roffey Social & Sports Club
HORS RH12 .... 229 K4
Roger Black Gallery
CROY/NA CR0 .... 4 D5
Roke Primary School
PUR/KEN CR8 .... 87 M4
Roman Industrial Estate
CROY/NA CR0 .... 5 G1
Romans Business Park
FNM GU9 .... 134 A6
Ronald Rose Primary School
WIM/MER SW19 .... 29 G1
Rosary RC Junior School
HEST TW5 .... 16 C1
Rosebery School
EPSOM KT18 .... 83 M4

Roselands Clinic
NWMAL KT3 .... 45 M4
Rosemead Preparatory School
DUL SE21 .... 31 M3
Rosendale Junior & Infant School
DUL SE21 .... 31 M1
Rosslyn Park Rugbyfootball
Club
PUT/ROE SW15 .... 19 J6
Rowan High School
MTCM CR4 .... 48 F2
Rowans School
RYNPK SW20 .... 28 D8
The Rowans Surgery
STRHM/NOR SW16 .... 48 F1
Rowfant Business Centre
CRAWE RH10 .... 214 B3
Rowledge C of E First School
RFNM GU10 .... 155 G6
The Royal Alexandra &
Albert School
REIG RH2 .... 126 B3
Royal Army Medical Corps
ALDT GU11 .... 113 G5
Royal Ascot Golf Club
ASC SL5 .... 36 D2
Royal Ashdown Forest
Golf Club
FROW RH18 .... 217 K8
Royal Borough of Kingston
Upon Thames Health Clinic
NWMAL KT3 .... 45 M3
Royal Grammar School
GU GU1 .... 9 H5
Royal Holloway College
EGH TW20 .... 21 G5
Royal Holloway College
EGH TW20 .... 39 G1
Royal Holloway University
of London
EGH TW20 .... 21 G7
Royal Horticultural Society's
Gardens
RPLY/SEND GU23 .... 79 H8
Royal Hospital
RCH/KEW TW9 .... 18 A5
Royal Hospital for
Neuro-disability
PUT/ROE SW15 .... 28 E2
Royal Hospital & Home
PUT/ROE SW15 .... 28 E1
Royal Kent First & Middle School
LHD/OX KT22 .... 81 M4
Royal Logistocs Corps Museum
FRIM GU16 .... 94 A1
Royal Marsden Hospital
BELMT SM2 .... 65 M8
The Royal School
HASM GU27 .... 199 K7
Royal & Sunalliance Sports Club
HORS RH12 .... 229 H3
Royal Surrey County Hospital
GUW GU2 .... 116 B8
Royston Primary School
BECK BR3 .... 51 G1
R T R Healthcare NHS Trust
PUT/ROE SW15 .... 19 K8
Rudgwick Medical Centre
HORS RH12 .... 225 M2
Rudgwick School
HORS RH12 .... 226 A2
Rufus Business Centre
WAND/EARL SW18 .... 29 L3
Rugby Club
COB KT11 .... 81 G2
Rugby Club
COUL/CHIP CR5 .... 107 K2
Rugby Club
EGRIN RH19 .... 215 M4
The Rugby Club
CHOB/PIR GU24 .... 56 B8
Runnymede Borough Council
CHERT KT16 .... 40 D7
Runnymede Hospital
CHERT KT16 .... 58 A2
Runnymede Medical Practice
WDSR SL4 .... 20 D1
Rushey Green Group Practice
CAT SE6 .... 33 K2
Rushmoor Borough Council
FARN GU14 .... 92 E6
Rusper School
HORS RH12 .... 209 M2
The Russell JMI School
RCHPK/HAM TW10 .... 27 G3
The Russell School
RCHPK/HAM TW10 .... 27 G2
Rutlish School
RYNPK SW20 .... 47 J2
Rydens County Senior School
WOT/HER KT12 .... 60 F3
Rydes Hill Preparatory School
GUW GU2 .... 116 C6
Ryelands Primary School
SNWD SE25 .... 50 B4
Sackville Galleries
EGRIN RH19 .... 196 D8
Sacred Heart RC Primary School
NWMAL KT3 .... 46 D4
Sacred Heart RC School
TEDD TW11 .... 26 E8
St Agathas RC Primary School
KUTN/CMB KT2 .... 3 H1
St Albans Primary School
E/WMO/HCT KT8 .... 43 L5
St Andrews C of E Secondary
School
COB KT11 .... 80 F3
St Andrews Primary School
CRAWE RH10 .... 212 D5
St Andrews RC School
LHD/OX KT22 .... 102 F2
St Andrews RC School
STRHM/NOR SW16 .... 31 H6
St Andrews School
CROY/NA CR0 .... 4 A8
St Andrews School
WOKN/KNAP GU21 .... 6 B3

St Annes Primary School
CHERT KT16 .... 40 D8
St Annes Primary School
STWL/WRAY TW19 .... 23 H1
St Annes RC Primary School
BNSTD SM7 .... 85 K6
St Annes School
MRDN SM4 .... 47 L5
St Anns Heath County
Junior School
VW GU25 .... 39 J5
St Anslems RC Primary School
TOOT SW17 .... 30 D4
St Anthony RC School
PGE/AN SE20 .... 50 E1
St Anthonys Hospital
WPK KT4 .... 47 G8
St Augustines R C
Primary School
CAT SE6 .... 33 L6
St Bartholomews C of E School
HASM GU27 .... 219 M1
St Bartholomews
Middle School
HASM GU27 .... 219 M2
St Bartholomews Primary
School
SYD SE26 .... 32 F5
St Bedes C of E Junior School
RPLY/SEND GU23 .... 98 A6
St Bedes Primary School
BAL SW12 .... 31 G2
St Bernadettes RC Primary
School
FARN GU14 .... 92 D4
St Boniface RC School
TOOT SW17 .... 30 B6
St Brelades Surgery
DORK RH4 .... 144 D4
St Catherines RC Middle School
NWMAL KT3 .... 46 F5
St Catherines School
CBLY GU15 .... 72 F5
St Catherines School
SHGR GU5 .... 161 J2
St Catherines School
TWK TW1 .... 26 C3
St Cecilias RC School
WPK KT4 .... 65 G1
St Chads RC Primary School
SNWD SE25 .... 50 B5
St Charles RC Primary School
WEY KT13 .... 59 K2
St Christophers School
BECK BR3 .... 51 M2
St Christophers School
EPSOM KT18 .... 84 B4
St Clare Business Park
HPTN TW12 .... 25 M7
St Clements School
EW KT17 .... 64 C7
St Cuthbert Mayne RC
Primary School
CRAN GU6 .... 185 H6
St Cuthberts RC Primary School
EGH TW20 .... 20 F8
St Davids College
WWKM BR4 .... 51 L7
St Davids Group Practise
FELT TW13 .... 24 D3
St Davids Health Centre
STWL/WRAY TW19 .... 23 G1
St Davids School
ASHF TW15 .... 23 J4
St Davids School
PUR/KEN CR8 .... 87 J1
St Dominics School
MFD/CHID GU8 .... 181 M8
St Dunstans C of E Primary
School
CHEAM SM3 .... 65 G6
St Dunstans College
CAT SE6 .... 33 J1
St Dunstans RC Primary School
WOKS/MYFD GU22 .... 7 H5
St Edmunds RC Primary School
RGODL GU7 .... 160 C6
St Edmunds RC Primary School
WHTN TW2 .... 25 L1
St Edmunds School
GSHT GU26 .... 199 C8
St Elizabeths RC School
RCHPK/HAM TW10 .... 18 C7
St Elpheges RC School
WLGTN SM6 .... 67 H5
St Francis Middle School
CRAWE RH10 .... 212 B4
St Francis RC Primary School
CTHM CR3 .... 108 C3
St Francis RC School
ASC SL5 .... 36 D6
St Georges Business Park
WEY KT13 .... 59 K7
St Georges College
ADL/WDHM KT15 .... 59 G2
St Georges Hospital
TOOT SW17 .... 30 A5
St Georges Industrial Estate
CBLY GU15 .... 72 E6
St Georges Industrial Estate
KUTN/CMB KT2 .... 27 G6
St Georges School
ASC SL5 .... 36 E4
St Giles C of E Primary School
ASHTD KT21 .... 83 J8
St Giles School
CROY/NA CR0 .... 67 L5
St Hugh of Lincoln RC First School
WOKN/KNAP GU21 .... 96 A1
St Ignatius RC Primary School
SUN TW16 .... 42 D1
St James C of E Primary School
MFD/CHID GU8 .... 157 M6
St James C of E Primary School
WEY KT13 .... 59 M2
St James Medical Centre
CROY/NA CR0 .... 4 F2
St James's School
WHTN TW2 .... 26 B4

St James the Great School
THHTH CR7 .... 49 L2
St John Baptist School
BMLY BR1 .... 33 M5
St John Fisher RC Primary School
NWMAL KT3 .... 46 F5
St John Rigby School
WWKM BR4 .... 70 A3
St Johns C of E First School
NFNM GU10 .... 178 B8
St Johns CP School
WOKN/KNAP GU21 .... 76 B8
St Johns Infant School
CTHM CR3 .... 108 E7
St Johns Junior School
CTHM CR3 .... 108 E8
St Johns Primary School
KUT KT1 .... 2 F9
St Johns Primary School
REDH RH1 .... 148 B2
St Johns RC Primary School
HORS RH12 .... 228 D7
St Johns School
LHD/OX KT22 .... 102 E3
St John the Baptist RC
Comprehensive School
WOKS/MYFD GU22 .... 97 K1
St Josephs Catholic
Primary School
EPSOM KT18 .... 83 M4
St Josephs College
STRHM/NOR SW16 .... 31 L7
St Josephs Gm RC Primary
School
ALDT GU11 .... 134 C1
St Josephs Infant School
NRWD SE19 .... 31 M7
St Josephs RC Junior School
NRWD SE19 .... 31 M7
St Josephs RC Primary School
BRAK RG12 .... 35 G2
St Josephs RC Primary School
DORK RH4 .... 144 D2
St Josephs RC Primary School
KUT KT1 .... 3 G7
St Josephs School
CRAN GU6 .... 185 J3
St Josephs School
REDH RH1 .... 126 B7
St Judes C of E School
EGH TW20 .... 20 F7
St Lawrence Business Centre
FELT TW13 .... 24 E3
St Lawrence Catholic School
FELT TW13 .... 24 E2
St Lawrence C of E Junior School
E/WMO/HCT KT8 .... 44 A3
St Lawrence CP School
EHSLY KT24 .... 121 G1
St Leonards C of E Primary
School
STRHM/NOR SW16 .... 31 G6
St Leonards County Infants
School
SWTR RH13 .... 229 G7
St Lukes C of E Primary School
KUTN/CMB KT2 .... 3 L1
St Lukes School
THHTH CR7 .... 49 K4
St Lukes Surgery
GU GU1 .... 9 L6
St Margaret Clitherow
Primary School
BRAK RG12 .... 34 C7
St Margarets C of E Primary
School
CRAWW RH11 .... 211 L2
St Margarets Medical Practice
TWK TW1 .... 17 L7
St Marks C of E Aided Primary
School
RGODL GU7 .... 159 L6
St Marks C of E Primary School
FARN GU14 .... 113 G1
St Marks C of E School
SNWD SE25 .... 50 D4
St Marks Primary School
MTCM CR4 .... 48 C2
St Marks RC School
HSLW TW3 .... 16 C5
St Martin In the Fields
High School
BRXS/STRHM SW2 .... 31 L2
St Martins C of E Junior School
EPSOM KT18 .... 84 A5
St Martins C of E School
DORK RH4 .... 144 C1
St Martins House Business
Centre
EHSLY KT24 .... 120 B3
St Mary Magdelens Primary
School
MORT/ESHN SW14 .... 19 G5
St Marys C of E First School
MFD/CHID GU8 .... 201 L6
St Marys C of E Infant School
LHD/OX KT22 .... 102 F4
St Marys C of E Primary School
BF/WBF KT14 .... 79 H3
St Marys C of E Primary School
CHSGTN KT9 .... 63 H5
St Marys C of E Primary School
THDIT KT7 .... 44 E8
St Marys C of E School
EGRIN RH19 .... 196 A7
St Marys C of E School
TWK TW1 .... 26 D1
St Marys Infant School
CAR SM5 .... 66 B3
St Marys Middle School
OXTED RH8 .... 130 B2
St Marys Primary School
BECK BR3 .... 33 M8
St Marys Primary School
HORS RH12 .... 228 E8
St Mary's RC Infant School
CROY/NA CR0 .... 4 E3
St Marys RC Junior School
CAR SM5 .... 66 C3

St Marys RC Primary School
WIM/MER SW19 .... **29** K8
St Marys & St. Peters C of E
  Primary School
TEDD TW11 .... **26** C6
St Marys School
ASC SL5 .... **36** E7
St Marys Tutorial College
GUW GU2 .... **8** F9
St Marys University College
TWK TW1 .... **26** C4
St Matthews C of E First School
COB KT11 .... **80** E8
St Matthews C of E Primary
  School
REDH RH1 .... **126** C6
St Matthews C of E Primary
  School
SURB KT6 .... **45** H7
St Maurs School
WEY KT13 .... **59** L2
St Michaels Abbey
FARN GU14 .... **92** F4
St Michaels C of E Controlled
  Secondary School
ALDT GU11 .... **134** E1
St Michaels C of E Infant School
ALDT GU11 .... **134** E1
St Michael's C of E School
SYD SE26 .... **33** H5
St Michaels School
BRAK RG12 .... **34** D5
St Michaels RC School
ASHF TW15 .... **23** K6
St Michaels School
HSLWW TW4 .... **16** C5
St Michael's School
WAND/EARL SW18 .... **29** J1
St Nicholas C of E First School
GUW GU2 .... **8** E8
St Nicholas C of E JMI School
SHPTN TW17 .... **41** L6
St Nicholas Middle School
CRAN GU6 .... **185** C6
St Nicholas School
PUR/KEN CR8 .... **87** J3
St Nicholas Special School
REDH RH1 .... **127** G3
St Nicks Art Gallery
SUT SM1 .... **65** L4
St Nicolas School
MFD/CHID GU8 .... **203** J3
St Omer Barracks
ALDT GU11 .... **113** G5
St Osmunds RC Primary School
BARN SW13 .... **19** J3
St Patricks RC School
FARN GU14 .... **93** G5
St Pauls Catholic School
SUN TW16 .... **42** D1
St Pauls C of E Primary School
DORK RH4 .... **144** E2
St Pauls C of E First School
NFNM GU10 .... **135** K2
St Pauls C of E Junior School
KUTN/CMB KT2 .... **3** K3
St Pauls C of E Primary School
BTFD TW8 .... **18** A1
St Pauls Middle School
ADL/WDHM KT15 .... **58** D3
St Pauls RC Primary School
ESH/CLAY KT10 .... **44** B7
St Pauls School
CHSGTN KT9 .... **63** H3
St Peter & St Paul RC
  Primary School
MTCM CR4 .... **48** C4
St Peters Catholic
  Comprehensive School
GU GU1 .... **117** M7
St Peters C of E Middle School
FNM GU9 .... **10** B6
St Peters Junior School
FARN GU14 .... **92** F5
St Peters RC Primary School
LHD/OX KT22 .... **102** F2
St Peters RC School
EGRIN RH19 .... **195** M8
St Peters & St. Paul C of E
  Primary School
CTHM CR3 .... **107** K7
St Peters School
SAND/SEL CR2 .... **68** A5
St Philips School
CHSGTN KT9 .... **63** G5
St Phillips Infant School
SYD SE26 .... **32** E5
St Philomenas School
CAR SM5 .... **66** B4
St Polycarps RC Primary School
FNM GU9 .... **11** J1
St Raphaels Hospice
WPK KT4 .... **65** G1
St Richards with St. Andrews
  C of E Primary School
RCHPK/HAM TW10 .... **26** E4
St Robert Southwell RC
  First School
HORS RH12 .... **229** K3
St Stephens C of E Junior
  School
TWK TW1 .... **17** K8
St Stephens C of E Primary
  School
GDST RH9 .... **151** J3
St Teresas Preparatory School
EHSLY KT24 .... **121** G2
St Teresas School
RDKG RH5 .... **121** G6
St Thomas of Canterbury RC
  Middle School
MTCM CR4 .... **48** D3
St Walter & St John Sports
  Ground
TOOT SW17 .... **30** B2
St Wilfrids RC School
CRAWW RH11 .... **211** L4
St William of York School
FSTH SE23 .... **33** H2

Salesian College
CHERT KT16 .... **40** D8
Salesian College
FARN GU14 .... **93** G8
Salesian School
CHERT KT16 .... **58** B1
Salfords First School
REDH RH1 .... **148** D6
Salfords Industrial Estate
REDH RH1 .... **148** D8
Sampson Business Park
CBLY GU15 .... **72** E6
The Samuel Cody School
ALDT GU11 .... **112** E2
Sandcross School
REIG RH2 .... **147** J3
Sandfield CP School
GU GU1 .... **9** G5
Sandhurst College Town
  County Junior School
SHST GU47 .... **72** B1
Sandhurst School
SHST GU47 .... **72** A1
Sandiford Industrial Estate
CHEAM SM3 .... **65** J1
Sandown Industrial Park
ESH/CLAY KT10 .... **61** K1
Sandy Lane Junior School
BNFD RG42 .... **34** F1
Sangers County Middle School
HORL RH6 .... **170** C6
Saxon Business Centre
WIM/MER SW19 .... **47** M2
Saxon CP School
SHPTN TW17 .... **41** J5
Sayer Clinic
CROY/NA CR0 .... **67** J3
Sayes Court Junior School
ADL/WDHM KT15 .... **58** E4
S C C Clinic
REDH RH1 .... **126** F3
School of Art College
REIG RH2 .... **126** A8
School of the Good Shepherd
CROY/NA CR0 .... **69** L6
Scott Broadwood School
RDKG RH5 .... **187** M5
Scott Broadwood School
RDKG RH5 .... **189** G3
The Scott Gallery
HORL RH6 .... **170** D7
The Scott Gallery
REDH RH1 .... **148** D1
Seaton House School
BELMT SM2 .... **66** A8
Secombe Theatre
SUT SM1 .... **65** K4
Secretarial College
BECK BR3 .... **51** H1
Sedgehill School
CAT SE6 .... **33** L6
The Selhurst Medical Centre
SNWD SE25 .... **50** A6
Sellincourt School
TOOT SW17 .... **30** C7
Selsdon CP School
SAND/SEL CR2 .... **68** F7
Selsdon High School
SAND/SEL CR2 .... **69** G6
The Selsdon Park Medical
  Practice
SAND/SEL CR2 .... **68** E8
Send C of E First School
RPLY/SEND GU23 .... **98** A6
Send Cricket Club
RPLY/SEND GU23 .... **97** L6
Send Surgery
RPLY/SEND GU23 .... **97** M5
Seymour First & Middle School
CRAWW RH11 .... **211** L7
Shalford County First School
RGUE GU4 .... **139** H6
Shanghai Traditional Chinese
  Medical Centre
TWK TW1 .... **18** A3
Shannon Corner Retail Park
NWMAL KT3 .... **46** C4
Shawfield County Infant School
ASHV GU12 .... **113** K6
Shawley County First &
  Middle School
EPSOM KT18 .... **84** F8
Sheen Lane Health Centre
MORT/ESHN SW14 .... **18** F5
Sheen Mount Primary School
RCHPK/HAM TW10 .... **18** E7
Sheen Sports Centre
MORT/ESHN SW14 .... **19** H6
Shelly Primary School
HORS RH12 .... **228** B6
Shene School
MORT/ESHN SW14 .... **19** G6
Shepperton Business Park
SHPTN TW17 .... **41** M5
Shepperton Health Centre
SHPTN TW17 .... **41** L5
Shere C of E Primary School
SHGR GU5 .... **141** K5
Shere Surgery & Dispensary
SHGR GU5 .... **141** L5
Sheringdale Primary School
WAND/EARL SW18 .... **29** J2
Sherwood First School
MTCM CR4 .... **48** F4
Sherwood Park School
WLGTN SM6 .... **67** G2
Shillinglee Park Golf Club
MFD/CHID GU8 .... **222** A3
The Ship Street Surgery
EGRIN RH19 .... **216** B1
Shirley Clinic
CROY/NA CR0 .... **50** F8
Shirley High School
CROY/NA CR0 .... **69** G2
Shirley Medical Centre
CROY/NA CR0 .... **69** H1
Shirley Wanderers
  Rugby Football Club
WWKM BR4 .... **69** M3

Shopping Trolley Gallery
BECK BR3 .... **33** J8
Shortwood County Infant School
STA TW18 .... **22** E4
Shotfield Health Clinic
WLGTN SM6 .... **66** E5
Shottermill County Middle School
HASM GU27 .... **219** J2
Shree Ghanapathy Temple
WIM/MER SW19 .... **29** M7
Shree Swaminarayan Temple
STRHM/NOR SW16 .... **49** H1
Silverglade Business Park
CHSGTN KT9 .... **82** F2
Silver Wing Industrial Estate
CROY/NA CR0 .... **67** J5
Singlegate First School
WIM/MER SW19 .... **30** A8
Sir William Perkins School
CHERT KT16 .... **40** C8
The Sixth Form College
FARN GU14 .... **92** E2
Skimped Hill Health Centre
BRAK RG12 .... **34** E1
Sky Business Park
EGH TW20 .... **39** M2
Slinfold C of E Primary School
SWTR RH13 .... **227** G5
Slinfold Park Golf &
  Country Club
SWTR RH13 .... **226** E6
Smallberry Green School
ISLW TW7 .... **17** K4
Smallwood Primary School
TOOT SW17 .... **30** A5
Smitham Primary School
COUL/CHIP CR5 .... **86** F6
Smithbrook Clinic
CRAN GU6 .... **184** A6
The Smith Gallery
TEDD TW11 .... **26** D6
Snowhill Business Centre
CRAWE RH10 .... **194** D5
South Bookham School
GT/LBKH KT23 .... **121** M1
Southborough School
SURB KT6 .... **63** H2
South Croydon Medical Centre
SAND/SEL CR2 .... **67** M6
South Croydon Medical Practice
SAND/SEL CR2 .... **67** M5
South Croydon Sports Club
SAND/SEL CR2 .... **68** B4
Southern Clinic
REIG RH2 .... **147** M1
South Farnborough
  County Junior School
FARN GU14 .... **93** G7
South Farnborough
  Infant School
FARN GU14 .... **113** G1
South Farnham Middle School
FNM GU9 .... **11** K1
Southfields Community College
WAND/EARL SW18 .... **29** K2
Southfields Group Practice
WAND/EARL SW18 .... **29** K3
Southgate First School
CRAWE RH10 .... **212** A6
Southgate Middle School
CRAWE RH10 .... **212** A5
Southgate School
CRAWW RH11 .... **211** M5
Southlands College
PUT/ROE SW15 .... **19** J6
Southlea Surgery
ALDT GU11 .... **134** E2
South Lewisham Health Centre
CAT SE6 .... **33** M5
South London Liberal
  Synagogue
STRHM/NOR SW16 .... **31** G4
South London Tamil School
CROY/NA CR0 .... **4** D1
South London Theatre Centre
WNWD SE27 .... **31** L4
Southmead Primary School
WIM/MER SW19 .... **29** H2
South Norwood Hill
  Medical Centre
SNWD SE25 .... **50** B2
South Norwood Medical Centre
SNWD SE25 .... **50** B4
South Norwood Primary School
SNWD SE25 .... **50** D4
South Nutfield Cricket Club
REDH RH1 .... **149** J2
South Thames College /
  Wandsworth Adult College
PUT/ROE SW15 .... **19** J8
Southview Surgery
WOKS/MYFD GU22 .... **6** D8
Southville Junior School
EBED/NFELT TW14 .... **24** C2
Southwark Sports Ground
DUL SE21 .... **32** C2
South West Surrey
  Business Centre
GU GU1 .... **9** H5
Southwood Golf Club
FARN GU14 .... **92** B7
Sparrow Farm County
  Junior School
EW KT17 .... **64** G4
Sparrow Farm Infant School
EBED/NFELT TW14 .... **24** F1
Sparrow Farm Junior School
EBED/NFELT TW14 .... **24** F1
Spelthorne Borough Council
STA TW18 .... **22** D7
Spelthorne Clinic
ASHF TW15 .... **24** B7
Spelthorne College
ASHF TW15 .... **23** J5
Spelthorne Council for
  Voluntary Services
STA TW18 .... **22** B5
Spelthorne County School
ASHF TW15 .... **24** A7

Spelthorne Leisure Centre
STA TW18 .... **22** D6
Spelthorne Museum
STA TW18 .... **22** B6
Spelthorne Sports Club
ASHF TW15 .... **24** A8
Sports Club
ESH/CLAY KT10 .... **61** J5
Sports Club
LHD/OX KT22 .... **81** M4
Sports Club
LHD/OX KT22 .... **102** B3
Sports Ground
THHTH CR7 .... **49** L2
Sports Ground
TOOT SW17 .... **30** B4
Springfield Hospital
TOOT SW17 .... **30** B4
Springfield Primary School
SUN TW16 .... **42** C1
Spring Grove Primary School
ISLW TW7 .... **17** G4
Springlake Country Club
ASHV GU12 .... **113** H5
Spring Park School
CROY/NA CR0 .... **69** K2
Springwell Junior School
HEST TW5 .... **16** B2
Sprint Industrial Estate
BF/WBF KT14 .... **79** G1
Spurgeons College
SNWD SE25 .... **50** B2
Staff College
CBLY GU15 .... **72** F2
Stafford Cross Business Park
CROY/NA CR0 .... **67** J4
Staines County Court
STA TW18 .... **22** D6
Staines & District Synagogue
STA TW18 .... **22** C6
Staines Preparatory School
STA TW18 .... **22** D6
Staines Rugby Football Club
FELT TW13 .... **24** D5
Staines Town Football Club
STA TW18 .... **22** D8
Staines Youth Sports Centre
STA TW18 .... **22** D5
Stamford Green
  Primary School
HOR/WEW KT19 .... **83** L2
Stammerham Business Centre
HORS RH12 .... **209** H2
Stanford Middle School
STRHM/NOR SW16 .... **49** G1
Stanley Infant School
TEDD TW11 .... **26** B5
Stanley Junior School
WHTN TW2 .... **26** B5
Stanley Park High School
CAR SM5 .... **66** D5
Stanley Park Infant School
CAR SM5 .... **66** C6
Stanley Technical High School
SNWD SE25 .... **50** C3
Stanton Square Industrial Estate
CAT SE6 .... **33** J5
Stanway School
DORK RH4 .... **122** E7
Starhurst School
RDKG RH5 .... **144** F4
Station Road Surgery
FRIM GU16 .... **93** G1
Station Yard
KWD/TDW/WH KT20 .... **105** J3
Stepgates Primary School
CHERT KT16 .... **40** E7
Stewart Fleming School
SNWD SE25 .... **50** F3
Stirling Way Industrial Estates
CROY/NA CR0 .... **49** H7
Stoke Hill CP School
GU GU1 .... **116** F5
Stonecot Surgery
MRDN SM4 .... **47** J7
Stoneleigh Galleries
EW KT17 .... **64** D4
Stoughton County Junior School
GUW GU2 .... **116** E5
Stowford College
BELMT SM2 .... **65** M6
Strand on the Green Junior &
  Infant School
CHSWK W4 .... **18** D1
Strathmore School
RCHPK/HAM TW10 .... **27** G2
Streatham & Croydon
  Rugby Football Club
THHTH CR7 .... **49** K5
Streatham Hill & Clapham
  High School
BRXS/STRHM SW2 .... **31** J2
Streatham Hill & Clapham
  High School
STRHM/NOR SW16 .... **30** F4
Streatham Ice Rink
STRHM/NOR SW16 .... **31** H6
Streatham Modern School
STRHM/NOR SW16 .... **31** H7
Streatham Park Surgery
STRHM/NOR SW16 .... **30** F6
Streatham Swimming Pool
STRHM/NOR SW16 .... **31** H6
Streatham Vale Sports Club
STRHM/NOR SW16 .... **30** F8
Streatham Wells Primary School
BRXS/STRHM SW2 .... **31** J3
Streete Court School
GDST RH9 .... **129** H4
Strodes College
EGH TW20 .... **21** J6
Stubbs Industrial Estate
ALDT GU11 .... **113** H4
Students Gallery
RYNPK SW20 .... **47** J1
Studholme Medical Centre
ASHF TW15 .... **23** J5
Study Preparatory School
WIM/MER SW19 .... **29** G6

The Study School
NWMAL KT3 .... **46** B5
Sturt Priory Hospital
KWD/TDW/WH KT20 .... **104** D8
Summit Business Park
SUN TW16 .... **24** D8
Sunbury Business Centre
SUN TW16 .... **42** B1
Sunbury Health Centre
SUN TW16 .... **42** D2
Sunbury Leisure Centre
SUN TW16 .... **42** C1
Sunbury Manor School
SUN TW16 .... **42** C1
Sunningdale Golf Coursel
ASC SL5 .... **55** K1
Sunningdale School
ASC SL5 .... **37** H6
Sunnydown School
CTHM CR3 .... **108** C3
Sunnyhill Primary School
STRHM/NOR SW16 .... **31** J5
Sunny Meed Surgery
WOKS/MYFD GU22 .... **6** F7
Surbiton Business Centre
SURB KT6 .... **45** C6
Surbiton High School for Girls
KUT KT6 .... **45** H4
Surbiton Hospital
SURB KT6 .... **45** H6
Surbiton Natural Health Centre
SURB KT6 .... **45** H6
Surex Swimming Pools
BH/WHM TN16 .... **91** C5
Surgery on the Green
MFD/CHID GU8 .... **158** A5
Surrey County Council
ADL/WDHM KT15 .... **58** F1
Surrey County Council
BNSTD SM7 .... **85** J5
Surrey County Council
E/WMO/HCT KT8 .... **43** K4
Surrey County Council
EW KT17 .... **64** D7
Surrey County Council
EW KT17 .... **84** B2
Surrey County Council
HOR/WEW KT19 .... **64** B7
Surrey County Council
HOR/WEW KT19 .... **84** A1
Surrey County Council
KUT KT1 .... **2** D9
Surrey County Council
LHD/OX KT22 .... **102** D2
Surrey County Council
LHD/OX KT22 .... **102** D4
Surrey County Council
THDIT KT7 .... **44** D6
Surrey County Council
WEY KT13 .... **59** J3
Surrey County Council
WEY KT13 .... **59** L3
Surrey County Council
WOKN/KNAP GU21 .... **6** F4
Surrey County Council
WOKN/KNAP GU21 .... **96** C5
Surrey County Council
WOT/HER KT12 .... **60** E1
Surrey Heartlands NHS Trust
HOR/WEW KT19 .... **63** M7
Surrey Probation Service
GU GU1 .... **8** F5
Surrey Welfare Court Service
GU GU1 .... **8** F6
Sussex Manor Business Park
CRAWE RH10 .... **192** D7
Sutton Alternative Health
  Centre
SUT SM1 .... **65** M4
Sutton Bowling Club
BELMT SM2 .... **65** K7
Sutton General Hospital
BELMT SM2 .... **65** L8
Sutton Grammar School for
  Boys
SUT SM1 .... **65** M4
Sutton High School for Girls
SUT SM1 .... **65** L5
Sutton Station Chiropractic
  Health Centre
BELMT SM2 .... **65** L5
Sutton Superbowl
SUT SM1 .... **65** L4
Sutton United Football Club
SUT SM1 .... **65** K3
Swansmere School
WOT/HER KT12 .... **42** F8
Swedish School
CRAWE RH10 .... **212** C5
Swinley CP School
ASC SL5 .... **36** D5
Swinley Forest Golf Club
ASC SL5 .... **36** C7
Sydenham High School
SYD SE26 .... **32** E6
Sydenham High School
SYD SE26 .... **32** E6
Sydenham Pre-school
FSTH SE23 .... **32** E3
Sydenham Secondary School
SYD SE26 .... **32** E4
Synagogue
SURB KT6 .... **45** C5
The Synagogue
E/WMO/HCT KT8 .... **45** C5
Syon House
BTFD TW8 .... **17** M3
Sythwood County
  Primary School
WOKN/KNAP GU21 .... **76** E6
Tadworth County
  Primary School
KWD/TDW/WH KT20 .... **105** C4
Tadworth Farm Surgery
KWD/TDW/WH KT20 .... **104** E2
Tait Road Industrial Estate
CROY/NA CR0 .... **5** C1
Talavera County Junior &
  Infant School
ALDT GU11 .... **112** E6

Tamworth Manor High School
STRHM/NOR SW16 .... 49 G3
Tanbridge House School
HORS RH12 .... 228 E8
Tanbridge Retail Park
HORS RH12 .... 228 E8
Tandridge Golf Club
OXTED RH8 .... 129 M5
Tandridge Primary School
GDST RH9 .... 129 K7
Tatsfield Primary School
BH/WHM TN16 .... 111 G3
Tattenham Health Centre
EPSOM KT18 .... 84 E8
Teddington Business Park
TEDD TW11 .... 26 C6
Teddington Clinic
TEDD TW11 .... 26 B7
Teddington Memorial Hospital
TEDD TW11 .... 26 B7
Teddington School
TEDD TW11 .... 2 C1
Teddington Swimming Pool
TEDD TW11 .... 26 B6
The Teddington Theatre Club
E/WMO/HCT KT8 .... 44 A4
The Teddington Theatre Club
HPTN TW12 .... 25 L8
Thames Ditton County
First School
THDIT KT7 .... 44 C6
Thames Ditton Junior School
THDIT KT7 .... 44 C7
Thamesmead County
Secondary School
SHPTN TW17 .... 42 A6
Theatre Magenta
LHD/OX KT22 .... 102 D2
Theatre of the Dispossessed
WIM/MER SW19 .... 29 G2
The Theatre on the Hill
CTHM CR3 .... 108 B4
Therapia Trading Estate
CROY/NA CR0 .... 49 G7
Therfield County
Secondary School
LHD/OX KT22 .... 102 C1
Thomas Becket RC
Primary School
SNWD SE25 .... 50 D6
Thomas Bennett
Community College
CRAWW RH11 .... 212 A6
Thorkhill Surgery
THDIT KT7 .... 44 E8
Thorn Chase & Grove School
GU GU1 .... 117 M8
Thornton Heath Baths
THHTH CR7 .... 50 A4
Thornton Heath Health Centre
THHTH CR7 .... 49 M4
Thornton Road Industrial Estate
CROY/NA CR0 .... 49 J6
Thornton Road Surgery
CROY/NA CR0 .... 49 J6
Thorpe C of E Infant School
EGH TW20 .... 39 M3
Thorpe Cricket Club
EGH TW20 .... 39 J4
Thorpe Lea Primary School
EGH TW20 .... 22 A7
Three Bridge County
Middle School
CRAWE RH10 .... 212 C3
Three Bridges Cricket Club
CRAWE RH10 .... 212 D3
Three Bridges First School
CRAWE RH10 .... 212 D2
Three Bridges Football Club
CRAWE RH10 .... 212 D3
Thurlow Park School
WNWD SE27 .... 31 L3
Tiffin Girls School
KUTN/CMB KT2 .... 27 H6
Tiffin School
KUTN/CMB KT2 .... 3 G6
Tilgate Forest Business Centre
CRAWW RH11 .... 212 A8
Tilgate Forest Golf Club
CRAWE RH10 .... 212 D7
Tillingbourne County Secondary
School
RGUE GU4 .... 139 L7
Tobias School of Art
EGRIN RH19 .... 216 B3
Tolgate School
CROY/NA CR0 .... 50 E6
Tolworth CP School
SURB KT6 .... 45 J8
Tolworth Recreation Centre
CHSGTN KT9 .... 63 J2
Tolworth Secondary Girls School
SURB KT6 .... 63 J2
Tomlinscote School
FRIM GU16 .... 73 J7
Tooting Bec Surgery
TOOT SW17 .... 30 D4
Tooting & Mitcham
United Football Club
MTCM CR4 .... 48 D1
Tormead School
GU GU1 .... 9 M3
Tower Hill CP School
FARN GU14 .... 92 C6
Tower House Preparatory
School for Boys
MORT/ESHN SW14 .... 18 F6
Tower Industrial Estate
SNWD SE25 .... 50 D4
Town Farm County
Primary School
STWL/WRAY TW19 .... 23 G1
Trafalgar County Infant School
HORS RH12 .... 228 E5
Trafalgar Junior School
WHTN TW2 .... 26 A3
Trident Business Centre
TOOT SW17 .... 30 C6
Trident Industrial Estate
DTCH/LGLY SL3 .... 13 H5

Trinity St Marys C of E Primary
School
BAL SW12 .... 30 D2
The Trinity Surgery
WAND/EARL SW18 .... 30 A1
Trumps Green County
First School
VW GU25 .... 39 G6
Tudor Lodge Health Centre
WIM/MER SW19 .... 29 G1
Turners Hill C of E School
CRAWE RH10 .... 214 D6
Turney School
DUL SE21 .... 31 M1
Tweedale Infant School
CAR SM5 .... 48 A7
Tweedale Junior School
CAR SM5 .... 48 A7
Twickenham Park Health Centre
TWK TW1 .... 17 M8
Twickenham Rugby
Football Ground
WHTN TW2 .... 17 H8
Twickenham Trading Estate
TWK TW1 .... 17 J8
Twin Bridges Business Park
SAND/SEL CR2 .... 68 A5
Two Rivers Retail Park
STA TW18 .... 22 B5
U C I Cinema
BRAK RG12 .... 34 E2
Ullswater Business Park
COUL/CHIP CR5 .... 87 H6
The Ullswater Business Park
COUL/CHIP CR5 .... 87 H6
Ullswater Trading Estate
COUL/CHIP CR5 .... 87 H6
Unicorn School
RCH/KEW TW9 .... 18 C3
Unicorn Trading Estate
HASM GU27 .... 219 L3
Union Buildings Playschool
ALDT GU11 .... 112 D6
United Services Sports Ground
CHSWK W4 .... 19 H3
University of Surrey
GUW GU2 .... 8 C4
University of Westminster
CHSWK W4 .... 18 F3
University Vandals Rugby
Football Club
WOT/HER KT12 .... 42 A8
Upper Selsdon Road Surgery
SAND/SEL CR2 .... 68 E8
Upper Tooting Independent
High School
TOOT SW17 .... 30 B3
Ursuline High School
RYNPK SW20 .... 29 G8
The Vale Medical Centre
FSTH SE23 .... 33 H3
Vale Primary School
EPSOM KT18 .... 104 A1
Valley End C of E Infant School
CHOB/PIR GU24 .... 55 K5
Valley End Cricket Club
CHOB/PIR GU24 .... 55 K6
Vicarage Lane Clinic
HASM GU27 .... 219 J3
Vicarage School
RCHPK/HAM TW10 .... 18 A8
Victoria Clinic
WOKN/KNAP GU21 .... 6 F4
Victoria Junior School
FELT TW13 .... 24 E2
Victor Seymour School
CAR SM5 .... 66 C2
Victory Business Centre
ISLW TW7 .... 17 J6
Village Surgery
NWMAL KT3 .... 46 B4
The Vine Clinic
KUTN/CMB KT2 .... 2 E1
Vine Medical Centre
E/WMO/HCT KT8 .... 43 M3
Vineyard Hill Road Surgery
WIM/MER SW19 .... 29 K4
Virgin Multiplex Cinema
CRAWW RH11 .... 212 A2
Virgo Fidelis Convent Schools
NRWD SE19 .... 31 M7
Viscount Industrial Estate
DTCH/LGLY SL3 .... 13 H5
Vulcan Business Centre
CROY/NA CR0 .... 70 B7
Waddon Clinic
CROY/NA CR0 .... 67 K4
Waddon Infant School
CROY/NA CR0 .... 67 K4
The Waldegrave Clinic
TEDD TW11 .... 26 C6
Waldegrave School
WHTN TW2 .... 26 A4
Waldorf School of S W London
STRHM/NOR SW16 .... 30 F3
Waldorf Steiner School of S W
London
STRHM/NOR SW16 .... 31 G5
Wallace Fields County
First School
EW KT17 .... 84 D2
Wallace Fields CP School
EW KT17 .... 84 D2
Wallbrook Business Centre
HSLWW TW4 .... 15 L5
Wallington County
Grammar School
WLGTN SM6 .... 66 C4
Wallington High School for Girls
WLGTN SM6 .... 66 E7
Walsh C of E First &
Middle School
ASHV GU12 .... 113 J8
Walton Business Centre
WOT/HER KT12 .... 42 E7
Walton Casuals Football Club
WOT/HER KT12 .... 42 E8
Walton Community Hospital
WOT/HER KT12 .... 60 E1

Walton Heath Golf Club Shop
KWD/TDW/WH KT20 .... 104 E7
Walton & Hersham Football Club
WOT/HER KT12 .... 60 D1
Walton Leigh School
WEY KT13 .... 60 C3
Walton-on-Thames Cricket Club
WOT/HER KT12 .... 42 C8
Walton-on-the-hill C of E
Junior School
KWD/TDW/WH KT20 .... 104 D7
Walton-on-the-hill CP School
KWD/TDW/WH KT20 .... 104 E6
Walton Swimming Pool
WOT/HER KT12 .... 42 E8
Walton & Weybridge
Urban District Council
WEY KT13 .... 59 K3
Wandle Primary School
WAND/EARL SW18 .... 29 L2
Wandsworth Adult College
TOOT SW17 .... 30 B5
Wandsworth Borough Council
TOOT SW17 .... 30 C6
Wandsworth Borough Council
WAND/EARL SW18 .... 29 L1
Wandsworth Community
Health Trust
TOOT SW17 .... 30 D6
Wandsworth Public Baths
TOOT SW17 .... 30 D3
Wandsworth Trading Estate
WAND/EARL SW18 .... 29 L1
Warehouse Theatre
CROY/NA CR0 .... 4 E6
Warlingham County
Junior School
WARL CR6 .... 89 G7
Warlingham County
Secondary School
WARL CR6 .... 88 E6
Warlingham Park Hospital
WARL CR6 .... 89 K6
Warlingham Park School
WARL CR6 .... 89 K6
Warlingham Rugby
Football Club
WARL CR6 .... 89 J7
Warlingham Sports Club
WARL CR6 .... 89 G7
War Memorial Sports Ground
SUT SM1 .... 66 B3
Warner Bros Cinema
CROY/NA CR0 .... 67 J1
Warnham C of E School
HORS RH12 .... 228 C1
Warnham Court School
HORS RH12 .... 228 C3
Warren Mead Infant School
BNSTD SM7 .... 84 F5
Warren Mead Junior School
BNSTD SM7 .... 85 G5
The Warwick School
REDH RH1 .... 126 D7
Watchetts County Middle
School
CBLY GU15 .... 72 F7
Waterden Road Private
Medical Clinic
GU GU1 .... 9 K5
Waterfield School
CRAWW RH11 .... 211 H5
Watermans Business Park
STA TW18 .... 22 B5
Watermeads High School
MRDN SM4 .... 48 A6
Watermill Museum
LING RH7 .... 174 F1
Waterside Business Centre
ISLW TW7 .... 17 L6
Wattenden Primary School
PUR/KEN CR8 .... 87 K6
Watts Gallery
RGUW GU3 .... 137 L5
The Wavell School
ALDT GU11 .... 112 E2
Waverley Abbey C of E School
NFNM GU10 .... 156 F4
Waverley Abbey Ho
FNM GU9 .... 156 E1
The Weald C of E Middle School
RDKG RH5 .... 167 G6
Websters Art Gallery
LHD/OX KT22 .... 81 M3
Wellington Primary School
HSLW TW3 .... 16 C4
Wellington Shopping Centre
ALDT GU11 .... 112 D7
The Wells Park Practice
SYD SE26 .... 32 E4
West Ashtead CP School
ASHTD KT21 .... 103 H2
Westbourne Primary School
SUT SM1 .... 65 K2
West Byfleet County
Infant School
BF/WBF KT14 .... 78 E2
West Byfleet Health Centre
BF/WBF KT14 .... 78 D3
West Byfleet Physiotherapy
Clinic
BF/WBF KT14 .... 78 D2
Westcott School
DORK RH4 .... 143 M3
The Westcroft Leisure Centre
CAR SM5 .... 66 D3
West Dene School
PUR/KEN CR8 .... 87 J3
Westend County Infant School
ALDT GU11 .... 112 C7
West Ewell County Infant School
HOR/WEW KT19 .... 64 A4
Westfield Primary School
WOKS/MYFD GU22 .... 97 H3
Westfields School
BARN SW13 .... 19 J5
Westfield Surgery
WOKS/MYFD GU22 .... 97 H3
West Green County First School
CRAWW RH11 .... 211 M2

West Hill School
LHD/OX KT22 .... 82 D8
West Lambeth Health Authority
STRHM/NOR SW16 .... 31 H7
West Middlesex Hospital
ISLW TW7 .... 17 K4
Westmoor Community Clinic
PUT/ROE SW15 .... 28 D1
West Norwood Clinic
WNWD SE27 .... 31 M3
West Surrey Golf Club
MFD/CHID GU8 .... 181 L3
West Suuex County Council
CBLY GU15 .... 72 E4
West Thames College
ISLW TW7 .... 17 H4
West Thornton Primary School
CROY/NA CR0 .... 49 J7
The Westway Clinic
REDH RH1 .... 126 B7
West Wickham Swimming Baths
WWKM BR4 .... 51 M8
Westwood High School for Girls
NRWD SE19 .... 31 M8
Weybourne County
Infant School
FNM GU9 .... 134 B3
Weybridge Business Park
ADL/WDHM KT15 .... 59 H3
Weybridge Cricket Club
WEY KT13 .... 60 B1
Weybridge Hospital &
Primary Care Centre
WEY KT13 .... 59 K3
Weydon County
Secondary School
FNM GU9 .... 10 B5
Weydown Industrial Estate
HASM GU27 .... 219 L2
Weyfield Primary School
GU GU1 .... 117 G5
Wey House School
SHGR GU5 .... 161 H1
White Hart Industrial Estate
BLKW GU17 .... 72 B4
Whitehorse Manor Junior School
THHTH CR7 .... 50 A4
White House Gallery
WAND/EARL SW18 .... 29 L2
The Whitgift Galleries
CROY/NA CR0 .... 67 M3
Whitgift School
SAND/SEL CR2 .... 67 M4
Whitton Health Centre
WHTN TW2 .... 25 M2
Whitton Health Clinic
WHTN TW2 .... 25 L2
Whitton School
WHTN TW2 .... 25 L3
Wholist Health Centre
SAND/SEL CR2 .... 67 M4
Whyteleafe Football Club
CTHM CR3 .... 108 C1
Whyteleafe School
CTHM CR3 .... 88 C8
Wickham Theatre
WWKM BR4 .... 70 A2
Wide Way Health Clinic
MTCM CR4 .... 49 G3
Wildridings CP School
BRAK RG12 .... 34 D4
The Wildwood Golf Club Plc
CRAN GU6 .... 204 D7
Willards Gallery
MFD/CHID GU8 .... 203 H5
William Byrd School
HYS/HAR UB3 .... 14 F1
William Cobbett County
Junior School
FNM GU9 .... 134 B3
William Morris Middle School
MTCM CR4 .... 49 G3
Willington School
WIM/MER SW19 .... 29 J7
Willow Business Centre
MTCM CR4 .... 48 C5
Willow Business Park
SYD SE26 .... 32 F4
Wilsons Grammar School
WLCTN SM6 .... 67 H5
Wimbledon Chase Middle School
RYNPK SW20 .... 47 H1
Wimbledon College for Boys
WIM/MER SW19 .... 29 G8
Wimbledon Common
Preparatory School for Boys
WIM/MER SW19 .... 28 F8
Wimbledon Football Club
SNWD SE25 .... 50 B4
Wimbledon High School for Girls
WIM/MER SW19 .... 29 H7
Wimbledon House School
WIM/MER SW19 .... 47 K1
Wimbledon Magistrates Court
WIM/MER SW19 .... 29 K7
Wimbledon Park First School
WIM/MER SW19 .... 29 L3
Wimbledon Rugby Club
RYNPK SW20 .... 28 C8
Wimbledon School of Art
WIM/MER SW19 .... 29 K8
Wimbledon School of Art
WIM/MER SW19 .... 47 K1
Wimbledon Stadium
Business Centre
WIM/MER SW19 .... 29 L4
Wimbledon Synagogue
WIM/MER SW19 .... 29 G3
Wimbledon Theatre
WIM/MER SW19 .... 29 L8
Windlesham Golf Club
BAGS GU19 .... 54 C5
Windmill Trading Estate
MTCM CR4 .... 48 F5
The Winston Churchill School
WOKN/KNAP GU21 .... 76 B8
Wishmore Cross School
CHOB/PIR GU24 .... 56 B8
Wispers School
HASM GU27 .... 199 M8

Witley Surgery
MFD/CHID GU8 .... 181 H4
Woking Arts Council
WOKN/KNAP GU21 .... 6 D5
Woking Borough Council
WOKN/KNAP GU21 .... 6 D5
Woking Borough Council
WOKN/KNAP GU21 .... 78 A4
Woking Business Park
WOKN/KNAP GU21 .... 7 K1
Woking College
WOKS/MYFD GU22 .... 97 K2
Woking Community Hospital
WOKS/MYFD GU22 .... 6 E7
Woking Football Club
WOKS/MYFD GU22 .... 97 J2
Woking Leisure Centre
WOKS/MYFD GU22 .... 6 F9
Woking Nuffield Hospital
WOKN/KNAP GU21 .... 77 H4
Woldingham School
GDST RH9 .... 109 H7
Wolfson Medical Centre
RYNPK SW20 .... 28 D8
Wolfs Wood Primary School
OXTED RH8 .... 130 D6
Wonersh & Shamley Green C of E
School
SHGR GU5 .... 161 M4
Wonersh Surgery
SHGR GU5 .... 161 L2
Woodbridge Business Park
GU GU1 .... 8 E2
Woodbrook School
BECK BR3 .... 51 J1
Woodcote Group Practice
PUR/KEN CR8 .... 87 J1
Woodcote High School
COUL/CHIP CR5 .... 87 G3
Woodcote House School
BFOR GU20 .... 54 E4
Woodcote Junior &
Infant School
COUL/CHIP CR5 .... 86 F4
Woodfield School
REDH RH1 .... 127 H3
Woodlands School
LHD/OX KT22 .... 102 F4
Woodlands Surgery
CRAWE RH10 .... 212 B6
Woodlea Primary School
CTHM CR3 .... 109 J4
Woodmansterne CP School
BNSTD SM7 .... 86 C4
Woodmansterne Primary
School
STRHM/NOR SW16 .... 49 G1
Woodmansterne Sports Club
BNSTD SM7 .... 86 B5
Woodside Health Centre
SNWD SE25 .... 50 E5
Woodside Junior School
CROY/NA CR0 .... 5 L1
Wood Street County
Infant School
RGUW GU3 .... 115 M6
The Woodvill School
LHD/OX KT22 .... 102 E2
Woolmer Hill School
HASM GU27 .... 219 G2
World Business Centre
Heathrow
HTHAIR TW6 .... 14 F3
Worlsey Bridge Junior
Mixed School
BECK BR3 .... 33 K8
Worple Primary School
ISLW TW7 .... 17 K6
Worplesdon CP School
RGUW GU3 .... 116 A4
Worton Hall Industrial Estate
ISLW TW7 .... 17 K4
Wray Common County
Middle School
REIG RH2 .... 126 A7
Wray Common County
Primary School
REDH RH1 .... 126 A7
Wraysbury Combined School
STWL/WRAY TW19 .... 12 B8
Wraysbury Medical Centre
STWL/WRAY TW19 .... 12 C8
The Wrythe Green Surgery
SUT SM1 .... 66 B2
Wyke CP School
RGUW GU3 .... 114 C5
Xanadu Theatres
WEY KT13 .... 59 H8
Yattenden Middle School
HORL RH6 .... 170 D5
Yehudi Menuhin School
COB KT11 .... 101 K1
York Clinic
WOKN/KNAP GU21 .... 6 D6
York Galleries
TWK TW1 .... 26 D2
York House Medical Centre
WOKS/MYFD GU22 .... 6 E7
Yvonne Arnaud Theatre
GUW GU2 .... 9 G8
Zenith Gallery
BAL SW12 .... 30 E1
Zennor Road Industrial Estate
BAL SW12 .... 30 F2

Page 15

G2
1 Grampian Cl
2 Mendip Cl
3 Pondside Cl
4 Providence La
5 Quantock Cl
6 Warner Cl
J6
1 Steam Farm La
L3
1 Bath Rd
2 Community Cl
3 Lynchen Cl
4 Meadowbank Gdns
5 Pine Tree Cl
6 Woodfield Rd
M8
1 Byward Av

Page 16

B4
1 Poole Court Rd
2 St Paul's Cl
3 Scott Trimmer Wy
C1
1 Walnut Tree Rd
D1
1 Hopes Cl
D3
1 Hardwicke Av
2 Palmer Cl
3 Willow Gdns
E4
1 Concorde Cl
2 Lampton Park Rd
E5
1 Balfour Rd
2 Douglas Rd
3 Hanworth Rd
4 Lansdowne Rd
E6
1 Clarence Ter
2 Ivy Rd
3 Wareham Cl
E7
1 Angelfield
2 Lanigan Dr
3 Maswell Park Rd
4 Sandra Cl
F3
1 Colwyn Crs
2 Gladstone Gdns
F5
1 Crown Yd
2 Fair St
3 Gilbert St
F6
1 Atcham Rd
F7
1 Church St
2 Leamington Cl
3 Park Cl
F8
1 Vicarage Rd

Page 17

G7
1 Bracken End
2 Heather Cl
3 Ploughmans End
4 Reapers Wy
H3
1 Moreton Av
2 Ravenswood Ct
3 St Christopher's Cl
4 Stanleycroft Cl
5 Weston Gdns
H5
1 Abinger Gdns
J8
1 Blyth Cl
2 Butterfield Cl
3 Palmerston Rd
4 Russell Rd
K4
1 Ferney Meade Wy
2 Thackeray Cl
K6
1 Heddon Cl
2 Honeywood Rd
3 Twickenham Rd
L3
1 Birch Cl
2 Hawthorn Rd
3 Hazel Cl
L5
1 Manor House Wy
L7
1 Normanhurst Dr
L8
1 Amyand Cottages
2 Baronsfield Rd
3 Bridge Rd
4 Bridle La
5 Cumberland Cl
6 Downes Cl
7 King's Rd
8 Norfolk Cl
9 South Western Cl
10 Sussex Cl
11 Westmorland Cl
M1
1 Brent Rd
2 The Dell
3 Upper Butts
M2
1 Brickfield Cl
M7
1 Arlington Cl
2 Willoughby Rd
M8
1 Kelvin Dr
2 St Stephen's Gdns
3 Wayside Ct

Page 18

A1
1 Albany Rd
2 Albany Rd
3 Alexandra Rd
4 Brockshot Cl
5 Brook La North
6 Half Acre Ms
7 Hamilton Rd
8 Sidney Gdns
9 Westbury Pl
A2
1 Augustus Cl
2 Brent Wy
3 Dock Rd
4 Town Meadow
A3
1 Castle Yd
2 Duke St
3 Hunters Ct
4 King St
5 Lewis Rd
6 Retreat Rd
7 St James's Cottages
8 Victoria Pl
9 Wakefield Rd
10 The Wardrobe
11 Warrington Rd
12 Whittaker Av
B6
1 Catherine Dr
2 Clarence St
3 Drummonds Pl
4 Duncan Rd
5 Larkfield Rd
6 The Quadrant
7 St John's St
8 St John's La
9 Salisbury Rd
10 Sydney Rd
B8
1 Lancaster Ms
2 Montague Rd
3 Richmond Hl
C5
1 Beaumont Av
2 Gaston Bell Cl
3 Stanmore Gdns
4 Topiary Sq
5 Trinity Rd
6 Wyndham St
C7
1 Albany Rd
2 Audley Rd
3 Beatrice Rd
4 Connaught Rd
5 Hyde Rd
6 Lorne Rd
7 Marchmont Rd
8 Winter Box Wk
9 York Rd
C8
1 Grove Rd
2 Manning Pl
3 Pyrland Rd
4 Reynolds Pl
D3
1 Lonsdale Ms
2 North Av
3 Station Ap
D4
1 Garrick Rd
2 South Av
D5
1 Chilton Rd
2 Garden Rd
3 Niton Rd
E1
1 Deans Cl
2 Harvard Hl
E4
1 Courtlands Av
E5
1 Elsinore Wy
2 Tangier Rd
E6
1 Coval Gdns
2 Langdale Cl
E7
1 Uplands Cl
F1
1 Florence Gdns
2 Nightingale Cl
F2
1 Huntingdon Gdns
2 Ranelagh Gdns
3 Russell Kerr Cl
4 Station Gdns
5 Windrush Cl
F5
1 The Lindens
F6
1 Beechcroft Rd
2 Cromwell Pl
3 Eastbourne Gdns
4 Hanson Cl
5 Langdon Pl
6 Moore Cl
7 Waldeck Rd
F6
1 Medcroft Gdns
2 Penrhyn Crs
3 Wellside Gdns
F7
1 Martindale
2 Spencer Gdns

Page 19

G5
1 Bulls Alley
2 Chestnut Av
3 Fitzgerald Rd
4 Glendower Gdns
5 Glendower Rd
6 Trehern Rd
H1
1 Bedford Cl
2 Boston Gdns
3 Chiswick Sq
4 Devonshire Rd
5 Langham Pl
J1
1 Gwynne Whf
J3
1 Coniston Cl
J3
1 The Hermitage
2 St Anns Rd
J5
1 Beverley Gdns
2 Leconfield Av
3 Priory Gdns
4 Westwood Gdns
K6
1 Beloe Cl
2 Ellenborough Pl
3 Gibbon Wk
4 Roehampton Cl
L5
1 Beauchamp Ter
L6
1 Fairdale Gdns
2 The Pleasance
3 Queensgate Gdns
L7
1 Greenstead Gdns
2 Hobbes Wk
3 Kingslawn Cl
4 Laneway
5 Montolieu Gdns
6 St Margaret's Crs
M1
1 Wingrave Gdns
M2
1 Rowberry Cl
2 Wheatsheaf La
M3
1 Stockhurst Cl
M5
1 Abbotstone Rd
2 Stanbridge Rd
M6
1 Pettiward Cl
M7
1 Whitnell Wy
M8
1 Pullman Gdns

Page 21

J6
1 Blue Ball La
2 Fairhaven
3 Langham Pl
4 Stoneyland Ct
5 Strodes College La
6 Wetton Pl
L8
1 Borrowdale Cl
2 Buttermere Wk
3 Coniston Wy
4 Grasmere Ct
5 Thirlmere Cl
6 Windermere Cl
M7
1 Mead Ct
2 Wards Pl

Page 22

B6
1 Boleyn Cl
2 Farmer's Rd
3 The Fernery
4 Simmons Pl
C7
1 St Peter's Cl
C7
1 Priory Ms
2 Turners Cl
M1
1 Willowdene Cl
M2
1 Hereford Gdns
2 Percy Wy

Page 23

G2
1 Buttercup Sq
2 Windermere Cl
G8
1 Greene Fielde End
2 King's Cl
3 Tavistock Cl
H1
1 Cranford Cl
2 Elsinore Av
3 Hadrian Cl
4 Hadrian Wy
M6
1 Romney Cl
2 St Paul's Cl
3 Sundown Rd
M7
1 Woodlands Pde
M8
1 Ashdene Cl
2 Corneside
3 Oxford Cl
4 Thorne Cl

Page 24

A7
1 Alexandra Ct
2 Cheyne Rd
3 Saville Crs
4 Staveley Rd
5 Templecroft
C7
1 Adelaide Rd
2 Bullard Rd
3 The Causeway
4 The Cedars
5 Elleray Rd
6 Middle La
7 Park La
8 St Mary's Av
9 White Heron Ms
D1
1 Cheltenham Av
2 Devoncroft Gdns
3 March Rd
4 Mary's Ter
5 Oak La
6 Railway Ap
7 Station Yd
8 Strafford Rd
D2
1 Arragon Rd
2 Copthall Gdns
3 Cornwall Rd
4 Flood La
C6
1 Cumbernauld Gdns
D1
1 Glebelands Rd
D1
1 Brassey Cl
2 Eastleigh Wy
3 St Catherines Ct
4 Sydney Rd
5 Tynan Cl
6 Westmacott Dr
D7
1 Blackmore's Gv
2 Chadwick Cl
3 Davenport Cl
4 Taylors Ct
D1
1 Charleston Cl
2 Chervil Cl
3 Parkfield Av
4 Sherringham Av
E2
1 Little Ferry Rd
E4
1 Ferrymoor
2 Rushmead
E5
1 Thamesgate Cl

Page 25

G3
1 Newgate Cl
H5
1 Burgess Cl
2 Crosby Cl
3 Dunmow Cl
4 Gabriel Cl
5 Hazlitt Cl
6 Swinfield Cl
H3
1 Blagdon Wk
2 Broomfield Rd
3 Canford Pl
F8
1 Conifers Cl

Page 26

C6
1 Alice Ms
2 Boucher Cl
3 Bychurch End
4 Hall Ct
5 Latimer Rd
6 Sydney Rd
7 Walpole Crs
8 Walpole Rd
C7
1 Chadwick Av
C7
1 Ashbourne Ter
2 Derby Rd
3 Gladstone Rd
4 Granville Rd
5 Harcourt Rd
6 Palmerston Gv
7 Palmerston Rd
8 Sir Cyril Black Wy
D2
1 Esparto Cl
2 Farlton Rd
3 Wardley St
L2
1 Thornsett Rd
2 Willow Tree Cl
L1
1 Archway Cl
D1
1 Dowman Cl
2 Hamilton Road Ms
3 Stane Cl
M1
1 Dingwall Rd
2 Whitehead Cl
M2
1 Capern Rd
J1
1 Aldrich Ter
2 St Andrew's Ct
3 Thorndean St
K1
1 Bridford St
2 Hopwood Cl
3 Rosemary Rd
M7
1 Abingdon Cl
2 Ashbury Pl
3 Battle Cl
4 Sunlight Cl
5 Tintern Cl
6 Woburn Cl
M8
1 Norman Rd
2 Olive Rd
3 Pincott Rd

Page 27

G6
1 Debden Cl
2 Hornchurch Cl
3 Horsley Dr
4 Tangmere Gv
G7
1 The Albany
2 Albany Ms
3 Grosvenor Gdns
J1
1 Atherley Wy
2 Daniel Cl
J3
1 Edmund Gv
J4
1 Sunrise Cl
B6
1 Aldis Ms
2 Ivy Rd
3 Recovery St
J7
1 Bramble La
2 Chichester Cl
3 Hawley Cl
4 Homewood Cl
5 Langridge Ms
6 Orpwood Cl
7 Stanborough Cl
8 Stanford Cl
9 Tulip Cl
10 Walker Cl
K4
1 Sekhon Ter
K7
1 Begonia Pl
2 Cyclamen Cl
3 Daffodil Cl
4 Gladioli Cl
5 Hyacinth Cl
6 Marlborough Rd
7 Snowdrop Cl
L2
1 Cranbrook Dr
L5
1 Hartland Rd
2 The Wilderness
L7
1 Acorn Cl
2 Birchwood Cl
3 Jeffs Cl
4 Kingswood Av
M1
1 Willowdene Cl
M2
1 Hereford Gdns
2 Percy Wy
M6
1 Cranebrook
2 Portugal Gdns
H1
1 Albert Rd
2 Deerhurst Rd
3 Edward Cl
4 Fitz Wygram Cl
5 Radcliff Ms
6 Sanders Cl
7 Tudor Cl
8 Vincent Rw
M7
1 School Road Av

Page 28

B8
1 Alphea Cl
2 Holmbury Ct
3 Rutland Rd
4 Tudor Pl
C1
1 Jaggard Wy
2 Mayford Cl
C3
1 Old Hospital Cl

Page 29

G2
1 Lewesdon Cl
2 Montfort Pl
3 Pilsden Cl
4 Sandringham Cl
5 Swanton Gdns
6 Wainford Cl
G4
1 Carnegie Pl
2 Heath Mead
3 Lawson Cl
G5
1 Lampton House Cl
G7
1 Homefield Rd
2 Wilberforce Wy
G8
1 Cumberland Cl
2 Lansdowne Cl
3 Southridge Pl
4 Thackeray Cl
5 Thaxted Pl
H1
1 George Wyver Cl
2 Girdwood Rd
H3
1 Bedgebury Gdns
2 Gonston Cl
3 Winterfold Cl
H7
1 Draxmont
2 Walham Ri
J6
1 Bernard Gdns
2 Helme Cl
3 Springfield Rd
J7
1 Francis Gv
2 Raymond Rd
3 St Mark's Pl
4 Wimbledon Br
5 Worple Road Ms
K1
1 Avening Rd
2 Colliston Rd
3 Lainson St
K4
1 Farquhar Rd
2 Strathmore Rd
K6
1 Anchorage Cl
2 Bradshaw Cl
3 Rostrevor Rd

Page 30

A1
1 Heathfield Av
A2
1 Broadgates Rd
A3
1 Dawnay Gdns
A4
1 Glentanner Wy
A5
1 Thurso St
A7
1 Burns Cl
2 Keats Cl
3 North Rd
4 Pope Cl
5 Shelley Wy
6 Waterfall Rd
B2
1 Burntwood Cl
2 Lyminge Gdns
3 Marham Gdns

Page 31

G1
1 Bowie Cl
2 Langholm Cl
G3
1 Goodman Crs
G4
1 The Spinney
2 Tarrington Cl
3 Woodfield Gv
G5
1 Babington Rd
2 Campbell Cl
G6
1 Gleneagle Ms
2 Gleneagle Rd
3 Keens Cl
4 Swallow Gdns
G7
1 Brunswick Ms
2 Edgington Rd
3 Plane St
4 Rotherhill Av
G8
1 Broadview Rd
2 Drakewood Rd
3 Nettlewood Rd
H1
1 Brixton Hill Pl
2 Rodmill La
H3
1 Barhill Rd
2 Broadlands Cl
3 Goodman St
H4
1 Blakemore Rd
2 Brancaster Rd
3 Cherry Tree Dr
4 Moorcroft Rd
H5
1 Gleneldon Ms
2 Newcome Gdns
H7
1 Westwell Road Ap
H8
1 Rochester Cl
J1
1 Saxonfield Cl
2 Wirnbart Rd
J2
1 Claremont Cl
2 Huggins Pl
3 Limetree Cl
4 Presentation Ms
J3
1 Normanhurst Rd
J4
1 Leigh Orchard Cl
J5
1 Francis Barber Cl

Page 32

A6
1 Georgetown Cl
2 Gibbs Cl
3 Gibbs Sq
4 Montserrat Cl
B5
1 Baird Gdns
2 Bell Meadow
3 Hunters Meadow
4 Rockwell Gdns
5 Surrey Ms
B7
1 Childs La
2 New Green Pl
3 Paddock Gdns
4 Victory Pl
5 Woodland Cl
F6
1 Aldenham Ter
2 Blackmeadows
3 Denham Gv
4 Hanworth Cl
5 Rickman Ct
6 Wagbullock Ri

Page 28 (cont.)

C4
1 Morven Rd
C5
1 St Cyprian's St
C6
1 Granada St
D1
1 Otterburn St
D3
1 Dovedale Ri
2 Kenmare Dr
3 North Pl
4 Shrewton Rd
5 Woodley Cl
D1
1 Churchcroft Cl
D2
1 Pakenham Cl
D3
1 Cheriton Sq
D4
1 Netherfield Rd
2 Wheatlands Rd
D5
1 Barringer Sq
D6
1 Abbey Dr
2 Carlisle Wy
3 Okeburn Rd
4 St Benedict's Cl
5 Southview Cl
D7
1 Freshwater Cl
2 Knapton Ms
3 St Nicholas Glebe
4 Sirdar Rd
5 Stanley Gdns
E1
1 Kenilford Rd
2 Lammermoor Rd
3 Royal Ms
4 Verran Rd
E3
1 Ethelbert St
2 Hildreth St
3 Rostella Rd
E4
1 Manville Gdns
E5
1 Molyneux Dr
E7
1 Vectis Gdns
E8
1 The Bungalows
F1
1 Anfield Cl
2 Limerick Cl
F2
1 Zennor Rd
F3
1 Brierley Rd
F6
1 Penrith St
2 Rackham Ms
F8
1 Bencroft Rd
2 Summerene Cl

Page 33

G3
1 Alexander Evans Ms
2 Perry V
3 Treviso Rd
H2
1 Steucers La
K7
1 Holland Av
2 Normandy Cl
3 Shaw's Cottages

Page 32 (cont.)

J6
1 Cricketers Wk
2 Raymond Cl
F8
1 Blenheim Rd
2 Gladstone Ms
3 Heath Gv
4 Montrave Rd
5 Osprings Cl
J8
1 Courtland Av
2 Hermitage La
K1
1 Estoria Cl
2 Scotia Rd
K2
1 Bannister Cl
2 Rickard Cl
3 Skiffington Cl
K4
1 Dodbrooke Rd
2 Knolly's Cl
3 St Peter's Gdns
K5
1 Fawcett Cl
2 St Julian's Cl
3 South Oak Rd
K6
1 Monarch Ms
2 Normington Cl
L2
1 Jarrett Cl
L3
1 Lupin Cl
2 Parade Ms
3 Station Ri
L4
1 Bloom Gv
2 Chartham Gv
3 Friar Ms
4 Hannen Rd
5 Lansdowne Wood Cl
6 Nettlefold Pl
7 Pyrmont Gv
L5
1 Beadman Pl
2 Cotswold St
3 Knight's Hill Sq
4 Millhouse Pl
5 Saints Cl
6 Tredwell Rd
7 Weaver Wk
L6
1 Holderness Wy
2 St Vincent Cl
3 Woodcote Pl
L8
1 Covington Wy
M2
1 Coney Acre
M3
1 Lords Cl
M5
1 Advance Rd
2 Curnick's La
3 Durkirk St
4 Hobbs Rd
5 Langmead St
6 Waring St
7 Windsor Cl
8 Windsor Gv
M7
1 Wedgwood Wy
M8
1 Downsview Gdns
2 Founders Gdns
3 Hermitage Gdns
F1
1 Edmonds Ct
F5
1 Buttermere Gdns

Page 34

B1
1 Simmonds Cl
2 Warren Down
B6
1 Compton Cl
2 Flexford Gn
3 Ramsbury Cl
4 Wickham V
D1
1 Appletree Pl
2 Portman Cl
3 Priestwood Court Rd
4 Windlebrook Gn
E3
1 Boxford Rdg
2 Friendship Wy
3 Leverkusen Rd
4 Old Bracknell Cl
E7
1 Jackson Cl
2 Pendline Rd
3 Peregrine Cl
4 Swancote Gn
F1
1 Edmonds Ct
F5
1 Buttermere Gdns
F6
1 Nightingale Rd
2 Paxton Cl
F8
1 Cheriton Ct
2 Cottimore La
3 Edgehill Cl
4 Lansdown Cl
5 Marston Ct
6 Newark Ct
7 Regency Gdns
8 Rodney Cl
9 Stratton Cl
H2
1 Kimmeridge Rd
2 Loughborough

Page 35

G2
1 Drayton Cl
2 Farnham Cl
3 Forest Cn
4 Kenton Cl
5 Tebbit Cl
H2
1 Basemoors
2 Freeborn Wy
3 Lambourne Cn
4 Lichfields
5 Perry Wy
H3
1 Dartmouth Cl
2 Drothwich Cl
3 Foresters Sq
4 Northampton Cl
5 Quadrant Cl
H4
1 Tarleton Gdns
H5
1 Crassmount
2 Heathedge
H6
1 Brickwood Cl
2 Hassocks Cl
3 Plane St
4 Rowland Gv
H7
1 Bradford Cl
2 Churchley Rd
3 Cable Ct
4 Hensford Gdns
5 Markwell Cl
H8
1 Burbage Gv
2 East Stratton Cl
3 Froxfield Down
4 Lytchet Minster Cl
5 Popham Cl
6 Sandford Down
7 Stokeford Cl

Page 40

C8
1 Charles St
2 Fox La South
3 Guildford Rd
4 Pannells Ct
D7
1 Beomonds Rw
2 Blacksmiths La
3 Chertsey Wk
4 Foundry Cl
5 Galsworthy Rd
6 Cogmore La
7 Guildford St
8 White Hart Rw
E1
1 The Close
2 Kingswood Cl
3 Mountcombe Cl
4 Oakenhaye Cl
5 Oak Hill Cfs
H8
1 Dunton Cl
2 Southborough Cl (The Lane)

Page 41

G2
1 Harrison Ct
2 Pearmain Cl
3 Shepperton Court Dr
M2
1 Crosswell Cl
2 Harrow Wy
3 Lodge Wy
4 Queen Mary Rd

Page 42

B3
1 Allington Cl
2 Bramley Av
3 Coxs Av
4 Keswick Av
5 Shalston Vls
B4
1 Annett Cl
2 Blackberry Cl
3 Charlton La
D2
1 Heathlands Cl
D7
1 Harvey Cl
2 Montague Cl
3 Sullivans Reach
4 Thames Mead
D8
1 Osborne Rd
E1
1 The Chase
2 Laburnum Cl
3 Summer Trees
E7
1 Cottimore Ter
2 Florence Cl
3 Kingsbridge Rd
E8
1 Crutchfield La
2 Kings Cl
F2
1 Ilex Cl
F3
1 The Pennards
F6
1 Thorneycroft Cl
2 Viners Cl
L8
1 Austyn Gdns
2 Oakleigh Wy
M1
1 Lord Chancellor Wk
M2
1 Dickerage Rd
2 The Triangle
M3
1 Ashcombe Sq
2 Lincoln Rd
3 Rosemont Rd
4 Warwick Rd
M4
1 Nevada Cl
2 Oregon Cl
3 Virginia Cl

Page 43

J4
1 Central Sq
2 Hollingworth Cl
3 Minster Gdns
4 Redland Gdns
5 Sovereign Ct
6 Tonbridge Rd
7 Weldon Dr
K2
1 Thames Meadow
L4
1 Avern Rd
2 Dunvegan Cl
3 The Forum

Page 44

D1
1 Lyndale Hampton Court Wy
E6
1 Thames Side

Page 45

G1
1 Station Rd
2 Thames Side
H2
1 Bath Pas
2 Bishop's Hall
3 Clarence St
4 St James's Rd
H3
1 Blewburton Wk
2 Brook Dr
3 Heathermount
H6
1 East La
2 Kennington Gdns
G4
1 Bridle Cl
2 Home Park Wk
G5
1 Cumbrae Gdns
H2
1 Castle St
2 Fife Rd
3 Littlefield Cl
4 Weston Pk
H4
1 Bellevue Rd
2 Fairfield Rd
3 Watersplash Cl
H5
1 Ardmay Gdns
2 Maplehurst Cl
3 Sheppard Cl
4 Surbiton Hall Cl
H6
1 Ardmay Gdns
H7
1 Ardmay Gdns

Page 46

A1
1 Coombe House Cha
A3
1 Fairmead
A4
1 South La West
2 Stratford Ct
A5
1 Allan Cl
2 Hawkhurst Wy
3 Maria Theresa Cl
B2
1 Selborne Rd
B3
1 Jacaranda Cl
2 Station Av
B4
1 Balgowan Cl
2 Cadmer Cl
3 Closter Rd
4 Kingston Lodge
5 Sussex Rd
6 Tregarron Gdns
B5
1 Coombefield Cl
2 Oxleigh Cl
3 Ranelagh Pl
B6
1 Canford Gdns
B8
1 Yew Tree Cl
C4
1 Alverstone Rd
2 Cocks Crs
3 Walton Cl
C5
1 Chatsworth Gdns
2 College Gdns
3 Malden Wy
4 Tadworth Av
5 Welbeck Cl
6 Wickham Cl
C7
1 Greenlaw Gdns
2 Stroudes Cl
C8
1 Keble Cl
D2
1 Huntley Wy
D3
1 Stourhead Gdns
D7
1 Hughenden Rd
D8
1 Beverley Gdns
2 Brookside Crs
3 Station Ap
E1
1 Cranford Cl
E2
1 Farnham Gdns
2 Grayswood Gdns
E3
1 Hidcote Gdns
2 Nymans Gdns
3 Petworth Gdns
E8
1 Hazelmere Gdns
2 Sutherland Gdns
F2
1 Lambton Rd
F3
1 Berrylands
2 Coppice Cl
3 Michaelmas Cl
F8
1 Wimborne Cl

Page 47

G1
1 Delamere Rd
2 Mason Cl
G4
1 Woodlands
G8
1 Buttermere Cl
2 Rosebery Cl
J2
1 Handside Cl
2 Stanton Cl
H1
1 Pentney Rd
H4
1 Cherry Cl
2 Hillside Cl
3 Northernhay Wk
H6
1 Cardinal Cl
H7
1 Cleveland Ri
2 Nova Ms
H8
1 Stonecot Cl
H1
1 Epsom Rd
2 Stonecot Hl
3 Tudor Dr
K1
1 Charles Rd
K4
1 Goodwood Cl
2 Hatherleigh Cl
3 Queen Elizabeth Gdns
4 Queen's Pl
5 Queens Rd
K5
1 Ashley Av
K6
1 Glastonbury Cl
K7
1 Glastonbury Rd
2 Wentworth Cl
A1
1 Bathurst Av
2 The Path
3 Queensland Av
4 Rowland Wy
J1
1 Parkleigh Rd
J3
1 Harland Cl
L6
1 Alnwick Gv
2 Bordesley Rd
L7
1 Dore Gdns
2 Garendon Gdns
L8
1 Hove Gdns
M1
1 Rodney Pl
M4
1 Buckland Wk
M5
1 Calder Rd
2 Cartmel Gdns
3 Chester Gdns
4 Langdon Wk
M6
1 Croxden Wk
2 Darley Gdns
3 Leominster Wk
4 Malling Gdns
5 Marham Gdns
6 Missenden Gdns
7 Neath Gdns
M7
1 Lovett Dr
2 Newbiggin Wk
3 Newhouse Wk
4 St Benet's Gv

Page 48

A1
1 Landseer Cl
2 Littlers Cl
3 Stubbs Wy
4 Thorburn Wy
5 Yarborough Rd
A2
1 Horner La
2 Sycamore La
3 Varley Wy
A3
1 Chantry Wy
2 Gale Cl
3 Phipp's Bridge Rd
4 Saxonbury Cl
A4
1 Deer Park Gdns
2 Hatfield Cl
3 Rawnsley Av
A6
1 Alphabet Gdns
2 Beadlow Cl
3 Olveston Wk
B1
1 Lister Cl
2 Longfield Dr
B2
1 Gilpin Cl
2 Lulworth Crs
B3
1 Benedict Whf
2 Blake Rd
3 Morland Cl
4 Taffy's How
5 Walnut Tree Av
B7
1 Assembly Wk
2 Neville Wk
3 Nevil Wk
4 Thornton Rd
5 Welbeck Rd
B8
1 Welbeck Cl
C1
1 Camomile Av
2 Mason's Pl
C2
1 Montrose Gdns
2 Sibthorp Rd
3 Upper Gn East
4 Upper Gn West